THE GARDENING YEAR

PUBLISHED BY THE READER'S DIGEST ASSOCIATION LIMITED

Fourth edition © Copyright 1982
Reprinted 1983
The Reader's Digest Association Limited

Printed and bound in Great Britain by
W. S. Cowell Ltd., Ipswich.

The Reader's Digest

THE GARDENING YEAR

Edited and designed by The Reader's Digest Association Limited,
25 Berkeley Square, London W1X 6AB

The Publishers express their gratitude for contributions by the following people and organisations:

Roy Hay, MBE, VMH (consultant editor)

Bob Woolley (revisions consultant)

Authors

J. R. McBain Allan, BSc (Hort), NDH
Alan Bloom
P. R. Chapman, ARPS, FRHS
Anthony Derrick
M. T. Drake, BSc (Hort)
Ian Greenfield, BSc (Agric), MIBiol
S. J. Grubb
Denis Hardwicke
Lowell Hartley, FJI
John Hayhurst
Bill Heritage

Will Ingwersen, VMH
Leslie Johns, BA
M. E. Leeburn
F. R. McQuown, MA, FLS
David K. Mann
Margaret J. Martin, MSc, ARIC
Frances Perry, MBE, FLS
Noel J. Prockter
Ray Procter, AHRHS
Henry John Randall, CBE
H. C. Russell
Kay N. Sanecki

Fred Shepherd
O. Slocock
L. P. Smith, BA
Violet Stevenson
Ian P. C. Unwin
Brian Walkden
John Warren, NDH
T. Wellsted
J. P. Wood, NDH
Bob Woolley
W. John Wright, BSc (Hort), NDH

Artists and Photographers

John Barber, LSIA
Norman G. Barber
Stewart R. Black
Leonora Box
David Bryant
Ann Buckmaster
Julia Clements
R. G. Corbin
Kathleen Dance
J. E. Downward
Valerie Finnis
The Flowers and Plants Council
John Gapp

Ian Garrard
Roy Grubb
Hargrave Hands, MSIA
Veronica Heywood
Peter Hunt, FLS
David Hutter
I.C.I. Ltd
David Jones
Peter Kesteven
Ronald Maiden
Elsa M. Megson
Murphy Chemical Co Ltd
L. Hugh Newman
D. W. Ovenden

W. Francis Phillips
Charles Pickard, ARAC
Charles Raymond
Carol Russell
Shell International Petroleum
    Company Ltd
Harry Smith
Kathleen Smith, MSIA
Glenn Steward
Sutton & Sons Ltd
Syndication International
Leo E. Walmsley, NDD, ATD
Elsie Wrigley, ATD, DA (Manc)

A plan for all seasons

THE gardener's most valuable aid is time—time to coax a lawn from the bare earth, to tend seedlings to their perfection of bloom, to prepare the ground thoroughly for a succession of vegetables, or to prune trees for a rich crop of sun-ripe fruit. Any book which aims to give constructive help to today's gardeners, with all their other commitments, must assume that few will have sufficient time for all the labours which guarantee success.

The heart of *The Gardening Year* is therefore a work plan, *Twelve Months of Gardening*, beginning in March when the first spring flowers bloom and the ground becomes workable after the frosts of winter.

The decision to organise the book in this way was the outcome of major re-thinking by the editors and their expert consultants on the purpose and style of a modern gardening book. In *The Gardening Year* are many new devices designed to make a complete easy-to-use manual for novices as well as experienced gardeners.

The Gardening Year has signposts on every page. Monthly tags on the corners of each page speed the process of finding information, and bold headings pick out the 25 subdivisions of each month's work.

The book is deliberately repetitive. All the advice needed for good husbandry is contained in the monthly work sections; it is repeated in brief outline at the start of each month, and gathered together in panel form in the *At a Glance* tables in the glossary.

The central core of the book includes not only the main chronological work section, but also nearly as many pages of plant descriptions and illustrations. These give details of herbaceous plants to fill borders, trees and shrubs to screen gardens from the outside world, trailing plants to decorate window-sills and boxes, greenhouse and indoor plants for colour in the winter months.

The Gardening Year divides the gardener's interests into 25 different subsections, always dealt with in the same order under each monthly heading. Most gardens have a lawn, and nearly every garden has roses, so these two subjects head each of the twelve monthly programmes. Although fruit and vegetables are found near the end of the month's work, they are no less important: inflated prices more than anything else have emphasised the advantages to be gained from home production.

Following a portrait of the weather that can be expected, each monthly programme begins with a summary of the month's tasks. Then follows the main detailed section, describing the jobs to be done, with illustrations showing how they are accomplished.

To find in which month of the year any job should be done, turn to the *Glossary* towards the back of the book, on pages 413-515. Here, arranged in alphabetical order, are *At a Glance* charts, one for each of the 25 divisions of *Twelve Months of Gardening*.

Suppose you are doubtful when to prune your roses: turn to the letter R in the *Glossary* to find the *At a Glance* chart on roses (p. 488). At once you will see that roses should be pruned in March. You can now turn to the March section of *Twelve Months of Gardening*, where you will find stage-by-stage drawings which show you how to prune the different kinds of rose. Or refer to the general index at the back of the book. There, under roses, you will also find page references to pruning. In the August rose section are illustrations and brief descriptions of the main types of roses, and a short list of recommended varieties expertly chosen from the hundreds of varieties on the market.

The treatment necessary to prolong the life of cut flowers and considerations to be borne in mind when planning a garden are explained on pp. 412 and 516.

The British climate varies considerably from one part of the country to another. *The Gardening Year* includes weather maps and information which enable the reader to time activities—sowing, planting and so on—to fit in with local weather conditions. Most of the plants we grow in our gardens are surprisingly adaptable: if seeds of vegetables or flowers are sown a few weeks late, when the soil has begun to warm up, they will catch up with those sown earlier under less favourable conditions.

The ultimate height and spread that plants will attain, and consequently the distance apart at which they should be planted to avoid eventual overcrowding, are obviously of prime importance. This information is meticulously provided in *The Gardening Year*. So, too, is advice about soil conditions needed by the different plants, and instructions on propagating them.

Gardening is an everlasting battle against the weather, adverse soil or atmospheric conditions, and pests and diseases. In every garden, every year, some plants will suffer from some pests or diseases. A dismaying list of such troubles (and the remedies for them) appears in this book, although gardeners rarely have to deal with more than a few of them. It is a waste of time to fight the weather and other imponderables. Rather than making the garden fit the plants, choose plants to suit your garden.

The Gardening Year is designed for all manner of gardeners in all manner of gardens. Whether yours is large or small, in town or country, whether you are a devoted gardener or just want to keep the place presentable, with a few flowers to cut for the house, *The Gardening Year* will lead you to the best results for the most economical expenditure of time and energy.

Contents

Illustrated plant descriptions

Pests and diseases. The gardener's enemies, and how to deal with them

Cut flowers. Treatment to make them last in water

Glossary. An encyclopaedia of gardening terms

THE YEAR AT A GLANCE

SPECIAL FEATURES

Garden design. Making the most of the area available

Plant and general index

Metric conversion tables

LENGTH				AREA				VOLUME		CAPACITY		WEIGHT			
Inches	Milli-metres	Feet	Metres	Square feet	Square metres	Square yards	Square metres	Cubic feet	Cubic metres	Pints	Litres	Ounces	Grams	Pounds	Kilos
1	25	1	0.3	1	0.1	1	0.8	1	0.03	1	0.57	1	28.4	1	0.45
2	51	2	0.6	2	0.2	2	1.7	2	0.06	2	1.14	2	56.7	2	0.91
3	76	3	0.9	3	0.3	3	2.5	3	0.09	3	1.71	3	85.1	3	1.36
4	102	4	1.2	4	0.4	4	3.3	4	0.11	4	2.27	4	113.4	4	1.81
5	127	5	1.5	5	0.5	5	4.2	5	0.14	5	2.84	5	141.8	5	2.27
6	152	6	1.8	6	0.6	6	5	6	0.17	6	3.41	6	170.1	6	2.72
7	178	7	2.1	7	0.7	7	5.9	7	0.2	7	3.98	7	198.5	7	3.18
8	203	8	2.4	8	0.7	8	6.7	8	0.23	8	4.55	8	226.8	8	3.63
9	229	9	2.7	9	0.8	9	7.5	9	0.25	9	5.11	9	255.2	9	4.08
10	254	10	3	10	0.9	10	8.4	10	0.28	10	5.7	10	283.5	10	4.54
11	279	11	3.4	11	1	11	9.2	11	0.31			11	311.8		
12	305	12	3.7	12	1.1	12	10	12	0.34			12	340.2		

LENGTH				AREA				VOLUME		CAPACITY		WEIGHT			
Milli-metres	Inches	Metres	Feet	Square metres	Square feet	Square metres	Square yards	Cubic metres	Cubic feet	Litres	Pints	Grams	Ounces	Kilos	Pounds
1	0.04	1	3.28	1	10.76	1	1.2	1	35.31	1	1.76	10	0.35	1	2.2
2	0.08	2	6.56	2	21.53	2	2.39	2	70.63	2	3.52	15	0.53	2	4.41
3	0.12	3	9.84	3	32.29	3	3.59	3	105.94	3	5.28	20	0.71	3	6.61
4	0.16	4	13.12	4	43.06	4	4.78	4	141.26	4	7.04	25	0.88	4	8.82
5	0.2	5	16.4	5	53.82	5	5.98	5	176.57	5	8.8	30	1.06	5	11.02
6	0.24	6	19.69	6	64.58	6	7.18	6	211.89	6	10.56	35	1.24	6	13.23
7	0.28	7	22.97	7	75.35	7	8.37	7	247.2	7	12.32	40	1.41	7	15.43
8	0.32	8	26.25	8	86.11	8	9.57	8	282.52	8	14.08	45	1.59	8	17.64
9	0.35	9	29.53	9	96.88	9	10.76	9	317.83	9	15.84	50	1.76	9	19.84
10	0.39	10	32.81	10	107.64	10	11.96	10	353.15	10	17.6	55	1.94	10	22.05
11	0.43	11	36.09	11	118.4	11	13.16	11	388.46			60	2.12		
12	0.47	12	39.37	12	129.17	12	14.35	12	423.78			65	2.29		

MARCH

APRIL

MAY

JUNE

JANUARY & FEBRUARY

Twelve Months of Flowers

A PANORAMA OF COLOUR

This opening section of colour pictures shows the rewards the gardener can expect from the programme of work given in *The Gardening Year*. It suggests the variety of shrubs, herbaceous perennials, annuals and alpines which today offer an endless choice for a year-long succession of constantly changing flowers and foliage. The whites and yellows of spring give way to the brilliant blooms of summer; dull winter days can be brightened with berries and variegated leaves

JULY

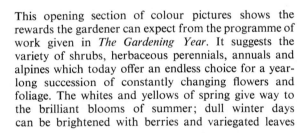

JULY

DECEMBER

NOVEMBER

OCTOBER

SEPTEMBER

AUGUST

March
FORERUNNER OF SPRING

After months of cold, unpleasant weather, the flowers of early spring are appreciated more than any others. Polyanthuses, Dutch crocuses and forsythias should be making a colourful show in most areas. Although the main display of tulips is yet to come, the varieties of the small *Tulipa kaufmanniana*, which are not so well known, will be opening their starry flowers. Freesias, grown in slightly heated greenhouses from corms planted the previous August, are now producing their fragrant flowers

Clivia miniata. Greenhouse evergreen perennial. Height 12–18 in. Plant or pot February

Hamamelis mollis (witch hazel). Hardy deciduous tree. Height 12 ft. Plant in autumn

Iris danfordiae. Hardy bulbous iris for the rock garden. Height 6 in. Plant in autumn

Narcissus 'Beryl' (cyclamineus daffodil). Hardy bulb. Height 8 in. Plant in autumn

Saxifraga apiculata. Hardy perennial alpine. Height 4 in. Plant in spring or autumn

Forsythia intermedia spectabilis. Hardy deciduous shrub. Height 8 ft. Plant in autumn

Helleborus corsicus. Hardy evergreen perennial. Height 24 in. Plant in autumn

Crocus tomasinianus. Hardy bulb. Height 3½ in. Plant in September or October

Prunus cerasifera. Deciduous tree. Height up to 20 ft. Plant in autumn and winter

Primula veris (polyanthus). Hardy perennial. Height 9 in. Sow seed March, plant in autumn

Chaenomeles japonica. Hardy deciduous shrub. Height 3–8 ft. Plant autumn, winter

Narcissus 'Carlton' (large-cupped daffodil). Hardy bulb. Height 16 in. Plant early autumn

Ribes 'Pulborough Scarlet'. Hardy deciduous shrub. Height 6 ft. Plant in autumn or winter

Freesia. Greenhouse corm with fragrant flowers. Height 12–24 in. Pot in August

Tulipa kaufmanniana 'Shakespeare'. Hardy bulb. Height 6 in. Plant in November

Corylopsis pauciflora. Tender deciduous shrub, requiring shelter. Height 4 ft. Plant in autumn

11

April
THE SEASON OF BULBS

More and more flowers will be opening as spring gets under way; they are always especially effective if grouped in masses of contrasting colours. Yellow daffodils look well in front of mauve honesty; or blue grape hyacinths (muscari) around the base of the pink flowering cherry, *Prunus* 'Kanzan'. One of the loveliest of dwarf bulbs is the erythronium or trout lily. Just as distinctive are the dainty cyclamineus narcissi, so called because their perianths turn right back, like the cyclamen

Lunaria biennis (honesty). Hardy biennial. Height 2–3 ft. Plant in early autumn

Magnolia soulangiana. Hardy deciduous tree. Height up to 30 ft. Plant in late winter

Muscari (grape hyacinth). Hardy bulb. Height 6–12 in. Plant late summer or autumn

Tulipa fosteriana. Hardy bulb. Height 16 in. Plant in autumn in permanent position

Erythronium revolutum 'White Beauty' (trout lily). Hardy bulb. Height 10 in. Plant August

Camellia japonica 'Elegans'. Evergreen shrub. Height 10 ft. Plant in autumn or spring

Aubrieta (purple rock cress). Hardy perennial. Height 3 in. Plant in late autumn or spring

12

ronicum 'Harpur Crewe'. Hardy perennial.
ight 3 ft. Plant in autumn or spring

Triteleia uniflora (spring starflower). Hardy
bulb. Height 12 in. Plant in autumn

Primula pubescens 'Mrs. J. H. Wilson'. Hardy
perennial. Height 3 in. Plant in spring

rgenia cordifolia purpurea. Hardy perennial.
ight 12 in. Plant in September

Prunus 'Kanzan'. Hardy deciduous tree.
Height 25–30 ft. Plant in autumn or winter

Alyssum saxatile. Hardy perennial alpine.
Height 6 in. Plant in autumn or spring

heiranthus cheiri (wallflower). Hardy
ennial. Height 12–24 in. Plant in autumn

Magnolia stellata. Hardy deciduous shrub.
Height up to 12 ft. Plant February or March

Rhododendron 'Pink Pearl'. Hardy evergreen
shrub. Height 10 ft. Plant autumn or spring

13

May
VARIETY IN FLOWERING SHRUBS

Geranium endressii. Hardy perennial. Height 20 in. Plant in autumn or spring

This is the month of rhododendrons and showy azaleas. In addition to the deciduous azaleas such as the very fine variety 'Silver Slipper' shown here, there are also evergreen species, bearing pink, red or white blossoms. The evergreen shrub *Pieris forrestii* is less known. It has clusters of white flowers, like those of lily-of-the-valley, and bright red foliage on the young shoots. Many paeonies, both single and double, are now in bloom, and flowering syringas enliven the spring border with their fragrance

Fritillaria imperialis (crown imperial). Hardy bulb. Height 4 ft. Plant in autumn

Phlox subulata 'Vivid'. Hardy perennial alpine. Height 3 in. Plant in autumn or spring

Cytisus praecox (broom). Hardy deciduous shrub. Height 5 ft. Plant in autumn or winter

Pieris forrestii. Hardy evergreen shrub. Height 8–10 ft. Plant in autumn or spring

Cytisus ardoinii (broom). Hardy deciduous shrub. Height 4–5 in. Plant autumn or winter

Pyrethrum 'Eileen May Robinson'. Hardy perennial. Height 3 ft. Plant in spring

quilegia hybrida (columbine). Hardy peren-
ial. Height 3 ft. Plant in autumn or spring

Weigela rosea. Deciduous shrub. Height 6–8 ft.
Plant in autumn or winter

Azalea 'Silver Slipper'. Hardy deciduous
shrub. Height 5 ft. Plant in autumn or winter

rollius 'Pritchard's Giant'. Herbaceous
erennial. Height 2½ ft. Plant in autumn

Myosotis alpestris 'Royal Blue' (forget-me-
not). Biennial. Height 6 in. Plant in autumn

Paeonia hybrida. Hardy herbaceous perennial.
Height 2½ ft. Plant in autumn or late winter

ulsatilla vulgaris (pasque flower). Hardy
erennial. Height 8–12 in. Plant in autumn

Tulipa 'Landseadel's Supreme' (Darwin tulip).
Hardy bulb. Height 2 ft. Plant in autumn

Syringa prestoniae 'Isabella'. Hardy deciduous
shrub. Height 12 ft. Plant autumn or winter

15

June
THE ROSE DISPLAY BEGINS

Roses commence their summer show of bloom this month. Beds of the floribunda varieties are especially effective. Hybrid tea roses, apart from their decorative value in the garden, are also excellent as cut flowers. 'Zephirine Drouhin' is a good choice where a climbing rose is required. It has thornless stems, and carmine-pink blooms of great fragrance. One of the most popular barberries, *Berberis darwinii*, bears plum-coloured berries in the autumn and carries its holly-like leaves throughout the year

Genista lydia. Hardy deciduous shrub. Height 2½ ft. Plant in autumn or late winter

Deutzia gracilis. Hardy deciduous shrub. Height 4 ft. Plant in autumn or winter

Dianthus 'Sweet Wivelsfield' (pink). Hardy biennial. Height 12–15 in. Plant in autumn

Campanula muralis (syn. *portenschlagiana*). Hardy perennial. Height 4 in. Plant in autumn

Rose 'Fragrant Cloud'. Hybrid tea bush rose. Height 3 ft. Plant in autumn or winter

Alchemilla mollis. Hardy perennial. Height 12–18 in. Plant in autumn or spring

Rose 'Anne Harkness'. Floribunda bush rose. Height 4 ft. Plant in autumn or winter

Papaver orientale (oriental poppy). Hardy perennial. Height 3 ft. Plant in autumn or spring

Begonia rex. Greenhouse perennial. Height 12 in. Plant or pot in spring or summer

Rose 'Zephirine Drouhin'. Hardy climber. Height 10–15 ft. Plant in autumn or winter

Viburnum tomentosum plicatum. Hardy deciduous shrub. Height 8 ft. Plant autumn

Berberis darwinii. Hardy evergreen shrub. Height 8–10 ft. Plant autumn or early spring

Iris germanica 'Limelight'. Hardy perennial. Height 3 ft. Plant in early autumn

Laburnum vossii. Hardy deciduous tree. Height 20 ft. Plant in autumn or winter

Campanula media (Canterbury bell). Hardy biennial. Height 1½–2½ ft. Plant in autumn

Gaillardia 'Goblin'. Hardy perennial. Height 9 in. Plant in March or April

17

July
THE BRILLIANCE OF ANNUALS

Most of the hardy annuals sown outside in March and April, and the half-hardy types planted in the open in early June, will be in flower this month. Eschscholzias, petunias, sweet peas and nasturtiums are all annuals, and are among the most colourful flowers in the garden. They can be put to good use in a variety of ways. In new gardens, for instance, they will provide a brilliant display in a short time, while in established gardens they are valuable for filling bare spaces between shrubs and other plants

Delphinium ajacis hybridum (larkspur). Hardy annual. Height 1-4 ft. Sow outside, September

Iberis hybrida (candytuft). Hardy annual. Height 9–15 in. Sow outside in spring

Rose 'Nevada'. Hardy shrub rose. Height 7–10 ft. Plant in autumn or winter

Hosta crispula (plantain lily). Hardy perennial. Height 2½ ft. Plant in autumn or spring

Kniphofia 'John Benary' (red hot poker). Hardy perennial. Height 4 ft. Plant in spring

Erigeron (fleabane). Hardy perennial. Height 24 in. Plant in autumn or spring

Petunia 'Starfire'. Half-hardy annual. Height 15 in. Plant in late May or early June

Eschscholzia hybrida. Hardy annual. Height 6–12 in. Sow seed outside in spring

Mesembryanthemum criniflorum. Half-hardy annual. Height 3 in. Plant May, June or July

Digitalis hybrida (foxglove). Hardy biennial. Height 4 ft. Plant out in early autumn

Salvia 'May Night' (sage). Hardy perennial. Height 18 in. Plant in autumn or spring

Lathyrus odoratus 'Bijou' (dwarf sweet pea). Hardy annual. Height 12 in. Plant in April

Clematis 'Nelly Moser'. Hardy climber. Height 12 ft. Plant autumn, winter or spring

Tropaeolum majus (nasturtium). Hardy annual. Height 5–8 ft. Sow in spring

Lilium 'Black Dragon' (lily). Hardy bulb. Height 5–6 ft. Plant in autumn or early spring

Astilbe 'Rhineland'. Hardy perennial. Height 2 ft. Plant in autumn or spring

Geranium 'Johnson's Blue'. Hardy perennial. Height 18 in. Plant in autumn or early spring

Rose 'Grandpa Dickson'. Hybrid tea bush rose. Height 3–4 ft. Plant in autumn or winter

Hydrangea hortensia. Hardy deciduous shrub. Height 3–4 ft. Plant in autumn or spring

Lilium 'Stardust' (lily). Hardy bulb. Height 4–5 ft. Plant in autumn or late winter

Delphinium. Hardy perennial. Height 3–5 ft. Plant in autumn or late winter

Lavatera trimestris. Hardy annual. Height 2–3 ft. Sow seed in the open in spring

Phlox 'Gaiety', Hardy perennial. Height 2½ ft. Plant in autumn or spring

Anthemis 'Grallagh Gold'. Hardy perennial. Height 24 in. Plant in autumn or spring

Lilium 'Enchantment' (lily). Hardy bulb. Height 3–4 ft. Plant in autumn or early spring

Rose 'Elizabeth of Glamis'. Floribunda. Height 3½ ft. Plant in late autumn or winter

Geranium armenum. Hardy perennial. Height 3 ft. Plant in autumn or spring

Antirrhinum nanum. Hardy perennial, treated as an annual. Height 15 in. Plant in April

Hemerocallis 'Cartwheels'. Hardy perennial. Height 3 ft. Plant in autumn or spring

Helianthemum (rock rose). Hardy perennial. Height 3–6 in. Plant in autumn or winter

Potentilla fruticosa. Hardy deciduous shrub. Height 3–4 ft. Plant in autumn or winter

Rose 'Iceberg'. Floribunda bush rose. Height 4 ft. Plant in late autumn or winter

Tradescantia 'Purewell Giant'. Hardy perennial. Height 24 in. Plant autumn or spring

Dianthus hybrida (pink). Hardy perennial. Height 12 in. Plant in autumn or spring

August
FORERUNNER OF AUTUMN TINTS

Though gardens tend to be neglected this month while their owners are away, many plants are at their best. In the south the outdoor early-flowering chrysanthemums are in bloom, as are many herbaceous perennials, such as heleniums and sidalceas. Late annuals, such as sturdy tagetes and calendulas, add bright splashes of yellow to the border. The hardy fuchsias should be covered in flowers, and the striking bowl-shaped flowers of *Lilium auratum* are releasing their heavy scent

Chrysanthemum 'Parasol'. Reflexed decorative chrysanthemum. Height 3½ ft. Plant in May

Scabiosa caucasica (scabious). Hardy perennial. Height 2–3 ft. Plant in March

Eucomis comosa. Half-hardy bulb. Height 24 in. Plant in spring, protect in winter

Cosmos bipinnatus. Half-hardy annual. Height 3 ft. Plant or sow in late May or June

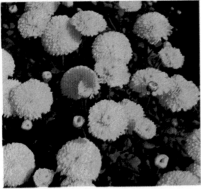

Chrysanthemum 'Golden Bouquet'. Pompon chrysanthemum. Height 2½ ft. Plant in May

Chrysanthemum 'Hansel'. American spoon chrysanthemum. Height 1½–2 ft. Plant May

Nymphaea 'Mrs. Richmond' (water lily). Plant in May on pool bottom

Begonia semperflorens. Half-hardy perennial. Height 6–12 in. Plant late May or early June

Helianthus hybrida (sunflower). Hardy annual. Height 6–10 ft. Sow in the open in spring

Helenium 'Wyndley' (orange) and 'Moerheim Beauty' (red). Hardy perennials. Height 3 ft.

Tagetes 'Orange Winner'. (French marigold). Half-hardy annual. Height 8 in. Sow in April

Sidalcea hybrida. Hardy perennial. Height 3 ft. Plant in autumn or spring

Echium hybrida (viper's bugloss). Hardy annual. Height 12 in. Sow in May or June

Fuchsia 'Dr. Foster'. Hardy deciduous shrub. Height 2–4 ft. Plant in late May

Calendula 'Radio' (pot marigold). Hardy annual. Height 24 in. Sow outside in spring

Lilium auratum (lily). Hardy bulb. Height 5–8 ft. Plant in autumn or spring

23

September
WHEN DAHLIAS DOMINATE

Dahlias and early-flowering chrysanthemums are the most prominent flowers in the garden. Dahlias are available in a great variety of forms, from the huge blooms of the giant decoratives to dainty and graceful cactus and pompon varieties. The appearance of colchicum blooms is a reminder that autumn is not far away: they are curious in that the flowers appear before the leaves. In the herbaceous border the flat flower heads of *Sedum spectabile* will attract butterflies on sunny days

Venidio-arctotis. Half-hardy perennial bedding plant. Height 24 in. Plant in May

Dahlia 'Pwll Coch'. Small semi-cactus dahlia. Height 3½–4 ft. Plant in early June

Aconitum 'Bressingham Spire'. Hardy perennial. Height 24 in. Plant in autumn or spring

Callistephus 'Ostrich Plume' (aster). Half-hardy annual. Height 18 in. Plant in late May

Anemone japonica (Japanese anemone). Hardy perennial. Height 24 in. Plant autumn, spring

Rudbeckia 'Goldsturm'. Hardy perennial. Height 24 in. Plant in autumn or early spring

Colchicum autumnale (naked boys). Hardy tuber. Height 6–8 in. Plant in July or August

24

Viburnum opulus xanthocarpum. Hardy deciduous shrub. Height 12 ft. Plant autumn

Aster (dwarf michaelmas daisy). Hardy perennial. Height 18 in. Plant autumn or spring

Chrysanthemum 'Bronze Fairie'. Pompon chrysanthemum. Height 12 in. Plant in May

Pelargonium 'Mrs. Quilter' (dwarf pelargonium). Tender perennial. Plant June

Gladiolus hybrida (butterfly gladiolus). Hardy corm. Height 3 ft. Plant in April or May

Aster 'Freda Ballard'. Hardy perennial. Height 2½ ft. Plant in autumn or early spring

Sedum spectabile 'Autumn Joy'. Hardy perennial. Height 24 in. Plant autumn or spring

Cyclamen neapolitanum. Hardy tuber. Height 4 in. Plant in July or August

Dahlia 'Holland Festival'. Giant decorative dahlia. Height 4½ ft. Plant in early June

October
BEAUTY IN AUTUMN LEAVES

The intensity of colour in autumn foliage appears to depend on weather conditions. After a hot, dry summer the colour always seems more brilliant. There are many trees and shrubs noted for their colourful autumn foliage, *Rhus cotinoides* and *Acer capillipes* being two which have wonderful autumn tints and are suitable for small gardens. The stately, silvery-white plumes of pampas grass (cortaderia) make a fine contrast to the red, yellow and pink hues of the autumn foliage

Arbutus unedo (strawberry tree). Hardy evergreen. Height 12–15 ft. Plant autumn, spring

Euonymus europaeus. Hardy deciduous tree. Height 9 ft. Plant in autumn or winter

Rose moyesii. Hardy shrub rose. Height 8 ft. Plant in autumn or winter

Acer capillipes (maple). Hardy deciduous tree. Height 30 ft. Plant in autumn or winter

Cotinus obovatus. Hardy deciduous shrub. Height 12 ft. Plant in autumn or winter

Skimmia japonica. Hardy evergreen shrub. Height 3 ft. Plant in autumn or spring

Amaryllis belladonna (belladonna lily). Hardy bulb. Height 1½–2 ft. Plant in July

Fothergilla monticola. Hardy deciduous shrub. Height 6–8 ft. Plant in autumn or winter

Nerine bowdenii. Hardy bulb. Height 1½–2 ft. Plant August or September in warm place

Cotinus coggygria (smoke tree). Hardy deciduous tree. Height 12 ft. Plant in autumn or winter

Gentiana sino-ornata. Hardy perennial alpine. Height 3–4 in. Plant in autumn or spring

Nyssa sylvatica (tupelo). Hardy deciduous tree. Height 60–100 ft. Plant in autumn or winter

Cortaderia (pampas grass). Hardy perennial grass. Height 7 ft. Plant in autumn or spring

Cornus alba sibirica variegata. Hardy deciduous shrub. Height 10 ft. Plant in autumn

Cotoneaster 'Cornubia'. Hardy deciduous tree. Height 15-20 ft. Plant in autumn

Acer japonicum (maple). Hardy deciduous tree. Height 10–20 ft. Plant in autumn or winter

November
COLOURFUL FRUITS AND BERRIES

In addition to colourful foliage, many shrubs have berries which make a wonderful display at this time of year. The firethorns (pyracantha) produce masses of red, yellow or orange berries. These tough evergreen shrubs can be trained on walls or grown as hedges. Ornamental crab apples have fine fruits, as do the deciduous barberries—thorny shrubs that do well even in the poorest soil. Pernettyas are low-growing evergreens that make a garden bright with pink, white and crimson berries

Pernettya mucronata. Hardy evergreen shrub. Height 2-3 ft. Plant in autumn or spring

Sorbus matsumurana. Hardy deciduous tree. Height 20 ft. Plant in autumn or winter

Callicarpa giraldiana. Hardy deciduous shrub. Height 6 ft. Plant in autumn or winter

Malus 'Yellow Siberian'. Hardy deciduous tree. Height 20 ft. Plant in autumn or winter

Viburnum betulifolium. Hardy deciduous tree. Height 8–12 ft. Plant in autumn or winter

Malus 'Veitch's Scarlet'. Hardy deciduous tree. Height 20 ft. Plant in autumn or winter

Capsicum annuum (red pepper). Greenhouse annual. Height 2½ ft. Sow seed in April

Lindera benzoin (spice bush). Hardy deciduous shrub. Height 10 ft. Plant in autumn or winter

Parthenocissus quinquefolia (Virginia creeper). Deciduous climber. Plant in autumn or winter

Abies spectabilis (Himalayan fir). Evergreen. Height up to 150 ft. Plant in autumn or spring

Garrya elliptica. Hardy evergreen shrub. Height 8–12 ft. Plant in autumn or spring

Cornus alba sibirica. Hardy deciduous shrub. Height 8–10 ft. Plant in autumn or winter

Pyracantha watereri. Hardy evergreen shrub. Height 8–10 ft. Plant in autumn or spring

Berberis rubrostilla. Hardy deciduous shrub. Height 4 ft. Plant in autumn or winter

Vitis coignetiae (Japanese vine). Deciduous climber. Height 20 ft. Plant autumn or winter

Pyracantha rogersiana aurantiaca. Hardy evergreen shrub. Height 10 ft. Plant autumn, spring

29

December

EVERGREENS TO BRIGHTEN WINTER

Plants with colourful, evergreen foliage are particularly valuable during the dull days of winter. There are many varieties of holly (*Ilex aquifolium*) that have attractive, variegated leaves. Two good kinds are 'Golden King' and 'Silver Queen'. *Mahonia bealei*, another evergreen, has attractive leaves which are large and leathery. It may be possible to find a few soft blue flowers among the grass-like leaves of *Iris unguicularis*. The first of the winter heathers, *Erica carnea*, will now be flowering

Ilex aquifolium 'Golden King'. Hardy evergreen tree. Ht. 6–10 ft. Plant autumn or spring

Chamaecyparis lawsoniana lutea. Evergreen conifer. Height 30 ft. Plant autumn or spring

Iris unguicularis (winter iris). Hardy perennial. Height 15 in. Plant in September

Primula kewensis. Greenhouse perennial. Height 9 in. Plant in pots, spring and summer

Cyclamen persicum 'Shell Pink'. Greenhouse perennial. Height 12 in. Sow August, February

Fittonia argyroneura. Greenhouse perennial. Height 6 in. Plant in pots, spring and summer

Erica carnea (heather). Hardy evergreen shrub. Height 6–9 in. Plant autumn, spring

Jasminum nudiflorum. Hardy deciduous climber. Height 5–10 ft. Plant autumn or winter

Azalea indica (Indian azalea). Greenhouse evergreen shrub. Height 2–4 ft. Pot in spring

Aphelandra squarrosa louisae. Greenhouse evergreen shrub. Height 2–3 ft. Pot in spring

Mahonia bealei. Hardy evergreen shrub. Height 6–7 ft. Plant in autumn or spring

Primula obconica. Greenhouse perennial treated as annual. Height 9 in. Sow in spring

Begonia 'Queen Juliana'. Warm greenhouse perennial. Height 18 in. Pot in spring, summer

Peperomia sandersii. Greenhouse perennial. Height 9 in. Pot in spring and summer

Euphorbia pulcherrima. Greenhouse perennial. Height 1–6 ft. Pot in spring and summer

Codiaeum (croton). Warm greenhouse evergreen shrub. Height 3–10 ft. Pot in spring

January and February
COLOUR IN A COLD CLIMATE

Depending on the weather, it should be possible to pick a varied posy of flowers from the garden. The yellow winter jasmine, *Jasminum nudiflorum*, will have been in flower for several weeks, and there should be blooms to pick of the Christmas rose, *Helleborus niger*. Two shrubs that flower in winter are *Daphne mezereum* and *Chimonanthus fragrans*, often known as winter sweet; both have sweetly scented blossoms. The Chinese witch hazel, *Hamamelis mollis*, produces its yellow flowers right into March

Helleborus niger. Hardy evergreen perennial. Height 6–15 in. Plant in autumn or spring

Daphne mezereum. Hardy deciduous shrub. Height 3–4 ft. Plant in autumn or winter

Sempervivum (houseleek). Hardy perennial alpine. Height 2–6 in. Plant in spring

Chimonanthus fragrans (winter sweet). Hardy deciduous shrub. Height 8 ft. Plant winter

Hyacinthus hybrida (hyacinth). Hardy bulb. Height 12 in. Plant in early autumn

Eranthis hyemalis (winter aconite). Hardy tuber. Height 3 in. Plant in autumn or winter

Solanum capsicastrum. Greenhouse shrub. Height 12–24 in. Pot in spring and summer

Twelve months of gardening

A PLAN OF WORK FOR THE YEAR

The gardener works to the rhythms of nature, in an annual cycle. This section of the book is organised accordingly, giving all the advice needed for successful gardening month-by-month. The gardener's activity begins in March, when most plants start to grow after their winter dormancy. Each monthly section begins with an analysis of the weather—the major influence on the timing of garden tasks. Plant descriptions are included when possible in the planting month. Schedules of work are included under these headings, in the same order each month:

Lawns
Roses
Hardy herbaceous
    plants
Dahlias
Chrysanthemums
Gladioli
Irises
Lilies
Carnations and
    pinks

Sweet peas
Flowers from
    seed
Bulbs
Alpines
Water plants and
    pools
Greenhouses and
    frames
Trees and shrubs

Rhododendrons
    and azaleas
Hedges
Heathers
Fruit
Vegetables
Herbs
Patios and town
    gardens
House plants
General tasks

March

As the days lengthen and a stronger sun dries out the soil, planting begins and the gardener's year gets under way

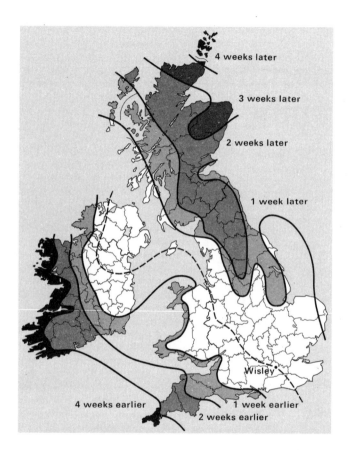

PROGRESS OF THE SEASON

The season in an average March may be earlier or later than at the Royal Horticultural Society's Gardens at Wisley, Surrey. The broken line joins places where the season is as advanced as it is at Wisley. As a rough guide, gardeners in the white areas can begin their programme at the beginning of March and can start sowing and planting out in mid-March. Gardeners to the north should wait for the number of weeks indicated. In the south-west, gardeners can begin before March. There is a time-lag of about two days for every 100 ft. rise in height

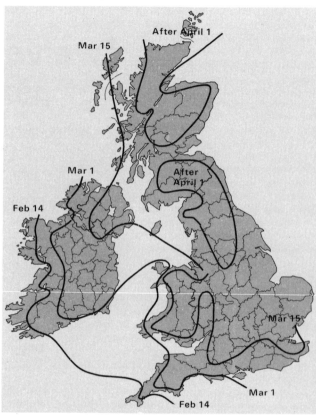

THE START OF SPRING

Over much of the British Isles spring arrives in March. After their winter resting period, plants resume growth when the daily mean temperature rises above 6°C (43°F), and the map shows the dates in an average year when this happens. To a gardener this means the time when the lawn starts to grow again, and sowing and planting out can begin. Spring arrives about mid-March in lowland England, but earlier in the west and south. In hilly country and the north it is usually April before plants begin to grow strongly in the garden

The weather in March

This month has the most pronounced variations from day to day, and the widest variations from year to year. The contrast between weather in the north and south is at its greatest.

In March depressions from across the Atlantic usually bring cold, strong, north-westerly winds, which can often reach gale force, especially on the western coasts. These winds may bring hail, sleet or snow showers to northern regions, and especially to high ground. The sun's rays are now beginning to grow stronger and sunshine hours are increasing, so that out of the wind, in the bright sun, it is warm. Mid-day temperatures at sea-level are about 10°C (50°F) in the midlands; but at night temperatures fall below 2°C (36°F), and there may be fog.

Occasionally warmer westerly to south-westerly winds arrive with a depression, and afternoon temperatures average 11–12°C (52–54°F) in the south; but although it is spring in the lowlands in Cornwall, it is still winter in northern Scotland. Widespread showers occur, but there is often less rain in March than in January and February; the second week of the month is sometimes one of the driest of the year in central and south-east England.

At other times cold north-easterly to easterly winds bring low, grey cloud to all areas, and snow to eastern regions and high ground. Afternoon temperatures seldom rise above 7°C (45°F); at night temperatures fall well below −1°C (30°F), and air frost is widespread and especially likely on high ground and in exposed places.

Frost is possible on most nights in March, because of the clear skies associated with the north-westerly winds and because of the north-easterly influence.

The gardener must take every advantage of dry spells in March to complete his spring cultivations; he must not be misled by short periods of warm weather into thinking that spring has finally arrived. It is often safer to delay sowings or plantings than to be caught by a subsequent cold spell.

A summary of the month's work

LAWNS

New lawns. Rake and treat seed bed, and apply pre-seeding fertiliser. Choose suitable seed mixture, and sow it at 1–2 oz. per sq. yd. Give the first mowing when the grass is 3 in. high.

Established lawns. Re-seed worn areas, and repair lawn edges which have crumbled. Aerate the lawn with a wire rake. Apply spring fertiliser. Cut grass when it is 2½–3 in. high. Control worms. Apply selective weedkillers when grass is growing actively. Control moss by improving drainage and aeration, and dress with mercurised moss compounds.

ROSES

Complete planting as soon as possible. Prune hybrid teas, floribundas, established miniatures, repeat-flowering climbers and repeat-flowering shrubs. Begin at the start of the month in the south; at the end of the month elsewhere. Cut out diseased or frost-damaged wood.

Under glass. Maintain ventilation. Water systemic insecticide into the soil. Feed with liquid or soluble plant food.

HARDY HERBACEOUS PLANTS

Check plant labels before they are obscured by new growth. If weather is dry, spread fertiliser on winter-dug ground and rake it in. Unpack plants on arrival from nurseries and dip roots in water if dry. If they cannot be planted, bed them in boxes of moist sand, peat or soil, or heel them in. If weather is mild and soil dry on the surface, plant home-raised seedlings, new plants and plants needing a move. Dig up host plants to get rid of perennial weeds. Watch for slugs in mild weather.

DAHLIAS

Prepare ground for dahlias by digging and dressing with bone-meal. Select a place where the dahlias will be in full sun and will not have to compete with other plants.

Under glass. Remove old tubers from storage and spray with tepid water to encourage new shoots, to be rooted as cuttings. Sow dahlia seeds.

CHRYSANTHEMUMS

Dig ground in preparation for planting, test for acidity, and add manure. Leave ground rough-dug until April or early May.

Under glass. In the south, move plants from the greenhouse to cold frames, covering against frost as necessary. Start to propagate most varieties, taking cuttings from old stools and rooting them in pots or boxes. Transfer cuttings to 3½ in. pots as soon as rooted.

GLADIOLI

Plant gladiolus corms, in rows for exhibition purposes, in colonies for decorating mixed borders. Plant a succession, to provide a continuous supply of blooms. Plant cormlets 2 in. deep in rows.

IRISES

Pull dead leaves off bearded irises and cut away brown spots or tips from new leaves. Examine rhizomes, cut away diseased parts, and dust cuts with dry powdered Bordeaux mixture. Loosen surface of soil around the plants and give a general fertiliser. Apply slug pellets: place them under foliage or a flat stone to hide them from birds and small mammals. Pick blooms of *I. unguicularis* regularly to avoid bird damage. Watch for virus symptoms among bulbous irises and burn affected plants.

LILIES

Mulch established beds. Protect young shoots from frost with cloches. Sow lily seeds outdoors in the south. Complete planting of bulbs. Prepare beds for lilies to be planted in autumn, following annuals during summer.

Under glass. Plant imported lilies in pots. Cease feeding forced lilies when the buds are about to open.

CARNATIONS AND PINKS

Order plants and seeds. Complete preparation of beds for spring planting. Stop modern pinks that are running to flower without making good side shoots. Dress plants put in last autumn with sulphate of potash or bonfire ash. Plant pot-grown border carnations and pinks. Spray against aphids, thrips, caterpillars and carnation flies. Apply zineb against rust and leaf spot.

Under glass. Prick out seedlings of annual and perpetual flowering carnations. Give perpetuals their first or second potting and their first stopping, as applicable. Cut blooms and disbud flower stems. Control pests, using HCH sprays or smokes against aphids and caterpillars, dicofol combination spray against red spiders. Control rust and leaf spot with zineb or benomyl.

SWEET PEAS

Plant out autumn-sown seedlings, in double rows where they are to be grown on the cordon system. Plant bush-grown seedlings in double rows, supported by 6 ft. sticks. Put slug bait round plants.

Under glass. Make spring sowings.

FLOWERS FROM SEED

Complete seed orders. Plant out hardy perennials raised from seed. Sow the hardier sorts of hardy annuals outdoors. Fork over ground to be sown with hardy annuals and give a fertiliser dressing. Sow seeds in rows to make thinning and hoeing easier. Thin seedlings when they have two or three leaves.

Under glass. Sow half-hardy annuals. Move forward batches of half-hardy annuals to cold frames. Protect frames containing tender plants from severe frosts.

BULBS

Choose new varieties for planting in late summer. Remove flower heads from daffodils as they fade. Plant out bulbs grown in pots which have finished flowering. Plant acidantheras in mild districts. Lift, divide, and re-plant crowded snowdrops. In cold districts plant de Caen and St. Brigid anemones.

Under glass. Give adequate water and fertiliser to hippeastrums and clivias in flower.

ALPINES

Firm plants loosened by frost. Apply slug pellets: place them under foliage or flat stones to hide them from birds and small mammals. Watch for germination in boxes of seeds placed outside for weathering, and move the choicer kinds to an unheated greenhouse or frame. Plant nursery-raised alpines as soon as possible after delivery. Plants that flower from June onwards may show signs of die-back after winter, so propagate by division where possible. Renew by division carpeting plants such as arenarias and raoulias.

Under glass. Plant out root cuttings in pots or boxes when they make leaves. Sow seeds of quicker-growing alpines in a frame or cold greenhouse.

WATER PLANTS AND POOLS

When the ice has thawed, drain three-quarters of the water and replace with fresh. Remove algae. Remove the tops of marginal plants that were left on for winter protection. Top-dress water lilies and marginals, if growth was poor last year. Plant a new bog garden. Begin regular feeding of fish if they are lively. Construct new garden pools in an open, sunny position.

GREENHOUSES AND FRAMES

Pot on over-wintered annuals such as schizanthus and antirrhinums from 3 in. pots into 5 in. pots. Remove old wood and overcrowded shoots from abutilons. Sow tomatoes for planting in an unheated house in May. Prepare a bed in a cool greenhouse for planting tomatoes in April. Start canna roots into growth in moist compost. Plant hippeastrum bulbs in 6 in. pots. Give liquid fertiliser every ten days to regal and zonal pelargoniums. Control insect pests with HCH and derris sprays. Near the end of the month, pot on begonias and gloxinias into 5 in. pots. Transfer *Campanula pyramidalis* plants to 9 in. pots. Prick out all seedlings when large enough to handle.

TREES AND SHRUBS

Plant deciduous trees and shrubs until the end of the month in fine weather. Top-dress young and newly planted trees and shrubs with old manure, peat or compost. Plant pot-grown clematis and other wall shrubs. Begin planting evergreens in prepared ground at the end of the month.

Propagation in the open. Layer shoots of amelanchier, chimonanthus, celastrus, rhus and syringa in pots of sandy loam sunk near the parent plants. Sever offsets from *Amelanchier canadensis* and pot up. Divide roots of *Hypericum calycinum* and lathyrus, and re-plant. Separate rooted suckers of kerria and plant in flowering positions.

Under glass. Sow seeds of clematis, cotoneaster and other shrubs in a cold frame or cool greenhouse. Sow seeds of eccremocarpus and *Lavatera olbia rosea*. Prick out seedlings in pots and keep in a cold frame until autumn, watering well in dry weather. Increase camellias by leaf cuttings. Take root cuttings of *Campsis radicans, Rhus typhina* and romneya.

Pruning. Lightly prune shrubs damaged by heavy snowfalls and frost, removing dead and damaged wood. Thin out old wood from berberis, hedera and *Hypericum patulum henryi*. Cut hard back previous year's shoots of *Caryopteris clandonensis*, deciduous ceanothus and *Hypericum calycinum*. Cut fuchsia and *Lavatera olbia rosea* back to live wood. Lightly prune *Lonicera fragrantissima* when it has finished flowering. Cut hard back willows grown for winter bark colour.

RHODODENDRONS AND AZALEAS

Prepare ground for planting. Start planting as soon as cold weather ceases. Water young plants when growth starts, if weather is dry.

HEDGES

Plant all types of hedges, except broad-leaved evergreens. Evenly space the plants, in a straight line, in holes adequate for their roots. Remove weeds from hedge bottoms by pulling, hoeing or using paraquat-diquat weedkiller. Remove brambles and unwanted tree seedlings. Complete hard pruning of old hedges.

HEATHERS

Plant heathers between now and May, selecting an open position with neutral or acid soil, except for lime-tolerant species. Prepare ground by digging, removing perennial weeds, and incorporating peat and bone-meal. Space the plants 12–18 in. apart, according to type, and plant firmly. Propagate heathers by layering or taking heel cuttings.

FRUIT

Complete planning of new fruit gardens. Complete planting as soon as soil conditions permit, particularly of trees which were heeled in. Firm trees and bushes lifted by frost. Complete pruning of trees and bushes. Feed established trees and bushes growing in cultivated soil. Spray apples, cherries, peaches and nectarines, pears, plums and damsons. Train new shoots of blackberries and loganberries on to wires. Protect flowers on wall-trained peaches and nectarines and pollinate artificially if insects are scarce. Plant raspberries and strawberries.

VEGETABLES

Sow seeds for main crop of Brussels sprouts, and set out hardened-off plants. In the north, plant out over-wintered Brussels sprouts. Sow parsnips. In the south, plant early potatoes from the middle of the month. Sow salad onions and radishes. Sow seeds of late summer cabbages. Continue sowing early, round-seeded peas. Sow leeks if raising your own plants. Sow summer spinach.
Under glass. Sow carrots under cloches, after dressing the seed.
Less common vegetables. Complete shallot planting. Sow kohl rabi seeds. Plant asparagus. Dress established asparagus beds with farmyard manure. Plant Jerusalem artichokes.

HERBS

Prepare a seed bed as soon as soil is warm. Sow small amounts of chervil, chives, dill, marjoram, parsley and sorrel. Layer shoots of pot marjoram and divide fennel roots. Split old clumps of bergamot and sorrel.
Under glass. Sow basil in a seed box at 13°C (55°F).

PATIOS AND TOWN GARDENS

Choose containers for patio gardening. Raise window boxes above sills with wooden blocks to help drainage and discourage pests. Fasten them in position securely, and fit a drip tray where water might mark walls. Construct raised beds, and leave soil-filled gaps in paving. Move container-grown plants into prominent positions as they come into bloom. Buy or mix soil in preparation for spring planting. Treat wooden boxes and troughs with preservative, and paint all metal parts. Place layers of crocks, washed clinker and turves in containers, then fill with soil. Plunge a succession of potted plants in larger containers to provide a constantly changing display.

HOUSE PLANTS

Give a little more water to plants as days lengthen. Move delicate plants or those in flower from south-facing to west-facing windows. Apply liquid fertiliser sparingly to plants in bud or flower. Prune climbers by cutting out weak or diseased shoots, tie in long growths, and remove dead leaves. Pot on plants which have become too large for their pots. Remove offsets from such plants as *Vriesia fenestralis* and pot them separately. Plunge the pots of those plants which like humid conditions inside larger containers and fill the space between with moist peat in readiness for warmer weather.

GENERAL TASKS

Complete all digging. Kill weeds on paths and drives with paraquat-diquat and keep them clean with a total weedkiller. Destroy moss on paths with a 4 per cent tar-oil wash. Apply slug pellets: place them under foliage or flat stones to hide them from birds and small mammals. Check ties securing plants.

Plants to enjoy in March

Border and rock garden plants in flower	Pieris japonica
Bergenia	Prunus cerasifera
Chionodoxa	Ribes (flowering currant)
Crocus	Spiraea thunbergii
Eranthis (winter aconite)	
Erythronium	**House plants in flower, depending on position and culture**
Galanthus (snowdrop)	Aphelandra
Helleborus corsicus	Begonia semperflorens
Helleborus niger	Cyclamen persicum
Helleborus orientalis	Impatiens petersiana
Hyacinthus	Saintpaulia
Iris danfordiae	
Muscari (grape hyacinth)	**Greenhouse plants in flower**
Narcissus	Calceolaria
Polyanthus	Cineraria
Saxifraga	Clivia
Scilla	Freesia
Tulipa kaufmanniana	Hippeastrum
	Mimosa (acacia)
Trees and shrubs in flower	Primula kewensis
Camellia japonica	Primula malacoides
Chaenomeles japonica	Primula obconica
(Japanese quince)	
Corylopsis	**Vegetables in season**
Daphne mezereum	Artichoke, Jerusalem
Forsythia	Broccoli, purple-sprouting
Hamamelis	Brussels sprouts
Lonicera fragrantissima	Carrots
Magnolia stellata	Leek
Mahonia	Radish
Parrotia	Spinach

Lawns

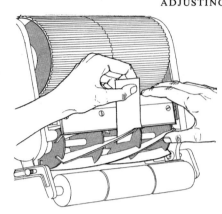

Turn the cylinder to check whether it will cut paper evenly along its length. Tighten or slacken the adjusting screws as necessary

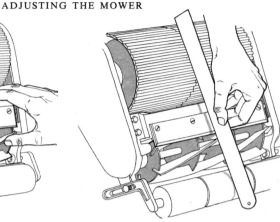

To determine cutting height, lay a rule across the front and rear rollers, and measure between the rule and the fixed blade

NEW LAWNS

After the preliminary autumn digging (see NOVEMBER), the lawn seed bed should be ready for its final preparation. The winter frosts will have broken down the soil, making it easy to produce a good tilth. If, however, you have been unable to give the ground an autumn digging, thoroughly dig the site over on a fine dry day. Turn old rough grass face downwards and remove the roots of perennial weeds such as bindweed and couch grass.

Rake the seed bed several times in different directions to produce a fine tilth and level surface. (For seed bed preparation see NOVEMBER.) This will also remove many stones and kill annual weeds. Thoroughly tread the soil to consolidate the ground and produce a firm, even surface.

Some weed seeds may germinate after the seed bed has been prepared but before the seed is sown. These can most safely be cleared by watering with paraquat weedkiller.

To aid establishment of the new seedlings apply a pre-seeding fertiliser evenly over the seed bed area and lightly rake it into the surface. A suitable pre-seeding mixture is: sulphate of ammonia 2 parts, superphosphate 4 parts, bonemeal 4 parts, sulphate of potash 1 part.

Apply the fertiliser evenly at 3 oz. per sq. yd. and rake it into the top inch or so of the soil surface.

Seed mixtures

When selecting a seed mixture, consider the amount of wear anticipated, the degree of shade and the cost of the seed. Most mixtures consist of three or four species, usually blends of tufted and creeping grasses, which will grow well together and mature at different seasons. Coarse ryegrass mixtures are suitable if the lawn is to be subjected to heavy wear and tear. Crested dogstail in a mixture improves the quality of a lawn. New hybrid ryegrasses, such as 'Hunter', can make a good-looking, drought-resistant, hard-wearing lawn. A number of leading seed firms supply balanced mixtures for both general and special purposes. Alternatively, if you prefer to have one mixed specially, the accompanying table shows suitable blends for a variety of purposes.

About a week after applying the fertiliser, sow the seed at 1–2 oz. per sq. yd. after making a final check that the seed bed is level and free from stones, and

GRASS SEED PERCENTAGES FOR LAWNS

	Top quality lawns		Good domestic lawns		Shaded situations		Lawns in town centres
	(alternatives)		wet soil	dry soil	wet soil	dry soil	
Agrostis tenuis	30	30	10	20		30	
Chewing's fescue	70	30	60	40			
S59 fescue		40	10	20			
Fine-leaved fescue						20	
Crested dogstail			10	20			
Timothy			10				
Agrostis stolonifera					20		
Ryegrass S23					50		40
Poa trivalis					30		30
Poa annua							30
Sheep's fescue						40	
Creeping red fescue						10	

has a good fine tilth. Delay until the weather is beginning to warm up, possibly towards the end of the month. Broadcast the seed, distributing half in one direction and the remainder at right angles. Lightly rake the surface to cover the seed to a depth of not more than $\frac{1}{4}$ in. On light soils, under dry conditions, give a final rolling, but do not roll on heavy soils, since there is a danger that the soil and seed will be picked up by the roller unless the soil is extremely dry.

Disease symptoms

The seed will germinate in about 14 days. If it has been already dressed with a bird repellent, little trouble may be expected from birds.

Keep a careful watch for any sign of post-germination damping-off, which may be recognised by the appearance of brightly-coloured red and purple patches of collapsed grass. Damping-off is encouraged by humid weather when seed has been sown too thickly. Dressing the seed with thiram or captan powder before sowing will reduce the risk of this disease. When it does occur, it is difficult to control, but watering the whole area with a proprietary brand of Cheshunt compound, using 1 oz. to $\frac{1}{2}$ gall. of water per sq. yd., will help to check its spread.

First mowing

When the grass is about 3 in. high, give the first light mowing. This will firm the seedlings in the ground, but if there is any tendency to pull the seedlings out, the ground may be too wet or the mower not sharp enough.

Check the sharpness and adjustment of the mower by placing a piece of newspaper between the cutting cylinder and the sole plate. If the paper is cut easily, the mower is sharp enough and correctly adjusted. Use a side-wheel mower for preference and remove only the top $\frac{1}{2}$ in. of leaf. This encourages tillering (branching from the base of the grass), thereby ensuring that it spreads over the soil surface.

To save time when handling grass clippings, place one or more large squares of hessian or polythene in convenient places and empty the grass-box on to them. When mowing is completed these are easily carried away for composting or for use as a mulch. Alternatively, collect in plastic bags.

ESTABLISHED LAWNS

Re-seed worn areas in the lawn, first levelling any depressions and providing a fine tilth. Follow the instructions given for seeding a new lawn.

Continue aerating the lawn, raking it vigorously a number of times in directions at right angles to each other. This will help to scatter worm casts, remove dead grass, debris and moss, and allow air and water to enter the surface of the turf. This treatment is important to maintain a healthy turf surface and aid drainage, so that rain is not allowed to remain on the surface and become absorbed by the debris, creating conditions ideal for disease.

Fertiliser dressing

Towards the end of the month, if the weather is warm, apply a spring fertiliser, preferably using a hand distributor set to provide an even application at the correct rate. Uneven application will produce local scorching and an uneven growth of grass. There are many suitable proprietary mixtures. Apply according to the manufacturer's instructions.

Straightening edges

To cut a clean, straight edge where border and lawn meet, place a plank on the grass beside the border, stand on this, and cut the grass with an edging tool, using the plank as a guide and sloping the cut away from you slightly to prevent crumbling.

COMMON ERRORS IN APPLYING FERTILISER

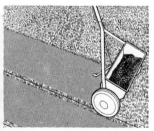

Bands of grass will remain untreated unless wheel tracks (shown by straight lines) overlap

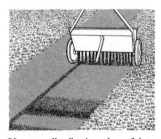

Uneven distribution, harmful to grass, results from jerky motion or from stopping and starting

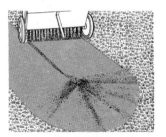

Avoid sharp turns. Instead, close the hopper, or lift it off the ground, at the ends of the rows

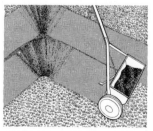

Right-angle turns, too, lead to gaps and overlaps. Always work in straight overlapping strips

REPAIRING A DAMAGED LAWN EDGE

Using a board as a guide, cut round the damaged area with a half-moon edging tool

Cut the strip into sections about 18 in. long and lift the turves with a spade or turfing iron

Replace the turves, turning them round so that their damaged edges face inwards

Cut a fresh edge. Make good damaged areas with sifted soil. Sow seed on bare patches

To straighten a wavering edge, lay a garden line tautly in the correct position. Cut away a 3 in. strip of lawn and move this level with the line. Fill in the bare space left with sifted soil and grass seed, level, and firm with your feet.

Where a lawn edge has crumbled or become worn, cut out the damaged area as a square or rectangle and turn it round so that there is sound turf at the edge. Sow grass seed on the bare patch and cover lightly with sifted soil.

First spring mowing
Cut the grass when it is about $2\frac{1}{2}$–3 in. high, setting the blades high. The weather should be dry. First scatter any worm casts with a cane or rake. Check the mower for correct adjustment and ensure that the blades are sharp; this is essential to produce an even cut. Always mow with the box on at this time of year, as cuttings left on the turf surface will encourage disease.

Fusarium patch disease can occur at this time of the year and may be recognised by collapsed areas of fawn-coloured, waterlogged, dead grass which develop under damp conditions. Sometimes the patches, which may be from 1 to 12 in. in diameter, fuse and a fine pinky-white mass of fungal threads develops over the patch. It is an indication that drainage and general turf management need improving.

Treatment of fusarium
Fusarium, recognised by the grass blades turning brown and collapsing and by a white mould, is the most common disease. Treat patches that appear, and surrounding areas, with benomyl. To harden the grass and make it more resistant to disease, apply sulphate of iron at $\frac{1}{4}$ oz. per sq. yd., mixed with 4 oz. sand.

Worms may be troublesome at this time of the year, throwing up a large number of casts on the surface. Control worms with a proprietary brand of derris, carbaryl or chlordane (see OCTOBER).

Selective weedkillers
A variety of selective weedkillers will control most lawn weeds. Apply one or two weeks after the spring fertiliser application. Most of the selective weedkillers are based on mixtures of MCPA, 2,4-D, 2,4,5-T and CMPP. Many lawn weeds, including creeping buttercups, plantains, dandelions and daisies, can be eliminated with one, or at most two, applications. Others, such as pearlwort, clover and ragwort, may sometimes require double doses and/or repeated applications.

To get the best effect, apply selective weedkillers during periods of active growth in damp, warm conditions, and take care that they do not drift on to vegetable or flower beds, where crops and plants can be damaged or killed.

Controlling moss
Selective weedkillers have no effect on moss, the presence of which is an indication of bad physical conditions, such as waterlogging and compaction of the turf, and indicates that attention should be paid to better drainage, aeration and general management. Use a mercurised moss control, which may be best applied at this time of the year and will usually control moss for a year or even longer.

Roses

Complete planting as early in the month as possible, preferably in beds prepared during the autumn or winter (see OCTOBER). If the beds have not been prepared, dig them to spade depth, incorporating garden compost, proprietary forest bark or peat, and a handful of bone-meal to each foot run of trench. Prune bush and standard roses before planting to make them easier to handle, and also cut back damaged roots and roots more than 12 in. long.

Make each planting hole wide enough to take the spread-out roots, and of such a depth that the point where the green stem emerges from the brown rootstock is 1 in. below the level of the surrounding soil. Incorporate a mixture of peat and bone-meal in the bottoms of the holes (for detailed planting advice, see NOVEMBER).

UNDER GLASS

On dry, frost-free days maintain ventilation to keep a circulation of fresh air, but try to maintain a day temperature of 21°C (70°F) and a night temperature of 16°C (61°F).

Spray during the day

On bright days spray the plants with clean water during the morning or afternoon so as to induce a moist atmosphere and encourage dormant buds to break into growth. Do not spray during the evening, because the foliage should be dry by the time the temperature has dropped at nightfall.

A systemic insecticide watered into the soil will keep plants free from greenfly for a month.

Feed once a week with a proprietary liquid or soluble plant food. To obtain top-quality blooms, also spray the foliage with the plant food solution once every two weeks.

PRUNING: THE RIGHT WAY TO CUT

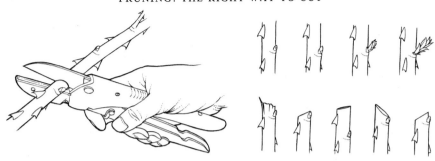

Slant the cut from ¼ in. above a dormant bud to bring the cut level with the top of the outward-facing bud on opposite side of the stem

Top row: Prune to buds resembling the two on the left; the others are too far advanced. *Bottom row:* Only the final cut is correct

Pruning programme

In the south, in western coastal areas of England and Wales and on the south-west coast of Scotland, start pruning early in March, in frost-free weather. In north-east England and central and north-east Scotland, and in gardens subject to late, hard frosts, delay pruning until the end of the month.

If roses were not pruned every year they would become unshapely, tangled masses of diseased and dead wood, with their blooms becoming progressively smaller, on weak shoots, and their lives shortened considerably. Pruning encourages healthy, shapely growth.

Prune newly planted and established hybrid tea and floribunda bushes, established repeat-flowering shrub roses and repeat-flowering climbers. Established miniature roses should also be pruned now, as well as newly planted and established standards. Climbers and weeping standards which bloom only once in summer should not be pruned (see colour section, AUGUST).

When pruning, use sharp secateurs to ensure a clean cut. Make each cut slope back from ¼ in. above a dormant bud to a point on the opposite side of the stem level with the top of the bud.

Make the cut at an angle to shed rain, which might otherwise set up disease, or it might become frozen in winter and damage the wood.

Prune to an outward-pointing dormant bud so that, as the new stem develops, it will also grow outwards and leave the centre of the plant open. Stems allowed to grow inwards, filling the centre of the plant, become a breeding-ground in summer for pests and diseases, disfiguring the foliage and the blooms.

Cut out completely any dead, diseased or frost-damaged wood. In healthy wood the pruning cut is a creamy-green colour; a brown cut shows that the wood is diseased or frost-damaged, and further cuts must be made until healthy wood is reached or the stem removed completely. Frost-damaged wood is also much lighter in weight than healthy wood and the thorns are brown and brittle, like dead wood.

Signs of disease

Look out for small brown disease patches in otherwise healthy green stems. If the stems have been slow to drop their leaves, following a mild autumn, frozen rain lodged in the angle of leaf-stalk and stem is liable to damage

41

PRUNING AN ESTABLISHED HYBRID TEA

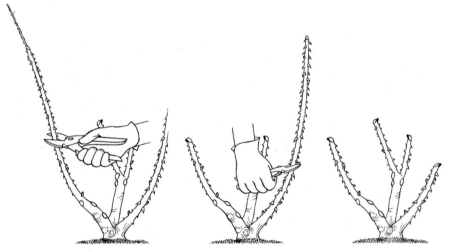

In addition to main stems, an established bush will have a number of twiggy shoots and perhaps some diseased growth

First remove dead, diseased or frost-damaged growths; also crossing stems. Cut twiggy shoots back to the main stem

Prune main stems to half their length, except for one, which should be cut to 6 in. above ground level (*centre illustration*)

Pruning completed (*right*) with each of the main stems cut back to an outward-pointing bud, so that the shape is maintained

the dormant bud and set up disease. Prune to healthy wood below any sign of disease.

Cut thin, twiggy side shoots back to the main stem. A side shoot is always thinner than the stem from which it grows, so aim to leave sturdy stems to produce the new growth.

When pruning roses, line the wheelbarrow with a large sheet of strong polythene and throw the trimmings into this, cutting longer pieces in half. It is a simple matter to lift out the polythene by the corners and tip the prunings on to the bonfire heap.

In cool northern areas and in wet western areas, paint pruning cuts which are more than $\frac{1}{2}$ in. across with a protective sealing compound.

Bearing these basic general rules in mind, carry out your pruning for the various types of roses as follows:

Hybrid tea bushes
Newly planted
Prune to dormant buds 4–6 in. above ground level. This hard pruning will enable the root system to become established before new, strong shoots grow from the base to form the bush.

Established
Cut out dead, diseased or damaged wood.
Prune twiggy side shoots back to the main stem. Prune strong, healthy stems back to half or a third of their length, except for one which should be pruned down to a dormant bud 4–6 in. above ground level to encourage vigorous new growth from the base.

Floribunda bushes
Newly planted
Prune to dormant buds 6 in. above ground level. This hard pruning will enable the root system to become established before new, strong shoots grow from the base to form the bush.

PRUNING A NEWLY PLANTED FLORIBUNDA

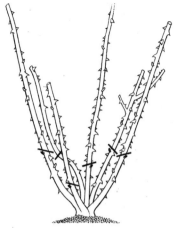

Pruned hard back, a newly planted floribunda will make fresh root growth before producing new shoots from near the base. The illustra-

tions show a typical nursery-grown bush before and after being pruned hard back to dormant buds 6 in. above ground level

PRUNING AN ESTABLISHED FLORIBUNDA

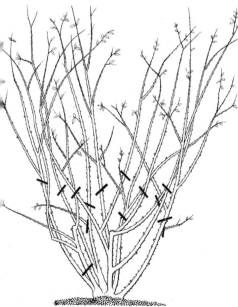

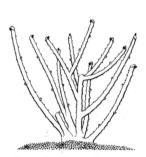

A variety of only moderate vigour, 'Lilac Charm', before and after pruning. The first step was to remove the large number of

twiggy and crossing shoots. To encourage new growth, main stems have been cut back harder than with a stronger-growing variety

Established

Cut out dead, diseased or frost-damaged wood.

Prune twiggy side shoots back to the main stem. Prune about a third of the growth from new green shoots which grew from close to ground level last year.

Prune older, darker-coloured stems back to about half their length, except for one which should be pruned to a dormant bud about 6 in. above ground level to encourage new growth.

Shrub bushes, repeat-flowering
Newly planted
No pruning is required.

Established
Cut out dead or frost-damaged wood. No other pruning is necessary other than occasionally to keep them to the shape and space desired. An old plant that has been allowed to grow too tall and tends to be bare of foliage lower down should have one or two of the main stems pruned to 12 in. from the ground to encourage new shoots to grow from the base.

Climbers, repeat-flowering
Newly planted
No pruning, apart from the removal of dead tips from the stems.

Established
Cut out dead, diseased or frost-damaged wood. Prune twiggy side shoots back to the main stem. Prune thicker side shoots back to about half their length.

Miniature roses
Newly planted
No pruning, apart from the removal of dead or diseased twigs.

Established
Prune main stems back to about half their length. Cut out any remaining dead, diseased or frost-damaged wood.

Hybrid tea and floribunda standards

Newly planted

Prune main stems of the top growth back to 6–8 in. and side shoots to 1–2 in., pruning to dormant buds pointing outwards or upwards in the directions in which new shoots are needed to form a shapely, balanced head.

Established

Cut out dead, diseased or frost-damaged wood. Prune twiggy side shoots back to the main stem. Cut all remaining stems back to about half their length, pruning to dormant buds pointing outwards or upwards in the directions in which new shoots are needed to maintain a shapely, balanced head.

Climbers, ramblers and weeping standards

Varieties, such as 'American Pillar' and 'Excelsa', which have only one flush of flowers during summer should not be pruned until September. These types of roses will flower the following summer on the new, non-flowering shoots which are produced in the current season.

PRUNING A STANDARD

This floribunda standard, 'Iceberg', has a number of twiggy side shoots which require cutting back to the main stems. *Centre:* All but one of the main stems have been pruned to half their length, the cuts being made to outward-pointing buds. *Right:* After pruning

Hardy herbaceous plants

A properly planned herbaceous border can be the focal point of any garden, giving a succession of blooms from early spring to the frosts of late autumn. Tough, virtually disease-free and lasting for years in the same position, the hardy herbaceous plants need the minimum of work for the maximum of results, from the lofty spires of delphiniums and lupins to the sweet-scented mats of pinks round the edge of the border.

This month, begin by checking plant labels before they are obscured by new growth.

Clear dead sticks which have blown on to paths adjoining herbaceous beds or borders from nearby trees. Prune trees, shrubs or hedges which overhang herbaceous beds or borders, if this has not already been done (see DECEMBER).

Apply fertiliser

If the weather is dry enough, apply fertiliser over winter-dug ground, and rake it in (see FEBRUARY). Avoid treading on naturally heavy, wet soil or on soil that is sticky from thawing frost or rain. Footmarks compress the soil, which will become wetter still if there is more rain, or will dry hard if there is a period of dry weather, because the essential air spaces within the soil have been lost.

Unpacking and heeling in

Unpack immediately plants arriving from nurserymen by post or rail. If the roots feel or appear dry, dip them at once in water. If the plants are not to be planted at once, bed them temporarily in a box of moistened sand, soil or peat, and place them outdoors in a shady place protected from the wind.

TREATMENT OF NEW PLANTS

Remove the wrapping as soon as possible after delivery, and dip the roots in a bucket of water if they appear dry

If you cannot plant them at once, lay the plants in a V-shaped trench, opened with a spade, with their roots well below soil level

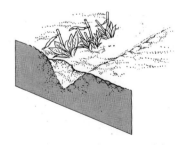

Replace the soil over the roots, applying water when they are partly covered if the roots or soil are dry, and firming with the foot

Alternatively, place the plants in a trench deep and wide enough to take the roots comfortably. Place the plants in the trench with their roots well down. If they are dry, water them when the soil is partly replaced.

If the weather is mild and the soil is reasonably dry on the surface, begin to plant home-raised seedlings, new plants and existing plants in need of re-planting which show signs of early growth. These are most likely to be kinds that flower in early summer, including delphiniums, pyrethrums, geums and lupins. March is the best of the spring planting months, except for late-flowering and slightly tender kinds and those that are slow to recover from winter dormancy (see APRIL). (The OCTOBER section gives general planting advice, but there are certain differences between autumn and spring planting.)

The need for water

In spring, the process of extraction of moisture by roots as well as by evaporation begins, but the soil is usually moist enough in March to make the watering of new plantings unnecessary. On light soils, however, especially in the east, it can be so dry that the continuing loss of moisture from the soil must be taken into account. The dry soil may trickle back into the plant hole, and the plants may suffer if there is no rain for a week or two. Watering the soil surface is seldom satisfactory.

It is much safer and in the end less troublesome to puddle them in at the time of planting. Make planting holes large enough to take the roots, and fill them with water from a spouted watering can. After watering, some soil will fall back into the holes, and should be removed. Insert the plant, and replace the damp soil round the roots, firming with your fingers as you go. Then firm 1 or 2 in. of dry topsoil round the plants.

STAGES IN PLANTING

Using a trowel, take out a hole sufficiently broad and deep to hold the plant's roots without cramping them

On light, dry soil, fill the hole with water. Watering is seldom needed this month on medium or heavy soil, as the soil is still damp

When the water has drained away, set the plant in position, and firm damp soil round the roots with your fingers

Draw drier soil round the base of the plant, firming it so as to leave the surface level

Renewed growth may reveal the presence of perennial weeds among old plants in the border. Weeds such as ground elder, couch and creeping grass often lurk in old plants, and the only way to destroy them is to dig up the host plants. Shake the plants fairly free of soil and, if they are large and tough, carefully divide them using two forks back to back as levers. Re-plant the divisions only when no vestige of the weed remains. It is better to destroy a whole plant than to harbour the smallest piece of a weed which may become a nucleus of further infestation.

In the second week of March, remove the protective covering of leaves from tender plants (see NOVEMBER).

Destroy slugs

Watch out for slugs during mild spring weather. The smaller grey slugs are the most frequent destroyers of herbaceous plants. They usually retreat to the nearest cover during the day. They eat the young leaves of plants, and leave a trail of white mucous film—the distinguishing mark of both slugs and snails —while foraging at night. Destroy the pests by putting down slug pellets or methiocarb.

Make a note of plants or groups which have become overgrown, invasive or diseased, so that you remember to re-plant or replace them with other kinds. Record interesting plants seen at shows, or on visits to gardens, which you may wish to order.

Dahlias

Dahlias provide some of the most brilliant colour in the garden, from July until the first frosts of October. The colours range from the deepest crimson to yellow and brilliant white, and the shapes vary from the broad rays of the cactus varieties to the tight-packed

blooms of the pompons. But they do not grow well if they are planted in a mixed border of herbaceous plants. So, whether they are to be grown to provide colour in the garden or cut flowers for the house, find a place for them where they will not have to compete with other plants. They prefer to grow in full sun.

Dahlias will thrive in any soil that is neither too acid nor too alkaline, but they are gross feeders. Dig plenty of organic material, such as compost, into the soil and give a dressing of about 8 oz. of bone-meal per sq. yd.

Planting time is towards the end of May in sheltered and warm areas, or by the first fortnight in June in the north of England and in Scotland.

UNDER GLASS

Remove the old tubers from storage in your shed or garage and spray them lightly as often as possible (every day is ideal) with tepid water. This will encourage them to produce new shoots for rooting in a heated greenhouse or frame.

When the shoots are 3–4 in. long, cut them off carefully with a sharp knife,

TAKING DAHLIA CUTTINGS

Remove short, sturdy shoots, 3–4 in. long, cutting them off as near the base as possible with a sharp knife or razor blade

Remove the lower pair of leaves, and make a clean cut across the stem just below the joint from which they were growing

Dip the base of each cutting in hormone rooting powder and insert 1 in. deep in boxes or small pots, using a proprietary compost

To conserve moisture and warmth, place polythene bags over the pots or boxes, or place the containers in large boxes covered with glass

as near the base as possible. Then remove any lower leaves and cut the stem
cleanly across just below a joint. Dip
the cuttings in hormone rooting powder
and insert about 1 in. deep in John
Innes potting compost No. 1, or a proprietary soil-less compost, in boxes or
singly in small pots. Water them in, and
keep them shaded and watered until
they have begun to root.

They will root more quickly if the
pots or boxes are placed in a large box
covered by a pane of glass, or in a transparent polythene bag, to conserve
warmth and moisture. On hot days place
brown paper over the glass.

Near the end of the month, sow home-
saved or nurseryman's dahlia seeds—bedding, cactus, decorative and pompom
types (see SEPTEMBER and OCTOBER) — in
pans or boxes of John Innes seed compost
or a proprietary soil-less compost. Scatter
the seeds thinly and cover with a further
$\frac{1}{4}$ in. of compost. Place the containers in
plastic bags and stand them in a greenhouse or propagating frame heated to
16–18°C (61–64°F). Remove the plastic
bags as soon as the seeds germinate,
pricking out the seedlings into boxes
when they are large enough to handle.

Chrysanthemums

Chrysanthemums grow best in soil well
supplied with organic matter, such as
farmyard manure, moist peat, spent hops
or well composted garden refuse. Now
is the time to dig the ground, make a
test for lime, and apply the chosen
manure. A 2 in. dressing each year is
about right, but take care not to bury it
more than 6 in. deep.

Chrysanthemums do not like soil which
is very acid (below pH 5·0) or very
alkaline (above pH 7·5); pH 6·8 is ideal.
Spent mushroom compost, which contains chalk, is not suitable for chrysanthemums, unless the soil needs lime.

CHRYSANTHEMUM CUTTINGS

Cuttings taken near soil level are best.
Choose healthy shoots about $2\frac{1}{2}$ in. long,
severing them $\frac{1}{2}$ in. above the soil surface

Remove the lower pair of leaves and cut
across the stem just beneath the bottom leaf
joint. Dip the end in hormone rooting powder

Leave the ground rough-dug, waiting
until April or early May, depending on
the weather, for the final preparation.

UNDER GLASS

In the south, move plants in small pots
from the greenhouse to a cold frame as
soon as possible (see FEBRUARY), but
have mats or sacking ready to cover the
frames at night in case of frost.

March is the main month for chrysanthemum propagation, although indoor
exhibition varieties should have been
propagated earlier, in January and
February, and some of the early-flowering and late-planted Christmas varieties
are left until April and May. (In chrysanthemum terminology 'exhibition'
refers to a group of large-flowered
varieties, not necessarily grown to be
exhibited.) Cuttings of mid-season and
late varieties grown in the greenhouse
border are propagated in June.

All chrysanthemums are best grown
from newly rooted cuttings. Plants increased by division will be inferior.

Cuttings are taken from the old plant
or stool. Select shoots about $\frac{1}{8}$ in. in
diameter and $2\frac{1}{2}$ in. long, with evenly
spaced leaves of good colour. They must

be free from insects and obvious disease,
with no signs of buds at the tips.

Cuttings taken from old plants at or
very near to ground level tend to root
more quickly and make the best plants,
but stem cuttings also give satisfactory
results. Cuttings must not be tough and
wiry. If in doubt, remove the cuttings
by breaking them off the old plant
rather than cutting them off. If they are
too tough to break, they are unsuitable.

Rooting cuttings

Root the chrysanthemum cuttings in
pots or boxes containing a mixture, by
volume, of two-thirds fine peat and one-
third washed sharp sand or perlite. Add 1
oz. of garden lime and $\frac{1}{2}$ oz. of a balanced
general fertiliser per bushel. Thoroughly
moisten the peat and mix the ingredients
carefully.

Remove the bottom leaves from each
cutting and trim the lower end, just below
the joint. Dip the lower ends of the
cuttings in a hormone rooting powder.
This aids the formation of an even root
system.

Using a stick or unsharpened pencil to
make the holes, insert the cuttings $\frac{3}{4}$ in.
deep and $2\frac{1}{2}$ in. apart in the rooting

mixture. Settle them in by soaking them gently, using a fine rose until the water lies on top of the compost.

Stand the cuttings over gentle heat—about 13°C (55°F)—and shade them in sunny weather. Cover with a sheet of transparent polythene to conserve moisture and heat. During sunny weather spray the cuttings lightly with clean water, morning and early afternoon.

At the beginning of the rooting period the cuttings will appear limp, but they will eventually look greener and show signs of growth. When this happens, but not before, water them again.

Pot cuttings

Transfer cuttings to 3 in. or $3\frac{1}{2}$ in. pots as soon as they are rooted, except for plants propagated in April and May, which can be planted direct into their flowering quarters. Pot cuttings before the roots become long and straggly. An inch of root all round the base of each stem is ample. Take care not to damage these tender roots by pressing them too firmly into the compost.

Crocks for drainage

Place a piece of broken pot, concave side downwards, over the drainage hole in the bottom of the pot to prevent the compost blocking the hole. For this first potting, use John Innes potting compost No. 1 or a proprietary soil-less compost.

Bury the roots without covering any part of the main stem. Leave the top $\frac{1}{2}$ in. of the pot unfilled (up to 1 in. or more when later you pot into larger containers) and fill the pot to the brim whenever the plant needs water. A good soaking will keep the compost moist for several days. Plastic pots are non-porous, and therefore need less frequent watering.

Label each pot with the name of the plant and the dates of rooting and

potting and stand them on a free-draining base where they will get plenty of light and air. Protect them from draughts and maintain an average temperature of 7°C (45°F).

Potting on

Pot on, into 4 in. or 5 in. pots, rooted cuttings first potted during January and February. If left too long in the smaller containers they will suffer a check. The important thing is to keep them growing steadily all the time.

Gladioli

Weather and soil conditions permitting, plant gladiolus corms between the second and fourth weeks of this month.

For exhibition purposes, plant the corms in either single or double rows. Allow $1\frac{1}{2}$–2 ft. between single rows; space double rows 12 in. apart, with a 2–3 ft. gap between each pair of rows.

For ordinary decorative purposes in a mixed border, plant the corms 4–6 in. apart in colonies. To provide cut blooms for household arrangements, plant in rows 12–15 in. apart.

Depth of planting

Allow 5–6 in. between corms planted in rows and plant them 4–6 in. deep: the lighter the soil the greater the depth. Planting insufficiently deep leads to collapse of the flower spikes. When planting, either make individual holes with a trowel or draw out deep drills with the point of a hoe. The base of each corm must rest firmly on the soil.

Three or four successive plantings of the same variety, at fortnightly intervals, will provide a continuous supply of blooms throughout the summer.

If you have saved cormlets from last year, plant them 2 in. deep in rows 4–6 in. apart. They can be set so that they are almost touching one another.

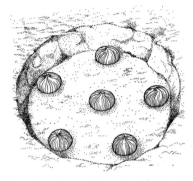

For garden display in the mixed border, plant the corms in clumps. One method is to set them 4–6 in. apart in a flat-bottomed hole

Alternatively, plant the corms in holes 4–6 in. deep. On heavy soil, set each corm on a base of sharp sand to aid drainage

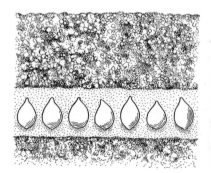

Set cormlets close together in rows, placing a layer of sand above and below to help growth and facilitate lifting

GLADIOLI VARIETIES

Large-flowered varieties are unsurpassed for a garden display. Primulinus, miniature and the butterfly gladioli are ideal as cut flowers

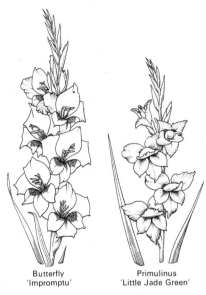

Butterfly
'Impromptu'

Primulinus
'Little Jade Green'

Medium-flowered
'Magic Frills'

Large-flowered
'Friendship'

Irises

Bearded irises are notable for their easy culture and for the kaleidoscope of brilliant colours which they provide during the spring and early summer. The genus also includes winter-flowering species and others which thrive as water-side plants.

This month, pull off dead leaves from bearded irises, taking care not to disturb the roots in the soil. Cut away any brown spots or tips on the newer leaves. Examine the rhizomes without disturbing them, cutting away any diseased parts with a knife and dusting the cut surfaces with dry powdered Bordeaux mixture to protect against fungus infection.

Loosen the surface of the soil around the plants and, towards the end of the month, apply a general fertiliser at the rate of 4 oz. per sq. yd. Give the same top-dressing of fertiliser to plants of *Iris sibirica*.

Planting and protection

Apply proprietary slug pellets to kill slugs and snails: place the pellets under foliage or flat stones to hide them from birds and small mammals.

Plant summer-flowering Dutch iris bulbs, sold as 'specially prepared', 3 in. deep and 4 in. apart in good garden soil.

Place cloches over spring-flowering Dutch irises to protect the blooms (see FEBRUARY).

Pick *I. unguicularis* regularly, otherwise birds will damage the blooms. In a late season the flowers will continue well into this month.

Look for symptoms of virus disease on bulbous irises, and burn affected plants to prevent the trouble from spreading. The danger signs are stunted growth, yellow streaks on the leaves and flower stems, and unusually dark patches on the flower petals.

Lilies

Spread a light mulch of leaf-mould or well rotted compost over established lily beds. Use cloches to protect young shoots against frost damage at night. In the south, sow lily seeds outdoors 1 in. apart and $\frac{1}{2}$ in. deep, in boxes 6–9 in. deep. In cold districts wait until April.

PROTECTING LILIES

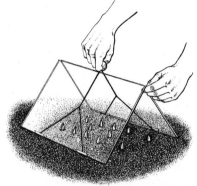

Tender young lily shoots are sometimes damaged by frost. Protect them with cloches

Complete the planting of lily bulbs by the end of the month, setting each bulb two and a half times deeper than its height. Lilies require well drained, deeply cultivated beds containing plenty of humus, preferably with at least 18 in. of good soil. Though lilies object to fresh manure, impoverished soil does not suit them either. The best material is well rotted compost, either left on the surface or mixed with the soil several inches under the bulbs.

Raised bed

In very heavy clay, deep cultivation of a small area may turn it into a drainage sump. If this seems likely, or if your soil is very alkaline, use good loam to make raised beds some 9–15 in. above the general level.

49

Spring-purchased bulbs, especially cheap ones of uncertain quality, are often grown in pots or boxes until the autumn. This allows time for the basal roots to make fresh growth and will reveal diseased stock without the risk of contaminating outdoor beds. However, the beds can be prepared at any time between now and August. If it suits you to do the job early rather than late, sow or plant the beds with annuals to provide colour during the summer.

UNDER GLASS

Plant imported lilies in pots (see FEBRUARY). Seed boxes sown earlier can go outdoors if greenhouse space is restricted. When the buds of forced lilies are ready to open, stop giving fertiliser; reduce the temperature (see JANUARY and FEBRUARY) to 13°C (55°F).

Carnations and Pinks

With their perfection of form and rich colouring, carnations and pinks are among the most popular of garden flowers. Both plants are members of the dianthus family and many varieties have a heady fragrance. Pinks, border carnations and annual carnations are grown outdoors; perpetual flowering carnations, familiar in florists' shops, are grown under glass.

Prepare planting sites

Now is the time to order plants and seeds (see colour section, MAY) and complete the preparation of beds for spring planting. Choose a sunny, open site, raising the bed about 6 in. above the level of the surrounding soil if the drainage is poor. Dig the site one spit deep and bury farmyard manure or compost below the top spit. Make a soil test and apply lime if it is below pH 6·5. Hoe

50

bone-meal, at 4 oz. per sq. yd., into the top 4 in., but if lime has been applied wait a month before doing so.

Stop pinks

Stop modern pinks that show signs of running to flower without making good side shoots. When the plant has developed about ten joints, hold it between your finger and thumb at the seventh joint, and with your other hand bend the top of the plant sharply at a right angle to snap off the top. If the top does not snap off easily cut it cleanly just above the joint. Tops snap off best in the early morning in damp weather.

If you are uncertain whether a pink is old-fashioned or modern it is advisable to stop any young pink that tries to run up to bloom without making good side shoots, even though this may prevent old-fashioned pinks from flowering for a season.

Apply fertilisers

Apply sulphate of potash at 2 oz. per sq. yd., or bonfire ash at 8 oz. per sq. yd., to stock planted last autumn. Apply a proprietary high-potash fertiliser to older plants at the rate recommended by the manufacturers. Apply this also to young plants if the pre-planting manuring (see AUGUST) was not carried out.

Plant pot-grown border carnations and pinks if this was not done in October, making sure that the soil ball is moist before planting, and keeping it intact.

Pest control

Watch for pests and diseases, taking action as necessary. The chief pests of pinks and border carnations are aphids, thrips, caterpillars, froghopper larvae and carnation flies. Control aphids and thrips by spraying with HCH or malathion when the pests are seen. These chemicals are also effective against caterpillars. Use a derris spray to control froghopper larvae.

Carnation flies lay eggs on the leaves. The grubs that hatch burrow first into the leaves, leaving a whitish streak, and then into the stems. Young plants, particularly seedlings, are susceptible, but the pests do not occur under glass. Pick off affected leaves and deter further attacks by dusting with HCH.

Rust and leaf spot

Most modern hardy outdoor carnations and hybrid pinks are resistant to, or have a tolerance of, rust disease. Older varieties are also susceptible to this fungal disease, which usually starts near the base of the plant and causes small yellow blisters to develop. These burst and discharge a reddish brown powder.

Leaf spot disease usually shows first on older leaves as light brown spots with purple margins extending to light straw or white discoloration along the leaf.

Control of both diseases is by fortnightly sprays of thiram or zineb. These fungicides are also effective on cuttings in frames that develop a grey mould.

Incurable diseases

Stem rot at ground level results from either over-deep planting or bad drainage and cannot be cured. Wilt disease, where the plant wilts and dies, is rare outdoors. Carefully remove affected plants, complete with roots, and burn.

UNDER GLASS

Continue to prick out seedlings of perpetual flowering and annual carnations (see JANUARY). Continue with the first and second potting of perpetual flowering carnations (see DECEMBER) and also the first stopping (see FEBRUARY).

Maintain a temperature of 7°C (45°F) for perpetual flowering carnations, increasing the ventilation in warm weather.

Cut blooms and disbud flower stems as necessary (see SEPTEMBER).

Order plants for delivery next month (see colour section, MAY).

Watch for pests and diseases, taking action as necessary. Smoke dispensers or powders are better than sprays for controlling pests under glass, particularly during the winter. Use HCH sprays or smokes for aphids and caterpillars; azobenzene smokes for red spiders.

Destroy plants infected with wilt and virus disease. Control rust and leaf spot with zineb (see opposite).

Sweet peas

As soon as soil and weather conditions permit, plant autumn-sown seedlings which have over-wintered in pots or boxes. For growing exhibition-quality blooms on the cordon system, set out the plants in double rows at least 12 in. apart, with a 4 ft. pathway between each pair of rows. Allow 8 in. between plants. (For construction of the supporting framework, see FEBRUARY.)

PLANTING SWEET PEAS

Using a trowel, dig a hole large enough to take the spread-out roots. Replace the soil, firming it evenly over the roots

Sweet peas are often grown on this system to provide long-stemmed cut flowers. In this case, grow a few plants naturally as well, up twiggy sticks, to provide foliage, tendrils and buds for cutting and arranging.

SUPPORTING EXHIBITION SWEET PEAS

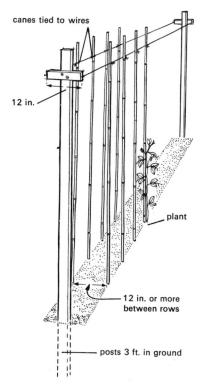

canes tied to wires

12 in.

plant

12 in. or more between rows

posts 3 ft. in ground

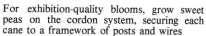

For exhibition-quality blooms, grow sweet peas on the cordon system, securing each cane to a framework of posts and wires

For garden display, sweet peas are especially effective when grown in clumps, supported with pea sticks or cylinders of netting

Use a trowel or dibber for planting, spreading the roots well out in the hole and planting firmly. Discard all plants which have a brown collar on the white part of the stem above the seed. If planted, they invariably collapse. Place small supporting twigs around each plant.

With naturally grown (bush-grown) sweet peas, plant in single rows wherever this is practicable. Plant in pairs, with 6

in. between each pair. To support the plants, use sticks or branches, wire or twine netting 6 ft. high for tall varieties and 3 ft. high for the new semi-dwarf multiflora types 'Knee-hi' and 'Jet-Set'. The Patio types grow only 15 in. high—a tent-shaped length of netting over a row will keep the birds off while plants are young. The peas will soon grow up through the mesh and cover it sufficiently to hide it.

51

MARCH

SUPPORTING NATURALLY GROWN SWEET PEAS

Branching sticks make good supports for naturally grown sweet peas. Set them beside the plants, inclining the tops inwards

As an alternative to branching sticks, use wire or string netting stretched between posts to support rows of naturally grown sweet peas

Put slug bait around the plants immediately after setting them out. If you are growing sweet peas on the cordon system, insert an 8 ft. cane alongside each plant. Tie the canes to the supporting framework (see FEBRUARY) to hold them steady.

UNDER GLASS

Make spring sowings as early in the month as possible, setting the containers in a cold frame or greenhouse. (For the method of sowing, see OCTOBER.)

52

Flowers from seed

Complete seed orders as soon as possible, otherwise varieties in short supply may be sold out.

When the weather is fine and the soil is dry, plant out hardy perennials raised from seed if this was not done in October or November.

Sow the hardier sorts of hardy annuals (see tables, pages 80–81) outdoors if weather and soil conditions are favourable. Sowing in cold, ill-prepared soil is a waste of time and seed. (For preparation of seed bed, see NOVEMBER.) The first signs of spring growth on the lawn show that the soil is warming up.

Seed dressing

To help both seeds and seedlings combat pests and diseases in the early stages, dress the seeds before sowing with a proprietary powder, shaking the powder and seeds together in the packet. These dressings usually make the seeds lighter in colour and easier to see against the soil, facilitating thin sowing. In addition to saving seed, this makes subsequent thinning-out of the seedlings less finicky and gives the small plants space to make sturdy, bushy growth right from the start.

Fertiliser dressing

If ground to be sown with hardy annuals has not already been lightly forked over, do this now and mix in a dressing of general flower fertiliser at the rate recommended. Rake in a similar dressing to beds forked over in February. Annuals have only a short season to grow and flower, but do not need generous feeding.

Some annuals are especially effective when sown in conjunction with contrasting sorts. When sowing shirley poppies, mix a few tall ornamental grasses among them and let them grow together, to provide contrasting material for both garden and indoor decoration.

Before sowing, work the soil down to a fine tilth by treading lightly and raking. Sow the seed in drills which are so spaced that the plants will just touch when fully grown. This is more satisfactory than broadcast sowing, as it enables you to cover the seeds to an even depth and makes for easier thinning-out and hoeing. Sow a few radish seeds in the drills at the same time. Radishes germinate very rapidly and will show you the positions of the rows if hoeing is needed before the annuals appear.

Take out the drills with one corner of a draw hoe blade, adjusting the depth of the drill to suit the size of the seeds. If small seeds are sown too deeply, they will not get through the soil. Large seeds will lack moisture if they are sown too near the surface. When drawing the drills, bear in mind that the raised soil along the sides makes them look deeper than they really are.

Sowing methods

Sow the seeds with a shaking action straight from the packet, in pinches picked from the palm of the hand, or with the aid of a patent sower. Do not use lumpy soil from the ridges at the sides of the drills to cover the seeds. A swan-necked hoe is useful for this job. Draw a corner of the blade along one side of the drill in the case of small seeds, or along both sides in the case of larger seeds, to move fine, moist soil over the seeds. On light or fairly dry land, firm the soil gently over the seeds, either with the back of a hoe or rake or by treading lightly, to help preserve moisture around the seeds and assist germination.

Keep weeds down by frequent hoeing as soon as the rows of seedlings appear. Where necessary, thin out the seedlings when they have two or three leaves, so

FOUR METHODS OF MAKING DRILLS

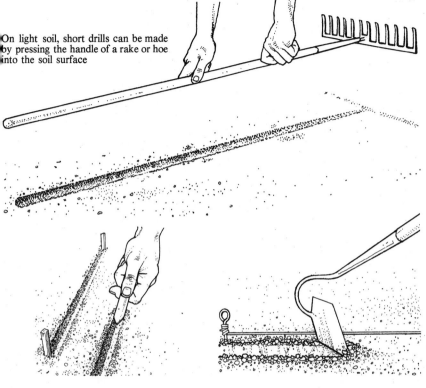

On light soil, short drills can be made by pressing the handle of a rake or hoe into the soil surface

Another method, also suitable for short lengths of drill, is to scratch the furrow with the pointed end of a plant label

For longer drills, use the corner of a draw hoe blade, with a garden line, stretched tight between two pegs, as a guide

Satisfactory drills can also be drawn with a rake, provided the head has sharply angled corners and is not too unwieldy

that they have sufficient space to develop laterally and make bushy growth.

UNDER GLASS

Many half-hardy annuals can be sown this month (see tables, pages 80–81). Sow seeds in plastic or clay pots or pans, cleaning the containers thoroughly before use. Fill with John Innes seed compost or a proprietary soil-less compost, give this a good watering, and leave the pots to stand for a short time before sowing.

It is well worth treating seeds with a proprietary dressing to help prevent damping-off, shaking the seeds and powder together in the seed packet. Sow the seeds thinly on the surface of the compost, covering all but the smallest, such as begonias and lobelias, with finely sieved compost, coarse silver sand or horticultural vermiculite.

Cover the containers

After sowing, give a light watering or spraying, then place each container in a polythene bag, or cover it with a sheet of glass, and place a sheet of paper over the top to prevent overheating. An even temperature of 13–18 °C (55–64 °F) is needed for germination.

Remove the paper covering as soon as the seedlings appear, otherwise they will become drawn and useless. Leave the polythene or glass on for a day or two.

Pricking out

When the seedlings are large enough to handle, prick them out into seed boxes containing John Innes potting compost No. 1 or a proprietary soil-less compost. Handle them carefully by their seed leaves, inserting them in holes made with a pencil or dibber and firming them in carefully so that their roots are not left in air pockets. Prick out 30 or 35 seedlings to each box (five rows, with either six or seven seedlings in each row).

PROTECTION FROM BIRDS

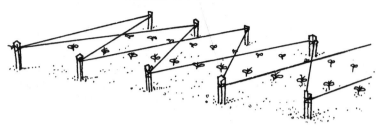

Black cotton criss-crossed between short pegs is effective, being almost invisible against the soil. Tie it securely to each peg

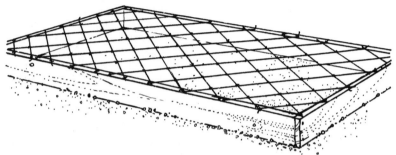

For small areas, a timber frame covered with close-mesh netting or black cotton provides complete protection. Make the frame sufficiently high to prevent birds pecking the plants through the netting

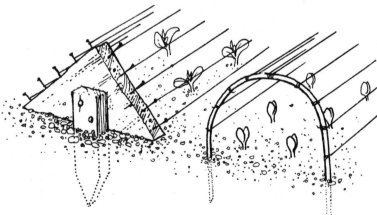

Protect rows of seedlings with black cotton, securing the ends to triangular wooden sections or hoops of wire. Hoops can be purchased bent to shape

After pricking out, water the seed boxes and place them in a shaded part of the greenhouse until the young plants are growing strongly. From this stage onwards give them plenty of light and ventilation. Excessive warmth will lead to soft, lanky plants.

Hardening-off
Move to a cold frame any well grown batches of early-sown half-hardy annuals (see FEBRUARY). Keep the frame closed at first, opening it progressively as the weather improves and the plants become hardened.

Take special care with the more tender plants. In the case of such frost-susceptible subjects as dahlias and ageratums, cover the frame with sacking in the late afternoon or early evening if a hard frost is forecast. If the weather is exceptionally hard at the beginning of the month, delay putting the plants in the frame, especially if the wind remains in the north or east.

Bulbs

Many kinds of bulbs are now at their best. A visit to one or more spring flower shows will help you to choose new varieties for planting in the late summer.

Remove flower heads from daffodils as they fade. This conserves the strength of the bulbs and prevents fungus spores from multiplying on the withering blooms.

The last of the bulbs grown in pots or bowls for indoor decoration will finish flowering this month. Plant them out at once, removing intact the bulbs and the fibre in which they were grown to encourage growth that will replenish the bulbs for future flowering. As such bulbs are unsuitable for forcing again, place them in clumps between shrubs, herbaceous plants or alpines, depending on their size. Daffodils and narcissi of all kinds, hyacinths, crocuses, and some of the smaller irises can all be planted out in this way to flower again two years later and in subsequent springs.

Tulips are less likely to succeed, but may well flower again for a year or two.

Plant acidantheras

In mild districts plant acidantheras 2–3 in. deep and 4–6 in. apart in a sheltered position. If snowdrops are crowded and need re-planting, lift them before the leaves die down, separate the bulbs, and re-plant at the same depth as before.

In cold districts plant de Caen and St. Brigid anemones for flowering during the summer.

UNDER GLASS AND INDOORS

Give adequate water and liquid fertiliser to clivias and hippeastrums in flower or in full growth.

SPLITTING SNOWDROPS

Snowdrops are best left undisturbed for at least four years. If they are then becoming overcrowded, use a fork to lift the clump out of the ground when the tips of the leaves are turning yellow, separate the bulbs, and re-plant them without delay at the same depth as they were previously.

Alpines

Firm into place any plants or labels loosened by frost (see FEBRUARY). Place slug pellets under foliage or flat stones and renew as necessary. As the soil surface becomes drier, hoe lightly between the plants to kill newly germinated weed seedlings. A dressing of fine gravel or stone chippings will suppress most weeds, but will also preclude use of a hoe on those that do appear.

Where chippings are not used, a short-handled onion hoe, with a blade 2–3 in. wide, is the best implement for working among alpines. But some weeds, such as annual grasses and groundsel, which carry a good deal of soil among their roots when pulled out, are better cut off with an old knife just below ground level.

Germinating seeds

If you have boxes or pans of seeds placed outside for weathering (see DECEMBER), watch carefully for signs of germination early in the month. Apply a fresh sifting of sand if heavy rain has exposed the seeds. Once they show signs of growth, move particularly choice or slow-growing alpines to an unheated greenhouse or frame if you wish to nurse them or hurry them along before pricking-off. Use a fine spray to water seed boxes which show signs of drying out, or soak them from beneath by standing the lower halves of the containers in water.

Plant alpines

Plant nursery-raised alpines as soon as possible after delivery, unless the soil is frozen (see FEBRUARY). Do not plant slow-growing alpines next to those which grow rapidly (see plant descriptions, NOVEMBER). If you have ordered a general collection, segregate the plants into sections according to spread, and

WEEDING ALPINES

Where the soil is not covered with chippings, a short-handled hoe is ideal for weeding and for loosening the soil between the plants

plant each section in a different part of the rock garden to minimise harmful competition.

A number of plants that flower from June onwards may show signs of die-back as a result of wintry weather. Lift those that can be propagated by division (see plant descriptions, NOVEMBER) and split the healthiest portions into compact pieces 1–2 in. across. Dig the ground from which they were lifted, adding peat or fresh soil in which bone-meal or a general fertiliser has been mixed at the rate of 1 part in 40 or 50, and then re-plant the divided portions.

Divide carpeting plants

Some carpeting plants, such as arenarias, androsaces, frankenias, raoulias and sedums, may also be in need of this treatment, and it is useful with others which tend to wander below ground beyond their allotted space.

UNDER GLASS

Plant out rooted cuttings (see FEBRUARY) into pots or boxes when they have produced small tufts of leaves.

Sow seeds of the quicker-growing

DAMPING SEED BOXES

If seed boxes start to dry out, stand the lower halves of the boxes in water until the compost appears moist all the way through

alpines in a frame or cold greenhouse. Some will germinate in three or four weeks and must then be hardened-off before the seedlings become leggy. Use a sterilised sandy compost, placing about four seeds per sq. in. Sift more compost over the seeds to a depth equal to their own thickness.

Water plants and pools

March is an important month in the water garden, whether you are looking ahead to a summer display of water lilies in an existing pool, planning new schemes for the bog garden, or starting a pool from the beginning.

When the ice on your pond has thawed with the approach of warm weather, drain about three-quarters of the water off and replace with clean fresh water. This will reduce the concentration of salts and toxic material accumulated during the winter from the decomposition of plant remains, and will benefit the fish in the pool.

While the water is half drained, remove any small masses of algae (blanketweed)

—the minute plants which multiply in standing water and turn it green. Remove the tops of marginal plants that were left to give winter protection. Take care not to throw out water snails, which clean the pool of plant and animal remains, or the turions (winter buds) of *Hydrocharis morsus-ranae* (frogbit) or *Utricularia vulgaris* (bladderwort).

If growth the previous season was poor, scrape away some of the mud around the water lilies and marginal plants and top dress with good fresh soil mixed with John Innes base fertiliser (1 oz. per bucketful).

Bog gardens

The end of March is an ideal period for planting a bog garden with most waterside plants such as ferns and primulas.

The soil for the bog garden should consist of loam mixed with an equal bulk of sphagnum peat of medium or coarse texture, with a dusting of seaweed fertiliser at 3 oz. per sq. yd. Plants in the bog garden may be set a little closer than normal spacing, so that the ground is covered quickly; in this way weeds are also discouraged.

If fish are lively, begin regular feeding with protein foods.

Protect children

Young children are always a problem in any garden with a pool. A thick planting of marginal plants will discourage children from trying to paddle, or a fine-mesh nylon net can be stretched over the pool at the beginning of the season. This will give complete safety, and the water lilies and other plants can grow up through it.

CONSTRUCTING A GARDEN POOL

Now is the time to begin the construction of new water gardens, to be in ample time for early spring planting. All pools

should have two depths, one averaging $1\frac{1}{2}$–2 ft. for water lilies, oxygenating plants and fish, and the other a depth of 6–9 in. for marginal plants.

Position

The best site for a pool is an open one. The water should be in full sun for at least eight hours a day in summer, to encourage all plants to flower well. The floating foliage of water lilies and other aquatics reduces the amount of sunlight entering the water, but the plants themselves need sunlight, and the pool must not be shaded. Site the pool well away from trees, or falling leaves will decay and pollute it.

Size and shape

Within the limits imposed by the garden layout, the larger the pool the better. Any pool intended to contain fish should have at least 15 sq. ft. of surface area, and 60 sq. ft. would be nearer the average, even for gardens of modest size.

Before excavating the site, mark out the proposed shape on the ground, using a length of cord or garden hose. Decide whether the size is adequate, the shape appropriate, and the position clearly visible from important viewpoints. You can then experiment to achieve the most satisfying result before turf or soil is disturbed.

Minimum depth

Water plants dislike sharp temperature changes, and no pool should have a central depth of less than 15 in. Make the pool sides steeply sloping, to achieve an adequate volume of contained water in relation to the surface area. Moreover, vertical walls are undesirable for constructional reasons. Make the slope 20° from the vertical.

Some water lily varieties will tolerate a water depth of 3 ft., but few need so much. A pool depth of 18 in. is perfectly satisfactory, allowing 4–5 in. of

GLASS FIBRE POOLS

Prefabricated glass fibre pools are sold in a variety of shapes and sizes, complete with shelves for placing marginal plants. They are extremely durable and much easier to install, though more expensive, than concrete pools

Plants and overlapping paving stones conceal the edges of the pool, which are set level with the surrounding ground. In pools of all types, the water level should be maintained almost to the brim, concealing the artificial lining material

Materials

Concrete, the traditional material, is far from ideal. Concrete construction is always laborious and frequently disappointing, because the rigid shell lacks tensile strength and is liable to fracture under the stresses imposed by ice pressure or soil movement. If, however, you wish to use concrete, first excavate a hole considerably larger than the size of the finished pool, to allow for a minimum thickness of 5 in. of concrete and rendering, with another 2 in. at the bottom for the rammed hard-core foundation.

Accurately measure the ingredients (3 parts coarse aggregate, 2 parts sand and 1 part cement), and mix them thoroughly with water to a firm, even consistency. Lay the concrete 4 in. thick over the floor and walls, using shuttering to retain the walls in position until the mix is set. Apply a rendering coat (3 parts sharp sand to 1 part cement) 1 in. thick. Waterproofing powder may be added to the cement, but will not compensate for inaccurate or uneven mixing.

Concrete contains free lime, from which plants and fish must be protected by painting the pool with a neutralising agent such as Silglaze. Alternatively, bleach out the lime by filling the pool with water, leaving for a week, and emptying. Repeat this process. The third filling will be virtually lime-free, and safe for plants and fish. Potassium permanganate is useless.

Plastic materials do not suffer from the drawbacks of concrete. The better sorts are not only easy to handle, but make pools with a greater expectation of useful life than the average concrete pool. (This is not true of polythene, which is easily punctured and not easily repaired.)

The most satisfactory plastic materials for pool construction are as follows.

Glass fibre
Very strong; rigid, but with enough 'give' to take up the pressure of ice expansion.

soil and a little over a foot of water. The maximum depth may be increased to 2 ft. or 2½ ft. for pools over 100 sq. ft. in surface area, but need never be greater. (There is no justification for the belief that a depth of several feet gives fish extra protection in winter.)

Shelves for marginals
To accommodate marginal plants such as water irises and arrowheads, which

like their roots in shallow water, make a shelf 8 or 9 in. below the surface of the pool, and 8–12 in. wide. The shelf itself may be continuous or interrupted, and in total length it may vary from a third to a half of the pool's perimeter.

The two depths—that of the shelf and that of the main pool—will meet all plant requirements (particularly if the pool is to be planted up with aquatic baskets and containers).

57

To install, dig a hole slightly larger than the pool, then back-fill with sand or soil to give firm, even support. Disadvantages are high cost and limitation of choice to the manufacturers' range of designs, none of which is very large.

Butyl rubber

A very strong elastic material available in sheets under various brand names. No size limit.

Plastolene

A sandwich of Terylene net between layers of PVC, making a sheet combining elasticity with great tensile strength. No size limit.

Polyvinylchloride (PVC)

PVC sheet, sold under various brand names, looks like polythene but is far superior, being thicker and elastic. No size limit.

Estimate the area of butyl rubber, Plastolene or PVC as follows. The length of the liner should be the overall length of the pool, plus twice the maximum depth; and the width should be the overall width of the pool, plus twice the maximum depth. Thus a pool 10 ft. long, 8 ft. wide and 18 in. deep needs a plastic liner 13 ft. long by 11 ft. wide.

The strength and elasticity of these materials permit a stretch-fitting technique which minimises wrinkling. After lining the excavation with a layer of sand or sifted soil, stretch the pool liner over the hole, weight the edges with stone, and run water on to it. As well as pulling the edges inwards, the weight of water stretches the liner and moulds it to the contours of the hole. Water pressure holds the liner firmly in place, and it does not require fixing.

For the sake of a neat finish, and to prevent the edges flapping back into the pool, trim off the excess plastic, leaving a flange 6–9 in. wide all the way round the pool. Bury the flange below the edge

1 Mark out the site with a garden line. Cut the edges with a spade or half-moon edging tool, then make the excavation, complete with shelves for marginal plants, sloping the sides at an angle of 20°

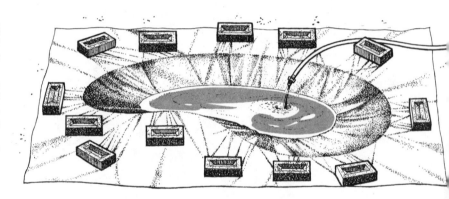

2 After placing sand on the bottom and sides of the hole, stretch the plastic liner over it, weighting the edges with stones or bricks. Direct a hose on to the centre of the sheet. The weight of water will stretch the liner and press it down, moulding it to the contours of the hole

of the turf, or alternatively cover it with crazy paving set in cement.

Plastic pools require no seasoning and may be stocked immediately.

Drains and overflows

There is no need for drain plugs and overflow fittings. Water draining away under a pool leads to erosion and subsidence risk, and there should be no constant inflow of water to make an overflow necessary.

Fountains, waterfalls and pumps

Fountains and waterfalls give the garden a special character. They also help to oxygenate the water and cool it in hot weather, to the great benefit of the fish. Water lilies and most other ornamental aquatic plants prefer static water, so currents and water movement must not be too great. A trickle gives as pleasing a sound as a torrent, and is much less disturbing to the plants.

WITH PLASTIC SHEETING AS A BASE

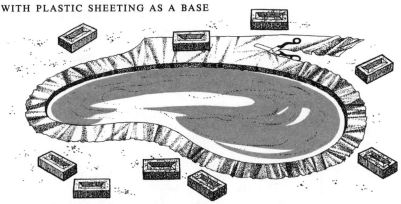

3 Fill the pool to within 1 in. of the surface; remove the bricks and trim the liner, leaving a 6–9 in. flap all round. Tuck the edges under the turf or cover them with crazy paving set in cement

4 The finished pool, with paving stones set flush with the turf and jutting over the edge of the finished pool to conceal the plastic liner

A waterfall or fountain should always be fed by water circulated from the pool itself. For this you need a pump.

Pump installation
Installation of pumps should always be carried out by a qualified electrician. A submersible pump stands in the pool, completely submerged in water. It has a length of waterproof cable, sealed into the pump, long enough to reach out of the water. A weatherproof connector joins the pump cable to an additional length reaching back to the nearest electricity outlet. Some submersible pumps are capable of producing fountains and waterfalls simultaneously.

For a fountain, place the pump in the water with the outlet section just above the water level. Push a fountain head or rose on to the outlet section, and the fountain is ready.

Surface pumps
For multiple-outlet installations on any but the smallest scale it is usually more economical to use a surface pump. This is housed outside the pool, in a weatherproof but not air-tight chamber. Water has to be drawn from the pool to the pump and then delivered to the fountain and waterfall outlets through polythene delivery pipes. Each of these pipes should have a stopcock for individual control.

Fountains and watercourses
Ornamental fountains in the form of statues can be connected to the outlet pipe of the surface pump, or by a short length of pipe to the outlet section of a submersible pump. A wide range of fountain jets or heads is available on the specialist's market, to produce a variety of water patterns.

The watercourse can be made with concrete, but it is difficult to make a watertight joint between concrete and rockery stone. To prevent leakage, first make a continuous waterproof concrete shell, bedded in firm soil to avoid the risk of subsidence. When the shell has set, place natural stone and more concrete on this to form the watercourse channels.

Glass-fibre channels
It is much easier to install glass-fibre units, in the form of stream channels and small pools with pouring lips, fashioned and coloured to simulate Westmorland stone.

The course for the water should be cut out to form an irregular or meandering route. If large rocks are available, a deep, bold face can be built up over which the water can pour. Effects can be enhanced if the water is allowed to fall on to a series of natural or simulated outcrops of rock. If moulded, glass-fibre units are used, disguise these with natural rocks and a number of moisture-loving,

59

FOUNTAINS AND WATERFALLS

Some submersible electric pumps will circulate water to a fountain and a waterfall simultaneously. Waterfalls can be formed from stone or concrete, or purchased as prefabricated glass fibre units. A surface pump is preferable to a submersible pump for large installations

creeping rock plants. Always try to position these pool basins in such a manner that an effective route and flow of water can be maintained. For large pool basins or for features where a lot of water is required, it will be necessary to install a large-capacity pump.

Pool heater

Fish do not die in winter from cold, but can be poisoned by gases accumulating under a persistent layer of ice. The best winter protection for fish is a small immersion heater, suspended from a float, which will keep a hole open in the severest weather. This will allow the poisonous gases to escape.

60

Aquatic baskets and crates

Specially designed containers for pond plants have mesh sides and are made from plastic. The sides are open, and sizes range from 8 to 12 in. across.

A PLASTIC CONTAINER

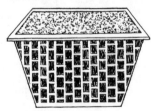

Perforated plastic containers allow removal of aquatics and check excessive root spread

Greenhouses and frames

A greenhouse adds a new dimension to gardening, enabling tender and exotic plants to be grown and providing colour and interest throughout the year. This is particularly welcome during the drab winter months, when most gardens contain little to please the eye. Though a considerable range of plants can be grown in even an unheated greenhouse, the possibilities are vastly increased if a minimum temperature of about 7°C (45°F) is maintained during the winter. Not the least value of a greenhouse is the interest derived from propagating a wide range of plants from seeds, bulbs and cuttings. The warmer weather of March sees a considerable increase in such activities.

Pot on annuals

Such annuals as schizanthus, nemesias and antirrhinums, which have been over-wintered in 3 in. pots on a shelf near the glass, grow rapidly at this time of year. Pot them on into 5 in. pots containing John Innes potting compost No. 2, inserting a supporting stake for taller plants. Stand the pots on the staging.

Remove old wood and crowded shoots from abutilons, taking cuttings if you wish to increase your stock. Choose young, sturdy shoots and root them round the sides of a 3 in. pot containing John Innes potting compost No. 1. Transfer the rooted cuttings individually into 3 in. pots, potting on progressively during the summer until the plants are in 10 in. pots. For the intermediate stages use John Innes potting compost No. 2, and No. 3 for the large pots. Cuttings can also be taken in September.

Sow tomatoes

Tomato plants grown from a February sowing now need extra space to prevent them from becoming drawn and spindly. Where practicable, stand the pots on the greenhouse border where they are to be planted. Otherwise, space them out on the staging.

If you wish to plant tomatoes in an unheated greenhouse in May, and have a heated propagating frame, sow the seeds this month in John Innes seed compost, in a temperature of 16°C (61°F), covering the seeds with a thin layer of sifted compost. Pot the seedlings individually into 3 in. pots of John Innes potting compost No. 2 as soon as the seed leaves are fully developed.

In a cool greenhouse, prepare the bed for planting tomatoes next month. Dig in plenty of well rotted manure or compost and apply 4 oz. per sq. yd. of a proprietary tomato base fertiliser.

Sow acacia seeds $\frac{1}{4}$ in. deep in a mixture of sand and peat, later transferring the seedlings to 3 in. pots.

Divide and pot canna roots

Start canna roots into growth in boxes of moist compost, first dividing any that are large. Pot them individually in May into 8 in. pots of John Innes potting compost No. 3.

Take cuttings of coleus at any time between now and September, inserting them in sandy compost at a temperature of 10–16°C (50–61°F). Take cuttings of zonal pelargoniums to produce plants for flowering next winter. Also take fuchsia cuttings this month (see AUGUST).

Plant hippeastrum bulbs in 6 in. pots containing John Innes potting compost No. 2. Bury only the lower half of each bulb. Provide a temperature of 10–13°C (50–55°F) and water sparingly until flower buds are showing. Maintain a humid atmosphere.

Take cuttings of *Tibouchina semidecandra* at any time between this month and September, using young side shoots and inserting them in

PLANTING A HIPPEASTRUM

In spite of their large size, hippeastrum bulbs can be planted in 6 in. pots. Bury only the lower half of the bulbs

sandy compost at a temperature of about 21°C (70°F).

Sow seeds of *Campanula isophylla* in a temperature of 13°C (55°F). Cuttings of this plant may be taken at any time from now until August.

Apply liquid fertiliser every ten days to regal and zonal pelargoniums, heliotropes, fuchsias and annuals in pots.

Warmer weather brings an increase in insect activity. For whitefly and aphids use smokes or sprays containing HCH. For greenhouse red spider mites, which will be at their worst after an early spring, spray with derris.

Towards the end of the month, pot on begonias and gloxinias into 5 in. pots containing John Innes potting compost No. 2, with peat added at the rate of 1 part peat to 9 parts compost.

Tranfer plants of July-flowering *Campanula pyramidalis* to 9 in. pots.

Sow seeds of *Primula kewensis* and *P. obconica*. Stand the box on the staging at normal greenhouse temperature.

Prick out all seedlings as soon as they are large enough to handle—preferably in the seed leaf stage.

Trees and shrubs

Flowering trees and shrubs deserve a place in every garden. Few plants offer such a varied beauty for so little work. Evergreens remain attractive right through the year, even with snow on the ground, and lend an air of maturity to a garden after they have been growing for a few years. They are especially effective when planted at a focal point or used as a permanent screen.

Take into consideration the ultimate height and spread of trees and shrubs. Do not plant tall-growing evergreens on the south or west boundaries of a small garden, otherwise shadows will be cast over a wide area—particularly when the sun is low in winter.

Plant deciduous trees and shrubs until the end of the month, except in severe weather or when the ground is frozen or waterlogged. Container-grown shrubs and trees, which are planted with an unbroken soil ball, can be put in now, or at almost any other time. These are obtainable at garden centres and are particularly useful for filling gaps in existing shrubberies.

Surface dressing

Top-dress young and newly planted trees and shrubs with old manure, composted forest bark, peat or garden compost. If these are not available, give a sprinkling of hop manure. Avoid quick-acting fertilisers.

Plant pot-grown clematis and other decorative wall shrubs. All trees and shrubs are planted in much the same way. Dig a hole large enough to hold the roots comfortably, making sure that the topmost roots will be covered by 4 in. of soil. Then position the shrub carefully, with its stem vertical, and gently replace the soil, firming it down as you go and finally treading round it. Planting is easier if you have someone to help.

61

Until the shrub is settled and growing strongly, it should be secured to a stake driven into the ground beside it. Soft and durable ties for staking trees can be made from old nylon stockings, torn plastic raincoats or plastic furnishing material.

Some newly planted shrubs, including campsis, caryopteris, cistus, garrya, hydrangea, hypericum and spartium, are tender in the young stage and need protection with old sacking, straw or netting. Tie stout polythene securely round three or four supporting stakes. This will act as a windbreak from the strong spring gales.

Windbreak for new trees

A good windbreak to protect newly planted trees can also be made by using large-mesh wire or plastic netting laced with pine branches, bracken or any small-leaved evergreen.

Towards the end of the month begin planting evergreens in well prepared ground (see SEPTEMBER).

PROPAGATION

In the open

Layer shoots of *Amelanchier canadensis,* chimonanthus, celastrus, all species of rhus (except *R. typhina*) and syringa in pots of sandy loam, sunk in the soil round the parent plants. The rooting process normally takes a year or more, and layers should not be separated from the parent plants until then.

Amelanchier canadensis produces offsets which can easily be severed from the parent plant. Pot the offsets in sandy soil until the autumn, and then transplant them to the positions in which they are to flower.

Divide roots of *Hypericum calycinum* and lathyrus and re-plant the separated pieces in their flowering positions.

Separate rooted suckers of kerria and plant out in permanent positions.

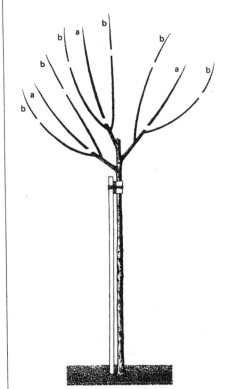

First-year growths (a) on a young standard tree are cut hard back. Second-year growths (b) are reduced by one-third

HOW TO PRUNE DECIDUOU

For pruning purposes, deciduous shrubs c be split into two groups—those that flower the current season's growth and others t flower on wood made the previous year. Pru the former in spring; the latter after floweri For general pruning principles, see page 48.

For shrubs flowering on this season's grow like *Hydrangea paniculata*, remove all bt few inches of last year's shoots

Under glass

Some shrubs are easily raised from seeds which can be sown now in a cold frame or a cool greenhouse. Sow seeds of *Amelanchier canadensis*, clematis, cotoneaster, genista, laburnum and wisteria in pans or boxes of sandy soil, lightly covering the seeds with sifted soil. Place the pans in a closed cold frame.

Seeds of eccremocarpus and *Lavatera olbia rosea*, sown in the same manner and placed in a greenhouse propagating frame with a temperature of 13–18°C (55–64°F), will germinate quicker than those sown in a cold frame.

When the seedlings are large enough to handle, prick them out singly into $2\frac{1}{2}$–$3\frac{1}{2}$ in. pots of potting compost and grow the seedlings on in an open cold frame until the autumn. Water well during dry weather.

Camellia japonica can be increased by leaf cuttings, 1 in. long, inserted in sandy peat and placed in a propagating

TREES AND SHRUBS

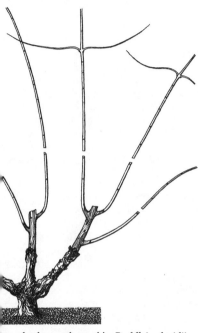

Some shrubs, such as this *Buddleia davidii*, flower on new shoots produced from old wood. Prune these shoots hard back

The weigela illustrated is one of many shrubs that flower on growth made during the previous season. After flowering, cut back to the base of a new shoot. Shrubs of this type also need occasional thinning of crowded branches

wood and damaged or weak shoots. This applies in particular to cistus, hebe, *Hydrangea macrophylla*, laburnum and potentilla.

Other shrubs, such as berberis, hedera and *Hypericum patulum henryi*, will produce more vigorous growth after a light thinning out of old wood to keep the shrubs in shape.

Caryopteris clandonensis, the deciduous species of ceanothus and *Hypericum calycinum* should have the previous year's shoots removed almost to the ground.

Cut fuchsias and *Lavatera olbia rosea* hard back to live wood at the base from which new shoots will appear.

Lightly prune *Lonicera fragrantissima* after flowering.

Cut hard back willows (*salix*) grown for winter bark colour. This will not only keep the trees under control but will also promote the lavish growth of brightly coloured stems.

Rhododendrons and azaleas

These popular flowering shrubs vary from forest giants to midgets. *R. falconeri* is a forest tree growing 40–50 ft., and *R. repens* crawls among the rocks; *R. sinogrande* has leaves 3 ft. long, and *R. radicans* has $\frac{1}{4}$ in. leaves creeping on the ground.

Among the azaleas (all in fact belonging to the genus *Rhododendron*) are the Christmas-flowering soft azaleas, which will not grow outdoors in this country; the so-called Japanese azaleas; and the deciduous azaleas, from the honey-scented yellow to the numerous coloured hybrids. Between these extremes lie a host of species and hybrids, evergreen and deciduous, that include some of our best garden plants.

frame. Maintain a temperature of 13–16°C (55–61°F) until the cuttings are well rooted. Place the rooted cuttings singly in 3 in. pots of potting compost and keep them in a cold, shaded frame. Plant out the following spring.

Take root cuttings, 2–3 in. long, of *Campsis radicans, Rhus typhina* and romneya. Insert the cuttings singly in pots of sandy compost and place these in a propagating frame where a temperature of 13°C (55°F) can be maintained.

When the cuttings have rooted, re-pot the new plants and leave them in an open cold frame to grow on before planting out into permanent positions the following spring.

PRUNING

If the winter has been severe, with hard frosts and heavy snowfalls, some of the more tender deciduous shrubs will need to be lightly pruned by removing dead

RHODODENDRONS IN TUBS

Where the garden soil is too alkaline for rhododendrons, dwarf varieties can be grown in tubs, using peaty compost

Rhododendrons thrive in areas where heather and pine flourish. They need acid soil, and are unsuitable for alkaline chalk areas. They do not object to partial shade, but cannot be grown in swampy conditions. On alkaline soil rhododendrons and azaleas can be grown successfully on a substantial mound of peat. Do not attempt to dig out a hole and fill it with peat, as alkaline moisture from the surrounding soil will seep in. Water only with rain water: local mains water is almost certain to be alkaline. If rhododendrons are unsuited to their surroundings, their leaves turn yellow. Sometimes sequestrene compounds, which provide iron for the roots in an easily assimilable form, will restore their health.

Prepare planting sites

This month is the last chance to prepare the ground for planting. Dig the ground deeply, incorporating plenty of manure or lime-free compost.

As soon as the warm spring weather arrives, start planting. Have ready plenty of peat or leaf-mould. Dig a hole big enough to take the root ball to a depth which ensures that the collar of the plant (or old planting-mark) will be level with the soil surface after planting. Surround the roots with plenty of the peat or leaf-mould, then fill in with soil and tread well in. If the roots are dry before planting, damp them but do not water excessively plants which are not growing. Water when growth starts if a dry period occurs.

Arrange by height

Arrange the plants so that the taller-growing specimens are at the back with plenty of room for growth, the medium growers next and the semi-dwarfs in the front. As a general guide, the spread of a rhododendron is roughly equal to its ultimate height.

Hedges

A well chosen hedge, forming a living boundary to the garden, is the ideal background for flowering plants and shrubs. It will also afford privacy and act as a windbreak. When selecting hedging plants, remember that many suitable shrubs have colourful flowers and foliage (see plant descriptions, SEPTEMBER), giving better value than the ubiquitous privet.

Planting deadline

With the exception of broad-leaved evergreens (see APRIL), this is the last winter month for planting hedges. If planted later, the young growth already on the plants may wilt and die during the time that it takes for the roots to become established.

When planting, use a measuring rod to ensure even spacing, and a garden line for straightness. Make each hole wide enough to take the spread-out roots and deep enough for the plants to be buried to the same depth as before, as shown by the old soil marks on the stems. Make sure that the roots are spread outwards and point downwards.

Cover the roots with the soil removed from the hole, or from the next hole, having first broken it up if it is not already in a fine, crumbly condition. Make sure that there are no empty gaps around the roots, firming them in first with your fingers and then with your heel. Break up the surface clods and leave the soil level. This not only improves the appearance of the newly planted hedge but also makes subsequent hoeing easier.

Weed removal

Weeds begin to grow in most parts of the country this month. Remove them from the bottoms of all hedges by pulling them up or by hoeing. Use a Dutch hoe for preference, as it is easier to push one of these tools round the hedging plants than to use a draw hoe, which requires a chopping action. Pull up large, deep-rooted weeds by hand. If chemical weed control is preferred, use paraquat-diquat, taking care to keep the liquid off the leaves and stems of the hedging plants.

It is particularly important to keep newly planted hedges free from weeds, which compete with the plants by taking moisture and nourishment from the soil. Weeds may also shade the lower branches of hedging plants and either kill them or reduce their growth.

Brambles, or the seedlings of unwanted trees such as ash, elder, sycamore and quickthorn, can also be a serious nuisance in hedges. Pull them up or cut them off below ground level.

Complete the hard pruning of any large old hedges not finished last month (see FEBRUARY).

Heathers

Compared with more aristocratic garden plants, heathers have a refreshingly natural quality. They are hardy, easy to grow and entail little work. By planting several species, flowers can be obtained throughout most of the year, even during the winter.

Plant clear of trees

Heathers can be planted during the spring from March until May, and in the autumn during October and November. Select an open position, well clear of overhanging trees. For all except lime-tolerant species (see plant descriptions, JANUARY) it is essential to plant in

PLANTING HEATHERS

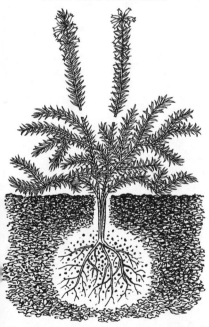

Plant deeply, setting the roots in crumbly soil and adding moist peat if the ground is dry. Clip off old flower stems where they emerge from the main mass of foliage

acid or neutral soil. Dig the ground thoroughly, removing the roots of perennial weeds and adding a dressing of peat at least 2 in. thick, forking this into the top 2 in. of soil. Unless the soil is known to be fertile, apply bone-meal at 4 oz. per sq. yd., mixing it thoroughly with the peat and topsoil. Heathers do not need feeding with farmyard manure.

Add peat

Apply extra peat if you are planting lime-tolerant heathers on an alkaline soil. The layer can be up to 4 in. thick on really chalky soils. If bracken peat is used, remove any live roots of bracken fern before planting.

Planting distances

Planting distances vary for different types of heather and depend, too, on the speed with which you wish to obtain complete ground coverage. Allow about 12 in. between small kinds and 18 in. between taller spreading varieties. Soak the roots of the plants if they appear dry. If the soil is dry, add a little moist peat round the roots of each plant. Plant deeply, with the whole of each stem buried and the lower foliage resting on the soil.

Surround the roots with loose, crumbly soil. Very firm planting is unnecessary, but the plants should be set sufficiently firmly to resist a gentle pull. Clip off old flower stems close to the main mass of foliage.

Layering technique

Propagate heathers this month from layers or cuttings if you wish to increase your stock. For layers, select healthy stems on the outside of a plant, bend them down to soil level, and either peg them down with bent wires or place stones to hold them in position. Providing the base of each layered stem is bent at an acute angle, there is no need to make cuts or notches. Leave the layers

LAYERING HEATHERS

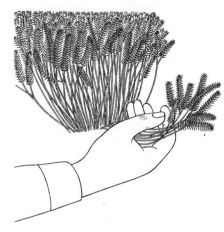

Select healthy stems on the outside of the plant. Prepare the adjacent soil by forking the surface and removing weeds. Bend the ends of the stems sharply upwards

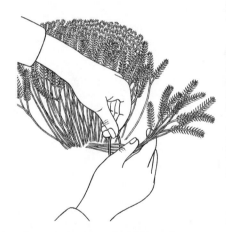

Peg the stems into the soil with bent wires, or secure them with stones. Left undisturbed for a year, the layers will have made their own roots and can then be severed from the parent plant

undisturbed for a year, by which time they will be well rooted and ready for detaching from the parent plant and setting out individually.

CUTTINGS IN A CLOSED FRAME

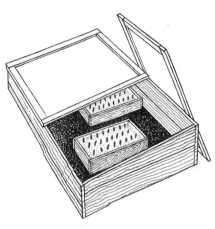

Place cuttings in a closed frame to reduce moisture loss while they are rooting. Left uncovered, they may wilt and die

CUTTINGS UNDER A CLOCHE

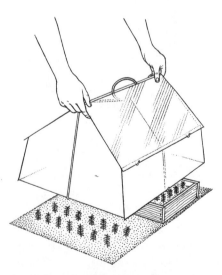

As an alternative to frame protection, cuttings rooted in the ground, or in boxes, can be covered with a cloche, with the ends closed

66

Heather cuttings

For cuttings, use short side shoots which have new growth at their tips. Choose shoots about 2 in. long (or up to 6 in. long if you have a mist propagator), pulling them away from the stem, together with small heels of old wood, and inserting them in pans or boxes filled with 2 parts sharp sand and 1 part finely sifted peat.

Unless you have a mist propagator, cover the containers with glass or keep them in a closed frame until the cuttings have rooted. Small plots of a similar rooting medium can be prepared in the open in a shady position. Insert the cuttings, water them thoroughly, and protect them with a cloche with the ends closed, or with a bottomless box covered with a sheet of glass.

When they have rooted, transfer the cuttings to outdoor nursery beds, planting them in their permanent positions when they are about 3 in. high.

Fruit

The planning of a fruit garden is most important, especially if fruit trees which will continue growing for 40 years or more are to be planted. The size of the garden and the time available for tending it must be taken into account when deciding which fruits to grow. Fruit trees require a lot of space, unless they are grown in restricted form, when they need more attention. In a small garden, therefore, it may be wise to grow only one row of apples or pears and to devote the rest of the garden to soft fruits.

Complete planting

In most seasons this is the last opportunity for planting, so try to complete planting as soon as soil conditions permit. This is particularly important for those plants that have been heeled in or kept under cover (see NOVEMBER).

Trees and bushes delivered during March are often behind established plants in growth and can be planted later in spring.

Firm trees and bushes planted in the autumn if they have been lifted by frost.

Finish pruning

Finish pruning established trees and bushes as soon as possible in the month (see NOVEMBER), and in any case before bud-burst. Prune autumn-planted trees and bushes now if this has not already been done, and prune spring-planted ones not later than the end of the month (see DECEMBER).

Feed established trees and bushes growing in cultivated soil. All soft fruit, except strawberry, will benefit from dressings of farmyard manure. Further details of feeding are given under the individual fruits. Tree roots become active before bud-burst and can absorb food before shoot growth begins. Do not feed trees in grass until May, and feed then only if fruit set is good. Newly planted trees and bushes should not be fed in their first season after planting if the ground has been properly prepared.

Apple

At bud-burst stage control apple scab by spraying with benomyl or captan, and control newly hatched pests (apple blossom weevil, capsid bug, greenfly and winter moth caterpillar) by spraying with HCH. If the fruit trees have been winter-washed (see DECEMBER), use only anti-scab spray. Every year, feed trees in open ground with $\frac{1}{2}$ oz. sulphate of ammonia or Nitro-chalk per sq. yd., but do not feed trained trees with nitrogen (as hoof and horn) unless vigour is lacking.

Blackberry, loganberry and hybrid berries

In windy situations, shoots produced during the last season may be damaged during the winter, so train these shoots on to the supporting wires now before bud growth is far advanced, rather than in the winter months. Use wire re-inforced paper strips which fasten easily, twisting the ends to tie the shoots to the framework. Feed every year with 1–2 oz. of sulphate of ammonia or Nitro-chalk per sq. yd.

Black currant

This fruit can still be planted (see NOVEMBER), and it is important to prune hard after planting (see DECEM-BER). Feed every year with nitrogen (as sulphate of ammonia or Nitro-chalk) applied at the rate of 1 oz. per sq. yd., and every other year with 1 oz. of sulphate of potash.

Cherry

Feed in the same way as apple, except fan-trained 'Morello' cherry grown in cultivated soil, which should be fed with up to 1 oz. of hoof and horn per sq. yd. according to vigour. At bud-burst control greenfly, winter moth cater-pillar and cherry fruit moth by spraying with derris.

Gooseberry, red currant and white currant

Prune currants or gooseberries which have been attacked by birds by cutting back to undamaged buds (see NOVEM-BER). Feed every year with 1 oz. of sulphate of potash per sq. yd., and apply about $\frac{1}{2}$ oz. of nitrogenous fertiliser if necessary to stimulate vigour. Cordon gooseberries need only $\frac{1}{2}$–1 oz. of sulphate of potash each year and are unlikely to need additional nitrogen.

Peach and nectarine

Wall-trained trees flower early and are easily frost-damaged, so protect the flowers with tiffany or similar material; a double thickness of garden netting may be sufficient protection. If pollinat-ing insects are scarce, pollinate flowers artificially with cotton wool on a stick. At bud-swelling stage, spray against

FRUIT BUD STAGES

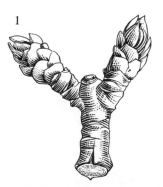

1

Bud-burst: the tips of the bud scales begin to separate

Green cluster: small green flower buds in the centre of the opening foliage

Pink or white bud: flowers not yet open but showing pink or white

4

Petal fall: the stage when nearly all the blossom has fallen

5

Fruitlets: they appear after all the blossom has fallen

A KEY TO SPRAY TIMING

The stages of bud development provide a key to the timing of spray applications for controlling pests and diseases. These may be ineffective if carried out at the wrong time. It is impracticable to determine spraying dates by the calendar, as the rate of growth varies considerably from season to season

peach leaf curl with Bordeaux mixture. Repeat ten days later. Feed bush trees in the same way as apple, and fan-trained trees with up to 1 oz. of hoof and horn per sq. yd.

Pear

Feed in the same way as apple. At green cluster and white bud stage, control pear scab by spraying with benomyl or dispersible sulphur, and control newly hatched pests (winter moth caterpillar, greenfly and pear midge) with BHC sprays. If the trees have previously been winter-washed (see DECEMBER), use only the anti-scab spray.

Plum and damson

Select leaders on newly planted bush trees and cut these back by half at bud-burst. If greenfly or winter moth caterpillar are a problem and the trees have not been winter-washed (see DECEMBER), use trichlorphon or derris at bud-burst or white bud stage to control newly hatched pests. Feed in the same way as apple, but increase sulphate of ammonia to $1\frac{1}{2}$–2 oz. per sq. yd.

Raspberry

Raspberries can still be planted (see NOVEMBER) and must be pruned hard after planting (see DECEMBER). Feed every year with $\frac{1}{2}$–1 oz. of sulphate of potash per sq. yd.

Strawberry

On heavy cold soils, or in districts where hard winters are expected, plant strawberries in the spring to avoid severe winter losses (see NOVEMBER). They will not fruit this season, except in the case of autumn-fruiting varieties, which will establish themselves during the summer. Work farmyard manure or a suitable substitute into the soil before planting to save further feeding. Feed established plants with sulphate of ammonia or Nitro-chalk, using small amounts ($\frac{1}{2}$ oz. per sq. yd.) or the foliage will be too heavy.

68

PRUNING A VINE

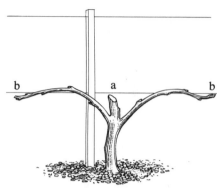

Cut the main stem hard back (a) to leave two strong shoots. Prune each of these shoots just beyond the fifth bud (b) and train them to the wires in opposite directions

Vine (outdoor)

Prune the main stem on established vines hard back to leave only two strong shoots. Bend these fruiting shoots horizontally and train them in opposite directions along wires 12 in. above ground level. These are necessary to support the shoots which will later carry the grape bunches (see recommended varieties, NOVEMBER). Prune each of these selected shoots back to five buds.

VINES IN POTS

Vines can also be grown in pots 14–16 in. deep, training the shoots on canes or stout wires bent over to form an arch

Vegetables

Vegetables picked fresh from the garden have a flavour unequalled by shop produce. There are, too, many delectable kinds, such as asparagus, globe artichokes and salsify, which are costly or even difficult to buy. Most vegetable growers also find a special satisfaction in growing and harvesting their crops, as distinct from the purely visual appeal of the flower garden.

This is an excellent month to start growing vegetables (see charts on pp. 130–1). If you cannot spare the space for a variety of crops, grow salads and some of the less common sorts.

Brussels sprouts

To grow an early crop of Brussels sprouts in the south, purchase hardened-off plants from a nursery or specialist grower and plant them in fertile soil after raking in a general fertiliser at 3 oz. per sq. yd. In the north, plant out Brussels sprouts which have been over-wintered outdoors (see AUGUST and OCTOBER), after applying a similar quantity of fertiliser. Do not loosen the soil below the surface. Plant with a trowel, retaining as much soil as possible round the roots and sprinkling calomel dust into each hole as a precaution against club root disease. Firm each plant in with your heel, and water.

For the main crop of Brussels sprouts, sow the seeds early in the month in drills $\frac{1}{2}$ in. deep and 6 in. apart, first dusting the drills with calomel as a precaution against club root disease. In the north, at the end of the month sow Brussels sprouts outdoors in a prepared seed bed to provide plants for setting out by the beginning of May.

Parsnips

Early in the month in the south, and towards the end of the month in the north, sow parsnip seed in ground well manured for a previous crop. Before sowing, rake in a general fertiliser at 4 oz. per sq. yd., or a mixture of 2 parts bone-meal and 1 part sulphate of potash at 3 oz. per sq. yd. Sow the seeds thinly in drills ½ in. deep and 15 in. apart, later thinning to 6 in. spacings. Lift the roots as required during the winter.

Potatoes

In the south, plant early potatoes (see FEBRUARY) from the middle of the month onwards, provided the soil is not saturated. Plant in trenches 12 in. wide and 9 in. deep, lining the trenches with 2–3 in. of well rotted manure, or garden compost or leaf-mould enriched with a proprietary potato fertiliser. Space the tubers 12–14 in. apart on the manure, covering them with soil to form a ridge over the top of each row. Sometimes burrowing slugs attack the tubers. If this trouble has occurred previously, sprinkle over the trench, when this has been filled in to ground level, a mixture of 1 oz. of copper sulphate and 4 oz. of sulphate of potash

PLANTING POTATOES

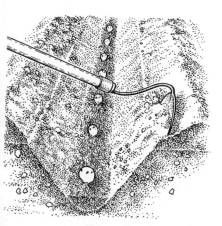

After setting potatoes on manure laid in trenches, draw soil over the tubers with a hoe to form a series of low ridges

for each 30 ft. of row. Then complete drawing up the ridge.

Onions

Onions are easy to grow from sets (the small bulbs sold by all garden shops). Plant them this month or in early April, following the method described for shallots (see JANUARY). Draw a little soil over the sets with the hand or a hoe to anchor them, otherwise birds may pull them up.

Salad crops

In the south, select a sheltered, moisture-retentive site to sow salad onions ('White Lisbon'), lettuce ('All The Year Round' or 'Webb's Wonderful') and radishes ('French Breakfast' or 'Scarlet Globe'). Sow all these seeds ½ in. deep in drills 12 in. apart, first dressing the soil with a general fertiliser at 3 oz. per sq. yd. Sow the seeds sparingly to reduce the work of thinning the seedlings.

Other vegetables

Sow seeds of late summer cabbages ('Winnigstadt', 'Stonehead' or 'Primo') in a nursery bed for planting out next month. Sow in drills 6 in. apart, covering the seeds ½ in. deep.

There is still time to sow early, round-seeded peas (see JANUARY).

If you prefer to grow your leek plants from seed rather than buy them from a nursery or garden shop, sow the seeds ½ in. deep in firm, fairly rich soil. Plant the seedlings in June.

Sow summer spinach, to give pickings during May and early June, in drills 1 in. deep and 9 in. apart. Allow 1½ in. between the seeds, later thinning to 6 in. spacings.

UNDER GLASS

In the south, sow carrots if cloches and a fertile, sheltered site are available. Suitable varieties include 'Champion

Scarlet Horn' and 'Early Horn'. Sow the seeds in two rows, 9 in. apart, covering them ½ in. deep. Use a proprietary seed dressing, following the manufacturer's directions, to prevent attack by the carrot fly.

LESS COMMON VEGETABLES
Shallots

Complete shallot planting as soon as possible (see JANUARY) if this was not done earlier.

Jerusalem artichokes

Plant Jerusalem artichokes towards the end of the month or early in April. Dig holes 12 in. square, 12 in. deep and 18 in. apart, placing half a forkful of manure or compost in each. Place a tuber on top of the manure in each hole and return the soil.

Kohl rabi

Kohl rabi, which has a bulging, turnip-like stem above ground, does well in moist, fertile soil where plants have not shown signs of club root disease. In the south, sow the seeds in drills 12–15 in. apart and ½ in. deep. Use a proprietary dressing to protect the seeds from flea beetles, and dust the drills with calomel as a precaution against club root disease.

Asparagus

Asparagus plants ordered earlier (see FEBRUARY) should arrive this month. Plant them at once unless the ground is saturated. If planting is impossible, make a shallow trench and bury the roots under 4–6 in. of soil, marking their positions with pegs.

If 5½ doz. plants were ordered, as recommended (see FEBRUARY), dig a bed measuring 30 ft. by 6 ft., then set a garden line 21 in. inside one of the longer edges. Using the line as a guide, set the plants 15 in. apart, with the plants at the

PLANTING ASPARAGUS

Make each hole large enough to spread the roots out fanwise, with the crown of the plant approximately 3 in. below ground level

extremities 15 in. from the ends of the row. Make the holes with a trowel, spreading the roots fanwise, with the crowns 3 in. below ground level. There will be sufficient plants for two more rows spaced 15 in. apart. Do not cut any asparagus during the first year and only a little during the following year.

During the early part of the month apply a 3–4 in. layer of well rotted farmyard manure to established asparagus beds or apply a general fertiliser at 4 oz. per sq. yd. Follow this with a 3 in. layer of good topsoil. At the end of the month, or early in April, give a similar treatment to new beds.

Herbs

Prepare a seed bed as soon as the air temperature is high enough to warm up the soil. Roll or tread the rough ground, then rake repeatedly to create a fine surface covering. With a draw hoe or the handle of the rake, take out seed drills 1 in. deep and about 8 in. apart.

Sow small amounts of chervil, chives, dill, pot marjoram, parsley and sorrel. Chervil should be sown at monthly or six-weekly intervals throughout the summer in order to maintain a succession of crisp, fresh leaves. In northern gardens delay sowing until the end of the month.

Amount to sow

Generally, only a pinch of seasoning is needed for successful cookery, but if the herbs are intended for drying and storing, sow more than the required amount. It needs a considerable bulk of fresh herbs to provide an adequate amount of dried herbs.

Layer shoots of pot marjoram, and divide the roots of fennel as soon as the shoots show above ground. Re-plant fennel 12 in. apart in its new position. Split old clumps of bergamot and sorrel,

SEPARATING CHIVES

Separate the offsets from clumps of chives, setting out the small, individual plants 10–12 in. apart in rich soil

and re-plant 12 in. apart in rich moist soil in full sun.

Separate the small new plants (or offsets) of chives from the parent plant and re-plant 10–12 in. apart in rich soil.

UNDER GLASS

In a cool greenhouse, at 13°C (55°F), sow basil in a seed box. Use a fine seed compost and cover the box with glass and brown paper.

Patios and town gardens

A paved patio or terrace, bright with flowering plants, provides a delightful sitting-out area for summer days. Shelter and seclusion can be enhanced by the use of modern screening materials, and climbers can be planted against these and the house walls to soften harsh outlines.

In town gardens, a courtyard layout makes much better use of limited space than a scaled-down garden of conventional design. Management raises few problems beyond the need for frequent watering in summer. As most of the smaller plants and shrubs described in the different sections of this book can be grown in containers, only a limited number have been suggested in this outline of monthly work.

New containers

Troughs, pots, window-boxes and tubs are obtainable in a wide range of materials and shapes. When choosing new containers, bear in mind the situation and the kinds of plants it is proposed to grow. Antique or rustic styles generally suit the traditional garden; modern materials and shapes, especially containers made of moulded asbestos, fit better into the more formal lines of a patio or courtyard. Check that containers intended for outdoor use have drainage holes in the base.

Raised beds

Not all the plants in a courtyard or patio need to be in portable containers. As an alternative, leave a soil-filled gap in the paving, and plant directly in this. Where space permits, raised beds in a courtyard enable the elderly or infirm to enjoy gardening without the strain of stooping. Permanent beds of this nature can be used for a succession of plants to provide colour for much of the year.

Containers on castors

Make the most of container-grown plants by moving them to prominent positions as they come into full flower. If large containers are likely to be moved frequently, place them on small platforms mounted on wheels or castors. Alternatively, make a stretcher with two stout poles and lift the container on to this for removal to the new site.

Buy or mix the soil for containers in readiness for spring planting. John

PERMANENT PLANTING SITES

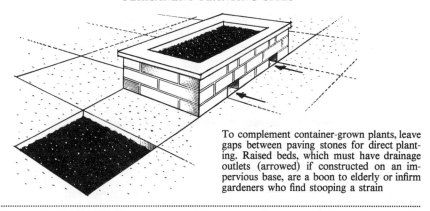

To complement container-grown plants, leave gaps between paving stones for direct planting. Raised beds, which must have drainage outlets (arrowed) if constructed on an impervious base, are a boon to elderly or infirm gardeners who find stooping a strain

Innes potting compost No. 2 suits most plants, as do proprietary soil-less composts. If ordinary garden soil is used, add peat to assist moisture retention, together with sharp sand if the soil is heavy. Soak the peat thoroughly before mixing it with the soil. Add a handful of bone-meal and 1 oz. of general fertiliser to each bucketful of soil and peat.

If timber boxes or troughs are used and the timber has not already been treated with a preservative, do this before filling them. Paint the outside with any preservative other than creosote, which is damaging to plants, so long as

VARIETY IN CONTAINERS

Square tubs, often made of cedar wood, make attractive containers, especially with overhanging plants to break the severe outline

If frequent moves are envisaged for large containers, avoid heavy lifting by placing them on platforms fitted with castors

Concrete troughs are durable and need no maintenance. They are particularly suitable for use in formal surroundings

71

INSTALLING A WINDOW-BOX

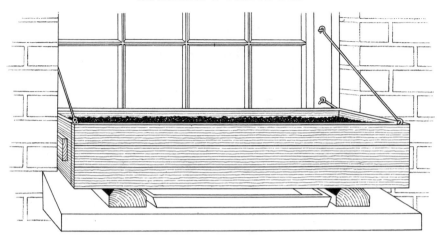

Stand the box on two wooden blocks to aid drainage, if necessary with a drip tray beneath. Fit the box closely in its space, securing it with wedges or hooks. Give boxes that project additional support by fastening them to the window frame

it will not discolour the container. The interior can also be painted with preservative or it can be charred. To do this, paint the inside with a liberal coat of paraffin and set light to this. Let it burn for a few minutes, then turn the container over to extinguish the flames. Paint all metals parts, such as hoops, or treat them with a rust inhibitor.

Fill containers

When filling containers with soil, first make sure that the drainage holes are not clogged. Place crocks over the holes to ensure that they remain open, followed by a layer of washed clinker or rubble to occupy about a quarter of the depth of the container. Over this material place a thin layer of turves, grass side down, or even a length of rag, to prevent soil being washed into the drainage layer. Then fill with soil, finishing with the surface about 1 in. below the top of the container.

If you require a constantly changing display of plant material, plunge plastic or terracotta pots inside the larger containers instead of planting direct. It is then easy to replace fading plants with fresh material, or simply to ring the changes between a number of containers. Pack peat around the pots, keeping this moist to prevent them drying out and reduce the time required for watering.

Raise window-boxes

Use wooden blocks to raise window-boxes above the sill to allow for drainage and to discourage insect pests. The boxes should fit the space closely and be secured by means of wedges driven between the ends of the box and the side walls or with hooks fastened to eyelets in the window frame. As the boxes will be heavy when filled with soil, fasten them in position while they are empty. In situations where excess water from the drainage holes could prove troublesome or mark the walls, stand the box over a drip tray, taking care when watering not to allow this to overflow.

House plants

Even non-gardeners appreciate the beauty and ever-changing interest of house plants. Some bear bright flowers; others have intriguing foliage. Without exception they bring a natural charm to their surroundings.

Seasonal management

As with outdoor plants, care and management must follow the seasons. For instance, now that the days are lengthening and the light is getting stronger, give a little more water to the plants, though continuing to keep most of them on the dry side. (For exceptions see plant descriptions, DECEMBER.) During sunny weather, transfer from a south-facing window to one facing west any plants that are flowering or have delicate foliage. Apply liquid fertiliser in solution sparingly to plants in bud or in flower, or any that are beginning to send out new shoots.

Prune climbers by cutting out weak or diseased shoots. Tie in long growth that needs support. Remove dead leaves and keep the soil at the base of the plant clear of any leaves that have fallen.

Potting-on

If any plant looks too large for its pot or if water passes through the pot too quickly, potting-on may be needed. Knock the plant from its pot by placing your fingers over the soil, turning the pot upside down, and tapping the edge of the pot on a firm surface. If the roots appear to take up all or nearly all the space in the pot, the plant needs transferring to a larger pot.

Choose a clean pot one size larger and put broken crocks or a perforated disc over the drainage hole. Rest the plant in the pot on a layer of John Innes potting compost No. 2 or a proprietary soil-less compost, so that the top of the root ball

'POTTING-ON

A larger container is needed if roots are seen to cover most of the soil ball when a plant is knocked out of its pot

....

reaches just below the pot rim. Fill in the space round the root ball with the compost, firming it evenly. Water well and allow the pot to drain. Do not water again until the soil surface is dry.

Some plants, such as *Vriesia fenestralis*, may have produced young plants

REMOVING OFFSETS

Plants such as this vriesia can be propagated by removing a basal offset and planting this on its own in a small pot

or offsets at the base of the mother plant. Remove these and pot them individually. Knock the plant from its pot, gently remove some of the soil, and pull or cut away the young plants, retaining as much as possible of the root system. Pot up the young plants, using as small a pot as they will conveniently fit. Water well and allow to drain before replacing in the room. Normally, vriesias and most other bromeliads should be watered merely by filling the vase formed by the leaves and keeping this topped up.

PREPARING FOR WARMER WEATHER

Placed in a larger pot, with moist peat packed between, many plants benefit from the extra humidity around their leaves

....

Provide humidity

Plants that need humid conditions can be prepared for warmer weather by plunging their pots inside another, larger container, with moist peat packed between the two. Keep this layer of peat always moist: the water vapour rising from it will provide sufficient humidity round the plant. The peat layer will also absorb any excess moisture through over-watering, the commonest cause of trouble with house plants.

General tasks

Complete all digging as soon as possible.

Kill weeds

Kill weeds on paths and drives with paraquat-diquat, then apply a total weed-killer to keep them free from weeds for the rest of the season. Moss on paths may be destroyed by watering them with 4 per cent tar-oil wash as used for spraying fruit trees—1 gallon for about 10 sq. yd. Kill weeds growing between paving stones or in drystone walls by watering them with paraquat-diquat. A second or third treatment will be needed if they are well established. This chemical kills growth of all types, so do not let it fall on either the stems or leaves of cultivated plants or on lawns.

Check ties

Check all ties that secure plants to wires or stakes, because March gales can cause much damage. Check also the strings attaching labels to trees or shrubs. Many nurserymen use nylon string which lasts for years. If the branch swells, and the string cuts into the bark, the branch may die.

Slug bait

Slugs begin to be troublesome in March. Place slug pellets under foliage or flat stones among tulips and delphiniums. Use only pellets containing methiocarb or 4 or 5 per cent metaldehyde. The old pellets contained only 3 per cent, which stupefied the slugs without killing them. One or two slug pellets under a grapefruit or orange skin will attract slugs and kill many of them. The skins also prevent birds from finding either the pellets or the slugs.

To protect young plants from slug attack, place over them tins without tops and bottoms. They can stay in position as long as you like.

73

Annuals to sow in March

The following varieties are likely to be found in most seed catalogues, though the colours may vary. New introductions, listed as 'F1 hybrids', often give flower colours that cannot be obtained in any other way. It is therefore best to choose from the genera in which several colours are available. The heights may be taken as a general planting guide.

Ageratum
Half-hardy. An attractive bedder, also useful for edging. The blue varieties mix well with yellow flowers. Included in the fine varieties are F1 hybrids 'Adriatic' (mid-blue—8 in.), 'Blue Blazer' (bluish-mauve—5 in.), 'Blue Surf' (soft blue—7 in.), 'Spindthrift' (white—7 in.).

Alyssum
Hardy or half-hardy. Rockery and edging varieties include the white 'Snowdrift', purple 'Royal Carpet' and pink 'Rosie O'Day' (all 3 in.). Good bedding plants are 'Little Dorrit' and 'Oriental Night' (both 6 in.), 'Wonderland' (rosy-red— 3 in.). 'Dorrit', 'Oriental Night' (both 6 in.). Good bedding plants: 'Little Dorrit' and 'Oriental Night' (both 6 in.), 'Wonderland' (rosy-red—3 in.).

Antirrhinum (snapdragon)
Half-hardy. The rock hybrids, 'Magic Carpet' (8 in.), and the 'Tom Thumb' varieties (10 in.), including 'Floral Carpet', are useful for edging and rock gardens. The 15–18 in. semi-dwarf, intermediate and majestic groups include a number of F1 hybrids. The tetraploids (24 in.) have larger, often bicoloured, flowers. Of the tall varieties (3½ ft.) suitable for cutting, the F1 hybrid 'Rockets' types are the best. 'Coronette' (24 in.), a hybrid bedding strain resistant to disease and rain, has uniform plants with 8–12 spikes that bloom together.

Aster: see **Callistephus**

Begonia (fibrous-rooted)
Half-hardy. Needs an early start and a temperature of not less than 15°C (60°F) for success, but results are most rewarding. One of the best bedding plants. Excellent F1 hybrid strains are 'Organdie' (6 in.), 'Thousand Wonders' (8 in.), 'Danica' (14 in.).

Calendula (pot marigold)
Hardy. Easy to grow and often self-seeding. 'Orange King' (18 in.), and the quill-petalled 'Radio' (24 in.) have flowers of brilliant orange, and the 'Pacific Beauty' varieties (24 in.) give a good mixing of pastel colours. 'Fiesta Gitana' is a richly coloured compact mixture (12 in.).

Callistephus (aster)
Hardy or half-hardy. These come in many varieties and forms: 'Pinocchio' (8 in.), 'Milady' (10 in.), quill-petalled 'Pompone' (15 in.), 'Teisa Stars' (8 in.), 'Lilli-put' (15 in.), curly petalled 'Ostrich Plume' (2 ft.), quill-centred 'Super Princess' (2—2½ ft.), and a long-stemmed 'Super Chinensis' (2½ ft.).

Candytuft: see **Iberis**

Centaurea (cornflower)
Hardy. The tall varieties (3 ft.) in various colours are good for cutting. 'Snowball', pure white, and 'Polka Dot Mixed' (12 in.) are good for bedding.

Chrysanthemum
Hardy. The *C. carinatum* or 'Tricolor' varieties (24 in.) are easy and profuse flowering. *C. spectabile* 'Cecilia' (2½ ft.) is a bicoloured yellow and white, and the double, button-like *C. coronarium* 'Golden Gem' and 'Lemon Gem' are 18 in. high. *C. indorum* 'Bridal Robe' (12 in.) is long-lasting as a cut flower.

Ageratum

Alyssum

Antirrhinum

Begonia

Calendula

Callistephus

Centaurea

Chrysanthemum

Clarkia
Hardy. Easy to grow. Semi-double and double flowering types. 'Salmon Queen' is an out-standing variety. Height 1–2 ft.

Convolvulus
Hardy. *C. tricolor* (*minor*) varieties are easy to grow. 'Royal Ensign' (15 in.) has ultramarine flowers with white and yellow throats. The mixed selection (height and spread 15 in.) has light blue, crimson, pink and white flowers.

Cornflower: see **Centaurea**

Cosmos
Hardy or half-hardy. The tall (3–3½ ft.) 'Sensation' mixture and 'Gloria' (rose-pink), 'Sun-set' (vermilion) and 'Psyche' (frilled flowers in mixed colours) are good for the back of the border. 'Candy-stripe' (2½ ft.) is the earliest to flower. 'Diablo' (2 ft.) is rich glowing orange. Grow in a sunny spot. (Illus-tration, p. 22.)

Dahlia
Half-hardy. Many good bedding forms can be raised from seed—the dwarf 'Rigoletto' (12 in.), semi-double with bronze foliage; 'Redskin' (18 in.) collarette; 'Dandy' (2 ft.) with single blooms containing a distinctive inner collar of small petals; 'Pompon' (3 ft.); and 'Cactus-flowered' (4 ft.).

Delphinium, annual (larkspur)
Hardy. Larkspurs (*D. ajacis*) all require good soil and a long

growing season. Sow before the soil gets too warm. They make excel-lent cut flowers. The stock-flowered and 'Giant Imperial' (3½–4 ft.) varieties are prolific. In small gardens the single-stemmed dwarf hyacinth-flowered (12 in.) form is most useful.

Dimorphotheca
Hardy or half-hardy. The *D. aurantiaca* hybrids (12 in.) con-tain some of the most attractive pastel-shaded single flowers, in

Clarkia

Convolvulus

Dahlia

Delphinium

Dimorphotheca

Eschscholzia

Gaillardia

Godetia

apricot, lemon, primrose, white and salmon. 'Goliath' (15 in.) has large, glossy-petalled, bright orange flowers.

Echium (viper's bugloss)
Hardy. A good annual for poor soil, flowering for a long time. 'Blue Bedder' (15 in.) has bright blue flowers, while those of 'Mixture' are blue, pink, mauve and white. (Illustration, p. 23.)

Eschscholzia
Hardy. This plant thrives in a bright sunny spot, and will often self-seed. Brilliant colours in red, yellow, crimson, orange and other vivid shades. The single varieties are surpassed by the 'Double Art Shade' (12 in.).

Gaillardia
Hardy or half-hardy. Best treated as a half-hardy plant, as outdoor germination can be difficult. The single *G. picta* 'Indian Chief' (18 in.) has striking bronze-red flowers. Two of the best bicoloured forms are the double *G. p. lorenziana* (18 in.) and the new dwarf version 'Lollipop' (12 in.).

Godetia
Hardy. Good for bedding in dwarf forms such as 'Monarch Dwarf Bedding' (12 in.), and the double

azalea-flowered (18 in.) mixtures. Needs thinning to give room for a bushy plant. Good single-flowered varieties are 'Crimson Glow', and 'Sybil Sherwood' (18 in.), which is salmon pink, edged with white. The tall double mixed godetias (2½ ft.) need support.

Gypsophila
Hardy. *G. elegans* 'Covent Garden White' (18 in.) has profuse large flowers, and *G. rosea* (15 in.) has sprays of small delicate blooms. Thrive in chalky soil.

Helianthus (sunflower)
Hardy. The tall double varieties, which range from 6–10 ft., are the best known. More useful are the compact varieties, such as 'Dwarf Sungold' (24 in.), which have several flowers to a plant.

Helichrysum
Hardy or half-hardy. Plant these everlasting flowers in a sunny part of the garden. For drying, cut the flowers before they are fully open. The tall double mixed kinds grow to about 3 ft., and the dwarf Bikini strain to 12 in.

Iberis (candytuft)
Hardy. An easy annual. For edging, 'Fairy Mixed' (8 in.) and 'Red Flash' (10 in.). For cutting,

the hyacinth-flowered 'White Pinnacle' (12 in.).

Ipomoea (morning glory)
Half-hardy. The beautiful climbing 'Heavenly Blue' is justly named. Plant in mid-June in a sheltered, sunny spot and support it. 'Flying Saucers' is blue and white and 'Wedding Bells' a soft pink.

Larkspur: see **Delphinium**

Lavatera
Hardy. 'Loveliness' (pink—3 ft.), 'Mont Blanc' (white—2 ft.) and 'Silver Cup' (rose—2½ ft.) are bushy with large trumpet flowers.

Linum (flax)
Hardy. The scarlet *L. grandiflorum rubrum* (15 in.) is easy to grow in any soil and flowers well for a long period.

Lobelia
Half-hardy. One of the most widely grown bedding plants. The compact 6 in. varieties cover a range of blue shades—'Crystal Palace', 'Mid-Blue', 'Mrs. Clibran' (which has a white eye) and 'Cambridge Blue'. 'Rosamond' is carmine with a white eye, and 'White Lady' is a pure white.

Marigold: see **Calendula**; **Tagetes**

Matthiola (stock)
Hardy or half-hardy. The stock's scent is one of its great attractions. The 'Ten Week' (12 in.) selections provide a good range of colours. The 'Column' (24 in.) varieties are single-stemmed and make excellent cut flowers.

Mesembryanthemum
Half-hardy. Suited to a hot, dry, sunny position. It opens well only when the sun is out. The *M. criniflorum* 'Mixed' (3 in.) selection is spectacular.

Mimulus (musk)
Half-hardy. Does well in shaded positions, but tends to burn up in strong sun. 'Queen's Prize Mixed' (10 in.) has spotted and self-coloured flowers.

Morning glory: see **Ipomoea**

Nasturtium: see **Tropaeolum majus**

Nemesia
Half-hardy. Flowers best in cool, moist positions. Plant as soon as the garden is frost-free. The 'Dwarf Compact' and 'Triumph' (4 in.) strains give excellent mixtures, and 'Fire King' and 'Orange Prince' (9 in.) are brightly coloured. 'Carnival Mixed' (10 in.) is larger-flowered in a wider range of colours

Gypsophila

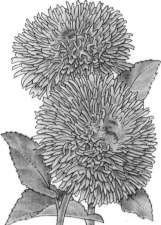

Helianthus

Helichrysum

Iberis

Nicotiana (tobacco plant)

Half-hardy. Valued for their fragrance in the evening. Plant in a sunny place. 'Tinkerbell' (10 in.) and F1 hybrid 'Nicki' (12 in.) are mixtures with pink, red, lime and white flowers that remain open all day. 'Crimson Rock' (18 in.) and 'Lime Green' (2 ft.) are distinctive for floral decoration.

Nigella (love-in-a-mist)

Hardy. Nigella benefits from an early sowing and produces flowers

good for cutting. There are blue varieties, 'Miss Jekyll' and 'Miss Jekyll Dark Blue' (18 in.). Other varieties are 'Persian Rose' and the mixed 'Persian Jewels' (15 in.).

Papaver (poppy)

Hardy. The double and single 'Shirley' poppies (24 in.) have some of the most delicate petals and colours of all annuals. They are profuse, long-flowering and easy to grow if sprayed to control blackfly. The 'Carnation-flowered'

and 'Paeony' (3 ft.) mixtures are large double-flowered forms useful in clumps in the border.

Petunia

Half-hardy. One of the most brilliant of bedding subjects for a sunny, sheltered spot away from the rain. There are good F1 hybrids in both *multiflora* and *grandiflora* forms. In the garden grow such *multiflora* varieties as the 9 in. 'Starfire' (deep rose marked with a white star), the 8

in. 'Sugar Plum' (veined orchid-purple), the 'Satin' (9 in.) series, and the more rain-tolerant 'Resisto' (10 in.) group. For window boxes and other containers the *grandiflora* 'Cascade' varieties are excellent.

Phlox

Hardy or half-hardy. Free-flowering. Dwarf varieties such as 'Beauty' (9 in.) and 'Cecily Mixed' (8 in.) will flower for a long time. The 'Twinkle Mixed' (8 in.) group

Ipomoea

Lavatera

Linum

Lobelia

Matthiola

Mesembryanthemum

Mimulus

Nemesia

has small star-like flowers in various colours.

Poppy: see **Papaver**

Rudbeckia
Half-hardy. Gives colour to the border in late summer and autumn. Recommended are 'Marmalade', rich orange, and 'Rustic Dwarfs', gold, bronze and mahogany (both 18 in.), and 'Autumn leaves' (2–2½ ft.). Tallest are the single and double 'Gloriosa Daisy', with 7 in. flowers on 3 ft. tall plants.

Salvia (sage)
Half-hardy. The brilliant colours are indicated by the names of 'Scarlet Pygmy' (10 in.) and 'Blaze of Fire' (12 in.). The darker 'Royal Purple' (12 in.) blends well with yellows in bedding schemes.

Scabiosa (scabious)
Hardy or half-hardy. Flowers late and is best raised as half-hardy. The 'Monarch Cockade' (2½ ft.) and the large-flowered double (2½ ft.) mixtures have long flower

stems and double blooms in a good colour range.

Snapdragon: see **Antirrhinum**

Stock: see **Matthiola**

Sunflower: see **Helianthus**

Tagetes (African and French marigolds)
Hardy or half-hardy. Tagetes are sub-divided into the large-flowered African types (*T. erecta*) and the smaller-flowered French forms (*T. patula*). The African

varieties have been much improved by the F1 hybrids such as 'Climax' (3 ft.), 'Jubilee' (24 in.) and 'Gold Coin' (3 ft.). Best of the non-hybrids are the 'Crackerjack Mixture' (2½ ft.) and the smaller orange 'Hawaii' (24 in.). The dwarf bedding 'Golden Age' (10 in.) is early. 'Dwarf' French marigolds have single, double or super-crested flowers. Excellent free-flowering singles are 'Pascal' (6 in.) and 'Naughty Marietta' (12 in.). Double and super-crested varie-

Nicotiana

Nigella

Papaver

Petunia

Phlox

Rudbeckia

Salvia

Scabiosa

ties have long-lasting, freely produced flowers. Recommended
varieties include the 'Boy' series
'Golden', 'Harmony', 'Yellow'
and 'Orange' (6 in.), the 'Petite'
mixture (9 in.), 'Orange Winner'
(8 in.), and 'Goldfinch', 'Honeycomb', 'Queen Bee' and 'Yellow
Jacket' (10–12 in.). From F1 hybrid crosses between the African
and French types are the compact
large-flowered 'Seven Star Red',
'NellGwyn'and'Showboat'(12in.).

Tropaeolum majus
(nasturtium)
Hardy. Excellent in poor soil and
hot dry places. Gleam hybrids
are semi-trailing. Good compact
varieties are 'Cherry Rose', 'Baby
Salmon', 'Jewell Mixed', 'Whirl-
bird', 'Red Roulette' and the
cream and green foliage 'Alaska.'

Verbena
Half-hardy. Richly colourful
plants that do well in wet or

sunny positions for edging, bedding and window boxes. 'Springtime', 'Sparkle', and 'Rainbow'
are compact mixtures (6—10 in.).
'Amethyst', violet blue, and
'Venosa', deep lilac (12 in.), contrast with yellow bedding plants.

Zinnia
Half-hardy. Do not like root disturbance. Sow singly in pots or
blocks under glass in warm sheltered gardens: sow outdoors in

mid-May. Dwarf varieties first
into flower are 'Thumbelina' (6
in.), 'Peter Pan' (10 in.), and the
miniature pompon 'Lilliput' (12
in.). They are followed by the F1
hybrid 'Ruffles' series (2 ft.), pink,
scarlet and yellow. 'Persian Carpet' (15 in.), with small bi-colou-
red double flowers, and 'Early
Wonder' (18 in.) are more rain
resistant than most. The giant
dahlia-flowered varieties ($2\frac{1}{2}$ ft.)
are later into flower.

Tagetes

Tropaeolum

Verbena

Zinnia

Annuals : guide

Key:
E = Edging 1–6 in.
D = Dwarf bedding 1–9 in.
M = Medium bedding 9–18 in.
T = Tall bedding. Over 18 in.
B = Back of border. Over 24 in.
○ = Sun
◐ = Partial shade
● = Full shade

	Use in garden	Colours	Flowering period	Planting distance in inches	Situation	Half-hardy. Sow in frame or greenhouse at 18°C (64°F)	Half-hardy. Sow in frame or greenhouse at 10°C (50°F)	Half-hardy. Sow in cold greenhouse, frame or cloche	Hardy. Direct sown in flowering position	Good for cutting	Dead-heading	Pinching out
Ageratum	D M	Blue, white, pink	Jul–Oct	6–12	○◐●	Apr	Mar–Apr			†	†	
Alyssum	E	White, pink, purple	Jun–Sep	6–12	○	Apr	Mar–Apr	Apr	Apr–May, Sep			
Antirrhinum	D M T B	Various, mixed	Jul–Aug	9–18	○◐	Feb–Mar	Feb–Mar			†	†	†
Begonia	E D	Pink, red, white, mixed	Jun–Sep	4–6	○◐●	Jan–Feb	Jan–Feb					
Calendula (pot marigold)	T	Orange, yellow, cream, mixed	May–Aug	12	○◐		Apr	Mar	Mar–May, Sep	†	†	†
Callistephus (aster)	E D M T	Various, mixed	Jul–Sep	12–18	○◐	Apr	Mar–Apr	Mar	Apr–May	†	†	†
Centaurea (cornflower)	M B	Red, blue, pink, white, mixed	Jun–Sep	12–18	○◐				Mar–Apr, Sep	†	†	†
Chrysanthemum (annual)	E T B	Various, mixed	Jul–Sep	12–18	○◐	Apr	Mar–Apr	Apr	Apr	†	†	†
Clarkia	T	Red, pink, mixed	Jul–Aug	12	○				Mar–Apr	†		†
Convolvulus	M	Red, crimson, mixed	May–Sep	12	○◐				Mar–Apr, Sep			
Cosmos	T B	Pink, red, white, orange, mixed	Jul–Sep	12–24	○◐	Apr	Mar–Apr		Apr–May	†	†	†
Dahlia (annual)	M T B	Various, mixed	Jul–Oct	12–24	○◐	Apr	Mar–Apr	Apr	May	†	†	†
Delphinium, annual (larkspur)	M B	Red, pink, blue, white, mixed	Jun–Sep	12–18	○◐				Sep	†	†	
Dimorphotheca	M	Orange, white, mixed	Jul–Sep	12	○	Apr	Mar–Apr	Apr	Apr–May		†	
Echium (viper's bugloss)	M	Blue, mixed	Jul–Aug	12–18	○◐				Mar–Apr, Sep			
Eschscholzia	M	Various, mixed	Jun–Aug	9–12	○				Mar–Apr, Sep			
Gaillardia	M	Various, mixed	Jul–Oct	12	○	Apr	Mar–Apr	Apr	Apr–May	†	†	†
Godetia	M T	Various, mixed	Jun–Aug	12–18	○◐				Mar–Apr, Sep	†	†	
Gypsophila	M	Pink, red, white, mixed	Jun–Sep	9–12	○				Mar–Apr, Sep	†		
Helianthus (sunflower)	T B	Yellow, mixed	Jul–Sep	24	○◐				Apr	†		
Helichrysum	M T B	Various, mixed	Jul–Sep	12	○	Apr	Mar–Apr	Apr	Apr	†	†	

sowing

= Edging 1–6 in.
= Dwarf bedding 1–9 in.
= Medium bedding 9–18 in.
= Tall bedding. Over 18 in.
= Back of border. Over 24 in.
○ = Sun
= Partial shade
= Full shade

	Use in garden	Colours	Flowering period	Planting distance in inches	Situation	Half-hardy. Sow in frame or greenhouse at 18°C (64°F)	Half-hardy. Sow in frame or greenhouse at 10°C (50°F)	Half-hardy. Sow in cold greenhouse, frame or cloche	Hardy. Direct sown in flowering position	Good for cutting	Dead-heading	Pinching out
Iberis (candytuft)	D M	Pink, lilac, white, red, mixed	May–Sep	6–9	○				Mar–May, Sep	†		
Ipomoea (morning glory)	B	Blue, pink, white, mixed	Jul–Oct	12	○	Apr	Apr	Apr	June			
Lavatera	B	Pink, white	Jul–Sep	18–24	○◐				Apr			
Linum (flax)	M	Red, white	Jul–Aug	9	○◐				Mar–Apr			
Lobelia	E D	Blue, white, carmine, mixed	Jul–Oct	6–9	○◐	Feb–Mar	Feb–Mar					
Matthiola (stock)	M T	Various, mixed	Jun–Sep	12	○	Mar–Apr	Mar	Apr	Apr	†	†	†
Mesembryanthemum	E D	Mixed	Jul–Oct	12	○	Apr	Mar–Apr		Apr–May		†	
Mimulus	D	Red, mixed	Jul–Oct	12	◐●	Apr	Mar–Apr				†	
Nemesia	D	Blue, red, orange, mixed	Jul–Sep	6–9	○◐	Apr	Mar–Apr	Apr	May	†	†	†
Nicotiana (tobacco plant)	T B	Red, white, lime, mixed	Jul–Oct	18	○◐	Apr	Mar–Apr			†	†	†
Nigella (love-in-a-mist)	M T	Blue, rose, white, mixed	May–Aug	9	○◐				Mar–Apr, Sep	†	†	
Papaver (poppy)	T B	Various, mixed	Jun–Sep	12–18	○◐				Mar–Apr, Sep		†	
Petunia	M	Various, mixed	Jul–Oct	12	○	Mar–Apr	Mar–Apr					†
Phlox	D M	Various, mixed	Jul–Oct	9	○◐	Apr	Mar–Apr	Apr	Apr–May		†	
Rudbeckia	M T B	Gold, brown, mixed	Aug–Oct	12–18	○	Mar–Apr	Mar–Apr			†	†	†
Salvia (sage)	D M	Red, pink, salmon, purple	Jul–Oct	12	○	Mar	Feb–Mar				†	
Scabiosa	T B	Various, mixed	Aug–Oct	12	○◐	Apr	Mar–Apr	Apr	Apr	†	†	
Tagetes (African and French marigolds)	EDM TB	Gold, lemon	Jul–Oct	9–12	○	Apr	Mar–Apr		Apr–May			
Tropaeolum majus (nasturtium)	M	Red, yellow, orange, mixed	Jul–Sep	12	○◐				Apr–May	†		
Verbena	D M	Various, mixed	Jul–Oct	12	○	Mar–Apr	Mar				†	†
Zinnia	E D M T	Various, mixed	Jul–Sep	9–18	○	Apr	Mar–Apr	Apr	May	†	†	

April

Spring spreads right across the country this month, bringing colourful
displays of bulbs, and the start of regular lawn-mowing

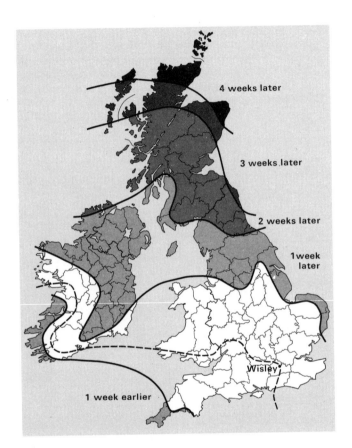

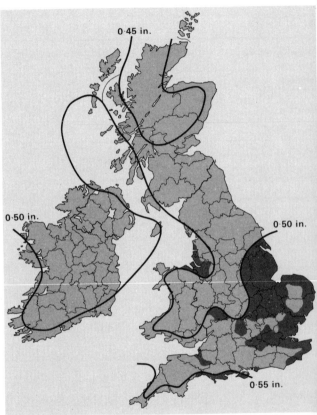

PROGRESS OF THE SEASON

As the year advances into spring, the differences between weather in
the south and north decrease, though differences are still quite great.
The map shows the earliness or lateness of the season in an average
April at places in the British Isles compared with the Royal Horticultural
Society's Gardens at Wisley. Gardeners in the white areas can often
begin the April sowing and planting-out programme at the beginning of
the month. Those to the north should wait the number of weeks
indicated; gardeners to the south may begin the programme earlier

WATER NEEDED BY A GARDEN IN APRIL

The total water used by a garden—an amount known as the potential
transpiration—is shown in inches per average week in April. In some areas
rainfall does not equal potential transpiration and, to ensure the
availability of all the moisture needed by plants, watering is necessary:
the shaded areas are those where this is likely to occur. Assessing the
amount of watering needed, the gardener must consider the local
rainfall. Water without delay in dry spells: do not wait until plants wilt.
(See GLOSSARY, *Weather*)

The weather in April

The general weather is much the same as in March, and differences between south and north are still quite great. Showers, sometimes of sleet or snow, are common when the wind is in the north or north-west. Snow is by no means unusual, but it rarely lasts long. Cold, grey weather is again possible. The best April days are those bringing warm rains from the west, or the occasional southerly wind with the promise of summer to come. Severe ground frost is possible at night, especially if the ground is dry. Because the sun is strong enough to mitigate the effects of the cold nights, daytime temperatures are nearly always above 10°C (50°F) in southern England, and widespread fog is rare.

Occasional periods of anticyclone weather with warm, dry, sunny conditions occur in April, and at least one day with a maximum temperature of over 21°C (70°F) can be expected in the south. A ground frost at night may follow these hot days, especially in sheltered valleys and hollows.

Inland thunderstorms with heavy rain are to be expected once or twice during April, sometimes with sleet or hail.

During this month the gardener may be blessed with intervals of soft, moist, cloudy weather.

April is a busy time in the garden, with much to do and little time available. Wet weekends can cause considerable hold-ups in the general work. A dry month can be helpful, but extra care must be taken to see that the young plants do not run short of soil moisture.

A summary of the month's work

LAWNS

New lawns. Mow twice a week if necessary. Roll to firm seedlings if required.

Established lawns. Mow, aerate, apply spring fertiliser, and scarify. Continue mowing frequently, lowering the blades at each successive cut, down to a minimum of $\frac{1}{2}$ in. Level humps and fill in hollows. Treat fusarium patch if present. Apply selective weed-killers and mercurised moss compounds.

ROSES

Complete pruning. Feed with rose fertiliser and hoe it into the surface soil. Tie new growths of climbers and ramblers to a separate cane to simplify pruning later. Water newly planted roses during prolonged dry weather. Mulch rose beds with manure, garden compost or moist peat, or apply $\frac{1}{2}$ in. of grass cuttings. Water beds with paraquat-diquat or a simazine rose-bed weed-killer. Buy and plant container-grown roses from garden centres.

Under glass. Keep temperature to 21°C (70°F) during the day and to 16°C (61°F) at night. Water pot-grown roses and feed once a week with liquid fertiliser. Shade the glass of the greenhouse and keep ventilators open. Spray foliage with dinocap.

HARDY HERBACEOUS PLANTS

Plant late-flowering herbaceous plants and those slow to make new growth. Lift and divide old clumps of michaelmas daisies, re-planting on well dug and manured ground. Treat rudbeckias, helianthuses and monardas similarly. Hoe between plants to control weeds. Stake and tie delphiniums late in the month.

DAHLIAS

Plant out healthy dormant tubers in mild areas towards the end of the month. Prepare the soil as for young plants, and protect the new shoots from spring frosts when they appear above ground. Divide clumps of tubers to increase stock.

Under glass. Pot rooted dahlia cuttings and insert more cuttings. Sow home-saved seeds and those of bedding varieties in an unheated greenhouse. Harden-off rooted cuttings and seedlings in a cold frame. Cover them with newspaper if nights are cold, but ventilate the frame during the day.

CHRYSANTHEMUMS

Rake a balanced general fertiliser into ground prepared for planting. Move pots of outdoor-flowering varieties outdoors. Some early-flowering varieties may need stopping. Prepare standing-out ground for late varieties.

Under glass. Order or prepare John Innes potting compost No. 3, ready for final potting of greenhouse varieties. Move outdoors greenhouse-flowering varieties already in 5 in. pots. Pot late decoratives propagated in March into 3 in. pots. Some large exhibition varieties will be ready for stopping. Control aphids with malathion, HCH or a systemic insecticide. Control leaf miners with malathion or HCH. Keep stools growing steadily to provide cuttings for growing in the greenhouse border for Christmas flowers.

GLADIOLI

Begin hoeing and dress the soil with fish manure beforehand.

IRISES

Cut blooms of bearded irises early in the morning and stand in hot water before transferring to cold. Remove flower stems from early-flowering plants after blooming. Renew slug pellets. Watch for leaf spot disease on bearded irises, and spray with Bordeaux mixture or apply zineb.

LILIES

Finish planting bulbs. Keep beds weeded. Sow seeds in boxes outdoors. Spray fortnightly with Bordeaux mixture against botrytis. Spray monthly with a systemic insecticide to control virus-carrying aphids.

Under glass. Spray with a systemic insecticide against aphids. Plant forced lilies outdoors after flowering. Sow seeds of *Lilium auratum, L. speciosum* and *L. sargentiae.*

CARNATIONS AND PINKS

Apply fertiliser to growing and mature plants. Continue planting pinks and border carnations. Stop modern pinks if necessary. Take action against pests. Stake pinks with branching twigs.

Under glass. Sow seeds of border carnations and pinks in boxes in a cold frame or greenhouse. Prick out the seedlings later, then plant in the open border when they have formed bushy plants. Put perpetual flowering carnations delivered from nurseries this month into a light, well ventilated greenhouse. Pot the plants in 4 in. pots and later move into 6 in. pots, using John Innes potting compost No. 2. Stop side shoots resulting from the first stopping, when they are 7 in. long, removing about 2 in. at the tips. Pot second-year plants into 8 in. pots. Set perpetual flowering carnations on slatted staging. Support plants with bamboo canes and wire rings. Third-year plants, if too large for greenhouses, may be planted outdoors to flower in a warm sheltered place. Water perpetuals sparingly. Give an overhead spray about once a fortnight. Feed rooted plants every fortnight in the warm months and every month the rest of the year.

SWEET PEAS

Plant out spring-sown seedlings. Start restricting growth on plants grown as cordons, removing all tendrils and side shoots.

FLOWERS FROM SEED

Complete seed purchases. Sow hardy annuals outdoors. Dress seed before sowing and fork in a general fertiliser.

Under glass. Complete sowings of half-hardy annuals. Move forward batches of half-hardy perennials to cold frames. Cover frames containing tender plants if severe frost threatens. Spray with systemic insecticide, HCH or malathion if aphids or thrips are seen. Plants with yellowing leaves may be starving, so give a liquid fertiliser weekly.

BULBS

Hand-weed beds of daffodils and tulips grown for cut flowers. Remove faded flowers from early-flowering bulbs. Water bulbous plants copiously in dry weather. Plant arum lilies in open ground in mild districts. Leave seed pods intact on scillas, muscari and other small bulbs to seed themselves and produce more new plants. Split old schizostylis clumps.

Under glass. Continue watering and feeding clivias. Pot up tuberoses for flowering under glass or indoors.

ALPINES

Re-plant plants which lack vigour, or which have been lifted slightly out of the ground. Dig the ground and apply a general fertiliser after lifting these plants. Be careful not to damage self sown seedlings around some short-lived plants.

Under glass. Prick out seedlings raised from seeds sown in December or March. Move outdoors seedlings raised under glass after middle of the month.

WATER PLANTS AND POOLS

Start planting in pools when weather is warm. Saturate all soil before planting. Set rhizomes or tubers of water lilies at about 15° to the horizontal; push the lower ends of the stems of oxygenators $\frac{1}{2}$–1 in. into soft soil; plant iris and calla rhizomes horizontally; and place floating plants on the surface of the water.

GREENHOUSES AND FRAMES

In sunny spells, shade young seedlings and newly potted plants, and keep the house well ventilated. Increase water supply to newly potted plants, and continue feeding established plants. Water hydrangeas generously, feed every ten days, and take cuttings. Plant tomatoes in a cool greenhouse in the bed prepared last month. Support tomato plants with canes or strings. To help them set, spray lightly at mid-day in sunny weather, or brush or shake the flowers in dull weather. Remove all side shoots from leaf axils. Sow seeds of tomatoes to be planted outdoors, later potting into 3 in. pots. Sow seeds of *Solanum capsicastrum* and *Campanula pyramidalis.* Feed herbaceous calceolarias every ten days, and train the stems outwards on split bamboos. Pot on begonias and gloxinias into 5 in. pots. Move half-hardy plants into a cold frame to harden-off. Sow melons and cucumbers in a temperature of 16–18°C (61–64°F), and sweet corn at 10°C (50°F). Plant cucumbers on mounds of manure and soil. Increase water supply to hippeastrums. Water plants in frames regularly. Give extra ventilation on sunny days. Scatter slug pellets.

TREES AND SHRUBS

Plant evergreen shrubs during showery weather. Continue planting pot-grown wall shrubs. Water newly planted trees and shrubs in dry weather and mulch with lawn mowings or black polythene sheeting.

Propagation. Sow seeds of *Cytisus scoparius* and genista where they are to flower. Layer shoots of *Hydrangea paniculata grandiflora* in pots of peaty soil. Layer young magnolia shoots by pegging into peaty soil.

Pruning. Lightly prune trees and shrubs which have finished flowering. Cut back *Forsythia suspensa* after flowering to within two buds of old growth. Sever rooted stems and re-plant elsewhere. Cut hard back those shrubs which flower on current season's growth, such as *Buddleia davidii* and *Hydrangea paniculata grandiflora.* Cut romneya shoots back to ground level and shorten growths of *Spartium junceum.* Cut back straggly branches of lavenders and *Magnolia grandiflora,* and remove weak shoots from evergreen olearia, euonymus and viburnum.

RHODODENDRONS AND AZALEAS

Transplant plants that need moving. Complete planting new bushes. Water newly planted bushes if weather is dry. Remove dead heads on early-flowering plants.

HEDGES

Plant evergreen hedging plants. Continue to weed and hoe ground under hedges. Straighten and firm newly planted hedging plants loosened by wind.

HEATHERS

Complete planting this month. Continue propagating by layers and heel cuttings. Cut back all heathers that have finished flowering.

FRUIT

Watch flowering and setting of apples, pears, plums and cherries to ascertain probable size of crop. Keep a watch for pests on flowers and fruitlets. Check that cross pollination is effective. Protect wall trees and soft fruit bushes against frost while in bloom. Plant late-flowering strawberries on frost-prone sites. Check tree ties and stakes to prevent rocking. Mulch round trees and water newly planted fruit. Spray apples, black currants, peaches and nectarines, pears, plums and strawberries. Give a fine spray of water to open peach and nectarine flowers to help setting. Ensure that pollinating insects can reach flowers on cloched strawberries. Remove flowers from immature and autumn-fruiting runners.

VEGETABLES

Plant onion sets and sow salad crops. In the north, plant early potatoes. Sow late summer cauliflowers. Sow wrinkle-seeded peas. Sow maincrop carrots. Cover potato foliage if frost threatens. Sow globe beetroot. Plant out late summer cabbages. Sow winter cabbages, and purple-sprouting and spring-heading broccoli. Order tomato plants for planting outdoors in June. Remove rhubarb flowers as soon as seen.
Under glass. In the south, sow french beans and cover with cloches.
Less common vegetables. Replace soil on earthed-up globe artichokes by manure or compost, and plant new artichokes. Cut asparagus from beds at least two years old.

HERBS

Sow small amounts of dill, fennel, hyssop, marjoram, rue and thyme, and make a further sowing of parsley. Thin seeds sown in March and hoe herb border to control weeds. Plant out rooted cuttings of bay, hyssop, lavender, mint, rosemary, rue and sage taken last August. Plant lavender or rosemary to form a shelter belt. Plant violets as an edging round the herb garden. Layer the creeping stems of thyme. Cut back weak, straggly stems of established rue plants.
Under glass. Make a further sowing of basil. Harden off seedlings sown in March and prick out.

PATIOS AND TOWN GARDENS

Complete preparation of tubs, boxes and troughs for planting. Plant alpines in sinks and troughs. Sow seeds of hardy annuals.

HOUSE PLANTS

Give plants their spring clean, removing dead leaves and washing off dust. Slightly increase the rate of watering again. Give cacti their first watering of the season. Give a liquid house-plant fertiliser to all plants you have had for more than six months. Propagate house plants by cuttings, division, offsets or layering.

GENERAL TASKS

Mulch beds and borders when they have warmed up, after destroying weeds with the hoe and making sure ground is moist. Ensure that tender plants which are frosted thaw out gradually by covering them with paper or spraying with cold water. Order seedlings, such as antirrhinums, dahlias and tomato plants.

Plants to enjoy in April

Border and rock garden plants in flower	
Alyssum	Magnolia soulangiana
Arabis	Magnolia stellata
Aubrieta	Malus
Bergenia	Pieris forrestii
Cheiranthus	Prunus 'Kanzan'
Convallaria (lily-of-the-valley)	Prunus persica
Dicentra	Rhododendron
Doronicum	Ribes
Erythronium	Spiraea arguta
Fritillaria	Spiraea thunbergii
Gentiana	Viburnum
Helleborus corsicus	
Hyacinthus	**Water garden plants in flower**
Leucojum	Caltha (marsh marigold)
Lunaria	Orontium (golden club)
Muscari (grape hyacinth)	
Narcissus	**Greenhouse plants in flower**
Primula	Acacia (mimosa)
Pulsatilla	Calceolaria
Saxifraga	Cineraria
Sparaxis	Hippeastrum
Triteleia	Primula kewensis
Tulipa	Primula malacoides
Trees and shrubs in flower	**House plants in flower, depending on position and culture**
Amelanchier	Anthurium
Aucuba japonica	Begonia semperflorens
Berberis darwinii	Cyclamen persicum
Camellia japonica	Impatiens
Chaenomeles japonica	Solanum capsicastrum
Clematis armandii	Zygocactus (Christmas cactus)
Cytisus praecox	
Cytisus scoparius	**Vegetables in season**
Forsythia	Asparagus
Fothergilla	Broccoli
	Lettuce
	Radish

Lawns

NEW LAWNS

If bad weather has delayed sowing, carry out pre-seeding operations and broadcast seed now (see MARCH).

Watch carefully for signs of bird damage and damping-off disease. Apply remedial measures (see MARCH) and sow fresh seed to repair bare patches.

Adjust the cutting height of the mower to 2 in., determined by laying the mower on its side, placing a straight edge across the front and rear rollers and measuring to the cutting edge of the fixed blade. If the grass is growing quickly, mow twice a week. Annual weeds will disappear as mowing continues.

If the seedlings tend to lift, use a light roller to firm the roots in the soil.

ESTABLISHED LAWNS

To improve old and worn-out lawns, mow, aerate, apply spring fertiliser, scarify and, where necessary, over-seed at $\frac{1}{2}$ oz. per sq. yd. Apply a light top dressing of loamy soil $\frac{1}{8}-\frac{1}{4}$ in. deep. Roll the lawn if dry, but leave it if wet.

Apply spring fertiliser to all established lawns if this has not been done already.

SCARIFYING A LAWN

Scarifying with a rake improves neglected lawns by removing dead growth and admitting light and air to the grass

EDGING A LAWN WITH METAL OR PLASTIC STRIP

Metal or plastic strip, inserted in a slot cut with a spade, keeps lawn edges neat without the need for frequent trueing-up

Firm the strip into place with a mallet, laying a wooden block on the upper edge to prevent distortion and damage to the strip

Continue to mow little and often, especially if the weather is warm and showery. Lower the cutting blades $\frac{1}{4}$ in. at a time at each successive mowing, but do not cut the grass shorter than $\frac{3}{8}-\frac{1}{2}$ in. high (the lower height for very fine turf). Use a light roller to firm the surface of the turf if the mower roller is inadequate, but remember that over-use of the roller tends to compact the surface and keep out water and air. On heavy soils roll very seldom.

Levelling a hump

To level a hump or fill a hollow in the lawn, make an H-shaped cut in the grass, with the crosspiece of the H over the hump or hollow. Roll back the turf and remove or add soil as necessary. Replace the grass, tamp down well and sift a little soil into the cracks.

Apply fungicides for the control of fusarium disease (see MARCH).

Weed and disease control

Some seven to ten days after applying a fertiliser, and at least three days before or after mowing, apply selective weed-killers. Remove persistent perennial weeds and coarse grasses by hand.

Use a plastic detergent container to simplify spot treatment of weeds in lawns. Squeeze the empty bottle with the nozzle in the solution. When pressure is released the solution will be drawn into the container. Squirt small jets at individual weeds, but be careful how much you apply, as too much can harm the surrounding grass.

Apply moss control compounds if necessary (see MARCH).

LEVELLING A LAWN

To level a hump, make an H-shaped cut in the turf, roll it back and remove the excess soil

Roses

Complete outstanding pruning as soon as possible (see MARCH).

Feed established roses with a proprietary rose fertiliser, scattering a handful to the square yard over the surface of the beds, except for a 6 in. circle round the main stem of each tree. Hoe the fertiliser into the surface soil.

Insert canes near ramblers

To simplify the removal later in the year of old flowering stems on climbing and rambler roses (see SEPTEMBER), insert a strong bamboo cane near the plant. As new, non-flowering stems appear, tie them to the cane, thus separating them from the old wood. You will then be able to remove the old stems more easily in the autumn. Afterwards, transfer the new growths to the permanent support and remove the bamboo.

Mulching with manure is an excellent way to encourage the production of new non-flowering stems.

Water and mulch

During prolonged dry weather, water new planted roses, a gallon to each plant, to keep the stems from shrivelling. Syringe the stems with water in the evenings.

Mulch established rose beds by covering the soil with a 1 in. thick layer of well rotted manure, proprietary forest bark, garden compost or moist peat. Horse manure will help to lighten heavy clay soil, whereas cow or pig manure is most useful on light, sandy soil. Alternatively, a ½ in. layer of grass mowings may be used. Do not use mowings from a lawn treated with weedkiller. Use moist peat for newly planted roses, as they do not need the fertiliser content of manure or compost at this stage.

Careless hoeing can damage shallow roots. Control weeds by applying a simazine rose-bed weedkiller, which remains effective for a season, or a paraquat-diquat weedkiller. Whichever chemical you use, take care to ensure that it does not come in contact with the rose stems.

Container-grown roses

Although the normal planting season is past, container-grown roses may be purchased from garden centres for transplanting into the open garden.

UNDER GLASS

Try to keep the temperature at around 21°C (70°F) during the day and 16°C (61°F) at night.

Water pot-grown roses more frequently as growth quickens, and feed once a week with a proprietary fertiliser, either liquid or soluble.

Shading methods

Shade the glass by fixing slatted blinds, muslin or green polythene to the inside of the sash bars or by spraying the outside of the glass with a proprietary shading compound.

Unless the weather is frosty, keep ventilators slightly open to maintain a circulation of fresh air.

Spray leaves on both sides with dinocap or benomyl to prevent and control powdery mildew.

Hardy herbaceous plants

Plant late-flowering herbaceous plants and those which are slow to make new growth, such as schizostylis, kniphofias, and *Aster novi-belgii* (michaelmas daisies).

Divide old clumps

Michaelmas daisies deteriorate fairly quickly, and much finer flowers and healthier growth come from young plants. Lift and divide old clumps this month. When dividing them, use only the healthiest outside shoots. Two or three single shoots planted together will make a good show in autumn. The dwarf kinds often spread more quickly and, though less liable to deteriorate with age, may need curbing.

Always dig the ground deeply where old plants are to be replaced by young, and either mix in a little manure or compost, or dust with 2 oz. per sq. yd. of John Innes base fertiliser, bone-meal, hoof and horn, or any organic fertiliser fairly high in phosphates and potash but low in nitrogen.

Re-plant tall perennials

The taller rudbeckias, helianthuses, monardas and heleniums need similar treatment. These plants, by exhausting the soil, produce progressively smaller flowers and often lose their lower leaves. Re-planting revitalises them: during the first season at least growth will not be so tall, but it will be greener and the flowers will be larger.

Hoe between the plants to keep down weeds while they are still small. Even if the soil between plants has been dug and raked over, a fresh crop of annual weeds will soon germinate.

Stake delphiniums

Stake delphiniums late in the month. This is more likely to be needed in borders backed by a hedge, wall or fence than in an open site. The tall delphiniums with their heavy flower spikes need early attention. Support the spikes before the plants reach half their expected height, either with pea sticks up to 6 ft. high according to the variety or, preferably, with a bamboo cane or a 1 in. sq. stake driven into the ground beside each delphinium.

Tie green raffia or string round the stake once with a single knot, and then make a knotted loop round the spike,

DIVIDING CLUMPS OF HERBACEOUS PLANTS

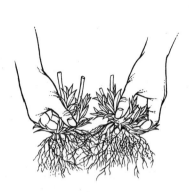

Whenever possible, divide herbaceous plants by pulling them apart. Plant well rooted pieces from the outside of the clump

Clumps which are larger and tougher can be split by thrusting in two forks, back to back, and levering them apart

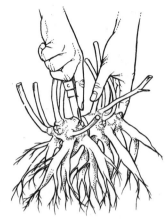

Use a strong, sharp knife to divide plants which have thick, fleshy root growths similar to this paeony

---

allowing ample room for expansion. As the spikes lengthen, tie them at intervals of about 18 in. Metal hoops with detachable legs and metal linking stakes are quicker to use and most effective.

Place shorter pea sticks in and around other weak-stemmed plants such as pyrethrums. Once kinks develop in weak stems, they can never be straightened, and the effect of supporting later in the season is unsightly.

Fill gaps in borders

By the end of the month most plants have emerged from winter dormancy, so that winter losses can usually be assessed by then. Make arrangements to fill such gaps with other plants, if necessary with annual flowers or bedding plants. Some perennials, mostly those with tuberous roots, do not emerge from dormancy until May. Before assuming that they are dead, feel for new shoots gently but thoroughly with your fingers.

STAKING METHODS FOR PERENNIALS

Twiggy pea sticks pushed into the ground around the clump make good supports

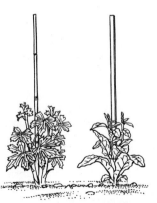

Insert canes or stakes behind tall, spiked plants such as delphiniums and verbascums

When canes are used, secure the plants to them with a loose figure-of-eight loop

Support large clumps by inserting three or four canes and securing string between them

Dahlias

Towards the end of the month in warm and sheltered areas, plant out healthy dormant tubers in the garden. You can tell which tubers are useless, because they are completely shrivelled, or have rotted at the crown (see OCTOBER).

Prepare the soil

Prepare the soil as you would for young plants (see MARCH). Plant the old tubers so that each crown is 3 or 4 in. below the surface of the soil. They should be 2½–3 ft. apart, with the same distance between the rows. If shoots appear above ground and you expect spring frosts, draw some soil well over them. In the north, and on light soil inland in the midlands, it is wise to delay planting old tubers until mid-May because of the likelihood of late frosts.

Divide clumps

If you wish to increase your stock of dahlias, divide each clump of tubers into sections. Each section must carry a bud or growing shoot.

UNDER GLASS

Pot dahlia cuttings that have already rooted into 4 or 5 in. pots, using John Innes potting compost No. 1 or a proprietary soil-less compost. Insert more cuttings in boxes or pots (see MARCH).

Home-saved and commercial strains of dahlia seeds (see OCTOBER) and seeds of bedding varieties can be sown in a heated greenhouse (see MARCH). Prick out seedlings raised from sowings made last month in a heated greenhouse or frame.

Gradually harden-off rooted cuttings, and also seedlings raised from March sowings, by placing them in a cold frame at the end of April or early in May. Protect them from slug damage by making use of proprietary slug pellets. If nights are

DIVIDING DAHLIAS

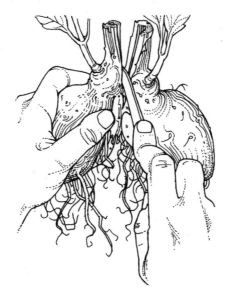

Split clumps of tubers with a sharp knife, ensuring that each section has a bud or a shoot that is already growing

cold, cover the plants with newspaper, and the frame with dry sacks or matting. Ventilate the frame by propping up the light an inch or two during the warmest part of the day.

Chrysanthemums

Rake in a balanced general fertiliser, at the rate suggested by the manufacturer, to land dug earlier (see MARCH) in readiness for putting out the outdoor-flowering varieties.

Sites for pot-grown plants

Prepare the area on which pot-grown plants will stand in the open from May until early September, choosing an open site with a well drained base. Weathered ash or clinker is best, but boards are satisfactory. Do not stand the pots directly on the soil, as worms will enter them through the drainage holes. Some shelter from strong winds is advantageous, but not too much shade.

Clear the ground of weeds and rubbish. Drive in a stout stake at each end of the proposed rows, which should run from north to south, and run a wire between the posts for anchoring the plants' supporting canes.

Move to the open garden pots of outdoor-flowering varieties which will be planted in a few weeks time in sheltered southern gardens. They need protection from frost and cold winds. Some of the very early-flowering varieties will need stopping before the end of the month.

Stopping

Stopping consists of removing the growing tip of a plant to encourage the growth of side shoots from the leaf axils. These side shoots will eventually grow into the flower-bearing stems. Breaking off the tip of the main growing shoot is sufficient for decorative and cut-flower purposes, but there are special rules for stopping to produce exhibition blooms on the required dates. Stopping is carried out one or two weeks earlier in the north than in the south.

UNDER GLASS

Order or prepare John Innes potting compost No. 3, which will be needed next month for the final potting of greenhouse-flowering varieties, or use a proprietary soil-less compost.

Prepare pots

Have 8 in. or 9 in. pots ready and clean. Scrub clay pots if necessary to get rid of last year's grime. Wash the drainage crocks as well. In the south, move outdoors greenhouse-flowering varieties which are already in 5 in. pots (see MARCH). Protect them from frost, heavy rain and strong winds.

STOPPING CHRYSANTHEMUMS

Removal of the tip of the main growing shoot stimulates development of side shoots from the leaf axils on the stem

a   b

The young plant (a) has just been stopped. In (b) this has led to the development of shoots, each terminating in a bud

....

Pot the late decorative plants which were propagated in March, using 3 in. pots (see MARCH).

Some of the large exhibition greenhouse-flowering varieties may be ready for their first stop during this month, and many of the exhibition incurves are also best stopped at about the middle of the month.

Stopping dates

It is not possible to lay down exact stopping dates, but the following is a general guide for the midlands and south.

Large exhibition varieties must either make a natural break or be stopped before the last week in May. This will enable the plants to make sufficient growth for the buds to be secured (see AUGUST) during the two middle weeks in August.

'Natural break' is the term used when a plant produces its side shoots without being stopped. All plants will do this sooner or later, but stopping speeds the process in those that are slow to break naturally.

The procedure is somewhat different for exhibition incurves, which are mostly stopped twice, once in mid-April and once in mid-June.

Decoratives receive the same treatment as large exhibition varieties, except that stopping is delayed until the third week in June, assuming that a natural break has not occurred.

Control pests

If aphids (greenfly) are seen on the plants, spray with malathion or BHC. Use malathion or BHC to control leaf miners, which often start to tunnel through the leaves this month.

Water pots early in the day, taking special care not to over-water newly potted plants. The development of strong, healthy roots is soon impaired by soggy compost.

If you plan to grow mid- and late-season varieties in the greenhouse border to flower at Christmas, keep the stools cool and growing steadily to provide cuttings for rooting in June.

Gladioli

Commence regular, shallow hoeing once the young shoots appear through the soil. This will check weed growth and keep the soil aerated. Immediately before the first hoeing give a light top dressing of fish manure. Do not water gladioli before the secondary roots have formed, about the end of this month.

GLADIOLI IN TUBS

The smaller gladioli can be grown successfully in tubs. Plant the corms early in the month, 3 in. deep and $\frac{3}{4}$ in. apart.

Irises

Bearded irises are in active growth this month, and the dwarf varieties are in bloom. Flowers cut for indoor decoration will last longer if removed in the early morning or in the cool of the evening, and stood at first in hot water before being transferred to a vase of cold water.

When the early-flowering irises have finished blooming, remove the stems.

Renew slug pellets as necessary.

Inspect leaves of bearded irises for signs of leaf spot disease (brown spots with yellow margins, enlarging quickly and turning grey). If this disease appears before flowering, spray with Bordeaux mixture or dust with zineb.

Mosaic virus spread by aphids is common amongst bearded and bulb irises. Yellowing of the leaves occurs, and in severe attacks there may be stunting of growth and colour changes in the flowers.

Lilies

All lily bulbs should be planted by now, though those temporarily potted up can wait until May, if necessary, or even until September if kept watered (see MARCH). Keep lily beds weeded, but be careful not to damage emerging shoots.

Sow lily seed in boxes outdoors.

In muggy weather spray fortnightly against botrytis with Bordeaux mixture.

Spray monthly with a systemic insecticide to control aphids, which spread virus diseases among lilies (see JUNE).

UNDER GLASS

Use a systemic insecticide to control aphids on pot-grown lilies, and keep the pots adequately watered.

Plant forced lilies outdoors when they have finished blooming. Do not force bulbs for two years in succession.

Sow seeds of *Lilium auratum*, *L. speciosum* and *L. sargentiae*. Keep the seedlings in the greenhouse until they can be established in their permanent positions at 18 months to two years old.

Carnations and pinks

Apply fertiliser to growing and mature plants if this was not done in March, and continue planting border carnations and pinks up to the middle of the month (see MARCH and OCTOBER).

Stop modern pinks if necessary (see MARCH).

Watch for pests and diseases, taking action as necessary (see MARCH).

Stake pinks, if necessary, by pushing branching twigs into the ground so that the flower stems can grow up through them. Staking is most likely to be needed with tall-growing varieties, especially on rich soil and in areas subject to heavy rainfall or strong winds.

UNDER GLASS

After the middle of the month sow seeds of border carnations and pinks in boxes in a cold greenhouse or frame. Space the seeds $\frac{1}{4}$ in. apart and cover with a thin layer of fine soil. When the first true leaves (not the seed leaves, which appear first) are $\frac{1}{2}$–1 in. long, prick out the seedlings 2 in. apart into seed boxes and from then on treat them as hardy perennials, planting them in the open border when they have formed bushy plants.

Perpetual flowering carnation plants are delivered by nurseries this month

SUPPORTING PINKS

Support tall pinks by inserting twiggy sticks close to the clump so that the stems can grow up through and around the supports

and early in May. They require a greenhouse with full light and plenty of ventilation. Keep the plants growing steadily throughout the year without forcing them, avoiding high temperatures when the light is poor. Maintain a minimum temperature of 7°C (45°F). Apply shading to the glass during the warmest part of the day. Damping down and increased ventilation are necessary during really hot weather.

Newly purchased plants, generally grown in 3 in. or $3\frac{1}{2}$ in. pots, will already have had their first stopping and will have made side shoots. Home-propagated plants should be at the same stage.

Potting-on

Pot the plants into 4 in. pots, moving them on into 6 in. containers as soon as the roots reach the sides of the pots. In each case use John Innes potting compost No. 2. The first flowers will be produced while they are in the 6 in. pots.

Stopping side shoots

The side shoots produced as a result of the first stopping will themselves normally require stopping. The time at which this is done controls the time that the first flowers appear. Stopping up to the middle of June produces autumn flowers. Stopping from then until the middle of July produces winter flowers. Stopping from mid-July to the end of August produces early spring flowers, though if plants are not ready for stopping by mid-July they are often left unstopped to flower in late summer. After the second stopping, cutting the blooms acts as a further stopping.

The side shoots are ready for stopping when they are 7 in. long, about 5 in. being left after the tops have been removed as described under the first stopping (see FEBRUARY).

During April and May, pot second-year plants into 8 in. pots, using John Innes potting compost No. 3.

Perpetual flowering carnations

As perpetual flowering carnations may grow 4–5 ft. tall in their second year, set the pots on slatted staging a few inches from the ground. This will ensure free movement of air around the plants. Support the plants with bamboo canes and proprietary wire rings which clip on to the canes.

Third-year plants are too big for most greenhouses, but in warm, sheltered gardens they may be planted out in beds to flower outdoors in summer and early autumn.

Perpetual flowering carnations should not be kept continuously wet. Wait until the soil is nearly dry, then water thoroughly. Give an overhead spray of plain water about once a fortnight during the warm months, but discontinue during the colder part of the year. Do not spray open or opening blooms.

Feed plants in 6 in. and 8 in. pots when their roots are well through to the sides of the pots. Apply weak, high-potash liquid fertiliser every fortnight during the warm months and every month during the rest of the year. Give no fertiliser at all during prolonged dull weather. The soil should be moist at the time of application.

Watch for pests and diseases, taking action as necessary (see MARCH).

Sweet peas

Plant spring-sown seedlings as soon as they are growing strongly.

Start restricting growth on cordon-grown plants when they are 9–12 in. high. Select the strongest shoot (leader) on each plant, and carefully cut off the remainder with a knife or scissors. Tie the leader loosely to the cane, leaving ample room for the haulm to thicken out. From this stage onwards, carefully remove while they are still small all the tendrils and side shoots which will form in every leaf axil.

RESTRICTING GROWTH
ON CORDON SWEET PEAS

Having selected the strongest shoot on each plant, cut off the remainder of the growths

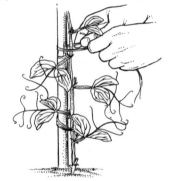

Tie the selected shoot, known as the leader, to the cane, allowing space for thickening

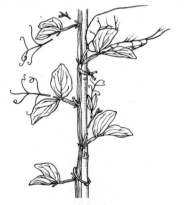

Raffia, twine or metal ring ties are useful for securing sweet peas. Remove all tendrils and side shoots as soon as they are big enough

Naturally-grown plants (see MARCH) need no restriction. Only routine hoeing is needed until the plants have finished flowering.

Remove the cloches from rows of sweet peas sown outdoors in October.

Flowers from seed

Complete your seed purchases as soon as possible.

Many hardy annuals can be sown outdoors this month if weather and soil conditions are favourable (see tables, MARCH). Dress the seeds before sowing and fork into the soil a dressing of general flower fertiliser if this was not done earlier (see MARCH).

Colour from annuals

Hardy annuals are particularly useful for providing colour on bare ground which is due to be planted out with shrubs or herbaceous perennials in the autumn.

Many make delightful ground-cover plants and help to stifle weeds. For instance, sow drifts of dwarf nasturtiums under ornamental cherries or other spring-blossoming trees. Trailing nasturtiums provide rapid ground cover in awkward spaces or gaps.

UNDER GLASS

Complete the indoor sowings of half-hardy annuals (see tables and sowing instructions, MARCH).

Move to a cold frame any well grown early-sown half-hardy annuals. Keep the frame closed at first, opening it progressively as the weather improves and the plants become hardened.

Take special care with the more tender plants. In the case of marigolds, dahlias and ageratums, cover the cold frame with sacking if a hard frost is forecast. There is more frost protection near the centre of the frame than round the edges.

Spray with insecticides

Later in the month, a spell of warm weather may lead to attacks from aphids or thrips on plants in frames. Keep an especially close watch on annual asters, salvias and dahlias, and spray with a systemic insecticide, or with HCH or malathion, as soon as these insects are seen. The first spray is the most valuable of the season. A monthly spraying with a systemic insecticide controls aphids and other sap-sucking insects.

Yellowing of the leaves may occur among some boxes of plants in frames. This often indicates slight starvation and is best overcome by watering weekly with a liquid flower fertiliser.

Sow biennials and perennials (see MAY).

Bulbs

Hand weeding may be necessary where daffodils and tulips are being grown in special beds to produce cut flowers, though autumn application of a residual herbicide should have prevented much weed growth (see OCTOBER).

Remove the faded flowers from early-flowering bulbs to prevent them wasting their energy in producing seed. Leave the flowers on snowdrops, crocuses or other plants you wish to increase by seed.

Water copiously

In dry weather water bulbous plants copiously. They can only fatten up their bulbs between the fading of the flowers and the withering of the foliage.

In mild districts plant arum lilies in open ground, or set them 2–3 ft. deep in a pool to grow and flower as water plants.

The smaller bulbs, such as scillas, chionodoxas, crocuses, galanthuses and muscaris, will soon be producing their seed pods. Leave these intact and allow the seed to fall and produce a further supply of plants. Split old schizostylis clumps and re-plant in rows or groups.

UNDER GLASS AND INDOORS

Continue watering and feeding greenhouse and indoor bulbs. Pot up a few tuberoses for flowering under glass, or in the window of a warm room, during June and July.

Alpines

Plants which appear less vigorous than they did last year, or seem to be lifting slightly out of the ground, may need re-planting. Other indications include partial loss of foliage and the exposure of more basal growth than previously, together with discoloured leaves and even completely dead patches. Reference to the descriptive list (see NOVEMBER) will tell you whether to divide and re-plant at once or wait until after flowering. If you have more than one plant of a particular kind, compromise by re-planting one now and the other later.

Re-plant and fertilise

After lifting affected plants, dig the ground and apply a sprinkling of general fertiliser. Alpines which have grown out of the ground must be set deeper than before. During dry weather fill the planting holes with water and insert the plants when it has soaked away, firming the wet soil around the stems, and finishing with dry soil.

Some plants may have died altogether, due to excessive cold or wet, or simply to old age. Take care not to damage the self-sown seedlings which will probably appear around some of the short-lived rock plants, though they must be kept within bounds.

UNDER GLASS

Prick out seedlings raised from seeds sown in December or March as soon as they have three or four leaves. Seedlings raised under glass can be moved outdoors from the middle of the month.

Water plants and pools

This month many plants in water really begin to grow. The ferns and primulas planted in March should be well established. A start can be made on planting a pool towards the end of the month if the weather is suitably warm.

Like all other plants, aquatics require a balanced food supply. Plant them in a sufficient depth of good soil covered with an adequate depth of water. There are several ways of doing this.

1. Put a 4–6 in. layer of soil on any areas where plants are to be grown.

2. Put a shallow soil layer 2 in. thick on the base (sufficient for oxygenating plants), use 4–6 in. deep slatted-sided containers for the water lilies, and place 4 in. of soil on the shallow shelves of the pool for marginal plants.

3. Use slatted-sided containers of varying sizes for all types of water plants.

With this last method the pool often takes longer to become properly established, as the many small forms of animal life, which are an essential part of the pool, will not multiply until there is a reasonable amount of sediment on the base, offering them food and shelter.

PLANTING WITHOUT CONTAINERS

Cross-section of a pool, with soil 4 in. deep on the shelves for marginal plants, and 4–6 in. deep on the bottom for planting water lilies

Soil selection

Whatever method is adopted, use soil of good quality. Fertile garden soil is suitable—preferably neutral or slightly alkaline. Acid soils should have ground

PLANTING A GARDEN POOL

Pockets for individual plants can be made by enclosing the soil with bricks or stones placed on the bottom of the pool

If plants are not set in containers, minimise root disturbance by directing the hose into a pot, rather than on to the bottom of the pool

chalk added. This is especially important with plastic pools; concrete pools have their own supply of calcium always available. Heavy soils, even clays, are normally better than light soils, as they are often richer in plant foods. Avoid fibrous materials, peat and strawy manure, and very soluble fertilisers. Poor

94

soils may be enriched with John Innes base fertiliser at about ½ oz. per bucketful of soil. Very chalky soils should also be avoided if possible, as they frequently encourage heavy algae growth.

Whether in containers or in the pool itself, the soil should be in a saturated state before planting. Stand containers in water for 10–15 minutes, and flood the soil in the pool to expel all air and so prevent plants from floating.

Plant water lilies

Set the rhizomes or tubers of water lilies at an angle of about 15° to the horizontal, with the growing point or crown just below the surface of the soil. Oxygenating plants, which are usually supplied as small bunches of unrooted cuttings, should have the lower ends of the stems pushed ½–1 in. into the soft soil. Spread the roots of marginal plants and push them downwards into the soil. The rhizomes of plants such as iris and calla (bog arum) should be more or less horizontal. Floating plants are merely placed on the water surface where they will grow more quickly.

Propagation

Plant out self-sown seedlings of water hawthorn and the young plants produced on stolons of nymphaeoides.

Sow seeds of primula in boxes for planting out in August or September. Seeds of mimulus sown now will produce plants for flowering in July.

Lift and divide overgrown lilies. Rampant parts of the plants can be carefully cut off with a sharp knife at any time during the summer.

PLANT QUANTITIES

Water lilies to grow in 12–18 in. of water will spread over approximately 4–6 sq. ft. in two or three seasons. Those for 1½–2 ft. of water will cover 8–12 sq. ft., while the very strong ones will extend over 15–25 sq. ft.

PLANTING IN A CONTAINER

Fill the container with loam or fairly heavy soil, mixing bone-meal with it at the rate of a double handful to each bucket of soil. Set the plant firmly, then cover the surface with a thin layer of gravel to keep the soil in place

Plant one oxygenating plant to every 2 sq. ft. of water surface in pools up to 50 sq. ft. in area. Reduce this to one to every 3 or 4 sq. ft. in larger pools.

Plant one floating plant to every 10 sq. ft. of surface.

As a rough guide, allow one marginal plant to every sq. ft. of shallow water.

Greenhouses and frames

The changeable weather often experienced this month can cause violent temperature fluctuations in the greenhouse. During sunny weather, shade young seedlings and newly potted plants with butter muslin or sheets of paper. Keep the house well ventilated, opening the lights only on the leeward side if there is a risk of squalls or hailstorms.

Give extra water

Give increasing amounts of water to plants re-potted in March, which should now be established and growing rapidly. Continue to feed established plants such

SUPPORTING TOMATOES

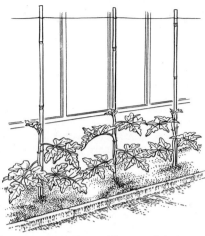

Support tomato plants with canes. Insert one alongside each plant, just outside the soil ball

TOMATO RING CULTURE

Tomatoes grown in this way develop fibrous feeding roots in the containers, where fertiliser is applied, and coarser, water-seeking roots in the layer of aggregate underneath

as zonal and regal pelargoniums, annuals in pots, fuchsias and heliotropes. Apply liquid fertilisers at ten-day intervals.

Hydrangeas in pots, now in active growth, require a temperature of 10°C

(50°F). Spray them frequently with water (daily if possible), water the pots generously, and apply liquid fertiliser every ten days. If you wish to increase your stock, take cuttings from the plants, choosing sturdy, non-flowering shoots, about 3 in. long, and rooting them in a propagating frame heated to 16°C (61°F).

Plant tomatoes

In a cool greenhouse, plant tomatoes in the bed prepared last month, allowing 15 in. between plants or in peat growing bags. Before planting, make sure that the compost in the pot is moist. If you are growing plants on the ring culture system, use John Innes potting compost No. 3 and bottomless containers which are 8 in. deep and 9–10 in. in diameter. Keep the aggregate base moist after planting, watering the containers just sufficiently to keep the plants growing.

Once the roots have penetrated into the aggregate, no further watering of the containers will be needed, except when the plants are fed.

Support tomato plants with tall canes or with strings. Tie the upper ends of the strings to wires secured to the glazing bars and the lower ends to hooks of thick wire pushed into the soil alongside the plants.

From the time the first tomato flowers open, spray the plants lightly at about mid-day during sunny weather. During dull weather, dust the flowers with a feather duster or a camel-hair brush, or give the supporting string or cane a sharp rap with a stick, to dislodge the pollen. Remove all side shoots, when they are 1 in. long, from the axils of the leaves.

Sow the seeds for outdoor tomato plants in a shallow pan of John Innes seed compost, covering the seeds with a thin layer of compost. Make sure that you choose a variety suitable for outdoor culture. Germinate at 16°C (61°F) and pot the seedlings individually into

DE-SHOOTING TOMATOES

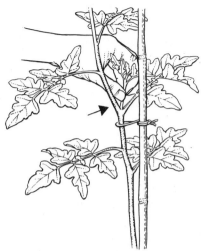

Removal of side shoots, which grow from the leaf axils of tomato plants, must continue throughout the spring and summer

3 in. pots of John Innes potting compost No. 2 when the seed leaves are developed.

Sow seeds of *Solanum capsicastrum* (winter cherry) following the procedure outlined for tomatoes.

Sow seeds of *Campanula pyramidalis*, using John Innes seed compost, potting the seedlings individually into 3 in. pots when they are large enough to handle.

Herbaceous calceolarias make rapid growth during April, so apply liquid fertiliser every ten days. To maintain shapely plants, train the growths outwards from the centre on split bamboos.

Pot on begonias and gloxinias into 5 in. pots of John Innes potting compost No. 2, if this was not done last month.

Hardening-off

Move half-hardy plants into a cold frame for hardening-off. This will also provide space for sowing melons, cucumbers and sweet corn at the end of the month or early in May. Cucumbers are a worthwhile greenhouse crop, though

95

a single plant, grown at the end opposite the door, will be sufficient for the average amateur. 'Butcher's Disease Resister' is an excellent variety. Melons of the cantaloupe type are usually grown in a cold frame or under cloches, and sweet corn can be planted in the open at the end of May or early in June.

Melons and cucumbers

Sow melons and cucumbers in a temperature of 16–18°C (61–64°F) and sweet corn in a temperature of 10°C (50°F). In each case sow the seeds individually about 1 in. deep in 3 in. pots of John Innes potting compost No. 1.

Where a single cucumber plant is being grown, plant it on a mound 12 in. high and 24 in. in diameter, made up of 1 part well rotted manure and 2 parts good soil. Add John Innes base fertiliser at the rate of one 3 in. pot to a barrowload of the mixture. For two or more plants, make a raised bed 12 in. high and 18 in. wide, allowing 3 ft. between plants. Fasten wires horizontally to the glazing bars, at 12 in. intervals, for training the laterals, tying the main stem to a cane

PLANTING CUCUMBERS

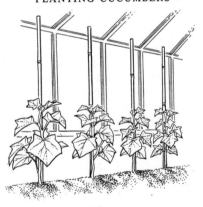

Canes provide initial support for cucumber plants. From these they are trained on wires fastened horizontally to the glazing bars

inserted alongside the plant in the early stages. Stop the main stem when it reaches the apex of the roof, tying the side shoots to the wires as they develop.

Hippeastrums started into growth in March will required more water as growth accelerates.

Plants in frames require regular watering, with the lights propped open to give extra ventilation on sunny days. If necessary, move the tallest plants to the back of the frame so that they do not touch the glass. Scatter slug pellets among the plants.

Trees and shrubs

Plant evergreen shrubs during showery weather (see MARCH).

Continue to plant pot-grown wall shrubs, such as ceanothus, clematis, vitis (decorative vines), lonicera (honeysuckle), jasmine and wisteria.

Plant rosemary on the top of a low retaining wall to cascade over it. It will enjoy the warmth of the stones and will flower more freely than on the ground.

Water newly planted trees and shrubs during dry spells. Trees and shrubs in hot dry sites often need care immediately after planting. To help them keep cool and moist at the roots, cover the watered soil with black polythene sheeting or a mulch of lawn mowings. Both will also help to keep down weeds.

PROPAGATION

Sow seeds of *Cytisus scoparius* and genista where the plants are intended to flower.

Layer shoots of *Hydrangea paniculata grandiflora* into pots of peaty soil. Sever these layers from the parent plants when sufficient strong roots have formed, after about a year.

Layer young magnolia shoots by cutting away a thin piece of bark, about

9 in. long, and pegging the shoots down into peaty soil. After two years sufficient roots should have formed for the layers to be severed from the parent plant and re-planted in their flowering positions. After transplanting, protect the young plants from cold winds, and water in dry hot weather until well established.

PRUNING

Trees and shrubs which have finished flowering may require some light pruning. Shorten branches and cut off dead flower spikes and old weak shoots of *Chaenomeles japonica*, spring-flowering clematis and rosemary.

Cut back *Forsythia suspensa* after flowering to within a bud or two of the old wood. The arching stems often root of their own accord where they come in contact with the ground. Sever the rooted pieces from the parent plant and plant them elsewhere.

Some flowering deciduous shrubs, such as *Buddleia davidii* and *Hydrangea paniculata grandiflora*, produce their flowers on current year's growths, and must be cut hard back now (see illustrations, pp. 62 and 63). *Rhus typhina* will produce strong young shoots if pruned in the same manner. Cut back to ground level all shoots of the summer-flowering romneya, and shorten branches of *Spartium junceum*, as it grows leggy.

Cut back straggly branches of overgrown evergreens, such as lavender and *Magnolia grandiflora*. Light pruning by removing weak or leggy shoots should be carried out on evergreen species of euonymus, olearia and viburnum.

Rhododendrons and azaleas

Transfer plants that have grown too large and require moving. This is also the last chance for planting new bushes (see MARCH). Water plants put in last month if the weather is dry.

Remove dead heads on the early-flowering plants.

Hedges

Plant evergreen hedging plants such as hollies, laurels and escallonias (see plant descriptions, SEPTEMBER). Escallonias are particularly suited to the milder climate of the west and south-west.

All evergreens do well if planted now; but if they are planted earlier in the year, when root growth is slow, the leaves may become desiccated during dry cold weather. On quick-draining soils water the plants during dry spells (see MAY).

Weed and hoe

Continue to weed and hoe the ground under hedges, particularly those recently planted (see MARCH).

If plants in newly planted hedges have been loosened by the wind, straighten them and firm the soil round their stems.

Heathers

Complete planting this month, if possible, and continue to propagate heathers from layers and cuttings (see MARCH).

Cut back all heathers that have finished flowering.

Fruit

Apple, pear, plum and cherry will start flowering in April. Watch flowering closely, because the first essential for fruit formation is that there should be flowers on the trees. As long as only 5–10 per cent of the flowers set fruit there will be a satisfactory crop; if every flower of a blossom sets fruit

there would be too many small fruits.

Start looking for pests on the flowers or fruitlets.

During blossom time keep a careful check on varieties planted for pollination (see recommended varieties, NOVEMBER). Make sure that there are flowers open, that they are healthy and not damaged by pests, and that there is an overlap of flowering times. In a normal season varieties recommended for cross-pollination will have overlapping flowering periods.

Pollination by bees

Honey bees do not fly actively if the temperature is much below 16 °C (61 °F), but if the hives are near the fruit garden, the bees will be active during short periods of good weather, especially if the garden is well sheltered from the wind. Many wild insects are useful pollinators below these temperatures. Do not spray open flowers with insecticides, which will harm pollinators.

If you are in doubt about pollination, try a simple test now before planting in the autumn. Fasten flowering branches from the same type of tree (not the same variety) in water near the tree you wish to pollinate when it is in flower, so that insects can transfer pollen between the two. If the crop is improved, it suggests that existing pollination is not adequate.

Bud protection from frost

The greatest hazard at this time of the year is frost damage to the flowers. Protect wall trees and soft fruit bushes against slight frost by covering with tiffany or muslin. Frost risk may be reduced if the soil is kept bare, firm and damp, since this type of soil absorbs the sun's heat better than dry soil, whether weed-covered or cultivated, and will release any absorbed heat at night. Water dry soil, especially for low-growing crops like strawberries. On sites susceptible to frost, plant late-flowering varieties (see varieties, NOVEMBER).

Check tree ties

Recently planted fruit trees and bushes are now at a critical stage. The buds will have burst, and while water is being lost by the tops the intake from the soil is still uncertain. Roots should be in firm contact with the soil, so check tree ties to stop rocking. If the soil round trees is moist but tending to dry out, give a mulch of straw or compost to form a shallow cover over the soil round the tree; for bushes do not mulch until May. In drying winds, water newly planted fruit, giving not less than 5 gal. per sq. yd. at a time.

Apple

If bad weather has delayed growth so that bud-burst takes place in April, apply a spring spray (see MARCH). Spray also against apple scab, at pink bud stage, with benomyl or captan, especially if the month is wet, with periods of rain and high temperatures.

Black currant

Spray with benomyl against big bud mite when the first flowers open (the late grape stage), and repeat three weeks later. Also spray with malathion against capsid bug and caterpillars.

Cherry

Prune now, cutting out crossing branches and keeping the tree moderately open. On fan-trained trees, cut out branches growing into or away from the wall. Spray with malathion or a systemic insecticide to control blackfly.

Peach and nectarine

Water open flowers with a fine spray to help setting. If red spider mites are seen, spray at petal-fall with derris. Prune fan-trained trees as for cherry.

Pear

Spray with benomyl against pear scab at early white bud stage, and also spray with malathion if greenfly or caterpillars are a problem.

Plum and damson

On fan-trained trees, cut out shoots growing directly towards or away from the wall as new growth starts. Prune bush and standard trees later in the season (see JULY). Spray with malathion to control greenfly.

Strawberry

Make sure that pollinating insects can reach the flowers on plants under cloches. Remove flowers from runners that are not well enough established to fruit this year, and from autumn-fruiting varieties. Watch for greenfly and spray with malathion if necessary. Top-dress with sulphate of ammonia or Nitro-chalk if the plants are slow to get away, but keep the rate low or the foliage will be too heavy.

Vegetables

Plant onion sets and sow parsley and salad crops when the soil is sufficiently dry to work to a fine tilth (see charts on pp. 130–1). In the north, plant early potatoes. (For sowing and planting details, see MARCH.)

Sow seeds of late summer cauliflowers ('Veitch's Autumn Giant', 'All the Year Round' or 'Dominant') in a nursery bed for planting out next month. Sow the seeds $\frac{1}{2}$ in. deep in drills 6 in. apart.

Sow peas of wrinkle-seeded varieties. They should be ready for picking in 12 weeks. Suitable varieties are 'Onward' (24 in.) and 'Gradus' (3–4 ft.). (For sowing instructions, see JANUARY.)

Maincrop carrots

About the middle of the month, sow maincrop carrots (intermediate varieties) for eating during the winter. Sow in drills $\frac{1}{2}$ in. deep and 15 in. apart, later thinning the seedlings to 6 in. spacings. Grow carrots on land manured for the previous crop, raking in 4 oz. per sq. yd. of a

general fertiliser before sowing. Lift and store in September.

Protect potatoes

From the middle of the month onwards be ready to cover potato leaves to protect them from frost. When the leaves first show through the soil, use a draw hoe to move the earth over them, forming higher, sharper ridges. When the ridges can be made no higher, have straw at hand to cover the plants if frost threatens, removing it the next morning when the frost has thawed.

Towards the end of the month sow beetroot (any globe-shaped variety) in soil that has received a medium dressing of manure, first soaking the seeds in water overnight. Sow the seeds in drills 1 in. deep and 9–12 in. apart, spacing the seeds 2 in. apart and later thinning them to 4–6 in.

Plant cabbages

Set out plants of late summer cabbages, sown last month, planting them 18 in. apart in rows 24 in. apart. Plant with a dibber, dusting calomel into each hole as a precaution against club root disease. Set the plants with their bottom leaves at soil level, firming them in with your heel and watering them in immediately afterwards.

Sow winter cabbages ('Christmas Drumhead', 'January King' and savoys), and both purple-sprouting and spring-heading broccoli, for planting out in June. Sow all these seeds $\frac{1}{2}$ in. deep in drills 6 in. apart.

Order tomato plants, for planting outdoors in early June.

As soon as rhubarb flowers are seen, cut them out near the base. If left, they absorb food and energy from the plant.

UNDER GLASS

From the middle of the month onwards in the south, unless the weather is unseasonably cold, sow seeds of french

beans 2–3 in. deep and 4–6 in. apart, in two rows 8 in. apart in a flat-bottomed drill 9 in. wide, and cover with cloches. In the north, and in the south if the weather is cold, wait until early May.

LESS COMMON VEGETABLES

Early in the month, remove the soil from globe artichokes earthed up last November, replacing it with a layer of manure or compost. If compost is used, first sprinkle sulphate of ammonia over the ground at 2 oz. per sq. yd. Plant globe artichokes (either newly purchased or rooted from suckers last November) in soil that has been manured recently. Set them 3 ft. apart in rows 3 ft. apart, with the crowns at soil level.

Cut asparagus, from beds that are at least two years old, when the growths are 4–6 in. above the soil. Use a sharp knife, cutting about 2–3 in. below ground and going over the bed two or three times each week.

In the north if the soil is workable, sow kohl rabi outdoors towards the end of the month (see MARCH).

CUTTING ASPARAGUS

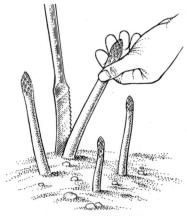

Cut asparagus stems obliquely about 3 in. below ground level, taking care not to damage other stems which are still developing. A serrated asparagus knife is the best tool

Herbs

Sow small amounts of dill, fennel, hyssop, pot marjoram, rue and thyme, and make a further sowing of parsley (see MARCH). Parsley may take as long as nine or ten weeks to germinate. Sow radish seed in the parsley rows at the same time to act as a marker crop.

Thin seedlings sown in March to 6 in. apart, and hoe to keep the weeds down.

Plant rooted cuttings

Cuttings taken last August of bay, hyssop, lavender, mint, rosemary, rue and sage should now be well rooted and ready to plant out into their permanent positions. Plant the rooted sage cuttings 12 in. apart in light dry soil.

Shelter and edging plants

Lavender (for plant description see *Trees and Shrubs*, SEPTEMBER), though not a herb, is often planted in the herb garden to provide a shelter belt. It grows best in poor soil. Plant 2–3 ft. apart in full sun. Rosemary is a useful shelter plant when planted 3 ft. apart on a dry sunny bank.

Plant violets 4 in. apart round the herb garden as an edging plant, or to separate individual beds.

Layer thyme

Layer the creeping stems of thyme by burying the runners in fine soil; the tiny roots at each joint will quickly establish themselves and can then be separated from the parent plant.

Cut weak and straggly shoots of well established rue plants hard back to encourage new strong growth.

UNDER GLASS

Make a further sowing of basil in fine seed compost and under glass (see MARCH). Harden-off seedlings of March-sown basil outdoors. At the end of the month prick out the seedlings, 3 in. apart, into boxes of potting compost.

Patios and town gardens

Complete the preparation of tubs, boxes and troughs in readiness for spring planting (see MARCH).

Decide which plants are to be grown in each container and where the latter are to be placed. Almost any plant can be chosen, including immature specimens of large trees and shrubs.

Plants to avoid are very tall types that require staking, and sorts that need a constantly moist or boggy soil. If you particularly want the latter, block the drainage holes and keep the water level topped up. Do not grow tall plants with heavy foliage in narrow-based containers which could be knocked over by gusts of wind.

Sow hardy annuals

Sow seeds of hardy annuals this month and in May directly into the containers where they are to flower. Choose containers in which perennials or shrubs are already growing, as the annuals will not flower until the summer. Sow as sparingly as possible, if necessary thinning the seedlings further as soon as they can be handled easily.

All types of hardy annuals are suitable, provided they are not too tall in proportion to the container.

Perennials tend to be somewhat uninteresting for much of the time, though they are useful where time cannot be spared for regular re-planting.

Plants for window-boxes

For window-boxes choose plants that will stand up to the wind that whistles round the corners of buildings. Choose sun-loving plants for south aspects; shade-lovers for north-facing walls.

Most alpines grow well in containers, either on their own or alongside taller subjects. Choose low-growing kinds, planting them now in free-draining compost and placing the container in a sunny position. Alpines look particularly effective in miniature rock gardens built in sinks and troughs. Suitable sorts are achilleas, androsaces, arenarias, aubrietas, *Gypsophila repens*, myosotis, potentillas, sempervivums and sedums.

House plants

Although room temperatures in the average home will not yet have risen a great deal, house plants will now be responding to the longer hours of daylight. This is the time to prepare them for vigorous growth during the summer.

Examine each plant carefully, removing dead or disfiguring leaves. Wash off any dust that may have accumulated during the winter. Take small-leaved plants into the bathroom and to the sink and spray them with clean, tepid water. Gently sponge the foliage of large-leaved plants with tepid water. Never apply olive oil, furniture polish or milk to give the leaves an extra shine, as these clog the pores. There are proprietary preparations to add shine to large leaves.

Give more water

Slightly increase the rate of watering again (see MARCH). Give any cacti kept indoors their first good watering since the autumn. This will plump them up and help to induce flowering.

Apply a proprietary liquid house-plant fertiliser to any plants that you have had for more than six months, applying it at half the recommended rate.

Propagation methods

This is a good time to propagate house plants. New plants can be obtained from cuttings, by division, from offsets (see MARCH) and by layering.

The simplest method of taking cuttings is in a jar of water. Ivy, tradescantia (wandering jew), philodendron, rhoicissus (grape ivy), impatiens (busy lizzie), chlorophytum (spider plant), saintpaulia (African violet), *Begonia semperflorens* and peperomia can all be rooted in this way. Choose a healthy, strong-growing tip and cut or break off 2–4 in. Strip away the lower leaves and rest the cutting in the water. In a few weeks roots will be seen. When these are strong enough, pot the new plant, selecting a clean pot no larger than is necessary to accommodate the roots and using John Innes potting compost No. 2 or a proprietary soil-less compost.

Rooting cuttings

Alternatively, cuttings may be inserted directly in the soil. In this case rooting will be quicker and more certain if slight extra warmth and humidity can be provided. This is best given by means of a propagating case in the greenhouse, but a simple substitute is to slip the pot or tray containing the cuttings into a polythene bag. Seal the open end of the bag with a rubber band and stand the pot in a warm place, such as above a radiator or in an airing cupboard. Normal room temperature will usually be sufficient to ensure rapid growth.

If the soil or compost is too moist, there may be excessive condensation inside the bag, with the consequent risk of damping-off. To prevent this, remove the pot or box when heavy condensation becomes apparent, turn the bag inside out, and replace the container.

Some plants, such as saintpaulia and *Begonia rex*, are propagated from leaf cuttings. There are two methods.

Leaf cuttings

To take leaf cuttings of saintpaulias, cut off healthy leaves with 1–2 in. of stalk and push them into a pot containing equal parts of peat and sand. Remove and plant in individual pots the new plants that will appear. The leaf cutting will root more easily if the pot is covered with a polythene bag or glass jar.

One or two other plants with rougher leaves, such as *Begonia rex*, are propagated from different leaf cuttings. The entire leaf is removed, and is laid flat on a box containing a similar sand and peat mixture. Cut the major ribs through at the points where veins meet, holding the entire leaf down firmly on the soil surface with pebbles or hairpins. New plants will grow from the slashed places.

Leaves in squares

Alternatively, cut the leaf into pieces 1 in. square, ensuring that two veins meet on some of the edges. Lay them on the surface of the prepared compost. New plants, which form on one or more of the edges, can later be potted up. A temperature of about 16°C (61°F) is required for both types of leaf cuttings.

Some plants, such as ivy, will send up so many new shoots at the base that the original plant can be divided to make several new plants. Knock the plant from its pot, separate the shoots as carefully as possible, and re-plant them in separate, smaller pots.

Propagate by layering

Some house plants, such as *Fatshedera lizei*, grow quite large on a single woody stem, almost like a tree. They can be propagated by layering. Train a branch downwards so that it rests on the soil surface of a smaller pot, peg it down, and a new plant will root itself in the pot. Other plants, such as chlorophytum, throw out long stems which carry tiny plantlets. These can also be layered.

This method of layering is not suitable for a tall plant with a single stem, such as *Ficus elastica decora* (rubber plant), but a similar process called air layering is employed. In this case the new plant is produced on the stem instead of in the soil.

Air layering

If a young ficus has lost its lower leaves, perhaps due to over-watering, it will be left with a long, naked stem and a few leaves right at the top. About 3–4 in. below this top-knot of leaves, cut away a strip of bark 1 in. wide right round the main stem. Dust this area with hormone rooting powder and wrap it in a fist-sized ball of moist sphagnum moss. Tie this round the stem with string and wrap it in a strip of polythene, tying it firmly at the top and bottom so that the moist moss cannot dry out.

Roots will grow into the moss after approximately 10 weeks. When this new growth is seen at the top, cut away the plant just below the polythene wrapping, remove the polythene and moss, and pot up the new plant in a suitable compost (see illustration, p. 479).

General tasks

As the ground begins to warm up, apply mulching material to beds and borders. Good mulches are mushroom and garden compost, half-decayed leaves, chopped straw and proprietary forest bark. Hoe the ground free of weeds, and see that it is thoroughly moist before applying the mulch. Birds often scratch about in the mulch and scatter it on adjoining paths. To prevent this, lay a length of wire netting about 12 in. wide along the edge of the border and cover it with the mulching material. The birds' claws catch in the wire and they move elsewhere.

If any tender plants become frosted, try to get to them before the sun reaches them. Cover them with papers or sacking, or spray cold water on them; this allows them to thaw out gradually.

Order boxes of seedlings, such as asters and antirrhinums, and also dahlias. Order tomato plants for planting when danger of frost is past.

May

In the sunny, dry days of May, rhododendrons and azaleas reach perfection,
and the garden makes up for the checks of a cold spring

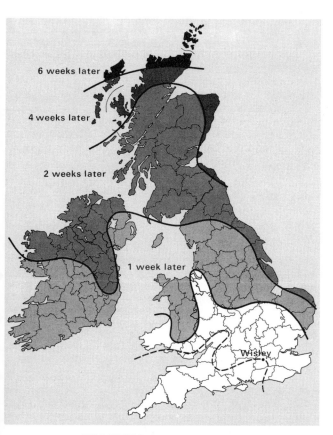

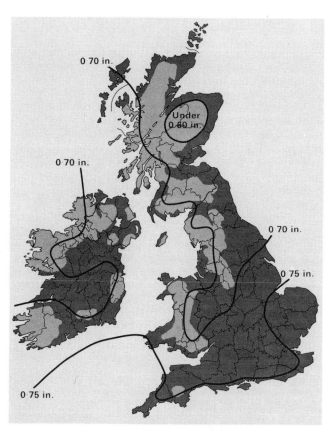

PROGRESS OF THE SEASON

In May much of southern England is subject to the same temperatures, but the north of the British Isles is lagging well behind in the approach of summer. The map shows the earliness or lateness of the season in an average May at places in the British Isles compared with conditions at the Royal Horticultural Society's Gardens at Wisley. At places along the broken line the season is as advanced as at Wisley. As a rough guide, gardeners in the white areas can start the programme of sowing and planting out given for May at the beginning of the month. Gardeners to the north should wait the number of weeks indicated. As in previous months, the gardener should take into account local conditions.

WATER NEEDED BY A GARDEN IN MAY

The total water used by a garden—an amount known as potential transpiration—is shown in inches per average week in May. In many areas of the British Isles the month is often dry, and on average weekly rainfall is less than potential transpiration. These areas are shaded on the map, and here some watering will usually be necessary in an average year if the plants are to receive all the moisture they need. Gardeners in all areas should be prepared to water in May, especially during hot sunny spells and periods of drying north-easterly weather. Amounts of watering can be calculated from rainfall and potential transpiration. (See GLOSSARY, *Weather*)

The weather in May

In the British Isles during May the gardener can expect all kinds of weather. Atlantic depressions are weak, so that damp westerly airstreams are less likely than at any other time, and the month is often dry. On average the second week of May is one of the five driest weeks of the year and also one of the sunniest in southern England, while the third week of May is the sunniest of the year in Ireland. Thunderstorms are much more frequent than in April and are often accompanied by hail and violent squally winds.

The weather in May is often influenced by a northerly or north-easterly airstream. As in April, this may bring snow showers to Scotland, northern England and high ground farther south; but snow cover does not usually persist, and snowfalls are rare in the south. On the whole, however, the north-easterly winds bring cool rather than cold weather, dry and with clear sunny skies. In south-east England mid-day temperatures average 13°C (55°F).

Anticyclone conditions give hot, tranquil weather in May;

daytime temperatures reach a maximum of 27°C (80°F) in southern England, and winds are light and skies clear.

Late May frosts are the bane of all gardeners. They are especially likely when night skies are clear—which is usually the case for much of the month—and when April has been drier than usual.

Eastern districts of England and Scotland may experience several grey, chilly days when morning fog or low cloud comes surging inland. Usually the sun is strong enough to clear skies by the middle of the day, but sometimes the fog or cloud persists for several days at a time.

May is often a stabilising month, for after a late spring it makes up for lost time, and plants respond quickly to the milder conditions.

As the danger of night frost diminishes, apply mulches to the soil to help to conserve moisture in the soil. On warm days in May, temperatures under glass cover can become excessive, so take care with ventilation.

A summary of the month's work

LAWNS

New lawns. Cultivate new sites for autumn sowing and leave rough during the summer.

Established lawns. Apply a high nitrogen fertiliser. Continue regular mowing. Apply fungicides for disease control. Continue to apply weedkiller.

ROSES

Spray regularly against greenfly, using a systemic insecticide. Spray with captan against black spot, with dinocap against mildew, and with zineb against rust. Spray with benomyl if black spot or mildew appears. Remove rolled-up leaves containing tortrix caterpillar or sawfly grub and destroy.

Under glass. Damp down on sunny days and ventilate well. Cease feeding when flower buds colour. After flowering, move roses outdoors.

HARDY HERBACEOUS PLANTS

Hoe between plants to control weeds. Continue staking tall plants such as delphiniums. Pinch out the tips of plants which tend to grow tall. Thin out shoots of plants more than three years old, removing weaker shoots from the centre of the plant. Puddle in plants planted during dry weather. Water newly planted beds.

DAHLIAS

Plant out young dahlias when danger of frost is past. Drive 5 ft. stakes 12 in. into the ground and label each plant. Protect young plants with newspaper if the weather is cold.

Under glass. Keep pots of rooted cuttings in cold frames well watered. Watch for aphids. Gradually increase ventilation.

CHRYSANTHEMUMS

Plant out garden-flowering varieties. Plant out pompons and koreans intended for garden decoration. Apply slug pellets under foliage and flat stones. Stop decorative plants in the north. In the south, discard any seriously damaged stools over-wintered outdoors. Carefully fork the ground around the healthy stools, fertilise, water, and reduce new shoots to six.

Under glass. Pot on late-flowering varieties into final pots (except in the north). In the south, set out pots on standing ground about a week later; in the north wait until June.

GLADIOLI

Continue regular hoeing. Water plants thoroughly in dry weather.

IRISES

Remove dead flower stems from dwarf irises and dead flowers from intermediates. Water occasionally in dry weather. Order bearded irises for planting in July–August. Renew slug pellets. Cut bearded irises for indoor decoration. Inspect bearded irises for signs of leaf spot disease. Water summer-flowering Dutch irises in dry weather.

LILIES

Spray monthly with a systemic insecticide against aphids and fortnightly with Bordeaux mixture against botrytis. Watch for signs of basal rot and fusarium disease.

Under glass. Control aphids with a systemic insecticide Plant forced lilies in the garden after flowering.

CARNATIONS AND PINKS

Support border carnations and straggly pinks. Plant out annual carnations. Take any action necessary to deal with pests and diseases.

Under glass. Continue potting-on perpetual flowering carnations. Shade glass and damp down during hot weather. Continue with second stopping to secure autumn blooms. Pot second-year plants in 8 in. pots. Cut blooms and disbud flower stems. Take action against pests and diseases. Continue to sow seeds of border carnations and pinks.

SWEET PEAS

Hoe round the plants frequently. Mulch the plants in dry weather. Tie cordons regularly as they grow.

FLOWERS FROM SEED

Make sowings of hardy and half-hardy annuals. Plant out half-hardy annuals when risk of frost has passed. Prepare a planting plan and water borders before planting. Sow hardy biennials in drills in a nursery bed, or in pans or boxes in a greenhouse or cold frame.

Under glass. Move boxes of well grown half-hardy annuals to cold frames. Spray monthly with a systemic insecticide. Apply a liquid fertiliser to boxed plants if they start to turn yellow. Sow hardy perennials in a frame or greenhouse. Prick out germinated seedlings. Transfer greenhouse-raised plants to a frame to harden-off when they have five or six leaves.

BULBS

Remove dead blooms from daffodils and hyacinths. Lift daffodils and tulips from beds to make way for summer bedding. Heel in bulbs to die back gradually. Weed rows of bulbs grown for cutting, and water in dry spells. Plant crinum bulbs in a south-facing border or in tubs.

ALPINES

Control weeds by hoeing or hand pulling. Trim aubrietas and other plants after flowering to prevent seeding and prolong flowering period. Dust soil mixture between rosettes of saxifrages which have become ragged.

WATER PLANTS AND POOLS

Plant all types of water plants. Control algae by removing with a stick. Thin overgrown clumps of water lilies and re-plant the crowns in new soil. In warm dry weather, flood the pool occasionally to keep plants in the bog garden cool and moist.

GREENHOUSES AND FRAMES

Sow cineraria seeds for flowers next December, and pot seedlings into 3 in. pots when large enough. Sow cucumbers, melons and sweet corn. Move tuberous begonias and gloxinias into 5 in. pots. On warm days, shade plants in flower, using plastic blinds or shading painted on the glass. Water vigorously-growing plants generously and give them a weekly liquid feed. Take cuttings of regal pelargoniums. Pot on canna roots into 8 in. pots. Move large *Campanula pyramidalis* plants to a sheltered position outdoors, supporting the flower spikes with canes. Stop laterals growing from the main stems of cucumbers, and remove all male flowers and tendrils. Continue to support tomato stems with strings or canes, and remove side shoots regularly. Feed tomatoes every week or ten days after the fruits begin to swell. In a cold greenhouse plant tomatoes in a border or peat growing bags, or in rings on aggregate.

TREES AND SHRUBS

Plant out shrubs that are tender when young (arbutus, choisya, fuchsia and hydrangea) and keep well watered until established. Complete planting evergreens in showery weather. Keep newly planted shrubs moist at the roots and spray foliage with water in dry weather. Keep lilacs to a single stem and mulch heavily to induce them to flower.

Pruning. Cut off dead flower heads and thin out weak shoots from shrubs that have finished flowering. Remove dead wood and and thin shoots to keep old forsythias shapely and within bounds. Clip *Laurus nobilis* (bay) where grown as a formal bush.

RHODODENDRONS AND AZALEAS

Pick off dead flowers. Water newly planted bushes in dry weather. Mulch with peat, leaf-mould or proprietary forest bark.

HEDGES

Clip *Lonicera nitida* hedges monthly until September to keep them shapely. Clip privet regularly. Clip forsythia and flowering currant hedges after flowering. Spread hessian or plastic sheeting alongside hedges to catch the clippings. In dry weather give newly planted hedges a soaking. Weed and hoe under hedges.

HEATHERS

Complete remaining planting. Mulch bare ground with peat or proprietary forest bark, and top-dress older plants.

FRUIT

Watch for pests and control as necessary. Water fruit trees and bushes in dry weather while fruit is swelling. Bark ring apples and pears if necessary to encourage fruiting. Feed apples, pears, cherries, blackberries, loganberries, black currants, gooseberries, peaches and nectarines, plums, damsons, raspberries and red currants. Spray apples, pears, cherries, black currants, gooseberries, peaches and nectarines, and strawberries. Tie up new growth on blackberries and loganberries. Control weeds around trees and bushes grown in cultivated soil. Start thinning fruit on wall-trained trees. Remove overcrowded and surplus shoots from raspberries and apply a mulch. Protect strawberry fruits with straw or paper collars and scatter slug bait. De-blossom immature and autumn-fruiting runners. Start summer pruning vines.

VEGETABLES

Cover potatoes if frost threatens. Prepare sites for growing marrows and pumpkins outdoors, sowing and thinning the seeds later in the month. Prepare planting sites for outdoor tomatoes. Sow french beans outdoors. Set out late summer cauliflowers. In the north, plant out Brussels sprouts. Make further sowings of summer spinach and salad crops. Sow long-rooted beetroot for storing for winter use. Sow runner beans and erect canes or poles to support them.

Under glass. Gradually remove cloches from spring cabbages, carrots, lettuces and broad beans. Prepare sites for growing cucumbers in frames or under cloches. In the north, sow runner beans under glass for planting out in June.

Less common vegetables. Continue cutting asparagus. Order self-blanching celery plants for June planting. Sow seakale beet, scorzonera, salsify and sweet corn.

HERBS

Make further sowings of chervil, dill, fennel, hyssop and parsley, and thin out April-sown herbs. Plant out basil seedlings and sow basil seed in drills. Take cuttings of pot marjoram, rosemary, sage and thyme. Divide thyme and mint if the plants are straggly. Plant out herbs in newly made herb gardens.

PATIOS AND TOWN GARDENS

Plant tender plants in containers after hardening-off. Complete sowing hardy annuals. Arrange containers on patios and erect supporting material for climbing plants. Lift spring-flowering bulbs after flowering, and plant in a spare corner of the garden, setting summer bedding plants in their place. Plant hanging baskets and set them in position. Water frequently in hot weather and soak in a tub of water if allowed to become over-dry.

HOUSE PLANTS

Water all plants liberally from now until autumn. Give liquid fertiliser. Avoid standing plants in a direct draught. See that plants, apart from succulents, do not remain on south-facing window-sills at mid-day. Pinch back long, straggly shoots and replace supporting canes when longer ones are needed. Re-pot older plants as they outgrow their pots.

GENERAL TASKS

Remove suckers from lilacs and fruit trees. Control slugs with metaldehyde or methiocarb pellets. Spray roses, fruit bushes and broad beans weekly against aphids and caterpillars. Water generously according to requirements. Apply liquid feeds or dress with quick-acting fertiliser and water in.

Plants to enjoy in May

Border and rock garden plants in flower	Trollius	Caltha (marsh marigold)
Achillea	Tulipa	Hottonia (water violet)
Ajuga	Veronica	Orontium (golden club)
Aquilegia	Vinca	
Aubrieta		**Greenhouse plants in flower**
Bergenia	**Trees and shrubs in flower**	Calceolaria
Calendula (pot marigold)	Aesculus hippocastanum (horse chestnut)	Cineraria
Campanula	Azalea	Pelargonium (regal)
Centaurea (cornflower)	Buddleia globosa	Pelargonium (zonal)
Cheiranthus (wallflower)	Choisya	Primula obconica
Convallaria (lily-of-the-valley)	Cistus	Schizanthus
Convolvulus	Clematis montana	
Dicentra	Crataegus (hawthorn)	**House plants in flower, depending on position and culture**
Fritillaria	Cytisus	Aphelandra
Gaillardia	Deutzia	Chloryphytum
Gentiana	Fothergilla	Euphorbia pulcherrima (poinsettia)
Geranium endressii	Genista (broom)	Saintpaulia
Geum	Laburnum	Saxifraga stolonifera
Gypsophila	Malus (crab apple)	Spathiphyllum wallisii
Iberis	Paeonia (tree paeony)	
Myosotis	Pernettya	**Vegetables in season**
Nigella	Pieris	Asparagus
Paeonia	Rhododendron	Beans, broad
Papaver (poppy)	Syringa (lilac)	Cabbage (spring)
Phlox subulata	Viburnum	Kohl rabi
Pulsatilla	Weigela	Leek
Pyrethrum	Wisteria	Lettuce
Scilla		Onion (salad)
Tiarella	**Water garden plants in flower**	Radish
	Calla (bog arum)	Spinach (summer)

Carnations and pinks

Selected varieties

Border carnations: 'Alice Forbes', white, marked rose cerise; 'Consul', orange apricot; 'Fiery Cross', scarlet; 'Lavender Clove', lavender-grey, scented; 'Scarlet Fragrance', fine scarlet self-colour.

Perpetual flowering carnations: 'Bailey's Delight', pink; 'Bonnie Charlie', orange; 'Fragrant Ann', white; 'Joker', crimson; 'Margaret', purple.

Old-fashioned pinks: 'Earl of Essex', rose-pink; 'Inchmery', pale pink, semi-double; 'Mrs. Sinkins', white.

Modern pinks: 'Bovey Belle', bright purple; 'Christopher', deep pink; 'Doris', pale pink with red eye; 'Haytor', white.

Miniature pinks: 'Bombardier', red; 'Dainty Maid', crimson, edged white; 'Pikes Pink', pale pink; 'Mars', crimson.

Harmony (border carnation)

Doris (modern pink)

Wink (miniature pink)

Scania (perpetual flowering carnation)

Sweet peas

Start to train these varieties in May

'White Leamington' (exhibition), white; 'Cream Beauty' (exhibition) cream; 'Red Ensign' (exhibition) scarlet; 'Leamington' (exhibition) lilac; 'Noel Sutton' (exhibition) rich blue; 'Southbourne' (exhibition) almond blossom pink; 'Mrs. R. Bolton' (exhibition) rich cream pink; 'Southampton' (exhibition) clear lavender; 'Crimson Excelsior' (exhibition) crimson; 'Elizabeth Collins' (exhibition) rose pink; 'Rosy Frills', white-edged rose; 'The Doctor', mauve; 'Galaxy Mixed', multiflora type.

The new semi-dwarf Knee-Hi and 'Jet-Set' mixed selections can be grown on netting or pea sticks with little trouble.

Those recommended for exhibition are also suitable for garden and home decoration.

Dorothy Sutton

Sunset (exhibition)

Reward (exhibition)

Biennials to sow in May

Some biennials, such as wallflowers, are available in such a wide range of varieties and colours that it is best to make a selection from seed catalogues. In the case of plants with a more limited choice of varieties, a selection of the best forms is given in the descriptions that follow. The heights quoted are a general guide only, as growth is subject to variable factors such as soil, aspect and weather. Some of the plants described can be grown as annuals if sown early in the spring. Examples are digitalis and cynoglossum. (For sowing and planting table, see p. 122).

Bellis (double daisy)
The 'Giant' or 'Super Enorma' selections, and the dainty 'Pomponette' forms, produce a profusion of double flowers in spring, large or small according to variety. The plants are compact and 4–6 in. high. F1 'Fairy Carpet' varieties are outstanding for the quantity and quality of their flowers.

Campanula
The popular *C. medium* (Canterbury bell) flowers later than most biennials and is best grown in clumps in the border rather than with spring bedding. The 'Cup and Saucer' varieties (3 ft.) are widely grown, but there are good double, single and dwarf bedding varieties.

Cheiranthus (wallflower)
C. allionii (Siberian wallflower). Pleasantly scented and makes a vivid splash of spring colour. The varieties 'Golden Bedder', 'Apricot Delight' and 'Lemon Delight' (12 in.) are recommended. *C. cheiri* is taller (1½–2 ft.) and has numerous varieties in shades of red, orange, pink, yellow, primrose and white. The dwarf series of 'Primrose', 'Orange', 'Golden' and 'Scarlet Bedder' (12 in.) make excellent bedding plants. 'Tom Thumb' (9 in.) is even more compact.

Cynoglossum
The varieties 'Blue Bird' (18 in.) and 'Firmament' (12 in.) have soft blue, myosotis-like flowers in incurling sprays. If sown in greenhouse in March, planted out in May, will flower in August.

Dianthus
D. barbatus (sweet william) is available in a range of crimson, scarlet, pink and white selections (all 1½–2ft.). The zoned flowers of the auricula-eyed varieties are particularly striking. 'Messenger Mixed' is a fortnight earlier than other varieties and is good for cut flowers. 'Sweet Wivelsfield' (12–15 in.) is a hybrid between *D. barbatus* and *D. allwoodii*. Useful for bedding are 'Indian Carpet' (9 in.) and 'Dwarf Double' (10 in.).

Digitalis (foxglove)
This beautiful, stately plant thrives in a shaded position. The best strain is the 'Excelsior' selection (4–5 ft.) which produces flowers all around the spike. The dwarf 'Foxy' (3 ft.) will flower as an annual but also does well as a biennial.

Lunaria
L. annua (syn. *biennis*) (honesty) is grown both for its flowers and for its seed heads, which make everlasting decorative material when dried. 'Munstead Purple' (3 ft.) has purple seed heads.

Matthiola (stock)
The Brompton and East Lothian stocks (1½–2 ft.) are derived from *M. incana*. They come in mixed and single colours making large, profusely flowered plants with rich colouring and a pleasant scent.

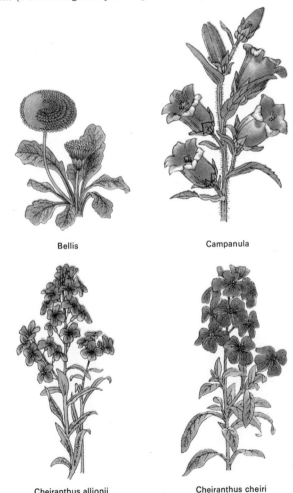

Bellis

Campanula

Cheiranthus allionii

Cheiranthus cheiri

Myosotis (forget-me-not)
M. alpestris. Easy plant which often seeds itself; useful both for bedding and for interplanting among bulbs. Several varieties are available in differing heights and shades of blue, including 'Blue Ball' (8 in.), 'Marine' (6 in.), 'Royal Blue' (12 in.) and 'Blue Bouquet' (12 in.).

Papaver (poppy)
The *P. nudicaule* (Iceland poppy) and all the 'Coonara' mixtures

(1½–2 ft.) have soft pastel shadings and a profusion of delicate blooms. They may also be grown as annuals if sown in early spring.

Primula
P. veris (polyanthus) is a perennial, but to get the best results the plants should be grown as biennials. A shaded, moist position is best, although they will grow well in other situations. Among the most outstanding selections are the

'Pacific Super Giants', 'New Century F1 hybrids' and 'Barnhaven Silver Dollars' (12 in.). These strains have the largest blooms and the most striking range of colours, from eye-catching brilliance to subtle pastel shades.

Viola
Most varieties of *V. cornuta* (viola) have flowers which are smaller than those of the pansy and not so rounded. They are, however, colourful and produced in profusion, especially

in 'Bambini' (6 in.) and 'Funny Face Mixed' (6 in.). The large-flowered mixtures have more self-colours than the others. *V. tricolor* (pansy) can be grown as an annual (especially the F1 'Majestic Giants'); but to get the best results treat pansies as biennials, and take care to remove the fading flowers. In addition to many giant and large-flowered strains, there is the brilliant, self-coloured 'Clear Crystals' type. All varieties grow to 6–8 in.

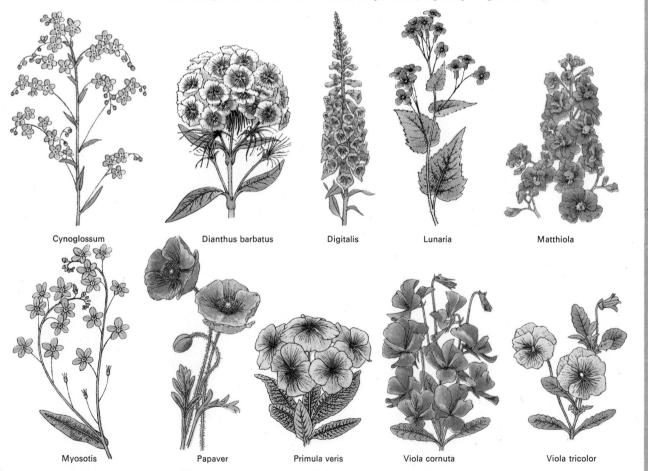

Cynoglossum   Dianthus barbatus   Digitalis   Lunaria   Matthiola

Myosotis   Papaver   Primula veris   Viola cornuta   Viola tricolor

Chrysanthemums to plant out in May

The following is a small selection from the thousands of varieties available for outdoor and greenhouse culture.

As new varieties are introduced each year, it is advisable to study the catalogues of specialist growers before ordering.

Outdoor varieties for exhibition and general culture

Large incurved: 'Ermine', white, September. Medium incurved: 'Peter Rowe', deep yellow, September. Large reflexed: 'Parasol', pink, September. Large intermediate: 'Woolley Magic', white, September. Medium intermediate: 'Gingernut', bronze, September.

Greenhouse varieties for exhibition and general culture

Large exhibition: 'Elizabeth Shoesmith', purple with silver reverse, November. Large incurved decorative: 'Shirley Model', mauve-purple, November. Medium incurved decorative: 'John Hughes', white, November. Medium reflexed decorative: 'Princess Anne', pink, October–November. Large intermediate decorative: 'Balcombe Perfection', amber-bronze, November–December. Medium intermediate decorative: 'Loveliness', pink with silver reverse, November–December. Large Single: 'Red Glory', reddish scarlet, November–December. Medium single: 'Alice Fitton', purple-rose, November.

Outdoor varieties for decoration and cut flowers

Medium incurved: 'Peter Rowe', deep yellow, September. Medium intermediate: 'Keystone', purple with silver reverse, September. Medium reflexed: 'Joyce Stevenson', red, August–September. Spray: 'Gerrie Hoek', deep rose pink, August–September.

Greenhouse varieties for decoration and cut flowers

Medium incurved decorative: 'Dorothy Hyman', golden amber, October–November; 'Reliant', mid-yellow, November. Medium reflexed decorative: 'Golden Princess Anne', deep gold, October–November. Large intermediate decorative: 'Balcombe Perfection', amber-bronze, November–December.

Low-growing varieties for garden decoration

Large intermediate: 'Bessie Davies' (3 ft.), pink with silver centre, August–September. Large reflexed: 'Bruera' (3½ ft.), white, September. Medium reflexed: 'Timmy Gray' (2½ ft.), pink. Aug.–Sept.

Tracey Waller.
Large reflexed.
Outdoor, September

Eve Gray.
Medium reflexed.
Outdoor, August–September

Sunsprite.
Large intermediate.
Outdoor, August

Salmon Fairie.
Pompon.
Outdoor, August

Cameo.
Pompon.
Outdoor, August–September

Golden Orfe.
Spray.
Outdoor, September

Lilian Hoek.
Spray.
Outdoor, August–September

Pennine Post.
Single spray.
Outdoor August–September

Pennine Tryst.
Single spray.
Outdoor, August–September

Natalie.
Double spray.
Outdoor, September

Gretel.
Spoon.
Outdoor, September–October

Tickled Pink.
Spoon.
Outdoor, September

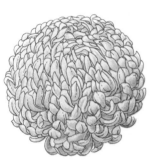

Incurved Primrose Evelyn Bush.
Incurved decorative.
Outdoor, September

Long Island Beauty.
Anemone-centred.
Greenhouse, December

Red Woolman's Glory.
Large-flowered single.
Greenhouse, November

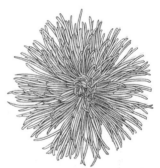

Primrose.
Rayonnante.
Greenhouse, October–November

Margaret Shoesmith.
Large exhibition.
Greenhouse, November

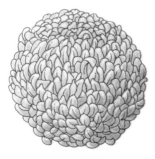

Goldfoil.
Large intermediate decorative.
Greenhouse, November

Shoesmith's Salmon.
Large reflexed decorative
Greenhouse. November

Rival's Rival.
Large intermediate decorative.
Greenhouse, November

Decorative dahlias to plant in May

There are few more rewarding dual-purpose plants than the dahlia for garden decoration. If the varieties are well chosen, suitably sited, and not jammed in with other plants, they will flower continuously from August until the first frosts.

The largest of the decorative and cactus varieties are suitable only for parks and large gardens, though many amateurs derive pleasure from producing blooms a foot across to win prizes at local flower shows.

For garden decoration and for use in flower arrangements, the most popular dahlias are the medium and small decorative varieties, the medium and small cactus and semi-cactus, ball, pompon and dwarf bedding varieties.

Giant decorative

Diameter of blooms usually over 254 mm. (10 in.). Flowering period early September until frosted. Average planting distance 4 ft. apart each way:

'Hamari Girl'; rose-pink, 3 ft. 'Holland Festival'; rich orange, tipped white, 4½ ft. 'Lavengro'; lavender, 4 ft. 'Liberator'; crimson, 4 ft. 'Trelawny'; apricot-orange, 4 ft. 'White Alvas', white, 4 ft.

Large decorative

Diameter of blooms usually 203–254 mm. (8–10 in.). Flowering period late August until frosted. Average planting distance 4 ft. apart each way:

'Hamari Boldness'; deep red, 4½ ft. 'Lifesize'; canary yellow, 3½ ft. 'Mrs. MacDonald Quill'; crimson and white, 4 ft. 'Polyand'; lavender, 4 ft. 'Silver City'; pure white, 4½ ft.

Medium decorative

Diameter of blooms usually 152–203 mm. (6–8 in.). Flowering period mid-August until frosted. Average planting distance 3 ft. apart each way:

'Barbara Rooke'; apricot-orange, 4 ft. 'Cyclone'; cyclamen pink, 4 ft. 'Hamari Approval'; golden-bronze, 3½ ft. 'Terpo'; red. 4 ft.

Small decorative

Diameter of blooms usually 102–152 mm. (4–6 in.). Flowering period early August until frosted. Average planting distance 2½ ft. apart each way:

'Alltami Serene'; creamy white, 4½ ft. 'Amethyst'; mauve and white, 4½ ft. 'Dedham'; lilac and white, 3½ ft. 'Frank Hornsey'; orange and yellow, 3½ ft. 'Leverton Chippy'; crimson and gold, 4 ft.

Miniature decorative

Diameter of blooms not usually over 102 mm. (4 in.). Flowering period early August until frosted. Average planting distance 2½ ft. apart each way:

'Brunton'; red and orange, 4 ft. 'David Howard'; deep yellow, 3½ ft. 'Horn of Plenty'; flame red, 4½ ft. 'Jo's Choice'; red, 3 ft. 'Mistill Delight'; white, 3 ft.

Giant cactus (gc) and Giant semi-cactus (gsc)

Diameter of blooms usually over 254 mm. (10 in.). Flowering period early September until frosted. Average planting distance 4 ft. apart each way:

'Arab Queen' (gsc); amber, coral-pink and yellow, 4 ft. 'Cocorico' (gsc); blood red, 4½ ft. 'Daleko Polonia' (gsc); apricot, 5 ft. 'Polar Sight' (gc); pure white, 4½ ft. 'Respectable' (gsc); autumn orange, 4 ft.

Large cactus (lc) and Large semi-cactus (lsc)

Diameter of blooms 203–254 mm. (8–10 in.). Flowering period late August until frosted. Average planting distance 4 ft. apart each way:

'Drakenburg' (lc); bronze-salmon and mauve, 4½ ft. 'Nantenan' (lsc); sulphur yellow, 4½ ft. 'Pride of Holland' (lc); rose-pink, 4 ft. 'Reginald Keene' (lsc); golden apricot, 4 ft.

Medium cactus (mc) and Medium semi-cactus (msc)

Diameter of blooms usually 152–203 mm. (6–8 in.). Flowering period mid-August until frosted. Average planting distance 3 ft. apart each way:

'Hamari Bride' (msc); white, 4 ft. 'Lavender Symbol' (msc), lavender, 4 ft. 'Othello' (msc); purple-red, 4 ft. 'Raiser's Pride' (mc); salmon pink, 4 ft. 'Rotterdam' (msc); crimson, 4 ft.

Small cactus (sc) and Small semi-cactus (ssc)

Diameter of blooms usually 102–152 mm. (4–6 in.). Flowering period early August until frosted. Average planting distance 2½ ft. apart each way:

'Alltami Cheer' (ssc); crimson scarlet, 4½ ft. 'Doris Day' (sc); deep red, 3½ ft. 'Freestyle' (sc); bright purple, 4 ft. 'Klankstad Kerkrade' (sc); yellow, 4 ft. 'Paul Chester' (sc); tangerine, 3 ft.

Small (sb) and Miniature ball (mb) and Pompon (p)

Blooms of honeycomb formation. Small ball diameter is 4–6 in., miniature ball up to 4 in., pompon not more than 2 in. Flowering period early August until frosted. Average planting distance 2½ ft. apart each way:

'Alltami Cherry' (sb); cherry red, 3½ ft. 'Nettie' (mb); primrose yellow, 3 ft. 'Jean Lister' (mb); white, 3½ ft. 'Diana Gregory' (p); mauve, 3 ft. 'Noreen' (p); pink, 3 ft. 'Small World' (p); white, 3½ ft.

Dwarf bedding

Free flowering from early July until frosted. Average planting distance 18 in. apart each way:

'Border Triumph'; orange-scarlet, 2 ft. 'East Count'; orange, 18 in. 'Park Delight'; white, 2½ ft. 'Park Princess'; pink, 2 ft. 'Piper's Pink'; rose-pink, 2½ ft. 'Preston Park'; scarlet, 18 in. 'Rothesay Castle'; cream and rose, 2 ft.

Lavengro. 4 ft.
Giant decorative

Blithe Spirit. 3½ ft.
Large decorative

Terpo. 4 ft.
Medium decorative

Rosemary Webb. 3½ ft.
Small decorative

Kochelsee. 3½ ft.
Miniature decorative

Fascination. 18 in.
Dwarf bedding

Diana Gregory. 3 ft.
Pompon

Drakenburg. 4½ ft.
Large cactus

Rotterdam. 4 ft.
Medium semi-cactus

Preference. 3½ ft.
Small semi-cactus

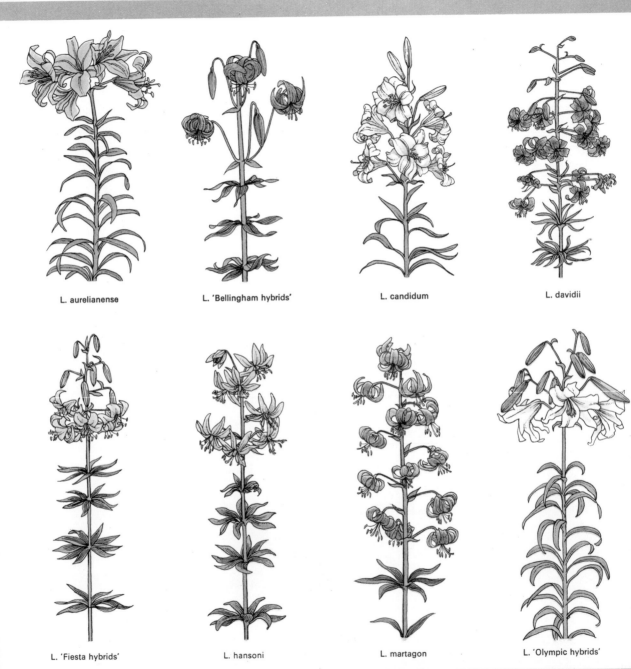

L. aurelianense

L. 'Bellingham hybrids'

L. candidum

L. davidii

L. 'Fiesta hybrids'

L. hansoni

L. martagon

L. 'Olympic hybrids'

Stately lilies to plant in May

With the relatively recent introduction of many beautiful species of lilies, and with the development of the modern hybrid lily, hundreds of robust, disease-resistant kinds are obtainable in scores of colours and shapes, from the large, pure white trumpet lilies to small-flowered turkscaps.

It is important to distinguish between stem-rooting lilies, which produce roots from the stem above the bulb as well as from the base, and basal-rooting kinds, which root only from the base. The former require deep planting, and soil must be drawn over roots that are seen above ground.

Lilium amabile
Height 4 ft. Bright red, recurved, nodding flowers with reddish pollen, June–July. Unpleasant scent. Light shade in ordinary soil. Planting distance 18 in., depth 5 in. Stem-rooting.

L. auratum
Height 5–8 ft. Fragrant, bowl-shaped flowers, petals pure white with yellow bands and wine-coloured spots, August–September. Lower part of stem should be in shade in lime-free soil. Planting distance 12 in., depth 6–9 in. Stem-rooting.

L. aurelianense
Height 4–7 ft. Large bowl- or trumpet-shaped flowers, others with strap-like petals, bicoloured, white, cream, golden-yellow or pink, August. Grows best in a sunny position. Planting distance 12 in., depth 9 in. Stem-rooting.

L. 'Backhouse hybrids'
Height 5 ft. Turkscap flowers, ivory, gold, orange or wine, some freckled with pink, June–July. Whorled leaves. Ordinary soil in light shade to preserve colours of the flowers. Hardy. Planting distance 9 in., depth 6 in. Basal-rooting.

L. 'Bellingham hybrids'
Height 5–7 ft. Orange-yellow bell-shaped flowers, July. Leaves often whorled. Sunny position in ordinary soil. Planting distance 9 in., depth 6 in. Among the most handsome lilies. When well situated will increase annually. Basal- and stem-rooting.

L. 'Black Dragon'
Height 5–6 ft. Large trumpet flowers, pure white inside, with rich purple-brown markings outside, July. The bulb can carry up to a dozen sweetly scented flowers. Full sun or partial shade in ordinary soil. Planting distance 9–10 in., depth 4 in. Stem-rooting.

L. brownii
Height 3–4 ft. Large creamy-white trumpet flowers, shaded with purple or green on the outside, July. Partial shade in ordinary soil, though it will tolerate some lime. Half-hardy only, and rarely sets seeds. Planting distance 9 in., depth 5–6 in. Stem-rooting.

L. canadense
Height 3–6 ft. Pendent, recurved flowers, yellow or orange-red with brown spots, July. Light shade in lime-free soil. Planting distance 9 in., depth 6 in. Basal-rooting.

L. candidum (madonna lily)
Height 4–5 ft. Pure white trumpet flowers with golden-yellow pollen, June–July. Sunny position in ordinary soil. Difficult to establish, and it should not be disturbed. Planting distance 9 in., depth 2 in. Basal-rooting. L. c. salonikae has smaller trumpet flowers and blooms earlier.

L. cernuum
Height 1½–3 ft. Fragrant, lilac-pink turkscap flowers with lilac pollen, June–July. Sunny position, will tolerate some lime. Planting distance 8 in., depth 5 in. Stem-rooting.

L. chalcedonicum (old scarlet turkscap)
Height 4 ft. Shiny, bright scarlet flowers with scarlet pollen, July. Sunny position in ordinary soil. Difficult to establish. Planting distance 9 in., depth 4 in. Stem-rooting.

L. concolor
Height 1½–2 ft. Upward-facing, star-shaped red flowers, June–July. Sunny position and ordinary soil. Easy to germinate from seed. Planting distance 6 in., depth 4 in. Basal-rooting.

L. dauricum
Height 1½–2 ft. Cup-shaped bright red flowers spotted with brown, July–August. Sunny position in lime-free soil. Hardy. Planting distance 8 in., depth 4 in. Stem-rooting.

L. davidii
Height 1–2½ ft. Orange turkscap flowers with purple-black spots, July–August. Sunny position in ordinary soil, roots in light shade. Parent of a number of beautiful hybrid lilies. Easily propagated from seed. Planting distance 9 in., depth 6 in. Stem-rooting.

L. 'Enchantment'
Height 3–4 ft. Large, upturned, nasturtium-red flowers, July. Sunny position in ordinary soil. Long-lasting and easy to establish. Planting distance 8 in., depth 5 in. Stem-rooting.

L. 'Fiesta hybrids'
Height 3–5 ft. Bright, recurved flowers in shades from lemon to damson, July. Some varieties have deep green, whorled leaves. Sunny position in ordinary soil. Neat plants, very free-flowering, good for planting in a mixed border. Planting distance 12 in., depth 5 in. Stem-rooting.

L. formosanum
Height 4–6 ft. Narrow white trumpet flowers, often marked with purple on the outside, yellow pollen, August–September. Light shade in lime-free soil. Half-hardy, but easily raised from seed. Virus-prone. Planting distance 12 in., depth 6 in. Stem-rooting.

L. giganteum (syn. *Cardiocrinum giganteum*)
Height 6–10 ft. Richly fragrant, funnel-shaped flowers, creamy white tinged with green, August. Glossy dark green, heart-shaped leaves. Each bulb bears flowers once only, but it is easily propagated by offsets which take four years to reach flowering stage. Partial shade in rich, well-drained soil. Planting distance 12 in., depth 1–2 in. Stem-rooting.

L. hansoni
Height 5 ft. Fragrant, pale orange turkscap with thick, waxy petals, sometimes spotted with brown, June–July. The leaves are whorled. Plant in a shaded position, as full sun may bleach the flowers. Dislikes lime, but easy to grow. Planting distance 10 in., depth 6–8 in. Stem-rooting.

L. henryi
Height 8 ft. Recurved, soft-apricot flowers with red spots, August–September. Lime-tolerant. Plant in light shade to preserve pale colours. Stake carefully. Planting distance 12 in., depth 8 in. Stem-rooting.

L. hollandicum
Height 1½–4 ft. Cup-shaped flowers, yellow to dark crimson, June–July. Sunny position in ordinary, well-manured soil. Planting distance 9 in., depth 4–6 in. Stem-rooting.

L. imperiale
Height 6 ft. White trumpet flowers, shaded with purple and with yellow centres, July. Easy to grow in full sun and ordinary soil. Planting distance 10 in., depth 6 in. Stem-rooting.

L. japonicum
Height 3 ft. Fragrant trumpet flowers, shading from white buds to rose-pink petals, June–July. Not hardy, and best grown as a pot plant and overwintered in a cool greenhouse. Plant in partial shade and sandy, lime-free soil. Virus-prone. Planting distance 9 in., depth 6 in. Stem-rooting.

L. lankongense
Height 2–4 ft. Fragrant pink turkscap flowers with reddish pollen, July–August. Semi-shaded position in lime-free soil. Planting distance 8 in., depth 4 in. Stem-rooting.

L. longiflorum
Height 1½–3 ft. Long white trumpet flowers with golden pollen, July–August. Plant in light shade in ordinary soil. Half-hardy, easily raised from seed. Makes a good pot plant. Planting distance 10 in., depth 6–9 in. Stem-rooting.

L. maculatum
Height 1–2 ft. Cross between *L. dauricum* and *L. concolor*, and the parent of *L. hollandicum*. Large, cup-shaped flowers are lemon-yellow, orange or deep red, June–July. There are numerous named varieties and hybrids. Easy to grow in full sun and lime-free soil. Planting distance 9 in., depth 4–6 in. Stem-rooting.

L. martagon
Height 5 ft. The common turkscap lily. Dark-spotted, rosy-purple flowers with unpleasant scent, July. Hardy in ordinary soil and light shade. Often seeds itself. The attractive white variety is vigorous and extremely free-flowering. Planting distance 9 in., depth 4 in. Basal-rooting.

L. 'Midcentury hybrids'
Height 3–5 ft. Large, variously shaped flowers, colours ranging from golden to yellow and red, July. Semi-shaded position in ordinary soil. Extremely hardy. Planting distance 12 in., depth 5 in. Stem-rooting.

L. monadelphum
Height 3 ft. Large, pendent, pale yellow flowers, faintly speckled with purple, June. Lightly shaded position in ordinary soil. The variety *L. m. szovitzianum* is similar, with reflexed yellow flowers, spotted with purple or black. Planting distance 9 in., depth 5 in. Stem-rooting.

L. 'Olympic hybrids'
Height 5–7 ft. Fragrant trumpet flowers, similar to *L. regale*, are cream, pale green or fuchsia pink, July. Full sun in ordinary soil. Planting distance 10 in., depth 6 in. One of the most imposing of modern introductions. The blooms are much in demand for flower arrangements. Stem-rooting.

L. pardalinum
Height 5–7 ft. Recurved red flowers with yellow centres and orange-brown spots, July. Sunny position in lime-free soil. Planting distance 12 in., depth 5 in. Basal-rooting.

L. parkmanni
Height 3–5 ft. Flat, open rose-crimson flowers edged with white, August. Light shade in lime-free soil. Tender lily, and best grown as a pot plant. Planting distance 12 in., depth 6 in. Stem-rooting.

L. 'Patterson hybrids'
Height 3 ft. Rose-pink, cream or lilac turkscap flowers, June. Sunny position in any soil. Very hardy. The varieties 'Edith Cecilia' with rose-lilac flowers, and 'Rosalind', rose-pink, are recommended. Planting distance 9 in., depth 4 in. Stem-rooting.

L. pomponium
Height 3–4 ft. Similar to, but smaller than, *L. chalcedonicum*. Bright red, recurved flowers with purple spots, June–July. Easily grown in full sun and heavy, limy soil. Planting distance 9 in., depth 4 in. Stem-rooting.

L. pumilum
Height 2–4 ft. Bright red turkscap flowers, June. Full sun in ordinary soil. Easily raised from seed. Planting distance 6 in., depth 4 in. Stem-rooting.

L. pyrenaicum
Height 2–3 ft. Bright yellow turkscap flowers with black spots and reddish pollen, June. Sunny position in ordinary soil. The earliest outdoor lily to bloom. Unpleasant scent. Planting distance 9 in., depth 5 in. Basal-rooting.

L. regale
Height 4–6 ft. White trumpet flowers, yellow centred and shaded with purple on the outside, July. Full sun in ordinary soil. Easily propagated from seed. Planting distance 12 in., depth 6–9 in. Stem-rooting.

L. rubellum
Height 1–1½ ft. Fragrant small pink trumpet flowers with golden-yellow pollen. Not hardy, and is best grown as a pot plant in a cool greenhouse or in partial shade in lime-free soil outdoors. Planting distance 6 in., depth 4–6 in. Stem-rooting.

L. sargentiae
Height 4–5 ft. Similar to *L. regale* with white trumpet flowers, shaded purple on the outside, and brown pollen, July. Sunny position in lime-free soil. Propagate by stem bulbils. Planting distance 12 in., depth 6–9 in. Stem-rooting.

L. speciosum
Height 4–6 ft. Fragrant, recurved white flowers, heavily shaded with rose-crimson, August. Partly shaded position in lime-free soil. Best grown as a pot plant. Planting distance 12 in., depth 6 in. Stem-rooting.

L. 'Stardust'
Height 4–5 ft. The flowers are semi-pendent, 6 in. across, pure white with a bright orange star in the centre, July–August. Very free-flowering: each stem can carry as many as 18–20 flowers. Full sun or partial shade in ordinary soil. Planting distance 9–10 in., depth 4 in. Stem-rooting.

L. 'T. A. Havemeyer'
Height 5–8 ft. Bowl-shaped ivory flowers with apricot centres and brown pollen, August–September. Sunny position in lime-free soil. Planting distance 12 in., depth 6 in. Stem-rooting.

L. testaceum
Height 4–6 ft. Recurved apricot-yellow pendent flowers with red pollen, July. Full sun and ordinary, limy soil. Planting distance 9 in., depth 4 in. Basal-rooting.

L. tigrinum (tiger lily)
Height 3–6 ft. Large, orange-red turkscap flowers spotted with purple, August-September. Full sun and lime-free soil. Easily raised from stem bulbils. Can carry virus disease without showing symptoms. *L. t. fortunei* flowers in early autumn. Planting distance 9 in., depth 6 in. Stem-rooting.

Lawns

NEW LAWNS

Plan cultivation and pre-seeding operations, and remedy defective drainage (see OCTOBER), where autumn sowing is intended. Thoroughly turn the site with a fork or cultivator and vigorously rake in several directions. Leave the ground rough during the summer.

ESTABLISHED LAWNS

Apply a high nitrogen liquid, soluble or granulated fertiliser to encourage a lush green appearance. A flow-through container attachment to the hose makes distribution of liquid feed simple. Watering is important in dry weather.

Continue regular mowing, but first check the mower blades for sharpness and correct the setting if necessary. Height of cut should not be lower than $\frac{1}{2}$ in.

Control fungus disease

Apply fungicides for disease control. In the west, dollar spot may be serious. Fescues are more susceptible to this disease, which usually occurs on poor, infertile, nitrogen-starved soil. Regular, circular, brown or bleached patches of collapsed grass, which may vary between 1 and 2 in. in diameter, sometimes fusing together, are typical of this disease. For serious attacks, treat with mercuric fungicides every month between May and October. In addition, apply sulphate of ammonia at $\frac{1}{2}$ oz. per sq. yd.

In good growing weather continue to deal with weeds (see APRIL).

Roses

Be prepared to spray regularly to combat rose pests. Spray both sides of the leaves and the stems, using a sprayer that delivers a fine, mist-like spray.

For greenfly, use a systemic rose insecticide. This kills initially by contact and is then absorbed through the leaves and stems into the sap stream of the rose, killing any greenflies that suck the sap during the next three to four weeks.

Pests and diseases

Leaves that become rolled up contain either a small green caterpillar of the tortrix moth or a small grey-green grub of the sawfly. Pick the leaves off and burn them, or tread them under foot.

Spray with captan against black spot, dinocap against mildew, and zineb against rust. Should black spot or mildew appear, spray with benomyl. Combined insecticides and fungicides should be sprayed on to roses every seven to ten days.

UNDER GLASS

Water the path between the greenhouse staging on sunny days, and maintain good ventilation.

Discontinue feeding when the flower buds start to show colour.

When flowering has finished, move pot roses outdoors and stand them on concrete or ashes. Continue watering during dry weather.

Hardy herbaceous plants

Continue hoeing between plants to kill the weeds while they are still small. Continue to stake and support tall plants, such as delphiniums, which are liable to suffer from damage by wind and rain when near flowering time (see APRIL). Do not stake dwarf plants or those that are naturally a little floppy near the front of the bed or border; these plants look more attractive if unregimented.

To check the growth of plants that are inclined to grow too tall, and to make the plants branch out, pinch out

STOPPING TALL PLANTS

To encourage a more bushy, branching form of growth, pinch out the tips of border plants that tend to grow too tall

the tips. Plants which respond to this treatment are generally those that make a leafy clump opening into heads of flowers—like heleniums, the tall rudbeckias, solidago (golden rod), phlox, michaelmas daisies and other members of the daisy family.

Pinch out the tips

When the plant has grown to approximately a quarter of its expected height, and at least a month before flowering time, pinch out the leading shoots. This may reduce the ultimate height by a quarter. Although it may retard flowering by a week or two, and in cold northern districts may make it undesirably late, it will not shorten the flowering period. However, if plants are more than three years old and are producing a large number of shoots, it is better to thin out some of these shoots, so that those left on the plant become more vigorous.

THINNING OLD PLANTS

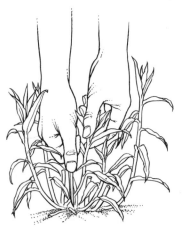

Use a sharp knife to remove surplus shoots from the inside of older plants, cutting the growths as close to the ground as possible

WATERING NEW PLANTS

When watering young but established plants, first scrape soil away from them to form a low bank, levelling the soil again after watering

Remove central shoots

Thin out the shoots at the same time as pinching out shoot tips or, preferably, a little earlier. Always thin out the weakest shoots, concentrating on those on the inside. Where the shoots are dense, take out up to half the total, severing them as near the ground as possible.

Puddle young plants

If the weather is dry and only a few new kinds have been planted among established plants, use the puddling method of watering. Scrape away about 1 in. of the dry topsoil to make a low bank all round the plant or group, and fill the trough once with water, or twice if the soil is dry. When the water has soaked away, push the dry soil back with a small-toothed rake or a hoe.

If a newly planted bed is too dry, use a sprinkler or a rose on a can or hose. Make sure that the water comes out as a fine spray and not in large drops which tend to pan the surface and may even

cause erosion. It is the roots of plants that need water, so be prepared to water the ground a second or even a third time if the moisture has not penetrated deeply enough. As soon as the surface begins to dry a little, scratch over with a fine rake to restore the tilth necessary for aeration. Surface panning (the formation of a dry crust on the soil surface) is always harmful.

Make a note of any plants that could be placed to better advantage elsewhere in the border when the time comes for re-planting.

Dahlias

Plant out young dahlias, either your own rooted cuttings or bought plants, when danger of frost is past—from about May 20 onwards in the southern half of England, and up to the end of the first fortnight in June in the north and in Scotland. Young dahlia plants are

usually about 8–10 in. high when the are supplied by the nursery. (For plan ing distances, see p. 110.)

Plant dahlias $2\frac{1}{2}$–3 ft. apart, with t same distance between rows. Take out hole with a trowel, deep enough to receiv the ball of soil around the plant's root Place two or three handfuls of moist pe round the ball of soil and plant firml leaving a shallow depression round t plant to collect rain. If the weather is dr apply water by can or hose into the sauce which will direct it down to the roots.

Stake dahlias

All dahlias (except the dwarf varieti that grow only to about $2\frac{1}{2}$ ft. high an are usually raised from seed each yea need staking, as their 3 ft. stems a usually too weak to support the heav flower heads. For each plant drive stout 5 ft. stake 12 in. into the groun Drive in the stakes before making t holes for the young dahlias, whic should be loosely tied to the stakes wi loops of soft green string or raffia.

Fasten a label showing the name the variety to the top of each stake wi plastic-covered wire, so that it can b seen throughout the growing season.

If night frost is forecast, protect t young plants with sheets of newspape removing these in the morning.

UNDER GLASS

If you have pots of rooted cuttings in cold frame, keep them well watered, an feed them once a week with a liqui fertiliser. Examine the young plants car fully and regularly for greenfly. If an are seen, spray with HCH. Alternative provide continued protection by sprayin monthly with a systemic insecticide.

The frame light may be opened mor and more each day as the weather im proves in May, and eventually proppe open at night if there is no risk of fros Leave it off altogether for a few nigh before the young dahlias are planted ou

Chrysanthemums

Plant out the garden-flowering varieties this month. Weather permitting, the first week is the ideal time in the south, but wait a little longer in the midlands and north.

After raking the bed prepared in March and April, set the plants in the ground at exactly the same depth as they were in the pots. Planting too deep checks subsequent growth. As each plant is removed from its pot, turn it upside down and dip the entire plant in a weak solution of insecticide. Firm the plants just enough to keep them upright, but not so hard as to damage the tender young roots.

Support chrysanthemums

The most convenient way to grow flowers for cutting is to use welded wire mesh with 8 in. squares. Lay this flat on the ground and attach it to stout posts at the corners. Plant in the centre of each square or each alternate square,

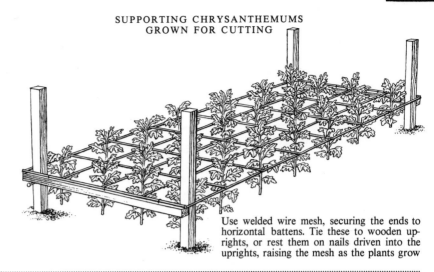

SUPPORTING CHRYSANTHEMUMS
GROWN FOR CUTTING

Use welded wire mesh, securing the ends to horizontal battens. Tie these to wooden uprights, or rest them on nails driven into the uprights, raising the mesh as the plants grow

and raise the mesh to support the plants as they grow.

Set plants for garden decoration, including pompons and koreans, 12–18 in. apart in any direction. Insert stout canes or stakes close to the plants and tie the plants loosely to them. Pass the raffia or soft twine gently around the plant, then around the cane, and tie there. Leave plenty of the material so that it can be loosened as the plant grows more bushy. Water each plant

PLANTING AND SUPPORTING BORDER CHRYSANTHEMUMS

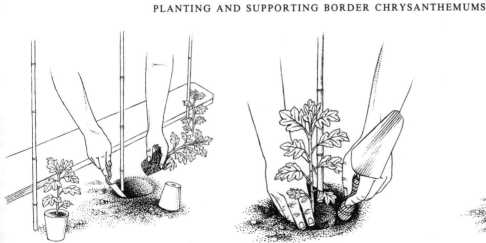

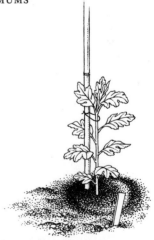

After inserting a 4 ft. cane alongside each planting position, set the plants at the same depth as they were previously in the pots

Firm the plants in with a trowel handle, leaving a shallow depression in the soil around the plants as an aid to watering

Tie each plant loosely to its cane, looping raffia or soft twine round the stems and securing it to the support thoroughly. Give no further water for several days, but spray lightly to counteract the effects of sun or drying winds.

Apply slug bait among the plants, renewing it as necessary until the plants are well established and the stems have become hard. In the north, plants grown for decorative purposes can be stopped from the middle of the month onwards (see JUNE).

Discard damaged stools

In southern gardens where stools have remained in the open all winter, discard any that appear seriously damaged by pests or the weather. Lightly fork the ground round each plant, give a scattering of general fertiliser, and water it in. If there are a large number of new ground shoots on the stools, retain the best six shoots and cut the remainder off at ground level.

Insert stout canes or sticks close to the plants and tie the new growth lightly to them with raffia.

UNDER GLASS

Except in the north (see JUNE) pot on late-flowering varieties into their final 8 in. or 9 in. pots. To ensure free drainage, place a layer of broken pot in the base of clay or hard plastic pots; use coarse fibre or plastic netting in pots made of soft plastic or compressed paper.

Final potting

For this final potting use John Innes potting compost No. 3 or a proprietary soil-less compost.

One-third fill the pots with compost, firming it down. Knock a plant out of its pot, complete with the ball of soil, by inverting it over one hand, with the stem of the plant between two fingers. Stand it upright in the centre of the part-filled larger pot so that the top of the soil ball is 1 in. below the rim. Fill in around the plant with new compost, firming it as you go, until it is level with the top of the soil ball. Fill the pot to the top with water and allow it to drain

through. Do not water again for seven to ten days, but spray with clean water at mid-day during warm weather.

Support with canes

Insert three 5 ft. canes, equally spaced into each pot as soon as potting is complete, and tie the main stem of the plant loosely to one cane.

In the south, after seven to ten days set out the pots 9–12 in. apart on their summer standing ground (see APRIL). In the north, wait until June. Take care not to damage the developing side shoots of plants which were stopped in April.

Continue to care for stools of late varieties which will provide cuttings for Christmas-flowering plants (see JUNE).

Gladioli

Continue routine hoeing to check weed growth and conserve soil moisture, taking care not to damage the stems. Give the plants a thorough watering if prolonged dry weather occurs.

Irises

Intermediate irises should flower this month, followed by the tall ones.

Remove dead flower stems from dwarf irises, and also dead flowers from the intermediates. In dry weather give an occasional watering to keep the plants growing well.

Order bearded irises for planting in July or August.

Renew slug pellets as necessary.

Cut bearded irises for indoor decoration (see APRIL).

Inspect leaves of bearded irises for signs of leaf spot disease (see APRIL).

Water summer-flowering Dutch irises if the weather is dry.

RE-POTTING AND STAKING CHRYSANTHEMUMS

Above: To remove a plant from its pot before final planting, turn it upside down, with the stem between your fingers, and tap the pot gently against the bench or staging
Right: Tie the main stem of pot-grown plants loosely to one of the supporting canes

Lilies

Plant out those lily bulbs which were temporarily potted up (see MARCH). Spray fortnightly with Bordeaux mixture during damp, mild weather. Spray monthly with a systemic insecticide.

Fusarium disease

Watch for signs of basal rot or fusarium disease, which affects the flat piece of tissue between the scales and the roots of a lily. Called the basal plate, this is actually a greatly compressed stem. Once it takes hold, this brown rot will kill the whole plant. But you may save the lily by cutting out the affected tissue, dusting the wound with a fungicide, and planting the bulb in a pot.

BASAL PLATE OF A LILY BULB

Basal rot may occur on the flat piece of tissue the basal plate) between the scales and roots of a lily. Cut out the affected tissue

Ideally, lift other bulbs from the affected bed and plant them elsewhere, growing no more lilies in the original bed for the next four years. However, you can take a chance if the lilies are not particularly valuable, leaving them in the bed as long as they look healthy.

UNDER GLASS

Use a systemic insecticide to control aphids on pot-grown lilies. Keep the pots adequately watered. Plant in the garden forced lilies which have finished flowering, but leave ordinary pot-grown lilies in their pots. They can remain in the containers for two or three years. As the foliage dies away, remove the soil to expose the tips of the bulbs, and replace with fresh material.

Carnations and pinks

Stake border carnations with 3 ft. bamboo canes. Rings of thin wire are sufficient to secure the single stems of first year plants; older plants need either proprietary wire rings which clip to the stakes, or loops of string secured round their stems.

Plant out annual carnations as bedding plants in the south and west. In cold northern gardens, annual carnations may be late in flowering: 'Knight' strain, an improvement, is recommended.

Watch for pests and diseases, taking action as necessary (see MARCH).

UNDER GLASS

Continue to pot perpetual flowering carnations from 3 in. and $3\frac{1}{2}$ in. pots into 4 in. pots, and from 4 in. into 6 in. pots. Apply shading to glass and attend to damping down in hot weather.

Continue with the second stopping to secure autumn blooms (see APRIL).

Pot second-year plants into 8 in. pots.

Plant third-year plants out in warm, sheltered beds to flower during summer.

Watch for pests and diseases, taking action as necessary (see MARCH).

Cut blooms and disbud flower stems (see SEPTEMBER).

Continue to sow seeds of border carnations and pinks (see APRIL).

STAKING A BORDER CARNATION

Support border carnations, often grown in pots, with 3 ft. bamboo canes, securing first-year plants with rings of wire. For older plants use string, or patent rings clipped to the canes

Sweet peas

Frequent hoeing around the plants keeps weeds in check and conserves moisture. Make it a routine operation throughout the season, whether the plants are grown naturally or on the cordon system. During prolonged dry weather, especially if the soil is on the light side, remove all weeds, water thoroughly, and then place a mulch of peat or well decayed manure around cordon plants. This keeps the roots cool, conserves moisture, and restricts weed growth.

Tie cordon-grown plants to their canes as they grow, using twine, raffia or galvanised wire rings. Pinch out side shoots and tendrils as they appear. Pinch out the first few flowers while they are tiny, but leave the little stems, bearing four buds, which will soon appear.

Flowers from seed

There is still time to make outdoor sowings of some hardy and half-hardy annuals (see tables and sowing instructions, MARCH).

In mild districts, planting of half-hardy annuals can begin as soon as the risk of local frost has passed. If in doubt, wait until the beginning of June. Water borders cleared of spring bedding before setting out half-hardy annuals.

Remove from seed boxes

Give the hardened-off plants a good watering. Remove them from the boxes or other containers with as much root as possible. To remove plants from a seed box, loosen the soil and root block by bumping it down from one end of the tray. Separate the plants by cutting them apart with an old knife or by easing the plants apart with your fingers.

Position the plants

Lay the plants in the proposed positions on the soil, then stand back to see whether the placing is balanced. When you have adjusted them to your satisfaction, use a trowel to make holes of appropriate depth and stand the plants in them. Thoroughly water the sides of the planting holes with a hose, or a watering can without a rose. This will ensure that the roots get plenty of moisture and that the soil is washed in among them.

Work in batches

Leave these plants to stand while you lay out, plant, and water the next batch. Then go back to the first plants and fill in the remaining small holes around them, using a trowel or hand fork. If you follow this method the plants will stand well for some time, even in hot weather. But if dry weather persists, give the plants a good soaking with a sprinkler to help settle them in.

120

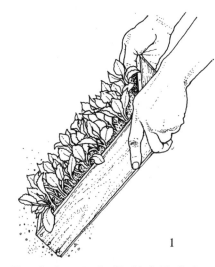

Though plants can be lifted individually from the seed box, it is easier to separate them if the whole mass of soil and roots is first removed. Hold the container at an angle, knock the sides and ends on the ground (1) and then toss the contents out as a complete block (2) taking great care that it does not turn upside down and crush the young plants beneath it

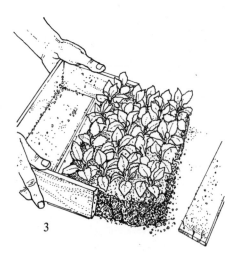

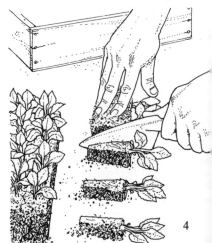

If you doubt your ability to toss the soil block on to the ground, as in (2), remove one side of the box and slide the contents out (3). Separate the plants with your fingers or cut them apart with a trowel (4) or an old knife retaining as much soil as possible round the roots, and planting without delay to prevent them from drying out

LAYING OUT AND PLANTING

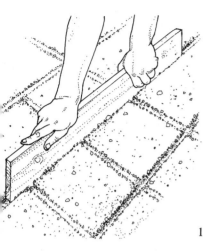

1

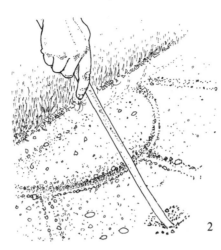

3

4

If your border plan has a regular design, use a board to mark out the planting positions, setting plants either at the intersections or in the centres of the squares

For less regular designs, mark the planting areas with a stick, varying their size and shape. If possible, stand on the grass while marking out; otherwise use a plank

After laying the plants in position and satisfying yourself that the placings are balanced, dig holes sufficiently deep for the roots and set the plants in position

A light sprinkling will not penetrate to the roots and may cause harm by attracting them to the surface.

Sow hardy biennials

Sow hardy biennials this month or next. The usual method is to sow the seeds in drills in a nursery bed. Choose fertile, weed-free soil and allow a minimum of 6 in. between the drills.

Alternatively, sow in pans or seed boxes in a greenhouse or cold frame, or in rows directly into the soil of a cold frame, and prick out the seedlings into seed boxes before eventually planting them out in a nursery bed (see JUNE).

This method gives greater control during germination and early growth, and is also useful if the weather is cold or wet. It leads to more rapid growth, so delay sowing for a few weeks.

A further alternative in the case of

5

With a hose, or a watering can without a rose, wash soil from the sides of the planting holes on to the roots. Leave while the water soaks in

When the water has drained away, fill in the remaining small holes round the plants. Level the soil surface after you have finished planting

Flowers from seed: biennials
guide to sowing and planting

	Use in garden	Colours	Flowering period	Transplanting distance in nursery rows (inches)	Final planting distance (inches)	Situation	Sow in green-house, frame or cloche	Sow in nursery border	Sow in flowering position	Good for cutting	Dead-heading
Bellis (double daisy)	D	Red, pink white, mixed	May–Jul	3	6	○ ◐	Jun	May–Jun		†	†
Campanula medium (Canterbury bell)	TB	Blue. pink, white, purple, mixed	Jun–Aug	6	9–12	○ ◐	Jun	May–Jun			†
Cheiranthus allionii (Siberian wallflower)	M	Orange, yellow	May–Jun	4	9–12	○ ◐	Jun–Jul	Jun			
Cheiranthus cheiri (wallflower)	MT	Various, mixed	Apr–May	4	9–12	○ ◐	Jun	May–Jun	Jul	†	
Cynoglossum	M	Blue	May–Jun	6	9	○ ◐	Jun–Jul	Jun–Jul		†	
Dianthus barbatus (sweet william)	MT	Various, mixed	Jun–Jul	6	9–12	○ ◐	Jun–Jul	Jun–Jul	Jul	†	†
Digitalis (foxglove)	B	Mixed	Jun–Jul	6	12–18	◐	Jun	May–Jun	Jul	†	†
Lunaria (honesty)	B	White, purple	May–Jul	4	12	○ ◐	Jun	May	Jun	†	
Matthiola (stock)	T	Various, mixed	Jun–Jul	6	9	○ ◐	Jul	Jul		†	†
Myosotis (forget-me-not)	DM	Blue, pink	Apr–May	4	6–8	○ ◐	Jun	May–Jun	Jun–Jul	†	
Papaver nudicaule 'Iceland' (poppy)	T	Various, mixed	Jun	4	9–12	○	Jun–Jul	Jun–Jul			
Primula veris (polyanthus)	M	Various, mixed	Apr–May	4–6	6–8	◐ ● ○	Apr–May	Mar–May		†	†
Viola cornuta (viola)	D	Various, mixed	Mar–Aug	4	6	○ ◐	Jun–Jul	Jun–Jul		†	†
Viola tricolour (pansy)	D	Various, mixed	Mar–Aug	4	6–8	○ ◐ ●	Jun–Jul	Jun–Jul		†	†

D = Dwarf bedding 1–9 in.
M = Medium bedding 9–18 in.
T = Tall bedding 18–30 in.
B = Back of border over 30 in.
○ = Sun
◐ = Partial shade
● = Full shade

wallflowers and sweet williams, especially if the plants are to be used for cutting, is to sow the seeds in drills in their flowering positions. As the seedlings will not be held back by a transplanting check, delay sowing until late June or early July.

Sow hardy perennials

If no frame or greenhouse is available, sow hardy perennials thinly in a nursery bed outdoors. Choose a lightly shaded, moist spot and be ready to water with a sprinkler during prolonged dry weather.

UNDER GLASS

Move boxes of well grown half-hardy annuals to a cold frame. Keep the frame closed at first, opening it progressively as the weather improves and the plants become hardened. Leave the top off altogether eventually, replacing it only if frost is forecast.

Spray monthly with a systemic insecticide to control aphids and other sap-sucking insects.

Apply a liquid flower fertiliser to boxed plants if the leaves show signs of yellowing (see APRIL).

Hardy perennials under glass

Sow hardy perennials in a frame or greenhouse, following the same procedure as for half-hardy annuals (see MARCH). Some types, such as alyssum, geum, primula and sidalcea, benefit from being placed in a refrigerator for a week after sowing to awaken them from dormancy. Afterwards, return the boxes to the frame or greenhouse. Keep the frame shaded and closed down unless it gets very hot. If ventilation is needed, keep the soil evenly moist. This is essential for good germination.

Prick out the germinated seedlings at the rate of 30 to a seed box (six rows of seedlings, five in a row). Transfer greenhouse-raised plants to a frame when they have five or six leaves.

Bulbs

Remove the dead blooms from daffodils and hyacinths as they finish flowering.

Bulbs such as tulips or daffodils are over now, and it may be necessary to lift them from the beds or borders to make way for summer bedding.

Heel in the bulbs to die back gradually. To do this, first take out a trench about 1 ft. deep. Lay a length of wire netting in the bottom and then lay the bulbs on the netting at an angle of about 20°. Fill the trench with soil so that it covers the lower half of the stems. By early July the stems and leaves will have shrivelled. When this has happened, take hold of one end of the wire netting and get a helper to take the other end. A good sharp pull will lift all the bulbs at once.

Cleaning and storing

Clean the bulbs and store them in shallow trays in a cool airy shed for re-planting in October. Burn or bury diseased tulip bulbs; if they are placed on a compost heap they may carry disease to fresh plantings.

Continue to weed rows of bulbs grown for cutting. Give them a thorough watering if a dry spell occurs before the leaves begin to turn yellow, particularly to daffodils in light, sandy soil.

Plant crinum bulbs 6–8 in. deep in a south-facing border. Alternatively, set them in tubs which can be moved under cover during the autumn in cold districts (see OCTOBER).

Alpines

This is the peak month for colour, but weeds are growing strongly, too. Weed seedlings are easily disposed of by hoeing during dry weather, but it is better to remove and burn any larger weeds, such as groundsel, shepherd's purse, mayweed or dandelions, which escaped notice

TRIMMING ALPINES

After they have flowered, trim such plants as aubrietas and mossy saxifrages to promote fresh, compact growth

earlier on and are now just about to shed their seeds.

Self-sown seedlings of aubrietas and mossy saxifrages can also be a nuisance. Trimming the plants after flowering not only prevents self-seeding but also prolongs the flowering period of aubrietas and promotes growth on mossy saxifrages. Dust a mixture of fine soil,

PROMOTING GROWTH

Such plants as sedums and saxifrages will benefit from a sprinkling of fine soil and fertiliser worked in among the rosettes

sand, peat and fertiliser among the green rosettes of sedums and saxifrages if they appear ragged, or, if the weather is damp, lift the plants, dig and fertilise the soil, and re-plant them deeper than previously in close-set bunches. If you adopt the former course, which is also beneficial to other carpeting or mounded plants, allow the mixture to trickle on to the plants through your fingers. Then use your ˈfingers to work it in below the leaves or stems, pushing further material underneath trailing stems.

Alpines seen at shows may have been forced in order to advance their flowering date. Before ordering new plants for your collection, ascertain the natural time of flowering from exhibitors in case this differs sufficiently to cause gaps in the seasonal display. Enquire, too, whether the plants that attract you are fully hardy and if they need any special treatment.

Water plants and pools

Plant all types of water plants this month. All the operations described in APRIL may also be carried out now. In most seasons floating plants will not be available until the middle of the month, and some, such as *Eichhornia crassipes* (water hyacinth) and *Trapa natans* (water chestnut) are not suitable for putting in an outdoor pool until early June.

Spreading algae

Until the leaves of water lilies are sufficiently large and numerous, and the floating plants have grown and multiplied, most of the water surface will be exposed to full light conditions and algae will probably become a nuisance. Algae (blanketweed or silkweed) are simple plants which grow rapidly in light, warm conditions. They produce masses of

fine filaments which restrict the growth of other plants under water.

Control algae

Deal with algae by removing as much as possible with a net, a roughened stick, or by hand. Chemicals such as copper sulphate, potassium permanganate and preparations based on paraquat will kill algae. However, even small concentrations are toxic to other plants and to fish, so follow the maker's instructions extremely carefully. Unless you have an exact knowledge of the cubic capacity of your pool, you may get the proportion of chemicals slightly wrong, leading to the death of some or all of your plants.

Remove dead algae

If you do use chemicals, however, remove the algae masses as soon as they have turned brown, to prevent them from blanketing other plants, and also to avoid an oxygen deficiency in the water.

Divide water lilies

Thin overgrown clumps of water lilies. After draining the pool, select as many plants as are required, and with a sharp knife sever the rhizomes about 6

DIVIDING WATER LILIES

After severing the rhizomes about 6 in. from the growing point, keep them cool and moist before re-planting in fresh soil

in. back from the crown or growing point. Cut the fleshy white roots underneath and remove the plants, keeping them in the shade either floating in water or stored in a box covered with wet sacking. Re-plant the crowns in fresh soil as described in APRIL.

If the weather is warm and dry, flood the pool occasionally to keep the plants in the bog garden cool and moist.

Re-plant marginals

Divide and re-plant large clumps of marginal aquatics in the same manner as described for water lilies. Surplus growth may be cut off with a sharp knife or secateurs during the summer.

Greenhouses and frames

Sow cineraria seeds to produce plants that will flower from December onwards. Sow the seeds thinly in pans of John Innes seed compost, cover lightly with finely sifted compost, and germinate in a temperature of 10–13°C (50–55°F). Pot the seedlings individually into 3 in. pots of John Innes potting compost No. 1 as soon as they are large enough to handle and keep them watered and shaded throughout the summer.

Sow cucumbers, melons and sweet corn as soon as possible.

Transfer tuberous begonias and gloxinias without delay to 5 in. pots if this was not done in March or April.

Provide shade

On warm days, provide shade for plants now in flower, such as calceolarias, zonal and regal pelargoniums, cinerarias, primulas and hydrangeas. Spring-loaded plastic blinds on the inside of the roof, or slatted wooden blinds outside, are ideal. Alternatively, paint the glass with a proprietary shading

GREENHOUSE SHADING

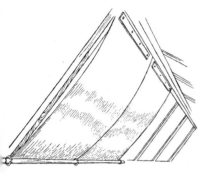

Green polythene, secured by battening at the top and fastened to a broom handle at the bottom, provides a convenient form of shading

material, taking care not to apply it too thickly. Increase the humidity by damping down the staging and floor. Provide adequate ventilation, but do not open side or top ventilators on the windward side of the house on windy days.

Give plenty of water, and a weekly liquid feed, to vigorous plants.

Pinch out fuchsias

When fuchsias are 4–5 in. high, pinch out the growing point of each plant to encourage bushy growth. Later, pinch out the side shoots as necessary to give a symmetrical shape. To train a plant as a pyramid, allow the centre shoot to grow until it reaches the required height, then pinch out the growing point. Allow all side shoots to grow, pinching them out as required to form a pyramidal shape. To form standard plants, take out the lower side shoots until the main stem reaches the required height; then pinch out the growing point and allow the top five or six side shoots to develop.

Detach plantlets from the leaves of *Asplenium bulbiferum*, setting them individually in 3 in. pots of John Innes potting compost No. 1.

Canna roots started into growth in boxes earlier in the year (see MARCH) will now be ready for potting into 8 in. pots containing John Innes potting compost No. 3.

Move plants of *Campanula pyramidalis*, lifted from the open ground last autumn and potted into 9 in. pots during March, to a sheltered spot outdoors. Support the flower spikes with thin canes.

Pinch out cucumber laterals

Stop laterals growing from the main stems of cucumbers at two leaves beyond the first or second fruit. Pinch out subsequent sub-laterals as soon as they have made two leaves beyond their first fruit. Remove all male flowers (those without an embryo fruit) and tendrils.

Twist the stems of tomato plants round the supporting strings, or tie them to the canes, and remove side shoots regularly. Feed the plants every week or ten days from the time the fruits on the first trusses begin to swell.

In a cold greenhouse, plant tomatoes in the border, in peat growing bags or in bottomless containers placed on an aggregate base (see APRIL).

STOPPING A MELON

Pinch out the growing points of melons, grown in cold frames, when each plant has produced four or five leaves

Plant out melons

Plant out into cold frames melons raised from an April sowing, one plant to each frame light. Set each plant on a mound of soil mixed with manure or compost. Pinch out the growing point when the plant has developed four or five leaves. Avoid splashing or damaging the main stem at soil level, or damping-off may occur.

Trees and shrubs

Plant out shrubs that are tender in the young stage, including arbutus, *Cytisus scoparius* (yellow broom), choisya, *Clematis armandii*, fuchsia and hydrangea. (These shrubs are not recommended for exposed northern gardens.) Keep the shrubs watered until established.

During showery weather, complete the planting of evergreens, although pot-grown plants may be planted at almost any time. Keep the newly planted shrubs moist at the roots, and spray the foliage with water in the evenings during dry or windy weather.

To induce a lilac to flower, keep the plant down to a single stem or trunk. Heavy mulches of weed-killer free lawn mowings at the base will reduce the tendency to send up suckers.

PRUNING

Cut off dead flower heads, shorten long shoots, and thin out or completely remove weak shoots of shrubs that have finished flowering. This light pruning applies to kerria, pieris, *Prunus triloba multiplex*, ribes and spring-flowering species of spiraea.

Well established or old shrubs of *Forsythia intermedia* may have outgrown their sites. Cut out all dead wood and thin shoots to retain shape.

Begin to clip *Laurus nobilis* (bay tree) if it is grown as a formal bush.

Rhododendrons and azaleas

This month many of the finest rhododendrons and azaleas are in flower, provided there are no freak frosts. In cool north-east areas they are not usually at their best until the first half of June.

DEAD-HEADING RHODODENDRONS

To avoid injury to the young growth, snap off the dead flowers with your finger and thumb. Secateurs are liable to damage the shoots

Pick off dead flowers. This will allow new growth to develop and form next year's flower buds. Normally, rhododendrons require no pruning.

Water newly planted bushes in dry weather. While the soil is damp, mulch bushes with peat or leaf-mould to prevent the soil drying out rapidly. Continue picking off faded flowers from the earlier-flowering plants.

Hedges

Clip hedges of *Lonicera nitida* monthly from now until the end of September to keep them neatly shaped and prevent them breaking open as they grow. Some other hedges, such as the commonly grown oval-leaved privet, also need regular clipping to look their best. (For times of clipping, see table, SEPTEMBER.)

Clip hedges of forsythia and flowering currants after the flowers have died. Do not clip them again until the following year, otherwise the flower buds will be removed and the spring display lost.

Before clipping, decide on the shape of each hedge. This can be modified, if desired, in the case of established hedges, but new ones need careful shaping from the beginning.

Trimming hedges

A rounded, lightly trimmed hedge is often appropriate in less formal parts of the garden, and many flowering hedges are so shaped. But straight lines may be preferred near the house, the ideal shape in this case being a hedge which has a broad base, sloping to a narrow top. A cross-section would appear as a thin isosceles triangle. This will ensure that the lower branches get some light and will continue to produce new leaves and shoots, while weeds will to some extent be smothered. Hedges with narrow tops are the least susceptible to snow damage and form the best wind-breaks. Though the thick base provides complete shelter at ground level, the thinner top filters the wind, resulting in less turbulence on the leeward side.

Clipping new hedges

When clipping new hedges or those which need reshaping, lay a garden line along the ground parallel to the row of plants and at the same distance from them as the required width of the lower branches. With sharp shears or a mechanical trimmer, cut about 12 in. up the side of the hedge, level with the line. Then insert rods or sticks to mark the desired height and clip along the top. Finally, complete clipping the sides, sloping them in to the top.

Alternative hedge shapes include those with vertical sides and with flat, rounded or angled tops.

Old yews and some other hedges may, over the years, become uneven in width and height as a result of careless clipping.

This is usually caused by clipping closely where the branches are short or weak but failing to clip the stronger branches as hard as necessary. A good straight hedge can be achieved in time, but sometimes such hedges are more attractive when left in their natural shape.

When cutting hedges, spread hessian or a plastic sheet to catch the clippings. Move it along as you work, and you will not have to sweep up the clippings when you have finished.

Watering new hedges

Dry spells this month can check or kill newly planted hedges. If the soil does become dry and the plants cease to grow, give them one really good watering, applying about five gallons of water to each yard of hedge. This quantity will rarely penetrate the soil at one watering unless applied slowly with a sprinkler. If you use a can or a hose, water the soil until the surface becomes puddled, then move on to a fresh stretch, returning to the original plants when the surface water has drained away. Repeat the watering only if the dry weather continues and the soil dries out again.

In very dry conditions, after watering dig two or three holes adjacent to the plants to make sure that there is not a layer of dry soil within the area of root growth.

Continue to weed or hoe hedge bottoms (see MARCH).

Heathers

Complete any remaining planting as early in the month as possible (see MARCH).

Spread peat or proprietary forest bark as a mulch on bare ground between heathers planted earlier. Older plants will benefit from a top dressing of peat worked into the base of the stems after the plants have been cut back.

Fruit

There is still a risk of frost damage, especially inland and in northern districts, but trees are now making more growth which will protect the flowers, and soil temperatures are rising so that low-growing fruits are less likely to be frosted than in April.

Most fruits contain a high proportion of water, and will benefit from watering in dry spells. Apart from its direct effect on the size and quality of the fruit, water applied when the trees and bushes are short of it will produce more growth and result in a larger plant, which will bear bigger crops in later years. To avoid producing too much growth, water mainly after flowering during the fruit-swelling stage. Water strawberries during ripening.

Relate watering to rainfall

Applications of water should be related to the amount of rainfall. Where the crop covers the ground, the rate of water loss is 4–5 gal. per sq. yd. every ten days. Even allowing for rainfall (it would take continuous moderate rain to replace this amount in 24 hours), the amount to apply artificially will depend on the rooting area of the plant and the type of soil. Fruit trees, for example, can withstand a greater shortage than bush fruits, since they have more extensive root systems. Heavy soils have a greater holding capacity than light ones, and will support plants for longer, provided that root run is unrestricted. Applications of less than 2 gal. per sq. yd. are wasteful and uneconomic. Strawberries are unlikely to benefit from more than 4–5 gal. per sq. yd., but other fruits will need 8–10 gal. per sq. yd. at a time. If the use of water is restricted or time is short, give one application in May or June to promote shoot growth, and another in June or July at the fruit-swelling stage.

Bark ringing

Bark ringing of trees (apple and pear only) is an alternative to root pruning and is probably more effective in forming fruit buds. If a ring of bark is taken out at blossom time, the normal food supply is partially or completely cut off, and the sap concentrated in the branches. A slight check is given by cutting through the bark in a ring round the tree without removing any bark; the most severe check is the removal of a complete ring.

Bark ring either the trunk or side branches, making the ring $\frac{1}{4}$ in. wide on large trees and decreasing the width for smaller trees and branches. Before going to the extreme, try removing two overlapping semi-circles of bark, $\frac{1}{4}$ in. wide and 2–3 in. apart, using a sharp knife to cut through the bark down to the wood. Always bind the cuts immediately with several turns of adhesive tape. The cuts need to heal quickly, and will not do so if they have dried out.

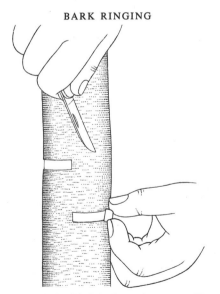

BARK RINGING

The growth of fruit buds can be promoted by removing overlapping semi-circles of bark. Afterwards, bind the cuts with tape

Apple, pear and sweet cherry

If fruit set appears good, apply $\frac{1}{2}$–1 oz. of sulphate of ammonia or Nitro-chalk per sq. yd. This will help to swell the fruit and form fruit buds for next year. Food and moisture shortage at this time causes reduced fruit size; if the shortage is severe, fruit bud formation (which takes place up to mid-July) will also be affected, and next year's crop reduced. Do not feed if the trees are not fruiting, or they will make too much growth. Young trees should not carry too much fruit, so limit the crop by rubbing out flower clusters or removing the fruitlets by hand, leaving the leaf clusters to build up the tree.

Apple and pear scab

Continue to spray apple against apple scab every 10–14 days, especially in a wet spring, if complete protection is required, and against apple blossom weevil, caterpillars and greenfly, especially if a winter-wash (see DECEMBER) or bud-burst spray (see MARCH) have been missed. At petal-fall stage, control sawfly with HCH, red spider mite with malathion or a systemic insecticide, and woolly aphis with malathion or HCH.

Continue to spray pear against pear scab at intervals of 10–14 days (see MARCH) and with malathion or systemic insecticide against greenfly.

Blackberry, loganberry and hybrid berries

New growth, which will give next year's crop, should now be coming away from the base of the plant. To check the spread of disease from the old canes to the new, keep them separate as much as possible. Use half-rounds of wire hooked at either end so that they can be attached to the framework on which the fruiting plants are growing (see recommended varieties, NOVEMBER) and moved up to higher wires as the shoots grow; two or three half-rounds will be needed for each plant. Train new shoots to grow up one side of the plant and inside the half-rounds. In early May feed in the same way as raspberries, increasing the amount of nitrogen to 2 oz. per sq. yd.

Black currant

If fruit set appears good, apply 1 oz. of sulphate of ammonia or Nitro-chalk per sq. yd. Apply benomyl three weeks after the first spray against big bud mite.

Gooseberry

Feed now with up to $\frac{1}{2}$ oz. of dried blood per sq. yd. on cordons, and up to 1 oz. of sulphate of ammonia or Nitro-chalk per sq. yd. on bushes; this is especially important for young bushes. Control weeds by careful hoeing, or by spraying with paraquat. Apply derris just before the flowers open to control sawfly, which starts attacking the centres of the bushes, and apply dinocap to control American gooseberry mildew.

Peach, nectarine and acid cherry

Watch for attacks of red spider mite and greenfly, and spray with malathion or derris as necessary. If fruit set is good, apply $\frac{1}{2}$–1 oz. of sulphate of ammonia or Nitro-chalk, or up to $\frac{1}{2}$ oz. of dried

THINNING PEACHES

Left unthinned, peaches may bear numerous small fruits of indifferent quality. These illustrations show a wall-trained tree before and after thinning, with surplus fruits removed to leave a space of 3–4 in. Further thinning, to 9 in. spacings, will be needed next month

blood per sq. yd. to wall-trained fruits. Start thinning fruit on wall-trained trees, removing the small or mis-shapen fruits with sharp scissors or finger and thumb so that the fruits are 3–4 in. apart. On newly planted fan-trained trees, allow the shoot from the end bud of each branch to grow out, and also two well placed shoots on the top side and one on the underside. Remove the rest of the shoots. On established trees repeat the treatment recommended after planting, until a good framework has been built up. On bush peaches remove crowded and crossing branches, and cut out the tips of shoots that have died back to a good bud.

Plum and damson

If fruit set appears good, apply $\frac{1}{2}$–1 oz. of sulphate of ammonia or Nitro-chalk per sq. yd. Watch for greenfly, especially

FAN-TRAINING A PEACH TREE

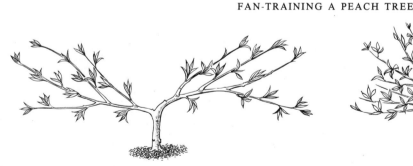

On recently planted trees, where both leaders were shortened to 12–18 in. during February, allow the end shoots to develop, together with two upward-growing shoots and one on the underside

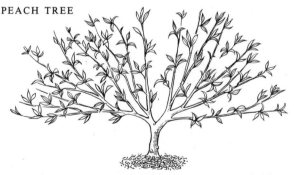

On established fan trees, repeat the treatment recommended for newly planted trees until a sufficient, evenly spaced framework has developed. Tie fan-trained branches to wires spaced 6 in. apart

meavy plum aphis on the undersides of leaves; these pests cause down-curling. The first signs of attack may be mould growing on the upper sides of leaves.

Raspberry

New canes should now be growing up strongly. Carefully pull out unwanted shoots which are causing overcrowding in the row or growing out into the space between the rows. Control weeds by careful hoeing or by spraying with paraquat. If fruit set appears good, a surface mulch will help to conserve moisture. Apply up to 1 oz. of sulphate of ammonia or Nitro-chalk per sq. yd.

Red and white currants

Apply up to ½ oz. of dried blood per sq. yd. before mid-May if fruit set is good.

Strawberry

Apply captan to the open flowers to protect the fruit against grey mould. As soon as there is no more risk of frost damage, and if possible before the swelling fruit has become splashed with soil, protect the fruit either by putting down chopped straw or using bituminised paper collars. This cover also provides protection for slugs, so put down slug bait at the same time. Keep weeds under control, especially if the plants are protected with straw, or the weeds will get out of hand during fruit picking. Continue to de-blossom spring-planted runners and autumn-fruiting varieties (see APRIL).

Vine (outdoor)

Start summer pruning (see JUNE) by rubbing out unwanted shoots. Control weeds round the plants.

Vegetables

Be ready to cover potatoes if frost is forecast (see APRIL).

Sow maincrop carrots, if not already done (see APRIL).

Prepare sites for outdoor crops

If you wish to grow outdoors crops of marrows, squashes, pumpkins or courgettes, prepare the sites early in the month by digging holes 12 in. square, 12 in. deep and 3 ft. apart, placing a forkful of well rotted manure in each and replacing the soil. As an alternative to the manure, mix two double handfuls of dried sewage sludge or proprietary hop manure with the soil when replacing it. Firm the soil and draw earth from the surrounding area to form a mound over each site. At the end of May sow three seeds on each site, later removing two of the seedlings and leaving the strongest to grow on. If you are buying the plants, set one on each mound during early June.

Marrow plants are sold by most garden shops, but it is generally necessary to raise squashes, pumpkins and courgettes from seed. Squashes are in many respects similar to marrows, but some varieties have round fruits and all are more delicately flavoured. Courgettes are small marrows, delicious when sliced and fried.

Sow runner beans

During the second half of the month sow runner beans, preferably on a site prepared earlier (see DECEMBER). If a site has not been prepared, dig a strip 18 in. wide and one spit deep, incorporating manure or compost and treading firmly before sowing. Sow the seeds 3 in. deep and 9–12 in. apart in two rows 12–15 in. apart. Provide bean poles alongside the plants, setting them at an angle. Tie opposing poles together near their tops and if necessary strengthen with horizontal struts. Alternatively, sow the seeds alongside 6 ft. canes erected in the form of a wigwam and tied

STAKING RUNNER BEANS

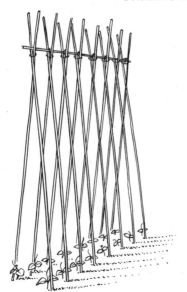

For added strength and rigidity, lay horizontal struts where opposing bean poles cross, securing these to the uprights

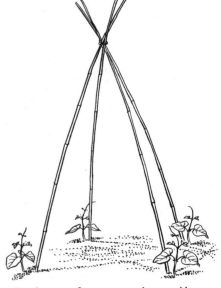

A wigwam of canes or poles provides an alternative means of support where space cannot be spared for a bean row

Vegetables : Guide

	Period of use	Sow	Depth (inches)	Plant or transplant	Space between rows (inches)	Space between plants (inches)	Chief pests and diseases	General comments
Artichokes, globe	Jul–Oct			Apr	36	36		Sufficiently decorative to grow among flowers when space is limited
Artichokes, Jerusalem	Nov–Mar			Mar–Apr	24	12		
Asparagus	Apr–Jun			Mar	15	15	Asparagus beetle	Weed as necessary during the growing season
Beans, broad	May–Jul	Nov, Jan, Feb	2½–3		7	6	Black bean aphids	Start picking when the pods are finger-thick, slicing them as for french or runner beans
Beans, dwarf french Under cloches Outdoor	Jul–Oct Jul–Oct	Apr May–Jul	2–3 2–3		8 24	6 6	Black bean aphids Black bean aphids	Pick every few days, before the beans become tough and stringy
Beans, runner	Jul–Sep	May	3		12–15	9–12	Black bean aphids	Pick every few days, before the beans become tough. Can make an ornamental screen
Beetroot	Jul onwards	Apr, May	1		9–12	4–6		Start using the roots of globe varieties when they reach the size of tennis balls
Beet, seakale	Aug–Dec	May	1–1½		12–15	4		Pull the leaves by their stems so that they break off at the base. Cook stems separately, serving with white sauce. Treat leaves as spinach
Broccoli, heading or spring	Feb–May	Apr–May	½	Jun–Jul	30	18	Flea beetle, cabbage fly, caterpillars. Club root	To make the best use of space, only winter and spring varieties are recommended
Broccoli, purple-sprouting	Mar–Jun	Apr–May	½	Jun	30	18	Flea beetle, cabbage fly, caterpillars. Club root	Pick the side shoots when they are no more than 6 in. long
Brussels sprouts	Oct–May	Jan, Mar, Aug	½	Mar, May, Jun, Jul, Oct	36	30	Flea beetle, cabbage fly, caterpillars. Club root	Remove three or four sprouts at a time from each plant
Cabbages Spring Under cloches Late summer Winter	Apr–Jun Apr–Jun Sep–Dec Dec–Feb	Aug Aug Mar Apr	½ ½ ½ ½	Sep–Oct Sep–Oct Apr Jun–Jul	24 12 24 24	18 12 18 18	Flea beetle, cabbage fly, caterpillars. Club root	Savoys and drumheads will withstand hard frosts for up to two months
Carrots Cloches Frame Maincrop	Mar–Aug May–Aug Sep onwards	Mar, Sep Feb Apr	½ ½ ½		6 15	3 6	Carrot fly Carrot fly Carrot fly	Remove cloches in late May. Frames may be cleared in May. Store the roots in a box filled with sand after twisting off the tops
Cauliflowers	Sep–Oct	Apr	½	May	24	24	Flea beetle, cabbage fly, caterpillars. Club root	
Celery, self-blanching	Aug–Oct			Jun	18	12	Celery fly	Weed often in the early stages. Give plenty of water
Chicory	Nov–Mar	Jun	1		15–18	12		
Cucumbers Under glass	Jul–Sep	May	½	May		36		Water frequently. Cut fruits regularly
Kohl rabi	May onwards	Mar, Apr	½		12–15	6–12	Flea beetle, cabbage fly, caterpillars. Club root	

to cultivation

	Period of use	Sow	Depth (inches)	Plant or transplant	Space between rows (inches)	Space between plants (inches)	Chief pests and diseases	General comments
Leeks	Dec–May	Mar	½	Jun, Jul	12	6		
Lettuce								
Summer and autumn	May–Oct	Mar–Aug	½		12	9	Aphids, slugs and snails. Grey mould	Choose varieties suited to the time of year and method of cultivation
Winter (outdoors)	May–Jun	Aug, Sep	½	Oct	12	9		
Winter (under glass)	Apr–May	Oct, Nov	½		12	9		
Marrows (bush)	Jul–Dec	May	½	May, Jun		36	Mildew	Ideally, cut fruits when they are 8–12 in. long. For storage, leave fruits to ripen on the plants until early October
Onions								
Salad	May onwards	Mar	½		12		Onion fly. Mildew	Sow sparingly, using the thinnings for salads
Maincrop (sets)	Aug onwards			Mar, Apr	12	9	Onion fly. Mildew	Sow sparingly, using the thinnings for salads
Parsnips	Nov onwards	Mar	½		15	9		
Peas	Jun–Sep	Jan–Jul	2½		3	2	Pea moth	Support tall kinds with wire netting or brushwood
Potatoes, early	Late Jun onwards		6	Mar, Apr	24	10–12		Lift as required when the tubers are large enough
Radishes								
Salad	Mar–Sep	Mar–Jul	½		12	12	Flea beetle. Club root	Make frequent sowings for succession
Winter	Oct onwards	Jul	1		12	6		
Rhubarb	Feb onwards			Jan		36		Remove stems by pulling from the base. Remove flower heads by cutting
Salsify	Dec–Apr	May	1–1½		15	8		Scrape or peel immediately before cooking as the flesh discolours rapidly
Scorzonera	Dec–Apr	May	1–1½		15	8		
Shallots	Jul onwards			Jan–Mar	12	9	Onion fly. Mildew	
Spinach, summer	May–Jul	Mar–May	1		9	6	Mildew. Black bean aphids	Pull the plants up by their roots when they are 5–6 in. high
Spinach beet	Aug onwards	Jun–Jul	1		9–12	4–6		Pick the leaves by breaking the stems at the base, about two at a time from each plant
Swedes	Nov onwards	Jun, Jul	½		18	9–12	Flea beetle. Club root, mildew	Keep well watered in a dry season
Sweet corn	Aug–Nov	May	1½		18	18		
Tomatoes	Sep onwards			Jun	24	15–18	Potato blight	Remove side shoots regularly and cut off the top of each plant just above the fourth flower truss
Turnips (late-sown)	Oct–Feb	Jul	½		12	9	Flea beetle. Club root mildew	

together near their tops. The former method produces the heavier crop; the latter is more decorative and can be adopted on any vacant patch. Several types of long-lasting and decorative metal supports on the wig-wam principle are available.

Tomatoes

Early in the month prepare sites for out-door tomatoes, following the method described for marrows but spacing the holes 15–18 in. apart, with 24 in. between the rows.

French beans

About the second week in the month, sow french beans for growing outdoors. Set the seeds 2–3 in. deep and 6 in. apart in drills 24 in. apart.

Cauliflowers

Set out plants of late summer cauli-flowers, sown last month, planting them 24 in. apart in rows 24 in. apart. Plant with a dibber, dusting calomel into each hole as a precaution against club root disease. Set the plants with their bottom leaves at soil level, firming them in with your heel and watering immedi-ately afterwards.

Other crops

Plant out Brussels sprouts in cool areas of the north and in Scotland.

Make further sowings of summer spinach and salad crops to maintain the supply (see MARCH).

Towards the end of the month sow seeds of long-rooted beetroot, such as 'Cheltenham Green Top'. The crop can be stored for use during the winter. Sow as globe beetroot (see APRIL).

UNDER GLASS

Remove cloches from spring cabbages, carrots, lettuces and broad beans. Carry this out in several stages, over three weeks, so that the plants harden-off

132

gradually. First move the cloches 2 in. apart, increasing the gap by an inch or two at intervals of four or five days.

Prepare sites for cucumbers

To grow cucumbers under cloches or in frames, prepare sites as already de-scribed this month for marrows. Sow the seeds a week or two afterwards, water-ing them in and covering with the cloches or frame lights. When the seeds have germinated and surplus plants have been removed, ventilate the cloches or frames during the day.

In cool northern areas sow runner beans under glass in mid-May for planting out in the open during the second week of June.

LESS COMMON VEGETABLES

Continue cutting asparagus (see APRIL).

Order plants of self-blanching celery for planting in early June.

Sow seakale beet after soaking the seeds overnight to speed germination. Cover the seeds 1–1½ in. deep in drills 12–15 in. apart. Allow 2 in. between the seeds, later thinning out alternate plants.

Salsify and scorzonera

Salsify, a root vegetable which can be left in the ground during the winter and which grows best in light, fertile soil, has a distinctive, oyster-like taste. Sow the seeds 1–1½ in. deep in drills 15 in. apart, at intervals of 4 in., and later remove every alternate plant. Scorzonera, another winter-hardy root vegetable, has a less distinctive flavour. It is grown in the same way as salsify.

Sweet corn

Towards the end of the month sow sweet corn in soil that has been manured recently. Sow the seeds 1½ in. deep in groups of three, at intervals of 18 in., later removing two plants from each station to leave the strongest. The crop is best grown in a number of short rows

arranged in a rectangular block to facilitate pollination.

Sweet corn is not successful in cool areas of north-east England and Scotland unless the summer is exceptionally warm.

Herbs

Make further sowings of chervil, dill, fennel, hyssop and parsley (see MARCH), and thin out seedlings of April-sown herbs to 3 in. apart.

Plant out basil seedlings about 15 in. apart and water well in the early stages, until the plants are established. Later in the month, sow basil seeds 1 in. deep in seed drills, or directly into a cold frame.

Take cuttings

Take cuttings 3–4 in. long of pot mar-joram, rosemary, sage and thyme from the previous year's growth. Remove the lower leaves from the cutting, and with

STEM CUTTINGS OF HERBS

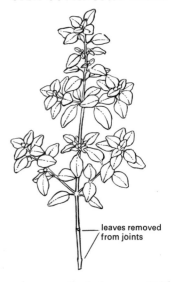

leaves removed from joints

Thyme is among the herbs propagated from cuttings. Insert in sand after removing the lower leaves and trimming below a joint

PROPAGATING FROM RUNNERS

Herbs which make runners, such as mint, can be separated at the points shown and re-planted. Young, vigorous roots are best

a sharp knife cut straight across the stem below a joint. Insert the cuttings round the edge of a sand-filled pot or into open, sandy soil. If the weather is cold or windy, give cloche protection.

Divide mint and thyme again if the plants are at all straggly. The tiny roots at each joint on the runners will strike readily if they are buried in fine soil.

If a new herb garden is being started, now is the time to plant out herbs into their permanent positions according to the designs made during the winter (see JANUARY).

Patios and town gardens

In the south, during the last week or ten days of the month, set out in containers tender plants that have been hardened-off in a cold frame. In the north, wait until the beginning of June.

Complete the sowing of hardy annuals direct into containers (see APRIL).

Prepare the patio or courtyard for the period when it will get most use, arranging the containers to allow plenty of space for outdoor living. Erect supporting material, such as wires or plastic netting, for vines and climbers.

Lift bulbs after flowering

As spring-flowering bulbs in window-boxes and other containers begin to fade, lift them and plant them temporarily in a spare corner of the garden. When the foliage has died down, clean and store the bulbs ready for autumn planting. Replace the bulbs with summer bedding plants, choosing annuals of a height to suit the container.

For positions in full sun, choose petunias, marigolds, zinnias, antirrhinums, lobelias, alyssums or verbenas. Water the containers frequently during hot weather—twice daily if this proves necessary to prevent the compost drying out. For places that are in shade for much of the day, try begonias, pansies and calceolarias.

Hanging baskets

Hanging baskets make charming decorations for courtyards or town houses. Plant them and set them in position now, making sure that the brackets from which they hang are strong, and are securely attached to the wall. Site the baskets where they will be seen to advantage and can be watered easily, but where drips will not be a nuisance. Avoid draughts or heavy shade.

To prepare a hanging basket, first line the inside with moss, with thin turves placed grass-side inwards, or with coarse sacking. Fill the interior with John Innes potting compost No. 3, or a proprietary soil-less compost. Use fairly mature plants, otherwise you will have to wait a good many weeks for the display to start.

Place the plants so that some trail over the edges, hiding the framework

PLANTING A HANGING BASKET

Hold the basket steady on a pot or bucket, and line it with moss, thin turves or sacking

Part fill with John Innes potting compost No. 3 before placing the plants in position

Add further compost after planting, leaving a shallow depression in the centre

133

of the basket. Insert a few plants, or sow nasturtium seeds, through holes in the lining.

Suitable flowering plants for hanging baskets include alyssums, lobelias, dwarf nasturtiums and begonias; for foliage there are small-leaved ivies, tradescantias and zebrinas. Some fuchsias and pelargoniums hang attractively.

Keep the baskets moist

Hanging baskets dry out very quickly and in hot weather may require a good soaking as often as three times a day. This task becomes a great deal easier if the baskets are suspended from a rope and pulley so that they can be lowered for watering and hoisted into position again afterwards.

When a basket has been allowed to get too dry, the first watering may not be absorbed by the compost. In this case, lower the basket into a tub or basin of water, allowing it to remain until the soil is well soaked. Wait for the surplus water to drain away before replacing the basket.

House plants

From now until the autumn water all plants liberally, though never allowing the compost to become soggy. Apply a liquid fertiliser at the recommended rate, or halve both the strength of the solution and the interval between applications. Make sure that no plant stands in a direct draught, though ensure that they all get a reasonable amount of fresh air. Never allow any plants other than succulents to stand in a south window during the hottest part of the day in sunny weather.

Control growth

In the case of plants which are growing rapidly, keep growth within bounds by nipping off over-long shoots or by

tying in the tips of such plants as rhoicissus and cissus. Where tall-growing, single-stemmed plants, such as ficus or fatshedera, outgrow their supporting canes, replace them with taller canes or lash extensions on to them, making fresh ties as necessary.

Re-pot old plants

Although, given reasonable care, most house plants will grow for several years in their original pots, they cannot be expected to do this for ever. Watch older plants carefully and re-pot when this appears necessary—if the soil dries out rapidly, if the roots are growing through the drainage hole, or if the plant has ceased to grow vigorously and loses condition.

General tasks

This month roses, lilacs, fruit trees and many other plants produce suckers—young shoots coming up through the ground, sometimes several feet away from the parent plant. Remove these, because they can weaken the parent. Cut them off with a sharp knife at the point where they leave the root system, first scraping away the soil. Alternatively, water them with a paraquat solution. This will kill the suckers without harming the parent plant. Heavy mulches of weed-killer free lawn clippings discourage lilacs from sending up suckers.

Trim lawn edges after mowing, using either shears or an edging tool.

Pest control

Pests become really active in May. Control slugs and snails by placing pellets wherever slug damage may arise. Spray roses, fruit bushes and broad beans once a week against aphids and caterpillars. A combined insecticide and fungicide will control most pests and diseases.

Importance of watering

Water is of paramount importance to all plants at this time. In a dry May a check to growth can be disastrous to crops grown from seed, and even established plants will not make normal growth unless they have enough water. Apply at least 1 gal. per sq. yd. at each watering. If you have applied a mulch, apply $\frac{1}{4}$ gal. per sq. yd. to wet the mulch, and then 1 gal. more to wet the ground underneath.

Give plants a liquid feed or a dressing of a quick-acting fertiliser and water it well in.

TRIMMING LAWN EDGES

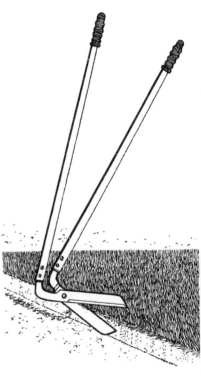

Trim lawn edges regularly after mowing, using either a pair of long-handled shears or a mechanical edging tool

June

Midsummer heat-waves give the chance for the gardener to relax and enjoy the rose display, but make it essential to water and mulch the borders

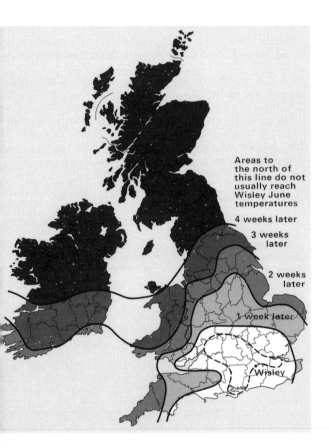

Areas to
the north of
this line do not
usually reach
Wisley June
temperatures

4 weeks later

3 weeks
later

2 weeks
later

1 week later

Wisley

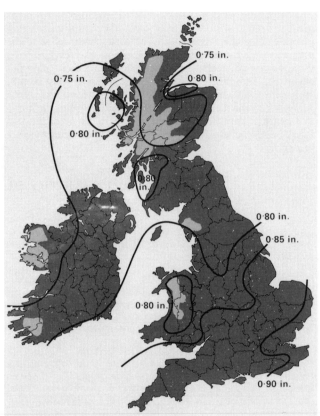

0·75 in.

0·75 in.

0·80 in.

0·80 in.

0·80
in.

0·80 in.

0·85 in.

0·80 in.

0·90 in.

PROGRESS OF THE SEASON

n June the north of the British Isles lags far behind southern England in he onset of summer conditions. The north does not often reach the varmth of average conditions in southern England, except during ery warm summers. The map shows the lateness of the season in an verage June in places in the British Isles compared with conditions at he Royal Horticultural Society's Gardens at Wisley. As a rough guide, ardeners in the white areas can begin sowing and planting out at the eginning of the month; those to the north should wait until later

WATER NEEDED BY A GARDEN IN JUNE

Over most of the British Isles gardeners will need to do some watering during June. The map shows the total water used by a garden (the potential transpiration) in inches per average week in June. In the shaded areas, weekly rainfall is on average less than potential transpiration, and watering will be necessary. Gardeners everywhere should pay attention to water requirements, especially during long, sunny spells. In June there is often heavy, thundery rain, not all of which enters the soil. (See GLOSSARY, *Weather*)

The weather in June

Westerly influences return to the British Isles in June. Depressions from the Atlantic once more frequently pass to the north-west, but winds are light, and June and July have fewer gales than any other months. Periods of widespread rain and warm, cloudy, muggy weather are followed by brighter, clearer weather brought by north-westerly winds.

Anticyclone weather is more likely in June than in any other month. Light, westerly winds cross the country, bringing generally cloudless conditions, with many hours of sunshine each day. Afternoon temperatures reach at least 27°C (80°F) throughout the region, but night temperatures may fall below 10°C (50°F). On average, June is the sunniest month, except in north-west Scotland and Ireland, where May is the sunniest. On the whole, June is also the driest month, but in the afternoons cumulus clouds may develop to great heights inland, and thunderstorms are likely to put an end to most fine spells.

Sometimes during June a light, warm, southerly wind from the sea brings coastal fog to the south coast, Devon, Cornwall and Wales. A similar south-west wind brings low, grey cloud to the north, and drizzle may occur in mountain districts in north-west England and south-west Scotland. Much of the sun's heat reaches the earth through clouds, and conditions can be oppressive.

During the first half of the month the north-easterly wind of the previous month may persist. Temperatures do not rise above 13°C (55°F) during the day, and at night they may fall nearly to freezing point in valley bottoms and sheltered places in the north.

The sun is at its strongest during June, and every care must be taken to keep down weeds and to maintain soil moisture. Pests and diseases must be checked whenever they show the first signs of infesting the garden: early action can do much to keep these enemies under control.

A summary of the month's work

LAWNS
Established lawns. Continue mowing, raising blades during very dry weather. Spike the lawn to allow water to penetrate. Apply fungicides for control of dollar spot and corticium. Treat with weedkillers if necessary.

ROSES
For quality blooms, remove small side buds from flower shoots. Hoe regularly. Pull away brier shoots and suckers. Water miniatures growing in tubs. Spray with systemic insecticide against aphids, and also spray against black spot, mildew and rust.

HARDY HERBACEOUS PLANTS
Cut back early-flowering plants to within 3 in. of soil level after flowering. Divide primroses for re-planting. Apply a 1 in. mulch of peat or leaf-mould between moisture- or shade-loving plants.

DAHLIAS
Plant out young dahlias in Scotland and the north of England. Pinch out the tips when they start to grow to make them bushy, and tie them to stakes. When aphids appear, control with alternate sprays of derris and HCH or a long-lasting systemic insecticide. Apply a mulch to conserve moisture and prevent weeds.

CHRYSANTHEMUMS
Stop plants set out in May. Remove tips from plants grown for decorative purposes. Stop pompons and spray varieties, to encourage bushy growth. Water plants thoroughly once a week and spray overhead with water in hot weather. Hoe in a dressing of sulphate of ammonia or Nitro-chalk. Spray regularly to control aphids and leaf miners.
Under glass. Take cuttings of mid- and late-season varieties to plant direct in greenhouse borders in July. In the north, move greenhouse-flowering varieties into their final pots and move to standing-out ground. Give second stopping to exhibition incurves and singles.

GLADIOLI
Give plants a good soaking in dry weather.

IRISES
Tie flower stems of bearded irises to light canes, and cut blooms for indoor decoration. Cut back stems after flowering and top dress poor soils with a general fertiliser. Inspect bearded irises for leaf spot disease. Prepare a sunny, well drained plot for planting in July–August. Dress summer-flowering Dutch irises with Nitro-chalk when flower buds show. Cut back the leaves of *I. unguicularis* to let the sun ripen the rhizomes.

LILIES
Spray monthly with a systemic insecticide and fortnightly with Bordeaux mixture. Burn virus-infected lilies.
Under glass. Control aphids with a systemic insecticide. Keep pot-grown lilies well watered.

CARNATIONS AND PINKS
Stake border carnations if not already done and disbud flower stems. Take action against pests and diseases. Plant old perpetual

flowering carnations outdoors to finish flowering. Order border carnations and pinks for autumn delivery.
Under glass. Take cuttings of pinks, inserting them in $3\frac{1}{2}$ in. pots in a cold frame. When they root, increase ventilation and eventually plant them out or pot them singly. Continue potting young perpetual flowering carnations into 6 in. or 8 in. pots. Renew shading on glass. Continue with second stopping to secure autumn or winter blooms. Take action against pests and diseases. Cut blooms and disbud flower stems.

SWEET PEAS
Syringe the plants with a mist-like spray of water in dry weather. Spray monthly with a systemic insecticide against sap-sucking insects. Remove any plants whose leaves turn yellow or brown. Continue to pinch out side shoots and tendrils from cordons.

FLOWERS FROM SEED·
Complete planting of half-hardy annuals. Water recently planted half-hardy annuals thoroughly in dry spells. Support taller-growing annuals. Spray monthly with a systemic insecticide. Hoe weeds among bedding plants. Sow hardy annuals. Set out seedlings of hardy biennials in a nursery bed, preferably during showery weather. Sow hardy perennials outdoors. Sow wallflowers and sweet williams in drills in their flowering positions. **Under glass.** Sow hardy perennials in a heated greenhouse.

BULBS
Start lifting spring bulbs whose foliage has turned yellow. Place bulbs in shallow boxes and dry in a well ventilated shed. When dry, remove dead leaves, roots and skins, then store in a cool, dry shed. Plant de Caen anemone corms for autumn and winter flowering in mild districts. Plant out arum lilies, or stand pots outdoors for their summer rest.
Under glass. Dry off lachenalias flowered in pots. Pot or re-pot vallota bulbs.

ALPINES
Continue weeding and hoeing. Trim dead flowers from aubrietas and saxifrages to prevent seeding, and clip other plants to keep them tidy. In showery weather, transplant recently planted alpines which have been wrongly sited. Water plants in dry weather, preferably using a fine mist in the evening.

WATER PLANTS AND POOLS
Finish planting aquatics this month for a display in their first season. In sultry weather, keep the water oxygenated by occasionally adding fresh water from a hose and spray. Watch for the appearance of aphids and deal with them immediately, being careful how chemicals are used where fish are present. Control *Chironomas* midge, which eats the leaves of water lilies and aponogeton. Continue to remove algae before large masses form. Reduce the growth of surface plants to allow light to penetrate to underwater plants. Prick out seedlings of February-sown primulas in seed boxes, ready for planting in September. Divide clumps of *Orontium aquaticum* and re-plant.

GREENHOUSES AND FRAMES
Water the greenhouse and damp down to maintain a humid atmosphere. Transfer as many plants as possible to cold frames to reduce watering. Plunge plants which have finished flowering in the garden. Sow cineraria seeds. Pot on streptocarpus plants, and make a further sowing. Transfer cyclamen sown last August to 5 in. pots. Give them a liquid feed every ten days. Remove faded flowers from plants now in flower, give a liquid feed every ten days, and control aphids with a systemic insecticide. Pot polyanthuses in 3 in. pots for greenhouse decoration next winter, and stand in shade outdoors. Move *Campanula pyramidalis* seedlings into 5 in. pots. Propagate saintpaulias and *Begonia rex* from leaf cuttings. Spray *Solanum capsicastrum* plants daily in warm weather to help set fruits. Pinch out all but four side shoots on melons planted last month, pollinate flowers, and shade glass in hot weather. Cease giving artificial heat; clean out the boiler, or store the oil heater in a dry shed. Maintain a humid atmosphere for cucumbers by regular spraying. If main stems of tomatoes are becoming thin, give extra nitrogen. Give some ventilation at night in warm weather.

TREES AND SHRUBS
Keep a space 4 ft. in diameter clear of grass around newly planted trees and shrubs. Remove self-sown ash and sycamore seedlings.
Propagation in the open. Layer shoots of chaenomeles and clematis in pots of sandy peat, severing a year later.
Under glass. Take soft or half-ripe cuttings and insert in sandy soil in an open, shaded cold frame. Root cuttings of fuchsia and philadelphus in a greenhouse propagating frame at 16°C (61°F). Take half-ripe cuttings of magnolia and viburnum.
Pruning. Cut out shoots which have just flowered from deciduous shrubs such as deutzia. Cut hard back flowering shoots of brooms to prevent them seeding. Remove spent flower heads from lilacs and thin out weak shoots. Remove dead flower clusters from laburnums. Remove flower buds from senecio.

RHODODENDRONS AND AZALEAS
Watch for Japanese lace-wing fly and control with contact or systemic insecticide. Watch for bud blast. Remove affected shoots and burn them or spray with a non-lime fungicide. Water young plants in dry weather.

HEDGES
Trim escallonia hedges for a display of flowers in late summer. Continue weeding and hoeing hedge bottoms.

HEATHERS
Use young shoots of *Erica carnea* as cuttings and trim back remaining growth. Top-dress with peat.

FRUIT
Watch for pests and diseases. Thin fruits if crop is heavy, allowing for natural dropping. Harvest strawberries. Spray apples and pears, blackberries, loganberries, gooseberries, peaches and

nectarines, plums and damsons, cherries and raspberries. Water and mulch to ensure sufficient water supply to apples, pears and black currants. Check weeds around trees and bushes growing in cultivated soil. Tie sacking round apple and pear trunks to catch apple blossom weevils. Destroy fruits attacked by sawfly. Train in new blackberry and loganberry shoots. Summer prune gooseberries. Tie in new wall-trained peach and nectarine shoots. Protect fruiting plum, damson and cherry trees, red currants, raspberries and strawberries against birds. Anchor healthy strawberry runners so that they form new plants. Summer prune outdoor vines.

VEGETABLES

Plant Brussels sprouts, winter cabbages, savoys, and purple-sprouting and spring-heading broccoli. Plant marrows if seeds were not sown earlier. Plant outdoor tomatoes on prepared sites and support with 4 ft. canes, except for bush varieties. Continue sowing salad crops, peas and french beans. In the north, sow swedes, dusting drills and seedlings with an insecticide powder against flea beetles. Plant leeks. Water lettuces and other salad crops if prolonged dry weather is forecast. Sow spinach beet.
Under glass. Shade frames and cloches with whitewash or shading liquid. Remove the tips from cucumber plants when seven leaves have formed and give a weekly feed of liquid manure.
Less common vegetables. Plant self-blanching celery. Sow

chicory. Cease cutting asparagus and support the developing ferny growth by means of canes and string.

HERBS

Sow further rows of chervil and dill and thin established seedlings. Control weeds by frequent hoeing. Take and insert more rosemary and sage cuttings. Start picking herbs, including those wanted for deep-freezing.

PATIOS AND TOWN GARDENS

Water containers at least once a day, if not top-dressed with damp peat. Remove dead flowers and discard plants past their best.

HOUSE PLANTS

Continue watering and feeding at the summer rate. Open some windows on humid days to allow plants to benefit from this humidity. Stand plants outside to benefit from light warm rain. Spray plants lightly with clean tepid water when humidity is too low. Water plants before you go away for a few days and remove them from sunny windows. Control aphids and other pests with derris or malathion, or sponge the leaves with soapy water.

GENERAL TASKS

Continue weekly spraying against pests and diseases. Stake herbaceous plants as necessary. Control weeds with paraquat and by hoeing. Water the garden in dry spells.

Plants to enjoy in June

Border and rock garden plants in flower	Trees and shrubs in flower		House plants in flower, depending on position and culture
Alchemilla mollis	Hypericum	Genista	Aphelandra
Allium	Iberis	Hebe	Begonia semperflorens
Alyssum	Iris germanica	Laburnum	Impatiens petersiana
Aquilegia	Lavatera	Paeonia	Saintpaulia
Aster	Lupinus	Passiflora	
Aubrieta	Matthiola (stock)	Philadelphus	
Begonia	Nigella	Rhododendron	Fruit in season
Calendula (pot marigold)	Paeonia	Viburnum tomentosum	Gooseberry
Campanula	Papaver orientale	Weigela	Strawberry
Centaurea (cornflower)	Pyrethrum		
Convolvulus	Rodgersia	Water garden plants in flower	
Delphinium ajacis (larkspur)	Rose (floribunda and hybrid tea	Aponogeton (water hawthorn)	Vegetables in season
Dianthus	bushes and climbers)	Butomus (flowering rush)	Asparagus
Dicentra	Sedum	Hemerocallis (day lily)	Beans, broad
Digitalis (foxglove)	Tiarella	Iris	Broccoli
Erigeron	Verbascum	Primula	Cabbage (spring)
Eschscholzia	Veronica		Kohl rabi
Fritillaria		Greenhouse plants in flower	Lettuce
Gaillardia	Trees and shrubs in flower	Achimenes	Onion (salad) and Japanese bulb
Geranium	Berberis darwinii	Begonia	Peas
Geum	Buddleia alternifolia	Calceolaria	Potatoes (early)
Godetia	Buddleia globosa	Fuchsia	Radish
Gypsophila	Choisya	Gloxinia	Spinach (summer)
Heliopsis	Cistus	Heliotropium	
	Cornus kousa	Pelargonium domesticum	
	Deutzia	Streptocarpus	

awns

ESTABLISHED LAWNS

Apply a supplementary fertiliser if not given in May.

Between June and October regulate the height of mower blades according to the weather. During drought, raise the blades and cut without the box; the clippings will help to retain moisture.

Avoiding drought damage

Summer drought can cause significant damage to a lawn, so spike well in June and July to enable rain or hose water to penetrate deeply to the roots. Do this when the soil is soft after rain or watering.

Fungus diseases

Apply fungicides for the control of dollar spot (see MAY) and corticium. The latter disease affects a number of grasses, including meadow grasses, bents, fescues and perennial ryegrass, generally tending to become more severe and prevalent in large areas of turf each year.

It is caused by a readily visible pink fungus, *Corticium fuciforme*. In the early stages regular patches of bleached grass are covered with a red, thread-like fungus. The thin pink needles on the tips of the dead grass break off and spread the disease. Grass in poor condition is more susceptible to attack, so in addition to using fungicides and fertilisers, carry out renovation treatment, including aeration, scarifying and over-seeding to increase fertility (see APRIL).

Continue treatment with weedkillers if necessary, except during a drought.

Roses

Many hybrid tea roses have flowering shoots on which two or three side buds are produced in addition to the main bud at the top. If you want quality blooms or

DISBUDDING A ROSE

Removal of side buds from flowering shoots of hybrid teas results in better quality blooms from the terminal buds that are left

blooms with long stems for cutting, remove the small side buds as soon as it is possible to pick them off with finger and thumb. This procedure is called disbudding.

Hoe the soil to improve aeration and remove weeds.

Do not use lawn mowings as a mulch if the lawn has been treated with weedkiller (see APRIL).

Remove brier shoots and suckers

Pull away brier shoots on the main stems of standard roses at the point where the growth emerges. Remove briers appearing through the soil in rose beds, after tracing them back to their source.

Rose suckers which appear at a distance from the bush are often difficult to trace back to the rootstock. Spraying with paraquat will kill the sucker without damage to the bush.

During dry weather, water miniature roses growing in tubs, window-boxes or troughs.

Spray with a systemic rose insecticide if greenfly appear.

REMOVING ROSE SUCKERS

Sever suckers at the points where they grow from the brier rootstock, if necessary scraping away the soil to determine their point of origin

Mildew, black spot and rust diseases

All these diseases are becoming widespread. Spraying every two or three weeks gives some protection and control. Many modern fungicides are available. Dinocap and triforine are effective against mildew only; captan combats black spot only; thiram and zineb are for use against rust; benomyl and thiophanate-methyl are each useful against mildew and black spot.

Carbendamin + maneb, available only in combination, is effective against all three diseases.

Hardy herbaceous plants

The herbaceous border should remain colourful from June until September if the plants have been carefully chosen (see AUGUST).

Where early-flowering kinds are fading, cut them off within 3 in. of ground level, and clear away any support sticks.

This encourages a fresh crop of foliage, which will provide ground cover for the rest of the summer. Oriental poppies are inclined to leave a bare gap if left untrimmed after flowering, but hardy geraniums and centaureas make good patches of new leaves. Use any surplus sticks for such late-flowering kinds as the taller michaelmas daisies.

If primroses have been planted and the weather is showery, divide and replant them this month.

Conserve moisture

Apply a 1 in. coating of peat or leaf-mould between moisture- or shade-loving plants to hold in the moisture and keep down weeds.

Dahlias

In Scotland and the north of England plant out young dahlias by the middle of the month.

When dahlias have begun to grow, two or three weeks after planting, pinch out the tip of each leading shoot. This will

STOPPING A DAHLIA

Promote bushy growth, with a number of flowering shoots, by pinching out the tip of the main stem two or three weeks after planting

encourage the production of several side growths and make fine bushy plants that will give a long succession of flowers. When they have reached a height of about 18 in., tie them to the stakes with loose loops of raffia or soft string.

Pest control

Pests such as greenfly may appear on the plants from June onwards, so spray them about every 14 days with a proprietary insecticide. Use two different insecticides—say, derris and HCH—alternately. This stop the pests building up resistance to a particular spray. Alternatively, give continued protection by spraying monthly with a systemic insecticide.

Apply a mulch

Dahlias need plenty of water in the growing season. A mulch or layer an inch or two thick of peat, half-decayed leaves, garden compost, straw or sawdust will help to prevent evaporation and will stop weeds from germinating. Clear all weeds, and water well before applying the mulch.

Chrysanthemums

Outdoor-flowering plants set out in May will now be ready for stopping (see APRIL).

Stopping

Plants grown for decorative purposes will give good results if the growing tips of the plants are removed at the time when the little breaks are just showing in the leaf axils of the main stems. Do this at any time between the middle of May and the middle of June, the earlier the better in the north. For plants which are to flower in the open, do not delay this stop later than June 21, otherwise the flowers will be of poor quality and too late to avoid the autumn frosts.

Stop plants of the pompon and spra varieties in the middle of the month encourage bushy growth.

Water, spray and feed

Do not allow plants to become dry their roots. Water thoroughly once week in periods of little or no rain, a if possible give an overhead spray clean water at the end of hot sunny day During the second week of the mont hoe in a dressing of sulphate of ammon or Nitro-chalk at $\frac{1}{2}$ oz. per sq. yd. produce the fast growth necessary f plants which are to flower in the ope

Spray regularly to control aphids a leaf miners (see APRIL).

Take care not to over-water plar standing outside in pots, as their ro systems are not yet fully developed.

UNDER GLASS

Take cuttings of mid- and late-seas varieties for planting direct into t greenhouse border in July.

In the north, move greenhouse-flow ing varieties into their final 9 in. p before moving them to the summ standing ground (see APRIL and MAY).

Stop exhibition varieties

About the middle of this month give second stopping to exhibition incurv and single varieties, which are intend for showing in November. These shou have had their first stopping in April.

Gladioli

During most seasons there are sufficie showers to keep the ground moist up the time the first flower buds appe but watering is generally essential if d weather sets in after the flower spik can be felt. In this case give the plants really good soaking—at least 2 gal. p sq. yd. A light sprinkling encourages t roots to stay near the surface.

rises

all bearded irises are at their best this month. Tie tall stems, or stems in exposed positions, to light canes to keep them upright; or insert canes round a group of irises, linking the canes with garden twine. Cut blooms for indoor decoration as required (see APRIL), removing the remainder as they die so that the new flowers have ample space.

Cut back stems

Cut back the stems when flowering has finished and, on poor soils, give a top dressing of general fertiliser, 4 oz. per sq. yd., to encourage sturdy growth for the following year.

Trim leaves

Early in the month cut back with shears the grassy leaves of *Iris unguicularis* (better known as *I. stylosa*), trimming the leaves nearly to soil level. This will let in the sun to ripen the rhizomes. This sun-baking is essential for good flowering.

CUTTING BACK AN IRIS

Trimming the leaves of *Iris unguicularis* assists ripening of the plants, which is essential for prolific flowering during the following winter

Inspect leaves of bearded irises for signs of leaf spot disease (see APRIL).

Dig well rotted manure or compost, together with a general fertiliser or bonemeal, into land earmarked for planting with irises in July or August. The site must be sunny and well drained.

When flower buds show in summer-flowering Dutch irises, apply a fertiliser dressing of Nitro-chalk, at the rate of 1 oz. per sq. yd. and lightly rake in. This will improve flower colour.

Lilies

Spray fortnightly with Bordeaux mixture against botrytis disease if the weather is damp or muggy.

Spray monthly with a systemic insecticide to control aphids, which may spread virus diseases. Lilies are subject to attack by at least three viruses, the following being some of the symptoms.

Virus symptoms

1. Yellow streaks or mottlings on the leaves, though this can be also caused by excessive watering, insect damage or too much lime.
2. Telescoping of the stalk, with the leaves crowding together unnaturally and the top bent over like a walking stick.
3. Unnatural twisting of the leaves or petals, sometimes with the tips of the petals sticking together.
4. Purple-coloured leaves and stems.

Other causes

However, twisted leaves may also be due to insect damage; the sticking together of petals to an escape of nectar, mingled with dust; and leaves may be naturally dark or suffering from lack of water. It follows that a single symptom may not necessarily be due to virus, though it should be regarded with suspicion.

Burn virus-affected lilies, and wash your hands before you touch other lilies, as the virus is carried in the sap. Tiger lilies can carry the virus without visible symptoms, so either avoid them altogether or spray them regularly with a systemic insecticide.

UNDER GLASS

Continue to control aphids with a systemic insecticide and keep pot-grown lilies adequately watered.

Carnations and pinks

Stake border carnations if this was not done last month, and disbud the flower stems. The main stem of a young border carnation has a bud at the top (the crown bud) and side shoots about 4 in. long, with buds at their tips, lower down the main stem. Retain the crown bud and the end buds on the side shoots, but remove all other buds by rubbing them out when they are about $\frac{1}{4}$ in. long. Do this over a period of a week or ten days.

Encourage modern pinks to make side shoots by pinching out the growing point of the main stem. This will give a succession of blooms. Do not disbud pinks.

Other tasks

Watch for pests and diseases, taking action as necessary (see MARCH).

Plant old perpetual flowering carnations outdoors in a spare bed to finish flowering.

Order border carnations and pinks for autumn delivery (see colour section, MAY).

UNDER GLASS

Take cuttings of pinks. Select vigorous, compact side shoots with four or five fully developed pairs of leaves. Remove the lowest pair by pulling downwards, and cut with a sharp blade just below the

TAKING CUTTINGS OF PINKS

(1) Remove side shoots with four or five pairs of leaves. (2) Pull off the lowest pair. (3) Place the shoot on a pad of paper to minimise bruising, and cut the stem cleanly just below the joint from which the leaves were removed

INSERTING THE CUTTINGS

Insert the prepared cuttings up to the base of the next pair of leaves, placing nine or ten cuttings in each 3½ in. pot of sandy soil

joint. Insert the cuttings up to, but not above, the base of the next pair of leaves in sandy soil in 3½ in. pots at the rate of nine or ten cuttings per pot. Water them in and place the pots in a shaded cold frame.

Renewed growth after about three weeks indicates that the cuttings are rooting satisfactorily. Increase the ventilation gradually over the next week or so.

PLACING THE POTS

Place the pots in an open box, about 10 in. deep, in shade; or stand them in a shaded frame

After a fortnight plant out the rooted cuttings or pot them individually into 3½ in. pots of John Innes potting compost No. 1.

Pot on perpetuals

Continue to pot young perpetual flowering carnations into 6 in. pots and year-old plants into 8 in. pots. Renew the shading on glass if necessary and damp down in hot weather.

Second stopping

Continue with the second stopping until the middle of the month to give autumn blooms, and from the middle of the month until mid-July for winter blooms (see APRIL).

Watch for pests and diseases, taking action as necessary (see MARCH).

Cut blooms and disbud flower stems (see SEPTEMBER).

Sweet peas

During warm, settled weather it is better to syringe the plants with a mist-like spray of clean, soft water than to water the soil. Do this after sunset or in the early morning. Otherwise, if watering is really necessary, give the ground a good soaking—about 3 gal. per sq. yd —at not less than ten-day intervals.

Pests and diseases

Spray monthly with a systemic insecticide to control sap-sucking insects.

If plants begin to die, with the leaves first turning yellow and then brown, either soil pests or disease are responsible. Whatever the cause, there is no cure at this stage, and such plants must be removed and burnt.

Bud-dropping

Bud-dropping, when the buds turn yellow and fall before opening, is not a disease at all, and is usually only a brief phase. Too much moisture at the roots, over-feeding, lime deficiency, too little sun, and abnormally cold or changeable weather may all cause bud-dropping. Do not apply water or fertiliser until the phase passes. Even then this should seldom be necessary if the bed was prepared correctly in the first place (see NOVEMBER). Continue to tie in the main stem to supporting canes and to pinch out side shoots and tendrils on cordon-grown plants (see APRIL).

Flowers from seed

Complete the planting of half-hardy annuals this month, waiting until the risk of frost has passed in northern areas and in low-lying spots notorious for late frosts. Water the cleared borders and the hardened-off plants thoroughly before setting these out in their flowering positions (see MAY).

Water in dry weather

During prolonged dry weather, water thoroughly the recently planted half-hardy annuals, and hardy annuals sown earlier, to help them make sufficient growth before flowering starts. Avoid over-watering, however, especially on rich soils, as this may lead to excessive leaf growth at the expense of flowers.

Support taller plants

Give support to the taller-growing annuals when they reach a height of 6–9 in. This is especially important in exposed situations. Use twiggy pea sticks slightly smaller than the eventual height of the plants, pushing them in among the individual clumps so that the plants conceal them while at the same time gaining support from them. If pea sticks are not available, use thin canes, preferably green, with green garden twine looped between them. Again, keep canes and twine within the plant clump.

Control of insects and weeds

Spray monthly with a systemic insecticide to control aphids and other sap-sucking insects.

Hoe regularly to control weeds among the bedding plants. Hoeing is easiest when the soil is slightly damp, and most effective if carried out before the weeds appear.

Hardy biennials

Sow hardy biennials if this was not done last month. They can be raised outdoors or under glass (see MAY).

As soon as they reach manageable size, set out in a nursery bed seedlings of hardy biennials which are at present in seed boxes or outdoor seed beds. Plant them 6–9 in. apart, in rows 12 in. apart, so that they have space to make sturdy, bushy plants for setting out in their final positions in September.

Ideally, carry out this transplanting during showery weather. Failing this, use a sprinkler to water the plants in after their move.

Sow wallflowers

At the end of the month, or early in July, seeds of wallflowers and sweet williams can be sown in drills in their flowering positions. This is a convenient method if they are to be used for cutting the following spring. Sow thinly, later removing surplus plants by chopping them out with a hoe or a knife.

Sow perennials

If no frame or greenhouse is available, sow hardy perennials outdoors (see MAY), and plant in nursery rows any plants which are large enough.

UNDER GLASS

Sow hardy perennials in a heated greenhouse, following the same sowing procedure as for half-hardy annuals (see MARCH and MAY).

Bulbs

Towards the end of the month in warm districts start lifting spring bulbs on which the leaves have turned yellow. Tulips need to be lifted regularly but most other bulbs, including daffodils, require dividing and re-planting in fresh soil only if show-quality flowers are desired or if the plants have become so crowded that they produce only masses of leaves.

LIFTING BULBS

To avoid damaging the bulbs, insert the fork well clear of the clump and sufficiently deep to get right under the roots

Dig well clear of the bulbs with a spade or fork, inserting it deep enough to get right under the clump. Place the bulbs in shallow boxes and dry them in a well ventilated shed.

Trim and store bulbs

When the bulbs are really dry, remove the dead leaves, roots and skins. Discard the smallest bulbs, unless you wish to increase your stock, and destroy any rotten or damaged bulbs, and the dried debris, by burning. Place the dried and

143

cleaned bulbs in trays or boxes, with not more than three or four layers of bulbs in each box. Store the boxes in a cool, dry shed.

DRYING BULBS AFTER LIFTING

After lifting, spread the bulbs out to dry in shallow boxes, and place in a well ventilated shed until all moisture has evaporated

CLEANING BULBS

Remove the dead skins, and also cut off the roots and shrivelled leaves, after the bulbs have been thoroughly dried. Store in a cool shed

144

REMOVING OFFSETS

Some bulbs, such as narcissi, multiply by off-sets. Store these separately, planting them later in a nursery bed until they have reached flowering size after two or three years

Plant anemones

In mild districts plant de Caen anemone corms for autumn and winter flowering. Set the corms 1–2 in. deep and 4–6 in. apart in rows if they are required for cutting, or in groups if they are intended as part of the general garden display.

Plant out arum lilies, or stand the pots outdoors, for their summer rest.

UNDER GLASS AND INDOORS

Dry off lachenalias flowered in pots, withholding water until September. Pot or re-pot vallota bulbs in 6–8 in. pots; use John Innes potting compost No. 1 and place the tops of the bulbs just below the surface.

Alpines

Continue with weeding and hoeing, placing weeds straight into a box or pail to reduce the chances of seeds dropping on to the ground. Use an old knife to sever annual grasses just below soil level. If you pull them out and shake the soil from their roots, their seeds may be scattered over a wide area.

Dead-heading

Trim dead flowers from aubrietas and saxifrages to prevent self-seeding. Dead-heading of other plants is not essential, but clipping with a small pair of shears keeps the rock garden tidy.

Trim trailing plants

At the same time, trim back excessive growth on trailing plants. In the case of alpines which root as they spread, trim back with an old knife thrust vertically into the soil, then pull or fork out the severed portions.

Re-plant vigorous plants

Where a rock garden or bed has recently been planted, errors in placing may now be apparent. In particular, vigorous kinds may be too close to slow-growing plants. They can be moved around now if the weather is showery. Otherwise, take note of what needs doing so that the plants can be re-positioned in late September or early October.

Drought conditions

If dry weather is affecting the plants, you must decide whether or not to irrigate. Watering calls for great care, as the plants will suffer if too much is given. Make random holes to find out how far below the surface the drought has penetrated. If you find moist soil at a depth of 1–1½ in., defer watering for a week, but water any areas which are dry to a depth of 2 in. or more, at the rate of 2 gal. per sq. yd.

Ideally, use a sprinkler that delivers a fine spray. Large drops of water will erode the soil. If you use a watering can fit a fine rose to the spout.

Water alpines in the evening, and apply sufficient to soak down to the existing moisture level, checking the depth of penetration an hour later and if necessary giving more water.

Water plants and pools

Finish planting aquatics this month if you want a display the first season.

In sultry weather keep the water well oxygenated by occasionally adding fresh water from a hose fitted with a spray. This will lower the water temperature, and is especially important in shallow pools where water evaporates quickly.

Propagation

Divide large, overgrown clumps of orontium and re-plant.

Control aphids

Keep a constant check for the first appearance of aphids, and deal with them immediately. If you keep fish, take care when you apply insecticides, which may be lethal to them. On a warm, still day spray carefully; use a pressurised container and allow the spray to fall on the leaves only. The aphids are killed quickly and dry on the leaves, instead of falling into the water and polluting it.

Harmful midges

Often one species of midge (*Chironomas*) can be a greater pest than the aphids. The larvae are difficult to see, being only $\frac{1}{8}$ in. long, not much thicker than a hair and greenish in colour. They attack the upper- and undersurfaces of leaves of water lilies, *Aponogeton distachyon* (water hawthorn) and some underwater plants, eating away the living tissue and leaving the foliage in skeleton form and ready to decay. In bad cases plants may be completely defoliated. Treatment is difficult, but the methods used against aphids may have some effect.

Other tasks

Continue to remove algae before large masses form, but keep an eye open for young fish. If surface plants are growing too rapidly, reduce them enough to allow light to penetrate to the underwater plants.

Prick out seedlings of February-sown primulas in 3 in. deep seed boxes using John Innes potting compost No. 1. These will be ready for planting out in September. Alternatively, prepare a shaded area of the garden with sphagnum peat and sharp sand dug into the top 6 in., together with a dressing of a general fertiliser at 3 oz. per sq. yd. Keep the bed or boxes moist, and shade from direct sunlight.

Greenhouses and frames

This month, pay particular attention to watering. Plants in earthenware pots may need two or more applications daily during hot weather. Maintain a humid atmosphere by frequent damping down, otherwise red spider mites may prove troublesome.

Reduce the time required for watering by transferring as many plants as possible to cold frames. Young cyclamens, seedling cinerarias, calceolarias, primulas and solanums will grow steadily throughout the summer in a lightly shaded cold frame. Place the pots on an ash base kept permanently moist.

Plunge azaleas

Other plants which have finished flowering, including azaleas, hydrangeas and regal pelargoniums, can be stood in the open garden and the pots plunged to their rims in ashes. They will require much less water than if left under glass.

Cut back pelargoniums

Cut back shoots on regal pelargoniums by about half. The young growths of camellias are easily damaged by strong sunshine if the plants are allowed to

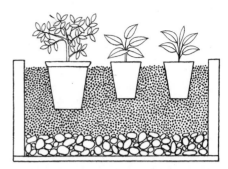

Build a timber or brick frame to contain ashes for plunging pots. Place the ashes on a 4 in. layer of clinker

become dry at the roots. They do best in partial shade on the northern side of a wall or hedge.

Sow cineraria seeds, if this was not done last month, to produce plants that will flower next winter and spring; also seeds of *Primula malacoides*.

Tend streptocarpus plants

Pot on streptocarpus plants, raised from a January or February sowing, to 5 or 6 in. pots of John Innes potting compost No. 2. Handle the leaves carefully, as they are brittle and easily damaged. Make a further sowing to provide plants for flowering early next year, sowing the seeds in shallow pans of John Innes seed compost in a temperature of 16–18°C (61–64°F).

Pot on cyclamens

Transfer to 5 in. pots cyclamens sown last August, which are due to flower during the coming autumn and winter. Use John Innes potting compost No. 2, standing the pots in a cold frame as soon as they show signs of renewed growth. Apply liquid fertiliser every ten days throughout the summer, using a high-potash mixture.

Plants such as hydrangeas, zonal pelargoniums and fuchsias, which are now flowering in the greenhouse, require careful management this month to keep them in good condition and prolong the flowering period. Remove faded flowers regularly, apply liquid fertiliser every ten days, and keep a sharp look-out for aphids. A routine watering or spraying with a systemic insecticide will keep these pests in check.

Polyanthuses in pots

Modern strains of polyanthuses make admirable pot plants for the cool greenhouse. When young plants for growing outdoors are being set out in nursery rows, pot a few strong specimens into 3 in. pots of John Innes potting compost No. 1 to provide greenhouse flowers next winter. Stand them in partial shade and keep them well watered throughout the summer. Bring them into the greenhouse in early January for flowering in February.

Campanula seedlings

Transfer seedlings of *Campanula pyramidalis* to 5 in. pots when their roots start to outgrow the 3 in. pots in which they were pricked out (see APRIL). Keep them growing steadily until next March, then move them to 9 in. containers for flowering during the summer. Alternatively, plant them from the 3 in. pots direct into the open garden, lifting them in the autumn and planting in pots sufficiently large to contain the roots. During the winter keep the plants growing steadily in the greenhouse and move them on into 9 in. pots in March.

Propagate from leaf cuttings

Propagate saintpaulias and *Begonia rex* from leaf cuttings. Insert the saintpaulia leaves, complete with 1–2 in. of stalk, vertically in pots containing a mixture of equal parts peat and sand. Lay the begonia leaves flat on pans containing the same mixture, after cutting the undersides of the leaf veins in several

places, and secure them with small stones or hairpins. Stand the containers in a propagating frame, maintaining a temperature of 16–18°C (61–64°F), until small plants are produced at the slashed points.

Spray plants of *Solanum capsicastrum* daily during warm weather.

Pollinate melons

Pinch out all but four side shoots on melons planted last month in cold frames, stopping these shoots when they have reached the corners of the frame. Wait until there is a female flower open on each shoot, then transfer pollen to them from the male flowers. Female flowers are distinguishable by their embryo fruits. Apply shading to the glass during hot weather.

Cease artificial heating

Towards the end of the month artificial heat can be dispensed with in a cool greenhouse. If it has a solid fuel heating

TAKING LEAF CUTTINGS FROM BEGONIA REX

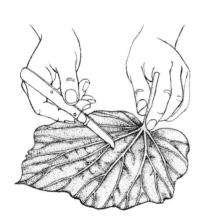

Remove a leaf, turn it upside down and make several cuts at the junctions of veins, using a sharp knife or a razor blade

Lay the leaf face upwards on a pan containing equal parts of peat and sand. Secure it with hairpins, bent wires or small stones

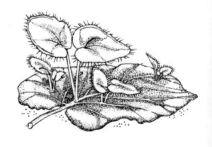

Placed in a propagating frame, the leaf will produce a rooted plantlet at some or each of the points where the veins were severed

POLLINATING A MELON

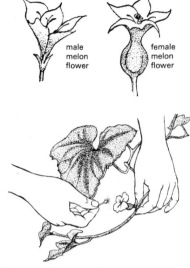

male
melon
flower

female
melon
flower

When female melon flowers have opened, pollinate by brushing them with the anthers of male flowers from which the petals have been removed

system, clean out the boiler and flue and leave the boiler doors open to allow a free circulation of air. If you use an oil heater, store it in a dry shed or garage until the autumn, after emptying the fuel tank and cleaning the burner parts carefully.

Pick cucumbers

Maintain a humid atmosphere for cucumber plants by regular spraying, picking the fruits when they are about 12 in. long.

Examine the main stems of tomato plants. If they are starting to become thin, change to a liquid fertiliser containing extra nitrogen.

If the weather is very warm towards the end of the month, leave the top ventilators on the leeward side of the house open a little way at night.

Trees and shrubs

Do not allow grass to grow right up to the trunk of a newly planted tree or shrub. For the first two years keep a clear space about 4 ft. in diameter around the base. Keep this area well mulched. In time the grass may be allowed to grow nearer.

Remove self-sown trees

Self-sown trees, usually sycamore or ash, frequently appear in a wall or against a house, and can do damage to the foundations if they are not removed quickly. If one has been left to grow, or if any other tree is growing too near a house, cut it down and paint the cut surface with an equal mixture of paraffin and brushwood killer. This will kill the roots and prevent re-growth.

PROPAGATION

In the open

Layer shoots of *Chaenomeles japonica* and clematis in pots of sandy peat. Do not sever from the parent plants for about a year, when the layers should be well rooted. Divide overgrown clumps of *arundinaria* (bamboo) and re-plant.

Under glass

Begin to take cuttings, 4–6 in. long, of softwood or half-ripe side shoots. With a sharp knife cut straight across the stems just below a joint, and insert the cuttings in sandy soil in an open, shaded cold frame. Water the cuttings freely during dry weather and, when roots have formed by early autumn, pot the cuttings singly in $2\frac{1}{2}$–$3\frac{1}{2}$ in. pots of potting compost. Leave the potted cuttings in a closed cold frame during winter and transplant next spring.

Cuttings of cotoneaster and deutzia should be treated in the manner described above, but cuttings of hybrid clematis, fuchsia and philadelphus will do better if placed in a greenhouse propagating frame at a temperature of 16°C (61°F) until well rooted.

Take half-ripe cuttings of magnolia and viburnum with a slip of old wood (or heel) attached. Treat these cuttings as described above, but leave young magnolia plants in the cold frame for at least a year before transplanting into flowering positions.

PRUNING

Prune deciduous shrubs, such as deutzia, cutting out shoots that have just flowered. This will encourage strong new growth to develop and ripen for next year.

Cut brooms hard back

As soon as brooms have finished flowering, the shoots must be cut hard back to prevent the shrubs seeding themselves. Be careful not to cut into the old wood when pruning.

Remove spent flower heads from lilacs and thin out weak shoots with secateurs.

Dead-head laburnums

Because laburnum seeds are poisonous, remove the dead flower clusters as soon as possible after flowering. Laburnum leaves are also poisonous, so never plant a tree too near a pool in case leaves blow in and kill the fish.

If you grow senecio mainly for the effect of its silver-grey foliage, you can keep the leaves finer and the plant bushier and in better shape by removing the flower buds as soon as they appear.

Rhododendrons and azaleas

Keep a watch for the Japanese lacewing fly which hatches in June. The larvae feed on the undersides of leaves, causing them to turn spotty and yellow.

They are easily seen in clusters under the leaves. If left to reach the adult stage, they will get up into the new growth of the plant and lay eggs on the mid-rib under the leaves. Spray with a systemic and contact insecticide. Control is usually complete after two sprays, three or four weeks apart, since not all lace-wing flies hatch at the same time.

Bud blast disease

Watch also for bud blast, a disease in which flower buds blacken and fail to flower. It is caused by a fungus which attacks the bud and rots it. The fungus travels up with the young growth, and is then ready to attack next year's buds. It is probably carried from plant to plant by the leaf hopper (see JULY). Control of bud blast is not easy. If possible, remove affected shoots and burn them; but if this is too big a task, spray with a recommended non-lime fungicide while the plants are in growth.

Water young plants well in dry weather (at least 2 gal. per sq. yd.).

Hedges

Many hedges need the first trim of the year (see table, SEPTEMBER). Escallonia hedges, if trimmed now, will produce a fine show of pink or white flowers on new growth during August and September.

Continue to weed or hoe hedge bottoms (see MARCH).

Heathers

Winter-flowering varieties of *Erica carnea* make a lot of new growth at this time of year. Use these shoots as cuttings if you require extra plants (see MARCH). After taking the cuttings, trim back the remaining growth with shears and mulch the plants with peat.

Fruit

The eventual size of most fruits can be improved by thinning with the thumb and forefinger, or with scissors if the crop is heavy, but many types of fruit have their own means of limiting the crop by dropping fruit, so allow for this by thinning in several stages.

Some fruits, such as strawberries, can be harvested this month.

Apple and pear

Watch for greenfly, which can be controlled by a systemic insecticide, and also for red spider mite, controlled by derris. Bronzing and early falling leaves indicate fruit tree red spider mite, which is encouraged by the use of persistent insecticides. Continue spraying regularly with benomyl or captan for apple or pear scab; apply malathion against codling moth caterpillar and tortrix caterpillar on apple. Where the set is heavy, thin out the fruits for the first time, but remember that there can be a heavy June drop (which in fact usually takes place in July), and do not over-thin at this stage. Make sure that the roots are receiving an even water supply, possibly by watering or by mulching after rain. Check weeds by shallow hoeing, or apply paraquat. Keep grass short by mowing.

Watch that newly planted trees do not dry out, and slacken ties as the trees grow and the stems expand.

Tie pieces of sacking about 6 in. wide round the trunks of the trees not later than the middle of the month, to catch apple blossom weevils. Destroy apples attacked by sawfly.

Fasten down young shoots that are required to form fruit buds into a nearly horizontal position.

Blackberry, loganberry and hybrid berries

Train in new shoots so that they are away from the old ones (see MAY). Apply derris or malathion, ten days after flowering, against raspberry beetle.

Black currant

Encourage new growth by watering if necessary, or by mulching with farm-yard manure or compost. Control weeds by shallow cultivation only.

PROTECTION AGAINST BIRDS

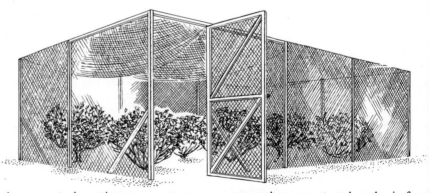

A permanent wire netting cage, or a temporary covering of string or nylon netting laid over a timber frame, will protect soft fruit crops such as currants and raspberries from damage done by birds. Make the structure tall enough to allow for fruit picking and hoeing

Gooseberry

If the bushes are carrying a heavy crop, thin the fruit, to improve the size of the remaining fruit, and use for cooking. At the end of the month, nip out the tips of the longest new lateral shoots to about five leaves to encourage the energy of the bush into fruit bud formation. Clear weeds by shallow cultivation or by directed spraying. Gooseberry sawfly starts in the centres of bushes and can quickly defoliate them unless eliminated with derris. Be prepared to spray with dinocap against gooseberry mildew, which can make the fruit inedible.

Peach and nectarine

If the de-shooting of wall-trained trees has been started properly (see MAY), the remaining shoots will need tying in to the framework as they develop. Thin the fruits to their final spacing of about 9 in. apart (not quite so far apart for nectarine). Watch for greenfly, and spray with derris or a systemic insecticide if necessary.

Plum, damson and cherry

Watch for attacks of greenfly, which can become serious if not checked by early spraying with malathion or a systemic insecticide. The leaves of shoots affected by silver leaf have a metallic appearance. If the branches are fruiting, pick the fruit and cut out affected branches until there is no brown stain visible on the cut surface. If the stain goes into the main stem, there is no cure and the tree must be removed. During this month the disease starts to spread from dead and dying branches left on trees or lying about, so be careful to burn affected branches.

On fan-trained trees, pinch out the tips of laterals not required for extension or as replacements, when they have made six or seven leaves. Protect fruiting trees wherever possible against bird attacks, either with netting or cotton.

Raspberry

Control weeds by shallow cultivation. Apply paraquat to control weeds, but do not let it touch leaves or stems of young growth. Apply derris or malathion ten days after flowering to prevent raspberry beetle attacking the fruit. Net the fruit against birds. Water well as the fruit swells if the weather is dry.

Red and white currants

Protect against birds by stringing cotton between the branches or covering with a wire cage. First fruits ripen this month.

Strawberry

Destroy fruit attacked by grey mould, which is common in damp weather. Examine fruit which has been attacked by pests. Damage by birds, slugs and beetles looks alike but can be distinguished. Birds attack the exposed sides of fruit and leave a dry wound with jagged edges. Slugs, which can be controlled by slug bait, usually attack protected sides of fruit, and leave a soft smooth cavity, wider at the surface than inside. Beetles also prefer the

PRUNING A VINE

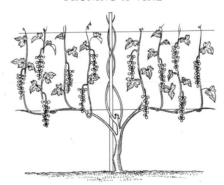

Cut back to the top wire new shoots from the five buds left on each lateral. Secure to the wires which are 2 ft. above ground level

LAYERING A STRAWBERRY

To assist root formation insert compost-filled pots round the parent plant, securing the runners in the pots with bent wires or small stones

undersides of berries, and make a dry cavity, narrower on the surface than inside; trap beetles by sinking jam jars to their rims at intervals over the bed.

Protect the fruit against birds, using netting—$\frac{3}{4}$ in. mesh nylon netting is ideal—held above the rows on wooden posts topped with inverted jam jars to prevent catching.

Young plants not carrying a crop must be kept clean. If growing isolated plants (see recommended varieties, NOVEMBER), remove all runners as they form; and to make matted rows, train runners along the row and let them root. In order to increase healthy stock, anchor the runners as they form with a stone, soil or a bent metal pin, and for early planting root the runners into pots containing soil or compost sunk up to their rims around the parent plant. The soil should be shallow-cultivated, and watered at intervals to encourage rooting. Remove any surplus runners that form.

Vine (outdoor)

Rub out unwanted buds and cut the new shoots back to about 24 in. as they grow beyond this length. Leave at full length the two replacement shoots which will later be trained horizontally to carry next year's laterals.

149

Vegetables

Plant Brussels sprouts for picking in late winter; also cabbages ('Christmas Drumhead', 'January King' and savoys) and both purple-sprouting and spring-heading broccolis. Plants can generally be purchased if seeds were not sown in April. Sprinkle hoof and horn meal on the ground at 3 oz. per sq. yd., raking it into the surface before planting. Do not loosen more than the top inch or so as these plants require firm soil.

Plant marrows

Plant marrows if seeds were not sown on the stations prepared earlier (see MAY). Plant with a trowel, retaining as much of the soil ball as possible, and water the plants immediately.

Outdoor tomatoes

Plant outdoor tomatoes in the stations prepared last month, setting the plants so that the tops of the soil balls are about 1 in. below the surface. Firm the ground round each plant, leaving a slight depression, and water in thoroughly. Insert a 4 ft. bamboo cane alongside each plant, tying the stem loosely to this at intervals during the season to provide support for the growing plant. Bush varieties do not require supporting. Give further waterings at intervals of a few days if the weather remains dry. In the colder exposed areas of the north, outdoor tomatoes are late in ripening. Recommended varieties are 'Sigmabush', 'Minibel' and 'Sleaford Abundance', which crop well and early in a sunny situation.

Water tomato roots

When planting outdoor tomatoes, insert a 4 in. pot in the ground beside each plant, with the top just at soil level. Fill the pots with water each time the plants are tended and the roots will benefit directly instead of the surrounding soil.

Continue to sow salad crops (see MARCH) to maintain supplies during the late summer. There is still time to sow further batches of peas (see JANUARY) and french beans (see MAY).

Sow swedes

In the north, sow swedes for eating during the winter. Sow thinly in drills $\frac{1}{2}$ in. deep and 18 in. apart, first dusting the drills with calomel as a precaution against club root disease. Dust the young seedlings with HCH to protect them from flea beetles, thinning the crop at an early stage to leave the plants 9–12 in. apart.

Plant leeks

Plant leeks, choosing the thickest seedlings if you have a surplus and cutting the tops back by a quarter of their length and the roots by about half. Leeks are often grown in ground cleared of early potatoes. Set the plants at 6 in. intervals in rows 12 in. apart, making holes with a dibber and simply dropping the plants in. Do not firm them into place, but water the plants immediately so that soil is washed over the roots.

If prolonged dry weather is forecast, water crops of marrows, lettuce and other salads, summer spinach, peas and runner beans. Other vegetables growing at this time of year, including the less common kinds, withstand drought fairly well. Always give the plants sufficient water to penetrate to the roots. A light watering may do more harm than good.

Sow spinach beet

Towards the end of the month sow spinach beet for eating during the autumn, winter and spring, following the method described earlier for beetroot (see APRIL).

UNDER GLASS

During hot weather, apply whitewash or a proprietary shading liquid to cloches or frames, lightly flecking the outside of the glass.

Pinch out the tips of cucumber plants when seven leaves have formed. Water

STAKING A TOMATO PLANT

Use bamboo canes to support tomato plants, securing them at intervals with twine looped loosely to allow for expansion of the stem

PLANTING LEEKS

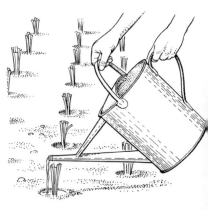

After dropping leek plants into holes made with a dibber, apply water from a can to wash soil round the roots from the sides of the holes

the plants regularly, using a fine rose on the can to avoid washing soil away from the roots. Feed weekly with liquid manure once the first fruits have started to grow.

LESS COMMON VEGETABLES

Plant self-blanching celery early in the month in well manured soil, retaining as much soil as possible round the roots.

Set the plants 12 in. apart, in rows 18 in. apart. Towards the end of the month, erect a surround of boards to prevent the outer plants from sprawling.

Sow chicory by the middle of the month, spacing the drills 15–18 in. apart and sowing thinly. 'Brussels Witloof' and 'Giant Witloof' are recommended varieties. Thin the seedlings to about 12 in. apart, using the thinnings for salads.

Complete asparagus cutting by the middle of the month, leaving the tops to grow on without restriction. Insert canes round the bed and link them with string to hold the ferny growths upright, otherwise the crowns may be damaged.

Herbs

Sow further rows of chervil and dill, and thin established seedlings from 6 in. to 2 or 3 ft., according to the eventual height of the plants.

Keep weeds down by frequent hoeing. Do not water the herb garden. Most herbs come from the dry Mediterranean countries and will not suffer from a little dryness at the roots.

Take and insert further cuttings of rosemary and sage (see MAY).

Most herbs will now be ready for picking. Use the fresh leaves of mint, sage and thyme, and begin also to gather herbs for deep-freezing. Several of the soft-leafed plants, such as chives, mint, fennel, parsley and sorrel, keep well this way.

Cut small sprigs from the plants and wash the leaves free of dust; chop up chives now rather than when they are later taken from the freezer. Place the sprigs in a colander (enamel if possible) and blanch the herbs for one minute by dipping the colander into rapidly boiling water. Rinse them in cold water and pack them into plastic bags or waxed cartons; label and put into the freezer at once. These herbs will not be crisp when taken out and are suitable only for flavouring.

Patios and town gardens

In dry weather water all containers once a day. If daily watering is impossible, top-dress the containers with damp peat. Remove dead flowers daily and discard any plants past their best. If necessary, the latter can be replaced by plants dug carefully from the border, retaining as much soil as possible round the roots.

House plants

Continue watering and feeding at the summer rate (see MAY). On warm, humid days open some windows to give the plants the benefit of this humidity, but do not allow them to stand in a draught. If there is light, warm rain, take outdoors any plants that can conveniently be carried.

On the other hand, if many successive days are dry, bright and sunny, there may be too little humidity for the plants. In this case spray them lightly with clean, tepid water.

Holiday care

If you go away for the day or a weekend make sure that no plants are in need of watering before you go and that none stand in a south or west window where they are likely to get direct sunshine during the hottest part of the day. Move them a little way into the room.

At this time of year and through the summer there is always the possibility of attack by pests, usually greenfly. Though it is possible to see these insects, it is more likely that they will escape detection until a yellowing or twisting of the foliage, usually at the succulent tips, becomes apparent.

Take immediate steps to clear all infested plants of greenfly. Use derris or malathion, preferably in an aerosol applicator, after covering adjacent walls and furniture with newspaper. Take care not to breathe the fine mist. Open doors and windows afterwards.

If you prefer not to use a toxic spray in the house, or even to bring into the house a plant that has been sprayed in the garden, sponge the leaves with soapy water.

General tasks

Pests and diseases can be even more troublesome than in April or May. The aphids multiply more quickly and moulds or mildews spread very fast, so keep up the weekly spraying.

Make sure that herbaceous plants are properly staked. Check ties on climbing roses or other plants growing on walls, fences, arches and pergolas. There may be heavy storms in July, and if plants are torn away from their supports, much time will be spent tying them up again.

This is the worst month of the year as far as weed control is concerned. An odd hour spent loosening the soil with a hoe pays off handsomely. Kill weeds by watering with a solution of paraquat under hedges, among shrubs or roses, and on paths and crazy paving.

Watering in dry spells is as important now as in May. Plants transpire at a greater rate, and more moisture is lost from the soil by evaporation as the sun's heat increases.

July

The hottest month of the year brightens the flower border with annuals,
and brings dry days for energetic constructional tasks

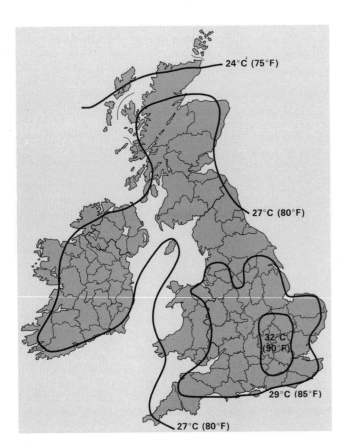

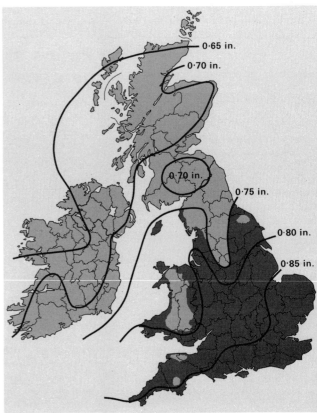

THE HIGHEST TEMPERATURES OF THE YEAR

The hottest days of the year often occur in July. The map shows the maximum temperatures of the year likely to be exceeded only one year in five. The highest temperatures occur inland in the Home Counties and Fen District. Coastal areas are cooler, especially in the north and west. During all hot spells planting out of seedlings and cuttings should be avoided and special attention paid to the water requirements of the garden. Lids of frames should be lifted, and in the greenhouse there must be ventilation, and shelter for young plants

WATER NEEDED BY A GARDEN IN JULY

The map shows the total water used by a garden (the potential transpiration) in inches per average week in July. In the shaded areas, rainfall is on average less than potential transpiration, and gardeners should pay particular attention to water requirements of the garden. In long spells of sunny weather gardeners everywhere should be prepared to water two or three times a week. Amounts of watering needed in the garden can be calculated from rainfall measurements and potential transpiration. (See GLOSSARY, *Weather*)

The weather in July

July is often the warmest month of the year in the British Isles, especially in inland areas in southern England, where temperatures in most years are likely to reach 24°C (75°F).

July can also be the wettest month of summer. Depressions from across the Atlantic can be frequent, and westerly winds may bring rain for many hours at a time. This rain is especially heavy in the hilly areas of the north and west, where temperatures may not rise above 18°C (65°F). Heavy showers or thunderstorms are also probable in all areas. When the wind veers towards the north-west the weather is usually drier and sunnier, and night temperatures may fall to about 10°C (50°F). Occasionally hot, moist air from the south arrives with a depression, bringing a humid, hazy spell which is often enervating; both day and night temperatures are high.

The best July weather occurs when the barometer is high and the wind is from the west or south-west. During these hot, sunny days, afternoon temperatures exceed 21°C (70°F) in the south, but during such spells the weather is often sultry and usually breaks down in thunderstorms after one or two days. These generally appear first along the south coast of England and move slowly northwards over the country, and can be accompanied by damaging hail.

The high humidity and fairly frequent rain of July produce favourable conditions for the spread of plant diseases. Precautions in the form of dusting or spraying must be taken early if proper control is to be maintained. Once a disease has taken a firm hold in the garden, it is usually too late to expect control measures to succeed.

A summary of the month's work

LAWNS
New and established lawns. Water copiously in dry weather. Aerate surface of lawn. Apply fungicides to control fusarium, dollar spot and corticium.

ROSES
Cut blooms for home decoration and remove dead heads as they appear. After the first flush of blooms, feed rose bushes with rose fertiliser and hoe it into the soil. Continue to spray against greenfly, black spot, mildew and rust.

HARDY HERBACEOUS PLANTS
Continue cutting back early-flowering plants and dead-heading where there are still flowers. Remove dead flowers from paeonies. Cut lupins and delphiniums to ground level in mild districts to encourage a second display. Hoe in a further application of fertiliser around michaelmas daisies lacking in vigour, and dust those liable to mildew with flowers of sulphur. Cut off and burn leaves of *Campanula persicifolia* infected with rust fungus. Plan position and shape of new beds to be made in the autumn, choosing an open site away from trees and fences. Begin preparing beds for autumn planting.

DAHLIAS
Continue tying young stems to their stakes. Feed plants which are slow to grow with a liquid fertiliser once a fortnight. Disbud at least some of the stems to obtain longer stems and better flowers. Regularly remove faded flowers.

CHRYSANTHEMUMS
Reduce the number of shoots per plant to five, except on pompons and spray varieties. Water plants thoroughly, and attend to tying and supporting once a week. Apply a balanced fertiliser in the middle of the month. Disbud early-flowering varieties if they show buds. Spray regularly to control pests. Reduce large exhibition varieties to three stems, exhibition incurves and decoratives to four.
Under glass. Dig and rake greenhouse borders to receive mid- and late-season varieties propagated last month.

GLADIOLI
Stake plants individually to provide straight stems for exhibition. Control gladiolus thrips with malathion or HCH.

IRISES
Dig up and divide dwarf, intermediate and bearded irises that have been undisturbed for three years. Select the best single rhizomes for re-planting in newly enriched soil. Leave the tops of the rhizomes above the soil. Cut off the top halves of the leaves. Plant irises obtained from nurseries. Water newly planted rhizomes in dry weather and pull off dead leaves. Order bulbous irises for autumn planting. Dress summer-flowering Dutch irises with Nitro-chalk. Lift bulbous irises when their leaves die down if they need moving. Dry them off and divide them for re-planting.

LILIES
Pick off dead flower heads, unless you wish to save seeds. Spray with Bordeaux mixture and with systemic insecticide. Keep beds weeded and watered.
Under glass. Control aphids, and water adequately.

CARNATIONS AND PINKS
Continue disbudding border carnations. Take action against pests and diseases. Order border carnations and pinks for autumn

planting. Remove old flower stems from pinks, water them if dry, and give a high-potash fertiliser. Propagate border carnations by layering. After six weeks sever each layer from its parent plant, and three or four weeks after this lift them and pot or plant out separately.

Under glass. Renew shading on glass and damp down in hot weather. Continue to give second stoppings to provide winter flowers. Cut blooms and disbud flower stems. Continue to take cuttings of pinks and harden-off rooted cuttings. Take action against pests and diseases.

SWEET PEAS

A liquid feed may be necessary every 12 days. Spray monthly with a systemic insecticide against sap-sucking insects. Continue pinching out tendrils and side shoots from cordons. Layer cordon-grown plants when they reach 5 ft. tall.

FLOWERS FROM SEED

Remove old flower heads from annuals to keep them flowering. Water liberally in dry weather. Support taller-growing annuals. Sow wallflowers and sweet williams in drills in their flowering positions. Spray monthly with a systemic insecticide. Hoe regularly. Set out seedlings of hardy biennials in a nursery bed.

BULBS

Lift and store tulips and daffodils. Remove from storage and burn any bulbs that are infested with eelworms and bulb fly grubs. Plant autumn-flowering bulbs, especially *Amaryllis belladonna*. Plant *Nerine bowdenii* outdoors; also autumn crocus, *Sternbergia lutea* and colchicum. Prepare ground for planting bulbs which are to provide cut flowers in the spring, by digging, removing weeds, and applying fertiliser, particularly potash.

ALPINES

Continue weeding and trimming. Water if necessary. Mounded or carpeting plants not showing new growth should have soil mixture and fertiliser worked into them. Save seeds of aquilegias, primulas and other short-lived alpines. Sow primula seed as soon as it is ripe. Store other seeds in a dry place.

WATER PLANTS AND POOLS

Continue to spray against aphids and other pests. In warm weather, replace water lost by evaporation, from a garden hose fitted with a spray. Cut off large water lily leaves hiding the flowers. Thin heavy growth of oxygenating plants. Remove weeds regularly from the bog garden.

GREENHOUSES AND FRAMES

Water and damp down during hot weather. Sow cinerarias. Pick tomato fruits regularly, keep stems supported, remove side shoots, and feed every ten days. Pick cucumbers regularly, remove male

flowers, and top-dress bed when a mass of white roots is seen. Shade plants which are in bloom and give adequate ventilation. Take cuttings of regal pelargoniums. Damp down borders, paths and staging at least once a day in warm weather, and water plants as required. Insert hydrangea cuttings individually in 3 in. pots, choosing well ripened, non-flowering shoots.

TREES AND SHRUBS

Keep an eye on hedges for aphids, whitefly and other pests, and control.

Propagation. Layer passiflora and wisteria shoots in sandy loam. Root cuttings of *Buddleia alternifolia* and callicarpa in a cold frame. Root cuttings of *Camellia japonica* and *Elaeagnus pungens* in pots of sandy soil in a propagating frame at 13–16°C (55–61°F). Insert heel cuttings of hibiscus and *Jasminum officinale* in pots of sandy soil in a cold frame.

Pruning. Prune deciduous shrubs such as jasmine and philadelphus after flowering by removing spent flowers and weak shoots.

RHODODENDRONS AND AZALEAS

Spray against Japanese lace-wing fly and bud blast. Watch for leaf hopper and control with malathion. Remove suckers on grafted plants.

HEDGES

Trim quickthorn hedges. Continue hoeing and weeding hedge bottoms. Control aphids and whitefly on hedges.

HEATHERS

Remove weeds and renew peat mulch where necessary.

FRUIT

Pick soft fruits. Summer prune trees grown in restricted form. Support heavily cropping branches of apples, pears and plums. Spray apples, pears, blackberries, loganberries, plums and damsons. Complete thinning apple and pear fruits. Check that ties on trained trees are not too tight. Train in new blackberry and loganberry shoots. Check weeds around trees and bushes growing in cultivated soil. Pick black currant fruit and prune bushes. Destroy bushes infected with reversion virus. Tie in replacement shoots on peaches and nectarines. Protect peaches against birds, wasps and earwigs. Support heavily laden plum branches. Prune trees after picking. Pick raspberries, cut down old canes and remove weak new shoots. Tie in new shoots and control weeds. Tidy up strawberry beds and discard plants which have given three crops. Continue summer pruning of vines.

VEGETABLES

Complete leek planting. In the south, sow swedes or hardy turnips. Complete planting late Brussels sprouts, winter cabbages, sprouting and spring broccoli. Sow spinach beet. Pinch out side shoots from tomatoes, except on bush varieties, which should be

strawed to keep the fruits clean. Make late sowings of round-seeded peas and globe beetroot. Continue watering shallow-rooted crops in dry weather. Start to lift and store onions.
Under glass. Cut cucumbers as they swell.
Less common vegetables. Lift and dry off shallots as their tops yellow, separate the bulb clusters, remove the loose skins and store in bags in a dry, cool shed or room. Sow winter radishes and thin to 6 in. apart.

HERBS

Make further sowings of chervil, dill and parsley. Harvest herbs just before they come into full bloom. Dry herbs in an airing cupboard. Cut lavender for drying and storing.

PATIOS AND TOWN GARDENS

Water container-grown plants at least once a day, if not top-dressed with damp peat. Remove dead flowers and discard plants past their best.

HOUSE PLANTS

Continue watering and feeding at the summer rate. Provide as much humidity as possible for all plants on hot days by standing them near pans of water. Clean foliage of plants standing near open windows.

GENERAL TASKS

Between now and the autumn carry out such constructional tasks as paving, wall building and concreting. Repair and paint greenhouses and frames. Remove dead heads from flowers weekly. Before going on holiday, cut the lawn, hoe all round, check plant ties and leave the hose ready for your neighbour to water for you. Instruct him to pick sweet peas and vegetables.

Plants to enjoy in July

Border and rock garden plants in flower			
Ageratum	Lathyrus (sweet pea)	Passiflora	Heliotropium
Alchemilla mollis	Lavatera	Philadelphus	Pelargonium domesticum
Althaea (hollyhock)	Lilium	Potentilla	Streptocarpus
Alyssum	Linum		Tibouchina
Anthemis	Lobelia	**Water garden plants in flower**	
Antirrhinum	Matthiola (stock)	Cyperus vegetus	
Astilbe	Mesembryanthemum	Eichhornia (floating water hyacinth)	**Fruit in season**
Begonia	Mimulus	Hemerocallis (day lily)	Black currant
Calendula (pot marigold)	Nemesia	Hosta	Gooseberry
Centaurea (cornflower)	Nicotiana (tobacco plant)	Hydrocharis (frogbit)	Raspberry
Chrysanthemum	Petunia	Mimulus	Red currant
Clarkia	Phlox	Nymphaea (water lily)	Strawberry
Convolvulus	Rodgersia	Sagittaria japonica	
Dahlia	Rose (floribunda and	Utricularia (bladderwort)	
Delphinium ajacis (larkspur)	hybrid tea)		**Vegetables in season**
Dianthus	Salvia	**House plants in flower, depending**	Artichoke, globe
Digitalis (foxglove)	Sedum	**on position and culture**	Beans, broad
Dimorphotheca	Tagetes (French marigold)	Anthurium	Beans, dwarf french
Erigeron	Tradescantia	Euphorbia pulcherrima (poinsettia)	Beans, runner
Eschscholzia	Tropaeolum (nasturtium)	Pelargonium	Beetroot
Gaillardia	Verbascum	Saxifraga stolonifera	Carrots
Gazania	Verbena		Cucumber
Geranium			Kohl rabi
Godetia	**Trees and shrubs in flower**	**Greenhouse plants in flower**	Lettuce
Gypsophila	Clematis	Achimenes	Marrow
Helianthemum	Cistus	Begonia	Onion (salad)
Helianthus (sunflower)	Hebe	Calceolaria	Peas
Helichrysum	Hydrangea	Campanula pyramidalis	Potatoes
Iberis	Hypericum	Canna	Radish
Ipomoea (morning glory)	Lavandula (lavender)	Celosia	Shallot
Kniphofia	Liriodendron (tulip tree)	Fuchsia	Spinach (summer)
	Olearia	Gloxinia	Squash

Lawns

During dry weather, water lawns as soon as a slackening growth rate shows that the soil is drying out. After brown patches appear, it is too late to restore the green appearance of the grass. A wide selection of irrigation equipment is available; either perforated plastic hose or the rotary sprinkler types are suitable. Liquid fertiliser may be introduced in some systems.

Aeration

If the lawn surface is compacted, open it up with aeration equipment or a garden fork so that water may penetrate. Do not water in bright sunlight; morning or evening is preferable. A light watering which only wets the top $\frac{1}{2}$ in. of the soil is useless; penetration to a depth of at least 6 in. is necessary. For the best results 2–4 gall. of water per sq. yd. is necessary, but requirements vary with soil type and climate. Sandy soils require half the volume of water needed for clay soils.

Disease control

Apply fungicides for the control of fusarium, dollar spot and corticium diseases, particularly if the weather is hot and humid. If a second crop of weeds has developed or earlier applications have been missed, apply selective weedkillers under warm, moist growing conditions (see MARCH).

Roses

Summer pruning consists of cutting blooms for home decoration, and dead-heading—the removal of faded blooms. When carried out correctly, both procedures encourage new, strong shoots to grow in the directions required to maintain shapely plants. They also assist the next crop of blooms to develop quickly.

As leaves produce the food needed to build up a plant, remove only short stems, with as few leaves as possible, from newly planted roses and any that are not growing strongly. Always cut back to a compound leaf that has five leaflets. These larger leaves have good flower buds in the axils.

Cutting blooms

When cutting blooms from established roses (those which have flowered for one or more years) do not cut stems longer than required. Ideally, remove only one-third of the flowering stem produced this season. Cut off faded blooms with one or, at most, two of the lower leaves.

Always use sharp secateurs, making each cut slope back from $\frac{1}{4}$ in. above a leaf and point in the direction you wish the new shoot to grow. Keep the centre of the plant open. Delay in removing faded blooms will retard the second crop of blooms.

When dead-heading roses, lay a square of polythene on the bed or lawn and throw the flower trimmings on to it. Pull it along as you proceed, then carry the sheet and dead flowers to the bonfire heap when dead-heading is finished.

Feed and spray

As soon as the first flush of blooms is over, feed both established and newly planted roses with a proprietary rose fertiliser, scattering a handful to the square yard over the surface of the beds, except for a 6 in. circle round the main stem of each tree. Hoe the fertiliser into the surface soil.

Spray with a systemic rose insecticide if greenfly appear.

Continue to spray every two or three

ASSISTING WATER PENETRATION

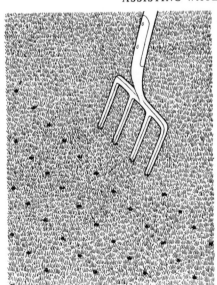

If the soil surface is compacted, spike the turf with a fork or proprietary aerator before watering. Though forking is satisfactory on

small lawns, a wheeled aerator saves time and effort. The type illustrated has spring-loaded tines which do not tear the turf

SUMMER PRUNING A ROSE

Cut roses for decoration with stems as short as possible, and make each sloping cut above a leaf. This will encourage new shoots

....

weeks against mildew, black spot and rust diseases (see JUNE). As some strains of fungi build up tolerance of specific chemical controls, especially benomyl, it is beneficial to change the fungicide used rather than continue using the same one throughout the season.

Hardy herbaceous plants

Continue cutting back early-flowering kinds and dead-heading where flowering is incomplete. Scabious, gaillardia, anthemis, *Chrysanthemum maximum,* sidalcea and achillea are among the plants which will flower longer if cut as they fade, or if cut for use in the house. Some kinds, such as *Achillea taygetea* and *Salvia superba* and its varieties, will produce a second crop if cut back quite severely just before flowering is over.

Dead-heading paeonies

Do not cut back paeonies that have flowered; simply remove the dead flower heads. The foliage is ornamental, and paeonies need to die back naturally, as part of the ripening process.

In warm, sheltered gardens, delphiniums and lupins may sometimes flower again if cut down to ground level.

If michaelmas daisies appear lacking in vigour, hoe in a further application of organic fertiliser round the plants (see FEBRUARY). Both the tall and dwarf varieties are liable to mildew, which produces a whitish film on the foliage. Prevent by spraying with dinocap or benomyl.

Control rust disease

Rust may begin to attack *Campanula persicifolia* and its varieties. It often affects the new leaves forming at the base after flowering, and is difficult to check. Cut off the leaves and burn them; then hoe all round the plants.

Plan new borders

Decide now on the position and shape of any new beds or borders for autumn planting. If possible choose an open site, preferably an island plot that is accessible all round. Only about 10 per cent of the plants in an island bed should need staking; it is also easier to maintain, and the plants can be seen from all sides. By scaling down the height of the plants, the bed can be as small as 40 sq. ft. This type of bed is easy to fit into most parts of the garden away from the boundary. An open position is the most suitable for an island bed and, since most herbaceous perennials prefer sun, a wide choice of plants is available. If the garden is laid out formally, choose a rectangular, oval or circular shape.

There is a limit to the varieties that can be grown in a dry, shady place. Avoid if possible a site in which tree roots are active, as it will be dry in summer. If the new border is backed by an established hedge, leave at least 3 ft. for its roots to feed in, or they will take nutriment from the plants. Any backing, whether wall, hedge or fence, reduces light and air, so that the plants grow taller and with weaker stems. In

DEAD-HEADING A PAEONY

Remove dead flower heads with secateurs or a knife, allowing the foliage to die back naturally as part of the ripening process

....

such a border more than half the subjects must be staked unless dwarf, stiff-growing kinds are selected.

Border shapes

If possible, avoid making the border so narrow that it makes tall plants look incongruous, but remember also that a wide, one-sided border is difficult to maintain. If the bed is backed by a straight or formal hedge or wall, choose either a straight-fronted border or a regular curve, either circular or elliptical. A scalloped or wavy edge is unattractive, and a zigzag is difficult to maintain.

Once the site and type of bed have been chosen, begin at once to prepare it for planting in the autumn.

Kill weeds

First, kill the weeds. To destroy annual weeds, such as groundsel, fat hen, sow-thistle and others that increase only by seeding, use a spray that kills surface growth but does not penetrate the soil or remain active for more than a few hours. Follow the spraying instructions closely. After a few days, when the weeds have started to wither, either burn them after they have been mown or hoed, or simply dig them in.

Dig the ground over roughly and, after shaking the weeds free of soil, leave them for a week or two to perish on top of the soil. Sun is the most effective killer of the more persistent perennial weeds, such as couch, ground elder, nettle, thistle and bindweed. They may have to be shaken again, or removed and burnt if the weather is showery. Weeds may not shake free of soil so easily if it is hard or heavy, but, if the surface is left lumpy, the weather will break it up by the autumn.

Light soil can be dug as soon as weeds are cleared, ready for autumn planting. A heavy clay soil, however, often needs autumn rain to make deep digging possible, and as it usually needs the weathering effect of winter frost it is safer to plan for spring planting.

Add manure
Once the weeds have been destroyed, dig in any manure that is needed, if possible farmyard manure or compost. If peat is used, combine it with John Innes base or organic fertiliser. To save the trouble of mixing with the peat, sprinkle the fertiliser at 2–3 oz. per sq. yd. before digging. Place the peat or manure in a convenient spot to avoid unnecessary carrying.

Digging the bed
First, take out a trench across one end of the bed and put the soil from it at the other end, ready to fill in the last trench. Loosen the bottom of the trench with a fork if the soil is stiff or hard. This helps to drain and aerate the soil, especially if the ground has not been cultivated for

some time. Do not turn the bottom of the trench over if there is any sign of subsoil, clay, chalk, marl, sand or gravel. Spread the manure, compost or peat evenly at the bottom of the trench and then turn over the next strip. Remove the roots of weeds such as thistle and bindweed, or any missed in the initial cleaning operation.

Manure will be more easily reached by the roots of the plants if it lies on the newly turned soil that trickles back after the first trench has been covered, rather than if it is jammed in the narrow V at the bottom of the trench.

Always dig across the width of a bed or border, and try to level up low places.

Dahlias

Continue to tie the young stems to their stakes with raffia or soft string.

If the plants are not growing as strongly as you would wish—by the middle of July most dahlias should have reached a height of about 2 ft.—a feed once every 14 days with a liquid fertiliser will be helpful. Always apply the feed to the soil when it is damp. In dry weather, water the soil first.

Disbudding
To obtain long clean stems and good flowers, disbud at least a proportion of the stems, otherwise flower stems may be a little too short to permit easy arranging in a vase. At the top of each main shoot there will be a flower bud, with two smaller buds immediately below. Remove the two lower buds. Alternatively, to obtain a large number of smaller flowers, remove the top bud, leaving the two lower buds to grow on.

Remove faded flowers regularly. If you want to try raising new varieties from your own dahlia seed, leave a few faded flowers on the plants to form seed pods.

DISBUDDING A DAHLIA

If large, long-stemmed flowers are needed for arranging, remove the two smaller buds on each main stem, leaving only the terminal bud

Chrysanthemums

Outdoor-flowering plants make very rapid growth this month, often producing too many shoots. Where large flowers are required, reduce the number of shoots to five per plant by breaking off the weaker ones. This is unnecessary on pompon and spray varieties.

In dry weather, water plants thoroughly once a week (see JUNE).

Attend weekly to tying and supporting. If welded wire mesh is being used (see MAY) raise it as the plants grow so as to keep it 9 in. below the tips.

Apply fertiliser
About the middle of the month apply a balanced fertiliser, in liquid or solid form, at the rate recommended by the

anufacturers. Keep dry fertiliser off
e foliage. If plants appear soft and
licate, water with a solution of $\frac{1}{2}$ oz.
lphate of potash per gallon of water,
the rate of $\frac{1}{4}$ pint per plant. If the
eather is dry, water the plants both
fore and after the application.

Towards the end of the month some
ry early-flowering outdoor varieties
ll begin to show their buds and may be
sbudded (see AUGUST).

Continue to spray against pests.

NDER GLASS

n large exhibition varieties, reduce
e number of flowering stems to three
r plant; on exhibition incurves and
hibition decoratives, reduce to four.

Lightly dig and rake greenhouse
rders in which the mid- and late-
ason varieties propagated last month
e to be planted.

Gladioli

ake the plants individually if you
quire perfectly straight stems for
hibition work. Use rings, twine or raffia
r securing the plants to the stakes.
ere is no need to support the plants
you are growing them simply for gar-
n decoration or to provide cut flowers.

SUPPORTING GLADIOLI

ants grown for garden decoration do not
ed staking, though in exposed gardens it is
pful to draw soil round the stems

STAKING EXHIBITION GLADIOLI

Insert a cane on the opposite side of the stem
to the developing florets, which will open in the
same direction as the forward-bending tip.
Secure to the stake with rings, twine or raffia

Spray against thrips

Be alert for signs of gladiolus thrips.
These pests cause a brown and silver
chequer-board pattern on the foliage,
with the buds shrivelling and failing to
open in severe attacks. Spray with
malathion or HCH, repeating every
three weeks to ensure control.

Irises

Early in the month dig up and divide
dwarf and intermediate bearded irises if
they have been undisturbed for three
years. Tall bearded irises need the same
treatment from the end of the month
onwards. Division can be carried out
annually or every other year, but plants
are best left undisturbed for three years.

Divide clumps

When re-planting, cut the best single
rhizomes from the old clumps and plant

them in soil which has had old manure
or compost, together with general fertiliser or bone-meal, dug into the top spit.
Leave the tops of the rhizomes above
ground level and press the soil firmly on
to the roots below. Plant dwarf irises
about 6 in. apart, intermediates at 8 in.
and tall irises at about 10 in.

After planting, cut off the top halves
of the leaves. This will lessen evaporation and possible loosening in the soil by
wind rocking.

New plants obtained from nurseries
must be similarly planted. Always plant
bearded irises in sunny, well drained
positions; never in damp or shady
places. In dry weather water the newly
planted rhizomes until they become
established. Pull off any leaves which die
in the natural course of plant growth.

Order bulbous irises now for autumn
planting.

Feed summer-flowering Dutch irises
with a dressing of Nitro-chalk, at the
rate of 1 oz. per sq. yd. Raked into the
surface of the soil, this will improve
flower colour.

HOW IRISES DEVELOP

Dwarf, intermediate and tall bearded irises will
have developed in this fashion when lifted after
growing undisturbed for two or three years

159

REMOVING AN IRIS RHIZOME

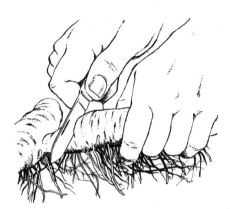

Using a sharp knife, sever the best single rhizomes from the old clump, making the cuts 2–3 in. back from the new growths

TRIMMING THE LEAVES

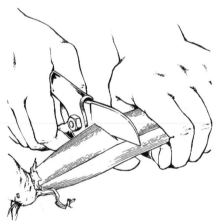

To reduce moisture loss and minimise wind resistance, cut off the upper halves of the leaves before or after planting the rhizomes

A SEPARATED IRIS RHIZOME

Each section of rhizome cut from the clump will have its own root system, together with a growing point and leaves at one end

RE-PLANTING THE RHIZOMES

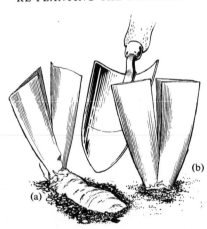

When planting, set the upper parts of the rhizomes above ground (a) on heavy soil, but just under the surface (b) on light soil

---

Lift bulbous plants

Lift bulbous irises when their leaves die down if they are becoming over-crowded or if you need to move them. Dry off in an airy shed, divide the bulbs and, as an anti-disease precaution, strip off their outer skin before re-planting in September.

Spray or dust with trichlorphon or derris any irises on which caterpillars are seen.

Lilies

This is one of the peak months of the lily display. Pick off dead flower heads unless you wish to save the seeds (see AUGUST).

Spray with Bordeaux mixture fortnightly against botrytis disease if the weather is damp or muggy. Spray monthly with a systemic insecticide against aphids which help to spread virus diseases (see JUNE). Keep the beds weeded and water thoroughly if the weather is exceptionally dry.

Fungus disease

Botrytis elliptica is a disabling fungus disease of lilies. Though not necessarily fatal in itself, it has a weakening effect which decreases resistance to other diseases. Damp, muggy weather encourages the spready of botrytis. The symptoms are brownish-red spots, or grey mouldy patches, or both. The spores, which can over-winter on the surface of the soil, multiply on bare damp surfaces. The risk of this disease is much reduced by sunny weather and by spraying with a fungicide. If it does occur, burn the affected foliage.

UNDER GLASS

Continue to control aphids with a systemic spray and keep the pots watered

Carnations and pinks

Continue to disbud border carnations this was not completed last month.

Watch for pests and diseases, taking action as necessary (see MARCH).

Order carnations and pinks for autumn planting (see colour section, MAY).

Remove old flower stems from pinks water the plants thoroughly if dry, and apply a high-potash liquid fertiliser. Do not feed border carnations.

LAYERING A BORDER CARNATION

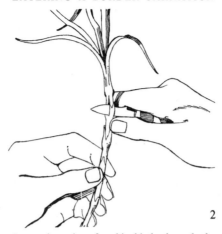

Select a vigorous side shoot, stripping off the lower leaves so that between four and six fully developed pairs of leaves remain at the tip

Insert the point of a thin blade through the stem just below the lowest leaves, cutting along the centre of stem and through the joint below

Twisting the knife, cut through the stem just below the joint, leaving a tongue which opens out away from the parent plant

Bend down the top of the layer, keeping it upright, with the cut open. Press the cut into a bed of prepared soil and secure with a pin

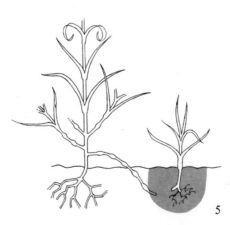

Six weeks later, when the layer will have made its own roots, sever it from the parent plant, cutting close to the new stem, and leave to grow on

Layer border carnations

Propagate border carnations by layering. This is the easiest method of increase and it is in any case advisable to replace plants after their second year. Young plants give the best layers; but do not spoil plants by taking an unneccesary number of layers.

Prepare the soil round the parent plant by mixing equal volumes of damp peat and sharp sand into the top 2 in. of soil. Strip lower leaves off vigorous side shoots, leaving four to six fully developed pairs of leaves at the tip. Push the point of a thin knife through the centre of the stem just below the lowest joint where the leaves have been left, cut downwards along the centre of the stem through the joint below, turn the knife sideways, and bring it out just below the joint, leaving a tongue which opens out away from the centre of the parent plant. Bring down the tops of the side shoots (from now on called layers), keeping them upright, and press them into the prepared soil, opening out the cut as you do so. If the stem attaching the layer to the parent plant is stiff, bruise it between leaf joints with pliers or your thumb-nail.

Press the base of the layer about 1 in. into the soil and secure it with a layering pin (a 6 in. length of thick galvanised wire bent over to form a hook at the top). Water in with a fine-rosed can, and make sure that the soil does not dry out during rooting.

After six weeks sever the layer from

161

the parent plant, cutting close to the layer, and after a further three or four weeks lift for planting or potting.

UNDER GLASS

Renew shading on glass if necessary and damp down in hot weather.

Continue to give second stoppings until the middle of the month to provide winter flowers (see APRIL).

Cut blooms and disbud flower stems (see SEPTEMBER).

Continue to take cuttings of pinks and to harden-off rooted cuttings (see JUNE).

Watch for pests and diseases, taking action as necessary (see MARCH).

Sweet peas

Feeding and watering should seldom be necessary if the bed was dug and manured correctly in the first place (see NOVEMBER). In any case, do not feed or water until the plants are well in flower. If eventually it proves necessary to feed the plants, one application every 12 days is sufficient, using a proprietary liquid fertiliser. It is important not to over-feed cordon-grown plants.

Spray monthly with a systemic insecticide to control sap-sucking insects.

Pinch out tendrils and side shoots on cordon-grown plants (see APRIL).

Layering cordons

A technique known as layering is often carried out with cordon-grown plants. (This is not layering as applied to propagation.) It results in blooms of improved quality but must be done at least two weeks before flowers are required for exhibition. It is also necessary in the case of exceptionally tall-growing plants.

Layer the plants when they are about 5 ft. high. Starting at one end of an outside row, unfasten all the ties on the first four to six plants and lay the plants

LAYERING CORDON SWEET PEAS

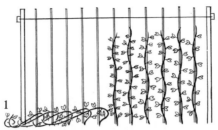

1 Where cordon plants are grown in a pair of adjacent rows (as illustrated in MARCH), unfasten the ties on the end plants of one row, laying the plants on the ground

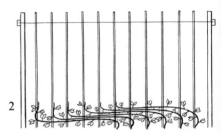

2 Lay the next plant in the row close to the canes and tie it to the first cane. Secure the remaining plants to successive canes, taking care not to damage the stems

3 Secure the stem of each plant with two or three raffia ties. At this stage, the end plants, which were the first to be unfastened from their canes, are still left on the ground

4 Bring the first plants from the second row round the end post and tie them to the vacant canes. Finally, secure the untied first row plants to the vacant second-row canes

on the ground. Then, taking care not to break the haulm, lay the next plant along the ground close to the canes and gently bend its top 12–15 in. up the first cane in the row, fastening the top with two or three raffia ties. Fasten the next plant to the second cane, and so on until the end of the row is reached.

Plant positions

Layer the first few plants in the next row to take the places of the last plants of the previous row. Secure the first plants of the first row to the last canes of the second row.

Flowers from seed

The lives of many annual flowers are shortened if they are allowed to form seed heads. Removing the old flower heads as they fade also keeps the border colourful and attractive. In very dry weather, liberal watering will extend the flowering period, but do not give so much water that leaf growth is encouraged at the expense of the flowers.

Give support to the taller-growing annuals when they reach a height of 6–9 in. (see JUNE).

Early in the month, wallflowers and sweet williams can be sown in drills in their flowering positions. This is a convenient method if they are to be used for cutting. Sow thinly, later removing surplus plants by chopping them out with a hoe.

Control insects and weeds

Spray monthly with a systemic insecticide to control aphids and other sap-sucking insects.

Hoe regularly to control weeds among the bedding plants. Hoeing is easiest and most effective if done before the weeds appear.

As soon as they reach manageable size, set out in a nursery bed seedlings of hardy biennials and hardy perennials which are at present in seed boxes or outdoor seed beds (see JUNE).

Bulbs

This is the chief month for lifting and storing spring-flowering bulbs such as tulips, daffodils, hyacinths and many other small bulbs which require dividing and re-planting (see JUNE).

Tulips and bedding hyacinths need lifting annually; daffodils grown for cutting, every two or three years; most others, much less frequently.

Daffodil pests

Eelworms and the grubs of bulb flies are serious pests of daffodils. It is evidence of eelworms if bulbs which feel slightly soft show concentric rings of brown and paler tissue when cut across. They sometimes have a woolly substance at the base. Bulb fly grubs eat away the centres of the bulbs, leaving them soft and rotten.

Commercially, immersion in hot water is used to control both pests, but special equipment is needed. On a garden scale, small numbers of bulbs can be dealt with by removal and burning. Otherwise, the only practical course is to destroy the entire stock and plant fresh bulbs in clean ground.

Plant bulbs for autumn

Plant autumn-flowering bulbs this month. They provide a touch of unusual form and colour among shrubs and trees at an otherwise dull time of the year. The first, and one of the most striking, is *Amaryllis belladonna*, which carries several trumpet-shaped scented pink flowers on the top of $1\frac{1}{2}$–2 ft. stems from late August to October. Plant them so that the tops of the bulbs are 4–6 in. below the soil surface, shallowest in warm situations in the south and deepest in the coldest districts. They are best close to a wall facing south, where they are protected from the coldest weather and where they can dry out and ripen during the summer.

Plant nerines

Nerines have rather similar but smaller flowers with more reflexed petals. Only *Nerine bowdenii* and its varieties are really hardy enough to stand outside, and then only in the south. Plant them with the tops of the bulbs just covered with soil. The leaves of both amaryllis and nerine follow the flowers and continue to grow through the spring months.

Autumn crocuses

Different in form and colour are the various crocus-like flowers which bloom from late September almost to Christmas. Most have mauve or white flowers. There are a dozen or more kinds of the true autumn crocus. Plant them 2–3 in. deep in soil which will not be disturbed by cultivation, or in grass which can be cut after planting in July–August, and then not again until the leaves have died down in the following May–June.

Sternbergia lutea has a rather similar flower to the crocuses, but has leaves which grow at the same time as the flowers and does not therefore delay grass cutting in the spring.

The colchicum or meadow saffron also has crocus-like flowers in pinkish mauve and white, but its large broad leaves can be out of place in a neat lawn or small flower bed. So plant them in rough grass or in small groups near the front of shrub borders, where the flowers can be seen in the autumn and the leaves will not be too obtrusive in the spring.

Planting preparations

Prepare ground for planting bulbs which are to provide cut flowers in spring. Dig deeply, remove all weeds, and break up any clods. Apply fertiliser before the final cultivation. Bulbs benefit especially from potash, so use either 4–6 oz. per sq. yd. of a high-potash compound, or 2 oz. each of sulphate of potash and superphosphate and 1 oz. sulphate of ammonia, per sq. yd.

If bulb catalogues are late arriving, give priority to ordering daffodils, as they benefit from early planting and should be put out not later than September.

Alpines

Continue with the routine tasks of weeding and trimming (see MAY and JUNE). Water the plants if tests show that this is necessary (see JUNE).

If mounded or carpeting plants are failing to show renewed growth after flowering, rub in fine soil to which peat, sand and a little fertiliser have been added (see MAY).

Late-flowering plants

From now until October is the most difficult time to provide continuity of colour in the rock garden. Visits to summer shows and to gardens open to the public provide excellent opportunities to see late-flowering alpines in bloom. Take note of those that appeal to you so that you can purchase plants to replace any early-flowering specimens that have proved unsatisfactory. Remember that some alpine varieties will not come true to colour from seed and will have to be increased by cuttings.

Collect and store seeds

Save seeds of aquilegias, primulas and other rock garden plants which are not long-lived. When collecting the seeds, either shake out the ripe seeds by bending the seed heads into a large envelope or polythene bag, or place the seed heads in a bag and let the seeds fall out of their own accord, as they will within a few days. Primula seeds should be sown as soon as they are ripe, during the summer. Store other seeds in a dry place but do not put them in airtight tins (see DECEMBER and MARCH for sowing instructions).

Water plants and pools

Continue to spray against aphids and other pests (see JUNE).

In warm weather, replace water lost by evaporation, using a garden hose fitted with a spray. This also helps to aerate the pool.

Defoliate water lilies

If large water lily leaves are hiding the flowers, cut the leaves off well below the water surface. Otherwise allow them to decay naturally on the base of the pool during the summer months.

Thin oxygenators

Thin heavy growths of oxygenating plants from time to time, always taking care not to remove young fish with the plant growth.

Remove weeds regularly from moisture-loving plants in the bog garden.

Greenhouses and frames

Continue to pay special attention to watering and damping down during hot weather (see JUNE).

There is still time to make another sowing of cinerarias (see MAY).

Herbaceous calceolarias should also be sown this month, in pans of John Innes seed compost, and placed in shade in a greenhouse or a cold frame. When the seedlings are large enough to handle, pot them individually in 3 in. pots containing John Innes potting compost No. 1.

Pick tomatoes and cucumbers

Tomato plants should be in full bearing, with a few fruits requiring picking almost every day. Twist the stems round the supporting strings, or tie them to the canes, and remove side shoots regularly. Apply liquid fertiliser every week or ten days.

Cucumbers should also be in full production; continue picking the fruits when they are about 12 in. long, and removing the male flowers as soon as they appear. When a mass of white roots appears on the surface of the bed, apply a top dressing of well-rotted manure or fibrous loam, or a mixture of the two about 2 in. deep.

Encourage blooming

Among the many plants which should now be in full flower are begonias, gloxinias, fuchsias, campanulas, heliotrope and zonal pelargoniums. To encourage prolonged blooming, shade the plant during sunny weather and give ample ventilation, especially in the early morning when delay in opening the side ventilators may cause excessively high temperatures. Except during unusually cold or windy weather, leave the roof ventilators open a little way throughout the night, on the leeward side of the house.

Regal pelargoniums which were cut back during June will now be carrying an abundance of new growth. Take cuttings from these as required. Choose short-jointed shoots about 4 in. long

WATERING POT PLANTS

As it is important not to splash the foliage, apply water gently from a can with a long spout, close to the rim of the pot. If necessary, wedge a sliver of wood in the spout to reduce the flow

TAKING HALF-RIPE HEEL CUTTINGS

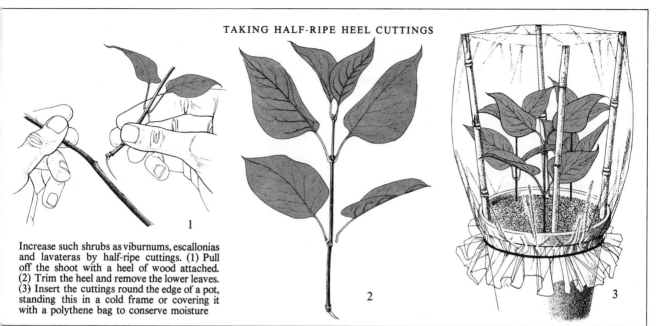

Increase such shrubs as viburnums, escallonias and lavateras by half-ripe cuttings. (1) Pull off the shoot with a heel of wood attached. (2) Trim the heel and remove the lower leaves. (3) Insert the cuttings round the edge of a pot, standing this in a cold frame or covering it with a polythene bag to conserve moisture

inserting them round the edge of a 5 in. pot, five or six cuttings in each pot, in sandy, free-draining compost.

Watering requirements

Damp down the borders, path and staging at least once a day during warm weather, but do not spray overhead, as the water droplets may mark the flowers. Unless the plants are standing on a capillary bench which waters them automatically, most will require watering daily and possibly two or three times a day during hot weather. To determine whether a plant needs water, press the compost lightly with your fingertips. Moist compost is soft and resilient, but dry compost feels hard and gritty. With a little experience, the water content of a pot can be gauged by lifting it to determine its weight. The important thing is not to withhold water until the plants are actually flagging, but to attend to watering daily.

Propagate hydrangeas and acacias

Insert cuttings of hydrangeas individually in 3 in. pots, choosing well ripened, non-flowering shoots of medium thickness. Ripe shoots are greeny-brown, whereas unripe shoots are light green. Make the cuttings about 3 in. long, severing them immediately below a leaf joint and removing the lower leaves. Stand the pots on the greenhouse bench. These later plants are grown on without stopping to produce a single head.

Take semi-ripe cuttings of acacias, inserting them in an equal parts mixture of sand and peat. Transfer the cuttings individually to 3 in. pots when rooted.

Greenhouse hygiene

Hygiene in the greenhouse is especially important at this time of year. Remove all plant debris and other rubbish, emptying old compost out of pots and boxes and scrubbing the containers before storage or re-use.

Trees and shrubs

Aphids and other pests can breed on hedges and quite tall shrubs. They do little apparent damage, but they are a powerful source of infestation, and migrate to other plants where they can do much harm. So, when spraying roses or other plants, keep an eye on hedges and shrubs. Beech hedges sometimes become infested with whitefly. They do not cause a great deal of damage, but it is safer to spray the hedge with insecticide.

PROPAGATION

In the open

Layer passiflora and wisteria shoots in sandy loam. Pot when good roots have formed and grown on in pots for a year before planting out in permanent positions in spring.

Put cuttings of the following in a cold frame to root: *Buddleia alternifolia*, callicarpa, *Campsis radicans, Chamae-cyparis lawsoniana*, cistus, clematis, cotoneaster, deutzia, escallonia, euonymus, *Hydrangea paniculata grandiflora, H. petiolaris, Lavatera olbia rosea*, mahonia, spiraea and viburnum.

Under glass

Cuttings of *Camellia japonica, Elaeagnus pungens,* hypericum, lonicera, pyracantha and *Cotinus coggygria* should be rooted in pots of sandy soil in a propagating frame at a temperature of 13–16°C (55–61°F) before being re-potted and placed in a cold frame (see JUNE). Over-winter the tender cuttings of passiflora in a frost-free greenhouse. Grow on cuttings of *Camellia japonica*, individually potted, for 18 months in a cold frame before planting out.

Take cuttings of hibiscus and *Jasminum officinale* with a heel and insert singly in pots of sandy soil. Place in a cold frame to root.

PRUNING

After flowering prune such deciduous shrubs as *Choisya ternata* (Mexican orange), jasmine and philadelphus by removing spent flowers and cutting out thin and weak shoots.

Rhododendrons and azaleas

Spray insecticide on plants infested with Japanese lace-wing fly (see JUNE). Continue to watch for bud blast and to remove infested shoots or spray with a non-lime fungicide.

Watch for the leaf hopper, an active insect which hides under leaves and jumps from plant to plant. Since it is thought to be a carrier of bud blast disease, spray with malathion. It kills leaf hopper; but if it is used too early,

166

red spider, normally kept in check by the leaf hopper, may become prevalent.

Watch for suckers on grafted plants. In bad cases, the wild rhododendron stock (*R. ponticum*) will take over completely. Remove all the wild growth, and the grafted plant will thrive.

Hedges

This is the best month to trim quickthorn hedges. If they are cut earlier, the new growth will require further trimming before the end of the summer; if left until later, the shoots will be more difficult to cut, and the outlines of the hedge more difficult to follow.

Continue weeding

Continue to weed or hoe hedge bottoms (see MARCH).

If a new hedge is needed, study neighbouring gardens before ordering the plants, preferably choosing types that are thriving near by on similar soil. You can also gain valuable advice at agricultural and horticultural shows where nurserymen are exhibiting.

Pests of hedges

Aphids and other pests often breed on hedging plants. Beech hedges are sometimes infested with whitefly. These pests do little apparent damage, but they may migrate to other plants with more serious results. When spraying roses and other flowering plants, keep an eye on hedges and spray them if pests are seen.

Heathers

There is little to do in the heather garden this month, apart from removing any weeds and, if necessary, renewing the peat or forest bark mulch.

Fruit

Most of the soft fruits are bearing fruit now and will need attention after picking. Others are nearing maturity.

Trees being grown in a restricted form need summer pruning. This keeps the parts of the tree above ground down to a small size, without encouraging new growth. Prune to open up the trees and bushes to make spraying and picking easier; and to let in light and air so that the colour of the fruit is improved.

SUPPORTING FRUIT TREES

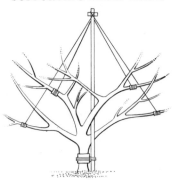

When fastening supporting ties from a centre post, wrap sacking or rubber round each of the branches to prevent friction

An easier but less tidy method is to support heavily-laden branches with stout stakes deeply forked at the top

Apple and pear

Growth is slowing down now, and attention can be given to the fruit. Modern pruning encourages early fruiting, often before the branches have become rigid. Support heavy cropping trees, either by a stake for each branch or by ties from a centre post.

It is less important from now on to keep weeds or grass under the trees in check.

Continue to watch for red spider mite, and also for codling moth on apple (see JUNE). Injury caused by codling moth can now be seen, and damaged fruit should be destroyed. Make sure that sack bands are securely tied round trunks (see JUNE): they will now also attract codling moth caterpillars.

The white covering produced by woolly aphis becomes thicker as the season proceeds. Treat small outbreaks by brushing with dilute malathion.

If the fruit has been well protected until now against apple and pear scab, later attacks will not mark it seriously, and further spraying is unnecessary.

Thin fruit and summer prune

Complete fruit thinning as soon as the natural drop is over (see JUNE). Reduce the number of fruits to one in every flower cluster, with a final spacing of 4–6 in.; larger fruit and cooking varieties should be spaced more widely. Summer prune cordon, espalier and dwarf pyramid trees, pruning the pear trees first because they are ready before the apples, and spread the job of pruning over the next two months. As the bases of this year's shoots start to get woody (this can be tested by bending them between thumb and forefinger), cut back with secateurs to about five leaves. Do not prune leading shoots, or those selected to extend the branch framework, until the tree has filled its allotted space. While summer pruning is essential

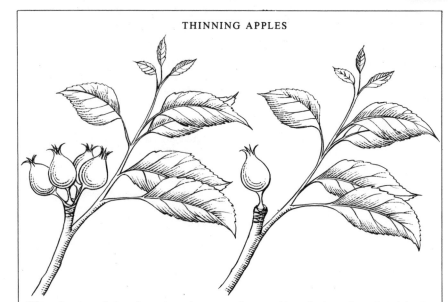

THINNING APPLES

When the natural drop has taken place, examine the trees to see whether more thinning is necessary. Reduce to one fruit in each cluster, with a final spacing of 4–6 in. for dessert apples of average size, and a little more for large varieties and cooking apples

to control trained trees, it can also be carried out on bush trees, although it is too drastic for unhealthy trees.

While working on trained trees, check that the ties are not cutting into stems and branches.

Blackberry, loganberry and hybrid berries

Train in new shoots, keeping them separate from the fruiting shoots to reduce the spread of disease. Apply derris or malathion for raspberry beetle ten days after flowering, repeating the application 14 days later if attacks in previous years have been serious. Control weeds, water if dry, and repair the surface mulch if one has been applied (see APRIL).

Black currant

Pick fruit as it matures: many varieties do not hang long on the bush once they are ripe. The extent of next year's crop depends largely on how much growth is made in the current year; the most useful new fruit-bearing shoots are those coming from below ground level. It is possible but not essential to prune black currants after picking, leaving in the robust new shoots. Keep weeds under control by careful hoeing.

Reversion virus

Vigorous and healthy looking bushes which are unfruitful may have reversion virus. The presence of enlarged buds in early spring due to big bud mite, which is the carrier of this disease, helps to confirm this. The leaves on reverted shoots are coarse with few serrations round the edges of the leaves. There is no cure for this quickly spreading disease, so burn affected bushes, and replace them with certified stock in winter.

167

SUMMER PRUNING APPLES AND PEARS

Summer pruning, essential for controlling trained trees, also admits light and air to the fruits. It consists of cutting back new laterals, except those needed to extend the branch framework, to about five leaves. The leading shoots should be left unpruned

Cherry

Rub out unwanted buds on standard trees to produce a good shape.

Gooseberry

Pick the fruit as it matures. Keep watching for sawfly attacks (see MAY). Control weeds.

Peach and nectarine

Continue to tie in new growths which are being kept as replacements on wall-trained trees (see JUNE). Protect the fruit against birds, earwigs and wasps by placing muslin or paper bags on individual fruits.

Plum and damson

Support trees which are heavily laden to prevent the branches from splitting, especially those of 'Victoria' plums, and also to prevent silver leaf infection, which usually affects large wounds. If necessary, spray with a systemic insecticide against mealy plum aphis.

As soon as picking has been completed, prune the trees. This is done now because large wounds heal rapidly at this time of year. Keep the centres of bush trees open, if necessary by taking out one or two large branches, and cut out dead, diseased, broken and crossing branches. Shorten the leaders on restricted trees according to vigour, and cut the laterals to about 6 in. Prune fan-trained trees by cutting back by half those laterals which have already been pinched to six or seven leaves (see JUNE). Remove any dead wood and tie new shoots into the framework to fill up the available space or replace worn-out shoots.

Raspberry

Pick the fruit as it ripens. Once the fruit has been picked, cut off the old canes close to the ground to leave room for the new growths which will carry next year's crop; and also remove weak new shoots, so that the row will not be crowded. As the remaining shoots reach the supporting framework, tie them to it. Control weeds and pull out suckers (shoots arising from the root below ground) which are too far from the row itself.

Strawberry

Tidy up the beds after picking, and dry the netting before storing it. Where three crops have been produced, remove the plants unless they are particularly vigorous and healthy. Younger beds can be tidied quickly by cutting off the old leaves and burning them. Burn any straw round the plants when it is dry enough. New leaves will be produced in 10–14 days. 'Rabunda' 'Gento' and 'Aromel' are among the new varieties that give a good crop in August and September. Apply a complete fertiliser at the rate of 2 oz. per sq. yd. after tidying up. Remove runners, unless required to produce more plants in a matted row. Control weeds by shallow cultivation.

Vine (outdoor)

Continue to rub out unwanted buds and cut back new shoots from the laterals to about 24 in. Do not prune the replacement shoots (see JUNE).

Vegetables

Complete leek planting as soon a possible if this was not done last month (see JUNE).

In the south, sow swedes by the middle of the month (see JUNE). Alternatively, sow hardy turnips, such as 'Golden Ball' or 'Manchester Market' in drills $\frac{1}{2}$ in. deep and 12 in. apart. In cold northern areas the turnips should be lifted in December.

Complete the planting of late Brussels sprouts, winter cabbages, and both sprouting and spring broccoli, by the middle of the month (see JUNE).

PLANTING BRASSICAS

When planting out late brassicas during dry weather, set the plants in shallow trenches to ensure maximum benefit from watering

Spinach beet can still be sown until the middle of the month (see JUNE).

Pinch out the side shoots which grow from the leaf axils of tomato plants. This must be done regularly throughout the growing season. Do not pinch out the side shoots on bush varieties, but cover the ground beneath with straw or peat to keep the fruits off the soil.

Late sowings of round-seeded peas (see JANUARY) and globe beetroot (see APRIL) will mature in October.

During dry weather, continue to water shallow-rooted crops (see JUNE).

At the end of the month or early in August, lift and store onions in the same way as shallots. (See LESS COMMON VEGETABLES section for this month.)

UNDER GLASS

Cut cucumbers about a fortnight after the fruits start to swell.

LESS COMMON VEGETABLES

Early this month the tops of shallots will be yellowing and bending over.

When this happens, ease the clusters of bulbs out of the ground with a fork, removing the soil and spreading the bulbs out to dry until the tops are crisp and can be rubbed off easily. A flat shed roof and a concrete terrace are good places for drying the bulbs. Turn them every day or two and move them under cover if rain threatens. When dry, separate the bulb clusters, rub off the loose skins, and store the bulbs in a box or paper bag in a dry, cool but frost-proof shed or room.

Sow winter radishes

This is the month to sow large winter radishes. These radishes have a strong flavour and can be cooked like turnips, sliced and fried, or used in salads. They are not harmed by frost. Suitable varieties are 'Long Black Spanish', 'Round Black Spanish', 'Chinese Rose' and 'Mino'. Sow early in the month in the north, later in the south, covering the seeds 1 in. deep in drills 12 in. apart and dusting calomel in the drills to prevent club root disease. Thin the seedlings to 6 in. spacings.

Herbs

Make further sowings of chervil, dill and parsley in open ground.

To retain their flavour and aroma, herbs must be harvested at the right time and in the right condition, whether flower, seed, leaf or stem is being used. Generally the correct time is just before the plant comes into full bloom, and when it is dry.

Harvest for storing

Pick only a small portion at a time. Lay cut herbs in flat containers, and dry immediately to prevent decomposition. Always keep one type of herb separate from another, or the aromas will be

PICKING HERBS

Pick only a small quantity at a time. Take care to keep the different types separate, to prevent their aromas becoming mixed

PREPARING HERBS FOR STORAGE

Rub the dried herbs in your hands, and store them in clean, airtight containers after discarding the stems and other chaff

mixed. Dry the herbs in an airing cupboard, the warming drawer of a cooker or a spare room equipped with an electric heater and a ventilator fan. Use flat cardboard boxes, sheets of brown paper,

STORING HERBS

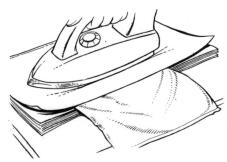

To seal a polythene bag used for storage, place it under a sheet of paper and press hard with the edge of a hot iron

DRYING LAVENDER

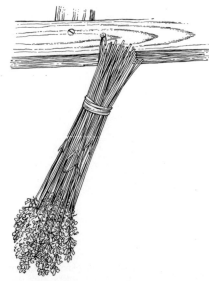

Cut lavender stalks just before the flowers are fully open. Tie in small, loose bundles and hang in a greenhouse or warm shed to dry

hessian, muslin or nylon tacked to wooden frames to make trays on which to spread out the herbs.

Handle the herbs as little as possible

while drying: a daily turning is enough. The aroma should be very faint. Maintain a temperature of 32°C (90°F) for 24 hours, reducing it to 21°C (70°F) until the drying process is complete. Herbs are ready for storing when they are brittle and rattle lightly when touched.

Prepare lavender

The first week of the month is usually the best time to cut lavender for drying and storing. Cut the whole stalk when the flowers are showing colour, but are not fully opened. Tie the stalks in loose bundles and hang them up in a greenhouse or warm shed to dry, or spread them on trays or in shallow boxes in the airing cupboard for a few days. When the flower buds are completely dry, rub them free of stalk and calyx, and put the lavender in small muslin bags.

Patios and town gardens

Continue to water all container-grown plants at least once a day. If daily watering is impossible, top-dress the containers with damp peat. Remove dead flowers daily and discard and replace plants that are past their best.

House plants

Continue watering and feeding at the summer rate (see MAY). Some plants will require more water than others, because of their nature or their position in the home. Provide as much humidity as possible for all plants on hot, sunny days, placing near them an open pan filled with water. Evaporation from the pan will benefit the plants.

Wash off dust

Where doors and windows are open a good deal there may be a considerable

amount of dust in the atmosphere, and the foliage of some of the plants will require frequent cleaning. Standing the plants out in the garden on a mild, rainy day will simultaneously clean the leaves and water the plants.

General tasks

Between now and the autumn carry out constructional or maintenance jobs, especially those involving concreting. Paving or wall building may be carried out over a period of time. Repair and paint greenhouses and frames, and treat wooden surfaces with a proprietary wood preservative.

Tidy up

Once a week, go around the garden and remove all dead heads from flowers, and clear away all vegetables that have finished cropping.

Holiday precautions

Take precautions before going on holiday, so that the garden is not a complete wilderness on your return. Hoe between plants. Make cutting the lawn the last job. Check all ties of plants growing against walls and fences, and reinforce them if necessary. If you have a helpful neighbour who will water your garden while you are away, leave the hosepipe already laid out for him. Tell him to help himself to any flowers, fruit or vegetables he pleases. The more he picks of your sweet peas, french beans and marrows, the more you will get. If these plants are not picked regularly they will stop producing flowers, pods or marrows.

If you have a greenhouse but no friendly neighbour who will water the plants, install a capillary bench, supplied either from the mains or from a large container, such as an old oil drum.

Water plants to enjoy in July

There are three main categories of plants for the water garden: the deep-water plants, such as lilies, for the deepest part of the pool; shallow-water plants or marginals, like the bulrush, which grow in a few inches of water; and the moisture-loving plants, like day lilies and ferns. In addition, there are the floating plants and the oxygenators.

Plants for deep water

NYMPHAEA (WATER LILY)

Suitable, according to variety, for water 1–5 ft. deep. Some varieties may be grown in a few inches of water, while others are more suited for lake planting. Flowers, though lasting four or five days only, are produced from June to September, once the plants are established. Colours range from white to pink, red, yellow or copper. Some varieties are sweetly scented. Propagate water lilies by division in April or May. Thin overcrowded clumps by removing surplus parts of the plants with a sharp knife during the summer.

Tall growers

(for water up to 5 ft. deep): 'Attraction', deep red, tipped with white. 'Charles de Meurville', magnolia-shaped, wine-red flowers up to 10 in. across. 'Colossea', large pale pink with golden stamens; 'Glastoniana', large white flowers, and leaves which may exceed $1\frac{1}{2}$ ft. across. 'Mrs. Richmond', large cup-shaped blooms, deep rose-pink.

Medium growers

(for water depth up to 3 ft.): 'Escarboucle', the most brilliant red water lily. The flowers are large, but few; it needs plenty of root run. 'Hermine', pure white, tulip-shaped flowers. 'James Brydon', large cup-shaped rose-crimson flowers and small maroon leaves. *N. marliacea chromatella*, symmetrical, starry flowers, deep primrose yellow and maroon foliage.

Small growers

(for water up to $1\frac{1}{2}$ ft. deep): 'Candidissima', small heart-shaped leaves and white flowers. 'Ellisiana', bright red flowers, tipped with white, are freely produced. 'Froebelii', lightly scented blooms of deep wine-red. 'Graziella', cup-shaped flowers, opening to pale yellow and changing to red copper. *N. odorata* 'Rose Arey', large strongly scented flowers of deep glowing pink. 'William Falconer', ruby-red flowers, with deep golden stamens.

LILY-LIKE PLANTS

Aponogeton distachyon (water hawthorn)
Suitable for water 1–3 ft. deep. The floating leaves are long and glossy green. Pure white, forked flowers, with waxy petals and black anthers, are sweetly scented, May–October. Propagate by transplanting self-sown seedlings in July–August.

Nymphaeoides peltatum (syn. *Villarsia nymphaeoides*) (water fringe)
Hardy aquatic. Will grow in water from 6 in. to 5 ft. deep. Floating leaves similar to those of the water lily. Bright yellow flowers, fringed at the edges, are produced in clusters at the end of the stems, June–July. Propagate in April or May by re-planting young plants produced on stolons.

Orontium aquaticum (golden club)
Requires deep soil and 6–9 in. of water. Oval pointed leaves have a blue-green metallic sheen. White stems carry narrow, club-like bright yellow flowers, May–June. Propagate by seed or division in June.

OXYGENATING PLANTS

These submerged aquatics are suitable for a water depth of 1–3 ft. and are essential to any pool. They encourage the growth of beneficial microscopic animal life, supplement the oxygen in the water and use up some of the carbon dioxide exhaled by fish. Oxygenating plants grow prolifically during summer and need thinning out in late autumn. Propagate all species by division in April–August.

Anacharis (syn. *Elodea*) **canadensis** (Canadian pond weed)
Vigorous plant with small, dark green leaves.

Ceratophyllum demersum (hornwort)
Fine, bristly, dark green leaves. Having no true roots, it anchors itself in the mud.

Hottonia palustris (water violet)
Whorls of pale lilac flowers on 9–12 in. stems above the water in May. The pale green, ferny foliage is active from October until May.

Lagarosiphon major (syn. *Elodea crispa*) (curled anacharis)
Reflexed deep green leaves are arranged in whorls along branching stems.

Myriophyllum (milfoil)
The most suitable species is *M. spicatum*, with red-green stems and leaves. It is active during most of the year.

Potamogeton crispus (curled pond weed)
The wavy-edged, reddish-green leaves resemble seaweed.

Ranunculus aquatilis

Ranunculus aquatilis (water buttercup, water crowfoot)
Clusters of small, pure white flowers in May above finely divided underwater leaves.

FLOATING PLANTS

Suitable for water 1–3 ft. deep. Some species, such as the common duckweed, are surface floating, while others, like bladderwort, are submerged. Surface-floating plants are useful in the control of algae; they spread rapidly and should not be introduced to a pool from which they cannot be removed.

Azolla caroliniana (fairy moss)
Surface-floating fern, forming mats of light green foliage, often tinged with red. Spreads quickly, but may be killed by frosts.

Eichhornia crassipes (floating water hyacinth)
The lavender flowers, with a conspicuous yellow eye, last for one day only. The curious leaves, whose swollen stems act as floats, are a bright shiny green. The plant is not hardy in Britain, but may be kept in a pool from June until late September. In winter it can be floated in a tank with an inch of soil and a few inches of water, heated to 10°C (50°F).

Hydrocharis morsus-ranae (frogbit)
Small three-petalled white flowers in July and August above round, surface-floating leaves. The plant increases by means of turions (winter buds), which are formed on the stolons in late summer. The buds sink to the bottom of the pool, and appear on the surface the following May.

Stratiotes aloides (water soldier)
The submerged rosettes of hardy, fleshy leaves with tough saw-toothed edges resemble the top of a pineapple. In the second season the plants thrust the upper part of the leaves above the water while small white flowers are produced, June–August. During the winter the plants are dormant on the pool bottom.

Trapa natans (water chestnut)
Annual, surface-floating plant with large, spiny black seeds. These germinate in late spring sending out long shoots to the surface. The rosettes of shiny green foliage which then develop, produce small, white flowers in summer.

Utricularia vulgaris (bladderwort)
Insectivorous plant with finely divided leaves on long trailing stems just below the water surface. Attached to the stems are tiny, insect-trapping sacs or bladders which also assist the plant in floating. Yellow snapdragon flowers are carried on 6 in. stems above the water in July and August.

Plants for shallow water

These plants, which grow at the margin or shallow edge of the pond, are known as marginal aquatics. The majority of species will grow well in 4 in. of soil covered by 3 in. of water. Propagation is by division and re-planting in May. Thinning by removing surplus growth with a sharp knife or secateurs may be done during the summer.

Cyperus vegetus

Acorus (sweet flag)
Decorative foliage plants. *A. calamus variegatus* (height 2–2½ ft.) has green iris-like leaves edged with creamy white. It remains attractive until October frosts.

Butomus umbellatus (flowering rush)
Height 1½–3 ft. Narrow, erect deep green foliage. Umbels of pink, cup-shaped flowers in June. Will grow in water up to 15 in. deep.

Calla palustris (bog arum)
Height 6 in. The creeping stems carry dark green and glossy, heart-shaped leaves. Pure white arum-like flowers in May and June are succeeded in late summer by brilliant red seed heads. Propagate by division of rhizomes.

Caltha (marsh marigold)
Height 9–12 in. *C. palustris* with its golden flowers is often the first plant to bloom in the water garden. *C. p. plena*, is smaller and covered with double deep yellow flowers, April–May. *C. p. alba*, the white marsh marigold, blooms in spring and again in late summer. All calthas grow best in either shallow water or wet soil.

Cyperus
Height 3–4 ft. *C. longus* has deep green, grassy leaves and red-brown flowers in August. *C. vegetus* (height 2 ft.) has pale green, shiny foliage and tufted green heads in July and August.

Eriophorum (cotton grass)
Height 12 in. *E. angustifolium* forms attractive clumps. It carries white, cotton-wool tufts in May and June above dark green, spiky leaves.

Glyceria (manna grass)
Height 1½–3 ft. *G. aquatica variegata* has golden leaves with thin green stripes and graceful, grassy flower heads. Its rampant growth may be controlled by planting in a container, but annual re-planting is necessary.

Iris (water iris)
Height 1½–2 ft. *I. laevigata* and its varieties are suitable for the small pool. The species has mid-blue flowers, but lighter and darker named varieties exist: *I. l. alba* is a white, three-petalled form; 'Snowdrift' has pure white, six-petalled flowers; *I. l. colchesteri* is purple-blue with white edging; *I. l. variegata*, silver and green leaves and pale blue flowers. All flower in June. *I. pseudacorus* (yellow flag). Height 3–5 ft. Small, bright golden yellow flowers are

Typha minima

freely produced in June. *I. p. marginatus* is a variegated form with golden edged leaves.

Mimulus (water musk)
M. luteus (yellow water musk) (height 1 ft.) bears deep golden tubular flowers in June. The double form *M. l.* 'Hose-in-Hose' and the brown-spotted *M. l. guttatus* are more suited to wet soil. *M. ringens* (height 1½ ft.) has pale lavender-blue flowers.

Myosotis (water forget-me-not)
Height 9 in. Sky-blue flowers in June and July. *M. palustris* 'Mermaid' has china-blue flowers with a deep yellow eye.

Pontederia cordata (pickerel)
Height 1½–2 ft. Deep green heart-shaped leaves. Spikes of blue flowers with golden eyes in August and September.

Sagittaria (arrowhead)
S. sagittifolia (height 1½–2 ft.) has thick fleshy, arrow-shaped leaves and white flowers with a central boss of black stamens, July–August. *S. japonica* has pale green, arrow-shaped foliage and larger, pure white flowers with golden stamens. *S. j. plena* is a double form.

Scirpus (true bulrush)
S. albescens (height 4 ft.) has tall cylindrical, sulphur-white stems

Water plants to enjoy in July

Butomus umbellatus

Hottonia palustris

Trapa natans

Utricularia vulgaris

Aponogeton distachyon

Nymphaea 'Escarboucle'

Eichhornia crassipes

Hydrocharis morsus-ranae

Caltha palustris

Nymphaea 'James Brydon'

Pontederia cordata

Sagittaria japonica

Iris kaempferi

with green vertical stripes. *S. zebrinus* (zebra rush), 2 ft. high stems, alternately banded green and white.

Typha (reedmace)
T. latifolia is the bulrush of the country pond. *T. stenophylla* is more suitable for the garden pool. Height 3–4 ft. Brown, cigar-shaped heads in August and September. *T. minima* (height 12–18 in.) has grassy foliage and small rounded heads of dark brown in June and July.

Moisture-loving plants

The soil round an artificial pool is often dry, but can be improved by the addition of large amounts of sphagnum peat. This, after a thorough soaking, will retain water for a considerable period. Propagate the following species of moisture-loving plants by division from October to March.

Lysichitum americanum

Astilbe
Height 1½–4 ft. Clumps of ferny foliage and plumes of small white, pink or red flowers in July.

Hemerocallis (day lily)
Height 1–3 ft. Yellow, pink or red flowers in July and August above luxuriant, weed-smothering foliage. The modern varieties have large blooms with broad petals. Some of

the older sorts, such as the deep butter-yellow 'Hyperion', are still worth growing. 'Pink Charm', 'Pink Damask', 'Tejas', 'Black Magic', 'Golden Orchid' and 'Helios' are all good.

Hosta (plantain lily)
The hostas form large tufts of foliage of ovate outline. The pendent, bell-like flowers, mostly purple-blue, are carried on slender stems in July and August. *H. glauca* (height 2–2½ ft.) has blue-grey, ribbed leaves 12–15 in. long and nearly as broad. *H. lancifolia* has green, smaller leaves. There are also varieties with glaucous, green or variegated foliage.

Iris
Many species and varieties do well in moist conditions. The clematis-flowered iris of Japan, *I. kaempferi* (height 2–2½ ft.), has large, flat flowers of white, pale to deep blue or purple-red. Most are beautifully netted or veined with another colour or shade. *I. siberica* (height 2–3 ft.) has slender, green leaves and an abundance of flowers in June. 'Emperor' is violet; 'Perrys Blue', 'Mountain Lake' and 'Cool Springs' are all sky-blue, while 'Wisley White' is a creamy-white with yellow markings.

Lysichitum
L. americanum is suitable beside the large pool. Large flowers, like butter-yellow arum lilies, appear in April before the foliage. *L. camschatcense* is smaller, with glaucous leaves and pure white flowers.

Peltiphyllum peltatum (umbrella plant)
Height 18 in. Ideal for very wet, heavy soil. Heads of pink flowers are produced in April before the circular, glossy leaves.

Primula (primrose)
Many species, varieties and selected strains are suitable for the water garden. The earliest to flower is *P. rosea* (height 9 in.) with pink flowers in April and early May. Other varieties include the

Primula 'Bartley Strain'

cerise *P. japonica* and its several forms: *P. pulverulenta* (red) and 'Bartley Strain' (pink). The 'candelabra' types are perhaps the most colourful. Other primula colours include white and orange. Propagate by seed sown in March or April.

Moisture-loving ferns

Many fern species are often grown in shade, but the following all require moist soil and atmosphere. March and April are the best planting times. Propagate by division or from spores.

Blechnum spicant

Blechnum spicant (hard fern)
Prostrate rosettes of dark green, shiny fronds up to 12 in. across. Erect spore-bearing fronds are produced in late summer.

Dryopteris
D. dilatata (height 2 ft.) has mid-green fronds, clothed with brown scales when young. Lasts well when cut. *D. thelypteris* (height 12 in.), erect, finely cut fronds of pale green.

Matteuccia struthiopteris (syn. *Struthiopteris germanica*) (shuttlecock fern)
Height 2½–3 ft. Suitable for a heavy wet soil. Pale green fronds rise from a central crown and open gradually like a giant shuttlecock.

Matteuccia struthiopteris

Onoclea sensibilis (sensitive fern)
Height 1½ ft. Grows well in very wet soil or shallow water. Creeping rhizomes send up red stems with fronds of pale powdery green.

Osmunda regalis (royal fern)
Height 2–6 ft. Wide, arching fronds hang gracefully over water. The fronds turn fox-red in autumn.

Scolopendrium (syn. *Phyllitis*) (hart's tongue fern)
One of the best evergreen ferns. *S. vulgare* has glossy, strap-shaped fronds, 18 in. long. There are many forms, including *S. v. crispum* with wavy-edged fronds.

Irises to re-plant in July

The iris family is large and varied, with both rhizomatous and bulbous forms. There are countless hybrids, in addition to over 200 different wild species. Many of the bulbous irises flower in mid-winter and need the minimum of attention. The bulbous group includes the spring- and summer-flowering Dutch, Spanish and English irises, with blooms in shades of blue, white and yellow. They flower between May and July, the Dutch first and the English last.

In addition, some suppliers sell 'specially-prepared' bulbs of Dutch irises for summer flowering.

Bearded irises are the most numerous and popular group. Dwarf bearded irises flower early in the spring for a short period. They are followed by the intermediate bearded irises, which have more flowers on each stem and provide a finer show than the dwarfs. Most spectacular are the tall bearded varieties.

I. danfordiae
A dwarf bulbous iris bearing bright yellow flowers in early February. Suitable for rock gardens. Also grown in pots or bowls under glass for early flowering. Height 6–12 in.

I. histrioides
Dwarf bulbous iris with blue, white or yellow flowers in late January. Suitable for pot culture under glass; plant the bulbs in September and provide gentle warmth during January. Height 12 in.

I. plicata
A group of hybrid bearded irises flowering in May and June. Plant in full sun in well drained soil. Height 24 in.

I. pumila
Blue, pale yellow and white flowers are produced in April and May on this bearded rhizomatous iris. Height 9 in.

I. reticulata
A February-flowering bulbous iris, with violet-blue scented flowers. Plant in September, outdoors or under glass. Height 9 in.

I. sibirica
Beardless rhizomatous iris, best grown near a pool. Blue or white flowers in May and June. Plant in September. Height 3 ft.

I. tingitana
Tender, bulbous iris generally grown in pots or bowls under glass for early flowering. The flowers are lilac blue, deep blue or yellow. Plant in September, giving gentle warmth from January onwards. Height 24 in.

I. unguicularis (syn. **stylosa**)
Rhizomatous iris requiring poor, alkaline, well drained soil in a warm sheltered position. Light lilac flowers in January and February. Plant in September. Height 12 in.

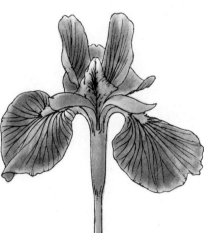

Iris germanica (barbata) 'Olympic Torch'

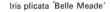
Iris plicata 'Belle Meade'

Iris sibirica 'Mountain Lake'

Hanging baskets and window-boxe

Imaginatively planted with gay summer flowers, hanging baskets will brighten a porch or forecourt for many months of the year. When choosing the plants, remember that the baskets will usually be viewed from below and should include trailing flowers and foliage. As frequent watering is essential, hang the baskets where they can be reached easily with a can. Regular dead-heading will keep the baskets trim and tidy and prolong the flowering period.

1. Trailing nasturtiums and lobelias provide this cascade of colour. Both are adaptable, trouble-free plants, needing little attention

2. Zebrinas, pendulous fuchsias and a begonia make up this varied planting for a hanging basket in a partially shaded position

3. Given a sunny position, petunias produce their showy flowers throughout the summer. There are many single and double varieties

4. Ivy-leaved pelargoniums and *Lysimachia nummularia* (creeping jenny), both trailing plants, combine with upright-growing coleus

for colour in July

Some of these boxes illustrate displays at particular seasons. In others, the aspect is the determining factor, because plants in window-boxes are inevitably more subject to extremes of heat, or lack of light. As a general rule, avoid obvious contrasts, choosing instead plants that provide a harmonious effect. Where colours tend to be garish, grey foliage provides a useful foil. The overall appearance can also be enhanced by trailing plants.

Spring. Trailing *Lysimachia nummularia* (creeping jenny); a camellia; gay *kaufmanniana* tulips and *Vinca minor* (periwinkle)

Summer. *Lysimachia nummularia* (creeping jenny); a potentilla; petunias and ageratums; *Vinca minor* (periwinkle)

Autumn–winter. Hardy, winter-flowering heather; trailing, evergreen ivy; a pot-grown *Solanum capsicastrum* (winter cherry)

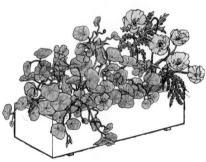

North. Trailing nasturtiums and taller Iceland poppies, both producing plenty of colour even where there is little sunshine

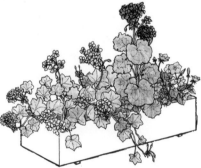

South. The attractive flowers and foliage of ivy-leaved and zonal pelargoniums blend well with *Campanula carpatica*

East. Bright calceolarias grouped with taller, formal marguerites and the vivid colours of free-flowering begonias

West. Achimenes, which flower for weeks on end, planted with a sweetly scented heliotrope and colourful fuchsias

For a windy corner. Hydrangeas, alyssums and marigolds are hardy and will stand up to wind better than most plants

Containers and tubs for town gardens

Almost any plant, from an alpine to a shrub, can be grown in a tub or trough. Soil can be chosen to suit the needs of particular plants, so that lime-hating rhododendrons, for example, can be grown in areas where the soil is chalky. Good drainage is essential, otherwise the soil will become waterlogged during wet weather. If the container has no

A shallow bowl planted with daffodils, scented hyacinths and bright crocuses. Such containers are generally made from asbestos

Sweet williams make a good foil to low-growing pansies, which provide a bright display from spring until late summer

Stately hemerocallis (day lilies) and the arching stems of chlorophytum are well suited to the lines of this pottery jar

Hydrangeas need frequent watering in warm weather. The rate of drying out can be reduced by mulching with damp peat

Graceful agapanthuses, with dainty nemophilas at their feet—an example of contrasting forms providing a harmonious effect

drainage holes, fill the lower third with such materials as broken crocks, shingle or charcoal. Water sparingly, unless the weather is hot and dry. During prolonged dry spells, containers of all types need frequent watering, though mulching with damp peat will reduce the rate of evaporation. If possible, move containers to a position in shade before you go on holiday, making sure that the compost and peat are thoroughly moist. Trees grown in containers must either be dwarf forms, or else transferred to open soil when they grow too large.

A bay tree, bought trained to shape, towers above tall and dwarf tulips. Leaves picked from the bay tree can be used for seasoning

In this ornamental vase the grassy foliage of a dracaena overhangs pelargoniums. A small-leaved ivy trails down the sculptured stem

August

The gardener can go on holiday with no worries, provided he has mown the lawn,
watered thoroughly, and asked a friend to pick the fruit and vegetables

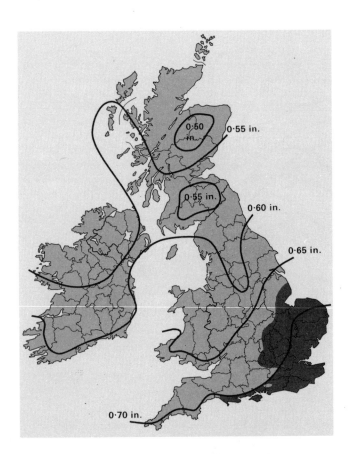

WATER NEEDED BY A GARDEN IN AUGUST

The map shows the total water used by a garden (an amount known as
the potential transpiration) in inches per average week in August. In
some areas rainfall does not equal potential transpiration, and watering
is necessary; the shaded areas are those where this is likely to occur.
Local conditions of aspect must be taken into account: during sunny
weather an unshaded garden on a southward-facing slope will need
more water than a garden which is shaded or has a different aspect.
The amount of water required can be calculated from rainfall measurements and potential transpiration. (See GLOSSARY, *Weather*)

The weather in August

Weather in August is often the same as in July: if July is wet,
August is likely to be wet as well. As in July, westerly winds
arriving with a depression often bring long periods of dull
weather with much rain. This rain is heaviest in the north and
west, especially in hilly areas, and south-east England often
escapes the worst of these wet spells.

Warm spells of anticyclone weather in August tend to be
very warm indeed, with temperatures over 27°C (80°F). They
often end in severe thunderstorms.

Nights are lengthening noticeably in August, and night
temperatures are lower. Dewfall can be heavy, thus complicat-
ing plant disease problems. However, if the wind swings round
to the north or north-east, dry, cool, clear nights may occur,
and over wide areas of the north temperatures approaching
freezing point may occur in sheltered valleys and hollows. In
Scotland, August is really an autumn month. Wind speeds
begin to increase at this time of year; towards the end of the
month gales are not unknown and bring a foretaste of autumn
even to the south.

As in Scotland, August in the north of Ireland is an autumn
month. Gardeners there and in northern England will need to
start the September programme in August (see map, *Progress
of the season*, p. 201).

Hedges should be cut in August, so that any subsequent
growth can harden enough to resist the winter cold. All gaps
in hedges and fences should be repaired, so that the garden is
protected against the autumn gales.

A summary of the month's work

LAWNS

New lawns. Apply fertiliser dressings to sites for new lawns.
A week after this sow grass seed.
Established lawns. Inspect, and decide which areas need
renovation. Continue applying weedkillers and fungicides.

ROSES

Remove blooms as they fade. Cease applying fertilisers. Continue
spraying. Place orders for new roses for November delivery.

HARDY HERBACEOUS PLANTS
Continue dead-heading. Remove supports from plants which have finished flowering and cut off tall, weak stems. Dig over old beds needing a complete overhaul. Plan arrangement of flowers to be planted in the autumn before ordering them from a nursery.

DAHLIAS
Continue to spray against pests. Inspect plants for symptoms of virus infection, and mark for later destruction. Feed with liquid fertiliser, and keep plants tied to their stakes as they grow.

CHRYSANTHEMUMS
Disbud where large blooms are wanted, leaving one bud per stem. Complete disbudding of outdoor-flowering varieties. Water once a week in dry weather. Apply fertiliser to fatten buds. Keep plants well supported. Prevent earwigs entering flowers by smearing Vaseline round stems. Water pot-grown plants and give balanced fertiliser every 10–14 days. Disbud large exhibition and October-flowering varieties.
Under glass. Water late-flowering varieties in greenhouse borders as necessary and reduce to three shoots per plant.

GLADIOLI
Cut gladioli for indoor decoration, but leave at least four leaves on each plant. Control gladiolus thrips as necessary.

IRISES
Complete planting or re-planting of bearded irises. Order bulbous irises for autumn planting. Examine iris bulbs which have been lifted and burn any which show signs of rotting. Spray or dust irises with trichlorphon or derris if caterpillars are present.

LILIES
Plant *L. candidum*. Order lilies for autumn delivery. Spray with Bordeaux mixture against botrytis and with systemic insecticide against aphids. Gather bulbils from *L. tigrinum* and *L. sargentiae*. Sow home-saved seed as soon as ripe.
Under glass. Control aphids with a systemic insecticide. Keep pots adequately watered.

CARNATIONS AND PINKS
Take action against pests and diseases. Continue to layer border carnations, and sever rooted layers. Remove dead flower stems. Order border carnations and pinks for autumn planting and prepare beds for them. Dig and manure the site. Dress with lime if below pH 6·5. Put dry soil under cover for use in autumn plantings.
Under glass. Renew shading on glass and damp down during hot weather. Watch for pests and diseases. Continue feeding. Cut blooms and disbud flower stems. Continue taking cuttings of pinks and harden-off rooted cuttings.

SWEET PEAS
Mulch, feed and water if necessary. Hoe regularly if no mulch has been applied. Cut blooms regularly, to prevent formation of seed.

Spray monthly with a systemic insecticide against sap-sucking insects, such as aphids.

FLOWERS FROM SEED
Plant out well grown perennial seedlings in nursery beds. Spray monthly with a systemic insecticide. Remove dead flower heads.

BULBS
Complete any outstanding bulb lifting. Plant daffodils. Complete orders for spring-flowering bulbs to be planted this autumn in bowls, for bedding or cutting.

ALPINES
Take cuttings of alpines, such as helianthemum and dianthus, which have outgrown their vigour, and insert in prepared soil in a frame or under a cloche. Spray cuttings daily in hot weather, shade from hot sun, and exclude draughts.

WATER PLANTS AND POOLS
Continue to spray against aphids and other pests. In sultry weather, keep the water oxygenated by adding fresh water from a hose and spray. Cut off large water lily leaves if they hide the flowers. Thin heavy growth of oxygenating plants and weed the bog garden.

GREENHOUSES AND FRAMES
Repair and paint the greenhouse in readiness for winter, and overhaul the heating system. Store hippeastrums which have now dried off. Take cuttings of regal pelargoniums. Remove growing points of tomatoes if the plants are to be followed by chrysanthemums; discontinue feeding and reduce watering. Sow cyclamen seeds. Insert cuttings of fuchsias to be grown as standards. Root zonal pelargonium cuttings. Raise *Campanula isophylla* plants from cuttings.

TREES AND SHRUBS
Continue taking cuttings of such plants as callicarpa, cistus and escallonia.
Under glass. Insert softwood cuttings of choisya and *Polygonum baldschuanicum* in pots of sandy soil in a cold frame. Put half-ripe cuttings of garrya and wisteria in pots of sandy loam in a propagating frame at 13–16°C (55–61°F), transferring to a cold frame when rooted. Take stem cuttings of *Hydrangea macrophylla*, using a shaded, closed frame and giving ventilation as they root.
Pruning. Prune shrubs that have finished flowering. Cut back established wisterias, taking out the tips of young shoots when they have made three or four leaves.

RHODODENDRONS AND AZALEAS
Propagate rhododendrons by layering. Layers will root sufficiently for planting out separately in two to three years.

HEDGES
Continue to trim fast-growing hedges. Continue hoeing and weeding hedge bottoms.

HEATHERS

Take cuttings if more plants are wanted for the heather garden.

FRUIT

Pick early apples and pears while under-ripe. Summer prune restricted forms of apples and pears. Pick loganberries, cut out fruited shoots, and tie in new shoots. Spray black currants and cherries. Prune fruited shoots of wall-trained peaches. Support heavily laden plum branches and complete pruning. Protect September-fruiting raspberries against birds and wasps. Plant rooted strawberry runners. Protect ripening grapes with glass.

VEGETABLES

Sow seeds of spring cabbages. Sow lettuces for early winter use. In the north, sow lettuces for over-wintering without cloche protection, and Brussels sprouts. Sow Japanese onions.
Less common vegetables. Pick sweet corn cobs.

HERBS

Take cuttings of bay, hyssop, lavender, mint, rosemary, rue and sage, and insert in sandy soil in open ground, or in pots in a cold frame. Divide chives every fourth year. Collect and dry dill and fennel seeds. Store dried herbs before they have had time to re-absorb moisture.

PATIOS AND TOWN GARDENS

Water containers daily, remove dead flowers, and replace plants past their best. Before going on holiday, move containers to a shady spot. Order bulbs for autumn planting.

HOUSE PLANTS

Continue watering and feeding at the summer rate. If you go on holiday make arrangements for the plants to be cared for by a local nurseryman or a neighbour. Otherwise water them thoroughly and slip them into a polythene bag; fix up a capillary watering device; or plunge the pots inside larger containers, filling the space between with moist peat.

GENERAL TASKS

Take and root cuttings of shrubs, heathers, hydrangeas, geraniums and fuchsias. Check all labels and renew as necessary. Continue to spray against pests and diseases.

Plants to enjoy in August

Border and rock garden plants in flower	Lavatera	Olearia	Impatiens
Agapanthus	Lilium auratum	Passiflora	Saintpaulia
Ageratum	Linum		Solanum capsicastrum
Alstroemeria	Lobelia	**Water garden plants in flower**	
Alyssum	Matthiola (stock)	Hosta	**Fruit in season**
Anthemis	Mesembryanthemum	Hydrocharis (frogbit)	Apple
Antirrhinum	Mimulus	Ligularia	Blackberry
Aster	Montbretia	Nymphaea (water lily)	Cherry
Begonia	Nemesia	Pontederia (pickerel weed)	Currant, black
Calendula (pot marigold)	Nicotiana (tobacco plant)	Sagittaria japonica	Currant, red
Centaurea (cornflower)	Nigella	Utricularia (bladderwort)	Currant, white
Chrysanthemum	Papaver (poppy)		Gooseberry
Clarkia	Petunia	**Greenhouse plants in flower**	Loganberry
Convolvulus	Phlox	Abutilon	Pear
Cosmos	Rose (floribunda and hybrid tea)	Acidanthera	Plum
Cyclamen neapolitanum	Rudbeckia	Achimenes	Raspberry
Dahlia	Salvia	Begonia	
Delphinium ajacis (larkspur)	Scabiosa	Campanula isophylla	**Vegetables in season**
Dimorphotheca	Sedum	(star of Bethlehem)	Artichoke, globe
Echium	Sidalcea	Campanula pyramidalis	Beans, dwarf french
Erigeron	Solidago	Canna	Beans, runner
Eschscholzia	Tagetes (French and	Celosia	Beet, seakale
Eucomis comosa	African marigolds)	Fuchsia	Celery
Gaillardia	Thyme	Gloxinia	Cucumber
Godetia	Tropaeolum (nasturtium)	Heliotropium	Lettuce
Gypsophila	Verbascum	Pelargonium domesticum	Marrow
Helenium	Verbena	Streptocarpus	Onion
Helianthus (sunflower)		Tibouchina	Peas
Helichrysum	**Trees and shrubs in flower**		Radish
Iberis	Fuchsia	**House plants in flower, depending**	Shallot
Ipomoea (morning glory)	Hibiscus	**on position and culture**	Spinach beet
	Hydrangea	Anthurium	Sweet corn
	Hypericum	Begonia semperflorens	

Lawns

NEW LAWNS

Major sub-surface drainage operations will have been carried out during the previous autumn and winter. Now apply top dressings appropriate to the soil: peat and organic dressings on light soils (at 3–4 lb. per sq. yd.), gypsum (1 lb. per sq. yd.) and coarse sharp sand (3–4 lb. per sq. yd.) on heavy soils.

Top-dress and fertilise

Incorporate the top dressings thoroughly and evenly into the top few inches of soil, and finish by raking to leave a level surface. Apply pre-seeding fertiliser (see MARCH) and rake again in several directions to produce a fine, even, moist tilth in which to sow the seed a week after the fertiliser application. If the seed bed has become fluffy during preparation in the summer months, roll lightly or tread the area. Only carry out rolling and seeding in dry, fine weather.

ESTABLISHED LAWNS

Inspect the lawn and make preparations for renovation of worn areas (see MARCH and APRIL).

Continue to apply fungicides for disease control, and apply selective weed-killers during good growing weather.

Roses

Remove blooms as they fade. Blooms required for home decoration should be cut as short as possible (see JULY).

Do not apply rose fertilisers after the end of July, as they would encourage late, soft growth that would not mature before winter.

Spray against greenfly

If greenfly appear, spray with a systemic rose insecticide (see MAY).

Spray fortnightly with the appropriate fungicide against mildew, black spot and rust (see JUNE). Pick up and burn infected fallen leaves.

Place orders now for new roses to obtain delivery early in November.

Hardy herbaceous plants

Continue dead-heading (see JUNE and JULY). Consider whether the plant will look less unsightly if left alone, because plants flowering after July are unlikely to flower a second time if cut back. Most kinds will show new growth at ground level even while still in flower, and these do not need cutting back. Anthemis, gaillardia and a few more kinds, however, are weakened by their profusion of flowers and make little or no new basal growth as flowering comes to an end, so cut them hard back after flowering. Remove supports from plants which have finished flowering, and cut off tall weak stems.

Overhaul old beds

Dig over an old bed that needs a complete overhaul because of weeds or because the plants have grown too large, using the same method as for a new bed (see JULY). This may mean sacrificing the remaining flowers, but it will enable sun and wind to kill all unwanted growth.

Plan for autumn

Before ordering plants for autumn planting from your nurseryman, consult the plant descriptions (see OCTOBER), and plan the arrangement of the flowers in accordance with their height, spread and time of flowering. A number of borders are illustrated in the OCTOBER colour section. Order as early as possible, because a nurseryman usually executes orders in rotation. If he cannot guarantee delivery by the end of October, ask for a spring delivery instead.

First estimate the area of the bed in square yards, and allow an average of five plants per sq. yd., remembering to allow more space between robust-growing kinds than between slow-growing ones. Planting distances are given in the plant descriptions, OCTOBER. Plant a little closer if groups of three or more of a kind are used, to allow 25 per cent more space around the group than between the individual plants in it. To avoid trouble, keep groups with a similar growth-spread next to one another. This is important, since some kinds grow five times as quickly as others.

Choose plants

Alternatively, decide first how many kinds the bed or border is to contain, based on an average of five plants per sq. yd., and then allot each kind a space in keeping with the planting distances.

Limit the height of selected plants to half the width of the bed or border, not including, in the case of the backed border, the 3 ft. left between the backing and the border (see JULY). In a one-sided border, grade down the height of plants from the back to the front, and in an island bed from the centre to the outside. To avoid flatness or too much regularity, intersperse plants like heleniums, which have a flat-topped appearance when in full growth and flower, with those that produce spikes, like sidalceas. Here and there, near the front, place plants of statuesque appearance, such as hostas and kniphofias, so that their ornamental foliage and flowers can be fully appreciated.

Continuous flower display

Time of flowering is also important to ensure continuity of display. As far as possible, plant kinds with different flowering periods in adjoining groups, to avoid having areas bare of colour both before and after flowering. The flowering period for herbaceous perennials extends from April to November, so it is possible to select plants to flower for any given period—for spring, early, mid or late summer, or autumn.

Make a scale plan

When a selection of plants has been made, draw a plan of the border or bed to scale on graph paper. Remember to make allowances for those plants which are best planted in the spring (see MARCH and APRIL).

Dahlias

Continue to spray against pests (see JUNE).

Inspect the plants for mottling or discoloration of the foliage. This may indicate the presence of virus disease, especially if the plant's growth is stunted. Mark any suspected plants, so that they can be destroyed in the autumn and not kept for producing cuttings the next year. Such cuttings would themselves be affected by disease.

Feed with liquid fertiliser, and keep the plants carefully tied to avoid wind damage.

Chrysanthemums

Buds will form very rapidly during this month on outdoor-flowering varieties. If large blooms are required, disbud the plants to one flower per stem.

Disbudding is sometimes called securing the bud or taking the bud. It entails removing the side shoots which appear where each leaf joins the stem; they appear at the same time as a bud forms at the tip of the stem.

Allow the shoots to grow about $\frac{3}{4}$ in. long before removing them, otherwise the main stem will be damaged, causing malformation of the flower when it opens. Remove the unwanted shoots with a sharp, sideways pull. Do not pinch them out with your finger-nails or break them off with a downward pull.

Complete the disbudding of outdoor-flowering varieties by August 21, to ensure blooming before autumn is too far advanced.

In dry weather water these plants once a week. When the buds have been secured, apply fertiliser (see JULY) to help fatten them. Do not apply fertiliser after the buds show colour.

Support and disbud

Keep the plants well supported, to allow for the increasing weight of the flowering stems. Many varieties will be in flower before the end of the month. Prevent earwigs from eating the opening florets by smearing a $\frac{1}{2}$ in. ring of Vaseline around the stem below the flower.

Water the pot-grown plants and feed with a balanced fertiliser (see JULY) every 10–14 days to keep the growth steady and even.

Disbud the large exhibition and October-flowering varieties towards the end of the month. It is important to delay this until after August 15, and varieties which form their buds earlier than this must be run on. This means removing the buds at the tips of the stems and allowing the best side shoots to grow on in their place. This delays flowering by about 14 days and prevents the flowers from opening with hard, green centres.

UNDER GLASS

Keep late-flowering plants in the greenhouse border supplied with water. They will make rapid growth and must be reduced to three shoots (see JULY) by the end of the month.

Gladioli

Cut gladioli for indoor decoration when the first flower on the spike is just opening. With exhibition plants, timing depends on variety.

CUTTING GLADIOLI

Cut into the stem with a sharp knife above the fourth or fifth leaf, jerking the stem gently each way and twisting until it snaps

Leave at least four or five leaves when cutting a flower spike, otherwise the new corm will be deprived of its source of nourishment. To cut a flower spike without damaging the plant, insert a sharp knife low down in the stem, give the spike a gentle jerk each way and twist. The stem will snap and can then be withdrawn from its sheath of leaves.

Be alert for signs of gladiolus thrips (see JULY) and spray if necessary.

Irises

Complete the planting or re-planting of bearded irises by the end of the month (see JULY).

Order bulbous irises now for autumn planting.

Examine iris bulbs which have been lifted and are awaiting re-planting in September. Burn any which have inky-black blotches on them. This is caused by a rot fungus for which there is no cure. Also burn any iris bulbs which are soft and look as if the basal plate is rotting—a trouble known as green mould or bulb rot.

Spray or dust with trichlorphon or derris if caterpillars are seen.

Lilies

Plant *L. candidum* (madonna lily) as soon as possible, with not more than 2 in. of soil above each bulb.

Order lilies for autumn delivery as soon as possible, bearing in mind the nature of your garden soil when choosing varieties. It is a mistake to attempt oriental and other lime-hating lilies (see colour section, MAY) in an alkaline soil, though they can be grown in pots, tubs and deep boxes in John Innes potting compost No. 1.

In damp, warm weather spray with Bordeaux mixture against botrytis. Spray with a systemic insecticide to control aphids.

Plant lily bulbils

Tiger lilies, *L. sargentiae* and some hybrids produce bulbils between the leaves and the stem. Gather the bulbils when they fall at a touch and plant them about 2 in. apart in a deep seed box. Either cover the small bulbs with ½ in. of soil or just press them into the surface with your fingertips.

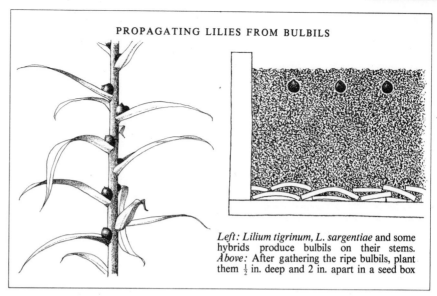

PROPAGATING LILIES FROM BULBILS

Left: Lilium tigrinum, L. sargentiae and some hybrids produce bulbils on their stems. *Above:* After gathering the ripe bulbils, plant them ½ in. deep and 2 in. apart in a seed box

Sow home-saved seed as soon as it is ripe. At this stage the capsule will have swollen to about the size of a walnut, will be fawn-coloured and beginning to crack slightly at the top. Save one or two pods of *L. pumilum* and *L. regale* for sowing soon. They will flower two or three years after germinating.

UNDER GLASS

Continue to control aphids with a systemic spray and keep the pots watered.

Carnations and pinks

Order border carnations and pinks for autumn planting (see colour section, MAY) and prepare the beds. Choose a sunny, open site, raising the bed about 6 in. above the level of the surrounding soil if the drainage is suspect. To test the drainage, dig a hole 18 in. deep during the winter. If water remains in it for

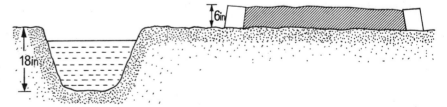

CARNATIONS AND PINKS ON WET SOIL

Where drainage tends to be poor, plant pinks and border carnations in a raised bed, supporting the sides with bricks, stones or concrete. To make a positive test for drainage, dig a hole 18 in. deep during the winter. Raised beds or improved drainage are necessary if the water remains for long periods less than about 12 in. from the surface

long periods closer than 12 in. to the surface, improved drainage or raising the bed are necessary.

Test the soil

Dig the site one spit deep and bury farmyard manure or compost below the top spit. Make a soil test with a proprietary testing kit and apply lime if it is below pH 6·5. Hoe bone-meal, at 4 oz. per sq. yd., into the top 4 in., but if lime has been applied wait a month before doing so.

Wait until the spring before applying a potash fertiliser; autumn application makes the stems brittle. However, it is safe to apply 2 oz. sulphate of potash, or 8 oz. bonfire ash, per sq. yd., to beds prepared in winter for spring planting.

Continue layering

Continue to layer border carnations if this was not done last month. Test layers put down six weeks ago by easing the layering pin and pulling very gently on the stem of the layer. If you can feel that it has rooted, push the layering pin back again and cut through the stem joining the layer to the old plant, leaving about $\frac{1}{2}$ in. of stem attached to the layer. Leave the severed layer three or four weeks before transplanting.

Watch for pests and diseases, taking action as necessary (see MARCH).

Put some dry soil under cover for use when planting border carnations and pinks in the autumn.

UNDER GLASS

Renew shading if necessary and damp down during hot weather.

Watch for pests and diseases (see MARCH). Continue feeding (see APRIL).

Cut blooms and disbud flower stems (see SEPTEMBER).

Continue to take cuttings of pinks and to harden-off rooted cuttings (see JUNE).

Sweet peas

Mulching (see MAY) and, if necessary, feeding and watering (see JUNE and JULY), encourage flowering over a long period. Hoe regularly if you have not applied a mulch.

Cut the blooms regularly, whichever system of growing you have adopted. Never allow blooms to fade and droop on the plants, or to form seed pods, otherwise the flowering period will be reduced drastically.

Spray monthly with a systemic insecticide to control sap-sucking aphids.

Flowers from seed

Plant out well grown perennial seedlings into nursery beds and water them in, following the same procedure as for biennials (see JUNE). They will be ready for planting out in their final positions in the herbaceous border during the autumn or next spring.

Spray monthly with a systemic insecticide to control aphids.

Remove dead flower heads regularly (see JULY).

If the summer is damp, hoe regularly to keep weeds under control.

Bulbs

If bulb lifting was not completed last month, finish the job as soon as possible (see JUNE).

Plant daffodils

Plant daffodils by the end of the month, except where they are to be used for spring displays in beds which cannot be cleared of summer bedding until next month or later. Daffodils recommence their root growth in late summer, and these roots should grow into soil from which they can draw moisture and plant food. Plant all but the smallest bulb 6 in. deep.

Order bulbs for spring

Complete your orders for spring-flowering bulbs which are to be planted this autumn. For growing in bowls or pots for winter flowering indoors, choose hyacinths, small irises, dwarf early tulips, crocuses, chionodoxas, scillas snowdrops and miniature daffodils. For spring bedding or for cutting, order tulips, hyacinths and daffodils. Bulbs suitable for planting in borders and rock gardens are alliums, hardy cyclamens, eranthis, erythroniums, galtonias, ixias, leucojums, muscaris, ornithogalums and tritonias.

Alpines

UNDER GLASS

Take cuttings of rock plants that become unthrifty with age. Examples are helianthemums, dianthuses, achilleas, mossy saxifrages and most of the sub-shrubby kinds. All these have flowered by now.

A shaded frame or even cloches will provide sufficient protection, a greenhouse being unsuitable unless you have a mist propagation outfit. Dig the ground, reducing it to a fine tilth. Lighten heavy soil by adding sand. If necessary, water dry clods until they soften. Spread $\frac{1}{2}$–1 in. of sharp sand on the surface and give a light watering.

Types of cuttings

The descriptions of alpine plants (see NOVEMBER) refer to four main types of cuttings:

1. Tip cuttings. These are the top sections of non-flowering shoots cut off cleanly just below a leaf joint (node) Lengths vary from $1\frac{1}{2}$–3 in., depending on the habit of the plant. Trim leaves from the lower half, cutting upwards

ALPINE CUTTINGS

The four types of cuttings used for propagating alpines. (a) Tip cutting. (b) Heel cutting. (c) Basal cutting. (d) Root cutting

INSERTING CUTTINGS

Insert the lower halves of tip, heel and basal cuttings in holes made with a dibber, firming them in gently with your fingers

COVERING CUTTINGS

Unless cuttings are grown in a frame, protect them with a cloche, closing the ends and covering with sacking or other shading material

4. Root cuttings. Pieces of fleshy root, cut while the plant is dormant (see FEBRUARY). Prepare by cutting the root into sections about 2 in. long.

Planting cuttings

Insert the lower halves of tip cuttings, heel cuttings and basal cuttings into holes made with a dibber or pencil, firming them in with your forefinger and thumb. Level the surface of the bed and water thoroughly.

Spray the cuttings daily during hot weather, keep them shaded, and exclude draughts. Gradually increase the ventilation and remove the glass altogether when the cuttings have rooted and are beginning to grow.

Water plants and pools

Continue to spray against aphids and other pests (see JUNE).

In sultry weather keep the water well oxygenated by occasionally adding fresh water from a hose and spray.

Cut off large water lily leaves if they are hiding the flowers. Otherwise allow them to decay naturally on the base of the pool during the summer months.

Thin heavy growths of oxygenating plants from time to time, always taking care not to remove young fish while doing so.

Remove weeds regularly from the bog garden.

Greenhouses and frames

This is a good month to repair and paint the greenhouse in readiness for the winter. Broken panes and drips from the roof, which are only minor irritations during the summer, can become a serious menace to plant health

towards the stem tip, to avoid damage to the stem.

2. Heel cuttings. Obtained by pulling off short growths from a larger branch. Pulled gently downwards, they will come away with a little tailpiece (heel). Pare away any ragged wood and

trim the leaves from the lower half of the shoot, cutting upwards towards the tip of the stem.

3. Basal cuttings. Obtained by severing shoots at, or just below, ground level. These need little trimming and may already show traces of new roots.

187

during the autumn and winter. Paint wooden greenhouses before heavy autumn dews soak into the timber. Mastic tapes are excellent for placing over glazing bars to cure stubborn leaks. Carry out repairs or modifications to heating systems before heating is required in October.

Hippeastrums should now have completed their growth, and the foliage will have died down. Store the bulbs just as they are in their pots, under the staging of a cool greenhouse, until required again in early spring.

Continue to take cuttings of regal pelargoniums (see JULY).

Speed tomato development

Where tomatoes are to be followed by chrysanthemums, remove the growing point of each tomato plant by the middle of the month to encourage rapid development of the fruits on the top

REMOVING GROWING POINTS
FROM TOMATOES

Where tomatoes are to be followed by chrysanthemums in the greenhouse, pinch out their growing points to speed development of the top trusses. This will allow earlier picking

trusses. At the end of the month discontinue feeding and reduce watering. This helps to prevent splitting of the fruits. If the nights turn chilly, close the ventilators early in the evening.

Sow cyclamen seeds at a temperature of 16°C (61°F) for flowering the winter after next. Use John Innes seed compost, spacing the seeds $\frac{1}{2}$ in. apart and covering them $\frac{1}{4}$ in. deep. When the first leaves have expanded, prick out the seedlings, 2 in. apart in both directions, into boxes containing John Innes potting compost No. 1.

Fuchsia cuttings

During the second half of the month insert fuchsia cuttings if young plants are required for growing on as standards next summer. Choose sturdy young shoots about 3 in. long, cut them through immediately below a leaf joint, and insert them round the edge of a 3 in. pot in a mixture of equal parts peat and sand. They will root in three or four weeks on the greenhouse staging, or considerably quicker if placed in a propagating frame. When rooted, pot the cuttings individually into 3 in. pots of John Innes potting compost No. 1 and grow them on in a temperature of 7°C (45°F) during the winter.

Pelargonium cuttings

Zonal pelargonium cuttings can also be rooted during August. Choose firm, medium-sized growths, with 3 in. of stem, from healthy plants. The careful selection of parent plants helps to maintain the health and vigour of the stock. Potting and subsequent care is the same as for fuchsias, described above.

Fresh stocks of *Campanula isophylla* can be raised from cuttings this month. Insert three or four cuttings, each 3 in. long, round the edge of a 2 in. pot containing John Innes seed compost, standing the pot on the greenhouse staging.

As soon as the cuttings have rooted, repot without separating the individual plants into a 3 in. pot of John Innes potting compost No. 2.

Trees and shrubs

Continue to take cuttings of callicarpa cistus, escallonia, euonymus, hypericum *Jasminum officinale,* lonicera, pyracantha, *Cotinus coggygria,* spiraea, viburnum

PROPAGATION
Under glass

Take cuttings, 4–6 in. long, of half-ripe wood from current year's growths of the following shrubs: *Buddleia davidii Caryopteris clandonensis,* fuchsia, hebe hedera, ilex, *Laurus nobilis* (bay) lavender, *Olearia haastii,* pernettya pieris, rosemary, senecio, *Skimmia japonica* and syringa. Insert the cutting either singly in pots or directly into sandy soil in an open but shaded cold frame. Keep the roots moist but do not over-water, and close the frame during cold or windy weather. Leave the cuttings in the cold frame for the winter. Plant the rooted cuttings out in their permanent flowering positions in late spring of the following year.

Insert 3–4 in. cuttings of half-ripe wood, taken with a heel, of ceanothus cytisus, genista and solanum. Treat these cuttings as described above until the following spring, when they should be potted and left to grow on in the cold frame. Plant out in late May or June the following year.

Place 3 in. long softwood cuttings of *Choisya ternata* and *Polygonum baldschuanicum* (Russian vine) singly in well drained pots of sandy soil and leave in a cold propagating frame for the winter. Transplant the cuttings to their permanent positions in the spring.

Take cuttings of half-ripe wood of garrya (3 in. long) and wisteria (4–6 in. long). Insert the cuttings in pots of sandy loam and place in a propagating frame. Maintain a temperature of 13–16°C (55–61°F) until the cuttings are well rooted. Pot the cuttings singly in 3 in. pots and grow on in a cold frame for a year or more before transplanting into their final positions.

Insert 3–4 in. cuttings, taken from the points of firm shoots of *Hydrangea macrophylla*, singly into 2½ in. pots of sandy loam. Place the cuttings in a shaded, closed frame and spray them daily with tepid water. Once the cuttings are rooted, give them ventilation. Pot the cuttings early the following spring and transplant in June.

PRUNING

Continue to prune shrubs that have finished flowering by shortening the flowering shoots and thinning out old and weak wood. Shrubs needing this attention include evergreen ceanothus, escallonia, lavender, deciduous species of lonicera, and senecio.

Well established, vigorous wisteria may need cutting back. Take out the tips of young shoots after they have made three or four leaves.

Rhododendrons and azaleas

Propagate rhododendrons this month by layering. Choose a healthy looking plant shoot and cut it half through, or twist it sharply upwards, about 1 ft. below the growing point. Pin the cut portion firmly into the soil with a layering pin 6 in. long made of galvanised wire. After two or three years the layered shoot will have made enough root growth to be severed from the parent plant and planted in its final position; make the cut close to the new plant.

FOUR STAGES IN LAYERING A RHODODENDRON

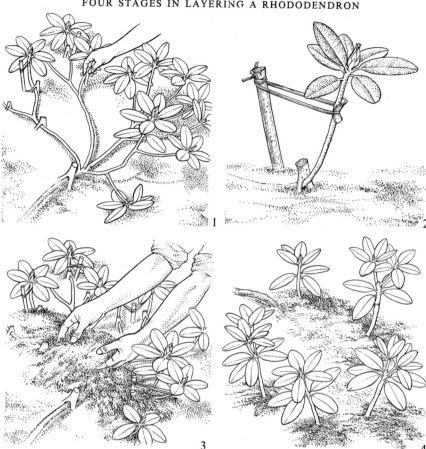

(1) Select a low-growing branch and cut each shoot to be layered half through. Secure the cut portions into the soil with wires or wooden pegs
(2) Secure the tips of the layered shoots in an upright position to further pegs

(3) To encourage rooting, and preserve moisture, cover all but the upright tips with peat
(4) The shoots will be growing strongly on their own roots after two or three years. They are then ready for severing from the parent plant and for planting out

Hedges

Continue to trim fast-growing hedges such as privet and lonicera (see MAY).

Continue to hoe or weed hedge bottoms (see MARCH).

Heathers

If you require extra heather plants, take cuttings this month when short side growths are available with new growth at their tips (see MARCH).

Fruit

Early top-fruit varieties are beginning to ripen now, and soft fruits are ending.

Prepare ladders for picking, and check that they are safe.

Apple and pear

Watch early-maturing varieties carefully and pick them while slightly underripe, because they retain their best flavour for only a short period. Test fruit for near-ripeness by lifting and twisting gently; when it is ready it parts easily from the spur. Protect ripening fruit against birds and wasps.

Continue to summer prune restricted trees (see JULY).

Blackberry, loganberry, and hybrid berries

Pick loganberries when perfectly ripe and dark crimson. Continue to train new shoots (see MAY). When harvesting has finished, cut out shoots that have fruited. On windy sites, keep new growths bundled up for protection during the winter.

PRUNING A PEACH

When picking is finished, prune the shoots that bore the fruit, leaving intact the new growths selected as replacement shoots

Black currant

Keep the leaves on the bushes healthy so that they continue to feed the present season's shoots as long as possible. Control leaf spot, which is most likely to cause leaf fall, by spraying with zineb or thiophanate-methyl. Burn fallen leaves.

Cherry

In mid-August spray with a copper fungicide to control bacterial canker.

Peach, nectarine and acid cherry

When the fruit from wall-trained trees has been picked, prune the shoots that have borne fruit, leaving in the current season's growth that has been selected to replace them. Re-tie new shoots where necessary to make the best use of space and to encourage the growth to ripen. In mid-August, spray acid cherry with a copper fungicide against canker.

Plum and damson

Continue to support heavily laden trees, and finish pruning (see JULY).

Raspberry

Protect September-fruiting plants against birds, and try to protect the fruit further by destroying near-by wasp nests.

Strawberry

Plant rooted runners now to ensure a good crop in the following year. Later planting reduces the crop, and runners planted in late October or early November should not be allowed to fruit at all the following year.

Runners rooted into pots (see JUNE) are the most successful and are ideal for cloches. In most areas runners planted before the middle of the month give leaf at the expense of fruit when they are covered.

Vine (outdoor)

Protect ripening fruit with glass or polythene, if at all possible.

Vegetables

Early in the month sow seeds of spring cabbage $\frac{1}{2}$ in. deep in drills 6 in. apart, first dusting the drills with calomel as a precaution against club root disease. Make the seed bed in ground that has not been manured since the previous autumn. Recommended varieties include 'Durham Early', 'Harbinger', 'Flower of Spring' and 'Wheeler's Imperial'.

Sow lettuces and Brussels sprouts

Until the middle of the month sow lettuces ('All The Year Round') for cutting in early winter. Sow the seeds very thinly, singling the seedlings to 6–8 in. In the north, for a spring lettuce crop to over-winter without cloche protection, sow 'Imperial Winter' or 'Arctic King', setting the plants out in early October. Sow the seeds $\frac{1}{4}$ in. deep in drills 6 in. apart.

Sow seed of Japanese hardy onions in moist shallow drills to form bulbs early next summer. 'Express', 'Imai', and 'Senshui' are recommended varieties. In the north, sow in the second week of August.

LESS COMMON VEGETABLES

Pick cobs of sweet corn when the tassels on the ends have withered and the seeds are firm but exude 'milk' when pressed with your thumb-nail. Gather the cobs by breaking them off the stems.

Start to use self-blanching celery as soon as there are sizeable plants. The crop should be cleared before the first frosts.

Herbs

Take cuttings of bay, hyssop, lavender, mint, rosemary, rue and sage, and insert in sandy soil in open ground. For the first two weeks protect the cuttings from sun and winds with a cloche, and water in the evenings until the roots have

ormed. Alternatively, put the cuttings in
 pot filled with sand and place in a cold
 rame, or simply insert in sandy soil in
 he frame itself.

Divide chives

Every four years chives need dividing.
 ift the clumps and cut into segments
 with a sharp knife, taking care that each
 egment retains a number of roots, and
lant out 12 in. apart.

Collect and dry the seeds of dill and
 ennel. Gather the dry seeds of chervil
 nd re-sow at once in 1 in. deep seed
 rills.

Store dried herbs

 tore dried herbs before they have had
 me to re-absorb moisture from the air.
 llow the herbs to cool after drying, then
 ub them between the hands, discarding
 ems and other chaff, and store at once
  prevent dust collecting. Use wooden
 rs with tight-fitting lids or screw caps,
  plastic bags firmly sealed. Glass jars
 ith screw tops are suitable only for
 mall amounts of herbs intended for
 mmediate use.

Patios and town gardens

 ontinue to water containers daily, to
 move dead flowers, and to replace
lants that are past their best.

If you leave home for a holiday, move
 e containers, if possible, to a spot
 at is in the shade for most of the day.
 ack damp peat around the plants to
 onserve as much moisture as possible.

Order bulbs for autumn planting and
 e spring display (see OCTOBER).
 hoose varieties that will not grow too
 ll, particularly if they are required for
 indow-boxes. Tall tulips and daffodils,
  example, will almost certainly be
 apped off by gusts of wind.

House plants

Continue watering and feeding at the
summer rate (see MAY).

If you leave home for a summer holiday, make sure that your plants will not
suffer while you are away. The ideal
plan is to have a local nurseryman collect your plants and keep them in a
greenhouse while you are away. Alternatively, arrange for a friend or neighbour to water them during your absence.

Holiday care

If you cannot arrange for your plants
to be cared for, there are ways of ensuring their welfare. Some of the smaller
plants can be watered thoroughly and
then slipped into a polythene bag. Blow
into the top of the bag to extend it and
prevent it from touching the foliage,
then seal it tightly with a rubber band.
Placed out of direct sunlight, most
plants treated in this way will remain in
good health for two or three weeks.

In the case of a larger plant, place the
pot inside another, larger container
which has no drainage holes, filling the
space between the two containers with
peat. If you water the peat until it is
quite wet, but not sodden, moisture will
be released gradually to the pot. This
method is more successful with clay pots
than with plastic, for the moisture is then
absorbed through the sides as well as
through the drainage holes in the base.

Automatic watering

Several proprietary systems of automatic watering are available. Some
make use of a storage tank or bottle
which gradually releases its contents to
give a drip feed or to keep a sand-
covered tray uniformly moist. Other
methods use wicks of glass fibre to feed
water from a reservoir into the pot. In
other systems, several plants are placed
above a tank of water, each having a

wick leading from the water into the
base of the pot.

Simple capillary watering

One of the simplest, least expensive
and most satisfactory methods is to fill
a bucket with water and stand it in the
centre of the room on a low stool or box.
Place the plants on the floor around the
bucket, standing each pot on a saucer to
keep the floor dry. Buy as many long
bootlaces as you have plants and tie a
small stone to one end of each, placing
this end of each lace in the bucket so
that the stone rests on the bottom. Take
the other end down to the surface of the
pot below, pressing the metal end of the
lace into the soil surface. Water will
creep by capillary action down the lace
and into the pot.

If the bucket is large enough a considerable number of pots can be watered
automatically in this manner at very
little expense and with an almost complete guarantee of success. Place the
bucket and pots out of direct sunlight.

Whichever method of watering you
choose, let the plants do without fertiliser while you are away. They are unlikely to suffer from starvation for so
short a period, but could well be affected
by over-feeding.

General tasks

This is a good month to take and root
cuttings of shrubs and heathers, hydrangeas, geraniums and fuchsias.

Check all labels on plants, trees or
shrubs, and renew any that have become
illegible. Write on plastic labels with an
ink that contains a little acid. The
writing will be etched into the label and
will last for many years.

Pests can still cause trouble, especially
on dahlias and chrysanthemums, so
keep up the regular spraying programme.
For holiday precautions, see JULY.

The rose's varied forms

Roses are as different in form as the gardens in which they grow. The compact bush roses are today's most popular border plants. For other situations there are the charming miniatures or the upright and weeping standards. Where a wall or screen needs to be concealed, or a pergola brightened up, there are wide-spreading climbers and ramblers. There is hardly anywhere in the garden where roses cannot be grown to advantage. August is the month in which to make your choice and place your orders for autumn delivery.

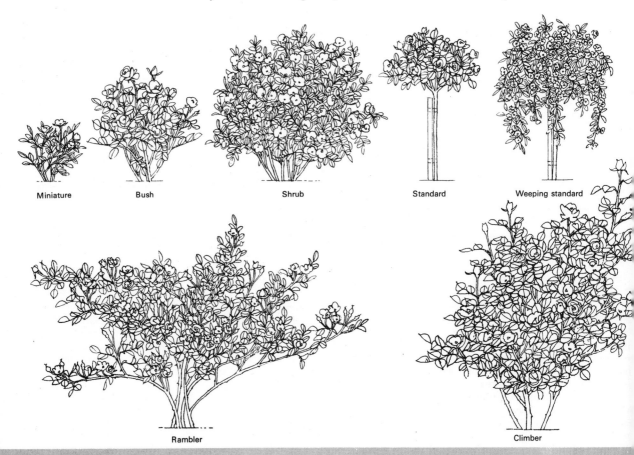

Miniature   Bush   Shrub   Standard   Weeping standard

Rambler

Climber

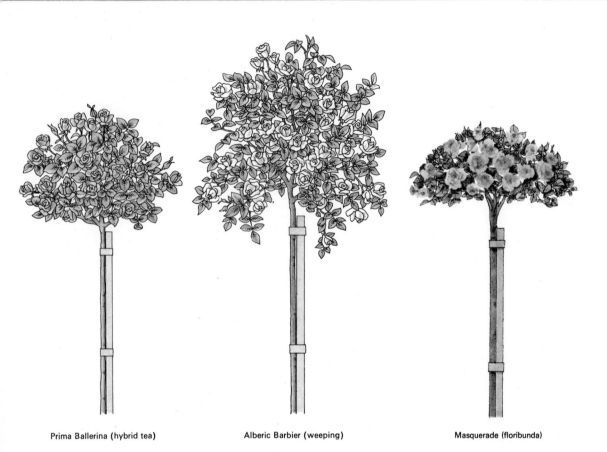

Prima Ballerina (hybrid tea) Alberic Barbier (weeping) Masquerade (floribunda)

Standards

These striking roses are formed from hybrid tea and floribunda varieties budded on 3–3½ ft. brier stems. Half-standards are 2–2½ ft. high. Rambler varieties are used for weeping standards, which have 5–6 ft. stems and trailing growths reaching almost to ground level. Plant standards at least 4 ft. apart, or up to 3 ft. from bush roses. Weeping varieties need to be 6 ft. apart. Yellow varieties tend to have short lives as standards and are not recommended. Pruning of hybrid teas and floribunda standards follows the same procedure as for bush roses. New growth on weeping standards is trained in annually after cutting out old wood.

Among recommended varieties are:

Excelsa. W Bright rosy crimson
Minnehaha. W Deep pink

Alberic Barbier. W Cream ❋
Dorothy Perkins. W Rose-pink
Emily Gray. W Golden-buff

Alec's Red. HT Deep red ❋
Blessings. HT Coral pink ❋
Fragrant Cloud. HT Geranium lake ❋
National Trust. HT Crimson scarlet
Pascali. HT White
Piccadilly. HT Scarlet and yellow
Prima Ballerina. HT Deep pink ❋
Allgold. F Unfading golden-yellow
City of Leeds. F Rich salmon
Iceberg. F Pure white
Red Gold. F Red inside, gold outside
Rob Roy. F Crimson scarlet
Regensberg. F Pink and white
Sunsilk. F Lemon yellow

HT = hybrid tea   F = floribunda
W = weeping   ❋ = fragrant

Wendy Cussons   Peace   Ernest H. Morse

Hybrid teas

Hybrid tea roses, now often listed as 'large-flowered', are unsurpassed for the beauty of their large and shapely individual blooms. The buds are long and graceful. Many hybrid teas are sweetly scented. Heights vary from $2\frac{1}{2}$–4 ft., a point to bear in mind when planting beds of mixed varieties. Plant 2 ft. apart, except Peace, which needs a planting distance of 3 ft. either way.

Among recommended varieties are:

Alec's Red. Cherry red $2\frac{1}{2}$ ft. ❋
Alexander. Orange-vermilion 4 ft. ❋
Bobby Charlton. Pink $2\frac{1}{2}$ ft. ❋
Blessings. Coral pink $2\frac{1}{2}$ ft. ❋
Blue Moon. Silvery lilac $2\frac{1}{2}$ ft.
Bonsoir. Peach pink $2\frac{1}{2}$ ft. ❋
City of Bath. Candy pink, lighter
   reverse $2\frac{1}{2}$ ft. ❋

Blue Moon

Alexander

Sunblest

Derek Nimmo. Salmon 3 ft.
Diorama. Apricot yellow 3 ft.
Ernest H. Morse. Turkey red 3 ft.❋
Fragrant Cloud. Dark coral red 3 ft.❋
Fred Gibson. Amber to apricot 3 ft.
Grandpa Dickson. Yellow to cream 3½ ft.
Josephine Bruce. Velvety crimson 2½ ft.❋
Just Joey. Coppery orange 3 ft.

King's Ransom. Yellow 3 ft.
Mischief. Vermilion and pale orange 3½ ft.
Mullard Jubilee. Cerise 3 ft.❋
National Trust. Crimson scarlet 4 ft.
Pascali. Pure white 2½ ft.
Peace. Yellow, edged pink 4 ft.
Piccadilly. Scarlet and yellow 3 ft.
Pink Favourite. Deep rose pink 3 ft.

Prima Ballerina. Deep pink 3 ft.❋
Red Devil. Scarlet, lighter reverse 3 ft.❋
Royal Highness. Soft pale pink 3 ft. ❋
Sunblest. Golden-yellow 3½ ft.❋
Wendy Cussons. Deep cerise 2½ ft.❋
Yorkshire Bank. White 3 ft.❋

❋ = fragrant

King Arthur

Iceberg

Allgold

Floribundas

The colourful and popular floribundas are derived from *R. multiflora*. 'Multi-flora', meaning 'many-flowered', had as its Greek equivalent 'polyantha', and thus the multiflora roses were also known as polyanthas. They have the free-flowering characteristic of *R. multiflora*, and some have the elegant shape of hybrid tea blooms. The majority have single (five-petalled) or semi-double rosette-type blooms, the flowers being borne in large trusses from June until the autumn. For the best effect, plant in groups of a single variety. Heights are 18 in.– 7 ft. Plant 2 ft. apart, except Dearest, Iceberg and Masquerade, which need 3 ft. Floribundas are now classified in some lists as 'cluster-flowered'.

Among recommended varieties are:

Allgold. Golden yellow 2 ft.
Anne Cocker. Vermilion 2½ ft.
Arthur Bell. Creamy yellow 2½ ft.
Chinatown. Yellow 4 ft.
City of Belfast. Bright red 3 ft.
City of Leeds. Rich salmon 3 ft.
Dearest. Rosy salmon 4 ft.
Dorothy Wheatcroft. Bright scarlet 4 ft.
Elizabeth of Glamis. Salmon 2 ft.❋

Queen Elizabeth   Anne Cocker   Sir Lancelot

Escapade. Magenta, white reverse 2½ ft.
Evelyn Fison. Scarlet 2 ft.
Eye Paint. Scarlet and white 3½ ft.
Glenfiddich. Amber 3 ft.
Iceberg. Pure white 4 ft.
Iced Ginger. Apricot and copper 2½ ft.
Irish Mist. Orange salmon 3 ft.
Kerryman. Cream to pink 2 ft.
King Arthur. Clear salmon pink 3½ ft.
Lilli Marlene. Scarlet 3 ft.
Marlena. Bright red 2 ft.
Masquerade. Yellow, pink and red 4 ft.

Molly McGredy. Rose red, silver reverse
   3 ft.
News. Beetroot red shaded purple 3 ft.
Orange Sensation. Red and orange 3 ft.❀
Orange Silk. Orange vermilion 2½ ft.
Paddy McGredy. Carmine, brighter
   reverse 2 ft.
Picasso. Carmine, silver reverse 2 ft.
Pineapple Poll. Yellow flushed orange 2 ft.
Pink Parfait. Pink, with yellow base 3 ft.
Priscilla Burton. Silver, carmine 2 ft.
Queen Elizabeth. Clear pink 6–7 ft.

Redgold. Gold, edged cherry-red 2 ft.
Satchmo. Scarlet 2½ ft.
Scented Air. Salmon pink 3 ft.❀
Sea Pearl. Soft pink and yellow 3 ft.
Stephen Langdon. Deep scarlet 2½ ft.
Sue Lawley. Pink and white, 3 ft.
Tip Top. Warm pink 18 in.
Topsi. Orange scarlet 2 ft.
Trumpeter. Scarlet 2½ ft.
Young Venturer. Apricot gold 3 ft. ❀
Woburn Abbey. Tangerine 3½ ft.
❀ = fragrant

American Pillar (rambler)   The New Dawn (climber)   Emily Gray (rambler)   Zephirine Drouhin (climber)

Climbers and ramblers

The true climbing roses, including climbing hybrid teas and climbing floribundas, have sturdier, more erect growth than the ramblers. They are suitable for walls and tall fences, whereas ramblers are better for relatively low screens and pillars. Ramblers have small blooms and flower briefly in early summer; they are pruned in September. Climbers have large blooms and those listed are all repeat-flowering; prune in March. Plant both climbers and ramblers 8 ft. apart.

Among recommended varieties are:

Autumn Sunlight. C Orange vermilion
Casino. C Soft yellow
Danse du Feu. C Orange scarlet

Elegance. C Pale yellow
Golden Showers. C Golden yellow ❋
Handel. C Cream, edged rose pink

Parkdirektor Riggers. C Blood red
Pink Perpetué. C Clear pink with carmine
Royal Gold. C Golden yellow
Swan Lake. C White ❋
The New Dawn. C Flesh pink ❋
Zephirine Drouhin. C Bright carmine pink ❋
Albertine. R Coppery pink ❋
American Pillar. R Bright rose, white centre
Dr. W. van Fleet. R Flesh pink ❋
Emily Gray. R Golden buff
Excelsa. R Bright rosy crimson
Paul's Scarlet. R Bright scarlet crimson

C = climber   R = rambler   ❋ = fragrant

Double Yellow

R. centifolia bullata

Charles de Mills

Shrub roses

This classification includes many old and showy types of roses, such as hybrid musks and moss roses, but also modern types. Many are richly fragrant. Plant individually, either as specimen shrubs or in a mixed border, as they can make large bushes up to 6 ft. or more high. Even poor soils are suitable and little pruning is needed except to cut out dead wood. Shrub roses can be used for informal hedges. Those listed are repeat-flowering, except *Rosa centifolia bullata*.

Among recommended varieties are:

Blanc Double de Coubert. White 6 ft. ❋
Bonn. Orange scarlet 6 ft.
Charles de Mills. Velvety crimson 4–5 ft. ❋

Chinatown. Yellow, edged cherry 6 ft.
Cornelia. Apricot, flushed pink 5–6 ft. ❋
Double Yellow. Buttercup yellow 3 ft.

Elmshorn. Light crimson 5 ft.
Felicia. Rose pink, shaded yellow 6 ft.❋
Fred Loads. Vermilion orange 5–6 ft.❋
Heidelberg. Bright red 6 ft.
Joseph's Coat. Yellow, orange and red 5–6 ft.
Kassel. Cherry red 6 ft.
Nevada. Cream, can be tinted pink 7–10 ft.
Penelope. Pale pink, shaded salmon 5 ft. ❋
Prosperity. White 6 ft.
R. centifolia bullata. Rich pink $2\frac{1}{2}$ ft. ❋
Roseraie de l'Hay. Purplish crimson 7 ft. ❋
Wilhelm. Rich crimson 6 ft.
❋ = fragrant

Species roses

The species roses grown as shrubs in the garden derive from the wild roses found all over the world. They go back to the earliest gardens of which we have record: *R. gallica*, the Red Rose of Lancaster, was cultivated by the ancient Greeks, and *R. alba*, the White Rose of York, was probably brought to Britain by the Romans. The flowering period of these old-fashioned roses is brief; many have attractive foliage and colourful hips.

1 Rosa moyesii
Vigorous and free-flowering, 8 ft. high. Has large bottle-shaped hips in autumn.

2 Rosa rubrifolia
Almost thornless; 4–8 ft. high. Grown principally for its distinctive foliage.

Miniature roses

These delightful little plants are ideal subjects for tubs and window-boxes, or for growing in a rock garden. There are numerous varieties, some more compact than others. Pot-grown specimens in bloom can be brought indoors, but should remain outdoors at other times.

1 Rosemarin
Free-flowering and of loose, spreading habit. Suitable for small borders or rock gardens

2 Pour toi
Vigorous and bushy, this miniature grows 9–10 in. high. The flowers are semi-double

3 Rosina
A free-flowering variety growing up to 18 in. high. The flowers are slightly fragrant

September

As the fruit ripens and dahlias and chrysanthemums come into full bloom, shortening days and early morning frosts give a foretaste of autumn

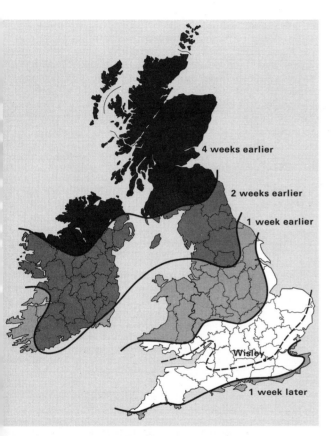

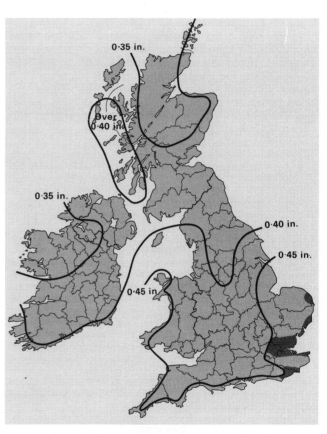

PROGRESS OF THE SEASON

This map shows the earliness or lateness of the season in an average September at places in the British Isles, compared with the Royal Horticultural Society's Gardens at Wisley. The broken line joins places where the season is as advanced as at Wisley. As a rough guide, gardeners in the white areas should begin their September gardening programme at the beginning of the month. Gardeners to the north are advised to start the programme even earlier. Coastal areas tend to be milder, especially in the west and south, and autumn there may not be as advanced as it is farther inland. Autumn arrives some two days earlier for every 100 ft. rise in height

WATER NEEDED BY A GARDEN IN SEPTEMBER

The map shows the total water used by a garden (the potential transpiration) in inches per average week in September. In some areas of eastern England the month is often dry, and the average weekly rainfall is less than potential transpiration. These areas are shaded on the map, and here some watering will usually be necessary if plants are to receive all the moisture they need. Gardeners in all areas of eastern Britain and in the east of Ireland should be prepared to water in September, especially during sunny weather. Amounts of watering needed can be calculated from rainfall measurements and potential transpiration. (See GLOSSARY, *Weather*)

The weather in September

This is the first of the autumn months, although after the occasional outstanding summer it can still provide spells of warm, dry weather. The effects of shortening days are much more noticeable. The warmth of the sun is decreasing, so that temperatures are rarely high; and the difference between north and south is much more pronounced than in August. The nights are appreciably cooler, and often very humid.

In good years, high pressure can occur over the British Isles during September. Calm, warm, sunny days result, and afternoon temperatures may occasionally reach 21°C (70°F) in south-east England, though they are much lower in northern Scotland. During dry, still nights, with no blanketing cloud cover, dew and mist form readily, and early morning frost may once more be a hazard for the gardener. This occurs sporadically inland in valley bottoms and sheltered

pockets, especially in northern areas, and may catch the gardener unawares, as surrounding hillsides and higher garden slopes usually remain well above freezing point.

During this month depressions usually bring periods of cool, wet, windy weather to the west, but drier, sunnier weather to the east, particularly to east Scotland. The weather is often unsettled in the closing days of the month, and strong winds bring rain to all areas.

Occasionally north to north-easterly winds bring much colder and drier weather, particularly in the second half of the month, and over much of inland Britain gardeners should expect their first widespread ground frost of the season.

During September the gardener must take precautions against gales by ensuring that stakes and ties are secure, and be prepared to move plants indoors if frost is forecast.

A summary of the month's work

LAWNS
Aerate, apply sharp sand or compost, and scarify to remove debris. Re-seed worn patches. Apply autumn fertiliser. Control weeds, fungal infections and moss.

ROSES
Remove faded blooms. Continue to spray against mildew and greenfly. For quality blooms on hybrid teas, remove small side buds from flower stems. Scatter wood ash or sulphate of potash on the rose beds and hoe it in. Tie the shoots of climbers into a fan shape. Prune climbers and ramblers which have only one flush of blooms, and also weeping standards. Take cuttings of mature side shoots from climbers and ramblers; and of this year's growth from floribundas and hybrid teas. Continue to spray fortnightly against black spot and rust diseases.

HARDY HERBACEOUS PLANTS
Continue dead-heading and cutting back. Finish preparing new beds, and hoe beds already prepared.

DAHLIAS
Check ties, as autumn gales can cause damage. Feed once a fortnight with a liquid fertiliser to produce good blooms and build up strong tubers. Save dahlia seeds, and dry in a cool cupboard.

CHRYSANTHEMUMS
Select best outdoor varieties and label for propagating. Protect blooms with greaseproof bags, dusting the insides with HCH to deter insects.
Under glass. Bring pot-grown varieties into the greenhouse by the middle of the month, preparing a level floor and cleaning the

glass. Spray the plants with a combined insecticide and fungicide. Ventilate well, disbud late varieties, and control aphids as necessary.

GLADIOLI
Leave new corms undisturbed until fully matured.

IRISES
Cut off and burn leaves infected with leaf spot disease. Plant Dutch, Spanish and English irises for flowering from May to July, choosing a sunny, well drained site. Plant *I. reticulata* in rows for cutting. Plant *I. unguicularis* in poor, well drained soil in a sheltered position. Plant *I. sibirica* in moist soil along margins of ponds. Spray trichlorphon or derris against caterpillars.
Under glass. Plant bulbous irises (Dutch, Spanish, English, *I. danfordiae*) in pots, and stand in a cold frame.

LILIES
Spray against aphids and botrytis. Start planting bulbs as soon as available. Lift small bulbs from around *L. auratum* and grow on in pots. Transplant well grown pots of seedlings. Sow seeds now or in spring. Propagate healthy scales broken off during transplanting.

CARNATIONS AND PINKS
Prepare beds for border carnations and pinks if not already done. Sever rooted layers from parent plants. Continue to harden-off rooted pink cuttings and plant out those that are now growing strongly. Stop newly planted pinks that start to run to flower. Put sifted bonfire ash in bags under cover to serve as a spring dressing, and store sifted dry soil to help with autumn planting.

Under glass. Continue feeding perpetual flowering carnations. Remove shading from the glass this month. Damp down in hot spells. Disbud flower stems. Keep water from falling on opening blooms, and wire calyces of blooms which threaten to split. Cut blooms with long stems and stand them up to their necks in water in a cool place for 12 hours before arranging them in vases. Take action against pests and diseases.

SWEET PEAS

Purchase seed for sowing next month. Include some of the old-fashioned varieties to provide scent among the modern ones.

FLOWERS FROM SEED

Remove fading annuals to make way for spring bedding. Sow the hardiest annuals to over-winter outdoors. Plant hardy biennials.

BULBS

Plant bulbs between shrubs or herbaceous plants, on rock gardens or in lawns, preferably in groups. Remove summer bedding as it fades and replace with bulbs. First plan the layout, then plant from the centre outwards. Where interplanting, set the plants first and put in the bulbs afterwards.

Indoors and under glass. Re-pot arum lilies for winter flowering. Prepare pots and bowls of bulbs to flower from Christmas to Easter, using bulb fibre. Ensure that indoor bulbs fill their pots or bowls with roots before they are forced, by putting them in dark, moist conditions for two to three months.

ALPINES

Transplant any plants which need re-siting. Start making a new rockery; but first consider whether a raised alpine bed might not be better. Choose an open, well drained position, away from trees. Allow several weeks to pass for soil and rocks to settle before planting.

WATER PLANTS AND POOLS

Collect the winter buds of hydrocharis and utricularia before they sink to the bottom of the pool, and keep them in an unsealed jar of water in a cool place until spring. Pot up waterside primulas pricked out in June, or plant them in their permanent positions. Feed the fish, as live food is now becoming scarce and they must build up their reserves for the winter.

GREENHOUSES AND FRAMES

Start giving artificial heat towards the end of the month. Sow annuals for a spring display in the greenhouse, potting the seedlings separately in 3 in. pots. Take cuttings of fuchsias, zonal pelargoniums and many other greenhouse plants. Remove permanent shading from the glass. Bring pot primulas and other plants into the greenhouse from cold frames.

TREES AND SHRUBS

Prepare ground for planting later in the month or in October. Start planting evergreen shrubs during showery weather at the end of the month. Support standard shrubs with stakes until they become established. Water newly planted shrubs during dry weather and spray their foliage with water.

Propagation under glass. Take hardwood and half-ripe cuttings of berberis, juniper and privet, rooting them in sandy soil in a cold frame. Leave them to grow on in the frame during the winter. In open ground, cover with cloches during cold weather.

Pruning. Lightly prune such shrubs as phlomis and senecio after flowering.

RHODODENDRONS AND AZALEAS

During rainy weather, transplant bushes which need moving. Continue to increase stock by layering. Heel in plants arriving from nurseries if the ground is not ready for planting, but do not allow them to become dry.

HEDGES

Clip new growth for the last time this season. Remove remaining weeds and burn or compost them. Prepare sites for new hedges. Plant evergreen hedges from mid-September to mid-October.

HEATHERS

Prepare ground for planting, selecting an open position.

FRUIT

Plan for new planting season, and order trees. Choose late-flowering varieties for frosty areas. Grass down established trees. Remove trees infected with honey fungus. Prepare storage places for apples and pears, and pick fruit in cool conditions before fully mature. Complete summer pruning of apples and pears. Harvest blackberries and loganberries, cut away old growth, and tie in new. Prune wall-trained peaches and tie in new shoots. Spray cherries. Pick plums and damsons, and prune trees. Pick September-fruiting raspberries. Protect autumn-fruiting strawberries against birds and slugs, and cover with cloches in cold weather.

VEGETABLES

In the south, sow lettuces for over-wintering with cloche protection. In the north, plant spring cabbages. Lift maincrop carrots and store sound ones in layers in deep boxes.

Under glass. Protect lettuces and spring cabbages with cloches. Sow carrots under cloches.

Less common vegetables. Cut off the tops of chicory before blanching.

HERBS

Sow parsley and chervil to provide a spring crop. Divide and re-plant clumps of bergamot.

Under glass. Take cuttings of bay and rue. Take cuttings of lavender and protect with a frame or cloche.

PATIOS AND TOWN GARDENS

Continue frequent watering and remove dead flowers. Discard plants past their best. Prepare containers for planting spring bulbs. Empty compost from containers not required during the winter.

SEPTEMBER

HOUSE PLANTS

Slightly reduce watering and feeding. Keep tender plants away from windows on cold nights. Transfer plants liking plenty of light from a west to a south window. Reduce the amount of water given to cacti. Complete re-potting and pruning. Examine plants for signs of over-watering or of pest attacks. Control red spider mites with derris or malathion. As these pests are encouraged by a dry atmosphere, try to increase atmospheric humidity round the plants.

GENERAL TASKS

Clear away remains of crops that have finished. Order bulbs, roses, herbaceous plants, shrubs and fruit bushes. Take cuttings of evergreen shrubs, geraniums and hydrangeas. Control mildew, especially on michaelmas daisies, with fungicide. Check that electrical installations are in working order before the winter. Complete major construction jobs, particularly concreting. Check that gutters and drains are free of leaves and other debris.

Plants to enjoy in September

Border and rock garden plants in flower	**Trees and shrubs in flower**	Canna
Aconitum	Campsis·radicans	Fuchsia
Agapanthus	Clematis jackmanii	Heliotropium
Ageratum	Hibiscus	Pelargonium
Alyssum	Hydrangea	Plumbago capensis
Anemone japonica	Passiflora	Tibouchina
Aster		
Begonia	**Trees and shrubs with colourful foliage**	**House plants in flower, depending on position and culture**
Centaurea (cornflower)	Amelanchier	Anthurium
Chrysanthemum	Azalea (deciduous)	Begonia semperflorens
Colchicum (autumn crocus)	Callicarpa	Impatiens
Convolvulus	Euonymus	Saintpaulia
Cyclamen neapolitanum	Fothergilla	
Dahlia	Nyssa	**Fruit in season**
Dimorphotheca	Parrotia	Apple
Erigeron	Parthenocissus	Apricot
Gaillardia	Prunus	Blackberry
Gladiolus	Rhus (Cotinus)	Cherry
Gypsophila	Sorbus	Currant, black
Helenium	Viburnum	Damson
Helianthus (sunflower)		Loganberry
Helichrysum	**Trees and shrubs with colourful fruits**	Peach
Iberis	Berberis rubrostilla	Pear
Ipomoea (morning glory)	Chaenomeles	Plum
Lavatera	Cotoneaster	Raspberry
Lobelia	Crataegus (hawthorn)	
Matthiola (stock)	Euonymus	**Vegetables in season**
Mesembryanthemum	Lindera benzoin	Artichoke, globe
Mimulus	Malus	Beans, dwarf french
Nemesia	Pernettya	Beans, runner
Nicotiana (tobacco plant)	Pyracantha	Beetroot
Papaver (poppy)	Sorbus (mountain ash)	Beet, seakale
Pelargonium	Symphoricarpos (snowberry)	Cabbage
Petunia	Viburnum	Carrots
Phlox		Cauliflower
Rose (floribunda and hybrid tea)	**Water garden plants in flower**	Celery
Rudbeckia	Aponogeton distachyon	Cucumber
Salvia	Caltha (marsh marigold)	Lettuce
Scabiosa	Nymphaea (water lily)	Marrow
Sedum	Pontederia (pickerel weed)	Onion
Solidago	Typha	Peas
Tagetes (French and African marigolds)		Radish
Tropaeolum (nasturtium)	**Greenhouse plants in flower**	Shallot
Venidio-arctotis	Abutilon	Spinach beet
Verbena	Begonia	Sweet corn
Viola	Campanula isophylla (star of Bethlehem)	Tomato
Zauschneria	Campanula pyramidalis	

Lawns

Using a hand fork or turf aerator, spike or hollow tine the lawn. Apply a dressing of sharp sand or compost, depending on the soil type, and brush it in well. Repair damaged areas in the lawn by re-seeding (see MARCH) or by laying turves (see OCTOBER).

Scarify or rake the lawn vigorously in two directions to remove debris and open up the turf surface. In addition to letting air and water into the soil, this exerts a pruning action on both leaves and roots and allows the nitrifying bacteria in the soil to function properly.

Fertiliser dressing

Apply a proprietary autumn fertiliser in two directions at 2 oz. per sq. yd. Autumn fertilisers contain smaller amounts of nitrogen (excess of which renders the grass liable to disease attack) and more phosphate and potash.

Continue to treat areas affected by disease (see MAY and JUNE), and to control weeds and moss (see MARCH).

Roses

Remove faded blooms, using sharp secateurs to make a cut sloping back from $\frac{1}{4}$ in. above a leaf (see JULY). On weak plants cut the stem above the first leaf down the stem from the faded bloom: on vigorous plants make the cut above the second or third leaf down the stem from the bloom. Cut flowers required for home decoration in the same manner.

Mildew is often troublesome on young foliage. Spray fortnightly with dinocap as a prevention. If mildew appears, spray with benomyl.

If ·greenfly are present, spray with a systemic rose insecticide.

Disbud hybrid teas

Towards autumn, hybrid tea roses tend to become as free-flowering as flori-bundas. To maintain the quality of the blooms, remove the two small side buds from each cluster of three buds as soon as it is possible to pick them off with the finger and thumb. This is known as disbudding.

To assist new wood to mature and withstand winter frosts, scatter a handful of sulphate of potash to the square yard, or a double handful of wood ash, over the surface of rose beds, except for a 6 in. circle round each tree, and hoe it lightly into the surface soil.

Train climbers

Tie in with garden twine new growths on climbers. Do this regularly as loose shoots are vulnerable to wind damage. Train long shoots growing from ground level into a fan shape, bending them over horizontally to encourage the production of flowering side shoots. Make ties sufficiently loose to allow for the thickening of the stems as they develop.

Prune climbers and ramblers

Wear gardening gloves and use sharp secateurs to prune climbing and rambling roses which have only one flush of blooms in summer (see colour section, AUGUST). These types of roses will flower best the following year on the

TO RENOVATE A WORN PATCH

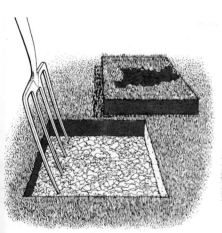

Re-seeding is a satisfactory alternative to laying fresh turves. Cut out the area of damaged turf and loosen the soil beneath

Fill the hole with sieved soil, firming gently and adding more soil to bring the surface level. Sow $1\frac{1}{2}$–2 oz. seed per sq. yd.

Sift a mixture of soil and peat over the seed. Protect the seed bed from birds by criss-crossing black cotton between short pegs

205

A PREPARED ROSE CUTTING

A 9–12 in. shoot, trimmed top and bottom, after its thorns and all but the upper pair of leaves have been removed

non-flowering shoots produced in the current season, so the object in pruning is to remove old growth which has finished flowering this year.

Where several new long non-flowering stems have grown from ground level, retain these to flower next year and cut back to ground level the old long stems which have flowered. However, if any

206

of the old stems has a strong new side shoot growing away from it about 12–24 in. above the ground, cut the old stem away just above the point where the side shoot joins it. These new side shoots will flower next year just like the ground-level shoots.

Encourage new shoots

If a rose has failed to throw new long stems from the base it will be necessary to retain the strongest of the old long stems, but to prune to 3 in. the side shoots which have flowered so that new side shoots will grow to provide next year's flowers.

Prune weeping standards

Weeping standards, which are summer-flowering climbers and ramblers growing on standard brier stems, are pruned in the same way as climbers by removing stems which have flowered during the summer and leaving the new main stems to flower next year.

Take cuttings

Mature side shoots of wood pruned from climbers and ramblers will provide cuttings to propagate new plants. Select strong shoots, 9–12 in. long, cutting $\frac{1}{4}$ in. below the bottom leaf and, at an angle, $\frac{1}{4}$ in. above the top leaf. Snap off the thorns and cut off all leaves except the top two.

In a shady part of the garden where there is medium to light soil, open a V-trench by inserting a spade and pushing the handle backwards and forwards. Put coarse sand in the bottom of the trench. Place each cutting in the sand so that the lower leaf is just above soil level. Root formation can be aided by first dipping the lower ends of the cuttings into hormone rooting powder.

Place cuttings 6–8 in. apart, according to the space available. When all the cuttings have been inserted, fill the

INSERTING ROSE CUTTINGS

Insert the cuttings in a V-shaped trench, first placing a 1–2 in. layer of coarse sand in the bottom. Fill in with light soil

trench with light soil and tread it down firmly. Cuttings which root will be ready for planting out in 15 months.

Floribundas and the more vigorous hybrid teas may also be grown from similar ripe cuttings taken from this year's growth.

Black spot and rust diseases

Continue to control black spot and rust diseases by spraying with fungicides (see JUNE) and by removing, gathering up and burning infected leaves.

Hardy herbaceous plants

For the first two or three weeks continue dead-heading and cutting back (see JUNE), and finish preparing a new bed or re-planning an old one (see JULY and AUGUST). A new bed prepared in July or August will need hoeing within a month after deep digging, especially if rain has followed soon afterwards.

Dahlias

Check stakes and ties, as autumn gales can cause much damage.

Feed once a fortnight with liquid fertiliser, to maintain blooms of good quality and to build up strong tubers.

To save your own dahlia seed, cut off yellow seed pods (which are about walnut size) with stems 9 in. long. Tie them together in a bunch and label them clearly before hanging the bunches upside down in a cool cupboard to dry out. Remove the seeds later.

Chrysanthemums

Outdoor varieties of all types will be in full flower this month. Select the best for next year's stock and label them clearly as such.

Flowers for cutting

Allow flowers for cutting to become well developed on the plants first. Greaseproof bags are sometimes used to protect the blooms. In this case, dust the insides of the bags lightly with HCH powder to deter ants, earwigs and aphids, which also enjoy this shelter. Special woven nylon net protectors are also made for this purpose. When cut, stand the blooms in 10–12 in. of water in a cool place before arranging them, first stripping the stems of all leaves for the lower foot or so.

UNDER GLASS

Bring pot-grown varieties into the greenhouse before the middle of the month. Carry large plants into the greenhouse pot end first, to lessen risk of damage.

Prepare a level floor on which to stand the pots, and clean the glass so that the plants get as much light as possible. Clean the pots, remove all dead or damaged leaves, and give the plants a thorough spraying with a combined insecticide and fungicide. Water the pots the day before bringing them in and make sure that each pot stands firm and level, allowing at least 12 in. between them.

Ventilation

Keep the ventilators and, if possible, the doors open day and night for the first week or ten days. Keep the floor clean and dry and do not heat the greenhouse.

Continue to disbud the late varieties, and keep a sharp watch for aphids, spraying as necessary (see APRIL).

Plants will still benefit from applications of weak fertiliser until the buds show colour. Discontinue at this stage.

Plants growing in the greenhouse borders need a night temperature of 13°C (55°F) while the buds are forming towards the end of the month.

Gladioli

The corms that were planted in the spring will have been shrivelling throughout the growing season, but a new corm will have formed on top of each. Tiny bulblets will have formed, too, and these will produce flower spikes two or three years after propagation (see NOVEMBER and MARCH).

Once the flower spikes have been cut, the old corms shrivel rapidly. Leave the new corms undisturbed until they are fully matured (see OCTOBER).

Irises

Cut off and burn any leaves which have developed the brown spots of leaf spot disease since flowering. This autumn treatment is generally sufficient to keep the disease in check.

Plant Dutch, Spanish and English irises for flowering from May to July.

The Dutch are earliest. The Spanish flower about a fortnight later and make less growth. The English are last and have the most robust flowers. All are good for garden decoration and excellent for cutting.

Plant bulbous irises

Choose a sunny, well drained site containing plenty of organic matter. Plant 3 in. deep and 4–6 in. apart. Leave undisturbed until they become overcrowded (see JULY). If flowers are wanted for cutting, plant the bulbs in rows so that they can be covered with cloches later to secure earlier blooms of perfect quality. Plant five rows of bulbs 3 in. apart to go under a standard barn-type cloche (see FEBRUARY).

Plant *Iris reticulata* 2 in. deep and 2 in. apart in rows for cutting or subsequent cloche protection (see JANUARY).

Plant *I. unguicularis* in poor, well drained soil in a sheltered situation—against the south wall of the house is ideal. Add mortar rubble to provide lime or, if this is not available, some lump chalk.

PLANTING IRISES FOR CUTTING

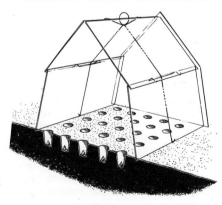

Set bulbous irises in rows, 3 in. apart, and protect with cloches during the winter. This will secure earlier and better blooms

Plant roots of *I. sibirica* in moist soil in places where they can remain undisturbed for some years. They are good plants for the margins of ponds or streams, flowering in May and June.

Spray or dust with trichlorphon or derris if caterpillars are seen.

UNDER GLASS

Plant bulbous irises in pots filled with a compost of equal parts loam, leaf-mould and silver sand. Stand the pots in a cold frame and give no water until growth shows. Plant the bulbs 2–3 in. deep, according to size, five bulbs to a 5 in. pot. The Dutch, Spanish and English irises may be treated in this way, also *I. danfordiae*, *I. histrioides*, *I. reticulata* and *I. tingitana*. Dutch, English and Spanish must have no artificial warmth, but the others may be given gentle warmth from January onwards.

Lilies

Continue to spray against aphids and botrytis (see APRIL). Begin planting as soon as the bulbs are available, giving priority to *L. candidum*. Plant this species with not more than 2 in. of soil above the bulbs, but cover others with a depth of soil equal to two and a half times their own height.

Plant basal-rooting lilies

Lilies which produce roots above the bulb, as well as below, transplant successfully in spring. But most lilies of European origin, and many American native lilies, root from the base of the bulb only. These sorts are best planted in the autumn. Base-rooting lilies to be grown in pots should be planted in the autumn.

Remove for indoor decoration the last of the blooms, as they may otherwise be

PLANTING LILY BULBS

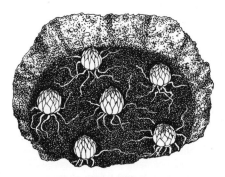

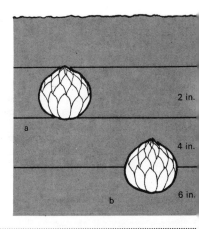

Above: For maximum effect, plant lilies in groups. *Right:* Set *L. candidum* bulbs (a) 2 in. deep; plant other species (b) at a depth equal to $2\frac{1}{2}$ times their height

spoiled by autumn gales. Cut them with a minimum of stalk.

Explore gently just below the surface of the soil close to the stems of healthy *L. auratum*. You will probably find several small rooted bulbs. Lift these

STEM-ROOTING LILIES

Some lilies produce stem roots, as well as roots beneath the bulb. Stem-rooting lilies can be transplanted successfully in spring

carefully and grow them on in pots or boxes. Left in the ground, they may be eaten by slugs.

Transplant well grown boxes of seedlings and overgrown clumps as soon as the foliage dies back.

UNDER GLASS

Seed can be sown now or kept until spring. To speed the growth of lilies with hypogeal (delayed) germination (see JANUARY) sow the seeds now and leave the containers in gentle warmth in a greenhouse for between six and 12 weeks. At the end of this period, move them outdoors to cool for six weeks, then bring them into the warmth again until they show above ground. Keep apparent failures for at least a year, then spread the discarded soil on a flower bed.

Propagate healthy scales broken off during transplanting. Lay a thin layer of sand on top of John Innes seed compost in a pot or seed box. Place the scales severed edges downwards in the sand, and add more sand to cover all but the tips. Stand the box in gentle warmth about 10°C (50°F), and keep it moist.

PROPAGATING LILY SCALES

Insert the broken edges of the scales in a thin layer of sand on top of the seed compost, then spread more sand to bury all but their tips

Carnations and pinks

Prepare beds for border carnations and pinks if this was not done last month.

Test carnation layers put down six weeks ago, severing them from the parent plants if they have rooted.

Continue to harden-off rooted pink cuttings and plant out those that are hardened and growing strongly.

Stopping pinks

Towards the end of the month, some young newly planted pinks may show signs of running to flower without making good side shoots. As this would spoil the plants for next season, they must be stopped. When the plant has developed about ten joints, hold it between your finger and thumb at the seventh joint, and with the other hand bend the top of the plant sharply at a right angle to snap off the top. If the top does not snap off easily, cut it cleanly just above the joint. Tops snap off best in the early morning in damp weather.

Modern pinks that are not stopped this month or next may need stopping in spring. If you are uncertain whether a pink is old-fashioned or modern, it is advisable to stop any young pink that tries to run up to bloom without making good side shoots, even though this may prevent old-fashioned pinks from flowering for a season.

Put sifted bonfire ashes in bags under cover to serve as a spring dressing, and also sifted dry soil to assist in autumn planting. Use a $\frac{1}{4}$ in. mesh screen in each case and store in a dry place.

UNDER GLASS

Continue to feed perpetual flowering carnations (see APRIL).

Remove shading

At the beginning of the month in Scotland and northern England, and towards the end of the month in the south, remove shading from the glass. Damp down in hot spells.

STOPPING A PINK

To stop a young pink, hold the stem at the seventh joint, then with your other hand bend the top sideways and snap it off

Disbud flower stems as they become ready. Perpetual flowering carnations are disbudded to leave only one bud per stem (the top or crown bud). Remove the other buds over a period as they become $\frac{1}{4}-\frac{1}{2}$ in. long.

Young plants stopped early will be coming into flower for the first time. Take care not to let water fall on the opening blooms. If any calyces (the tubular sheaths surrounding the petals) show signs of splitting, fix a split ring of thin wire round them.

Cut blooms

Cut the blooms with long stems, making the cut just above the side shoots at the base. Stand the cut blooms up to their necks in water in a cool place for at least 12 hours before arranging them.

Watch for pests and diseases, taking action as necessary (see MARCH).

Sweet peas

Purchase seed for sowing next month (see colour section, MAY). The colour range of sweet peas is almost limitless, yellow being the only colour which has proved elusive.

When growing modern sweet peas, plant a few of the old-fashioned varieties among them to provide extra fragrance.

Most catalogues list recommended exhibition varieties; but whether for exhibition or ordinary culture, choice is mainly a matter for individual taste.

Flowers from seed

Remove fading annuals to make room for spring bedding.

In mild districts and on well drained soils, sow the hardiest of the hardy annuals to over-winter outdoors (see tables, MARCH). Plants that are 2–3 in. high at the turn of the year stand the best chance of coming through hard weather.

Plant out hardy biennials, watering the rows of young plants the day before. Also thoroughly water the ground to be planted if the weather is dry. Set the plants out with a trowel and settle them in with a generous watering around their roots. In dry weather, water again with a sprinkler a few days later.

Bulbs

Plant bulbs between shrubs or herbaceous plants, in rock gardens and in lawns. As a guide to planting depth, bury each bulb twice as deep as its height. For instance, a daffodil bulb 2 in. tall is covered with 4 in. of soil.

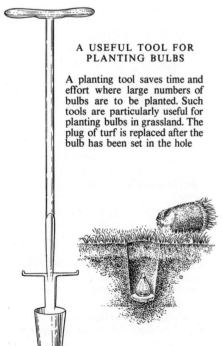

A USEFUL TOOL FOR PLANTING BULBS

A planting tool saves time and effort where large numbers of bulbs are to be planted. Such tools are particularly useful for planting bulbs in grassland. The plug of turf is replaced after the bulb has been set in the hole

Except where bulbs are grown as bedding plants or especially for cutting, irregular, informal groups look better than straight lines or regularly spaced arrangements. A good method is to scatter between half a dozen and 20 bulbs on the site to be planted and then to plant each where it fell. Use a trowel for small bulbs; a bulb-planting tool, or a small spade, for larger ones.

Easy planting method

An easy method of planting small bulbs, such as crocuses, snowdrops, winter aconites and scillas, in lawns, is to make holes 3–4 in. deep with a crowbar in the required irregular pattern. Fill the bottoms of the holes with peat or fine soil, place a bulb in each, then fill to the lawn surface with peat or sand. The grass will soon cover the tiny patches, and mowing can continue as long as necessary.

Such plantings need not necessarily interfere with spring mowing if early varieties are chosen. The flowers will come before the grass, which can be cut as usual and the bulbs replaced with fresh ones for the following season if they do not survive.

Prepare for early display

Towards the end of the month remove summer bedding when it becomes unattractive or frosted and replace with bulbs. Daffodils and hyacinths are best for an early display; tulips for later. Plant the bulbs on their own or between such plants as wallflowers, forget-me-nots and polyanthuses.

First plan the layout, then start planting in the centre and work outwards to the edges. If using bulbs alone, allow about 6 in. in each direction. When mixing bulbs with other plants, set the latter first and then insert the bulbs between them. Allow a rather wider spacing between bulbs when using them in this way.

UNDER GLASS AND INDOORS

Re-pot arums for winter flowering, using John Innes potting compost No. 3 and placing one plant in each 5–6 in. pot or three in each 8–9 in. pot.

Force bulbs

Prepare pots and bowls of bulbs to flower from Christmas until Easter using bulb fibre in containers which have no drainage holes. This fibre encourages root growth and allows enough moisture to be retained, without excluding air. Such bowls can stand on tables and other furniture without damaging the surface.

Flower pots with bottom drainage holes must be stood in saucers to avoid damage by water seepage or extruding roots. Fill with John Innes potting compost No. 1.

INDOOR HYACINTHS

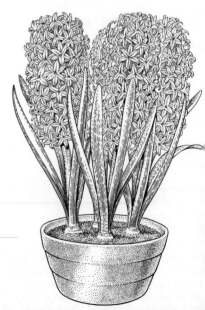

Hyacinths are among the most popular bulb for growing in bowls indoors. Choose containers deep enough to allow for root development

PLANTING BULBS IN A BOWL

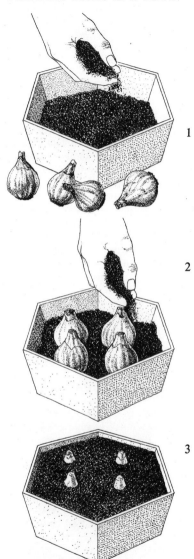

(1) Fill with fibre up to required planting depth. Small bulbs need a layer deep enough to bring their tops 1 in. below the rim; large bulbs should have their tops above the rim. (2) Fill in with more fibre. (3) Level the fibre ½ in. below the rim

Pack bulbs closely

With all indoor bulbs the aim is to produce a mass of colour, so use as many bulbs as the container will hold, packing them as closely as possible. Place a crock or piece of broken pot over the hole in the bottom of the pot and cover it with coarse peat, soil or moss to prevent the accumulation of stagnant water. No crocks are needed beneath the fibre in bowls without drainage holes.

Bulbs in pots and containers

Add compost or fibre so that small bulbs, when placed on the surface, have their tops about 1 in. below the rim of the bowl or pot; then cover with more compost or fibre until the surface is ½ in. below the rim. Stand large bulbs, such as hyacinths and daffodils, so that their tops are half out of the container, but again finish with the surface of the compost or fibre about ½ in. below the rim. If you fill to the rim when watering, this will moisten the whole container.

To obtain a spectacular show of daffodils or tulips, plant the bulbs in two layers in a 10 in. pot. Place one layer of bulbs half-way down the pot, almost covering them with fibre, then place another layer in the spaces on top. The bulbs will all flower together. This method is not applicable to hyacinths.

Plunge containers

With all indoor bulbs it is necessary for the bulbs to fill the bowl or pot with roots before the leaves and flower stems start into growth. This takes from two to three months and is best achieved in moist, dark, cool conditions. After filling and watering, wrap the bowls in sheets of newspaper and place them in the coolest available shed or room. Alternatively, place the containers outdoors against a north wall; cover them with 6 in. of peat, old ashes or soil or wrap each bowl in black polythene. This procedure is known as plunging.

PLANTING BULBS IN LAYERS

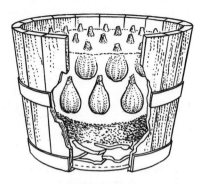

For a mass display of tulips or daffodils, plant the bulbs in two layers in a deep container. Set the upper layer above the spaces between the bulbs in the lower layer

WRAPPING FILLED BOWLS IN NEWSPAPER

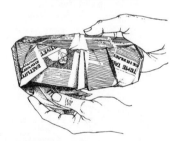

Covering the bowls with newspaper, and then standing them in a cool room or shed, serves the same purpose as plunging them outdoors

Alpines

Towards the end of the month, move plants that need repositioning, such as vigorous alpines that have been planted too close to slow-growing kinds.

This is the best month for making a rockery. Before you go ahead with the construction of a conventional rock garden, consider first whether an alpine bed, preferably raised, may not suit your purpose better. Contoured rock gardens, which should resemble natural

211

A RAISED ALPINE BED

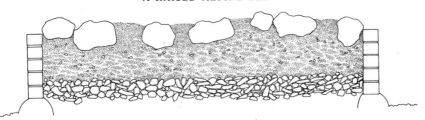

Section through a raised alpine bed, showing the layer of rubble at the base and the positioning of rocks on the surface. Such beds are easier to manage than conventional rock gardens and enable many plants to be grown in a small area

rock outcrops, often look incongruous in flat, suburban settings. Suitable stone is expensive, and routine maintenance tasks, such as weeding, are onerous.

An alpine bed

In contrast, an alpine bed is not intended as a natural feature. Only a few rocks are needed, and such tasks as weeding and planting present no difficulty if the bed is raised to 2 ft. above ground level. As many as 50 different kinds of alpines can be grown in a 6–8 sq. yd. bed.

Unless you require a rockery as a garden feature, an alpine bed may be the better choice, especially if the plants are your chief interest. Whether you prefer an alpine bed or a rock garden, select an open situation away from overhanging trees.

Alpine beds should be of regular shape, rectangular for preference. Old bricks are the best material for constructing the sides. On heavy or wet land, first remove the top spit of soil and fill the hole with hard-core or clinker. On lighter, well drained land, place a layer of rubble at ground level to aid drainage.

Soil to suit alpines

A suitable soil mixture for most common alpines consists of 2 parts loamy soil, 1 part coarse sand and 1 part leaf mould or peat, adding $\frac{1}{2}$ lb. John Innes base fertiliser to each barrow load. If the soil is heavy, add an additional part of limestone chippings, $\frac{1}{2}$ in. gravel or brick rubble broken down to pieces not larger than 1 in. across. This mixture is also suitable for slow-growing alpines, sometimes classified as scree plants (see colour section, NOVEMBER). Where these are grown, place $\frac{1}{2}$–1 in. of stone chippings or pea shingle on the surface.

After filling the bed with the soil mixture, half bury some small rocks in the surface.

Rock garden site

If you decide to build a conventional rock garden, avoid a site which is boggy or subject to flooding. Break up heavy soil with a fork, incorporating plenty of rubble, then cover the surface with a mound of smaller rubble.

How to choose rock

Selection of rock is straightforward if stone occurs naturally in your district. Local stone can be relied upon to blend with the surroundings, and costs less to transport. Otherwise you will have to buy stone from a garden centre or builders' merchant, remembering when you compare costs that some stones weigh considerably more than others. A ton of sandstone has twice the volume of a ton of Westmorland limestone.

AN ALPINE SINK GARDEN

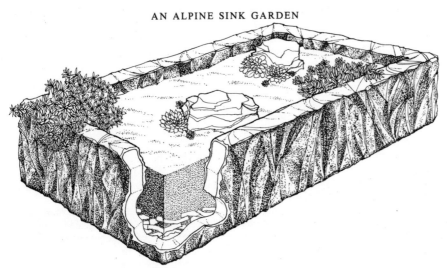

An old glazed sink, coated with cement to give it a stone-like appearance, is excellent for alpines. Cover the base with crocks, fill with compost, and set stones in the surface

212

On the other hand, some sandstone is less durable and is subject to frost damage. Limestone is little affected by frost and has a most attractive, weathered appearance.

Imitation boulders

Tufa stone is light in weight, porous and ideal for the rock garden, but it is sometimes difficult to obtain and always expensive. You can make your own imitation tufa boulders which have the requisite porosity. Mix 1 part cement with 2 parts sand and 2 parts peat. Wet the mixture until it is plastic.

An old cardboard box makes an excellent mould. Tear away the cardboard when the mixture has set, and with a knife or chisel smooth off any ridges and make the shape slightly less regular.

Place the rocks

If possible, select your own stones so as to secure a balance of large and small ones. A heap of soil dotted with small stones looks rather like an almond cake. A few large rocks, skilfully placed, should form the basis of the design. Before attempting to place them, study the stones carefully so as to determine their most attractive faces and how they can best complement one another.

ARRANGING THE ROCKS

Imitate nature as closely as possible, setting the rocks to resemble outcrops in roughly connected tiers. Pack each stone firmly and fill spaces between the rocks with earth

BUILDING A ROCK GARDEN

When constructing a tall rock face, place small stones between the large rocks to hold them apart and set plants in soil rammed into the crevices. Always place rocks with their weathered surfaces facing outwards

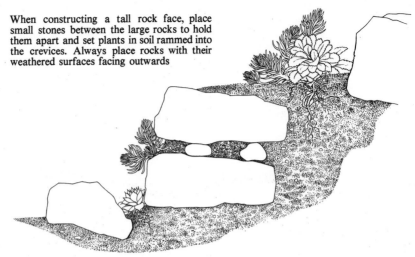

CROSS-SECTION OF A ROCK GARDEN

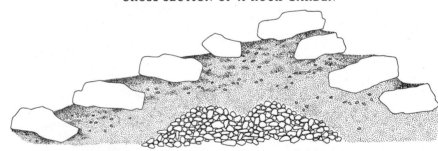

A section through a small rock garden. Note the drainage material at the base and the inward-sloping tilt of the rocks. Set at this angle, the rocks direct moisture inwards towards the plants' roots, which may be shielded by the rocks from direct watering

Incorporate shallow ravines or gullies for plants that require a fair amount of moisture. Avoid very steep slopes, which are subject to erosion. Minimise subsequent settlement by packing each stone firmly into place.

Always allow a week or two to pass before planting to give rocks and soil time to settle, otherwise air gaps are likely to appear and any plant roots in these will wither and die.

Alpines in a drystone wall

Where space is too limited to allow for a rock garden or an alpine bed, remember that many alpines will grow happily in a drystone wall or in a sink garden. If the wall already exists it will not be easy to plant, but tiny cuttings can be pushed into crevices where they will frequently root. To sow seeds in a drystone wall, place one or two in a tiny pellet of mud and squeeze the pellet into a crevice.

213

An alpine sink garden

Stone troughs are difficult to find and expensive to buy. Make your own from an old glazed kitchen sink. To enable a cement coating to stick to the glaze, first paint the sink surface with Polybond. Make up a slightly wet mixture of 1 part cement to 2 parts sand and 2 parts peat, and smear this (preferably by hand) over the surfaces of the sink. It will dry to a rough, stone-like appearance, and the highly glazed surface will be completely hidden. Crock the sink before filling with compost.

BUILDING A ROCK GARDEN ON LEVEL GROUND

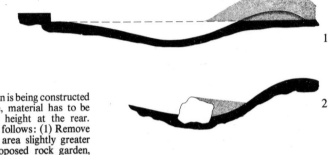

Unless the rock garden is being constructed on an existing slope, material has to be obtained to provide height at the rear. This can be done as follows: (1) Remove the topsoil from an area slightly greater than that of the proposed rock garden, stacking it on one side for returning later to the planting areas. Then excavate to a depth of 12 in. in front of the intended mound, using the soil as a base for the rock garden. (2) Place the first course of stones, then pull soil forwards to fill in the space behind. (3) When the first tier is well bedded down, place the second course, pulling soil forwards as before. (4) Continue to the required height, finally returning the topsoil to the planting areas. *Below:* A completed rock garden, with the stones placed to give a natural effect

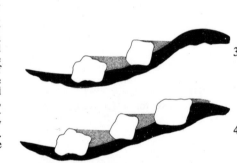

Water plants and pools

There is little to be done in the water garden this month. Water lilies make their final display in warm, sunny weather.

Collect the turions (winter buds) of hydrocharis (frogbit) and utricularia (bladderwort) before they sink to the bottom of the pool. Keep them in a small unsealed jar of water in a cool place until spring.

Pot up waterside primulas pricked out in June in John Innes potting compost No. 2, using 3 in. pots, or plant them in their permanent positions after clearing places for them in the bog garden.

Feeding fish

September and October are the most important months for fish feeding, as supplies of live food tend to decrease. Fish do not feed when the water is cold, and during the winter months exist on the store of nourishment in their own bodies. Give them a daily feed of a high-protein food, supplemented with dried *Daphnia* or other aquatic insects.

Greenhouses and frames

This is the key month in the greenhouse, as many plants can now be raised from seeds and cuttings. It is also the transition period from summer to autumn management. Towards the end of the month a little artificial heat may be needed. Leave electric heaters with the thermostat set at 7°C (45°F), but light solid-fuel boilers if there is a threat of frost or if the weather is excessively wet.

Sow annuals for spring

Annuals such as clarkias, cornflowers, nemesias, antirrhinums and calendulas, sown in September and grown in pots in a cool greenhouse, make a colourful display during spring and early summer. Sow the seeds in pans of John Innes seed compost, at a temperature of 13–16°C (55–61°F), and prick out the seedlings into 3 in. pots of John Innes potting compost No. 1 as soon as they are large enough to handle.

Prick out seedlings

Plant one seedling per pot in the case of vigorous plants such as godetias and clarkias, but plant three or four seedlings of the less vigorous kinds such as nemesias. Over-winter the plants on a shelf near the glass and re-pot them into 5 in. or 6 in. pots in February or March.

Schizanthus is one of the best plants for growing in this way. Pot the seedlings individually.

Take cuttings

Continue to take cuttings of regal pelargoniums (see JULY).

Take cuttings of fuchsias and zonal pelargoniums if this was not done last month (see AUGUST). Also abutilons (see MARCH).

Other greenhouse plants to propagate from cuttings this month include *Campanula isophylla* (see AUGUST), coleus, heliotropes, impatiens, shrubby calceolarias and *Plumbago capensis*. They will generally root satisfactorily in boxes or pots standing on the greenhouse staging, but speedier and more certain results can be obtained by placing them in a propagating frame or a mist propagator.

Remove permanent shading

Towards the end of the month remove any permanent shading from the glass. In sunny weather provide local shading for seedlings and cuttings, using paper or butter muslin.

Before the nights turn too cold, bring into the greenhouse cinerarias, primulas, cyclamens, *Solanum capsicastrum*, regal pelargoniums, begonias and gloxinias which have been standing out in frames. Discard any plants of indifferent quality.

Trees and shrubs

Early in the month dig the ground thoroughly before planting hardy evergreen shrubs at the end of the month or the beginning of October. Also prepare the ground for deciduous shrubs to be planted later in the autumn. Take care not to bring the subsoil to the surface while you dig, and work in garden compost, peat or well rotted manure. Slow-acting bone-meal at the rate of about 2–3 oz. for each shrub may also be used, but avoid any quick-acting fertilisers.

Plant evergreens

At the end of the month, and preferably during a showery spell, start planting evergreen shrubs. Disturb the ball of soil round the roots as little as possible.

Many standard shrubs need the support of a stake for a few years until they are established. Drive the stake into the planting hole before positioning the shrub, and tie the stem securely to the stake. Place a pad of hessian between stake and plant to prevent chafing of the young bark.

In the first months water newly planted shrubs freely during dry weather and spray the foliage to prevent young evergreens from shedding their leaves.

PROPAGATION
Under glass

Take hardwood and half-ripe cuttings of such evergreen and deciduous shrubs as berberis, griselinia, juniper, phlomis, potentilla and yew. They will all root readily in sandy soil in a shaded cold frame, or even in the open in a shady, sheltered place. Take pieces 6–9 in. long, complete with a slip of old wood (or heel), and insert the cuttings 2–3 in. deep in the soil, making them firm with a dibber and watering them in.

Cuttings of privet without a heel will root easily if treated in the same way.

Leave the cuttings to grow on in the frame during winter. In cold weather close the frame and place cloches over cuttings in the open. Plant cuttings of hardy species out in their permanent positions the following spring. Cuttings of tender or half-hardy species should be potted singly and kept in the cold frame before transplanting in May or June.

PRUNING

Prune phlomis lightly after flowering by removing spent flowers and thinning out old wood.

Rhododendrons and azaleas

During rainy weather, transplant any plants which need moving. (For planting instructions, see MARCH.)

Continue to increase your stock of plants by layering (see AUGUST).

Nurseries will start to deliver plants in wet weather, and these will be quite safe left unplanted for a week or two if the ground is not ready; but do not allow them to dry out. Heel them in if you are leaving them more than a fortnight.

Hedges

Clip, for the last time this season, any hedges which have produced new growth, except those that flower on their new shoots in the spring.

Pull out any remaining weeds before they seed and either burn them or put them on the compost heap. At this time of year they will take root again if left on the surface.

New sites

Prepare sites for any new hedges to be planted in the next six or seven months, first deciding on the line of the hedge. Dig the strip of ground one spit deep and 3 ft. wide (18 in. on either side of the pro-posed planting line), first marking the edges with a garden line. Skim off any turf growing on the site, burying it up-side down in the bottom of the trench as digging proceeds, and remove the roots of perennial weeds.

Plant evergreen hedges from the middle of the month until mid-October (see OCTOBER).

Heathers

Prepare the ground in which to plant heathers during October and November (see plant descriptions, JANUARY), selecting an open position well clear of overhanging trees (see MARCH). These two autumn months, and from March to May, are the best planting periods, but planting can continue, if necessary, throughout the winter during dry, frost-free weather.

Fruit

Start to plan now for the new planting season, and order new trees or bushes for autumn delivery, after consulting the list of recommended varieties (see NOVEMBER). If a new fruit garden is planned, try to fit in with the peculia-rities of the chosen site as far as possible. As a general rule south of the River Trent fruit trees like apple and pear will usually grow best in places not too near the sea and at altitudes below 400 ft. Exposed sites must be protected

216

PICKING AND STORING APPLES AND PEARS

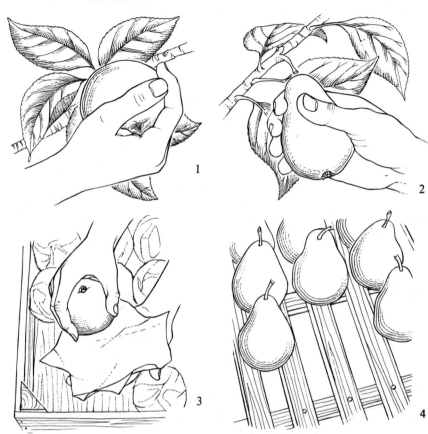

(1) Place your hand under the fruit and twist gently. (2) If the stalk is left attached to the tree, as here, the fruit will not store well.

(3) Wrap apples which are to be stored for a long time. (4) Place pears on slatted racks in a dry, moderately warm atmosphere

against the wind. High rainfall does not suit most fruit trees.

In valley bottoms, or where hedges and obstructions prevent cold air from flowing away to lower levels, frost hollows are a difficult problem; spring frosts damage tender blossoms, al-though dormant fruits can withstand winter cold. If the fruit garden is sited in a frost hollow, plant late-flowering kinds, such as 'Golden Noble' apple,

'Comice' and 'Winter Nelis' pears, 'Shropshire' damson, or any form of cultivated blackberry.

Grass the ground between established fruit trees for easier maintenance.

Honey fungus attack

The appearance of a ring of yellow-brown capped mushroom-like growths round the base of a tree in September, together with wilting leaves and even dead branches during the season, indicates that the tree has been attacked by honey fungus, *Armillaria mellea*. This is a soil-borne disease which attacks tree roots, spreads along them and affects the trunk. Even if the mushrooms have not appeared, on diseased trees the bark is loose and can often be pulled off with the hands; underneath, the trunk is covered in a white mould with a pronounced mushroom smell. There is no cure, so take out affected trees and remove as many roots as possible to prevent the fungus feeding on them while extending further underground; the spread from the mushrooms is not important. The main concern is to prevent further spread: applying a phenolic emulsion helps.

Apple and pear

Check that storage places are free from mice, and that clean trays are ready for the fruit. Leave any new containers outside to absorb moisture, otherwise they will take it from the fruit and cause it to shrivel. In the cool of the day pick the fruit before it has reached full maturity, when the fruits part easily from the spurs and the colour changes from green to yellow. Exposed fruit on the tops of trees will mature before that on the sides, and inside fruit matures last. Fruit which is to be stored for a long time should not be too large, should be free from blemishes, and should have its stalk intact. After picking wrap such fruits in paper or special oiled wrapping.

Complete summer pruning of pears and apples (see JULY). Destroy sack bands which were secured to the trees during the summer (see JUNE).

Blackberry, loganberry, and hybrid berries

Harvest the fruit as it ripens. When all the fruit has been gathered, prune old shoots and in protected situations train young growth on to the framework.

Cherry

In mid-September, spray with a copper fungicide against bacterial canker.

Peach and nectarine

After picking, prune wall-trained trees and re-tie new shoots (see AUGUST).

Plum and damson

Pick and use the fruit when it is ripe, as neither plums nor damsons can be stored for long. Prune the trees as soon as picking is over (see JULY); protect large wounds with bituminous paint.

Raspberry

Pick September-fruiting varieties.

Strawberry

Protect autumn-fruiting types against birds and slugs (see JUNE). Place cloches in position, so that the fruit can be covered when the weather turns cold.

Vegetables

In the south, for a spring lettuce crop to over-winter without cloche protection, sow 'Imperial', 'Arctic King' or 'Winter Density', setting the plants out in early October. Sow the seeds $\frac{1}{4}$ in. deep in drills 6 in. apart.

Spring cabbages in the north

In the north, plant spring cabbages in land that was manured for the previous crop. In damp, low-lying gardens, plant on ridges 9 in. high. Apply bone-meal at about 4 oz. per sq. yd. before planting, and dust the dibber holes with calomel. Set the plants with their bottom leaves at soil level, firming them in with your heel and then watering.

Lift maincrop carrots with a fork, cutting off the tops. Remove split roots for use as soon as possible and store the remainder in layers in deep boxes, with $\frac{1}{2}$ in. of sand between the layers. Place the boxes in a dry shed.

Marrows which are to be stored for use during the winter should be left on the plants until next month.

UNDER GLASS

Cloches will afford winter protection for a variety of crops, including lettuces, spring cabbages, broad beans and carrots. Protection will reduce losses during winter and hasten maturity in spring. If carrots are chosen, sow the seeds now on land that was manured for the previous crop, drawing the drills 6 in. apart and $\frac{1}{2}$ in. deep.

'Amsterdam Forcing' is a recommended variety. After sowing, apply a pre-emergence weedkiller. The other crops are sown or planted in October and November.

LESS COMMON VEGETABLES

If you have chicory growing in rows, prepare for blanching by cutting off the tops 1 in. above the roots and drawing the soil from either side to form a 9 in. ridge over the plants. Gather the white growths (chicons) which will eventually push through the ridges.

RIPENING MARROWS

To assist the ripening of marrows for storage, rest the fruits individually on platforms of glass or wood, supported by bricks

Herbs

Sow parsley and chervil now for a spring crop.

Divide and re-plant clumps of bergamot. Plant 1 ft. apart, preferably in a rich loam.

UNDER GLASS

Take cuttings of bay and rue, and root them in sandy soil in a shaded frame.

Lavender cuttings taken this month will need the protection of a frame or a cloche.

Patios and town gardens

Continue frequent watering of all plants in containers. Remove flowers that are fading.

Remove and discard plants that are past their best. As the containers are gradually emptied, prepare them for planting spring bulbs. Replenish the compost after making any necessary repairs to the containers (see MARCH). Plant the bulbs slightly deeper than normally recommended so that subjects that will provide colour during the winter can be planted on top (see NOVEMBER).

Empty dead plants and compost from containers that will not be used during the winter. Store timber containers under cover.

House plants

Though the days may appear to be almost as long and as warm as in high summer, house plants are less adaptable than humans to seasonal changes and some slight additional attention is needed.

Reduce watering and feeding slightly from the summer peak. Do not allow the more tender plants (see plant descriptions, DECEMBER) to stay too near

a cold window, particularly during the night. On the other hand, transfer plants which need plenty of light from a west to a south window. Begin to reduce the amount of water given to cacti and stand them where they will get as much sunshine as possible.

This is generally the last month to carry out any re-potting or pruning before growth slows for the winter.

Check for over-watering

During the next few weeks examine each of your plants. Look for signs of over-watering, apparent by yellowing or drooping leaves. If these are seen, let the plant dry out almost completely before watering again. Search, too, for signs of attack by red spider mites, indicated by yellowing and twisting of the leaves and by the presence of fine spiders' webs. The webs are so difficult to see that it is helpful in doubtful cases to sprinkle powder or cigarette ash over the affected part. The webs, if present, will retain the powder.

Red spider control

To eradicate red spider mites, spray with derris or malathion, making sure that every part of the plant is covered. If the plant is small and easily handled, dip it in insecticide. In the case of large plants, if spraying is inconvenient sponge both sides of the leaves with insecticide. If the infestation is severe, discard the plant and burn it, together with the soil.

Increase humidity

Red spider attacks are commonest where the atmosphere is too dry, so try to increase the atmospheric humidity around your plants. If possible, place one or two pans of water about the house in inconspicuous places, or hang proprietary humidifiers on the radiators. Plunge pots in larger containers, with moist peat between the two, or stand the plants on gravel trays which are always

kept moist. Even the occasional bowl of boiling water brought into the room and allowed to stay until the water cools will provide plants with extra humidity.

General tasks

Clear away any crops that have finished producing, such as stumps of summer cabbages or peas.

Order bulbs, roses, herbaceous plants, trees, shrubs and fruit bushes this month, otherwise you may not get the varieties you want.

Take cuttings of evergreen shrubs, hydrangeas and geraniums.

Control mildew

Mildew is the worst autumn trouble, affecting many plants, especially roses and michaelmas daisies. It can be controlled by spraying with fungicide, but varieties that habitually suffer from mildew should be marked for replacement by immune or resistant varieties.

Check electrical installations

If you have any electrical installations in frames or greenhouses, get an electrician to check them over every two years and make an earth leakage test. Insulation of cables can break down after a time in damp outdoor conditions, and it is infuriating to have a failure of the heating system just as the first frosts arrive.

Carry out construction jobs

Hasten on with any major constructional jobs, such as paving, walling and fence repairs. Once frosty weather arrives it is unwise to carry on with work involving concreting. If wet concrete is frozen it will disintegrate.

Check that gutters and drains are free from leaves or other debris. There are usually some heavy storms late in the month, and these can cause flooding.

Trees and shrubs to select in September

All the trees and shrubs described on the following pages are hardy in the British Isles unless otherwise stated. A few are described as semi-evergreen, which means that they retain their leaves in a mild winter but may shed them during a severe winter. The comment 'prune when necessary' means prune only to retain shape or restrict growth.

Abies (fir)
Evergreen coniferous trees of pyramidal or cylindrical habit. Plant in a moist position in any well drained soil. No pruning. *A. concolor* (Colorado fir). Height up to 100 ft. or more.

Abies concolor

Spread 15–20 ft. Long grey needles are set in two rows along the branches. Cylindrical cones are up to 5 in. long, green to purple becoming light brown. *A. spectabilis* (Himalayan fir). Height up to 150 ft. Glossy dark green leaves are silvery beneath.

Acer (maple)
A large family of deciduous trees and shrubs notable for their decorative foliage. They do best in light loam and peat, in an open position; Japanese varieties in warm, sheltered borders. No pruning. *A. capillipes*. Height and spread 30 ft. Marbled bark. Green, red-veined leaves turn crimson in autumn.

A. negundo elegantissimum. Height 25 ft. Spread 35 ft. Golden variegated leaves. Japanese maples include *A. japonicum* and *A. palmatum*. Height 10–20 ft. Spread 15–25 ft. There are many varieties, with pale green, crimson or bronze leaves, usually five-lobed, and some deeply cut. All assume splendid autumn colours. Purple flowers in June. *A. platanoides* (Norway maple). Height 60 ft. Spread 50 ft. Fast-growing tree with five-lobed, bright green leaves, turning yellow in autumn. Green-yellow flowers in April, and keys about 2 in. long. *A. pseudoplatanus* (sycamore). Height 70 ft. Spread 60 ft. Various forms have mottled or variegated foliage, or leaves edged with white. All are five-lobed and coarsely toothed. Green flowers are produced in drooping racemes in summer. Suitable for exposed position in any soil.

Acer platanoides

Actinidia
Deciduous twining plants. Thrive in good garden soil, against a fence or supported by trellis against a wall. Propagate by layers in November. No pruning. *A. chinensis* (Chinese gooseberry). Vigorous climber, covering an area of 6 sq. ft. within a couple of years. Hairy red shoots with large heart-shaped leaves. Small white flowers are unisexual. If plants of both sexes are grown, large gooseberry-like fruits are produced and may ripen in sheltered southern and western gardens.

Actinidia chinensis

Aesculus (horse chestnut)
Deciduous. Fruits, often prickly, contain one or more shiny brown seeds. Plant in sun or shade in ordinary, well drained soil. No pruning. *A. hippocastanum* (common horse chestnut). Height 80–100 ft. Spread 50–70 ft.

Aesculus hippocastanum

White flowers, with a red patch at the base of each petal, are borne on erect panicles in May. *A. carnea* (red horse chestnut). Height 35–50 ft. Spread 25–40 ft. Similar, but with pink flowers.

Amelanchier canadensis

Amelanchier

Hardy deciduous spring-flowering trees. Thrive in any soil, preferably moist, and in a sunny position. Suitable for town gardens. Propagate by seeds, layers or rooted offsets in March. No pruning. *A. canadensis* (snowy mespilus or June berry). Height and spread 25 ft. White trailing flowers in April are followed by purple berries in June. Oblong leaves, woolly on both sides when young, turn bronze-yellow in autumn.

Arbutus (strawberry tree)

Small family of large evergreen shrubs. Thrive on the coast in a sunny position, and on limy soil. No pruning. *A. unedo.* Height 15 ft. Spread 18 ft.

Arbutus unedo

Pitcher-shaped clusters of creamy-white, self-fertile flowers in autumn, with deep orange-red strawberry-like fruits produced from previous year's blooms. Dark glossy leaves. The form *rubra* has pink flowers.

Arundinaria (bamboo)

Evergreen shrubby grasses, rarely in flower. Plant in good moist soil and in sunny positions, sheltered from cold winds. Once established, bamboos are fast-growing. Propagate by division and replanting in June. *A. japonica* (Japanese bamboo). Height up to 15 ft. One of the

Arundinaria japonica

hardiest bamboos, suitable for forming a windbreak in exposed gardens, or a screen in more sheltered gardens.

Aucuba

Evergreen shrubs. Easily grown in any soil and in shady places beneath deciduous trees. Increase by hardwood cuttings in October. No pruning. Excellent for town and seaside gardens. *A. japonica* (spotted laurel). Height and spread 8 ft. Narrow, oval, leathery green leaves. Purple flowers in erect panicles in March and April. Both male and female plants are needed to produce red berries in autumn and winter. To get the best show of berries, plant three females to one male.

Aucuba japonica

Berberis (barberry)

A large family of evergreen and deciduous shrubs notable for a profusion of flowers and berries. They thrive in full sun and partial shade, and in almost any soil, including chalk, that is reasonably well drained. Propagate by hardwood cuttings in September. No pruning other than thinning out old wood in early spring. The following are evergreen forms: *B. darwinii.* Height and spread 8–10 ft. Orange-yellow flowers in May and June, purple-blue berries. Leaves are small, holly-like and glossy. *B. stenophylla.* Height 10 ft. Spread 12 ft. Golden flowers in April; blue berries, covered with white bloom. Entire, narrow leaves.

Berberis darwinii

Both are suitable hedging plants that need only light trimming to shape. The following are deciduous forms: *B. rubrostilla.* Height 4 ft. Spread 6–8 ft. Notable for its sprays of brilliant coral-red berries and ruby autumn foliage. *B. thunbergii.* Height 6 ft. Spread 8 ft. Pale yellow flowers in spring; berries and autumn foliage are brilliant red. The small green leaves are blue-grey beneath.

Betula (birch)

Deciduous trees, notable for the various bark colours. Plant in ordinary soil, in sun or shade.

Betula pendula

No pruning. Associate well with hardy heathers. *B. pendula* (common silver birch). Height 50–60 ft. Spread 15–20 ft. *B. p. dalecarlica* (Swedish birch). Height 50–70 ft. Spread 30–35 ft. An erect tree with pendulous branches and deeply cut leaves. *B. p. youngii.* Height 20–30 ft. Spread 25–35 ft. A dome-shaped weeping tree suitable for the lawn.

Buddleia

Deciduous, often fragrant, shrubs. Will grow in any light soil, such as chalk, in a sunny position. *B. alternifolia.* Height 15 ft. Spread 20 ft. Soft-purple flowers in graceful sprays during June and July. Small lance-shaped leaves are set alternately

Buddleia davidii

n slender arching stems. Propagate in July by softwood cuttings. Thin out old wood immediately after flowering. *B. davidii* (butterfly bush). Height 9–12 ft. Spread 12 ft. Purple spikes of flowers in late summer. Large lance-shaped leaves. Propagate in August by softwood cuttings, or in the autumn by half-ripe cuttings. Prune in April. There are several named, coloured forms. *B. globosa*. Height 12 ft. Spread 10 ft. Orange, ball-like flowers in May–June. Large lance-shaped leaves. Propagate in August by cuttings. Prune hard back after flowering.

Callicarpa

Deciduous shrubs, notable for their large clusters of berries and autumn foliage. Plant in well drained loamy soil in a sheltered, sunny position. Propagate by half-ripe cuttings in July and August. Thin out in February. *C. giraldiana*. Height

Callicarpa giraldiana

ft. Spread 4 ft. Small pink flowers in July, followed, when several shrubs are grown, by masses of bead-like violet berries. Rosy-violet tinted leaves in autumn.

Camellia

Hardy evergreen shrubs. Easily grown in lime-free, cool soil in sheltered positions, such as a woodland garden or against a north wall. In an east-facing

Camellia japonica

position the morning sun after a frosty night may ruin the blooms, and a south-facing wall may prove too hot for the roots. Propagate in March by leaf cuttings, or in July by half-ripe wood cuttings. No pruning. *C. japonica*. Height 6–20 ft. Spread 6–15 ft. Double or single blooms in March and April are red, pink, white or variegated. Glossy leaves. Red varieties: 'Adolphe Audusson', 'Fred Sander', 'Mars'. Pink: 'Elegans', 'Gloire de Nantes', 'Lady Clare'. White: *alba grandiflora* (double), *alba simplex* (single), *nobilissima* (double). Variegated varieties include: 'Apollo', red, flecked with white (semi-double); 'Contessa Lavinia Maggi', white, flushed with pink and speckled with carmine (single).

Campsis radicans

Campsis (trumpet creeper)

Deciduous vigorous self-clinging creepers. Thrive in southern gardens, against a wall in full sun and in loamy soil. Propagate in July by cuttings of young shoots, or in March by root cuttings. Prune in February. *C. radicans*. Height and spread up to 30 ft. Large, tubular vermilion trumpet flowers in August and September. Long, coarsely toothed leaflets are downy beneath. The variety 'Madame Gallen' is salmon-red.

Carpinus (hornbeam)

Deciduous trees commonly used for hedging. Plant 18 in. apart in ordinary soil, including chalk. Trim hedges in July or August. *C. betulus* (common hornbeam).

Carpinus betulus

Height up to 80 ft.; hedges to 20 ft. Double-toothed oval leaves will remain on branches throughout winter, until new leaves appear in spring.

Caryopteris (blue spiraea)

Deciduous shrubs, suitable for ordinary soil and full sun. Propagate by half-ripe cuttings in August or September. Prune in March. *C. clandonensis*. Height and spread 4–5 ft. Bright blue flowers in August and September, or later. Grey-green aromatic leaves.

Caryopteris clandonensis

Ceanothus

Large family of hardy and half-hardy evergreen and deciduous shrubs, with numerous small, usually blue flowers from July onwards. Do best trained against a south- or west-facing wall, and in ordinary, well drained soil. Propagate by heel cuttings in August. Prune evergreen species lightly after flowering; deciduous species should be cut back in March. Evergreen species include: *C. burkwoodii*. Height 10–20 ft. Spread 12–15 ft. Rich blue flowers in late summer and autumn. *C. prostratus*. Prostrate and up to 10 ft. wide. Bright blue flowers during summer; of creeping habit, and suitable for

Ceanothus burkwoodii

a sheltered, sunny bank. *C. thyrsiflorus*. Height 15–30 ft. Spread up to 15 ft. against a wall. Pale blue flowers in May. The hardiest species. Deciduous species include: *C. dentatus*. Height 8–10 ft. Spread 8–12 ft. Bright blue flowers. Among named hybrids are: 'Ceres', lilac-pink flowers throughout summer; 'Gloire de Versailles', fragrant powder blue flowers, June–October; 'Topaz', deep blue flowers during summer and autumn.

Celastrus

Deciduous twining plants. Plant in ordinary soil, against a wall or fence. Propagate by layers in March or October. Prune in February. *C. orbiculatus*. Height 40 ft. or more. Vigorous climber.

Celastrus orbiculatus

In late autumn and winter bears numerous pea-like fruits which split when ripe, revealing the deep yellow of the capsule and three bright red seeds.

Cercis

Small family of deciduous trees and shrubs. Plant in full sun in any reasonable soil, including chalk. No pruning. *C. siliquastrum* (Judas tree). Height up to 25 ft. Spread 20 ft. Rosy-lilac pea-flowers appear in May before the rounded light green leaves develop. *C. s. alba* has white flowers.

Cercis siliquastrum

Chaenomeles (flowering quince)

These deciduous early-flowering shrubs do best in full sun and in any reasonable soil. Propagate by layers in June. Prune after flowering. *C. japonica* (Japanese quince). Height 3–8 ft. Spread

Chaenomeles japonica

5–8 ft. Large orange-scarlet flowers in March. Oval, almost round, shiny green leaves. Apple-like fruits may be used for making jelly. Of spreading habit, it may be trained against a wall.

Chamaecyparis (false cypress)

Evergreen conifers. Plant in rich, preferably moist, soil as hedging plants (2 ft. apart) or as

a specimen for a lawn. Propagate by cuttings from July to September. No pruning when grown as a specimen. Hedges should be trimmed in May or June. *C. lawsoniana* (Lawson's cypress). Height 40 ft. Spread 10 ft. Of pyramidal habit, with red-brown bark and variable foliage. Round glaucous cones turn brown. Suitable as a hedging plant. More ornamental varieties, with foliage in shades of green, grey, glaucous, silver and golden, include *C. l. allumii*. Height 40 ft. Spread 10 ft.

Chamaecyparis lawsoniana

Glaucous-blue foliage. *C. l. fletcheri*. Height 15–20 ft. Spread 6–8 ft. Grey-blue feathery foliage. Suitable as a specimen tree. *C. l. lutea*. Height 30 ft. Spread 9–12 ft. Cone-shaped tree with bright golden foliage.

Chimonanthus (winter sweet)

Deciduous shrubs, flowering when well established. Plant in well drained loamy soil, and against a sunny south or west wall. Propagate by layers in March. Prune after flowering. *C. praecox* (syn. *C. fragrans*). Height 8–10 ft. Spread 10–12 ft. Fragrant flowers, waxy cream with purple centres, are borne on naked branches in December and January. Young plants need protection against frost until established.

Chimonanthus praecox

Choisya (Mexican orange)

Evergreen single species. *C. ternata*. Height 6–9 ft. Spread 7–10 ft. Fragrant clusters of white flowers in May and June. Suitable for any well drained soil, including chalk, in a sheltered, sunny corner. The glossy green foliage is liable to damage from cold winds and late spring frost. Propagate in August by softwood cuttings. Prune lightly after flowering.

Choisya ternata

Cistus (rock rose)

Evergreen shrubs, free-flowering from May to July. Hardy in southern gardens, they thrive in dry soil, and in hot sun.

Cistus laurifolius

Deciduous. Purple-blue flowers, July–September. Green ovate leaflets. There are many summer-flowering named hybrids, including the soft pink 'Comtesse de Bouchard' and 'Nelly Moser', mauve-pink with deep carmine bar. C. macropetala. Height 5 ft. Deciduous. Pendent heads of violet-blue flowers in May. Leaves lance-shaped, coarsely toothed. C. montana. Height 20 ft. Deciduous. Profusion of star-shaped white flowers in May. Ovate pointed leaflets. C. patens. Height 12 ft. Deciduous.

positions. Propagate in July or August by cuttings of half-ripe wood. No pruning, except for removal of damaged parts in March after a hard winter. C. corbariensis. Height 2–3 ft. Spread 5–8 ft. White flowers, yellow at base. C. ladaniferus (gum cistus). Height 5 ft. Spread ? ft. White flowers with crimson blotches at base. C. laurifolius. Height 6 ft. Spread 5 ft. White flowers, yellow at base of petals; the hardiest species. 'Silver Pink' (height 3–4 ft.) has soft pink flowers; 'Sunset' (height 2–3 ft.) has purple-red flowers.

Clematis
Large family of hardy, deciduous and evergreen climbers. Plant in limy soil with plenty of leaf-mould to keep the roots moist, and in sun or partial shade. Propagate species by seed in March or by layering in June or early July. Named hybrids may also be increased by layering or cuttings in July. Prune summer-flowering varieties in February; spring-flowering species after flowering. Suitable for training against walls, pergolas and old tree-trunks. C. armandii. Height 10–20 ft. Evergreen. Clusters of white flowers in April. Dark, glossy green narrow leaves. Requires a sheltered wall. C. jackmanii. Height up to 10 ft.

Clematis 'Nelly Moser'

Large violet-mauve flowers in May and June. Ovate pointed leaves. C. tangutica. Height 10 ft. Deciduous. Hanging bell-shaped yellow flowers in July.

Cornus (dogwood or cornel)
A large family of decorative shrubs or small trees. Those listed are all deciduous. Prefer moist soil in sun or partial shade. No pruning. C. alba sibirica. Height 8–10 ft. Spread 9–12 ft. Stems are coral red. Clusters of small yellow flowers. Green leaves. The variety variegata has silver edges to green-grey leaves. C. kousa. Height 20 ft. Spread 25 ft. Large creamy-white bracts in June, followed by strawberry-like fruits on spreading, horizontal branches. Ovate leaves with crimson

Cornus kousa

autumn foliage. The variety chinensis has larger bracts, is taller and of more open habit. C. mas (cornelian cherry). Height up to 20 ft. Spread 25 ft. Small yellow flowers in February before dull green leaves and cherry-like red berries.

Corylopsis
These deciduous early-flowering shrubs do well in any good soil, including sand, and in a position sheltered from morning sun which may damage the flowers after a frosty night. Propagate by layers in October. No pruning. C. pauciflora. Height and spread 4–6 ft. Tender, except in warm

Corylopsis spicata

districts. Fragrant yellow flowers in February and March. C. spicata. Height 6 ft. Spread 6–8 ft. Hardier than C. pauciflora. Pendent clusters of pale yellow, fragrant flowers in spring.

Cotoneaster
A large family of deciduous and evergreen shrubs, mainly remarkable for their berries and some for their autumn foliage. Heights vary from prostrate species to 20 ft. or more. Spread indefinite. Small white or rose-tinted flowers in May or June. Easily grown in any well drained soil and in open or shaded positions. Propagate by seed in March, or by cuttings of half-ripe wood in June and July. Prune straggling growths in winter. C. adpressa. Height 1 ft. Deciduous. Scarlet leaves and red berries in autumn. Ideal for

Cotoneaster horizontalis

the rock garden. C. bullata. Height and spread 15 ft. Deciduous. Arching branches with clusters of cherry-like red berries and large corrugated leaves. 'Cornubia' is a well-known variety. C. frigida. Height 20 ft. Spread 25 ft. Deciduous. Vigorous, quick-growing screening shrub with clusters of bright red berries. C. horizontalis. Height 3 ft.; against a wall 10 ft. Spread 8–10 ft. Deciduous. Brilliant red berries on the herring-bone branches last well into winter. *C. microphylla*. Height 3 ft. Indefinite spread. Evergreen. Slender pointed leaves and large red berries in autumn.

Crataegus (hawthorn or may) Deciduous small trees with white or pale pink flowers in May. Will grow in any soil and in an open sunny position. No pruning. *C. monogyna* (quickthorn). Height 15–20 ft. Spread 20–25 ft. Plant 1 ft. apart to form a dense hedge. Clusters of white flowers in May and June,

Crataegus coccinea plena

followed by red berries. Prune hedges to shape from June onwards. *C. oxyacantha*. Height and spread 20–25 ft. Numerous decorative forms include: *coccinea plena* (Paul's double scarlet thorn), double scarlet flowers; 'Maskei', double pale rose; *plena*, double white; *rosea flore pleno*, double pink.

Cytisus (broom) Deciduous free-flowering shrubs. Do well in full sun, and even in poor soil. Propagate by seed in February or April, or by heel cuttings in August. Prune directly after flowering. *C. ardoinii* (dwarf broom). Height 4–6 in. Of spreading habit, and suitable for the rock garden. Clusters of small bright yellow flowers in April and May. *C. praecox*.

Cytisus scoparius

Height 6 ft. Spread 6–8 ft. Buttercup-yellow flowers in April and early May. *C. scoparius* (common yellow broom). Height and spread 8 ft. Fragrant yellow flowers, April to July. The parent of many hybrids: 'Andreanus', yellow and crimson; 'Firefly', yellow and bronze-crimson; 'Windlesham Ruby', red. Brooms go well with hardy heathers.

Daphne Evergreen and deciduous fragrant shrubs. Suitable for a rock garden with moist, well drained loamy soil, in sun or partial shade. Leaf-mould or peat will help to keep the roots cool.

Daphne cneorum

Propagate by layers in autumn. No pruning. *D. cneorum* (garland flower). Height 1 ft. Spread 3 ft. Evergreen. Rose-pink flowers in May. Does not object to lime. *D. mezereum*. Height 3–4 ft. Spread 4 ft. Deciduous. Pale pink flowers in February and March on erect branches before leaves appear. Bright red berries. Grows best in full sun. There is also a white form.

Deutzia These deciduous free-flowering shrubs can be grown in almost any soil, preferably with some lime, and in sun or dappled shade. Propagate by softwood cuttings in June or July, or by hardwood cuttings in October.

Deutzia gracilis

Prune after flowering. *D. elegantissima*. Height 5 ft. Spread 6 ft. Rose-pink fragrant flowers in May. *D. gracilis*. Height 4 ft. Spread 5 ft. White flowers on arching stems in May and June. *D. pulchra*. Height 6–8 ft. Spread 6–9 ft. Large pendent panicles of white flowers in May. Grey-green foliage.

Eccremocarpus Deciduous tendril climbers, hardy in warm districts, but not suitable for cold, exposed northern gardens. Plant in light soil against a warm south or southwest wall. Easily propagated by

Eccremocarpus scaber

seeds in March. No pruning. *E. scaber* (Chilean glory flower). Height 6–8 ft. Fast-growing. Clusters of tubular red or orange flowers from June to September. Suitable for training against trellis or wire to cover screens and fences. Frost often kills the plants.

Elaeagnus Evergreen and deciduous shrubs notable for their foliage. Thrive in full sun and in poor, well drained soil. Propagate by half-ripe cuttings in July, or by hardwood cuttings in November. No pruning. *E. pungens*. Height ft. Spread 10–15 ft. Evergreen.

Elaeagnus pungens aureo-variegata

ragrant yellow-white flowers
autumn. Suitable hedging
lant. The variegated forms.
ich as *E. p. aureo-variegata*,
ith rich gold and glossy green
aves, are preferable to the
ecies. Remove entirely shoots
hich revert to green.

Escallonia macrantha

scallonia
vergreen free-flowering shrubs.
uitable hedging plants for
easide gardens. Some varieties
re reasonably hardy inland.
n northern gardens they may
e grown on a south-facing wall.
hrive in any good garden soil,
cid or alkaline. Propagate by
alf-ripe cuttings in July and
ugust, or by ripe hardwood
uttings in October and Novem-
er. Prune after flowering. *E.
iacrantha*. Height up to 6 ft.;
gainst a wall 10 ft. Spread 10 ft.
tosy-crimson flowers from June
nwards, and glossy foliage.
Iybrid varieties, suitable as
edging plants, include: 'C. F.
tall'. Height and spread 9–12 ft.
.arge tubular scarlet flowers in
une and July; pale green leaves.
Donard Seedling'. Height and
pread 9–12 ft. Fragrant pale
ink flowers in June.

Euonymus (spindle)
vergreen and deciduous hardy
hrubs. They thrive on chalk,
ut will grow in almost any

soil in sun or shade. Propagate
evergreen varieties by cuttings
of half-ripe wood in July or
August. Prune evergreen varieties in April. *E. alata*. Height 6 ft.
Spread 8 ft. In autumn deciduous green leaves turn pink.
Corky bark. *E. europaeus* (common spindle tree). Height 9 ft.
Spread 12 ft. Deciduous foliage
has brilliant autumn colours and
bright red fruits, which open
up to show orange-red seeds. *E.
fortunei* (syn. *E. radicans*). Prostrate evergreen, useful as ground
cover in sun or shade. Propagate
by division in October. *E. japonica*. Height 12 ft. Spread 10 ft.
Evergreen with leathery, dark
green leaves and pink fruits.
Suitable as a hedging plant for
coastal or town gardens.

Euonymus japonica

Fagus (beech)
Deciduous trees. Plant in sandy,
chalky or ordinary, well drained
soil, in open sunny positions.
No pruning. *F. sylvatica* (common beech). Height 80–100 ft.
Spread 70–80 ft. Round clusters
of green flowers appear in spring
after oval wavy-edged leaves.
Suitable as specimen trees or for
hedges; the latter, when trimmed
in July or August, retain the
leaves until the following spring.
Varieties include *purpurea*, purple beech; *cuprea*, copper beech;
pendula, weeping beech.

Fagus sylvatica

Forsythia
Deciduous, easily grown and
early-flowering shrubs. Plant in
sun or partial shade in ordinary
soil. Propagate by hardwood
cuttings in October. *F. intermedia*. Height 8 ft. Spread 8–12 ft.
Golden-yellow flowers in March
and April. The variety *spectabilis* is of erect habit with larger, bright yellow flowers and
is suitable as a hedging plant.
No pruning when grown as a
specimen; trim hedges hard
back in April. *F. suspensa*.
Height and spread 10–15 ft. Primrose-yellow pendulous flowers
in April. Suitable for a north-

Forsythia intermedia
spectabilis

facing wall. The drooping branches often root where they touch
the ground; these rooted pieces
can easily be severed from the
parent plant. Prune in April.
One of the most vigorous forms
is *fortunei*.

Fothergilla
Deciduous slow-growing flowering shrubs, notable for their
autumn colours of orange and
crimson. Plant in light lime-free
soil and in a sunny position.
Propagate by cuttings in August,

Fothergilla monticola

or by layers in October. No
pruning *F. gardenii*. Height and
spread 3 ft. Fragrant white tufts
of long stamens in May. *F.
monticola*. Height 6–8 ft. Spread
5–7 ft. Large flower spikes of
fragrant cream-white stamens in
April and May.

Fuchsia
Deciduous hardy shrubs flowering through the summer into
autumn. Height 2–4 ft. Spread
3–5 ft. Plant in sun or partial
shade in any good garden soil.
In northern districts the roots
need protection in winter. Propagate by cuttings in June or
August. Cut back in March.
Good hybrids are 'Dr. Foster',
scarlet and cyclamen-purple
flowers; 'Graf Witte', carmine
and soft violet-blue, 'Madame

Fuchsia

Cornelissen' (semi-double), white and deep rose-carmine; 'Mrs. Popple', carmine and deep violet. 'Tom Thumb', with violet and carmine flowers, rarely exceeds 2 ft. and is suitable for the rock garden. *F. magellanica*. Height 2–5 ft. Suitable as a flowering hedge in mild or seaside districts. Profusion of carmine and crimson flowers throughout summer. No pruning, but thin established hedges lightly in March. The variety *riccartonii* is the hardiest.

Garrya
Strongly-growing evergreen shrubs. Male and female flowers (or catkins) are produced on

Garrya elliptica

separate trees. Thrive in ordinary, well drained soil, in a sheltered position against a wall, and in sun or partial shade. Propagate by cuttings in August. Prune only to maintain shape. *G. elliptica*. Height 8–12 ft. Spread 8–12 ft. Grey-green male catkins, 9 in. long, are freely produced in January and February. Female catkins are less spectacular, but produce clusters of black fruits if male and female plants are grown.

Genista
Broom-like deciduous flowering shrubs. Easily grown in light, well drained soil and full sun. Propagate by seed in March or April, or by heel cuttings in August; young, pot-grown plants are the best for

Genista lydia

transplanting. No pruning. *G. hispanica* (Spanish broom). Height about 2 ft. Spread 6 ft. Clusters of bright yellow flowers in May and June. Excellent shrub for a dry bank. *G. lydia*. Height 2–3 ft. Spread 6–8 ft. Bright yellow flowers on slender, pendulous, grey-green branches in May and June. Suitable for a dry wall or a sunny rock garden. *G. tinctoria* (dyer's greenwood). Height 1–2 ft. Spread 6 ft. Deep-yellow pea-like flowers in June and July. The prostrate form, *flore pleno*, has double yellow flowers.

Ginkgo biloba

Ginkgo (maindenhair tree)
Deciduous slow-growing conifer. Plant in sheltered position (in southern gardens as a lawn specimen), and in ordinary soil. No pruning. *G. biloba*. Height 60–80 ft. Spread 30–40 ft. Light green leathery leaves, resembling those of the maidenhair fern, turn clear yellow in autumn. Catkin-like flowers in spring.

Griselinia
Evergreen shrubs, slightly tender in frost-prone inland gardens. Suitable as hedging shrubs in ordinary or chalky soil, especially in seaside gardens, or as a hedge beneath deciduous trees. Propagate in September by

Griselinia littoralis

half-ripe cuttings. Trim light in April. *G. littoralis*. Height to 20 ft. Small green flowers an rounded triangular leaves.

Hamamelis (witch-hazel)
Deciduous shrubs, winter-flowering. Their narrow-petalled fragrant flowers are in shades yellow, gold and rusty-orange Large hazel-like leaves oft assume colourful autumn tint Plant in sun or partial shade, lime-free, well drained an moist soil. No pruning. *japonica*. Height 10–15 Spread 15 ft. Bright yellow

Hamamelis mollis

flowers from January onward *H. mollis*. Height 10–12 Spread 12–15 ft. Rich golde yellow flowers from Decemb to February. Leaves turn simil colour in autumn.

Hebe (veronica)
Evergreen tender shrubs. Flow spikes in shades of white, pin blue, lilac or mauve are pr duced throughout the summe Most adaptable for frost-fr maritime districts or inla sheltered gardens, where th thrive in well drained soil a in full sun. Propagate by ha ripe cuttings in August. pruning except to remove fro damaged shoots in March. *speciosa*. Height 2 ft. Spread 3

Hebe speciosa

decorative than the gold and silver variegated forms. Will grow in any soil, and in shade or partial sun. Propagate by half-ripe cuttings in August or September, or by hardwood cuttings in November. Trim in April when necessary. Suitable as cover for a north-facing wall.

Hibiscus (tree mallow or tree hollyhock)

These deciduous summer-flowering shrubs thrive in well drained rich soil and in full sun. Propagate by heel cuttings of half-ripe shoots in July. Little pruning unless trained against a wall, when these specimens should be

'Midsummer Beauty' has lavender-blue flower spikes from June . August. *H. cupressoides*. eight 2–3 ft. Spread 3–4 ft. Pale ue flowers in June and July. laucous-blue leaves. Hardy in e south. *H. hulkeana*. Height d spread 5–6 ft. Panicles of le lavender flowers, up to ft. long, in May and June. eds wall protection.

edera (ivy)

vergreen self-clinging climbers ground-cover plants. *H. lchica variegata* is an attractive d strongly-growing ivy. The mmon ivy, *H. helix*, is less

Hibiscus syriacus

cut back after flowering. *H. syriacus* (bush mallow). Height 8 ft. Spread 8–10 ft. Mallow-like flowers, 2 in. or more across, in shades of blue, purple, pink and white in August and September. Among leading varieties are 'Blue Bird', the best single blue; 'Snowdrift', large single white; 'Woodbridge', large single red.

Hydrangea

Deciduous shrubs, hardy in the south and west. Most varieties thrive in sun or partial shade and in almost any soil, kept amply moist during the growing season. *H. macrophylla* (syn. *H. hortensia* and *H. opuloides*).

Hedera helix

Height and spread 3–4 ft. Large flower heads in shades of blue, pink, red or white in summer and autumn. Hortensia varieties have round heads of sterile flowers; lacecap forms have flat flower heads composed of a centre of small fertile flowers, surrounded by larger sterile florets. Propagate by cuttings in August. Thin out weak shoots during March.

Hydrangea macrophylla

H. paniculata grandiflora. Height 6–7 ft. Spread 6–8 ft. Large panicles of creamy-white flowers on erect, semi-arching stems in August and September. Propagate by half-ripe cuttings in July or by layering in April. Prune in April. *H. petiolaris*. Self-clinging climber up to 50 ft. high. Suitable for north-, east- or west-facing walls. Flat heads of white flowers in June. Heart-shaped dark green leaves. Propagate by half-ripe cuttings in July or August. No pruning.

Hypericum (St. John's wort)

Evergreen and deciduous late summer and autumn-flowering shrubs, all with yellow or golden flowers. Plant in a sunny position in any well drained soil. Propagate by softwood or hardwood cuttings in July and August. *H. calycinum* (rose of Sharon). Height 1–1½ ft. Indefinite spread. Evergreen. A good ground-cover

Hypericum calycinum

plant for sun or dry shade, with individual flowers 3 in. across. Propagate by division in March. Cut hard back in March. *H. patulum henryi*. Height and spread 3–4 ft. Semi-evergreen. Cup-shaped golden flowers in July and August. Prune lightly in March.

Ilex (holly)

Evergreens. Slow-growing in any soil and suitable for exposed or town gardens. They do not transplant readily, and must be lifted with a ball of soil attached in September, October or April. Propagate by half-ripe cuttings in August. No pruning. *I. aquifolium* (common holly).

Ilex aquifolium 'Golden King'

Height 40–50 ft. Spread 30–35 ft. Variegated varieties: 'Golden King'. Height 6–10 ft. Spread 12 ft. Wide, bright yellow margins to leaves. 'Silver Queen'. Height 8–10 ft. Spread 12 ft. Broad leaves with creamy-white variegations. *I. aquifolium* is suitable for a hedge and should be trimmed in April or winter-pruned in September. The variegated forms make fine specimen shrubs.

Jasminum (jasmine)
Deciduous climbing plants. Easily cultivated in any well drained soil and against a wall facing east, south or south-west. *J. nudiflorum* (winter jasmine). Height 5–10 ft. Spread 8–10 ft.

Jasminum nudiflorum

Sprays of yellow flowers from November to February. Does well on a north-facing wall. Propagate by hardwood cuttings in November. Prune after flowering. *J. officinale.* Height and spread up to 20 ft. Fragrant white sprays from June to September. Propagate by half-ripe heel cuttings in July and August. Prune after flowering and thin out in winter.

Juniperus
Conifers of erect and spreading habit. Thrive in an open position and in any soil, particularly

Juniperus communis
compressa

chalk. Propagate by cuttings of young shoots in September or October. No pruning. *J. communis compressa* (Noah's ark juniper). Height 2½ ft. Spread 1 ft. Slow-growing; suitable for the rock garden, where it forms a blue-grey pillar. *J. communis hibernica* (Irish juniper). Height 10–15 ft. Spread 2 ft. Erect tree with dark green glaucous foliage. *J. sabina tamariscifolia.* Prostrate, spreading to 10 ft. Rich green foliage is suitable for covering a sunny bank or a large rock garden.

Kerria (jew's mallow)
These deciduous spring-flowering shrubs thrive in almost any

Kerria japonica

soil in semi-shade or sun. Propagate by division and replanting in March, or by hardwood cuttings in October or November. Prune immediately after flowering. *K. japonica.* Height 4–6 ft. Spread 4–8 ft. Golden-yellow flowers in May. Small leaves on bright green graceful stems. The double flowered variety, *pleniflora*, is less hardy and is better when planted against even a north-facing wall where it will grow to about 7 ft. 'Picta' is a silver-variegated dwarf form.

Laburnum
Deciduous trees with long racemes of golden flowers in May. Height up to 25 ft. Spread 25–30 ft. Grow best in a sunny

Laburnum vossii

position and in any soil. Propagate in March by seeds which are poisonous. Prune by thinning out weak shoots in early spring; remove spent flower heads after flowering. *L. vossii.* Extremely long racemes of yellow flowers in May and June.

Lathyrus
Perennial hardy tendril climbers. Plant in rich, well manured soil, in sunny borders against a fence or trained to form a temporary screen during summer. Propagate by division in March or by sowing seeds in October.

Lathyrus latifolius

No pruning. *L. latifolius* (everlasting pea). Height up to 6 ft. Purple, rose, pink or white flowers from June onwards. These perennial sweet peas die back in winter, but new shoots will develop the following spring.

Laurus (bay tree)
Reasonably hardy, evergreen shrubs. Will grow in any soil, in sun or partial shade. Propagate by half-ripe cuttings in August. *L. nobilis* (sweet bay). Height and spread 20 ft. or more. Aromatic glossy leaves are used in cooking. May be clipped during summer to form a dense bush. Can also be grown in tubs.

Laurus nobilis

Lavandula vera

Lavandula (lavender)
Evergreens with fragrant spikes of blue or purple flowers in July. Plant in a sunny position in well drained soil. Propagate by cuttings of half-ripe wood in August. Trim off old flower spikes in late summer, and prune old bushes in April. Associates well with rosemary. *L. spica* (old English lavender). Height and spread 3–4 ft. Grey foliage and blue flowers. *L. vera* (Dutch lavender). Similar to *L. spica*, but smaller and of more spreading habit.

Lavatera olbia rosea

Lavatera (tree mallow)
Deciduous flowering shrubs. Thrive in a sunny position in well drained soil. Propagate by seed in March, or by half-ripe cuttings in July. Prune in March. *L. olbia rosea*. Height 5–6 ft. Spread 6–7 ft. Hollyhock-like soft pink flowers from July to October. Leaves are grey-green and fig-shaped. Prune back to live wood in March.

Ligustrum ovalifolium

Ligustrum (privet)
Deciduous and semi-evergreen shrubs extensively used as hedging plants. Thrive in ordinary, even poor soil, and in sunny, shady or windy positions. Propagate by half-ripe cuttings in September. Trim hedges from May to August. *L. ovalifolium*. Height 10–20 ft. Evergreen. Dirty white flowers with unpleasant scent in July and August. Black berries. Though privet is evergreen, the oval-shaped leaves may drop in cold and windy districts. There are also some variegated forms.

Lindera
Deciduous and evergreen aromatic shrubs. Do well in lime-free soil, and in open, sunny positions. Propagate by cuttings in October. Little pruning, except

Lindera benzoin

trimming to shape when necessary. *L. benzoin* (spice bush). Height 6–12 ft. Spread 6–8 ft. Deciduous. Of rounded habit. Clusters of small green-yellow flowers in early spring. Oblong red berries and clear yellow leaves in autumn.

Liriodendron (tulip tree)
Deciduous flowering tree. Plant in a sunny position in any ordinary, well drained soil. No

Liriodendron tulipifera

pruning. *L. tulipifera*. Height up to 90 ft. Spread 40 ft. Tulip-like yellow-green, fragrant flowers produced on 15-year-old trees

in July. Leaves of unusual shape, with the apex cut off almost square; they turn glowing yellow in autumn.

Lonicera (honeysuckle)
Evergreen and deciduous shrubs, used as twining and hedging plants. Shrubby varieties will grow in any good soil in full sun, but twining varieties do best in partial shade. Propagate shrubby species by hardwood cuttings in October; twining species by cuttings of the current year's growths in July or August. Prune all honeysuckles after flowering. *L. fragrantissima*. Height 6–7 ft. Spread 6–9 ft. Deciduous. Cream-white, small fragrant flowers in February and March. The following are twining forms: *L. japonica*. Strong-growing, evergreen climber. Fragrant creamy-white flowers in summer. *L. nitida*. Bush honeysuckle,

Lonicera periclymenum

useful as a hedging plant. *L. periclymenum* (woodbine). Deciduous. Creamy-white, flushed pink, fragrant flowers from June to August; the variety *belgica* (early Dutch) bears flowers, deep red outside, yellow inside, during May and June; *serotina* (late Dutch) has similar flowers from July onwards.

Magnolia

Evergreen and deciduous flowering trees and shrubs. Any well cultivated garden soil is suitable, with the addition of leaf-mould or peat on light sandy soils. Propagate by heel cuttings in June or July, or by layering in April. Little pruning is necessary, although *M. grandiflora* may occasionally require hard pruning in April. *M. grandiflora*. Height 20 ft. or more as a wall shrub. Spread 25 ft. Evergreen. Glossy leaves. Large, globular, creamy-white fragrant flowers from July to September. *M. sieboldii* (syn. *M. parviflora*). Height 10–20 ft. Spread 20–25 ft. Deciduous. Pendent white flowers with wine-coloured stamens, May to July. *M. soulangiana*. Height up to 30 ft. Spread 30–40 ft. Deciduous. Large pure-white flowers, stained rosy-purple at base, are produced

Magnolia soulangiana

freely in April and May. *M. stellata*. Height 10–12 ft. Spread 15–20 ft. Deciduous. Star-shaped semi-double fragrant white flowers in March and April. Slow-growing, but flowers when quite young. Does not object to chalky soil.

Mahonia

Evergreen flowering shrubs with large, compound, glossy green leaves. Thrive in sun or partial

Mahonia lomariifolia

shade and in almost any soil. Propagate by half-ripe cuttings in July. No pruning. *M. bealei*. Height 6–7 ft. Spread 8–12 ft. Fragrant lemon-yellow flowers in erect racemes in February and March. *M. japonica*. Similar to *M. bealei*, but yellow flowers are set in long pendent racemes. *M. lomariifolia*. Height 8–10 ft. Spread 8–12 ft. Deep yellow fragrant flowers on erect racemes in late winter. Large, compound, sea-green leaves. Not hardy, but does well in sheltered, south-western coastal gardens.

Malus (flowering crab apple)

Deciduous flowering trees. Usually grown as standard or half-standard trees, and thrive in any good soil, in a sunny position. Newly planted specimens should be securely staked. Prune in winter when necessary. *M. floribunda* (Japanese crab). Height 25 ft. Spread 35 ft. Crimson buds on arching branches open to pale pink flowers in May. Bright yellow and red fruits. *M. lemoinei*. Height 30 ft. Spread 35 ft. Deep wine-red flowers in April and May. Leaves, purple in spring, turn coppery-green. *M. prunifolia* (Siberian crab apple). Height 20 ft. Spread 25 ft. Rose-coloured buds develop into white flowers in April. Scarlet

or yellow fruits. The variety 'Yellow Siberian' has bright yellow fruits. *M. pumila* (wild crab apple). Height 20–30 ft. Spread 20 ft. White or pink flowers in April. Large yellow fruits in autumn. The variety 'Veitch's Scarlet' has white flowers, followed by large, scarlet fruits. *M. purpurea*. Height and spread 30 ft. Rose-crimson flowers in April, May. Purple-green leaves and light crimson-purple fruits.

Malus prunifolia

Nyssa (tupelo)

Deciduous trees. Plant in moist, lime-free soil. Propagate by layering in October. No pruning. *N. sylvatica*. Height 60–100 ft. Spread 25–35 ft. Erect tree, chiefly grown for its fine autumn colour of brilliant scarlet. (Illustration, p. 27.)

Olearia (daisy bush)

Evergreen flowering shrubs. Plant in a sunny position, in well drained sandy or chalky soil. Propagate by half-ripe cuttings in July. Prune in April. *O. albida*. Height and spread 6–10 ft. Daisy-like white flowers in July and August. Dull green entire leaves. Suitable as hedging plants for coastal gardens. *O. ilicifolia*. Height and spread 6–10 ft. Sweetly fragrant clusters of white flowers during summer.

Olearia ilicifolia

Pale green holly-like leaves. Suitable for training as a hedge. *O. haastii*. Height and spread 6–8 ft. White fragrant flowers in July and August. Small dark green leaves are white beneath. Propagate by half-ripe cuttings in August. Suitable for most town gardens. *O. semidentata*. Height 6–9 ft. Spread 8–10 ft. Pale lilac flowers with purple centres. Silvery elongated leaves.

Paeonia (tree paeony)

Deciduous flowering shrubs. Plant in a sunny or shaded position in deep rich soil, top-dressed

Paeonia suffruticosa

spring with well rotted man-
re. The young shoots in early
pring need protection from
ost and early morning sun.
No pruning. Once planted, leave
ndisturbed. *P. suffruticosa*
(Moutan tree paeony). Height
–5 ft. Spread 9–12 ft. Rose-
urple flowers in May and June.

arrotia
Deciduous tree. Thrives in any
ood soil, in sun or dappled
hade. No pruning. *P. persica.*
Height 10–25 ft. Spread 30–40 ft.
mall flowers with red stamens
n March. Upper branches are
lmost horizontal; amber and
rimson foliage in autumn.

Parrotia persica

Parthenocissus
Deciduous shrubs notable for
heir foliage. Self-climbing by
neans of tendrils on walls or
ree-trunks. Slow-growing at
irst, they may after a few
ears cover a two-storey build-
ng. Plant in ordinary soil,
against a wall. Propagate by
hardwood cuttings in March, or
y softwood cuttings in July.
No pruning. *P. henryana* (syn.
Vitis henryana). Dark green
oliage, variegated with white or
pink, turns red in autumn. Suit-
ble for north or other shaded
walls. *P. quinquefolia* (syn. *Vitis
quinquefolia*) and *P. tricuspidata*
syn. *Ampelopsis veitchii* or

Parthenocissus henryana

Vitis inconstans). Both are
known as Virginia creeper, but
the former is the true native
form. Both have large leaves
which assume purple, rich red
and pale yellow autumn tints.

Passiflora (passion flower)
Deciduous vigorous climbers.
Plant in ordinary, well drained
soil against a sheltered, sunny
wall. Propagate by layers or
cuttings in July. No pruning.
P. caerulea. Height 20–25 ft.
Large blue and white flowers are
freely produced from June to
September. Does well in poor,
well drained soil, but is not
suitable for cold districts. Evergreen in mild western gardens.
'Constance Elliott' is an ivory-
white form.

Passiflora caerulea

Pernettya
Evergreen shrubs with clusters
of berries in autumn and winter.
Do well only in lime-free moist
soil and in partial shade or sun.
Propagate by cuttings in August,
or by layering in spring. No
pruning. *P. mucronata.* Height
5–7 ft. Spread indefinite. Small
white heath-like flowers in May
and June are followed by clusters of large marble-like berries,
when plants of both sexes are
grown. There are various named
varieties with berries in shades
of deep plum, pink and white.

Pernettya mucronata

Philadelphus (mock orange)
Deciduous shrubs with fragrant
flowers in June and July. Easily
grown in any good soil, including
chalk, and in sun or partial
shade. Propagate by cuttings of
half-ripe side shoots in June and
July, or by hardwood cuttings
in October. Prune immediately
after flowering. Among numerous named varieties are: 'Belle
Etoile'. Height 8–10 ft. Spread
10–12 ft. Large chalice-shaped
white flowers with purple blotches at base of petals. 'Silver
Showers' has pure white, scented
flowers in great profusion.
'Sybille'. Height 4 ft. Spread 3
ft. Arching branches bearing
single white flowers with purple
centres.

Philadelphus

Phlomis
Evergreen shrubs, suitable for
a well drained soil, including
chalk, and a sunny position,
particularly in seaside gardens.
Propagate by half-ripe cuttings
in September. Cut back in late
autumn after flowering. *P.
fruticosa* (Jerusalem sage).
Height 2½–3½ ft. Spread 4–5 ft.
Spikes of yellow flowers from
June onwards. Leaves and shoots
are grey, soft and woolly.

Phlomis fruticosa

Pieris
Evergreen shrubs with sprays of
white flowers, resembling lilies-
of-the-valley. Deep green and
leathery leaves. Plant in shaded,

Pieris japonica

sheltered position and in lime-free soil. Propagate by half-ripe cuttings in August. Little pruning except to remove dead flower spikes. Associate well with rhododendrons. *P. formosa*. Height 15–20 ft. Spread 10–15 ft. Panicles of white flowers in May. Young growths are copper-tinted. *P. forrestii*. Height 8–10 ft. Spread 6–8 ft. Fragrant pendulous white flowers in April before brilliant red, new foliage. *P. japonica*. Height 4–6 ft. Spread 5–6 ft. Bell-shaped panicles of waxy white flowers in March.

Polygonum
Deciduous rapid climbers and scramblers. Plant in ordinary

Polygonum baldschuanicum

soil, in a sunny position against a fence or wall with space for growth. Propagate by softwood cuttings in August. No pruning. *P. baldschuanicum* (Russian vine). Height 20–50 ft. Sprays of small white flowers from July onwards.

Populus (poplar)
Deciduous trees with catkin-like flowers in March and April. Easily grown in ordinary garden soil, and even in heavy cold soils. Do not plant near buildings, as the spreading surface roots may damage foundations and drainpipes. Propagate by suckers in October or February, or by hardwood cuttings in

Populus nigra italica

November. No pruning. *P. nigra italica* (Lombardy poplar). Height up to 120 ft. Spread 20–25 ft. An erect, fast-growing tree suitable for an avenue or where vertical effect is desired. *P. tacamahaca* (syn. *P. balsamifera*, balsam poplar). Height 50–70 ft. Spread 25–35 ft. In spring, the unfolding leaves have a pleasant balsam scent.

Potentilla (shrubby cinque-foil)
Deciduous summer-flowering shrubs of compact habit. Thrive in well drained soil and a sunny position. Propagate by half-ripe

cuttings in September. No pruning except to remove dead shoots in March. *P. fruticosa*. Height and spread 3–4 ft. Golden-yellow flowers from May to September. *P. f. farreri*. Height 2 ft., and of spreading habit. Golden-yellow flowers throughout summer.

Potentilla fruticosa

Prunus (ornamental almond, cherry, peach, plum)
A large family of ornamental trees, mainly deciduous. Thrive in any good garden soil, and in a sunny position. Cherries and plums do well on chalky soil. Generally no pruning.

Ornamental peaches and almonds: *P. amygdalus* (syn. *P. communis*, common almond). Height 15–20 ft. Spread 20–25 ft. Small pink flowers in February and March before leaves appear. *P. persica* (peach). Height 12–18 ft. Spread 18–20 ft. Single pale pink flowers in April. Varieties include 'Clara Meyer', double peach-pink flowers. *P. triloba multiplex* (almond). Height and spread 7–9 ft. Slender branches with rosettes of double pink flowers in March and April. Usually grown as half-standards. Prune in May.

Ornamental cherries: *P. avium* (gean). Height 50–60 ft. Spread 30–40 ft. Single white flowers

in April. Colourful autumn foliage tints. The variety *plena* is a double white form. *P. subhirtella autumnalis*. Height and spread 20–25 ft. Semi-double, small and pure white flowers intermittently from November to March. *P. serrulata* (Japanese cherry). Height and spread 20–40 ft. White, pink or rose, single and double flowers in April and May. The variety 'Kanzan' has large clusters of double purple-pink flowers; foliage turns orange-red in autumn.

Ornamental plums: *P. cerasifera* (myrobalan). Height and spread up to 20 ft. White flowers in February and March, before purple-coloured leaves appear. Suitable as hedging plants. *P. spinosa purpurea* (purple-leaf sloe). Height 12–15 ft. Spread 15–18 ft. Pink flowers in March and April. Leaves bronze-red.

Prunus triloba multiplex

Ornamental cherry laurels: *P. laurocerasus* (common laurel). Height 20–25 ft. when left unpruned. Spread 20–30 ft. Evergreen, with large glossy leaves. *P. lusitanica* (Portugal laurel). Height 10–15 ft. Spread 15–20 ft. Evergreen. Small, pointed, dark green leaves. Makes a good hedge for exposed positions. Prune in late summer or early autumn.

Pyracantha (firethorn)
Evergreen and extremely hardy shrubs, suitable for walls or as hedging plants. Green-cream flowers in June, and bright red or orange berries throughout autumn and winter. Do well in any good soil, particularly chalk, and in full sun or partial shade. Propagate by cuttings in July and August. No pruning when grown as specimens; as a hedge trim between May and July. *P. angustifolia*. Height 8 ft. Spread 12 ft. Narrow leaves, grey beneath. Orange-yellow berries. *P. atalantioides*. Height 15–18 ft. Upright habit. Clusters of white flowers in June. Deep red berries. *P. coccinea lalandei*. Height 15 ft. Spread 18 ft. Large orange-red berries. *P. crenulata flava* (syn. *P. rogersiana*). Height 8–10 ft. Spread 12–15 ft. Small leaves and large bright yellow berries; the variety *P. r. aurantiaca* has orange-yellow berries. *P. watereri*. Height 8–10 ft. Spread 9–12 ft. Masses of pure white flowers. Bright red berries.

Pyracantha atalantioides

Quercus (oak)
Large family of hardy deciduous and evergreen trees. Plant in ordinary well drained and moist soil, in sun or shade. No pruning. *Q. borealis maxima* (red oak). Height up to 100 ft. Spread 50–70 ft. Deciduous. Dull red oval

Quercus borealis maxima

leaves turn red-brown in autumn. *Q. ilex* (evergreen or holm oak). Height 50–70 ft. Spread 40–60 ft. Narrowly oval, dark green glossy leaves, grey felted beneath. Suitable as a hedging plant for coastal and other windswept districts.

Rhus (sumach) (Cotinus)
Deciduous, easily grown shrubs notable for their autumn foliage colouring. Plant in a sunny position in any ordinary soil; not recommended for exposed northern gardens. Propagate by layers in March, or by cuttings in July and August. No pruning. *C. obovatus*. Height and spread 12–15 ft. Blue-tinted

Rhus cotinus

green leaves assume autumn shades of purple, orange and scarlet. *C. coggygria* (smoke tree). Height and spread 12–15 ft. Dense smoky-grey flowers in June and July. Leaves brilliant yellow in autumn. *R. typhina* (stag's horn sumach). Height 10–15 ft. Spread 12–16 ft. Leaves, 1–2 ft. long, assume bright orange and red tints in autumn. Propagate by root cuttings in March or by layers in October. Prune in April.

Ribes (flowering currant)
These deciduous spring-flowering shrubs thrive in most soils, in a sunny position or partial shade. Propagate by hardwood cuttings from November to February. Prune in May after flowering. *R. aureum* (golden or buffalo currant). Height 4–5 ft. Spread 4 ft. Fragrant yellow flowers in April. *R. sanguineum*. Height 6 ft. Spread 7 ft. Fragrant rosy-red flowers in March and April. Varieties include 'King Edward VII', deep crimson; 'Pulborough Scarlet', rich red.

Ribes sanguineum

Robinia (false acacia)
Deciduous summer-flowering trees and shrubs. Plant in a sunny position in ordinary soil. Propagate by layers in October. No pruning. *R. hispida* (rose

Robinia pseudoacacia

acacia). Height 6 ft. Spread 8 ft. Rose-pink flowers in drooping clusters in June. *R. pseudoacacia* (common acacia). Height 40 ft. or more. Spread 25–30 ft. Racemes of white flowers in June are slightly fragrant. The variety 'Frisia' has golden foliage.

Romneya (Californian tree poppy)
Deciduous flowering shrubs, hardy in the south, but not recommended for north-east England or north-east Scotland. Fragrant white flowers in late summer. Plant in a sunny position in well drained soil. Propagate by root cuttings in March. Prune in April. Once established do not disturb. *R. coulteri*. Height 5–6 ft.

Romneya coulteri

Spread indefinite. Large fragrant satin-white flowers with golden stamens from July onwards. Glaucous green leaves and stems.

Rosmarinus officinalis

Rosmarinus (rosemary)
Evergreen spring-flowering shrubs with aromatic foliage. Thrive in full sun and a well drained soil, including chalk. Propagate by half-ripe cuttings in August. Trim off dead shoots in April. Associate well with heathers. *R. officinalis*. Height 5–6 ft. Spread 6–7 ft. Blue flowers in May. Suitable for an informal hedge. There is a white form.

Salix babylonica

Salix (willow)
Deciduous trees. Plant in heavy damp soil, preferably at the margin of a pond or pool. Propagate by hardwood cuttings in November. No pruning except to remove dead wood. *S. babylonica*. Height and spread up to 40 ft. The most common weeping willow. *S. caprea* (palm or goat willow). Height 15–20 ft. Spread 18–25 ft. Silvery-grey female catkins and yellow male catkins in early spring. *S. repens argentea*. Height 4–6 ft. Spread 8–10 ft. Prostrate shrub with arching branches up to 6 ft. long. Silvery foliage and yellow catkins.

Senecio greyi

Senecio
Evergreen shrubs notable for their foliage. Do best in coastal gardens, planted in a sunny position and a well drained chalky soil. Propagate by half-ripe cuttings in August or September. Prune in August. *S. greyi*. Height 3–4 ft. Spread 4–6 ft. Yellow daisy-like flowers in June and July. Deeply cut silvery-grey leaves. *S. laxifolius* has similar flowers, but with large oval leaves.

Skimmia
Evergreen ornamental shrubs. Easily grown in town gardens,

in well drained loamy or peaty soil, in full sun or partial shade. Propagate by half-ripe cuttings in August. No pruning. *S. japonica*. Height 3–4 ft. Spread 5–6 ft. Panicles of dull white flowers in April. When plants of both sexes are grown, clusters of bright red berries are produced throughout winter. The variety 'Fortunei' is bisexual and has bright crimson berries. Does best in full shade.

Skimmia japonica

Solanum
Deciduous tender climbers. Plant in loamy soil with added leaf-mould, and in a sheltered position against a warm south wall.

Solanum jasminoides

Suitable only for the mildest parts of the country. Propagate by heel cuttings of young shoots in August. Prune in February. *S. jasminoides*. Height 15–20 ft. Clusters of pale blue flowers like those of the potato from June to August. There is also a white form.

Sorbus aucuparia

Sorbus
Deciduous trees notable for autumn berries and foliage. Plant in a sunny position in any ordinary garden soil. No pruning. *S. aria* (whitebeam). Height 30–50 ft. Spread 30–40 ft. White flowers in May followed by scarlet fruits. Silvery foliage almost pure white on the underside. Suitable for chalky soil. *S. aucuparia* (mountain ash or rowan). Height 30–50 ft. Spread 30–40 ft. Milky white flowers in May and June, followed by drooping clusters of scarlet fleshy fruits in August and September. *S. hupehensis*. Height 25–30 ft. Spread 20–25 ft. Glistening white clusters of berries turn pale pink in late autumn. *S. matsumurana* (Japanese mountain ash). Height and spread up to 20 ft. Orange-red berries. *S. vilmorinii*. Height 15–20 ft. Spread 18–20 ft. Red fruits change in autumn to white with a pink tint

Spartium junceum

partium
eciduous flowering shrubs. lant in porous soil on a dry unny bank; hardy in seaside ardens. Propagate by seed in ebruary or March. Prune in April. *S. junceum* (Spanish room). Height 8–10 ft. Spread –9 ft. Sprays of golden-yellow agrant flowers on slender, lmost leafless branches from une to August.

piraea
eciduous summer-flowering hrubs. Thrive in a sunny posi- on in ordinary good soil. Pro- agate by half-ripe cuttings in uly and August, or by division

Spiraea bumalda

or hardwood cuttings in October. Prune spring-flowering varieties immediately after flowering, summer-flowering varieties in February. *S. arguta* (bridal wreath). Height and spread 6–8 ft. Dainty white flowers in April and May. Narrow, pointed, bright green leaves on slender stems. *S. bumalda* 'Anthony Waterer'. Height 3–4 ft. Spread 4–5 ft. Flat heads of deep crim- son flowers in July and August. *S. japonica*. Height 3–5 ft. Spread 4–6 ft. Large flat heads of pink flowers in July and August. *S. thunbergii*. Height 5–6 ft. Spread 6–8 ft. Sprays of small star-like white flowers in March and April. The bright green foliage assumes glowing yellow and apricot autumn tints.

Symphoricarpos albus

Symphoricarpos (snowberry)
Deciduous spreading shrubs with small pink or rose flowers in July, and large round white fruits from October to February. Plant in ordinary soil, in sun or shade. Propagate by rooted suckers or hardwood cuttings in October. Thin out old wood occasionally. *S. albus* (syn. *S. racemosus*, common snowberry). Height 7–10 ft. The form *laevi- gatus* has clusters of large white berries on slender branches. *S. orbiculatus* (coral berry or Indian currant). Height 5–6 ft. Clusters

of pink fruits during winter. There is also a prostrate form.

Syringa (lilac)
Deciduous shrubs. Clusters of fragrant flowers in late April and early May. Thrive in full sun and in a deep loamy soil. Propa- gate by layers in March or by cuttings of half-ripe wood in

Syringa
'Souvenir de Louis Spaeth'

August. No pruning except to remove dead flower heads and to thin out weak shoots. *S. vulgaris* (common lilac). Height 12–18 ft. Spread 10–12 ft. Fragrant flowers in May. Named single- flowered hybrids include: 'Maud Notcutt', white; 'Souvenir de Louis Spaeth', wine red; 'Congo', deep purple. Some good double- flowered hybrids are; 'Katherine Havemayer', soft mauve; 'Charles Joly', deep purple; 'Madame Lemoine', white; 'Paul Thirion', rosy red; 'Michael Buchner', clear lilac. New Canadian-raised hybrid lilacs (*S. prestoniae*) include the variety 'Isabella', with loose panicles of mallow-purple flowers.

Tamarix (tamarisk)
Deciduous flowering shrubs. Plant in full sun, and in any soil except chalk. Suitable as hedg- ing plants for seaside gardens, but will also grow in sheltered inland districts. Propagate by hardwood cuttings in October.

Tamarix pentandra

Prune in February. *T. pentandra*. Height 12–15 ft. Spread 15–18 ft. Graceful slender branches covered in rosy-pink scented flowers in July and August. There is also a deep rose form.

Taxus (yew)
Evergreen conifers. Dark green narrow leaves are poisonous, as are the fleshy red fruits. Plant in ordinary soil, including chalk, and in a shaded or sunny shrub- bery. Propagate by half-ripe cuttings in September. No pruning. *T. baccata* (common yew). Height 30–40 ft. Spread 40 ft. Suitable as a hedging plant, which must be trimmed in

Taxus baccata

August and September. Varieties include the golden yew, *elegantissima*, and the erect Irish yew, *fastigiata*.

Thuja plicata

Thuja (arbor-vitae)
Spreading conifers, suitable as hedging or screening plants. Thrive in well drained, moist soil and in a sunny position. Trim hedges in September. *T. plicata* (syn. *T. lobbii*). Height, when grown as a hedge, up to 20 ft.; as a screen, up to 35 ft. Erect tree with spreading branches. Not wind-resistant, and grows best in lime-free soil.

Tilia (lime)
Deciduous trees with small dull white or yellow flowers from

Tilia platyphyllos rubra

June to August. Plant in loamy moist soil, in full sun or semishade. Easily trained as pollarded (mop-headed) specimens or as a pleached (interwoven) screen. No pruning when allowed to grow naturally. *T. platyphyllos rubra* (red-twigged lime). Height up to 120 ft. Spread 40–60 ft. Young upright shoots are bright red in winter. Branches are semipendulous on mature trees.

Ulmus glabra

Ulmus (elm)
Deciduous hardy trees. Plant in an open position in ordinary well drained soil. No pruning. *U. glabra* (wych or Scotch elm). Height up to 100 ft. Spread 40–50 ft. Foliage turns a pleasing yellow in autumn. *U. g. pendula* (weeping wych elm). Height 15–20 ft. Spread 20 ft. Domeshaped tree with stiffly pendulous branches. Good specimen for a lawn.

Viburnum
Evergreen and deciduous flowering shrubs. Thrive in rich moist soil, preferably in a sunny position, though some species do well in partial shade. Propagate by heel-cuttings of half-ripe wood from June to August. Prune evergreen varieties in April; deciduous kinds occasionally need thinning out of old wood. Evergreen varieties include: *V.*

burkwoodii. Height 8–10 ft. Spread 9–12 ft. Pink buds develop into fragrant white flower heads in April. Deep green oval leaves. Best planted in shade. *V. davidii*. Height 2–3 ft. Spread 4–5 ft. Clusters of rose-coloured flowers in June. Large, oval and leathery dark green leaves. Bright turquoise berries in autumn if several plants are grown together for pollination purposes. *V. rhytidophyllum*. Height 10–15 ft. Spread 10–12 ft. Large heads of white to pale rose flowers in May and June. Long glossy leaves, deeply furrowed above. Will grow in partial shade. *V. tinus* (laurustinus). Height 7–10 ft. Spread 8–10 ft. Pink-budded white flowers throughout winter and spring. Oval dark green leaves. Suitable as a hedging plant. Deciduous varieties include: *V. betulifolium*. Height and spread 8–12 ft. Clusters of white flowers in June. When mature, masses of currant-like red berries in autumn. *V. bodnantense*. Height and spread 9–12 ft. Clusters of fragrant pink flowers from December to

Viburnum davidii

February. Vigorous and frosthardy. *V. carlesii*. Height and spread 4–6 ft. Rounded heads of fragrant flushed pink flowers, becoming white, in April and May. Does best in light shade.

V. fragrans. Height and spread 9–12 ft. Fragrant white flowers tinged with pink from November to February. Thrives in light shade. *V. opulus* (guelder rose). Height 10–15 ft. Spread 12–18 ft. Fragrant white flowers in May and June, followed by clusters of bright red berries. Foliage turns red in autumn. The variety *xanthocarpum* has amber-yellow berries. *V. tomentosum*. Height 8–10 ft. Spread 10–15 ft. White hydrangea-like flowers on wide spreading branches in June. Leaves turn rich crimson in autumn. *V. t. plicatum* (Japanese snowball tree). Large round heads of white sterile flowers are borne in pairs along the branches.

Vitis coignetiae

Vitis
Deciduous climbers, notable for their ornamental foliage. Slow growing at first, they may eventually cover a whole building. Thrive in ordinary soil, against a south or west wall, or trained on trellis or wire fences to form a screen. Though self-climbing, shoots should be tied into position. No pruning. *V. coignetiae* (Japanese vine). Height up to 20 ft. Large leathery leaves turn yellow, orange, crimson and red in autumn.

Weigela florida variegata

Weigela

Deciduous shrubs, flowering in May and June. Plant in rich moist soil and in full sun. Propagate by half-ripe cuttings in July, or by hardwood cuttings in October. Prune after flowering. *W. florida*. Height and spread 6–8 ft. Trumpet-shaped flowers, rose-pink on the outside, paler within, on arching stems. The variety *variegata* is of more compact habit. *W. rosea*. Height and spread 8–9 ft. Arching stems with masses of rose-pink flowers.

Wisteria

Deciduous vigorous climbers, needing support if grown on a

Wisteria floribunda

wall, self-climbing over a pergola. Easily grown in good loamy garden soil and in a sunny position. Propagate by layers in July, by half-ripe cuttings in August, or by seed in March. Prune from January to March, and vigorous climbers again in August. *W. floribunda*. Height 20 ft. or more Spread indefinite. Long clusters of violet-blue flowers in May and June. *W. sinensis*. Height 20 ft. or more. Spread indefinite. Racemes of fragrant mauve flowers in May and June. *W. venusta*. Height 30 ft. or more. Indefinite spread. Racemes of fragrant pure white large flowers in May and June.

Trees and shrubs for special purposes

Autumn foliage
Acer · Amelanchier
Azalea (deciduous)
Berberis rubrostilla
Berberis thunbergii
Callicarpa
Cornus kousa
Cotinus · Euonymus
Fothergilla · Ginkgo
Hamamelis
Lindera benzoin
Nyssa · Parrotia
Parthenocissus
Prunus · Rhus
Sorbus · Viburnum

Chalky soils
Berberis · Buddleia
Cercis · Chaenomeles
Choisya · Cistus
Clematis · Cornus
Cytisus · Deutzia
Escallonia · Euonymus
Fagus · Forsythia
Griselinia
Hamamelis · Hebe
Hypericum · Juniperus
Kerria · Laburnum
Lavandula · Malus
Philadelphus · Phlomis
Potentilla · Prunus
Pyracantha · Ribes
Rosmarinus · Senecio

Sorbus aria · Spiraea
Symphoricarpos
Syringa · Viburnum

Colourful fruits
Amelanchier · Arbutus
Aucuba · Berberis
Chaenomeles
Cotoneaster
Crataegus · Euonymus
Lindera benzoin
Malus · Pernettya
Pyracantha
Skimmia japonica
Sorbus
Symphoricarpos
Viburnum

Damp, wet sites
Arundinaria · Cornus
Hydrangea
Populus · Salix
Spiraea bumalda
Viburnum opulus

Fragrance
Azalea
Chimonanthus
Choisya · Corylopsis
Daphne · Fothergilla
Hamamelis
Jasminum officinale

Lavandula · Lonicera
Olearia ilicifolia
Philadelphus · Ribes
Romneya coulteri
Rosmarinus · Syringa
Viburnum
Wisteria

Ground cover
Ceanothus prostratus
Cotoneaster adpressa
Cytisus ardoinii
Euonymus fortunei
Genista · Hedera
Hypericum
Mahonia
Pernettya

Hedges
Berberis darwinii
Berberis stenophylla
Carpinus · Crataegus
Escallonia
Euonymus japonica
Fagus
Fuchsia magellanica
Griselinia
Ilex aquifolium
Ligustrum
Olearia
Prunus cerasifera
Taxus baccata
Thuja

Hot, dry sites
Berberis · Caryopteris
Chaenomeles · Cistus
Cotoneaster · Cytisus
Euonymus · Genista
Hebe · Hedera
Hypericum
Lavandula
Olearia · Pernettya
Phlomis · Potentilla
Rhus · Robinia
Rosmarinus
Senecio · Spartium
Spirea · Tamarix

Peat and acid soil
Acer · Arbutus
Azalea · Callicarpa
Camellia · Escallonia
Hydrangea · Ilex
Laurus · Magnolia
Parrotia · Pernettya
Pieris · Rhododendron
Skimmia

Seaside gardens
Arbutus · Aucuba
Berberis · Cornus
Escallonia
Euonymus japonica
Fuchsia magellanica
Griselinia · Lavandula

Mahonia lomariifolia
Olearia albida
Phlomis · Rosmarinus
Salix · Senecio
Spartium · Tamarix

Shady sites
Aucuba · Berberis
Camellia · Cornus
Euonymus · Garrya
Hedera · Hydrangea
Hypericum · Ilex
Jasminum · Kerria
Mahonia · Pernettya
Pieris · Rhododendron
Skimmia
Symphoricarpos
Viburnum

Town gardens
Amelanchier · Aucuba
Cercis · Chaenomeles
Cotinus · Cotoneaster
Crataegus · Deutzia
Euonymus japonica
Forsythia · Hypericum
Ilex · Kerria
Laburnum
Magnolia · Malus
Olearia haastii
Philadelphus · Prunus
Rhododendron · Rhus

Ribes · Skimmia
Symphoricarpos
Syringa · Viburnum

Walls and screens
Actinidia · Campsis
Celastrus · Clematis
Cotoneaster
    horizontalis
Eccremocarpus
Hedera · Hibiscus
Hydrangea petiolaris
Jasminum · Lathyrus
Lonicera
Magnolia grandiflora
Parthenocissus
Passiflora
Polygonum · Solanum
Vitis · Wisteria

Winter flowers
Arbutus (autumn)
Chaenomeles
Chimonanthus
Cornus mas
Corylopsis
Daphne mezereum
Garrya · Hamamelis
Jasminum
    nudiflorum
Lonicera · Mahonia
Prunus · Viburnum

Rhododendrons and azaleas to plant in September

In addition to scores of species, there are hundreds of named rhododendron hybrids. Growth habit varies from compact, dwarf forms to tall, rambling shrubs or small trees. The flowering period lasts from winter to late summer. There is no botanical distinction between rhododendrons and azaleas, and they both require lime-free soil. Garden azaleas are divided into deciduous varieties and the evergreen or Japanese kinds. All the plants mentioned are hardy in most areas of Britain, unless otherwise stated. (See also colour section, TREES AND SHRUBS, pp. 241-8.)

RHODODENDRONS

R. 'Albatross'
Height 15 ft. Spread 10–12 ft. Pointed leaves, 7–10 in. long. White or very pale pink flowers in large trusses, June.

R. 'Armantine'
Height 8–12 ft. in the open. Spread 8–10 ft. Dark green leaves, 8–10 in. long. Free-flowering, deep lilac-rose flowers in large trusses, March.

R. augustinii
Height 12 ft. Spread 6 ft. Small pointed leaves, 2–3 in. long. Large flowers, nearest to blue of any rhododendron, late April and early May.

Rhododendron
'Blue Tit'

R. 'Azor'
Height 8–12 ft. Spread 8–10 ft. Pointed leaves, 7–9 in. long. Trumpet-shaped, salmon-pink flowers, 4–5 in. across, in large trusses, June.

R. 'Betty Wormald'
Height 8–10 ft. Spread 6–8 ft. Leaves 6–9 in. long. Strong-growing with rosy-pink flowers of the 'Pink Pearl' type in very large trusses, May.

R. 'Blue Diamond'
Height 6 ft. Spread 4–5 ft. Tiny, rounded leaves. Violet flowers, April.

R. 'Blue Tit'
Height 5 ft. Spread 5 ft. Tiny leaves. Pale violet flowers freely produced, April–May. Easily grown, and suitable for seaside gardens.

R. 'Bric-a-brac'
Height 2–3 ft. Spread 2–3 ft. Rounded leaves, 1–1½ in. long. Striking, clear white flowers with chocolate-coloured stamens in small trusses, February.

R. 'Britannia'
Height 5 ft. Spread 5 ft. Rounded leaves, 6–8 in. long. Scarlet-crimson flowers in big trusses on a thick bush, June.

R. canadense
Height 2–3 ft. Spread 2–2½ ft. Tiny leaves. Small, star-shaped lilac flowers in small trusses, April. Deciduous.

R. cilipinense
Height 5 ft. Spread 5 ft. Rounded leaves, 2–3 in. long. Pink flowers fading to white, March.

R. 'Cornubia'
Height 6–10 ft. Spread 6 ft. Rounded leaves, 6–8 in. long in open, larger in woodland. Fine trusses of blood-red flowers, March.

R. 'Elizabeth'
Height 3 ft. Spread 3 ft. Pointed leaves, 4–5 in. long. Scarlet flowers in large trusses, April. Slightly tender.

R. falconeri
Height 40–50 ft. Spread 45 ft. Leaves 12 in. long, with brown indumentum (furry under-surface). Yellow flowers with a purple blotch, March. Plant in oak or fir forest.

R. 'Furnival's Daughter'
Height 10 ft. Spread 10 ft. Strong, dark leaves, 5–6 in. long. Pale pink flowers with very dark red markings, mid-May.

R. 'Goldsworth Crimson'
Height 14 ft. Spread 10 ft. Leaves 4–6 in. long. Bright scarlet flowers, late April.

R. 'Goldsworth Yellow'
Height 4–6 ft. in open. Spread 4–6 ft. Rounded leaves, 5–6 in. long. Apricot-pink buds opening to a gradually deepening yellow, May.

R. 'Hugh Koster'
Height 10–15 ft. Spread 5–8 ft. Pointed leaves, 6–7 in. long. Scarlet flowers, late May.

R. 'Lady C. Mitford'
Height 15 ft. Spread 15 ft. Leaves 4–6 in. long, rough on upper surface. Peach pink flowers in trusses, June.

R. 'Lavender Girl'
Height 15 ft. Spread 15 ft. Rounded leaves, 6–8 in. long. Very close-growing bush with sweet scented lavender-coloured flowers with green throats, in large trusses, May.

R. 'Lees Scarlet'
Height 6 ft. Spread 6 ft. Leaves 5–7 in. long. Scarlet buds opening to pink flowers. Always the first rhododendron to bloom, in December or January.

R. 'Letty Edwards'
Height 10–12 ft. Spread 8–10 ft. Rounded leaves, 4–6 in. long. Pale yellow flowers tinged pink in the bud, May. So free-flowering that some buds may have to be removed in autumn.

R. leucaspis
Height 1–2 ft. Spread 1–2 ft. Small, rounded leaves, 1 in. long. Florin-sized flowers, cream with brown stamens, February.

R. loderi
Height 20 ft. Spread 20 ft. Leaves 8–10 in. long. Flowers

in. across, sometimes in conical trusses, April. Good varieties are: 'King George', nearly pure white, 'Venus', pale pink, and 'Pink Diamond', pink.

. lutescens
Height 4–6 ft. Spread 8–12 ft. In woodland, but narrower in open. Pointed, bronze leaves, in. long; young growth has red leaves and shoots. Primrose-yellow flowers, March–April (February in mild years).

. 'Moser's Maroon'
Height 15 ft. Spread 8–10 ft. Leaves 6–8 in. long, remaining reddish through most of the summer. Maroon flowers in large trusses, June.

. moupinense
Height 1–2 ft. Spread 1½–2 ft. Small, slightly rounded leaves, in. long. Slightly spotted, white or pale pink flowers, February.

. 'Mrs. G. W. Leak'
Height 8–10 ft. Spread 5–7 ft. Pointed leaves, 6–7 in. long. Close-growing bush with pale pink, star-shaped flowers with prominent brown-purple blotches, April–May.

Rhododendron
'Mrs. G. W. Leak'

R. 'Mrs. W. C. Slocock'
Height 6 ft. Spread 6 ft. Rounded leaves, 4–6 in. long. Apricot flowers fading through pink to yellow, May. Close-growing.

R. mucronulatum
Height 4–6 ft. Spread 4–5 ft. Small leaves, 1½ in. long. Rosy lilac flowers in trusses, January.

R. nobleanum 'Scarlet'
Height 4 ft. Spread 4 ft. Leaves have silvery indumentum (furry under-surface). Red to deep rosy-red flowers, early January. May grow much taller in thick cover.

R. 'Pink Pearl'
Height 10 ft. Spread 12 ft. Pointed leaves, 6–8 in. long. Rose-pink flowers in large conical trusses, May.

R. 'Polar Bear'
Height 20–30 ft. Spread 20–25 ft. Leaves 7–10 in. long. Large, white, scented flowers, July.

R. sinogrande
Height 30 ft. Spread 20–30 ft. Leaves up to 2 ft. long; dark green with light indumentum (furry under-surface). Creamy-white flowers with a crimson blotch, March. Grows in oak or fir forest.

R. 'Susan'
Height 15 ft. Spread 15 ft. Slightly rounded leaves, 6–7 in. long. Pale lavender-blue flowers, darker in the bud, in large trusses, April.

R. 'Unique'
Height 6 ft. Spread 6 ft. Very close-growing. Rounded, dark leaves, 4–6 in. long. Pale creamy-pink flowers, fading to ivory, April.

R. williamsianum
Height 2 ft. Spread 2–3 ft. Rounded, leathery leaves, 1–2 in. long. Large, bell-shaped, rose-red to pale pink flowers in small trusses during April and May. Of dense and spreading habit.

R. 'Yellowhammer'
Height 6 ft. Spread 3–4 ft. Small pointed leaves. Tiny, bright yellow, funnel-shaped flowers, March and October.

JAPANESE AZALEAS

R. obtusum (var. amoenum)
Height 4–6 ft. Spread 4–6 ft. Tiny leaves. Small, star-shaped, deep magenta flowers, May. Grows in tiers, taking a long time to reach its full height.

Azalea
'Hi-no-degiri'

R. o. 'Hi-no-degiri'
Height 1½ ft. Spread 1½ ft. Small rounded leaves. Crimson flowers, growing one inside another (hose-in-hose), May. Not very hardy. Cover with bracken in winter.

R. o. 'Toreador'
Height 4–6 ft. Spread 4–5 ft. Small leaves. Bright rose-red flowers, May. Similar in growth to R. o. amoenum.

JAPANESE AZALEA HYBRIDS

R. 'Betty'
Height 4 ft. Spread 4 ft. Small leaves. Large, soft pink flowers carried in profusion during May.

R. 'John Cairns'
Height 3–4 ft. Spread 2–3 ft. Small leaves. Large, pure white single flowers, May.

DECIDUOUS AZALEAS

R. molle (syn. Azalea mollis)
Height 6 ft. Spread 4 ft. Leaves 4–6 in. long, sometimes blue underneath. Golden-yellow flowers, May. 'Dr. M. Oosthoek', large, dark red, shaded with orange. 'Golden Sunlight', large, golden yellow. 'Koster's Brilliant Red', bright orange red. 'Queen Emma', large orange. 'Mrs. Oliver Slocock', large orange with pink backs. 'Samuel T. Coleridge', brilliant pink.

AZALEA 'KNAP HILL' VARIETIES
Height 6–8 ft. Spread 4–6 ft. Leaves sometimes smaller than molle; bright autumn colours. Flowers in May. 'Annabella', mustard-yellow flowers, fine foliage. 'Berry Rose', pink with a yellow eye. 'Homebush', double violet-pink flowers in rounded trusses. 'Satan', dark scarlet flowers; free-flowering when mature. 'Silver Slipper', white with yellow blotches. 'Tangerine', brilliant orange.

'Knap Hill' azalea
'Annabella'

PLANTS FOR HEDGES	Deciduous or Evergreen	Planting months	Planting distance	Trim	General comments
Berberis darwinii Berberis stenophylla	E	Oct–Nov or Mar	18 in.	May–Jun after flowering	Prickly, with yellow flowers. Make useful boundary hedges, where space is not limited. Need little trimming
Carpinus betulus (common hornbeam)	D winter brown	Oct–Mar	18 in.	Jul–Aug	Makes massive solid hedges. Particularly suitable for light, dry soil
Crataegus monogyna Crataegus oxyacantha (quickthorn, hawthorn, whitethorn)	D	Oct–Mar	12 in.	Jun–Aug	The cheapest thorny boundary hedges. Suit almost any conditions except close to the sea
Escallonia macrantha	E	Oct–Apr	24 in.	Jun	Escallonias are among the best of hedges for the seaside. They thrive best in mild winters and high rainfall, and are salt-resistant
Euonymus japonica (spindle tree)	E	Mar–May	24 in.	Jul	Stands salt spray and industrial pollution. Thrives best by the sea, but also makes a useful hedge in towns
Fagus sylvatica (common beech)	D winter brown	Oct–Mar	24 in.	Jul–Aug	Excellent in chalky soils. Attractive hedge, with pale green leaves in spring and persistent brown leaves all the winter
Fuchsia magellanica	D	Oct–Mar	12 in.	Oct or Mar	A colourful hedge for the mildest climates. Not hardy as a hedge inland, where it is often cut to the ground in winter
Griselinia littoralis	E	Mar–Apr	3 ft.	Jun–Jul	Large, pale-leaved shrub suitable for hedges in mild areas, particularly in the semi-shade of larger trees
Ilex aquifolium (common holly)	E	Apr–May	24 in.	April	Hardy, prickly hedge for almost all parts of the country. Plant one holly to five crataegus to make a permanent boundary hedge
Ligustrum ovalifolium (oval-leaved privet)	E	Oct–Apr	18 in.	May–Jun and Jul–Aug	The cheapest hedge plant. Quick-growing and needs proper trimming. Not always evergreen in the worst conditions
Olearia albida	E	Oct–Mar	18 in.	Jul–Aug	Useful hedge plant for coastal gardens
Prunus cerasifera (myrobalan plum)	D	Oct–Mar	18 in.	Jul	Quick-growing, slightly thorny plant, useful on poor soils
Taxus baccata (common yew)	E	Apr–May	24 in.	Aug–Sept	The best long-lived dividing hedge. Provides a dark background for flower beds and borders
Thuja plicata (western red cedar)	E	Apr–May	24 in.	Jun–Jul	A fairly quick-growing conifer. Needs plenty of space and lime-free soil. Does not need much trimming

Trees and shrubs

selected for their beauty, shape and screening value

...alus lemoinei 30 ft. Flowers April–May

Syringa vulgaris 12–18 ft. May

Buddleia globosa 12 ft. May–June

Prunus persica 12–18 ft. April

Elaeagnus pungens 12 ft. Autumn

Sorbus vilmorinii 15–20 ft. Ma...

Rhododendrons May–June

Viburnum tomentosum 8–10 ft. Jun...

...drons

Cytisus praecox 6 ft. April

Rhododendrons May–June

Rosmarinus officinalis (rosemary) 5–6 ft. May

Euonymus fortunei (prostrate)

Daphne cneorum 1 ft. May

Juniperus sabina tamariscifolia (prostrate)

Azalea. May–June

Azalea. May–June

241

A succession of gay colou

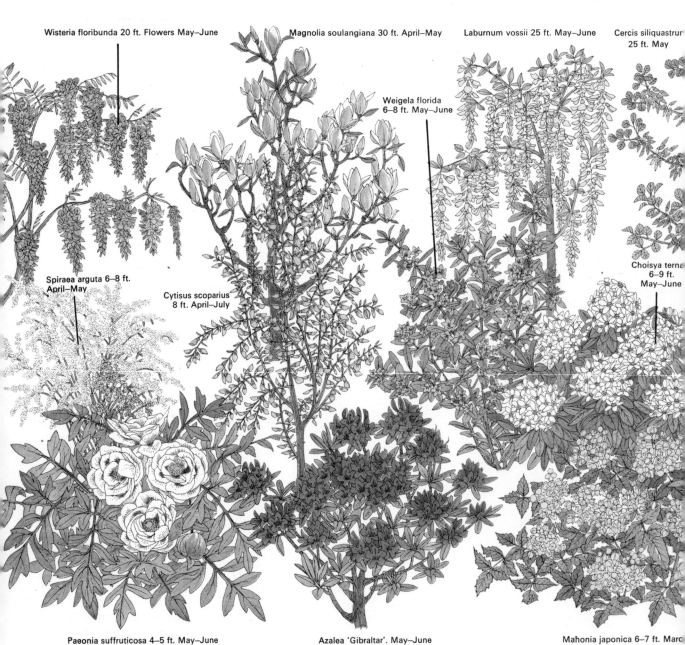

Wisteria floribunda 20 ft. Flowers May–June

Magnolia soulangiana 30 ft. April–May

Laburnum vossii 25 ft. May–June

Cercis siliquastru
25 ft. May

Weigela florida
6–8 ft. May–June

Spiraea arguta 6–8 ft.
April–May

Cytisus scoparius
8 ft. April–July

Choisya terna
6–9 ft.
May–June

Paeonia suffruticosa 4–5 ft. May–June

Azalea 'Gibraltar'. May–June

Mahonia japonica 6–7 ft. Marc

n spring and early summer

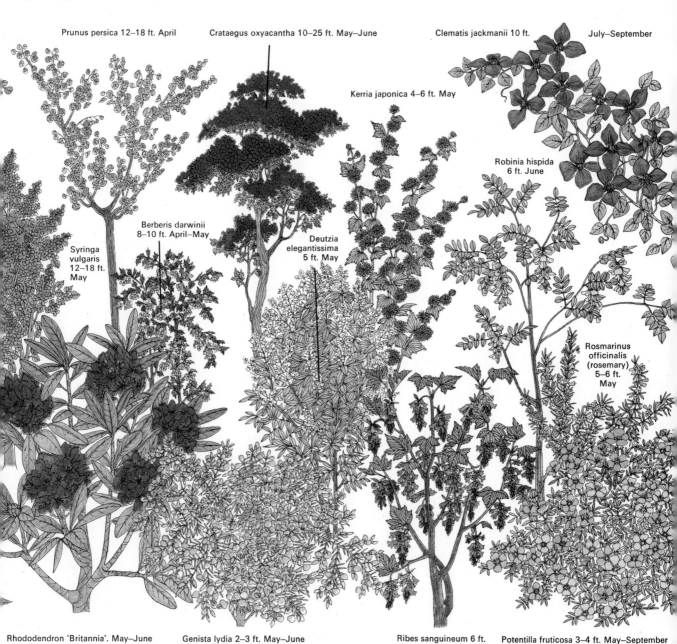

Prunus persica 12–18 ft. April

Crataegus oxyacantha 10–25 ft. May–June

Clematis jackmanii 10 ft.

July–September

Kerria japonica 4–6 ft. May

Robinia hispida
6 ft. June

Syringa
vulgaris
12–18 ft.
May

Berberis darwinii
8–10 ft. April–May

Deutzia
elegantissima
5 ft. May

Rosmarinus
officinalis
(rosemary)
5–6 ft.
May

Rhododendron 'Britannia'. May–June

Genista lydia 2–3 ft. May–June

Ribes sanguineum 6 ft.
March–April

Potentilla fruticosa 3–4 ft. May–September

243

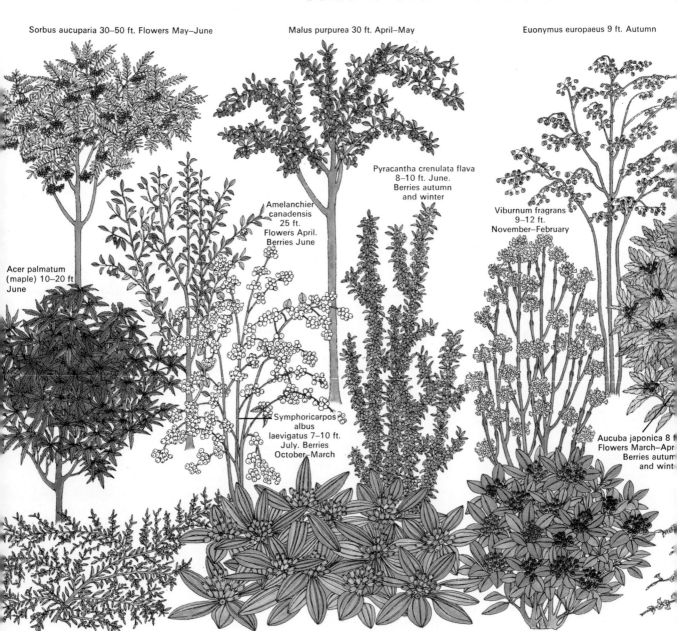

Colourful autumn tints and winter berrie

Sorbus aucuparia 30–50 ft. Flowers May–June

Malus purpurea 30 ft. April–May

Euonymus europaeus 9 ft. Autumn

Pyracantha crenulata flava
8–10 ft. June.
Berries autumn
and winter

Amelanchier
canadensis
25 ft.
Flowers April.
Berries June

Viburnum fragrans
9–12 ft.
November–February

Acer palmatum
(maple) 10–20 ft
June

Symphoricarpos
albus
laevigatus 7–10 ft.
July. Berries
October–March

Aucuba japonica 8 f
Flowers March–Apr
Berries autum
and wint

Cotoneaster horizontalis 3 ft. Berries winter

Viburnum davidii 2–3 ft. June. Berries autumn

Skimmia japonica foremanii. April. Berries winter

followed by forerunners of spring

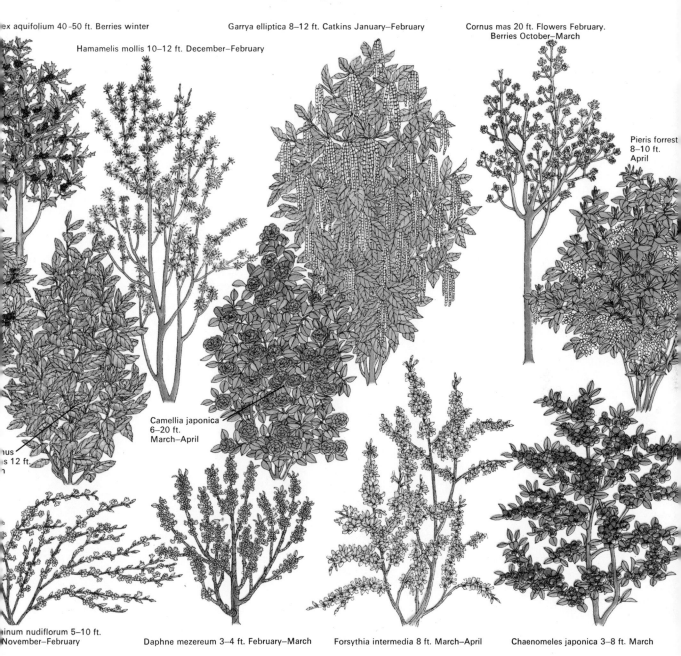

ex aquifolium 40–50 ft. Berries winter

Hamamelis mollis 10–12 ft. December–February

Garrya elliptica 8–12 ft. Catkins January–February

Cornus mas 20 ft. Flowers February.
Berries October–March

Pieris forrest
8–10 ft.
April

Camellia japonica
6–20 ft.
March–April

nus
s 12 ft.

inum nudiflorum 5–10 ft.
November–February

Daphne mezereum 3–4 ft. February–March

Forsythia intermedia 8 ft. March–April

Chaenomeles japonica 3–8 ft. March

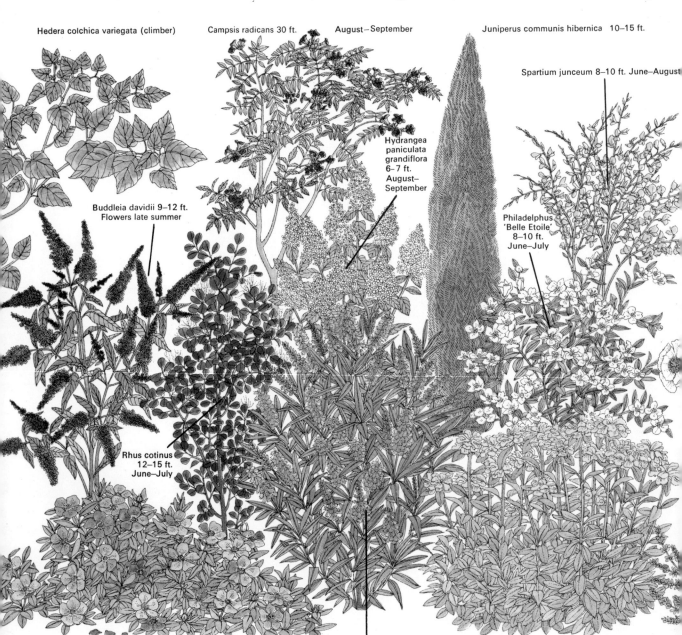

Slender evergreen columns and arching tre

Hedera colchica variegata (climber)

Campis radicans 30 ft.

August–September

Juniperus communis hibernica 10–15 ft.

Spartium junceum 8–10 ft. June–August

Hydrangea paniculata grandiflora 6–7 ft. August–September

Buddleia davidii 9–12 ft. Flowers late summer

Philadelphus 'Belle Etoile' 8–10 ft. June–July

Rhus cotinus 12–15 ft. June–July

Cistus 'Sunset' 2–3 ft. May–July

Hebe 'Midsummer Beauty' 2 ft. June–August

Phlomis fruticosa 2½–3½ ft. June–September

ntrast vividly with low-growing shrubs

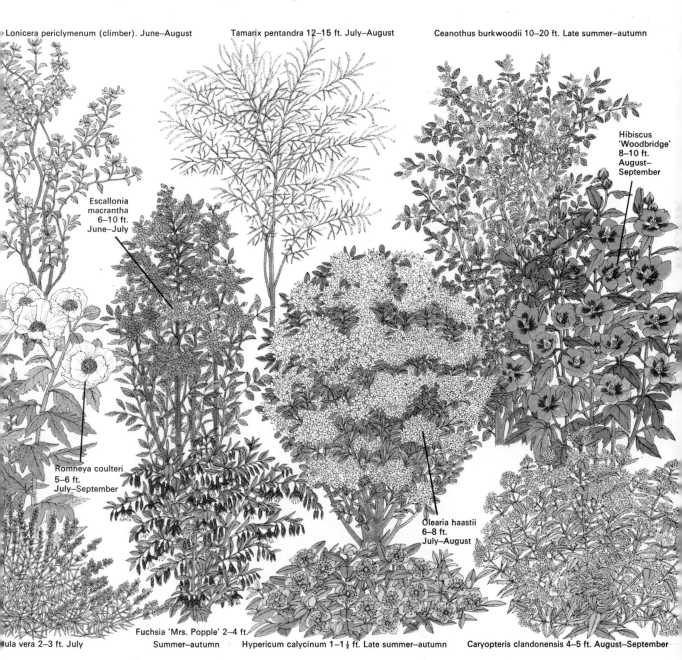

Lonicera periclymenum (climber). June–August

Tamarix pentandra 12–15 ft. July–August

Ceanothus burkwoodii 10–20 ft. Late summer–autumn

Hibiscus 'Woodbridge' 8–10 ft. August–September

Escallonia macrantha 6–10 ft. June–July

Romneya coulteri 5–6 ft. July–September

Olearia haastii 6–8 ft. July–August

Fuchsia 'Mrs. Popple' 2–4 ft. Summer–autumn

tula vera 2–3 ft. July

Hypericum calycinum 1–1½ ft. Late summer–autumn

Caryopteris clandonensis 4–5 ft. August–September

247

A screen of evergreens and climbers to ensure privacy

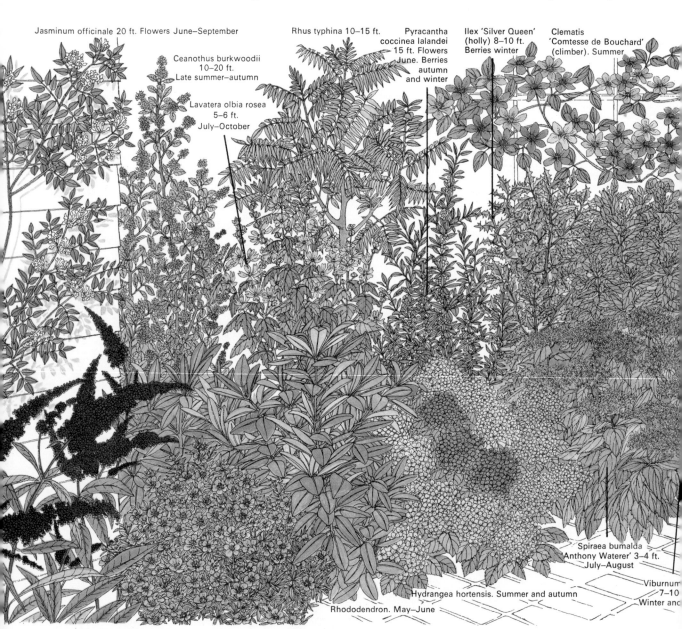

Jasminum officinale 20 ft. Flowers June–September

Ceanothus burkwoodii 10–20 ft. Late summer–autumn

Lavatera olbia rosea 5–6 ft. July–October

Rhus typhina 10–15 ft.

Pyracantha coccinea lalandei 15 ft. Flowers June. Berries autumn and winter

Ilex 'Silver Queen' (holly) 8–10 ft. Berries winter

Clematis 'Comtesse de Bouchard' (climber). Summer

Spiraea bumalda 'Anthony Waterer' 3–4 ft. July–August

Viburnum 7–10 Winter and

Hydrangea hortensis. Summer and autumn

Rhododendron. May–June

Buddleia davidii 9–12 ft. Late summer

Potentilla fruticosa 3–4 ft. May–September

October

A mellow Indian summer is the time to carry out autum digging, to collect leaves for compost, and to divide plants in the herbaceous border

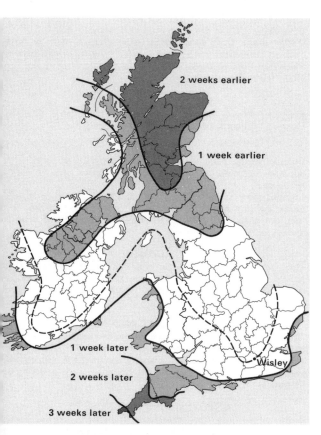

The weather in October

Rain, wind and cloud characterise the weather this month, which is sometimes the wettest of the year. But there is often an Indian summer about the middle of the month, when a short spell of mellow anticyclonic weather similar to that of September occurs. In such weather it is much calmer and drier, but at night fog is more likely than in September, and frost is a serious hazard for the gardener.

South to south-westerly winds arriving with a depression usually bring long periods of cool, dull days, with much low cloud and widespread rain that is especially heavy against the hills of the west; afternoon temperatures average 16–18°C (61–64°F) in south-east England, but are considerably lower in northern Scotland. Fresh west to north-west winds often follow, with scattered showers and, in the east, sunny periods; afternoon temperatures in the south-east average 13°C (55°F). The first air frost of the winter usually occurs this month.

The end of October and the beginning of November form one of the most consistently stormy periods of the year. Gales and rain sweep across the country, and outdoor work is severely restricted, especially on heavier land. The ground is approaching saturation point, and heavy or continuous rains can bring autumn floods to valley areas.

Every opportunity must be taken in fine October weather to carry out autumn digging. Soil which is dug over early in the autumn gets the maximum benefit from the winter frosts, and is broken down into good condition for spring planting.

A summary of the month's work

LAWNS

New lawns. Mow when 3 in. high. Roll to firm seedlings if loose.
Established lawns. Remedy defective drainage and lay new drains if necessary. Aerate, scarify, hollow-tine and treat with autumn fertiliser. Treat lawn against earthworms.
Turfing. Prepare weed-free turf bed, allow to settle, and rake in fertiliser. Select turf of adequate quality. Lay turves as soon as possible after delivery, making sure that they are of uniform thickness. Begin laying turves from corner of plot, bonding them like bricks. Finally, trim all edges evenly.

249

ROSES

Prepare new rose beds for planting, digging well and mixing in plenty of fertilising material. Continue to spray against greenfly and fungus diseases.

HARDY HERBACEOUS PLANTS

Begin planting herbaceous perennials. Transplant plants needing moving. Tidy beds and borders, remove dead heads and keep down seedling weeds. Divide old clumps of perennials and replant the vigorous outer shoots. Dig ground for March planting to weather during winter. Dig over old borders which need a complete overhaul. Remove turf from site chosen for new bed, using it to rot down into potting soil.

DAHLIAS

Cut down the top growth of dahlias as soon as it is blackened by frost, then lift dahlias carefully with a fork. Stand tubers upside down in a frost-free place to dry out, then place them in boxes and cover them with very slightly damp peat after dusting the crowns with flowers of sulphur. Store in a frost-free greenhouse or shed for the winter. Examine the tubers several times during the winter. If they are shrivelled, plunge them in a bucket of tepid water overnight to make them plump again. Remove seeds from seed pods and store in matchboxes until sowing time in March.

CHRYSANTHEMUMS

Over-winter plants by leaving them in the garden; or lift them, bedding them in a cold frame or housing them in the greenhouse.
Under glass. Ventilate well, but give gentle heat if necessary. Water sparingly. Dust with captan against mildew if necessary. Disbud the later-flowering varieties. Cease feeding large exhibition and incurved varieties when they show colour.

GLADIOLI

Lift corms before the winter frosts, cutting off all but $\frac{1}{2}$ in. of stem and placing in a dry, airy place. When dry, store the clean corms in trays or shallow boxes.

IRISES

Tidy bearded iris beds before winter. Remove dead leaves and weeds and trim longer leaves by a quarter.
Under glass. Complete planting of bulbous irises in pots.

LILIES

Plant as many of your lilies as possible. Allow lily stems to die down naturally. Lift some lily bulbs from the garden and pot up to grow as pot plants; then plunge them 4 in. deep in ashes.
Under glass. Bring newly potted lilies wanted for forcing into the greenhouse three months before flowers are required.

CARNATIONS AND PINKS

Plant border carnations and pinks in beds prepared earlier, except in districts with heavy soil, where they should be kept in pots in a cold frame until March. Prepare beds for spring planting. Continue cutting away layers of border carnations. Stop modern pinks. Clear leaves and rubbish from around stems. Protect plants against birds, using black cotton. In mild spells firm soil around plants lifted by frost.
Under glass. Maintain a temperature of 7°C (45°F) for perpetual flowering carnations, and give some ventilation at all times. Water and feed sparingly. Cut blooms and disbud flower stems. Take action against pests and diseases.

SWEET PEAS

Sow sweet peas in the open ground if desired.
Under glass. Sow sweet peas under glass in pots or boxes, treating them beforehand with a proprietary fungicidal dressing. Place the pots or boxes in a cold frame and remove the light when the seedlings appear.

FLOWERS FROM SEED

Remove annuals before they become bedraggled. Plant out biennials and hardy perennials raised from seed.

BULBS

Complete bulb planting. Hoe beds of daffodils or spray with contact herbicide to control weeds. Follow with a residual herbicide.
Indoors and under glass. Lift half-hardy summer-flowering bulbs and dry as quickly as possible. Store them in a cool, frost-free, dry place in shallow boxes. Examine forced bulbs in bowls and water if fibre is dry.

ALPINES

Plant seedlings or rooted cuttings this month, except for pot-grown plants, which can go in at any time. Water plants in if soil is dry. Renew writing on labels. Scatter slug pellets in damp weather.

WATER PLANTS AND POOLS

Thin out underwater oxygenating plants and remove old water lily leaves. If the water appears dark, drain off half of it and replace with fresh. Remove old leaves and debris from the bottom. Plant waterside plants in the bog garden. Continue feeding fish as long as they are eating.

GREENHOUSES AND FRAMES

Bring plants into the greenhouse from cold frames. Reduce watering and damping down. Fumigate houses where tomatoes have contracted fungus diseases. Thin out shoots of greenhouse climbers. Line the greenhouse with polythene sheeting to conserve heat. Leave a little ventilation permanently where an oil heater is used. Gradually dry off cannas. Control slugs with pellets placed under foliage or flat stones. Close frames at night.

TREES AND SHRUBS

Start planting deciduous trees and shrubs towards the end of the month, but avoid frosty or wet conditions. Untie plants arriving from nurseries during inclement weather and stand them in a dry

hed, protecting their roots with straw or sacking. Plant scrambing plants as ground cover. Stake standard trees.

Propagation. Take hardwood cuttings of *Buddleia davidii*, forsythia and philadelphus, inserting them in sandy soil in a cold frame or in the open. Layer shoots of *Daphne cneorum* and fothergilla in pots of peaty loam plunged round the parent plants. Separate and re-plant rooted suckers of poplar, forsythia and *Rhus typhina*. Divide and re-plant *Euonymus fortunei* and spiraea.

Pruning. Cut back wall-trained hibiscus after flowering.

RHODODENDRONS AND AZALEAS

Prepare ground for planting, and plant new bushes. Feed plants which are not making healthy growth with peat, leaf-mould and well rotted manure. Spray buds with a bird deterrent.

HEDGES

Prepare hedge sites, if not already done. Plant evergreens as soon as received, though deciduous plants may be heeled in. Complete planting evergreens by the middle of the month.

HEATHERS

Lightly fork ground prepared for planting, then set the plants, soaking their roots if they are dry. Plants delivered in weather unsuitable for planting should be put close together in trays of peat, until planting is possible.

FRUIT

Order fruit trees and bushes for autumn delivery. Prepare planting sites, breaking up the subsoil to ensure good drainage. Work fertiliser into the soil while digging. Ground previously occupied by fruit should be chemically sterilised. Control weeds around established trees. Put grease bands round apple and cherry trees to catch winter moths. Pick and store apples and pears as they mature. Cut out fruited blackberry and loganberry canes and train in new shoots. Spray cherries, peaches and nectarines. Take gooseberry cuttings. Pick autumn-fruiting strawberries.

VEGETABLES

In the south, plant out spring cabbages. Pick and take indoors the last of the tomatoes. Plant winter and spring lettuces. Cut remaining marrows and store in a dry, frost-proof place. Clear away pea and bean haulm and dig vacant ground. Lift beetroot and store in a clamp covered with straw. In the north, set out Brussels sprout plants in a nursery bed.

Under glass. Sow lettuces for growing under cloches. Cover spring cabbages and early carrots with cloches. Force rhubarb.

Less common vegetables. Store winter radishes in a clamp.

HERBS

Take more cuttings of bay, lavender and rue, putting them in pots of sand in a cold frame. Divide clumps of chives in mild weather.

Plants to enjoy in October

Border and rock garden plants in flower	Trees and shrubs with colourful foliage	Cotoneaster	Saintpaulia
Ageratum	Acer (maple)	Crataegus (hawthorn)	Solanum capsicastrum
Amaryllis belladonna	Amelanchier	Lindera benzoin	**Fruit in season**
Antirrhinum	Azalea (deciduous)	Malus	Apple
Aster	Berberis	Pernettya	Grape
Cortaderia	Callicarpa	Pyracantha	Peach
Cyclamen alpinum	Cornus kousa	Skimmia japonica	Pear
Dahlia	Cotoneaster adpressa	Shrub roses	Plum
Erigeron	Euonymus	Sorbus (mountain ash)	Strawberry
Gaillardia	Fothergilla	Symphoricarpos (snowberry)	
Gentiana sino-ornata	Ginkgo	Viburnum	**Vegetables in season**
Helenium	Hamamelis		Artichoke, globe
Ipomoea (morning glory)	Lindera benzoin	**Greenhouse plants in flower**	Beans, dwarf french
Lobelia	Nyssa	Abutilon	Beet, seakale
Mesembryanthemum	Parrotia	Campanula isophylla (star of Bethlehem)	Brussels sprouts
Mimulus	Parthenocissus	Canna	Cabbage
Nerine	Prunus	Fuchsia	Carrots
Nicotiana (tobacco plant)	Rhus	Heliotropium	Cauliflower
Petunia	Sorbus (mountain ash)	Pelargonium	Celery
Phlox		Plumbago capensis	Lettuce
Rudbeckia	**Trees and shrubs with colourful fruits**	Tibouchina	Marrow
Salvia	Amelanchier		Onion
Scabiosa	Arbutus	**House plants in flower, depending on position and culture**	Peas
Schizostylis	Berberis rubrostilla	Anthurium	Radish
Solidago	Callicarpa	Aphelandra	Spinach beet
Tagetes	Chaenomeles	Chlorophytum	Sweet corn
Verbena		Euphorbia pulcherrima (poinsettia)	Tomato
			Turnip

Divide roots of mint, re-planting some and potting others to grow in the greenhouse. Dig up fennel and place in boxes of peat to force in a cool greenhouse.

PATIOS AND TOWN GARDENS

Remove plants that are past their best. Pot up tender plants and bring indoors. Move trees and shrubs in containers to a less exposed position, or protect with straw or bracken. Plant containers with dwarf conifers, heathers and skimmias and underplant with bulbs.

HOUSE PLANTS

Soak newly acquired plants in a bucket of water. Place plants where they will be warm but not subject to direct heat; where they will get plenty of light but be out of draughts. Keep them away from frosty windows at night.

GENERAL TASKS

Remove summer bedding plants soon enough to plant spring bedding and get it established before severe weather begins. Do not manure flower borders at this time of year, but give a dressing of 4 oz. per sq. yd. of bone-meal. Spread a net over the garden pool to catch fallen leaves, lifting this off every week or two. Rotting leaves produce poisonous gases which may kill fish during the winter. Clear fallen leaves from rock plants and lawns. Stack them to decompose.

Lawns

NEW LAWNS

Treat newly seeded areas as described in MARCH and APRIL.

ESTABLISHED LAWNS

Now is the time to remedy defective drainage. Investigate areas which have been susceptible to flooding and slow dispersal of water after heavy rain. Trouble may be due to an old drainage system with blocked or broken pipes preventing the water from running away and forcing it to come to the surface. Consult previous drainage plans where these are available.

Sub-surface drainage

On domestic lawns the installation of a tile drainage system to deal with sub-surface drainage is not usually justified. However, if the water table is near the surface or water runs down a slope on to the lawn, lay a line of tile drains at 90° to the general flow, $1\frac{1}{2}$–2 ft. deep, overlaid to within 6–9 in. of the surface with fine washed clinker or other porous material such as stone or gravel to trap the water. Provided that there is a fall into a ditch or other outlet, the water will be carried away. Afterwards take care to replace the soil and turves firmly, otherwise subsidence may later lead to an uneven lawn surface.

As an alternative to tile drains, dig narrow trenches leading to the outlet and lay rubble or large stones in the base.

Cover the rubble with a layer of small stones or gravel, or with strips of polythene overlaid with a 1 in. concrete layer, before replacing the soil and turves.

Surface drainage

On many lawns surface drainage is the problem. On heavy soils, particularly those subjected to a great deal of traffic, compaction of the surface occurs, forming an impervious layer which

LAYING TILE DRAINS

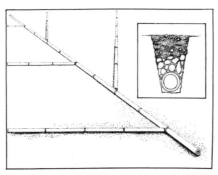

A herringbone pattern of drainage tiles, laid with a gentle fall to the outlet, will effectively drain a large lawn. Cover the tiles with porous materials to within 6–9 in. of the surface

prevents water percolating downward so that pools of water stand on the surface. This type of impeded drainage is comparatively easy to remedy. First thoroughly rake or scarify the area; then open up the surface, preferably with a hollow-tined fork, making holes some 4 in. deep and 2–3 in. apart. Apply sharp sand and gypsum liberally and work them thoroughly into the turf surface. Finally, treat with an autumn fertiliser to encourage growth. Prevent foot traffic or wear on the turf during wet weather.

In difficult cases, consult a drainage expert. The installation of tile or open drains can be unnecessarily expensive and may do more harm than good if carried out incorrectly.

Turfing

October is the best month for laying turf, since the sods can then settle and root into the underlying soil before winter. Prepare a weed-free turf bed in the same manner as for a seed bed (see MAY and AUGUST); a coarse tilth is adequate for turf. Allow the soil to settle before laying the turf, and tread in dry weather. Apply fertiliser to the turf bed at $2\frac{1}{2}$ oz. per sq. yd. and lightly rake into the surface. The following is a suitable mixture: bone-meal 4 parts, superphosphate 4 parts, sulphate of potash 1 part.

STAGES IN LAYING TURVES

1. Position the first row to protrude beyond a line marking the eventual lawn edge

2. Leave periodic gaps, slightly smaller than the standard turf size, for filling as shown

3. Gentle treading will press the centre down and exert lateral pressure on adjacent turves

4. Firm the second row of turves against the first by kicking with the side of your foot

5. When turf laying is completed, place soil in any remaining gaps to bring the surface level

6. Firm the turves into place by thumping them with a rake head held horizontally

7. Return to the first edge. If the line has moved, lift, and let it snap back into place

8. Trim the edge, using the line as a guide. Repeat the process on the other three edges

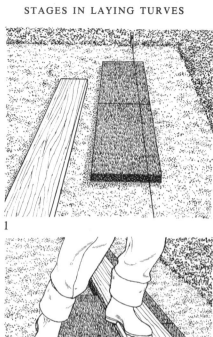

1

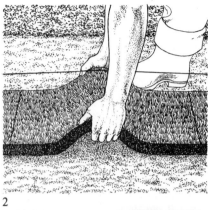

2

3

4

5

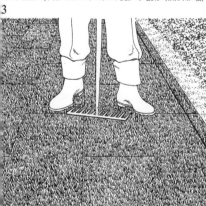

6

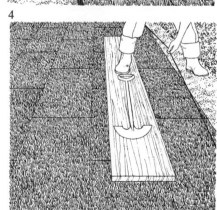

7

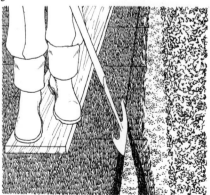

8

Quality of turf

Good turf is expensive and difficult to maintain. Although sea-washed turf is ideal in appearance, it requires expert management and even then is subject to rapid deterioration due to the change from its natural environment. Good weed-free parkland turf is best for domestic lawns, but is again difficult to obtain. Much garden turf is nowadays secured from meadowland which has been close-mown and treated with weed-killer to promote the finer grasses. Buy from a reputable supplier.

Turf dimensions

Turves are supplied either 1 ft. by 3 ft. or 1 ft. square and should be of uniform size and thickness (about $1\frac{1}{2}$ in.). Do not stack them in rolls, but lay them as soon as possible after delivery.

If the turves are not of uniform thickness, make a three-sided box, $1\frac{1}{2}$ in. deep, of the required dimensions. Lay each turf in the box, grass downwards, and trim off any soil that protrudes above the sides. If the turves are too thin, place them on one side to be used where there is a slightly higher soil level.

Laying the turves

Start at one corner of the site, using a plank to kneel on and moving forward over the laid area. Lay the turves in staggered rows in the same way as brickwork and fill any depressions in the soil with lightly sieved soil. Fit the turves closely and firmly together to help root development through the autumn and winter.

Continue with aeration and renovation treatment, and continue to apply fertilisers and preventive and curative fungicides (see MARCH).

Worms and weeds

Earthworms are a nuisance in the lawn. Worm casts are not only unsightly but when flattened cause bare patches in the grass and provide ideal sites for weed and moss colonisation. Treat the lawn during dull, moist, warm weather, using carbaryl, derris or chlorane. Mowrah meal, which was formerly recommended for use as a worm eradicator, is no longer available. Whichever chemical you use, follow the manufacturer's directions regarding precautions and rates of use.

Continue treatment for weeds and moss where necessary (see MARCH).

Roses

If new roses have been ordered, prepare the ground so that it will have time to settle for planting next month. Thorough preparation is the key to success with roses.

Ideally, new beds must be double-dug —that is, dug two spits deep—mixing any of the following materials generously with the soil.

New beds on light soil

On light soils, suitable materials for mixing with the lower spit include chopped turves, hop manure, leaf-mould, clay soil, manure, old rags, peat, torn-up sacking, sawdust, seaweed, spent hops from a brewery and wool shoddy, together with a large handful of bone-meal to each foot run of trench. For the top spit, use chopped turves, garden compost, peat or leaf-mould, plus a large handful of bone-meal to each foot run of trench.

New beds on heavy soil

On medium loam or heavier soils, put clinker, gravel, gypsum, pebbles or sand in the lower spit, together with such materials as coarse peat, hop manure, balls of paper, leaves, manure, old rags, torn-up sacking, seaweed, spent hops from a brewery, straw, top growth from hardy herbaceous plants or wool shoddy, also a handful of bone-meal to each foot run of trench. You can also work clinker, gravel, gypsum, pebbles or sand into the top spit, together with chopped turves, garden compost, peat or leaf-mould. Add a large handful of bone-meal to each foot run of trench.

Add extra topsoil

In some places a ridge of chalk lies under the topsoil. If the topsoil is less than two spits deep, add more topsoil or dig out a hole at each planting site and mix in some of the materials listed above.

Roses enjoy a slightly acid soil, so it is not usually necessary to lime the land. If a soil-testing kit shows it to be strongly acid, spread lime lightly over the surface at 4 oz. to the sq. yd.

If possible, put some light soil under cover to keep it dry until required for planting new roses next month.

Pests and diseases

Spray with a systemic rose insecticide if greenfly appear.

Continue fortnightly spraying to keep black spot and rust diseases under control. Gather up and burn infested fallen leaves.

Hardy herbaceous plants

October, when the soil is warm and not too wet and plants make new roots quickly, is the best month for planting most herbaceous perennials, except in cold wet parts of the country.

If the plants you have ordered (see AUGUST) arrive during a wet period, lessen the harmful effects of treading by using short boards to walk on while planting.

Lay out the plants in their correct places (see AUGUST). If the weather is sunny or windy, leave the wrappings on until you are ready to begin planting. Then unwrap each plant and, after assessing the depth and size of the hole needed according to the length or spread of the roots, make a hole with a trowel. If the soil is rather dry, puddle in the plants as you would for spring planting (see MARCH).

Planting techniques

Insert the plant upright, put the soil back so that it falls between as well as on the roots until levelled off. Firm the soil, either with the fingers if the soil is moist and lumpy, or with the heel if it is fairly loose and dry. Make sure that the plant when firmed is no more than 1 in. deeper than it was before being dug up—the soil line indicating its previous depth is marked by a change in colour where the plant has a stem or foliage—or no more than 1 in. below the surface if the plant consists of roots and dormant buds, like paeonies, or of crowns, like hostas.

Plant positions

Some kinds will show no sign of growth until well into the spring, so if you have not made a plan showing the name of each plant in its correct position (see AUGUST), mark the position of plants by labelling, by placing a short stick against each plant, or by drawing a furrow about 1 in. deep with the point of the trowel round a group of plants, or even round a single plant. Use metal or pointed wood labels, and write the names in indelible pencil or ink. There are also patent labels on the market on to which names can be scratched or etched. The labels must be at least 9 in. long if stuck into the ground, but can be shorter if wired to a 12 in. cane or stiff wire rod. String and most wooden peg labels will eventually rot.

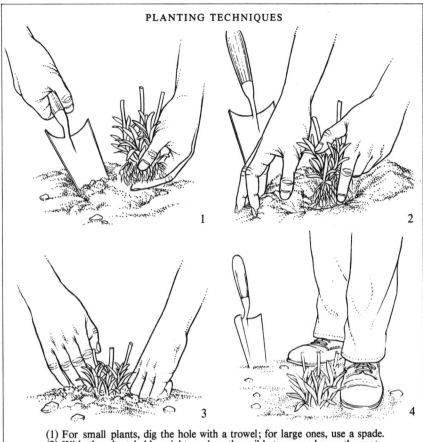

PLANTING TECHNIQUES

(1) For small plants, dig the hole with a trowel; for large ones, use a spade. (2) With the plant held upright, replace the soil between and over the roots. (3) Firm with your fingers if the soil is moist or lumpy. (4) On soil that is loose or tends to be dry, firm with your foot or puddle in

If for any reason a plant needs moving from its original position, re-plant it in October after it has flowered once.

Tidy the beds and borders, but do not cut back faded growth if it is not unsightly. Continue dead-heading for the first half of the month at least, and always keep down young seedling weeds whenever the weather is dry enough.

Divide and re-plant old clumps (except soft-foliaged kinds such as pyrethrum and achillea) that finished flowering in early summer (see MARCH).

Preparing borders

Dig for winter weathering and March planting (expecially on heavy soil) any new bed or border where the soil has previously been too hard, using the same method as for autumn planting (see JULY). Also, dig over old borders which need a complete overhaul because of

255

weeds, or because the plants have grown too large. It is better to do this earlier in the year (see AUGUST); but if you have left it until now, dig up all growth, shake it, and discard as weeds all but the healthy plants or pieces of plant which are to be used again. Then dig deeply and manure as for bare ground (see JULY), making sure that roots of perennial weeds are picked out and destroyed. Green annual weeds can be dug in if covered by 9 in. of soil.

Laying out new beds

If grass is growing on the site chosen for the new bed, the ground is likely to be too dry or hard for digging until October or even later. Pare off the turf, which may be needed for re-laying elsewhere, with a sharp spade or turfing iron into strips $1\frac{1}{2}$ in. thick and 1 ft. wide. If the soil underneath is richer, use less manure or compost, but still use fertiliser (see JULY).

Turf not needed for re-laying makes excellent potting soil if stacked in a neat square or oblong heap where it can rot down. It can also be used for layering in with home-made compost, or can simply be dug in if it is first pared or chipped off and then chopped into 2 in. thick pieces about the size of the palm of your hand. Large lumps of turf will rot slowly and leave air pockets to cause drought conditions in spring.

Surface cultivation

A rotary hoe set to dig 2–3 in. deep will chop the surface so well that the loose pieces can be pushed in trench by trench when the ground is dug over. Rotary cultivation should be regarded only as a surface conditioner before deep, hard digging. Cultivators do not bury rubbish or dig deeply enough, and they leave any soil out of their reach as a hard pan which will impede drainage and make the surface too fine and loose.

256

Dahlias

As soon as the first frost blackens the foliage and stems, cut them down to about 6 in. above ground. Then, with a fork, carefully dig up the plants without damaging any of the fleshy tubers. If any tubers are accidentally damaged, cut the damaged parts away cleanly with a sharp knife, and dust the cuts with flowers of sulphur. Remove as much soil as possible, then stand the plants upside down in a frost-free place for about a week, to allow the sap in the stems to dry out.

Place the plants in shallow boxes and just cover the tubers with slightly damp

peat, but take care not to allow any peat to come into contact with the crown of the plant (the point where the tubers join the stem). It is from this point that new growth will appear next spring, and it is vital that no rotting takes place here. Dust the crown with captan or flowers of sulphur as a precaution. Shoots are not produced from the fat fleshy tubers, which are merely food reservoirs.

Storing tubers

Place the boxes of tubers in a frost-free shed or greenhouse. A spare room in the home will be just as satisfactory.

Dahlias may also be stored through

CUTTING DOWN DAHLIAS

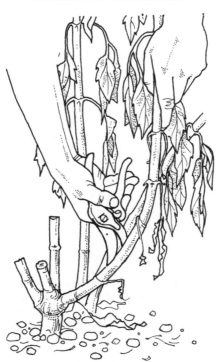

After frost, dahlia foliage becomes limp and black. When this occurs, cut back the stems to 6 in. and carefully lift the plants with a fork

STORING DAHLIA TUBERS

When the stems have dried out, place the tubers in shallow boxes and cover with slightly damp peat, taking care not to cover the crowns

STORING IN VERMICULITE

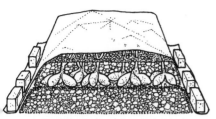

Storing dahlia tubers under cover in vermiculite, with an overall covering of polythene, is a sound alternative to storing in boxes

....

the winter in horticultural vermiculite, which has excellent insulating properties. Spread a layer of vermiculite 1 ft. thick on the floor of your shed or garage. After the stems have been allowed to dry, place the dahlias upright on the vermiculite. Then cover them all over with another layer of the vermiculite, at least 1 ft. thick. Spread a sheet of thin polythene tightly over the whole heap. The dahlias should then be safe until the following spring.

Inspection of tubers

Examine the tubers once or twice during the winter and, if they are shrivelling, plunge them in a bucket of water for a night to plump them up again. Dry them off thoroughly and replace them in the vermiculite. Inspect dahlias stored in boxes every few weeks and, if the tubers show signs of shrivelling, moisten the peat or plunge the tubers overnight in tepid water.

In cold weather, do not put the tubers in a bucket of water outside, but in a reasonably warm place.

Storing seeds

Remove seed from dried seed pods. The seeds, which resemble dry tea-leaves about $\frac{1}{2}$ in. long, will keep safely in a matchbox until wanted for sowing in March.

Chrysanthemums

As plants stop flowering, decide which of the three following methods of over-wintering is most suitable and take appropriate action.

1. Leave them in the garden

Most modern varieties will survive in an average winter in southern England, provided they are in well drained ground which is not infested with slugs. Clear all the rubbish and dead leaves away from around them, but do not cut down the top growth until spring, apart from

CUTTING DOWN CHRYSANTHEMUMS

If plants are not to be left in the garden, remove the canes and use secateurs to cut the main stems down to within 6 in. of ground level

....

removing dead flowers. Collect the supporting stakes and store them until the spring.

2. Lift them out and bed them in a cold frame

Cut the plants down to about 6 in. and cut off all green, flowering shoots at ground level. Label the stools carefully, lift them, and wash thoroughly in clean

LABELLING THE STOOLS

Before lifting the plants, cut off the green shoots at ground level, write fresh labels, and tie them securely to the stems

....

water before bedding or boxing them in 3 in. of John Innes potting compost No. 1 or a proprietary soil-less compost. The cold frame must be well drained and protected against frosts by matting, and should preferably face south.

OVER-WINTERING CHRYSANTHEMUM STOOLS

Wash the stools thoroughly before storing them in compost in a protected cold frame or in compost-filled boxes in a greenhouse

3. Lift them and house them in the greenhouse

Treat the stools as in (2) and put them in compost-filled boxes on a shelf in the greenhouse where they will get plenty of light and air. Plant the stools at the same depth as they were growing in the garden and water them in.

Clear away and burn unwanted stools.

UNDER GLASS

The first of the mid-season varieties will come into flower by the middle of the month. They need a dry atmosphere and abundant light. Keep the greenhouse ventilated at all times, even in cold wet weather when gentle heat is necessary. A cold, stagnant atmosphere is damaging to chrysanthemums in flower.

Attend to watering with extra care, being sparing rather than too generous. Avoid spilling water on the floor or on the foliage.

Discoloration

If brown spots appear on the petals, increase the temperature immediately to 13°C (55°F) and dust the plants with captan.

Continue to disbud the very late-flowering varieties, including the greenhouse border plants.

Stop feeding large exhibition and incurved varieties when they begin to show colour.

Gladioli

It is not safe to leave gladioli in the ground through the winter. Like dahlias, they must be lifted before the first hard frosts. Do this about the middle of the month, when the foliage is beginning to turn yellowish-brown. Lift the corms with a fork, taking care not to bruise them. Remove any soil adhering to them.

Cut off all but $\frac{1}{2}$ in. of the main stem,

258

LIFTING GLADIOLI

When the foliage begins to turn yellowish-brown, lift gladiolus corms with a fork, taking care not to bruise them

then place the corms in a dry, airy place for a week or ten days.

When the corms are absolutely dry, store them in trays or shallow boxes in a room or greenhouse that is dry and frostproof. Too warm an atmosphere

TRIMMING GLADIOLUS STEMS

After lifting gladioli, use secateurs to cut off all but about $\frac{1}{2}$ in. of each stem before placing the corms in a dry, airy place to dry out

will cause them to shrivel. The corms can be cleaned at the time they are stored or left until later when there is little work to be done in the garden (see NOVEMBER).

Irises

Tidy the bearded iris bed before the onset of winter, raking off dead leaves and other debris. Weed carefully and trim back the longer leaves, cutting off about a quarter of their length.

UNDER GLASS

Complete the planting of bulbous irises in pots as soon as possible (see SEPTEMBER).

Lilies

Plant as many of your lilies as possible this month, staking the late-flowering kinds, which may be damaged by autumn gales, at the time of planting. Cover the bulbs with a depth of soil equal to two and a half times their own height. This generally means about 4 in. of soil.

Most lilies like well drained, fairly rich, moist soil which is neutral or very slightly acid (pH 6.5). When in doubt, and on very heavy soil, rather shallow planting is advisable.

Lilies for cut flowers

If you wish to plant lilies for cutting, order three times as many bulbs as the number of blooms you are likely to need. Cut the blooms from only a third of the bulbs each year, allowing them a minimum of two years to recover. Do not cut more than a third of each stem.

Allow lily stems to die down naturally, unless they are showing signs of disease. In this case cut them down while they are green. To grow lilies as pot plants, lift some of the bulbs from the garden as soon as the stems begin to die down, and put them in 6–10 in. pots, depending on their eventual size. Plunge the pots in ashes, covering them 3–4 in. deep, or place them in a sheltered spot and cover with a similar depth of peat.

UNDER GLASS

If newly potted lilies are required for forcing, bring the pots into the greenhouse about 13 weeks before flowers are needed. Maintain a temperature of 7–10°C (45–50°F) until they have started into growth, then increase to 16–21°C (61–70°F) (see JANUARY and FEBRUARY). This will ensure that a good root system is established before top growth is encouraged.

Carnations and pinks

Plant border carnations and pinks in beds prepared during August or September. Space border carnations 15–18 in. apart, and pinks 12 in. apart. In cold districts with very heavy soil the plants should be potted into 4 in. pots, kept in a cold frame, and planted out in March.

Planting method

Spread the roots and firm the soil over them thoroughly, mixing in dry, sifted soil if the ground is wet. Keep the bottom pairs of leaves just clear of the soil, and secure each plant with a 6 in. stake and a split ring of thin wire.

Prepare beds for spring planting following the method described in AUGUST.

Continue to cut away layers of border carnations and to stop modern pinks as necessary (see SEPTEMBER).

Clear away leaves and rubbish from around stems. Protect plants with black cotton against birds. In mild spells, firm the soil around plants, if it has been loosened by frost.

UNDER GLASS

Maintain a temperature of 7°C (45°F) for perpetual flowering carnations and give some ventilation at all times.

Water and feed sparingly (see APRIL).

Cut blooms and disbud flower stems (see SEPTEMBER).

Watch for pests and diseases, taking action as necessary (see MARCH).

Sweet peas

Lose no time if you wish to sow sweet peas direct in the ground outdoors. This method is suitable only for naturally-grown plants (see MARCH) but is successful in three seasons out of four in mild districts and on well drained land. Sow at the rate of 1 oz. of seed for a row 10 yd. long. This allows approximately 1 in. between seeds. Treat the seeds first with a proprietary fungicidal dressing, shaking the seeds and powder together.

UNDER GLASS

Sow sweet peas under glass by the middle of the month. Before sowing, treat the seeds with a proprietary fungicidal dressing by shaking the dust and seeds together in the packet.

Seed sowing

Sow the seeds in John Innes seed compost, a proprietary soil-less compost or a mixture of 4 parts loam and 1 part each of sand and peat. The compost must be moist when the seed is sown.

Use pots or seed boxes, placing crocks (pieces of broken pot) in the bottoms of pots. Sow the seeds ½ in. deep. Allow eight to twelve seeds to a 5 in. pot, or space them 1½–2 in. either way in seed boxes. Water moderately after sowing, but thereafter water only if absolutely necessary.

Treatment of seedlings

Place the pots or boxes in a cold frame, preferably plunging pots up to their rims in peat. When the seedlings appear,

SOWING SWEET PEAS IN POTS

Make the holes ½ in. deep, using a marked stick, or one with an adjustable depth gauge. Allow eight to twelve seeds to a 5 in. pot

Drop one seed into each hole, afterwards covering them with compost and applying water from a can fitted with a fine rose

259

OVER-WINTERING SWEET PEAS

After sowing sweet peas, stand the pots in a cold frame, removing the lights as soon as the seedlings appear through the compost

remove the frame lights entirely and replace them only during very wet weather or when a hard frost is imminent. Light frost will not harm the young seedlings. Set mouse traps. Use netting to protect the seedlings from birds.

Sweet peas may be sown early in the month about 1 in. apart in a double row, allowing about 8 in. between the rows. Cover with cloches, which can remain in position until late April. Sow extra seeds in pots or boxes to replace young plants eaten by mice or slugs.

Flowers from seed

Remove all annuals before they become too bedraggled. In a mild autumn, retaining the plants for their last few flowers may delay the planting of other bedding subjects.

Plant out hardy perennials raised from seed. The sooner this job is completed, the longer the plants have to become established before winter.

Plant out any remaining hardy biennials.

Bulbs

Complete the programme of bulb planting started last month.

Hoe beds of daffodils, except in the very mildest districts, where growth may have already started. Alternatively, spray with a contact herbicide to destroy weed seedlings and follow with a residual herbicide which will inhibit further growth of weed seedlings.

Plant tulips and hyacinths this month and next. The leaves of tulips planted earlier may be damaged by frost, and are more susceptible to tulip fire disease.

UNDER GLASS AND INDOORS

Lift half-hardy summer-flowering bulbs such as acidantheras, ixias, chincher-inchees, schizostylis and sparaxis, and in cold districts take inside tubs and large pots of amaryllis, crinums and nerines to protect them from winter frost. When lifting bulbs and corms at this time of the year, dry them as quickly as possible. Damp soil, roots and leaves left on the bulbs will cause them to rot.

Drying bulbs and corms

A few days in shallow boxes in an airing cupboard or other really warm spot will dry the bulbs completely and make it easy to separate bulbs and corms from the rubbish. Then store them in shallow boxes, in a cool, dry place but out of reach of frost.

Inspection of forced bulbs

Examine bulbs in bowls which are standing in a shed or cool room and water if the bulb fibre is at all dry. Bowls plunged in the open (see SEPTEMBER) should not need such attention.

Alpines

Plant seedlings or rooted cuttings by the third week of this month, except for pot-grown plants which can go in at almost any time. Seedlings or cuttings planted too late may have their roots exposed by frost, but pot-grown plants set out with a complete soil ball do not suffer in this way. If you are moving established plants to a fresh site, retain as much soil as possible on the roots.

Water the plants in if the soil is dry.

PROTECTION FOR ALPINES

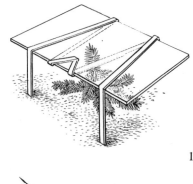

1

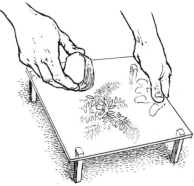

2

Alpines with woolly or hairy leaves need protection from winter rain. The illustrations show: (1) A pane of glass held over the plant by a strip of bent metal; thick wire would serve as well. (2) A pane of glass supported by four wooden pegs and held in place with a stone

Avoid leaving footmarks on wet soil, if necessary placing boards or stepping stones on which to stand.

Renew the writing on labels that are difficult to read, before winter rain makes them illegible.

Apply slug pellets if the weather is damp, placing them under foliage or flat stones close to evergreen, trailing and shrubby plants, or rough grass, where slugs are most likely to lurk.

Water plants and pools

Towards the end of the month prepare for the winter by drastically thinning out underwater oxygenating plants and removing old water lily leaves. This will avoid the presence of a great deal of decaying vegetation on the base of the pool when the water is iced over, and will minimise the formation of toxic gases and prevent a shortage of oxygen.

If the water looks dark green or blackish, drain off half the volume and

REMOVING LEAVES FROM A POOL

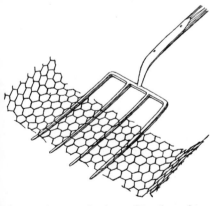

A scoop for removing leaves from the surface of a pool can be made by fitting wire netting over a garden fork. Use the scoop with care if the pool is lined with a plastic sheet

replace with fresh water. While the pool is half drained, take the opportunity to remove old leaves and debris from the base, but leave most of the mud, which contains aquatic insects and the resting buds of some plants.

In the bog garden and in areas surrounding the pool, divide and plant waterside subjects as described in APRIL.

Continue feeding fish as long as it is obvious that the food is being eaten and they are eager for it.

Greenhouses and frames

Bring into the greenhouse without delay any plants still standing outdoors in frames. Frost and autumn gales can ruin them overnight.

In the greenhouse, reduce syringing, damping down and watering progressively as the days get shorter and the nights become colder. Where possible, carry out any necessary watering and damping down before mid-day. Check the heating occasionally during the evening to make sure that it is working properly and that thermostats are operating at the required temperature.

Fumigate the greenhouse

Where tomatoes have suffered from fungus diseases, and if the house can be emptied of all other plants, fumigate with a sulphur candle to kill the spores on the old tomato plants and on the fabric of the house. Light the candle in the evening after closing the ventilators and plugging all obvious leaks. Keep the house closed until next morning, then open the door for a while before going in. A $\frac{1}{2}$ lb. candle will fumigate 500 cu. ft.

Thin out the shoots of climbing plants such as plumbagos, passifloras and *Tibouchina semidecandra* to admit more light and air during the winter.

LINING A GREENHOUSE

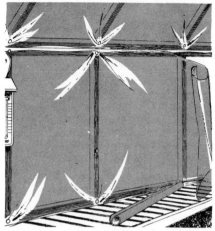

Lining a greenhouse with polythene sheeting to conserve heat enables higher temperatures to be maintained and reduces fuel bills

Conserve heat

Line the greenhouse with polythene sheeting, to within 12 in. of the ridge on either side of the roof, to conserve heat during the winter, covering the ventilators separately. Where an oil heater is used, leave the ventilators on the leeward side of the roof open about $\frac{1}{4}$ in. the whole time, to allow fumes and moisture-vapour created by the heater to escape. To minimise loss of light, clean the glass before fastening the polythene lining.

Dry off cannas

Gradually withhold water from cannas to dry them off before storing them for the winter under the greenhouse staging, but do not allow the compost to become dust-dry.

Keep a sharp look-out for slug damage and for the slimy trails of these pests, scattering slug pellets as necessary and renewing them if they disintegrate.

Make sure that the frames are closed each night in case of a sudden, unexpected frost.

Trees and shrubs

Towards the end of the month start planting hardy deciduous trees and shrubs of all kinds in well prepared ground (see SEPTEMBER). Do not plant in frosty or wet weather, or when a strong north or north-east wind is blowing. If shrubs arrive from the nursery during a spell of bad weather, untie the plants and stand them in a dry shed with straw or sacking round the roots, until the weather improves.

Heel in new plants

If the bad weather seems to have set in, or you cannot plant for a few weeks, heel the shrubs in by making a V-shaped trench in the soil, inserting the shrubs so that their roots are covered, and firming down the soil. If necessary, the plants will survive until the spring planting season.

When moving evergreens in the autumn, spray the entire plant with the waterborne plastic S600, which considerably reduces respiration and so lessens the risk of flagging. It can also be used for deciduous trees if they have to be moved while in leaf. The almost invisible plastic coating disintegrates and disappears after a month or two.

Stake standards

Newly planted standard trees must be firmly staked and tied. Drive the stake into the ground close to the tree before covering the roots with soil, otherwise damage may be done to the roots.

A clematis cone

Make a clematis cone by planting one, two or three plants at the base of a stout central pole surrounded by four or five heavily galvanised wires leading from a foot or so from the base up to the top.

To bring colour to an old tree, a small copse or group of trees, plant one or more clematis and allow it to wander up into the branches in the same way as the wild species, old man's beard or traveller's joy.

To hide a manhole in the garden, plant beside it a low-growing spreading plant such as *Contoneaster horizontalis*. If the shrub is grown in a container, this can then be pushed to one side to remove the cover.

If plants fail to grow because of dogs in the front garden, plant a thick bed of *Hypericum calycinum* (rose of Sharon). These low, evergreen shrubs will give a continuous display of yellow flowers from June to September. Excellent as ground cover they will smother all weeds, and are never troubled by dogs.

Contrasting climbers

For striking beauty and contrast, to clothe an old tree or to cover a wall, fence or building, plant a *Polygonum baldschuanicum* (Russian vine) and a *Parthenocissus quinquefolia* (Virginia creeper) and let them climb and mingle together.

Many plants which are allowed only to climb (when they have to be trained and secured) will also make splendid ground cover if instead they are allowed to sprawl. These include clematis, *Hydrangea petiolaris*, ivy and winter jasmine.

Orange berries

If you have many birds in your garden, yet wish to keep the berries on your shrubs for as long as possible, grow those which have orange fruits. These include pyracantha, viburnum and holly.

PROPAGATION

Take hardwood cuttings of *Aucuba japonica, Buddleia davidii*, deutzia, escallonia, kerria, spring-flowering lonicera, lindera, philadelphus, spiraea, tamarisk and weigela. Select strong, firm shoots, about 1 ft. long, and insert them in sandy soil, either in a cold frame or in the open. Make the cut with a sharp knife immediately below a joint, at the same time removing the lower leaves on the part of the stem which will be in the soil. Treat the cuttings as described in SEPTEMBER.

Propagate *Daphne cneorum* and fothergilla by layering young shoots in pots of peaty loam, plunged round the parent plants. By the following spring these layers should have formed sufficient roots to be severed from the parent plants and to be planted out.

Separate rooted suckers of celastrus, *Forsythia suspensa*, poplar, *Rhus typhina*, robinia and snowberry from their parent plants. Re-plant these rooted pieces in their permanent growing places and give support where necessary.

Divide *Euonymus fortunei* and spiraea and re-plant.

PRUNING

Cut back the spurs of wall-trained hibiscus after flowering.

Rhododendrons and azaleas

Dig ground where bushes are to be planted (see FEBRUARY). Plant new plants in prepared ground (see MARCH).

Feed plants which are not producing good leaves and flowers or making healthy growth. Add peat or leaf-mould and well rotted manure to the top few inches of soil. The young feeding roots of rhododendrons are active at this time.

Tits can be troublesome during the winter months, since they peck at the buds and disfigure the flowers. To discourage them, spray or paint the buds with a bird deterrent.

PRUNING A LARGE BRANCH

Crossing branches or diseased wood on established, deciduous trees (including fruit) should be pruned flush with the main stem and the wounds covered with bituminous paint

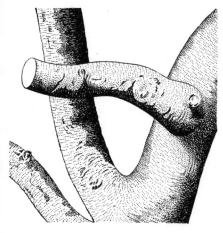

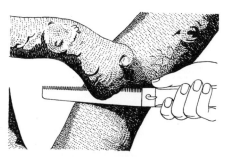

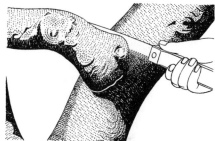

1. To make the branch lighter, sever it 18 in. from where the final cut is to be made

2. Before making the final cut, saw through the underside of the branch to prevent splitting

3. Saw through the top of the branch to meet the cut made on the underside of the branch

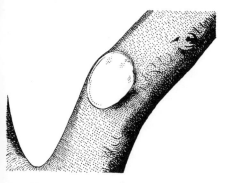

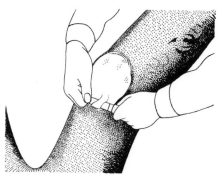

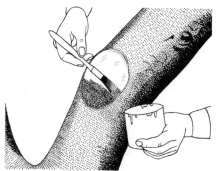

4. With care, the two cuts will meet to give a perfectly level surface, as here. Careless sawing will leave an unsightly ridge

5. Use a sharp knife to trim away any ragged edges of bark or wood which may remain round the outside of the cut

6. Immediately after sawing and trimming, protect the cut surface from disease spores by painting with a proprietary sealing compound

Hedges

Prepare hedge sites if this was not done last month (see SEPTEMBER).

Hedging plants ordered in good time may be delivered this month. Though evergreens should be planted immediately, deciduous plants can be heeled in temporarily. Separate the plants in the bundles and bury the roots in shallow trenches, laying the plants at an angle so that they are not blown about too much while awaiting planting. If the weather is showery try to complete the planting of evergreen hedges by the middle of the month, otherwise planting must be delayed until the following spring, and the plants must be heeled in.

Planting method

When planting, use a measuring rod to ensure even spacing, and a garden line for straightness. If the root balls are not more than 8 in. wide or deep, and if the soil is reasonably fine, use a trowel to take out the holes. If the root balls are larger or if the soil is lumpy, use a spade. Make each hole wide enough to take the spread-out

263

roots and deep enough for the plants to be buried to the same depth as previously, as shown by the old soil marks. Make sure that the roots are spread outwards and point downwards.

Firm roots

Cover the roots with the soil removed from the hole, or from the next hole, having first broken it up if it is not already in a fine, crumbly condition. Make sure that there are no empty gaps around the roots, firming them in first with your fingers and then with your heel. Break up the surface clods and leave the soil level. This not only improves the appearance of the newly planted hedge, but also makes subsequent hoeing easier.

Heathers

Lightly fork over the ground which was prepared in September, removing any weeds which have appeared and also any bracken which may have been left if bracken peat was used as a dressing.

All kinds of heathers can be planted during this month, provided the soil is not frozen or saturated. First soak the roots thoroughly if they appear dry. If plants are delivered during weather which is unsuitable for planting, unpack them and set them close together in shallow boxes or trays, covering their roots with soil or peat. Stand the boxes in a position sheltered from cold, drying winds until planting is possible.

Planting sites

Choose an open position, well clear of overhanging trees. All heathers, except those which are lime-tolerant (see plant descriptions, JANUARY), must be planted in acid or neutral soil. On an alkaline soil lime-tolerant species will benefit from extra peat; on a very chalky soil the layer of peat can be up to 4 in. thick.

Set all plants deeply so that the lower foliage rests on the soil. Clip off old flower stems.

Planting distances vary according to species (see plant descriptions, JANUARY), but as a general guide a distance of 12 in. between small kinds and 18 in. between the larger varieties is suitable.

Fruit

Order fruit trees and bushes for autumn delivery (see recommended varieties, NOVEMBER), if this has not already been done.

Begin to prepare the planting site. Most fruits will succeed on a wide range of soil types, but the ideal soil is a deep, well drained, medium loam, preferably slightly acid. The particular type of soil suited to each fruit is given before the lists of varieties.

Soil improvement

To open heavy soils and to improve the water-holding capacity of light soils, break up and improve the subsoil by thoroughly incorporating organic matter or compost into it. No fruit will tolerate bad drainage, and on heavy clay soil it may be necessary to dig trenches and put in tile drains. Always fill the trenches with porous materials through which the water can percolate. If drainage is restricted, but tile draining is not justified, plant on a mound of soil above the surrounding level to improve drainage.

Add fertiliser

Inorganic fertilisers are also necessary to supply nutrients. Except on good garden soils which have been regularly manured, a balanced inorganic general fertiliser or John Innes base fertiliser should be worked into the soil while digging the planting site.

Soil sterilisation

If the site chosen has previously been used for a fruit garden, bear in mind that fruits of the same type re-planted on the same soil within five to seven years will not grow successfully unless the site has been treated with a chemical sterilising agent. Fruit trees and bushes may have been killed by honey fungus (see SEPTEMBER), and re-planting trees of any sort within about five years is likely to fail because the fungus will attack again, particularly if adverse growing conditions cause a check to the re-planted tree or bush.

Trees in grass

It is not always necessary to plant fruit in cultivated soil; but if trees are planted in grass, make sure that they have adequate water during the first growing season. This can be done by mowing, by mulching round young trees with a shallow layer of strawy compost or farmyard manure, or by watering them in the early summer months. Soft fruits are not suitable for growing in grass, because the grass gets in among the shoots and cannot easily be controlled.

Trees in cultivated soil

In cultivated soil, weed control with hand tools can damage roots; but the use of weedkillers combined with mulching gives good results, because the roots are encouraged to grow up to the warm rich surface layers without risk of breaking. If perennial weeds are removed before planting, annual weeds can be killed by paraquat. The soil round most fruits can be kept free of further weed growth by an application of simazine to moist soil in spring before new weed growth starts, and this will be effective for months if the soil is not disturbed. However, simazine should be used only on established fruit. It is not suitable for use round stone fruits,

ROOT PRUNING A PLUM OR DAMSON TREE

To root prune an unfruitful older tree, first dig a trench half way round it at a distance of about 2–4 ft. from the trunk

When digging the trench and removing the soil, take care not to damage the thin feeding roots which will be exposed

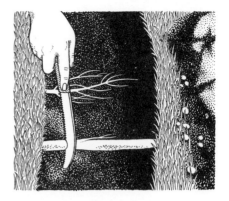

Sever the thick roots, then cut under the tree to break the tap roots. Prune the other half of the tree the following autumn

---

or on raspberries when new growths are near the soil surface in spring, or on strawberries.

Tidy the ground round established trees to get rid of weeds. Treatment with a paraquat spray will usually control annual weeds and grasses for a long period.

Apply a band of vegetable grease to the trunks of apple and cherry trees to catch wingless female winter moths climbing up to lay eggs on the twigs and spurs.

Apple and pear

Continue to pick the fruit of different varieties as they mature. Some of the longest-keeping varieties of apple and most late pears will not mature on the tree, but should be left as long as possible before they are picked and stored. Pick the fruit early in the day (see SEPTEMBER). Storing in polythene bags, which are closed without being completely sealed, helps to retain moisture and prolongs storage life. Store in an even temperature of 2–4 °C (36–39 °F).

Blackberry, loganberry and hybrid berries

Cut out canes that have fruited, and train new shoots on to the supporting framework, preferably with wire re-inforced paper ties. Collect the wire hoops that have been used to train up the new growths (see MAY) and put them away for use next year. Clear away weeds from the soil round the plants in preparation for the winter.

Cherry

In mid-October, spray with a copper fungicide as a precaution against bacterial canker.

Gooseberry

This is one of the few fruits that can be propagated with safety from garden stock if the bushes are bearing well and they appear healthy. Prepare cuttings 10–12 in. long from well ripened wood of the current season. Remove buds on the part of the cutting that will be underground. For best results, take the cuttings early, even before leaf-fall.

Peach and nectarine

At leaf-fall, spray the trees with Bordeaux mixture or some other copper fungicide to control peach leaf curl.

Plum and damson

Root prune unfruitful trees after leaf-fall, cutting vigorous roots but leaving the fine feeding roots intact. A young tree can be lifted completely and re-planted. When dealing with an older tree, take out a trench round it about 2–4 ft. away from the tree, cutting cleanly through any thick roots growing outwards. Then cut under the tree to break the tap roots, re-fill the trench, and stake the tree. To prevent the tree suffering too much shock, this operation can be spread over two winters, cutting half way round the tree each time.

Strawberry

Pick the autumn fruit, and protect ripening fruit with cloches. Complete planting of runners for fruiting next year (see AUGUST). Finally, tidy established beds.

Vegetables

In the south, plant out spring cabbages during the first week of the month (see SEPTEMBER).

Early in the month pick and take indoors the last of the tomatoes, including those that are still green. The latter can be made into chutney or placed in a warm, light place to continue ripening.

Winter lettuces

Plant winter and spring lettuces early in the month after raking in bone-meal at 4 oz. per sq. yd. Set the plants out with a trowel, spacing them 9 in. apart in rows 12 in. apart. When planting lettuces, take care not to damage the seed leaves. These should be just above the soil surface after planting, never buried.

STORING MARROWS

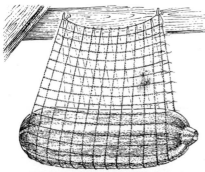

Ripe marrows may be hung in nets suspended from the roof or placed on the shelves of a dry, frost-proof room or shed

Cut any remaining marrows and store in a dry, frost-proof place. They should be eaten by the end of the year.

Clear away the growth of peas and beans as picking is completed; start to dig this and other vacant ground.

266

TOPPING BEETROOT

Before storing beetroot, twist the tops off an inch or two above the roots. If they are trimmed too closely, the roots will not store well

Incorporate farmyard manure or garden compost at about 5–6 lb. per sq. yd. (a layer 1 in. thick), dried sewage sludge at 2 lb. per sq. yd., or a proprietary hop manure applied 'as instructed by the manufacturers. Leave the soil rough.

Storing beetroot

Lift beetroot with a fork and twist the tops off. Store them in a convenient corner of the garden, on a base of brushwood or straw, covering them first with straw and then a layer of soil.

In the north, set out in a nursery bed Brussels sprout plants grown from an August sowing. Choose poorish soil, dusting the dibber holes with calomel and allowing 10–12 in. between both the plants and the rows.

UNDER GLASS

Sow lettuces for growing under cloches. 'Imperial Winter', 'Arctic King', 'Kwiek', 'Premier' and 'Valdor' are all recommended. Sow $\frac{1}{4}$ in. deep on well manured land in two rows 12 in. apart, afterwards applying a pre-

emergence weedkiller and putting the cloches in place. At the end of the month, thin the plants to 9–10 in. apart and cover the ends of the rows with glass.

Place cloches over spring cabbages and early carrots, closing the ends of the rows with glass.

In a heated greenhouse, at a temperature of 10–13°C (50–55°F) force rhubarb under the staging. Lift the crowns and pack them with a little moist soil in boxes. Cover with a box and black polythene until the young shoots appear. The crowns will have to be discarded after forcing.

FORCING RHUBARB

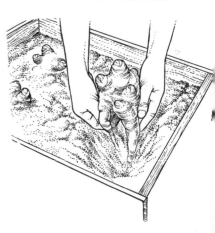

Packed in a large box, with moist soil between, rhubarb crowns will produce young shoots within about four weeks

LESS COMMON VEGETABLES

Winter radishes (see JULY) are generally hardy enough to be left outdoors during the winter. However, if left in the ground they may become coarse and it is preferable, especially in the north, to lift and store them, at the end of this month or in early November, as described for beetroot.

Herbs

Take further cuttings of bay, lavender and rue, and insert them round the rim of a pot filled with sand. Protect these cuttings either under a cloche or in a frame.

Divide clumps of chives if the weather is mild (see AUGUST).

UNDER GLASS

Divide roots of mint, planting some in the open and potting or boxing up the remainder in the greenhouse to force for winter use.

Lift fennel and put into boxes of peat to force in a cool greenhouse, at a temperature of 13 °C (55 °F).

MINT FOR WINTER USE

Lengths of mint root, planted 2 in. deep in a box and forced in a greenhouse, will provide fresh young shoots during the winter

Patios and town gardens

Continue to empty containers of plants that are past their best or that will not last the winter. Lift and pot tender plants, such as pelargoniums, and bring them indoors for the winter. If possible move trees and shrubs planted in large containers to a position where they will be least affected by cold winds and heavy falls of snow. Alternatively, tie a loose wrapping of straw or bracken around the plants.

Store timber containers under cover.

Add winter colour

Instead of emptying all containers so that the patio is devoid of plant life, leave some in position and plant them with such subjects as dwarf conifers, ivies, winter-flowering heathers, aucubas and skimmias. Plant bulbs beneath the shrubs. They will send up their shoots around or among the shrub foliage and will flower in the early spring.

As wind is one of the chief hazards of tub and window-box plants, choose bulbs that will not grow too tall. Hyacinths, species tulips and crocuses, snowdrops and short-stemmed daffodils are all suitable.

House plants

Plants bought this month will have time to acclimatise themselves before the cold short days set in.

Give new plants a thorough watering before they are placed in their positions in the home, immersing the entire pot in a bucket of water warmed to room temperature. Keep it submerged until bubbles have ceased to rise from the surface of the soil, then lift it out and allow it to drain for a few minutes.

Place plants where they will be warm but not subject to direct heat; where they will be out of draughts and will receive plenty of light. However, do not place tender plants too near a cold window, especially at night, in case they are harmed by night frosts.

Continue to watch for red spider mites and take action as necessary (see SEPTEMBER).

General tasks

When the weather is kind in the autumn and the frosts arrive late, leave summer bedding plants like marigolds, begonias and geraniums as long as they have any flowers on them. Often there is no frost severe enough to ruin the summer bedding until November.

Remove summer bedding plants from the border where you intend to plant out wallflowers, myosotis and other plants for a spring display. Plant them this month, while the soil is still warm and they can make new roots before the hard weather sets in. If they are planted later they will almost certainly suffer during periods of severe frost or, even more, through searing cold east winds. The leaves shrivel because the plant has not made sufficient roots to supply them with enough moisture. At best they will suffer a severe check.

Do not manure beds or borders for spring-flowering bedding plants at this time of year. This would only encourage soft growth that would be very vulnerable to frost damage. Work into the top 6 in. of soil 4 oz. of bone-meal per sq. yd. This is a slow-acting fertiliser, and the plants will be able to make use of it in the spring when growth begins again.

Spread a net over your garden pool or rock garden to catch fallen leaves, and lift it off every week or so. If leaves fall or blow into a pond they may kill the fish, as they rot and produce poisonous gases. If leaves lie thickly over small rock garden plants, or for more than a week or so on a lawn, they can choke and kill the plants, and cause yellow patches on the lawn.

Stack leaves and allow them to rot down to make leaf-mould for digging into the ground or using as a mulch. Ask the local road-sweepers to drop off a load of leaves if you have enough room to stack them.

Herbaceous borders to plant in October

Beds or borders of perennials should be regarded as an investment. They bring the greatest possible joy at the least cost and trouble of maintenance.

Preparing the site

The first thing is to ensure that the bed is placed where it will be in harmony with the rest of the garden, and that it has been well prepared. Though a selection of plants can be made for out-of-the-ordinary sites—damp, dry, shady or exposed—most plants like an open, mainly sunny spot. Thorough preparation may entail hard work, especially in the clearance of perennial weeds; but unless destroyed in advance, these weeds will spoil all your efforts. The ground should be dug and, if necessary, dressed with manure. Peat and spent hops are good substitutes for manure, but apply fertiliser as well.

Decide what kind of bed or border you wish to have, bearing in mind that the shape, size or aspect of the garden may limit your choice. For instance, a one-sided border (pp. 280–1) is not the best for display or easy maintenance. Access to the rear of the bed is difficult, and the backing wall or fence often restricts light and air, leading to soft, lanky growth. An island bed is more effective for display, since it can be viewed from all sides. Island beds can range from midget layouts (p. 284) to more ambitious designs of any desired shape (pp. 272–3). They should be of regular shape (pp. 269, 274–5) in gardens with formal lines, but can have less formal outlines (pp. 282–3) if these harmonise with surrounding trees and shrubberies.

Soil and situation

Care is needed when choosing plants for beds or borders in shade. This is not especially troublesome for sites with moist soil (pp. 270–1), but a shaded bed with dry soil (pp. 278–9) is the most difficult situation of all to fill.

If you prefer to combine perennials with shrubs (pp. 276–7), always give the perennials plenty of space to prevent harmful competition from the shrubs.

Bear soil and situation in mind when choosing the plants. Although most are quite adaptable, there are some that do not flourish in heavy clay, or in chalky soil. These points are covered in the plant descriptions (pp. 285–307), which should be studied in conjunction with a nurseryman's catalogue. Always buy your plants from a specialist grower of hardy perennials.

Continuous display

If you aim for a continuous display, choose plants that flower in spring, as well as those that bloom in summer and autumn. Avoid having too many of a type, all flowering at the same period, as this will inevitably cause the bed to look bare at other times. However, it is by no means difficult to arrange for a display with one predominant colour, or for an effect which owes much of its attraction to foliage (pp. 274–5).

For display purposes, the grouping of at least three plants of a kind is most effective, and far preferable to having single plants dotted about.

The planning of a bed or border must also take account of the height of each plant. Tall kinds are apt to look out of proportion in narrow borders. As a rough guide to the maximum suitable height, measure the width of the bed, whether island or one-sided, and then halve the resulting figure. For example, if the bed is 8 ft. wide, do not select plants which grow more than 4 ft. high.

Placing tall plants

As a general rule, the tallest kinds should be placed at the rear of a one-sided border but in the centre of an island bed. However, you can enhance the effect by placing spiky plants here and there between those of flatter or more rounded habit. Also keep plants of especially rapid or slow growth in their own groups. Refer to the plant descriptions for planting distances, as a means of assessing probable growth spread. When planting in groups, allow 25 per cent more space between groups than between member plants of a group.

When to plant

The best months for planting are October and March. If conditions are sticky or wet, do not tread directly on the surface, but use short pieces of board for standing on. If the soil is dry, puddle the plants in as described on p. 45. Do not unwrap individual plants until they are correctly spaced out. If possible mark out in advance the allotted space with sticks, or with permanent labels so that when the plants arrive you can insert them at once.

You may make one or two errors in siting plants at the first attempt. However, any errors can be corrected the following autumn, after you have had a season to observe the plants coming into flower.

Circular island bed

A graceful wisteria set in the centre of the bed provides a foil to the roses' close-set foliage, and gives colour in late spring before the main flower display begins. An artemisia (No. 1 on the plan) and a hosta (No. 10) do not appear, as they are hidden behind the taller roses. The diameter of the bed is 12 ft. H=height. PD=planting distance.

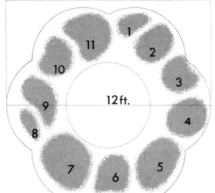

Key to plan
1 Artemisia schmidtii nana
2 Rose spinosissima 'Stanwell Perpetual'
3 Hosta sieboldiana
4 Rose 'Prince Charles'
5 Rose 'La Reine Victoria'
6 Hosta plantaginea
7 Rose 'Zigeuner Knabe'
8 Artemisia schmidtii nana
9 Rose alba 'Celestial'
10 Hosta crispula
11 Rose rugosa 'Roseraie de l'Hay'
12 Wisteria

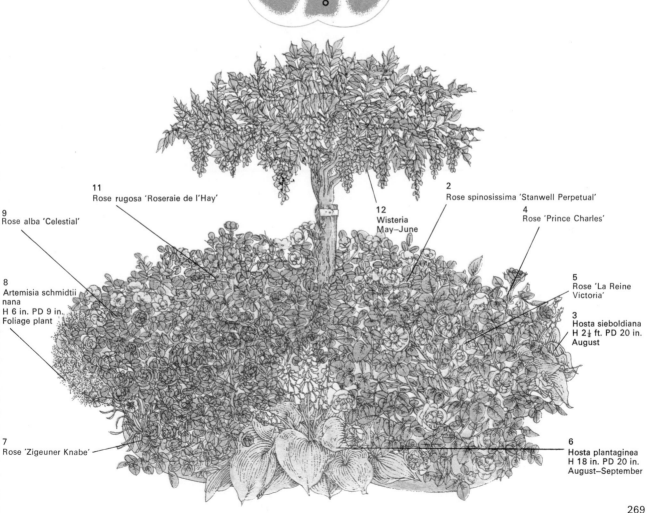

11
Rose rugosa 'Roseraie de l'Hay'

9
Rose alba 'Celestial'

8
Artemisia schmidtii nana
H 6 in. PD 9 in.
Foliage plant

7
Rose 'Zigeuner Knabe'

12
Wisteria
May–June

2
Rose spinosissima 'Stanwell Perpetual'

4
Rose 'Prince Charles'

5
Rose 'La Reine Victoria'

3
Hosta sieboldiana
H 2½ ft. PD 20 in.
August

6
Hosta plantaginea
H 18 in. PD 20 in.
August–September

269

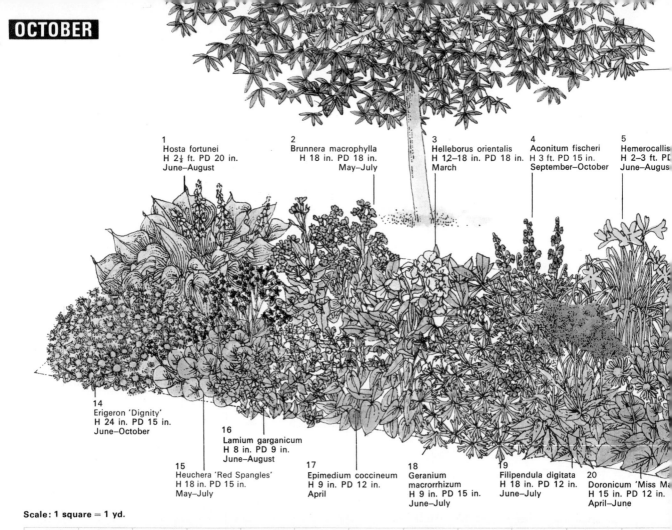

1
Hosta fortunei
H 2½ ft. PD 20 in.
June–August

2
Brunnera macrophylla
H 18 in. PD 18 in.
May–July

3
Helleborus orientalis
H 12–18 in. PD 18 in.
March

4
Aconitum fischeri
H 3 ft. PD 15 in.
September–October

5
Hemerocallis
H 2–3 ft. PD
June–August

14
Erigeron 'Dignity'
H 24 in. PD 15 in.
June–October

16
Lamium garganicum
H 8 in. PD 9 in.
June–August

15
Heuchera 'Red Spangles'
H 18 in. PD 15 in.
May–July

17
Epimedium coccineum
H 9 in. PD 12 in.
April

18
Geranium
macrorrhizum
H 9 in. PD 15 in.
June–July

19
Filipendula digitata
H 18 in. PD 12 in.
June–July

20
Doronicum 'Miss Ma
H 15 in. PD 12 in.
April–June

Scale: 1 square = 1 yd.

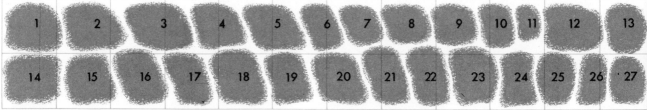

Key to Plan
1 Hosta fortunei
2 Brunnera macrophylla
3 Helleborus orientalis
4 Aconitum fischeri
5 Hemerocallis
6 Veronica gentianoides

7 Polygonatum multiflorum
8 Meconopsis baileyi
9 Iris foetidissima
10 Digitalis ambigua
11 Lamium orvala
12 Geranium sylvaticum
13 Bergenia cordifolia

14 Erigeron 'Dignity'
15 Heuchera 'Red Spangles'
16 Lamium garganicum
17 Epimedium coccineum
18 Geranium macrorrhizum
19 Filipendula digitata
20 Doronicum 'Miss Mason'

21 Mertensia virginica
22 Gentiana asclepiadea
23 Hosta undulata medio-variegata
24 Ajuga pyramidalis
25 Heucherella 'Bridget Bloom'
26 Pulmonaria angustifolia azurea
27 Calamintha nepetoides

Narrow border in shade

These herbaceous plants will do best in soil that remains reasonably moist during the summer. The border illustrated measures 36 ft. by 6 ft., allowing space for three plants in each group. H=height. PD=planting distance

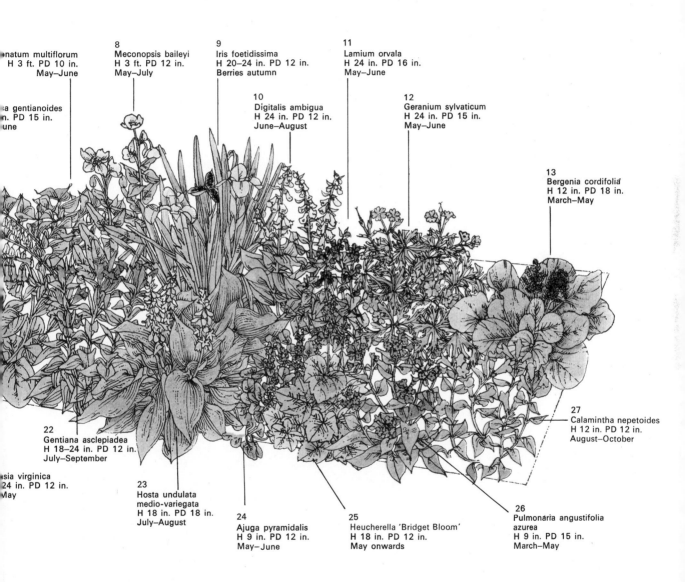

natum multiflorum
H 3 ft. PD 10 in.
May–June

a gentianoides
n. PD 15 in.
une

8
Meconopsis baileyi
H 3 ft. PD 12 in.
May–July

9
Iris foetidissima
H 20–24 in. PD 12 in.
Berries autumn

10
Digitalis ambigua
H 24 in. PD 12 in.
June–August

11
Lamium orvala
H 24 in. PD 16 in.
May–June

12
Geranium sylvaticum
H 24 in. PD 15 in.
May–June

13
Bergenia cordifolia
H 12 in. PD 18 in.
March–May

27
Calamintha nepetoides
H 12 in. PD 12 in.
August–October

22
Gentiana asclepiadea
H 18–24 in. PD 12 in.
July–September

sia virginica
24 in. PD 12 in.
May

23
Hosta undulata
medio-variegata
H 18 in. PD 18 in.
July–August

24
Ajuga pyramidalis
H 9 in. PD 12 in.
May–June

25
Heucherella 'Bridget Bloom'
H 18 in. PD 12 in.
May onwards

26
Pulmonaria angustifolia
azurea
H 9 in. PD 15 in.
March–May

271

Oval island bed

A selection of perennials to provide colour and interest from spring until late autumn. The bed illustrated measures 30 ft. by 12 ft., allowing space for five plants in each group. H = height. PD = planting distance

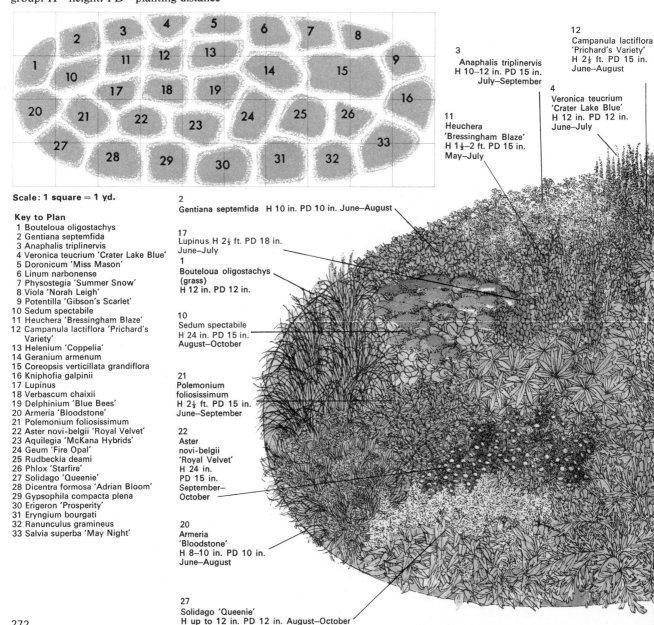

Scale: 1 square = 1 yd.

Key to Plan

1 Bouteloua oligostachys
2 Gentiana septemfida
3 Anaphalis triplinervis
4 Veronica teucrium 'Crater Lake Blue'
5 Doronicum 'Miss Mason'
6 Linum narbonense
7 Physostegia 'Summer Snow'
8 Viola 'Norah Leigh'
9 Potentilla 'Gibson's Scarlet'
10 Sedum spectabile
11 Heuchera 'Bressingham Blaze'
12 Campanula lactiflora 'Prichard's Variety'
13 Helenium 'Coppelia'
14 Geranium armenum
15 Coreopsis verticillata grandiflora
16 Kniphofia galpinii
17 Lupinus
18 Verbascum chaixii
19 Delphinium 'Blue Bees'
20 Armeria 'Bloodstone'
21 Polemonium foliosissimum
22 Aster novi-belgii 'Royal Velvet'
23 Aquilegia 'McKana Hybrids'
24 Geum 'Fire Opal'
25 Rudbeckia deami
26 Phlox 'Starfire'
27 Solidago 'Queenie'
28 Dicentra formosa 'Adrian Bloom'
29 Gypsophila compacta plena
30 Erigeron 'Prosperity'
31 Eryngium bourgati
32 Ranunculus gramineus
33 Salvia superba 'May Night'

3
Anaphalis triplinervis
H 10–12 in. PD 15 in.
July–September

12
Campanula lactiflora
'Prichard's Variety'
H 2½ ft. PD 15 in.
June–August

4
Veronica teucrium
'Crater Lake Blue'
H 12 in. PD 12 in.
June–July

11
Heuchera
'Bressingham Blaze'
H 1½–2 ft. PD 15 in.
May–July

2
Gentiana septemfida H 10 in. PD 10 in. June–August

17
Lupinus H 2½ ft. PD 18 in.
June–July

1
Bouteloua oligostachys
(grass)
H 12 in. PD 12 in.

10
Sedum spectabile
H 24 in. PD 15 in.
August–October

21
Polemonium
foliosissimum
H 2½ ft. PD 15 in.
June–September

22
Aster
novi-belgii
'Royal Velvet'
H 24 in.
PD 15 in.
September–
October

20
Armeria
'Bloodstone'
H 8–10 in. PD 10 in.
June–August

27
Solidago 'Queenie'
H up to 12 in. PD 12 in. August–October

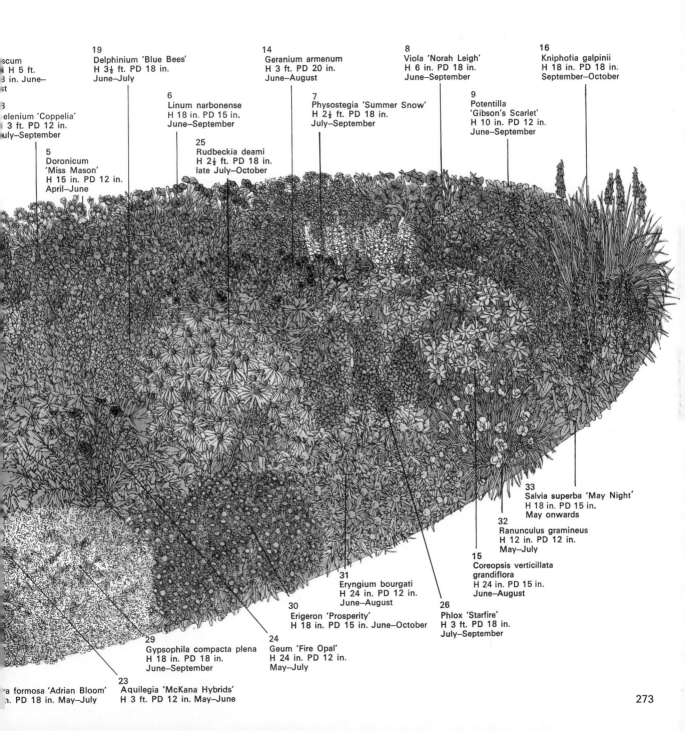

scum
H 5 ft.
3 in. June–
st

3
elenium 'Coppelia'
3 ft. PD 12 in.
uly–September

5
Doronicum
'Miss Mason'
H 15 in. PD 12 in.
April–June

19
Delphinium 'Blue Bees'
H 3½ ft. PD 18 in.
June–July

6
Linum narbonense
H 18 in. PD 15 in.
June–September

25
Rudbeckia deami
H 2½ ft. PD 18 in.
late July–October

14
Geranium armenum
H 3 ft. PD 20 in.
June–August

7
Physostegia 'Summer Snow'
H 2½ ft. PD 18 in.
July–September

8
Viola 'Norah Leigh'
H 6 in. PD 18 in.
June–September

9
Potentilla
'Gibson's Scarlet'
H 10 in. PD 12 in.
June–September

16
Kniphofia galpinii
H 18 in. PD 18 in.
September–October

33
Salvia superba 'May Night'
H 18 in. PD 15 in.
May onwards

32
Ranunculus gramineus
H 12 in. PD 12 in.
May–July

15
Coreopsis verticillata
grandiflora
H 24 in. PD 15 in.
June–August

31
Eryngium bourgati
H 24 in. PD 12 in.
June–August

30
Erigeron 'Prosperity'
H 18 in. PD 15 in. June–October

26
Phlox 'Starfire'
H 3 ft. PD 18 in.
July–September

29
Gypsophila compacta plena
H 18 in. PD 18 in.
June–September

24
Geum 'Fire Opal'
H 24 in. PD 12 in.
May–July

a formosa 'Adrian Bloom'
. PD 18 in. May–July

23
Aquilegia 'McKana Hybrids'
. H 3 ft. PD 12 in. May–June

273

White and silver border

Striking plants for edging a lawn or garden path. The border illustrated measures 33 ft. by 9 ft., allowing five plants per square yd. H = height. PD = planting distance

Key to Plan
1 Delphinium
2 Iris pseudacorus variegatus
3 Tiarella cordifolia
4 Anaphalis nubigena
5 Cimicifuga racemosa 'Elstead'
6 Eryngium planum
7 Physostegia 'Summer Snow'
8 Achillea 'Moonshine'
9 Verbascum bombyciferum
10 Aster novi-belgii 'White Choristers'
11 Bergenia cordifolia
12 Morina longifolia
13 Phalaris arundinacea picta
14 Geranium pratense album plenum
15 Phlox 'Mia Ruys'
16 Cynara scolymus
17 Senecio 'White Diamond'
18 Heuchera 'Pearl Drops'
19 Campanula persicifolia
20 Paeonia lactiflora 'Duchesse de Nemours'
21 Epimedium niveum
22 Buddleia
23 Astilbe 'Irrlicht'
24 Nepeta mussinii
25 Aruncus sylvester
26 Filipendula hexapetala plena
27 Stachys lanata
28 Ruta graveolens
29 Holcus mollis variegatus
30 Iris ochroleuca
31 Anthemis cupaniana
32 Artemisia lactiflora
33 Achillea ptarmica 'The Pearl'
34 Hosta sieboldiana

Scale: 1 square = 1 yd.

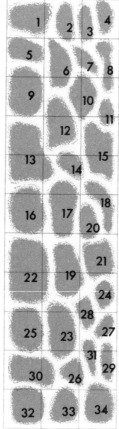

1
Delphinium
H 3–5 ft. PD 20 in.
June–July

5
Cimicifuga racemosa 'Elstead'
H 5 ft. PD 18 in.
August–October

12
Morina longifolia
H 24 in. PD 12 in.
July–September

13
Phalaris arundinacea picta (grass)
H 24 in. PD 16 in.

16
Cynara scolymus
H 5 ft. PD 4 ft.
August–September

22
Buddleia
July–August

19
Campanula persicifolia
H 3 ft. PD 15 in.
June–July

25
Aruncus sylvester
H 6 ft. PD 20 in.
June

30
Iris ochroleuca
H 3–6 ft. PD 16 in.
June–July

26
Filipendula hexapetala plena
H 24 in. PD 15 in.
June–July

32
Artemisia lactiflora
H 4 ft. PD 18 in.
August–September

33
Achillea ptarmica 'The Pearl'
H 2½–3 ft. PD 15 in.
July–August

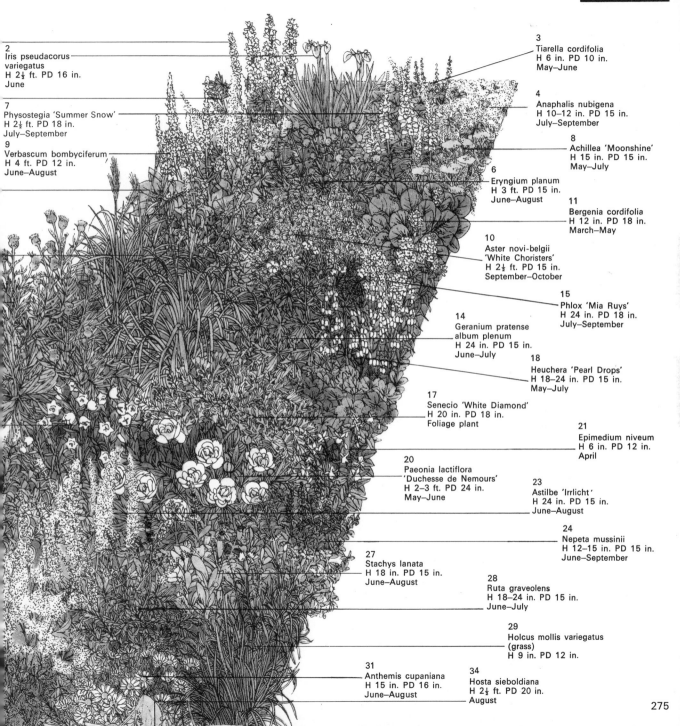

2
Iris pseudacorus
variegatus
H 2½ ft. PD 16 in.
June

7
Physostegia 'Summer Snow'
H 2½ ft. PD 18 in.
July–September

9
Verbascum bombyciferum
H 4 ft. PD 12 in.
June–August

3
Tiarella cordifolia
H 6 in. PD 10 in.
May–June

4
Anaphalis nubigena
H 10–12 in. PD 15 in.
July–September

8
Achillea 'Moonshine'
H 15 in. PD 15 in.
May–July

6
Eryngium planum
H 3 ft. PD 15 in.
June–August

11
Bergenia cordifolia
H 12 in. PD 18 in.
March–May

10
Aster novi-belgii
'White Choristers'
H 2½ ft. PD 15 in.
September–October

15
Phlox 'Mia Ruys'
H 24 in. PD 18 in.
July–September

14
Geranium pratense
album plenum
H 24 in. PD 15 in.
June–July

18
Heuchera 'Pearl Drops'
H 18–24 in. PD 15 in.
May–July

17
Senecio 'White Diamond'
H 20 in. PD 18 in.
Foliage plant

21
Epimedium niveum
H 6 in. PD 12 in.
April

20
Paeonia lactiflora
'Duchesse de Nemours'
H 2–3 ft. PD 24 in.
May–June

23
Astilbe 'Irrlicht'
H 24 in. PD 15 in.
June–August

24
Nepeta mussinii
H 12–15 in. PD 15 in.
June–September

27
Stachys lanata
H 18 in. PD 15 in.
June–August

28
Ruta graveolens
H 18–24 in. PD 15 in.
June–July

29
Holcus mollis variegatus
(grass)
H 9 in. PD 12 in.

31
Anthemis cupaniana
H 15 in. PD 16 in.
June–August

34
Hosta sieboldiana
H 2½ ft. PD 20 in.
August

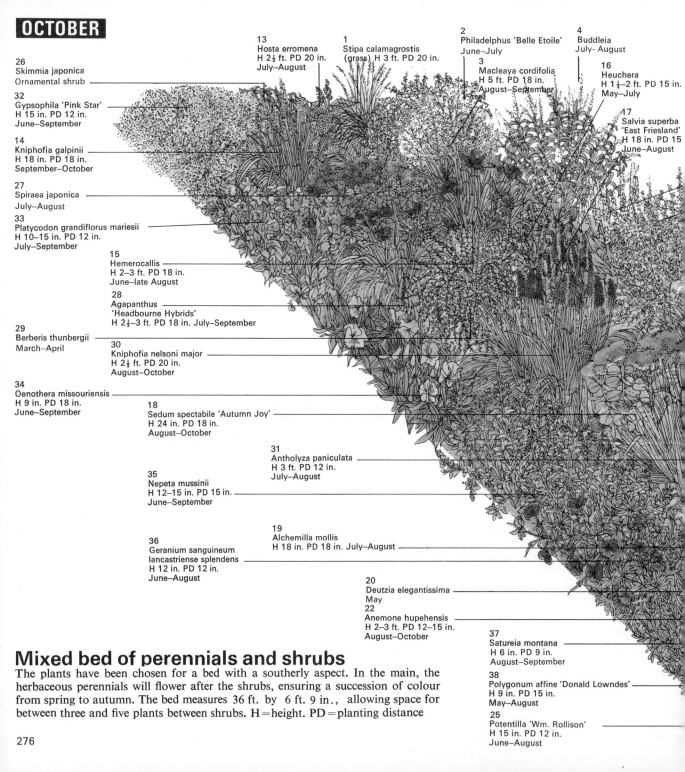

26
Skimmia japonica
Ornamental shrub

32
Gypsophila 'Pink Star'
H 15 in. PD 12 in.
June–September

14
Kniphofia galpinii
H 18 in. PD 18 in.
September–October

27
Spiraea japonica
July–August

33
Platycodon grandiflorus mariesii
H 10–15 in. PD 12 in.
July–September

15
Hemerocallis
H 2–3 ft. PD 18 in.
June–late August

28
Agapanthus
'Headbourne Hybrids'
H 2½–3 ft. PD 18 in. July–September

29
Berberis thunbergii
March–April

30
Kniphofia nelsoni major
H 2½ ft. PD 20 in.
August–October

34
Oenothera missouriensis
H 9 in. PD 18 in.
June–September

18
Sedum spectabile 'Autumn Joy'
H 24 in. PD 18 in.
August–October

31
Antholyza paniculata
H 3 ft. PD 12 in.
July–August

35
Nepeta mussinii
H 12–15 in. PD 15 in.
June–September

36
Geranium sanguineum
lancastriense splendens
H 12 in. PD 12 in.
June–August

19
Alchemilla mollis
H 18 in. PD 18 in. July–August

13
Hosta erromena
H 2½ ft. PD 20 in.
July–August

1
Stipa calamagrostis
(grass) H 3 ft. PD 20 in.

2
Philadelphus 'Belle Etoile'
June–July

3
Macleaya cordifolia
H 5 ft. PD 18 in.
August–September

4
Buddleia
July–August

16
Heuchera
H 1½–2 ft. PD 15 in.
May–July

17
Salvia superba
'East Friesland'
H 18 in. PD 15
June–August

20
Deutzia elegantissima
May

22
Anemone hupehensis
H 2–3 ft. PD 12–15 in.
August–October

37
Satureia montana
H 6 in. PD 9 in.
August–September

38
Polygonum affine 'Donald Lowndes'
H 9 in. PD 15 in.
May–August

25
Potentilla 'Wm. Rollison'
H 15 in. PD 12 in.
June–August

Mixed bed of perennials and shrubs

The plants have been chosen for a bed with a southerly aspect. In the main, the
herbaceous perennials will flower after the shrubs, ensuring a succession of colour
from spring to autumn. The bed measures 36 ft. by 6 ft. 9 in., allowing space for
between three and five plants between shrubs. H = height. PD = planting distance

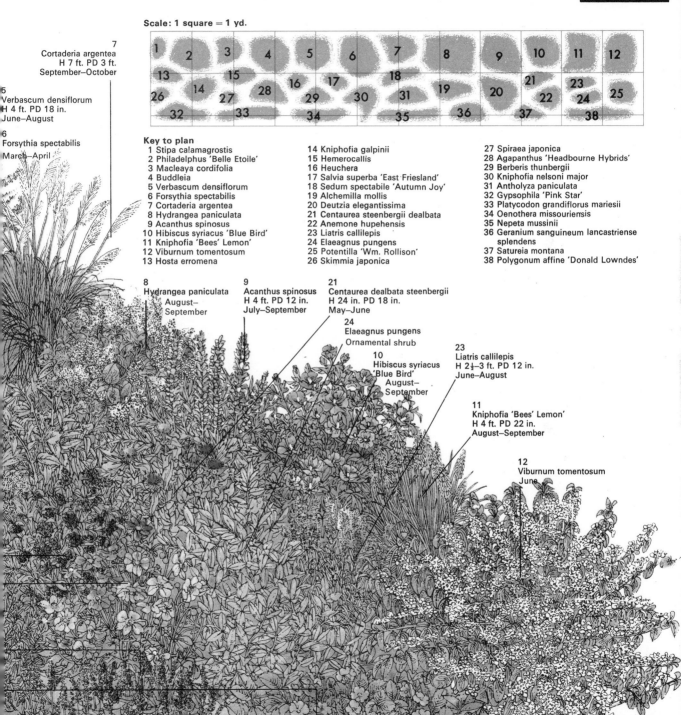

Scale: 1 square = 1 yd.

7
Cortaderia argentea
H 7 ft. PD 3 ft.
September–October

5
Verbascum densiflorum
H 4 ft. PD 18 in.
June–August

6
Forsythia spectabilis
March–April

Key to plan

1 Stipa calamagrostis
2 Philadelphus 'Belle Etoile'
3 Macleaya cordifolia
4 Buddleia
5 Verbascum densiflorum
6 Forsythia spectabilis
7 Cortaderia argentea
8 Hydrangea paniculata
9 Acanthus spinosus
10 Hibiscus syriacus 'Blue Bird'
11 Kniphofia 'Bees' Lemon'
12 Viburnum tomentosum
13 Hosta erromena

14 Kniphofia galpinii
15 Hemerocallis
16 Heuchera
17 Salvia superba 'East Friesland'
18 Sedum spectabile 'Autumn Joy'
19 Alchemilla mollis
20 Deutzia elegantissima
21 Centaurea steenbergii dealbata
22 Anemone hupehensis
23 Liatris callilepis
24 Elaeagnus pungens
25 Potentilla 'Wm. Rollison'
26 Skimmia japonica

27 Spiraea japonica
28 Agapanthus 'Headbourne Hybrids'
29 Berberis thunbergii
30 Kniphofia nelsoni major
31 Antholyza paniculata
32 Gypsophila 'Pink Star'
33 Platycodon grandiflorus mariesii
34 Oenothera missouriensis
35 Nepeta mussinii
36 Geranium sanguineum lancastriense
   splendens
37 Satureia montana
38 Polygonum affine 'Donald Lowndes'

8
Hydrangea paniculata
August–
September

9
Acanthus spinosus
H 4 ft. PD 12 in.
July–September

21
Centaurea dealbata steenbergii
H 24 in. PD 18 in.
May–June

24
Elaeagnus pungens
Ornamental shrub

10
Hibiscus syriacus
'Blue Bird'
August–
September

23
Liatris callilepis
H 2½–3 ft. PD 12 in.
June–August

11
Kniphofia 'Bees' Lemon'
H 4 ft. PD 22 in.
August–September

12
Viburnum tomentosum
June

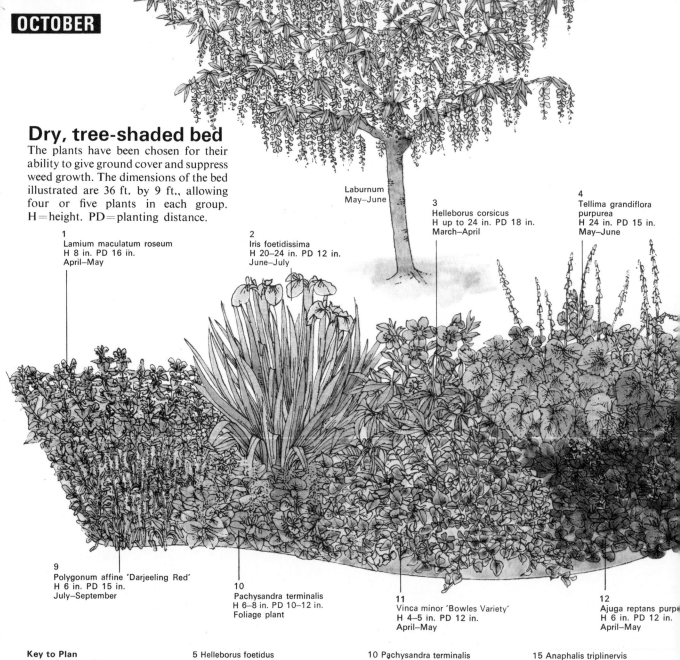

Dry, tree-shaded bed

The plants have been chosen for their ability to give ground cover and suppress weed growth. The dimensions of the bed illustrated are 36 ft. by 9 ft., allowing four or five plants in each group. H = height. PD = planting distance.

Laburnum
May–June

1
Lamium maculatum roseum
H 8 in. PD 16 in.
April–May

2
Iris foetidissima
H 20–24 in. PD 12 in.
June–July

3
Helleborus corsicus
H up to 24 in. PD 18 in.
March–April

4
Tellima grandiflora purpurea
H 24 in. PD 15 in.
May–June

9
Polygonum affine 'Darjeeling Red'
H 6 in. PD 15 in.
July–September

10
Pachysandra terminalis
H 6–8 in. PD 10–12 in.
Foliage plant

11
Vinca minor 'Bowles Variety'
H 4–5 in. PD 12 in.
April–May

12
Ajuga reptans purp
H 6 in. PD 12 in.
April–May

Key to Plan

1 Lamium maculatum roseum
2 Iris foetidissima
3 Helleborus corsicus
4 Tellima grandiflora purpurea

5 Helleborus foetidus
6 Hypericum calycinum
7 Digitalis 'Excelsior'
8 Luzula sylvatica
9 Polygonum affine 'Darjeeling Red'

10 Pachysandra terminalis
11 Vinca minor 'Bowles Variety'
12 Ajuga reptans purpurea
13 Saxifraga umbrosa
14 Vinca major variegata

15 Anaphalis triplinervis
16 Pulmonaria saccharata 'Bowles Variety'
17 Lamium galeobdolon variegatum

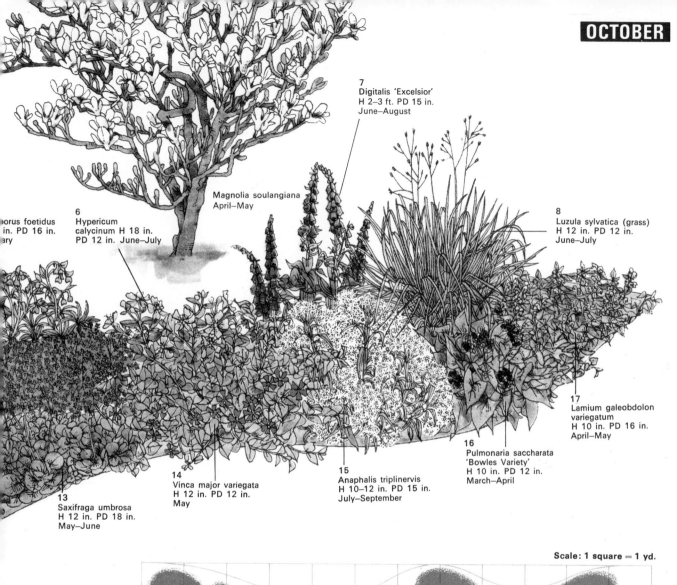

7
Digitalis 'Excelsior'
H 2–3 ft. PD 15 in.
June–August

Magnolia soulangiana
April–May

...orus foetidus
...in. PD 16 in.
...ary

6
Hypericum
calycinum H 18 in.
PD 12 in. June–July

8
Luzula sylvatica (grass)
H 12 in. PD 12 in.
June–July

17
Lamium galeobdolon
variegatum
H 10 in. PD 16 in.
April–May

16
Pulmonaria saccharata
'Bowles Variety'
H 10 in. PD 12 in.
March–April

15
Anaphalis triplinervis
H 10–12 in. PD 15 in.
July–September

14
Vinca major variegata
H 12 in. PD 12 in.
May

13
Saxifraga umbrosa
H 12 in. PD 18 in.
May–June

Scale: 1 square = 1 yd.

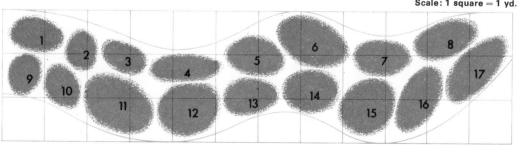

279

Border backed by climbers

This planting scheme is suggested for positions where island beds, generally to be preferred, are impractical. The border illustrated measures 36 ft. by 6 ft. Allow five plants for each group. H=height. PD=planting distance

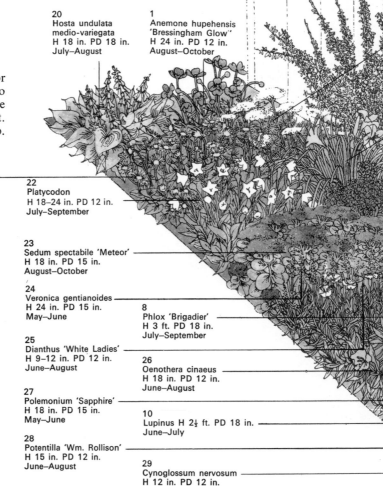

20
Hosta undulata medio-variegata
H 18 in. PD 18 in.
July–August

1
Anemone hupehensis 'Bressingham Glow'
H 24 in. PD 12 in.
August–October

2
Achillea
H 18 in. PD
June–August

3
Forsyth
March–

4
Heme
H 2–
PD 1
June–

5
Euph
griffi
'Fireg
H 24
PD 1
May–

21
Doronicum 'Spring Beauty'
H 15 in. PD 12 in.
April–June

22
Platycodon
H 18–24 in. PD 12 in.
July–September

Key to plan
1 Anemone hupehensis 'Bressingham Glow'
2 Achillea
3 Forsythia
4 Hemerocallis
5 Euphorbia griffithii 'Fireglow'
6 Salvia superba 'Lubeca'
7 Iris germanica 'Aline'
8 Phlox 'Brigadier'
9 Lonicera serotina
10 Lupinus
11 Scabiosa caucasica 'Clive Greaves'
12 Aster acris
13 Chaenomeles japonica
14 Chrysanthemum maximum 'Wirral Supreme'
15 Solidago 'Golden Shower'
16 Rudbeckia deami
17 Aconitum arendsii
18 Clematis jackmanii
19 Kniphofia 'Bees' Sunset'
20 Hosta undulata medio-variegata
21 Doronicum 'Spring Beauty'
22 Platycodon
23 Sedum spectabile 'Meteor'
24 Veronica gentianoides
25 Dianthus
26 Oenothera cinaeus
27 Polemonium 'Sapphire'
28 Potentilla 'Wm. Rollison'
29 Cynoglossum nervosum
30 Lychnis coronaria
31 Aster novi-belgii 'Autumn Princess'
32 Geum borisii·
33 Geranium renardii

23
Sedum spectabile 'Meteor'
H 18 in. PD 15 in.
August–October

24
Veronica gentianoides
H 24 in. PD 15 in.
May–June

8
Phlox 'Brigadier'
H 3 ft. PD 18 in.
July–September

25
Dianthus 'White Ladies'
H 9–12 in. PD 12 in.
June–August

26
Oenothera cinaeus
H 18 in. PD 12 in.
June–August

27
Polemonium 'Sapphire'
H 18 in. PD 15 in.
May–June

10
Lupinus H 2½ ft. PD 18 in.
June–July

28
Potentilla 'Wm. Rollison'
H 15 in. PD 12 in.
June–August

29
Cynoglossum nervosum
H 12 in. PD 12 in.
June–August

Scale: 1 square = 1 yd.

16
Rudbeckia deami
H 2½ ft. PD 18 in.
July–October

31
Aster novi-belgii
'Autumn Princess'
H 12 in. PD 12–15 in.
September–October

30
Lychnis coro
H 18 in. PD
June–August

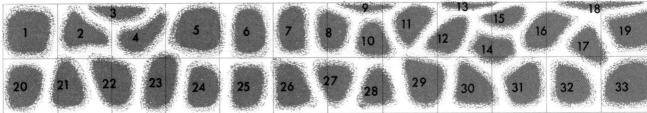

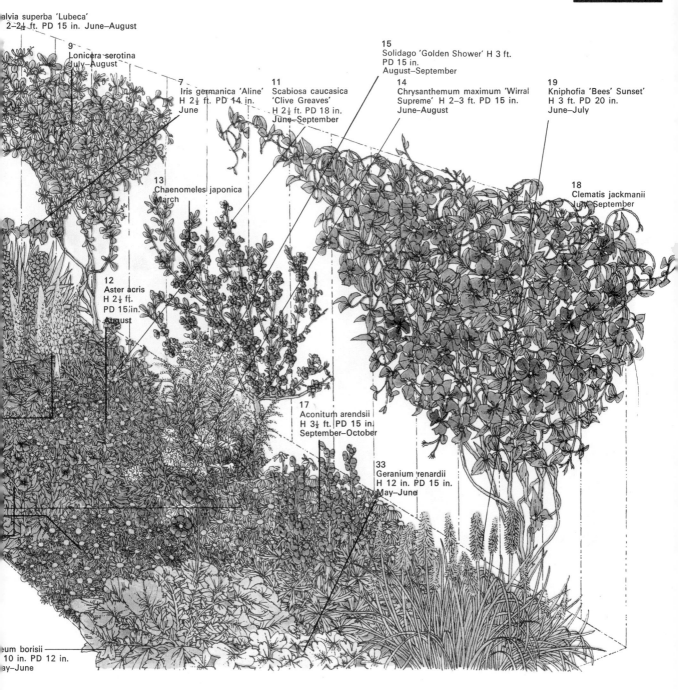

alvia superba 'Lubeca'
2–2½ ft. PD 15 in. June–August

9
Lonicera serotina
July–August

7
Iris germanica 'Aline'
H 2½ ft. PD 14 in.
June

11
Scabiosa caucasica
'Clive Greaves'
H 2½ ft. PD 18 in.
June–September

15
Solidago 'Golden Shower' H 3 ft.
PD 15 in.
August–September

14
Chrysanthemum maximum 'Wirral
Supreme' H 2–3 ft. PD 15 in.
June–August

19
Kniphofia 'Bees' Sunset'
H 3 ft. PD 20 in.
June–July

13
Chaenomeles japonica
March

18
Clematis jackmanii
July–September

12
Aster acris
H 2½ ft.
PD 15 in.
August

17
Aconitum arendsii
H 3½ ft. PD 15 in.
September–October

33
Geranium renardii
H 12 in. PD 15 in.
May–June

eum borisii
10 in. PD 12 in.
ay–June

Informal island bed

Island beds can have free-flowing, asymmetrical lines where such a design harmonises with surrounding trees or a shrubbery. The bed illustrated measures 24 ft. by 12 ft. overall. H = height. PD = planting distance

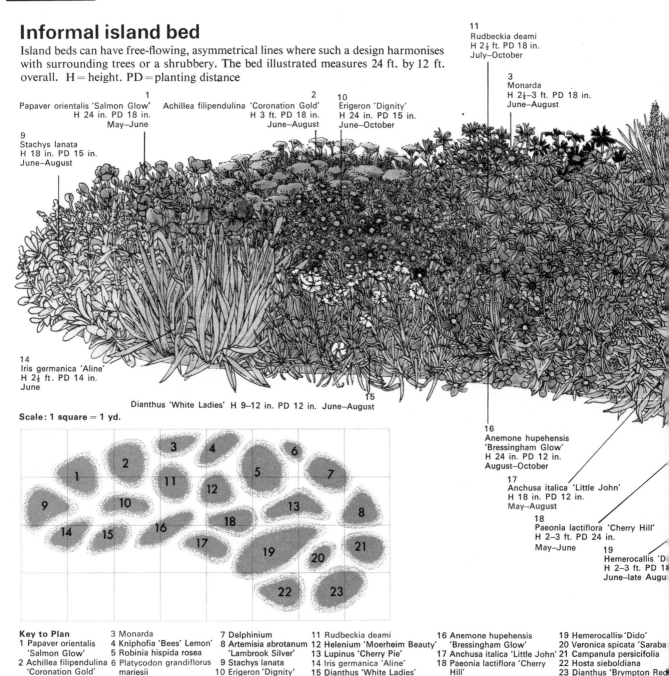

11
Rudbeckia deamii
H 2½ ft. PD 18 in.
July–October

3
Monarda
H 2½–3 ft. PD 18 in.
June–August

1
Papaver orientalis 'Salmon Glow'
H 24 in. PD 18 in.
May–June

2
Achillea filipendulina 'Coronation Gold'
H 3 ft. PD 18 in.
June–August

10
Erigeron 'Dignity'
H 24 in. PD 15 in.
June–October

9
Stachys lanata
H 18 in. PD 15 in.
June–August

14
Iris germanica 'Aline'
H 2½ ft. PD 14 in.
June

Dianthus 'White Ladies' H 9–12 in. PD 12 in. June–August

16
Anemone hupehensis
'Bressingham Glow'
H 24 in. PD 12 in.
August–October

17
Anchusa italica 'Little John'
H 18 in. PD 12 in.
May–August

18
Paeonia lactiflora 'Cherry Hill'
H 2–3 ft. PD 24 in.
May–June

19
Hemerocallis 'D
H 2–3 ft. PD 1
June–late Augu

Scale: 1 square = 1 yd.

Key to Plan

1 Papaver orientalis 'Salmon Glow'	3 Monarda
2 Achillea filipendulina 'Coronation Gold'	4 Kniphofia 'Bees' Lemon'
	5 Robinia hispida rosea
	6 Platycodon grandiflorus mariesii

7 Delphinium
8 Artemisia abrotanum 'Lambrook Silver'
9 Stachys lanata
10 Erigeron 'Dignity'

11 Rudbeckia deamii
12 Helenium 'Moerheim Beauty'
13 Lupinus 'Cherry Pie'
14 Iris germanica 'Aline'
15 Dianthus 'White Ladies'

16 Anemone hupehensis 'Bressingham Glow'
17 Anchusa italica 'Little John'
18 Paeonia lactiflora 'Cherry Hill'

19 Hemerocallis 'Dido'
20 Veronica spicata 'Saraba
21 Campanula persicifolia
22 Hosta sieboldiana
23 Dianthus 'Brympton Red'

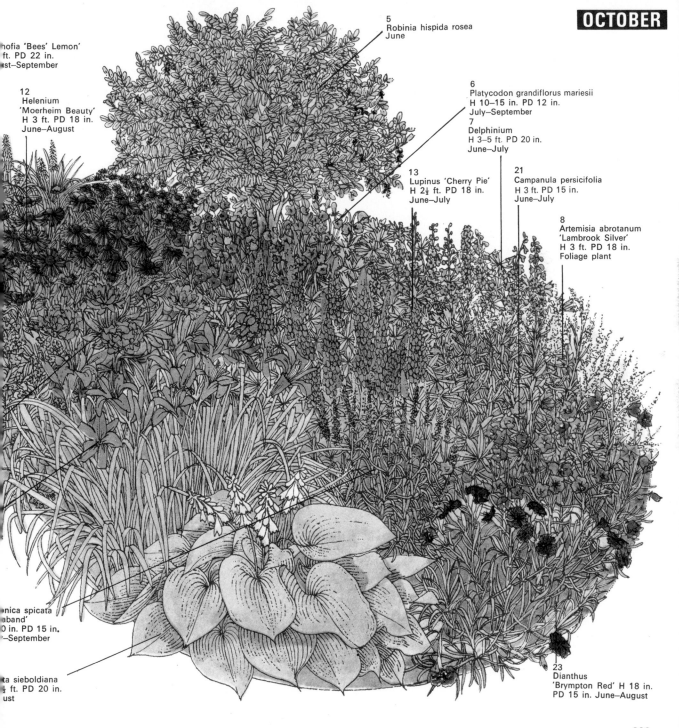

5
Robinia hispida rosea
June

hofia 'Bees' Lemon'
ft. PD 22 in.
ust—September

12
Helenium
'Moerheim Beauty'
H 3 ft. PD 18 in.
June—August

6
Platycodon grandiflorus mariesii
H 10—15 in. PD 12 in.
July—September
7
Delphinium
H 3—5 ft. PD 20 in.
June—July

13
Lupinus 'Cherry Pie'
H 2½ ft. PD 18 in.
June—July

21
Campanula persicifolia
H 3 ft. PD 15 in.
June—July

8
Artemisia abrotanum
'Lambrook Silver'
H 3 ft. PD 18 in.
Foliage plant

nica spicata
aband'
0 in. PD 15 in.
—September

ta sieboldiana
ft. PD 20 in.
ust

23
Dianthus
'Brympton Red' H 18 in.
PD 15 in. June—August

283

Midget island bed

A planting scheme to make maximum
use of limited space. The bed illustrated measures 12 ft. by 6 ft.,
providing room for a single plant in
each position. H = height. PD =
planting distance

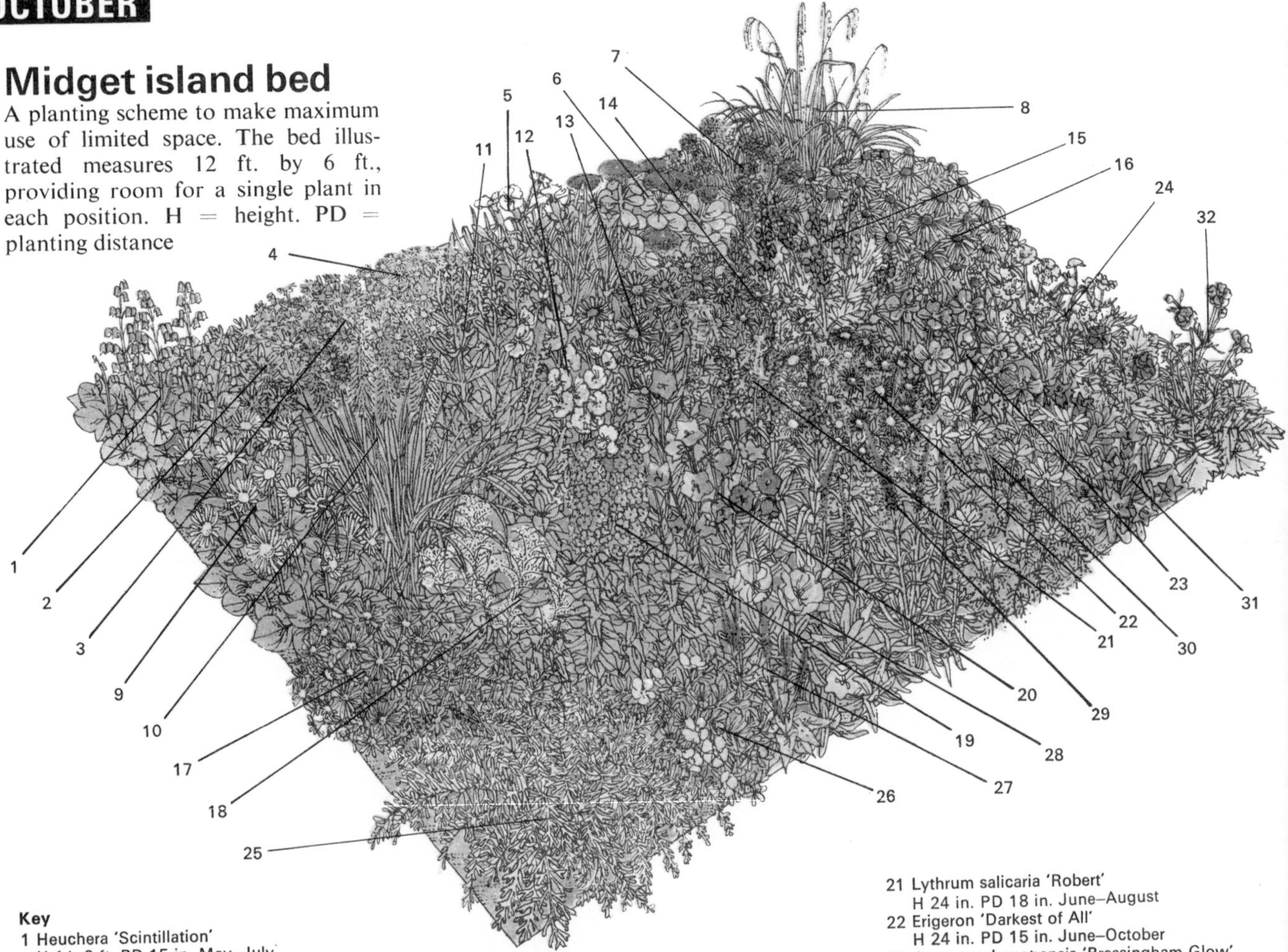

Key

1 Heuchera 'Scintillation'
  H 1½–2 ft. PD 15 in. May–July
2 Stokesia laevis
  'Blue Star' H 15 in. PD 12 in. July–September
3 Aster tibeticus
  H 12 in. PD 10 in. May–June
4 Inula ensifolia compacta
  H 10 in. PD 10 in. June–September
5 Dianthus
  June–August
6 Sedum spectabile 'Meteor'
  H 18 in. PD 15 in. August–October
7 Armeria 'Bloodstone'
  H 8–10 in. PD 10 in. June–August
8 Pennisetum orientale
  (grass) H 10 in. PD 12 in. July–October
9 Doronicum 'Spring Beauty'
  H 15 in. PD 12 in. April–June
10 Kniphofia macowanii
  H 2½ ft. PD 20 in. September–October
11 Salvia superba
  H 3½ ft. PD 18 in. June–August

12 Sidalcea 'Puck'
  H 24 in. PD 15 in. June–September
13 Helenium 'Wyndley'
  H 24 in. PD 18 in. July
14 Aster novi-belgii 'Blue Bouquet'
  H 15 in. PD 12–15 in. September–October
15 Aconitum napellus 'Blue Sceptre'
  H 2–2½ ft. PD 12 in. July–August
16 Rudbeckia speciosa 'Goldsturm'
  H 24 in. PD 18 in. August–October
17 Aster acris nanus
  H 18 in. PD 12 in. August–October
18 Solidago 'Goldenmosa'
  H 2½ ft. PD 15 in. August–September
19 Phlox 'Prince of Orange'
  H 3 ft. PD 18 in. June–September
20 Campanula trachelium 'Bernice'
  H 18–20 in. PD 10 in. June–July

21 Lythrum salicaria 'Robert'
  H 24 in. PD 18 in. June–August
22 Erigeron 'Darkest of All'
  H 24 in. PD 15 in. June–October
23 Anemone hupehensis 'Bressingham Glow'
  H 24 in. PD 12 in. August–October
24 Scabiosa graminifolia
  H 10 in. PD 10 in. June–September
25 Centaurea hypoleuca
  H 12 in. PD 12 in. May–July
26 Potentilla 'Wm. Rollison'
  H 15 in. PD 12 in. June–August
27 Polygonum carneum
  H 24 in. PD 18 in. June–August
28 Oenothera cinaeus
  H 18 in. PD 12 in. June–August
29 Veronica teucrium 'Shirley Blue'
  H 9 in. PD 10 in. June–July
30 Coreopsis verticillata
  H 20 in. PD 15 in. June–August
31 Gentiana septemfida
  H 10 in. PD 10 in. June–August
32 Geum 'Red Wings'
  H 24 in. PD 12 in. May–July

Hardy herbaceous plants to set out in October

The planting distance (PD) is that required in average soil to achieve a good spread in the second growing season after planting. Plant a little closer when using groups of three or more of a kind, allowing 25 per cent more space around the group than between the individual plants. Heights (H) are the average achieved under normal growing conditions.

Acanthus (bear's breeches)

Stately plants with dark green, deeply incised leaves arching out from a central crown. Plant in March or April in full sun and light soil; propagate by division in October or March or by cuttings of the fleshy roots. *A. longifolius* (H 3 ft. PD 24 in.), white and lilac lipped flowers, July–September. *A. spinosus* (H 4 ft. PD 12 in.), similar in colour, with sharply spined spikes; flowers, July–September.

Achillea ptarmica 'The Pearl'

Acanthus spinosus

Achillea (yarrow)

Types differ, but all like sun and most prefer dry soil. Plant in October or March; divide in spring. *A. clypeolata* (H 18 in. PD 15 in.), 4 in. heads of deep yellow flowers, June–August; silvery woolly leaves. *A. filipendulina* 'Coronation Gold' (H 3 ft. PD 18 in.), 4 in. heads of deep yellow flowers, June–August; green filigree leaves. *A. f.* 'Gold Plate' (H 4–5 ft. PD 18 in.), similar but more erect, with larger leaves. Both are useful for cutting but have astringent, aromatic foliage. They can be dried for winter if cut before fading begins.

A. 'Moonshine' (H 15 in. PD 15 in.), more reliably hardy, lemon-yellow flower heads, May–July; silver-grey leaves. *A. ptarmica* 'The Pearl' (H 2½–3 ft. PD 15 in.), ½ in. double white button flowers carried on loose heads, July–August; shiny, dark green, saw-edged leaves. The spreading underground shoots need annual curbing. *A. serrata* 'W. B. Child', similar to *A. ptarmica* 'The Pearl', but with single flowers. *A. sibirica* 'Perry's White', similar to *A. p.* 'The Pearl'. *A. taygetea* (H 18 in. PD 12 in.), 3 in. heads of light yellow flowers, June–August; grey leaves.

Aconitum (monkshood)

These plants grow from small crowns which are poisonous. They produce handsome spikes of hooded flowers rather like delphiniums from June–October; easy to grow in sun or partial shade. Divide and plant in October or March. *A. arendsii* (H 3½ ft. PD 15 in.), a fine hybrid, with large amethyst-blue flowers on strong stems in September and October. *A. fischeri* (H 3 ft. PD 15 in.), similar to *A. arendsii*. *A. napellus bicolor* (H 3½ ft. PD 15 in.), open spikes of blue and white flowers in July and August. Other varieties of this species are: 'Blue Sceptre' (H 2–2½ ft. PD 12 in.), similar to 'Bressingham Spire' but the flowers are blue and white; 'Bressingham Spire' (H 2½–3 ft. PD 12 in.), violet-blue flowers set closely on stiff, tapering spikes in July and August; 'Newry Blue' (H 3½ ft. PD 15 in.), deep blue flowers on closely set spikes in June and July; 'Spark's Variety' (H 4 ft. PD 15 in.), deep blue flowers on branching spikes in July and August.

Agapanthus

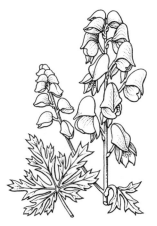

Aconitum arendsii

Agapanthus (African lily)

These perennials grow from congested, clumpy plants. They have smooth stems hung with 1 in. wide trumpet- or lily-shaped blue flowers, July–September, and bladed leaves 6–8 in. long. Plant in well drained, fertile soil, choosing a sheltered situation in colder areas. Although these plants are quite hardy in the south and west, protect against severe frost by covering from November until mid-March with a mound of litter 6–9 in. deep; divide in

April or early May. A. 'Head-bourne Hybrids' (H 2½–3 ft. PD 18 in.), variable shades of blue. A. 'Isis' (H 2½ ft. PD 18 in.), rich deep blue.

Ajuga (bugle)
Although by nature shade-loving, most of these plants will grow in almost any soil and position. Divide at any time when the soil is moist. A. pyramidalis (H 9 in. PD 12 in.), spikes of gentian-blue flowers in May and June. It forms dense, dark-leaved tufts, and prefers dampish soil and shade. A. reptans purpurea (H 6 in. PD 12 in.), deep blue spikes in April and May; makes purple-green mats, spreading by runners.

Alchemilla
A. mollis (H 18 in. PD 18 in.), tiny sulphur-yellow flowers in loose sprays in July and August; round, saw-edged, light green leaves. Excellent ground cover in any but hot, dry situations; easily grown from seed or by division in spring; valuable as a foil for other plants.

Alchemilla mollis

Alstroemeria
A. ligtu (Peruvian lily) (H 2½ ft. PD 8 in.), terminal heads of trumpet-shaped flowers, June–August, colours ranging from light pink to yellow, flame and orange. The roots, which are difficult to establish, need light deep soil in a sunny, sheltered position. Transplant in autumn when the tubers are dormant.

Althaea rosea

Althaea
A. rosea (hollyhock) (H 8 ft. PD 15 in.), is still popular in borders. The seeds of both double- and single-flowered varieties will come true to colour. Sow in April in a frame for transplanting in October to flower the following June–September. Plant in full sun and in dry soil.

Anaphalis
These plants have ½ in. wide, ivory-white flowers of a papery

Anaphalis triplinervis

texture on loose heads, July–September; silvery-grey foliage. They make fresh roots in the course of spreading close to the ground and give ground cover for most of the year. Plant in fairly dry situations in sun or partial shade; divide in spring or sow seeds in spring in a cold frame. A. margaritacea (H 18 in. PD 18 in.), a vigorous plant. A. nubigena and A. triplinervis (H 10–12 in. PD 15 in.), are much alike and make good frontal or edging plants. A. yedoensis (H 24 in. PD 15 in.), closely set heads of flowers, at the ends of silver-leaved stems, which are good for cutting and winter drying. This anaphalis spreads from underground shoots and makes a densely growing and erect bush.

Anchusa
These plants prefer a dry, sunny situation and are liable to rot in winter where damp. A. angustifolia (H 10 in. PD 12 in.),

Anchusa italica 'Little John'

brilliant gentian-blue flowers, May–August; short-lived. Propagate from basal cuttings in February–March. The italica varieties have thick, branching stems of small, bright blue flowers, May–July; large, tongue-shaped, hairy leaves and thick, fleshy roots. Increase by

root cuttings in early spring. 'Little John' (H 18 in. PD 12 in.), is less bright than the taller varieties, but flowers for much longer. 'Loddon Royalist' (H 3 ft. PD 15 in.), deep blue; 'Morning Glory' (H 4 ft. PD 15 in.), similar to 'Loddon Royalist'; 'Opal' (H 4 ft. PD 15 in.), sky blue.

Anemone hupehensis splendens

Anemone (windflower)
The varieties of A. hupehensis or A. japonica have open flowers, 2–3 in. across, on erect but branching stems, August–October. They make good border plants, needing sun and good drainage, and grow into shapely plants that spread from secondary roots. Divide in winter or early spring.

'Bressingham Glow' (H 24 in. PD 12 in.), semi-double, with deep rose-red flowers on erect stems; expands slowly. 'Lady Gilmour' (H 24 in. PD 15 in.), large - flowered, semi - double, pink. 'Louise Uhink' (H 3 ft. PD 15 in.), very large white flowers. 'Max Vogel' (H 2½ ft. PD 15 in.), clear pink. 'Profusion' is similar to 'Bressingham Glow', but the flowers are slightly deeper and richer in colour. 'Queen Charlotte' is similar to 'Max Vogel'. 'September Charm' (H 24 in. PD 12 in.), large, soft pink flowers. A. h. splendens (H 18 in. PD 12 in.), rose-pink flowers.

Anthemis 'Grallagh Gold'

Anthemis

These plants are very free-flowering and are best in full sun. Increase by division in spring or from basal cuttings. *A. cupaniana* (H 15 in. PD 16 in.), white daisy-like flowers, June–August, on rather sprawling growth; prefers well drained soil. *A.* 'Sancti-Johannis' (H 20 in. PD 12 in.), deep yellow flowers; neat growing. Varieties of *A. tinctoria* make open, bushy growth from a woody rootstock and produce branching stems carrying daisy-like flowers 2 in. across, June–August. 'Mrs. Buxton' (H 2½ ft. PD 15 in.),

Antholyza paniculata

primrose-yellow flowers; 'Grallagh Gold' (H 24 in. PD 15 in.), bright yellow flowers.

Antholyza

A. paniculata (H 3 ft. PD 12 in.), deep orange trumpet flowers in July and August; like a very robust montbretia with broad, ribbed, sword-like leaves and wiry stems. Grows best in a sunny place. The rounded corms grow in congested clumps which are easily divided in February or March.

Aquilegia 'McKana hybrids'

Aquilegia (columbine)

These popular perennials are not very long-lived, but often seed themselves. They make a bright display in May and June with their graceful, branching stems and spurred flowers. Sow seeds in spring under glass to produce large-flowering plants a year later, or sow outdoors in May in a sunny position and in moist soil. *A. caerulea* (H 24 in. PD 12 in.), clear blue flowers. *A.* 'Crimson Star' (H 18 in. PD 12 in.), red and white flowers. The McKana hybrids (H 3 ft. PD 12 in.) have a wide variation in colour.

Armeria (thrift)

These tufty evergreen plants for edging a border carry rounded flowers on short stems. Plant in a sunny position; divide in September or October. *A.* 'Bloodstone' (H 8–10 in. PD 10 in.), deep rosy-red flowers June–August. *A. maritima* 'Vindictive' (H 6 in. PD 9 in.), bright pink flowers. *A.* 'Ruby Glow', similar to 'Bloodstone'.

Armeria 'Vindictive'

Arnebia

A. echioides (prophet flower) (H up to 8 in. PD 12 in.), a fleshy rooted plant, with hairy, tongue-shaped leaves, and sprays of bright yellow flowers, April–May. Easy to grow in light, good soil in a sunny position. Increase by division, August–September.

Artemisia (wormwood)

The silver-leaved artemisias thrive in a sunny position and in well drained soil. Divide in spring. *A. abrotanum* 'Lambrook Silver' (H up to 3 ft. PD 18 in.), ferny foliage improved by cutting out whitish flower stems. *A. nutans* (H 24 in. PD 15 in.), more erect, filigree silver leaves. *A. lactiflora* (H 4 ft. PD 18 in.), the only artemisia grown for its flowers, having creamy white plumes on stiff stems in August and September; green jagged foliage. Plant in moist soil.

Artemisia lactiflora

Aruncus (goat's beard)

A. sylvester (H 6 ft. where moist. PD 20 in.), large, ivory plumes of tiny white flowers in June; deeply cut foliage. Prefers some shade but dislikes dry soils; propagation by seed.

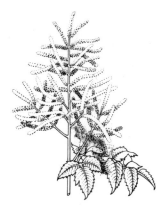

Aruncus sylvester

Asphodelus (asphodel lily)

These plants prefer a sunny position. Divide in spring. *A. liburnicus* (H 4 ft. PD 15 in.), small shiny yellow flowers, June–August; grass-like glaucous foliage.

A. luteus (H 3½ ft. PD 15 in.), sulphur-yellow flowers, broad-leaved spikes, June–August.

Asphodelus luteus

Aster

Although asters are often collectively referred to as michaelmas daisies, this name strictly applies only to *A. novi-belgii*. *A. acris* (H 2½ ft. PD 15 in.), small lavender-blue flowers in August and September; makes a dense bush. The dwarf form *nanus* (H 18 in. PD 12 in.) is similar. *A. amellus* (H 2–3 ft. PD 15 in.) is less vigorous than the michaelmas daisies but is disease-free; it seldom needs support and usually flowers August–October; the leaves are greyish-green and the stems are woody. Plant in April and leave undisturbed after flowering. Although plants can be left alone for several years, they are easy to divide. Good varieties are: *A. a. frikartii* (H 3 ft. PD 15 in.), light blue flowers, July–October; 'King George' (H 12 in. PD 15 in.), violet-blue; 'Lady Hindlip' (H 2–2½ ft. PD 15 in.), pink; 'Nocturne' (H 2½ ft. PD 15 in.), rosy-lavender; 'Sonia', similar to 'Lady Hindlip'. *A. farreri* 'Berggarten' (H 20 in. PD 12 in.),

violet-blue flowers in June; easy to grow, forms a mat; divide in September or March. *A. linosyris* (H 2½ ft. PD 12 in.), deep yellow flowers on wiry stems, August and September; propagation by division. *A. novae-angliae* has clumpy roots and slightly greyish, heavy-leaved stems which become woody by the time the flowers open in September; leaves may shrivel prematurely in a dry position. Two good varieties are 'Harrington's Pink' (H 4 ft. PD 20 in.), yellow-centred, salmon-pink flowers, September–October; 'September Ruby' (H 4 ft. PD 20 in.), almost red flowers, September. Divide in March.

A. novi-belgii are highly bred plants and are subject to attacks of mildew and verticillium wilt; mark those which die off and wilt before the normal flowering period in September and October, so that they can be dug up and burnt. Stem cuttings taken in April, rooted under glass and planted in fresh soil, are generally free from virus disease, even if the parent stock was affected. Young plants always produce the finest flowers, so replace old healthy plants with small divisions taken in March or April from the outer portions of the plant, discarding the rest. There are innumerable varieties, and the following (all PD 15 in.), which all flower September–October, are recommended. Red shades: 'Crimson Brocade' (H 3 ft.), large-flowered; 'Freda Ballard' (H 2½ ft.), semi-double; 'Winston Churchill', (H 3 ft.), small-flowered. Pink shades: 'Fellowship' (H 3 ft.); 'Flamingo' (H 3 ft.), semi-double; 'Rembrandt' (H 3½ ft.), nearly double. Blue and purple shades: 'Blandie' (H 4 ft.), semi-double; 'Blue Radiance' (H 2½ ft.); 'Marie Ballard' (H 3 ft.); 'Moderator' (H 3½ ft.); 'Royal Velvet' (H 24 in.), neat. White: 'White Choristers' (H 2½ ft.), bushy. The dwarf michaelmas

daisies, which range in height from 9–18 in., are popular and less subject to disease. Good varieties (PD 12–15 in.) are 'Autumn Princess' (H 12 in.), clear blue; 'Blue Bouquet' (H 15 in.); 'Dandy' (H 12 in.), purple-red; 'Lady in Blue' (H 10 in.); 'Little Pink Baby' (H 10 in.); 'Little Red Boy' (H 15 in.), light beetroot-red; 'Jenny' (H 15 in.), semi-double, maroon-purple; 'Rose Bonnet' (H 10 in.), misty-pink.

Aster amellus 'King George'

A. thompsoni nana (H 15 in. PD 10 in.) forms a little greyish bush covered in blue flowers 1½ in. across, July–September; prefers well drained soil; divide only in spring. *A. tibeticus* (H 12 in. PD 10 in.), sprays of light blue flowers in May and June. Grows easily in sun and well drained soil. Divide in March, August or September.

Astilbe

Although suitable only for shady positions and rich, moist soil, these lovely plants, with erect spikes rising above deep green foliage, are remarkable for their colour and graceful habit. They flower from June to August, forming strong clumps of woody crowns which can be divided in early spring. Old plants respond

Astilbe

to mulching in September ar October. Recommended vari ties: 'Bressingham Pink' (2½–3 ft. PD 12 in.); 'Cattley (H 3 ft. PD 12 in.), orchid-pin 'Fanal' (H 24 in. PD 15 in. red; 'Federsee' (H 24 in. P 15 in.), rosy-red; 'Fire' (H 2 ft. PD 18 in.), salmon re 'Irrlicht' (H 24 in. PD 15 in. white; 'Rhineland' (H 24 i PD 18 in.), carmine-pink. *simplicifolia* varieties (H 9–1 in. PD 12 in.), pink shades. *tacqueti superba* (H 4 ft. PD in.), deep lilac.

Astrantia (masterwort)

These are easy plants to gro though they do not like dry position. They form lar clumps, which should be divide in March. *A. major* (H 2½ PD 16 in.), flattish heads rayed, starry, greenish-pink flo ers, June–July. *A. maxim* (H 3 ft. PD 16 in.) has large pinker flowers, June–August.

Avens: see **Geum**

Bellflower: see **Campanula**

Bergamot: see **Monarda**

Bergenia (bear's ears)
Having large, shiny, dark green, cabbage-like leaves, which are more or less evergreen, these plants give good ground spread. The flowers dangle from short spikes, March–May, and are followed by new leaves. Easy to grow in any soil and in partial shade. Divide and re-plant in

Bergenia cordifolia

September or October. B. 'Ballawley' (H 18 in. PD 18 in.) has deep pink flowers and very large leaves. B. cordifolia (H 12 in. PD 18 in.), bright pink flowers, leaves 6 in. across; B. c. purpurea, pink flowers, purple-tinged leaves. B. crassifolia (H 12 in. PD 15 in.), light pink flowers, wavy-edged leaves. B. 'Silberlicht' (H 10 in. PD 14 in.), sprays of white flowers in April and May.

Bocconia: see **Macleaya**

Brunnera
B. macrophylla (syn. Anchusa myosotidiflora) (H 18 in. PD 18 in.), small, bright sky-blue flowers in sprays like forget-me-nots, May–July; large greyish green leaves in spring. It is easy to grow, but needs ample space. Divide in spring.

Bugbane: see **Cimicifuga**

Calamintha
Grow best in a position which is not too dry and sunny. Divide in spring when new growth has

Brunnera macrophylla

begun. C. nepetoides (H 12 in. PD 12 in.), a long succession of small, light blue flowers, August–October. By July or August it is a rounded bush of light green leaves.

Campanula glomerata

Campanula (bellflower)
A large genus containing several types suitable for both rock gardens and borders. Easy to grow in sun or partial shade, they can be planted in spring or autumn and nearly all are increased by division. C. glom-erata (H 12–18 in. PD 18 in.), clustered blue flowers, hairy leaves. Varieties include: 'Joan Elliott' (H 18 in. PD 15 in.), violet-blue flowers in May and June; nana alba (H 18 in. PD 12 in.), white flowers in June and July; 'Purple Pixie' (H 15 in. PD 10 in.), lavender-violet

Catananche caerulea

flowers in July and August, very neat-growing; superba (H 3 ft. PD 18 in.), heads of large violet bells on leafy stems in June and July; C. lactiflora (H 3 ft. PD 18 in.), heads of up-turned bell-shaped blue flowers, June–August; graceful branching stems. Varieties include: 'Loddon Anna' (H 4–5 ft. PD 18 in.), pale pink; 'Pouffe' (H 12 in. PD 16 in.), light lavender flowers on spreading mounds; 'Prichard's Variety' (H 2½ ft. PD 15 in.), deep lavender-blue flowers. C. latiloba 'Percy Piper' (H 3 ft. PD 15 in.), rich blue saucer flowers, 3 in. wide, in June and July; forms light green rosettes. C. persicifolia is similar to C. latiloba but more fragile, with dark green leaves; the bowl-shaped flowers are in shades of blue and white. Mixed colours can be raised from seed. C. trachelium 'Bernice' (H 18–20 in. PD 10 in.), double powder-blue flowers, June and July.

Campion: see **Lychnis**

Catananche (cupid's dart)
These plants have fragile fleshy roots from which root cuttings can be taken in spring. Always plant in well drained soil and cut hard back after flowering. C. caerulea (H 24 in. PD 18 in.), has blue flowers, quilled and papery, carried in great profusion on wiry stems over a long period from June to August.

Catmint: see **Nepeta**

Centaurea
These are easy plants to grow in sun and well drained soil. Divide in autumn or spring. C. dealbata steenbergii (H 24 in. PD 18 in.), deep pink flowers, May and June; a robust leafy plant. The variety 'John Coutts' is similar, but has larger, clear pink flowers. C. hypoleuca (H 12 in. PD 12 in.), pink flowers, May–July; grey leaves. C. macrocephala (H 4–5 ft. PD 20 in.), flowers appear as yellow quilled globes, June–August; very leafy and robust plant. C. rigidifolia (H 18 in. PD 15 in.), close sprays of pink, tufty

Centaurea dealbata

flowers, June–August. *C. ruth-enica* (H 4 ft. PD 18 in.), canary-yellow flowers, June–August, on wiry stems.

Cephalaria
C. tatarica (giant yellow sca-bious) (H 5–6 ft. PD 24 in.), short-stemmed, light yellow flowers, 3 in. across, with quilled petals, June–August. Makes busy growth. The long-lived roots can be divided in March.

Chelone (turtle-head)
These plants are easy to grow in the open; divide in spring. *C. barbatus:* see PENSTEMON. *C. obliqua* (H 2½ ft. PD 15 in.),

Chelone obliqua

purple-red and white snap-dragon-like flowers on stiff glossy-leaved spikes, July-September.

Chinese lantern: see **Physalis**

Christmas rose: see **Helleborus**

Chrysanthemum
(All H 2–3 ft. and PD 15 in.) *C. maximum* (shasta daisy), white, single or double flowers, June–August. Easy to grow; divide in March or September. The best single variety is 'Everest'. Doubles include 'Cobham Gold', with a flushed yellow centre, 'Esther Read' and 'Wirral Supreme'.

Chrysanthemum maximum
'Esther Read'

Cimicifuga (bugbane)
All these plants have handsome tapering spikes of white or ivory flowers, August–October, and finely cut foliage. They need good, deep, fairly moist soil and like partial shade. Divide in February or March. *C. cordi-folia* (H 4 ft. PD 15 in.), white spikes in September and Octo-ber. *C. racemosa* 'White Pearl' (H 4½ ft. PD 18 in.), very strik-ing in autumn. *C. r.* 'Elstead' (H 5 ft. PD 18 in.), creamy white flowers in autumn.

Cimicifuga racemosa

Columbine: see **Aquilegia**

Cone flower: see **Rudbeckia**

Coreopsis
These are sun-loving plants with a long flowering season. Easy to raise from seed. *C. grandiflora* (H 2½ ft. PD 18 in.), single deep yellow flowers, 1½ in. across, on wiry stems, June–September; usually survives only two seasons. The variety 'Goldfink' (H 8 in. PD 10 in.) is similar, but if cut back in September can be divided in spring. *C. verticillata* (H 20 in. PD 15 in.), golden starry flowers, 1 in. across, cover the perfectly shaped bushes, June–August. Very reliable and easy to grow; creeping roots. *C. v. grandiflora* is similar but slightly taller and has larger flowers.

Coreopsis verticillata

Cornflower: see **Centuarea**

Cortaderia (pampas grass)
C. argentea (H 7 ft. PD 3 ft.), produces silvery-white plumes, September–October, from a large plant with long, narrow, sharp-edged leaves. Does best in a sunny position in isolation or between shrubs; as an established plant can spread 4–5 ft. Divide in April, and trim off dead foliage in March. (For other grasses, see GRASSES.)

Cranesbill: see **Geranium**

Crocosmia
C. masonorum (H 2½ ft. PD 10 in.), deep orange flowers, 1½ in. across, as a terminal spray, July–September; 24 in. sword-blade leaves. Plant in sun and light soil; the corms increase by producing rhizomes. Excellent for cutting.

Crocosmia masonorum

Cynara
C. scolymus (globe artichoke) (H 5 ft. PD 4 ft.), small thistle-like, light purple flowers; silver foliage; large tough roots. A handsome border plant. Plant in April in full sun; divide only in April. *C. s. glauca* (H 6 ft. PD 2½ ft.) is a decorative form, with wide-spreading, grey-ish leaves and strong stems. The rounded flower heads have violet-blue tufts of narrow petals during August–Septem-ber. Needs deep, light soil and winter protection in cold dis-tricts. Do not divide or plant until new growth begins in April.

Cynoglossum
These plants are easy to grow in any soil, in sun or partial shade. Divide in March. *C. nervosum* (H 12 in. PD 12 in.), small blue drooping flowers, June–August. Greyish tongue-shaped leaves and fleshy roots.

Day lily: see **Hemerocallis**

Dead nettle: see **Lamium**

Delphinium 'Giant Pacific'

Delphinium, perennial

These superlative border plants need rich, deep soil and a sunny position; must be staked in late April. Mixed colours can be raised from seed sown under glass in March or April and, if transplanted in June, make good plants the following year, flowering June–July. 'Giant Pacific Hybrids' (H 4½–6 ft. PD 18 in.) include many doubles which will sometimes flower the first year if sown early, but these and other strains can also be sown outdoors in May. Named varieties are best increased from basal cuttings in March. Old plants can be divided in March, but these are not the best material.

New plants can be expensive, and for borders the smaller varieties (H 3–5 ft. PD 20 in.) are preferable to the tall ones, which may reach 6–7 ft. Consult specialist catalogues if you wish to make a selection from the many varieties that exist in shades of blue and white. Reduce the flower spikes to three per plant in the first year by pinching out weaklings, and repeat this process each year in April, leaving about six spikes

the second year, with a limit of 12 after that on large plants. Feed annually with a general organic fertiliser in March after making sure that new plantings are on really fertile deep soil. Watch for slugs in autumn and spring. The 'Belladonna' delphiniums have smaller flowers and leaves, and shorter, more branching spikes, 3–4 ft. long. They can be supported by pea sticks, unlike the large-spiked varieties which need staking, and are more suitable for cutting. Colours range from light to deep blue, with 'Blue Bees' (H 3½ ft. PD 18 in.), and 'Wendy' (H 4 ft. PD 18 in.), being particularly good.

Dianthus

Dianthus (pink)

Pinks are excellent for the front of sunny borders. The single and double carnation-like flowers rise on 6–18 in. stems from bluish-silver hummocks. All flower June–August. Increase by stem cuttings after flowering, or divide in autumn and replant deeply. Sow the seed of mixed strains under glass in March or April and transplant in June. Named varieties include: 'Brympton Red' (H 18 in. PD 15 in.), single deep red

flowers; 'Excelsior' (H 9 in. PD 12 in.), double pale pink flowers; 'Inchmery' (H 10 in. PD 12 in.), double pink flowers; 'Ipswich Crimson' (H 12 in. PD 12 in.), double; 'Isolde' (H 18 in. PD 12 in.), double pink flowers with maroon centre; 'Mrs. Sinkins' (H 9–12 in. PD 15 in.), double white; 'Susan' (H 10 in. PD 12 in.), similar to 'Isolde'; 'White Ladies' (H 9–12 in. PD 12 in.), double white.

Dicentra spectabilis

Dicentra

D. formosa (H 15 in. PD 18 in.), small sprays of crimson flowers in May and June; ferny foliage. The variety 'Adrian Bloom' has larger, brighter and longer-lasting flowers. Plant in sun or half shade and divide in early March. *D. spectabilis* (bleeding heart) (H 2–2½ ft. PD 18 in.), arching stems carry red and white locket-shaped flowers from April to June; tender foliage but hardy, fangy root. A beautiful plant for good, deep soil and a fairly sheltered position. It is difficult to increase, though old plants can be divided, using a sharp knife.

Dictamnus

D. fraxinella (burning bush) (H 3 ft. PD 15 in.), strong spikes of lilac-pink flowers in June and July; grows bushily. Plant in full sun on well drained soil and do not disturb; increase by seed.

Dictamnus fraxinella

Dierama

D. pendulum 'Fairy's Wand' (H 2½–3 ft. PD 20 in.) has long, rushy leaves forming a dense clump; sprays of pink trumpet flowers, June–August. Likes moist but not wet soil, sandy or peaty, but with no lime, and is not fully hardy in cold districts. Divide or plant in April. *D. pulcherrimum* is another popular dierama.

Digitalis (foxglove)

The perennial kinds are worth growing in sun or half shade.

Digitalis ambigua

Propagate by division or by seed sown in April or May. *D. ambigua* (H 24 in. PD 12 in.), soft yellow flowers, June–August. The best mixture is the 'Excelsior' hybrid strain (PD 15 in.). Raise from seed sown outdoors in May, and transplant to flowering position during early autumn. *D. mertonensis* (H 2½ ft. PD 12 in.), large strawberry-pink trumpets on heavy spikes, May–July.

Doronicum (leopard's bane)
These popular plants produce their yellow-rayed, daisy-like flowers early in the year. Plant in sun or half-shade and divide every two or three years in September. Recommended varieties are: 'Harpur Crewe' (H 3 ft. PD 15 in.), large single yellow flowers in May and June; 'Miss Mason' (H 15 in. PD 12 in.), bright yellow flowers, 3 in. across, April–June; 'Spring Beauty', similar to 'Miss Mason' but the flowers are fully double.

Doronicum 'Harpur Crewe'

Echinacea: see Rudbeckia

Echinops (globe thistle)
These stocky plants penetrate deeply and need space for development. They are strong and bushy, and the woody stems carry rounded, prickly thistle

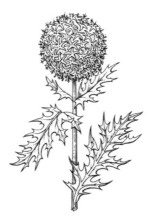

Echinops ritro

heads in June and July, greyish jagged leaves. Divide in autumn or spring, but old plants will shoot again from the roots left in the ground. *E. humilis* 'Taplow Blue' (H 4½ ft. PD 22 in.), light blue flowers. *E. h.* 'Veitch's Blue' (H 4 ft. PD 22 in.), steely-blue flowers. *E. ritro* (H 3½ ft. PD 20 in.), deep blue rounded flowers—the most compact kind.

Epimedium
These are valuable ground cover plants in shady or open positions where the soil is moist. The slow-creeping rhizomes send up sprays of flowers in April, followed by pretty rounded

Epimedium niveum

leaves which make a good canopy for many months of the year. Divide in October or February. *E. coccineum* (H 9 in. PD 12 in.), rosy-red flowers; leaves die in late autumn. *E. macranthum* (H 8–15 in. PD 12 in.), pink starry flowers, leaves 6–8 in. high which die in late autumn. *E. niveum* (H 6 in. PD 12 in.), ivory-white flowers; striking foliage. *E. perralderianum* (H 12 in. PD 18 in.), with yellow flowers on 9 in. sprays, is more robust. *E. pinnatum sulphureum* (H 9–12 in. PD 15 in.), sulphur-yellow flowers. *E. warleyense* (H 10 in. PD 15 in.), coppery-orange flowers.

Erigeron 'Quakeress'

Erigeron (fleabane)
All these plants have daisy-like flowers with orange centres, June–October, and some are nearly double; easy to grow in sun. Divide and plant in spring. Recommended varieties are: 'Amity', lilac-pink; 'Darkest of All', violet-blue; 'Dignity', deep violet-blue; and 'Felicity', pink (all H 24 in. PD 15 in., with 2 in. wide single flowers); 'Foerster's Liebling' (H 18 in. PD 15 in.), semi-double, bright pink; 'Lilofee' (H 2½ ft. PD 15 in.), semi-double, lavender-blue;

'Prosperity' (H 18 in. PD 15 in.) nearly double, mauve-blue 'Quakeress' (H 2½ ft. PD 15 in.) single, mauve-pink.

Eryngium (sea holly)
These plants have a prickly appearance, and in most case

Eryngium planum

both the stems and the curious flower bracts are blue. Plant in open positions and propagate by root cuttings in early spring They are valuable for cutting *E. alpinum* (H 2½ ft. PD 15 in.) large, rich amethyst-blue flowers June–August. *E. bourgatii* (H 24 in. PD 12 in.), silvery-blue flowers, June–August. *E. planum* (H 3 ft. PD 15 in.), small blue bracts, June–August; green leaves. *E. variefolium* (H 2½ ft. PD 15 in.), violet-blue spikes July–September.

Eupatorium
E. purpurescens (H 6 ft. PD 20 in.) has strong, stately stems with broad flat heads of small purple-rose flowers, August–September. Long-lived. Does best in rich, deep soil. Divide in October or March. *E. rugosum* (H 3½ ft. PD 20 in.) grows more bushily and has many small heads of white flowers, July–September.

Euphorbia (spurge)

These are showy, easy, long-living plants which prefer to be left undisturbed. Plant in sun or partial shade. Propagate by root division in October or April. *E. epithymoides* (syn. *E. polychroma*) (H 24 in. PD 15 in.), comes through in March, making a brave show of mounded sulphur-yellow heads in April; continues as a green bush until the autumn after the flowers fade. *E. griffithii* 'Fireglow' (H 24 in. PD 15 in.), deep orange heads 3 in. across in May and June; also continues as a green bush after the flowers fade. *E. palustris* (H 3½ ft. where moist. PD 18 in.), grows into a tall plant after producing a show of sulphur-yellow flowers in May and June.

Euphorbia epithymoides

Filipendula (meadowsweet)

These plants need moisture and rich soil, and some require shade; otherwise they are easy and hardy. Divide in spring. *F. digitata* (H 18 in. PD 12 in.), pink flower heads on leafy stems. *F. elegantissima* (H 3 ft. PD 18 in.), covered in light pink flower heads in June and July; grows bushily. *F. hexapetala plena* (H 24 in. PD 15 in.), heads of ivory-white in June and July; ferny, dark green leaves; requires open, dry position.

Filipendula hexapetala plena

F. purpurea (syn. *Spiraea palmata rubra*) (H 3 ft. PD 15 in.), beautiful cerise-red heads, 4 in. wide, in June and July. *F. rubra* (formerly *Spiraea venusta magnifica*) (H 4–5 ft. PD 18 in.), glistening pink heads in July and August on strong stems. *F. ulmaria* (H 2–4 ft. PD 18 in.), the true meadowsweet; can be obtained in double white form.

Flax: see Linum

Foxglove: see Digitalis

Gaillardia 'Ipswich Beauty'

Gaillardia (blanket flower)

These plants exhaust themselves by flowering too profusely, so cut them hard back in late August or in September after flowering. All flower from June until late August and, with the exception of 'Goblin', reach about 2½ ft. They need sun and good drainage. Propagate by root cuttings in spring, or by seed. Sow the seedlings, which vary in colour, outdoors in May or June to flower the following year. Recommended are: 'Croftway Yellow' (PD 15 in.), deep yellow self-colour; 'Goblin' (H 9 in. PD 12 in.), yellow and red, a neat-growing variety; 'Ipswich Beauty' (PD 15 in.), which has the typical gaillardia browny-red centre, the outer half of the petals being yellow; 'Mandarin' (PD 15 in.), suffusion of flame-orange and red; 'Wirral Flame' (PD 15 in.), deep browny-red.

Galega officinalis

Galega

G. officinalis (goat's rue) (H 3–4 ft. PD 20 in.), short flower spikes of lilac, mauve and sometimes white; flowers profusely and makes a stout green bush. Plant in dry sunny places; propagate by seed.

Gentiana

Most summer-flowering gentians are easy to grow in a sunny position in any soil. Seed sown outdoors in autumn or winter will flower when two years old, after being pricked off outdoors. *G. asclepiadea* (H 1½–2 ft. PD 12 in.), deep blue trumpets, July–September; arching, willow-leaved stems; does not do well in sun, lime and dry soil. *G. septemfida*, and its variety *hascombensis*, (H 10 in. PD 10 in.), rich blue trumpets on rather lax stems, June–August.

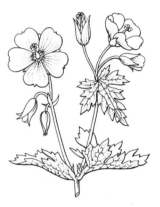

Geranium ibericum

Geranium (cranesbill)

True geraniums are usually hardy and perennial. They grow in sun or partial shade, need no special soil, and are easily divided in autumn or early spring. The taller varieties need cutting back hard after flowering to promote a new canopy of foliage. *G. armenum* (H 3 ft. PD 20 in.), vivid magenta flowers, 1½ in. across, June–August, on dense, bushy growth. *G. endressii* (H 20 in. PD 18 in.), clear pink flowers, June–August, on lax, mounded growth. Named varieties of this only differ slightly, but 'Johnson's Blue' (H 18 in. PD 15 in.), a mass of blue flowers, 1 in. wide, late May–July, is excellent. *G. ibericum* (H 24 in. PD 15 in.)

large deep blue flowers, late May–July. *G. macrorrhizum* (H 9 in. PD 15 in.), sprays of pale lilac flowers, June–July, and aromatic leaves. Gives good ground cover in sun or shade. Divide in October or March. *G. pratense* (the true cranesbill) (H 24 in. PD 15 in.), light blue flowers in June and July; there is a fine double blue *plenum* and a double white *album plenum*. *G. renardii* (H 12 in. PD 15 in.), veined lilac flowers in May and June, followed by a mound of soft greenery. *G. sanguineum* (H 12 in. PD 15 in.) forms a dense hummock covered in magenta flowers, June–August. *G. s. lancastriense splendens* (H 12 in. PD 12 in.), clear rose-pink flowers. *G. sylvaticum* (H 24 in. PD 15 in.), abundant foliage tipped by light lavender-blue, saucer-shaped flowers, May–June. Good forms are *G. s.* 'Mayflower' and the white *G. s. album* (both H 24 in. PD 15 in.). All thrive in sun or partial shade. Divide in October or March.

Geum

Geum (avens)

These plants grow easily in a sunny place, but some are short-lived unless divided and re-planted every two years in early spring or in September. *G. borisii* (H 10 in. PD 12 in.), bright orange flowers in May and June, makes leafy mats, and

is more reliable. Named varieties, which need cutting back after flowering and are reliable if re-planted every two years, include: 'Dolly North' (H 24 in. PD 12 in.), semi-double orange flowers on arching stems, May–July; 'Fire Opal', flame orange, 'Rubin' and 'Red Wings', scarlet-red, all of which are similar in habit to 'Dolly North'. The following varieties will seldom live beyond three years and can be propagated only by seed sown in spring to flower the following year: 'Lady Stratheden' (H 24 in. PD 12 in.), double yellow flowers, May–August; 'Mrs. Bradshaw' (H 12 in. PD 12 in.), red flowers, May- August.

Globe flower: see **Trollius**

Golden rod: see **Solidago**

Grasses

Some grasses are good perennials and blend well with border plants. They can also be used as edging plants or between shrubs. Easy to divide in spring when new growth is beginning. None of the following is invasive, either from spread or self-seeding. *Avena candida* (H 2½–3 ft. PD 22 in.), bluish evergreen growth, making large tufts with graceful sprays in June. *Bouteloua oligostachys* (mosquito grass) (H 12 in. PD 12 in.), produces curious hairy seed pods held obliquely on its stems; makes neat tufts, July–November. *Carex morrowii* (H 12 in. PD 15 in.), greenish-yellow flower sprays in March and April; striped gold evergreen leaves, 6–9 in. long. *Festuca glauca* (fescue grass) (H 9 in. PD 10–12 in.), blue-grey densely leaved evergreen tufts, good for edging or a bank. *Holcus mollis variegatus* (H 9 in. PD 12 in.), densely clustered blades, variegated buff and blue-green; a spreading, tufty grass, useful for edging. *Luzula sylvatica* (H 12 in. PD 12 in.),

greenish flower sprays in June and July; an evergreen grass of rushy habit which requires shade. *Miscanthus sinensis* (H 3 ft. PD 20 in.), upright-growing blades with a whitish midrib, May–November; *M. s. gracillimus*, much narrower foliage; *M. s. variegatus*, very bright, striped green and buff foliage. *Pennisetum alopecuroides* (H 3 ft. PD 22 in.), graceful feathery plumes in autumn, rather like a compact pampas grass; *P. orientale* (H 10 in. PD 12 in.), hairy, poker-shaped, brownish-green flowers, July–October. *Phalaris arundinacea picta* (gardener's garters) (H 24 in. PD 16 in.), brightly variegated leaves; a rampant grass difficult to keep in check. Divide in March or April. *Stipa calamogrostis* (H 3 ft. PD 20 in.), erect ivory-buff waving plumes, June–September; *S. gigantea* (H 3 ft. PD 20 in.), handsome purplish plumes in June and July; dark evergreen foliage. (See also CORTADERIA and Ornamental Grasses, p. 478).

Gypsophila paniculata 'Bristol Fairy'

Gypsophila (baby's breath)

These deep-rooting, long-lived plants need sun and must have

plenty of space for the summe[r] spread of their often tangle[d] growth and myriads of sma[ll] flowers. All flower from Jun[e] to September. *G. paniculata* ([H] 3 ft. PD 24 in.), clouds of singl[e] white flowers. Increase by seed[.] The variety 'Bristol Fairy' [is] similar but with double whit[e] flowers, while *compacta plen[a]* (H 18 in. PD 18 in.) is a smalle[r] double white, suitable for mixe[d] borders. *G.* 'Pink Star' (H 15 in[.] PD 12 in.), clouds of double pal[e] pink flowers on lax blue-gree[n] growth; propagate all these b[y] cuttings.

Helenium 'Moerheim Beauty'

Helenium (sneezewort, henbane)

Heleniums grow from congeste[d] rosettes, which are easily divide[d] in April. Plant in sun and an[y] ordinary soil. The flowers, 1½–[2?] in. across, have a mounded con[e] and soft petals which tend t[o] turn down in hot weather o[r] when about to fade. Older plant[s] respond to thinning out. Th[e] tallest varieties are less attractiv[e] and often lose their leaves befor[e] flowering is over. Recommende[d] kinds are: 'Bruno' (H 3 ft. P[D] 12 in.), chestnut-red, August–October; 'Butterpat' (H 3 ft[.] PD 12 in.), warm yellow

August–October; 'Coppelia' (H
3 ft. PD 12 in.), coppery-orange,
July – September; 'Crimson
Beauty', (H 24 in. PD 15 in.),
browny-red, June – August;
'Golden Youth' (H 2½ ft. PD
15 in.), yellow, June–August;
'Gold Fox' (H 3 ft. PD 18 in.),
large orange flowers streaked
with brown, July–September;
'Moerheim Beauty' (H 3 ft. PD
18 in.), tawny-red, June–August;
'Wyndley' (H 24 in. PD 18 in.),
orange streaked with copper,
July; bushy habit.

Helianthus 'Capenoch Star'

Helianthus (sunflower)
The perennial varieties which
have running underground roots
should be avoided. Plant in deep
rich soil and divide in spring.
The following grow from stout
compact clumps into quite
massive bushes topped with
short-stemmed yellow flowers,
July–September: 'Loddon Gold'
(H 5 ft. PD 20 in.), flowers 3 in.
across, the finest fully double
kind; 'Capenoch Star' (H 4 ft.
PD 20 in.), similar but single
flowered; 'Triomphe de Gand',
semi-double.

Heliopsis
These are better border plants
than helianthuses, since they are

Heliopsis 'Golden Plume'

more compact and trouble-free.
All are best in sun, but will thrive
in almost any soil. They have
a long flowering period, late
June–September. Divide in February or March. H. gigantea (H
5 ft. PD 18 in.), single deep
yellow flowers 2½ in. across; the
tallest. H. 'Golden Plume' (H
3 ft. PD 18 in.), large deep
yellow flowers; the finest double
kind. H. 'Gold Greenheart' (H
3½ ft. PD 18 in.), double chrome-
yellow flowers tinged with green
at the centre. H. patula (H 3 ft.
PD 18 in.), warm yellow, smaller
single flowers.

Helleborus
H. atrorubens (H 12–18 in. PD
18 in.), deep purplish-rose
flowers, February–April; slow-
growing and does not seed.
H. corsicus (H up to 24 in. PD
18 in.), wide heads of attractive
pale apple-green flowers in
March and April. Easy to grow,
but requires some shade. Propagate by seed or by division in
autumn. H. foetidus (H 24 in.
PD 16 in.), spikes of greenish
flowers in February; leafy, dark
green bushes. Will grow in any
soil in shade. Plant in October or
March. Increase only by seed

sown in the open as soon as ripe.
H. niger (Christmas rose) (H
6–15 in. PD 18 in.), usually
flowers January–March; it needs
shade and good deep soil, and
although unsuitable for a mixed
border can be grown on the
shady side of shrubs or a wall;
responds to mulching with peat
after flowering. Can be raised
from slow germinating seed or
by division of old plants. H.
orientalis (Lenten rose) (H
12–18 in. PD 18 in.), cup-shaped
flowers in March, varying in
colour from greenish-white to
pink and plum-purple; it loses
its leaves just before flowering,
but new leaves follow the flowers
and maintain a deep green
canopy 12 in. high. Easy to grow
where shady but not too dry.
Seedlings vary in colour; old
plants will divide in October.

Helleborus niger

Hemerocallis (day lily)
Day lilies have been highly bred,
and hundreds of varieties exist.
They are easy to grow in any
good soil, but normally require
sun. Divide in October, February or March. Each flower
lasts only one day, but the
clustered heads keep opening to
give a long flowering season
from June to late August.
Among named varieties (H
2–3 ft. PD 18 in.) are: 'Black
Magic', ruby-red; 'Cartwheels',
light orange; 'Dido', apricot;
'Doubloon', golden yellow;
'Fandango', orange; 'Golden
Orchid'; 'Hyperion', canary-

Hemerocallis

yellow; 'Morocco Red', deep
red with yellow centre; 'Pink
Damask', almost pink; 'Sirius',
lemon-yellow; 'Stafford', ma-
hogany-red.

Heuchera (coral flower)
These are charming plants, with
slender spikes bearing sprays of
little bell-shaped flowers from
May–July in a wide range of
colours. The compact, drought-
resisting root also produces
mounds of overlapping evergreen leaves. They need sun and
light soil.
    The tendency of heucheras
to grow out of the ground when
the crowns become old and

Heuchera 'Oakington Jewel'

woody can be offset by mulching between the crowns or by dividing and re-planting the most vigorous crowns more deeply every three or four years. Seedlings are slow to raise and produce only mixed shades. Some good named varieties (H 1½–2 ft. PD 15 in.) are: 'Bressingham Blaze', deep coral-flame; 'Damask', carmine; 'Ibis', deep rose-pink; 'Oakington Jewel', deep coral flowers, bronzy leaves; 'Pearl Drops', white; 'Red Spangles', blood red; 'Scintillation', pink, red-tipped; 'Sunset', salmon-scarlet.

Heucherella 'Bridget Bloom'

Heucherella
This plant is a bigeneric cross between heuchera and tiarella, and has the merits of both parents. Easy to grow in sun or half shade. Both the following divide easily in August, September, February or March. *H.* 'Bridget Bloom' (H 18 in. PD 12 in.), a neatly mounded plant producing spikes of deep pink, white-centred flowers from early May onwards; will often flower again in autumn if planted in well drained but not dry soil. *H. tiarelloides* (H 12 in. PD 15 in.), short spikes of bright pink flowers in May and June; it

makes good ground cover with a mat of golden-green leaves.

Himalayan blue poppy : see Meconopsis

Hollyhock : see Althaea rosea

Hosta lancifolia

Hosta (plantain lily)
These plants are becoming increasingly popular for their reliability, handsome foliage and small, trumpet-lily flowers. Although they are easy to grow in any good soil, they grow best in one that is moist and rich; they also need some shade. A rich soil will help to compensate for lack of moisture, but plants with variegated leaves may be spoiled where it is dry or sunny. Plants become large with age, so divide them with two forks or cut through with a sharp spade in autumn or spring. *H. crispula* (H 2½ ft. PD 20 in.), mauve flowers, July–August; wavy-edged leaves, 12 in. long, 6 in. wide, with a yellow band. *H. fortunei* (H 2½ ft. PD 20 in.), lavender-lilac flowers, June–August; pointed glaucous leaves 15 in. long. *H. f. picta* is similar, but has richly variegated leaves

in spring. *H. lancifolia* (H 24 in. PD 18 in.), lilac flowers in July and August; deep green overlapping leaves. *H. plantaginea* (H 18 in. PD 20 in.), light green leaves and spikes of scented white flowers, August–September. Flowers more freely in an open position. *H. rectifolia* (H 3–4 ft. PD 22 in.), purple-mauve flowers, July–September; green leaves. *H. sieboldiana* (H 2½ ft. PD 20 in.), nearly white flowers in August, rounded glaucous-blue leaves; *H. s. elegans* (H 2½–3 ft. PD 24 in.), is a larger-leaved form. *H. undulata medio-variegata* (H 18 in. PD 18 in.), mauve flowers in July and August; smaller wavy-edged leaves streaked with yellow. *H. undulata erromena* is a similar, green form. *H. ventricosa* (H 3 ft. PD 20 in.), bold spikes of lavender-purple, July–September; large green leaves; *H. v. variegata*, a brightly variegated form, is particularly good.

Hypericum
H. calycinum (rose of Sharon) (H 18 in. PD 12 in.), yellow flowers, 1½ in. across, in June and July; dark green foliage gives almost complete coverage. Roots creep considerably. Ground cover plant for shade or sun, tolerating quite dry conditions and any soil; divide in spring.

Incarvillea delavayi

Incarvillea
These plants have exotic-looking trumpet flowers, 3 in. long and 1½ in. wide, which appear before the leaves. Plant in open, well drained positions. They can be raised from seed, but take two years to reach flowering size. The fangy roots will not divide. Both the following are late to appear in spring: *I. delavayi* (H 24 in. PD 15 in.) deep pink flowers in June and July; long jagged leaves; *I. grandiflora* (H 10 in. PD 12 in.) large, deep rose-pink flowers appear in May.

Inula orientalis

Inula (fleabane)
All these sun-loving plants have finely rayed yellow flowers. They need no special care. Propagate by seed, or by division of roots in October or March. *I. barbata* (H 18 in. PD 18 in.), 2 in. wide, golden-yellow flowers, June–September; makes a dense low bush and spreads rather quickly. *I. ensifolia compacta* (H 10 in. PD 10 in.), deep yellow flowers, June–September; tufty growth forming small bushes. *I.* 'Golden Beauty' (H 24 in. PD 15 in.), deep yellow flowers, 1½ in. across, on short stems, June–September; compact and upright. *I. hookeri* (H 2½ ft. PD 20

in.), similar to *I. barbata*. *I. orientalis* (H 12–18 in. PD 15 in.), golden-yellow flowers up to 4 in. across in June and July; grows erectly. *I. magnifica* (H up to 6 ft. PD 24 in.), branching yellow-flowered spikes, June–August; very large leaves.

Iris

I. foetidissima (gladwyn iris) (H 20–24 in. PD 12 in.), small yellow flowers, but the seed pods open to reveal orange berries in autumn; dark evergreen foliage. Grows well in dense, dry shade but is tolerant of some sun; easy to divide at almost any time, but best in February or March. *I. f. variegata* is also evergreen but handsomely variegated; outstanding in winter. *I. germanica* 'Aline' (H 2½ ft. PD 14 in.), sky-blue flowers; one of the best June-flowering irises; 'Limelight' (H 3 ft. PD 16 in.), pale yellow, June–July. *I. ochroleuca* (H 3–6 ft. PD 16 in.), deep yellow flowers in June and July, upstanding leaves form a dense clump. Easy to grow in sun where not parched; divide in September or October. *I. pseudacorus* (water flag iris) (H 3 ft. PD 16 in.), yellow flowers in June, bold clumps of sword-like leaves; needs only moisture, but will grow in up to 6 in. of water. Plant or divide in September or October.

Jacob's ladder: see **Polemonium**

Kaffir lily: see **Schizostylis**

Kirengeshoma

K. palmata (H 2½ ft. PD 20 in.), a rarely seen but charming plant with light green foliage and soft yellow flowers which do not fully open, July–September. Divide in March. Though hardy, new growth is sometimes nipped by late spring frosts.

Kniphofia (red hot poker)

Not all kniphofias are red, and a selection of named varieties

Kniphofia galpinii

can give a flowering season from June–October in colours varying from white through all shades of yellow and flame-orange. Heights vary from 1½–6 ft. All prefer full sun and well drained soil. Plant in September or early October, or wait until the new growth begins in April. Old plants are easily divided in April; kniphofias can also be propagated from seed sown in drills outdoors in May or June for flowering the following year. Plants raised from seed vary in height and colour from the parent plants. In cold districts, tie leaves at the top to prevent snow from damaging the crowns and, especially when newly planted, place mulch round each plant beneath the leaves from late November until mid-March. Named varieties make excellent groups above smaller plants in borders. Varieties of kniphofia include: 'Bees' Lemon' (H 4 ft. PD 2? in.), heavy spikes of luminous lemon-yellow in August and September; 'Bees' Sunset' (H 3 ft. PD 20 in.), orange-flame in June and July; *galpinii* (H 18 in. PD 18 in.), charming dainty spikes of soft orange-yellow in September and October; 'Gold Else' (H 3 ft. PD 20 in.), deep yellow in June

and July; 'John Benary' (H 4 ft. PD 22 in.), brilliant red, July–August; *macowanii* (H 2½ ft. PD 20 in.), orange-yellow pokers in September and October; 'Maid of Orleans' (H 3½ ft. PD 22 in.), creamy-white, July–September; 'Modesta' (H 24 in. PD 18 in.), ivory, tipped with rose, July and August; *nelsonii major* (H 2½ ft. PD 20 in.), deep orange-flame, August–October; 'Royal Standard' (H 3 ft. PD 20 in.), yellow and red, July–September; 'Samuel's Sensation' (H 6 ft. PD 24 in.), giant spikes of coral-red in September and October; 'Springtime' (H 4 ft. PD 24 in.), creamy-yellow and red, July and August; *tubergenii* (H 3 ft. PD 20 in.), primrose-lemon in June and July.

Lamb's ears: see **Stachys**

Lamium (dead nettle)

L. galeobdolon variegatum (H 10 in. PD 16 in.), spikes of yellow flowers in April and May, light green foliage; increasing from runners; a rampant dead nettle for any shady place. Plant in autumn, divide in October. Trim in August or September to prevent encroachment. *L. garganicum* (H 8 in. PD 9 in.), clear pink flowers, June–August. Best in shade, and dislikes dry soil. Divide in March. *L. maculatum roseum* (H 8 in. PD 16 in.), spikes of pink flowers in April–May; quick spreading striped leaves, mounted growth. Plant and divide as *L. galeobdolon*. *L. orvala* (H 24 in. PD 16 in.), thick-set spikes of deep rose flowers, May–June. The top growth dies back in autumn to a strong, dormant root. Does well in shade, and dislikes dry soil. Increase by seed or by division and re-planting in March.

Larkspur: see **Delphinium**

Lathyrus

L. vernus (H 12 in. PD 16 in.), makes a low, bushy plant from a strong, clumpy root. Pea-

shaped flowers vary in colour from pale pink to purple, blue and white, July–September. Divide in March. Though hardy, new growth is sometimes nipped by late spring frosts.

Lavatera (tree mallow)

L. olbia rosea (H 6 ft. PD 24 in.) has a long succession of pink, saucer-like flowers, 3 in. across, June–October. A useful shrubby plant for dry or starved soil, preferably in a sunny position. Not long-lived; but heeled cuttings in September will root under glass.

Lenten rose: see **Helleborus**

Liatris callilepis

Liatris (gay feather)

These plants grow from fleshy, corm-like roots and produce sturdy spikes covered in drooping, blade-like leaves. The flowers open first at the top of the long poker-like spike and are good for cutting. Easily grown in full sun. Divide in March. *L. callilepis* (H 2½–3 ft. PD 12 in.), intense lilac flowers which are closely set and cover the spike for a third of its length, June–August. *L. c.* 'Kobold' (H up to 2 ft. PD 12 in.) is smaller, but similar.

Ligularia (ragwort)

The common name strictly applies only to a meadow weed which is quite unlike the cultivated species. The kinds mentioned below do not thrive in dry conditions but give a bright display in good moist soil. All of them become quite large plants, which can be divided in March.

L. clivorum (H 3–5 ft. PD 24 in.), branching spikes of yellow flowers, July and August; massive rounded leaves. Varieties of *L. clivorum* include: 'Desdemona' (H 4 ft. PD 24 in.),

Limonium latifolium

Ligularia clivorum

spikes of orange flowers, 2½ in. across, July–September; handsome purplish leaves; 'Gregynog Gold' (H 3 ft. PD 24 in.), orange flowers in July and August; *hessei* (H 5 ft. PD 24 in.), deep yellow flowers, July–September. *L. hodgsonii* (H 24 in. PD 18 in.), bright orange flowers in June and July. *L. pryzwalskii* (H 5 ft. PD 20 in.), many small yellow flowers on tapering spikes in July and August; jagged leaves and black stems; the variety 'Rocket' is similar but more striking.

Limonium (sea lavender)

These long-lived plants require sunny positions and ordinary soil. They can be raised from seed. *L. latifolium* (H 2–3 ft. PD 20 in.), tiny lavender-blue flowers on stiff, widely branched sprays, July–September; dark green, aspidistra-like leaves; a deep-rooting plant. The varieties 'Blue Cloud', a larger-flowered form, and 'Violetta', violet-blue flowers, are finer than most seedlings. They can be increased only from root cuttings taken in spring; these take two or three years to reach flowering size.

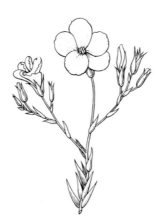

Linum narbonense

Linum (flax)

These long-flowering plants prefer full sun and good drainage. Plant in October or March. Propagate by seed sown under glass in spring. *L. dolomiticum* (H 18 in. PD 15 in.), shining yellow flowers on flattish heads, June–August; rather leafy in growth; *L. narbonense* (H 18 in. PD 15 in.), the best blue species, with very bright flowers, June–September, on wiry bushy growth.

London pride: see Saxifraga

Lungwort: see Pulmonaria

Lupinus 'Tom Reeves'

Lupinus (lupin)

These popular plants flower the first year from seed, if this is sown under glass in late February or early March and transplanted in May. They can also be sown outdoors in May or June to flower the following year. Lupins tend to revert to the less brilliant blues and pinks if self-sown seedlings are allowed to flower, so always buy branded seed. The parent plants themselves do not revert. Lupins do not usually live for more than two or three years, especially on limy soils, and do not like

manure round the roots. All flower in June and July, and flowering can be extended by cutting out terminal spikes as soon as they are over. Cut off the rest of the spike before the seed ripens, to prevent self-germination. Divide old plants in March, cutting away and discarding all but the young shoots with white roots, which should then be re-planted deeply and firmly. Named varieties are sometimes affected by an incurable virus disease, but this happens more often in nurseries than in gardens. Good varieties (H 2½ ft. or more, PD 18 in.) are: 'Blue Jacket', blue and white; 'Cherry Pie', 'Flaming June', 'Guardsman' and 'Orange Flame', all with red flowers; 'Rapture', pink; 'Thunder-cloud', purple; 'Tom Reeves' and 'Wheatsheaf', yellow.

Lychnis chalcedonica

Lychnis (campion)

The types of lychnis vary, but all need sun and require no special soil. Propagate by seed or by division in spring. *L. chalcedonica* (H 2½–3 ft. PD 15 in.) is a compact plant, with heads of upfacing scarlet flowers on leafy stems in June and July. *L. coronaria* (H 18 in. PD 15 in.), branching stems carrying open-petalled, bright pink or magenta-carmine flowers, ¾ in. across, June–August; soft, silver-grey mounded foliage. *L. viscaria splendens plena* (H 12 in. PD 12 in.), intense carmine-pink double flowers, 1 in. across, in June and July; dark green narrow leaves.

Lysimachia (yellow loose-strife)
These are easy plants to grow in sun or partial shade, where conditions are not hot nor dry. Divide in autumn or spring. *L. clethroides* (H 3 ft. PD 15 in.), outward-curving spikes (like a small buddleia) of white flowers in August and September at the ends of strong, dark-leaved stems; matted roots. *L. nummularia aurea* (creeping jenny), trailing stems of vivid yellow flowers in summer. *L. punctata* (H 3 ft. PD 20 in.), heavy spikes with whorls of yellow flowers, ½ in. across, June–August; spreads rapidly in moist soil.

Lysimachia punctata

Lythrum (purple loosestrife)
These plants prefer moisture but are adaptable, long-lived and reliable. All have a woody root-stock and make erect bushes carrying pointed leaves and a profusion of brightly coloured flower spikes, June–August.

Lythrum virgatum 'Rose Queen'

Old plants are easily divided in October or April. *L. salicaria* 'Brightness' (H 2½ ft. PD 18 in.), deep rose; 'Robert' (H 24 in. PD 18 in.), clear pink; 'The Beacon' (H 3 ft. PD 18 in.), rosy-red. The varieties of *L. virgatum* have thinner spikes: 'Rose Queen' (H 24 in. PD 15 in.), light pink; 'The Rocket' (H 2½ ft. PD 18 in.), deep pink.

Macleaya microcarpa 'Coral Plume'

Macleaya
These plants prefer sun or partial shade and are effective

among tall shrubs. Propagate by cuttings in summer. Both the following kinds grow from fleshy roots, which tend to spread considerably and may need curbing. *M. cordifolia* (syn. *Bocconia cordifolia*) (H 5 ft. PD 18 in.), small but attractive ivory-white tubular flowers in August and September on strong spikes; large glaucous leaves. *M. microcarpa* 'Coral Plume' (H 6 ft. PD 18 in.), very small individual flowers in August and September; the coppery-purple sheen of the plumes, emphasised by the silvery foliage, is attractive.

Malva (mallow)
M. alcea fastigiata (H 4 ft. PD 18 in.) produces clear pink saucer-like flowers, June–August. Needs full sun and light soil. Increase from seed sown in spring.

Meadowsweet: see **Filipendula**

Meconopsis
The perennial species prefer a shady but not dry position and soil with peat or ample humus. Increase by seed wintered out-doors and pricked off in March, and then grown on in pots to flower the following year. *M. betonicifolia* 'Bailey's Variety' (Himalayan blue poppy) (H 3 ft. PD 12 in.), bright blue saucer flowers, 3 in. across, May–July, on erect stems; grey hairy leaves, fibrous roots.

Mertensia
Most of these plants grow easily in partial shade and can be propagated in autumn by seed or division. *M. ciliata* (H 24 in. PD 15 in.), sprays of little blue bells in June and July. More glaucous and less fragile than *M. virginica* (Virginian cowslip) (H 1½–2 ft. PD 12 in.), purple-green shoots in March, rich blue bells dangling from arching stems

in April and May, followed by a long dormant period; a fragile plant.

Mertensia virginica

Mimulus (musk)
M. 'A. T. Johnson' (H 15 in. PD 15 in.) forms matted rosettes with spikes of large, yellow, brown-speckled flowers, June–July. Does best in rich, damp soil. Divide for re-planting every two years.

Monarda 'Croftway'

Monarda (bergamot)
These aromatic, leafy bushes are tipped with curiously shaped flowers on terminal branching heads from June to late August. Their height varies from $2\frac{1}{2}$–3 ft., depending on the richness and moisture of the soil. To ensure a continuing display, divide and re-plant the wide, mat-like roots every two to three years in April. The following (all PD 18 in.) are recommended: 'Adam', cerise-red; 'Blue Stocking', violet-purple; 'Cambridge Scarlet'; 'Croftway' and 'Melissa', both bright pink; 'Prairie Glow', salmon-red.

Morina
These plants grow best in full sun and in a well drained soil. Plant in spring. Increase by seed sown under glass in spring. *M. longifolia* (H 24 in. PD 12 in.), flower spikes carrying pink-lipped flowers from July–September; semi-evergreen rosettes with long, glossy, prickly leaves.

Mullein: see **Verbascum**

Musk: see **Mimulus**

Nepeta (catmint)
These are adaptable plants for sun or semi-shade, dislike wet

Nepeta 'Six Hills Giant'

ground in winter. Propagate by cuttings or by division in March. *N.* 'Blue Beauty' (H 24 in. PD 15 in.), large lavender-blue flowers, June–August; pungent foliage, erect spikes and spreading roots. *N. mussinii* (H 12–15 in. PD 15 in.), a profusion of spikes of lavender-blue flowers on soft grey-green growth, June–September; suitable for beds and borders. *N.* 'Six Hills Giant' (H 2–$2\frac{1}{2}$ ft. PD 18 in.), violet-blue flowers; a taller variety of *N. mussinii.*

Obedient plant: see **Physostegia**

Oenothera cinaeus

Oenothera (evening primrose)
The common name strictly applies only to *O. odorata*, a biennial. Perennial kinds are easy to grow in sun, and make compact plants that divide freely in spring. *O. cinaeus* (H 18 in. PD 12 in.), highly coloured pink, yellow and bronze shoots in spring, followed by sheaves of large, cupped, bright yellow flowers, June–August. *O.* 'Fireworks' (H 18 in. PD 12 in.), flowers like *O. cinaeus;* purplish foliage in spring. *O. fruticosa* 'Yellow River', similar to *O. cinaeus* but has green foliage. *O. missouriensis* (H 9 in. PD 18 in.), canary-yellow flowers, 3 in. wide, June–September. Good for a sunny bank.

Omphalodes (navelwort)
A long-lived perennial for shade or half shade where conditions are not too dry. Divide in September or October. *O. cappadocica* (H 6 in. PD 10 in.), sprays of small, bright blue forget-me-not flowers in April and May; greyish-green, oval leaves form dense carpets of modest spread.

Origanum
O. laevigatum (H 15 in. PD 12 in.), blue-green foliage during the summer develops into a haze of tiny, purple flowers, August–October. Does best in a sunny position. Divide in March.

Pachysandra
These plants require shady places beneath trees in any soil. Plant or divide in September, October or March. *P. terminalis* (H 6–8 in. PD 10–12 in.), insignificant flowers, glossy foliage; an evergreen ground cover plant which is trouble-free and permanent but rather slow to become established. *P. t. variegatus* is similar but has light yellow blotches on the leaves.

Paeonia (paeony rose)
Paeonies require rich, deep soil and need to be left undisturbed to grow in large clumps. Plant them carefully in an open position 24 in. or more apart, preferably in September or October, although it is safe to do so until new shoots appear above the ground in March. They will not flower freely and may not flower at all if planted too deeply, and dormant buds should not be more than 1 in. below the surface. Feed with an organic fertiliser, mixed with fine soil or peat, either in September–October or February–March. Division needs skill and patience; always use a sturdy knife to separate the roots so that the pieces for planting have roots, and either eyes or buds, intact. Use only well

established plants for cut flowers, and leave the foliage on the plant until September. There are numerous double and single flowered varieties of *P. lactiflora* (Chinese paeony), mostly perfumed, all H 2–3 ft. and flowering from late May to late June. Good doubles are: 'Alice Harding', creamy-white; 'Cherry Hill', red; 'Duchesse de Nemours', white; 'Felix Crousse', carmine; 'M. Jules Elie', lilac-pink; 'Neomie Demay', flesh pink; 'Sarah Bernhardt', soft pink; 'Solange', salmon-rose; 'Wiesbaden' bluish-pink. Singles can be obtained in similar colours. *P. mlokosewitschii* (H 2 ft.), single yellow flowers in April. *P. officinalis*, which is taller and earlier flowering, has double white, pink, and red varieties.

Paeonia mlokosewitschii

Papaver (poppy)
All the varieties of *P. orientale* (the oriental poppy) are easy to grow in sun on well drained soil. They have huge flowers, up to 5–6 in. across, in May and June on stems which often need supporting. The roots are fangy and the foliage coarse and hairy. Cut back plants after flowering to promote new leaves and to avoid having a bare gap in the border in late summer. Propagate by division

of old plants or by root cuttings in February or March. The following varieties (all PD 18 in.), are recommended: 'Goliath' (H 3 ft.), crimson-red, does not need staking; 'Indian Chief' (H 3 ft.), deep browny-red; 'Marcus Perry' (H 3 ft.), the best scarlet, does not need staking; 'Perry's White' (H 2½ ft.), a good white; 'Salmon Glow' (H 24 in.), double, salmon-orange; 'Sultana' (H 2½ ft.), fine peach-pink.

Papaver orientale
'Perry's White'

Pasque flower: see **Pulsatilla**

Peltiphyllum
P. peltatum (H 18 in. PD 20 in.), pale pink clusters of flowers in spring followed by a canopy of umbrella-like leaves up to 3 ft. tall. A good waterside plant, forming a slowly creeping mat of roots. Divide or plant in February–March.

Penstemon
Only a few of this large and colourful genus are reliably hardy or long-lived. All like a fair amount of sun and light soil. Plants usually live three or four years, but seed is not difficult to raise in spring. P. barbatus (syn. Chelone barbatus) (H 24 in. PD 15 in.), salmon, red or pink tubular flowers dangling from slender spikes,

June–August; makes a low mat of evergreen leaves. P. deustus (H 18 in. PD 15 in.), yellowish-white flowers, June–August; grows rather like P. barbatus. There is a group of penstemons which are more suitable for summer bedding than borders. If started from young plants in spring they give a fine display from July–October, when cuttings should be taken to keep under glass until spring. They are useful for filling up gaps in borders in late spring, but are hardy only in very mild districts. A few others of similar habit are much hardier, but have smaller flowers. These include: P. hartwegii 'Firebird' (syn. schonholzeri) (H 24 in. PD 15 in.), bright scarlet-red trumpets on bushy growth, July–September; P. h. 'Garnet' (H 2½ ft. PD 15 in.), very deep red flowers, July–September.

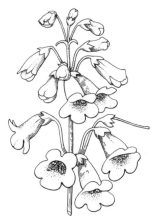

Penstemon barbatus

Periwinkle: see **Vinca**

Perowskia (Russian sage)
This shrub makes a good border plant, since it needs to be cut back annually to 1½–2 ft. in March or early April. Easy to grow where sunny. Propagate by

Perowskia atriplicifolia

cuttings in July. P. atriplicifolia (H 3½ ft. PD 20 in.), tapering, grey-leaved spikes of small but attractive lavender-blue flowers, August–October, on the current year's growth. P. 'Blue Haze' is similar, but has flowers of a lighter blue, which appear three weeks earlier.

Phlox
These indispensable plants are obtainable in a wide range of colours, and flower from July to September. They prefer a light, not too dry soil and respond well to a light mulching and feeding in April or May. Phlox are liable to be attacked by eelworms, which eat their way inside the stems, causing distortion, wilting and yellowing of the leaves, which becomes visible during the summer. There is no cure, so remove and burn the affected plants and do not plant phlox in the same ground for several years. Since top cuttings or divisions contain eelworms, propagate by root cuttings taken from the fibrous roots of healthy young plants. Do not plant woody plants deficient in fibrous roots, as these may be divisions of old or infected stock. A selection of the best modern varieties (PD 18 in.) are: 'Balmoral' (H 2½

ft.), rosy-lavender; 'Brigadier' (H 3 ft.), orange; 'Endurance' (H 2½ ft.), salmon-pink, red eye; 'Firefly' (H 3 ft.), pink, red eye; 'Gaiety' (H 2½ ft.), cherry-red; 'Little Lovely' (H 24 in.), light lavender, white eye; 'Marl-borough' (H 3 ft.), deep purple, dark foliage; 'Mia Ruys' (H 24 in.), dwarf white; 'Mies Copijn' (H 3 ft.), soft pink; 'Mother of Pearl' (H 2½ ft.), tinged pink, long-flowering; 'Prince of Orange' (H 3 ft.), orange-scarlet; 'Red Indian' (H 3 ft.), crimson-purple; 'Russian Violet' (H 3 ft.); 'Starfire' (H 3 ft.), bright crimson; 'White Admiral' (H 2½ ft.); 'Windsor' (H 24 in.), carmine-red.

Phlox 'White Admiral'

Phygelius (Cape figwort)
These shrubs are best grown in full sun and can be propagated by seed or by cuttings. P. aequalis (H 2½ ft. PD 18 in.), pendent buff-rose flowers, June–August; a little-known species. P. capensis (H 2½ ft. PD 18 in.), scarlet tubular flowers dangling from widely branched, dark-leaved spikes, July–September. Sub-shrubby, grows from slowly creeping roots.

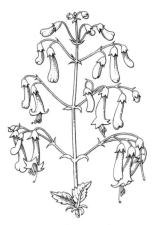

Phygelius capensis

Physalis (Chinese lantern, Cape gooseberry)

These plants require a rich soil and a sunny, well drained border. Plant in March or April, and propagate by seed or division in April. *P. franchetii* (H 2–3 ft. PD 15 in.), nondescript flowers on leafy stems, followed by ornamental, bright orange fruits in autumn. If left after November, the skins surrounding the fruits become skeletons. Roots run considerably but are not difficult to check. Useful for indoor decoration in winter.

Physalis franchetii

Physostegia (obedient plant)

If the close-set tubular flowers, on pyramidal spikes, are pushed to one side, they will stay in that position—hence the common name. These plants have shiny, dark-leaved stems, and the creeping roots spread fairly rapidly. Plant in sun or partial shade. Propagate by root division or by cuttings of young shoots in spring. The garden varieties originate from *P. speciosa* and *P. virginiana*: 'Rose Bouquet' (H 2½ ft. PD 18 in.), pinkish-lilac tubular flowers, July–September; 'Summer Snow' (H 2½ ft. PD 18 in.), white flowers, July–September; more slender spikes; 'Vivid' (H 18 in. PD 18 in.), deep rose flowers, August–September.

Physostegia virginiana 'Vivid'

Pink: see Dianthus

Plantain lily: see Hosta

Platycodon (balloon flower)

The white fleshy roots of these plants grow slowly, but platycodons will succeed in any well drained soil. Propagate by seed or by careful division of old plants. *P. grandiflorus* (H 1½–2 ft. PD 12 in.) has buds like little balloons opening into

Platycodon grandiflorus

light blue, pointed-petalled flowers, July–September; glaucous foliage. *P. g. mariesii* (H 10–15 in. PD 12 in.) is a deeper blue.

Polemonium (Jacob's ladder)

The common name of this plant refers to the double row of secondary leaves attached to the midrib. These plants are easy to grow in sun or a little shade, but some kinds are short-lived and become a nuisance when they

Polemonium

seed themselves. Divide in March. The best are: 'Blue Pearl' (H 12 in. PD 15 in.), sprays of flowers ½ in. across in May and June; *P. foliosissimum* (H 2½ ft. PD 15 in.), fine heads of lavender blue, June–September; 'Pink Dawn' (H 10 in. PD 15 in.), pale pink flowers, June–August, dark leaves; 'Sapphire' (H 18 in. PD 15 in.), light blue flowers in May and June.

Polygonatum

P. multiflorum (Solomon's seal) (H 3 ft. PD 10 in.), dangling white bells on arching sprays in May and June. Grows in any ordinary soil in cool shade. Divide the slowly-creeping rhizomes in October or November and plant horizontally 3 in. below the surface.

Polygonum campanulatum

Polygonum (knotweed)

All polygonums are easy to grow in sun or partial shade; they can be divided in February or March. The following are among the best of this large family which includes some weedy kinds: *P. affine* 'Darjeeling Red' (H 6 in. PD 15 in.), deep rose pink spikes, July–September, narrow leaves making a spreading mat. *P. a.* 'Donald Lowndes

'H 9 in. PD 15 in.), short, poker-like pink spikes, May–August and often in October as well; a rapid but not invasive spread of fingery leaves, which remain russet-brown all winter. This is an excellent carpeting plant, useful for planting under flowering shrubs. *P. amplexicaule atrosanguineum* (PD 22 in.), thin red spikes from June, when the plant is 18 in. high, until September, when it has reached 4 ft.; bushy growth; *P. a.* 'Firetail', is similar but scarlet-red. *P. bistorta superbum* (H 3 ft. PD 20 in.), clear pink bottle-brush spikes in May and June and often again in autumn. Makes spreading mats; needs moist soil. *P. campanulatum* (H 3–4 ft. PD 22 in.), covered from June–September with heads of shell-pink flowers; grows into quite a large bush where moist. *P. carneum* (H 24 in. PD 18 in.), a profusion of pink pokers, June–August; makes neat but strong tufts of shiny green.

Poppy: see **Papaver**

Potentilla
These plants grow best in full sun. Divide and plant in autumn or spring. *P.* 'Gibson's Scarlet' (H 10 in. PD 12 in.), floppy sprays of bright red flowers, June–September; strawberry-type leaves. 'Flamenco' (H 20 in. PD 18 in.) has larger flowers of similar colour, June–August. 'M. Rouillard' (H 18 in. PD 15 in.) has semi-double, mahogany-crimson flowers, 2 in. across, June–August. 'Tom Rollison' (H 18 in. PD 15 in.), flame orange flowers, June–July. 'Yellow Queen' (H 15 in. PD 15 in.), semi-double, pure yellow flowers, June–July. 'Wm. Rollison' (H 15 in. PD 12 in.), the best orange variety; semi-double flowers on loose sprays, June–August.

Poterium
P. obtusum (H 2½ ft. PD 18 in.) has pink, bottle-brush flowers,

June–August, with glaucous-green leaves. Does best in sun. Divide in October or March.

Prunella 'Loveliness'

Prunella (self-heal)
These dwarf, mat-forming plants are easy to grow in a sunny position and produce short spikes from June–August. Divide in October or March. *P. grandiflora* (H 12 in. PD 15 in.), pink spikes for a long period. *P. incisa* (H 9 in. PD 15 in.), purple spikes; *P.* 'Loveliness' (H 9 in. PD 15 in.) has pink, lilac and white forms.

Pulmonaria angustifolia
azurea

Pulmonaria (lungwort)
These plants make a bright display from March–May, and are easy to grow in shade or semi-shade. Divide in September or October. *P. angustifolia azurea* (H 9 in. PD 15 in.), sprays of small, brilliant blue, bell-shaped flowers; makes narrow-leaved clumps. 'Mawson's Variety' is somewhat shorter and flowers a little later. *P. saccharata* 'Bowles Variety' (H 10 in. PD 12 in.), sprays of red flowers in March and April, coarse heavy leaves. *P.* 'Pink Dawn' (H 12 in. PD 18 in.), pink and blue flowers in April and May; large, light green leaves spotted with silver-green.

Pulsatilla vulgaris

Pulsatilla
P. vulgaris (pasque flower) (H 8–12 in. PD 15 in.), attractive seed heads; hoary, chalice-like mauve, violet or crimson flowers, according to variety, in April and May followed by ferny greyish foliage. Needs lime and a sunny, well drained situation; does not divide successfully; sow seed outdoors as soon as ripe.

Pyrethrum (red ox-eye daisy)
These brightly coloured daisies are popular flowers for cutting;

often need supporting. They require light soil and full sun. Divide in March, June or July, discarding all but the non-woody rooted sections. Cut back soon after flowering (late June) so that the tall, dark green, carroty leaves make a neat mound; they will flower again if the plants are young. Recommended single varieties (all PD 16–18 in.) are: 'Bellarion' (H 2½ ft.), salmon-red; 'Brenda' (H 2½–3 ft.), cerise-pink; 'Bressingham Red' (H 2½ ft.), crimson-scarlet; 'Eileen May Robinson' (H 3 ft.), clear pink; 'Inferno' (H 24 in.), salmon-scarlet; 'Kelway's Glorious' (H 2½ ft.), crimson; 'Silver Challenger' (H 3 ft.), white. Recommended double varieties, usually less vigorous than the singles, are: 'Apollo' (H 24 in.), warm cherry-pink; 'Captain Nares' and 'J. N. Twerdy' (H 24 in.), deep red; 'Vanessa' (H 2½ ft.), pink, flushed gold in centre; 'Venus' (H 24 in.), clear shell pink.

Pyrethrum 'Brenda'

Ragwort: see **Ligularia**;
Senecio

Ranunculus (buttercup)
All these plants like sun and a well drained soil. Propagate by seed or division in autumn. *R. acris plenus* (H 24 in. PD 15 in.),

fully double yellow flowers, ½ in. across, on sprays in June and July. Mat-forming but not invasive; a widely grown species. *R. gramineus* (H 12 in. PD 12 in.), sprays of shiny yellow flowers on graceful stems, May–July; glaucous, grassy leaves.

Ranunculus acris plenus

Red ox-eye daisy: see Pyrethrum

Rhazya
R. orientalis (H 18 in. PD 16 in.) produces a large number of willowy stems and leaves tipped with clusters of small, starry, light-blue flowers, June–August. Easily grown and long-lived, it needs sun or partial shade. Divide in October or March.

Rodgersia
These are fine plants for moist soil and some shade. Propagate by seed or by division in spring. *R. pinnata* (H 3–4 ft. PD 20 in.), arching sprays of creamy-white flowers in June and July; large ornamental leaves, not unlike those of a horse chestnut. Stout roots, with slowly expanding crowns. *R. p. superba* has sprays of flesh pink flowers and bronzy-purple foliage.

Rodgersia pinnata superba

Rose of Sharon: see Hypericum

Rudbeckia (cone flower)
All rudbeckias, except the double-flowered varieties, have a central cone above the petals, which are inclined to droop. Plants need good, well drained, but not dry soil. Propagate by seed or by division in April. The older kinds are too tall for most gardens and it is the shorter kinds which are more highly recommended. *R.* 'Autumn Sun' ('Herbstsonne') (H 6 ft. PD 18 in.), yellow flowers, 3 in. across, in August and September. *R. deami* (H 2½ ft. PD 18 in.), similar to *R. speciosa* but flowers more freely and lasts from late July–October. *R.* 'Golden Glow' (H 6 ft. PD 20 in.), double lemon-yellow flowers from August–October; invariably becomes top-heavy and needs staking. *R.* 'Goldquelle' (H 3 ft. PD 18 in.), double chrome-yellow flowers on leafy bushes, August–October; neater than *R.* 'Golden Glow'. *R. purpurea* (syn. *Echinacea purpurea*, purple cone flower) (H 3–4 ft. PD 15 in.), flowers with rayed, rosy-

purple petals and a golden-hued cone, July–September; rough hairy leaves, slightly branched stems. 'Bressingham Hybrids' vary slightly in colour but grow erectly. 'The King', rosy-red flowers, is the best-known variety, but the stems do not always stand erect. 'Robert Bloom', reddish flowers, makes an upright bush. *R. speciosa* (black-eyed susan) (H 24 in. PD 18 in.), rayed, black-centred, yellow flowers, August–September; an old favourite. The variety 'Goldsturm' is similar, but flowers longer where the soil is good.

Rudbeckia 'Goldquelle'

Ruta (rue)
Plant in full sun and any well drained soil. Cuttings taken in March or April will root in a frame, but plants will not divide. Trim with shears in March. *R. graveolens* 'Jackman's Blue' (H 1½–2 ft. PD 15 in.), sulphur-yellow flower heads in June and July; blue-green aromatic foliage forms a neat dense bush.

Salvia (sage)
The members of this diverse genus are not difficult to grow in ordinary soil, either in sun or partial shade. *S. haematodes* (H 3–4 ft. PD 18 in.), full spikes of lavender-blue flowers, June–

August. A compact leafy plant; comes easily from seed. *S. superba* and its varieties are the most valuable for borders. *S. superba* (H 3½–4 ft. PD 18 in.), a profusion of erect branching spikes of small violet-blue flowers, June–August, which, if cut back as they die, will continue more or less all summer; stout and rather woody-rooted, but does not spread. Divide in spring or autumn. Varieties, all with violet-blue flowers, are: 'East Friesland' (H 18 in. PD 15 in.); 'Lubeca' (H 2–2½ ft. PD 15 in.); 'May Night' (H 18 in. PD 15 in.), a new, smaller variety which begins flowering in May. *S. turkestanica* (H 4 ft. PD 18 in.), white, pink-tinged flowers. Lives only two or three years; comes easily from seed.

Salvia superba

Saxifraga
S. fortunei (PD 12 in.), makes a canopy of copper-green foliage (purple-red in 'Wada's Variety'), 6 in. high throughout the summer, and then produces a sheaf of creamy-white flowers 12 in. high in October. Plant in good soil in a cool shady position.

propagate by division. In winter cover plants with leaves in cold districts. *S. umbrosa* (London pride) (H 12 in. PD 18 in.), makes evergreen carpeting rosettes and produces a good show of pink flowers in May and June. Grows in open positions or in dank or dry shady places where little else will thrive; propagate by division in spring.

Saxifraga umbrosa

Scabiosa (scabious)

These are deservedly popular plants, which provide blue flowers for cutting for many weeks from June onwards. They require an open position, light soil and lime. Plant in March. Old plants may die in patches, so divide a portion of a group every two years in March, using the younger sections. Mixed shades come from seed. Recommended varieties of *S. caucasica* are: 'Clive Greaves' (H 2½ ft. PD 18 in.), medium-blue, strong growing; 'Miss Willmott' (H 24 in. PD 15 in.), white; 'Moonstone' (H 3 ft. PD 18 in.), light blue; 'Penhill Blue' (H 3 ft. PD 18 in.), violet-blue. *S. graminifolia* (H 10 in. PD 10 in.), a profusion of lilac-blue pincushion flowers, June–September; greyish grassy leaves.

Scabiosa caucasica
'Clive Greaves'

S. g. 'Pinkushion' is similar but pink. *S. rumelica* (syn. *Knautia macedonica*) (H 24 in. PD 18 in.), short-stemmed, deep red flowers, June–September; makes a dense but sprawling bush.

Sea holly: see **Eryngium**

Sea lavender: see **Limonium**

Sedum (iceplant)

All these plants are easy to grow in mainly open positions and in ordinary soil; divide easily in March or April. *S.*

Sedum spectabile

rhodiola (rose root) (H 12 in. PD 15 in.), yellow flowers on small heads in May and June; blue-grey foliage on neat tufty growth. *S.* 'Ruby Glow' (H 10 in. PD 12 in.), very bright 2–4 in. heads of rosy-red flowers, July–September. *S. spectabile* (H 24 in. PD 15 in.), wide, round heads of pink flowers, up to 9 in. across, August–October; glaucous, fleshy foliage all summer. The best sedum for borders. 'Autumn Joy' (H 24 in. PD 18 in.) is the best variety, having even larger flower heads, changing from light pink to salmon and then finally to russet in late October; 'Brilliant' (H 18 in. PD 15 in.) is bright pink; 'Carmen' (H 18 in. PD 15 in.) is crimson-pink, and 'Meteor' is very similar.

Self-heal: see **Prunella**

Senecio (ragwort)

Both the following varieties are propagated by basal cuttings or division in April or May. *S. doronicum* 'Sunburst' (H 15 in. PD 15 in.), orange daisies, 2 in. across, in May and June on erect stems; grows best where moist. *S.* 'White Diamond' (H up to 20 in. PD 18 in.), the yellow flowers are of less consequence than the mounds of deeply cut, bright silver leaves which grow into a small bush by late summer; hardy in all but the coldest districts.

Sidalcea

These plants produce spiky flowers from June to September and mix well with flatter-headed kinds. All need a sunny position and can be divided in March. Cut back soon after flowering to encourage basal growth, which spreads slowly. Those under 3 ft. do not need staking. The following varieties (all PD 15 in.) are recommended: 'Croftway Red' (H 3 ft.), tapering spikes with rosy-red, open, mallow-type flowers, ½–1 in. across, June–August; 'Elsie Heugh'

(H 4 ft.), satiny pink, graceful; 'Oberon' (H 2½ ft.), large, rose-pink flowers, neat habit; 'Puck' (H 24 in.), clear pink, even neater; 'Rose Queen' (H 4 ft.), pink flowers, June–August, a robust plant; 'Wensleydale' (H 4 ft.), deep rose-red.

Sidalcea 'Rose Queen'

Solidago (golden rod)

These are easy plants in any soil if set in a fairly sunny position. Choose small varieties as some of the older tall varieties become weedy and invasive. Divide in February or March and thin out in May. 'Crown of Rays' (H 24 in. PD 18 in.), horizontal, bright yellow spikes on erect stems, July–August. 'Golden Gates' (H 3 ft. PD 15 in.), deep yellow plumed spikes in August and September. 'Golden Shower' is similar. 'Goldenmosa' (H 2½ ft. PD 15 in.), bunched spikes in August and September, bushily upright. 'Mimosa' (H 4 ft. PD 18 in.), deep yellow flowers in August and September; the best tall variety. 'Peter Pan' (H 3 ft. PD 18 in.), bright yellow, outward-branching spikes in July and August; grows stiffly. Dwarf varieties (H up to 12 in.) are: 'Cloth of Gold' (PD 18 in.),

Solidago 'Peter Pan'

full plumes of deep yellow in September and October; vigorous; 'Golden Thumb' (PD 12 in.), yellow flowers, August–October; more bushy with little spread; 'Laurin', similar to 'Cloth of Gold'; 'Queenie', similar to 'Golden Thumb'.

Solomon's seal: see **Polygonatum**

Speedwell: see **Veronica**

Spurge: see **Euphorbia**

Stachys
Most of these plants will thrive in any ordinary soil, and can

Stachys macrantha

easily be divided in March or April. *S. lanata* (lamb's ears, donkey's ears) (H 18 in. PD 15 in.), loose spikes of small pink flowers, June–August; makes mats of soft silvery leaves. Very easy to grow even where the soil is dry and poor, as is the non-flowering variety 'Silver Carpet', which makes excellent ground cover. *S. macrantha* (syn. *Betonica macrantha*) (H 24 in. PD 15 in.), dense spikes covered in bright rosy-purple lipped flowers, June–August; mat-forming plant. *S. nivea* (H 10 in. PD 12 in.), white flowers, June–September, contrast well with the dark green foliage; grows neatly. *S. spicata robusta* (H 18 in. PD 15 in.), leafy plant carrying many stiff, short, bright pink spikes, June–September.

Stokesia

Stokesia (Stokes' aster)
These plants grow best in full sun and light soil; divide in March or April. *S. laevis* (formerly *S. cyanea*) 'Blue Star' (H 15 in. PD 12 in.), branching sprays of 3 in. lavender-blue flowers, July–September; shiny, tongue-shaped leaves. *S. l.* 'Wyoming' is darker.

Sunflower: see **Helianthus**

Tellima
These plants are easy to grow and adaptable for sun or shade. Divide in September or February. *T. grandiflora purpurea* (H 24 in. PD 15 in.), greenish-gold sprays of flowers, May–June; rounded, purple-hued leaves make pretty mounds of greenery throughout the year.

Tellima grandiflora purpurea

Thalictrum (meadow rue)
These dainty plants, which vary greatly in height, prefer a rich moist soil; divide in March or April. All have attractive foliage, rather like maidenhair fern. *T. angustifolium* (H 5 ft. PD 18 in.), light yellow fluffy flowers on wide heads in June and July; grows stiffly. *T. aquilegifolium* (H 3–4 ft. PD 15 in.), clouds of mauve flowers, May–June. Varieties of this are: *T. a. album*, white; 'Dwarf Purple', purple-mauve; 'Thundercloud', deeper purple. *T. dipterocarpum* (H 4–5 ft. PD 15 in.), much branched and rather floppy sprays, with myriads of small, mauve, yellow centred flowers, July–September; usually needs staking; 'Hewitt's Double', a fine double-flowered, smaller variety; grows

Thalictrum dipterocarpum

slowly and needs rich soil and some shade. *T. flavum*, and its variety *glaucum* (H 5 ft. PD 18 in.), yellow flowers in June and July. *T. rocquebrunianum* (H 4–5 ft. PD 15 in.), rosy lilac flowers, ½ in. across, on branching sprays, June–July; fully erect with strong purplish-blue stems.

Thrift: see **Armeria**

Tiarella
These plants prefer a peaty or lime-free soil and a shady position which is not too dry. Divide in September. *T. cordifolia* (foam flower) (H 6 in. PD 10 in.), creamy-white flowers in May and June; golden-green leaves; spreads from runners.

Tradescantia
T. virginiana (trinity flower) (H 1½–2 ft. PD 15 in.), 1 in. wide three-petalled flowers opening on loose heads from June to early September above rushy dark green foliage. Easy to grow in sun or partial shade; requires a soil which is not too rich or moist. Divide in February or March. Varieties include: *T. v. caerulea flore plena*, one of the few doubles, sky blue; 'Isis', single, Oxford blue; 'Leonora',

Tradescantia virginiana 'Leonora'

 light blue; 'Osprey', large flowered, white with a centre crest;
'Purewell Giant', carmine-purple.

Trollius (globe flower)
Most of these plants, which
form compact fibrous clumps,
produce their globe-shaped buttercup-like flowers in May and
June and will flower again later
if cut back after flowering.
Require sun or only partial
shade and a good moist soil.
Divide in July or March.
Named varieties of *T. europaeus*
(all PD 15–16 in.) are: 'Canary
Bird' (H 2½–3 ft.), large canary-

Trollius 'Orange Princess'

yellow flowers; 'Earliest of All'
(H 24 in.), lemon-yellow; 'Fire-
globe' and 'First Lancers' (both
H 2½ ft.), very deep yellow;
'Orange Princess' (H 2½ ft.),
deep yellow; 'Prichard's Giant'
(H 2½–3 ft.), mid-yellow; *super-
bus*, similar to 'Earliest of All'.
T. ledebourii 'Golden Queen'
(H 2½–3 ft.), rich orange petals
which open to reveal a crest of
bright yellow stamens from late
June–August.

Venidio-arctotis
These tender hybrids are best
used as bedding plants in full
sun and ordinary soil. (H 24 in.
PD 10 in.) Increase by cuttings
only. Short-lived, daisy-like
flowers in shades of brown, red,
pink, orange and yellow are
produced in profusion, June–
October.

Verbascum 'Cotswold Beauty'

Verbascum (mullein)
These handsome spiked plants
grow from fangy roots and make
a tuft of large pointed leaves.
They need sun and good drainage, and can be increased only
from root cuttings taken in
February or March and placed
in a frame. *V. bombyciferum*
(syn. *V. broussa*) (H 4 ft. PD
12 in.), spikes of bright yellow

flowers, June–August; heavily
silvered foliage; a biennial
which will grow in any soil,
in sun or shade, and can be
increased only by seed sown in
March under glass. *V. chaixii*
(syn. *V. vernale*) (H 5 ft. PD
18 in.), tapering, branching
spikes of clear yellow, June–
August. *V. densiflorum* (H 4 ft.
PD 18 in.), clear yellow flowers,
June–August. Varieties flowering from June–August are:
'Cotswold' (H 3½–4 ft. PD 15
in.), with three variations,
'Beauty', 'Gem' and 'Queen', all
having flowers in varying suf-
fused shades of biscuit, terracotta, amber, purple and yellow
on branching stems; green leaves.

Veronica (speedwell)
Most herbaceous veronicas have
blue flowers and grow easily in
ordinary soil and mainly sunny
situations. Propagate by division
in autumn or spring and by seed
in spring. *V. exaltata* (H 4 ft.
PD 18 in.), small, mid-blue
flowers in August and September; pointed, saw-edged leaves
on slender tapering spikes. *V.
gentianoides* (H 24 in. PD 15
in.), spikes of light blue in May
and June; forms tufty mats of
shiny leaves. Easy in sun or
shade, it divides best in September or October. *V. incana*
(H 12 in. PD 15 in.), lax,
violet-blue spikes, June–August;
ash-grey mounded leaves; 'Wendy' (H 24 in. PD 15 in.) is similar
but less grey; stronger growing.
Varieties of *V. spicata* include:
'Barcarolle' (H 24 in. PD 12 in.),
deep pink spikes, July–September; green foliage; 'Minuet'
(H 18 in. PD 12 in.), clear pink
flower spikes, July–September;
grey leaves; 'Saraband' (H 20
in. PD 15 in.), violet-blue
spikes, July–September; free
flowering and erect. The following varieties of *V. teucrium* all
flower in June and July:
amethystina (H 24 in. PD 15 in.),
bright blue flowers; 'Blue Fountain' (H 24 in. PD 15 in.),
rich blue spikes; congested,

fibrous roots; makes sturdy
clumps; 'Crater Lake Blue' (H
12 in. PD 12 in.), very bright;
'Royal Blue' (H 18 in. PD 12 in.),
a little deeper in colour than
'Blue Fountain'; 'Shirley Blue'
(H 9 in. PD 10 in.), deep blue.

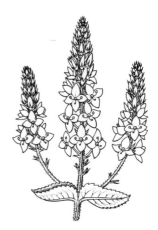

Veronica teucrium 'Royal Blue'

Vinca (periwinkle)
These plants will grow in any
ordinary soil and are useful
as ground cover in shady places.
V. major variegata (H 12 in.
PD 12 in.), sparse, light blue
flowers in May; brightly variegated leaves on stems which
will root down and become good
ground cover in time. Divide or
plant in October or March. *V.
minor* 'Bowles' Variety' (H 4–5
in. PD 12 in.), violet-blue
flowers in April and May; forms
dense clumps of dark evergreen
leaves. Spreads steadily; divide
or plant, October–November.

Viola
V. 'Norah Leigh' (H 6 in. PD
18 in.), good perennial variety
with light blue flowers, June–
September; clumpy growth.
Easy to grow; divide in March,
September or October.

Yarrow: see **Achillea**

Bulbs to plant in October

Bulbs provide some of the earliest and latest colour in the garden. Snowdrops and eranthis (winter aconites) bloom early in the New Year and are followed by crocus and early-flowering narcissi and tulips. In the late autumn outdoor cyclamens, colchicums and nerines add welcome colour to the shortening days. In this section corms as well as bulbs are included: a bulb is made up of fleshy scales, while a corm consists of a solid mass of starchy material.

Acidanthera bicolor

Allium neapolitanum

Alstroemeria aurantiaca

Amaryllis belladonna

Acidanthera
A. bicolor murieale. Height 2–3 ft. Strongly scented white flowers with purple blotch, August–October. Erect, gladiolus-like. Needs well drained soil and sheltered warm aspect in milder districts, or cool greenhouse in colder ones. Plant corms 2–3 in. deep, 4–6 in. apart, from March to May, according to district. Lift before sharp frosts occur, dry quickly, and store in dry, frost-free place. Corms should then flower year after year. Increase by growing-on the small cormlets which are produced round the base of the large corms. Plants raised from seeds will take 2–3 years to come into flower.

Allium
Bulbous plants, including leeks, onions and shallots. All have clusters of flowers at the top of thin stems; the erect leaves are rounded and hollow or thin and flat. All can be planted 2–3 in. deep in groups of half a dozen or more, 3–6 in. apart according to size. Leave to grow and flower year after year without moving. Increase by lifting and dividing the bulbs or plants soon after flowering, or by saving and sowing seed when it is ripe. *A. caeruleum.* Height 2–3 ft. Deep blue flowers, June to August. *A. moly.* Height 6–12 in. Yellow flowers, July. *A. neapolitanum.* Height 6–12 in. Whitish flowers, July. *A. nigrum.* Height 12-24 in. White and green striped flowers, May-June. *A. ostrowskianum.* Height 8–12 in. Rose-pink flowers, June. *A. roseum.* Height 9–15 in. Pink flowers, May. *A. schoeno prasum* (chives). Height 8–12 in. Purple flowers, May–July. The grass-like, tubular leaves are used for flavouring salads and egg dishes.

Alstroemeria
A group of plants with fleshy roots, and with small leaves from top to bottom of the flowering stems. Up to 50 or so flowers clustered at the top of the stems, June–August. Several species are available, and some colourful hybrids have been raised. Not entirely hardy particularly in colder districts but they have a better chance of survival if planted 8 in. or so deep in a warm sheltered spot and covered with a 6–8 in layer of straw in winter. Roots and shoots are easily damaged. Buy pot-grown plants and plant August–September then leave undisturbed for several years. *A. aurantiaca* Height 3–4 ft. Orange and yellow flowers. *A. ligtu.* Height $1\frac{1}{2}$–$2\frac{1}{2}$ ft. Pale pink, lilac, red or white flowers.

Anemone

Chionodoxa

Clivia

Colchicum

Convallaria

Crinum powellii

Amaryllis

A. belladonna (belladonna lily). Height 1½–2 ft. Three to six scented flowers to a stem; white, pale pink to deep rose, August–October. The strap-shaped leaves do not appear until late winter or early spring. Has large bulbs which will survive outdoors in most districts if planted at least 8 in. deep close to a south-facing wall. Grows well in the open in mild districts. Plant in July–August and leave undisturbed for several years.

Anemone

A group of mainly herbaceous and rock garden plants, also including the single de Caen and the double St. Brigid anemones, grown mainly from corms. Height 9–15 in. White, red, cerise or bluish-purple flowers; in the best conditions each plant has a succession of up to 20 flowers. In the mildest districts plant the corms 1–2 in. deep in June–August to flower October–May. Elsewhere plant in February–March to flower through the late spring and early summer. The corms will survive most winters in nearly all districts, but tend to die out after a few years.

Bluebell: see Scilla

Chionodoxa

A small genus of dwarf bulbs with bright blue, purple or sometimes white flowers produced in late winter and early spring. At their best when naturalised, but can be forced. Plant 1–2 in. deep in autumn in groups 3–4 in. apart. Leave pots or bowls in cool condition until the flowers are almost open, or these will be poor and leaf growth excessive. Increase by growing-on offsets. *C. gigantea.* Height up to 8 in. Flowers violet-blue with white centres; there is also a white variety. *C. luciliae.* Height 6 in. Flowers clear blue, white or pink.

Clivia

Height 12–18 in. Not hardy, but provide useful pot plants for home or greenhouse decoration. The strap-shaped leaves are evergreen and from 12–24 in. long. Clivias produce many open bell-shaped flowers, yellow, orange or red, in the late winter and spring, at the top of leafless stems. Pot clivias after flowering in containers that will allow them to remain for several years without disturbance. Water well and feed with liquid manure all the summer, after flowering, then reduce water and keep nearly dry until flower buds appear in the late winter. The variety *C. miniata* has scarlet and yellow flowers in spring and early summer.

Colchicum

A group of autumn-flowering plants with mauve or white flowers similar to crocuses. Plant the large corms 4 in. deep in July, preferably in a sunny spot where they can be left undisturbed for several years. If grown in pots, plant in July and stand in the open until flowers appear, then take inside. The leaves appear in the following spring, and in some cases are so large as to be obtrusive if planted in the company of smaller plants. *C. autumnale* grows wild in this country. Flowers up to 3 in. tall; lilac, purple and white, including some doubles. Narrow leaves 9–10 in. long. *C. byzantinum* produces up to 20 lilac-coloured flowers per corm in autumn, followed by broad leaves up to 15 in. long in spring. Has large corms. *C. speciosum* is similar, but has several varieties in a range of colours.

Convallaria (lily of the valley)

C. majalis. Height 6–9 in. Normally produces its bell-like white flowers in late April and May, but can be forced from specially prepared roots to flower at any time of the year. In addition to the common kind, there is a large-flowered variety and one with pinkish flowers. Leaves come immediately before

Crocus

Cyclamen

Dierama pulcherrimum

the flowers and then die down during summer. Plant in early autumn in partial shade and moist soil, adding leaf-mould, peat or other organic material. Leave undisturbed, but add more organic material each winter.

Crinum

A few of this genus from the tropics are near-hardy. Plant 6–8 in. deep in May in a south-facing border or large tub and water when soil is dry. Protect tops of bulbs in coldest period, or bring tubs inside for the winter. *C. bulbispermum*. Height 12–15 in. Flowers 3–4 in. across, up to a dozen on each stem, white inside, red outside, from midsummer onwards. Leaves 2–3 ft. long. Bulbs 3–4 in. across. *C. moorei*. Similar to *C. bulbispermum*, but with even larger bulbs. Has fewer, less colourful flowers, sometimes pure white, on taller stems. *C. powellii* is a hybrid between these two; flowers are pink to white.

Crocus

There are some 80 species and many varieties of these colourful autumn-, winter- and spring-flowering plants. They produce their yellow, purple or white flowers year after year without attention, if planted about 3 in. deep in early autumn in places where they need not be disturbed. Many kinds are useful in pots or bowls, provided they are not brought into the warmth of the house until the buds are showing colour. Plant in September–October as thickly as possible in bulb fibre in bowls, or in potting compost in pots with drainage holes, and place in the coolest available shed or outside against a north wall. Water in but do not saturate and do not allow to dry out. Move to a light cool position when the first signs of growth appear, and then indoors as colour shows. Plant out immediately the flowers finish, placing the whole bowlful 2–3 in. deep where they

Eranthis

can complete their leaf growth and then remain to flower year after year. Best places are rock gardens, or borders between but not completely sheltered by larger plants or shrubs. Plant fresh corms in the autumn in similar places, or in lawns and rough grass. The earliest spring kinds are best in well kept lawns, as their flowers are over and some leaf growth has been made by the first mowing.

Where permanent planting is required the lawn must be sacrificed, as mowing cannot start until the crocus leaves are beginning to yellow. Autumn-flowering: *C. byzantinus*, larger outer petals purple, inner smaller ones lilac. September–October. *C. kotschyanus*, lilac pink flowers, gold base, September. *C. speciosus*, many coloured varieties, September–October. Early spring-flowering: *C. biflorus*, several varieties, mostly white with streaks and flecks of purple or lilac, February onwards. *C. chrysanthus*, numerous varieties, mostly yellow but also purple and white, February. *C. laevigatus*, pale lilac, January. Spring-flowering: *C. tomasinianus*, several varieties, mostly shades of purple, March. *C. aureus*, shades of yellow, blue and purple, also white and striped, late February–April.

Cyclamen

Mediterranean plants propagated from seed and grown on by means of tuberous rootstocks. (The winter pot plants are varieties of *C. persicum*). The smaller hardy species grow in the open in autumn and spring, producing white, pink, deep rose or purple flowers. The leaves of most species are also attractive. Sow seed as soon as ripe in spring or early summer, in frames or pots; prick off when large enough to handle where they are to remain and flower. They grow in any good garden soil in the open, but are well suited to shade or semi-shade below trees or tall shrubs. *C. alpinum*. Height 3–4 in. Carmine flowers, October–November. *C. europaeum*. Height 4 in. Deep pink flowers, June–August. *C. neapolitanum*. Flowers rose-pink or white, from July until sharp frosts.

Daffodil: see Narcissus

Dierama

Hanging tubular flowers in clusters at the tops of tall, wiry stems, with grass-like leaves. Grow from large corms. Hardy in all but the coldest parts, best growing at the edge of a pond or through low-growing shrubs or herbaceous plants. Two species with several varieties, including some dwarf ones for small borders. *D. pendulum*. Height 3 ft. Flowers white, pink or purple, June–July. *D. pulcherrimum*. Height up to 4 ft. Flowers mostly purple and red, September–October.

Eranthis

E. hyemalis, the yellow winter aconite. Height 3–4 in. Buttercup-like flowers in February–March. The short foliage follows and dies down in early summer. Plant corms 2 in. deep in small clusters 3–4 in. apart in the rock garden, or in larger drifts in lawns. Also successful in moist soil in partial shade. The hybrid. *E. tubergeniana* has larger flowers on stronger stems

Erythronium dens-canis

Fritillaria

Galanthus

Erythronium (dog's tooth violet)

E. dens-canis. Height 4–8 in. Violet, purple and white flowers, March–May. The rounded leaves are attractively blotched and persist for some time after the flowers. Plant corms 3 in. deep in groups 6 in. apart in the rock garden, or at the front of the border, where they can remain undisturbed for years. *E. revolutum* is taller. 'White Beauty' (10 in.) has pure white flowers in March.

Eucomis (pineapple flower)

E. comosa. Height 24 in. South African bulb for a sheltered spot in a warm garden, or for the greenhouse. Greenish-cream and purple-spotted flowers, July–August, clustered round the top of purple-spotted stem. Broad, strap-shaped leaves, purple-spotted beneath. Plant the 2–3 in. diameter bulbs 5–6 in. deep in the open, or in deep pots in the autumn or early spring. Mulch outdoor bulbs in winter. Water lightly in winter, increasing water in spring and summer until after flowering. (Illustration, p. 22.)

Fritillaria

Spring-flowering plants of the lily family, with hanging, somewhat tulip-like flowers on leafy stems. They need thoroughly dry and warm conditions during their late-summer resting period, and ample lime in the soil to maintain non-acid conditions for their best growth. *F. imperialis* (crown imperial). Height up to 4 ft. Bronze, yellow and red flowers, April–May. Whorls of leaves, particularly near the top, from which the large nodding flowers appear. Plant the large bulbs 4–6 in. deep, 9 in. apart in early autumn. The leaves and stems die back soon after flowering and can be removed. In heavy, well limed soil undisturbed bulbs will flower annually for years; in lighter acid soil, or if disturbed by cultivation or transplanting, the bulbs will soon have to be replaced.

Galtonia candicans

Gloriosa

Hippeastrum

F. meleagris (snake's head fritillary). Height up to 15 in. Flowers mottled and veined in purple, green and white, April–early June. Thrive in riverside meadows. Best in similar garden conditions, where they can flower in short grass which need not be cut until July.

Galanthus (snowdrop)

The first of the bulbs to flower in the New Year. There are several species and numerous varieties, height 3–12 in., which can give a succession of blooms from November to March. All have the snowdrop shape, with white and green as the basic colours. A few are double. Bulbs will persist for years if planted 2–3 in. deep in grass or elsewhere where they will not be disturbed by cultivation. Move and re-plant just after flowering, before the leaves have died down. Usually bought in late summer; plant as soon as bulbs arrive. When grown in bowls or pots for Christmas plant in late summer and early autumn and keep cool until flower buds are showing. After flowering, plant bulbs in the garden.

Galtonia candicans

Height up to 4 ft. Hyacinth-like white flowers, July. The narrow leaves all grow from ground level, and spread up to 24 in. in length. Plant 6–8 in. deep, 12 in. apart in autumn in mild areas, or in spring in colder districts.

Gloriosa

A small group of lilies from the tropics, which produce yellow, red or purple flowers on climbing stems up to 6 ft. high in the summer. They can be grown outdoors in sheltered places, but are at their best in the warmth of a greenhouse or conservatory. Plant bulbs in well drained pots in February, give ample heat and water, and provide canes or trellis work for the plants to grow up. After flowering, the stems die back and the pots can be completely dried off by withholding water. Keep them

Hyacinthus

Ixia

Lachenalia

warm and undisturbed until they can be restarted into growth in warm and moist conditions in February–March.

Hippeastrum

Height 2–3 ft. There are some 70 species and many varieties of this magnificent greenhouse bulb. Large trumpet-shaped flowers in all shades of red, also white or striped white and green, February–May. To grow permanently requires a heated greenhouse, but a brilliant show of colour can be obtained from fully grown bulbs bought annually in the winter. Pot bulbs in John Innes potting compost No. 1, in 5 in. pots, leaving half the bulb above the soil level. Stand the pots in the warmth of a heated greenhouse, conservatory or warm room, and water well. Keep moist and warm for the rest of the growing period, which will cease in early autumn. The leaves will die down and water can be withheld until the following January.

Hyacinthus

Height 6–12 in. Hyacinths provide bold colour and scent from Christmas to Easter when grown in bowls or pots, and can also give fine displays in outdoor beds in March–April if planted in the autumn after the removal of the summer bedding plants. Flowers may be blue, purple, red, pink, white, cream or yellow. For winter flowering indoors, plant the bulbs from September onwards, singly in small 3 in. pots or as thick as they will go in larger pots or bowls. Use bulb fibre in bowls or pots without drainage holes at the bottom, and John Innes potting compost No. 1 in pots with drainage holes. Arrange the bulbs so that their tops are just showing above the top of the fibre or compost. Water, and keep cool and covered. Remove to a light position only when the leaves have emerged from the bulbs. Do not take into the warmth of a room until the leaves are spreading and the fat

Leucojum

Montbretia

Muscari

buds can be seen in their midst. For a succession of colour and scent, plant in bowls September–November and move into the house as the earlier flowers fade. After flowering, plant indoor and border hyacinths in odd corners of the garden, where they may flower for several years. They cannot successfully be lifted for forcing again in bowls or pots. Several smaller related species grow in the rock garden or narrow border. Plant them 2–3 in. deep in the autumn and leave them to flower.

Ixia

Height up to 18 in. Spikes of star-like flowers, red, pink, purple or white. Plant corms 2 in. deep, 2–3 in. apart, in October in mild districts for flowering April–May, and in the spring in most parts of the country for flowering June–July. Early flowers can be lifted in July–August and dried, cleaned and re-planted. Late flowering ones are unlikely to survive more than a year.

Lachenalia

Height up to 12 in. For a cool greenhouse or indoors. Flowers mostly yellow, but sometimes green, red, purple or bluish colours, carried on the top of bare stems. Leaves are strapshaped and tend to spread and hang down over the sides of the pots; many have purple spots and streaks on their glossy dark green surface. Pot bulbs in August–September, six or seven in a 5 in. pot, in John Innes potting compost No. 1. Water and keep cool until the cold weather comes, and then protect enough to keep out frost. Give no more water than is necessary to keep the soil just moist until the flower spikes appear, then water more generously until flowering is over. From then onwards reduce the water until about midsummer when the leaves will die down. Give no more water, but leave the bulbs until they are re-potted in August–September.

Leucojum (snowflake)

Like larger snowdrops, up to 18 in. high. Flowers mostly white or white and green, also one or two with pinkish flowers, April–May or September–October. Pink varieties need a sheltered site with well drained soil to survive. The rest grow well in almost all conditions, but do best in moist soils enriched with leaf-mould or peat, where they can be naturalised in the same way as snowdrops. Plant spring-flowering kinds 2–3 in. deep and 4–5 in. apart in early autumn, and autumn-flowering kinds in the summer.

Montbretia

Height 1–4 ft. Flowers orange, yellow or red, May–October, depending on the variety. Grow undisturbed in the milder parts of the country. In colder parts they need to be lifted in November before the sharpest frosts kill the corms. Plant 6 in. deep in early spring or in autumn in open spaces between but not under shrubs, or in mixed borders.

Muscari botryoides (grape hyacinth)

Height 6–12 in. Flowers generally blue, some white, February–June. Plant bulbs 2–3 in. deep and 4–6 in. apart as soon as available in late summer or early autumn. They shrivel and become mouldy if kept too long out of the ground. They will grow in any garden soil, but will increase rapidly in rich, well drained soil in milder districts. Lift the bulbs after the leaves die down in midsummer, and re-plant the numerous new bulbs at once. They can be left undisturbed for many years.

Narcissus

The botanical name for all the daffodils; also the common name usually given to the small-cupped single-flowered daffodils and those with two or more flowers on a stem. Over 1,000 varieties are commonly listed by specialist firms, ranging from tiny miniatures 1 in. across on 2 or 3 in. stems, to mighty trumpet daffodils with flowers 5–6 in. across on stems 18 in. or more in height. They are grouped in 11 divisions according to shape and colour, as follows:

Division I, trumpet narcissi. This is the group usually referred to as daffodils. Division II, large-cupped. Division III, small-cupped. Division IV, double. Division V, triandrus. Division VI, cyclamineus. Division VII, jonquilla. Division VIII, tazetta. Division IX, poeticus. Division X, wild species and varieties. Division XI, kinds which will not fit in elsewhere. Narcissi can be used for forcing, for bedding, for cutting and for naturalising. With different varieties and methods of cultivation, flowers are available from Christmas to the end of May. Narcissi are not the best of bulbs for forcing in bowls for indoor decoration, but a few, such as 'Cragford', 'Paper White' and 'Soleil d'Or', can be forced into flower long before Christmas. Place bulbs in bowls or pots in August–September, as close as possible and almost on the surface of the fibre or compost. Water and place in a cool dark place until the shoots appear, then take them straight into light, warm conditions where they will grow quickly into flower. Many of the miniatures can also be flowered indoors. They are best grown in potting compost, and the bulbs should be buried. Potted in September–October, they will flower from January onwards.

Early flowers of most of the larger narcissi can be obtained by forcing in pots or boxes. Pot or box in compost or good garden soil in September–October and place in a cool place under 6 in. of ashes. If the leaves are 2 in. or more in height after 6–8 weeks, remove the ashes and place the bulbs in full light in a greenhouse or frame. Keep the temperature low, at 7°C (45°F) for the first few

NARCISSUS (DAFFODIL)

Beersheba White

Mary Copeland (double)

Sun Chariot (large cup)

Liberty Bell (triandrus)

Frigid (small cup)

Peeping Tom (cyclamineus)

NARCISSUS (DAFFODIL)

Bulbocodium

Tittle Tattle (jonquilla)

Grand Soleil d'Or (tazetta)

Actaea (poeticus)

weeks, gradually rising to 13°C (55°F). Bulbs will then flower from Christmas to late February. The larger-flowered narcissi can give good displays in beds and borders in the early spring. Plant in September–October to provide colour until the summer bedding is planted out in early June. Remove the seed heads after flowering and lift the bulbs after the display has finished; line out the bulbs without damaging the leaves in a spare part of the garden, or plant them in shrub borders or elsewhere where they can remain and flower indefinitely. To produce high-quality flowers for cutting, narcissi are best re-planted every second or third year. The first year after planting the flowers are unlikely to be at their best; the second year should produce the best flowers; and in the third year there should be a large number of flowers of good quality.

Narcissi can also provide bright splashes of early spring colour in clumps between shrubs and herbaceous plants, and in less formal lawns. The smaller kinds, such as the cyclamineus narcissi, are valuable rock garden plants. Plant the larger bulbs which are to be left indefinitely 8–9 in. deep; this will allow cultivation to be carried out without harm to the bulbs. Plant smaller bulbs, 1 in. or less in diameter, 3–4 in. deep. Bulbs in grass mean that it cannot be cut until the bulb leaves are almost brown, and a lawn-like appearance cannot be achieved until late June or July, as the bulb leaves must be left to feed the bulbs in readiness for next season's growth.

Nerine
Height 18 in. Pink and red flowers, August–October. Only one nerine, *N. bowdenii*, is hardy. The rest are better as greenhouse or conservatory pot plants, although some of them will survive out of doors in the milder counties, in well drained soil at the foot of a south-facing wall or in some other warm sheltered situation. In winter, cover the bulbs with a layer of ashes or straw to protect them from sharp frosts. Plant in summer 3–4 in. apart, just covering the bulbs with soil. Do not lift or re-plant unless the bulbs become crowded. Under glass, plant the bulbs in July, almost touching in 6–12 in. pots, and half cover them with compost. Water when the flower buds appear. Keep watered until the flowers finish and the leaves, which follow the flowers, begin to die down. Then keep dry until new growth appears.

Ornithogalum
O. thyrsoides (chincherinchee). Height 18 in. White or yellow flowers, June. Suitable for a warm protected border. Lift bulbs and store in dry warmth during winter; re-plant March–April. For indoor display, plant in pots in February, keep in the dark for six weeks, then place in full sunlight. Water once a week. *O. umbellatum* (star of Bethlehem). Height 6–8 in. Six-petalled star-shaped white

Nerine

Ornithogalum

Polianthes

and green striped flowers in early summer. Does well outside in poor soil.

Polianthes (tuberose)

P. tuberosa. Height 3–4 ft. Highly scented white flowers, produced at almost any time of the year in a heated greenhouse or conservatory. For a cool or unheated greenhouse, buy the imported tuberous roots in the spring and plant a few at a time, three in a 6 in. pot or one in a 4 in. pot, in John Innes potting compost No. 1. Do not water until the shoots are well above the soil; then keep well watered until flowering is over. Tuberoses planted in April will take 8–10 weeks in warm summer conditions. The stems need canes to support them. The roots will be of little use the next year.

Schizostylis

S. coccinea. Height up to 3 ft. Many star-shaped red or pink flowers in October–November. Resembles an upward-facing gladiolus. Hardy only in the south-west. The erect narrow leaves last almost the year round and grow from small corm-like rootstocks. Split the clumps of plants in the spring, planting in groups 6 in. apart, in rows 18 in. apart, or in small clusters of two or three plants 9 in. apart. Leave to flower for two to three years before moving.

Scilla (bluebell)

Mainly spring-flowering, dwarf blue-flowered plants. Includes the common bluebell, *S. nutans,* which is at its best in partial shade and deep soil containing ample supplies of leaf-mould. *S. hispanica.* Height 6–9 in. Blue, pink or white flowers, May. Thrives in drier, warmer conditions. *S. sibirica* and *S. tubergeniana.* Height 6 in. Several wide-open, bright blue flowers on each stem. Can be used as pot plants for flowering from January onwards. Plant in bulb fibre in bowls or in potting compost in pots in September–October. Keep moist but cool

Schizostylis

Scilla

Sparaxis

until the leaves and buds are showing. Then take into the greenhouse or lightest part of a room. Plant out bulbs after flowering, and leave undisturbed for several years. Plant new bulbs in the autumn 2 in. deep and 2–3 in. apart in groups of half a dozen or more.

Snowdrop: see Galanthus

Sparaxis

Height 1½–2 ft. Six-petalled flowers, white through yellow and red to purple, often striped, April–July. They need hot dry conditions during the summer and are at their best in the lighter soils of the south-west of England. Can be grown in pots under glass or against south-facing walls in less favoured parts of the country. Plant 4–6 in. deep, 2–3 in. apart, in November in mild districts; or use prepared corms for planting in the same way in March in colder districts. Will not survive a second winter unless lifted and dried soon after flowering, since early growth will be killed by winter frosts. In colder areas it is usually necessary to buy new corms each year.

Sternbergia

S. lutea. Height 8 in. Yellow crocus-like flowers in September–October. Long narrow leaves which grow with the flowers. Useful for permanent planting in short grass which will not need cutting from flowering time until the spring, but which can then be cut without fear of damage to leaves. Plant the bulbs 6 in. deep in irregular groups 4–8 in. apart.

Triteleia (spring starflower)

T. uniflora. Height 6–10 in. Single pale lilac or blue flowers on slender stems, March–May. Plant small bulbs 3 in. deep in autumn in large groups 2–3 in. apart, between shrubs or among alpines in the rock garden. They should then flower for several years without being lifted. (Illustration, p. 13.)

Sternbergia lutea

Tritonia crocata

Tritonia

T. crocata. Height 12–24 in. Striking orange or red flowers in June–July. Only grows outdoors in warm sheltered situations or in the extreme west of England; best in pots in greenhouse or conservatory. Plant in late autumn at six to a 6 in. pot. Give little or no water until the growth is showing in the spring, then water well through the flowering season. When the leaves begin to die off, shake out and dry the corms, or leave in their pots for the rest period.

TULIPA

Golden Ducat (early double)

Keizerskroon (early single)

Parrot tulip

Aladdin (lily-flowered)

Vallota

Zantedeschia

Tulipa

Garden-raised tulips are grouped into several divisions according to time of flowering, height, shape of flower and whether self-coloured or striped. Flowers range from white through various yellows, pinks and reds to dark purple, April–June. The most useful of the groups are the single and double early tulips, which flower outdoors from mid-April and grow about 12 in. tall; the triumph tulips, which flower towards the end of April and are taller than the earlies but not as tall as the later ones; the lily-flowered tulips, with pointed petals which are usually reflexed or bent outwards at the top of the flower; cottage tulips, whose flowers are rounded or angular with a more or less flat top to the flower; darwin tulips, in which the base of the flower is rounded but the top is pointed.

There are also parrot tulips and various other hybrids. The parrots have wavy edges to the petals, which are also roughened and puckered. The single and double early tulips can make useful room plants from Christmas onwards. Plant bulbs in September in pots or containers under ashes or peat until shoots are 2–3 in. tall, then remove to warmer conditions in partial light from November onwards.

Keep well watered, but do not raise temperature above 16°C (61°F) until buds are showing among the leaves, and not above 18°C (64°F) at any time. For outdoor flowering, plant 4–6 in. deep, 5–6 in. apart in beds in October or November. Bulbs of a single colour are usually most effective in each bed, but striking contrasts can be obtained by planting two varieties with the same height and time of flowering. Few tulips survive for long if left year after year without lifting. The exceptions are the species such as *T. clusiana*, *T. fosteriana*, *T. greigii*, *T. kaufmanniana* and *T. praestans*. Plant bulbs of these and similar kinds 4–6 in. apart, 3–5 in. deep in groups in November, where they can be left undisturbed.

Vallota (Scarborough lily)

Height 18 in. Flowers scarlet, sometimes other shades of red, or white, July–August. The strap-shaped leaves are evergreen. Plant the bulbs in June, in 6–8 in. pots, just below the surface, in John Innes potting compost No. 1. Keep just damp in the autumn and winter, but use increasing amounts of water and liquid fertiliser in spring and summer. Leave undisturbed.

Zantedeschia (arum lily)

Height 1½–4 ft. Flowers white, yellow and various shades of red, in spring. The common arum (*Z. aethiopica*) is usually grown as a greenhouse plant, but can be grown in the open in the milder parts of the country and as a water plant in all but the coldest parts. Set out pot-grown plants in April, placing the corms 4–6 in. deep in rich soil, which must be kept moist at all times, or tie the plants in a weighted basket and drop into a pond or pool where the water is 12–24 in. deep. Pot-grown plants flower throughout the winter and spring in heated houses. They can then be stood in their pots or planted out in rich garden soil from June to September, when they are re-potted into large pots.

November

In spite of cold, raw days and frequent fog, this is a good month for planting shrubs and herbaceous plants, and for clearing up before the winter

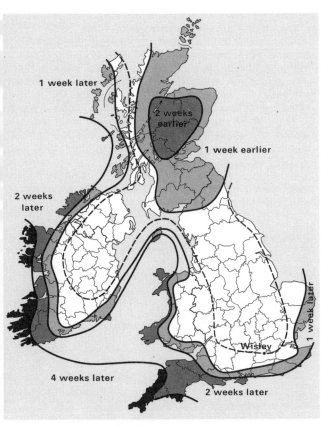

PROGRESS OF THE SEASON

The advantage of warmer conditions in the south-west is pronounced in November: the onset of winter weather lags well behind there. The map shows the earliness or lateness of the season in an average November at places in the British Isles, compared with the Royal Horticultural Society's Gardens at Wisley. The broken line joins places where the season is as advanced as at Wisley. Gardeners in the white areas should usually begin their November gardening programme at the beginning of the month. Gardeners to the north-east, where the season is more advanced, should start the programme earlier. In the west, gardeners can delay their programme, as indicated

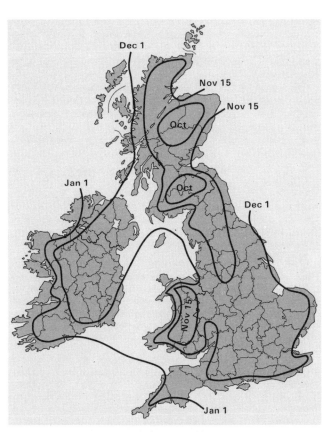

THE ARRIVAL OF WINTER

Autumn ends when plants begin their period of winter dormancy. Most plants cease to grow when the daily mean temperature falls below 6°C (43°F), and the map shows the dates in an average year when this happens. In much of lowland England and Ireland this occurs during the latter half of November, although frosts may have curtailed growth before this time. Winter comes earlier in the north, but much later in the south and west. As a rough guide, gardeners should aim to finish their November programme by the date given for their area. However, in the hills and on north-facing slopes winter arrives about two days earlier for every 100 ft. rise in height

317

The weather in November

November is often one of the wettest months of the year, but like the previous month, it often relents slightly for a few days to give us a last glance of summer sunshine.

The general weather brought by depressions in November is much the same as in October, but the shorter days and weaker sun result in lower temperatures. Rainfall may be heavier in the west than in October, and gales are often more frequent. Southerly airstreams may bring fog and mist, particularly to the built-up areas of the midlands and to south-east England, especially after a drier spell of cold easterly winds.

An onslaught of northerly winds in November will bring snow to all the northern hills. Snow can also fall over lower ground, but is unlikely to last for more than a few days before a return to milder conditions causes it to melt away.

Fogs are common. Anticyclones—which in summer bring the hottest days—are often responsible for these cold, raw spells. Fog forms inland during a cloudless, still night, and the sun may be too weak and not have enough time to clear it during the following day. If the still, calm conditions of the anticyclone persist, the fog may last for several days. It is densest in low-lying, sheltered valleys and in smoke-laden city air. This may be some slight help to the gardener, for a layer of fog often prevents temperatures from falling below freezing point. If the air is drier and no fog forms, hard frosts can occur in November.

Good gardening days are rare this month, which is all the more reason for taking the fullest advantage of the few suitable days. Clearing-up should be in full swing. The gardener should collect leaves for compost, but burn diseased leaves. Good garden hygiene in autumn can prevent many a disease outbreak the following summer.

A summary of the month's work

LAWNS

New lawns. Prepare sites for sowing next spring.
Established lawns. Complete laying of turf. Continue aeration. Apply autumn fertiliser. Make final cut, and bring in mowing machines for overhaul. Continue treatment against earthworms.

ROSES

Plant out roses, after preparing a planting mixture containing bone-meal and peat or other humus-forming material. Heel in plants which cannot be planted straight away. For standard roses, drive in a stout stake and secure near the head of the rose.
Under glass. Pot roses for flowering next April and May, and leave them outside in the garden until December.

HARDY HERBACEOUS PLANTS

Finish digging new beds and borders for winter weathering. Plant tops cut off now may be composted if cut into 6–12 in. lengths. New plants delivered late may still be planted in mild weather. Take precautions against slugs. Pack away supporting canes in a dry place. Begin digging between border plants on heavy soil to permit winter weathering. Collect fallen leaves lying on plants and use them for leaf-mould or to protect tender plants.

DAHLIAS

Examine stored tubers and plunge them in a bucket of tepid water overnight if they have shrivelled. Cut away portions of tubers that have rotted and dust the cuts with captan or flowers of sulphur.

CHRYSANTHEMUMS

Keep beds clear of weeds. Drain waterlogged stools outdoors by piercing soil deeply with a garden fork.

Under glass. Keep dormant stools moist and give full ventilation. Keep temperature for flowering varieties to 10°C (50°F). Dust with captan weekly to protect flowers. After flowering, cut stems back to 6 in. to encourage basal growths for cuttings. Late-flowering decoratives in the greenhouse border need a night temperature of 10°C (50°F). Water regularly and control leaf miners.

GLADIOLI

Clean the corms some time between drying-off and planting. Store cormlets separately if they are to be grown on. Dust corms with malathion or HCH against thrips if necessary. Discard corms diseased with dry rot, hard rot, fusarium rot or botrytis. Select the site for next year's gladioli, dig it over and incorporate manure or compost, and some bone-meal.

IRISES

Watch for buds on established plants of *I. unguicularis* and pick the flowers before birds damage them.

LILIES

Plant late-delivered bulbs if the ground is still easily worked.
Under glass. Pot bulbs which cannot be planted outdoors, or set them in trays of damp peat. Keep the trays frost-free and protect from mice, slugs and aphids.

CARNATIONS AND PINKS

Plant border carnations and pinks in mild weather. Test soil for lime content and add lime if below pH 6·5. In mild spells firm soil around plants loosened by frost. Clear rubbish from around stems

and make sure stakes and ties are secure. Protect plants against birds, using black cotton. Watch for signs of rust and the grubs of carnation flies. Order plants for setting out in March, and prepare beds.

Under glass. Maintain a temperature of 7°C (45°F) for perpetual flowering carnations, and give some ventilation at all times. Water and feed sparingly, cutting blooms and disbudding flower stems. Dust against rust and aphids.

SWEET PEAS

Prepare next season's planting site by double-digging. Apply 3–4 handfuls of bone-meal per sq. yd. to the top spit.

Under glass. Prick out seedlings from October sowings into 3 in. pots and grow on slowly.

FLOWERS FROM SEED

In suitable weather, plant out hardy perennials raised from seed. Dig beds to be used for annuals next year, working in a dressing of well rotted manure or compost. Send for seed catalogues to plan bedding programme.

BULBS

Complete planting of tulips and hyacinths.

Indoors and under glass. Examine pots and bowls of bulbs and move inside any with 1 in. shoots, placing them in cool conditions not exceeding 10°C (50°F). Give sufficient water. 'Paper White' and 'Soleil d'Or' narcissi may be taken straight into warmer conditions in a room or warm greenhouse.

ALPINES

Complete trimming and dead-heading, saving seeds if desired. Remove fallen leaves from the rock garden. Plant shrubs, heathers and pot-grown plants. Dress surface of level ground with small shingle or stone chippings, $\frac{1}{2}$–1 in. deep, or prick over the surface soil with a fork.

WATER PLANTS AND POOLS

Finish preparing for winter by removing old leaves and thinning oxygenating plants. Leave foliage on marginal reeds and rushes as a protection against severe weather. Protect the pool against falling leaves by covering it with small-mesh netting. Overhaul pumps used for waterfalls and fountains, removing submersible types from the water and storing them in a dry place.

GREENHOUSES AND FRAMES

Ventilate house freely on sunny days. Wash the glass to admit maximum light. Close house during foggy weather. Complete remaining potting, moving annuals and rooted cuttings into 3 in. pots. Store achimenes, fuchsias, heliotropes and hydrangeas under greenhouse staging after they have been dried off. Pinch back solanum shoots where they hide the berries. Control white-fly with HCH. Give cinerarias more space and keep them free from aphids. Lift hardy plants for gentle forcing. Water over-wintering annuals sparingly.

TREES AND SHRUBS

Continue planting deciduous trees and shrubs in fine weather. Protect tender species such as campsis and garrya with a screen of wire netting and bracken, or make a windbreak of stout poly-thene tied to three or four stakes.

Propagation. Take hardwood cuttings of ivy, poplar and ribes and insert in a cold frame or in the open ground. Layer firm young shoots of actinidia in pots sunk round the parent plant. Re-firm cuttings lifted by frost.

Propagation under glass. Take heel cuttings of winter jasmine and insert in a cold frame.

RHODODENDRONS AND AZALEAS

Spray buds with a bird deterrent. Continue planting in fine weather. Lift and pot small plants suitable for indoor decoration. After flowering, re-plant them outdoors.

HEDGES

Prepare hedge sites if not already done, and complete planting as soon as possible. Heel in plants if site is not ready for them

HEATHERS

Continue planting. Firm newly planted heathers lifted by frost and remove any weeds.

FRUIT

Plant fruit frees and bushes. In inclement weather, store trees in a frost-free shed or heel them in outdoors. Soak dry tree roots before planting. Plant firmly and at the same depth as the trees were in the nursery. Prune fruit trees after planting. Complete work on heavy soils. Clear weeds from around established trees and bushes. Start winter pruning established trees, but do not prune cherries, peaches, nectarines, plums or damsons. Check that ties are not cutting bark. Cut out cankers and control woolly aphis with malathion. Inspect stored fruit, and ripen pears at room temperature.

VEGETABLES

In the south, sow broad beans outdoors for an early crop.

Under glass. Apply a pre-emergence weedkiller to broad beans sown under cloches. In the south, complete sowings of lettuces. Force chicory under staging in a warm greenhouse.

Less common vegetables. Trim the outer growths of globe artichokes and draw soil round the crowns. To increase stock of globe artichokes, detach suckers from the plants, and grow on in pots in a cold frame or cold greenhouse until planting out in April.

HERBS

Clear basil, chervil and dill; also fennel and parsley which have grown for a second season. Dig over the cleared ground. Cover September-sown parsley and chervil with cloches.

PATIOS AND TOWN GARDENS

Plant trees and shrubs in containers, choosing compact varieties and using tubs with broad bases.

HOUSE PLANTS

Try to avoid drastic fluctuations of temperature. Reduce watering so that soil surface is almost dust-dry, but roots are slightly moist. Use fertiliser only on plants in flower or growing strongly. Give plants plenty of light, but do not leave them so close to a window that they can be damaged by night frosts.

GENERAL TASKS

Lift fuchsias, begonias and geraniums, and bring inside. Dig vacant ground and leave it rough for the frost to break down. Dress heavy soil with lime. Plant trees and shrubs arriving from nurseries. If weather is not fit for planting, heel them in. Clear up fallen leaves and cut down herbaceous plants to 18 in. above soil level.

Plants to enjoy in November

Border and rock garden plants in flower Cyclamen alpinum Galanthus (snowdrop) Gentiana farreri Gentiana sino-ornata Nerine bowdenii Schizostylis coccinea	**Trees and shrubs with colourful fruits** Amelanchier Arbutus Aucuba Berberis rubrostilla Callicarpa Chaenomeles Cotoneaster	**House plants in flower, depending on position and culture** Aphelandra Begonia semperflorens Cyclamen persicum Euphorbia pulcherrima (poinsettia) Impatiens petersiana Saintpaulia Saxifraga stolonifera
Shrub in flower Jasminum nudiflorum (winter jasmine)	Crataegus (hawthorn) Euonymus Malus Pernettya	
Trees and shrubs with colourful foliage Acer (maple) Amelanchier Berberis thunbergii Callicarpa Cornus kousa Cotoneaster adpressa Ginkgo Hamamelis Lindera benzoin Viburnum	Pyracantha Skimmia japonica Sorbus Symphoricarpos (snowberry) Viburnum **Greenhouse plants in flower** Abutilon Capsicum Cineraria	**Vegetables in season** Artichoke, Jerusalem Brussels sprouts Cabbage Carrots Chicory Marrow Parsnip Radish Spinach beet Swede Sweet corn

Lawns

NEW LAWNS

Try to complete laying turf this month, though laying can continue during the winter if the weather remains favourable.

Prepare for sowing

Prepare the ground for sowing a new lawn in the spring. Ideally, the site should be dug over two spits deep, but the area covered by the average lawn and the need to press on with other jobs makes this hardly feasible.

Thoroughly dig the ground, turning clods of old rough grass face downwards, and removing the roots of perennial weeds such as bindweed and couch grass. Leave the ground for the frosts to break it down, and wait until spring for making the final seed bed preparation (see MARCH).

Dig in well rotted manure or sewage sludge.

Levelling a sloping site

If your garden is on a slope, you may want to level off the site. First remove the topsoil and heap it up to one side, preferably on a large plastic or canvas sheet. A gentle slope can be levelled off by eye, or by using a long piece of wood as a straight-edge. A steep slope will need terracing. Do this by the cut-and-fill method. Begin at a point half way down the slope, and take subsoil from the upper half of the area down to the lower half, until the area appears level. When the main bulk of the work has been done, drive in pegs and check that the site is perfectly level by means of a plank and a spirit level. Finally replace the topsoil.

After terracing, you may be left with steep banks above and below the site. Such banks are difficult to mow, and it is better not to grass them, but to build retaining walls of brick or rockery stone and plant with alpines.

ESTABLISHED LAWNS

Continue drainage operations if the weather is suitable (see OCTOBER), and continue aeration treatment (see SEPTEMBER). Apply an autumn fertiliser if not already done (see SEPTEMBER).

Bring mowing machines in for overhaul, as in most cases the final cut for the winter will have been made.

Continue treatment for earthworms (see OCTOBER). Chlordane will also control leatherjackets.

Roses

Prepare the ground for planting if this was not done last month (see OCTOBER). This is the best time to plant roses, as the soil still has sufficient warmth to encourage root growth.

Heeling in

Roses which cannot be planted at once will come to no harm if left in the nurseryman's packing for up to a week. If planting has to be delayed still longer, remove the plants from the package, separate them, and heel them in by digging out a shallow trench sufficiently deep to contain the roots and 3 in. of the stems. Water the roots, replace the soil and firm it in.

Planting preparations

When planting can be carried out, first stand the roots in a bucket of water for an hour. Then mark out the planting positions with canes. (For distances see colour section, AUGUST.)

Prepare a planting mixture comprising a large handful of bone-meal to a 2 gal. pail of moist peat or a proprietary organic compost. This is sufficient for five roses.

Using sharp secateurs, cut off any leaves, blooms, fruits and twiggy side shoots; also cut back damaged roots and roots more than 1 ft. long.

Planting procedure

Dig out the first hole, placing the soil where the last rose will be planted. Make the hole wide enough to take the spread-out roots and of such a depth that the point where the green stems emerge from the brown rootstock is 1 in. below the level of the surrounding soil.

Mix a double handful of the planting mixture into the soil at the bottom of the hole and draw the soil up into a low mound in the centre. Sit the rose on the mound and spread out the roots. Cover

PLANTING A ROSE

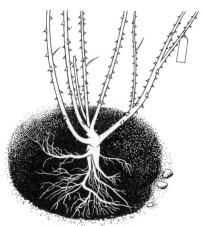

1. Dig a hole wide enough to take the spread-out roots without cramping or twisting them

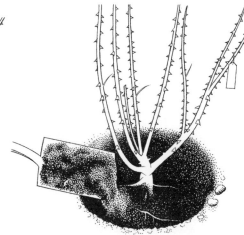

2. Shake the plant gently to ensure that the planting mixture settles between the roots

3. When the hole is partly filled, tread lightly to firm the soil over the roots

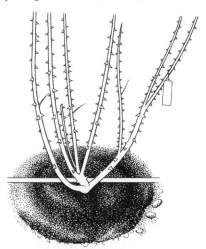

4. After firming, check that the union of stem and rootstock is 1 in. below soil level

the roots with planting mixture and loose soil, ideally using the soil that has been kept dry under cover for this purpose, as advised in OCTOBER.

Partially fill in the first hole with soil taken out to make the second planting hole. Firm in the rose by treading lightly inwards from the outside, keeping the correct planting depth, then fill in the hole level with the surrounding soil by taking more soil from the second hole. The second rose can then be planted.

321

HEELING IN BEFORE PLANTING

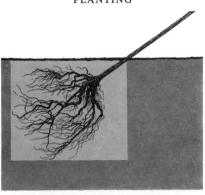

If rose planting has to be delayed for more than a week after delivery, remove the packaging, separate the roots, and set the plants outdoors in a trench. Insert standard roses at an angle to minimise wind resistance

Continue planting round the bed, filling each hole with the soil taken out to make the next hole.

Do not plant standard roses deeper than the old soil mark on the stem. Standards vary in height, so do not attempt to bring the tops level by planting some more deeply than others. First drive in a stout stake, at least 1 in thick, on the side from which the prevailing wind blows. Use a proprietary plastic strap to secure the top of the stake, which should be just below the head of the rose, to the main stem of the standard rose.

Planting climbers and ramblers

Do not plant climbing and rambling roses less than 15 in. from a wall or fence. To avoid dryness at the roots, slope the roots away from the wall. When planted, fan out the main stems and tie them loosely in position with garden twine.

When roses are being replaced in old beds that have grown roses for more than 15 years, fill in the planting holes with fresh soil taken from another part of the garden where roses have not previously been growing.

UNDER GLASS

If a greenhouse or glass conservatory is available in which to grow roses to flower in pots next April and May, now is the time to pot them up. Use either

TRAINING A WEEPING STANDARD

A wire training frame is necessary for weeping standards with stiff growth. Pull the shoots through the top and tie down

9 in. clay or plastic pots or the cheap fibre pots which are made specially for roses and which last for at least a year.

Cover the drainage holes with pieces of broken plant pots or slates and place 1 in. of peat and bone-meal planting

PLANTING A ROSE IN A POT

Cover the drainage hole of a 9 in. pot with broken pottery or slate, placing a layer of peat, mixed with bone-meal, on top

Before setting the rose in the pot, cut straggly roots back to about 6 in. This pruning is best done with secateurs

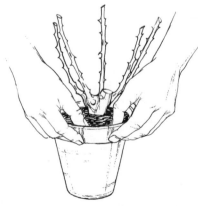

Pot the roses in John Innes potting compost No. 2, filling the container to within 1 in. of the top. Firm evenly over the roots

mixture on top. Prune the roots back to 6 in. and pot the rose into John Innes potting compost No. 2, filling the pot to within 1 in. of the top. Leave the potted roses outside in the garden, standing them on a base of concrete or ashes, until next month.

Hardy herbaceous plants

Finish digging new beds and borders where winter weathering is needed, using the same method as for autumn planting (see JULY), and continue to tidy existing borders and cut down tall plants.

Making compost

Dead tops of non-shrubby plants cut off now still have some sap left in them and make better compost than if left until fully dried off. If compost is needed, chop the tops into 6–12 in. lengths with a spade, and place in layers with damp peat or soil, adding either a rotting compound or sulphate of ammonia. Then tread the heap down firmly and cover with a final layer of soil. If dead tops are burnt, the ash is of little fertilising value.

If delivery of new plants has been delayed for some reason, it is still safe to plant them (see OCTOBER) as long as the soil is light and not inclined to pan down with treading.

Mild autumn weather encourages slugs, so take precautions against them (see MARCH).

Pack away support sticks or canes in a dry place to use again next year.

Winter dig heavy soil

On heavy soil that needs winter weathering, begin winter digging between plants in the middle of the month, provided the weather is mild and the ground is not sticky. The frost will reduce the rougher surface and restore it to a good texture by the spring. Use a flat-tined potato fork rather than a spade, except on the lightest sandy soils, and insert it obliquely so that its wide tines turn over a neat wedge of surface soil, burying any weeds, such as annual grass, nettle and chickweed, in the process.

Bury annual weeds

Take out only one or two forkfuls as you begin at one end of a bed or border, and work backwards, filling up each hole in turn with subsequent forkfuls. At the same time pick out weeds growing close to the plants and hook them with the points of the fork into the vacant hole, to ensure that they are buried. There is no need to dig more than 3 in. deep in the open spaces between the plants, and less if there are no weeds. Deep digging may harm the plant roots, which, if exposed during the digging, should be covered again with a little clean soil. Do not bury deep-rooted perennial weeds. They should be removed and burnt.

Collect fallen leaves

On a still day towards the end of the month collect fallen leaves which are lying on plants. Use them for rotting down into leaf-mould or, if they are from beech or oak, to protect tender plants, such as kniphofia, schizostylis, *Iris stylosa* and agapanthus, which need protection during a severe winter except in mild districts.

Place a 6 in. pile of oak or beech leaves—other leaves rot too quickly—round the base of the plants, leaving the tops uncovered if they are still green as it is only the crowns and roots that need protection. Then place sticks over the leaves to prevent them from blowing away, and leave the protective covering in place until the second week in March, except in a mild spring, when it can be removed a few weeks earlier.

Dahlias

Examine stored tubers. If they are shrivelling, plunge them in tepid water for the night, dry, and replace in the peat or vermiculite (see OCTOBER). Cut off with a sharp knife any parts of the tubers that show signs of rotting, and dust the cuts with flowers of sulphur or captan.

Chrysanthemums

Watch plants over-wintering in the garden for signs of waterlogging (see JANUARY) and keep beds clear of weeds which serve as host plants to pests (see FEBRUARY).

UNDER GLASS

Keep moist, but not wet, dormant stools in the greenhouse and cold frame. Give full ventilation except in windy or frosty weather, and restrict the temperature to a maximum of 10°C (50°F).

Greenhouse blooms

The large exhibition, incurved, single and anemone-centred varieties will flower this month. They all require a long time to develop their flowers and no attempt should be made to hurry them. Restrict the temperature to a maximum of 10°C (50°F) and do not close the ventilators completely except in frosty or very windy weather. Give a weekly dusting of captan (see OCTOBER) to prevent fungus damage to the flowers.

As the plants finish flowering, cut off all but 6 in. of the stems and foliage to allow light and air to reach the pots and encourage the growth of base cuttings for next season's propagation (see JANUARY and MARCH).

Late-flowering decoratives

The late-flowering decoratives in the greenhouse border will begin to show colour. They need a night temperature of 10°C (50°F), with some ventilation. Continue to water them weekly or every ten days, but keep the foliage dry. These and other plants in the warm greenhouse are susceptible to leaf miners, so spray with malathion or HCH before the signs appear, rather than waiting until damage occurs.

Gladioli

Clean the corms at any time from the drying-off stage until just before planting them next spring.

Discard old corms

Break away and discard the old, shrivelled corms. If the little bulblets are to be kept for propagation (see MARCH) remove these too and store them separately. Remove the tough outer skins from the large corms. If you see thrips on them (see JULY), or if there has been a severe attack of thrips during the growing season, dust the corms with malathion or HCH.

Destroy diseased corms

Discard any diseased corms. Small, pitted lesions indicate dry rot, which can cause serious losses if gladioli are grown on the same plot year after year.

Hard rot will produce large, black lesions on the corm, and in some cases the corm shrinks and dies. Fusarium rot, which usually causes the corm to disintegrate in the soil or in the store, shows itself as corrugated surface lesions. Corms affected with botrytis show a black, spongy rot.

Select next year's site

Select the site for growing gladioli next year. They do best in a medium soil that is neither excessively light nor excessively heavy. Gladioli require plenty of moisture, but are not successful in waterlogged soil. Dig the plot evenly, preferably two spits deep, incorporating a moderate dressing of well rotted manure or compost, also some bonemeal, in the top spit. Quick-acting fertilisers are unsuitable for gladioli at any stage of growth.

Irises

Watch for buds on *Iris unguicularis* (unlikely the first year after planting) and pick the flowers just before the buds open, thus forestalling the birds, which will otherwise spoil the flowers. The flowers soon open in water indoors.

Lilies

Though late summer is the ideal time for planting lilies, many lily bulbs are not received from the nurseries until November or even December. If the weather is still good, and the ground in an easily worked condition, plant the bulbs now (see SEPTEMBER and OCTOBER).

UNDER GLASS

If winter has set in early, preventing outdoor planting, pot bulbs in John Innes potting compost No. 1, or set them in trays of slightly damp peat with just the top of each bulb above the surface. Although the lily is a bulbous plant, it has no outer tunic of tough skin

CLEANING A GLADIOLUS CORM

Clean gladiolus corms after they have dried off, first removing the bulblets and storing them separately in paper bags

REMOVING THE OLD CORM

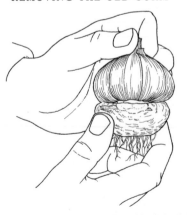

Break away and discard the old, shrivelled corm which will be found adhering to the base of each new corm formed this year

DISCARDING THE OUTER SKIN

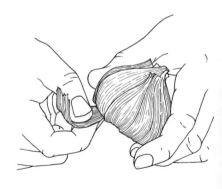

Remove the outer skin, dusting each corm with insecticide if thrips are seen or if they have been troublesome during the summer

to protect it against damage or drying. Losses will be minimised if it is treated like a dormant herbaceous plant.

Keep the pots or trays in a frost-proof greenhouse or shed. Protect with slug pellets and be ready to take action against mice and, possibly, aphids.

Carnations and pinks

Continue to plant border carnations and pinks in mild weather if this was not done last month. Test the soil for lime content and add lime if it is below pH 6·5.

After-care of new plants

In mild spells, firm the soil around any plants loosened by frost. Clear away rubbish from around the stems of plants and ensure that stakes and ties are secure. Protect with black cotton against birds.

Watch for signs of carnation rust and the grubs of carnation flies (see MARCH).

Order plants for setting out in March (see colour section, MAY) and prepare the beds (see AUGUST).

UNDER GLASS

Maintain a temperature of 7°C (45°F) for perpetual flowering carnations and give some ventilation at all times.

Water and feed sparingly (see APRIL), cutting blooms and disbudding flower stems as necessary (see SEPTEMBER).

Watch for carnation rust and aphids (see MARCH), using dusts in preference to sprays during the winter.

Sweet peas

Prepare next season's planting site, choosing an open, well drained, sunny position. Ideally, rectangular plots should run north to south.

Double-dig the plot, but do not apply manure if it is already in really fertile condition. Otherwise, especially if you are growing for exhibition, dig well rotted manure or compost into the second spit. Never mix manure with the top spit, as this will encourage shallow rooting. Apply three or four handfuls of bone-meal per sq. yd. to the top spit. Leave the surface rough to secure maximum benefit from winter weathering.

UNDER GLASS

It is not essential to prick out seedlings raised from last month's sowings, though some exhibitors pot them individually into 3 in. pots. This has the advantage of keeping the soil ball intact at planting time in the spring and is particularly advantageous on heavy land.

Whether or not you prick out, the essential thing is to grow all autumn-sown plants slowly, and to encourage hardiness.

Flowers from seed

If winter weather has not yet set in, hardy perennials raised from seed can still be planted in their final positions in the border. Otherwise, it is better to wait until March.

Prepare sites for annuals

Dig the beds to be used next year for hardy and half-hardy annuals, working in a dressing of well rotted manure or compost. If the land is left rough, winter weathering will break the soil down and will result in a fine tilth, or surface structure, for seed sowing. Autumn digging is especially beneficial on heavy land, but it is important to press on with the task before winter rain and snow make the soil too sticky to work.

Send for seed catalogues so that you can plan next year's bedding programme in good time.

Bulbs

Complete the planting of tulips and hyacinths as soon as possible.

UNDER GLASS AND INDOORS

Examine bowls and pots of bulbs and move inside any on which the growth is 1 in. or more in height. Place them in a cool greenhouse or frame for a few weeks, or in the window of a cool room where frost can be excluded but where the temperature will not exceed 10°C (50°F). Give sufficient water to prevent the fibre or compost becoming dry.

Take indoors

Exceptions may be made with 'Paper White' and 'Soleil d'Or' narcissi, which may be taken straight into a warmer greenhouse or room to flower, if required, well before Christmas.

Alpines

Complete any outstanding trimming and dead-heading, saving the seeds if desired (see JULY).

Remove fallen beech and oak leaves and save them either for compost-making or for mounding over tender plants. Place sticks over the mounds to prevent the leaves blowing away.

Shrubs, heathers and pot-grown alpines can still be planted.

Surface treatment

This is a good time to place a layer of small shingle or stone chippings, ½–1 in. deep, on clean, level ground between the plants. The covering will suppress most weed seedlings, but will also preclude use of a hoe. Otherwise, fork over the surface wherever it is bare of plants. A small hand fork, 6–9 in. long and 4 in. wide, with flat tines, is the best tool for this work. Carefully remove the roots of all perennial weeds.

Water plants and pools

Finish preparing for winter by thinning oxygenating plants (see OCTOBER).

Leave the foliage of marginal reeds and rushes, as it gives some protection during severe weather.

Protect the surface

If your pool is sited where leaves can fall or blow into it, cover the surface completely with small-mesh netting. If this is stretched on frames over the pool, it may easily be removed, together with the leaves.

Overhaul equipment

Overhaul pumps used for waterfalls and fountains. Remove submersible types from the water, and where possible clean and dry working parts before storing in a dry place. Disconnect the suction line from surface pumps and run for a few seconds only to empty the pump chamber. If possible, disconnect the pump from its ancillary fittings, clean and dry metal parts, and smear with grease before storing in a dry place.

Discontinue feeding the fish when the days become colder.

Greenhouses and frames

Ventilate the greenhouse freely on all sunny days; avoid cold draughts, and close the ventilators fairly early in the afternoon to trap some of the daytime warmth. Dirty glass excludes valuable light, so wash the glass, inside and out, with warm water containing detergent. Keep the greenhouse closed during foggy weather, covering the plants with newspaper if the fog persists.

Complete any outstanding potting early in the month. Annuals raised from seed sown in September will now be ready for moving to 3 in. pots of John Innes potting compost No. 1. Cuttings of zonal pelargoniums, fuchsias, heliotropes and campanulas, inserted in September, will now be rooted and ready for potting individually in 3 in. pots containing John Innes potting compost No. 1.

Storing in pots

Now that the foliage of achimenes has died down and the corms are at rest, store them in their pots under the greenhouse staging. A minimum winter temperature of 7°C (45°F) is needed. Dry off fuchsias, begonias, heliotropes and hydrangeas which have flowered during the summer and autumn. Store the pots under the staging in a cool greenhouse or in a frost-proof shed, but do not at any time allow the compost to become dust-dry.

Pinch back new growths on *Solanum capsicastrum* (winter cherry), which may otherwise hide the berries.

PINCHING BACK
A WINTER CHERRY

Pinch back any new growths on *Solanum capsicastrum* (winter cherry) which are tending to hide the shiny berries

Fumigate or spray

Whitefly are often troublesome in the greenhouse at this time of year. At the first signs of an attack, fumigate with an HCH smoke, or spray the plants with malathion or dimethoate.

Give room to cinerarias

When the earliest cinerarias begin developing their flower heads, give the plants extra space to allow them to grow freely and ensure that they get as much light as possible. Spray or fumigate regularly to ensure that they do not become infested with aphids.

Lift hardy plants

Many hardy plants will flower in the cool greenhouse if lifted now from the garden and potted into 6–7 in. pots, depending on the size of the roots. Examples are astilbes, *Dicentra spectabilis* (bleeding heart), polyanthuses, *Primula denticulata* and *Helleborus niger* (Christmas rose) which flowers at Christmas under glass.

Over-wintering annuals

Give water sparingly to annuals over-wintering in pots on a shelf in the cool greenhouse, and keep the atmosphere as dry as possible. Avoid high temperatures throughout the growing period or the seedlings will grow too lanky before repotting (see SEPTEMBER).

Trees and shrubs

During favourable weather continue to plant deciduous trees and shrubs (see OCTOBER). In severe weather the more tender species, such as campsis, caryopteris, cistus, garrya, hydrangea, hypericum and spartium, may need protection with a screen or wire netting to which bracken or old sacking is woven. Stout polythene also serves as a windbreak when tied securely round three or four supporting stakes. Make a lid of the same material to place over the windbreak to prevent snow damage.

PROPAGATION

Take hardwood cuttings (see OCTOBER) of *Elaeagnus pungens*, ivy, poplar, ribes and salix (willow) and insert in open ground or in a cold frame. Transplant the cuttings to their permanent positions the following spring.

Layer young firm shoots of actinidia in pots of peaty loam sunk into the ground round the parent plant. The following spring the layers should have made sufficient roots to be severed from the parent plants and transplanted.

Check that cuttings in cold frames or in open ground have not been loosened by frost. Firm the cuttings in again.

Under glass

Hardwood cuttings of winter jasmine should be taken with a heel and inserted in a cold frame.

Rhododendrons and azaleas

In the garden, take steps to discourage tits from pecking flower buds if you have not already done so (see OCTOBER).

Planting can continue in fine weather (see MARCH).

If you wish to enjoy some plants in the house during the winter, lift them now and pot them. Suitable plants are the dwarf or smaller-flowered species and hybrids. Japanese azaleas are particularly easy.

Select a pot which is big enough to take the root ball intact. Put crocks in the bottom for drainage and plant the bush in its own soil, topping off with a mixture of ordinary soil and peat. After the plant has flowered, re-plant it in its old quarters, and it will grow on.

Hedges

Prepare hedge sites if this work has not already been done (see SEPTEMBER) and complete planting as soon as possible (see OCTOBER). If the site is not ready when plants are delivered, separate the plants in the bundles and bury the roots in shallow trenches. Lay the plants at an angle so that they are not blown about too much while awaiting planting.

Heathers

Continue planting as necessary when the soil is in a suitable condition (see MARCH and OCTOBER).

Examine heathers planted last month, removing any weeds and gently firming into place any plants which have been partially lifted by frost.

Fruit

November is usually the best month for planting fruit. The soil is still workable, and is warm enough for roots to establish themselves before winter. It is, however, possible to plant at any time between leaf-fall and bud-burst when soil conditions are suitable and the ground is not too wet. Night frost need not stop planting, as long as the frozen surface crust of soil can be lifted off and the trees or bushes planted into reasonably dry unfrozen soil beneath. If planting is not immediately possible, either store the trees in a frost-free shed, covering the roots with sacks to stop drying out or frosting, or heel in with the tops leaning over at an angle, and cover the roots with well trodden soil so that it packs closely round them.

Prepare the holes for the trees immediately before planting, so that water cannot fill them, and keep the topsoil and subsoil separate.

If the roots are dry, soak them for a few hours before planting, and cut off any broken roots with secateurs. Large roots only anchor the plants, which depend on the new fine roots to absorb water and food.

Insert stakes before planting

Drive vertical stakes for fruit trees into the ground just before planting, so that the root system is not damaged. The stakes, which should be treated with preservative before use, will hold the tops steady while the roots are getting established. Many dwarfing rootstocks (see recommended varieties, pp. 348–50), are only poorly anchored, and the trees need staking throughout their life. Trained trees and bushes also need support.

Planting procedure

Spread the roots out in the prepared planting hole and re-fill it with layers of topsoil, shaking the trees and bushes to settle the soil round the roots. Firm the soil with the heel. Cover the next layer of roots with more topsoil and firm again, repeating the process until the level of the surrounding soil has been reached. If the soil is not too wet and sticky it can be firmed thoroughly at this stage without permanently affecting the soil structure, so that there will be little settling of the soil later. If you have any doubt that the soil is in firm contact with the roots, water in to settle the soil round the roots. After planting, insert sloping stakes, which will give greater rigidity to short-stemmed trees, with their tops towards the prevailing wind, and tie all stakes firmly to the trees with plastic ties.

Planting depths

As a general rule all fruits should be re-planted at the same depth as they were in the nursery. When planting trees on rootstocks, make sure that the union (easily distinguishable as a swelling on the stem, usually just above where the roots grow out) is well clear of the soil, so that the scion variety does not form its own roots and counteract the effect of the rootstock.

When planting trees on windy sites, set them with their best shoots growing into the prevailing wind, to assist formation of a more balanced tree.

Plant strawberries so that the flowers will all face south. They produce their main blossom on the opposite side of the plant to the runner connecting it with the parent, so the end of the runner should point away from the sun.

Prune after planting

Prune fruit trees after planting (see DECEMBER). Where older plants are moved, it is particularly important to compensate for the loss of roots by removing part of the top. Apples and pears planted in late spring should not be pruned until the autumn.

For further planting details see recommended varieties, pp. 348–50.

On heavy soils complete all work that entails treading on the ground.

Clear weeds from the soil round established trees and bushes, so that they will be tidy through the winter.

Winter pruning generally stimulates growth from close to where cuts are made, and dormant shoots can be cut away at any time between leaf-fall and bud-burst in spring, except during periods of hard frost.

Shaping the tree

Prune only enough to shape the tree and encourage shoots to grow where they are required, particularly when the main framework branches are being formed. In the early years remove branches growing at a narrow angle to the trunk, as they are weak and split easily at the junction with the trunk when bearing fruit. Cut just above a bud which points in the direction that a shoot is required.

Apple and pear

Winter pruning generally stimulates too much growth on restricted trees; but winter prune dwarf pyramids and espaliers for one or two seasons to establish the basic shape, and lightly prune cordon tip-bearing varieties, such as 'Worcester Pearmain', which produce fruit from buds at the tips of the shoots.

Prune established trees by tipping leaders, or shoots which have been selected to extend the branch framework; by removing badly placed shoots; and by thinning out spur systems on older trees. After four or five years stop tipping leaders. Thereafter, cut out crossing and rubbing branches, and dead and diseased wood. Keep secateurs sharp for cutting small branches,

PRUNING FRUIT TREES AFTER PLANTING

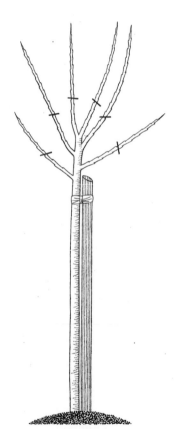
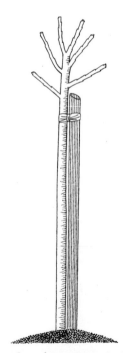

Prune apple and pear trees after planting, cutting back by about two-thirds the young shoots selected to form the framework. The illustrations show a two-year-old tree before and after pruning. Leave unpruned shoots not required for establishing the framework

PRUNING ESTABLISHED TREES

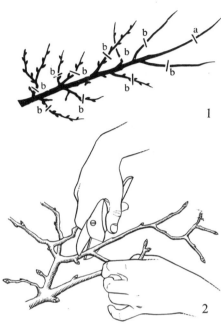

(1) Tip the leaders (a) until the trees are four or five years old. Where growth is required, also shorten new laterals (b) to four or five buds. (2) Fruit spurs are thinned to increase the size of the fruits next season

bearing down on them to open the cuts as they are made. For large branches use a saw, trim wounds with a knife, and cover with bituminous paint. Established pears should be pruned rather harder than apples, and trees that are to be winter-washed in December or January should be pruned before the spraying programme begins.

If birds are attacking the fruit buds, do not prune until the spring.

While pruning, check that ties are not cutting or chafing the bark.

Scrape and cut out cankers, and treat woolly aphis colonies with malathion if they cannot be pruned out.

Inspect stored fruit, and ripen pears from store at room temperature.

Blackberry, loganberry and hybrid berries

Complete pruning as soon as possible (see OCTOBER), and train new growths on to the supporting framework. In windy situations new loganberry shoots may be damaged during the winter, so leave them tied up until spring.

Black currant

Prune established bushes by removing some of the old wood and leaving in as much new growth as possible. No pruning is required at the end of the first season of growth after planting.

Cherry

This is not the time to prune cherry, peach, nectarine, plum or damson, because slowly healing wounds expose the trees to disease (see APRIL). If pruning is necessary—to remove split or

damaged branches, for instance—tidy up the wounds with a knife and protect with bituminous paint.

Gooseberry, red and white currants

Prune established bushes by shortening the leaders by half and the laterals to 2 in. (on older bushes prune the laterals harder). Prune cordons by shortening the leaders by one-third (on old gooseberry bushes prune the leaders harder) and the laterals by half. Remove weak growths on gooseberry.

Peach and nectarine: see Cherry

Plum and damson: see Cherry

Raspberry

Cut out all fruiting shoots which have carried this season's crop as soon as possible. Tie new canes to the supporting framework. In windy situations, if there is a lot of growth above the top wire, tie it to the wire to prevent damage. Remove weak and surplus shoots.

PRUNING AND SUPPORTING RASPBERRIES

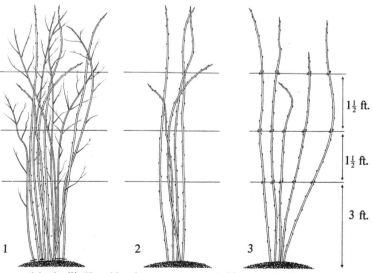

(1) An unpruned bush. (2) The older shoots which carried fruit this year have been removed. (3) The new shoots have been tied to an alternative method of wire support

Vegetables

For an early crop of broad beans (May–June) in the south, sow the seeds this month on a sheltered site. 'Aquadulce' and dwarf varieties 'The Sutton' and 'Bonny Lad' are recommended. The dwarfs are short enough to grow under cloches. Dust the seeds with a captan dressing and draw flat-bottomed drills 9 in. wide and $2\frac{1}{2}$–3 in. deep. Sow in two rows, 7 in. apart, allowing 6 in. between the seeds.

UNDER GLASS

If you sow 'The Sutton' broad beans to grow under cloches, apply a pre-emergence weedkiller afterwards. Cover the ends of the rows with glass.

In the south, complete sowings of cloched lettuce as early in the month as possible (see OCTOBER).

In a heated greenhouse, at 10–13°C (50–55°F), force chicory under the staging for eating during the winter. The roots will have to be discarded afterwards. Cut off all but 1 in. of the top growth of chicory, lift the roots of the plants and pack them closely, with a little moist soil between them, in large pots or boxes. Cover with other pots or boxes and then with a sheet of black polythene to exclude all light.

LESS COMMON VEGETABLES

Trim the outer growth on globe artichokes to within 2–3 in. of the crowns, taking care not to damage the centre growth. Draw soil up to the crowns in a ridge, leaving the top open. Pack straw 12 in. deep over the soil, again leaving the top open.

To increase your stock of globe artichokes, or to provide replacements for older plants that are past their best, detach suckers from plants that are at least two years old and plant them in pots containing good garden soil. Over-winter the plants in a cold frame or cold greenhouse and plant out in April.

Herbs

Clear basil, chervil and dill; and fennel and parsley which have grown for a second season. Dig over cleared ground before the end of the month.

Put cloches over September-sown parsley and chervil to encourage winter shoots and keep them clean.

Patios and town gardens

This is a suitable time to plant trees and shrubs in containers (see MARCH). Among low-growing evergreens which will provide winter colour are *Euonymus radicans variegatus*, *Hypericum calycinum* and *Vinca major* or *V. minor*.

Even for the largest containers, avoid trees and shrubs with a height or spread of more than 6 ft. Where a plant will reach these limits, the container should be at least 18 in. deep and wide. The container should also have a broad base or be sufficiently heavy not to be blown over by the wind.

Dwarfing effect

Because of the limited soil available to large plants in containers, most trees and shrubs tend to grow smaller than they would in open soil. It is possible to keep some specimens within bounds by pruning or pinching out the growing tips.

House plants

Few house plants will stand really cold conditions; on the other hand, few need more than a moderate amount of heat (see plant descriptions, DECEMBER). Most house plants thrive in normal living-room temperatures. Try to avoid drastic fluctuations, which may occur when a living-room becomes warm during the evening and then cold towards morning. The plants will do better where the temperature is more constant—the kitchen, perhaps, though not if gas is used there. Substantial changes in temperature are seldom a problem in centrally heated houses.

Cut down on watering now, so that for most of the time the soil is almost dust-dry on the surface, though slightly moist around the roots. Use fertiliser only on plants that are in flower or growing strongly. Allow plants to get as much light as possible, but do not have them so near to the window that night frosts can affect them. Supplement natural daylight with artificial light if you wish, but make sure that foliage is not so close to the light source that it burns.

General tasks

Lift fuchsias, begonias, geraniums and other tender plants.

Dig vacant ground this month, especially if the land is heavy. The winter frosts will break down heavy clay, and in the spring it will only be necessary to fork it over and rake it down to a fine tilth for sowing or planting. A dressing of $\frac{1}{2}$ lb. of lime per sq. yd. will help the breaking-down process.

Plant trees and shrubs

Trees, shrubs and roses will be arriving from the nurseries now and may be planted. If the roots are dry on arrival, soak them in a bucket of water. If the weekends are wet or frosty and planting has to be postponed, unpack the bundle and separate the plants. Take out a trench about 18 in. deep and heel the plants in. Cover their roots with soil and firm it well down.

Clear up fallen leaves and other rubbish. Cut the shrivelled stems of herbaceous plants down to about 18 in. above ground, and then cut them right down to ground level in March.

Alpine beds and rock gardens to plant in November

Hundreds of alpines need so little room in which to grow that a rock garden or alpine bed can provide the maximum interest in the minimum of space. However, certain principles must be observed to ensure success.

Selecting the site

Wherever possible choose a position open to sun and air, as the majority of alpines do best in a sunny position, and will withstand full exposure to wind. If you cannot provide a site open to the sun, you can still grow shade-loving alpines, providing the shade is not that of overhanging trees.

Rocks in terraces

A conventional rock garden is not particularly troublesome either to construct or to maintain. Avoid steeply sloping surfaces, which are subject to erosion, and remember that perennial weeds (including some weed-like alpines) are difficult to eradicate once their roots or shoots become established among the rocks. The rocks should be placed in the form of ledges or terraces.

The best way to grow alpines is in a raised bed (pp. 332–3), where the plants can be grown for their own sakes, rather than as decorations for an elaborate construction, with little or no rock. Such beds are easy to plant and maintain, and can be seen from all sides.

Having decided on a site and method of construction, make sure that the land is well drained and free from perennial weeds. Annual weeds can be controlled, but it is easier from the start to use a sterilised soil suitable for rock plants (see p. 212). Drainage is so important that on heavy, wet soils it will pay to lay brick rubble, coarse gravel or even land drains below the surface. As few alpines require damp conditions, it is better to err on the side of dryness, except where the soil is especially free-draining.

Choosing plants

Decide whether to go in for a wide variety of choice, slow-growing alpines, or whether to aim for plants that will provide masses of colour. It is quite feasible, if you have the space, to grow both, but the quick spreaders, which are often very showy, must be segregated from the slow-growing kinds. Use the spreads given in the plant descriptions (pp. 337–47) as a guide to planting distances. Avoid kinds which are weedy by nature, especially in small beds.

The flowering season for alpines is from February to October, the peak flowering time being April to June. Unless a careful selection is made, and late-flowering plants included, the bed may be bereft of colour in late summer and autumn. When selecting plants, always use a specialist grower's catalogue in conjunction with the plant descriptions.

Having made your alpine bed or rock garden, pot-grown plants (as sold by alpine specialists) can be planted with safety at almost any time, except when the ground is frozen or under snow. It is also better to avoid planting during very dry weather in the summer. However, if the soil is on the dry side, use the puddling method, rather than simply splashing water on the surface soil. Overhead watering may be needed at a later stage—sometimes, in a drought, even when plants are established—but be sure to use a fine spray under pressure from a sprinkler, or a fine-rosed can, preferably at the end of the day.

Contrasting shapes

Dwarf shrubs, especially conifers, can be used with good effect. They provide interest in the winter months and will break up any tendency to flatness in a raised bed. They should, however, be chosen with discretion, as in time they may become too large. The smaller the bed or garden, the more care is needed to choose slow-growing kinds, even if it takes several years for a shrub to stand out as a feature. Prostrate varieties are not advised for small areas, and should in any case be pruned as growth becomes excessive.

Pruning rock plants

Trimming is also necessary for such quick-growing alpines as alyssum, aubrietas and helianthemums. This can be done with shears or scissors, preferably just as flowering comes to an end and before any seed pods can ripen and shed their contents. Other quick-growing, mat- or rosette-forming kinds may need lifting, dividing and re-planting after their second season, in order to promote fresh growth and also to curb excessive spread.

Weeding should never be neglected. When annual weeds have germinated, use an onion hoe to avoid tedious hand weeding later on. If allowed to run to seed, annual grasses, groundsel or shepherd's purse can entirely spoil your efforts. A 1 in. layer of fine gravel or stone chippings will save much weeding.

Raised bed for alpines

A greater concentration of plants can be grown in a bed of this type than in a conventional rock garden. The bed illustrated measures 36 ft. by 3 ft., allowing space for three plants in each group, with additional plants set in the wall crevices. H=height; where no height is given, the plants are prostrate or trailing

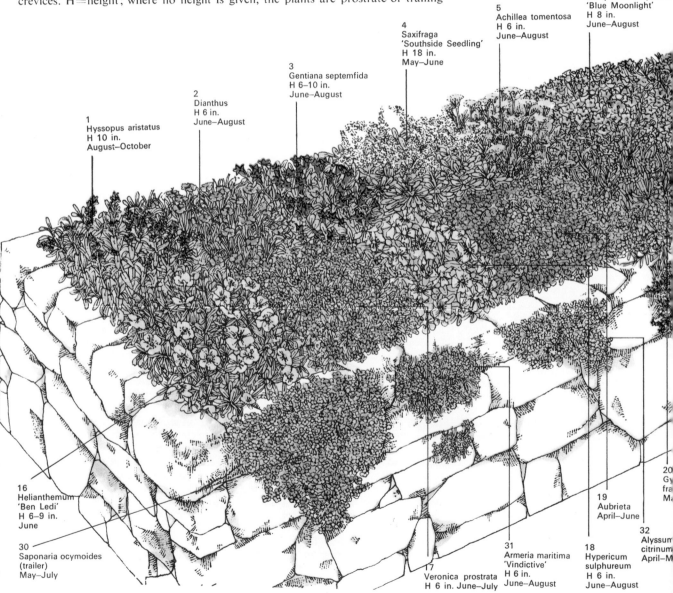

Geranium wlassowia
H 1
June–Septe

6
Campanula carpatica
'Blue Moonlight'
H 8 in.
June–August

5
Achillea tomentosa
H 6 in.
June–August

4
Saxifraga
'Southside Seedling'
H 18 in.
May–June

3
Gentiana septemfida
H 6–10 in.
June–August

2
Dianthus
H 6 in.
June–August

1
Hyssopus aristatus
H 10 in.
August–October

16
Helianthemum
'Ben Ledi'
H 6–9 in.
June

30
Saponaria ocymoides
(trailer)
May–July

17
Veronica prostrata
H 6 in. June–July

31
Armeria maritima
'Vindictive'
H 6 in.
June–August

19
Aubrieta
April–June

18
Hypericum
sulphureum
H 6 in.
June–August

20
Gy
fra
M

32
Alyssum
citrinum
April–M

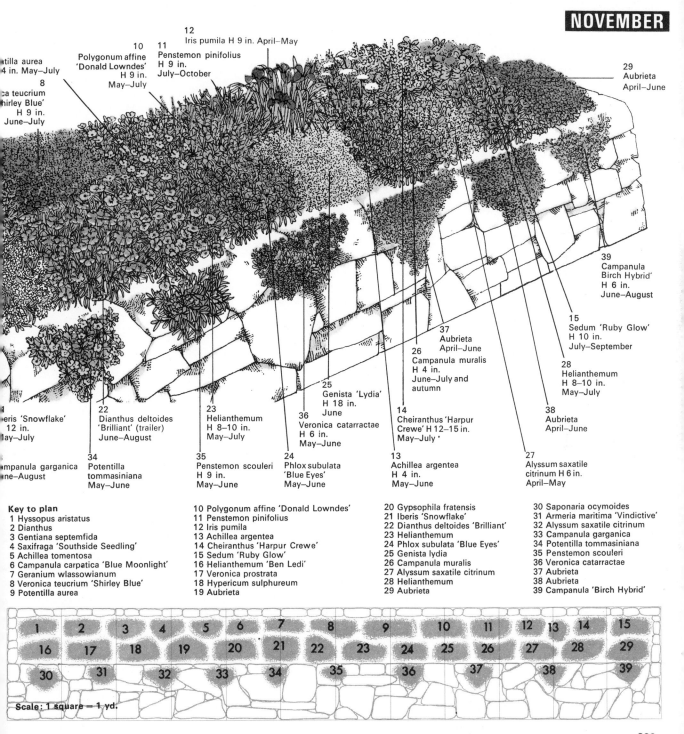

12
Iris pumila H 9 in. April–May

10
Polygonum affine
'Donald Lowndes'
H 9 in.
May–July

11
Penstemon pinifolius
H 9 in.
July–October

...tilla aurea
...4 in. May–July

8
...ca teucrium
...hirley Blue'
H 9 in.
June–July

29
Aubrieta
April–May

39
Campanula
'Birch Hybrid'
H 6 in.
June–August

15
Sedum 'Ruby Glow'
H 10 in.
July–September

37
Aubrieta
April–June

26
Campanula muralis
H 4 in.
June–July and
autumn

28
Helianthemum
H 8–10 in.
May–July

25
Genista 'Lydia'
H 18 in.
June

...eris 'Snowflake'
...12 in.
...ay–July

22
Dianthus deltoides
'Brilliant' (trailer)
June–August

23
Helianthemum
H 8–10 in.
May–July

36
Veronica catarractae
H 6 in.
May–June

14
Cheiranthus 'Harpur
Crewe' H 12–15 in.
May–July

38
Aubrieta
April–June

...mpanula gargarica
...ne–August

34
Potentilla
tommasiniana
May–June

35
Penstemon scouleri
H 9 in.
May–June

24
Phlox subulata
'Blue Eyes'
May–June

13
Achillea argentea
H 4 in.
May–June

27
Alyssum saxatile
citrinum H 6 in.
April–May

Key to plan

1 Hyssopus aristatus
2 Dianthus
3 Gentiana septemfida
4 Saxifraga 'Southside Seedling'
5 Achillea tomentosa
6 Campanula carpatica 'Blue Moonlight'
7 Geranium wlassowianum
8 Veronica teucrium 'Shirley Blue'
9 Potentilla aurea

10 Polygonum affine 'Donald Lowndes'
11 Penstemon pinifolius
12 Iris pumila
13 Achillea argentea
14 Cheiranthus 'Harpur Crewe'
15 Sedum 'Ruby Glow'
16 Helianthemum 'Ben Ledi'
17 Veronica prostrata
18 Hypericum sulphureum
19 Aubrieta

20 Gypsophila fratensis
21 Iberis 'Snowflake'
22 Dianthus deltoides 'Brilliant'
23 Helianthemum
24 Phlox subulata 'Blue Eyes'
25 Genista lydia
26 Campanula muralis
27 Alyssum saxatile citrinum
28 Helianthemum
29 Aubrieta

30 Saponaria ocymoides
31 Armeria maritima 'Vindictive'
32 Alyssum saxatile citrinum
33 Campanula gargarica
34 Potentilla tommasiniana
35 Penstemon scouleri
36 Veronica catarractae
37 Aubrieta
38 Aubrieta
39 Campanula 'Birch Hybrid'

Scale: 1 square = 1 yd.

333

Wall-raised alpine bed

This ambitious alpine bed, with stone side walls 18 in. high, measures 18 ft. by 7½ ft. overall. There is space for one plant of each kind. Paving stones have been included to provide standing space for weeding and planting. H=height; where no height is given, plants are rosetted or semi-prostrate

Key to plan

1 Helianthemum lunulatum
   H 6 in. June–July
2 Dianthus
   H 6 in. June–August
3 Viola cornuta nana
   H 3 in. May–August
4 Veronica catarractae
   H 6 in. May–June
5 Campanula garganica
   H 4–6 in. June–August
6 Phlox subulata 'Blue Eyes'
   May–June
7 Achillea 'King Edward'
   H 4–6 in. June–September
8 Allium cyaneum
   H 6 in. July–August
9 Geranium dalmaticum
   H 4 in. May–June
10 Potentilla aurea plena
   H 3–4 in. May–July
11 Aubrieta
   April–June
12 Aubrieta
   April–June
13 Geranium subcaulescens
   H 6 in. June–August
14 Sempervivum schlehanii
   rubrifolium
   Foliage plant
15 Asperula nitida
   H 2 in. June–July
16 Saxifraga 'Southside Seedling'
   H 18 in. May–June
17 Crepis incana
   H 9 in. May–July
18 Stachys lanata 'Silver Carpet'
   June–August
19 Silene acaulis pedunculata
   May–June
20 Iberis commutatum
   H 9 in. May–July
21 Thymus nitidus
   H 6 in. May–June
22 Tunica saxifraga 'Rosette'
   H 6 in. July–August
23 Gypsophila repens
   'Dorothy Teacher'
   May–July
24 Ranunculus gramineus
   H 12 in. May–July
25 Globularia incanescens
   H 1 in. May–June
26 Thymus doefleri
   May–June
27 Picea mariana nana (spruce)
28 Spiraea bullata
   H 12–18 in. June–July
29 Gentiana sino-ornata
   H 3–4 in. September–October

30 Asperula lilaciflora
   caespitosa
   H 3 in. June–September
31 Genista lydia
   H 18 in. June
32 Sedum tartarinowii
   H 4 in. August–September
33 Micromeria corsica
   H 4 in. June–September
34 Saxifraga primuloides
   H 6 in. April–May
35 Linum salsoloides nanum
   May–July
36 Sedum pluricaule
   H 4 in. July–September
37 Origanum laevigatum
   H 10–12 in. August–October
38 Dianthus June–August
39 Cotyledon simplicifolia
   H 6 in. June–August
40 Campanula carpatica
   H 3–4 in. June–August
41 Geranium cinereum 'Ballerina'
   H 6 in. June–August
42 Saxifraga 'Triumph'
   H 6 in. April–May
43 Arenaria caespitosa aurea
   May–June
44 Potentilla aurea
   H 3–4 in. May–July
45 Erinus alpinus 'Mrs. Boyle'
   H 3–4 in. May–July
46 Sempervivum 'Jubilee'
   Foliage plant
47 Thymus serpyllum
   H 3 in. June–July
48 Raoulia australis
   Foliage plant
49 Helichrysum
   May–July
50 Wulfenia amherstiana
   H 5 in. June–July
51 Potentilla tonguei
   June–September
52 Pulsatilla vulgaris
   H 6–12 in. April–May
53 Saxifraga oppositifolia
   March–April
54 Hutchinsia auerswaldii
   H 3 in. May–June
55 Leontopodium alpinum
   H 4–6 in. June–July
56 Acaena microphylla
   June–September
57 Phlox douglasii
   May–June
58 Polygonum vaccinifolium
   July–September
59 Saxifraga 'Gold Dust'
   H 3 in. February–April

60 Veronica prostrata
   'Loddon Blue'
   H 6 in. June–July
61 Linum extraxillare
   H 6 in. May–July
62 Campanula carpatica
   'Chewton Joy'
   H 6 in. June–August
63 Genista pilosa
   June–July
64 Helianthemum H 8in. May–July
65 Lychnis flos-jovis
   H 6 in. May–July
66 Hypericum polyphyllum
   H 6 in. June–August
67 Silene alpestris 'Bressingham'
   H 4 in. May–July
68 Sedum floriferum
   'Weihenstephaner Gold'
   H 4 in. June–August
69 Juniperus communis
   compressa
70 Hyssopus aristatus
   H 10 in. August–October
71 Silene schafta
   H 6 in. July–September
72 Aubrieta
   April–June
73 Scabiosa pterocephala
   H 3 in. June–September
74 Iberis 'Little Gem'
   H 6 in. May–July
75 Penstemon pinifolius
   H 9 in. July–October
76 Achillea argentea
   H 4 in. May–June
77 Dianthus 'White Ladies'
   H 9–12 in. June–August
78 Achillea tomentosa
   H 6 in. June–August
79 Prunella
   H 9 in. June–August
80 Hieraceum villosum
   H 6 in. June–August
81 Phlox subulata
   May–June
82 Veronica prostrata
   H 6 in. June–July
83 Gypsophila fratensis
   May–July
84 Helianthemum
   H 8 in. May–July
85 Campanula muralis
   H 4 in. June–July
86 Alyssum saxatile
   H 6 in. April–May
87 Aubrieta
   April–June

Scale: 1 square = 18 in.

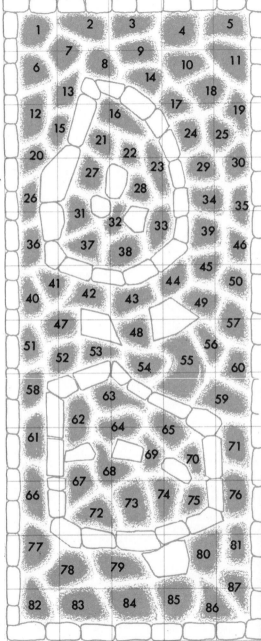

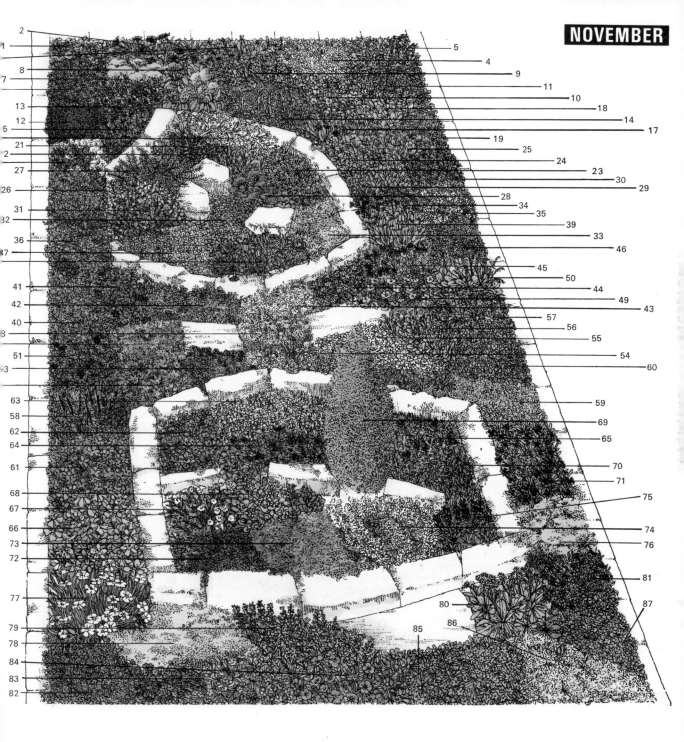

Alpines to plant in November

Unless otherwise stated, the plants described will grow satisfactorily year after year in ordinary, well drained soil with no special additions. H stands for the average flowering height. Spreads are the average after two seasons' growth from plants grown in 3 in. pots. SS is the perennial surface spread (not necessarily evergreen). AS is the approximate diameter of seasonal growth which dies back to the dormant plant. S is tufty or erect growth, which dies back in winter.

Acaena microphylla

Acaena
Long-lived carpeting plants that spread rapidly when grown in a sunny position. Propagate by division during the growing season. *A. buchanani* (SS 18 in.) is a light glaucous green, with insignificant green burrs when in flower. Useful between paving stones. *A. microphylla* is slower-growing. Bronze-purple leaves, red flower bracts, June–September. *A. novae-zealandiae* (New Zealand burr) (SS 18 in.) has coppery leaves; brownish flower heads, June–September. Useful between paving stones.

Achillea (yarrow)
Requires sunny position. Best divided and re-planted after flowering every two or three years to restore vitality. *A. argentea* (H 4 in. SS 10 in.) is bright silver, with heads of single white flowers, May–June. *A. chrysocoma* (H 6 in. SS 15 in.)

has woolly, grey-green mats; mustard-yellow flower heads, June–July. *A.* 'King Edward' (H 4–6 in. SS 8 in.) has a less vigorous, tufty habit; lemon-yellow flower heads, June–September. *A. tomentosa* (H 6 in. SS 12 in.) has green filigree mats; bright yellow flower heads, June–August.

Aethionema (burnt candytuft)
Excellent for a well drained, sunny position. Short-lived, except *A.* 'Warley Rose'. Propagate *A.* 'Warley Rose' by heel cuttings after flowering; others by seed in spring. *A. theodorum*, *A. pulchellum* and *A. grandiflorum* (all H 9 in. SS 10 in.) are twiggy, blue-grey bushes, covered with heads of clear pink flowers, June–July. *A.* 'Warley Rose' (H 4 in. SS 8 in.) is blue green; a mass of deep pink flowers, late May–July.

Ajuga (bugle)
These are mostly low-growing spreading plants, though easy to control. Useful as ground cover in a shady position, where they have a long life. Propagate by division during the growing season. *A. reptans multicolor* (syn. 'Rainbow') (H 6 in. SS 12 in.) has abundant foliage, variegated orange, bronze and purple; spikes of blue flowers, May–June. *A. purpurea* (H 4 in. SS 18 in.) has bronze-purple leaves. *A. metallica crispa* (H 2 in. SS 6 in.) grows very slowly, with tight mats of crinkled, shiny leaves; light blue flower spikes, May–

June. *A. pyramidalis* (H 8 in. SS 9 in.) is slow to spread. Dark, glossy leaves; rich gentian blue flower spikes, June–July.

Ajuga pyramidalis

Alyssum (gold dust)
Plants for a sunny, well drained position; will grow in poor, dry soil. All except *A. saxatile plena* are propagated by seed in spring. *A. saxatile* (H 6 in. SS 15 in.) is a greyish, spreading plant with masses of bright yellow flowers, April–May. Trim back after the second or third flowering to promote compactness. *A. s. citrinum* (H 6 in. SS 15 in.) has lemon-yellow flowers. Trim as above. *A. s. plena* (H 6 in. SS 12 in.) is slower to grow and can only be increased from heel cuttings taken August–September and rooted in a frame. Double yellow flowers. *A. spinosum* (H 6 in. SS 9 in.) makes small twiggy bushes; white or pale pink flowers, May–June.

Androsace (rock jasmine)
Require a sunny, well drained position. Sometimes succumb to excessively wet conditions in winter. Short-lived, they form grey, mounded rosettes; round flower heads, May–June, except *A. lanuginosa*. Divide and re-plant August–September if the plants show signs of dying. *A. lanuginosa* (SS 12 in.) has silvery trailing growths; light pink flowers spasmodically from July onwards. *A. microphylla* (H 3 in. SS 9 in.) forms small rosettes; pink flowers. *A. sarmentosa* and *A. sempervivoides* (both H 4 in. SS 9 in.) have rosettes 1–1½ in. across; light pink flowers. *A. vitaliana* (SS 3 in.) is cushion forming, with stemless yellow flowers, May–June.

Androsace sempervivoides

Aquilegia (columbine)
For a sunny or partially shaded position; not parched. Generally short-lived. Propagate by seed under glass, January–March, or

in the open in July. *A. bertoloni* (H 6 in. S 3 in.) has large, light blue flowers, May–June. *A. discolor* (H 4 in. S 3 in.) is blue and white. *A. ecalcarata* (H 9 in. S 3 in.) needs some shade and moisture; graceful sprays of reddish-purple flowers, June–July. *A. einsellana* (H 10 in. S 4 in.) has lilac-blue flowers, May–June. *A. flabellata* (H 10 in. S 4 in.) bears erect blue spikes, May–June. *A. f. alba* is a white form. *A. schockleyi* (H 12 in. S 4 in.) has yellow and red flowers, May–June.

Arabis (rock cress)
Require a sunny position; generally long-lived. Propagate by division or heel cuttings in October. *A. albida* (H 6 in. SS 18 in.) is popular for covering banks or as an edging, especially the double white form *plena* which flowers April–May. These are too coarse among most other alpines, but *A. a. variegata* (SS 12 in.) is a neater form with variegated leaves. *A. aubretioides* 'Rosabella' (H 6 in. SS 12 in.) makes leafy mounds and has sprays of light pink flowers, April–May.

Arenaria pinifolia

Arenaria (sandwort)
Dwarf, creeping plants for a sunny position. Propagate by division or seed in spring. *A. balearica* (SS 15 in.) makes a green mat, studded with small single white flowers, May–June. Best partially divided and replanted every April. *A. caespitosa aurea* (SS 15 in.) is golden green, with white flowers, May–June. Divide and re-plant every April. This and *A. balearica* are useful for paving. *A. montana*

(SS 12 in.) has bold masses of white flowers on trailing green stems, May–July. *A. pinifolia* (H 4 in. SS 9 in.) is more mounded and erect; white flowers, May–June.

Asperula (woodruff)
The species suitable for rock gardens require a sunny position. They are generally long-lived. Propagate by division in early spring. *A. capitata* (syn. *hirta*)

Asperula suberosa

(H 2 in. SS 12 in.) makes spreading, matted growth and is sometimes invasive; pale pink flowers, May–June. *A. lilaciflora caespitosa* (H 3 in. SS 9 in.) is an excellent rock garden plant, forming close green mats; clear pink flowers spasmodically, June–September. *A. nitida* (H 2 in. SS 9 in.) forms a dense cushion; stemless pink flowers, June–July. *A. pontica* (H 2 in. SS 10 in.) is similar but spreads more rapidly. *A. suberosa* (syn. *arcadiensis*) (H 3 in. S 5 in.) needs free-draining, gritty soil, and protection from winter rain in northern and western districts. It forms fragile tufts of greyish woolly stems, tipped by delicate clusters of clear pink tubular flowers, May–June.

Aster
Some of the dwarf perennial kinds are useful for rock gardens where the soil is not too dry. They require a sunny position and are generally long-lived. Propagate by division in March or after flowering *A. alpellus* 'Summer Greeting' (H 9 in. S 8 in.) makes neat clumps; sprays of pink daisies, June–

July. *A. a.* 'Triumph' is similar but blue flowered. Varieties of *A. alpinus* (H 9 in. S 6 in.) have similar clumpy growth, with stiff, upright daisies, 1½ in. across, May–June: 'Beechwood' is lavender blue; 'Joy' lilac blue; 'Wargrave' lilac pink; *A. tibeticus*, light blue and very free flowering. *A. sativus atrocaeruleus* (H 6 in. S 6 in.) has sky blue flowers, ½ in. across, on leafy tufts, June–September.

Astilbe
Suited only to moist, shady positions in soil containing ample humus. Long-lived. Propagate by division in March. *A. crispa* 'Perkeo' (H 8 in. AS 6 in.) has crisp, mounded dark green foliage; stumpy pink flower spikes, June–July. *A. glaberrima saxosa* (H 4 in. AS 4 in.) is a delightful miniature, with pretty dark foliage; sprays of tiny pale pink flowers, July–September. *A. simplicifolia compacta* (H 6 in. AS 6 in.) has shiny, light green leaves and sprays of light pink flowers, June–August. *A. s.* 'Bronze Elegance' (H 6 in. AS 6 in.) has bronze-green leaves and sprays; light salmon-pink flower sprays, June–August; 'Sprite' (H 9 in. AS 9 in.) is shell pink. *A. sinensis pumila* (H 10 in. AS 10 in.) spreads rapidly from underground shoots. Dark green, fern-like leaves; erect lilac-rose flower spikes, July–September.

Aubrieta (rock cress)
These plants become ragged if allowed to spread unchecked. Self-sown seedlings are recessive and may take control, even if large, rich-coloured varieties were planted originally. To prevent seeding and to maintain a compact shape, trim plants as soon as flowering is over.

Aubrietas require a sunny position, good drainage and lime. Seed-raised plants come in mixed shades. If from seed sown outdoors in April–May, set the young plants in their flowering positions by late

October. Divide old plants or take heel cuttings in October.

The following varieties flower April–June (all SS 10–14 in.): 'Belisha Beacon', 'Bressingham Red', 'Mrs. Rodewald', 'Magnificent', all rosy reds; 'Maurice Prichard', pale pink; 'Riverslea Pink', deep pink; 'Bressingham Pink' and 'Mary Poppins', both pink and double; 'Gurgedyke', deep purple; 'Wanda', double purple-red; 'Peter Barr', crimson purple; 'Dr. Mules' and 'Carnival', both violet blue; 'Lancashire Blue', 'Oakington Lavender' and 'Lilac Time', all lavender blue; 'Studland', pale blue; 'Triumphant', mid-blue.

Bellflower: see **Campanula**

Bugle: see **Ajuga**

Calamintha alpina

Calamintha
Require full sun or half shade. *C. grandiflora* and *C. nepetoides* are long-lived, but *C. alpina* is short-lived. Propagate by basal cuttings in spring. *C. alpina* (H 4 in. S 8 in.) has a long succession of mauve-blue flowers on trailing stems, June–August. *C. grandiflora* (H 6 in. SS 10 in.) has low bushy growth; small deep pink flowers, June–September. *C. nepetoides* (H 12 in. SS 10 in.) produces many light blue flowers on erect bushes, July–September. Not for dry soil.

Campanula (bellflower, harebell)

Valuable for continuing the rock garden display in late summer. Require a šunny position and good drainage. Length of life is varied. Propagate by division in March. The recommended kinds are grouped according to habit, some being slow-growing and compact while others spread rapidly.

The first group consists of non-spreading kinds which maintain a clumpy rootstock: 'Abundance' (H 6 in. S 8 in.) makes a mound set with lavender-blue bells, June–August. 'Molly Pinsent' (H 10 in. S 10 in.) is similar. 'Norman Grove' (H 4 in. S 8 in.) has golden-green mounded foliage; lavender bells, June–August.

Carpatica campanulas, the second group, grow as clumps, with flower bells 1–2 in. across, facing upwards and outwards, June–August: 'Blue Moonlight' (H 8 in. S 9 in.) is light blue; 'Chewton Joy' (H 6 in. S 8 in.) has small, porcelain-blue flowers; 'Hannah' (H 6 in. S 8 in.) is similar but has white flowers; 'Isobel' (H 10 in. S 12 in.) has large, deep blue flowers; 'Mrs. Frere' (H 6 in. S 10 in.), mid-blue, saucer-shaped flowers; 'Wheatley Violet' (H 6 in. S 10 in.), deep violet; 'White Star' (H 10 in. S 12 in.), large white blooms. C. garganica varieties (H 4–6 in. S 8–10 in.) make a compact evergreen tuft, sending out trailing sprays of starry flowers, June–August. Grow well on walls. Most varieties have light or mid-blue flowers.

In the third group are vigorous growing kinds with some degree of underground spread. 'E. K. Toogood' (H 12 in. S 12 in.) and 'Glandore' (H 4 in. S 8 in.) are clumpy plants which spread above ground during the summer; star-like blue flowers, June–August. C. poscharskyana (H 6–9 in. S 18–20 in.) is pretty but invasive and should not be planted with choicer kinds, especially in a wall. Leaves rounded; light blue flowers on small sprays, June–August. Useful varieties of C. rotundifolia are: 'Covadanga' (H 9 in. S 12 in.), deep blue flowers, June–August; 'Midnight Blue' (H 9 in. S 12 in.), deep violet, June–August; 'Spetchley White' (H 9 in. S 12 in.), June–August; 'Mist Maiden' (H 6 in. S 10 in.), grey leaves, deep blue flowers, June–August.

The fourth group consists of dwarf kinds which creep below ground: 'Blue Tit' (H 6 in. S 12 in.), upturned blue trumpets, June–July; 'Birch Hybrid' (H 6 in. S 10 in.), short sprays of deep blue flowers, June–August. Good for walls or edging; 'G. F. Wilson' (H 4 in. S 10 in.), violet-purple dangling bells 1 in. across, June–July; C. muralis (H 4 in. SS 10 in.), deep green tufts; short sprays of lavender-blue bells, June–July, and often in autumn; C. pilosa major (H 3 in. S 8 in.) has cup-shaped light blue flowers, May–June; C. pulla (H 3 in. S 12 in.) makes creeping growth below ground with violet-purple bells, June–July; C. pulloides (S 12 in.) is similar to C. pulla but is twice as tall; C. pusilla (S 12 in.) has thread-like roots which creep below ground to form mats set with dainty nodding bells, June–July; C. p. 'Oakington Hybrid' (H 4 in. S 12 in.) has rich blue flowers; C. p. hallii (H 4 in. S 12 in.) is white; C. p. 'Miranda' (H 4 in. S 12 in.), pale blue; C. warleyensis (H 4 in. S 8 in.) has sprays of double, powder-blue flowers, 1 in. across, July–August; C. wockii (H 4 in. S 8 in.) makes a low mound set with deep mauve drooping bells in July. Slow-growing.

Campion: see Lychnis

Cheiranthus (wallflower)

The perennial wallflowers will grow in the poorest soil and are useful for wall planting. Sunny

Cheiranthus 'Sunbright'

aspect. Propagate 'Constant Cheer' and 'Harpur Crewe' by heel cuttings after flowering; divide and re-plant 'Sunbright' every two or three years. 'Constant Cheer' (H 12–15 in. S 10 in.) flowers almost continuously; narrow foliage and sprays of lavender-amber flowers. 'Harpur Crewe' (H 12–15 in. S 9 in.) is longer-lived, with spikes of double yellow flowers, May–July. 'Sunbright' (H 6 in. SS 12 in.) makes a green mound covered with single yellow flowers, May–June.

Chrysogonum

For sun or half shade; long-lived. Propagate by division in spring or late summer after flowering. C. virginianum (H 9 in. S 9 in.) makes leafy tufts; short sprays of deep yellow flowers, $\frac{1}{2}$ in. across, May–September. Needs lime-free soil.

Chrysopsis

For a sunny position; long-lived. Propagate by heel cuttings in late summer. C. villosa (H 6 in. SS 12 in.) makes spreading sub-shrubby mounds set with yellow flowers, 1 in. across, June–August.

Cinquefoil: see Potentilla

Columbine: see Aquilegia

Cotula

For a sunny position; long-lived. Propagate by division during the growing season. C. squalida (S 18 in.) is invasive, though useful as a paving plant. Dense, bronze, saw-edged leaves; non-flowering.

Cotyledon

A long-lived plant for sun or partial shade. Propagate by division, August–October. C. simplicifolia (H 6 in. SS 8 in.) is a delightful plant, with leathery green rosettes throughout the year and beady yellow flowers drooping from arching sprays, June–August.

Crepis

For well drained soil and a sunny position. Propagate from root cuttings in March. C. incana (H 9 in. S 9 in.) grows like a narrow-leaved dandelion but with clear pink quilled flowers, May–July.

Dianthus 'Waithman's Beauty'

Dianthus

For a sunny position and well drained limy soil. D. deltoides is short-lived, but the others mostly have a fairly long life. Propagation of named varieties is by cuttings taken after flowering and inserted in a frame; by autumn division of quick-growing, mat-forming kinds; by seed sown under glass, February–March. *D. arvernensis* (H 2 in. SS 10 in.) has clear pink flowers on grey mats, June–July. 'La Bourbrille' (H 2 in. SS 10 in.) makes similar growth but flowers more freely. *D. lemsii* (H 4 in. SS 6 in.) has pink flowers, June–August. 'Blue Hills' (H 2 in. SS 6 in.) makes neat, blue-green tufts with carmine-magenta flowers. 'Fanal' (H 6 in. SS 8 in.) is a fiery red. 'Little Jock' (H 6 in. SS 8 in.) grows neatly, with large, semi-double pink flowers, June–August. 'Dubarry' is similar but double-flowered. 'Oakington Hybrid' (H 6 in. SS 9 in.) has double pink flowers. 'Scaynes Hill' (H 6 in. SS 9 in.), deep rose pink. 'Waithman's Beauty' (H 6 in. SS 10 in.) is red and white. *D. deltoides* (SS 12 in.) is trailing; bright carmine-pink flowers, June–July. *D. d.* 'Brilliant' (SS 12 in.) is bright pink; *D. d.* 'Flashing Light' (SS 9 in.), intense salmon red; *D. d.* 'Wisley Variety' (SS 9 in.), purplish leaves, deep red flowers.

Dodocatheon

Dodocatheon (shooting star)
Aptly named, for at the tip of smooth erect stems come clusters of flowers with reflexed petals and prominent yellow

stamens and pistils. They require shade and moist, though not boggy, soil. Long-lived. Propagate by seed or division in autumn. There are several species (all H 9–15 in. S 6 in.) which do not differ greatly.

Dryas octopetala

Dryas
Long-lived plants for a sunny position. Propagate by layers after flowering. *D. octopetala* (SS 16 in.) makes shrubby, prostrate mats of greenery, a few large white flowers, May–June. Easy to keep in check. *D. vestita* (SS 14 in.) also has white flowers but produces them more freely.

Edelweiss: see **Leontopodium**

Erinus alpinus

Erinus
Requires a sunny aspect; rather short-lived. Propagate by seed in spring. *E. alpinus* (H 3–4 in. SS 4–5 in.) forms neat hummocks which spread slowly; spikes of small, lilac-blue flowers, May–July. The variety *albus* is white; 'Dr. Hanelle' rosy red; 'Mrs. Boyle' clear pink.

Erodium
Generally long-lived if grown in a sunny position. Propagate by basal cuttings in late summer. *E. chamaedroides roseum* (H 2 in. SS 6 in.) forms bright green hummocks set with stemless bright pink flowers, May–August. *E. chrysanthum* (H 9 in. S 10 in.) has grey, ferny foliage; soft yellow flowers, June–September. *E. guttatum* (S 9 in.) is a low, grey-leaved plant; pale pink flowers with red markings, June–August.

Erodium chrysanthum

Genista
Long-lived in a sunny position. Propagate by heel cuttings after flowering. *G. pilosa* (SS 12 in.) is a fully prostrate broom, with deep green stems that spread slowly, and bright yellow flowers, June–July. *G. sagittalis* (SS 12 in.) is also prostrate, with flat-leaved stems and single yellow flowers, June–July.

G. tinctoria (H 9 in. S 10 in.) is a low, shrubby plant forming a sturdy clump; deep yellow flowers, June–July. *G. t. plena* is a double-flowered variety. *G.* 'Lydia' (H 18 in. S 18 in.) bears vivid yellow flowers, June.

Gentiana acaulis

Gentiana (gentian)
These can be divided into three groups: spring-flowering, summer-flowering and autumn-flowering.

Spring-flowering kinds require a sunny position and will grow in soils containing lime. Propagate *G. acaulis* by division after flowering; *G. verna* by freshly saved seed in the autumn. *G. acaulis* (SS 6 in.) bears large, blue, stemless trumpets, April–May. Flowering is sometimes sparse, though a light dressing of topsoil in the early autumn, with a little bone-meal added, is helpful. *G. verna* (H 3 in. S 4 in.) produces abundant blue flowers, April–May.

Summer-flowering gentians are the easiest to grow, with or without lime in the soil. They do best in a sunny position. Propagate by seed in November or March. Reliable species (all H 6–10 in.) include *G. doeringiana*, *G. bisetaea* and *G. lagodechiana* (all AS 6 in.);

G. septemfida and *G. hascombensis* (both AS 8 in.). All have blue flowers, June–August.

Autumn-flowering gentians grow with grassy stems, bearing trumpets in varying shades of blue. They require semi-shade and, with the exception of *G. farreri*, do not thrive in soils containing lime. Propagate by division; plants should in any case be divided every other year. Add extra peat to the soil when re-planting. *G. farreri* (H 6 in. AS 6 in.) has ice blue flowers, September–October. *G. sino-ornata* (H 3–4 in. AS 6 in.) has deep blue trumpets, September–October. 'Kidbrook Seedling' (H 3–4 in. AS 6 in.) bears brilliant blue flowers, August–September. 'Inverleith' (H 3–4 in. SS 6 in.), large, deep blue trumpets on trailing stems, August–September.

Geranium

Geranium (cranesbill)
Given a sunny position, these are reliable, long-lived plants. Propagate by division in early spring. *G. cinereum* (H 4 in. S 6 in.) makes mounded, ash-grey plants; pink, saucer-like flowers, June–July. *G. c.* 'Ballerina' (H 6 in. S 6 in.) flowers more freely, June–August, the lilac-coloured blooms having red veins. *G. dalmaticum* (H 4 in. S 8 in.) produces light pink flowers, May–June, from an expanding clump. *G. farreri* (H 4 in. AS 8 in.) has bright pink flowers 1 in. across, June–July. It needs a warm situation. *G. sanguineum lancastriense* (H 1½ in. AS 12 in.) spreads with some vigour and the mat is well covered with clear pink flowers, June–August. *G. subcaulescens* (H 6 in. S 8 in.) forms dense, grey-green tufts, with purple-red flowers, June–August. *G. s. splendens* (H 6 in. AS 15 in.) is less vigorous; the flowers are bright salmon-rose. *G. wlassowianum* (H 18 in. S 18 in.) has blue flowers.

Globularia (globe daisy)
Evergreen mat-forming plants for ordinary soil in a sunny position. Long-lived. Divide in September. *G. bellidifolia* (H 3 in. SS 8 in.) makes close, dark green mats, with light blue flowers, May–June. *G. cordifolia* (H 6 in. SS 9 in.) is similar in all but size. *G. incanescens* (H 1 in. S 4 in.) needs gritty soil; blue puff-ball flowers, May–June.

Gypsophila
The species described are all of trailing or creeping habit, good as wall plants, with narrow glaucous foliage and short sprays of flowers, May–July. They need a sunny position, and are long-lived. Propagate by seed in April. *G. dubia* (SS 10 in.) makes a subdued, purplish spread and has bright pink flowers. *G. fratensis* (SS 10 in.) trails more extensively from a central rootstock and carries a good show of clear pink flowers. *G. repens* 'Letchworth Rose' (SS 14 in.) is somewhat larger and coarser, with light pink flowers. *G. r.* 'Dorothy Teacher' has pink flowers, June–July.

Helianthemum (rock rose)
These popular, long-lived plants are not true roses but the flowers, both double and single, ½–1 in. in diameter, bear some resemblance to roses. They require an open, sunny position. Cut back with shears after flowering. Propagate by tip cuttings in September or March. There are many named varieties in white, pink, yellow, red and orange. Some grow close to the ground; others are erect and bushy, 10–12 in. high. Foliage varies from ash-grey to light and dark green. *H.* 'Ben Ledi' (H 6–9 in. S 12 in.) has brilliant red flowers, June. *H. lunulatum* (H 6 in. S 8 in.) has grey leaves and dangling yellow flowers, June–July. *H. serpyllifolium* (SS 15 in.) is prostrate and has a blaze of yellow flowers, May–June.

Helianthemum

Helichrysum (everlasting flower)
Sun-loving plants for well drained soil. Propagate by seed or cuttings in spring. *H. bellidioides* (SS 18 in.) has a prostrate habit, with white flowers, May–August. *H. marginatum* (syn. *milfordae*) (SS 9 in.) makes close silver cushions, with white flowers, May–July.

Hieraceum (hawkweed)
Easy to grow in a sunny position. Propagate by seed or division in spring. *H. villosum* (H 6 in. S 8 in.) has silvery, woolly leaves and yellow, dandelion-like flowers, June–August.

Houseleek: see **Sempervivum**

Hutchinsia
Requires partial shade; long-lived. Propagate by division after flowering. *H. alpina* (H 3 in. SS 6 in.) makes tight, deep

Hutchinsia alpina

green hummocks and bears sprays of pure white flowers, May–June. *H. auerswaldi* is very similar.

Hypericum (St. John's wort)
These need full sun and are good for walls. Not very long-lived.

Hypericum nummularium

Propagate by basal cuttings in August or February, or by seed in spring. *H. nummularium* (H up to 6 in. S 10 in.) has yellow flowers, May–June. *H. olympicum* and *H. polyphyllum* (both H 6 in. S 14 in.) are vigorous plants with glaucous leaves. Flowers are 1½ in. across, bright yellow, June–August. *H. orientale* (H 4 in. S 10 in.) is more compact; yellow flowers, June–August.

Hyssopus (hyssop)
For a dry, sunny position; fairly long-lived. Propagate by division in spring. *H. aristatus* (H 10 in. S 8 in.) forms an erect dark green bush; deep blue flowers, August–October.

Leontopodium

Iberis (candytuft)
Useful evergreen plants, especially for walls. Require sun and good drainage; long-lived. Propagate from seed in April in a cold frame, or from heel cuttings after flowering. *I. commutatum* (H 9 in. SS 15 in.) has deep green foliage and masses of pure white flower

heads, May–July. *I.* 'Snowflake' (H 12 in. SS 10 in.) is less vigorous but bears larger flower heads, May–July. 'Little Gem' (H 6 in. S 9 in.) makes a compact, non-trailing bush which is not fully evergreen but produces white flowers freely, May–July.

Leontopodium (edelweiss)
Easy to grow in a sunny position on light soil, but not long-lived. Propagate by seed under glass in March. *L. alpinum* (H 4–6 in. S 6 in.) has silvery tufts; soft white flower bracts, June–July. *L. a. souliei* (H 4–6 in. S 6 in.) and *L. crassense* (H 4 in. S 6 in.) have the same curious flowers but the leaves are duller. They are longer-lived than *L. alpinum*.

Linum (flax)
For full sunshine and well drained soil. Long-lived. Propagate from seed under glass in March or from cuttings after flowering in August. *L. extra-xillare* (H 6 in. S 12 in.) makes strong clumps, with semi-prosrate stems carrying light blue flowers, May–July. *L. salsoloides nanum* (S 12 in.) is quite prostrate, with white flowers on trailing stems, May–July.

Lithospermum prostratum

Lithospermum (gromwell)
These plants are long-lived if given a sunny position in suitable soil. *L. prostratum* requires acid conditions, but *L. graminifolium* needs lime. Propagate the latter by division in September or March; the former by heel or tip cuttings, July–August, under glass. *L. graminifolium* (H 6–8 in. S 8 in.) forms grey-leaved bushes; short sprays of deep blue flowers, May–July. *L. prostratum* 'Heavenly Blue' (SS 12 in.) makes dark green mats with intense blue tubular flowers, May–July.

Lychnis (campion)
For a sunny site and well drained soil. Fairly long-lived. Propagate by division in spring. *L. flos-jovis* (H 8 in. S 6 in.) makes silver-grey woolly mats, with bright pink flowers, May–July.

Mertensia

Mertensia
Needs a cool, shady position. Long-lived. Propagate by division in September. *M. echioides* (H 6 in. SS 10 in.) makes leafy

carpets that die back in autumn. Short sprays of deep blue flowers, April–May.

Micromeria
Requires a sunny position and well drained soil. Long-lived. Propagate by division in March or April. *M. corsica* (H 4 in. S 10 in.) makes neat grey mounds set with tiny pink flowers, June–September.

Mimulus

Mimulus (musk)
Require moist soil in a sunny position. Propagation, except of dwarf varieties, is by division every year in March or August. Dwarf varieties such as 'Red Emperor', 'Wisley Red' and 'Whitecroft Scarlet' (all H 4–6 in. S 6 in.), flower June–August. They are short-lived, but can be raised from seed sown under glass in March or from tip cuttings in August. *M. burnetii* (H 8 in. S 12 in.) has orange-brown flowers, June–August. *M. langsdorffii alpinus* (H 8 in. SS 12 in.) has bright yellow flowers, June–August. *M. primuloides* (H 4 in. S 6 in.) makes tiny mounds and has small yellow flowers, July to

September. It needs shade and moisture. These three species are fully perennial.

Nierembergia

Requires sun or half shade in soil that is not excessively dry. Given these conditions it is long-lived. Propagate by division in March. *N. rivularis* (H 1 in. S 14 in.) is mat-forming and spreads fairly rapidly. Large, white, cup-shaped flowers, June–August.

Nierembergia rivularis

Omphalodes (navelwort)

Good ground cover plants for a semi-shaded position; long-lived. Propagate by division in September. *O. cappadocica* (H 6 in. S 9 in.) has greyish leaves and sprays of bright blue flowers, April–May. *O. c.* 'Anthea Bloom' is similar, with sky-blue flowers and a compact habit.

Origanum

For ordinary soil and a sunny position. Long-lived. Propagate by division in spring. *O. laevigatum* (H 10–12 in. S 9 in.) has

Omphalodes cappadocica

sprays of small purple flowers, August–October.

Oxalis (shamrock)

Some species are invasive, their creeping growth spreading among surrounding plants. They require a sunny position, and are long-lived. *O. adenophylla* (H 3 in. AS 4 in.) produces a tuft of glaucous leaves, with rose-pink flowers, May–June. *O. floribunda* (H 6 in. S 9 in.) is not invasive, forming a green mound which carries pink flowers, June–August.

Penstemon

Require sun and good drainage. Propagate by division in spring. *P. davidsoni* (H 6 in. S 10 in.) is sub-shrubby, with ruby-red flowers, May–July. *P. pinifolius* (H 9 in. S 8 in.) makes neat, small-leaved bushes, with bright scarlet flowers, July–October. *P. scouleri* (H 9 in. S 8 in.) is of shrubby habit; lavender flowers, May–June.

Phlox

The alpine kinds are mat-forming. They are long-lived in

a sunny position with gritty soil. Propagate by division in March or heel cuttings in July. *P. douglasii* (SS 10 in.) has somewhat bristly foliage; stemless flowers, May–June. *P. d. effusa* (SS 10 in.) is rosy-pink; *rosea*, pink; 'May Snow', white. *P. subulata* varieties grow a little larger and less tidily but keep prostrate; the flowers are in small sprays, May–June. 'Benita' (SS 12 in.) is lavender mauve; 'Blue Eyes' (SS 12 in.), lavender blue; 'Brightness' (SS 10 in.), pink; 'Sensation' (SS 10 in.), rose pink; 'Temiscaming' (SS 12 in.), vivid rose red. The *P. verna* (syn. *stolonifera*) variety 'Blue Ridge' (SS 9 in.) has blue flower heads.

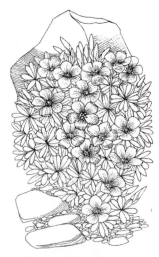

Oxalis adenophylla

Polygonum (knotweed)

Useful ground-cover mats for sun or shade. Long-lived. Propagate by division in spring or autumn. *P. affine* 'Darjeeling Red' (H 9 in. SS 18 in.) forms wide mats, green in summer and brown in winter; poker-like flower spikes, June–August. *P. a.* 'Donald Lowndes' (H 9 in. SS 12 in.) has stumpy, bright

pink spikes, May–July and September–October. *P. vaccinifolium* (SS 14 in.) is prostrate, with small pink spikes, July–September.

Potentilla nitida

Potentilla (cinquefoil)

Easily grown plants in a sunny position. Generally long-lived. Propagate by division in March. *P. aurea* (syn. *verna nana*), *P. crantzii* and *P. ternata* (syn. *chrysocraspeda*) (all H 3–4 in. SS 6 in.) make deep green tufts; yellow, strawberry-type flowers, May–July. *P. t. aurantiaca* is an orange-buff variation; *P. aurea plena* is double-flowered. *P. fragiformis* (H 9 in. S 6 in.) has soft grey leaves, with bright yellow flowers, May–June. *P. nitida* (H 2 in. S 5 in.) forms silver-leaved hummocks bearing pink flowers, May–June. *P. tommasiniana* (H 3 in. SS 14 in.) makes spreading, silvery-grey mats, covered in yellow flowers, May–June. *P. tonguei* (S 12–14 in.) forms strong tufts, prostrate sprays of buff and orange-brown, June–September.

Primula (primrose, cowslip)
A vast and varied genus, divided into the following four sections:

Bog primulas, with drooping flowers from terminal heads or spikes of candelabra formation. Mainly short-lived. Propagate by seed in December. Most species require sun and ample moisture. Flowers are up to 24 in. high, May–July.

Primula

Woodland primulas. Need semi-shade and damp, peaty soil. Propagate by seed in December. Flowering is from April–June, heights varying from 1–18 in.

Primroses. This section includes such well-known varieties as the purple-red 'Wanda', but there are many others with white, pink, yellow or crimson-purple flowers. Given heavy soil, they are easy to grow and long-lived. Propagate by division in June. The flowering period is March–May.

Auricula types. These make rosetted plants, often with whitish leaves; flower heads, 2–6 in. high, April–May. Require moist, gritty soil in a reasonably sunny position. Slow-growing. Propagate by division in September.

Pulsatilla
Require a sunny position, good drainage and soil containing lime. Propagate by seed sown outdoors as soon as ripe. *P. vulgaris* (pasque flower) (H 6–12 in. S 9 in.), flowers April–May; the blooms are goblet-shaped, with pointed petals, followed by ferny leaves and fluffy seed heads. The varieties are shaded from white to mauve, violet-purple and red, with golden anthers.

Raoulia
Require full sun. Propagate by division in April. *R. australis* (SS 10 in.) makes a close, silver, evergreen mat; insignificant, yellow-ochre flowers. Patches may die out in a cold winter. *R. tenuicaule* (SS 14 in.) is less colourful and rather rampant.

Raoulia

Rock cress: see **Arabis**; **Aubrieta**

Rockfoil: see **Saxifraga**

Saponaria ocymoides

Rock rose: see **Helianthemum**

St. John's wort: see **Hypericum**

Saponaria (soapwort)
S. ocymoides (SS 14 in.) is a vigorous trailer, suitable for sunny walls. Short-lived. Needs occasional trimming. Propagate by seed in spring. Bright pink flowers, May–July.

Satureia (winter savory)
Long-lived in sun or partial shade. Propagate by division in April. *S. montana* (H 6 in. SS 9 in.) forms low, aromatic bushes, with small, light blue flowers, August–September. *S. repanda* (H 3 in. AS 12 in.) dies back in winter. During the summer it makes a low green mat with white flowers, August–September.

Saxifraga (rockfoil)
This large genus is best divided into four sections:

Kabschia saxifrages. These form tight, rosetted cushions and need gritty, but not parched soil. An open aspect on a north-facing slope is ideal. Propagate by basal cuttings under glass in May. All flower February–April. *S. apiculata* (H 4 in. SS 6 in.) has green hummocks and yellow flowers. There is a white variety, *S. a. alba.* Varieties with a slower growth rate and neater form (all H 3 in. and in shades of light or golden yellow) are 'Boston Spa' (SS 5 in.), bright green cushions; 'Elisabethae' (SS 4 in.) and 'Gold Dust' (SS 5 in.). The following are silver-leaved, very slow-growing and all under 2 in. high: 'Cranbourne' (SS 4 in.), shell pink; 'Jenkinsae' (SS 3–4 in.), light pink; *obristi* (SS 3–4 in.) and *kewensis* (SS 4 in.), both white; *megasaeflora* (SS 3–4 in.), deep pink.

Encrusted or aizoon saxifrages. These are mostly silver, with larger rosettes. Though

Satureia montana

less demanding than the kabschia saxifrages, they do best in a sunny position and well drained soil. Long-lived. Propagate by basal cuttings after flowering. All flower May–June. *S. aizoon baldensis* (H 4 in. SS 6 in.) is compact, with a few white flower sprays; *rosea* (H 8 in. SS 6 in.) has pink flowers; *lutea* (H 8 in. SS 6 in.), yellow; 'Esther' (H 6 in. SS 6 in.), greyish foliage, light primrose coloured flowers on erect sprays. *S. burnatii* (H 9 in. SS 5 in.) has silvery foliage, white flower sprays. *S.* 'Kathleen Pinsent' (H 9 in. SS 4 in.) has delicate pink flowers. 'Whitehills' (H 6 in. SS 5 in.) has silvery rosettes and produces abundant white flowers. 'Southside Seedling' (H 18 in. SS 5 in.) bears sprays of white flowers, spotted pink.

Mossy saxifrages. Bright evergreen rosetted cushions, with a fair degree of spread. They require semi-shade and soil that is not over-dry. Propagate by division after flowering while the soil is damp. Division is in any case needed when the plants become ragged with age. All varieties flower April–May in sprays on erect stems. *S.* 'Carnival' (H 6 in. SS 6–9 in.) has carmine-rose flowers; 'Dubarry' (H 9 in. SS 6–9 in.), large crimson flowers; 'Gaiety' (H 6 in. SS 6–9 in.), warm pink; 'Pearly King' (H 4 in. SS 6–9 in.), white; 'Sprite' (H 4 in. SS 6–9 in.), deep pink; 'Triumph' (H 6 in. SS 6–9 in.), blood red; 'Winston Churchill' (H 6 in. SS 6–9 in.), clear pink; *whitlayii compacta* (H 4 in. SS 6–9 in.), close and mossy, with white flowers.

Other saxifrages include *S. oppositifolia* (S 6 in.), which forms low, dark green mats set with bright pink flowers, March–April. It needs similar conditions to the aizoon saxifrages. Propagate by division or basal cuttings after flowering. *S. primuloides* 'Elliott's Variety' (H 6 in. SS 6 in.) makes neat mounds of leathery green rosettes and has sprays of small, deep pink flowers, April–May. It is similar to, but smaller than, 'London Pride' (*S. umbrosa*).

Propagate by division or basal cuttings after flowering.

Scabiosa (scabious)

Drought-resistant plants for a sunny position. Long-lived. Propagate by division in March. *S. pterocephala* (syn. *parnassi*) (H 3 in. S 9 in.) has soft, grey-green mats, with pink flowers, June–September.

Sedum (stonecrop)

This large genus includes weedy kinds, as well as those described here which are useful for providing late flowers. A sunny position is needed. Propagate by division, March–April. *S.* 'Coral Carpet' (SS 9 in.) seldom flowers but makes colourful mats. Useful for paving. *S. floriferum* 'Weihenstephaner Gold' (H 4 in. SS 10 in.) makes clumpy plants, with deep yellow flower heads, June–August. *S. kamtschaticum* (H 4 in. S 6 in.) also has yellow flowers but is less vigorous. *S. lidakense* (H 6 in. AS 6 in.) has glaucous-blue summer foliage, is slow-growing and has semi-prostrate, deep rose flower heads, July–September. *S. pluricaule* and *S. cauticolum* (both H 4 in. AS 6 in.) have a similar habit, with bright pink flowers. *S.* 'Ruby Glow' (H 9 in. AS 9 in.) is more upright, with crowded, ruby-red heads, July–September. *S. pulchellum* (H 4 in. AS 6 in.) has bright pink flower heads, June–September. *S. spathulifolium* (H 4 in. SS 6 in.) makes bluish-purple rosettes and has deep yellow flowers, June–July. *S. spurium* 'Erdblut' and *S. s.* 'Schorbuser Blut' (both H 4 in. S 10 in.) form green mats, with sizeable heads of glistening, deep pink flowers, June–August. *S. tartarinowii* (H 4 in. AS 6 in.) is very neat, making low, bushy growth in summer, covered with light pink flowers, August–September.

Avoid planting *S. acre*, *S. dasyphyllum* and *S. album*, which are weed-like.

Sempervivum fimbriatum

Sempervivum (houseleek)

Evergreen rosettes of limited spread. Long-lived, they will flourish in poor soil, provided it is well drained and in a sunny position. Sempervivums will grow in walls, or outdoors in pans or troughs, with scarcely any attention. Diameter of the rosettes varies from ½–4 in., some of the smaller ones having a cobwebby appearance and the larger ones having purple and bronze-red shades in their leaves. The flowers are mostly pinkish, in erect or drooping sprays. Propagate by division at almost any time.

There are over 200 kinds in cultivation, and a selection is best made by examining the stock or catalogue of a specialist supplier. The following are among the most attractive: smaller cobwebby types include *S.* 'Jubilee' (SS 10 in.), 1 in. silvered rosettes; *laggeri* (SS 5 in.) is similar but smaller, with deep pink flowers. Examples with smooth rosettes of medium size are: *fimbriatum*, green rosettes with crimson tips;

'Granat', wine-red leaves, and 'Spinell', grey-green, tinged red, with purplish rosettes (the last two are both SS 6–7 in.); 'Commander Hay', overlapping rosettes, tinged rosy green; 'Mahogany', purplish brown-green; *schlehanii rubrifolium*, large, crimson-purple rosettes; 'Zircon', green rosettes, tinged brown. (All these are SS 8–9 in.)

Shamrock: see **Oxalis**

Silene (catchfly)

Given a sunny position, these plants have a long life. Propagate by seed in spring or heel cuttings after flowering. *S. acaulis pedunculata* (SS 10 in.) forms slow-creeping, bright green mats set with clear pink flowers, May–June. *S. alpestris* (H 4 in. S 8 in.) makes matted clumps, with sprays of small white flowers, May–July. *S. a.* 'Bressingham' is white, double-flowered. *S. schafta* (H 6 in. S 6 in.) makes tufty clumps, with bright pink flowers, July–September.

Silene schafta

Sisyrinchium
Alpine species have midget, iris-like growth, though the flowers are more open. Given a sunny position they are long-lived. Propagate by division in March. *S. bellum* and *S. bermudianum* (both H 6 in. S 4 in.) grow as bladed tufts, with violet-blue flowers, May–July.

Sisyrinchium bermudianum

Spiraea
Easily grown, long-lived plants for a sunny position. Propagate by cuttings in spring. *S. bullata* (H 12–18 in. S 12–15 in.) makes a rounded bush, with rose-red flowers, June–July.

Stonecrop: see Sedum

Thymus (thyme)
Most are useful carpeting plants, spreading fairly rapidly and having aromatic foliage. They require sun and are generally long-lived. Propagate by division in March. *T. citriodorus* (S 12 in.), known as lemon thyme, forms low bushes bearing insignificant flowers. *T. c. aureus* (S 10 in.) has golden-green foliage; 'Silver Queen' and 'Silver Posie' (both S 8 in.) are variegated in

lighter shades but tend to revert to green as they grow older. *T. doefleri* (SS 12 in.) makes close grey mats covered with small, bright pink flowers, May–June; *T. d.* 'Bressingham' is a little later. *T. herba-barona* (SS 14 in.) forms dark green, carroway-scented mats. *T.* 'Porlock' (H 8 in. SS 12 in.) makes spreading, bushy growth, with a good display of pink, May–June. *T. nitidus* (H 6 in. SS 6 in.) has light pink flowers, May–June. *T. drucei* (SS 15 in.), the wild thyme, has mauve-pink flowers and is useful for paving but too rampant for small beds. *T. serpyllum coccineus* (H 3 in. SS 12 in.) makes dark, purple-green mats covered with reddish flowers, June–July; the large forms *T. s. major* and *T. s.* 'Pink Chintz' (both SS 14 in.) have clear pink flowers and a similar habit. *T. lanuginosus* (SS 16 in.) is grey, woolly and very vigorous, and one of the best plants for carpeting or paving; the pink flowers are sparse.

Thymus serpyllum coccineus

Tiarella (foam flower)
Mounded, evergreen plants for a shady position where the soil is

Tiarella cordifolia

not excessively dry; long-lived. Propagate by division in March or September or by seed in spring. *T. cordifolia* (H 8 in. S 16 in.) is of spreading habit, with golden-green foliage and sprays of tiny cream flowers, May–July. *T. polyphylla* (H 10 in. S 8 in.) is more compact, with sprays of pearl-like flowers, May–July. *T. wherryi* (H 10 in. S 6 in.) has golden-green leaves, is not vigorous, but produces abundant sprays of creamy-white flowers, May–August.

Tunica
Needs a sunny position. Propagate *T. saxifraga* from seed in spring; *T. s.* 'Rosette' from basal cuttings in spring. *T. saxifraga* (H 6 in. AS 9 in.) makes grassy tufts with limited spread; pink flowers, July–August. Short-lived. 'Rosette' (H 6 in. AS 6 in.) is a more attractive, double-flowered variety.

Veronica (speedwell)
A large family of plants, including both shrubby and herbaceous types, some erect, some prostrate. Require an open position and well drained soil. Propagate by

division in September or March.
Shrubby types. *V. buchanani nana* (H 2–3 in. SS 6 in.) is the smallest, forming tiny golden evergreen bushes; insignificant flowers. *V. catarractae* (H 6 in. SS 10 in.) has lilac-pink flowers, May–June. *V. edinensis* (H 18 in. SS 10 in.) is deep green throughout the year; small white flowers, June–July. *V.* 'Karl Teschner' (H 12 in. S 9 in.) has bronze-purple foliage; short spikes of deep violet flowers, June–July. *V. loganoides* (H 6 in. SS 9 in.) is of golden hue. *V. pageana* (H 8 in. SS 9 in.) is a blue-grey evergreen bush, with white flower heads, June–July.

Non-shrubby evergreen types. *V. cinerea* (H 4 in. SS 10 in.) forms ash-grey mats and has spikes of violet-blue, May–June. *V. guthreana* (H 4 in. SS 10 in.) is dark green and mat-forming; blue flowers, May–June. *V. whittleyi* (H 4 in. SS 14 in.) forms vigorous grey-green mats, with masses of bright blue flower spikes, May–June.

Non-evergreen types. *V. prostrata* (syn. *rupestris*) (H 6 in. S 12 in.) makes sturdy, clumpy, prostrate growth and produces a fine

Tunica saxifraga

Vinca minor

show of violet-blue spikes, June–July. *V. p. bastardi* is similar but has light blue flowers. *V. p.* 'Loddon Blue' has larger flowers of a richer blue in May–June and spreads less rapidly. 'Mrs. Holt' is one of the best pink varieties, May–June. *V.* 'Shirley Blue' (H 9 in. AS 9 in.) has brilliant blue flowers in June.

Vinca (periwinkle)

These plants are adaptable to sun or shade. Because they will grow in dry shade where little else will flourish they are seldom used elsewhere. Vincas are excellent for ground cover, needing minimal attention; they spread by means of rooted runners. Easily propagated by cuttings in summer or autumn, and can be safely planted or divided between September and March. Of the two main groups, only *V. minor* is sufficiently dwarf and neat to be classed under alpines. *V. major* has its uses beneath trees and shrubs. All vincas flower in spring, rather sparsely or briefly, but *V. minor* 'Bowles Variety' makes quite a show with its clear blue

flowers nestling closely on the low evergreen foliage during April and May. It spreads more compactly and evenly than most other vincas (SS 15 in.). *V. m.* 'Multiflex' (SS 18 in.) has semi-double wine-purple flowers. Apart from the white flowered *V. minor alba* (SS 18 in.) there is a double blue form, *V. m. caerulea plena* (SS 18 in.). Some forms of *V. minor* have variegated leaves, silvery and green as *V. m. argentea variegata*, and *V. m. aurea variegata* (both SS 18 in.), which is a more golden hue. The one species which is not evergreen is *V. herbacea* (SS 15 in.). It dies back in autumn to a neat dormant root, and in spring it sends out trailing stems up to 15 in. long, on which appear the typical periwinkle flowers of a light blue shade. It is an uncommon species, well worth a place in the garden.

Viola

Most require a sunny position; they are free-flowering, but short-lived, unless propagated from basal cuttings in Septem-

Viola cornuta alba

Waldsteinia ternata

ber. Though many are sufficiently dwarf for growing as alpines, only the fully hardy and perennial types should be used. Hybrids derived from *V. gracilis* or *V. cornuta* are suitable (all H 3–6 in. AS 9 in.; May–August) and include 'Norah Leigh', light blue; 'Martin', purple-violet; 'Blue Carpet', and 'Buttercup', yellow. The less vigorous *V. gracilis* varieties (AS 8 in.), apart from the true purple-violet species which is now rare, include 'Moonlight' (H 3–6 in. AS 6 in.), primrose yellow. *V. cornuta* (H 3–6 in. AS 9 in.) is blue; there is a white form, *V. c. alba*, with small white flowers; *V. c. nana* is a light blue, miniature form (AS 6 in.). A useful species for fairly dry ground in shade is *V. labradorica purpurea* (H 3–6 in. S 5 in.), with purplish leaves and pink flowers, April–June.

Waldsteinia

For sun or shade. Long-lived. Propagate by division or tip cuttings after flowering. *W. ternata* (syn. *sibirica*) (H 4 in. S 14 in.) forms spreading evergreen mats,

with short spikes of bright yellow flowers, April–May. Useful for banks or walls.

Wallflower: see **Cheiranthus**

Wulfenia

Neat evergreen plants requiring moist soil and some shade. Long-lived. Propagate by division in spring. *W. amherstiana* (H 5 in. S 4 in.) forms neat rosettes of deep green toothed leaves; spikes of lavender-blue flowers, June–July.

Zauschneria

Require a sunny position and light soil. Given these conditions they are long-lived. Greyish-leaved, twiggy, bushy growth, with scarlet tubular flowers, August–October. Late to appear in spring but form mounds 12–18 in. high by autumn. In cold districts, protect with leaves during the winter. Propagate by tip cuttings under glass in July. The following species (all AS 15 in.) have the same general appearance: *Z. californica mexicana*, *Z. canescens* and *Z. microphylla*.

Zauschneria californica

Alpines for special purposes

Rock plants can be used to advantage in many places in the garden. Where space is too limited to allow a rock garden or a raised alpine bed, many alpines will grow well in odd crevices in a wall, between crazy paving, or in sinks and troughs. While the majority of rock plants grow best in a dry sunny position, a number prefer damp and shade. Before choosing your alpines from the following lists the plant descriptions (pp. 336–46) should be consulted as to which species are suitable for various sites. It should not be assumed that all members of a suggested genus are suitable.

Alpines for paving and crevices
Acaena
Androsace
Arenaria
Asperula
Campanula garganica
Campanula 'Birch Hybrid'
Cotula
Globularia
Helichrysum
Nierembergia
Raoulia
Saxifraga
Sedum
Silene
Thymus

Alpines for ground cover
(unless otherwise indicated, these should be in a dry sunny position)

Ajuga (shade)
Arabis
Asperula
Campanula
Chrysopsis
Cotula
Dianthus
Dryas
Genista 'Lydia'
Helianthemum
Nierembergia
Omphalodes (shade)
Oxalis
Polygonum
Potentilla
Raoulia
Saxifraga (shade)
Sedum
Thymus
Veronica
Vinca

Androsace lanuginosa

Alpines for damp, peaty and mainly shady sites
Aquilegia ecalcarata
Astilbe
Calamintha

Dodocatheon
Epimedium
Gentiana (autumn flowering species)
Lysimachia nummularia
Mertensia
Mimulus primuloides
Omphalodes
Phlox stolonifera·'Blue Ridge'
Primula
Saxifraga (most green-leaved species)
Sedum pulchellum
Tiarella

Alpines for dry sunny sites
Achillea
Aethionema
Anthemis
Arabis
Armeria
Artemisia
Aubrieta
Cheiranthus
Crepis
Dianthus
Dryas
Erinus
Erodium
Genista
Globularia
Gypsophila
Helianthemum
Helichrysum
Hypericum
Iberis
Linum
Micromeria
Penstemon
Phlox
Potentilla
Pulsatilla
Saponaria

Dianthus

Satureia
Scabiosa
Sedum
Sempervivum
Silene
Thymus
Tunica
Veronica (bushy types)
Zauschneria

Alpines for dry shady sites
Ajuga
Campanula muralis
Epimedium
Geranium
Lamium
Pachysandra
Polygonum affine
Pulmonaria
Saxifraga umbrosa
Tiarella
Vinca
Viola labradorica
Waldsteinia

Fruit varieties to plant in November

APPLE AND PEAR

A wide range of rootstocks (the root systems on to which scions of selected varieties are grafted or budded) is now available, especially for apples, so that the ultimate size of the tree can be chosen before planting, subject to soil conditions. When ordering, tell the nurseryman the size of tree you need and he will supply a tree on the correct rootstock.

Bush trees (planting distance 12–15 ft.) and dwarf bush trees (planting distance 10–12 ft.) have trunks 2–3 ft. high, and are usually bought when two years old. They bear fruit quickly and need little space; all parts of the tree are within easy reach of the ground for pruning and picking.

Cordons (planting distance 2½–3 ft., rows 6–10 ft.) are trained trees whose growth is restricted to a main stem which may be single or multiple, upright or oblique, and are usually bought when one year old. They are best for a small space, but must be summer pruned if they are to maintain their restricted growth, and may become difficult to manage if not pruned regularly. They are usually trained at an angle of 45° by being tied to two wires stretched at heights of about 2½ and 5 ft. between posts rising 7 ft. out of the ground and placed at intervals of 10 ft.

Dwarf pyramids (planting distance 3½–5 ft., rows 7–10 ft.) are trained trees of restricted height with branches radiating from an upright central trunk, and are usually bought when three or four years old. They need a poor soil and require less attention than cordons or espaliers, but more than dwarf bushes. Vigorous varieties, such as 'Bramley's Seedling', 'Blenheim Orange' and 'Newton Wonder', cannot be grown in this way. Fasten the trees to two wires stretched at about 18 in. and 3 ft. above ground level between posts placed at intervals of 10 ft.

Espaliers (planting distance 12–15 ft., rows 8–10 ft.) are trained trees with a central trunk and two or three tiers of horizontal branches, and are usually bought when three or four years old. Like cordons, they are good in a small space. The branches are usually already trained when the trees are bought, so treat the branches as individual cordons and tie them to wires stretched 24 in. apart.

Half-standards and standards (planting distance 25–30 ft., rows 30–40 ft.) have trunks 4 and 6 ft. high respectively, and are bought when three or four years old. These trees are suitable for large gardens, and take six to ten years to come into full bearing. They are less easy to work on than bush trees.

Apples and pears like a well drained deep soil, although pears are more difficult to suit than apples.

Early maturing dessert varieties have only a short life when ripe, so do not plant more than you can use, and unless you have good fruit storage do not plant too many varieties which mature after Christmas. Some of the top-quality dessert varieties demand good soil and regular attention. 'Cox's Orange Pippin' and 'James Grieve', for example, are prone to apple scab and canker on heavy soil and in wet climates. Early-flowering varieties are not generally recommended for cold northern gardens, because the flowers are more likely to be damaged by frost than those of the later-flowering varieties.

Some varieties of apple are self-fertile, but cropping will be more satisfactory if varieties which flower at the same period are chosen to provide cross-pollination (see list of varieties). When planting pears, it is more important to provide for cross-pollination. If you are only planting one pear, choose 'Conference' or 'Williams' Bon Chrétien'.

The useful life of a bush tree is about 30 years. The life of trained trees depends on how well they are cared for.

Recommended apples
D = Dessert   C = Cooking

'Ashmead's Kernel' (D), December–March. Greenish-yellow. First-class quality russet. Firm flesh. Moderate cropper. Flowers in mid-season.

'Bramley's Seedling' (C), November–March. Large, greenish-yellow. Keeps well, but flowers are susceptible to frost. Grows vigorously. Poor pollinator. Flowers in mid-season.

'Cox's Orange Pippin' (D), November–January. Dull brown-red russet. Firm and juicy. Susceptible to mildew and canker. Flowers in mid-season. Not recommended for cold northern gardens.

'Egremont Russet' (D), October–December. Yellow and russet. Distinctive flavour and firm flesh. Not susceptible to scab. Flowers early.

'George Cave' (D), mid-August. Brilliant red and yellow. Firm, juicy and sweet. Regular cropper. Flowers early.

'Golden Noble' (C), September–January. Yellow. Soft flesh with sharp flavour. Forms a prolific healthy tree. Flowers late.

'Gravenstein' (D), October–December. Yellow with red flush and streaks. Crisp and juicy. Vigorous variety. Poor pollinator, unsuitable for growing in restricted form. Flowers early.

'Grenadier' (C), August–September. Large, greenish-yellow. Crisp and acid. Good cropper. Scab-resistant. Flowers in mid-season.

'James Grieve' (D), September–October. Pale yellow with red flush and streaks. Good flavour, juicy. Liable to bruise. Susceptible to scab and canker. Flowers in mid-season.

'Laxton's Epicure' (D), end of August–early September. Greenish-yellow with red flush and streaks. Sweet and juicy. Very prolific cropper. Flowers in mid-season.

'Laxton's Fortune' (D), September–October. Yellow with red flush and streaks. Crisp and juicy. Regular cropper. Frost-resistant. Flowers in mid-season.

'Merton Worcester' (D), September–October. Golden yellow, covered with bright crimson flush. Sweet, slightly aromatic. Flowers in mid-season.

'Monarch' (C), October–January. Large, pale yellow with red flush. Soft, juicy and acid. Flowers late and tends to be irregular.

'Orleans Reinette' (D), January–February. Golden yellow with russet patches. Hardy and prolific. Best late variety.

'Ribston Pippin' (D), November–January. Greenish-yellow with russet. Crops regularly, often lightly. Choice fruit. Poor pollinator. Flowers early.

'St. Edmund's Russet' (D),

September–October. Covered with golden russet. Small fruit, good flavour. Flowers early.

Recommended pears

'Conference', October–November. Tapered, dark green with brown russet. Fruit melting, very juicy and sweet. Reliable cropper. Flowers in mid-season. Pollinated by 'Williams' Bon Chrétien' and 'Joséphine de Malines'.

'Doyenné du Comice', November. Pale yellow with red flush, some russet. One of the most delicious of all pears. Flowers late. Pollinated by 'Winter Nelis'.

'Joséphine de Malines', December–January. Small, greenish-yellow. Regular cropper. Flowers in mid-season. Pollinated by 'Williams' Bon Chrétien', 'Louise Bonne of Jersey' and 'Conference'.

'Louise Bonne of Jersey', October. Greenish-yellow flushed with deep red. Flesh melting. Regular cropper. Pollinated by 'Joséphine de Malines'.

'Williams' Bon Chrétien', September. Large, golden yellow dotted with russet. Juicy and sweet. Susceptible to scab. Flowers in mid-season. Pollinated by 'Conference' and 'Joséphine de Malines'.

'Winter Nelis', December. Dull green. Juicy, good flavour. Flowers late. Pollinated by 'Doyenné du Comice'.

BLACKBERRY, LOGANBERRY AND HYBRID BERRIES

Plant one-year-old blackberries 12–16 ft. apart, in rows 8–10 ft. apart, and the other berries 8–10 ft. between plants and rows. All or part of the fruited wood is cut out each autumn and new growth trained in. Growth is often vigorous. The loganberry is suitable if space is limited. Place strong posts at the ends of each row and tie new growths to wires stretched between the posts at intervals of 12 in., the top one at about 5½ ft.

These fruits will grow in any deep ordinary soil, will succeed in shady situations, and have a long cropping life.

Recommended blackberry

'Smoothstem', late August–October. Thornless and vigorous. Large fruit, heavy crop.

Recommended loganberry

'LY654 Clone', late July–August. Very large berries. Burgundy red colour when ripe.

Recommended hybrid berries

Boysenberry, July–August. Large, round, reddish-brown. Heavy cropper. Hardy. Tayberry, July–August. Bright crimson. Excellent flavour. Heavy crop. For dessert, freezing and jam making.

BLACK CURRANT

Plant two-year-old bushes deeply, 5–6 ft. apart, in rows 6–8 ft. apart, so that new growth comes from below the ground. Plant for succession.

Black currants like moisture-retaining but fairly well drained soil.

The bushes produce up to ten crops, but reversion disease often reduces cropping before that (see JULY).

Recommended black currants

'Mendip Cross', early. Large, slightly acid berries which will not hang long. 'Wellington XXX', mid-season. Large, sweet, good flavour. Moderately vigorous. 'Ben Lomond', late flowering and early ripening, so escapes frost. Large berries. Heavy crop.

CHERRY (acid)

Bush trees (planting distance 15–18 ft.) are usually bought when one year old. Fan-trained trees (planting distance 15–18 ft., rows 8–10 ft.) are usually partially trained when bought. Grow the trees against a wall, and space the wires horizontally about 6 in. apart. They will grow in border soil and even on a north-facing wall.

Many varieties, such as 'Morello', are self-fertile, and their useful life is 25–30 years.

Recommended acid cherry

'Morello', August–September. Roundish, deep red to black. Good small fruit. Self-fertile.

CHERRY (sweet)

Bush, half-standard and standard trees (planting distance 30–40 ft.) are usually bought when two years old. They make trees suitable for larger gardens. Fan-trained trees (planting distance 18–24 ft.) are difficult to manage because of their vigour.

All the trees are so subject to attack by birds that their main attraction will be the spring blossom, unless the whole tree can be covered, or sufficient trees are planted to make full-time bird scaring worth while.

Sweet cherries need deep, well drained soil, and light summer rainfall to prevent the fruit from cracking.

Treat varieties as self-sterile. The useful life is about 50 years.

Recommended sweet cherries

'Early Rivers', mid–late June. Reddish-black. Juicy. Vigorous. Pollinated by 'Merton Favourite', 'Merton Bigarreau' and 'Merton Bounty'.

'Merton Bigarreau', mid–late July. Almost black. Rich flavour. Vigorous and spreading. Pollinated by 'Early Rivers' and 'Morello' (acid).

'Merton Bounty', late June–early July. Dark crimson to black. Soft and juicy. Spreading tree. Pollinated by 'Early Rivers' and 'Morello' (acid).

'Merton Favourite', late July. Heart-shaped, black. Flesh dark crimson, sweet and very juicy. Pollinated by 'Early Rivers' and 'Morello' (acid).

GOOSEBERRY

Bushes (planting distance 5–6 ft., rows 6–8 ft.) are usually bought when two years old. They are normally grown on about 9 in. of clear stem below the branches.

Cordons (planting distance 1½–2 ft., rows 5–6 ft.) are also bought when two years old.

Gooseberries prefer a well drained, moist, loamy soil. The useful life is over 20 years.

Recommended gooseberries

'Green Gem', mid-season. Green, oval berries. Pick some berries early, leaving the rest to produce fruit of dessert size. 'Langley Gage', mid-season. Greenish-white. Delicious flavour. Compact upright habit. 'Leveller', mid-season. Large, yellowish-green. Good quality for cooking and dessert. Spreading growth. 'Whitesmith', late. Large, white. Excellent for dessert. Spreading growth.

PEACH AND NECTARINE

These fruits are traditionally fan-trained, but more bush trees are now being grown to save summer pruning, although the fruit on bush trees is difficult to protect against attacks by birds and insects. No dwarfing rootstocks are available; peaches and nectarines are not vigorous growers.

Bush trees (planting distance 18–20 ft.) are usually two years old when planted.

Fan-trained trees (planting distance 12–15 ft., rows 8–10 ft.) are usually partially trained when bought. Train them against a wall in the same way as acid cherries.

All these fruits need a well drained soil, and are liable to damage by spring frosts because they flower early. Bush peaches grow best in eastern counties; in other areas, plant peaches against a wall. Nectarines need a warm and sunny site outside.

The choice of variety is limited because of the climate. The life of these fruits is about 20 years.

Recommended peach

'Rochester', mid-August. Rich yellow. Flesh deep crimson. Good, hardy and prolific. Suitable for a bush tree. Self-fertile.

Recommended nectarines 'Early Rivers', mid-July. Greenish-yellow flushed with scarlet. Very tender and juicy. 'Lord Napier', early August. Large, yellowish-green with deep red flush. Rich flavour.

PLUM AND DAMSON
No dwarfing rootstocks are available for plums and damsons, so the trees tend to grow to a good size and will not start to flower for five years or more. Bush trees (planting distance 12–15 ft.) are usually two years old when planted. Half-standards and standards (planting distance 18–24 ft.) are also planted when two years old. Fan-trained trees (planting distance 12–15 ft., rows 8–10 ft.) are usually partially trained when bought. Train them against a wall in the same way as acid cherries.

These fruits do not like badly drained cold soils. They flower early, so plant them where they will be free from frost and sheltered from the wind.

Plant mainly dessert types, because even the choicest can be cooked when nearly ripe. Gages (included under plums) grow best in districts which are warm and dry in summer; in other districts grow them on a wall. Damsons are hardier and can be planted as shelter trees. Unfruitfulness is often a problem with plums. Cross-pollination is generally required, so bear this in mind when deciding which varieties to buy. If you are planting only one plum tree, choose 'Victoria' or 'Early Transparent Gage'. The useful life of a tree is about 40 years.

Recommended plums and gages 'Cambridge Gage', late August. Round, greenish-yellow. Excellent for dessert and canning. Pollinated by 'Early Transparent Gage', 'Victoria' and 'Kirke's Blue' plums, 'Merryweather' and 'Shropshire Prune' damsons.
'Coe's Golden Drop', September–October. Amber yellow, spotted red on sunny side. Sweet and rich. Good small

plum. Not a heavy cropper. Pollinated by 'Victoria' and 'Kirke's Blue' plums and 'Merryweather' damson.
'Early Transparent Gage', mid August. Apricot yellow with carmine spots and stripes. Excellent for jam making. Self-fertile.
'Jefferson's Gage', early September. Golden-yellow dotted with red, russet patches. Sweet, gage flavour. Pollinated by 'Victoria' plum.
'Kirke's Blue', mid-September. Dark purple with blue bloom. Sweet and juicy. Good small plum. Pollinated by 'Early Transparent Gage', 'Victoria' and 'Cambridge Gage'.
'Victoria', late August. Bright red, speckled with darker dots. Multi-purpose. Liable to branch splitting. Self-fertile.

Recommended damsons 'Merryweather', September. Large, black, with thin bloom and thick skin. Self-fertile. 'Shropshire Prune', October. Small, blue-black. Good for canning and bottling. Self-fertile.

RASPBERRY
Plant one-year-old bushes 18 in. apart in rows 5–8 ft. apart.

Established canes produce suckers and new canes every year, so if young canes are planted 18 in. apart a continuous band of plants arises. Support the canes by tying them to a wire 4 or 5 ft. from the ground stretched between posts set at 15 ft. intervals, or use two parallel wires separated by short horizontal pieces of wood attached to the end of the posts, and grow the canes between the wires.

Raspberries prefer a slightly acid soil, and should be sheltered from strong winds.

Plant a number of varieties for succession. The life of raspberry beds is usually limited by health and weeds.

Recommended raspberries 'Delight', mid-season. Virus resistant. High yield. 'Glen Clova',

early. Medium light red. Fine flavour. 'Malling Admiral', late. Disease resistant. Sheltered site. 'Malling Jewel'. early mid-season. Bright red becoming darker. Firm. Slow to increase. 'Zeva', autumn fruiting (not for northern gardens).

RED AND WHITE CURRANTS
These currants are like apples, in that they fruit on spurs on the established branches, whereas black currants fruit on the previous season's growth.

Bushes (planting distance 5–6 ft., rows 6–8 ft.) are bought when two years old.

Cordons (planting distance 1½–2 ft., rows 5–6 ft.) are also bought when two years old.

They like a moist but not badly drained soil, and are susceptible to lack of potassium.

The varieties are few but adequate for a choice, because the fruits have a limited use.

Recommended red and white currants
'Laxton's No. 1', early. Large, bright red. Regular and heavy cropper. Strong upright grower. 'White Versailles', early. Large, light yellow. Sweet berry carried in long bunches. Strong grower.

STRAWBERRY
Establish the bed by planting rooted runners. Then either restrict the plants by removing the runners as they form, or allow the runners to root down the row to form a matted bed of plants. Single plants produce large, high-quality fruit, while the matted rows produce a greater weight of fruit from the same area, although the fruit is usually smaller.

Plant strawberries 18 in. apart in rows 2½–3 ft. apart, but if the plants are to be protected with cloches in spring for earlier fruiting, plant them 9–12 in. apart in a single row. The crowns should be exactly level with the surface of the soil.

They grow best in a soil rich in humus. If farmyard manure

or compost is worked in before planting no further applications of fertiliser will be needed.

Summer- and autumn-fruiting types are available. The season can be extended by protecting the fruit in spring and again in the autumn.

The normal life of a bed is three crops, but allow protected plants one year under glass and one year outside.

Recommended strawberries 'Cambridge Favourite', mid-season. Large salmon-scarlet. Preserving and quick-freezing. 'Cambridge Vigour', second early. Medium crimson. Good flavour. 'Gento', successive crops on plants and runners July–October. Very large fruit. 'Redgauntlet', mid-season. Large, scarlet. Vigorous and compact. Highly recommended for cold northern districts. 'Royal Sovereign', early mid-season. Large, wedge-shaped, scarlet. Excellent flavour. Soft, and susceptible to grey mould.

VINE (outdoor)
The varieties of table grape currently available cannot be ripened successfully without protection in this country, but grapes for wine-making can be grown outdoors in the southern part of the country.

Plant one-year-old plants 24 in. apart in rows 3 ft. apart, or as a fan on a wall with 5 ft. between the plants.

Vines grow best in poor soils and in areas where the rainfall is not high.

Recommended vines for wine making
'Riesling Sylvaner', October. Light colour. Usually a good cropper. Makes excellent wine of Alsatian type. 'Siegerrebe', October. Large, golden. Fine muscat flavour.

December

Fruit trees can be pruned, plots tidied, and frost precautions taken before
the Christmas holiday puts a temporary stop to gardening

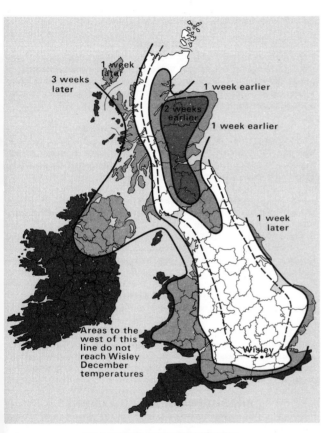

PROGRESS OF THE SEASON

The map shows the earliness or lateness of the season in an average
December at places in the British Isles, compared with conditions at
the Royal Horticultural Society's Gardens at Wisley in Surrey. The
broken line joins places where the season is as advanced as at Wisley.
In western areas temperatures never fall as low as those at Wisley, and
autumn conditions may persist in much of south-west Ireland and on
the coasts of Cornwall. Here gardeners will usually be able to leave their
December tasks until after the end of the month. Elsewhere, when the
weather permits, gardeners should carry on with their December
programme as soon as possible.

The weather in December

Usually there is little sunshine, and gales and rain are common,
with fog and frost inevitable when pressure rises during an
anticyclone and winds drop. December can be sometimes
the coldest month of the year, but it is rarely so in severe
winters. Cold spells which begin in early December seldom
persist for more than one or two weeks; but cold setting in at
the end of the month can presage a long, hard winter.

Occasionally in December south-westerly winds arriving
with a depression bring showers, and brighter intervals. In
the midlands afternoon temperatures average 7°C (45°F)
and night temperatures fall below 2°C (35°F), but it is much
colder in Scotland. More usually west winds, often reaching
gale force, bring heavy rain and, to the west, violent hailstorms; temperatures seldom rise above 4°C (40°F). Occasionally gentle, southerly winds cross the British Isles. Then low
cloud covers the country, and rainfall is heavy in the south-
west while drizzle occurs to the north and east. At other times
squally, cold, north-east winds bringing raw weather cross
the country. Temperatures may not rise above freezing
point all day.

Garden work is difficult in December, but every effort
should be made to tidy up the plots and to complete the
preparation of the ground. Care should be taken to eliminate
draughts in greenhouses and outhouses.

A summary of the month's work

LAWNS

Dig over areas to be seeded in the spring. Treat against leatherjackets. Clean and overhaul machines and equipment.

ROSES

Complete planting, but not if the soil is wet and sticky or if there
is frost or snow on the surface. If conditions are unsuitable, heel
the roses in or keep them in a frost-free place. Prepare established
rose beds for winter, shortening long growths to 2½ ft., collecting
and burning fallen leaves which show traces of black spot, and
chopping up the top inch of compacted soil. Ensure that
September-planted cuttings are firm in the ground.

Under glass. Bring pot roses into the greenhouse and prune hard.

HARDY HERBACEOUS PLANTS

Continue tidying beds and borders and digging between plants. Cut back invasive roots of trees and hedges. Replace worn turf beside a bed or border, and spread fresh gravel on flanking paths if necessary. Prune overhanging branches of trees and shrubs. Order seeds or plants for spring sowing or planting.

DAHLIAS

Examine stored tubers and plunge them in a bucket of tepid water overnight if they have shrivelled. Cut away portions of tubers that have rotted and dust the cuts with flowers of sulphur or captan.

CHRYSANTHEMUMS

Firm ground around over-wintering plants lifted by frost.
Under glass. Ventilate and maintain temperature of 10°C (50°F). Take cuttings of large exhibition varieties. Keep stools of garden varieties cool and not too wet.

GLADIOLI

Check stored corms and discard any which are diseased.

IRISES

Continue picking *I. unguicularis* regularly.
Under glass. Water bulbous irises in pots when growth begins and move earlier species to a cold greenhouse to encourage more rapid growth.

LILIES

Plant bulbs if soil is easily worked.
Under glass. Pot bulbs or set them in trays of damp peat if they cannot be planted outdoors. Bring in boxes of autumn-sown seedlings and also pots of lilies.

CARNATIONS AND PINKS

Test soil for lime content and add lime if below pH 6·5. Clear rubbish from around stems and ensure that stakes and ties are secure. Protect with black cotton against birds. Watch for signs of rust and the grubs of carnation flies. Order plants for setting out in March and prepare the beds for them, first testing the drainage of wet soils.
Under glass. Maintain a temperature of 7°C (45°F) for perpetual flowering carnations, and give some ventilation at all times. Water and feed sparingly, cutting blooms and disbudding flower stems. Use dusts if rust or aphids are present. Order plants and seeds. Propagate perpetual flowering carnations from cuttings. Put them in a closed frame and give more air when they start to grow. Ten to 14 days later, pot them up into $2\frac{1}{2}$ in. pots, later moving them to $3\frac{1}{2}$ in. pots.

SWEET PEAS

Cover frames with matting after severe frosts to avoid rapid thawing. Pinch out the tips of seedlings after the second or third pair of leaves has been formed.

FLOWERS FROM SEED

Plan seed requirements from new catalogues. Continue digging ground to be used for next year's annuals.

BULBS

Hoe beds of late-planted tulips or spray with a contact herbicide to control weeds. Follow with a residual herbicide.
Indoors and under glass. Examine bowls and pots of bulbs and move them indoors as they are ready. Give bowls or pots a quarter turn each day to ensure even growth.

ALPINES

Remove fallen leaves and dig vacant spaces between plants. Sow slow-germinating seeds and those that need exposure to frost to assist germination. Use clay pots, pans or shallow boxes. Do not water seed containers, but stand outdoors, choosing a hard surface away from worms and the drip from trees.

WATER PLANTS AND POOLS

Keep a small area of the pool free of ice to permit toxic gases to escape. Alternatively, cover a small area with boards or rush matting to prevent thick ice from forming. Melt ice if necessary by standing a can of boiling water on its surface.

GREENHOUSES AND FRAMES

Do not give too much heat while growth is at a low ebb. Give extra attention to plants to be in flower at Christmas. Keep plants not in flower fairly dry. Give some ventilation on sunny days. Remove all rubbish from the greenhouse, and wash pots and seed trays. Control slugs with pellets. Give hydrangeas a dry atmosphere and very little water.

TREES AND SHRUBS

Plant deciduous trees and shrubs during mild weather, making the soil firm round the roots. Re-firm soil around newly planted shrubs loosened by frost. Tie branches of young conifers together with sacking to prevent snow breaking them down. Gather leaves and put on compost heap to provide a top dressing next spring. Bring tub-grown fuchsias and hydrangeas into a cold greenhouse or shed in cold districts.

RHODODENDRONS AND AZALEAS

Planting is possible if weather is fine. Spray flower buds with a bird deterrent.

HEDGES

Complete planting of deciduous hedges. Plants received when ground is unfit for planting should be kept in a frost-free shed.

HEATHERS

Continue planting during suitable weather. Remove any weeds among newly planted heathers. Lightly trim established plants which have finished flowering, unless dead flowers are to be retained as a decoration.

FRUIT

Spray all fruit trees and bushes with tar-oil winter-wash when dormant. Continue planting in suitable conditions. Continue pruning. Apply nitrogenous fertiliser to trees grown in grass. Cut back newly planted apples, pears, blackberries, loganberries, currants, cherries, gooseberries and raspberries.

VEGETABLES

In the north, lift turnips and swedes and store in clamps. Prepare the site for next year's runner beans.
Under glass. Lift rhubarb and chicory for forcing.

HERBS

Protect bay, rosemary and marjoram from severe winter weather.

PATIOS AND TOWN GARDENS

Protect valuable trees and shrubs. Plant trees and shrubs in containers during fine weather.

HOUSE PLANTS

Keep plants on the dry side and give them plenty of light. Avoid both under- and over-watering. Give extra humidity to *Azalea indica, Solanum capsicastrum* and cyclamen. Keep pots of bulbs moist but not too hot, and plant them outdoors after they have flowered.

GENERAL TASKS

Control mice with traps or Warfarin if they steal peas or attack fruits and roots in store. Check gladiolus corms and begonia tubers, onions and other dormant bulbous plants, and stored fruits and roots before severe frosts begin, making sure they have adequate protection. Cover ground around newly planted camellias and rhododendrons with 12 in. of straw to prevent roots being frozen. Protect autumn-planted evergreen shrubs against east winds. Lag outdoor taps and water pipes. Shake heavy falls of snow off hedges and branches of trees and shrubs to help them keep their shape.

Plants to enjoy in December

Border and rock garden plants in flower Hyacinths Iris unguicularis Narcissus 'Paper White' Narcissus 'Soleil d'Or'	Callicarpa Ilex Pernettya Pyracantha Skimmia japonica Sorbus (mountain ash)	Cyclamen persicum Euphorbia pulcherrima Primula kewensis Primula obconica	Beet, seakale Brussels sprouts Cabbage Carrots Chicory
Trees and shrubs in flower Chimonanthus (wintersweet) Erica carnea (heather) Hamamelis mollis Jasminum nudiflorum (winter jasmine) Mahonia	**Water plant in flower** Aponogeton (water hawthorn)	**House plants in flower, depending on position and culture** Begonia semperflorens Chlorophytum Euphorbia pulcherrima Saintpaulia Solanum capsicastrum Zygocactus truncatus (Christmas cactus)	Leek Marrow Onion Parsnip Radish, winter Salsify Scorzonera Spinach beet
Trees and shrubs with colourful fruits Arbutus Aucuba	**Greenhouse plants in flower** Aphelandra Azalea indica Begonia Chrysanthemum Cineraria	**Vegetables in season** Artichoke, Jerusalem	Swede Turnip

Lawns

If you have not yet prepared a seed bed for areas to be seeded in the spring (see NOVEMBER), dig the site over and apply well rotted manure or sewage sludge. It is always a good idea to have a small area of turf specially sown for transfer to any damaged areas of the lawn.

Continue treatment against leatherjackets (see NOVEMBER), and also aeration treatment (see SEPTEMBER).

Clean and overhaul machines and equipment, putting them away well oiled in a dry place until the spring. An aerosol oil dispenser is useful for getting at intricate parts of machinery.

Roses

Roses may be planted if the soil is dry or just moist (see NOVEMBER) but not if it is wet and sticky, or if there is frost or snow on the surface. Roses which cannot be planted at once will come to no harm if left in the nurseryman's packing for up to a week. If planting has to be delayed still longer, remove the plants from the package and heel them in until suitable conditions occur (see NOVEMBER).

If the roses cannot be heeled in because there is ground frost or snow, open the package, cut off any leaves remaining on the plants, then wrap the roots and lower parts of the stems with moist sacking and keep them in a frost-free place.

Winter preparations

Prepare established rose beds for winter. Using sharp secateurs, shorten long growths on bush roses to about $2\frac{1}{2}$ ft.

353

high, to prevent wind damage. Collect and burn all fallen leaves where roses have been attacked by black spot disease. On heavy soils or where the ground has been walked over and compacted, use a spade to chip up the top inch of soil to expose it to the crumbling action of winter frosts.

Ensure that cuttings planted in September are firm in the ground. Those which root will be ready for lifting and planting a year from now.

UNDER GLASS

Bring pot roses into the greenhouse or conservatory and withhold water until they are pruned during the last fortnight of the month. Use sharp, clean secateurs and prune hard to outward-pointing dormant buds about 6 in. above soil level (see MARCH). Fill the pot to the top with water after pruning and maintain just sufficient heat to exclude frost.

Hardy herbaceous plants

Continue tidying beds and borders, and continue digging between plants (see NOVEMBER).

If the beds are close to trees, hedges or large shrubs, check harmful effects from tree roots, which will take much nutriment from plants if they invade a bed or border. Ash, elm, pine, birch and beech are particularly voracious, and can spread several feet during a summer. The more distant foraging roots are usually within 12 in. of the surface.

Keep roots in check

Cut back invasive roots each year by thrusting a sharp, deep-bladed spade into the soil around the edge of the bed, so that it penetrates deeply enough to sever the outlying roots. If a large

thick root is encountered, make a small hole to expose the root and cut it with a chopper or axe. The severed portion will die and rot away. It is unnecessary to dig the root out unless it is from an elm or from one of the plum trees, which tend to throw suckers.

Replace worn-down turf beside a bed or border, and spread fresh gravel on flanking paths if necessary.

Prune the branches of overhanging deciduous trees or bushes.

Order seeds or plants needed for spring sowing or planting in March.

Dahlias

Examine stored tubers. If they are shrivelling, plunge them in tepid water for the night, dry, and replace in the peat or vermiculite (see OCTOBER). Cut off any parts of the tubers that show signs of rotting, and dust the cuts liberally with flowers of sulphur or captan.

Chrysanthemums

After a frosty spell, re-firm the ground around over-wintering plants and attend to drainage (see JANUARY).

UNDER GLASS

The quality and duration of late flowers depends quite a lot on maintaining an even supply of moisture to the roots, a consistent temperature of 10°C (50°F) and a well ventilated atmosphere. Reduce the temperature by 2°C (4°F) during very dull weather.

Cuttings of the large exhibition varieties can be propagated towards the end of the month (see JANUARY and MARCH).

Keep cool and not too wet the resting stools of garden varieties which are in the greenhouse or cold frame. Cuttings will not be required from these stools until new growths appear in March.

Gladioli

Check stored corms for disease and discard any that are not healthy.

Irises

Continue to pick *Iris unguicularis* regularly. If conditions are favourable, an established clump will produce a continuing supply. As the flowers grow very quickly, make a daily inspection.

UNDER GLASS

Water bulbous irises in pots as necessary if growth has begun, and move the earlier species from the cold frame into a cold greenhouse if you wish to encourage more rapid growth.

Lilies

Providing both soil and weather are suitable, you can still plant bulbs which have arrived late (see OCTOBER).

UNDER GLASS

If conditions are unsuitable for planting outdoors, pot the bulbs in John Innes potting compost No. 1, or store them in trays of slightly damp peat in a frostproof greenhouse or shed. Protect them with slug pellets and be ready to take action against mice and aphids.

Bring in boxes of autumn-sown hypogeal (slow germinating) seeds (see JANUARY) and pots of lilies.

Carnations and pinks

Test the soil for lime content if this was not done earlier and add lime if it is below pH 6·5.

In mild spells firm the soil around any plants loosened by frost. Clear away rubbish from around the stems of plants and ensure that stakes and ties are secure. Protect with black cotton against birds.

Watch for signs of carnation rust and the grubs of carnation flies (see MARCH).

Order plants for setting out in March (see colour section, MAY) and, if the weather conditions are favourable, prepare the beds, first testing the drainage if the land tends to be wet (see AUGUST).

UNDER GLASS

Maintain a temperature of 7°C (45°F) for perpetual flowering carnations and give some ventilation at all times.

Water and feed sparingly (see APRIL), cutting blooms and disbudding flower stems as necessary (see SEPTEMBER).

Watch for carnation rust and aphids (see MARCH), using dusts in preference to sprays during the winter.

Order plants and seeds.

Take cuttings

Propagate perpetual flowering carnations from cuttings. Take side shoots from the lower part of the flowering stem on a recently watered plant, choosing strong shoots that have not begun to lengthen preparatory to flowering. Each cutting should have four or five fully developed pairs of leaves; pull off the pair of leaves below these and cut the stem cleanly just below the joint.

Insert and root cuttings

Space the cuttings 1 in. apart in a pan of sharp sand, inserting them almost up to the bottom pair of leaves, and place the pan in a propagating frame. If you do not have such a frame, a box covered with a piece of glass will do. Maintain a temperature of 13–16°C (55–61°F) and keep the frame closed.

When the tops of the cuttings begin to grow, admit more air gradually over

a period of a week or so, then remove the glass. Between ten days and a fortnight later, pot the cuttings into $2\frac{1}{2}$ in. pots of John Innes potting compost No. 1. When the roots are through to the sides of the pots, pot the cuttings on into $3\frac{1}{2}$ in. pots of the same compost.

A mist propagator is excellent for rooting cuttings. If you use one, maintain a sand temperature of 21°C (70°F) during the rooting period.

Sweet peas

UNDER GLASS

Place matting or straw over the frames if a severe frost is expected, or first thing after a frost. Rapid thawing will blacken the leaves and stems.

To encourage the formation of side shoots, pinch out the tips of the seedlings after the second or third pairs of leaves have formed.

PINCHING OUT THE TIPS OF
SEEDLING SWEET PEAS

Remove the growing point above the second or third pair of leaves in order to encourage the formation of vigorous side growths

Flowers from seed

With the seed catalogues now arriving, this is a good time to plan your seed requirements for the coming season.

Continue and, if possible, complete the digging of beds and borders in which next year's hardy and half-hardy annuals will be grown (see NOVEMBER). Try to complete as much digging as possible before the snow arrives.

Bulbs

Hoe beds of late-planted tulips and hyacinths, or spray them with a contact herbicide on a dry day to kill weed seedlings. Follow this with a residual herbicide to keep the surface weed-free for most of the rest of the season.

UNDER GLASS AND INDOORS

Continue to examine bowls and pots of bulbs and move them indoors as they are ready or as required. Bowls moved earlier to a cool greenhouse or room can be taken into the living-room when the buds are visible among the leaves. If bowls are placed near a window, give them a quarter turn every day to ensure even growth.

Study the catalogues and order bulbs to plant in the spring.

Alpines

Remove fallen leaves and fork over vacant spaces between plants with a small hand or onion fork. Remove perennial weeds.

Sow slow-germinating seeds and also those kinds that require exposure to frost to assist germination (see plant descriptions, NOVEMBER).

Sow the seeds in clay pots or pans, or in wooden boxes not more than 4 in. deep. Prepare the compost by mixing

2 parts of sterilised or weed-free soil with 1 part each of peat and sharp sand. Place a 1 in. layer of crocks, gravel or broken brick in the bottom of the container, then fill loosely with compost. Strike off the loose soil with a board, then press the surface with a block of wood or clean brick to leave it $\frac{1}{2}$ in. below the edge of the pot or box. Sprinkle a thin coating of pea shingle (the smallest possible grade of gravel) if you are sowing very small seeds. Failing this, use a film of coarse sand.

Sowing technique

Sow the seeds by tipping them from the packet into the palm of one hand, then pushing them off with the forefinger of your other hand so that they are distributed evenly. Try not to sow more than eight to ten small seeds per sq. in., and fewer if they are large. Give an overall dusting of sand, just sufficient to cover the seeds.

Stand containers outdoors

As the containers will spend the winter outdoors, there is no need to water them. Stand the boxes or pots on paving or a similar surface that will prevent entry of worms from below, preferably on the north side of a shed or wall. Avoid places subject to drip from overhanging trees or roof eaves.

In March, move the boxes to a cold frame to prevent them drying out. Germination should have begun by late March.

Water plants and pools

In severe weather a pool heater will keep a small area free of ice, allowing toxic gases to escape.

Alternatively, place boards or rush matting across a small area of the pool to prevent ice from forming too thickly.

PREVENTING DAMAGE FROM ICE

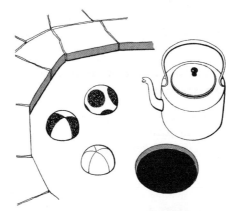

Float rubber balls on the surface of concrete-lined pools to absorb ice pressure, which might otherwise crack the sides. As fish may asphyxiate if ice persists for long, melt a hole by standing a container of boiling water on the surface

A third method is to stand an empty container on the ice and fill it with boiling water. Repeat the process until the container has melted a hole and penetrated to the water beneath the ice.

Do not break thick ice in a pool. Apart from the possibility of injuring fish, mixing the ice with the water will lower the temperature, and the insulating effect of the ice will be lost.

Greenhouses and frames

Plant growth is at its lowest ebb this month, due to the brief hours of daylight. It is a mistake to try to make plants grow more rapidly by raising the temperature, as the resulting growth will be too soft and sappy. Within reasonable limits temperature must be related to light conditions; a minimum night temperature of 7°C (45°F) is adequate for plants in the average greenhouse.

Early in the month give a little extra attention to plants that you hope to have in flower at Christmas. Select the warmest spot in the house for any cinerarias, cyclamens or primulas which appear to be a little backward. Move to a cooler spot any plants that appear to be too forward.

Ventilate slightly

Open ventilators a little on sunny days but close them again quite early in the afternoon. Most plants, except those actually in flower, must be kept fairly dry, but do not allow them to dry out so much that the soil begins to shrink from the sides of the pot.

Damping down

If floors and paths need damping down to increase humidity, do this during the early part of the day. This is unlikely to be required where an oil heater is used. Discontinue overhead spraying of the plants for the time being.

Throw away old seed packets, broken

SHELVES FOR PLANT DISPLAY

Slatted shelves, arranged in tiers on the staging, provide extra space for containers and are useful for displaying pot plants

boxes and any other rubbish which may harbour disease organisms. After emptying old compost from pots and seed boxes, scrub them thoroughly in readiness for the new season. When the seed boxes are dry, treat with a non-toxic wood preservative.

Destroy slugs

Scatter slug pellets at the first signs of damage to the leaves of plants, or if the slimy trails of slugs are seen.

Hydrangeas which have shed their leaves but are carrying plump buds require a dry atmosphere and only sufficient water to prevent the soil becoming dust-dry.

Trees and shrubs

Deciduous trees and shrubs can still be planted during mild weather. Make the soil firm round the roots, otherwise winter gales will rock the shrubs loose before they have had a chance to get settled and establish new roots. This is a common cause of failure.

Coping with frost and snow

Hard frost may loosen the soil around newly planted shrubs, so keep a check on these and tread the soil firm whenever necessary.

To prevent snow settling on the branches of young conifers and breaking them with its weight, wind strips of sacking around to hold the branches together. Remove the sacking when danger of snow has passed.

Leaves for compost

Gather leaves and place them on the compost heap to provide leaf-mould for top dressing in the spring. Oak and beech are the best; holly and rhododendron leaves, and pine needles, should not be placed on the compost heap.

Bring tub-grown hydrangeas and fuchsias into a cold greenhouse or shed, except in mild districts where they can over-winter in the open. Little water will be required until the spring.

Rhododendrons and azaleas

This is not a good month for work, although planting can be done if there is no frost or snow about (see MARCH).

If tits are pecking flower buds, spray with a bird deterrent.

Hedges

Complete the planting of deciduous hedges as soon as possible (see OCTOBER), first digging the ground if this was not done earlier (see SEPTEMBER). If hedging plants are delivered while the ground is frozen or wet, keep them in a frost-free shed with straw around and beneath their roots. Continue with planting as soon as the weather permits.

Heathers

Planting can continue this month if the ground is not waterlogged or frozen (see MARCH and OCTOBER), but unless the heathers have been lifted already it would be better to delay planting until the spring.

Weed and trim

Remove any weeds which have appeared among newly planted heathers. Established plants which have finished flowering can be lightly trimmed with shears, though this can be delayed until the early spring if you wish to retain the rich winter colours of the dead flowers. Complete trimming before the new growth is too far advanced.

Fruit

Inspect stored fruit and bring pears from store indoors to ripen at room temperature before use.

Winter-wash fruit trees

Spray all fruit trees and bushes with a tar-oil winter-wash when they are fully dormant. In most seasons the dormant period lasts from December to mid-January, although peach and nectarine, which reach bud-burst early, normally need spraying in December, and there is an alternative spray for apples and pears (see FEBRUARY). A 5 per cent tar-oil solution will kill pest eggs on the trees, remove the unsightly green growth of algae on trunks and branches, and scorch or remove annual weeds under the trees. Tar-oil can be applied to all fruit except strawberries.

Trees and bushes which are not going to be sprayed in the summer need spraying every winter. Spray other trees every second or third winter.

Plant, and check stakes

Continue planting if soil conditions are suitable (see NOVEMBER). If trees are received when the soil is not fit for planting, heel them in or keep them in a frost-free place (see NOVEMBER). Check stakes and ties on newly planted trees; gales may loosen the trees and can have a bad effect if the ties are not properly secured.

Examine all framework supports and wires for trained trees (see recommended varieties, NOVEMBER), and renew and tie in where necessary.

Burn prunings

Continue pruning (see NOVEMBER) except when there is a hard night frost.

Collect and burn prunings, scattering the ash around fruit trees before it becomes damp; red currants and gooseberries will benefit most.

Trees and bushes grown in grass should be fed with nitrogen before the middle of January, because grass roots become active early in spring and if feeds of nitrogen are not washed into the soil before then, they will mainly benefit the grass. Established trees grown in cultivated soil should be fed with nitrogen in March.

Fell old trees

Cut down old trees during the winter, if possible cutting off the trunk below soil level, so that the stump cannot be seen. Decay of the stump can be hastened by boring a grid of holes at 6 in. intervals, each 1 in. in diameter and 6 in. deep, and filling them with a ferti- liser mixture consisting of 3 parts Nitro- chalk to 1 part superphosphate. Plug the holes and cover the stump with turf if it is in grass.

Apple and pear

Feed established trees in grass every year with 1 oz. nitrogen (as sulphate of ammonia or Nitro-chalk) per sq. yd. Feed all trees every other year with 1 oz. sulphate of potash and every third year with 2 oz. superphosphate. Trained trees will also benefit from dressings of farmyard manure, which is rich in nitrogen; trees grown in grass do not need nitrogen (as hoof and horn), unless they are lacking in vigour.

Prune newly planted bush trees, standards and half-standards by cutting back shoots required to grow by two- thirds, leaving the other shoots and laterals full length; on newly planted dwarf pyramids cut back shoots requir- ed to grow to 8–10 in. On espaliers, trim the leaders on the lowest branches only; and on cordons, lightly trim tip- bearing varieties. Do not winter prune trained trees once they are established, otherwise they will grow too strongly. Summer prune to control vigour of trees grown in a restricted form (see JULY).

358

Blackberry, loganberry and hybrid berries

Cut newly planted bushes down to within 9–12 in. of the soil level.

Black currant

Cut newly planted bushes hard back after planting to encourage the development of the root system and the shoots below ground level. Cut to an outward- pointing bud within 2 in. of soil level, otherwise right down to soil level. Shoots removed from newly planted healthy bushes can be used as cuttings to produce more bushes. Shorten only the well ripened shoots to 10 or 12 in.,

CUTTING BACK BLACK CURRANTS

Prune black currants hard back after planting, to encourage the development of roots and the production of vigorous young shoots

and line them out 6 in. apart with a quarter of their length showing above the soil. After two seasons' growth, they can be used for further planting. Or plant three or four cuttings 6 in. apart in a clump to form a bush. Each cutting should root and in the following season produce shoots which will fruit in the second season.

Cherry

On newly planted standard trees cut selected leaders to 12–18 in.

Feed in the same way as apple, except fan-trained 'Morello' (acid) cherry, which should be fed in the same way as fan-trained peach.

Gooseberry, red currant and white currant

Prune newly planted bushes by cutting leading shoots by half. Cut the leading shoots on cordons by one-third.

Peach and nectarine

Feed bush trees in the same way as apple, and feed fan-trained trees every year with up to 1 oz. of hoof and horn per sq. yd. Feed all fan-trained trees every other year with 1 oz. of sulphate of potash. Dressings of farmyard manure are also beneficial.

Plum and damson

Feed in the same way as apple, but increase the rate of sulphate of ammonia for trees grown in grass.

Raspberry

Prune newly planted canes hard after planting (see black currant). Cut them down to within 9–12 in. of the soil level.

Vegetables

In the north, lift turnips and swedes as soon as possible and store them in the same manner as beetroot (see OCTOBER). In the south it is sufficient to draw soil round the plants.

During this month or early in January, prepare the site for next year's runner beans. Dig a trench 18 in. wide and about 12 in. deep, loosening the bottom with a fork and covering this with a 3–4 in. layer of manure or compost, together with a sprinkling of hoof and horn fertiliser or dried blood. Over this place 3–4 in. of soil and a further layer of manure and fertiliser before returning the remaining soil. Mark the site with pegs.

UNDER GLASS

Rhubarb and chicory can still be lifted for forcing (see OCTOBER and NOVEMBER).

Herbs

Herbs, generally, have a long dormant period, and some of them need protection during the winter. Bay, if grown in tubs, can be brought into the greenhouse or put on a sheltered patio away from cold winds. In the coldest districts marjoram and rosemary need a protective layer of peat, leaf-mould or straw, although rosemary will survive in the open if it is well established and away from northern and eastern winds.

Bergamot, chives and mint die down completely, leaving no trace above ground until the following spring. Clear away annual and biennial herbs, if not already done (see NOVEMBER).

Patios and town gardens

Heavy falls of snow may break slender branches of trees and shrubs. If possible, move the containers to a sheltered position or at least to a spot where they will not be covered by melting snow dropping from a roof. Tying some of the more vulnerable branches together will increase their resistance. In exposed positions, tie a loose wrapping of straw or bracken round the plants for added protection.

Unless it is freezing, shrubs and trees can still be planted in containers to provide a permanent display (see MARCH and NOVEMBER).

House plants

Continue to keep your plants on the dry side and give them as much light as possible. Yellowing and dropping of leaves can signify either over- or under-watering, so watch your plants carefully. Over-watering is the more common fault, and is the cause of most problems that arise with house plants.

House plants as gifts

This is the peak months for giving and receiving house plants, and certain plants are grown in huge numbers for the Christmas trade. Some require special care, in particular the colourful *Azalea indica* and *Solanum capsicastrum* (winter cherry), both of which need extra humidity. Spray them frequently with tepid water (rain water for preference). Many cyclamens are given as presents, and these too need a moist atmosphere. Always water cyclamens from the bottom; if water is allowed to settle on the top of the corms it may cause rotting. Cyclamens keep best in a cool room or hall where the temperature does not often rise above 16°C (61°F).

Tending bulbs

Large numbers of flowering bulbs, including hyacinths, daffodils and tulips, also appear as Christmas gifts. These have all been forced into early bloom but last surprisingly well if the soil is kept moist and the room in which they are kept is not too hot and stuffy. Plant the bulbs out in the garden when the flowers have died.

General tasks

Mice can be extremely annoying just now—burrowing under cloches to steal autumn-sown peas, and active in greenhouses and frames or among fruits and vegetables in store. Watch for them among plantings of small bulbs; they are partial to crocuses and prefer the choicer species. At the first sign of damage or mouse droppings, set mouse traps or put down Warfarin. Prop boards over the traps so that birds cannot be caught.

Storage check

Before the severe frosts begin, check gladiolus and begonia corms, onions, shallots, apples and stored root vegetables. If possible, bring them into the house, perhaps into a spare room or a cupboard under the stairs, where they can be certain to be safe from frost.

If you have planted young camellias or rhododendrons, cover the ground for 2 or 3 ft. around them with a layer of leaves or straw 1 ft. thick. Camellias are easily killed by a frost severe enough to penetrate 1 ft. or so into the ground. Protect autumn-planted evergreen shrubs against east winds. A sheet of thin polythene supported by two or three bamboo canes and draped round the young shrubs will save them from being withered by drying winds.

Protect water pipes

Lag any outdoor stand-pipes or taps. Better still, if you can turn off the water supply, drain the outdoor system dry.

After a heavy snowfall, go round the garden with a long cane and knock the snow off the branches of trees or shrubs, and especially off the tops of hedges. Snow may splay the hedges apart, making it necessary to put in stakes and wires to bring them back into shape.

If December is kind, keep on with the digging and clearing up.

House plants for indoor decoration

Many house plants are now available, offering a great variety of foliage and growth habit. The large leathery leaves of the rubber plant and the bright variegation of begonias are well known; but there are less known, more graceful house plants, like the neanthe, which are just as worth while. Though most are foliage plants, a few are grown for their flowers, such as the pink, mauve or white cyclamens, and the scarlet bracts of the euphorbia (see also descriptions of Greenhouse plants, pp. 382–5). The groupings show use of contrasting leaves: even that old Victorian favourite, the aspidistra, can be given a new look when surrounded by feathery ferns and trailing ivy.

Adiantum
A. cuneatum (maidenhair fern). One of the most attractive indoor ferns, with tiny, delicate, pale green leaves carried in sprays on thin stems. Difficult to grow, since it requires moist, pure air at all times. Water frequently with lime-free water, and keep away from draughts. Provide extra humidity in hot weather.

African violet: see Saintpaulia

Aglaonema
A. commutatum. Compact, attractive foliage plant with dark green, glossy, lance-shaped leaves about 6 in. long and 2 in. wide, marked with chevron-like silvery bands. Prefers warmth and moisture, but keep it fairly dry during the winter. Propagate by dividing the roots in spring.

Aloe
A. variegata (partridge-breasted aloe). A succulent, with fairly erect leaves arranged in three rows, keeled on the outside, dark green with white teeth along the edge, and having transverse rows of white spots in irregular bands. Red flowers on a loose spike about 12 in. high in April. Keep in a light position, where it will get the morning sun. Water well in spring and summer. In winter keep in a cool room and give little water.

Anthurium
A. scherzerianum (piggy-tail plant). Its name is derived from the red palette-shaped flower, from which rises a straight or curled tail. Hybrids have flowers of various colours, including white, pink and orange. The long glossy leaves should be sponged weekly. Fairly difficult to grow, since it needs plenty of light and warmth in order to flower.

Aphelandra
A. squarrosa louisae (zebra plant, saffron spike). A striking plant with dark green, shiny, lance-shaped leaves, about 9 in. long and 4½ in. across, carried in pairs, the main rib and side veins being emphasised by ivory-coloured stripes. Bright yellow flower bracts shaped like four-cornered pyramids emerge from the top pairs of leaves on each main branch, and each segment produces a tubular, ivory-coloured flower. After flowering, cut off the bract to the nearest pair of leaves to encourage the formation of new shoots. Keep in a warm, light position out of direct sun, and always keep moist in summer. In winter, use sufficient warm water to prevent the soil

Aglaonema commutatum

Anthurium scherzerianum

Aphelandra squarrosa louisae

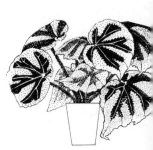

Begonia masoniana

Begonia rex

Chlorophytum elatum variegatum

Cissus antarctica

Codiaeum variegatum pictum

drying out completely. The plant will not stand temperatures below 10°C (50°F).

Asparagus
A. plumosus (asparagus fern). This plant provides the familiar feathery, light green foliage commonly used by florists for bouquets, buttonholes and floral arrangements. Water and feed regularly in spring and summer. Water sparingly in winter.

Aspidistra
A. elatior (parlour palm, cast-iron plant). A plant with large, dark green, rather oblong leaves and occasionally small purple flowers near soil level. It is extremely easy to grow, since it will tolerate bad light, gas fumes, and extremes of temperature. A position out of direct sunshine is best. In summer, water freely and wash the leaves occasionally; in winter keep the plant fairly warm and do not over-water.

Begonia
A large genus of widely different plants, some grown for their foliage, others for their flowers. *B. masoniana* (iron cross begonia), is a striking foliage plant with bright green, rather rounded leaves, attractively pointed at the tips, and bearing a clearly

defined purplish cross which gives the plant its common name. The leaf surface is covered with rounded nodules, which give the leaves a mossy look. Always keep moist and feed during the growing period, but do not over-water in winter. Keep in a draught-free light position, but out of direct sun. A minimum temperature of 13°C (55°F) is essential. Rather slow-growing. Propagate by leaf-cuttings. *B. rex* is the most decorative and popular begonia, with beautiful leaves in many different colour combinations of green, purple, pink and silver in intricate patterns. The leaf surface can be hairy, or smooth and almost metallic, and the edges are toothed. It prefers a humid atmosphere. Treat in the same way as *B. masoniana*. *B. semperflorens* is a compact, bushy plant for a sunny windowsill. The leaves are bright green or glistening bronze with a rather waxy surface. This fibrous-rooted begonia produces a profusion of pink, red or white flowers in summer and autumn, if given plenty of water, rich feeding and good light. In winter, reduce watering, and keep at a minimum temperature of 13°C (55°F). Propagate by stem cuttings. (See illustration p. 23.)

Busy lizzie: see **Impatiens**

Capsicum
The bushy little *C. annuum* (red pepper), which grows to about 10 in. high, relies for its beauty and appeal on its brightly coloured fruits, which are produced from August to early November.

The variety 'Chameleon' has short, somewhat conical fruits, which turn from cream to rich red as they mature; and there are thus fruits of different shades on the plant at the same time. Seed can be sown in April. Cultivation as for *Solanum capsicastrum*. (Illustration, p. 28.)

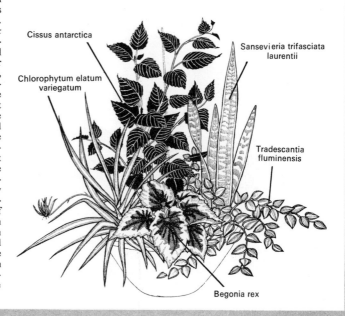

Cissus antarctica

Chlorophytum elatum variegatum

Sansevieria trifasciata laurentii

Tradescantia fluminensis

Begonia rex

Cyclamen persicum   Dieffenbachia amoena   Dizygotheca elegantissima   Dracaena terminalis   Fatshedera lizei

Chlorophytum

C. elatum variegatum (spider plant). An attractive foliage plant, with striped green and white grass-like leaves. It sends out long arching stems, with young plants at the end; these can be potted up to make new plants. Needs water and good light to retain its variegation.

Christmas cactus: see Zygocactus

Cissus

C. antarctica (kangaroo vine). An easy and popular climber or trailer, with dark green serrated leaves and stems which readily attach themselves to trellis, cane or string supports by means of tendrils. It can be trained to cover an entire wall and will tolerate almost any conditions except temperatures below 7°C (45°F). Prefers a semi-shaded position and plenty of water in summer, and more light and less water in winter. Feed regularly in spring and summer. Propagate by stem cuttings.

Codiaeum (croton)

C. variegatum pictum. A difficult plant that is well worth growing for even a few weeks of its wonderful multicoloured leaves, which range through all shades of yellow, orange, pink and scarlet, and are sometimes mottled or striped. The leaves are glossy and can be slender or broad, crimped or curled. Keep in a temperature above 13°C (55°F), away from draughts, and in a moist atmosphere. Keep evenly moist at all times and feed during the growing season. Propagate by stem cuttings.

Cordyline

C. terminalis. One of the most beautiful foliage plants, with tapering leaves up to 12 in. long and 4 in. wide, coloured bright red or pink, with green in irregular streaks and splashes. Needs a rich soil with plenty of peat or leaf-mould and a minimum temperature of 13–16°C (55–61°F) in summer, when it should be watered freely. Give less water in winter, when it will stand lower temperatures.

Croton: see Codiaeum

Cyclamen

C. persicum. A popular flowering plant, whose flowers, in shades of pink, red, mauve and white, sometimes spotted or frilled, provide cheerful colour throughout the winter. Stand the pot on a block of wood or an inverted saucer in a bowl of water to ensure a humid atmosphere, and water from the bottom, otherwise the corm tends to rot. Keep in an even temperature and in a light position, but do not leave near a window, where it will get cold at night. After the flowering period is over, reduce the amount of water and put the plant in a cool place; in May move it outside if possible. Re-pot in a mixture of 2 parts leaf-mould, 2 parts loam and 1 part peat. Leave plants outside until October, and introduce gradually to higher temperatures, increasing the amount of water.

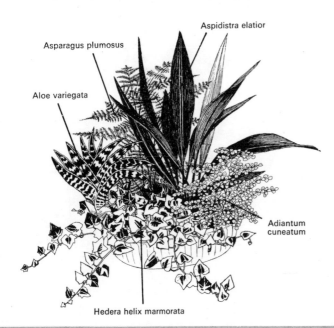

Aspidistra elatior

Asparagus plumosus

Aloe variegata

Adiantum cuneatum

Hedera helix marmorata

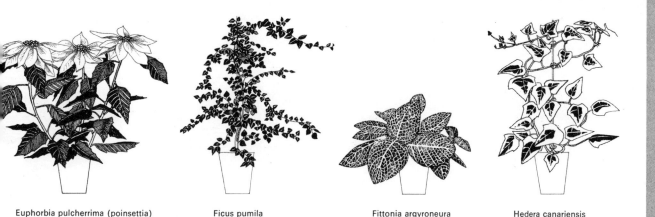

Euphorbia pulcherrima (poinsettia)   Ficus pumila   Fittonia argyroneura   Hedera canariensis

Dieffenbachia

D. amoena (dumb cane). Easily grown foliage plant. It has large green leaves, about 9 in. long and 4–5 in. wide, flecked and blotched with white or cream. It sheds the lower leaves from time to time, but produces new leaves at the top, and eventually develops into a palm-shaped 'tree'. The flesh and sap are poisonous. Ideally needs warmth and humidity to maintain growth but will withstand temperatures as low as 10°C (50°F), lower if kept dry at the roots.

Dizygotheca

D. elegantissima. A dainty foliage plant, with finely fingered, serrated leaves of a dark copper colour, carried on thin stems of the same colour but flecked with cream. Slow-growing, it needs a warm humid atmosphere. Regular syringing of the leaves helps to keep it in good condition.

Dracaena

D. terminalis (flaming dragon tree). A foliage plant with lance-shaped variegated leaves of different colours ranging from bright red and green to pale pink and green in irregular patterns. Rather delicate, really requiring greenhouse conditions, but will withstand temperatures as low as 10°C (50°F). Keep evenly moist, and provide humidity by plunging in peat. Hot dry conditions encourage attack by red spider mites.

Euphorbia

E. pulcherrima (poinsettia). A popular plant for Christmas decoration. The large bright red bracts surrounding tiny inconspicuous flowers, contrast with the bright green pointed leaves. Place in a south window, where it will not have to be moved about. Water well until the bracts fall, then give no more water. When the leaves fall cut the plant down to about 12 in. and apply powdered charcoal or cigarette ash to the wound, then move to a less light position. In April, after re-potting in rich compost, return the plant to its south window and start watering gradually, increasing the quantity as growth progresses. Feed regularly during the summer and, if preferred, plunge into the soil in a sunny place in the garden, but return to its old position indoors in September.

Fatshedera

F. lizei. A bigeneric hybrid between fatsia and hedera (ivy), this plant bears large glossy palmate leaves and will grow to 10 ft. or more. An easy plant, tolerant of most conditions. Give plenty of water, except in winter, and feed fortnightly during the summer. Regular sponging of leaves or standing the pot out in the rain is beneficial.

Ficus

This genus provides a wide range of popular house plants. *F. benjamina* (weeping fig) is an attractive plant with a single woody stem and numerous branches covered with small dark green leaves, giving the impression of a graceful weeping tree, rather like a small birch.

Cyclamen persicum
Solanum capsicastrum
Pteris umbrosa major
Zygocactus truncatus
Zebrina pendula

Hedera helix 'Glacier'

Helxine soleirollii

Impatiens petersiana

Maranta makoyana

Requires a minimum temperature of 10°C (50°F). Always keep moist in summer, but in winter allow almost to dry out between waterings. Prefers a semi-shaded position out of direct sunlight. Some yellowing and dropping of leaves may occur naturally in winter, but this loss will be more than replaced in the growing season. *F. elastica decora* (rubber plant) is a highly decorative and popular plant. It has dark green leathery leaves about 9–12 in. long and 5–7 in. wide, which are red on the underside and grow spirally from the upright stem. The dark red growing tip turns brown and falls off when the new leaf emerges. Remove it if it becomes lodged, as it may cause the new leaf to rot. Prefers temperatures between 13–16°C (55–61°F), but will tolerate much lower and higher temperatures, as long as it is protected from draughts. Keep evenly moist in spring and summer, but fairly dry in winter. Sponge the leaves regularly to remove all traces of dust and keep the plant out of direct sun, or the new leaves will be small and hard. Propagate rubber plants by air layering (see *House plants*, APRIL). *F. pumila* (creeping fig) is a climbing, creeping or trailing plant with thin stems and a thick growth of elongated, heart-shaped leaves about 1 in. long and ½ in. across, and is quite unlike other members of its family. The plant is best grown in a shaded or semi-shaded position. Always keep moist, and never let the soil dry out. Feed regularly, and give the leaves an occasional spraying to remove dust. Will withstand moderate to cool temperatures, and in a cool greenhouse the creeping fig will climb a wall rapidly, supported by its aerial roots.

Cordyline terminalis

Euphorbia pulcherrima

Aphelandra squarrosa louisae

Rhoeo discolor

Begonia masoniana

Pteris cretica

Fittonia

F. argyroneura (snake-skin plant). A prostrate-growing plant with roundish leaves 3–4 in. long, of medium green with silver veins, giving the effect of an intricate silver net. A rather delicate plant preferring deep shade and a minimum temperature of 13°C (55°F), although it cannot stand a hot room. A humid atmosphere is essential. Will quickly die if allowed to dry out, but over-watering will have the same effect.

Hedera (ivy)

One of the largest house plant families, of many shapes, forms and colours. Nearly all are easy to grow in the home. If they drop their leaves, most ivies can be put into the garden, where they will acclimatise themselves. All ivies are easily propagated by stem cuttings. *H. canariensis* (Canary Island ivy) is more tender than our common green-leaved varieties, but is still a fairly easy house plant. Place in good light, but not in direct sunlight.

Feed ivies regularly during the growing season and keep the soil moist, but in winter allow it to dry out between

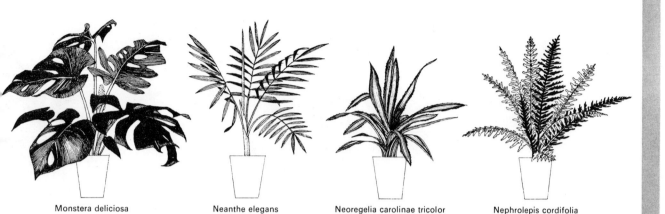

Monstera deliciosa   Neanthe elegans   Neoregelia carolinae tricolor   Nephrolepis cordifolia

waterings, since over-watering at this time causes parts of the leaves to turn brown. If the plant reverts to green growth in the winter, or produces thin spindly growth in early spring, cut it out as soon as the plant is growing vigorously.

H. helix 'Chicago', which has green leaves, is one of the most popular house plants, mainly because of its vigour and tolerance of rough treatment. It is a cultivated variety of the common English ivy. It can be grown as a climber or trailer, and benefits from restrictive pruning during the growing season. *H. h.* 'Glacier', with variegated leaves of silver-grey with a cream margin, is a good trailer which will withstand frost and therefore makes a good subject for window-boxes. Still easy, although slightly less tolerant of neglect than the green-leaved varieties, the variegated varieties should be kept away from any source of dry heat and given a good light position, particularly in winter, to retain the leaf colourings. Do not place in direct sun. Feed well during the growing season, but allow almost to dry out between waterings during the winter. *H. h. marmorata* (Irish marbled ivy),

which is slow growing, has fairly large leaves with patches of dark green on mid-green, or of green on ivory, giving a marbled effect, and attractive pink leaf stems. Treat in the same way as *H. h.* 'Glacier'.

Helxine
H. soleirollii (baby's tears). A little creeping plant with tiny, closely set, vivid green leaves, which will quickly cover the surface of a pot and creep down the sides. Easy to grow, it will thrive almost anywhere, although a moist cool situation in partial shade is best. Keep the pot in a saucer filled with water, and never allow the plant to dry out. Water on the leaves in winter can cause them to rot.

Hibiscus
H. rosa-sinensis. A shrubby plant suitable for growing in a large pot or tub. It produces abundant, large and showy rose-red, pink, scarlet or almost violet flowers on young shoots during summer and autumn. Keep almost dry and fairly cool in winter, at a temperature of 10°C (50°F). In spring cut the plant back to about half its size, re-pot in an open, rich soil mixture and give plenty of light. When growth

starts again water freely. At the same time begin spraying with water over the entire plant to help induce new shoots to develop, as these will produce the flowers. Pots can be taken outdoors to a terrace or a patio during the summer, but should never be allowed to dry out.

Impatiens
A quick-growing plant, which produces a succession of flowers over a long period. The more light the plant receives, the more flowers it will produce. Pinch out the tips occasionally to keep the plant bushy. Give plenty of water during the summer, watering twice a day if necessary in hot spells, but sparingly in winter. Feed regularly and often, about twice a week, while the plant is flowering. Take cuttings in summer to ensure succession through the winter (old plants are in any case often too large for a windowsill). Small shoots will quickly produce roots in water, and can be potted up in ordinary garden soil. *I. petersiana* (dusky lizzie). Has clear red flowers and brownish-purple leaves. In summer, stand outside in hot sun to encourage new flowers. *I. sultanii* (busy lizzie). Has green leaves, and white, pink, orange or red flowers.

Ivy: see **Hedera**

Maidenhair fern: see **Adiantum**

Maranta
M. makoyana (peacock plant). A small bushy plant with almost transparent, pale pink oval leaves, which are darker on the underside and marked on top with chocolate stripes and blotches. Keep this tender plant out of direct light and away from draughts, in a minimum temperature of 16°C (61°F) in the winter, and always in a moist atmosphere. A bottle garden is ideal. Water well and regularly in summer, and spray the foliage weekly with tepid water. Feeding in the summer months will improve the colour of the foliage.

Monstera
M. deliciosa (Gruyère cheese plant). An accommodating and popular plant, with a thick main stem and side stems 12-15 in. long bearing drooping, dark green leaves. These are 12 in. long and 10 in. wide, and are an elongated heart-shape, deeply cut almost to the mid-rib and, in mature plants, with holes near the mid-rib between the cuts. Both cuts and perforations are more marked in plants

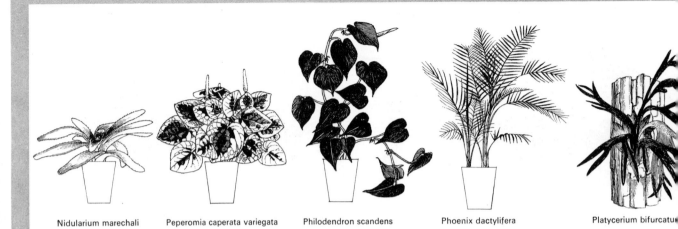

Nidularium marechali   Peperomia caperata variegata   Philodendron scandens   Phoenix dactylifera   Platycerium bifurcatu

grown in a greenhouse. Thick aerial roots grow from each leaf node. Train the lower ones down into the soil in the pot, and the higher ones on to a mossed stake. Re-pot in spring or early summer only if the plant is top-heavy; if fed and watered regularly the plant will continue to grow in a small pot. Place in shade or semi-shade and keep moist but never too wet, particularly in winter. A temperature of 16°C (61°F) or over is ideal, but the plant will withstand lower temperatures.

Mother-in-law's tongue: see Sansevieria

Neanthe
N. elegans (dwarf palm). A graceful little plant which is the best indoor palm for ordinary room conditions. It is very easy to grow, although in a hot and dry atmosphere the leaves will turn brown. Keep the plant out of direct sun, water well in summer, and spray or sponge the leaves occasionally. Keep out of draughts and water sparingly in the winter.

Neoregelia
N. carolinae tricolor. An easy plant with narrow, saw-toothed leaves, 12–15 in. long and 1–1½

in. wide, forming a cup-shaped depression in the centre of the plant. The central portion becomes pink, then a vivid, fiery scarlet, before the rather insignificant flowers appear. Prefers shade or semi-shade, but will tolerate a hot dry atmosphere. Keep the depression filled with water, and the plant will flourish; but allow the soil to dry out between waterings in winter. As the flowers die off, wash out the centre cup each day, or a pungent odour will arise.

Nephrolepis
N. cordifolia (ladder fern). A fern with leaves similar in shape to our common bracken, except that the fronds are more finely divided, and the edges are attractively crimped. Likes a shady position and a moist atmosphere away from draughts. Feed fortnightly in spring and summer, and keep the soil moist.

Nidularium
N. marechali. The dark green leaves of this plant form a depression in the centre, and the central portion turns scarlet when about to produce flowers. Keep the depression filled with water. Does not require a great deal of light and does well in a moderate, even temperature.

Peperomia
A popular small plant, with a neat compact habit. Quite easy to grow. There are several forms, with unusual markings and colours. All have fleshy leaves, which are likely to rot if overwatered, so avoid splashing the centre of the crown when watering. Does best in a warm, humid atmosphere away from strong light. Peperomias cannot tolerate gas fumes. Water frequently in summer; less often and in smaller quantities in winter. Feed during spring and summer. *P. caperata variegata* has small crinkled leaves with green and cream markings, and cream flower spikes. *P. sandersii* is a tender greenhouse plant.

Philodendron
P. scandens, the best-known of the philodendrons, is an easy and accommodating climber or trailer, with small, heart-shaped dark green leaves. The aerial roots make it a good subject for training up a mossed stake, when the leaves will be larger. Will survive in almost any conditions, but does best in warmth and humidity. Place in a semi-shaded position; water moderately and feed regularly in summer. Keep fairly dry in winter if in a cool position.

In spring, cut back growth made in winter to encourage fresh vigorous growth. Easily propagated by stem cuttings.

Phoenix
P. dactylifera. The common date palm, with arching, blue-green leaves. Grows quite well in the house and will retain a miniature form when grown as a pot plant, reaching a height of about 24 in. Plants can be raised by sowing date stones outdoors in summer and bringing the plants indoors before the winter. Give plenty of light, even direct sunlight, and water copiously; it should never stand in a pool of water. Keep almost dry in winter. Feed in summer only. Do not expose to extreme cold.

Platycerium
P. bifurcatum (stag's horn fern). This fern is best grown on a piece of wood, bark or cork, placed high on a wall so that its fronds, which vary in length from 8–15 in. and resemble a stag's antlers, can be seen to their best advantage. The smooth round leaves fold back to form a cup round the roots, preventing them from drying out. If the fern is grown on cork or wood, the roots must be held firm with copper wire in a

Plectranthus fruticosus

Pteris umbrosa major

Rhoicissus rhomboidea

Saxifraga sarmentosa

mixture of finely chopped moss, peat and loam placed in a hollow in the upper side of the cork or wood. Will grow quite well in the house in a warm, shaded position. When the leaves droop, stand the plant in water and soak the soil well. Do not water again until the leaves droop once more.

Plectranthus

P. fruticosus. An easy climber or trailer, with almost round, glossy, slightly crinkled leaves about the size of a half-crown. Grows rapidly and is best kept high on a wall, so that the trails can hang downwards and turn upwards at the tips. It likes plenty of water in summer when it is growing strongly, and an occasional feed will make the foliage larger and glossier. A light position out of direct sunlight is best. Keep warm, but away from all direct sources of heat. The plectranthus will root easily and quickly from cuttings. Nip off the end of a growing trail and insert the cutting in the parent soil, in another pot or even in plain water.

Poinsettia: see Euphorbia

Pteris

A popular group of ferns for growing in the house. *P. cretica*

(crested ribbon fern) and *P. umbrosa major* (ribbon fern) have ribbon-like, firm and rather leathery fronds. Both are sturdy and stand up well to the warm dry atmosphere of the average living-room; they are also able to withstand quite low temperatures, though they cannot stand frost. In summer, water well, spray the foliage regularly, and feed fortnightly.

Red pepper: see Capsicum

Rhoeo

R. discolor (boat lily). The long narrow leaves, dark green above and pinkish below, are carried in a rosette on a thick fleshy stem. Insignificant flowers appear at the base of the leaves in unusual boat-shaped bracts. Warm, moist conditions will deepen the pink colouring.

Rhoicissus

R. rhomboidea (grape ivy). An easy and accommodating climber that will live for years in the house in a cool, shady position and can be trained to cover an entire wall or screen. The leaf stalks, each with three leaflets on individual stalks, arise from a cluster of climbing stems. The deep green leaves, about $2\frac{1}{2}$ in. long and 2 in. wide, are

Saintpaulia ionantha

Ficus benjamina

Scindapsus aureus 'Marble Queen'

Rhoicissus rhomboidea

Hedera helix 'Chicago'

Ficus elastica decora

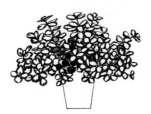

Sedum sieboldii variegatum

Solanum capsicastrum

Spathiphyllum wallisii

Syngonium podophyllum

nearly rhomboidal in shape, with toothed edges, and the growing tips are covered by a fine silvery down. Keep the soil just moist in summer and feed regularly. Pinch out the tips to make the plant bushy. Needs some warmth in winter and rather less water. Propagate by stem cuttings.

Rubber plant: see **Ficus**

Saintpaulia
S. ionantha (African violet). One of the most popular flowering house plants, with single or double violet-shaped flowers of white, pink, blue or purple. Not easy to keep in good condition, particularly in winter; but may flower all the year round if given warmth, moisture, a light but sun-free position, and absolute freedom from draughts, gas fumes, cold water and fluctuating temperatures. Propagate by leaf cuttings.

Sansevieria
S. trifasciata laurentii (mother-in-law's tongue). A popular plant with stiff, thick and fleshy sword-like leaves, marked with irregular horizontal bands of dark green and greyish green, and edged with a clear yellow margin. The size of the leaves,

varying from 6–24 in., or longer, by about 3 in. wide, depends on the size of the pot. Easy to grow if not over-watered, it will tolerate long periods of neglect. Keep in a sunny or shaded position in a hot, dry atmosphere. Water weekly in the summer and monthly in the winter, rather more in a hot, dry atmosphere. The plant's leaves will rot if exposed to frost or if the pot is allowed to become cold when wet. Side shoots thrown up from the rhizomatous roots can be cut off with some root attached and potted up separately. Support with a stick until rooted.

Saxifraga
S. sarmentosa (syn. *S. stolonifera*). A pretty little plant with attractive strawberry-like leaves, which sends out long, hair-like runners with young plants hanging at the end. These will root easily in a pot. Easy to grow, and does best under cool and moist conditions. Prefers a position out of direct sun.

Scindapsus
S. aureus. An attractive climbing or trailing plant with green and gold marbled heart-shaped leaves, somewhat similar to a philodendron. The foliage will

be larger and more luxuriant if the aerial roots are trained on to a mossed stake. Requires a warm, humid, draught-free position in semi-shade. Full light in winter will help the plant to maintain its variegation. Keep moist in summer, but avoid over-watering in winter. If the leaves droop when the soil is moist, allow to dry out before watering again. *S. a.* 'Marble Queen' has almost entirely white leaves flecked with green. Without plenty of light, the leaves will revert to all green; but avoid direct sunlight.

Sedum
S. sieboldii variegatum. An easy and attractive plant, with long sprays of glaucous blue-green leaves splashed with gold in the centre, and pinkish-red flowers in the autumn before the plant dies down. Also used in hanging baskets and window-boxes. If the plant becomes dry outdoors, the leaves take on a deep reddish tinge. Keep the plant dry in winter in a cool greenhouse or outside in a sheltered position. In early March re-pot into a pot one size larger, and water to start the plant into growth. Keep quite moist in a cool place and allow to dry out between waterings.

Solanum
S. capsicastrum (winter cherry). A bright little evergreen shrub with shiny red, white or yellow berries in autumn. These will remain for months if the plant is well watered and provided with a humid atmosphere by frequent spraying, or by being placed near a source of steam. Once the fruits have fallen, cut the plant back hard and re-pot in rich soil containing plenty of humus. To help fruit to set, spray the plant while it is in flower. Pinch out the tips of branches in late September.

Spathiphyllum
S. wallisii. An easy, bushy plant with dark green, shiny, lance-shaped leaves, 5–6 in. long and 1–1½ in. wide. The delicate white flowers rise up through the leaves on thin stems at intervals between spring and autumn, and are surrounded by white or green spathes rather like those of an arum lily. Prefers shade, warmth and humidity, but will tolerate temperatures down to 10°C (50°F), or a hot dry atmosphere. Water well and feed in summer; keep just moist in winter.

Spider plant: see **Chlorophytum**

Tradescantia fluminensis   Vriesia fenestralis   Zebrina pendula   Zygocactus truncatus

Syngonium

S. podophyllum (goose foot plant). Easily grown plant (height about 2 ft.), tolerating poor light and dry air. The leaves are produced on long stems and held horizontally to reveal their distinctive shape. 'Emerald Gem' has white lines delineating the main veins of the foliage. *S. vellozianum* is a larger and more vigorous plant. It will withstand difficult conditions for considerable periods, but does better if given warmth and protection from draughts. Place away from sun, but in good light, and give plenty of moisture to the roots in summer. Water sparingly in winter.

Tradescantia

T. fluminensis (wandering jew, wandering sailor). A trailing or creeping plant with small pointed leaves, usually striped, on long, fairly brittle stems. Gold and silver forms are available, and purple can be induced into the foliage if given sufficient light. To retain the bushy effect, break off the stems when they become bare and root them in the same pot. Keep moist, although it will stand dry periods. Grow in a poor soil and do not feed. Propagate by stem cuttings.

Vriesia

V. fenestralis. A bromeliad, with attractive apple-green strap-like leaves marked with fine horizontal lines of dark mauve. The showy flowers rise on short stalks from the centre of the rosette, which should be kept full of water. Prefers a shady position and even temperature.

Winter cherry: see **Solanum**

Zebrina

Z. pendula. This plant is so similar to tradescantia that the two are sometimes confused. Zebrina is fleshier, larger and more brightly coloured. Cultivation as for tradescantia.

Zygocactus

Z. truncatus (Christmas cactus, crab cactus). An epiphytic cactus with flattened, jointed stems hanging down in an umbrella - shape. Two - tipped bright carmine, scarlet or white flowers emerge from the ends of the stems in profusion in autumn and winter. An easy plant for a humid atmosphere, a shaded position and rich soil. Needs less water in summer and benefits from being put outside in the shade. Bring the plant indoors before the frost, and re-pot if it is pot-bound.

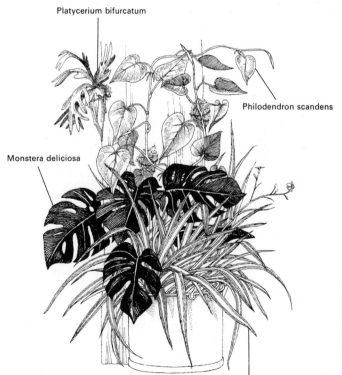

Platycerium bifurcatum

Philodendron scandens

Monstera deliciosa

Chlorophytum elatum variegatum

January

The coldest month is the time to plan ahead with seedsmen's catalogues,
and to send mowers and other equipment for servicing

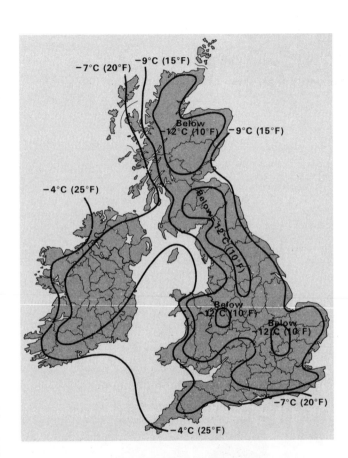

THE LOWEST TEMPERATURES OF THE YEAR

The coldest nights of the year usually occur at the end of January or the beginning of February. The map shows the minimum temperatures of the year, likely to be exceeded only one year in five. The lowest temperatures are usually attained in gardens well away from the coast. In mid-winter the sea is warmer than the land; coasts are warmer than inland localities, especially in the west and south. Gardens in large towns or cities are often several degrees warmer than those in open country. During severe cold the gardener can do little except check that greenhouses are draught-proof, and that heating systems are efficient.

The weather in January

In mild winters, gales and rain are common this month. As in December, depressions come sweeping inland from the Atlantic, accompanied by violent westerly winds, bringing continuous low, grey cloud and much rain. Brief periods of less stormy weather may bring brighter, showery conditions. But if the wind veers to a northerly quarter, it is considerably colder and snow falls on all high ground and on much of the northern half of the British Isles. Snow showers also penetrate into southern districts, but southern Ireland, south-west England and southern Wales often escape them.

Snowfalls usually occur more often in January and lie for longer than in December. The heaviest falls occur when the wind is from the south-east—from the cold continent of Europe. When bitter, strong east winds persist over the British Isles, less snow falls; but under grey skies temperatures throughout the country may never rise above freezing point. In the hardest winters these severe cold spells often persist for days at a time, and night temperatures are very low.

Although the sun's rays are getting stronger and the days are beginning to lengthen noticeably, the lowest temperatures of the year are likely to occur at the end of January or at the beginning of February. January is often the coldest month.

Little can be done in the garden in January, except to try to minimise the effects of adverse weather. Plants will often survive well under a complete cover of snow, but if they penetrate above the snow they can be badly frosted, and even so-called hardy plants can be affected. Heavy snow can break down branches, and it is wise to knock it off them.

A summary of the month's work

LAWNS

Check drainage outlets. Prepare top dressings for spring use. Continue aeration treatment. Lay turves in favourable weather.

ROSES

Complete planting, but not if the soil is wet or sticky or if there is frost or snow on the surface. If conditions are unsuitable for planting, heel the roses in. Support bushes lashed by winter gales

and firm the soil around them. Prepare ground for planting in February and March.
Under glass. Maintain a temperature of 5°C (41°F) and water roses once a week.

HARDY HERBACEOUS PLANTS

Clear dead tops of non-shrubby plants from borders. Fork over the surface of the soil between plants, and bury weeds. Continue digging heavy soils to be weathered by frost. Order new plants.

DAHLIAS

Examine stored tubers and plunge them in a bucket of tepid water overnight if they have shrivelled. Cut away portions of tubers that have rotted and dust the cuts with flowers of sulphur or captan.

CHRYSANTHEMUMS

Drain waterlogged stools outdoors by piercing soil deeply with a garden fork. Ventilate stools in frames.
Under glass. Take cuttings of large exhibition varieties. Remove shoots more than 3 in. long from stools of outdoor varieties. Control aphids and leaf miners as necessary. Pot on any large exhibition plants which are big enough. Take basal cuttings of very late varieties while they are in flower.

GLADIOLI

Order new corms in good time from a reputable supplier.

IRISES

Place cloches over rows of *I. reticulata* intended for cutting. Pick *I. unguicularis* regularly.
Under glass. Water bulbous irises in pots after growth has started. Transfer Dutch, Spanish and English irises to a cold greenhouse when growth is evident.

LILIES

Plant bulbs in mild weather.
Under glass. Sow lily seeds in boxes. Bring in boxes of slow-germinating lilies sown in autumn. Bring in pots of lilies for forcing for Easter. Lift surplus strong lilies from the garden for forcing.

CARNATIONS AND PINKS

Test soil for lime content and add lime if below pH 6·5. In mild spells firm soil around plants loosened by frost. Clear rubbish from around stems and ensure stakes and ties are secure. Protect plants with black cotton against birds. Order plants and seeds for spring planting, and prepare the beds.
Under glass. Maintain a temperature of 7°C (45°F) for perpetual flowering carnations, and give some ventilation at all times. Water and feed sparingly, cutting blooms and disbudding flower stems. Dust against rust and aphids. Continue propagating perpetual flowering carnations from cuttings and pot up rooted cuttings. Sow seeds of perpetual flowering and annual carnations, and place the boxes or pots in a propagating frame at a temperature of 16°C (61°F). After germination, harden them off and prick them out into 2 in. pots.

SWEET PEAS

Dress beds prepared for planting with hydrated lime.
Under glass. Sow seed in slight heat.

FLOWERS FROM SEED

Plan spring planting programme. Complete digging beds and borders to be used for annuals.

BULBS

Bring in bulbs for indoor flowering as they become ready. Plant those which have finished flowering in odd corners of the garden.

ALPINES

Remove remaining fallen leaves and dig vacant spaces between plants. Order nursery-grown plants for delivery in early spring. Complete sowing of alpines that require exposure to frost.

WATER PLANTS AND POOLS

Continue to protect pools from ice. Check water levels for indications of loss caused by cracking of the lining. Check the covering on any protected plants. Feed fish with light food such as daphnia in mild weather.

GREENHOUSES AND FRAMES

Plan the number and types of plants to be grown in the coming year. Remove faded blooms from plants in flower. Avoid over-watering annuals and other young plants. Remove diseased foliage from pelargonium cuttings. Sow begonias, gloxinias and streptocarpus in a heated propagating case. Bring pots of polyanthuses, which have stood in the open garden, indoors to flower.

TREES AND SHRUBS

Stand shrubs arriving from nurseries during hard weather in a frost-free shed with straw around their roots. Continue planting in suitable weather.
Propagation. Sow seeds of camellia, ginkgo and liriodendron under glass at 16°C (61°F).
Pruning. Thin out dead and diseased branches from established trees and shrubs. Winter prune wisterias by cutting back young shoots to within 3 in. of old wood.

RHODODENDRONS AND AZALEAS

Lightly cover dwarf rhododendrons and Japanese azaleas with dead bracken to protect from severe frost; remove protection during mild spells.

HEDGES

Plant deciduous hedges during mild dry weather. Plants received when ground is unfit for planting should be kept in a frost-free shed. Protect their roots with straw.

HEATHERS

Firm newly planted heathers lifted by frost. Heathers may still be planted during suitable weather.

FRUIT

Inspect stored fruit and discard any which has rotted. Continue spraying trees and bushes with tar-oil. Continue planting in suitable conditions. Check stakes and ties. Continue pruning, collecting and burning prunings. Apply a nitrogenous fertiliser to trees and bushes grown in grass. Cut down old, worn-out trees. Take black currant cuttings.

VEGETABLES

Plant rhubarb and spread strawy manure over each station after planting. Cover established crowns similarly. Cover plants with boxes to encourage early growth. Sow peas in sheltered southern districts. Sow broad beans for an early crop.
Less common vegetables. In the south, an early crop of shallots can be planted on well drained soil.

HERBS

Plan your new herb garden during the dormant period. Choose a suitable sunny, south-facing position. Order seeds in readiness for spring sowing. Some protection is needed from north and east winds, and a south-sloping site is ideal. Plant the smaller herbs at the bottom of the slope.

PATIOS AND TOWN GARDENS

Move containers to a sheltered position or provide other protection. Plant trees and shrubs in containers for a permanent display, except during frosty weather.

HOUSE PLANTS

Keep plants warm and supplied with plenty of light. Water lightly and do not feed unless they are flowering or growing strongly.

GENERAL TASKS

Order seeds, gladioli, onion sets and shallots, garden sundries, weedkillers and fertilisers. Send mowers, cultivators and shears for servicing and sharpening. Treat wooden seed boxes with preservatives and wash pots and plastic trays. Check pergolas and other wooden structures and repair if necessary.

Plants to enjoy in January

Border and rock garden plants in flower Crocus Eranthis Galanthus (snowdrop) Helleborus niger (Christmas rose) Sempervivum	Hamamelis Jasminum nudiflorum (winter jasmine) Lonicera fragrantissima Mahonia	Impatiens Saintpaulia Saxifraga stolonifera
Trees and shrubs with colourful fruits Aucuba Pernettya Pyracantha Skimmia japonica	**Greenhouse plants in flower** Acacia Azalea indica Cineraria Euphorbia pulcherrima Primula obconica Senecio	**Vegetables in season** Artichoke, Jerusalem Brussels sprouts Cabbage Carrots Chicory Leek Onion
Trees and shrubs in flower Chimonanthus (wintersweet) Daphne mezereum Garrya elliptica	**House plants in flower, depending on position and culture** Anthurium Aphelandra Cyclamen persicum	Parsnip Radish, winter Salsify Scorzonera Swede

Lawns

Check drainage outlets, and make a particular note of areas of turf where drainage is ineffective but where surface treatments may be adequate.

Prepare top dressings for use on seed beds in spring, provided this can be done on a concrete floor and under cover.

If the ground is not too wet, continue aeration treatment (see SEPTEMBER), applying coarse sand to wet, muddy surfaces and hand forking wet areas to allow water to run away.

Although late, turfing is still possible in favourable weather.

Roses

Roses may be planted if the soil is dry or just moist (see NOVEMBER), but not if it is wet and sticky, or if there is frost or snow on the surface.

Delayed planting

Roses which cannot be planted at once will come to no harm if left in the nurseryman's packing for up to a week. If the planting has to be delayed still longer, remove the plants and heel them in.

If the roses cannot be heeled in because there is ground frost or snow, open the package, cut off any leaves remaining on the plants, then wrap the roots and lower parts of the stems with moist sacking and keep them in a frost-free place.

Support with bamboos

Use bamboo canes to support rose bushes loosened by winter gales. Push the canes into the soil at an angle on each side so that they form a cross, with the bush resting against the cross. Firm the soil around the base of the bush and removing the canes at pruning time.

If not already done during the autumn, prepare the ground for planting in February and March (see OCTOBER).

UNDER GLASS

Maintain a temperature of 5°C (41°F). Keep a can of water to use on roses once a week with water at the same temperature as the air in the greenhouse.

Hardy herbaceous plants

Clear all dead tops of non-shrubby plants from borders, if this has not already been done, taking care to tread between the plants. On some light or loose soils the tops can be severed and cleared more cleanly if the ground is frostbound, although the dead tops will be fully dried off and will not make such good compost (see NOVEMBER). Once the tops are cleared, fork over the surface of the soil between the plants and bury annual weeds.

Heavy clay or loam soils should have been dug in November or December, but frosts in late January or February will probably still reduce lumpy soil to a workable looseness before the arrival of the dry spring winds. On lighter soils the need for weathering is much less important, but annual surface-growing weeds must be buried at whatever stage of growth, so that the soil is clean and easy to work in the spring. Do not bury deep-rooted perennial weeds. Both the top growth and the roots should be removed and burnt.

Order new plants

Order new plants, if this has not already been done. Bear in mind that nurserymen are unlikely to have their full range to offer at this time after completing autumn orders, and enclose a list of alternative plants.

Dahlias

Examine stored tubers. If they are shrivelling, plunge them in tepid water for the night, dry, and replace in the peat or vermiculite (see OCTOBER). Cut off any parts that show signs of rotting, and dust with flowers of sulphur or captan.

Chrysanthemums

Examine the soil around stools of outdoor-flowering varieties which have been left to over-winter in sheltered southern gardens. If there seems any possibility of waterlogging, pierce the ground around each stool several times with a digging fork inserted to its full depth. Tread ground loosened by frost to re-firm it around the roots.

Ventilate stools bedded in frames whenever it is not freezing or blowing a gale, but protect them from frost at night with sacks or matting. Take care not to over-water resting stools.

UNDER GLASS

Maintain a maximum temperature of 10°C (50°F). Take cuttings of large exhibition varieties (see MARCH) but remove from the stools of outdoor varieties any shoots longer than 3 in. This will keep the stock in good condition for propagation during March and April. Take action, as necessary, against leaf miners and aphids (see APRIL).

Pot exhibition plants

Towards the end of the month cuttings of some large exhibition plants will be ready for their first potting (see MARCH).

Flowers of the very late varieties will carry on well into this month in a cool, dry greenhouse. Basal cuttings can be taken of these now, provided the shoots are in good shape (see MARCH).

Gladioli

Order new corms in good time from a reputable supplier. When they arrive, unpack them for examination, then either lay them out in shallow boxes or trays or return them to the bags after cuttings holes to allow free ventilation. Put in a dry, frost-proof place.

The theory that the largest corms are best is quite erroneous. A young, plump, high-necked corm with a small root-base is preferable to a much larger, flatter, older corm with a broad root-base.

Three main categories

Gladioli fall into three main categories —large-flowered, primulinus and butterfly (see illustrations p. 49). The large-flowered are the tallest, growing to about 5 ft., and have always been popular for garden display, exhibition and as cut flowers for decoration. Primulinus are not quite so tall and have slimmer spikes with smaller florets that include a brilliant range of colours. Butterfly gladioli are increasingly becoming more popular. They also are not so tall as the large-flowered type and the florets are about half the size. They are dainty and strikingly coloured with distinctive flushes and markings. The newest butterflies, named 'Magic Frills', have very frilled florets and grow about 3 ft. in height.

Choice of varieties depends largely upon individual taste, and most catalogues carry good colour descriptions. The following are recommended.

Large-flowered

'Peter Pears', apricot-orange; 'Deciso', salmon-pink; 'Trader Horn', crimson scarlet; 'Green Woodpecker', greenish lemon; 'Impudence', white and scarlet; 'Misty Eyes', plum red; 'Flowering', yellow.

Primulinus hybrids

'Scarlet Knight', brick red; 'Chrysantha', rich yellow; 'Richard Unwin', velvety crimson; 'Katharine', rosy mauve; 'Rosella', rosy lilac; 'Dante', soft pink.

Butterflies

'Evening Song', red and white; 'Lucette', scarlet and yellow; 'St Patrick's Day', greenish yellow; 'Darling', cream striped purple.

Butterfly Magic Frills

'Cupido', cream and orange; 'Fortuna', apricot and salmon; 'Olympia', scarlet and primrose; 'Venus', green and crimson.

Irises

Place closed cloches over *Iris reticulata* planted in rows for cutting. This will advance the time of flowering and will protect the blooms from the weather.

Pick flowers of *I. unguicularis* regularly (see DECEMBER).

UNDER GLASS

Water bulbous irises in pots as necessary. *Iris tingitana* can be gently forced. Transfer Dutch, Spanish and English irises from the cold frame to a cold greenhouse when growth is evident.

Lilies

Lilies can be planted at any time until March, provided both soil and weather are suitable (see OCTOBER). Otherwise, it is safer to pot the bulbs (see NOVEMBER).

UNDER GLASS

Sow lily seeds $\frac{1}{2}$–1 in. apart and $\frac{1}{2}$ in. deep in boxes.

Bring in boxes of slow-germinating lilies sown in the autumn (see SEPTEMBER).

Germination

The seeds of some lilies germinate and appear above ground within a month of sowing, usually as little green loops similar to onion seedlings. This is known as epigeal germination. Others start by producing a tiny bulb, nothing appearing on the surface until possibly a year after sowing, when a small lance-shaped leaf appears. This is hypogeal germination.

Bring in pots of lilies for forcing for Easter, maintaining a temperature of 7–10°C (45–50°F) until growth is well started, then gradually raising it to 16–21°C (61–70°F). They should flower in 13 weeks.

Lift any surplus strong lilies from the garden for gentle forcing. Use 3 parts fibrous loam, 1 part leaf mould, 1 part well rotted manure and a little sand.

Carnations and pinks

Test soil for lime content and add lime if it is below pH 6·5.

In mild spells firm the soil around any plants loosened by frost. Clear away rubbish around plants, and ensure that stakes and ties are secure. Protect with black cotton against birds.

Order plants and seeds for spring planting (see colour section, MAY) and prepare the beds (see AUGUST).

UNDER GLASS

Maintain a temperature of 7°C (45°F) for perpetual flowering carnations and give some ventilation at all times.

Water and feed sparingly (see APRIL), cutting blooms and disbudding flower stems as necessary (see SEPTEMBER).

Winter protection

Watch for carnation rust and aphids (see MARCH), using dusts in preference to sprays during the winter.

Continue to propagate perpetual flowering carnations by cuttings, and pot up rooted cuttings (see DECEMBER).

Sow seeds of perpetual flowering and annual carnations in pans or seed boxes. Water the compost with Cheshunt compound, space the seeds $\frac{1}{4}$ in. apart, and cover them with a thin layer of fine soil. Cover the box or pan with a sheet of glass and maintain a temperature of 16°C (61°F).

Prick out seedlings

When the seedlings appear, gradually admit air to harden the plants off to the normal greenhouse temperature. Prick them out into 2 in. pots when the first true leaves (not the seed leaves, which appear first) are $\frac{1}{2}$ in. long. Thereafter, treat seedlings of perpetual flowering carnations in the same way as cuttings, but do not stop them. Treat annual carnations as bedding plants, though they are not recommended for growing in the open garden in cold areas in the north.

Order perpetual flowering carnations.

Sweet peas

Broadcast a light dressing of hydrated lime over the surface of outdoor beds dug earlier, unless lime was applied last year. In this case, scatter a light dressing of a general compound fertiliser or a proprietary sweet pea fertiliser.

UNDER GLASS

Seed can now be sown in slight heat, about 4°C (39°F), following the method outlined in OCTOBER.

Flowers from seed

Study the seed catalogues and plan your spring planting programme. Varieties in short supply may be sold out unless you order in good time.

If not already done, complete the digging of beds and borders in which the coming season's hardy and half-hardy annuals will be grown (see NOVEMBER).

UNDER GLASS

Sow *Begonia semperflorens*, which needs a long growing period, if a heated greenhouse or frame is available (see tables and sowing instructions, MARCH).

Bulbs

UNDER GLASS AND INDOORS

Continue to bring in bulbs for indoor flowering as they become ready for extra warmth (see DECEMBER). Bulbs which have finished flowering may be planted straight from their containers into odd corners of the garden (see MARCH). If the weather is too cold or wet, keep them watered in a frost-free greenhouse or frame until planting conditions are more favourable.

Alpines

Remove any remaining fallen leaves and dig vacant spaces between plants with a small hand fork or trowel.

Order nursery-grown plants for delivery in early spring. Up to 12 slow-growing plants will be needed for each sq. yd., but only four or five of sorts that spread rapidly.

Complete as soon as possible the sowing of alpines that require exposure to frost (see DECEMBER).

Water plants and pools

Continue with pool protection (see DECEMBER). Check the water level for indications of loss due to cracking. Check covering on protected plants.

If the weather is mild, give fish a little light food such as *Daphnia*.

Greenhouses and frames

Stocking a greenhouse with flowering plants is much easier if a plan is made each January, setting out how many of each kind will be required to fill the available space.

Remove faded flowers

Examine regularly plants in flower, such as primulas and cyclamens, removing any faded flowers or discoloured leaves. Take care when watering not to splash the flowers or to leave water lodging in the crowns of the plants.

Avoid over-watering annuals in pots and any other young plants in the greenhouse, or the roots may be damaged.

Check cuttings for mildew

Examine cuttings of zonal pelargoniums inserted in September. Remove any leaves showing signs of mildew, and discard cuttings which have diseased stems. Water the plants only when the soil in the pots shows signs of drying out.

If a propagating case is available to maintain a temperature of 16–18°C (61–64°F) during germination, towards the end of the month sow begonias, gloxinias and streptocarpus in pans of John Innes seed compost. Otherwise delay sowing until late February.

Bring polyanthuses indoors

Bring indoors pots of polyanthuses which were planted in June and have since been standing in the open garden. They should flower next month.

Trees and shrubs

If shrubs arrive from the nursery when the ground is frozen, keep them in a frost-free shed with straw around and beneath the roots. Continue with planting as soon as the weather permits.

PROPAGATION

Under glass

Seeds of camellia, ginkgo (maidenhair tree) and liriodendron (tulip tree) can be sown under glass at a temperature of 16°C (61°F). Though it is interesting to raise these trees from seed, results are slow and unpredictable. A tulip tree raised in this way may take 15–20 years to flower, and named varieties of camellia do not come true from seed.

PRUNING

Thin out dead and diseased branches from established trees and shrubs. Winter prune wisteria by cutting back to within 3 in. of the old wood all young shoots not needed to increase the size of the plant.

Rhododendrons and azaleas

Lightly cover dwarf rhododendrons and Japanese azaleas with dead bracken to a depth of about 8–10 in. if severe frost or snow threatens.

Hedges

During mild, dry weather it should still be possible to plant deciduous hedges on well drained land (see OCTOBER). If hedging plants are delivered when the ground is frozen or excessively wet, keep them in a frost-free shed with straw around and beneath their roots. Continue with planting as soon as possible.

Heathers

Firm into place any newly planted heathers that have been partially lifted by frost. Planting is still possible this month if the ground is not waterlogged or frozen (see MARCH and OCTOBER), but unless the heathers have been lifted already delay planting until the spring.

Fruit

Inspect stored fruit and discard any that has rotted.

Continue spraying fruit trees and bushes with a tar-oil winter-wash; see DECEMBER for strength of application.

Continue planting if soil conditions are suitable. If the soil is waterlogged heel the trees in; if it is frozen, keep them in a frost-free place until the coming of warmer weather.

Check stakes and ties, and renew framework supports and wires where necessary.

Continue pruning, and collect and burn the prunings.

Before the middle of the month, feed with nitrogen trees or bushes grown in grass (see DECEMBER).

Cut down old, worn-out trees, if possible cutting off the trunk below soil level.

Apple and pear
If not already done, feed established trees (see DECEMBER). Complete pruning of newly planted trees.

Blackberry, loganberry, and hybrid berries
Cut newly planted bushes down to within 9–12 in. of the soil level.

Black currant
Cut newly planted bushes hard back after planting. Use well ripened shoots as cuttings (see DECEMBER).

Cherry
On newly planted standard trees cut leaders to 12–18 in.

Feed in the same way as apple (see DECEMBER), except fan-trained 'Morello' cherry, which should be fed in the same way as fan-trained peach.

Gooseberry, red currant and white currant
Prune newly planted bushes by cutting leading shoots by half. Cut leading shoots on cordons by one-third.

Peach and nectarine
Feed bush trees in the same way as apple (see DECEMBER), and feed fan-trained trees every year with up to 1 oz. of hoof and horn per sq. yd.

Plum and damson
Feed in the same way as apple (see DECEMBER), but increase the rate of sulphate of ammonia for trees grown in grass.

Raspberry
Cut newly planted canes hard back to within 9–12 in. of the soil level.

Vegetables

Plant rhubarb roots, obtainable from most garden shops, 3 ft. apart in well manured soil. An alternative to manure is hoof and horn fertiliser applied at 4 oz. per sq. yd. Set the roots so that their tops are about 1 in. below soil level. If you have compost or strawy manure to spare, place a 3 in. layer over each station after planting, covering this with a sprinkling of soil to prevent

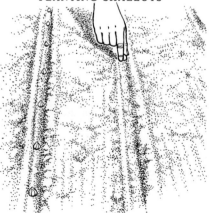

PLANTING SHALLOTS

Set the bulbs in shallow drills, afterwards covering all but the tips. Do not press them into the soil, as this may damage the bulbs

birds scratching it away. Do not gather rhubarb during the first season.

Early this month, cover established rhubarb plants with a similar layer of manure or garden compost. If compost is used, first sprinkle sulphate of ammonia round the crowns at 2 oz. per sq. yd. This feeds the plants and induces early growth. To encourage still earlier growth, cover the plants with large upturned boxes or other light-proof receptacles.

Sow peas in sheltered areas
In sheltered southern districts, sow peas for picking in May or June, first dressing the seeds with captan and applying hoof and horn fertiliser or bone-meal at 4 oz. per sq. yd. If spare cloches are available, place them over the rows, closing the ends with sheets of glass. Take out a flat-bottomed drill 9 in. wide and about 2½ in. deep, spacing the seeds 2 in. apart in three rows. Use a round-seeded variety, such as 'Feltham First', 'Meteor', 'Pilot' or 'Kelvedon Wonder'.

Sow broad beans
Also sow broad beans for an early crop. 'Aquadulce', 'Masterpiece Green Longpod' and 'The Sutton' are excellent. Follow the method for peas, but sow in rows 7 in. apart with 6 in. between the seeds.

LESS COMMON VEGETABLES
Shallots can be planted this month on well drained soil, though many gardeners prefer to wait until February or early March. Set the bulbs 9 in. apart, in rows 12 in. apart, choosing soil that was manured last autumn and leaving the tips at ground level. In cold northern gardens do not plant shallots outside until the end of February.

Lift Jerusalem artichokes for cooking as required, inserting a spade about 9 in. from each stem and pushing it under the clump of tubers to lift it intact.

Herbs

The dormant period of winter is the ideal time to plan your herb garden. Most herbs should be planted in a sunny, south-facing position and with some protection from north and east winds. A south-sloping plot of ground is ideal. The taller, sun-loving herbs can be planted at the back, and the smaller herbs, which do best in a moist soil, can be planted at the bottom of the slope.

Planning herb borders

Small herb borders, sufficient to provide flavouring, may be treated as an integral part of the vegetable garden. On a larger scale the herb border can virtually be a herbaceous border and may include many perennial herbs. A herbaceous herb garden needs careful planning, to give the most pleasing effect to the eye, and a natural or contrasting grouping of plants.

A small collection of herbs can be based on an old cartwheel laid on the ground; each segment is planted with a different herb. In a larger garden a round bed may be marked out in wedge-shaped segments, each for a different herb.

Where space permits, an attractive herb garden may be planned as a chess-board, each square containing one species. Alternate the patches with equal-sized squares, either paved or filled with gravel or granite chippings.

Elizabethan knot garden

More complicated designs, such as an imitation of the Elizabethan knot garden, must be carefully drawn up on paper. The pattern of the design is formed by planting in individual beds herbs whose leaf textures or colours contrast with those of the next bed. Each bed or shape may be outlined by box or violets.

When you have decided on the shape and size of the herb garden, order seeds in readiness for sowing in the spring, from your own seedsman or from a specialised herb nurseryman.

Patios and town gardens

Move containers to a sheltered position or provide some other form of protection, if this has not been done already (see DECEMBER).

Unless it is freezing, shrubs and trees can still be planted in containers to provide a permanent display (see MARCH and NOVEMBER).

House plants

Continue to keep plants warm, free from draughts, in as much light as possible and away from all direct heat. Water very lightly and do not feed unless the plant is growing strongly or is in flower.

General tasks

Order seeds, gladioli, onion sets and shallots, and garden sundries such as tree stakes, pea sticks, bean poles, canes, insecticides, fertilisers and weed-killers.

Maintenance and protection

Send mowers, cultivators, shears, secateurs and hedge-trimmers to be serviced or sharpened.

Wash plastic seed trays or flower pots. Treat wooden wheelbarrows and seed boxes with a preservative. Never use creosote for any woodwork that is likely to come into contact with plants. Even the fumes from a newly creosoted fence or pergola can be harmful. Check pergolas and other wooden structures. If they are weak or wobbly, repair them. A heavy snowfall may bring them down.

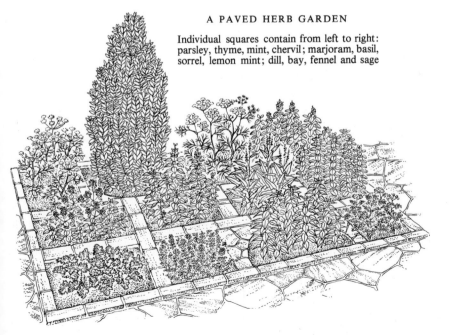

A PAVED HERB GARDEN

Individual squares contain from left to right: parsley, thyme, mint, chervil; marjoram, basil, sorrel, lemon mint; dill, bay, fennel and sage

Herbs to order in January

Apart from their uses in cooking, most herbs are also highly decorative. They will flourish on small patches of ground, preferably near the kitchen; or they can be grown more formally in a herb garden laid out to a pattern.

Basil, sweet or **common**
(Ocimum basilicum)
Height 2–3 ft. Spread 12 in. Annual. Light green aromatic leaves, green-grey beneath, or tinged purple. White flowers in late summer. Plant in well drained light soil, and in sheltered position. Propagate by seeds in May. Harvest leaves July–September, or before flowering if they are to be dried. Used for flavouring salads, beverages, soups and sauces, omelettes and summer drinks.

Bay

Basil

Bay (Laurus nobilis)
Height up to 30 ft. Spread up to 20 ft. Small evergreen tree of pyramidal form. Aromatic, slightly waxy leaves. Thrives in full sun in a sheltered position, and in ordinary soil. Propagate by cuttings, August–September. Dried leaves are used for flavouring soups, stews and fish dishes, and in *bouquet garni*.

Bergamot (Monarda didyma)
Height 1½–3 ft. Spread varied. Perennial. Dark aromatic leaves have serrated edges. Flower whorls in shades of red, pink, mauve or white, July–September. Plant in rich moist soil in full sun. Cut leaves for drying before plants flower, or use both leaves and flowers fresh for flavouring summer drinks. Clumps need splitting and re-planting in spring.

Chervil (Anthriscus cerefolium)
Height 12 in. Spread 6–9 in. Annual with feathery and fern-like leaves. White flower umbels, June–August of the second year. Plant in ordinary soil, in a semi-shaded position. Harvest leaves six to eight weeks after sowing the first year, and before flowering the second year. Use fresh or dried for flavouring salads, soups and sauces.

Chives (Allium schoenoprasum)
Height 6–10 in. Spread 6–8 in. Perennial. Grass-like tubular foliage is dark glaucous green. Pale mauve flower umbels in July and August; remove these before flowering. Thrives in medium loamy soil, and in semi-shade. Propagate by off-sets in March. Harvest leaves as required and use for flavouring salad dressings and egg dishes. They have a mild onion flavour, and are used in *sauce tartare*. Useful as edging plants to herb border.

Dill (Anethum graveolens)
Height 3 ft. Spread up to 24 in. Annuals with fine, thread-like blue-green foliage. Yellow flowers in small upright umbels in summer. Sow in a dry, sunny position in well drained, fine loamy soil. Propagate by seed each March. Harvest leaves before seed is set, and seeds when ripe. Use fresh or dried leaves

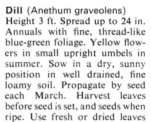

Chervil

Dill

for flavouring potatoes, beans, peas, poultry and *hors d'oeuvres*, and the stronger-flavoured seed in salad dressings and pickles.

Fennel (Foeniculum vulgare)
Height 1–4 ft. Spread 1½–2½ ft. Perennial, biennial or annual. Polished stems become slightly hollow with age. Blue-green feathery leaves wilt on cutting. Yellow flowers in July and August. Thrive in rich chalky soil, in a warm sunny position. Propagate by seed or division of roots in March. Leaves have a strong anise flavour and are used, fresh or dried, for flavouring cheese and fish dishes and for pickles and chutney. Roots and seeds, harvested at the end of July, are also used.

Hyssop (Hyssopus officinalis)
Height 2–4 ft. Spread 1½–2½ ft. Evergreen, hardy shrub. Dark green rough leaves and bright

Fennel

blue flower spikes, June–August. Plant in light soil in a sunny position. Propagate by seed in April, or by cuttings in August. Bitter, mint-flavoured flowers and tops are used with game, meat and salads.

Marjoram, pot (Origanum onites)

Height up to 12 in. Spread indefinite. Perennial. Small leaves with red stems; mauve flowers in July and August. Plant in a warm sunny position, in light dry soil, especially chalky. Propagate by seeds or layers in March. Harvest leaves July–September, and use fresh or dried in poultry stuffing.

Hyssop

Mint or spearmint (Mentha viridis, syn. M. spicata)

Height 12–24 in. Spread indefinite. Perennial. Shining dark green leaves are deeply veined. Mauve flowers in terminal spikes in August. Plant in rich moist soil and in a shady position. Propagate by division in March or by cuttings in August. Harvest leaves for drying at any time, or use fresh before or after the plants flower.

Parsley, curly (Petroselinum crispum)

Height 6–9 in. Spread 4–6 in. Biennial. Dark or light green leaves are crisply curled and deeply divided. Creamy-white flowers in summer of the second year. Thrives in sun or partial shade in a rich, fine and moist soil. Propagate by seed which germinates very slowly. Cut leaves before flowering, and use for garnishing and flavouring.

Marjoram

Rosemary (Rosmarinus officinalis)

Height up to 6 ft. Spread up to 7 ft. Evergreen lax shrub with grey-green aromatic leaves. Pale blue flowers in May. Plant in light, chalky, rather dry soil and in full sun. Propagate by cuttings in August or September. Harvest leaves all year round—for drying before flowering, or in August. Use as an infusion, in

Sage

fruit cups, or as flavouring for meat, poultry and egg dishes.

Rue (Ruta graveolens)

Height 2–3 ft. Spread 1½–2½ ft. Evergreen shrub. Blue-green, deeply divided thin foliage has unpleasant scent. Does well in ordinary soil in a sunny position. Propagate by seed in April or by cuttings in August. Chiefly grown for decorative purposes; 'Jackman's Blue' has blue flowers throughout the summer months.

Sage (Salvia officinalis)

Height and spread 4 ft. Evergreen shrubs. Grey crinkled leaves. Violet-blue flowers in June and July. Plant in light

Sorrel

chalky soil and in a sunny position. Propagate by cuttings in May. Harvest the leaves at any time for flavouring, or before flowering for drying. Use to flavour stuffing.

Sorrel, French (Rumex scutatus)

Height 2–2½ ft. Spread 12–18 in. Perennial. Dark green glossy leaves. Red flowers in clustered spikes, but plants should be dis-budded to encourage the production of young basal leaves, superior in flavour and texture. Thrives in moist, ordinary soil, and in a sunny or semi-shaded position. Propagate by seeds or division in March and April. Harvest leaves when young and use for flavouring in salads, sandwiches or soups. May also be used as a green vegetable early in the year.

Thyme

Thyme (Thymus vulgaris)

Height 4–10 in. Creeping and spreading evergreen. The small leaves are long and narrow. Mauve flowers appear in small heads in axils of leaves in June. Does best in a sunny position, in well drained chalky soil. Propagate by seeds, cuttings or division in April or May. Harvest shoots at any time for use fresh or dried in *bouquet garni* or to flavour soups, meat and fish. Useful as ground cover or as edging plants.

Heathers

The following heather species are subdivided into numerous named varieties, which vary greatly in habit of growth, and in flower colour from white through all shades of red to mauve. As a general guide to spread of plants, the ultimate spread of varieties less than 12 in. high is approximately three times the height—in other words, a heather 9 in. high will spread to something over 24 in., depending on soil and situation. The flowering times are also approximate. All heathers can be propagated by layers, division or cuttings, though cuttings are preferable.

Calluna vulgaris (ling)
Evergreen shrub. Height 6–24 in. Leaves in four longitudinal rows on the woody stems, densely overlapping. Flowers in terminal spikes, varying in colour according to variety, July–October. Grows in well drained, lime-free soil and open, sunny position.

Erica carnea
Height 6–9 in. Leaves vary from light green to dark purple-green. Flowers vary from white to crimson, winter. Will grow on alkaline soil. Plant in an open, sunny position.

Calluna vulgaris

Erica carnea

Erica ciliaris

E. ciliaris (Dorset heath)
Evergreen shrub. Height 6–12 in. Foliage mostly pale green, slightly sticky, in whorls. Flowers carried on terminal racemes, all facing one way, and varying in colour from white through all shades of pink to rose-red, July–September. Grows in lime-free soil. Does not like polluted air.

E. cinerea (scotch heather, bell heather)
Dwarf evergreen shrub. Height 6–12 in. Small, deep green leaves, in whorls of three. Numerous flowers in terminal umbels,

colour varying from white to deep purple-red, June–August. Grows in well drained, lime-free soil and full sun.

E. mediterranea
Shrub. Height 2–8 ft., according to variety. Small green leaves set in whorls of four on brittle, woody stems. Flowers, in racemes in the leaf axils, white, pink or deep purple according to variety, late winter and spring. Grows in good loamy soil, and does not object to a little lime. Needs shelter from cold north and east winds.

E. terminalis (syn. **E. stricta**)
Tree heather. Height 3–6 ft. Young leaves bright green, older ones dark green, in whorls of four or six. Rose-pink flowers, July–December. Will grow on lime. Prefers an open, sunny position.

E. tetralix (cross-leaved heath)
Evergreen shrub. Height 9–12 in. Tiny hairy leaves set in crosswise whorls of four, often grey in colour. Flowers cylindrical in shape, usually in groups of four or more on a stem, varying from white to crimson, June–October. Grows in lime-free soil.

Erica cinerea

Erica mediterranea

Erica terminalis

Erica tetralix

Less common vegetables

A selection of rewarding but seldom grown vegetables referred to in the VEGETABLES section month by month.

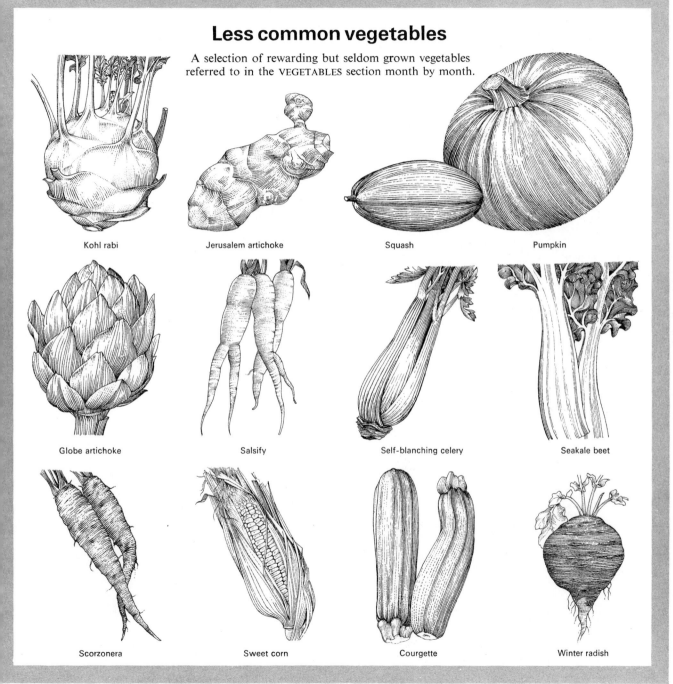

Kohl rabi

Jerusalem artichoke

Squash

Pumpkin

Globe artichoke

Salsify

Self-blanching celery

Seakale beet

Scorzonera

Sweet corn

Courgette

Winter radish

Greenhouse plants for winter colour

Some of the plants, especially annuals, mentioned in the monthly work sections for the greenhouse are described elsewhere in this book. *Begonia rex* and other foliage plants often grown as house plants are described on pp. 360–9. Passifloras are listed under TREES AND SHRUBS. Grow greenhouse plants at a temperature of about 6–7°C (43–45°F).

Abutilon

Abutilon (Indian mallow)
Several species of this half-hardy shrub are grown as greenhouse plants. They are often treated as climbers to show off the beautiful trumpet-like, pendulous flowers which appear between August and November. All grow to about 8 ft. Propagate from seed sown in February, or from stem cuttings rooted in September or March. In March, prune established specimens grown as pot plants, re-potting them at the same time if necessary. Recommended are: 'Boule de Neige', white flowers; 'Canary Bird' and 'Golden Fleece', yellow flowers; *A. megapotamicum*, red and yellow flowers; *A. milleri*, orange flowers, mottled foliage; *A. savitzii*, yellow and green foliage.

Acacia (mimosa)
These graceful greenhouse shrubs bear clusters of fluffy yellow balls in early spring. Though some species will grow to 30 ft. or more, plants grown in pots and pinched back each year after flowering can be restricted to about 20 in. Propagate from seeds in March or from cuttings of semi-ripe shoots rooted in July. Stand the plants outside from June to October. *A. armata* is probably the best species for growing in pots. *A. baileyana* makes a graceful and leafy small tree and is just as attractive as *A. dealbata*, the popular mimosa sold by florists, which is too large for most greenhouses.

Acacia dealbata

Achimenes (hot water plant)
A. hybrida. Height 12 in. Delightful tubular flowers in shades of red, pink, white, blue, violet and purple during the summer. Tuberous-rooted plants, which die down in autumn and remain dormant throughout the winter. Useful for hanging baskets. If sufficient heat is available, start the tubers into growth during February, but leave until March in a cool house.

Azalea
A. indica (Indian azalea). Popular evergreen and Christmas-flowering shrub. The flowers are mostly reds and pinks, but some varieties have white blooms. Height 2–4 ft. After flowering, keep the compost moist and syringe the leaves frequently to promote new growth. Stand the pots outdoors between June and October. Re-pot in peaty, lime-free compost every two years.

Achimenes

Begonia
B. tuberhybrida (tuberous-rooted begonia). Height 24 in. Beautifully formed flowers in subtle and delicate shades of red, pink, yellow and white, in a variety of single, double, and semi-double forms, some with picotee edges to the petals. All flower throughout the summer. Tuberous begonias are the easiest and best of this family for the cool greenhouse. Start the dormant tubers into growth in January if a propagating case is available, but under cooler conditions leave them until March. All begonias like an open compost and a free root run, so do not pot them too firmly. Maintain a moist atmosphere throughout the growing season, and shade the plants from full sun from early May onwards. Stake large plants, and remove the female

Azalea indica

Begonia tuberhybrida

(outer) flowers from plants for exhibition. After the plants have flowered, dry them off gradually and store the dormant tubers until the following spring. There are numerous varieties, and the pendulous varieties of the *lloydii* type are grown in hanging baskets.

Calceolaria

Calceolaria (slipper flower)
The herbaceous calceolaria hybrids are exotic and colourful plants, with pouch-like flowers, usually yellow with scarlet,

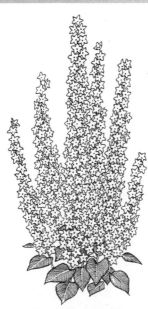

Campanula pyramidalis

black and brown blotches. Sow the seed in July and germinate in a cold frame or a cool greenhouse. The large-flowered types grow to about 18 in., and the *multiflora nana* hybrids, height 9–12 in., are particularly recommended.

Campanula isophylla

Campanula
C. pyramidalis (chimney bell-flower). Height 5 ft. Graceful spires of china-blue bells for several weeks from early July onwards. Sow the seed in a cold frame in April or May for plants to flower the following summer in July. A hardy plant which needs a minimum of heat, except in severe conditions. *C. isophylla* (star of Bethlehem). Height 4–6 in. Delightful pale blue flowers for a long period from August onwards. Can be grown as a pot plant to trail over the front of the staging in the greenhouse, or in a hanging basket. Propagate from seed sown in March or from cuttings taken in March or August. *C. i. alba* is a white variety.

Canna

Canna (Indian shot)
C. hybrida. Height 3 ft. Tropical herbs with a profusion of dazzling flowers in a range of colours from July onwards, and attractive bronze-brown and dark green foliage. Slightly tender. Propagate from seed sown in February or March, or from rhizomes dried off when the foliage dies down in autumn and restarted into growth in March.

Celosia

Celosia
C. plumosa. Height 15 in. Bright red, feathery, silky tassels in summer; the variety *aurea* is golden yellow. An attractive pot plant which must be kept growing steadily. Propagate from seed sown in February or March.

Cineraria
Cinerarias (botanically now *Senecio*) are easily grown plants bearing a profusion of daisy-like flowers in shades of red, blue, pink or white from

Cineraria

November to May. Propagate from seed sown in succession from April to July, so that the plants flower over a long period. Good strains are: *grandiflora*, height 18 in., large flowers 2 in. in diameter; *multiflora nana*, height 10 in., dwarf and compact; *stellata*, height up to 3 ft., star-like, narrow flowers.

Coleus
C. blumei. Height 1–3 ft. Grown for its attractive bronze-red leaves. Remove the flower spikes while they are still buds. Propagate from seed sown in a propagating case in February, or raise named varieties from cuttings at any time from March to September.

Coleus

Freesia
New vigorous varieties of these plants (height 24 in.) are constantly being produced. The fragrant flowers are borne on thin but fairly strong wiry stems, in colours ranging through pink, lavender, rose, yellow, creamy white, pure white and purple. Freesias can be had in flower in a cool greenhouse from November to March, if they are grown in successive batches. Good modern varieties are 'White Swan', 'Pink Giant', 'Rynvelds Golden Yellow' and 'Sapphire'. Seeds of mixed colours sown in April produce seedlings which can be grown on

Freesia

to flower the following February. Bulbs can be potted in August in 5 in. pots, at six bulbs per pot.

Fuchsia
These popular plants bear elegant, pendulous flowers in varying shades of pink, violet, crimson and orange throughout the summer and autumn. They need a good rich soil, good ventilation and a moist atmosphere. Young plants can be trained as standards, up to 4 or 5 ft., or as bushes or pyramids, height up to 24 in. (see *Greenhouses and frames*, MAY). Take cuttings of young shoots in March or August.

Fuchsia

Geranium: see **Pelargonium**

Gloxinia: see **Sinningia**

Heliotropium
H. peruvianum (cherry pie). Height 24 in. or more. Blue and white fragrant flowers from June to October. Propagate from seed sown in March or from cuttings taken in September. Plants raised from cuttings will grow up to 24 in. the following year, and if trained as standards (in the same way as fuchsias) will grow taller.

Heliotropium peruvianum

Pelargonium
Pelargoniums, commonly called geraniums, are easy to grow and are generally free from pests and diseases. There are several groups:

Zonal pelargoniums, the ordinary geraniums, are the hybrids or varieties of *P. zonale*. They produce vividly coloured flowers at almost all seasons, and make ideal plants for the cool greenhouse. Propagate from stem cuttings in August or September. Outstanding varieties, height 2½–3 ft., are 'Elizabeth Cartwright', large, carmine-red with a white eye; 'Gustav Emich' and 'Maxim Kovaleski', vermilion; 'Mrs. Henry Cox', orange-red, leaves marked with black, red, green and cream.

Pelargonium domesticum

Regal pelargoniums are the hybrids of *P. domesticum*. They produce single or double flowers, usually striped or blotched, in a wide range of colours from almost black, through violet, orange and magenta, to pale

Pelargonium zonale

pink and white. All flower during spring or early summer, and reach a height of 3 ft. or more. Propagate from stem cuttings taken in July, August or September. Interest in regal pelargoniums has recently been renewed by the introduction of varieties of the 'Irene' strain from America.

Plumbago capensis

Plumbago
P. capensis (cape leadwort). Height 10 ft. Delightful, soft blue, phlox-like flowers in September. Effective as a climber in the cool greenhouse, it needs tying and supporting. Can also be grown as a pot plant, if the shoot tips are pinched out. Propagate from stem cuttings in late summer. Prune the flowering shoots hard each February.

Primula
P. kewensis. Height 9 in. Rich yellow flowers in late spring

Primula kewensis

and early summer. Leaves covered with the milky white powder known as farina. A compact plant, which is almost hardy. Easily raised from seed sown in March. *P. malacoides* (fairy primula). Height 15 in. Dainty lilac flowers in spring. Almost hardy, and requires little heat. Propagate from seed sown in June or July. Modern varieties with much larger crimson, maroon, pink, lilac and white flowers are now available. *P. obconica*. Height 9 in. Compact flower heads appear intermittently throughout the year. Propagate from seed sown in March, April or May. Contact

Schizanthus

with these plants may cause skin irritation, and anyone allergic to them should wear gloves when handling them. There are white, pink, salmon, blue and crimson varieties.

Schizanthus (butterfly flower, poor man's orchid)
These graceful and elegant annuals are grown in pots and produce flowers in shades of pink, crimson, mauve and white from May to July. Propagate from seed sown in

Sinningia (gloxinia)

September or February. Many varieties and strains have been developed, including the large-flowered hybrids, height up to 4 ft., and the dwarf bouquet strains, height 12 in.

Senecio: see Cineraria

Sinningia (gloxinia)
These plants are hybrids or varieties of *S. speciosa*. They produce richly coloured, velvety, trumpet-like flowers in shades of red, blue, purple and white from midsummer until early

Streptocarpus

autumn. They need warm, moist conditions and shade from direct sunlight. Propagate from seed sown in February, or raise plants from corms started into growth in March.

Streptocarpus (cape primrose)
The streptocarpus hybrids, height 12–15 in., produce trumpet-like flowers, gracefully poised on wiry stems, in a wide range of colours, for several months from midsummer onwards. Seed sown in February will flower in late July or August, but for early flowering varieties sow seed the previous June. Plants can be kept for two or three years, but if possible grow fresh stock each year.

Tibouchina semidecandra

Tibouchina
T. semidecandra (glory bush). Height 6–8 ft. Distinctive rich purple flowers in summer and autumn. Propagate by cuttings of young side shoots in a propagating case at any time from March to September. When grown in a pot it can be restricted to about 24 in. by pruning and pinching out the tips of the growths.

February

Snowdrops and other bulbs in flower are a reminder that spring is near, and warmer spells allow the gardener to prepare the ground for planting

The weather in February

If the wind is in the east at the beginning of the month, winter is likely to remain for a further spell of some weeks; but if there are clouds and rain, the winter is virtually over, especially if the wind is westerly.

In a hard winter February is often the coldest month, and brings winter conditions even to the south coast of Ireland and the Cornish coasts. The sun has little warming effect on any wind reaching Britain from the cold continent of Europe. Cold east to north-east winds bring grey skies and heavy falls of snow, especially to eastern regions and high ground farther west. Afternoon temperatures may not rise above freezing point, except in the lowlands of south-west England and western Ireland. At other times long spells of northerly weather may occur. Blustery winds come sweeping down from the Arctic regions, bringing vigorous snow squalls and intense cold, particularly to northern Scotland. Still nights often occur during these spells, and then temperatures may fall exceptionally low; in Highland valleys temperatures as low as −23°C (−10°F) occasionally occur.

In a mild February, west to south-west winds occur frequently. Periods of heavy rain are broken by bright, sunny intervals and showers; in the midlands afternoon temperatures may reach 10°C (50°F), but it is much colder in Scotland. At night the wind often drops sufficiently for frost to occur. However, western coastal areas are milder than the rest of the country, and the first signs of spring are apparent. A short spell of southerly winds may bring unseasonable warmth to the whole of southern England, and temperatures there may reach 13°C (55°F), but it is always wise to ignore these false springs, for the spell rarely persists and cold weather is sure to return.

Preparation of the ground for spring planting can be carried out in February whenever the weather permits. The greatest possible use should be made of any available glass cover, making sure that the glass is clean, so that it admits the maximum possible light. Glass cover will not keep out frost in February in a severe winter, but in most years it affords reasonable protection against the night cold. It can also be placed over fallow soil to assist in the warming up of the earth, so that sowing can take place a week or two earlier.

A summary of the month's work

LAWNS

New lawns. Continue preparing spring seed beds.
Established lawns. Aerate and scarify in dry conditions. Apply worm-killing preparations and lawn sand. Treat moss with mercurised compounds.

ROSES

Complete planting, but not if the soil is wet and sticky or if there is frost or snow on the surface. If conditions are unsuitable for planting, heel the roses in. Support bushes lashed by winter gales and firm the soil around them.
Under glass. Maintain temperatures of 16°C (61°F) during the day and 7°C (45°F) at night. Water well once a week.

HARDY HERBACEOUS PLANTS

Clear dead tops of plants if not already done. Top-dress established borders with fertiliser, using John Innes base, hoof and horn, or other similar fertiliser. Where digging between plants has been deferred until now, spread fertiliser and then dig it in.

DAHLIAS

Examine stored tubers and plunge them in a bucket of tepid water overnight if they have shrivelled. Cut away portions of tubers that have rotted and dust the cuts with flowers of sulphur or captan.

CHRYSANTHEMUMS

Drain waterlogged stools outdoors. Keep beds clear of weeds and scatter slug pellets around stools.
Under glass. Propagate greenhouse decorative, single and anemone-flowered varieties. Finish potting exhibition varieties. Prepare frames to receive potted plants, scattering slug bait.

GLADIOLI

Sprout gladioli in a greenhouse at 10°C (50°F). Dust corms with HCH if aphids appear. Check stored corms.

IRISES

Order summer-flowering Dutch iris bulbs, sold as 'specially prepared'. Place cloches over rows of Dutch irises intended for

cutting, to protect the blooms from the weather. Protect early-flowering irises in the rock garden with panes of glass. Pick *I. unguicularis* regularly.

Under glass. Give gentle warmth to all bulbous irises in pots, except Dutch, Spanish and English types.

LILIES

Plant bulbs in mild weather. When buying, choose plump healthy bulbs which are not dried up. Outdoors protect emerging shoots against frost with cloches.

Under glass. Sow seed under glass. Pot imported lilies to raise as pot plants. Plant bulbs of stem-rooting lilies. When buds appear on forced lilies, raise temperature to 18–21°C (64–70°F) and feed weekly with dilute liquid manure.

CARNATIONS AND PINKS

Test soil for lime content and add lime if below pH 6·5. Clear rubbish from around stems and ensure stakes and ties are secure. Protect with black cotton against birds. Order plants for spring planting. Prepare beds, first testing the drainage of wet land.

Under glass. Maintain a temperature of 7°C (45°F) for perpetual flowering carnations, and give some ventilation at all times. Water and feed sparingly, cutting blooms and disbudding flower stems. Dust against rust and aphids if they are present. Continue to propagate perpetual flowering carnations from cuttings and pot up rooted cuttings. Pot on from 2 in. to 3½ in. pots cuttings which were taken earlier. Give well developed, rooted cuttings their first stopping when they have made 9–10 pairs of leaves. Continue sowing seeds of perpetual flowering and annual carnations, and prick them out when they are ready.

SWEET PEAS

Break down and tread soil on planting site. Erect supports for plants to be grown on the cordon system. Sow seeds outdoors in their flowering positions.

FLOWERS FROM SEED

Plan spring planting programme. Lightly fork beds prepared for annuals and work in bone-meal.

Under glass. Sow the first of the half-hardy annuals.

BULBS

Bring in the last of the bulbs for indoor flowering as they become ready. Plant those which have finished flowering in odd corners of the garden. If the weather is cold and wet, keep them in a frost-free greenhouse until planting conditions are better.

ALPINES

Firm into place any plants loosened by frost. Dress soil with fine stone chippings to suppress weeds. Press back into place labels loosened by frost, and renew writing if necessary. Remove annual grass and other weed seedlings. Apply slug pellets among plants in mild weather. Unpack plants delivered in frosty weather, stand them in shallow boxes, and pack them round with damp peat.

Under glass. Propagate some alpines by root cuttings. Root them in boxes of sandy compost in a cold frame and plant into pots or boxes when they have produced leaves.

WATER PLANTS AND POOLS

Continue to protect pools against ice. Remove weeds from the bog garden. Sow moisture-loving primulas in seed boxes.

GREENHOUSES AND FRAMES

Move dormant fuchsias, heliotropes and hydrangeas on to the staging and spray with water to encourage new growth. Sow seeds of cannas, coleus and gloxinias. Sow seeds of tomatoes for planting in a cool greenhouse in April. Start an early batch of achimenes. Prune greenhouse climbers. Keep watering to a minimum and ventilate freely on mild days. Remove dead and discoloured fronds from ferns and pot on or divide as necessary. Pot on over-wintered fuchsias, pelargoniums and coleus into 5 in. pots.

TREES AND SHRUBS

Continue planting deciduous trees and shrubs in favourable weather. Firm any which have been loosened by frost. Clear moss and lichen from tree trunks with tar-oil wash.

Propagation in the open. Separate and plant out rooted suckers of poplars.

Under glass. Sow seeds of cytisus and spartium in pots of sandy peat in a propagating frame at 18°C (64°F).

Pruning. Cut hard back summer-flowering varieties of clematis. Prune hard back to within a few inches of old wood such shrubs as *Campsis radicans*, spiraea and tamarisk. Cut back all shoots which have just flowered of chimonanthus and winter jasmine and thin old and weak wood from *Jasminum officinale*. Remove inward-growing branches of crab apples. Thin out climbers such as celastrus and solanum.

RHODODENDRONS AND AZALEAS

Prepare ground for planting during periods of fine weather.

HEDGES

Plant deciduous hedges in mild dry weather. Plants received when ground is not fit for planting should be kept in a frost-free shed. Protect their roots with straw. Cut back overgrown hedges towards the end of the month.

HEATHERS

Firm newly planted heathers lifted by frost. Plant during suitable weather.

FRUIT

Continue planting in suitable conditions, or store trees in a frost-free place. Continue pruning, except during hard frost. Apply simazine to soil round established trees and bushes. Spray apples and pears with DNOC. Prune newly planted fan-trained peaches and nectarines, plums, damsons and cherries. Spray peaches and nectarines against peach leaf curl. Cover with cloches strawberries planted for early fruiting.

VEGETABLES

Sow early peas and beans. Buy or order potato tubers for early crops, and sprout them in a light, frost-proof room or shed.
Under glass. Sow carrots in light, fertile soil in a cold frame.
Less common vegetables. In the north, plant shallots. Order asparagus plants.

HERBS

Prepare site for a new herb garden by digging it one spit deep. Incorporate peat and compost to lighten a heavy soil. Sow parsley if the weather is dry and not too cold. Propagate mint by runners.

PATIOS AND TOWN GARDENS

Plant trees and shrubs in containers during fine weather.

HOUSE PLANTS

Examine plants after winter to see whether they are worth keeping. Prune and re-pot the best, and replace the others.

GENERAL TASKS

Have a soil test carried out in a new garden. Destroy weeds under hedges with paraquat. Use dalapon against couch grass.

Plants to enjoy in February

Border and rock garden plants in flower	Trees and shrubs with colourful fruits	Solanum capsicastrum
Chionodoxa	Aucuba	Spathiphyllum wallisii
Crocus	Pernettya	Zygocactus truncatus (Christmas cactus)
Eranthis	Pyracantha	
Galanthus (snowdrop)	Skimmia japonica	**Vegetables in season**
Helleborus niger (Christmas rose)		Artichoke, Jerusalem
Iris reticulata	**Greenhouse plants in flower**	Broccoli, spring
Muscari (grape hyacinth)	Azalea indica	Brussels sprouts
Saxifraga	Cineraria	Cabbage
	Cyclamen	Carrots
	Hippeastrum	Chicory
Trees and shrubs in flower	Primula obconica	Leek
Chimonanthus (wintersweet)	Senecio	Onion
Daphne mezereum		Parsnip
Garrya elliptica		Radish, winter
Hamamelis	**House plants in flower, depending on position and culture**	Rhubarb
Jasminum nudiflorum (winter jasmine)	Begonia semperflorens	Salsify
Lonicera fragrantissima	Euphorbia pulcherrima	Scorzonera
Mahonia	Impatiens	Swede
Prunus cerasifera		Turnip

Lawns

NEW LAWNS

Under suitable and dry conditions, continue to cultivate spring seed beds, adding the appropriate top dressings and fertilisers. If the weather is wet, delay until later in the month, or until March.

ESTABLISHED LAWNS

Continue aeration, scarification and brushing treatments in dry conditions. Apply sharp sand to heavy wet soils, and loam and organic materials to light porous soils.

In dry weather scatter worm casts.

Apply worm-killing preparations in dull, mild weather (see OCTOBER).

Apply lawn sand towards the end of the month to control daisy and clover.

Moss invasion may be serious now. Try to discover the cause; it may be bad drainage or impoverished turf. Correct poor physical conditions and treat with a mercurised control.

Roses

Roses may be planted if the soil is dry or just moist (see NOVEMBER) but not if it is wet and sticky, or if there is frost or snow on the surface.

Roses which cannot be planted at once can be left in the nurseryman's packing for up to a week. If planting has to be delayed still longer, remove the plants from the package and heel them in.

If the roses cannot be heeled in because there is ground frost or snow, cut off any leaves on the plants, then wrap the roots and lower parts of the stems with moist sacking and keep in a frost-free place.

UNDER GLASS

Maintain a temperature of 16°C (61°F) during the day and 7°C (45°F) at night. Once a week, fill the pots to the top with water which is at the same temperature as the air in the greenhouse.

Hardy herbaceous plants

This is the last opportunity for clearing last year's dead tops (see JANUARY).

Unless the border was newly planted on well dug and manured ground, it will probably need an annual dressing of fertiliser in early spring. Use 2 oz. per sq. yd. of John Innes base fertiliser, bone-meal, hoof and horn, or any organic fertiliser fairly high in phosphates and potash but low in nitrogen.

Fertilise before digging

If digging between plants has been deferred until now (see NOVEMBER), spread the fertiliser just before digging and then turn it into the soil. Ground dug in autumn or early winter may also need an application of fertiliser if the surface is beginning to dry. Be careful to apply it before spring cultivations are given, so that, if the surface is being raked or hoed, the fertiliser will be worked into the top 2–3 in. of soil.

Dahlias

Examine stored tubers. If they are shrivelling, plunge them in tepid water for the night, dry, and replace them in the peat or vermiculite (see OCTOBER). Cut off any parts of the tubers that show signs of rotting, and dust the cuts with flowers of sulphur or captan.

Chrysanthemums

Attend to the drainage around stools in the open ground (see JANUARY). Keep the beds clear of weeds. Groundsel, chickweed and docks are particularly dangerous, as they are host plants for chrysanthemum eelworm.

Tread ground loosened by frost to re-firm it around the roots.

Destroy slugs

Scatter slug pellets around plants in the open ground and in frames. Choose a weather-resistant brand, or protect from the rain with an upturned box or a slate supported by bricks.

UNDER GLASS

Maintain a cool, ventilated atmosphere. Keep the stools just moist but avoid over-watering. Propagate greenhouse decoratives throughout the month (see MARCH). Single and anemone-centred types will also be ready towards the end of the month.

Inspect exhibition plants

Keep a close watch on large exhibition plants which are in $3\frac{1}{2}$ in. pots, as they dry out very quickly on sunny days. Pot any remaining exhibition plants.

Prepare space in a cold frame for the potted plants: a base of weathered ash or clinker is best, but wooden slats are a good substitute. Pots must be level.

Ventilate frames

Scatter slug bait in the frame before putting in the pots. Remove stupefied or dead slugs after the bait has been down for 24 hours. Ventilate the frame to prevent drops of moisture accumulating on the underside of the glass.

Gladioli

UNDER GLASS

Gladioli will flower earlier if sprouted in a greenhouse. Place single layers of corms in trays in a temperature of 10°C (50°F). The trays must be placed in full light. Watch for signs of aphids on the sprouts, which will soon appear, and dust the corms promptly with HCH if pests are seen. Plant the sprouted corms, 4–6 in. deep in colonies or in rows 12–15 in. apart (see MARCH).

Check stored corms and discard any that are diseased.

If ground has not been prepared for gladiolus planting, this must be done at the first opportunity (see NOVEMBER).

Irises

Order summer-flowering Dutch iris bulbs, sold as 'specially prepared', for planting in March or April. These are excellent for cutting or for filling gaps in borders.

Protect from the weather

Place cloches over Dutch irises planted in rows for cutting. This will secure only slightly earlier blooms but, being

CLOCHES FOR PROTECTION

Dutch irises planted for cutting may be protected with cloches. If the varieties are tall-growing, raise the cloches on bricks

protected from the weather, they will be of better quality. Bear in mind the ultimate height of the particular variety you are growing. If necessary, be ready to raise the cloches on bricks or boards to give adequate height.

Use a sheet of glass to make a roof over early-flowering irises in the rock garden. Alternatively, cover with a cloche. This will protect the fragile blooms from being beaten down and blown about in rough weather.

Pick flowers of *Iris unguicularis* regularly (see DECEMBER).

UNDER GLASS

Give all bulbous irises in pots, except the Dutch, Spanish and English types, gentle warmth, but do not overheat them.

Lilies

Lilies can still be planted if the weather and soil are suitable (see OCTOBER).

When buying from a store, choose plump, healthy looking bulbs and avoid dried-up specimens. Some otherwise good bulbs arrive in an over-dry condition. Revive these bulbs by setting them in trays of slightly damp peat in a frost-proof place, then potting them (see NOVEMBER) prior to planting out.

Some lilies will already be coming through in the garden. Use cloches to protect the shoots from frost. Many autumn-flowering lilies are the first to appear, while some early-flowering lilies appear surprisingly late.

POTTING LILY BULBS

When planting lily bulbs (1) place crocks at the bottom of the pot to allow for drainage. Plant stem-rooting lilies (2) 2 in. above the crocks to accommodate the stem roots

UNDER GLASS

Sow seed under glass (see JANUARY).

Many of the imported lily bulbs now on sale make splendid pot plants. Pot them in John Innes potting compost No. 1, using plenty of drainage material in the bottom of the pots. A 6 in. pot will hold three small lilies such as *L. pumilum*, or one medium-sized bulb such as 'Enchantment'. An 8 in. pot will accommodate three medium-sized lilies, or one large one such as *L. auratum*.

Plant stem-rooting lilies with the base of the bulb only 2 in. above the drainage material to leave space for adding soil around the stem roots.

When buds appear on forced lilies, raise the temperature to 18–21°C (64–70°F). Feed weekly with dilute liquid manure until the buds are ready to open. Most forced lilies flower six weeks after the appearance of the buds.

Carnations and pinks

Test the soil for lime content if this was not done earlier and add lime if it is below pH 6·5. Clear away rubbish from around the stems of plants and ensure that stakes and ties are secure.

Order plants for spring planting in outdoor beds and for greenhouse cultivation (see colour section, MAY). Prepare beds, first testing the drainage if the land tends to be wet (see AUGUST).

UNDER GLASS

Maintain a temperature of 7°C (45°F) for perpetual flowering carnations and give some ventilation at all times.

Water and feed sparingly (see APRIL), cutting blooms and disbudding flower stems as necessary (see SEPTEMBER).

Watch for carnation rust and aphids (see MARCH), using dusts in preference to sprays during the winter.

Continue to propagate perpetual flowering carnations by cuttings and pot up rooted cuttings (see DECEMBER). When the roots of young plants reach the sides of the 2 or 2½ in. pots, pot on into 3½ in. pots, using John Innes potting compost No. 1.

Stop plants

Give the plants their first stopping when they have made nine or ten pairs of fully developed leaves. Hold the stem firmly with your finger and thumb at the seventh joint and bend the top of the plant sideways with the other hand to break off the tip. If the top does not snap off cut it just above the seventh joint.

Continue to sow seeds of perpetual flowering and annual carnations and prick them out when ready (see JANUARY).

Sweet peas

If the weather and soil are suitable, fork over the area where sweet peas are to be planted. Break up any clods and pulverise the top few inches of soil. Treading helps to provide a firm, settled soil structure beneficial to rooting.

If you plan to grow plants on the cordon system (see MARCH), erect the supporting framework of wooden posts and cross-pieces, with stout strands of wire connecting them. Though design details are usually determined by the materials available, the structure must be sufficiently firm and rigid to withstand strong winds.

Make sure you have adequate canes for supporting the plants. Bamboo canes, 8 ft. long, are ideal, but osier rods or even strong netting will suffice.

Towards the end of the month, soil and weather conditions permitting, sow seeds outdoors in their flowering positions, following the method outlined for autumn sowing (see OCTOBER).

Flowers from seed

Study the seed catalogues and plan your spring planting programme. Varieties in short supply may be sold out unless you order in good time.

Provided that the soil does not become too compacted when walked on, lightly fork over beds which have been winter-dug (see NOVEMBER). Avoid bringing to the surface any soil that has not been weathered. If manure or compost has not been applied earlier, rake or hoe in a 4 oz. per sq. yd. dressing of bone-meal in the top 2 or 3 in. of soil.

UNDER GLASS

Though most half-hardy annuals are sown in March, some require a longer growing period and are sown this month (see tables and sowing instructions, MARCH).

Bulbs

UNDER GLASS AND INDOORS

Bring in the last of the bulbs for indoor flowering as they become ready for extra warmth (see DECEMBER). Bulbs which have finished flowering may be planted straight from their containers into odd corners of the garden (see MARCH). If the weather is too wet or cold, keep them watered in a frost-free greenhouse or frame until planting conditions are more favourable.

Alpines

The first flowers should appear this month, notably on the cushion (kabschia) saxifrages.

Firm after frost

If frost has loosened any plants, firm the soil around them with your fingers. A sprinkling of fine gravel or stone chip-pings will suppress most weed seedlings, but will also preclude use of a hoe on weeds that do appear.

Push back into place labels that have been loosened by frost and renew the writing if necessary.

Remove weeds

Remove small tufts of grass and the seedlings of annual weeds. These often germinate unnoticed during the autumn but become more prominent during a mild February. Should there be patches of heavy weed growth, lift any plants in danger of being smothered, free them from clinging weeds, and then bury the weeds by digging before replacing the plants.

Kill slugs

During mild weather, put down slug pellets among the plants: place them under foliage and flat stones to hide them from birds and small mammals.

If plants are delivered during frosty weather, unpack them and stand them upright in shallow boxes, packing damp peat between the plants. Place the boxes under cover until conditions are suitable for planting.

UNDER GLASS

Some alpines are propagated by root cuttings (see plant descriptions, NOVEMBER). These are pieces of fleshy root, prepared while the plant is dormant by cutting the root into sections about 2 in. long. Make the upper cut of each section horizontal, the lower cut slanting.

Root cuttings

Root them in boxes of sandy compost in a cold frame, inserting the sections vertically with the tops $\frac{1}{4}$ in. beneath the surface. Plant them into pots or boxes when they have produced small tufts of leaves. If they are not developed sufficiently until April, plant them direct into the open ground.

Water plants and pools

Continue with pool protection (see DECEMBER).

Remove weeds from the bog garden; this task is often easiest after light, drying frosts.

Sow primulas

Sow moisture-loving primulas, which germinate better after freezing. Fill seed boxes to within $\frac{3}{4}$ in. of the top with John Innes seed compost. Firm down with the fingers, especially at the corners and sides, and level off with a board. Sow the seeds thinly, then cover lightly with finely sifted compost. Water carefully, using a can fitted with a fine rose, or soak by standing the box in shallow water to within $\frac{1}{2}$ in. of the soil surface. Stand the boxes outside on a level site in light shade and allow them to freeze, but protect them from heavy rain.

Alternatively, put sown boxes inside polythene boxes and seal the ends until germination takes place.

Greenhouses and frames

Move dormant fuchsias, heliotropes and hydrangeas on to the greenhouse staging, if possible in a warm spot where a temperature of 10°C (50°F) can be maintained. Spray the plants with water on sunny days, and give them increasing amounts of water as growth becomes active.

Sow and prick out

Sow seeds of cannas, coleus, gloxinias, tuberous and fibrous begonias, celosias, abutilons and streptocarpus. Place the pans or seed boxes in a propagating frame heated to 16–18°C (61–64°F). When the seedlings are large enough to handle, prick them out individually into

PRUNING GREENHOUSE CLIMBERS

To prune climbers, such as plumbago (*left*) and passiflora (*right*), cut back shoots made the previous summer to within one or two buds of where the shoots join the old wood

3 in. pots of John Innes potting compost No. 1 and grow them on at normal cool house temperature.

Sow seeds of schizanthus (see SEPTEMBER) to provide plants for flowering in late spring.

Sow tomatoes

If you wish to plant tomatoes in a cool greenhouse during April, sow the seeds this month in pans or boxes of John Innes seed compost in a temperature of 16°C (61°F) (see MARCH).

Start an early batch of achimenes into growth by placing the corms into shallow boxes of moist peat and keeping them in a temperature of 13–16°C (55–61°F). When the shoots are an inch or so high, pot them into 5 in. pots containing John Innes potting compost No. 1, at the rate of five corms per pot.

Prune greenhouse climbers

Prune greenhouse climbers, such as plumbagos and passifloras. by cutting back the growths made last summer to within one or two buds of their point of origin.

Keep watering to a minimum and ventilate freely on mild days.

Care of ferns

Remove any dead and discoloured fronds from ferns, potting on into larger pots any that may require it. Potting on is needed if more roots than compost can be seen when the soil ball is tapped out of the pot. Use John Innes potting compost No. 1 or a mixture of 2 parts loam, 1 part peat, 1 part leaf-mould and 1 part sand. To increase your stock of ferns, divide old plants and pot the divisions separately into 3 in. pots. Use the vigorous crowns from the outsides of the old plants, discarding the weak ones from the centre.

Towards the end of the month transfer to 5 in. pots young plants of fuchsias, zonal and regal pelargoniums and coleus, which have been over-wintered in 3 in. pots, setting them in John Innes potting compost No. 2.

Trees and shrubs

When the weather and soil are favourable, continue to plant deciduous trees and shrubs. Check that newly planted standard trees have not become loosened in the soil, and tread down where necessary.

Tar-oil winter-wash will remove moss and lichen from tree trunks, but protect nearby plants with sacking or newspaper while the job is carried out.

PROPAGATION

In the open

Separate rooted suckers of poplar from the parent plant, and re-plant them in their permanent positions.

Under glass

Sow seeds of cytisus and spartium $\frac{1}{4}$ in. deep in pots of sandy peat and place in a propagating frame at a temperature of 18°C (64°F).

Pot seedlings of spartium singly as soon as they are large enough to handle. Transplant seedlings of both cytisus and spartium in late May or early June.

PRUNING

Prune such shrubs as callicarpa, *Campsis radicans*, spiraea and tamarisk hard back by cutting away the previous year's growth to within a few inches of the old wood. This will encourage new and vigorous shoots to develop.

Prune summer-flowering varieties of clematis hard back, either to 12 in. above ground, or to within two buds on young growth.

Prune after flowering

Cut back all the shoots that have just flowered of chimonanthus and *Jasminum nudiflorum* (winter jasmine); also thin out old, damaged and weak wood of *Jasminum officinale*.

Remove inward-growing branches of crab apples to keep the centres of the trees open.

Thin climbers such as celastrus and solanum by removing any weak growths, and shorten or pinch out the tips of main shoots.

Rhododendrons and azaleas

If the weather allows, prepare the ground in readiness for planting next month by deep digging, incorporating manure or lime-free compost. Leave the ground to settle.

Hedges

During mild, dry weather it should be possible to plant deciduous hedges on well drained land (see SEPTEMBER and OCTOBER). If hedging plants are delivered when the ground is frozen or excessively wet, keep them in a frost-free shed with straw around and beneath their roots. Continue with planting as soon as the weather permits.

Prune hedges

Cut back overgrown hedges towards the end of the month or early in March so that they produce new growth during the spring. If cut back earlier, the shoots may be killed by frosts or cold winds; if cut later, the dormant buds on the older wood may fail to produce new growth. Cut the top growth 1 ft. or more lower than the height ultimately required, so that there will be space for new growth to hide the old skeleton.

Use a sharp saw for the larger stems, checking both height and width as the work proceeds and dabbing each cut with bituminous paint to seal the ends.

Heathers

Firm into place any newly planted heathers that have been partially lifted by frost. Planting is still possible this month if the ground is not waterlogged or frozen (see MARCH and OCTOBER), but if possible, delay until March.

Fruit

Continue to plant if soil conditions are suitable, otherwise store the trees where they will not be harmed by frost.

Continue pruning, except when there are hard night frosts (see NOVEMBER).

In late February, apply simazine to moist soil round most established fruits to keep the soil clear of further weed growth (see OCTOBER).

Apple and pear

As an alternative to tar-oil winter-wash (see DECEMBER), apply DNOC in late February. This spray will control red spider eggs, which will make the dormant shoots look red if present in large numbers (see JUNE).

Peach and nectarine

Prune newly planted fan-trained trees by cutting back shoots to 12–18 in. Spray with copper fungicide or lime sulphur at bud-swelling stage against peach leaf curl.

Plum, damson and cherry

Prune newly planted fan-trained trees in the same way as peach.

Raspberry

Prune established autumn-fruiting varieties close to the ground before spring.

Strawberry

In the second half of the month place cloches over plants which have been planted for early fruiting (see AUGUST). If they are covered earlier, leaves rather than fruit will be encouraged.

Vegetables

Sow early crops of peas and broad beans, if this was not done last month (see JANUARY). In the north, except on the west coast, do not sow broad beans and early peas until March unless they can be covered with cloches.

Sprout potatoes

If you wish to grow early potatoes, buy the tubers as soon as possible, allowing 7 lb. for each 50 ft. length of row. Arrange the tubers in one layer in shallow boxes, with the eyes (embryo shoots) uppermost. Put these in a light, frost-proof shed or room to encourage the tubers to sprout.

UNDER GLASS

Carrots such as 'Early French Frame', 'Early Nantes' or 'Amsterdam Forcing', sown this month in light, fertile soil in a cold frame, should be ready in June. Keep the lights on for a week or two to warm the soil, then sprinkle the seed thinly over the surface and rake it in lightly. Keep the frame closed until the seed has germinated.

LESS COMMON VEGETABLES

Plant shallots if this was not done last month (see JANUARY). Draw a little soil over the sets to anchor them, otherwise birds may pull them up.

Buy asparagus plants

Order asparagus plants during the first half of the month if you wish to grow this long-lasting, comparatively trouble-free crop. Reserve a site measuring 30 ft. long and 6 ft. wide, the most practical size for easy management, on land manured last autumn. You will need $5\frac{1}{2}$ doz. plants for a plot this size.

If weather permits dig the site in preparation for planting out asparagus during next month (see MARCH).

Herbs

Prepare the site for the herb garden by digging the soil to a spade's depth. Lighten heavy soil by incorporating peat, wood ash or compost at the rate of two buckets per sq. yd. Herbs grow best in warm, still air, and a hedge of rosemary, lavender, sage or roses will provide a good shelter. A good temporary shelter can be made by planting annual sunflowers for a season or two.

Sow parsley

If the weather is dry and not too cold, sow a first batch of parsley in the open. Sow in seed drills 10 in. apart, in a damp, shady position.

Mint runners

Propagate mint by the long, rooted runners which form immediately below the soil. Uproot them, separate them from the parent plant, and plant them out on their own in rich, moist soil. If you plant mint with other plants in a window box, place a barrier of wood or tile near the plants to check the runners.

Patios and town gardens

Unless it is freezing or the soil is wet and sticky, deciduous shrubs and trees can be planted in containers this month to provide a permanent display (see MARCH and NOVEMBER).

Plants for a patio

When selecting plants for a patio, bear in mind that climbers can provide large areas of colour, and will hide drab walls, without occupying any more space than low-growing subjects. Some are self-clinging but most need support in the form of wires, trellis or mesh. Choose plants to suit the aspect. Remember that climbers trained against walls or fences will receive light on the side facing away from the wall only.

Choose climbers

Evergreen or winter-flowering climbers are preferable in positions which can be seen from the house. Hedera (ivy) is an evergreen climber with a wide range of leaf forms and colours. *Chimonanthus praecox* and *Jasminum nudiflorum* are easy and colourful winter-flowering subjects. Among the many attractive deciduous and summer-flowering climbers are *Actinidia chinensis, Campsis radicans,* clematis and *Hydrangea petiolaris.*

House plants

After the winter some house plants may not look their best. Examine them carefully to decide whether they can be rejuvenated by treatment during the coming spring (see MARCH), or whether they are better discarded and replaced. Among those likely to look poorly after the winter, and which are almost impossible to bring into attractive shape again, are codiaeums and dracaenas. Most other overgrown house plants can be pruned and re-potted into larger containers to give them a good start before active growth begins (see MARCH). Or give the plants a top dressing of good soil.

General tasks

If you have taken over a new garden, have a lime test and a soil analysis made. Firms will do this for you, or you can do it yourself with a soil-testing kit. The kit will show whether the soil in various parts of your garden is deficient in nitrogen, phosphate, potash or lime; and it contains information about the correct fertilisers and how much to apply if the tests reveal a shortage. Test the soil under the lawn.

Eradicate weeds

Destroy weeds under hedges by watering with paraquat-diquat. If couch grass alone is present, apply dalapon. Treat weeds among shrubs and soft fruit bushes in the same way. The dead weeds will disintegrate in a short time.

Pests
and diseases

This section will help you to recognise and combat the common pests and diseases of garden plants. Many are shown in colour on pp. 397–400. Where appropriate, related pests have been grouped under a single heading. For instance, descriptions of apple aphis, woolly aphis and four other species appear as sub-sections under the heading *Aphids*. Plant diseases have been grouped into broad divisions—for example, bacterial, deficiency, virus—depending on their cause or origin

Pests

ANTS

These small insects are often a nuisance in the garden. They swarm over plants infested with aphids in search of the honeydew excreted by them, and transport them bodily to fresh crops. Ants build nests in the soil of flower borders, and by tunnelling underground damage the roots of herbaceous plants, and often kill them. In frames and greenhouses they feed on newly sown seeds. Ripe fruits are often attacked by swarms of ants.

To control ants, dust the soil with HCH. Destroy nests by pouring liquid derris, petrol or boiling water on them or by spraying with trichlorphon.

APHIDS

Widespread pests, also known as greenflies or blackflies. They cause severe damage to many decorative plants and most fruits and vegetables.

The many different species of aphids attack the tissues of stems, leaves and fruit to suck out the sap. Direct damage to the plants includes leaf-curl and distortion of young shoots.

As virus-carriers, aphids indirectly damage many garden plants by sucking infected sap from a diseased plant and carrying it to a healthy one.

The spores of the sooty mould fungus germinate in the exreta of aphids, producing a thick sooty covering on the leaves of apples, plums, pears, phlox and asters. The mould does not harm the plants, but it is unsightly, and may spread to the fruit.

As soon as the first aphids are seen, they must be destroyed, as they multiply at an alarming speed and quickly build up large, dense colonies on young shoots and the undersides of leaves. In summer, spray or dust affected trees and shrubs, flowers and vegetables with any insecticide containing HCH, derris, malathion,

pirimicarb or nicotine. Or use a systemic insecticide, based on menazon, formothion, metasystox or dimethoate, and spray it on to the foliage, or water it in. It will become absorbed in the sap stream, making it toxic to aphids.

During the dormant period, control aphids on fruit trees and bushes by winter-washing with tar oil or DNOC; or spray in early spring with one of the insecticides listed above.

Apple aphids

There are several species that attack apple and pear trees. The small, shiny black eggs are clearly visible on twigs and branches in the autumn. To prevent these eggs hatching out and damaging the young leaves, flowers and fruitlets, spray the trees in winter with tar oil or DNOC. At bud-burst, applications of either HCH or malathion may be necessary.

Black bean aphis

Found on top growths of all types of beans and spinach. Similar black aphids occur on rhubarb, nasturtiums and dahlias. Attacks by this pest cause a check on growth and a subsequent poor crop. Spray with derris, malathion or a systemic insecticide.

Cabbage or mealy aphis

Attacks most brassicas, especially cabbages and Brussels sprouts. The tightly packed colonies must be destroyed early, while it is still possible to spray the developing hearts and buttons. Spray with malathion or nicotine, or use a systemic insecticide.

Root aphis

Chiefly infests the roots of autumn and winter lettuces. The main symptom is wilting of the plants. If this is recognised in time, applications of a root drench containing malathion, watered into the soil around the plants, may prevent further damage.

Rose aphis (greenfly)

Frequently attacks the leaves and flower buds of roses and scabious, causing stunted growth. Apply malathion or a systemic insecticide when the leaves appear, and repeat when necessary.

Woolly aphis

A pest of apple trees, and of related ornamental shrubs and trees, such as crab apples. The white woolly secretions on the bark often leave ugly, corky galls, leading to stunted or deformed growth. Paint individual colonies with a dilute solution of malathion or HCH, or apply a drenching spray of malathion insecticide in May. Winter-was with tar oil.

Aphids under glass

Colonies of aphids can build up more rapidly under glass than they can outdoors. Control methods in the greenhouse are the same as outdoors, but the use of greenhouse smokes is more effective. These contain insecticides, obtainable as a combustible mixture or in aerosol form.

BEETLES
Cockchafers (may bugs)

Both the adult beetles and the young larvae cause extensive damage to many plants. The adult beetles attack the leaves of many trees and shrubs, and the larvae feed on the roots of herbaceous plants, fruits and vegetables. The fat white larvae live in the soil for three to four years before attaining maturity. They are not easy to control, though HCH or bromophos dust raked into the soil can be effective. When the soil is dug over, the larvae can be picked up and killed.

Other grubs found in the soil include the larvae of the garden chafer and rose chafer, which feed on the roots of grass. The adults feed on the leaves and fruit of apples and pears, and on the

leaves of roses and shrubs. Control as for cockchafers.

Flea beetles

Numerous species of these small black and yellow beetles attack vegetables. They damage brassicas, often covering the leaves with holes, and they can destroy a whole seedling bed by chewing off the young plants at ground level. To prevent attacks, treat seeds with a proprietary seed dressing, or dust the seed drills with HCH before sowing. Spray or dust the seedlings at fortnightly intervals with these insecticides until the plants are well developed.

Raspberry beetle

The adult beetles appear in May, and feed on the flower buds of raspberries, loganberries and cultivated blackberries, where they lay their eggs. The larvae feed on the young fruitlets, and unless control measures are taken, much of the fruit will be maggoty. Apply derris or malathion ten days after flowering begins, and repeat a fortnight later.

CAPSID BUGS

A large family of sucking insects that chiefly attack fruit trees and herbaceous plants. They are seldom troublesome on vegetables or in the greenhouse.

The following are among the more common capsid bugs.

Apple capsid bug

Green nymphs hatch out in April and May, and feed on the sap of the foliage. These insects are related to aphids, but are larger (about $\frac{1}{4}$ in. long when mature) and do not cluster in colonies. The adult bugs are green, and after petal fall they begin to feed on the fruits, puncturing the skin and causing raised brown marks. Control by spraying the trees with DNOC in petroleum oil in winter, with malathion or HCH in spring and summer.

THE GARDENER'S ENEMIES

The unpleasant creatures and organisms that disfigure and kill your garden plants have to be controlled. Already systemic insecticides give protection to roses and other flowering shrubs against sap-sucking greenflies for several weeks. Chemical companies are producing mixed compounds that dispose of many fungi and blights with a single squirt of the garden spray. Plant breeders are constantly trying to produce varieties immune from or resistant to pests and diseases. Nevertheless, you cannot afford to relax. As the following pictures show, in spite of chemical break-throughs there are still plenty of enemies to be fought in every garden.

Antirrhinum rust. Spreads rapidly during wet weather, killing or deforming the plants

Aphis, black bean (blackfly). Attacks beans, root crops, rhubarb, nasturtiums and dahlias

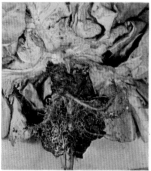

Aphis, root. Confined chiefly to winter lettuce. First symptoms are yellow and wilting leaves

Aphis, rose. Colour from green to pink. Infests shoots and buds. Attacks scabious and strawberries

Aphis, woolly. Found on apple trees. The 'wool' is a secretion of the sap-sucking aphids

Apple sawfly. This damage is caused in the early stages, when the larvae feed under the skin

Apple sawfly. The larvae cause extensive damage to the interiors and exteriors of developing fruit

Apple scab. Fungus disease, spoiling the fruit and damaging leaves and young shoots

Big bud mite. Causes swollen buds and often spreads reversion virus to black currants

Bishop bug. Holes the leaves and distorts blooms of chrysanthemums, zinnias and dahlias

397

Black spot. Common rose disease from midsummer on. Unsightly, and may kill bushes

Botrytis (grey mould). Occurs indoors and out in humid conditions; attacks plants and fruit

Cabbage root fly. The larvae attack brassica roots, causing wilting and collapse of the plants

Cabbage large white butterfly. Common in late summer. The caterpillars damage brassicas

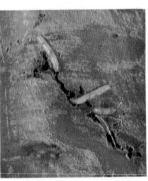

Carrot fly. The larvae hatch from eggs laid in May, and tunnel into the developing roots

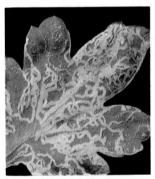

Chrysanthemum leaf miner. Causes disfigurement and loss of condition. Attacks cinerarias

Club root. Fungus disease, found in sour soil, that attacks most brassicas, wallflowers and stocks.

Cockchafer (may bug). Adults and grubs attack shrubs, perennials and vegetables

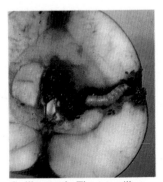

Codling moth. The caterpillars are the familiar maggots found in apples during the autumn

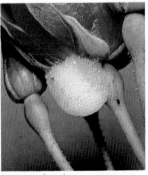

Common frog-hopper on a rose. The nymphs are protected by a secretion ('cuckoo spit')

Cutworm. The caterpillars of several different moths. Attack vegetables and flowers

Earwig. Attacks dahlias and chrysanthemums causing distorted flower heads and foliage

Flea beetle. Cause of the holes seen in the leaves of brassica, wallflower and alyssum seedlings

Leaf-cutting bee. Confined chiefly to roses. Causes disfigurement, but is seldom serious

Leatherjacket. The larvae of the crane fly, which eat the roots of herbaceous plants and vegetables

Mildew. Plants of many types are subject to attack, particularly in warm, humid conditions

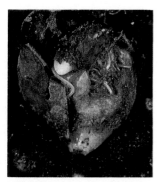

Millepede. Underground feeder, damaging seedlings. Also attacks tubers and bulbs, especially lilies

Moth caterpillar damage on rose. Four types of moth can cause this sort of damage to rose buds

Narcissus fly. Larvae over-winter in narcissus and other bulbs, leading to sickly growth and rot

Peach leaf curl. Fungus disease of peaches and almonds, causing premature leaf fall and debility

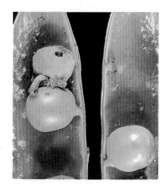

Pea moth. Maggoty peas are the result of pea moth eggs laid on or near the developing pods

Potato blight. Fungus disease which attacks the foliage and eventually causes tubers to rot

Potato blight. Tomatoes as well as potatoes are affected. Blight is troublesome in wet summers

Raspberry beetle. Larvae feed on the fruits of raspberries, blackberries and loganberries

399

Rose leaf-hopper. Causes rose leaves to become mottled and discoloured. Leaves may drop

Rose leaf-rolling sawfly. The larvae attack young leaves, which roll up lengthwise, then shrivel

Rose rust. Leaf distortion and die-back occur in severe cases. Spots may appear on the twigs

Snail. Feeds on foliage and flowers, especially in damp weather and shady places

Soft scale insect. Causes leaf damage to outdoor camellias. Also a serious greenhouse pest

Swift moth. The caterpillars feed on vegetable roots, and hollow out bulbs and tubers

Tomato leaf mould. This greenhouse disease spreads rapidly in high temperatures and humidity

Verticillium wilt (sleepy disease). Attacks greenhouse tomatoes. Wilting is followed by withering

Whitefly. Attacks tomatoes and other greenhouse plants. Mould develops on the secretions

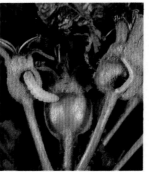

Winter moth. In spring, the caterpillars attack the buds and foliage of fruit trees and bushes

Wireworm. The larva of the click beetle. Causes serious damage to roots and tubers

Woodlouse. Nocturnal feeder on stems, foliage and roots, especially of plants under glass

Bishop bug (tarnished plant bug)
These bugs, which have a pattern like a bishop's mitre on their backs, infest the leaves and flower buds of chrysanthemums, dahlias and zinnias, disfiguring and stunting the shoots. As soon as any damage is seen, spray or dust with malathion or HCH.

Common green capsid bug (lygus)
The small wingless nymphs make holes in the leaves of currant bushes, gooseberries, blackberries, cherries, raspberries, strawberries, peaches and pears. After maturity, the green bugs leave the crop in June and July to feed on herbaceous plants or weeds. To control, apply winter-washes of DNOC in petroleum oil, or spray with malathion or HCH in spring.

CATERPILLARS
The soft-bodied larvae of numerous species of butterflies and moths, which themselves cause no damage to plant life. Caterpillars, however, are a considerable menace in the garden. They feed mainly on foliage, but also attack the roots, seeds and bark of a wide variety of crops. The life cycles of the various species are similar. Caterpillars hatch out from eggs in spring and begin to feed immediately. They pupate in early summer, sometimes in a tiny cavity in the soil, or suspended from a sheltered wall. The following spring the adults break out of the chrysalis to mate.

Buff-tip moth
The black-headed caterpillars, with downy, orange-striped bodies, hatch out on the foliage of fruit trees, especially cherries, and are voracious feeders in July and August. Pick off individual caterpillars or, if the attack is severe, spray with trichlorphon or derris.

Cabbage moth
The green, brown or grey caterpillars feed in early summer on the leaves and hearts of cabbages, and may completely strip the plants. These serious pests attack all types of brassicas, as well as flowering plants such as nasturtiums, wallflowers and stocks. Spray with trichlorphon or dust with derris when the pests appear, paying particular attention to the undersides of the leaves.

Codling moth
The small, pale pink caterpillars are serious pests of apples, boring into the fruits and making them maggoty. Codling moth caterpillars leave the fruits in the autumn to pupate on the bark of the tree. Apply malathion during warm weather in mid-June and mid-July. Or trap the cocoons by tying sacking round the trunk by mid-July for the caterpillars to pupate in. Remove and destroy the sacking with the cocoons inside before spring.

Cutworms
These fat caterpillars, which may be green or mud-coloured, inhabit the top layers of the soil during the day. At night they come up to feed on the roots, stems and leaves of numerous herbaceous plants, and of vegetables such as beet, carrots and onions. Control is not easy, as the pests are seldom detected until the damage has been done. Avoid severe infestations by control of weeds; if plants are attacked water the soil with a spray-strength solution of trichlorphon or HCH.

Pea moth
The pale yellow caterpillars attack pea pods, feeding on the peas and causing them to be maggoty. Sow early maturing varieties for picking by mid-July; sow late varieties after mid-June.

Swift moth
These large white caterpillars live in the soil, where they attack the roots of a wide range of plants. They attack most vegetables, strawberries, and herbaceous plants such as dahlias, paeonies, irises, daffodils and delphiniums.
Regular digging and forking of the ground provides the best control. Lift valuable perennial plants if they are being attacked and remove and kill the caterpillars before replanting. Discourage egg laying by the female moths by controlling weeds.

Tortrix moth
There are several species of tortrix moth caterpillars, with differing colours. All can be distinguished by their habit of wriggling backwards when disturbed. They feed on the foliage of ornamental trees and shrubs, and roses. The leaves are fastened together with a cobwebby substance, making it difficult to penetrate with a spray, and hand-picking is the easiest form of control. Spray fruit trees, especially apple and pear, with trichlorphon.

Vapourer moth
The hairy, bright yellow caterpillars occasionally infest the leaves of fruit trees and roses. Routine sprays with trichlorphon, HCH, derris or malathion are effective.

Winter moth
The green caterpillars are active early in the year on fruit trees and bushes, related ornamental trees and shrubs, and roses. They begin to feed as soon as the leaf buds break, and can cause considerable damage to young leaves and fruitlets in a short time. The best method of control is to spray with trichlorphon when leaf buds open in the spring. Apply greasebands to tree trunks in the autumn to prevent the wingless female moths from climbing up to lay eggs on the branches.

Under glass
Tomatoes and chrysanthemums are the plants most liable to attack by caterpillars. They feed voraciously on the foliage, and must be destroyed as soon as detected with sprays of HCH or malathion.

CUCKOO-SPIT INSECTS
These pale green or yellow nymphs are the larvae of the common froghopper. They produce frothy or spittle-like masses on leaves and shoots of roses, campanulas, geums, lavender, rudbeckias and solidagos. Inside these deposits are the larvae that suck the sap and cause wilting of leaves and malformation of young shoots. They are not serious pests. Destroy by syringing with clear water to remove the froth, then with derris or nicotine to kill the larvae.

EARWIGS
In damp, warm weather these insects will sometimes attack the leaves of dwarf beans, cauliflowers, cucumbers and tomatoes, and the flowers heads of chrysanthemums, dahlias and French marigolds. In the garden, earwigs seldom do severe damage, though occasionally they may completely strip the foliage. In the greenhouse, they can cause serious damage to flower heads. Earwigs are night feeders, and they are seldom discovered until damage is done. To minimise damage, dust or spray dahlias and chrysanthemums with HCH or trichlorphon.
If damage in the greenhouse is persistent, spray the affected plants and surrounding areas with trichlorphon. Keep the garden clear of rubbish, which provides shelter for earwigs.

EELWORMS
These minute, worm-like creatures are invisible to the naked eye. They are widely distributed in the soil, and attack a great variety of food crops and herbaceous plants.
Chemical control is impractical and difficult, and in nearly all cases the only remedy is to destroy the infested plants and avoid replanting the host plants in the same plot of land for at least three years.

Strawberry eelworm
The presence of strawberry eelworms is difficult to diagnose, as signs of attack are similar to those of various virus diseases. The chief symptoms of infestation by these pests are puckered strawberry leaves, silvery patches near

the abnormally thickened mid-ribs, and swollen leaf-stems. Onions, parsnips and narcissi are also attacked. Burn all plants in an infested bed, and do not plant any more strawberry plants in the same patch for at least three years.

Potato root eelworm
These are among the most serious potato pests, and in some parts of the country they are very common. They also attack tomatoes grown under glass. Affected potato plants are stunted, the leaves turn yellow, and the crop of tubers is severely reduced. The minute eggs are present in cysts (dead female eelworms), attached to roots and tubers. There is no adequate chemical control against potato eelworms. Rotation of crops is an effective cultural method.

Chrysanthemum eelworm
A fairly common and serious pest of chrysanthemums outdoors and under glass. The microscopic creatures live in the tissues of leaves and buds. Symptoms of attack are dark patches on the lower leaves, followed by drooping of the leaves and blind flowers. Asters, dahlias, and pyrethrums are also attacked. Dig up and burn all infested plants.

Stem and bulb eelworm
Narcissi, hyacinths, irises, daffodils, tulips and onions are the chief hosts of these serious pests; though rhubarb, and phlox and other herbaceous plants, are also attacked. The small eelworms survive in the soil, where they tunnel into bulbs and stems, causing twisted growth and deformed flowers and leaves. The leaves often show small swellings. Infested bulbs are soft to the touch and may have a white woolly substance on the base. A cut across the bulb will reveal dark rings in the white flesh. There is no effective chemical control, but healthy bulbs from reputable sources are usually sterilised against eelworm. Infested plants

must be dug up and burnt, and bulbs should not be planted in the same bed for three years.

Root knot eelworm
These small pests produce nodules or swellings on the roots of greenhouse plants such as cucumbers, gloxinias, lettuces and particularly tomatoes. The roots function poorly, producing poor growth. The nodules house female cysts, which release young eelworms into the soil to infest healthy plants. Unless the soil is treated, the cysts will survive to attack the next crop.

Infested tomato plants can be temporarily helped by a layer of peat round them, so that the aerial roots can develop in a healthy medium. In the autumn destroy the plants, and then sterilise the soil with dazomet or formaldehyde. In a small greenhouse, replace the soil altogether. Infested soil must not be deposited in the garden, otherwise the eelworms will spread to the roots of carrots, celery, parsnips and clematis in the open.

FLIES
Cabbage root flies
The white larvae of these flies tunnel into many root vegetables, such as turnips, swedes and radishes, making them useless. The larvae also attack the roots of newly planted cabbage and other brassica seedlings; the plants turn bluish, wilt and die. To control, apply HCH or bromophos round the base of the plants in late April, and within four days after transplanting seedlings; or dip the seedlings in calomel paste before planting in their permanent positions.

Carrot fly
The larvae tunnel into the carrot roots. Symptoms of damage are reddening and wilting of the foliage. In dry weather seedlings may be killed. Before sowing, dress the seeds with HCH and water spray-strength trichlorphon or bromophos into the soil in mid-May and end of July.

Celery fly
The small white larvae of these flies are the most serious pests of celery, and may also attack parsnips. They burrow into leaves, stunting the growth of stalks and hearts. Spray or dust seedlings with malathion. During very severe attacks, continue to apply at regular fortnightly intervals until August.

Leatherjackets
These large, earth-coloured grubs are the larvae of the cranefly or daddy-long-legs. They feed on the roots of grass, particularly in lawns, causing whole areas to grow weak and thin. Many plants in the herbaceous and vegetable gardens are also attacked by leatherjackets, especially after a wet autumn, as they need damp conditions to survive the winter.

Digging and hoeing the soil, destroying weeds, and filling in or draining low-lying places are effective cultural methods of control. Chemical control consists of treating infested lawns with HCH from mid-October to April. When new land is taken into cultivation dig thoroughly and control weeds.

Narcissus fly
Larvae, emerging from eggs laid near the necks of such bulbous plants as daffodils, narcissi, lilies and hyacinths, burrow into the bulbs and feed inside. Bulbs lifted with larvae inside have a soft skin, and should be burnt immediately. To prevent attack spray or dust the bulb necks with HCH at weekly intervals until the end of June.

Female narcissus flies lay eggs on bulbs in June by crawling down the holes left above the bulbs as the foliage dies down. Frequent cultivation of the soil around the bulbs will prevent this.

Onion fly
The larvae of these flies burrow into the bulbs of young onions and shallots, causing the plants to wilt and reducing the bulbs to pulp. Destroy attacked plants immediately.

Water a spray-strength solution

of trichlorphon into the soil around onion plants towards the end of May and repeat twice at 10-day intervals. Calomel dust, used for the control of white rot disease, will also help to reduce onion fly infestation, if the insecticide is sprayed on the surrounding soil.

Pea midges
The minute larvae are common on pea flowers and the inner surface of the pods, spoiling the quality of the crop. Routine applications of HCH or malathion to control pea moths and weevils will also kill off pea midges.

LEAF-CUTTING BEES
These insects resemble hive bees. They damage the foliage of roses, and also sometimes of laburnums, lilacs and rhododendrons, by cutting small pieces from the leaves and using them to line their nests. Severe damage is seldom caused. There is no chemical control. If damage is serious the nests should be traced and destroyed.

LEAF MINERS
These larvae of several species of insect feed on the tissues between the leaf surfaces of beet, celery and occasionally parsnips. Tomatoes and many pot plants under glass may also be attacked, as well as chrysanthemums and cinerarias. In severe cases whole leaves may be destroyed. The adult flies appear from April onwards, and lay eggs on the undersides of the leaves. The larvae or grubs mine or tunnel between the upper and lower surfaces, causing white wavy marks on the foliage. Eventually the whole leaf may be destroyed.

Spray with HCH, nicotine or malathion as soon as the damage is seen, and in severe cases repeat at fortnightly intervals. Do not use HCH on cucumbers, melons or other cucurbits.

MEALY BUGS
These pink or yellow insects, related to the scale insects, are common in greenhouses, where they feed on the leaf-sap or roots

of a wide range of plants. The bodies of the bugs are covered in a white wax; and their presence in the greenhouse is often denoted by sooty deposits on leaves. If not controlled they will spread rapidly, since they can breed throughout the year if the conditions are right for them under glass. Outdoors they infest flowering currants, ceanothus and laburnum.

Control is not easy, as they multiply rapidly under greenhouse heat, and the waxy coat is difficult to penetrate without a powerful spray. Apply tar oil during the dormant season, where this is possible. It may be necessary to fumigate the greenhouse to dislodge the pests from curled leaves and leaf axils. In the growing season spray with nicotine, white oil or malathion.

MILLEPEDES
These long, black, slow-moving creatures, with numerous legs, live in the soil. They feed on all vegetable matter, both dead and living, and do extensive damage by tunnelling into seeds, gnawing roots and chewing into tubers and bulbs, particularly lilies. They also extend the damage already done by slugs and snails, and prepare the way for attacks by fungi and bacterial diseases.

Control is not easy. Bait such as hollowed-out potatoes can be sunk just below the surface, crude naphthalene can be incorporated into the top spit of soil, or HCH can be dusted along the drills to protect young seedlings. Continuous hoeing to keep the soil disturbed will also help.

MITES
Microscopic creatures related to the spider family. Certain species are harmful pests in the garden; they produce as many as seven generations during a hot, dry summer, and unless controlled may cause a drastic reduction of crops. Certain insecticides which are lethal to true insects have no effect on mites, and may even help to increase their numbers by killing off insect predators on the mites.

Big bud mite (black currant gall mite)
These mites live in black currant leaf buds, which swell to an abnormal size, and eventually wither and fall off. Red and white currants may also be affected, but the buds do not swell before they die off.

It is important to control these mites, as they are responsible for the spread of the virus disease known as reversion, which causes a rapid falling off in cropping. Spray with benomyl at grape stage, just before the blossoms open. Some varieties of black currants are sulphur-shy, and should be sprayed with a weaker solution.

If bushes are badly attacked, they must be destroyed.

Bulb scale mite
These extremely small creatures infest the scales and young leaves of bulbous plants, such as daffodils, narcissi and amaryllis, particularly those that are being forced or stored under warm conditions.

Brown patches may be seen between the scales when the bulbs are lifted; other symptoms of attack are rust-coloured streaks on foliage and flower stalks, poor blooms and weak growth.

Always lift bulbs carefully to avoid splitting the skins, and store under cool conditions. Burn infested bulbs.

Fruit tree red spider mite
The minute red eggs are laid on the bark and young shoots of fruit trees, such as apples, pears, plums and quinces. When present in large numbers, the mites cause extensive damage to the foliage by feeding on the sap. In a bad attack, the leaves turn bronze and drop prematurely.

Destroy the eggs with a petroleum winter-wash before bud-break, or spray in summer with derris, malathion or dimethoate. Benomyl sprays, used to control scab on apples and pears, are also effective against red spider mites.

Gooseberry red spider mite
These pests chiefly suck the sap of gooseberry leaves, and related species infest other plants. The foliage turns pale or bronze-red, and fruits do not develop. Apply derris, nicotine, malathion or dimethoate after petal fall. If necessary, repeat two weeks later.

Greenhouse red spider mite
These are serious pests of many plants grown under glass. They attack tomatoes, melons, chrysanthemums, carnations, grapes, orchids and pot plants. The mites suck the sap from the foliage, causing a severe check on growth and vigour. Control, however, is difficult, but spray three times in May and June: use benomyl fungicide on the first and third occasions, but change to a derris spray for the second. Red spider mites dislike damp conditions: keeping the roots moist and regularly watering the foliage will help to prevent serious damage.

Strawberry mite
In April or May these creatures may attack strawberry foliage, causing it to shrivel and turn yellow. Spray or dust with a non-persistent insecticide such as a finely divided sulphur dust or nicotine when the air temperature is above $16°C$ ($61°F$). A late attack after harvesting is best controlled by burning off the leaves.

ROSE LEAF-HOPPERS
These small yellow sap-sucking insects can be seen in hot, dry weather on the undersides of rose leaves. The foliage becomes mottled and turns yellow; in severe attacks the plants may be completely defoliated. Spray the leaves, particularly the undersides, with either HCH, derris or malathion as soon as damage is seen, and repeat if necessary at fortnightly intervals.

SAWFLIES
The larvae or caterpillars of these small insects cause serious damage to fruit, vegetables and flowers.

Apple sawfly
Adult sawflies lay their eggs in apple and plum blossoms. The creamy-white, fat caterpillars begin to bore into the fruitlets in June, leaving ribbon-like scars across the fruits, which have an obnoxious smell when cut. Spray with HCH at petal fall. Applications in two succeeding years should be sufficient to get rid of these pests.

Gooseberry sawfly
The green and black-speckled larvae are serious pests on gooseberry bushes. They feed rapidly on the foliage, crippling the plants to such an extent that they will not fruit that season. As soon as the larvae are seen, spray or dust with derris or malathion, and if necessary repeat at monthly intervals.

Pear and cherry sawfly
Sometimes known as slugworms, these black caterpillars attack the upper surfaces of the leaves, stunting growth. Spray or dust with HCH at petal fall.

Rose leaf-rolling sawfly
The black, shiny larvae feed on the surface of rose leaves, which curl up, reducing growth. Pick off and burn infested leaves, or spray with HCH, derris or malathion. Sprays must be applied before the leaves curl.

Larvae of similar sawflies may infest the leaves of irises, rhododendrons, spiraea and polygonatum (Solomon's seal). Spray with derris or malathion.

SCALE INSECTS
Several species of these small, hard-coated insects suck the sap of ornamental and fruit trees, and herbaceous and greenhouse plants, often causing them to wilt. They are practically immobile, and resemble blisters on the bark, stems and leaves. Many species excrete honeydew, leading on to attack by sooty mould fungus.

To control all scale insects, winter-wash deciduous trees with tar oil, and spray ornamental trees and shrubs with white oil and nicotine, or with malathion.

Mussel scale insect
The trunks of neglected apple, pear, plum and cherry trees, and the stems of cotoneasters and ceanothus, may be infested by mussel scale insects.

Soft scale insect
In southern England ivy, holly and camellias are attacked by soft scale insects. They are also serious pests of greenhouse plants.

SLUGS AND SNAILS
These gastropods cause great damage. Field and garden slugs and snails eat the low-hanging foliage, and often the flower heads and upper leaves, of numerous herbaceous plants and vegetables. Underground, keeled slugs feed off bulbs, roots and tubers, causing widespread injury and loss of crop. On strawberries, slugs cause severe damage by eating large holes in the fruits. Slugs and snails are nocturnal feeders. By day they hide under stones, leaves and rubbish in dark, cool and moist places.

Destroy them with poisoned bait. This is made by mixing 1 part of metaldehyde with 3 parts of bran. Place the mixture on the ground near susceptible plants, and cover with a propped-up tile or piece of glass to protect it from rain. Slug pellets can be bought ready-made, or one of the proprietary liquid slug killers can be watered in. Lime is disliked by slugs and snails, and may be sprinkled round seedlings or valuable plants.

Slugworms: see Pear and cherry sawfly

SYMPHILIDS
Minute, barely visible soil pests occurring generally under glass, and on a number of outdoor crops in south-west England. They attack a wide variety of plants—tomatoes, lettuces, cucumbers, anemones, sweet peas and primulas—by chewing off the root hairs. With seedlings, this can result in crop failure. On infested mature plants, the lower leaves turn yellow and the top ones dark blue.

Work HCH into the soil before planting susceptible crops. Other methods, such as steam sterilisation, may be used on cucumber beds.

THRIPS
These tiny elongated insects infest greenhouse plants, and also attack herbaceous plants outdoors. They puncture and tear minute holes in leaves, which assume a silvery appearance. At a later stage they pierce the petals, producing white spots. Thrips may also transmit virus diseases, especially spotted wilt virus of tomatoes.

Gladiolus thrip
The thrips which attack gladioli, and sometimes irises, lilies and freesias, over-winter on the corms. When the young shoots break through, they show silvery streaks, and the flower petals have unsightly white spots. Dust the corms with HCH powder before planting, and dust or spray the young foliage with HCH or derris, malathion or nicotine.

Greenhouse thrip
Cyclamens, carnations, fuchsias, roses and tomatoes are the chief host plants. Control greenhouse thrips by fumigation with nicotine. Derris, dimethoate, malathion and HCH smokes or sprays may also be used. If necessary, repeat the applications.

Pea thrip
In dry, hot weather pea thrips are found in large numbers on young developing pea pods. They tear at the surface, and cause twisted growth and malformation, and silvery leaves. Spray or dust as soon as damage is first seen with HCH, malathion or nicotine. Repeat the dose after ten days during serious infestations. Allow an interval of two weeks before harvesting after applications of persistent chemicals.

WASPS
Wasps feed on most top fruits, gnawing holes in apples, pears and plums. The spoiled fruits are liable to attacks by fungal diseases, especially brown rot, which is difficult to control.

Control by destroying the wasp nests. The nests, often built in underground holes, in roofs or under the eaves, are best attacked in the evening when the wasps head for home. Place derris dust or carbaryl in the nests, and block the entrance holes with damp sacking or grass turves. The nests may also be destroyed by pouring carbon tetrachloride, paraffin or petrol into the entrance holes.

WEEVILS
A large family of small, active beetles. They are distinguished by elongated snouts. Both the adults and the larvae may damage fruits and plants.

Apple blossom weevil
In March, adult females deposit their eggs in the flower trusses of apples, pears and quinces. The cream-coloured grubs hatch at pink-bud stage and feed inside the buds, causing the petals to close over and form a brown cap.

HCH applied in early spring to kill aphids will also destroy apple blossom weevil at the same time. In June tie sacking round tree trunks to catch the grubs. Remove and destroy sacking in September.

Clay-coloured weevil
Adult weevils are destructive to the foliage, flowers and fruit buds of top and soft fruit, and rambler roses. They particularly attack the buds of newly grafted trees. They are nocturnal feeders, and are not easy to control. New grafts on trees can be protected by grease bands, or by HCH sprayed below the graft as soon as it is made. Spray a second time if further damage is evident.

Leaf-eating weevil
Considerable damage can be done in spring to fruit tree leaves and blossom by these insects. Routine sprays in spring of malathion or HCH should prevent infestation.

Pea and bean weevil
The adults are serious pests, biting regular segments from the edges of leaves. The growing shoots of the young plants are also attacked, and growth may be severely checked. One application of either HCH or malathion as soon as the damage is seen is usually sufficient.

Turnip gall weevil
The presence of this pest may be indicated by swellings on the roots of cabbage or cauliflower seedlings ready to plant out. The swellings, or galls, contain the weevil grubs, and such plants should be destroyed.

Vine weevil
The adult beetles feed at night on the foliage of a great number of greenhouse pot plants, and the larvae damage roots and underground stems. Outside, the weevils damage the foliage of polyanthuses and rhododendrons and the roots of many alpine plants. Spray with HCH in the greenhouse and outdoors; or trap the weevils in rolled-up corrugated paper or pieces of sacking. The insects will hide there and can then be destroyed.

WHITEFLIES
The adult whiteflies are small, white, moth-like insects. They are common in the greenhouse where they are found in dense clusters on the undersides of leaves. Adults and nymphs feed mainly on the foliage of tomatoes, though they attack other greenhouse plants as well. The leaves turn mottled and yellow, with subsequent loss of vigour. The nymphs also secrete a sticky honeydew, on which the sooty mould fungus develops to distort the plants still further.

Fumigate with HCH, or spray with resmethrin or permethrin. The pests are not easily eradicated, and repeated applications may be necessary.

Outdoors, especially in the south, whiteflies are significant only on brassicas, where they may attack the edible parts. Spray or dust with resmethrin.

WIREWORMS
The yellow, threadlike larvae of the click beetle, found in the soil of most gardens. The grubs feed on the underground parts of many plants, and are particularly troublesome in seedling beds. Symptoms of damage are yellowing and wilting. Young plants may die. Fork HCH or bromophos dust into the soil before planting or sowing.

WOODLICE
Grey, hard-skinned creatures, found in damp and shady parts of the garden, where they feed on decaying or dead vegetable matter. They are nocturnal feeders, and cause serious damage only in humid conditions under glass; or outdoors if they are present in large numbers. They feed on stems, leaves and roots.

Clear away all garden rubbish, and eliminate dark, damp nesting places. Dust or spray hiding-places and other infested areas with HCH, or trap the insects in hollowed-out potatoes and oranges.

Diseases

Bacterial diseases

Bacteria are simple forms of life consisting of minute rod-like bodies that reproduce by dividing in two.

Various types of bacteria attack many plants, causing considerable loss. They do not form over-wintering spores like fungi, but spend the winter in plant debris, tubers and bulbs, or in the soil. Some species can be transported from plant to plant in drops of water, but they are sensitive to drying out and cannot survive without moisture. All bacterial diseases are difficult to cure.

Bacterial canker
Bacterial canker on plums and cherries is a common and serious disease. Infection enters through a wound caused by pruning or, more commonly, at the scars left where the leaves fall off. The symptoms, which appear during summer, are brown spots on the leaves, later becoming small holes. The wood develops dark, elongated cankers that cause young shoots to curl over. In severe cases the infected trees must be destroyed. The disease may be temporarily checked by spraying with Bordeaux mixture or other copper fungicide in late autumn.

Crown gall
Crown gall is mainly a disease of woody plants. It is found on apples, pears, plums, peaches, loganberries and raspberries as swellings or tumours at ground level on the trunks or stems.

Roses, hollyhocks, dahlias, phlox and beetroot are sometimes affected. The tumours attack the roots and can cause pale foliage. There is no cure for this disease, but affected plants need not necessarily be destroyed.

Pear fireblight
Fireblight of pears is a serious disease which may suddenly attack pear blossoms and leaves (particularly 'Laxton's Superb') in spring. Odd branches, or often the whole tree, appear to have been scorched by fire. There is no chemical control of this disease, and infected trees must be cut down and destroyed. Fireblight is a notifiable disease and must be reported to the local authorities.

Carrots and other vegetables
Root vegetables are chiefly affected by bacteria. However, carrot bacteria infect not only carrots, but also celery, cucumbers, onions, potatoes, seakale and turnips. Infection results in soft slimy rot of the roots. When lifting root vegetables for storage be careful to store only sound roots. This should be done during dry weather to prevent the spread of any bacteria that might be present.

Celery heart rot
Heart rot in celery is more common in wet weather. The symptoms are a wet brown rot of the underground plant parts that eventually turns to a slimy mess. Turnips, swedes and onions are similarly affected. There is no chemical method of control. Treat the seedlings against attacks from slugs and other pests, as bacterial rot can enter only through a wound.

Potato rot
Blackleg of potatoes occasionally causes serious damage in northern districts. It occurs in June when the weather is wet. The plants have a stunted look, with pale foliage and stiff, erect leaves. When the plants are pulled up, the base of the stem will be found to be blackened and rotted. Infected plants will not produce any tubers, and should be dug up and burnt.

Rhubarb
Crown rot of rhubarb is caused by bacteria infecting the tissue of the crown just below the buds. The outward signs, not easily detected, are dull foliage, small sticks and dead buds; later the tops of the crowns can be knocked off. There is no cure, and infected plants should be destroyed.

Arum lilies
Arum corms often suffer from a slimy decay that first shows as a discoloration round the edges of the leaves. During dry weather the corms may recover, but if conditions are wet the damage may extend further. At the end of the growing season remove the corms from the pots, scrub them with a 2 per cent formalin solution and re-pot in fresh, sterilised soil.

Begonias
Bacterial blight can cause serious damage to winter-flowering begonias in the greenhouse. The infection spreads from the leaves, which are dotted with brown spots, through the stem and down to the corms. Drastic measures must be taken at once: destroy all plants and sterilise the house.

Hyacinths
Soft rot bacteria occasionally attack hyacinths grown in bowls. The decay of the bulbs is very rapid. The flowers fail to develop and topple over at soil level while still in bud. The disease is precipitated by moist, humid conditions and the use of heavy dressings of nitrogenous fertiliser.

Fungus diseases

Anthracnose: see Leaf spot (cucumbers)

BLIGHT
Blight is a common name for a number of different plant diseases, especially those that lead to sudden, serious leaf damage. Some of these diseases are caused by microscopic fungi.

Raspberries
Cane blight of raspberries causes the leaves to wilt, and the canes to become brittle and snap off easily. The variety 'Lloyd George' is very susceptible. Cut off the canes at the base and burn them.

Potatoes
Blight is probably the worst enemy of potatoes. The first signs of the disease are brown spots or blotches on the margins and tips of the leaves. As these spots

spread, the affected foliage dies, and the stems become black. Eventually the entire plant becomes an evil-smelling mass.

Warm, wet weather favours potato blight. The spores are washed down into the soil and infect the tubers, which then suffer from an evil-smelling wet rot. Infected tubers are unfit for eating. The disease also spreads to healthy potatoes in the clamp.

Blight can be prevented, if action is taken in time. By the time the symptoms are seen, it is usually too late for treatment. Preventive measures consist of spraying the foliage, including the underside, with copper fungicide. Repeat applications at three-week intervals from the beginning of July (or mid-June in damp western districts). If an attack of blight persists, the plants must be cut down to ground level, and the tubers dug up two or three weeks later.

Tomatoes
The potato fungus may attack and cause serious damage to tomatoes. Brown mottled spots appear on the ripening fruit. When blight is detected on potatoes, tomato plants must also be sprayed with copper fungicide.

BROWN ROT
Spores of this common fungus damage flower stalks and young shoots of apples, pears, peaches, plums, cherries and related ornamental trees. The brown lesions on the wood develop into cracks and cankers that may encircle the stems. Later the spores enter the fruitlets through wounds caused by wasps and other insects, hail and frost damage, or severe scab. Harvested fruit may also be attacked by brown rot fungi at the stalk end.

The infected fruits shrivel up, and in severe cases remain in a mummified condition on the trees, creating new sources of infection.

Regular winter washes will reduce the spores; but cultural control methods are more effective.

Cut off all diseased wood and remove cankers. Pick off dead and rotten fruits, fumigate store rooms and destroy wasp nests.

CANKER
The chief victims of this disease are fruit trees, especially apples. Cankers appear as sunken areas on the bark near a bud, or near a wound caused by scab, pruning or other mechanical damage. Fungus spores infect the wound edges, laying bare the wood and eventually encircling the whole branch. The disease extends upwards and downwards from the infected area, discolouring the wood and causing fruit spurs to wilt.

The type of rootstock on to which the trees are grafted influences their resistance to canker. Some varieties, such as 'Cox's Orange Pippin' and 'James Grieve', are susceptible, while 'Bramley's Seedling' is more resistant.

Cankers must be treated at the first sign. Cut the diseased area out with a knife, pare the wound clean, and paint with a fungicidal wound paint. If a branch is encircled, it must be cut back to below the infected area. Badly cankered trees must be destroyed.

Cankers on cherry, peach and related ornamental trees are caused by bacterial diseases or brown rot.

Cabbages
In the north, brown or purplish stem cankers on cabbages may occasionally occur and cause the plants to wilt. The disease is seedborne. Severely affected plants must be destroyed to prevent a build-up in the soil.

Roses
Several different fungi may cause rose canker. Crown cankers develop at the base of the plants and cause them to die back, while other fungi produce depressions near a wound on the wood and kill the stems. Prune away diseased wood and burn.

Tomato canker: see **Root rots**

DAMPING-OFF
A common disease that attacks young seedlings. The fungus infects the stems of young plants at ground level, causing them to collapse and die.

Several different fungi cause this disease, which is encouraged by wet, cold soils, and crowded sowings.

To prevent damping-off, water the compost with Cheshunt compound, or dust the seed boxes with a proprietary seed dressing.

GREY MOULD (BOTRYTIS)
Grey mould fungi attack practically every flower, vegetable and fruit in the garden, covering stems, foliage and fruit with soft, grey fluff, and seriously damaging crops.

The disease is more prevalent in the south and west than in the cooler and drier areas in the north and east.

The fungi are particularly active in the greenhouse, where they may destroy whole boxes of seedlings. Grey mould is encouraged by cold, wet conditions, and thrives on dead and rotting vegetation. It spreads rapidly among weak plants, and thrives during changes in temperature and humidity. The spores invade damaged plant tissues and often kill the plants. Benomyl fungicide provides an effective control.

Gooseberry die-back
Gooseberry die-back is caused by one of these fungi invading the main stems and branches, young shoots and leaves. The plant is defoliated, and in severe attacks cracks will appear in the bark. Cut down diseased branches well below the infected areas or, if necessary, dig up the plants and burn them.

Peaches
Peaches, too, may be attacked by botrytis, particularly under glass, where the spores are encouraged by too much moisture in the atmosphere. In the open the fungus may cause the fruit to rot during wet weather. Ventilate the

greenhouse and pick off infected fruit to keep the disease under control.

Raspberries
Grey mould fungus may attack raspberry fruits and canes. Severe loss is unlikely, but canes that are grey and whose surface skin is cracked should be thinned out.

Strawberries
Strawberries are the fruit most liable to attack by grey mould. During wet, cold weather at ripening time the fungus can destroy almost the whole crop. To prevent the disease, space plants widely and place straw under the fruit trusses to keep them from touching the soil; or spray with captan or thiram, beginning as soon as the first flowers open, and repeating every 7–10 days.

Cabbages and Brussels sprouts
Cabbages and Brussels sprouts attacked by botrytis display soft downy growths that rot the leaves and hearts. The disease flourishes during wet weather, and may be encouraged by too generous use of nitrogen fertilisers. There is no chemical cure, and attacked plants must be destroyed. Prevent attack by adding potash to the soil to counter-balance the nitrogen.

Dwarf french beans
On beans, particularly dwarf french beans, grey mould causes rotting of the tips of the pods. The risk of this trouble can be lessened by wide spacing of plants and rows.

Lettuce
Lettuce, especially under glass, suffers seriously from botrytis. In the greenhouse, grow a variety of upright habit whose leaves will not touch the soil. Fumigate with tecnazene at seedling stage, and keep well ventilated. Avoid overhead watering, but keep the roots moist by careful application of the hose between the plants. Outdoors rake quintozene or dicloran into the soil.

Tomatoes

Tomatoes, both under glass and outdoors, are attacked by botrytis rot. The growth will invade any jagged snags left after de-shooting. If the disease is not halted at once, it will spread to stems and leaves. The fruit stalks, too, may be infected, and cause the fruits to drop off. Fumigate with a tecnazene smoke, and spray outdoor plants with thiram or benomyl.

Flowers

The foliage and blooms of many flowers, such as anemones, antirrhinums, stocks and sweet peas, may be spoilt by grey mould fungi during wet and cold weather. The infection may spread from dead tissue to healthy plants, but unless the attack is severe, the disease may be halted by picking off infected leaves, or spraying with a proprietary fungicide.

Carnations and chrysanthemums

Carnations and chrysanthemum cuttings grown under glass are susceptible in the early stages. Ventilate the house to keep down humidity, and destroy diseased plants. Fumigate with tecnazene.

Narcissi and tulips

Bulbs, particularly narcissi and lilies, may be severely damaged by several leaf diseases caused by grey mould fungi. The symptoms are brown marks and stripes on the foliage, known as fire. The diseases are common in the south and west. In damp, muggy weather spray at fortnightly intervals with Bordeaux mixture to prevent the diseases. Tulip fire is even more serious, as it affects the blooms as well as the foliage and can destroy a whole bed. Irregular grey, scorched areas on the leaves turn brown and spread rapidly in wet weather. Spray as soon as the disease is seen with a fungicide such as zineb or captan. The resting bodies of the fungus live on bulb scales and may lie dormant in the soil. Do not re-plant bulbs in beds that have been infected. Alternatively, rake quintozene into the soil.

LEAF CURL (PEACH)

On the leaves of peaches, almonds and nectarines large blisters develop, which are at first red, then swell up and turn white. Many leaves may be completely curled, swollen and discoloured. They turn brown, wither and fall, and this premature defoliation leads to a reduction in tree vigour. Remove and burn affected leaves as soon as they are seen, then in the autumn spray the affected tree just before leaf-fall with Bordeaux mixture or some other copper fungicide, or with lime sulphur ($\frac{1}{2}$ pint in 2 gall. of water). Spray again at bud-swelling stage in early spring, and repeat ten days later.

LEAF MOULD (TOMATO)

Fungus disease is very common and serious on tomatoes grown under glass. The symptoms are yellow spots on the upper leaf surfaces and browny-green growths of spores on the undersides. The whole foliage can be affected, and cropping may be severely reduced. Ventilate the greenhouse, and increase the night temperature to prevent attacks of this disease. Fumigation with tecnazene is effective.

LEAF SPOT (RING SPOT)

A number of different fungi cause spotting or blotching of plant leaves. Spores settle on leaf surfaces, where they germinate and send out minute threads, known as hyphae. These invade plant tissues and destroy the cells, making the surfaces discoloured. An aggregate of hyphae appears as fluff or down on the leaves. These spots, seen on many garden plants, may spread all over the leaves and stems, causing severe damage.

Gooseberries and black currants

Both gooseberries and black currants may suffer from serious leaf infection after fruiting; this will cause early defoliation and failure to produce wood for next year's crop. Numerous dark spots on the leaves join together, and the foliage turns yellow and dies. Spray with zineb or benomyl from mid-June onwards, and with dinocap or a copper fungicide after the fruit is picked.

Strawberries

Red or purple patches on strawberry leaves seldom affect the plants' vitality. Burn the foliage together with the protective straw in autumn to get rid of fungal spores.

Celery

Celery is often attacked by a fungus which causes brown spots on the leaves. In wet weather the disease spreads rapidly from plant to plant, and may result in the foliage wilting completely. Spray early in the year with Bordeaux mixture or other copper fungicide, and buy seed that is pre-treated to kill the spores.

Cucumbers under glass

Leaf spot or anthracnose of cucumbers under glass can be serious. Pale, water-soaked spots appear on the foliage, causing it to turn brown and wither. Maintain strict hygiene in the greenhouse to prevent anthracnose, and dust regularly with sulphur.

Black spot on roses

Black spot is now widespread throughout the country. New rose bushes should be dipped in a solution of benomyl before they are planted. Dark brown spots on the foliage, twigs and leaf stalks cause early defoliation and general loss of vigour. The disease is not easy to control, especially during wet weather. Effective chemical control with captan or copper fungicide can be started from early spring onwards. If signs of the disease do develop, spray with benomyl or thiophanate-methyl.

MILDEW (POWDERY)

Powdery mildew, common on many garden plants, is caused by fungi. Infected plants have a white powdery coating on the foliage and stems, consisting of numerous spores and fungal threads that suck the sap from the plants, reducing their vitality. Later the coating turns brown and appears as a kind of felt, studded with minute black dots. These are new fruiting bodies that overwinter in the soil. Spores from these bodies will infect next year's crop.

Apple

Apple trees are particularly liable to this disease, which can cause serious losses. The leaves become narrow and curled, and remain small and pale. Diseased buds fail to set fruit, and shoots may be completely defoliated. The fungus may infect healthy parts of the tree. Routine spring spraying with dinocap or benomyl should control the disease.

Gooseberries and currants

Powdery mildew on gooseberries and currant bushes (known as American gooseberry mildew or blight) may greatly lessen the crop. The infection, which produces white powdery patches on the leaves, fruit and young wood, can be prevented by pruning to allow air through the framework. Spray with dinocap or benomyl before blossoming, and repeat immediately after the fruits have set and again three weeks later.

Strawberries

Mildew on strawberries first appears as grey blotches on the undersides of the foliage. The margins curl inwards, exposing the white fungus. From the leaves spores infect the flowers and later the fruits. Prevent infection by spraying with dinocap or benomyl from late April, and repeat spraying at intervals until the fruits develop or, if necessary, until harvested. In the autumn burn over the beds to destroy the spores.

Peas

Almost every year, pea plants in many gardens will be covered with white powdery down. The attack usually occurs after the crop has been picked, but later sowings must be protected with sulphur dust, as mildew is far more prevalent towards autumn.

Marrows
Marrows are similarly affected, and the ripening of the fruit may be checked if the leaves do not function well. Spray with dinocap or benomyl fortnightly.

Cucumbers under glass
Cucumbers under glass may occasionally be infected. White spotty areas on the leaves soon spread, until the whole plant is covered with a powder-like growth. Dust the plants with sulphur, or spray, dust or fumigate with dinocap. Keep the roots moist and the atmosphere dry.

Roses
The leaves and shoots of roses are often coated with white powdery spores. Spray the foliage regularly with dinocap or benomyl to control the disease.

Flowers
Most flowers are attacked by mildew fungi. Attacks are seldom serious on such plants as lupins, marigolds, phloxes, myosotis, scabiosa and campanulas.

MILDEW (DOWNY)
Downy mildew is caused by various species of fungi, different from those that produce powdery mildews. The fungal threads grow deeper into the tissues, especially on seedlings. They are encouraged by damp weather, and produce white mealy growths on the underside of the foliage. The disease is difficult to control, but may be prevented by giving adequate moisture to the roots, and dusting with a protective fungicide after watering.

Onions and leeks
In a wet season, onions and leeks may suffer from downy mildew. The tips of the leaves die back, and the diseased tissues become covered with a fine fungal growth

of minute grey hairs. From these, spores pass down into the soil to infect the roots. Spray or dust with a fungicide such as zineb.

Lettuces and cauliflowers
In frames and greenhouses, or under cloches, lettuces and cauliflowers show yellowing of the outer leaves and patches of fungal growth on the surface. Increase the ventilation, and pick off diseased leaves. Spray with thiram or zineb.

Flowers
Stocks, wallflowers and other cruciferous flowers can be affected by mildew. Dust with flowers of sulphur.

Antirrhinums
Antirrhinums may suffer seriously from downy mildew, which appears as fungal growths on the undersides of the leaves. Spore masses are produced in great numbers, and contamination of one plant by another is rapid. Spray young plants with copper sulphate or dinocap. Do not plant in the same bed in consecutive years, as the spores over-winter in the soil.

ROOT ROTS
The fungi causing root rots give no external decay symptoms until it is too late, and even then the symptoms are often similar to those of nutrition disorders or bad drainage. Sickly looking plants eventually wilt and die, and only by digging them up and examining the roots can the presence of these fungi be determined. Some root rot fungi attack plants at the seedling stage, causing them to shrivel and die before they have developed. Others attack root vegetables and render them useless.

Honey fungus
The most damaging of all fungi that attack fruit trees and bushes is *Armillaria mellea*, the bootlace or honey fungus. It can attack all types of plants. The underground fungus attacks the roots and lower parts of the stem, gradually weakening the trees until they die. When a diseased or dead tree is

pulled up, the roots will be found to be entwined with long black strands. Under the bark are white fan-like growths of the same fungus, destroying the tissues of the stem.

These black strands grow through the soil, and attack other healthy trees and bushes. The fungus may emerge many feet away as a honey-coloured toadstool, from which new spores are produced. The toadstools are often seen on dead tree stumps in reclaimed woodland. As there is no cure for this disease, such areas should not be re-planted with trees.

Dig up and burn diseased or infected trees and as many of the black strands as possible. Sinking a trench 24 in. deep round the area or drenching the soil with phenolic emulsion may prevent the disease spreading.

Carrots, beet and asparagus
Violet root rot is common on many root vegetables such as carrots and beet, and also attacks asparagus. The fungus, which is persistent and not easy to control, covers the underground parts with purple web-like strands.

Brassica club root
Brassicas are often infected with the persistent club root fungus. This slime fungus is active in rotten roots and debris. It attacks the roots, causing them to thicken and develop into large swollen masses. The plants are small and sickly. The disease is prevalent on sour, acid soils with bad drainage. and in plots where brassicas have been grown for years. Lime the land to reduce acidity, and ensure proper drainage. Rake in 4 per cent calomel dust. Before planting, dip roots of young plants into a paste of calomel, benomyl or thiophanate-methyl. Drenching the soil with a phenolic emulsion can also help.

Tomatoes and cucumbers
Tomatoes and cucumbers under glass are attacked by several fungal diseases of the roots.

Brown root rot can be prevented by sterilising the soil with dazomet. Verticillium wilt (sleepy disease) causes the plants to wilt and the lower leaves to droop on sunny days. To control the disease, raise the temperature to at least 24°C (75°F) for a fortnight and syringe the foliage with water. In severe attacks the plant must be uprooted. Water the planting hole with Cheshunt compound, and mulch the roots of new plants with peat. Fresh roots will grow into this mulch at a higher level. Apply the same methods to combat didymella disease (stem canker). This fungus is common under glass, and infects the main stems at the base, causing shrinking and cracking.

Onions
Neck rot of onions first appears as a brown softness at the necks of the bulbs. Stored onions with this disease develop a grey woolly growth, which can ruin the whole crop. Add fertilisers such as potash to the soil, and avoid nicking the bulbs when hoeing. Harvest ripe onions only, and store them in an airy shed.

Narcissi
Narcissi may be infected with white rot (*Rosellinia*). White fungal strands between the bulb scales of infected plants cause brown decay of the roots and base plates. The disease is associated with sour and waterlogged soil, which must be sterilised and adequately drained before being re-planted.

Asters
Foot rot or black leg is the most common disease of asters. The bases of the stems turn brown, and the plants usually keel over and die. If the trouble is widespread, water the soil with a 2 per cent formalin solution a month before re-planting, and spray seed boxes with Cheshunt compound.

Bedding plants
Many annuals such as petunias and nemesias, and biennials such

as pansies, are susceptible to root rot, particularly if they are grown in the same position in the border every year. Control as for asters.

RUST DISEASES
These fungal diseases are easily recognised by yellow, brown or orange pustules on the foliage, which assumes a rusty appearance. Many different rust fungi attack garden plants, but the damage is seldom fatal.

In dealing with rust diseases, it is important to know which fungus is at work. Rust fungi fall into two groups: those that complete their life cycles on the same plant (autoecious rusts), and those fungi that migrate to an alternate host for some of their spore stages (heteroecious rusts). Control of rust fungi may therefore include tracing of the different host plants.

Currants
Currant bushes may in early summer show clusters of small yellow pustules on the undersides of the leaves. This is a heteroecious rust fungus, which produces spores that infect some species of pine. From the resulting cankers new spores develop, and these are borne to the currant bushes in late summer. The foliage withers and drops prematurely, but applications of copper fungicide against leaf spot will also control rust.

Plums
Plum leaves, too, may be rusted with minute yellow spots on the upper surfaces. The undersides are brown, and contain spores that infect the leaves of healthy trees. The alternate host is the anemone, either cultivated or wild. Plum rust is not a serious disease, but repeated early defoliation will weaken the trees. Spray with Bordeaux mixture or thiram when the fruits are half-grown, and again after harvest. Remove any garden anemones.

Mint
Rust fungus can be troublesome on mint. Diseased plants have thickened, distorted shoots, which develop small orange-coloured cups in spring. The disease spreads rapidly, and may spoil the crop. In autumn, black spots on the plants release spores that are washed down in the soil to over-winter. Destroy diseased plants and spray with Bordeaux mixture. If the mint bed is badly affected, buy new healthy plants and set out in a different site.

Antirrhinums
Most flowers are attacked by rust fungus of one sort or another, the most seriously affected being antirrhinums. Some strains are now rust-resistant, but at the first sign of an attack, infected plants must be pulled up and destroyed.

Chrysanthemums
On chrysanthemums, rust can be more destructive than mildew. Infection results in lowered plant vitality, leading to weak plants and poor flowers. Spray with thiram or zineb as a preventive measure before the disease starts.

Sweet williams
Sweet williams are susceptible to rust disease, especially in the south. The symptoms are pale green spots on the upper leaf surfaces and brown spore masses on the undersides. Flowering is severely reduced, though the red varieties appear to be more resistant. Grow sweet williams in poor soil, as a rich soil encourages too much leaf and soft growth susceptible to rust.

Hollyhocks
Hollyhocks are nearly always affected by rust. The orange pustules can be seen on leaves, stems and seed pods. Though the disease is unsightly, the plants seldom die. The spores over-winter on the plants; to avoid new attacks, plant fresh hollyhocks each year. Spray seedlings with thiram.

Roses
Rust disease on roses—usually confined to the south-west of England—can be troublesome and difficult to control. The fungus lives inside the wood, where the life cycle is completed. Bright orange pustules on branches and leaves, and even on the hips, weaken the bushes and cause early defoliation. Spray regularly with a copper fungicide, thiram or zineb.

Bushes that have become badly diseased should be destroyed.

SCAB
There is no disease called scab: it is a term used to describe the damage caused by various fungi in the skin of many plants.

Apple and pear
Apple and pear scab is caused by one of the most destructive fungi. Infection appears as black spots on the young foliage and blisters on the bark of young shoots. The disease next spreads to the fruit, causing raised areas that eventually crack, thus reducing the crop that is suitable for storage.

Effective control methods must be employed early in the season to ensure vigorous growth. Spray apple trees with a fungicide, such as benomyl or captan, from bud burst until July, at intervals of 2–3 weeks. Make sure the spray covers the leaf surface.

The seriousness of infection depends on many factors—variety, soil type, manuring and pruning methods, and climatic conditions. The disease is more serious in wet areas, and soft, sappy growth is more susceptible than well grown foliage. Prune apple and pear trees so as to allow plenty of air to circulate round the branches. The fungus over-winters in fallen leaves, and these should be cleared in autumn to prevent re-infection.

Peaches
Peach scab is not serious on the leaves, but it may sometimes badly attack the fruits. Brown, scabby marks on the skins enlarge until they crack and exude gum. Control the fungus by cutting away diseased twigs. Under glass, give plenty of ventilation, and dust with sulphur. In the open, spray with Bordeaux mixture.

Beet and radishes
Beet and radishes may show ugly, raised marks; but the damage is only skin-deep, and can be corrected by cultural methods. Scab usually occurs when the vegetables are grown in lime-rich soil. Dig in compost or organic fertilisers to achieve a proper balance.

Potatoes
Potatoes are infected with both common scab and powdery scab. The symptoms of common scab are raised spots and patches on the skins of the tubers, which crack, leaving the whole surface covered in ragged edges. Powdery scab is less common: the spots are similar to those caused by common scab, but they may distort the tubers so badly that they are made inedible. At a later stage the spots burst, releasing a dry powder of new spores that over-winter in the soil to infect next year's crop. Effective control methods consist of adding plenty of organic material to the soil before planting, as the disease is more prevalent on light, hungry soils. Add only small quantities of lime, which is conducive to potato scab.

SILVER LEAF DISEASE
This fungal infection of stem and branches appears as a silvery sheen on the foliage of many fruit and ornamental trees. Silvered leaves alone are not enough to identify the disease: affected branches will show dark brown stains when cut across and, as severely infected trees die, bracket-like growths appear on the dead wood.

These growths are reproductive bodies from which spores will infect other healthy stock.

Plums and other fruit
It is a serious disease particularly on plum trees, though apples, pears, cherries, currants and gooseberries may also be attacked. There is no chemical control

method. All diseased wood must be cut back so far that no stained wood shows. In severe attacks, the tree must be dug up and burnt.

The disease is least active in early summer, and susceptible fruit trees should be pruned during this period. Paint the wounds carefully with a fungicidal paint to prevent spores entering.

Tulip fire: see **Grey mould (narcissi and tulips)**

WILT
Like scab, wilt is not a disease, but a symptom caused by various fungi. Although wilting may be caused by physiological disorders, the damage is more commonly attributable to root fungi that damage the water-conducting tissues inside the plant stems.

Cucumbers
Under glass and in high temperatures cucumbers may suffer and collapse from wilting, caused by a root fungus, fusarium. Plants affected by this disease must be dug up and burnt.

Tomato wilt: see **Root rots**

Carnations and chrysanthemums
Greenhouse carnations and chrysanthemums can be severely reduced by attacks of the root fungus, verticillium. The moisture-carrying cells become diseased, and the plants slowly droop and die. There are no preventive measures: once the disease is diagnosed the plants must be pulled up, and the house and soil sterilised.

Physiological disorders

In spite of care and attention, plants may still produce stunted growth, distorted flowers and inferior or useless crops. As well as pests and diseases, there are additional disorders, caused by poor environment and growing conditions, such as unsuitable soil, poor drainage and bad weather conditions. In addition, lack or excess of essential plant foods, moisture and lime can cause physiological disorders.

Unsuitable soil
Unsuitable soil can give rise to numerous disorders. If the soil is chiefly composed of heavy clay, the young roots will not be able to reach down and develop, and top growth will consequently be retarded. Roots also need air, and closely packed clay particles keep air from them. A light, sandy soil fails to retain the moisture necessary for root development. The roots reach far down in the soil in search of moisture. They dry out and cause the top growth to be weak and stunted.

Poor drainage
Poor drainage seriously affects plant growth. When excess moisture cannot drain away through the soil, water fills up the air pockets in the soil. Roots are denied oxygen and fail to develop; and the whole plant will eventually collapse and die.

Weather damage
Though the gardener has no control over the prevailing weather, preventive measures can be taken to reduce the damage caused by high winds, heavy rain, frosts, snow and excessive heat. Windbreaks and cloches will protect young, tender plants. Young trees should be securely staked. High winds will rock the trees and loosen the soil round the roots. This may result in severe root damage and facilitate the entry of bacteria and fungi.

Water: too little or too much
All growing plants need moisture. Without enough water, top growths wilt and droop, fruits fail to develop, and dry roots encourage attacks by fungi and root aphids, resulting in further deterioration due to disease organisms. Excess of moisture can be equally serious, particularly in the greenhouse. If the soil is too damp, the roots will rot, and over-watering often prevents seeds from germinating. Soaking the seed boxes will rot the seeds.

Lack of lime
Lime stabilises the acidity and alkalinity of the soil. Lack of lime results in acid conditions that discourage soil bacteria, earthworms and other living organisms. Lime enables the roots to absorb the elements needed for development. Some plants, such as azaleas, rhododendrons, heathers and camellias, are lime-haters. To grow them in alkaline soil, plant them in mounds of acid peat.

Chlorosis
Yellowing of the foliage may be due to a common disorder known as chlorosis. Green chlorophyll in the leaves enables plants to absorb food and assists growth; and lack of it may in severe cases kill the plants. Chlorosis may be caused by too much lime or too little iron in the soil, and may be counteracted by soil dressings of peat or leaf-mould to increase acidity, or the addition of a compound such as sequestrene.

Split plums and cherries
Plums and cherries may split after heavy rainfall following a dry spell. Fungi enter the damaged fruits and cause further damage.

Bitter pit
Storage troubles of apples and pears may be associated with weather conditions during the growing season. The brown spots of bitter pit, which spread from under the skin to the flesh, are more prevalent after a hot summer or a light crop. Lack of calcium may be the cause, and this deficiency can be corrected by spraying with calcium nitrate.

Water core
Apples with translucent or glassy flesh are suffering from water core, usually caused by alternating wet and dry periods and high temperatures. Apply only small amounts of nitrogenous fertiliser.

Cracked fruits
Russeting and cracking of fruits may be caused by frost and cold winds, or by high humidity and heavy rainfall.

Potato disorders
Potatoes may show symptoms of several functional disorders. The cause of rust spots in the flesh is unknown. A different variety should be grown if the trouble persists. Large cavities in the tubers (hollow heart) usually appear after heavy rainfall following drought. The same weather conditions may result in the eyes on the tubers growing into knots; or into chains, where the tubers produce stolons bearing secondary tubers. Healthy-looking potatoes occasionally turn black when being boiled; potash deficiency may be the cause.

Frosted brassicas
Grey foliage on brassicas and dead centres of spring cabbages are the indirect results of heavy frosts. Continual low temperatures reduce chlorophyll production; the plants may look sick and yellow, but will usually recover in warmer weather.

Split carrots
Carrot splitting may be due to sudden rain after a dry spell, or to excessive use of nitrogenous fertilisers. Compost and a balanced fertiliser provide carrots with the proper growing conditions. Fresh dung should never be applied.

Cankered carrots
Blue-black cankers (pit) on carrots reduce the value of the roots. The disorder is thought to be due to too heavy or too acid soils.

Parsnip canker
Large brown patches on the skin of parsnips just below soil level spread to the roots, which eventually rot. These cankers are associated with unsuitable soil conditions, although a number of fungi are the main cause of the trouble. Adequate amounts of

lime and potash should be added to the soil, and the seeds should not be sown before March. Without these precautions, disease organisms will enter the canker.

Tomato disorders
Tomatoes suffer from various functional disorders that chiefly affect the fruits. Circular brown patches at the blossom end of the fruits become sunken and flat and affect the flesh underneath. The probable cause is water shortage, which may also be responsible for blotchy ripening. This shows as large patches that remain green, making the fruits practically inedible.

Failure of the fruits to ripen near the stalk end is known as greenback. Potash deficiency may be one cause, as may scorching of the top of the fruits. To prevent scorching, tomatoes grown under glass should be shaded with lime wash during summer.

Deficiency diseases

All growing plants need essential elements to enable them to reach maturity, to set seeds, and to attain a certain size of flower, leaf or root.

These elements—nitrogen, phosphates and potash—can be supplemented with organic or inorganic fertilisers to improve vigour and increase the crop. Plants further require fairly large quantities of carbon, oxygen, hydrogen, calcium, magnesium and sulphur; and also traces of iron, manganese, boron, copper, zinc and molybdenum.

Nitrogen
Nitrogen is chiefly responsible for the increase in leaf area and the overall vigour of plants. The correct balance of nitrogen gives the foliage its dark green colour. Excess of nitrogen results in soft, sappy growth liable to fungus attack and frost damage; ripening of the fruit is retarded, and in general too much foliage is produced with inferior flowers and

fruits. Lack of nitrogen causes restricted growth with short, thin shoots. The plants grow spindly and upright, with small yellow leaves, small amounts of blossom, and premature leaf fall.

Phosphates
Phosphates are essential for root development, and the production and ripening of fruits and seeds. Phosphate deficiency leads to restricted root growth, resulting in small, dull, purple leaves. Blossom is reduced, and fruit set and seed production is poor.

Potash
Potash is important as a balancer of nitrogen; it hardens plants against frost and fungal diseases. Lack of potash leads to scorching of the leaf edges, particularly on fruit trees. Parts of the foliage may die or develop yellow spots. Deciduous plants lose their foliage early in the season.

Magnesium
Deficiency of minor chemicals in the soil is of little consequence, with the exception of magnesium. Magnesium is necessary for the production of chlorophyll, without which the foliage, especially on greenhouse tomatoes, turns brown and withers. Magnesium deficiency can be rectified by an application of Epsom salts.

Boron
Lack of boron may cause heart rot of beet, turnips, swedes, and sometimes potatoes. If the trouble persists, apply borax to the soil in small quantities.

Other trace elements
Most trace elements are found in organic animal manures, which should occasionally be used on the garden. Organic chemical compounds, such as sequestrene, can easily be applied to the soil to rectify some deficiency diseases.

Virus diseases

Viruses consist of minute particles that live in the sap of plants, and

are thus distributed throughout all the tissues.

The spread of virus diseases from plant to plant is most often carried out by sap-sucking insects, usually aphids. These virus carriers or vectors suck up virus particles from infected plants and pass the disease on to healthy tissues of other plants. Seeds of virus-infected plants are usually free of the disease, but plants that are vegetatively propagated will pass on the infection. As a safeguard against virus diseases, buy only certified plants and seeds.

Black currants
Reversion virus is a disease spread by big bud mites. The leaves on reverted shoots are coarse and have few serrations round the leaf edges. There is no chemical cure, and diseased bushes should be burnt and replaced with new, certified stock.

Raspberries
Mosaic is the most serious disease of raspberries. The symptoms are partial or general mottling, and curling and distortion of the foliage. Different viruses cause the varying symptoms, but all adversely affect the vigour of the canes, which will eventually cease to crop. Destroy all infected plants as soon as the disease is suspected, and control attack by aphids with regular sprayings of insecticide.

Strawberries
Strawberries are particularly prone to the two main virus diseases known as yellow edge and crinkle. Yellow edge virus infection appears as a dwarfing of the young leaves, which turn yellow and curl up at the edges, giving the whole plant a flattened look. 'Royal Sovereign' is a particularly susceptible variety. Aphids spread the disease from plant to plant. Crinkle virus shows as yellow spots on the foliage, which becomes wrinkled. Diseased plants must be removed and burnt, and new plants should be sprayed throughout the season with an insecticide to control the aphids.

Lettuces
Lettuce seedlings may be affected by the mosaic virus, which is carried in the seeds. When the disease does attack, the whole seed bed may be destroyed. Aphids carry the disease, which shows as mottled and puckered foliage and undeveloped hearts. Growth is so severely checked that the plants must be destroyed. Under glass, prevent attack by fumigating against aphids.

Tomatoes
Mosaic virus shows on the leaves as bright yellow blotches, and alternate areas of dark and light green; but strong-growing plants in the open may recover. Plants that look too sickly must be destroyed. Streaks and stripes are symptoms of different viruses that affect the leaves and later cause brown sunken pits on the fruits. The plants may recover with adequate feeding, but badly damaged plants should be destroyed.

Spotted wilt is a serious virus disease. Attacks on young tomato plants in the greenhouse may spread to such plants as gloxinias, cinerarias, primulas, schizanthus and zinnias.

On tomatoes the disease appears as a bronzing of the lower leaves. Circular brown spots sometimes develop on all the foliage, which droops and becomes oily-looking. The tops of the plants and flower trusses fail to develop. Diseased plants must be destroyed immediately, and care should be taken not to spread the disease to other susceptible plants.

Flowers
A number of virus diseases may infect decorative plants. The diseases, mainly of the mosaic type, chiefly attack the foliage, reducing the vigour of the plants. Flower heads may be distorted, or the petals may show white streaks. Mottling of the foliage occurs on irises, nasturtiums and sweet peas; the flowers may fail to develop.

Any sickly-looking plants should be pulled up and destroyed before the disease spreads.

Getting the best from cut flowers

Flowers which have been cared for correctly from the moment they are cut last the longest. Flowers of all types should be hardened (given the opportunity to become absolutely firm) before they are arranged. For this purpose they should be placed up to their necks in water for at least an hour, using a deep container. There are a number of flowers, such as forced tulips, which wilt as soon as they are brought into the dry warmth of the average living room unless given this treatment. However, quite shallow containers may suffice once the flowers are taking water properly.

Ways of treating stems

There are various ways of treating stems in order to speed the passage of water to the leaves and petals before they begin to dry out. The essential points are to expel any air bubbles from the stems, and to expose the inner tissues to water. Both objects can be achieved by splitting the ends of the stems upwards for $\frac{1}{2}$ in. or more—the taller the stem, the longer the cut. Exceptions to this rule are hollow-stemmed plants, such as delphiniums, which are not easy to arrange if they are split. Such stems are best cut on a slant while the end of the stem is held under water.

Immediately after treating the ends of the stems, stand them in water to cover as much of their length as possible. In many cases it is an advantage if the foliage is covered; this prevents loss of moisture from the leaf or petal surfaces, so that even a flower that has begun to wilt soon becomes firm. However, if the foliage of forced roses is submerged for any length of time and then brought into a room with a warm, dry atmosphere, it will become brittle

and papery. In this case it is better to strip the lower part of the stems and stand them under water.

Place in heated water

Flowers placed in tepid water (21°C, 70°F) shortly after cutting are less likely to wilt than flowers placed in cold water. Others, particularly shrubs, absorb water more readily if the ends of the stems are stood in about 2 in. of boiling water and allowed to remain there until they have become quite firm. This boiling water treatment is good for plants which are notoriously reluctant to take water—hollyhocks, euphorbias, viburnums and young hydrangeas.

Some shrubs—lilacs and young viburnums, for example—will not take water while sprays of foliage remain on the stems. These should be cut off and arranged separately. Partial or complete defoliation may also be necessary in the case of such shrubs as philadelphus, which have leaves growing among their flowers. Similar treatment may be necessary for flowers with tough-fibred stems, such as wallflowers and stocks. These ought always to have two-thirds of their stems in water.

Complete immersion

In some instances, only complete immersion is effective. Examples are branches of newly opened foliage; also finely cut mature foliage, such as ferns and hydrangeas. Generally, it is also necessary to split the ends of the stems. Frail flowers, such as annual gypsophila, can be drawn through water and then shaken to release surplus moisture. On the other hand, some flowers must be kept dry. Sweet peas, primroses and pansies suffer disfigurement if moisture remains on their petals. Cut them only in dry weather.

After arrangement, some flowers benefit from being sprayed; violets, mimosa and carnations are examples.

Early-flowering shrubs cut for forcing should either be immersed for a quarter of an hour or sprayed with an atomiser before being stood in tepid water in a warm place.

Some flowers—notably narcissi and bluebells—exude a slimy sap soon after they are cut. For this reason they should be kept apart from other flowers at this stage and the water changed frequently.

Flowers should not be crowded during the hardening stage because this can cause loss of colour. Bronze or red chrysanthemums become dull if jammed together in an inadequate container.

Care after arranging

Continuing care is necessary after the flowers have been arranged. Although it is unnecessary to change the water in the vases daily, try to ensure that it remains clean and fresh. Always strip the leaves from portions of stems which will be under water, to prevent decomposition, and add fresh water daily to keep the level high, using rain water if possible.

Glass containers are not ideal if they are likely to be stood in sunshine. The admission of light promotes considerable bacterial activity, causing the water to become foul. Bacterial activity is least troublesome in metal containers.

Adequate humidity is as essential for cut flowers indoors as it is for pot plants. Increased humidity is generated by natural evaporation of the water from a container, and because of this it is an advantage to certain flowers, such as snowdrops and other hardy winter flowers, to be arranged in containers with a large surface area.

Glossary of gardening terms

This section supplements the information given in the remainder of *The Gardening Year*. It defines a great many technical terms—words used to describe the parts of flowers, the shapes of leaves, or the intricacies of propagation. It also contains major entries on subjects as varied as children's gardens, soils and manures, and tools and equipment. (You will find a full list in the *Contents* at the start of the book.) The glossary also includes *At a Glance* tables, boxed off from the rest of the entries, summarising the whole year's work for each of the 25 subjects covered month by month in the *Twelve Months of Gardening* section

A

Acaricide
Chemical used to control mites.

Accelerator
A fertiliser, often nitrogenous, added to the compost heap to hasten rotting.

Acclimatisation
Accustoming plants to different (usually cooler and less protected) conditions from those under which they have been previously grown. Tomato plants, for example, should be stood in a cold frame for a day or two before being planted outdoors, to avoid a sudden check to their growth.

Acuminate: see Leaf shapes

Acute: see Leaf shapes

Adventitious
Applied to a root or shoot which forms where it would not normally be expected. Usually the result of cutting back the stem or root of a plant. When a branch is cut back, shoots may form from the stump, although no dormant buds were present.

Adventitious shoots

Aerator: see Tools

Aerial root
A root that grows from the stem of a plant, and does not usually root into the soil. Such roots absorb moisture from the atmosphere

Aerial roots

and may help to support the plant. An example is ivy, which clings by means of its aerial roots.

Algae
Primitive green plants that form a green scum on damp rocks, paths and flower pots, or choke stagnant pools with their threads. Controlled with an algicide.

Alginate
Chemical soil conditioner made from seaweed. It is used to bind together the fine particles in a heavy soil to produce a more crumbly texture.

Alpine
Strictly, a plant that grows naturally in the Alps or similar mountains. Alpines are adapted to mountainous environments by their dwarf, compact habit and deep, extensive root systems. The term usually refers to any plant suitable for growing in rock gardens, and includes dwarf forms of shrubs and conifers.

Alternate
Applied to leaves that are placed singly at different heights and on alternate sides of the stem.

Alternate leaves

Ammonium sulphamate: see Weeds and weedkillers

Annual
A plant, such as calendula or godetia, that germinates, grows, flowers and sets seeds within the space of one growing season.
Annual, half-hardy. Annual, such as ageratum or tagetes, that will not withstand frost and must either be raised from seed under glass and planted out when danger of frost is past, or must be sown outdoors in late May or early June.
Annual, hardy. Annual, such as centaurea

(cornflower) or delphinium (larkspur), that will stand frost. May be sown outdoors in September–October and over-wintered, or sown outdoors in March–April (clarkia).
Annual, tender. Annual that usually requires constant greenhouse cultivation, such as celosia or schizanthus.

Anther
The pollen-bearing terminal point of the stalk or filament, that forms the flower's male organ, the stamen. See **Flower parts**.

Apex
The tip of a shoot or branch. A shoot situated at the apex of a plant is termed 'apical'.

Aquatic
Plant adapted to live in water. It may float on the surface and root in the mud at the bottom of a pool or stream, like nymphaea (water lily), be free-floating, like eichhornia (water hyacinth), or be completely submerged, like myriophyllum, which is also an oxygenator.

Arboretum
A collection of species of trees and shrubs grown for their botanical rather than their decorative interest. There are well-known arboreta at Kew; at Wisley, Surrey; at Bedgebury, Kent; at Westonbirt, Gloucestershire; and at Winkworth, Surrey.

Attenuate: see Leaf shapes

Axil
The angle between a leaf stalk and the stem to which it is joined. This angle often contains a leaf bud or flower bud.

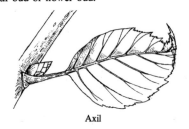

Axil

Azaleodendron
Cross between a rhododendron and an azalea. Flowers in May.

THE YEAR AT A GLANCE

Alpines

MARCH

Firm plants or labels loosened by frost.
Scatter slug pellets.
Hoe lightly between plants to kill weed seedlings, using a short-handled onion hoe.
Watch for signs of germination in boxes of seeds placed outside for weathering, and move the choicer kinds to an unheated greenhouse or frame.
Plant nursery-raised alpines as soon as possible after delivery. Plants that flower from June onwards may show signs of die-back after winter, so propagate by division where possible.
Renew by division carpeting plants such as arenarias and raoulias.

Under glass

Plant out root cuttings in pots or boxes when they have made leaves.
Sow seeds of quicker-growing alpines in a frame or cold greenhouse.

APRIL

Re-plant plants which lack vigour, or which have been lifted slightly out of the ground.
Dig the ground and apply a general ferti-liser after lifting these plants. Be careful not to damage self-sown seedlings around some short-lived plants.

Under glass

Prick out seedlings raised from seeds sown in December or March.
Move outdoors seedlings raised under glass after the middle of the month.

MAY

Control weeds by hoeing or hand pulling.
Trim aubrietas and other plants after flowering to prevent seeding.

Dust soil mixture between rosettes of saxifrages which have become ragged.

JUNE

Continue weeding and hoeing.
Trim dead flowers from aubrietas and saxifrages to prevent seeding, and clip other plants to keep them tidy.
In showery weather, transplant recently planted alpines which have been wrongly sited.
Irrigate plants in dry weather, preferably using a fine mist in the evening.

JULY

Continue weeding and trimming.
Water if necessary.
Mounded or carpeting plants not showing new growth should have soil mixture and fertiliser worked into them.
Save seeds of aquilegias, primulas and other short-lived alpines.
Sow primula seed as soon as it is ripe.
Store other seeds in a dry place.

AUGUST

Take cuttings of alpines, such as heli-anthemum and dianthus, which have out-grown their vigour, and insert in prepared soil in a frame or under a cloche.
Spray cuttings daily in hot weather, shade from hot sun, and exclude draughts.
Increase ventilation as they grow.

SEPTEMBER

Transplant any plants which need re-siting.
Start making a new rockery; but first consider whether a raised alpine bed might not be better. Choose an open, well drained position, away from trees. Allow several weeks to pass for soil and rocks to settle before planting.

OCTOBER

Plant seedlings or rooted cuttings this month, except for pot-grown plants, which can go in at any time.
Water plants in if soil is dry.
Renew writing on labels.
Apply slug pellets in damp weather.

NOVEMBER

Complete trimming and dead-heading, saving seeds if desired.
Remove fallen leaves from the rock garden.
Plant shrubs, heathers and pot-grown plants.
Dress surface of level ground with small shingle or stone chippings $\frac{1}{2}$–1 in. deep, or fork over the surface soil.

DECEMBER

Remove fallen leaves and dig vacant spaces between plants.
Sow slow-germinating seeds and those that need exposure to frost to assist germination. Use clay pots, pans or shallow boxes.
Do not water seed containers, but stand outdoors, choosing a hard surface where worms cannot reach them and away from the drip from trees.

JANUARY

Remove remaining fallen leaves and dig vacant spaces between plants.
Order nursery-grown plants for delivery in early spring.
Complete sowing of alpines that require exposure to frost.

FEBRUARY

Firm into place any plants loosened by frost.
Dress soil with fine stone chippings to sup-press weeds.
Press back into place labels loosened by frost, and renew writing if necessary.
Remove annual grass and other weed seedlings.
Apply slug pellets among plants.
Unpack plants delivered in frosty weather, stand them in shallow boxes, and pack them round with damp peat.

Under glass

Propagate some alpines by root cuttings. Root them in boxes of sandy compost in a cold frame and plant into pots or boxes when they have produced leaves.

B

Ball

The compact mass of roots and soil of a well rooted, pot-grown plant. A plant will become established more readily if the ball is not broken when the plant is transplanted. Nursery-grown shrubs, sold as balled specimens, have their roots wrapped in sacking.

Ball

Bark-bound

Applied to trees that are stunted in growth due to lack of moisture or plant foods. The bark becomes hard and unyielding, and further growth is restricted. A bark-bound tree may cure itself by splitting naturally along the length of the trunk; otherwise the bark should be cut with a sharp knife, and the wound sealed with grafting wax.

Bark ringing

The removal of a partial or complete ring of bark from an apple or pear tree. This restricts growth but encourages formation of fruit buds. See also *Fruit* MAY.

Semi-circles overlap

Protective binding

Basal

Applied to a shoot or bud arising from the base of a plant.

Basal-rooting. Term describing a bulb that roots from the base only. Most European and American species of lilies are basal-rooting.

Basal-rooting lily bulb

Basic slag: see **Fertilisers and manures**

Bastard trenching: see **Soil (Soil operations)**

Batter

Method of trimming a hedge or building a retaining wall so that the sides slope inwards to make the top narrower than the base. Such a hedge will keep its shape better than one with vertical sides, particularly when weighed down with snow.

Batter

Beard

Dense growth of long hairs, usually yellow, which occurs at the upper end of the falls of flag irises.

Beaumont period: see **Weather**

Bed

Any clearly defined plot of cultivated ground within a garden. It may be set in grass or a paved surround, and may be used for a particular purpose, such as a rose bed.

Island bed. Isolated bed, usually of an informal, curved shape, arranged with the taller flowers in the centre and low-growing specimens near the edge.

Raised bed. Specially constructed bed, used particularly for growing alpines. The two main purposes are to provide the plants with well drained conditions, and to display them more effectively nearer to eye-level.

Bedding plants

Any plants raised in quantity for a temporary garden display. A wide range of hardy and half-hardy annuals, biennials and perennials and some tender species can be used. Planting or **bedding out**, is done twice a year: in late spring and in early autumn.

Benomyl

A systemic chemical fungicide that controls a wide range of diseases. It can penetrate the leaves to enter the plant sap and is effective on mildews, rose black spot, botrytis, fruit scab and lawn fungus diseases. Should not be used exclusively: some fungi can build up tolerance.

Berry

Fruit in which the seeds are protected only by a fleshy outer covering, such as gooseberries and black currants.

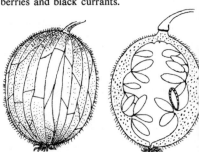

Berry. External and internal diagram of a gooseberry, showing the fleshy outer covering protecting the seeds within

BHC: see **HCH**

Biennial

Plant that completes its life-cycle in two growing seasons. Digitalis (foxglove), for example, germinates and forms a rosette of leaves in its first season. The second year it produces a flower stem, after which it flowers, sets seeds, and dies.

Biennial bearing

The habit of bearing alternately light and heavy fruit crops. The habit may start as a result of frost killing the blossoms one year, resulting in a heavy crop the following year.

Bigeneric

Applied to a hybrid which combines genetic factors of two different genera. Most hybrids are the result of crossing plants of different species, but of the same genus. For instance *Fatshedera lizei* is a bigeneric hybrid between *Hedera helix* (ivy) and *Fatsia japonica* (figleaf palm)—different genera, but both members of the plant family *Araliaceae*.

Bipinnate: see Leaf shapes

Bisexual

Applied to a plant that has both stamens and pistil in the same flower.

Blanching

Excluding light from the stems of celery and leeks, and from the leaves of chicory and seakale. This makes them more palatable and tender for eating by preventing the formation of chlorophyll. The parts to be blanched can be earthed up, wrapped in thick paper, or covered with a flower pot.

Flower-pot blanching

Bleeding

Excessive loss of sap from a tree or plant after being cut. This is more apparent in spring when the sap is rising; vines should not be pruned then. Beetroots whose skin is damaged during lifting will also bleed, and lose their red pigment.

Blind

Applied to a plant without a terminal growth or flower bud. This is usually due to physical damage or disease, and results in cessation of growth.

Bog garden

Artificial garden, constructed in association with a stream or water garden. The marshy soil, which must be permanently wet, is suitable for growing such plants as water irises and rushes.

Bolting

Running to seed, particularly prematurely. Lettuce may bolt in hot, dry weather, either before or as soon as the hearts have been formed.

Bolting (lettuce)

Bone-meal: see Fertilisers and manures

Bonsai

A dwarf tree. The dwarfing technique, invented by the Japanese, consists in severe

Bonsai (conifer)

Bonsai (conifer)

root restriction, and pruning and pinching back of growing shoots. Pine, larch and maple are suitable subjects for bonsai training. The gnarled appearance of a bonsai tree, which should be grown in a shallow container to restrict root growth, is achieved by cutting back the main stem repeatedly over a number of years. The shape of the tree is induced by careful training on wires and strings.

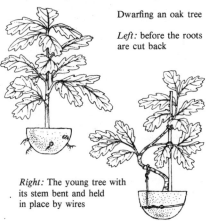

Dwarfing an oak tree

Left: before the roots are cut back

Right: The young tree with its stem bent and held in place by wires

Bordeaux mixture

General-purpose protective fungicide which will prevent a number of fungus diseases, such as tomato and potato blight, and leaf spot on celery and chrysanthemums. Commercial preparations can be bought in powder or paste form to mix with water, or a mixture can be made up as follows: 1 lb. of copper sulphate to $1\frac{1}{4}$ lb. of hydrated lime and 10 gal. of water, mixed in a non-metallic container. The preparation must be used immediately on the foliage, as its effectiveness is quickly lost.

Border
A cultivated rectangular area of a garden, running beside a path, boundary fence or wall. Borders are chiefly planted with herbaceous subjects; but roses, fruit bushes (with fruit trees trained against the boundary wall) and annual flowers in front are equally effective.

Border, marking out: see Weights and measures

Bract
A modified leaf at the base of a flower stalk. Bracts are often brightly coloured, like the scarlet bracts of poinsettias, and may be mistaken for petals. The true flowers of poinsettias are yellow and insignificant.

Bract (poinsettia)

Brassica
Generic term for members of the cabbage family, such as broccoli, Brussels sprouts, cabbages, cauliflowers, kales, savoys, swedes and turnips.

Break
Side growth or shoot formed from the main stem of a plant. Formation of these shoots

Break (chrysanthemum)

occurs naturally in such plants as chrysanthemums. Artificial stopping or pinching out of the growing tips encourages new shoots earlier than when the plant is left to grow naturally.

Breastwood
Vigorous shoots on mature branches, the result of hard pruning of older trees. They are of no permanent value and should be cut out completely during summer.

Broadcast
Seeds sown broadcast are spread evenly over an area of ground, rather than in drills. Grass seed is sown in this way, as are annuals for irregular groups.

Bromeliads
A family of stemless or short-stemmed plants with stiff, channelled leaves that direct water inwards to the crown. A number of bromeliads are grown as house plants, including *Nidularium marechali* and *Vriesia splendens*.

Bud
Embryo growing point of a shoot from which leaves or flowers will develop.
Axillary bud. One situated in the axil of a leaf.

Axillary bud

Crown bud. Flower bud at the tip of a shoot and surrounded by other flower buds.
Dormant bud. One that is inactive, especially on trees.
Fruit bud. One from which, on fruit trees, leaves, flowers and eventually fruits will develop.
Fruit buds are larger than **growth buds** from which leaves or a shoot will appear.
Terminal bud. One at the end of a shoot, from which a further shoot will develop, with its own terminal bud.

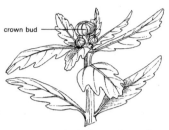

Crown bud (chrysanthemum)

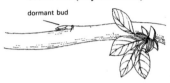

Dormant bud (fruit tree)

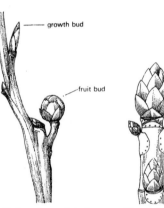

Fruit and growth bud   Terminal bud
(pear tree)   (horse chestnut)

Bud burst: see Bud stages

Budding: see Propagation

Bud nicking
Cutting a small crescent of bark from beneath a bud of a fruit tree to stop the bud 'bursting' and so affect the shape of the tree.

Bud notching
Cutting a small crescent of bark from above a bud to stimulate growth and to produce a wide and strong angle between the shoot and the main branch. Bud nicking and

notching may be used in the early stages of training fruit trees, to encourage branches to form where they are wanted.

Bud notching

Bud rubbing
The removal of fruit buds by hand in order to limit the crop. Allow the buds to develop to pink-bud stage (see **Bud stages**), and remove them just before they open. The leaves, which help to feed the tree, should be left intact.

Bud stages
Different stages of fruit-tree growth, from late winter through early spring. It is important to recognise the various stages, as spray applications are determined by growth development rather than the date. When dormant—or apparently inactive—buds start to increase in size and the outer scales begin to loosen, the buds are said to be **swelling.** This is followed by the **breaking stage,** when green leaves can be seen at the apex of the buds. At **bud burst** these leaves begin to separate. At **green-cluster stage** the bud

Bud stages

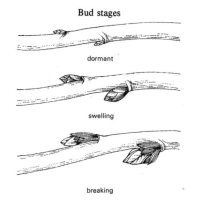

dormant

swelling

breaking

Bud stages (apple tree)

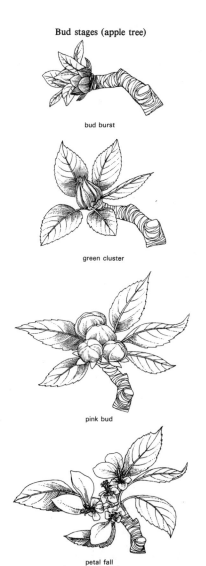

bud burst

green cluster

pink bud

petal fall

scales have dropped off, and a tight cluster of green flower buds can be seen in each leaf rosette. This is succeeded by **pink-bud stage,** when the flower buds are not yet open, but display a trace of pink or white. **Petal fall** occurs after full blossom and before the formation of fruitlets (see also illustration under *Fruit,* MARCH).

Bulb
Swollen, underground bud with fleshy scales. The scales, which are the storage organs, may completely encircle the bulb and be enclosed in thin, drier scales (daffodils, narcissi), or they may be smaller, numerous and gaping (lilies). At the centre of the bulb are the embryo leaves and flowers for the next growing season. Some bulbs, such as tulips, die as the season advances, but are replaced by two or more new bulbs at the base of the old one. Other bulbs, such as narcissi, decrease in size, but swell again as the foliage dies down, and also produce one or more offsets or bulbils.

Bulbs. Daffodil and lily

Bulb fibre
Medium in which bulbs are grown for indoor decoration, consisting of peat, oyster shell and charcoal. Bulbs grown in this mixture live on the food stored within themselves, and are exhausted after flowering.

Bulblet, bulbil
Tiny bulb which forms on a parent bulb. On *Lilium tigrinum* bulblets also form in the leaf axils. Detached from the parent bulb, bulblets can be grown on separately and will in time reach flowering size.

Bush
Low shrub with no definite leader, and with branches all arising near ground level.
Bush tree. Usually a fruit tree, with a trunk of 3 ft. or less before the lowest branches.

THE YEAR AT A GLANCE

Bulbs

MARCH

Choose new varieties for planting in late summer.

Remove flower heads from daffodils as they fade.

Plant out bulbs grown in pots which have finished flowering. Plant acidantheras in mild districts. Lift, divide, and re-plant crowded snowdrops. In cold districts plant de Caen and St. Brigid anemones for summer flowering.

Under glass

Give adequate water and fertiliser to hippeastrums and clivias in flower.

APRIL

Hand-weed beds of daffodils and tulips grown for cut flowers.

Remove faded flowers from early-flowering bulbs.

Water bulbous plants copiously in dry weather.

Plant arum lilies in open ground in mild districts.

Leave seed pods intact on scillas, muscaris and other small bulbs to seed themselves and produce more new bulbs.

Divide schizostylis clumps.

Under glass

Continue watering and feeding hippeastrums and clivias.

Pot up tuberoses for flowering under glass or indoors.

MAY

Remove dead blooms from daffodils and hyacinths.

Lift daffodils and tulips from beds to make way for summer bedding. Heel in bulbs to die back gradually.

Weed rows of bulbs grown for cutting, and water in dry spells.

Plant crinum bulbs in a south-facing border or in tubs.

JUNE

Start lifting spring bulbs whose foliage has turned yellow. Place bulbs in shallow boxes and dry in a well ventilated shed. When dry remove dead leaves, roots and skins, then store in a cool, dry shed.

Plant de Caen anemone corms for autumn and winter flowering in mild districts.

Plant out arum lilies, or stand pots outdoors for their summer rest.

Under glass

Dry off lachenalias flowered in pots.

Pot or re-pot vallota bulbs.

JULY

Lift and store tulips and daffodils.

Control eelworms and bulb fly grubs by removing and burning infested bulbs.

Plant autumn-flowering bulbs, especially *Amaryllis belladonna*. Plant *Nerine bowdenii* outdoors; also autumn crocus and *Sternbergia lutea*. Plant colchicum in small clumps in rough grass.

Prepare ground for planting bulbs which are to provide cut flowers in the spring, by digging, removing weeds, and applying fertiliser, particularly potash.

AUGUST

Complete any outstanding bulb lifting.

Plant daffodils by the end of the month.

Complete orders for spring-flowering bulbs to be planted this autumn in bowls, for bedding or cutting.

SEPTEMBER

Plant bulbs between shrubs or herbaceous plants, on rock gardens or in lawns, preferably in groups.

Remove summer bedding as it fades and replace with bulbs. First plan the layout, then plant from the centre outwards. Where interplanting, set the plants first and put in the bulbs afterwards.

Indoors and under glass

Re-pot arum lilies for winter flowering.

Prepare pots and bowls of bulbs to flower from Christmas to Easter, using bulb fibre.

OCTOBER

Complete bulb planting.

Hoe beds of daffodils or spray with a contact herbicide to control weeds. Follow with a residual herbicide.

Indoors and under glass

Lift half-hardy summer-flowering bulbs and dry as quickly as possible. Store them in a cool, frost-free, dry place in shallow boxes. Examine bulbs and bowls, and water if fibre is dry.

NOVEMBER

Complete planting of tulips.

Indoors and under glass

Examine pots and bowls of bulbs and move inside any with 1 in. shoots, placing them in cool conditions not exceeding 10°C (50°F). Give sufficient water. 'Paper White' and 'Soleil d'Or' narcissi may be taken straight into warmer conditions.

DECEMBER

Hoe beds of late-planted tulips or spray with a contact herbicide to control weeds. Follow with a residual herbicide.

Indoors and under glass

Examine bowls and pots of bulbs and move them indoors as they are ready.

Give bowls or pots a quarter turn each day to ensure even growth.

Study catalogues and order bulbs for spring planting.

JANUARY

Bring in bulbs for indoor flowering as they become ready.

Plant those which have finished flowering in odd corners of the garden.

FEBRUARY

Bring in the last of the bulbs for indoor flowering as they become ready. Plant those which have finished flowering in odd corners of the garden. If the weather is cold and wet, keep them in a frost-free greenhouse until planting conditions are better.

C

Cacti and other succulents

Succulent plants have become adapted to survive periods of drought. Many are inhabitants of deserts, although some come from other regions, where for one reason or another water is not always available. The best known are the American cacti, all of which belong to the same family. There are also many succulent plants found in the desert regions of South Africa, distributed among a number of families. On the whole, these plants need slightly warmer conditions in the winter than the cacti, and suffer less from being grown in a heated living-room.

Most growers have a mixed collection of succulent plants. The following cultivation hints will suit most of them. Desert plants need as much light as possible. If you grow your plants on a window-sill, stand them outdoors from May until September. Cacti need a cool, dry winter rest if they are to flower well the next year. A winter temperature of 5°C (41°F) is adequate for most succulents. A good compost is 1 part grit and 3 parts John Innes potting compost No. 2. When grown in this open compost, succulents can be watered freely during the summer; from April to September they should not be allowed to dry out. After September, gradually reduce watering and leave plants dry during December and January. As the light improves in February, gradually re-start watering.

Many cacti and succulents may be pro-pagated quite easily from cuttings, preferably in spring and summer. Where offsets can be easily detached, they can be potted up at once; but when a stem has to be cut off, it should be allowed to dry for a few days before being potted, or it may rot.

Many of these plants can be grown from seed. The most common types are often available from the larger seedsmen, and specialist nurseries supply a wide selection. A good compost may be made from 3 parts of well sterilised John Innes seed compost to 1 part of sharp sand. Place this on plenty of crocks in pots or pans, and carefully smooth it down on the surface. Do not compress. Scatter the seeds on the surface; most seeds should not be covered, but large seeds can have a light covering of sand. Very large seeds, such as those of opuntia and stapelia, should be pressed individually into the surface of the compost and planted edge-on. Soak the pots in water, cover them with glass or plastic, and place in a temperature of 21–27°C (70–81°F). The plants need light when germination starts, but should be shaded from direct sunlight. If heat is available, sow seed early in the year; if not, wait until late spring.

Like other greenhouse plants, cacti and succulents are prone to some pests and diseases. The most common pest is the mealy bug—a small, whitish creature, which often leaves a woolly deposit on the stem. It can be controlled by a nicotine spray, or malathion. The root mealy bug attacks the roots of plants, and is controlled by regular re-potting, and watering with a nicotine solution.

The most likely disease is rotting, due to too much water in the resting period, or too low a temperature in winter in the case of some more delicate species. If the rot takes place at the base and is not too extensive, cut off the top and treat it as a cutting. The cut surfaces may be dusted with flowers of sulphur or captan to prevent infection.

In the following descriptions, C = cactus, S = succulent.

Aporocactus (C)

A. flagelliformis, the rat's tail cactus, originates from Mexico. The stems are long, thin, cylindrical and pendent; the cerise flowers appear in the spring. It needs a sunny position, and plenty of water in the growing season. It should be watched carefully as the long 'tails', which may reach 3 ft., are a favourite feeding ground for the mealy bug pest. Propagate by cutting the tails, drying for a few days, and potting up. Long tails may be divided.

Astrophytum (C)

A. myriostigma is found at high altitudes in Mexico. It grows to about 6 in.; the entire body is covered with silvery scales, and the shiny yellow flowers, which may be sweetly scented, flower in summer and autumn. Astrophytums are solitary, but grow rapidly from seed, which often germinates within two or three days. These plants come from very dry regions, and require an extra-porous compost and careful watering.

Chamaecereus (C)

C. silvestrii (peanut cactus) originated in

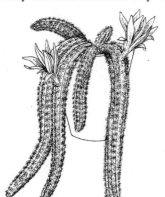

Aporocactus flagelliformis

Astrophytum myriostigma

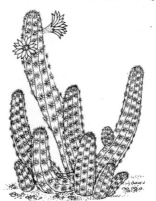

Chamaecereus silvestrii

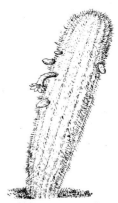

Cleistocactus strausii

Crassula lycopodiodes

Echeveria derenbergii

Echinocactus grusonii

Echinocereus knippelianus

Argentina. The plant consists of many stem segments about $\frac{1}{2}$ in. thick and 2–3 in. long; the segments are easily detached and can be re-rooted to produce fresh plants. The fiery red flowers are produced freely in the early summer. If kept dry in winter, it is quite hardy; a cold, dry winter rest improves the flowering. Propagate by shoots easily removed from main stems.

Cleistocactus (C)
C. strausii comes from the mountains of Bolivia, and is hardy if kept dry in winter. It forms a column about 2 in. in diameter, densely covered in fine white spines, giving a silvery effect. Specimens above 3 ft. in height may flower. The dark red blooms (rarely produced), about 5 in. long and only partially open, appear in summer on the sides of the upper stem. Propagate from seed, or by cutting off branches at the base.

Crassula (S)
C. lycopodiodes is an easily grown and popular plant, native to Cape Province. The stems are long and thin, covered with crowded, scale-like leaves. Insignificant yellow flowers are formed in summer. Propagate by removing branches and potting up.

Echeveria (S)
E. derenbergii is one of a large group of rosette plants from Mexico. The pale green leaves are covered with a whitish waxy coating, and each leaf has a red point. Although many echeverias have long flower stems, those of this plant are quite short; the reddish-yellow flowers appear in spring. It is an attractive plant, although after the winter it may

become leggy. It should be beheaded in the spring and the top re-rooted. Offsets are readily formed.

Echinocactus (C)
E. grusonii is a golden, ball-shaped plant from Mexico. It is very slow-growing, and many years would be needed to produce a plant 6 in. across from seed. The 24 in. diameter specimens sometimes seen in botanical gardens are of an immense age. However, the small plants are most attractive with their dense, pale yellow spines. The small yellow flowers are formed only on large plants, and rarely in our climate, where the sunlight is not usually intense enough to stimulate bud formation. Propagate from seed.

Echinocereus (C)
E. knippelianus, a five-ribbed, dark green cactus, with insignificant spines, is found in Central Mexico. It is slow-growing, and will eventually reach a diameter of 2 in. The pale pink flowers are small for this family—about $1\frac{1}{2}$ in. across—and appear in the early summer. Water carefully. Propagate from seed.

Echinopsis (C)
E. rhodotricha, a native of Argentina and Paraguay, is one of the larger-growing echinopsis, reaching 12–24 in. in height. It will flower in spring, when only 6 in. tall. The long, tubular, white flowers open in the evening and last through the following day. Hardy if kept dry in the winter months. Propagate by offsets.

Epiphyllum (C)
The easiest epiphyllums to flower are the scarlet hybrids, sold as *E. ackermannii*. They

need a rich soil, with plenty of leaf-mould, and generous watering during the summer. All cultivated epiphyllums are hybrids (except for some in specialist collections); the original plants come from tropical forests. They need some protection from full sun, and should be kept above 5°C (41°F) in winter; they will survive lower temperatures, but will bloom less freely. Do not allow them to dry out completely. The flowers, which may be 6 in. across, open about May or June. Propagate by cutting stems.

Eriocactus (C)
E. leninghausii, although coming from Brazil, is comparatively hardy. It is a cylindrical plant, covered in long, golden, bristly spines. Yellow flowers are produced in spring and summer on the tops of old specimens, which also produce side shoots, although younger plants are solitary. Rather a slow grower.

Euphorbia (S)
E. meloformis is one of the extremely succulent euphorbias from Cape Province. The grey-green plant body is globular, with deep ribs. The persistent flower stalks become woody and spine-like. Male and female flowers occur on separate plants. Tiny, greenish flowers are produced in spring and summer. Propagate by seed, which germinates readily if fresh.

Faucaria (S)
F. tigrina, a South African desert plant, has several pairs of crowded, toothed leaves. They may be up to 2 in. long and 1 in. wide at the base, and are covered with white dots. The flowers are golden-yellow, about 2 in. across,

Echinopsis rhodotricha

Epiphyllum (hybrid)

Eriocactus leninghausii

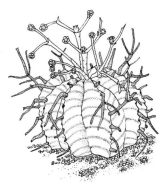

Euphorbia meloformis

and produced in the autumn. Plants should be rested in winter and early spring. Watering may be re-started about May. Propagate by splitting, or from seed.

Gasteria (S)

G. verrucosa, a native of South Africa, has leaves about 6 in. long, covered with white warts; it is almost stemless. The small, reddish, bell-shaped flowers are carried on the long, straggly leaves mainly in summer and autumn. Gasterias hybridise easily, and plants are usually propagated by removing the small offsets formed at the base of the plant.

Gymnocalycium (C)

G. multiflorum, found mainly in Argentina, is a bluish-green cactus. A large specimen may be 6 in. across and up to 4 in. in height; flowering size is 3–4 in. The ribs are cut into

prominent, chin-like warts (characteristic of gymnocalyciums in general). The spines are spreading, thick and sharp, and the funnel-shaped flowers are nearly 2 in. long, brownish-green outside and whitish-pink inside. Propagate by seed.

Hamatocactus (C)

H. setispinus is a free-flowering plant from Mexico and Texas. Specimens less than 2 in. across bear large golden flowers with red throats in summer. Grows to about 5 in. The stout, hooked central spines give the plant an attractive appearance, even when it is out of flower. If kept dry, it is comparatively hardy in winter. Propagate from seed or basal shoots.

Haworthia (S)

H. reinwartii is an attractive, succulent plant

from Cape Province. The leaves form an elongated rosette, and are covered with pearly tubercles. It grows to about 6 in., and the small, whitish flowers, borne on long stems, are produced over a long period, mainly in summer. Propagation is by small, rooted offsets.

Lithops (S)

L. olivacea is one of the stone mimicry plants from the South African deserts. The plant bodies occur in clumps, but each consists of only two leaves, very thick and with attractive markings on the tops. They grow to about $1–1\frac{1}{2}$ in. The colour is dark olive-green to brownish, and the bright yellow flowers are produced in autumn. A well drained soil is essential. The growing period is from spring to late autumn, after which water should be

Faucaria tigrina

Gasteria verrucosa

Gymnocalycium multiflorum

Hamatocactus setispinus

423

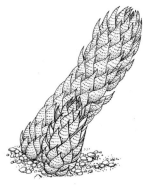

Haworthia reinwartii

Lithops olivacea

Lobivia hertrichiana

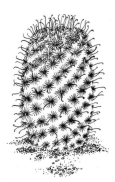

Mammillaria bombycina

reduced, and none given until the following spring. Wait until the old leaves have completely shrivelled away before resuming watering. By this time, new leaves will have formed. Propagate by splitting clumps, or from seed.

Lobivia (C)
Though lobivia is an anagram of Bolivia, *L. hertrichiana* comes in fact from Peru. It forms large clumps, although individual heads are not more than 2 in. across, and grows up to 4 in. high. The offsets may be removed and will root easily; in fact, many will already have roots. The bright red flowers last only one day, but are produced profusely in summer.

Mammillaria (C)
M. bombycina, a native of Mexico, has bright green clustering stems, at first globular but becoming elongated, growing to about 2½ in.; white woolly tufts are produced at the top. Some of the spines are white and glossy, and others are reddish-yellow and hooked at the tips. The bright red flowers are produced in rings at the top of the plant in spring and summer. Propagate from offsets or seed. *M. zeilmanniana*, also from Mexico, is one of the few red-flowered mammillarias to bloom as a young plant. It branches quite freely, and the stems, which grow to 2 in., are covered with whitish spines. The rings of purplish-red flowers, produced in spring and summer, are almost fluorescent in their brilliance. One of the most beautiful of all mammillarias. Propagate from offsets or seed.

Notocactus (C)
N. tabularis will eventually make a spherical plant about 5 in. across. The many-ribbed body, growing to about 3 in., is dark green and covered with fine spines. The large, golden flowers have red throats and are freely produced in early summer. The plants grow readily from seed and bloom when quite young. A native of Uruguay, it is hardy if kept dry in winter.

Opuntia (C)
O. microdasys rufida is one of the Mexican prickly pears. The bright green pads, which are really stem segments, are dotted with pincushion-like, dark red areoles; these are spineless, but contain many tiny barbed bristles (glochids), and care must be taken in handling the plant, as the glochids can irritate the skin. An attractive plant up to 12 in. high can be grown in a 6 in. pot, although the yellow flowers are rarely produced in pot-grown specimens. A winter temperature

Mammillaria zeilmanniana

Notocactus tabularis

Opuntia cylindrica

Opuntia microdasys rufida

Pachyphytum oviferum

Parodia aureispina

Rebutia minuscula

Schlumbergera gaertneri

of 5°C (41°F) is sufficient, but disfiguring spots may develop; these can be avoided with slightly higher temperatures. The ordinary *O. microdasys* has yellow areoles, and the variety *albispina* has white ones. Propagate by removing 'pads', or from seed. *O. cylindrica*, which comes from Ecuador and Peru, is not of the prickly pear type. The stems are up to 3 ft. high, and cylindrical, and seldom branch naturally, though branching specimens can be produced by beheading the plant. The bright green stems are covered with flat warts, and small cylindrical leaves appear on the new growth.

Pachyphytum (S)
P. oviferum (the sugar almond plant), a native of Mexico, makes a tiny, branched shrub up to 3–4 in. high, with fat, egg-shaped leaves which are covered with white 'meal' and

Stapelia variegata

sometimes flushed pink. When watering, do not splash the leaves, since they mark easily. Be careful not to touch them, or the bloom will rub off, leaving a disfiguring mark. Propagate by splitting off branches and re-rooting.

Parodia (C)
P. aureispina, found in Argentina, is a slow-growing cactus which will eventually make a plant about 6 in. high. It is almost globular and covered with pale gold spines. The deep golden flowers are produced in large quantities during the early summer. Parodias readily lose their roots if they do not have very good drainage. Propagate from seed.

Rebutia (C)
The rebutias are small cacti, free-flowering and easy to grow. *R. minuscula* grows among the grasslands of Argentina; sometimes it blooms so profusely that it will shrivel and

Trichocereus spachianus

die afterwards. The flowers, produced in spring, are red and self-fertile; seedlings are often found around the parent plant. The adult is about 2 in. across and 1–1½ in. high, and clusters freely. Propagate by offsets or seed.

Schlumbergera (C)
S. gaertneri (syn. *Rhipsalidopsis gaertneri*), the Easter cactus, has scarlet flowers on 6 in. stems, opening around Easter. It comes from the jungles of Brazil, and needs some warmth and moisture all the year round. During summer, place it outdoors in semi-shade. It is an excellent plant for a hanging basket. Propagate from stem segments.

Stapelia (S)
S. variegata is a spreading, densely clustered plant, with grey-green stems about 4 in. high, and without leaves. It is found in desert regions of South Africa, where it is pollinated by flies. For this reason, the flowers, although attractively marked in brown and yellow, are evil-smelling. The flowers open in late summer, and are followed by very elongated seed pods. The seeds are wind-dispersed. Propagate by splitting clumps or by seed, which germinates rapidly.

Trichocereus (C)
Of the many *Trichocerei*, *T. spachianus* is one of the most attractive and most frequently grown. It is native to Argentina, and is a tall, cylindrical plant, branching freely from the base. It can grow to 4 ft., but 12–18 in. is more common. The stem is bright green and ribbed, with yellowish-brown spines. For those who wish to graft cacti, this is one of the best grafting stocks.

Calcifuge
Plant which will not grow in limy soil. Examples are rhododendrons, camellias and many heathers.

Callus
Tissue which forms over a wounded surface, especially where a limb has been cut off a tree. Callus also forms at the base of a cutting to heal the wound before roots are produced.

Calomel (mercurous chloride)
Effective as an insecticide against cabbage-root fly and onion fly, or as a fungicide to control club-root disease of brassicas, and some turf diseases. Calomel is usually compounded as a 4 per cent dust which can be spread along seed drills, or used as a dip for seedlings before transplanting. The dust is harmful to fish and should be kept away from ponds.

Calyx
The outer green ring or whorl of a flower, consisting of a number of sepals which enclose the petals. The tubular calyx of a vigorous carnation or pink bloom may burst and produce a shapeless flower. This can be overcome by placing an elastic band round the calyx at an early stage in its development. See **Flower parts.**

Cambium
The narrow layer of growing tissue between the bark and the wood of most plants. The moist, bright green tissue forms the callus and roots on cuttings, heals wounds, and causes grafts and inserted buds to unite.

Cambium layer

Capillary watering: see Greenhouses

Capsule
Seed case with divisions that give it a number of compartments. The seed heads of irises and poppies are the better-known examples of capsules.

Capsule (poppy), cut away to show seeds

Captan
Protective fungicide, used to combat apple and pear scab, and grey mould on strawberries. Dusting bulbs, such as begonias, gloxinias and tulips, will protect the bulbs against a number of fungus diseases. Captan, which can be obtained as a spray or dust, is poisonous to fish, and should not be used near a pond unless the pond is given a temporary cover, such as a plastic sheet.

Carpel
One of the divisions of a pistil.

Catch crop
Fast-growing crop grown on a piece of ground in the interval between harvesting one main crop and sowing or planting the next. A crop of lettuces or radishes can be grown on a plot which has carried early potatoes, before spring cabbages are planted on it.

Catkin
Flower spike, often pendulous, which is composed of stalkless, unisexual flowers. Birch, hazel and willow bear catkins.

Catkin (hazel)

Cell
The basic unit of all plant tissue. It consists of a nucleus embedded in protoplasm and cell sap, surrounded by a membranous cell wall. Plant growth is caused by cells at the growing points increasing by division.

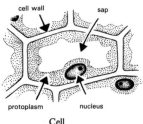

Cell

Cement mixes: see Weights and measures

Certified stock
Applied to, for example, strawberries and seed potatoes which have been certified by the Ministry of Agriculture as being free of certain diseases and pests and true to name.

Chalk: see Soil

Cheshunt compound
Soluble copper compound used to control damping-off disease in seedlings. Seed boxes should be watered with the solution as germination takes place.

Children's gardens
It needs more than an out-of-the-way corner of the garden and a handful of left-over plants to encourage a child's interest in gardening. However small the plot, it must be well drained and fertile to ensure the maximum chance of success. It should also be in a prominent position, for children love to show off their gardens to visitors. The plants selected should be undemanding, yet capable of producing worthwhile flowers or fruits. Even if space cannot be spared in existing beds, a tub or window-box, or even some large pots, should be sufficient.

Flowers may appear the obvious choice, yet children often prefer to grow vegetables, or even fruit. The thought of growing something to eat can be a great incentive.

Flowers
Where flowers are grown from seed, annuals

are the best choice. They are inexpensive, give quick results and provide plenty of colour.

Choose hardy annuals, which can be sown where they are to flower. Suitable kinds include alyssum (coloured varieties as well as white), annual chrysanthemums, clarkia, candytuft, shirley poppies and nasturtiums. Half-hardy annuals, such as ageratums, petunias and asters, or biennials, such as pansies, are best bought as plants.

Bulbs are always a good choice, as they seldom fail to give a colourful show. Daffodils, tulips, crocuses and lilies-of-the-valley can be grown in the border, in pots, in tubs or in window-boxes. Indoors, there is special interest to be gained from growing hyacinths in glass containers, so that root development can be watched before the plants come into flower.

Containers sold for this purpose are so shaped that the bulb rests on a narrow neck over the water reservoir, but any glass jar will serve so long as the bulb is supported near the top. This can be done by filling the container almost to the top with pebbles, afterwards filling it with water to just below the surface of the pebbles.

Vegetables and fruit
Children love quick results, so radishes, which germinate speedily and can be harvested in about three weeks, are always popular. Lettuces, especially small varieties such as 'Tom Thumb', are another good choice. Bush tomatoes, which do not require staking or removal of side shoots, give worthwhile results for a minimum of work. The same applies to runner and french beans, and there is added interest to be gained by growing varieties with unusual colouring. 'Coco Bicolour', for instance, has purple foliage and flowers and blue pods, the latter turning green when cooked. The easiest and fastest-growing of all crops is mustard and cress, which reaches maturity within a fortnight of sowing. Sow the mustard seeds three days after the cress.

Most fruit crops take too long to mature for interest to be sustained, but a few strawberry plants, or a gooseberry bush from which a child can pick fruits without having to ask permission, are worth while.

Herbs
Most herbs will grow in a variety of soils, but do best in a south-facing plot sheltered from north and east winds. Easy herbs for kitchen use are mint, thyme, sage, marjoram and chives. Parsley is slow to germinate, though undemanding once the seedlings appear.

Tubs, pots and window-boxes
Bulbs are the best choice for spring, together with forget-me-nots and primroses, if contrasting plants are required. Annuals will give a colourful display during the summer. When growing annuals in a tub or pot, it is best to stick to one kind only, perhaps with a foliage plant in the centre to provide contrast.

When the annuals are finished, dwarf michaelmas daisies give a gay autumn display. Alternatively, dwarf dahlias will last until the frosts come. Neither of these plants is in the least demanding.

Chimaera: see **Variegated**

Chipping
Nicking the outer coat of a seed. Germination of hard seeds, such as those of sweet peas, is speeded up by chipping the seed coat with a sharp knife.

Chlorophyll
The green colouring matter in plant foliage. Its function is to carry out the chemical process that produces plant growth, using sunlight to synthesise the complex chemicals upon which plants feed (photosynthesis).

Chlorosis
The loss of chlorophyll in a leaf which causes it to become yellow. This may eventually kill the plant (see also PESTS AND DISEASES, **Physiological disorders**).

Chromosome
One of the numerous, rod-like bodies in plant cells, which carry the genetic characteristics of a plant.

Chrysalis
The stage in the life of an insect between the larva (or caterpillar) and the winged insect. It consists of a hard papery capsule within which the larva is completing its growth process into the perfect insect stage.

Chrysalis (large white butterfly)

Ciliate: see **Leaf shapes**

Clamp
A method of storing root crops in the open. A potato clamp is formed by heaping the potatoes into a pyramid and covering them first with a thatch of straw 12 in. thick and then with a layer of soil 9 in. thick, to keep out frosts. A 'chimney' of straw in the top of the clamp allows ventilation.

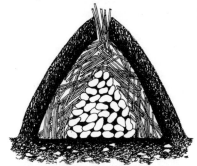

Clamp (potatoes)

Classification
The internationally accepted system of classifying and naming plants is chiefly of interest to botanists. Latin names are preferred to common ones, because a number of plants have no common name, because different plants are often known by the same common name, or because the same plant has different common names in different areas.

All plants are grouped according to family, genus, species and variety. The gardener should be familiar with all except the first in order to obtain the exact plants required. The genus is the basic unit, and may encompass a number of species with structural similarities, chiefly of flower, fruit and seed. The genus *Clematis* is divided into more than 200 different species, such as *Clematis jackmanii* and *C. patens*. Each species may again be subdivided into varieties: *C. patens* has a larger-flowered variety, *C. patens grandiflora*. A man-made variety produced by hybridisation is known as a cultivar and usually has a vernacular varietal name, chosen by the breeder, such as *C. patens* 'Nelly Moser'.

Clay: see **Soil**

Cleft: see **Leaf shapes**

427

Carnations and pinks

MARCH

Order plants and seeds.

Complete preparation of beds for spring planting.

Stop modern pinks that are running to flower without making good side shoots.

Dress plants put in last autumn with sulphate of potash or bonfire ash.

Plant pot-grown border carnations and pinks.

Spray against aphids, thrips, caterpillars, froghoppers and carnation flies. Apply zineb against rust and leaf spot.

Under glass

Prick out seedlings of annual and perpetual flowering carnations.

Give perpetuals their first or second potting and their first stopping, as applicable.

Increase ventilation in warm weather.

Cut blooms and disbud flower stems.

Order plants for delivery next month.

Control pest colonies, using HCH smokes against aphids and caterpillars, benomyl and derris against red spiders. Destroy plants infected with wilt or virus diseases.

APRIL

Apply fertiliser to growing and mature plants.

Continue planting pinks and border carnations.

Stop modern pinks if necessary.

Take action against pests.

Stake pinks with branching twigs.

Under glass

Sow seeds of border carnations and pinks in boxes in a cold frame or greenhouse.

Prick out the seedlings later, then plant in the open border when they have formed bushy plants.

Put perpetual flowering carnations delivered from nurseries this month into a light, well ventilated greenhouse.

Pot the plants in 4 in. pots and later move into 6 in. pots, using John Innes potting compost No. 2.

Stop side shoots resulting from the first stopping when they are 7 in. long, removing about 2 in. at the tips.

Pot second-year plants into 8 in. pots using John Innes No. 3.

Support plants with bamboo canes and wire rings.

Third-year plants, if too large for greenhouses, may be planted out to flower in a warm, sheltered place.

Water perpetuals sparingly. Give an overhead spray about once a fortnight.

Feed rooted plants in 6 in. and 8 in. pots with a weak, high-potash liquid fertiliser.

MAY

Stake border carnations.

Plant out annual carnations in warmer gardens.

Stake pinks if not already done.

Under glass

Continue potting on perpetual flowering carnations.

Shade glass and damp down during hot weather.

Continue with second stopping to secure autumn blooms.

Pot second-year plants into 8 in. pots.

Cut blooms and disbud flower stems.

Take action against pests and diseases.

Continue to sow seeds of border carnations and pinks.

JUNE

Stake border carnations if not already done and disbud flower stems.

Plant old perpetual flowering carnations outdoors to finish flowering.

Order border carnations and pinks for autumn delivery.

Under glass

Take cuttings of pinks, inserting them in $3\frac{1}{2}$ in. pots in a cold frame. When they root, increase ventilation and eventually plant them out or pot them singly.

Continue potting young perpetual flowering carnations into 6 in. or 8 in. pots.

Renew the shading on glass if necessary and damp down in hot weather.

Continue with second stopping to secure autumn or winter blooms.

Take action against pests and diseases.

Cut blooms and disbud flower stems.

JULY

Continue disbudding border carnations.

Order border carnations and pinks for autumn planting.

Remove old flower stems from pinks, water if weather is dry and apply a high-potash liquid fertiliser.

Propagate border carnations by layering.

Under glass

Continue to give second stoppings to provide winter flowers.

Cut blooms and disbud flower stems.

Continue to take cuttings of pinks and harden-off rooted cuttings.

Take action against pests and diseases.

AUGUST

Continue to layer border carnations, and sever rooted layers.

Remove dead flower stems.

Order border carnations and pinks for autumn planting and prepare beds for them.

Dig and manure the site.

Put dry soil under cover for use when planting in the autumn.

Under glass

Renew shading on glass and damp down during hot weather.

Watch for pests and diseases.

Continue feeding.

Cut blooms and disbud flower stems.

Continue taking cuttings of pinks and harden-off rooted cuttings.

SEPTEMBER

Prepare beds for border carnations and pinks if not already done.

Sever rooted layers from parent plants.

Continue to harden-off rooted pink cuttings and plant out those that are now growing strongly.

Stop newly planted pinks that start to run to flower.

Under glass

Continue feeding perpetual flowering carnations.

Remove shading from the glass this month.

Damp down in hot spells.

Disbud flower stems.

Keep water from falling on opening blooms; secure calyces of blooms which threaten to split.

Cut blooms with long stems and stand them up to their necks in water in a cool place for 12 hours before arranging them in vases.

Take action against pests and diseases.

OCTOBER

Plant border carnations and pinks in beds prepared earlier, except in districts with heavy soil, where they should be kept in pots in a cold frame until March.

Prepare beds for spring planting.

Continue cutting away layers of border carnations.

Stop modern pinks.

Clear leaves and rubbish from around stems.

Protect plants against birds, using black cotton.

In mild spells firm soil around plants lifted by frost.

Under glass

Maintain a temperature of 7°C (45°F) for perpetual flowering carnations, and give some ventilation at all times.

Water and feed sparingly.

Cut blooms and disbud flower stems.

Take action against pests and diseases.

NOVEMBER

Plant border carnations and pinks in mild weather.

In mild spells firm soil around plants loosened by frost.

Clear rubbish from around stems and make sure stakes and ties are secure.

Protect plants against birds, using black cotton.

Watch for signs of rust and the grubs of carnation flies.

Order plants for setting out in March.

Under glass

Maintain a temperature of 7°C (45°F) for perpetual flowering carnations, and give some ventilation at all times.

Water and feed sparingly, cutting blooms and disbudding flower stems.

Dust against rust and aphids.

DECEMBER

Under glass

Propagate perpetual flowering carnations from cuttings. Put them in a closed frame and give more air when they start to grow. Ten to 14 days later, pot them up.

JANUARY

In mild spells firm soil around plants loosened by frost.

Order plants and seeds for spring planting, and prepare the beds after testing the drainage of wet land.

Under glass

Maintain a temperature of 7°C (45°F) for perpetual flowering carnations, and give some ventilation at all times. Water and feed sparingly, cutting blooms and disbudding flower stems.

Use dusts against rust and aphids.

Continue to propagate perpetual flowering carnations from cuttings and pot up rooted cuttings. Pot on from 2 in. to $3\frac{1}{2}$ in. pots when pots are filled with roots.

Sow seeds of perpetual flowering and annual carnations. After germination, harden them off and prick them out into 2 in. pots.

Order perpetual flowering carnations for April delivery.

FEBRUARY

Order plants for spring planting.

Prepare beds, first testing the drainage of wet land.

Under glass

Give plants their first stopping when they have made 9–10 pairs of leaves.

Climber

A plant that ascends towards the light. Climbers may attach themselves to such supports as walls, fences and trellis by aerial roots, leaf stalks and tendrils. Other plants twine their stems round the supports, or may be self-clinging by means of sticky suckers.

Cloche: see Tools

Clone

The collective term for plants which have originated from one individual plant by vegetative means. All 'Bramley's Seedling' apple trees, for example, form a clone, since they are the result of grafting material of the original specimen on to rootstocks.

Clove

1. Strongly scented type of border carnation.
2. Small bulb in a cluster of young shallots or garlic.

Clove (garlic)

Composite

Member of the plant family *Compositae*, the daisy family. The apparently single flowers are made up of many smaller florets, either neuter or each with petals and stamens or stigma.

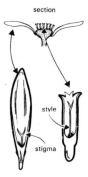

section

Composite (Michaelmas daisy). *Above:* flower head. *Right:* Cross-section through the head, and horizontal and vertical views of the stigma

style

stigma

Compost

This term is applied to two different substances. One is the garden compost produced from decomposed vegetable matter (see **Fertilisers and manures**); and the other is the soil mixture used for raising seedlings and growing pot plants.

Ordinary garden soil is unsuitable as a growing medium for seedlings raised in boxes and for pot-grown plants. It becomes compacted too easily, seldom contains sufficient nutritional elements, and is often inhabited by pests and disease organisms. A suitable compost is one which has been sterilised, and which is open and well drained. It should also contain the correct amount of nutrients to suit the plants to be raised in it.

Research carried out at the John Innes Horticultural Institution established that most plants can be grown in standard compost mixtures. Ready-mixed composts, obtainable from garden shops, are mixed to the John Innes formulae. The John Innes seed compost used for raising seedlings, and sometimes for rooting cuttings, consists of 2 parts sterilised medium loam, 1 part fibrous peat and 1 part coarse sand. To each bushel of this mixture is added $1\frac{1}{2}$ oz. superphosphate of lime and $\frac{3}{4}$ oz. ground chalk. In small prepacked sacks of John Innes seed compost, the fertilisers are usually contained in a separate sachet and must be mixed with the compost before use.

There are three John Innes potting composts. Each consists of 7 parts medium loam, 3 parts peat and 2 parts sand. The potting composts differ from one another in the amount of added fertilisers. To each bushel of potting mixture is added $\frac{3}{4}$ oz. ground chalk,

---

Chrysanthemums

MARCH

Dig ground in preparation for planting, test for acidity, and incorporate manure. Leave ground rough-dug until April or May.

Under glass

In the south, move plants from the greenhouse to cold frames, covering against frost as necessary.

Start to propagate most varieties, taking cuttings from old stools and rooting them in pots or boxes. Transfer cuttings to $3\frac{1}{2}$ in. pots as soon as rooted.

Pot on into 4–5 in. pots those cuttings first potted in January and February.

APRIL

Rake a balanced general fertiliser into ground prepared for planting.

Move pots of outdoor-flowering varieties outdoors.

Some early-flowering varieties may need stopping.

Prepare standing-out ground.

Under glass

Order or prepare John Innes potting compost No. 3, ready for final potting of greenhouse varieties.

Move outdoors greenhouse-flowering varieties already in 5 in. pots.

Pot late decoratives propagated in March into 3 in. pots.

Some large exhibition varieties will be ready for stopping.

Control aphids with malathion, HCH or a systemic insecticide.

Control leaf miners with malathion or HCH.

Keep stools growing steadily to provide cuttings for growing in the greenhouse border for Christmas flowers.

MAY

Plant out garden-flowering varieties.

Plant out pompons and koreans intended for garden decoration.

Apply slug pellets, hiding them under foliage and stones from birds and mammals.

Stop decorative plants in the north.

In the south, discard seriously damaged stools over-wintered outdoors.

Fork the ground around the healthy stools, fertilise, water, and reduce new shoots to six.

Under glass

Pot on late-flowering varieties into final pots (except in the north).

In the south, set out pots on standing-out ground about a week later; in the north wait until June.

JUNE

Stop plants set out in May. Remove tips from plants grown for decorative purposes. Stop pompons and the spray varieties to encourage bushy growth.

Water plants thoroughly once a week and spray overhead with water in hot weather.

Hoe in a dressing of sulphate of ammonia or Nitro-chalk.

Spray regularly to control aphids and leaf miners.

Under glass

Take cuttings of mid- and late-season varieties to plant direct in greenhouse borders in July.

In the north, move greenhouse-flowering varieties into their final pots.

Give second stopping to exhibition incurves and singles.

JULY

Reduce the number of shoots per plant to five, except on pompons and spray varieties.

Water plants thoroughly, and attend to tying and supporting once a week.

Apply a balanced fertiliser in the middle of the month.

Disbud early-flowering varieties if they show buds.

Spray regularly to control pests.

Reduce large exhibition varieties to three stems, exhibition incurves and decoratives to four.

and 4 oz. of a chemical mixture made up as follows: 2 parts of hoof and horn meal, 2 parts superphosphate of lime and 1 part sulphate of potash (all parts by weight). This mixture is the John Innes potting compost No. 1. No. 2 contains double the quantity of fertilisers, and No. 3 three times.

Composts may be mixed at home to the above proportions. An electric steriliser is needed; or sterilised loam can be bought.

The difficulty in obtaining suitable loams has led to soil-less (loamless) composts, such as vermiculite and composts based on peat.

There are various seedling and potting grades of these loamless composts. Peat-based composts should never be firmed too hard or allowed to dry out. Plants raised in soil-less compost should be pricked out and potted at an early stage of development.

Compost bin: see **Tools**

Compost heap: see **Fertilisers and manures**

Compound

Applied to a leaf, flower or fruit composed of several similar parts, such as a rose leaf, a daisy flower or a strawberry fruit.

Concrete mixes: see **Weights and measures**

Condensation

Beads of moisture that form beneath glass covering boxes of seedlings, and on the insides of greenhouses, frames and cloches. Condensation occurs when there is a marked difference between the internal and external temperatures. Glass should periodically be wiped to avoid damping-off.

Under glass

Dig and rake greenhouse borders to receive mid- and late-season varieties propagated last month.

AUGUST

Disbud where large blooms are wanted, leaving one bud per stem. Complete disbudding of outdoor-flowering varieties.
Water once a week in dry weather.
Apply fertiliser to fatten buds.
Prevent earwigs entering flowers by smearing Vaseline round stems.
Water pot-grown plants and give balanced fertiliser every 10–14 days.
Disbud large exhibition and October-flowering varieties.

Under glass

Water late-flowering varieties in greenhouse borders as necessary and reduce to three shoots per plant.

SEPTEMBER

Select best outdoor varieties and label for propagating.
Protect blooms with grease-proof bags, dusting the insides with HCH.

Under glass

Bring pot-grown varieties into the greenhouse by the middle of the month, preparing a level floor and cleaning the glass.
Spray the plants with a combined insecticide and fungicide.

Ventilate well, disbud late varieties, and control aphids as necessary.

OCTOBER

Over-winter plants by leaving them in the garden; or lift them, bedding them in a cold frame or housing them in the greenhouse.

Under glass

Ventilate well. Give gentle heat if needed.
Water sparingly.
Dust with captan against mildew if necessary.
Disbud the later-flowering varieties.
Cease feeding large exhibition and incurved varieties when they show colour.

NOVEMBER

Keep beds clear of weeds.
Drain waterlogged stools outdoors by piercing soil deeply with a garden fork.

Under glass

Keep dormant stools moist and give full ventilation.
Keep temperature for flowering varieties to 10°C (50°F). Dust with captan weekly to protect flowers. After flowering, cut stems back to 6 in. to encourage basal growth for cuttings.
Late-flowering decoratives in the greenhouse border need a night temperature of 10°C (50°F).
Water regularly and control leaf miners.

DECEMBER

Firm ground around over-wintering plants lifted by frost.

Under glass

Ventilate and maintain temperature of 10°C (50°F).
Take cuttings of large exhibition varieties.
Keep stools of garden varieties cool and not too wet.

JANUARY

Drain waterlogged stools outdoors by piercing soil deeply with a garden fork.
Ventilate stools in frames.

Under glass

Take cuttings of large exhibition varieties.
Remove shoots more than 3 in. long from stools of outdoor varieties.
Pot large exhibition plants.
Take basal cuttings of latest varieties while they are in flower.

FEBRUARY

Drain waterlogged stools outdoors.
Keep beds clear of weeds and scatter slug pellets around stools.

Under glass

Propagate greenhouse decorative, single and anemone-flowered varieties.
Finish potting exhibition varieties.
Prepare frames to receive potted plants, scattering slug bait.

Conifer

Tree or shrub, mainly evergreen, which bears its seeds in cones. Pines, firs and cedars are conifers. The cluster of flowers or fruits is a cone.

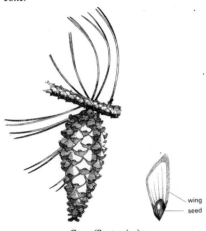

Cone (Scots pine)

Copper fungicide

A number of powerful fungicides are based on copper. They control potato blight, mildew and black spot of roses, raspberry cane spot, currant rust, bacterial canker of cherry and mildew on chrysanthemums, and are available in dust, powder or liquid form. Copper has a tendency to check and harden the foliage of some chrysanthemums, fruit and vegetables, and instructions with proprietary brands should be closely followed. Where copper is not suitable, an organic fungicide must be used instead.

Cordon

A form of tree developed by restricting the growth from the main stem and training all laterals to induce the formation of fruit spurs. This gives a high yield for a tree of such size. The stem may be erect, but it is often trained obliquely, and a double cordon will have two such stems. Apple and pear trees in cordon form are suitable for small gardens. Gooseberries and red currants are also frequently so trained.

Corm

Swollen and rounded underground stem of plants such as crocuses and gladioli. The stem is sometimes enclosed in a thin scale, thus giving the superficial appearance of a bulb. At the top of the corm is a bud, and at the corm bottom are the old roots. The bud produces the shoots and new roots, so that a new corm or cormlets appear at the base of the new growth. After flowering the old corm withers.

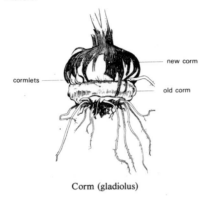

Corm (gladiolus)

Cormlet

One of the young corms which form round gladioli and crocus corms. Cormlets removed from the parent corm can be grown on for a year or two to produce flowering-sized corms.

Corolla

The inner ring or whorl of petals in a flower, enclosed within a whorl of sepals (the calyx). As the main function of the corolla is to attract pollinating insects, the petals are usually brightly coloured and often striped to guide the insects to the centres of the flowers. See **Flower parts.**

Corona

The cup or trumpet of a daffodil or narcissus.

Cotyledon

Seed leaf. Plants that are monocotyledons produce one seed leaf, and dicotyledonous plants have two. When the seed germinates, the first shoot (plumule) bears a simply shaped seed leaf, or a pair of such leaves, before the first true leaves appear. Some cotyledons, such as those of the broad bean, contain stored starch on which the seedlings live in the early stages.

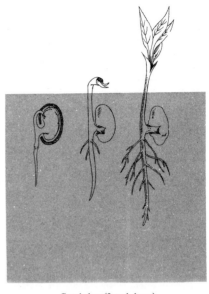

Cotyledon (french bean)

Crenate: see **Leaf shapes**

Crop rotation

System whereby different vegetable crops are grown on the same plot in consecutive years. This practice has a double purpose: it reduces the incidence of soil-dwelling pests and diseases, and it ensures that maximum use is made of the natural resources of the soil and of any fertilisers and manures applied. A simple three-year rotation plan is based on the division of crops into three groups: onions, peas and beans, brassicas and root crops.

Cross: see **Hybrid**

Crotch (or crutch)

The angle where the main branch joins the stem or trunk of a tree.

Crown

The upper part of a rootstock from which the shoots appear, found in rhubarb, paeonies and lupins. Also applied to rhubarb roots lifted for forcing.

Crown bud: see **Bud**

Cultivar

A cultivated variety of a plant, such as the French marigold 'Naughty Marietta'. A cultivar differs from a naturally occurring variety, such as *Berberis thunbergii atropurpurea*, the purple-leaved variety of Thunberg's barberry (see **Classification**).

Cultivators: see **Tools**

Cuneate: see **Leaf shapes**

Cuspidate: see **Leaf shapes**

Cutting: see **Propagation**

D

Dalapon: see **Weeds and weedkillers**

Damping down

Watering the floor and staging of a greenhouse to increase the humidity and reduce the temperature. The degree of damping down depends on the time of year, the outside weather conditions, the type of plants being grown and the maintained greenhouse temperature. In summer a greenhouse normally needs to be damped down morning and evening; in winter hardly at all.

Damping-off: see page 398

Dead-heading

Removing dead flower heads from plants, especially those in beds and borders. Dead-heading prevents the plants from setting seeds (which would divert their energies from producing further flowers), and gives a tidier appearance to the garden. Violas, paeonies, rhododendrons and roses should be regularly dead-headed.

Deciduous

Applied to plants which shed their foliage in winter. The term usually refers to trees and shrubs and contrasts with evergreen plants which retain their foliage throughout winter. Deciduous trees and shrubs should all be planted or transplanted when they are leafless, from the end of October to the beginning of April.

Decumbent

A botanical term used to describe plant stems which are prostrate for part of their length, but which turn upwards at the tips.

Deltoid: see **Leaf shapes**

Dentate: see **Leaf shapes**

Derris (Rotenone)

Insecticide which originates from the root of a tropical climbing plant. It is effective in the control of numerous plant pests, but is toxic to fish and should never be used near a pond. Derris, in dust or liquid form, is less effective than modern synthetic insecticides, but is valuable where the long-lasting effects of HCH are unacceptable, especially near cropping time.

Dibber: see **Tools**

Dichlofluanid

A sulphur based fungicide effective in the control of botrytis on lettuce and tomatoes. Allow not less than three weeks between spraying and harvesting.

Dicotyledon: see **Cotyledon**

Digging: see **Soil (soil operations)**

Digitate: see **Leaf shapes**

Dimethoate

Systemic insecticide destructive to aphids and other sap-sucking insects. It is sometimes mixed with synthetic insecticides, and such a combination provides a wide control of insect pests. Dimethoate is almost non-toxic to humans, but edible crops sprayed with it should not be harvested for a week.

Dinocap

Fungicide used to control powdery mildews on roses, apples, gooseberries, cucumbers and marrows. Dinocap should be sprayed immediately the disease appears, and a second application given three days later. To ensure continued protection, spray regularly at intervals of seven to ten days.

Dioecious

Applied to plants which have male and female flowers on separate plants.

Disbudding

Removing unwanted buds so as to direct the whole of a plant's energies into a few buds. It is done to produce exhibition-sized blooms of chrysanthemums, roses, carnations and dahlias. All buds but one on each stem are removed as soon as they can be handled, by

rubbing them out between thumb and forefinger or cutting them off with a knife. Disbudding also means the removal of buds on young shoots as an aid to shaping fruit trees.

Disbudding (dahlia)

Disk

The compact centre of a flower of the daisy family. It consists of many disk florets, each a small tube containing a stamen.

Distributor: see **Tools**

Division: see **Propagation**

DNOC (or DNC)

Chemical used in a compound with petroleum oil to destroy the eggs of fruit-tree pests, such as aphids, capsid bugs, red spider mites, scale insects and winter-moth caterpillars. DNOC is a poisonous yellow dye, toxic to plant tissues, and can be used only as a winter-wash of fruit trees and bushes. Care must be taken when using it: plants growing under the trees should be covered with newspaper. Do not apply during frosty or windy weather, or when the bark of trees is wet from rain.

Dormant

Applied to the inactive period during winter when plant growth temporarily ceases.

Dormant bud: see **Bud**

Dot plant

Tall-growing plant used as a single specimen in a formal flower bed to contrast in height, colour and texture with smaller plants.

Double

Applied to a flower with more than the usual

number of petals. Examples are double chrysanthemums and dahlias.

Double digging: see **Soil (soil operations)**

Drawn
Applied to plants or seedlings that are crowded, or grown away from the light. Under such conditions the shoots become thin and weak. To prevent this, sow seeds thinly, and place seedlings near the light.

Dried blood: see **Fertilisers and manures**

Drill
A straight, shallow furrow in which seeds are sown outdoors. Fine seeds, such as those of parsley, are sown in drills $\frac{1}{2}$ in. deep; coarse seeds, like broad beans, need drills $1-1\frac{1}{2}$ in. deep. Drills, which should always be of uniform depth, may be taken out with the corner of a draw-hoe blade, with a stick, or by merely pressing a tool handle horizontally into the surface of the ground. When the seeds have been sown, the drill is carefully filled by raking the soil over it and lightly firming.

Drought: see **Weather**

Drupe: see **Berry**

Dusters: see **Tools**

Dutch light: see **Greenhouses**

THE YEAR AT A GLANCE

Dahlias

MARCH
Prepare ground for dahlias by digging and dressing with bone-meal. Select a place in full sun where the dahlias will not have to compete with other plants.

Under glass
Remove old tubers from storage and spray with tepid water to encourage new shoots, to be rooted as cuttings.
Sow home-saved and commercial seed of bedding, cactus, decorative and pompon varieties in pans or boxes of John Innes or soilless seed compost.

APRIL
Plant out healthy dormant tubers in mild areas towards the end of the month.
Prepare the soil as for young plants, and protect the new shoots from spring frosts when they appear above ground.
Divide clumps of tubers to increase stock.

Under glass
Pot rooted cuttings and insert more.
Sow home-saved seed and that of commercial bedding and taller varieties in an unheated greenhouse.
Harden-off rooted cuttings and seedlings in a cold frame, protecting them from slugs with pellets.
Cover them with newspaper if nights are cold, but ventilate the frame during the day.

MAY
Plant out young dahlias when danger of frost is past.
Stake the plants with 5 ft. stakes driven 12 in. into the ground, and label each with the name of the variety.
Protect young plants with newspaper if the weather is cold.

Under glass
Keep pots of rooted cuttings in cold frames well watered.
Watch for aphids.
Gradually increase ventilation.

JUNE
Plant out young dahlias in Scotland and the north of England.
Pinch out the tips of dahlias when they start to grow, to make them bushy, and tie them to stakes.
Control aphids with a systemic insecticide or alternate sprays of derris and HCH.
Apply a mulch to conserve moisture and prevent weeds.

JULY
Continue tying young stems to their stakes.
Feed plants which are slow to grow with a liquid fertiliser once a fortnight.
Disbud at least some of the stems to obtain longer stems and better flowers.
Regularly remove faded flowers.

AUGUST
Continue to spray against pests.
Inspect plants for symptoms of virus infection, and mark for later destruction. Feed with liquid fertiliser, and keep plants tied to their stakes as they grow.

SEPTEMBER
Check ties, as autumn gales can cause damage.
Feed once a fortnight with a liquid fertiliser to produce good blooms and build up strong tubers.
Save dahlia seeds, and dry in a cool cupboard.

OCTOBER
Cut down the top growth of dahlias as soon as it is blackened by frost, then lift dahlias carefully with a fork.
Stand tubers upside down in a frost-free place for a week to dry out, then place them in boxes; cover with slightly damp peat after dusting the crowns with flowers of sulphur. Store in a frost-free greenhouse or shed for the winter.
Examine the tubers several times during the winter. If they are shrivelled, plunge them in a bucket of tepid water overnight to make them plump again.
Remove seeds from seed pods and store in matchboxes until sowing time in March.

NOVEMBER–FEBRUARY
Examine stored tubers and plunge them in a bucket of tepid water overnight if they have shrivelled.
Cut away portions of tubers that have rotted and dust the cuts with flowers of sulphur.

Dwarf pyramid

A trained fruit tree, especially apple and pear, of restricted height, with branches from an upright central trunk. Dwarf pyramids are suitable for small gardens.

Dwarf tree: see Bonsai

E

Earthing-up

Drawing soil round plants so that they are covered more deeply than in level soil. Potatoes are earthed up to prevent the tubers from turning green and tasting bitter through exposure to light. Earthing-up also protects the tubers from frost damage and from blight spores which may fall from the haulm or from the atmosphere. Celery and leeks may be earthed up to blanch them, and earthing-up Brussels sprouts and broccoli protects them against wind damage. The soil is drawn round the plants with a draw hoe or spade, and left with sloping sides to drain away surplus water.

Earthing up (celery)

Electricity

There are numerous uses for electricity in the garden. It provides a convenient source of power for lawn mowers (both mains and battery), lawn edgers, long grass cutters, hedge trimmers and pumps. Electricity is particularly valuable in greenhouses and garden frames, bringing the advantages of automation to temperature control, ventilation, soil warming and mist propagation.

All electrical installations in the garden should be carried out by an electrician experienced in this type of work and should be checked at regular intervals throughout their

working lives. See **Tools (hedge trimmers)** and **Greenhouses.**

Elliptic: see Leaf shapes

Emarginate: see Leaf shapes

Entire

Applied to leaves with smooth margins.

Epiphyte

A plant that grows upon another, though not parasitically. Lichen, mosses and many orchids are epiphytes. They grow naturally upon residues of decomposed vegetation in the crotches of trees, but take no nutriment from the trees themselves.

Epiphyte (lichen)

Ericaceous

Applied to plants of the family *Ericaceae,* for example ericas (heather), and to other lime-hating plants, such as rhododendrons. Such plants must be grown on acid soils and will not survive on limy soils.

Espalier

1. A trained fruit tree, especially an apple or pear. From the vertical trunk branches are trained in horizontal tiers about 15 in. apart. 2. The support of upright posts and horizontal wires on which a tree is trained.

Evergreen

Applied to trees and shrubs which are always clothed in foliage.

Everlasting

Applied to flowers with papery petals which retain their colours after being cut and dried. Helichrysum is the best-known everlasting flower. Pick the flowers just before full bloom, in dry weather, and hang them upside down in a cool, airy shed or loft until dry.

Exhibition

Term used of highly developed flowers, grown for exhibition purposes. The large show varieties of dahlias, chrysanthemums and roses are not suitable for exposure to wind and rain in the open garden.

Exotic

Any plant introduced from another country. An alien plant is always termed 'exotic', irrespective of the climate of the country of origin.

Eye

1. An undeveloped growth bud, such as the eyes of potato and dahlia tubers. 2. The centre

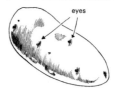

Eye (potato)

of some flowers, for example the disk in a member of the daisy family. The term is also applied to any flower centre differently coloured from the petals.

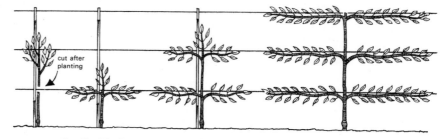

Espalier. The drawing shows different stages in the growth of a trained apple tree

F

Falls
The lower, pendulous petals of flag irises. Often different in colour from the ordinary upright petals.

Family
A group of related genera. (See **Classification**.)

Fan
A tree, usually a fruit tree, trained against a wall in a fan shape. Examples are plum, peach, cherry and apricot.

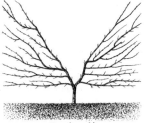
Fan (peach)

Fancy
Applied to some flowers, particularly exhibition carnations, which have variegated blooms. Opposed to the selfs, or blooms of one colour.

Farmyard manure: see **Fertilisers and manures**

Fasciation
Abnormal plant growth in which several stems become fused together. The flattened and swollen stems may be found on a wide range of flowers, including lilies, delphiniums

Fasciation (delphinium)

and forsythias. The deformity may disappear as mysteriously as it has appeared.

Fastigiate
Applied to trees and shrubs of erect habit. *Populus nigra italica* (Lombardy poplar) is the best-known fastigiate tree, but there are fastigiate forms of prunus (flowering cherry) and taxus (yew).

Fastigiate (poplar)

Feather
A lateral shoot produced on the current year's growth of a maiden (one-year-old) fruit tree.

Feather

Female flower
A flower bearing only the female reproductive organs, the pistils. Many plants bear bisexual flowers with both pistils and stamens, but in other species these occur separately. The hazel produces male pollen-bearing catkins, and small female flowers.

Fences
The enclosure of a garden serves several purposes: in addition to marking boundaries it reduces the harmful effects of wind damage, screens ugly views and affords privacy.

Fences of all kinds must be adequately supported to withstand wind pressure. Timber posts with a diameter of about 4 in. will support most fences, but in exposed gardens concrete supports may be more suitable. Posts should be spaced at intervals of approxi-

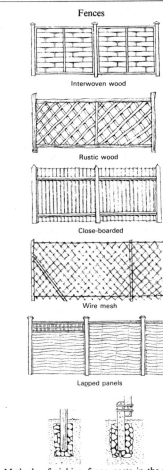
Fences

Interwoven wood

Rustic wood

Close-boarded

Wire mesh

Lapped panels

Methods of sinking fence posts in the ground *Left:* Packed with stones and rubble. *Right:* Concrete replacement for the rotted base of a wooden post.

mately 10 ft. and driven into the ground to a depth of 18 in. The bottoms of timber posts must be impregnated with a wood preservative, such as creosote, tar or copper, to protect them from rot. Soak the ends of the supports in the preservative for 24 hours before placing the posts in position. Pack the posts firmly in their holes with rubble and soil, fasten reinforcing struts to end posts and those at corners.

Fences must be erected in such a manner that the fence itself is on the boundary line, and the posts are on the owner's side of the land. Solid fences can be constructed of interwoven board and panels, or of weatherboard. The latter type requires horizontal rails let into the upright supports, and the fencing is nailed to the rails. Temporary fences consist of fine-mesh wire or chain-link netting. Barbed wire must never be used beside a public right of way. Ready-made fencing is available in many designs. All parts are cut to length, usually in sections 6 ft. long. Ugly fences can be hidden by growing a hedge against them or by planting a wide range of climbing plants or ramblers. A wooden fence can be camouflaged by painting with black, grey or green bituminous paint.

Fern

A non-flowering plant which reproduces by means of spores carried on the undersides of the fronds. Ferns generally grow best in an acid soil and in a moist, shady position.

Fern (*Polypodium*)

Fertile

1. Applied to a plant which produces abundantly. (See also **Self-fertile.**) 2. Applied to a rich soil that will yield good crops.

Fertilisation

The process whereby the male and female reproductive cells fuse. Pollination, either natural or artificial, is necessary to effect fertilisation, whereby flowering plants reproduce themselves and set fruits.

Fertilisers and manures

Most soils contain natural plant foods, in varying degrees. Because they are constantly being utilised for plant growth, and are also leached out of the soil, they have to be re-plenished with fertilisers and manures. Of the numerous chemical elements in the soil, nitrogen, phosphate, potassium, magnesium, calcium and sulphur are required in substantial quantities. Iron, boron, zinc, manganese, copper and molybdenum are present as minor or trace elements and are required only in small quantities. Nutrient materials are absorbed in solution by the roots of plants; of the six major elements, nitrogen, phosphate and potassium are the most important and must be available in the correct balance. Trace elements occur as impurities in the major elements and also naturally in garden compost and peat; only in the case of severe deficiencies do trace elements need to be supplemented (see **Pests and diseases**, *Deficiency diseases*).

A fertiliser is a substance which supplies one of the major nutrients—nitrogen, phosphate or potassium—to the soil. Manures supplement the plant nutrients already present, but also provide humus and improve the condition of the soil.

Fertilisers may be of organic or inorganic origin. They are derived from animal and/or vegetable matter, from mineral deposits or produced synthetically. Inorganic fertilisers are often termed 'artificial' or chemical fertilisers, but this does not imply an inferior quality. An important difference between organic and inorganic fertilisers is that the chemical elements in an organic fertiliser have to go through a process of conversion before they become available to plants; consequently an organic fertiliser is long-lasting. In an inorganic fertiliser the plant nutrients are readily available, and long-lasting inorganic fertilisers are now being developed, e.g., nitroform.

Manures are usually dug into the soil while plant growth is dormant, generally at the rate of a bucketful per sq. yd.; fertilisers may be applied either as a base dressing or as a top dressing. As a base dressing, fertiliser is applied to the top few inches of soil prior to sowing or planting. It is lightly raked or hoed in, following the manufacturer's recommended rates of application. When used as a top dressing, fertiliser is applied during the growing season; it should be spread evenly, not concentrated round the base of a plant, and hoed into the surface of the soil. It should not be allowed to fall on foliage.

Fertilisers
The use of any straight fertiliser—nitrogenous, phosphatic or potassic—is dependent on the crop grown and its need for a particular nutrient.

Nitrogen (N)

This chemical is the most essential element in plant nutrition. It is used up rapidly and must therefore be replaced frequently. Nitrogen promotes above-ground growth and dark green foliage, and is especially beneficial for such crops as cabbages, lettuces, spinach and rhubarb. Lack of nitrogen, more prevalent in light, free-draining soils, is apparent in stunted growth and pale green foliage. Excess nitrogen causes soft, sappy growth susceptible to pest and disease attack, and often prevents fruiting or delays ripening. Nitrogenous fertilisers should be applied more sparingly during the later stages of the growing season. Nitrogen may be used as a base dressing before sowing, or as a top dressing. The following are nitrogenous fertilisers.

Dried blood
Organic fertiliser containing about 13 per cent nitrogen, which is released fairly quickly and has a long-lasting effect. It is too expensive for widespread use outdoors, but is suitable as a top dressing for most greenhouse plants.

Hoof and horn
Organic, slow-acting fertiliser with an approximate nitrogen content of 14 per cent, releasing nitrogen steadily over a long period. It may be worked into the soil before sowing or planting, at a rate of 2–4 oz. per sq. yd.

Nitrate of soda
Chemical fertiliser which releases its nitrogen (16 per cent) very quickly, and is best used as a top dressing during summer. Average rate of application is $\frac{1}{2}$–1 oz. per sq. yd. Nitrate of soda should not be applied to a heavy clay soil, as it makes such soils harder to work.

Nitro-chalk
Quick-acting chemical fertiliser containing lime. It is applied as a top dressing at the rate of $\frac{1}{2}$–1 oz. per sq. yd. during summer, and is particularly useful on acid soils.

Nitroform
Slow-release, inorganic nitrogen fertiliser used in some lawn and rose fertilisers.

Sulphate of ammonia
Chemical fertiliser releasing its nitrogen

within 17 days of application. Chiefly used as an ingredient of compound fertilisers, or as a top dressing at the rate of $\frac{1}{2}$–1 oz. per sq. yd. Sulphate of ammonia uses up lime in the soil and should be applied only on adequately limed soils.

Urea

Chemical with a higher nitrogen content than any other nitrogenous fertiliser. It is quick-acting, and is often used in liquid fertilisers. Apply as a top dressing at the rate of $\frac{1}{4}$–$\frac{1}{2}$ oz. per sq. yd.

Phosphate (P_2O_5)

This substance is essential for the development of roots. It also encourages maturity and ripening of fruits and seeds. In acid soils phosphate does not break down in solution, and the soil must therefore be limed to obtain the correct balance before adding a phosphate fertiliser. Lack of this substance causes stunted growth, dull green or purple foliage and poor fruiting quality. Phosphate fertilisers are slow-acting, and applications (average 2 oz. per sq. yd.) should be lightly forked into the soil to bring the fertiliser nearer to the plants' roots. The following are phosphatic fertilisers.

Basic slag

The phosphate in this chemical is released slowly, but as it contains lime it is useful on acid and wet soils. Apply during autumn and winter at 4 oz. per sq. yd.

Bone-meal

Organic fertiliser, obtainable in coarse, medium or fine grades. Bone-meal, which also contains a small amount of nitrogen, is slow-acting and becomes soluble at a rate depending on the size of its particles and the action of organic acids in the soil. Bone-meal brings about an alkaline reaction in the soil and should not be used on acid-loving plants, such as rhododendrons and azaleas. Due to its slow but steady release it is an ideal fertiliser for slow-growing crops, shrubs and herbaceous plants.

Superphosphate of lime

Popular fertiliser with a readily available phosphatic content. It is used as a base fertiliser before sowing or planting in spring or early summer, at the rate of 2–4 oz. per sq. yd. The chemical is derived from treating mineral rock phosphate with sulphuric acid. As the end product is neutral, it does not affect soil acidity.

Potassium (K_2O)

This nutrient is essential for the production of flowers, and is of particular value to plants grown for their fruiting qualities. It balances the nitrogen content of the soil, promoting healthy plant growth and resistance to frost and fungal diseases. Lack of potassium shows itself by brown scorching on dark green foliage, by inferior flower colouring, and by small, immature fruits. The following are potassic fertilisers.

Muriate of potash

A concentrated form of potash. It is harmful to such crops as strawberries, currants and tomatoes. Apply during winter and spring at the same rate as sulphate of potash.

Sulphate of potash

Chemical fertiliser, high in potash content, derived from muriate of potash. Though it is quick-acting and soluble, it does not easily leach out of the soil. Sulphate of potash can be applied at any time of the year, at an average rate of $\frac{1}{2}$–1 oz. per sq. yd., as a base or top dressing. Beneficial to tomatoes.

Wood ash

The potash content of ash depends on the type of material burnt. Bracken, bean haulm and tree prunings provide the richest wood ash. Apply at any time of the year at a general rate of $\frac{1}{2}$ lb. per sq. yd. Heavy dressings of wood ash should be avoided on chalky soils.

Compound fertilisers

The most essential nutrients—nitrogen, phosphate and potash—may all be applied to the soil separately, but it is more convenient to apply a compound fertiliser which incorporates all three elements. Proprietary brands are readily available; several are produced to suit particular plants, for example tomato or rose fertiliser, while other compound fertilisers are intended for general garden use. Fork in compound fertilisers in the spring before sowing or planting.

The percentage of nitrogen, phosphate and potash is stated on proprietary compound fertilisers. The figures 5 : 5 : 10, for example, denote that the compound contains 5 per cent nitrogen, 5 per cent phosphate and 10 per cent potash. When selecting a compound, the ratio of the nutrients is as important as the percentage; the best fertiliser for general use is one which contains approximately equal amounts of nitrogen, phosphate and potash, expressed as 7 : 7 : 7.

Lime

Although calcium—the chief chemical element of lime—is an essential plant food, the main importance of lime is as a soil conditioner. Liming a heavy clay soil causes the fine soil particles to flocculate—to join together into larger granules—thereby improving soil texture. The most important effect of lime, however, is its ability to neutralise soil acidity and turn acid soils alkaline. Most plants react unfavourably to excessively acid soil: brassicas grown on a sour soil are liable to attack by the club root fungus. In too acid soils, essential plant foods, like nitrogen and phosphates, are either present in small quantities only or become insoluble. When testing a soil sample, a pH reading below 7·0 indicates acidity; follow the instructions on the soil-testing kit in respect of lime application. Autumn and winter are the best times for applying lime in the form of ground limestone or magnesium limestone: sprinkled on the surface of newly dug land, it is quickly washed down through the soil.

Liquid fertiliser

A highly concentrated form of compound fertiliser, containing nitrogen, phosphate and potash—and, in many cases, trace elements. Liquid feeds are particularly useful for greenhouse and other pot plants. The fertiliser, which must be diluted according to the maker's instructions, is readily available to the plants but its effects are relatively short lived.

Manures

Organic matter is essential for maintaining or improving soil fertility. Manures are all of organic origin; and, as they decompose in the soil, they not only improve the soil texture, but also become valuable food sources for plant growth. Farmyard manure, particularly, has a high nitrogen content which is released slowly on decomposition. In this way nitrogen becomes available to plants over a longer period than when a nitrogenous fertiliser is applied. The decomposed manure provides food for beneficial soil organisms; and, as it retains water and soluble nutrients, plants are more drought-resistant. When organic matter decomposes, weak acids are released which are necessary to make certain plant foods available in solution. These acids may render the soil sour and should be neutralised by the addition of lime.

Compost

The partly decomposed remains of garden waste provide useful plant food and humus. A compost heap has the added advantage that it disposes of most garden refuse. Choose an open site for your compost heap; a bin 4 ft. sq. is adequate for the average garden. The bin can be constructed, or obtained ready made, of wooden slats or either wire or plastic mesh.

Build up the heap with layers of garden waste—plant refuse, grass mowings, leaves and kitchen waste. The layers should not be more than 6 in. thick. If the material is dry, it must be saturated with water before a compost activator is sprinkled on to aid decay. Diseased plant material, tough weeds such as couch and ground elder, and woody materials should be burnt and not added to the compost heap. Straw is useful for composting, but must be thoroughly wetted first. Soil or bonfire ash may be added 1 in. thick between the waste layers. When the heap reaches a height of about 4 ft., a second compost heap should be started.

Air and water aid the process of decay, in the course of which heat is set up, and the proteins and carbohydrates in the material are released; bacteria then complete the production of plant nutrients. Decomposition may be speeded by turning the heap after two months, and forking the less decomposed material to the centre of the heap, the rotted compost being placed to the outside of the bin. A compost heap made in autumn should have rotted down for use by the following spring; if the winter is very wet, the heap may be protected by polythene sheeting to prevent the plant nutrients being washed away.

The decomposed compost is used as a manure by mixing it into the top spit of soil at the rate of a bucketful per sq. yd. When planting roses, shrubs and deep-rooting perennials, fork in compost to a depth of 2 ft. to supply humus and encourage root growth. During spring and summer, compost may also be used as a top dressing round plants to retain moisture and to prevent the roots from getting scorched.

Farmyard manure

Animal droppings mixed with litter, particularly useful for its humus-forming properties. The quality of the manure depends on the nature of the droppings, the food on which the animals were fed and the kind of litter used for their bedding. Manure which has been stacked for several months is preferable to fresh manure. Stable manure from straw-bedded animals is the richest, and is ideal for heavy clay soils. Cow and pig manure contain less nutrients than horse manure. Cow manure decomposes slowly and is most suitable for light, sandy soils.

One ton of farmyard manure contains about 10 lb. of nitrogen, 5 lb. of phosphates and 10 lb. of potash, as well as small quantities of the trace elements. All these nutrients become available to plants over a long period; a good dressing of farmyard manure may remain active in the soil for up to three years. Apply farmyard manure by forking it into the topsoil at the rate of a bucketful per sq. yd. or by placing it in 2 in. layers at the bottom of the trenches when digging in the autumn.

Hop manure

This is a dry form of spent hops, obtainable under brand names from horticultural sundriesmen. Proprietary hop manures have added ingredients to compensate for nutrients in which the hops are deficient. They should be dug in at the rates recommended by the manufacturers.

Leaf-mould

Compost derived from decayed leaves, decomposed oak and beech leaves providing the best humus. While the nutritional elements of leaf-mould are few, it greatly increases soil fertility. In the autumn, gather fallen leaves and stack them in 6 in. layers between layers of soil. A heap 2–3 ft. high will have decayed to a fibrous mould by the following autumn, when it may be dug into the top spit of soil at 5 lb. per sq. yd.

Poultry manure

The dried droppings of poultry and pigeons are rich in plant foods. Poultry manure contains four times as much nitrogen and phosphates as farmyard manure, but it supplies little or no humus-forming material to the soil. It may be used as a top dressing to leafy vegetable crops at 5 lb. per sq. yd.

Seaweed

Where this substance is available, seaweed provides a rich manure. It decomposes rapidly when dug into the soil (at the rate of 10 lb. per sq. yd.) and contains as much nitrogen as farmyard manure and more potash. These nutrients become rapidly available to the plants, but do not have a lasting effect. Dried seaweed meal may be purchased from sundriesmen and worked into the topsoil during the autumn.

Sewage sludge

Wet sewage sludge may be used as a substitute for farmyard manure, but although it has a high nitrogen and phosphate content, it contributes little humus-forming material to the soil. Dried sewage sludge is more pleasant to handle and may be used as a nitrogenous fertiliser.

Shoddy

Waste materials from wool factories, obtainable under proprietary brand names. Shoddy decomposes slowly and is a useful conditioner on light, sandy soil. Its chief value lies in its high nitrogen content, which is released slowly over as long a period as three years. Apply shoddy by forking it into the topsoil during autumn and winter at the rate of $\frac{1}{2}$–1 lb. per sq. yd.

F1 hybrid: see Hybrid

Filament

The stalk at the point of which is the anther in a male flower.

Filiform: see Leaf shapes

Fimbriate

Applied to petals with fringed margins.

Fimbriate (carnation)

Flaked

Applied to bicoloured carnations, in which the ground colour is streaked with broad bands of a second colour.

Flame gun: see Tools

Floret

One of the individual flowers in a compound inflorescence. The bellis (double daisy), for example, is composed of central disk florets and outer ray florets.

Flower parts

The primary purpose of flowers is sexual. They contain the male and/or female reproductive organs, including the seeds which, following fertilisation, develop to provide a new generation of plants. The illustration shows the main parts of a bisexual flower. These

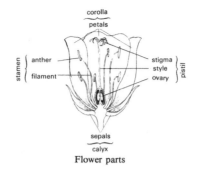

Flower parts

parts are described under their individual names.

Flowers, dried

A group of plants, known collectively as everlastings or immortelles, produce flowers with papery, tough or straw-like petals which remain on the plant and do not fall or wither. These plants belong mainly to the daisy family. As long as they are harvested at the correct time, they keep their shape, form and colour even after cutting, altering very little when dried.

THE YEAR AT A GLANCE

Flowers from seed

MARCH

Complete seed orders.
Plant out hardy perennials raised from seed.
Sow the hardier sorts of hardy annuals outdoors.
Dress seeds with a protective powder before sowing.
Fork over ground to be sown with hardy annuals and give a fertiliser dressing.
Work soil down to a good tilth, then sow seeds in rows to make thinning and hoeing easier.
Control weeds by frequent hoeing, and thin seedlings when they have two or three leaves.

Under glass

Sow half-hardy annuals.
Move forward batches of half-hardy annuals to cold frames.
Protect frames containing tender plants from severe frosts.

APRIL

Complete seed purchases.
Sow hardy annuals outdoors.
Dress seed before sowing and fork in a general fertiliser.

Under glass

Complete sowings of half-hardy annuals.
Move forward batches of half-hardy perennials to cold frames. Cover frames containing tender plants if severe frost threatens.
Spray with systemic insecticide, HCH or malathion if aphids or thrips are seen.
Plants with yellowing leaves may be starving, so give a liquid fertiliser weekly.

MAY

Sow hardy and half-hardy annuals.
Plant out half-hardy annuals when risk of frost has passed.
Prepare a planting plan and water borders before planting.
Sow hardy biennials in drills in a nursery bed, or in pans or boxes in a greenhouse or cold frame.

Under glass

Move boxes of well grown half-hardy annuals to cold frames.
Spray monthly with a systemic insecticide.
Apply a liquid fertiliser to boxed plants if they start to turn yellow.
Sow hardy perennials in a frame or greenhouse.
Prick out germinated seedlings.
Transfer greenhouse-raised plants to a frame to harden off when they have five or six leaves.

JUNE

Complete planting of half-hardy annuals.

Water recently planted half-hardy annuals thoroughly in dry spells.
Support taller-growing annuals.
Spray monthly with systemic insecticide.
Hoe weeds among bedding plants.
Sow hardy annuals. Set out seedlings of hardy biennials in a nursery bed, preferably during showery weather. Sow hardy perennials outdoors.
Sow wallflowers and sweet williams in drills in their flowering positions.

Under glass

Sow hardy perennials in a heated greenhouse.

JULY

Remove old flower heads from annuals to keep them flowering.
Water liberally in dry weather.
Support taller-growing annuals.
Sow wallflowers and sweet williams in drills in their flowering positions.
Spray monthly with a systemic insecticide.
Hoe regularly.
Set out seedlings of hardy biennials in a nursery bed.

AUGUST

Plant out well grown perennial seedlings in nursery beds.
Spray monthly with a systemic insecticide.
Remove dead flower heads regularly.
Hoe regularly in damp summers.

A second group consists of flowers, and such varied materials as foliage, buds, catkins, fruits, seed heads and stems, which, although not naturally dry like the everlastings, can be dried sufficiently for long-lasting winter decoration and for flower arrangements placed in hot, dry parts of the house. These are termed perpetuelles. Although many perpetuelles are well known and used frequently, it is worth experimenting with any flowers that you find attractive. Flowers such as moss roses, that dry on the bush, and double flowers such as paeonies, often dry successfully.

SEPTEMBER

Remove fading annuals to make way for spring bedding.
Sow the hardiest annuals to over-winter outdoors.
Plant out hardy biennials.

OCTOBER

Remove annuals before they become bedraggled.
Plant out perennials raised from seed.

NOVEMBER

In suitable weather, plant out hardy perennials raised from seed.
Dig beds to be used for annuals next year, working in a dressing of well rotted manure or compost.
Send for seed catalogues to plan bedding programme.

DECEMBER

Continue digging ground to be used for next year's annuals.

JANUARY

Plan spring planting programme.
Complete digging beds and borders.

FEBRUARY

Lightly fork beds prepared for annuals and work in bone-meal.

Under glass

Sow the first of the half-hardy annuals.

All such materials should be gathered on a dry day before the frosts begin, and then dried in complete darkness or in deep shade so that the flowers retain their true colour. Plants gathered during a wet season take longer to dry and should be tied in very small bunches or dried individually.

Everlastings

Cut all these plants when the flowers are at their prime so that the colour remains clear and the stems strong after drying. If they are cut when too young they become limp when dry; if they are too mature the flowers may go to seed and become fluffy or disintegrate.

Dry everlastings by tying them together in bunches, then hanging them in a cool airy place. The following are recommended.

Annuals. *Ammobium alatum* (sand flower); *Gomphrena globosa* (Spanish clover); *Helichrysum bracteatum* (straw daisy), in many varieties and a good range of colours; *Helipterum manglesii* (syn. *Rhodanthe manglesii*); *H. roseum* (syn. *H. acroclinium*); *Limonium suworowii*; *Lonas inodora* (African daisy); *Xeranthemum annuum*, *X. ligulosum* and *X. perligulosum*.

Perennials. *Anaphalis margaritacea* (pearly everlasting); *A. triplinervis*; *Catananche caerulea* (cupid's dart); *Limonium bonduellii* (syn. *Statice bonduellii*), *L. sinuatum*, *L. latifolium* and *L. incanum*.

Grasses

Cut grasses for drying when they are young, drying them in bunches in the same way as everlastings. The following are recommended.

Annuals. *Agrostis elegans*, *A. alba* and *A. nebulosa*; *Aira elegans* (syn. *A. capillaris*), suitable only for the greenhouse; *Avena sterilis* (animated oat); *Briza maxima* (pearl grass) and *B. gracilis* (quaking grass); *Bromus briziformis*; *Coix lacryma-jobi* (Job's tears); *Hordeum jubatum* (squirrel's-tail grass); *Lagurus ovatus* (hare's-tail grass).

Perennials. *Alopecurus lanatus* (lamb's-tail grass); *Anthoxanthum odoratum* (sweet vernal grass); *Phleum pratense* (cat's-tail or timothy grass). Barley, millet, oats and wheat are also recommended.

Perpetuelles

Dry these plants quickly in a dark, warm place such as an airing cupboard. Support flat, round flowers, such as zinnias, by con-

structing a rack of wire netting, with the blooms resting on the rack and the stems hanging down below it. Tie wires round the base of thick-stemmed flowers, such as delphiniums, hanging them singly, head downwards, from a rail in the cupboard.

Perpetuelles can also be dried by burying them in borax, in sand mixed with borax, or, preferably, in silica gel. Several pounds of silica gel crystals are needed to dry enough flowers for an average-sized arrangement, but the same crystals can be used many times.

The petals of such flowers as daisies and cornflowers, which tend to shatter after drying by this process, can be secured by placing a drop of gum arabic at their base before they are dried. Some flower stems may have to be shortened before drying and replaced later by false stems of wire or straw if the drying container is too small or the stem is weak.

First, pour a layer of the drying agent on to the floor of an airtight box. If the heads of the flowers are flat with the stems—as with pansies or narcissi—lay them face upwards on the drying agent. If the heads of the flowers are flat but at right angles to the stems, lay them head downwards. In each case pour more of the drying agent round the flowers until every crevice is filled and the flowers are completely covered. If the flowers are not flat, support them face upwards while the

A vase of dried hydrangeas, delphiniums, chrysanthemums, and beech and berberis leaves

441

drying agent is poured over them. Finally, close the lid of the container, sealing it if the lid does not fit closely.

After two days gently uncover a portion of the flowers to see if they are dry. The length of time needed to dry flowers by this process varies from one to five days, depending on the flowers' condition and on the weather. After drying, keep the flowers in a non-humid atmosphere. The following are recommended.

Annuals. *Amaranthus caudatus* (love-lies-bleeding); *Anthriscus cerefolium* (chervil); *Celosia cristata* (cockscomb); *Coriandrum sativum* (coriander); delphinium (larkspur); *Didiscus caeruleus* (blue lace-flower); salvia, many of the scarlet bedding types, and also the new varieties; tagetes; zinnia—all varieties are recommended except red.

Perennials. *Achillea filipendulina*, also its garden varieties; *A. ptarmica* (sneezewort), also its garden varieties; *A. millefolium* (yarrow); chrysanthemum, most pompon varieties are recommended, including those grown in the greenhouse; delphinium (larkspur); echinops (globe thistle); eryngium (sea holly); *Gypsophila paniculata*; *Salvia farinacea*; solidago (golden rod), a genus that provides a variety of shapes, from the older, plume-like type to the newest varieties, which have longer individual florets; *Stachys lanata* (lamb's tongues).

Shrub flowers. Buddleia; erica (heath); hydrangea; *Lavandula spica* (lavender); rambler roses.

Catkins. Alnus (alder); corylus (hazel); *Garrya elliptica*; salix (willow).

Coloured stems. Most species of cornus (dogwood) and salix (willow) have coloured stems, and should be cut in winter when the bark colour is at its best.

Trees and shrubs

Branches cut from deciduous and evergreen trees and shrubs can be treated to preserve the leaves and fruits. In the case of evergreens these must be mature, one-year-old growths, since new leaves do not absorb the solution properly. The branches of deciduous trees should be cut just before the leaves turn colour in the autumn.

Stand the branches firmly in a deep, narrow jar containing 2–3 in. of a boiled mixture made up of one-third glycerine and two-thirds water. Put the branches in the solution while it is still hot and leave them there for several

THE YEAR AT A GLANCE

Fruit

MARCH

Complete planning of new fruit gardens.
Complete planting as soon as soil conditions permit, particularly of trees which were heeled in.
Firm trees and bushes lifted by frost.
Complete pruning of trees and bushes.
Feed established trees and bushes growing in cultivated soil.
Spray apples, pears, cherries, peaches and nectarines, plums and damsons.
Train new shoots of blackberries and loganberries on to wires.
Protect flowers on wall-trained peaches and nectarines, and pollinate artificially if insects are scarce.
Plant raspberries and strawberries.

APRIL

Check flowering and setting of apples, pears, plums and cherries to ascertain probable size of crop.
Keep a watch for pests on flowers and fruitlets.
Protect wall trees and soft fruit bushes against frost while they are in bloom.
Plant late-flowering strawberries on suitable sites.
Check tree ties and stakes.
Mulch round trees, and water newly planted fruit.
Spray apples, pears, black currants, cherries, peaches and nectarines, plums and strawberries.
Give a fine spray of water to open peach and nectarine flowers to help setting.
Ensure that pollinating insects can reach flowers on cloched strawberries.
Remove flowers from immature and autumn-fruiting strawberry runners.

MAY

Watch for pests and control as necessary.

Water fruit trees and bushes in dry weather while fruit is swelling.
Bark ring apples and pears if necessary to encourage fruiting.
Feed apples, pears, cherries, blackberries, loganberries, black currants, gooseberries, peaches and nectarines, plums, damsons, raspberries and red currants.
Spray apples, pears, cherries, black currants, gooseberries, peaches and nectarines, and strawberries.
Tie up new growth on blackberries and loganberries.
Control weeds around trees and bushes grown in cultivated soil.
Start thinning fruit on wall-trained peaches.
Remove overcrowded and surplus shoots from raspberries, and apply a mulch.
Protect strawberry fruits with straw or paper collars and apply slug bait.
De-blossom immature and autumn-fruiting strawberries.
Start to summer prune vines.

JUNE

Watch for pests and diseases.
Thin top fruits if crop is heavy, allowing for natural dropping.
Harvest strawberries.
Spray apples and pears, blackberries, loganberries, gooseberries, peaches and nectarines, plums and damsons, cherries and raspberries.
Water and mulch to ensure sufficient water supply to apples, pears and black currants.
Check weeds around trees and bushes growing in cultivated soil.
Tie sacking round apple and pear trunks to catch apple blossom weevils.
Destroy apples attacked by sawfly.
Train in blackberry and loganberry shoots.
Summer prune gooseberries.
Tie in new wall-trained peach and nectarine shoots.
Protect fruiting plum, damson and cherry trees, red currants, raspberries and strawberries against birds.
Anchor healthy strawberry runners to form new plants.
Summer prune plum, damson, cherry and vines.

JULY

Pick soft fruits.

Complete thinning apple and pear fruits.

Summer prune cordon, espalier and dwarf pyramid apple and pear trees.

Support heavily cropping branches of apples, pears and plums.

Spray apples, pears, blackberries, loganberries, plums and damsons.

Check that ties on trained trees are not too tight.

Train in new blackberry and loganberry shoots.

Check weeds around trees and bushes growing in cultivated soil.

Pick black currant fruit and prune bushes.

Destroy black currant bushes infected with reversion virus.

Tie in replacement shoots on peaches and nectarines.

Protect peaches against birds, wasps and earwigs.

Prune plum and damson trees.

Pick raspberries, cut down old canes, and remove weak new shoots. Tie in strong new shoots and control weeds.

Tidy up strawberry beds and discard plants which have given three crops.

AUGUST

Pick early apples and pears while slightly under-ripe.

Summer prune restricted forms of apples and pears.

Pick loganberries, cut out fruited shoots, and tie in new shoots.

Spray black currants and cherries.

Prune fruited shoots of wall-trained peaches and re-tie new shoots.

Support heavily laden plum branches and complete pruning.

Protect September-fruiting raspberries against birds and wasps.

Plant rooted strawberry runners.

Protect ripening grapes with glass.

SEPTEMBER

Plan for new planting season, and order trees. Choose late-flowering varieties for frosty areas.

Grass down established trees.

Remove trees infected with honey fungus.

Prepare storage places for apples and pears, and pick fruit in cool conditions before fully mature.

Complete summer pruning of apples and pears.

Harvest blackberries and loganberries, cut away old growth, and tie in new.

Spray cherries.

Prune wall-trained peaches and tie in new shoots.

Pick plums and damsons, and prune trees.

Pick September-fruiting raspberries.

Protect autumn-fruiting strawberries against birds and slugs, and cover with cloches in cold weather.

OCTOBER

Order fruit trees and bushes for autumn delivery.

Prepare planting sites, breaking up the subsoil to ensure good drainage.

Work fertiliser into the soil while digging. Ground previously occupied by fruit should be chemically sterilised.

Control weeds around established trees.

Put grease bands round apple and cherry trees to catch winter moths.

Pick and store apples and pears as they mature.

Cut out fruited blackberry and loganberry canes and train in new shoots.

Spray cherries, peaches and nectarines.

Take gooseberry cuttings.

Root prune unfruitful plum and damson trees after leaf-fall.

Pick autumn-fruiting strawberries and complete planting runners.

NOVEMBER

Plant fruit trees and bushes. In inclement weather, store trees in a frost-free shed or heel them in outdoors. Soak dry tree roots before planting. Plant firmly and at the same depth as the trees were in the nursery. Stake trees.

Prune fruit trees after planting.

Plant strawberries.

Clear weeds from around established trees and bushes.

Start winter pruning established apple and pear trees.

Cut out cankers on apple and pear trees and control woolly aphis with malathion.

Inspect stored fruit, and ripen pears at room temperature.

Complete pruning and tie new growths of blackberry, loganberry, and raspberry.

DECEMBER

Inspect stored fruit, and ripen pears at room temperature.

Spray all fruit trees and bushes with tar-oil winter-wash when dormant.

Continue planting in suitable conditions.

Check stakes, ties and supports.

Continue pruning of apple and pear trees.

Apply nitrogenous fertiliser to trees grown in grass.

Cut back newly planted apples, pears, blackberries, loganberries, black, red and white currants, cherries, gooseberries and raspberries.

Use black currant prunings as cuttings.

JANUARY

Inspect stored fruit and discard any which have rotted.

Continue planting in suitable conditions.

Check stakes and ties.

Apply a nitrogenous fertiliser to trees and bushes grown in grass.

Cut down old trees.

Take black currant cuttings.

FEBRUARY

Continue planting in suitable conditions, or store trees in a frost-free place.

Continue pruning, except during hard frost.

Apply simazine to soil round established trees and bushes.

Spray apples and pears with DNOC.

Prune newly planted fan-trained peaches and nectarines, plums, damsons and cherries.

Spray peaches and nectarines against peach leaf curl.

Cover with cloches strawberries planted for early fruiting.

days. Deciduous plants must be left until the glycerine has spread over the surface of each leaf; but evergreens, which turn an attractive tan or brown colour and acquire a pleasant leathery texture, can be removed while some area of the original leaf colour still remains.

After removing the branches, either arrange them in a vase (containing no water), or store them in boxes or plastic bags until they are needed. The following are recommended.

Deciduous. Any trees or shrubs with tough leaves, including acer (maple), carpinus (hornbeam), and fagus (beech).

Evergreen. Any trees or shrubs with tough leaves, including camellia, elaeagnus, eucalyptus, laurus (laurel), and *Prunus lusitanica* (Portugal laurel).

Miscellaneous. Immature seedling stems, downy leaves (such as verbascum), and tough-textured foliage (such as gladiolus).

Forcing

Hastening plants into growth, flower or fruit before their time. This can be done by placing them in darkness and applying heat under glass. Narcissus bulbs cooled for a period of several weeks will force more quickly than untreated bulbs.

Forking: see **Soil (soil operations)**

Forks: see **Tools**

Form

A botanical term for a naturally occurring variety (see **Classification**). *Clematis patens grandiflora* is a large-flowered form of *C. patens*.

Formaldehyde (or formalin)

Chemical solution used for sterilising greenhouse soil. The soil is dug over and watered with the prescribed amount of formalin, which is a 40 per cent solution of formaldehyde gas in water. After digging over the soil again, the watering process is repeated one week later. All fumes must have dispersed before plants are moved back into the house. Formalin can also be used to sterilise potting soil, seed pots and boxes, and for washing down the inside of the greenhouse; but it is little used today and has largely been replaced by sterilants such as Jeyes Fluid.

Frame: see **Greenhouses** (page **459**)

Frond

One of the feathery leaf branches of a fern.

Frost: see **Weather**

Fruit

The seed-bearing organ of any plant, for example a bean pod or an apricot.

Fruit bud: see **Bud**

Fumigation

The exposure of pests and disease-carrying organisms in the greenhouse to poisonous, destructive fumes.

G

Gametes

Name given to the sexual reproductive cells of pollen (male) and ovule (female) in plants.

Gamma-BHC: see **HCH**

Gamopetalous

Definition of flowers that are more or less united to form a cup or tube, such as Canterbury Bells.

Garden law: see **Law**

Garden line: see **Tools**

Genes

The hereditary units in each plant chromosome. When a cell divides, the genetic characteristics of the plant (shape, height and colour of flowers and foliage) are transmitted to its progeny through the seeds or the cutting.

Genus

A group of closely related plant species. (See **Classification**.)

Glass: see **Greenhouses**

Grass trimmers

Petrol-driven, mains electric and battery-powered grass trimmers with a fast-rotating, hard nylon cord that enables the grass to be cut easily where mowers cannot reach, e.g., right up to walls.

Grafting: see **Propagation**

Grease band

Sticky band, 4 in. wide, of petroleum jelly, applied to the trunk of a fruit tree, about 3 ft. from ground level. The band traps the female winter-moth caterpillars as they crawl up the trunk to lay their eggs in early autumn. Remove and burn the bands the following March.

Green cluster: see **Bud stages**

Greenhouses and garden frames
Basic types of greenhouse

There are three basic types of garden greenhouse—span roof, lean-to and three-quarter span. Relatively recent variations of the span roof pattern are houses constructed from Dutch lights, or with panes the same size as those used in Dutch lights—generally 56 in. by 28 in. These houses generally have sides which slope outwards at the base. In addition, home extension structures are being used increasingly for growing plants, and there are also one or two aluminium structures of unconventional design.

Span roof

This is by far the most useful shape for a greenhouse. It has vertical sides and a sloping roof in the form of an inverted, slightly flattened V. If this type is to be used as a general-purpose house, with crops such as tomatoes or chrysanthemums growing in the greenhouse soil, the sides should be of glass almost

Span roof greenhouse

THE YEAR AT A GLANCE

General tasks

MARCH

Complete all digging.
Kill weeds on paths and drives with paraquat-diquat and keep them clean with a total weedkiller.
Destroy moss on paths with a 4 per cent tar-oil wash.
Check all ties securing plants to stakes and strings attaching labels.
Bait slugs with pellets hidden under foliage or flat stones.

APRIL

Mulch beds and borders when they have warmed up, after destroying weeds with the hoe and making sure ground is moist.
Ensure that tender plants which are frosted thaw out gradually by covering them with paper or spraying with cold water.
Order boxes of seedlings, such as antirrhinums and dahlias, and tomato plants.

MAY

Remove suckers from lilacs and fruit trees.
Control slugs with metaldehyde pellets.
Spray roses, fruit bushes and broad beans weekly against aphids and caterpillars.
Water all plants generously according to requirements.
Apply liquid feeds to plants or dress with quick-acting fertiliser and water in.

JUNE

Continue weekly spraying against pests and diseases.
Stake herbaceous plants as necessary.
Control weeds with paraquat-diquat and by hoeing.
Water the garden in dry spells.

JULY

Between now and the autumn carry out such constructional tasks as paving, wall building and concreting.
Repair and paint greenhouses and frames.
Remove dead heads from flowers weekly.
Before going on holiday, cut the lawn, hoe all round, check plant ties and leave the hose ready for your neighbour to water for you. Ask him to pick sweet peas, french beans and marrows.

AUGUST

Take and root cuttings of shrubs, heathers, hydrangeas, geraniums and fuchsias.
Check all labels and renew as necessary.
Continue to spray against pests and diseases.

SEPTEMBER

Clear away remains of crops that have finished.
Order bulbs, roses, herbaceous plants, shrubs and fruit bushes.
Take cuttings of evergreen shrubs, geraniums and hydrangeas.
Control mildew, especially on michaelmas daisies, with fungicide.
Check that electrical installations are in working order before the winter.
Complete major construction jobs, particularly concreting.
Check that gutters and drains are free of leaves and other debris.

OCTOBER

Remove summer bedding plants soon enough to plant spring bedding and get it established before severe weather begins.
Do not manure flower borders at this time of year, but give a dressing of 6–8 oz. of bone-meal per sq. yd.
Spread a net over the garden pool to catch fallen leaves. Clear fallen leaves from rock plants and lawns. Stack them to decompose.

NOVEMBER

Lift fuchsias, begonias and geraniums, and bring inside.
Dig vacant ground and leave it rough for the frost to break down.

Dress heavy soil with lime.
Plant trees and shrubs arriving from nurseries. If weather is not fit for planting, heel them in.
Clear up fallen leaves and cut down herbaceous plants to 18 in. above soil level.

DECEMBER

Control mice with traps or Warfarin if they steal peas or attack fruits and roots in store.
Check gladiolus corms and begonia tubers, onions, and other dormant bulbous plants, and stored fruits and roots before severe frosts begin, making sure they have adequate protection.
Cover ground around newly planted camellias and rhododendrons with 12 in. of straw to prevent roots being frozen.
Protect autumn-planted evergreen shrubs against east winds.
Lag outdoor taps and water pipes.
Shake heavy falls of snow off hedges and branches of trees and shrubs to help them keep their shape.
Leave a large heap of sand or ash near the front drive for spreading on paths in snowy weather.

JANUARY

Order seeds, gladioli, onion sets and shallots, garden sundries, weedkillers and fertilisers.
Send mowers, cultivators and shears for servicing and sharpening.
Treat wooden seed boxes with preservative, and wash pots and plastic trays.
Check pergolas and other wooden structures, and repair if necessary.

FEBRUARY

Have a soil test carried out in a new garden.
Destroy weeds under hedges with paraquat-diquat.
Use dalapon against couch grass.
Kill slug eggs in crevices of drystone walls with a blowlamp.

to ground level. If it is to be used exclusively for growing plants in pots on benches, the sides can be solid up to bench level.

Before deciding whether to buy a greenhouse with glass to the ground or with solid walls, the following considerations should be borne in mind. A greenhouse with solid walls costs slightly less to heat in the winter and is easier to keep cool in summer; but its use is limited to growing plants in pots on benches. A greenhouse which has glass to the ground will cost a little more to heat in winter and be more difficult to keep cool in summer; but it offers extra scope for plant growing.

Crops can be grown in the soil on both sides of the centre path, or a bench can be fitted along one side for pot plants, leaving the other side for tomatoes or chrysanthemums.

If desired, portable benches can be fitted along both sides for growing pot plants, and removed when not required, so that crops can be planted in the soil. In addition, ferns or other shade-loving plants can be grown in the space beneath the benches.

Lean-to

The standard lean-to greenhouse, which has a single sloping roof and is built against a wall or the side of a building, is the least expen-

Lean-to greenhouse

sive to buy or to heat. A disadvantage is that light can enter from one side only, so that plants growing in it have a tendency to develop in that direction. In spite of this, a lean-to can prove a most useful greenhouse and can be built facing any aspect, except due north.

If soundly constructed, a lean-to is relatively inexpensive to heat. Heat losses at night are greatly reduced by the insulating properties of the rear wall, and the wall also radiates warmth absorbed during the daytime.

Three-quarter span

The three-quarter span, lean-to greenhouse has a roof ridge, with a short span on the wall side at the back and a sloping roof of normal length at the front. It costs more to construct and maintain than a standard lean-to house, but affords extra light and increased headroom.

Three-quarter span houses are excellent for growing peaches and vines, or displaying plants, but for most amateurs an ordinary lean-to is adequate.

THE YEAR AT A GLANCE

Gladioli

MARCH

Plant gladiolus corms, in rows for cutting purposes, in colonies for decorating mixed borders. Plant a succession, to provide a continuous supply of blooms. Plant cormlets 2 in. deep in rows.

APRIL

Begin regular hoeing and dress the soil with fish manure beforehand.

MAY

Continue regular hoeing.
Water plants thoroughly in dry weather.

JUNE

Give plants a soaking in dry weather.

JULY

Stake plants individually to provide straight stems for exhibition.
Control gladiolus thrips with malathion or HCH.

AUGUST

Cut gladioli for indoor decoration, but leave at least four leaves on each plant.
Control gladiolus thrips as necessary.

SEPTEMBER

Cut spikes and leave corms undisturbed.

OCTOBER

Lift corms before the winter frosts, cutting off all but ½ in. of stem and placing in a dry, airy place.
When dry, store in trays or shallow boxes.

NOVEMBER

Clean the corms some time between drying-off and planting.

Store cormlets separately if they are to be grown on.
Dust corms with malathion or HCH against thrips if present.
Discard corms diseased with dry rot, hard rot, fusarium rot or botrytis.
Select the site for next year's gladioli, dig it over and incorporate manure or compost, and some bone-meal.

DECEMBER

Check stored corms and discard any which are diseased.

JANUARY

Order new corms.

FEBRUARY

Sprout gladioli in a greenhouse at 10°C (50°F).
Spray all corms with HCH if aphids appear.
Check stored corms and discard any which are diseased.

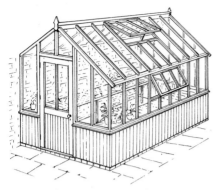

Three-quarter span greenhouse

Dutch light house

This design was first developed by commercial growers. It has the advantage of being relatively cheap and highly functional. A Dutch light is a single sheet of glass, measuring 56 in. long by 28 in. wide, surrounded by a simple wooden frame made from 2 in. by 2 in. timber. The glazed frames are built into a greenhouse by fixing them to a wooden or metal structure. In addition, several manufacturers are now making greenhouses to take glass of this size. These are called 'Dutch light type' houses, as distinct from true Dutch light structures built from individual lights.

Dutch light type greenhouse

Construction materials

Because of its relative cheapness and the ease

with which it can be worked, wood is the traditional material for building greenhouses. However, there is an increasing use of steel and aluminium. Metal houses, especially those made from aluminium, warrant close consideration.

Softwoods

Baltic red wood and Scots pine are satisfactory timbers for greenhouse construction, but need to be painted regularly, inside and out, if they are to resist decay. Unless you are prepared to spend time on this, or to pay for it to be done professionally, it is better to choose a more durable material.

Western red cedar

This has much greater resistance to decay than softwoods and is now used extensively for greenhouse manufacture. It does not require painting, although the timber may be treated with a special cedarwood colourant. It should be oiled every other year. Use brass screws or galvanised nails in the construction of cedar greenhouses. Western red cedar is attractive in appearance and requires a minimum of maintenance. It blends well with contemporary buildings, but, being less robust than softwoods, wood of larger cross-section has to be used.

Oak, teak

These hardwoods are excellent for greenhouse construction, being durable and tough. But they are for the most part ruled out on the score of cost. Teak is better than oak, having an almost unlimited life, and does not tend to twist and warp as oak does. There is, however, one satisfactory mass-produced greenhouse made from oak, braced with rustproof metal, which is competitive in price.

Aluminium alloy

Because it can be readily constructed into elaborate shapes, does not require any maintenance, and should last indefinitely, aluminium is now a popular material for greenhouse construction. The sections can be quite slender, so that greenhouses built from aluminium admit the maximum amount of light. With the development of plastic glazing strips and non-hardening compounds instead of the traditional putty, glazing is no longer a problem. The roof bars have channels in them, which conduct condensation down the inside of the bar to drip off under the eaves outside the greenhouse. In shape, aluminium houses are for the most part traditional, although

there is an exceptionally high-quality house on the market in the form of half a 16-sided figure. An exciting new development is a hexagonal aluminium greenhouse, which has something of the appearance of a space capsule. This could well be a standard design for greenhouses ten years hence.

Steel

The effectiveness of steel as a material for greenhouse construction depends entirely on the efficiency of the rust-proofing. If guaranteed by the manufacturers to last indefinitely, without rusting, under garden conditions, it is a first-class material, its strength allowing thinner struts than with other materials. It is relatively cheap and needs little maintenance, though some gardeners feel that steel greenhouses are not quite so attractive in appearance as those made from aluminium or timber.

Miscellaneous materials

There is a move towards the use of glass fibre and, possibly, rigid plastics for greenhouse construction. One day these may become standard materials. Concrete has been tried, with limited success, and a lot of experiment and development is being carried out to find a substitute for glass. However, for the present glass is the best available material.

Size, ventilation and siting

Take care not to underestimate your needs. Once a greenhouse is in use, it is a simple matter to grow and acquire more plants, so that a house that seemed large enough at the outset is soon grossly overcrowded, which is bad for the plants. Small greenhouses are more difficult to manage than larger ones, for they warm up too quickly in summer and cool down too quickly in winter. On the other hand, too large a house will be unnecessarily expensive to heat during the winter.

Width and height

Size also has a bearing on ease of working in a greenhouse. Narrow houses are extremely inconvenient. Generally, you need a path 2–3 ft. wide down the centre of the house; so that, if the house is 10 ft. wide, about $3\frac{1}{2}$ ft. is left on each side for borders or benches. This is a convenient width when working from the centre path. In greenhouses wider than 10 ft. it may be difficult to work from a centre path without wasting space. The average span roof greenhouse measures about 5 ft. to the eaves and 8 ft. to the ridge, which gives a convenient working height. The wider the house, the greater the height—at any rate, the height to the ridge. This will lead to increased heating costs.

Ventilators

A well designed greenhouse will have a ventilator on each side of the roof, and one in each of the side walls, for every 10 ft. of length. Ventilators on the leeward side can be opened during windy weather without admitting cold draughts to the house. During warm, still weather, the ventilators on both sides can be opened to keep the temperature in the house within bounds, provide fresh air for the plants, and control the humidity.

Automatic ventilation

Ventilation is extremely important to greenhouse plants; when adjusted and controlled automatically, it can be a great boon to the busy gardener. One method is to install a thermostatically controlled extractor fan. During the summer the thermostat controlling the fan is set at 10–13°C (50–55°F); during the winter the fan thermostat is set 5°C (10°F) higher than the thermostat controlling the heater.

As an alternative, automatic ventilators may be attached to the opening roof lights. There are two types, and they operate on a similar principle. One has a cylinder containing oil that expands and contracts with the changes in temperature: that actuates a piston that opens and closes the ventilator. In the other type, oil is replaced by a metal rod that is sensitive to temperature changes. Neither type needs an electricity supply. A separate unit is needed for each ventilator.

Doors

Greenhouse doors must be soundly constructed, well hung, and of a perfect fit, otherwise they are a source of draughts. A badly fitting door can add significantly to heat loss and, in consequence, to fuel bills.

Siting a greenhouse

No matter how well it is designed or constructed, a greenhouse cannot function properly in an unsuitable situation. For obvious reasons, it must not be built in the shadow of trees or buildings, and only sites which are in full sun for almost the whole of the day are suitable. On the other hand, a greenhouse must not be too exposed, particularly to the north and east. Cold winds will cool down a greenhouse much more rapidly than will still

THE YEAR AT A GLANCE

Greenhouses and frames

MARCH

Pot on over-wintered annuals such as schizanthus and antirrhinums from 3 in. pots into 5 in. pots.

Remove old wood and overcrowded shoots from abutilons and take cuttings.

Give extra space to tomato plants sown in February.

Sow tomatoes for planting in an unheated house in May.

Prepare a bed in a cool greenhouse for planting tomatoes in April.

Start canna roots into growth in moist compost. Plant hippeastrums in 6 in. pots.

Take cuttings of zonal pelargoniums.

Give liquid fertiliser every ten days to regal and zonal pelargoniums.

Control insect pests with HCH smokes and pirimiphos-methyl or derris sprays.

Near the end of the month, pot on begonias and gloxinias into 5 in. pots. Transfer *Campanula pyramidalis* to 9 in. pots.

Prick out all seedlings when large enough to handle.

APRIL

In sunny spells, shade young seedlings and newly potted plants, and keep the house well ventilated.

Increase water supply to newly potted plants, and continue feeding established plants. Water hydrangeas generously, feed every ten days, and take cuttings.

Plant tomatoes in a cool greenhouse in the bed prepared last month. Support tomato plants with canes or strings. To help them set, spray lightly at mid-day in sunny weather, or brush or shake the flowers in dull weather. Remove all side shoots from leaf axils. Sow seeds of tomatoes to be planted outdoors, later potting seedlings into 3 in. pots.

Sow seeds of *Solanum capsicastrum* and *Campanula pyramidalis*.

Feed herbaceous calceolarias every ten days, and train the stems outwards on split bamboos.

Pot on begonias and gloxinias into 5 in. pots.

Move half-hardy plants into a cold frame to harden-off.

Sow melons and cucumbers in a temperature of 16–18°C (61–64°F), and sweet corn at 10°C (50°F).

Plant cucumbers on mounds of manure and soil, and train the lateral shoots on wires fixed to the glazing bars.

Increase water supply to hippeastrums.

Water plants in frames regularly.

Give extra ventilation on sunny days.

MAY

Sow cineraria seeds for flowers next December, and pot seedlings into 3 in. pots when large enough. Sow cucumbers, melons and sweet corn.

Move tuberous begonias and gloxinias into 5 in. pots.

On warm days, shade plants in flower, using plastic blinds or shading painted on the glass.

Water vigorously-growing plants generously and give them a weekly liquid feed.

Take cuttings of regal pelargoniums.

Pot on canna roots into 8 in. pots.

Move large *Campanula pyramidalis* plants to a sheltered position outdoors, supporting the flower spikes with canes.

Stop laterals growing from the main stems of cucumbers, and remove all male flowers and tendrils.

Continue to support tomato stems with strings or canes, and remove side shoots regularly. Feed tomatoes every week or ten days after the fruits begin to swell.

Plant tomatoes in the border of a cold greenhouse, or in rings on aggregate.

Plant melons in cold frames.

JUNE

Water the greenhouse and damp down to maintain a humid atmosphere.

Transfer as many plants as possible to cold frames to reduce watering.

Plunge plants which have finished flowering out in the garden.

Sow cineraria seeds.

Pot on streptocarpus plants, and make a further sowing.

Transfer cyclamens sown last August to 5 in. pots. Give them a liquid feed every ten days. Remove faded flowers from plants now in flower, and control aphides with a systemic insecticide.

Pot polyanthuses in 3 in. pots for greenhouse decoration next winter, and stand in shade outdoors.

Move *Campanula pyramidalis* seedlings into 5 in. pots.

Propagate saintpaulias and *Begonia rex* from leaf cuttings.

Spray *Solanum capsicastrum* plants daily in warm weather to help set fruits.

Pinch out all but four side shoots on melons planted last month, pollinate flowers, and shade glass in hot weather.

Cease giving artificial heat; clean out the boiler, or store the oil heater in a dry shed.

Maintain a humid atmosphere for cucumbers by regular spraying.

If main stems of tomatoes are becoming thin, give extra nitrogen.

Give some ventilation at night in warm weather.

JULY

Water and damp down during hot weather.

Sow cinerarias.

Pick tomato fruits regularly, keep stems supported, remove side shoots, and feed every ten days.

Pick cucumbers regularly, remove male flowers, and top-dress bed when a mass of white roots is seen.

Shade plants which are in bloom and give adequate ventilation.

Take cuttings of regal pelargoniums.

Damp down borders, paths and staging at least once a day in warm weather, and water plants as required.

Insert hydrangea cuttings individually in 3 in. pots.

AUGUST

Repair and paint the greenhouse in readiness for winter, and overhaul the heating system.

Store hippeastrums which have dried off.

Take cuttings of regal pelargoniums.

Remove growing points of tomatoes if the plants are to be followed by chrysanthemums; discontinue feeding and reduce watering.

Sow cyclamen seeds.

Insert cuttings of fuchsias to be grown as standards.

Root zonal pelargonium cuttings.

Raise *Campanula isophylla* plants from cuttings.

SEPTEMBER

Start giving artificial heat towards the end of the month.

Sow annuals for a spring display in the greenhouse, potting the seedlings separately in 3 in. pots.

Take cuttings of fuchsias and zonal pelargoniums.

Remove permanent shading.

Bring primulas and other plants into the greenhouse from cold frames.

OCTOBER

Bring plants into the greenhouse from cold frames.

Reduce watering and damping down.

Fumigate houses where tomatoes have contracted fungus diseases.

Thin out shoots of greenhouse climbers.

Line the greenhouse with polythene sheeting to conserve heat. Leave a little ventilation permanently where an oil heater is used.

Gradually dry off cannas.

Control slugs with pellets.

Close frames at night against sudden frosts.

NOVEMBER

Ventilate house freely on sunny days.

Wash the glass to admit maximum light.

Close house during foggy weather.

Complete remaining potting, moving annuals and rooted cuttings into 3 in. pots.

Store achimenes, fuchsias, heliotropes and hydrangeas under greenhouse staging after they have been dried off.

Control whitefly with HCH.

Give cinerarias more space and keep them free from aphides.

Lift hardy plants for gentle forcing.

Water over-wintering annuals sparingly.

DECEMBER

Do not give too much heat while growth is at a low ebb.

Give extra attention to plants to be in flower at Christmas.

Give some ventilation on sunny days.

Remove all rubbish from the greenhouse, and wash pots and seed trays.

Control slugs with pellets.

Give hydrangeas a dry atmosphere and very little water.

JANUARY

Plan the number and types of plants to be grown in the coming year.

Remove faded blooms from plants in flower.

Avoid over-watering annuals and other young plants.

Remove diseased foliage from pelargonium cuttings.

Sow begonias, gloxinias and streptocarpus in a heated propagating case.

Bring pots of polyanthuses indoors.

FEBRUARY

Move dormant fuchsias, heliotropes and hydrangeas on to the staging and spray with water to encourage new growth.

Sow seeds of cannas, coleus and gloxinias.

Sow seeds of tomatoes for planting in a cool greenhouse in April.

Start an early batch of achimenes.

Prune greenhouse climbers.

Keep watering to a minimum and ventilate freely on mild days.

Remove dead and discoloured fronds from ferns and pot on or divide as necessary.

Pot on over-wintered fuchsias, pelargoniums and coleus into 5 in. pots.

air of the same temperature. A hedge or a fence sited to filter the wind and reduce its speed will give effective protection for up to six times its height. Such a barrier, 5 ft. high and placed 5–6 yd. from the greenhouse, will help to protect it from the chilling effect of cold winds.

In most gardens, such features as paths and boundaries will dictate the direction in which the greenhouse must be built. Otherwise, bear in mind that a greenhouse with its ridge running north to south receives more light, taking the year as a whole; but a house with the ridge running east to west will receive more light during the winter months—an important point for those who wish to raise seedlings and propagate plants during the early months of the year. The site must be well drained and sound foundations laid. An interior central path of concrete slabs or firm ash is essential inside the greenhouse, while there should be a firm path leading to it from the dwelling house. Choose a site as near as possible to water and electricity supplies.

Heating
Though even an unheated greenhouse can be a source of pleasure throughout the year, the range of plants that can be grown in it during the winter is strictly limited. The first step in greenhouse heating is to provide a source of warmth that will keep the temperature above freezing point. This will increase the usefulness of the greenhouse, but the range of plants that can be grown will still be restricted. A portable paraffin heater is usually sufficient to provide protection from frost.

For most gardeners a cool greenhouse—one in which a minimum temperature of about 6–7°C (43–45°F) is maintained—is the most satisfactory. To raise the minimum temperature of a greenhouse to 10°C (50°F) will almost double the fuel bill; to raise it to 16°C (61°F) will cost four times as much.

By combining soil warming and space heating it is possible to effect a considerable economy. With a root temperature provided by the soil-warming cables of 13°C (55°F), and an air temperature of 6–7°C (43–45°F), plants will grow very well.

Solid fuel
A solid fuel boiler, supplying 4 in. hot water pipes, is the traditional method of heating a greenhouse. Solid fuel is cheaper than electricity, while modern boilers are more

efficient than the older designs and can be fitted with a thermostatic control. Installation is straightforward if you follow the manufacturer's instructions. Install a boiler which has a sufficient capacity to maintain the required minimum temperature during severe cold spells. Always use the grade of fuel advised by the manufacturers.

Electric heating
Although it is more expensive than the alternative fuels, electricity has many advantages and is widely used by greenhouse owners. It is clean and reliable, can be completely automatic, and does not have to be ordered or stored. With the aid of a good rod-type thermostat, temperature control can be more precise than with any other form of heating. All electrical installations in greenhouses should be carried out by an electrician experienced in this type of work, and should be checked at regular intervals throughout their working life.

Tubular heaters
These consist of a bank of aluminium tubes containing elements which consume 60 watts of electricity for every foot of tube. Mounted round the greenhouse walls, they make a sound, permanent installation.

Fan heaters
These are extremely efficient electric heaters, which can be moved freely about the house. Warmth is distributed evenly throughout the structure.

Fan heater

Electric convector heaters
Inexpensive and reliable. No installation problems, but heat distribution is inferior to the two types of electric heaters already described.

Mineral-insulated cables
Copper-sheathed heating cables can be fixed to the sides of the house in the same way as tubular heaters. This is quite an efficient form of heating, but surface temperatures are high and the cables can burn if touched.

Electric soil-warming cables
In a cool greenhouse, mains voltage cables, laid in a sand bed on the staging, provide an inexpensive form of supplementary heating, especially for propagation. They are arranged to give a loading of 8 watts per sq. ft. Asbestos sheeting, roofing felt or heavy gauge polythene is first laid on the bench as a base, and boards 6 in. deep are fixed round the outside to form a trough. A 2 in. layer of soft sand is spread over the base, and the cable is laid on top of this and then covered with a further 2 in. of sand. The temperature can be controlled by a thermostat, or the current switched on and off by hand using a thermometer as a guide. A temperature of 13–16°C (55–61°F) is ideal in a cool greenhouse, where soil warming can be used as required throughout the year. In a cold greenhouse the use of soil-warming cables should not be started until April.

Soil warming can also be used to raise the temperature of the soil in the greenhouse border—an advantage when growing tomatoes and lettuces early in the year. In this case, low voltage soil-warming wires, fed from a transformer, are used. They are buried 10–12 in. deep, to avoid disturbance during normal cultivation. The wires are spaced to give an electrical loading of 6 watts for each sq. ft. of border.

Oil heaters
Portable paraffin heaters are excellent as a means of providing frost protection, but have limitations as a permanent source of heat in greenhouses. The chief problem is that the water vapour emitted as a product of combustion creates excessive condensation in the house, unless a little ventilation is left on the whole time. It is important to use the correct grade of paraffin and to keep the burner parts scrupulously clean. Do not leave the wick turned up too high. Always check 15 minutes after lighting that the wick is burning cleanly and correctly.

Miscellaneous equipment
Automatic watering
Capillary watering, or sub-irrigation, provides a simple but effective means of supplying water automatically to pots and boxes on the greenhouse staging. Its basis is a layer of sand, which is kept evenly moist by means of a supply tank or cistern. Placed on this moist sand, the pots extract the water they need by

capillary attraction. The system works equally well with clay or plastic pots, providing the compost in the pots makes good contact with the sand.

Where mains water is available, the supply to the sand bed is controlled through a cistern and ball valve. On a more modest scale, an inverted jar or bottle, with its outlet just above the base of the sand bed, is adequate. It releases its contents little by little whenever the water level in the tray drops below the neck of the bottle. Alternatively, a suitable bench can be constructed by laying a corrugated asbestos sheet as the base, with strips of glass fibre laid in the corrugations. The strips act as wicks, to conduct water along the bench from a tank at the side. The whole area is covered with a generous layer of sand. There are several relatively inexpensive proprietary systems on the market.

Trickle irrigation
This system of watering is semi-automatic, and can be used for supplying such plants as tomatoes growing in the soil in the greenhouse, and also for pot plants. The equipment consists of rubber tubes, through which the water passes, with nozzles set at regular intervals to dispense water very slowly to the base of each plant.

Mist propagation
This modern technique has revolutionised the rooting of cuttings, particularly hardwood types. While mist propagation is by no means essential, it makes a fascinating extra for the greenhouse owner who does a fair amount of propagation. The equipment dispenses a mist-like spray over the cuttings to keep them moist and prevent wilting. The frequency of the spray is controlled by a device, known as a 'leaf', mounted within the spray area, which dries out at the same speed as the leaves of the cuttings. Mist propagation is generally used in conjunction with soil-warming cables to provide the necessary rooting temperature.

Garden frames
A garden frame provides standing space for plants at times when the greenhouse is overcrowded. In the spring it can be used for hardening-off seedlings and cuttings which are waiting to be planted outside. During the summer, a main crop of cucumbers or melons can be grown, and cyclamens, cinerarias, primulas and solanums will grow satisfac-

torily, provided that a thin layer of shading material is applied to the glass. In autumn, the frame can be used for housing bulbs in pots and boxes, and for shrubs and herbaceous plants which are waiting to be taken into the greenhouse for forcing during the early months of the year. Lettuces planted in a frame during November will be ready by early spring.

Dutch lights
Of the several types of frame available, the Dutch light type is nowadays the most popular, being relatively cheap, easy to erect and light to handle. Two Dutch lights will cover a frame approximately 5 ft. sq. The frame walls should be about 18 in. deep at the back and 12 in. at the front. The walls can be built from timber, bricks or concrete blocks.

Metal frames
Lightweight frames, consisting of a metal framework with glazed sides and roof, are also popular. They are generally taller than Dutch light frames, and admit more light, but are colder during the winter than frames with thicker walls.

Glass substitutes
Many substitutes for glass are used in garden frames, but none are quite as good as glass in all respects. These substitutes weigh less than glass and are less brittle, but in most cases they do not transmit as much light or retain as much warmth inside the frame. Glass substitutes are safer than glass in gardens where there are small children.

Electricity in the garden frame
Electrical soil-warming cables add greatly to the usefulness of a garden frame, turning it into a hot bed for raising early crops such as lettuces, or into a heated propagating frame. To make an electrically heated hot bed, low voltage wires are laid under 6–8 in. of fertile soil to give an electrical loading of about 6 watts per sq. ft. Lettuces, such as 'Dandie', 'Kloek', 'Pius' and 'Premier', are sown in October and transplanted into the frame in December. They should be ready for harvesting by mid-March. The heat is usually switched on for 12 hours each night from a few days before the crop is planted until a few days before the first lettuces are ready for cutting.

If the frame is required for propagation, or for over-wintering plants, the cable is

installed in a similar fashion, but covered with 2 in. of sand instead of soil. In addition, a mains voltage cable is fastened round the sides of the frame above soil level to give a loading of 15 watts per sq. ft. of glass. The electricity supply to this cable is controlled by thermostat.

Ground cover
The planting of ground-covering plants to reduce or eliminate weeding and hoeing. Low-growing shrubs such as the periwinkles, *Vinca major*, dwarf hypericums, ivies and prostrate conifers are suitable for ground cover. Low-growing perennials include polygonums, sedums, *Stachys lanata*, aubrietas, *Saxifraga umbrosa* and London pride.

Growing point
The leading part of a shoot or branch from which a tree or shrub grows.

Growth substances
Chemicals, usually artificially synthesised in imitation of naturally occurring hormones. They are used in powder or liquid form to promote plant development.

H

Half-hardy
Applied to plants that cannot withstand frost. Such plants need the protection of a greenhouse or frame during the winter months.
Half-hardy annual. See Annual.

Half-standard: see Standard

Hardening-off
The practice of gradually accustoming plants raised under glass to outdoor conditions. Plants should first be moved from the greenhouse to a cold frame, where they are gradually given more ventilation until they are sufficiently toughened to be moved completely into the open.

Hardy
Applied to plants which are able to withstand frost during a normal winter. A bad winter with severe frost may kill some hardy plants.
Hardy annual. See Annual.

Hastate: see Leaf shapes

THE YEAR AT A GLANCE

Hardy herbaceous plants

MARCH

Check plant labels before they are obscured by new growth.

Prune trees, shrubs or hedges overhanging herbaceous borders.

If weather is dry, spread fertiliser on winter-dug ground and rake it in.

Unpack plants on arrival from nurseries and dip roots in water if dry.

If they, cannot be planted, bed plants in boxes of moist sand, peat or soil, or heel them in.

If weather is mild and soil dry on the surface, plant home-raised seedlings, new plants and plants needing a move.

Puddle in plants put in on light soils.

Dig up host plants to get rid of perennial weeds such as couch grass and ground elder.

Remove protective covering of leaves from tender plants.

Protect young growth from slugs in mild damp weather with slug pellets.

APRIL

Plant late-flowering herbaceous plants and those slow to make new growth.

Lift and divide old clumps of michaelmas daisies, re-planting on well dug and manured ground. Treat rudbeckias, helianthuses and monardas similarly.

Hoe between plants to control weeds.

Stake and tie delphiniums late in the month.

Place short pea sticks around weak-stemmed plants such as pyrethrums.

MAY

Hoe between plants to control weeds.

Continue staking tall plants such as delphiniums.

Pinch out the tips of plants which tend to grow tall.

Thin out shoots of plants more than three years old, removing weaker shoots from the centre of the plant.

Puddle in plants planted during dry weather.

Water newly planted beds with a sprinkler or rosed can.

JUNE

Cut back early-flowering plants to within 3 in. of soil level after flowering.

Divide primroses for re-planting.

Apply a 1 in. mulch of peat or leaf-mould between moisture- or shade-loving plants.

JULY

Continue cutting back early-flowering plants and dead-heading where there are still flowers.

Remove dead flowers from paeonies.

Cut lupins and delphiniums to ground level in mild districts to encourage a second display.

Hoe in a further application of fertiliser around michaelmas daisies lacking in vigour, and spray those liable to mildew with benomyl.

Cut off and burn leaves of *Campanula persicifolia* infected with rust fungus.

Plan position and shape of new beds to be made in the autumn, choosing an open site away from trees and fences.

Begin preparing beds for autumn planting, killing weeds with a contact weedkiller and digging ground to leave it rough.

AUGUST

Continue dead-heading.

Remove supports from plants which have finished flowering and cut off tall, weak stems.

Dig over old beds needing a complete overhaul.

Plan arrangement of flowers to be planted in the autumn before ordering them from a nursery.

SEPTEMBER

Continue dead-heading and cutting back.

Finish preparing new beds, and hoe beds already prepared.

OCTOBER

Begin planting herbaceous perennials.

Mark the position of plants showing no growth above ground.

Transplant plants which need moving.

Tidy beds and borders, remove dead heads and keep down seedling weeds.

Divide and re-plant old clumps of pyrethrum and achillea.

Dig ground for March planting to weather during winter.

Dig over old borders which need a complete overhaul. Remove turf from site chosen for new bed, using it to rot down into potting soil.

NOVEMBER

Finish digging new beds and borders for winter weathering.

Plant tops cut off now may be composted if cut into 6–12 in. lengths.

New plants delivered late may still be planted in mild weather.

Take precautions against slugs.

Begin digging between border plants on heavy soil to permit winter weathering.

Collect fallen leaves lying on plants and use them for leaf-mould or to protect tender plants.

DECEMBER

Cut back invasive roots of trees and hedges.

Replace worn turf beside a bed or border.

Prune overhanging branches.

Order seeds or plants for spring sowing or planting.

JANUARY

Clear dead tops of non-shrubby plants from borders.

Fork over the surface of the soil between plants, and bury weeds.

Continue digging heavy soils to be weathered by frost.

FEBRUARY

Top-dress established borders with fertiliser, using John Innes base, hoof and horn, or other similar fertiliser.

THE YEAR AT A GLANCE

Heathers

MARCH

Plant heathers between now and May, selecting an open position with a neutral or acid soil, except for lime-tolerant species.

Prepare ground by digging, removing perennial weeds, and incorporating peat and bone-meal.

Space the plants 12–18 in. apart, according to type, and plant firmly.

Propagate heathers by layering or taking heel cuttings.

APRIL

Complete planting this month.

Continue propagating by layers and heel cuttings.

Cut back all heathers that have finished flowering.

MAY

Complete remaining planting.

Mulch bare ground with peat, and top-dress older plants.

JUNE

Use young shoots of *Erica carnea* as cuttings and trim back remaining growth. Top-dress with peat.

JULY

Remove weeds and renew peat mulch where necessary.

AUGUST

Take cuttings if more plants are wanted.

SEPTEMBER

Prepare ground for planting, selecting an open position.

OCTOBER

Lightly fork ground prepared for planting, then set the plants, soaking their roots if they are dry.

Plants delivered in weather unsuitable for planting should be put close together in trays of peat, until planting is possible.

NOVEMBER

Continue planting.

Firm newly planted heathers lifted by frost and remove any weeds.

DECEMBER

Continue planting during suitable weather.

Remove weeds among new plants.

Lightly trim established plants which have finished flowering, unless dead flowers are to be retained as a decoration.

JANUARY–FEBRUARY

Firm new plants lifted by frost.

Plant heathers during suitable weather.

THE YEAR AT A GLANCE

Hedges

MARCH

Plant all types of hedges, except broad-leaved evergreens. Evenly space the plants in a straight line.

Remove weeds from hedge bottoms by pulling, hoeing or using paraquat weedkiller. Remove brambles and unwanted tree seedlings.

Complete hard pruning of old hedges.

APRIL

Plant evergreen hedging plants.

Straighten and firm newly planted hedging plants loosened by wind.

MAY

Clip *Lonicera nitida* hedges monthly until September to keep them shapely. Clip privet regularly. Clip forsythia and

flowering currant hedges after flowering. Spread hessian or plastic sheeting alongside hedges to catch the clippings.

Give newly planted hedges a good soaking in dry weather.

JUNE

Trim escallonia hedges for a display of flowers in late summer.

Continue weeding and hoeing hedge bottoms.

JULY

Trim quickthorn hedges.

Control aphids and whitefly on hedges.

AUGUST

Continue to trim fast-growing hedges.

Continue hoeing and weeding hedge bottoms.

SEPTEMBER

Clip new growth for the last time.

Remove remaining weeds and burn them.

Prepare sites for new hedges.

Plant evergreen hedges from mid-September to mid-October.

OCTOBER

Plant evergreens as soon as received, though deciduous plants may be heeled in.

Complete planting evergreens by the middle of the month.

NOVEMBER

Prepare hedge sites if not already done, and complete planting as soon as possible. Heel in plants if site is not ready for them.

DECEMBER–JANUARY

Plant deciduous hedges during mild, dry weather.

Plants received when ground is unfit for planting should be kept in a frost-free shed. Protect their roots with straw.

FEBRUARY

Complete planting of deciduous hedges.

Cut back overgrown hedges towards the end of the month.

THE YEAR AT A GLANCE

Herbs

MARCH

Prepare a seed bed as soon as soil is warm.
Sow small amounts of chervil, chives, dill, marjoram, parsley and sorrel.
Layer shoots of pot marjoram and divide fennel roots.
Split old clumps of bergamot and sorrel.

Under glass

Sow basil in a seed box at 13°C (55°F).

APRIL

Sow parsley, and small amounts of dill, fennel, hyssop, marjoram, rue and thyme.
Thin seeds sown in March.
Plant out rooted cuttings of bay, hyssop, lavender, mint, rosemary, rue and sage.
Plant lavender or rosemary to form a shelter belt.
Plant violets as an edging.
Layer the creeping stems of thyme.
Cut back weak, straggly stems of established rue plants.

Under glass

Make a further sowing of basil.
Harden-off seedlings sown in March, and prick out.

MAY

Make further sowings of chervil, dill, fennel, hyssop and parsley.
Plant out basil seedlings and sow basil seed in drills.
Take cuttings of pot marjoram, rosemary, sage and thyme.
Divide straggly thyme and mint.
Plant out herbs in new herb gardens.

JUNE

Sow further rows of chervil and dill, and thin established seedlings.
Control weeds by frequent hoeing.
Take and root more rosemary and sage cuttings.
Start picking herbs.

JULY

Make sowings of chervil, dill and parsley.
Harvest herbs just before they come into full bloom.
Dry herbs in an airing cupboard. Cut lavender for drying and storing.

AUGUST

Take cuttings of bay, hyssop, lavender, mint, rosemary, rue and sage.
Divide chives every fourth year.
Collect and dry dill and fennel seeds.
Store dried herbs.

SEPTEMBER

Sow parsley and chervil.
Divide and re-plant clumps of bergamot.

Under glass

Take cuttings of bay and rue.
Take cuttings of lavender and protect with a frame or cloche.

OCTOBER

Take cuttings of bay, lavender and rue; place in pots of sand in a cold frame.
Divide clumps of chives in mild weather.
Divide roots of mint, re-planting some and potting others to grow in the greenhouse.
Dig up fennel for forcing under glass.

NOVEMBER

Clear basil, chervil and dill; also fennel and parsley grown for a second season.
Cover September-sown parsley and chervil with cloches.

DECEMBER

Protect bay, rosemary and marjoram.

JANUARY

Plan your new herb garden.
Order seeds in readiness for spring sowing.

FEBRUARY

Prepare site for a new herb garden.
Sow parsley if the weather is dry and not too cold.
Propagate mint by rooted runners.

Haulm

The stems and foliage of some plants, particularly potatoes, runner beans and sweet peas.

HCH

A form of the synthetic chemical BHC. It is an effective insecticide against aphids, earwigs, leaf hoppers, thrips, woolly aphis and young caterpillars. It can be obtained in dust form, as a wettable powder, in liquid form or as a smoke. It should not be used on hydrangeas, beetroots, the cucumber family or black currants. Crops that have been sprayed with HCH—formerly known as lindane— should not be harvested less than two weeks after the last application.

Head

1. Cluster or spike of flowers crowded together at the end of the stalk. 2. The branch system of a standard or half-standard tree. 3. Fully developed cauliflower, lettuce or cabbage.

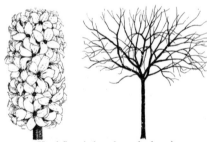

Head (hyacinth and standard tree)

Head (cabbage)

Heart-wood

The hard wood at the centre of the trunk or main branch of a tree.

Heating: see Greenhouses

Hedge trimmers: see Tools

Heeling-in

The temporary planting of trees, shrubs or plants until permanent planting can be done. If plants arrive from the nursery during frosty or wet weather, or if the ground has not been prepared for them, they can be placed in a shallow trench. The roots should be covered with soil and firmed in place with the foot. Larger plants and small trees are usually heeled-in at an angle, so that the wind will not blow them over.

Herbaceous

Applied to plants which produce soft, non-woody growth. Herbaceous plants usually die down in the winter, and grow again the following spring from basal shoots. The term is often loosely applied to perennials.

Hip (or hep)

The fleshy fruit of a rose, red or orange in colour. Some species, such as *Rosa moyesii*, are grown for their orange, bottle-shaped hips as well as for their flowers.

Hoeing: see **Soil (soil operations)**

Hoes: see **Tools**

THE YEAR AT A GLANCE

House plants

MARCH

Give a little more water to plants as days lengthen.
Move delicate plants or those in flower from south-facing to west-facing windows.
Apply liquid fertiliser sparingly to plants in bud or flower.
Prune climbers by cutting out weak or diseased shoots, tie in long growths, and remove dead leaves.
Pot on plants which have become too large for their pots.
Remove offsets from such plants as *Vriesia fenestralis* and pot them separately.
Plunge the pots of those plants which like humid conditions inside larger containers and fill the space between with moist peat ready for warmer weather.

APRIL

Give plants their spring clean, removing dead leaves and washing off dust.
Slightly increase the rate of watering.
Give cacti their first watering.
Give a liquid house-plant fertiliser to all plants you have had for more than six months.
Propagate house plants by stem or leaf cuttings, by division, offsets or layering.

MAY

Water all plants liberally from now until autumn.
Give liquid fertiliser.
Avoid standing plants in a direct draught.
See that plants, apart from succulents, do not remain on south-facing windows at mid-day.
Pinch back long, straggly shoots and replace supporting canes when necessary.
Re-pot plants as they outgrow their pots.

JUNE

Continue watering and feeding at the summer rate.
Stand plants outside to benefit from light warm rain.
Spray plants lightly with clean tepid water when humidity is too low.
Water plants if you are going away and remove them from sunny windows.
Control aphids and other pests.

JULY

Provide as much humidity as possible for all plants on hot days.

AUGUST

If you go on holiday, make arrangements for the plants to be cared for by a local nurseryman or a neighbour. Otherwise water them thoroughly and slip them into a polythene bag; fix up a capillary watering device; or plunge the pots inside larger containers of moist peat.

SEPTEMBER

Slightly reduce watering and feeding.
Keep tender plants away from windows on cold nights.
Transfer plants liking plenty of light from a west to a south window.
Reduce water given to cacti.
Examine plants for signs of over-watering or of pest attacks.
Control red spider mites with derris or pirimiphos-methyl.

OCTOBER

Soak newly acquired plants.
Place plants where they will be warm but not subject to direct heat; where they will get plenty of light but be out of draughts.

NOVEMBER

Try to avoid drastic temperature changes.
Reduce watering so that soil surface is almost dust-dry, but roots are slightly moist.
Use fertiliser only on plants in flower or growing strongly.
Give plants plenty of light, but avoid frosty windows.

DECEMBER

Keep plants on the dry side and give them plenty of light.
Give extra humidity to *Azalea indica*, *Solanum capsicastrum* and cyclamen.
Keep pots of bulbs moist but not too hot, and plant them outdoors after flowering.

JANUARY

Keep plants warm, free from draughts, and supplied with plenty of light.
Water lightly and do not feed unless they are flowering or growing strongly.

FEBRUARY

Examine plants to see whether they are worth keeping. Prune and re-pot the best, and replace the others.

Hooded

Applied to flowers, particularly those of gladioli, whose petal tips are curved inwards.

Hooded gladiolus flower

Hoof and horn: see **Fertilisers and manures**

Hop manure: see **Fertilisers and manures**

Hose-in-hose

An abnormal arrangement of the flowers in some primroses and cowslips. The flowers grow in pairs, one from the centre of the other.

Hoses: see **Tools**

Humidity: see **Weather**

Humus: see **Soil**

Hybrid

A plant which has resulted from crossing two different species, often of the same genus, and which contains some of the characteristics of each. Plants raised from the seeds of hybrids often do not breed true to type.

F1 hybrid. Plant raised from seeds produced by crossing two perfectly true parent strains. Pollination is done by hand in the greenhouse. F1 hybrids are vigorous and uniform. Seeds from these hybrids do not breed true to type.

Hydroponics

The practice of growing plants without soil, using dilute nutrient solutions. The plants are supported on fine wire-mesh netting, with their roots suspended in the solution. Plants, especially carnations, can also be grown in a sterile rooting medium and watered with the nutrient solution.

I

Immune

Applied to plants which by their nature are unaffected by certain pests or diseases. The term has a restricted application: immune varieties of potatoes are immune only to wart disease and may contract other diseases.

Incinerator: see **Tools**

Incised: see **Leaf shapes**

Incurved

Applied to the flower heads of certain chrysanthemums. The florets curve inwards to form a firm globe.

Inflorescence

The flowering part of a plant.

Inorganic

Applied to any chemical compound not containing carbon. Inorganic fertilisers are artificially synthesised, in contrast to organic fertilisers, which are produced from bones, blood, feathers or other formerly living matter.

Insecticide

Any substance or chemical compound that will destroy garden pests. Insecticides—in liquid, powder, smoke or vapour form—fall into two categories: contact poisons and stomach poisons. Some chemicals, such as HCH. combine both types. See also **Systemic Insecticides.**

Insectivorous

Insect-eating. The native wild plant *Drosera* (sundew) traps insects between its toothed

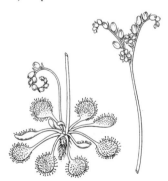

Insectivorous plant (drosera)

leaves. Insectivorous plants generally dissolve their prey in special secretions and absorb the result as food.

Intercrop

A crop which is grown between the rows of another crop, particularly while the latter is in the early stages of its growth and not taking up much space. Radishes may be sown between rows of peas, or lettuces between rows of onions.

Irrigation

The artificial application of water to stimulate growth. In the damp climate of Britain, irrigation has a limited use, but it is valuable for supplying vegetables and lawns with sufficient water during dry periods. Irrigation is best applied through an overhead revolving spray, or a soak-hose with small holes along its length, to give even coverage.

J

John Innes composts: see **Compost**

Joint: see **Node**

K

Key

The winged seed pod of the ash, lime and sycamore.

Key (sycamore)

L

Labels: see **Tools**

Lanceolate: see **Leaf shapes**

Latent

Sometimes applied to a dormant leaf bud (see **Bud**).

Lateral shoot

Shoot branching off from the leader or a main branch.

THE YEAR AT A GLANCE

Irises

MARCH

Pull dead leaves off bearded irises and cut away brown spots or tips from new leaves.
Examine rhizomes, cut away diseased parts, and dust cut surfaces with benomyl powder.
Loosen surface of the soil around the plants and apply a general fertiliser.
Apply slug pellets among the plants. Most of these pellets are lethal to birds and small mammals, so hide them under foliage, flat stones or pieces of slate.
Cover spring-flowering Dutch irises with cloches to protect the blooms.
Pick blooms of *I. unguicularis* regularly to avoid bird damage.
Watch for virus symptoms among bulbous irises and burn affected plants.

APRIL

Cut blooms of bearded irises early in the morning and stand in hot water before transferring to cold.
Remove flower stems from early-flowering plants after blooming.
Renew slug pellets.
Watch for leaf spot disease on bearded irises, and spray with Bordeaux mixture.

MAY

Remove dead flower stems from dwarf irises and dead flowers from intermediates.
Water occasionally in dry weather.
Order bearded irises for planting in July–August.
Renew slug pellets.
Cut bearded irises for indoor decoration.
Inspect bearded irises for signs of leaf spot disease.
Water summer-flowering Dutch irises in dry weather.

JUNE

Tie flower stems of bearded irises to light canes, and cut blooms for decoration.
Cut back stems after flowering and top-dress poor soils with a general fertiliser.
Inspect bearded irises for leaf spot disease.
Prepare a sunny, well drained plot for planting irises, in July–August, digging in manure, compost, bone-meal and fertiliser.
Dress summer-flowering Dutch irises with Nitro-chalk when flower buds show.
Cut back the leaves of *I. unguicularis*.

JULY

Dig up and divide dwarf, intermediate and bearded irises that have been undisturbed for three years.
Select the best single rhizomes for re-planting in newly enriched soil. Leave the tops of the rhizomes above the soil. Cut off the top halves of the leaves.
Plant irises obtained from nurseries.
Water newly planted rhizomes in dry weather and pull off dead leaves.
Order bulbous irises for autumn planting.
Dress summer-flowering Dutch irises with Nitro-chalk.
Lift bulbous irises when their leaves die down if they need moving.
Dry them off in an airy shed and divide them ready for re-planting in September.
Spray or dust irises with derris or trichlorphon against caterpillars.

AUGUST

Complete planting or re-planting of bearded irises.
Order bulbous irises for autumn planting.
Examine iris bulbs which have been lifted, and burn any which show signs of rotting.

SEPTEMBER

Cut off and burn leaves infected with leaf spot disease.
Plant Dutch, Spanish and English irises for flowering from May to July, choosing a sunny, well drained site. Plant *I. reticulata* in rows for cutting. Plant *I. unguicularis* in poor, well drained soil in a sheltered position. Plant *I. sibirica* in moist soil along margins of ponds or streams.

Spray or dust irises with derris or trichlorphon against caterpillars.

Under glass
Plant bulbous irises (Dutch, Spanish, English, *I. danfordiae*) in pots and stand in a cold frame.

OCTOBER

Tidy bearded iris beds before winter. Remove dead leaves and weeds and trim longer leaves by a quarter.

Under glass
Complete planting bulbous irises in pots.

NOVEMBER

Watch for buds on *I. unguicularis* and pick before birds damage the flowers.

DECEMBER

Continue picking *I. unguicularis* regularly.

Under glass
Water bulbous irises in pots when growth begins, and move earlier species to a cold greenhouse to encourage growth.

JANUARY

Place cloches over rows of *I. reticulata* intended for cutting.

Under glass
Water bulbous irises in pots after growth has started.
Transfer Dutch, Spanish and English irises to a cold greenhouse when new growth is evident.

FEBRUARY

Place cloches over rows of Dutch irises intended for cutting, to protect the blooms from the weather.
Protect early-flowering irises in the rock garden with panes of glass.

Under glass
Give warmth to all bulbous irises in pots, except Dutch, Spanish and English types.

457

Latin specific names

The use of Latin nomenclature for plants is internationally accepted. (See **Classification**.) Botanical names are made up of two or more words derived from Latin (or sometimes Greek). The first word, always written with an initial capital letter, gives the plant genus, for example, *Campanula*. This is followed by the specific name, for example, *latifolia*. Next comes the varietal name, which may be in Latin (as *alba*, when referring to a naturally occurring variety); or in the vernacular (as 'Brantwood', when occurring as a cultivated variety or cultivar). When ordering plants it is important to state the full plant name, such as *Campanula latifolia alba* or *Campanula latifolia* 'Brantwood'. The specific name, which always follows the gender of the genus (-*us* is masculine, -*um* neuter and -*a* feminine), often expresses some characteristic of the plant, its place of origin or the name of its discoverer.

acaulis	stemless
aculeatus	prickly, thorny
aestivalis	of summer
affinis	related to another species
alatus	winged
albus	white
alpestris	of mountains
alpinus	alpine
alternifolius	alternate (of leaves)
amabilis	lovely

americanus	American
amoenus	pleasing, lovely
angustifolius	narrow-leaved
annuus	annual
apiculatus	pointed at the tip (usually of leaves)
aquaticus	aquatic
aquifolius	pointed, holly-like (of leaves)
arborescens	tree like
argenteus	silvery
argutus	sharp
armatus	armed (with prickles or thorns)
arvensis	of fields
asiaticus	Asiatic
atro-	dark (prefix)
aurantiacus	orange
auratus, aureus	golden
auriculatus	ear-shaped, eared
australis	southern
autumnalis	autumnal
azureus	sky blue
baccatus	berried
barbarus	foreign
barbatus	bearded, barbed
bellus	beautiful
bicolor	two-coloured
bicornis	two-horned
biflorus	two-flowered
blandus	agreeable, pleasant
borealis	northern
brachy-	short (prefix)
bracteatus	with bracts
brevi-	short (prefix)
bulbosus	bulbous
caeruleus	blue
caespitosus	tufted
calcaratus	spurred
calcareus	chalky or limy
campanulatus	bell-shaped
campestris	of fields or plains
candicans	whitish
candidissimus	pure white

candidus	shining white
capensis	of the Cape of Good Hope
cardinalis	deep scarlet
carneus	flesh-coloured
chinensis	Chinese
cinereus	grey, ash-coloured
coccineus	scarlet
communis	common, growing in company
cordatus	heart-shaped
cordifolius	heart-shaped (of leaves)
cristatus	crested
cruentus	blood-red
cyaneus	blue
decurrens	leaves extending down the stem
dentatus	sharp-toothed
edulis	edible
elatus	tall
elegans	elegant
elegantissimus	very elegant
esculentus	edible
fastigiatus	erect, close-branched
flavescens	becoming yellow, yellowish
flavus	yellow
flore pleno	double-flowered
foetidus	bad-smelling
fragilis	brittle
fragrans	fragrant
fruticosus	shrubby
fulgens	glowing, shining
giganteus	very large
glaber, glabratus	hairless, smooth
glaucus	covered with a whitish or bluish-grey bloom
globosus	globular (usually of flower heads)
glomeratus	clustered
glutinosus	sticky
gracilis	slender
grandiflorus	large-flowered
grandifolius	large-leaved
grandis	large
hirsutus	long-haired

Law and the gardener
Birds, pests and animals

Birds

The Protection of Birds Acts 1954–1969 make it a criminal offence for anyone to destroy or interfere with any wild bird or its nest, subject to certain exceptions. The Acts list certain rare species which are given special protection, and also list harmful birds which may be lawfully killed by an owner or occupier. These lists can be varied by the Home Secretary, and any gardener who wishes to kill a wild bird should first consult either the police or the local authority, who are given powers under the 1967 Protection of Birds Act to publicise the provisions of the Acts. A gardener who is prosecuted will, in most cases, have a good defence if he can prove that his action prevented severe damage to crops or property.

Pests

The Minister of Agriculture, Fisheries and Food has powers to prevent both the importation and spread of destructive insects, fungi and pests in England and Wales. In Scotland this is the responsibility of the Department of Agriculture and Fisheries for Scotland, in Northern Ireland of the Department of Agriculture for Northern Ireland. Orders have been made against a number of pests and diseases, granting the Ministry powers to inspect gardens and to take necessary steps to control the spread of the pest or disease.

Pets

Damage caused by a pet belonging to a dangerous species—such as a python—is the responsibility of its owner; if a pet from a non-dangerous species, such as a dog, causes damage then its owner is liable for the damage, if this is of a kind that the animal, when unrestrained, was likely to cause and if the owner knew of that characteristic. If a dog injures farmyard animals or poultry, its owner is liable without proof of his knowledge or neglect, and if it worries livestock on agricultural land, the owner is guilty of an offence.

A landowner is expected to take reasonable precautions to prevent his livestock straying on to a neighbour's land, and he is liable in most cases for any damage it might be ex-

horizontalis	horizontal
hortensis	of gardens
hyemalis	of winter
imbricatus	overlapping
insignis	distinguished, remarkable
japonicus	Japanese
laciniatus	irregularly cut, jagged
laevigatus	smooth
lanatus	woolly
lanceolatus, lancifolius	lance-shaped (of leaves)
lati-	broad (prefix)
lutescens	becoming yellowish
luteus	yellow
macro-	large (prefix)
majalis	of the month of May
major	larger
majus	great
maritimus	of the sea
maximus	largest
mediterraneus	Mediterranean
mega-	large (prefix)
micro-	small (prefix)
minimus	smallest
minor	smaller
mollis	downy, soft
montanus	of mountains
mucronatus	short, sharp-tipped (of leaves)
multiflorus	many-flowered
muralis	of walls
nanus	dwarf
natans	floating, underwater
niger	black
nitidus	shining
nivalis	of snow
novae-angliae	of New England
novi-belgii	of New Belgium (old name for New York)
nutans	nodding
ob-	inverse (prefix)
obovatus	ovate leaves, with broad end farther from the stalk (see also *ovatus*)
obtusus	bluntly rounded (of leaves)
occidentalis	western
officinalis	medicinal
oppositifolius	leaves opposite, forming a pair one on each side of a node
orientalis	eastern
ovatus	ovate leaves, with broad end at the stalk (see also *obovatus*)
palmatus	lobed or divided like a hand (of leaves)
palustris	of marshes and boggy places
paniculatus	with flowers in panicles
patens	spreading
peltatus	shield-like (leaves), with stalk at or near the centre
perfoliatus	with leaves united round the stem
petiolatus	with leaf stalks
platy-	broad (prefix)
plenus	full or double flowered
poly-	many (prefix)
praecox	very early, precocious
pratensis	of meadows
prostratus	lying flat
pseudo-	false (prefix)
pubescens	downy
pulcher	handsome, beautiful
pulcherrimus	very handsome, very beautiful
pumilus	dwarf
purpureus	purple
racemosus	with flowers in racemes
radicans	rooting
repens, reptans	creeping
reticulatus	net-veined (of leaves)
rhodo-	rose, red (prefix)
rigidus	stiff
robustus	stout, strong
roseus	rose, rosy
rubens	red, ruddy
rugosus	wrinkled (of leaves)
rupestris	of rocks
sagittifolius	with arrow-shaped leaves
sanguineus	blood-red
scaber	rough
scandens	climbing
semperflorens	ever-flowering
sempervirens	evergreen
septentrionalis	northern
sessilis	stalkless
sibiricus	Siberian
sinensis	Chinese
sino-	Chinese (prefix)
speciosus	showy
spectabilis	spectacular
splendens	splendid, brilliant
stellatus	starry
suaveolens	sweet-scented
sub-	nearly or under (prefix)
suffruticosus	nearly shrubby
superbus	superb, superior
sylvaticus	forest-liking
sylvestris	of woods or forests, or growing wild
tomentosus	densely hairy
tri-	three (prefix)
tricolor	three-coloured
truncatus	cut off squarely (of leaves)
umbellatus	flowers in umbels
uni-	one (prefix)
vagans	wandering
variegatus	irregularly coloured
veris	of spring
vernalis, vernus	of spring
villosus	softly hairy
violaceus	violet
virens	green
virescens	becoming green, greenish
virginalis	virgin
virginianus or *virgineus*	of Virginia
viridiflorus	green-flowered
vulgaris	common, usual
zebrinus	striped
zonatus	banded, zoned

pected to do. If the straying animal is a cat or dog, however, the owner is not liable unless he has been negligent or it has attacked livestock. The owner is not expected to prevent his tame animals straying on to the highway.

No action can be brought against a person whose animal strays into a garden unless the owner has been negligent or unless the animal is a dog which damages livestock. If, however, an animal is taken on to the highway, its owner must take care that it does not cause any damage. The garden owner may recover damages if he can prove negligence.

Rats and mice
Local authorities have statutory powers to deal with rats and mice.

Wild rabbits
An order made under the Pests Act 1954 may require an occupier of land to destroy, or control in some way, any wild rabbits on his land.

Plants

Plants from abroad
The importation of plants is covered within the terms of the Importation of Plants, Plant Produce and Potatoes (Health) (Great Britain) Order 1971, and the Importation of Forest Trees (Prohibition) (Great Britain) Order 1965. The latter Order prohibits entry of certain species of forest trees and includes miniatures or 'bonsai' of these species, whilst the former Order imposes restrictions on the importation of other plants including the prohibition of annual or bi-annual plants from countries outside Europe.

Plants from Northern Ireland or the Irish Republic may, however, be brought into Great Britain without restriction, but no plant from the United Kingdom can be imported into the Irish Republic unless a licence is obtained and a plant health certificate produced.

Seeds
The Vegetable Seeds Regulations 1973 apply to most kinds of vegetable seed used in the British Isles. They provide that seed marketed must attain the standards laid down in the Regulations in respect of analytical purity, germination, and content of seed of other

plants. If the seed does not meet these standards, penalties can be imposed on the seller.

Buyers of grass seed are similarly protected under the Fodder Plant Seeds Regulations 1974, but there is no special legislation governing the sale of flower seeds, and buyers of these must rely on the skill, judgment and reputation of the seedsman.

Property rights and duties

Bonfires

Smoke from a bonfire may cause inconvenience to a neighbour, but an action for nuisance can be brought only if his enjoyment of his property or his comfort is interfered with substantially or unreasonably.

Smoke from bonfires is not forbidden under the 1956 Clean Air Act. Such smoke is unlikely to be a nuisance to a neighbour unless it is black smoke from a bonfire lit with paraffin. If the smoke spreads across the highway and causes an accident, the gardener may be held liable.

Damage

1. BY ROOTS AND BRANCHES OF TREES

A householder may be liable for any actual damage caused by roots or branches of trees which encroach on a neighbour's land, but comprehensive insurance policies can cover damage of this kind. A tenant may himself be liable to indemnify his landlord if he has agreed with him to keep the trees in proper condition and fails to do so.

2. BY SPRAYING

If a gardener's crops or land are injured in any way by spray from adjoining land, he can sue for damages, and can apply for an injunction to stop the spraying if it continues.

3. BY STEALING OR MALICIOUSLY DAMAGING

It is an offence to steal, or to destroy or damage with intent to steal, garden produce or any tree or shrub.

It is a criminal offence to damage plants,

THE YEAR AT A GLANCE

Lawns

MARCH

New lawns

Rake and treat seed bed, and apply pre-seeding fertiliser.
Choose suitable seed mixture, and sow it at 1–2 oz. per sq. yd.
Watch for symptoms of damping-off.
Mow when the grass is 3 in. high.

Established lawns

Re-seed worn areas.
Repair lawn edges which have crumbled.
Aerate the lawn with a wire rake.
Apply spring fertiliser.
Cut grass when it is $2\frac{1}{2}$–3 in. high.
Watch out for fusarium patch disease and treat with mercury fungicide.
Control worms.
Apply selective weedkillers when grass is growing actively.
Control moss by improving drainage and aeration, and dress with mercurised moss compounds.
Watch out for bird damage.

APRIL

New lawns

Mow twice a week if necessary.
Roll to firm seedlings if required.

Established lawns

Mow, aerate, apply spring fertiliser, and scarify.
Continue mowing frequently, lowering the blades at each successive cut, down to a minimum of $\frac{1}{2}$ in.
Level humps and fill in hollows.
Treat fusarium patch if present.
Apply selective weedkillers and mercurised moss compounds.

MAY

New lawns

Cultivate new sites for autumn sowing and leave rough during the summer.

Established lawns

Apply sulphate of ammonia.
Continue regular mowing.
Apply fungicides for disease control.
Continue to apply weedkiller.

JUNE

Established lawns

Continue mowing, raising blades during very dry weather.
Spike the lawn to allow water to penetrate.
Apply fungicides for control of dollar spot and corticium.
Treat with weedkillers if necessary.

JULY

New and established lawns

Water copiously in dry weather.
Aerate surface of lawn.

Apply fungicides to control fusarium, dollar spot and corticium.

AUGUST

New lawns

Apply top dressings to sites for new lawns.
A week after this sow grass seed.

Established lawns

Inspect, and decide which areas need renovation.
Continue applying weedkillers and fungicides as necessary.

SEPTEMBER

New lawns

Aerate, apply sharp sand or compost, and scarify to remove debris.
Apply autumn fertiliser.
Control weeds, fungal infections and moss.

OCTOBER

New lawns

Mow when grass is 3 in. high.
Roll to firm seedlings if loose.

Established lawns

Remedy defective drainage and lay new drains if necessary.
Aerate, scarify, hollow-tine, and treat with autumn fertiliser.

Turfing

Prepare weed-free turf bed, allow to settle, and rake in fertiliser.

trees, fences, stiles, gates or any other property if the person who did the damage intended to damage property, or was reckless as to whether it would be damaged.

The penalties for these offences vary widely, but fines and imprisonment can be imposed in most cases.

Dangerous or poisonous trees and hedges

If a tree or hedge is in a dangerous condition, and the owner knows this or should have known it, he is liable for any damage caused by the tree or hedge to the occupier of the adjoining land or to anyone using the highway. An occupier will also be liable for any

---

Select turf of adequate quality.
Lay turves as soon as possible after delivery.
Treat lawn against earthworms.

NOVEMBER

Complete laying turf.
Continue drainage operations.
Apply autumn fertiliser.
Make final cut, and bring in mowing machines for overhaul.
Continue treatment against earthworms.

DECEMBER

Dig over areas to be seeded in the spring.
Treat against leatherjackets.
Clean and overhaul machines and equipment.

JANUARY

Check drainage outlets.
Prepare top dressings for spring use.
Continue aeration treatment.
Lay turves in favourable weather.

FEBRUARY

New lawns

Continue preparing spring seed beds.

Established lawns

Aerate and scarify in dry conditions.
Apply worm-killing preparations and lawn sand.
Treat moss with mercurised compounds.

---

damage caused by poisonous trees which he allows to grow over a neighbour's land.

Fences

Although there is no general duty to erect fences round property, a landowner ought to do so, since he may become liable for injury caused to children he allows to trespass continually on his land, or for damage done by animals who stray off his land. Most sales of land for building do in fact contain covenants requiring owners to build and maintain fences.

If the title deeds of a house do not make it clear, either in writing or by 'T' marks on the plan, who owns and should repair a particular fence or hedge, the position of the supports of brick walls or fences (usually found on the owner's side), together with previous acts of ownership, such as repairs done by one owner, will help to indicate who is the owner. The fence may be owned in common with the owner of the adjoining property, in which case both owners are equally liable.

If a barbed-wire fence is a nuisance to the adjoining highway, the local authority may order the occupier to remove it and, if he fails to do so, a magistrates' court will order him to remove it.

Fixtures

A greenhouse built by a tenant (see *Greenhouses and garden sheds*) which is fixed to the ground becomes part of the landlord's property. A tenant who wishes to remove the building at the end of his tenancy must make sure that it merely rests on the ground by its own weight. Likewise a vendor cannot remove a fixed greenhouse after sale of his property, as it is part of the property, without prior agreement of the purchaser.

The courts have also decided that no fruit or rose trees, shrubs or plants can be removed by a tenant, even if he planted them himself.

Greenhouses and garden sheds

Before building a greenhouse or garden shed, the owner should provide the local authority with details of the proposed greenhouse so that they can decide whether consent is necessary and, if so, whether the plans conform with the sanitary requirements and standards specified under the building regulations made under the Public Health Acts. If consent

is not obtained, the owner may be committing an offence, and be asked to pull the building down. However, an order made under the Town and Country Planning Acts allows a 10 ft. high garden shed (12 ft. high if it has a ridged roof) to be built without consent.

A tenant who wishes to build a greenhouse may, under his tenancy agreement, have to obtain his landlord's consent.

Roots and branches of trees

A gardener may cut off the branches or roots of his neighbour's trees if they overhang or encroach into his garden. Although he need give their owner no notice of intention, he must cut the branches and roots from his own garden. The branches, and any fruit on them, belong to the owner of the tree. The owner himself may cut overhanging branches, but must do so with care and inform his neighbour if there is any likelihood that they may fall and injure his property. (See also *Damage*.)

Watering

Water supplied for domestic purposes can be used to water a garden if the water is drawn from a tap inside the house and no hose is used, but the water companies can, if they wish, increase the water rate if a gardener uses a hose or sprinkler, or draws water from an outside tap even if a hose is not used.

Weeds and rubbish

Under the Weeds Act 1959 the Minister of Agriculture, Fisheries and Food (in Wales the Minister of Agriculture, Fisheries and Food acting jointly with the Secretary of State for Wales) may in certain circumstances order an occupier to prevent the spread of certain injurious weeds (spear thistle, creeping or field thistle, curled or broad-leaved dock and ragwort). If the occupier fails to do this, he can be fined.

Also, under the Public Health Act 1961, a local authority can remove from a vacant site in a built-up area any rubbish detrimental to the local amenities, unless it has been put there in connection with a business.

Lawn edger: see **Tools**

Lawn rake: see **Tools**

Layering: see **Propagation**

Leaf shapes
There is immense variety in leaf shapes, from the arrow-shaped (hastate) leaves of *Polygonum baldschuanicum* to the three-leaved (trifoliate) form of clover. The main botanical classifications, used in plant descriptions, are illustrated on this page.

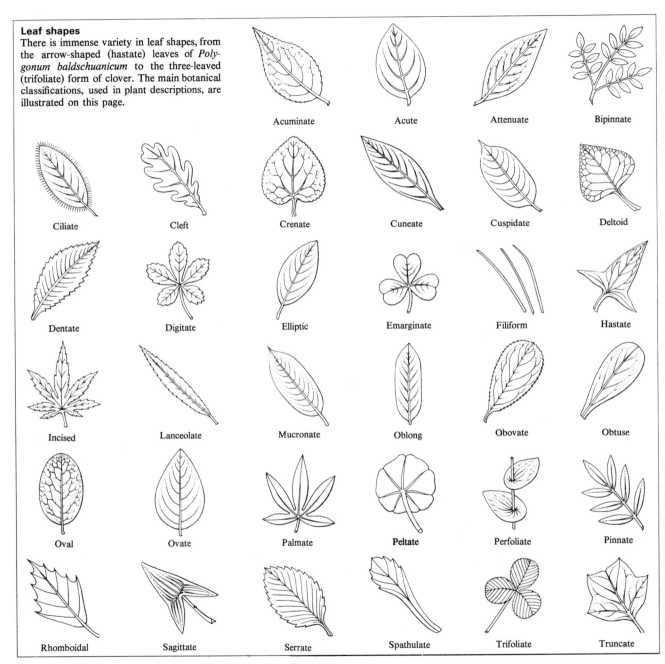

Acuminate	Acute	Attenuate	Bipinnate

Ciliate	Cleft	Crenate	Cuneate	Cuspidate	Deltoid
Dentate	Digitate	Elliptic	Emarginate	Filiform	Hastate
Incised	Lanceolate	Mucronate	Oblong	Obovate	Obtuse
Oval	Ovate	Palmate	**Peltate**	Perfoliate	Pinnate
Rhomboidal	Sagittate	Serrate	Spathulate	Trifoliate	Truncate

THE YEAR AT A GLANCE

Lilies

MARCH

Mulch established beds.
Protect young shoots from frost with cloches.
Sow lily seeds outdoors in the south.
Complete planting of bulbs.
Prepare beds for lilies to be planted in autumn, following annuals during summer.

Under glass

Plant imported lilies in pots.
Cease feeding forced lilies when the buds are about to open.

APRIL

Finish planting bulbs.
Keep beds weeded.
Sow seeds in boxes outdoors.
Spray fortnightly with Bordeaux mixture against botrytis. Spray monthly with a systemic insecticide to control virus-carrying aphids.

Under glass

Spray with a systemic insecticide against aphids.
Plant forced lilies outdoors after flowering.
Sow seeds of *L. auratum, L. speciosum* and *L. sargentiae.*

MAY

Complete bulb planting.
Spray monthly with a systemic insecticide against aphids and fortnightly with Bordeaux mixture against botrytis.
Watch for signs of basal rot and fusarium disease.

Under glass

Control aphids with a systemic insecticide.
Plant forced lilies in the garden after flowering.

JUNE

Spray monthly with systemic insecticide and fortnightly with Bordeaux mixture.

Burn virus-infected lilies.

Under glass

Control aphids with a systemic insecticide.
Keep pot-grown lilies well watered.

JULY

Pick off dead flower heads, unless you wish to save seeds.
Spray with Bordeaux mixture and with a systemic insecticide.
Keep beds weeded and watered.

Under glass

Control aphids.
Water adequately.

AUGUST

Plant *L. candidum.*
Order lilies for autumn delivery.
Spray with Bordeaux mixture against botrytis and with a systemic insecticide against aphids.
Gather bulbils from *L. tigrinum* and *L. sargentiae.*
Sow home-saved seed as soon as ripe.

Under glass

Control aphids with a systemic insecticide.
Keep pots adequately watered.

SEPTEMBER

Spray against aphids and botrytis.
Start planting bulbs as soon as available.
Lift small bulbs from around *L. auratum* and grow on in pots.
Transplant well grown pots of seedlings.
Sow seed now or in spring.
Propagate healthy scales broken off during transplanting.

OCTOBER

Plant as many of your lilies as possible.
Allow lily stems to die down naturally.
Lift some lily bulbs from the garden and pot up to grow as pot plants; then plunge them 4 in. deep in ashes.

Under glass

Bring newly potted lilies wanted for forcing into the greenhouse three months before flowers are required.

NOVEMBER

Plant late-delivered bulbs if ground is easily worked.

Under glass

Pot bulbs which cannot be planted outdoors, or set them in trays of damp peat.
Keep the trays frost-free and protect from mice, slugs and aphids.

DECEMBER

Plant bulbs if soil is easily worked.

Under glass

Pot bulbs or set them in trays of damp peat if they cannot be planted outdoors.
Bring in boxes of autumn-sown seedlings and also pots of lilies.

JANUARY

Plant bulbs in mild weather.

Under glass

Sow lily seeds in boxes.
Bring in boxes of slow-germinating lilies sown in autumn. Bring in pots of lilies for forcing for Easter.
Lift surplus strong lilies from the garden for forcing.

FEBRUARY

Plant bulbs in mild weather.
When buying, choose plump healthy bulbs which are not dried up.
Protect shoots against frost with cloches.

Under glass

Sow seed under glass.
Pot imported lilies to grow as pot plants.
Plant bulbs of stem-rooting lilies.
When buds appear on forced lilies, raise temperature to 18–21°C (64–70°F) and feed weekly with dilute liquid manure.

Leader

The main shoot extending the branch framework of a tree. If the shoot is badly shaped or otherwise unsuitable, a lateral shoot may be selected as a new leader by pruning away all growth beyond it.

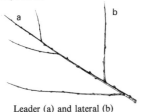

Leader (a) and lateral (b)

Leaf-mould: see **Fertilisers and manures**

Leaf shapes: see p. 462

Leaf sweeper: see **Tools**

Legume

Strictly, a botanical term for the type of seed pod found in plants of the pea family. Also loosely applied to a plant which is a member of the pea family, especially to food plants.

Levelling

Producing on a plot of ground an even, horizontal or gently sloping surface.

To level a slope, T-shaped boning rods are driven into the ground at regular intervals from the lowest to the highest points of the slope. The rods are sighted by eye and made level with each other. Discrepancies in the soil level will then show up. Indicate the point to which the soil should be levelled by marking an equal distance down from the cross-member of each rod, and move the soil roughly to these marks. Remove the boning rods and drive in pegs at intervals of a few feet, protruding 3–6 in. above the ground. Repeat the levelling process with the pegs, using a spirit level and a straight edge.

Where the plot is very uneven, levelling may bring inferior subsoil to the surface. To avoid this, remove the topsoil to one side and level the subsoil as described. When the plot is level, replace the topsoil evenly.

Lichen

Primitive plant growth often found on rocks or old trees. The grey-green encrustation, formed of algae and fungi, can be eradicated by spraying with a tar-oil wash.

Lifting

The digging up of all types of plants, including trees and shrubs, for planting elsewhere, and of bulbs and root crops to be stored. Take care not to damage the roots, bulbs or tubers, otherwise they will not re-establish or store satisfactorily.

Always lift plants during the most suitable season. Deciduous trees and shrubs are best moved in late autumn and early spring, but they may also be lifted successfully in open weather during winter. Evergreens should be moved in early October or late April to establish themselves before the arrival of cold, drying winter winds or spring drought. Fibrous rooted herbaceous plants should be lifted in March or April, and tap-rooted herbaceous subjects in September or October. Lift flag irises in July, after flowering. Lift bulbs as their foliage dies down.

Vegetables, particularly root crops like potatoes, carrots and beet, are lifted in the early autumn, when they have reached maturity and their foliage has started to wither.

Light

Adequate light is essential for plant growth. Energy from sunlight is used by plants to convert water and atmospheric carbon dioxide into simple sugars, which form the basis of the plants' tissues. This process is known as photosynthesis, and is dependent on the presence of chlorophyll.

Length of daylight also influences plants and controls flowering and bulb formation in many species. Onions, for example, form their bulbs after the longest day has passed, and chrysanthemums flower as the days become shorter. In the greenhouse short days are provided artificially by shading plants with black material for several hours each day if out-of-season chrysanthemums or certain other flowers are wanted.

Limb

A large branch on a mature tree.

Lime: see **Fertilisers and manures**

Lindane: see **HCH**

Liquid fertiliser: see **Fertilisers and manures**

Loam: see **Soil**

Lopping: see **Pruning**

M

Maiden tree

A fruit tree in its first year after grafting or budding. It consists of a single, unbranched stem.

Malathion

An insecticide effective in the destruction of many sap-sucking insects, such as aphids, leaf hoppers, thrips and adult whiteflies. It is obtainable as a dust or a spray, and is safe to use on most plants, but not on antirrhinums, ferns, petunias and zinnias. Malathion is less poisonous than other insecticides, and only a short delay need elapse between spraying and harvesting edible crops.

Male flower

A flower, such as the hazel catkin, bearing only the male, pollen-bearing organs, the stamens. The female flowers may occur on the same plant or on a separate female plant. Hollies, for example, are either male or female trees, and at least one of each is needed before berries can be produced.

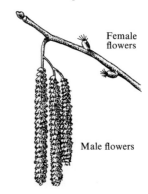

Female flowers

Male flowers

Maneb

Chemical fungicide, obtainable as a wettable powder. It is effective in the control of potato and tomato blight, tulip fire, and black spot on roses. After the last application, one week at least must elapse before harvesting edible crops.

Manure: see **Fertilisers and manures**

Manuring: see **Soil (soil operations)**

MCPA: see **Weeds and weedkillers**

Mecoprop: see **Weeds and weedkillers**

Menazon
Systemic insecticide, widely used against aphids. Combined with other insecticides, such as HCH, menazon is effective against most insects, and is quite safe to use. The last application should be given thirty days before harvesting.

Mice
These creatures can be a nuisance in the garden, where they feed on bulbs and tubers during the winter. Potatoes and carrots, newly sown seeds of peas and sometimes beans are the crops that suffer most. Peas can be protected against attack by dipping the seeds in paraffin and rolling them in red-lead powder before sowing. In greenhouses and frames mice can be caught by spring traps.

Micro-climate: see **Weather**

Mills period: see **Weather**

Mist propagation: see **Greenhouses**

Monocotyledon: see **Cotyledon**

Monoecious
Applied to plants which have separate male and female flowers on the same plant.

Moraine
The tumbled deposit of rocks and grit found at the end of glaciers. Certain alpine plants,

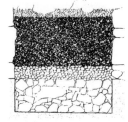

Moraine (cross-section)

such as *Engleria* saxifrages, will grow only in such conditions, which combine moisture with sharp drainage. A simulated moraine bed, consisting of small stone chippings fed with water from below, can be constructed as an adjunct to the rock garden. If lime-hating plants are to be grown, the chippings must be of sandstone or granite.

Moss
A non-flowering main division of the plant world. Moss can be a serious nuisance on lawns, where it grows in damp, stagnant and acid conditions. For immediate control apply mercurised lawn sand as a top-dressing; for long-term control, aerate the lawn and improve its texture and drainage by working sand into it.
Sphagnum moss. Used in air layering to retain moisture round newly forming roots. In its decayed form—sphagnum peat—it is widely used for mulching and for working into the soil to improve texture and water retention.

Mowers: see **Tools**

Mowing
The cutting of lawn grass. The effect of frequent mowing produces a close, even sward and eradicates coarser plants and grasses. Fine grass is encouraged, as are creeping and rosette-forming weeds, such as trefoil, plantain and dandelion. Such a lawn requires occasional feeding and weedkilling. Too close mowing should be avoided, as it tends to cause bare patches, which may be colonised by moss. Sports turf should contain hard-wearing grasses.

Mucronate: see **Leaf shapes**

Mulch
Any top-dressing of organic material—farmyard manure, straw, peat, compost, pulverised wood bark or spent hops. It is spread several inches thick, usually in spring or early summer, over the roots of plants, both to conserve moisture and to supply the roots with nutriment as the material decomposes. Avoid covering cold or frozen soil, and give dry soil a good soaking before mulching it. See also **Soil (soil operations)**.

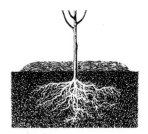

Mulch (over roots of tree)

Muriate of potash: see **Fertilisers and manures**

Mutation
A chance-occurring variation of a plant. A chrysanthemum, for example, may produce a shoot with flowers of a colour different from its type. If such a mutation, also known as 'sport', is thought valuable, it may be perpetuated by means of cuttings or by budding or grafting on to a suitable rootstock. Many climbing roses are mutations of bush forms.

N

Naturalise
To establish bulbs or other plants in the garden, usually in grass, so that they appear to be growing there naturally. Daffodils, crocuses and snowdrops are the most frequently naturalised bulbs, and after planting require no further attention for the next three years.

Nectar
A sweet liquid secreted by some flowers to attract pollinating insects. Bees make honey from the nectar they collect from flowers, and in the process carry pollen from the anthers of one flower to the stigma of another.

Nets: see **Tools**

Nicotine
Powerful insecticide, particularly against aphids. It can be used as a liquid spray, as a dust or as a fumigator, but is not effective at temperatures below 16°C (61°F). Nicotine is poisonous to humans and animals, and great care must be exercised when using it.

Nitrate of soda: see **Fertilisers and manures**

Nitro-chalk: see **Fertilisers and manures**

Nitrogen: see **Fertilisers and manures**

Node
The joint on a stem from which leaves or axillary buds arise.

O

Oblong: see **Leaf shapes**

Obovate: see **Leaf shapes**

Obtuse: see **Leaf shapes**

Offset: see **Propagation**

Oiler: see **Tools**

Opposite
Applied to leaves arranged in pairs on opposite sides of a stem.

Opposite leaves (lilac)

Organic
Any chemical compound containing carbon. Organic fertilisers, such as bone-meal, dried blood and fish manure, are of vegetable or animal rather than of artificial origin.

Organic matter: see **Soil**

Ornamental fish
All ornamental pools should contain a few fish, if only to keep down the mosquitoes which are invariably attracted to still water. The lively movements of fish, and their bright colours, are a constant source of interest. In addition to destroying mosquito larvae, they account for many plant pests, such as aphids, water-lily beetles and caddis worms. Fish fertilise water plants with their excreta and provide carbon dioxide, exhaled in breathing, which is used by submerged plants in the process of photosynthesis.

In garden pools, fish which swim near the surface are the most satisfactory, as they are easily seen and do not make the water muddy by constant rooting about in the bottom. They should not be introduced to a new pool until the plants have settled in and are starting to grow—six or seven weeks after planting.

Some shade is necessary for fish. In a mature pond this is generally supplied by means of waterside aquatics or the floating leaves of water lilies. A section $2-2\frac{1}{2}$ ft. deep in one part of the pool will provide a cool retreat in summer and an area which will not freeze solid even in the coldest winter.

Handle fish as little as possible, as they are sensitive to rough treatment. When newly purchased fish are delivered, open the container, lower the can or bag into the water, and let them swim out.

An abundance of underwater plants is essential, since they charge the water with oxygen and also use up carbon dioxide exhaled by the fish. In addition, the leaves and stems provide suitable nurseries for eggs and later protect the young fry from being eaten by the adults.

Feeding is rarely essential in large ponds if there is plenty of underwater vegetation, but if fish are fed they make larger specimens and become tame. Protein foods are beneficial in early spring when the fish are recovering from their winter fast, and again in autumn to prepare them for the winter. No food at all should be given between late November and early March, but during the rest of the year small feeds of proprietary fish foods, chopped earthworms and baked bread-crumbs will be welcome. Never give more food at any one time than the fish consume in approximately five minutes, otherwise it will lie on the mud and rot.

Running water, fountains or aerators are unnecessary for the fish described, provided the pool is not overstocked. Give them plenty of room, allowing 2–3 in. of fish per square foot of surface area, based on the adult size of the fish.

Snails are useful as scavengers, consuming fish excreta, algae and remnants of food. However, it is better to avoid the freshwater whelk (*Limnaea stagnalis*), which frequently damages water plants. If these snails occur, they can be trapped by placing a lettuce or cabbage stump in the pool, removing this frequently and shaking off the adhering snails.

Bitterling
Bitterling are rather small fish, the male rarely exceeding 3 in. in length and the female about 2 in. At breeding time the male is very colourful, with a mauve and green body and red fins edged with black. The female is more sombre; her back is greenish-brown, her sides are silvery, and she has a curious appendage in the shape of a reddish oviduct beneath her body. At spawning time this sometimes protrudes for as much as 1 in., and some authorities suggest that it is used for the act of depositing eggs inside the open shell of a pond mussel. The eggs hatch, and the young fry emerge when the mussel opens its shell to feed. Bitterling are hardy and associate well with other fish.

Carp, common
The common carp is eaten as food in parts of Europe and Asia and is believed to be unusually long-lived, some authorities quoting a life span of more than a century. It is dull brown and olive in colour and grows over 24 in. long and up to 50 lb. in weight.

Carp, hi-goi golden
A varietal form of the common bronze carp, bred by the Japanese for its deep orange-red colour, with or without black markings. Silvery white forms also occur. Hi-goi are very hardy fish and well suited to the larger pool or lake, where they will grow up to 24 in. in length and 10 lb. or more in weight. In common with other carp, hi-goi tend to be both bottom and surface feeders and are very partial to basking in the shallows, where they are easily seen. These fish are easily tamed with such bait as baked bread-crumbs, worms or any proprietary fish food, and they associate well with other hardy fish.

Carp, Japanese koi
In Japan, the production of these fish is a highly developed business. A wide variety of colours is produced—red, silver, blue, black, gold and cream, in many combinations. The

commoner shades, which are exported to England, have Japanese names: Koohaku are red and white; Shiro-muji, white; Sanke, three-coloured; Asagi, light blue; Kin-kabuto, light gold, with a deep gold helmet. Koi carp are perhaps the most highly prized fish for pools and lakes. They grow to about 24 in. and need the same conditions and treatment as goldfish. Purchasers should insist on Japanese-bred stock. Some specimens coming in from other Far Eastern countries are semi-tropical and not likely to prove hardy in an outside pool.

Carp, mirror

The mirror carp is a showy variety, having curious scales. Though there are only a few of these scales, they are large and glisten like small mirrors as the fish moves. Mirror carp tend to keep fairly low in the water and can grow up to 24 in. or more. The largest known mirror carp caught in this country weighed 44 lb. and is in the London Zoo aquarium.

Comets

These are really long-bodied, streamlined goldfish, and because of their slim shape are fast and graceful swimmers. They dart about rapidly, often with jerky movements, and at breeding time sometimes leap out of the water. Comets are perfectly hardy, provided the pool is deep enough not to freeze solid. Good specimens have bright eyes and bodies, and long, free-flowing tails and fins. They will grow to about 10 in. Comet shubunkins, with multi-coloured bodies, are also obtainable.

Golden orfe

Golden orfe and goldfish are two important fish for ornamental pools. They live together amicably, and both keep near the surface; but, while goldfish tend to hang around in ones and twos, orfe are constantly on the move and swim in shoals. They grow to about 24 in. In colour they are salmon-gold, sometimes flecked along the back with brown or black, and there is also a silver form. Orfe that are at least 12 in. long will breed in a lake or pool, provided there is a good depth of water. Feeding the fish on chopped worms or minced raw meat increases the chance of successful breeding.

Goldfish

Goldfish are of oriental origin. Both the Chinese and Japanese have bred varietal

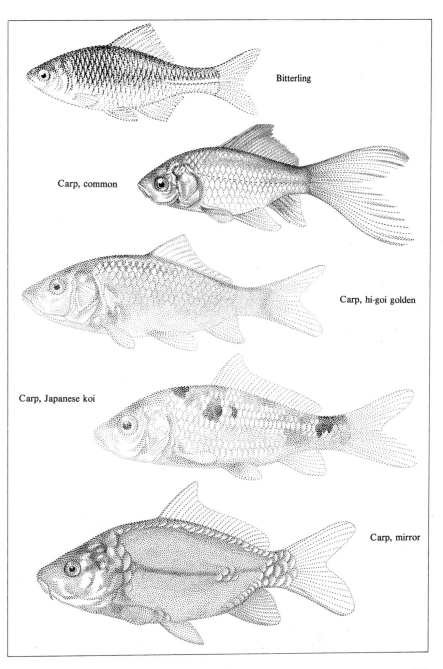

Bitterling

Carp, common

Carp, hi-goi golden

Carp, Japanese koi

Carp, mirror

467

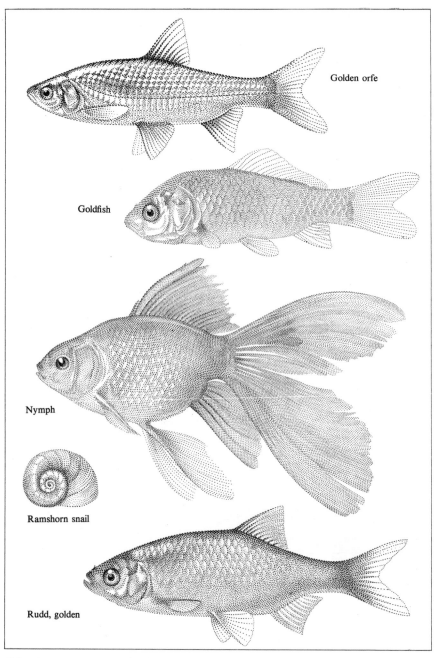

Golden orfe

Goldfish

Nymph

Ramshorn snail

Rudd, golden

forms, but whereas Chinese goldfish are often grotesque, with deformed heads and protruding eyes, the Japanese have concentrated on graceful lines and flowing, veil-like fins and tails. Ordinary goldfish breed freely and can be trained to eat from the hand. Points to look for are a short wide head, bright eyes, good colour and a stiff tail. This is the most popular fish for small ornamental pools, as it is hardy and colourful, and keeps near the surface. Good specimens grow to about 10 in.

Nymphs and veiltails

Nymphs and veiltails, both of Japanese origin, are frequently confused because they both have chunky, almost globular bodies and flowing tails. In the case of nymphs, however, the anal fins and tail are single, whereas in veiltails they are double. Having fewer appendages, nymphs are more active and consequently hardier. However, they are rarely bred separately, but are usually culled from broods of young veiltails. They will grow to 8–9 in. (including tail) and keep near the water surface. If constantly fed in one place, they soon become tame.

Ramshorn snail

This species (*Planorbis corneus*) has a shell shaped like a catherine wheel. It is the best of the pond molluscs and an excellent scavenger, consuming all sorts of debris, such as food remains, dead creatures, algae, fish excreta, etc. Normally it does not attack ornamental plants. A red-fleshed variety, called *rubra*, is more ornamental than the black species and breeds true if kept apart in the pond. There is also a white-bodied variety. These creatures are hermaphrodites; the eggs are laid in jelly-like masses on the backs of water lily leaves and the stems of submerged plants.

Rudd

The common rudd is olive-brown with silvery sides, sometimes tinged with gold. It has rough, coarse scales. The fins and eyes are bright red. It is similar in appearance to the roach, except for differences in the positioning of the fins; but unlike roach, which require running water, rudd can be kept in a pool. The golden rudd, which is deep red gold, is more striking than the common rudd. Both sorts feed on worms, small molluscs, vegetable matter and the larvae of insects. They need plenty of underwater vegetation and grow up to 9–10 in. long.

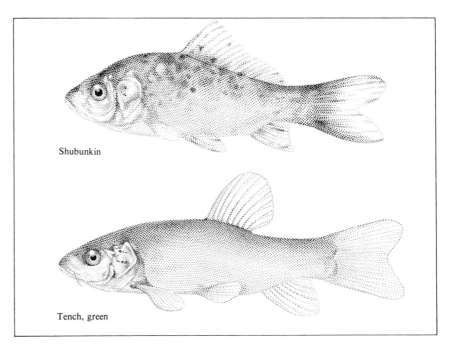

Shubunkin

Tench, green

Shubunkins

In form and size shubunkins resemble common goldfish, except that they have transparent scales, which give them a luminous appearance. They come in a miscellany of patterns and colours—red, black, brown, pearl, yellow, blue and lavender. No two fish are marked exactly the same, although broods will sometimes show a predominance of blues and purples, or be uniformly bright red with black or brown spots. The young fry are always white, but begin to colour up after 3–6 months. Shubunkins are hardy and very active in the pool. Because of their patchwork appearance, they are often called calico fish. They grow to about 8–9 in.

Tench

Both gold and green tench can be kept in large ponds, where, when well fed, they frequently grow to about 20 in. and weigh 4–5 lb. They come to the surface only in the early morning. They are also inclined to root about in the pond bottom, thus stirring up mud, which can be a nuisance in small pools. In winter they bury themselves deep in the mud and become practically dormant.

Ornamental grasses: see p. 470

Oval: see **Leaf shapes**

Ovary

The swelling at the base of the carpel. The ovary contains the female cells, or ovules, which when fertilised become the seeds or fruits.

Ovate: see **Leaf shapes**

Ovule: see **Ovary**

Oxygenator

An aquatic plant, such as *Hottonia* (water violet), which releases oxygen through its leaves. Oxygenating plants are necessary to the survival of fish in a pool.

P

Palmate: see **Leaf shapes**

Panicle

A compound flower cluster consisting of several branches, each with numerous stalked flowers. Lilac flower heads are panicles.

Panicle (lilac)

Paraquat: see **Weeds and weedkillers**

Parasite

Any living organism growing on and taking nourishment from another living organism. Mistletoe, for example, is chiefly parasitic on apple and poplar trees. Fungi and other living organisms growing on dead organisms are known as saprophytes.

Parterre

A formal garden of geometrical beds, completely carpeted with low-growing plants and often edged with dwarf, clipped box. A style much used in French and Italian garden designs of the sixteenth century. The beds may be formed of turf or gravel, and the design may be formed entirely of the edging plants.

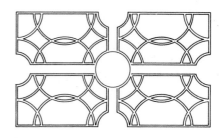

Parterre

Ornamental grasses

Bouteloua oligostachys

Carex morrowii

Festuca glauca

Helictotrichon sempervirens

Holcus mollis variegatus

Luzula sylvatica

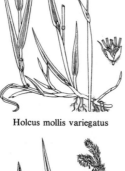

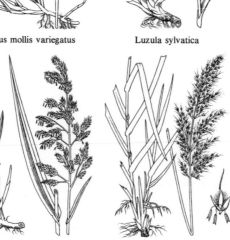

Miscanthus sinensis

Phalaris arundinacea picta

Stipa calamagrostis

THE YEAR AT A GLANCE

Patios and town gardens

MARCH

Choose containers for patio gardening.
Raise window boxes above sills with wooden blocks to help drainage.
Construct raised beds, and leave soil-filled gaps in paving.
Move container-grown plants into prominent positions as they come into bloom.
Buy or mix soil in preparation for spring planting.
Treat wooden boxes and troughs with preservative, and paint all metal parts.
Place layers of crocks, washed clinker and turves in containers, then fill with soil.
Plunge a succession of potted plants in larger containers to provide a constantly changing display.

APRIL

Complete preparation of tubs, boxes and troughs for planting.
Plant alpines in sinks and troughs to make miniature rock gardens.
Sow seeds of hardy annuals.

MAY

Plant tender plants in containers after hardening-off.
Complete sowing hardy annuals.
Arrange containers on patios and erect supporting material for climbing plants.
Lift spring-flowering bulbs after flowering, and plant in a spare corner of the garden, setting summer bedding plants in their place.
Plant hanging baskets and set them in position. Water frequently in hot weather and soak in a tub of water if they have become over-dry.

JUNE

Water containers at least once a day, if not top-dressed with damp peat.

Remove dead flowers daily and discard plants past their best.

JULY

Water container-grown plants at least once a day, if not top-dressed with damp peat.

AUGUST

Water containers daily, remove dead flowers and replace plants past their best.
Before going on holiday, move containers to a shady spot.
Order bulbs for autumn planting.

SEPTEMBER

Continue frequent watering and remove dead flowers.
Prepare containers for planting spring bulbs.
Empty compost from containers not required during the winter, storing wooden ones under cover.

OCTOBER

Remove plants that are past their best.
Pot up tender plants and bring indoors.
Move trees and shrubs in containers to a less exposed position, or protect with straw or bracken.
Plant containers with dwarf conifers, heathers and skimmias, and under-plant with bulbs.

NOVEMBER

Plant trees and shrubs in containers, choosing compact varieties and using tubs with broad bases.

DECEMBER–JANUARY

Move trees and shrubs in containers to a less exposed position and tie up vulnerable branches to avoid snow damage.
Plant trees and shrubs in containers during fine weather.

FEBRUARY

Plant trees and shrubs in containers during fine weather.

Paths

Paths form the framework of a garden. They are important both as a means of access to various parts of the garden, and as an element of artistic design. Paths must be wide enough to wheel a barrow and to allow people to pass; an average width of 3–4 ft. is suitable for most gardens.

Paths need good foundations of brick or clinker laid to a depth of at least 6 in. to provide good drainage and a solid foundation. Surfacing materials may be stone or pre-cast paving slabs, crazy paving slabs, brick, concrete (at least 2 in. thick), asphalt (1 in. thick) or gravel. Slabs, which can now be obtained in unusual shapes as well as the traditional rectangular, can be bedded in various designs on sand, ashes or cement.

Ready-made paving materials include cold black or brown tarmacadam, which is spread evenly over the path to a depth of about $\frac{1}{2}$–$\frac{3}{4}$ in. and rolled in. Chippings are provided for surface decoration, and the path is ready for use immediately.

Brick paths. The first two patterns do not require cut bricks, and are easier to lay than the right-hand example

Brick and concrete squares

Concrete slabs with cobbles

Stone slabs with gravel

Crazy paving

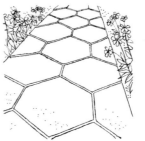

Hexagonal concrete slabs

Flat pebbles in concrete

PCNB: see **Quintozene**

Peat

Dead vegetable matter in a partially decomposed state. It is formed when plant remains from bogs (sphagnum peat) or heathland (sedge peat) are prevented from decaying beyond a certain point through lack of oxygen. Peat, which is generally free of fungus spores and weed seeds, is used in potting composts, as a mulch or a soil conditioner, and is the main constituent of soil-less composts. Its chief function lies in its moisture-retaining ability; it is purchased in a dry state and must be thoroughly saturated before use. Dusty peat, which will clog up the soil, should be avoided, and very acid peat is suitable only for rhododendrons, azaleas and members of the heather family.

Peltate: see **Leaf shapes**

Perennial

Applied to plants which live and flower for more than two years. Although trees and shrubs are perennial, the term is chiefly used of herbaceous perennials, such as lupins, delphiniums and paeonies, which live for many years. They die down each winter and shoot up again each spring.

Perfoliate: see **Leaf shapes**

Pergola

A series of arches consisting of larch or pine poles or squared timber to form a covered area. Usually climbing plants are trained over a pergola. The upright posts should be sunk 24 in. in the ground and have a height of about 8 ft. above ground level. Elaborate

Pergola (squared timber canopy)

designs can be constructed with concrete or brick pillars, with roofing formed from thick timber. A pergola can also be erected as a garden screen or partition, consisting of a single line of strong uprights connected by cross pieces of larch or western red cedar.

Pergola (larch partition)

Perianth

Botanical term for the corolla and calyx which surround the reproductive organs of many flowers.

Perpetual

Applied to flowering plants which produce blooms intermittently throughout the year. There are perpetual flowering carnations and pinks.

Petal

One of the separate, brightly coloured leaves of the corolla. The main function of the petals is to attract pollinating insects.

Petaloid

Applied to flower parts, notably the stamens, which have become modified to resemble petals.

Petroleum oil insecticides

Substances derived from lubricating oils and widely used as acaricides in crop protection. A winter-wash of petroleum oil, mixed with DNC, is used on fruit trees in late winter or early spring to destroy insects and the eggs of moth, capsid bug and red spider mite. Pure petroleum oil, applied as a summer wash to fruit-tree foliage, greenhouse plants and other tender foliage, is effective in the control of scale insects and red spider mites.

Phosphate: see **Fertilisers and manures**

Photosynthesis: see **Light**

pH scale: see **Soil (soil testing)**

Picotee

Applied to a type of carnation whose petals are narrowly edged with a colour on a white or yellow ground.

Pillar

A form of trained apple tree, grown in a limited space. A pillar tree has an upright, central trunk, 6–8 ft. high, from which is produced a succession of young fruit-bearing lateral shoots. The shoots are one or two years old, and are replaced by a system of renewal pruning. Roses, such as 'American Pillar', are termed pillar roses because they are frequently trained up the pillars of rose pergolas.

Pinching

Removing the tips of unwanted growing shoots. (See also **Break**.)

Pinching back: see **Pruning**

Pink bud: see **Bud stages**

Pinnate: see **Leaf shapes**

Piping: see **Propagation**

Pistil

The total female reproductive organs of a flower. The structure is composed of one or several fused carpels and contains the ovary, stigma and style.

Planting

Careful planting is essential if plants are to be successfully established. The soil must be in a suitable condition—not too wet and sticky, not too dry, and not cold. Set the plant at the correct depth, so that the roots are neither too deeply buried nor too near the surface. The depth is often indicated on a tree or shrub by the soil mark left on the plant when it was lifted.

Plant herbaceous subjects to the level of the crown where stems and roots join. Planting holes must be of such a size and shape that the roots will spread comfortably. Begin to firm a plant in as soon as the roots are covered with soil, add more soil, and work it down firmly. Continue this process until the planting hole is filled. A firmly planted subject will root quickly and absorb water and nutrients. The plant is also securely anchored against wind-rocking. The best tools for planting are a trowel for small plants and a spade for large ones.

Plumule
The initial shoot on a germinated seed. It carries the cotyledons.

Plunging
Burying pot-grown plants to the rims in soil or in a special plunge bed. Placing such plants in a bed of peat, ashes or sand prevents them from drying out and reduces the need for watering during the summer. Bulbs for indoor cultivation are placed in their bowls several inches deep in the plunge bed. Here they will make a strong root system before being taken into a high indoor temperature in late autumn.

Pod
A non-fleshy fruit containing several seeds, which splits open when ripe. The fruits of peas, beans and wallflowers are pods.

Pollarding: see Pruning

Pollen
The dust-like grains produced by the anther of a male flower. Pollen fertilises the seeds in the ovary if transmitted to the stigma.

Pollination
The transference of pollen from the anthers to the pistil to bring about fertilisation of the same or another flower.

Potassium: see Fertilisers and manures

Pots: see Tools

Potting
The act of placing plants in pots—either decorative pot plants, or young plants for later transplanting outdoors. The time of planting depends on the type of plant and its age, but most potting is done between February and May. The composts used for potting have been standardised: the John Innes range and proprietary brands of soil-less composts are most often used.

A few plants require special composts: cyclamens need more peat than is included in the John Innes mixtures; azaleas should be potted in pure peat with a little sand; and cacti require a very gritty mixture. Composts should always be thoroughly saturated before use, though not to such a degree that they are wet.

For potting, always use clean clay or plastic pots, and ensure adequate drainage by covering the drainage holes with a few crocks. Cover the crocks with coarse siftings from the compost before putting compost in the bottom of the pot. Stand the plant on the compost, holding it upright in the centre of the pot and at the right depth, and then fill compost round the plant to the rim of the pot. Plastic pots need to be filled with compost only. Tap the pot sharply on the bench to settle the soil, which should then be firm enough for young plants. The compost must be firmed to leave a space of $\frac{1}{2}$–1 in. below the rim of the pot for watering.

Older plants should be firmed with the fingers and have more compost added. Generally, the older or woodier the plant, the firmer it should be planted. Newly potted plants need warm, humid conditions for a few days until they have become established.

Pot (cross-section), with chrysanthemum

Potting on. Plants need potting on or re-potting when they are potbound—that is, when they have filled their pots with roots. Plants should be suspected of being potbound when the water drains through too quickly, or when they appear not to be making any growth. Turn the pot upside down and tap it briskly to release the plant with its soil ball intact. Prepare a new and larger pot as described, and place the moist soil ball on the compost. Trickle compost into the space between the pot and the roots and firm lightly with a stick.

Potting compost
A mixture of soil, peat, sand and other ingredients for potting plants. Soil-less potting compost consists of peat and chemical nutrients. (See also **Compost**.)

Pricking-out
Transplanting seedlings from the receptacle or seed bed in which they have been raised, to other receptacles or pots with more room.

Seedlings can be pricked out as soon as the cotyledons have appeared. Great care is needed to lift and plant these small, tender seedlings. If they are being moved to other boxes or pots, fill these with the same compost as that in which the seeds were germinated, having first covered the bottoms of the receptacles with crocks. If the seedlings are to be pricked out in a bed, the soil must first be broken down to a fine tilth, and manure or compound fertiliser incorporated.

Pricking-out seedlings

Make planting holes with a dibber, lift the seedlings carefully so as not to damage the fine roots, place them in the holes and firm the soil round the roots with the fingers. Prick out seedlings in rows, spacing them approximately 2 in. each way, and water thoroughly to settle the soil more firmly. After pricking out, the seedlings should be kept under slightly warmer and damper conditions for a few days until they have re-started growth.

Propagation
The increase of plants. The methods by which plants may be propagated are grouped under the two main categories of vegetative propagation and seminal propagation (seed). The increase of plants by vegetative means includes budding, cuttings, division, grafting and layering. Although plants that are produced vegetatively exist separately, they are in fact multiplications of one plant, and replicas of the parent. Plants increased by

seed are entirely new plants, and may differ from the parent plants.

Budding

A form of grafting, chiefly used to propagate roses. A well developed leaf bud with a sliver of bark attached is joined to an appropriate rootstock. Budding is carried out from mid-June until the end of August. One-year-old, well rooted stem cuttings of the wild brier rose and seedlings of *R. laxa* (obtained commercially) are suitable stocks for bush roses. Today, standard roses are usually budded on to *R. rugosa* stock. The leaf bud of a choice variety is inserted in a T-shaped incision in the bark of the stock and bound firmly with raffia or a stapled latex band. Standard roses are budded about 3½–4 ft. from ground level; weeping standards are budded at 5–7 ft. from ground level. On bush roses, the buds are inserted just below the soil level.

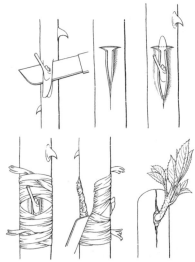

Stages in budding a rose. The back of the raffia is split one month after budding to allow for the swelling of bud and stock. The following spring the stock is cut back to about 1 in. above the bud

Cutting

Any portion of leaf, bud, stem or root removed from a plant and treated in such a way that it will form a replica of the parent plant. Propagation by cuttings is an easy, quick and cheap method of obtaining new plants with the same characteristics as the parent.

Cuttings from strong, healthy plants can be taken throughout the year, with the exception of root cuttings, which are best taken during the dormant season. Before the cuttings are inserted in a rooting medium, they must be trimmed cleanly with a sharp knife. Stem cuttings should be cut immediately below a node or joint. Leaves, stalks and buds should be removed from the portion of the cutting to be inserted, and the ends may be dipped in a root-promoting hormone substance.

Cuttings can be rooted in pots, pans, boxes, greenhouse propagating frames or outdoor frames. Ensure adequate drainage by filling the pots or boxes up to a third with crocks, and fill up with a compost. The rooting medium or compost depends on the type of cuttings to be inserted. Generally, the softer the cutting, the sandier the compost should be; but the John Innes seed compost is suitable for most types of cuttings.

Firm the soil and sprinkle a thin layer of coarse, dry sand on top so that, when the cutting is inserted, the sand will trickle down into the hole and aid the rooting process. Make a hole with a dibber and insert the cutting firmly, particularly at the base, to a depth of approximately 1½ in. Hardwood cuttings are usually inserted in outdoor beds to a depth of at least 5 in. Water the cuttings in with a fine rose fitted to the watering can; this will settle the soil round the cuttings further.

Most leaf cuttings, eye cuttings and some bud cuttings, such as those of camellia, are best propagated with the aid of some form of heat: in a warm greenhouse or propagating frame, preferably with mist propagation (see **Greenhouses**).

Cuttings will root successfully under conditions that supply them with adequate moisture, temperature and light. Softwood cuttings need a close, moist atmosphere in a closed propagating frame at an average temperature of 18°C (64°F), while half-ripe cuttings inserted under the same conditions will root at a temperature of 13–16°C (55–61°F). Cuttings in closed propagating frames should be inspected and watered daily; in hot weather the frames can be shaded with sheets of brown paper or newspaper. Soft cuttings propagated with bottom heat will root in 1–2 weeks; half-ripe cuttings take up to a month

to form roots; while hardwood cuttings—always taken in the autumn and inserted outdoors—cannot be expected to have formed strong roots before the following spring.

As soon as the cuttings are rooted, pot them on into clean pots or boxes filled with a light potting compost. Keep the new, small plants moist, and shade them from strong light at first. Gradually harden them off by moving them into colder temperatures and less shade, until they are finally planted out in their permanent positions. Hardwood cuttings in nursery beds should not be planted out until a year after inserting them.

Basal cutting

Young shoot severed at the base of the plant, at or just below ground level. Basal cuttings need little trimming and can be inserted outdoors straight into a shaded frame. Spray the cuttings daily during hot weather to keep the soil moist, and gradually increase ventilation. When the cuttings have rooted and started growth, the glass should be removed. Dahlias, chrysanthemums and many alpines are propagated by basal cuttings.

Bud cutting

Stem cutting of half-ripe wood with a leaf attached and a growth bud in the leaf axil. Insert the cutting so that the leaf and bud are just above the soil surface. Camellias are propagated by bud cuttings at gentle bottom heat until well rooted.

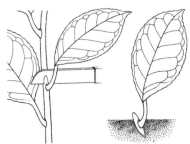

Bud cutting (camellia)

Eye cutting

Hardwood stem cutting, particularly of vines, taken in the dormant period during autumn and winter. The cutting should be about 1½ in. long with a single bud or eye. Remove a strip of bark on the side opposite to the bud and peg the cutting down in a turf block or a loamy rooting medium. Sprinkle the surface liberally with sand, and push in the cutting so that the eye protrudes just over the soil level. Root the cuttings in a propagating frame at a bottom heat temperature of 24°C (75°F), and keep the cuttings moist.

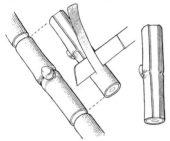

Eye cutting (vine)

Half-ripe cutting

Stem cutting taken in late summer of current year's wood. Take cuttings 2–4 in. long from side shoots or the tip of main shoots. Remove all leaves from the lower part of each cutting, and cut them straight across just below a node. Insert the cuttings firmly to a quarter of their length in John Innes seed compost, and place in a shaded, closed frame to root. Most shrubs and shrubby plants can be propagated by this method.

Hardwood cutting

Stem cutting from fully mature wood taken at the end of the growing season from current

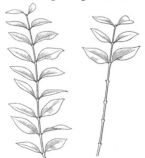

Hardwood cutting. The leaves are stripped from the part of the stem to be inserted

year's wood. Take cuttings, 10–12 in. long, and treat as other stem cuttings by removing the lower leaves and cutting the stems below a node. Hardwood cuttings are inserted in the open, to make roots before being planted in their permanent positions the following year.

First, take out a V-shaped trench, about 4 in. deep. Then sprinkle coarse sand at the bottom to encourage rooting, and place the cuttings against one side of the trench. Replace the soil and firm it round the cuttings by treading. This type of cutting requires no additional moisture. To give the cuttings some protection against severe weather, the trench can be taken out in an open frame. During the winter the trenches must be inspected, as severe frosts may loosen and raise the cuttings. Hardwood cuttings will remain dormant through the winter, but begin to produce roots the following spring. Hardy shrubs and trees, and soft fruits, are propagated by hardwood cuttings.

Heel cutting

Usually a half-ripe or hardwood cutting of a side shoot, pulled away from the main shoot with a strip of bark attached. Trim the ragged, heel-like portion with a knife before inserting the cutting, following the method used for other half-ripe or hardwood cuttings. Some cuttings appear to root more readily if taken with a heel, rather than cut below a node.

Heel cutting

Internodal cutting

A stem cutting of half-ripe wood cut between a pair of nodes instead of just below a node. Clematis cuttings are often internodal.

Irishman's cutting

Single shoot with a few roots, which is removed from the crown of a plant and planted out elsewhere. Early-flowering chrysanthemums are sometimes propagated in this manner.

Leaf cutting

Well developed leaf, complete with stalk, removed from a stem. Many greenhouse plants, such as begonias, gloxinias and saintpaulias, are propagated by leaf cuttings. Insert the leaf stalk in a compost of sand and peat moss, so that the leaf lies flat on the surface. Roots

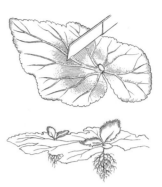

Leaf cutting (begonia)

will develop from the leaf axil. With some plants, such as *Begonia rex*, rooting is further encouraged by making a number of cuts with a sharp knife across the main veins on the back of the leaf. Roots are formed from each incision, and a number of new plants can be raised in this way from a single leaf. Leaf cuttings of saintpaulias are often left upright round the rim of the pot. Leaf cuttings should be rooted in a close, damp atmosphere; greenhouse plants require a temperature of 16–18°C (61–64°F).

Nodal cutting

Any stem cutting severed from the main shoot immediately below a node.

Root cutting

A section of a root cut into pieces 2–3 in. long. During the dormant season, lift such plants as phlox, verbascum, hollyhocks, romneyas and oriental poppies, and cut off pieces of the larger, fleshy roots. Cut the end nearer the crown of the plant straight across

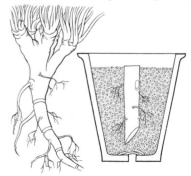

Root cutting

and the other end at a slant; plant the root cuttings with the slanting side down. Insert the cuttings in boxes of a rooting compost of loam, leafy soil, or peat and sand. The top of the root cuttings should be just below the soil level. Cuttings of thin roots, such as those of phlox, can be placed on top of the soil and covered with a thin layer of potting compost. This type of cutting can be rooted in an unheated frame or greenhouse. By spring roots will have formed, and buds and shoots will appear at the crown. Cuttings can be planted outdoors in a nursery bed by early summer.

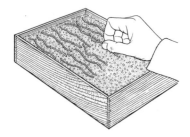

Root cuttings in a box

Softwood cutting

Young stem cutting taken early in the growing season, while the shoots are soft and sappy. The cuttings should average 2–2½ in. long and should be prepared as other stem cuttings, by removing the lower leaves and trimming the stems sharply with a knife just below a node. The moisture in these young cuttings evaporates rapidly, and they must therefore be rooted in a close and damp atmosphere. Insert the cuttings in a light

Softwood cutting

sandy compost in a propagating frame and maintain a temperature of 16–18°C (61–64°F) until roots have formed. As there is no plant nourishment in sand, softwood cuttings must be potted on as soon as they are rooted. Herbaceous plants, such as chrysanthemums, geraniums, delphiniums and lupins, are propagated by softwood cuttings.

Stem cutting

Any cutting taken from the tip of a main shoot or a side branch. Stem cuttings are divided into softwood, half-ripe wood and hardwood cuttings.

Tip cutting

Any stem cutting taken from the top growth of a non-flowering shoot or branch.

Top cutting

An alternative term for a stem cutting.

Division

Vegetative propagation method whereby plants are separated into smaller plants, each complete with roots and growth buds. Division is the easiest means of increase of most perennial plants and alpines, and is carried out during the winter dormant period, or at the beginning of the new growing season.

Plants that can be propagated by division fall into the following six groups:
1. Plants with a spreading, fibrous root system, and several stems arising from the crown. Examples are michaelmas daisies, phlox and heleniums.
2. Plants with woody crowns and growth buds, such as lupins and delphiniums.
3. Plants with rhizomatous roots, such as montbretias and the bearded irises.
4. Tuberous-rooted plants, such as potatoes, paeonies and dahlias.
5. Single-stemmed plants growing from bulbs or corms, and producing small offsets or bulbils beside the parent bulbs. Tulips, daffodils, gladioli and bulbous irises are propagated by offsets.
6. Shrubby plants, such as raspberries and lilacs, which send up suckers some distance from the parent plant.

Although the general principles for dividing plants are the same, the separation differs according to the type of growth. All plants to be divided should be lifted in either spring or autumn, and the separated pieces planted immediately into their permanent positions. (Small or rare plants may be potted up or grown on in a nursery bed.) Some offsets

lifted in the spring need a resting period before being re-planted.

1. PLANTS WITH FIBROUS ROOT SYSTEMS

Shake the soil off the root clump and pull it apart into several portions, each retaining a number of roots and growth buds. Tough clumps which are not easily torn apart can be divided with the aid of two forks. Drive the forks back to back through the clump and lever it apart. Discard the woody centres of old, overgrown plants and re-plant only those portions round the side with young, healthy roots and buds.

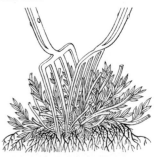

Division of a fibrous-rooted plant

2. PLANTS WITH WOODY CROWNS

Division of these plants, particularly delphiniums, is best done in spring. Wash the crowns in water, so that the growth buds are clearly visible, and with a sharp knife cut the crown into portions, each retaining a sound bud and roots. Small portions may be boxed up until the young plants are thoroughly established.

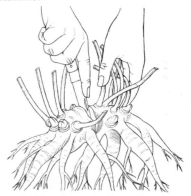

Division of a plant with woody crown

3. RHIZOMES

Divide these underground stems by cutting off portions 2–3 in. long, with strong new growths, from the outside. Throw away the old centres. Re-plant the sections horizontally and just below soil level. Bearded irises should be divided after flowering, usually in July.

Division of a rhizome

4. TUBERS

The method of dividing tuberous plants varies from plant to plant. Potatoes and Jerusalem artichokes can be propagated by cutting the tubers into pieces. Provided each section contains a bud or eye, new plants can be raised. Dahlia tubers are cut into vertical sections, so that each piece contains a portion of the stem and a strong growth bud.

Division of a dahlia tuber

5. OFFSETS

Small, complete plants produced by many bulbous plants. Offsets are attached to the parent bulbs or corms; when detached by hand and planted elsewhere, they will form large bulbs, which will flower after a couple of years. Most bulbs, such as tulips and daffodils, produce offsets alongside their bulbs. Gladiolus corms produce new corms on top of the old corm as well as side offsets, all of which may be removed and rooted.

Division by offsets

6. SUCKERS

Shoots arising from the roots of some shrubby plants. Sometimes, as with raspberries, the suckers appear some distance from the parent plant. As a quick and easy means of propagation, sucker growths can be dug up and severed from the parent with a sharp knife. This should be done at normal planting times, in spring and autumn. The severed shoots, which must retain some of the old roots, can be planted in their flowering positions immediately. Suckers from grafted shrubs, such as the named forms of lilac, will revert to the common form.

Grafting

The practice of joining two living parts of plants so that they form a permanent, growing union. One part, the stock (see **Rootstock**) consists of the rooting system and main stem; the other, called the scion, is a piece of the previous year's wood from another plant. A suitable rootstock will produce vigorous growth, and the scion will give the fruiting qualities of the selected choice variety. It is essential that the stock and scion should be compatible—that is, belong to the same genus—though in a few cases genera within the same plant family can be joined: syringa, for example, is often grafted on ligustrum (privet) stock.

This method of vegetative propagation is chiefly applied to fruit trees and some shrubs, although cacti and some woody herbaceous plants may also be propagated in the same manner. Grafting is normally carried out at the end of the dormant season. The stock should be young, disease-free and vigorous, though occasionally an old fruit tree, which has stopped bearing fruit, may be rejuvenated by grafting a choice scion on to it. The scions are selected from strong, one-year-old woody shoots. These are cut during the winter (December or January) and planted in cool soil against a wall or fence. Under these conditions, the shoots will remain dormant until the time of grafting, when the shoots are cut down to lengths containing three buds.

There are numerous methods of grafting, but the basic principles are the same. The thin green layer (cambium) between bark and wood contains plants cells, which will fuse with similar cells. In every form of successful grafting the cambium of the stock must therefore be placed in direct contact with the cambium of the scion. Graft unions are normally bound with raffia and sealed with grafting wax, or a proprietary bitumen emulsion.

Approach grafting

The joining of stock and scion before severing the scion from its own roots (also known as inarching). Usually stock and scion are grown in separate pots. Place the pots side by side, and remove a sliver of bark and wood from each, so that the two cambium layers are exposed. Fit the two wounded surfaces together and bind with raffia, before covering the union with grafting wax. After a couple of months the union should be complete. The top growth of the stock is removed above the union, and the scion is severed from its roots just below the union. Vines are sometimes grafted by this method.

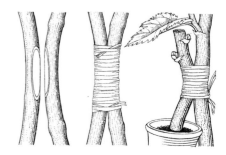

Approach grafting

Bridge grafting

A form of tree surgery used where a branch has been damaged by canker, or the bark destroyed by some natural cause. Prepare a scion of the same variety by making a slanting cut, 1–2 in. long, at both its ends. Make an incision above and below the damaged portion on the tree, and insert the scion so that it bridges the wound. Bind the incisions with raffia and seal with grafting wax.

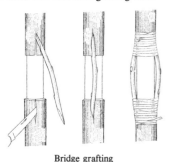

Bridge grafting

Cleft grafting

A method chiefly used for reworking old and cut-back trees. Two scions are usually inserted on the stock, which is a fair-sized limb. A small chopper or axe is used to split the end of the stock, which is kept open by the pointed end of a wedging tool. Cut the scions 3–4 in. long, and wedge-shaped, so that the cambium layers on each side of the scion will come into contact with the cambium layers of the split surfaces of the stock. Insert the scions and bind with raffia. Fill up the split stock with clay, and seal the graft with wax.

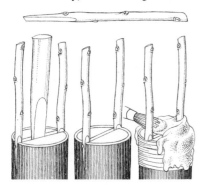

Cleft grafting

Crown or rind grafting

A method of grafting used in top-working old fruit trees. Several scions are inserted under the rind or ring of bark on the stumps left after heading back the tree, giving the effect of a crown. Cut each scion with a slanting end, about 1 in. long. Make vertical slits round the bark of the stock. Lift the edges of the bark, and insert the scions so that their cut surfaces rest against the cambium layer of the stock. Bind the wounds with raffia and cover with grafting wax.

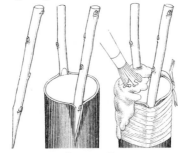

Crown grafting

Framework grafting

Used to convert the head of an established tree to another variety. The main branches are headed back, and most side branches removed. Scions of the new variety, each with at least six buds, are then inserted on the stumps of the existing branch system. Four methods of grafting are used for frameworking an established tree: 1. Bark grafting. 2. Oblique side grafting. 3. Side grafting. 4. Stub grafting.

1. BARK GRAFTING

Prepare the scion by making a long sloping cut at one side of the base and a shorter cut at the other side to form an uneven wedge. Make a reversed L-shaped incision in the bark of a limb. The two halves of the incision should make an oblique angle of about 150°. Lift the flap of bark, and insert the scion so that the long surface of the wedge lies against the exposed wood of the limb. Fix the scion in position by a thin nail through the bark and the scion, and seal with grafting wax.

2. OBLIQUE SIDE GRAFTING

Cut the scion to form a pointed wedge about 1 in. long, and insert the point into an oblique, 2 in. cut in the bark of a main branch. The point of the scion is held firmly in place by the bark, and can be placed at the angle at which the eventual lateral is required to grow. Seal the cut with grafting wax to make it entirely waterproof.

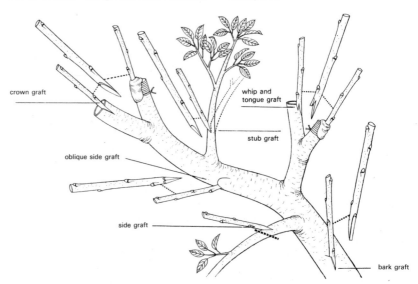

Grafting by six different methods

3. SIDE GRAFTING

Make an incision in the bark of a main branch, at an angle of 20°, and insert a scion cut to a wedge with unequal sides. After inserting the scion, trim the bark behind it, and seal all exposed cuts with wax.

4. STUB GRAFTING

This differs from the other three methods of frameworking, in that the scions are grafted on to the spurs or stubs of lateral branches as close as possible to the main branch. Make a downward incision in the upper surface of the lateral, and insert the scion, cut to form a short, uneven wedge. Bend the lateral gently back while pushing the scion into position; then allow the lateral to spring back and grip the scion firmly. Prune away the remainder of the lateral branch above the scion, and cover the whole wound with grafting wax.

Saddle grafting

A method of grafting often used to joint a named rhododendron variety to the common rhododendron stock. Stock and scion should be of equal size, and the scion should contain one terminal bud. Make two upward slanting incisions in the scion, to form an inverted V or saddle, and fit the scion in position over the stock, which is cut to match the saddle. Bind the union with raffia, and place in a warm, closed propagating frame. Saddle grafts require no grafting wax.

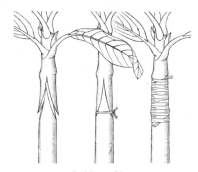

Saddle grafting

Splice grafting

Simple method of grafting which involves two slanting corresponding cuts, one each on stock and scion. Place the two cut surfaces together and bind with raffia. Broom, roses and clematis may be propagated by splice grafting.

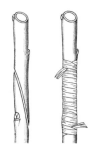

Splice grafting

Top working

Similar to framework grafting. The stock of an established tree is cut down to the trunk and stubs of main branches.

Whip and tongue grafting

The most frequently used method of grafting young fruit and ornamental trees. Trim the stock down to about 4 in. from ground level and make an upward slanting cut, $1\frac{1}{2}$ in. long; by making a downward cut just below the apex of the upward cut a tongue is formed. Prepare the scion, which should be of the same thickness as the stock, in a similar manner, so that the cuts on the scion correspond with those on the stock. Fit the tongue of the scion into the tongue of the stock, bind with raffia and seal with grafting wax.

Layering

A method of vegetative propagation whereby a stem attached to a plant is induced to form roots and eventually produce an independent plant. Natural examples of layering are strawberry runners and the tip layering of blackberries. Shrubs, such as forsythia, layer themselves where the low-sweeping branches come into contact with the soil. The constant rubbing of the branch against the ground causes an injury to the bark, and from the callus formed over the wound roots develop to anchor the branch. This natural means of increase is employed in propagating border carnations, clematis, magnolias, rhododendrons, syringas and a number of other ornamental shrubs.

Choose a young, non-flowering shoot, and check the flow of sap. This can be done by twisting or bending the stem at the point where it will make contact with the soil, or by making an incision just below a bud, so that a tongue is formed. Spread a layer of a prepared rooting medium round the plant to be layered to form a ridge 2–3 in. higher than the soil level. Strip off the leaves from that part of the stem or branch that will be in the soil, and bend the shoot down into the compost. Keep the cut open, and press the tongue or injured point into the soil. Anchor the shoot by fixing it with wooden or wire pegs, and cover the cut parts firmly with a further inch of soil before watering thoroughly.

When sufficient roots have formed, the layer is severed from the parent plant, and after a few days it can be planted out in its permanent position. Border carnations will root in 6–8 weeks; ornamental shrubs may take 6–12 months to root sufficiently; and magnolias and rhododendrons require up to two years before they can be severed from the parent plants. Shrubs are layered from midsummer to early autumn, border carnations in August.

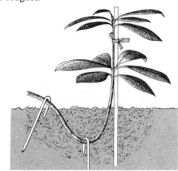

Layering (rhododendron)

Air layering or Chinese layering

A method used on branches that are too stiff or too high to be layered at soil level. Remove a ring of bark from the layer; or, better, make a $1\frac{1}{2}$ in. upward cut from just below a node or a leaf stalk. Treat the wounded surfaces with a root-promoting substance and keep the cut open with a twist of moss. Pass a tube of polythene over the cut, securing it tightly 3–4 in. below the cut with insulating tape. Pack the tube tightly with moist sphagnum moss, and seal the top. Ficus (rubber plant) is propagated by this method in April.

After about 10 weeks the layer should be rooted. Sever the shoot beneath the polythene packing and free the roots, before potting the new plant in a suitable compost. Place the potted layers in a closed frame for two weeks and keep them moist to allow the roots to become well established. Harden off the new plants, and plant out the following spring.

Air layering

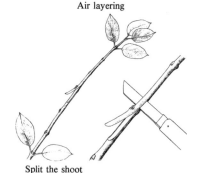

Split the shoot

Treat the cut with rooting hormone, and keep it open with a twist of moss

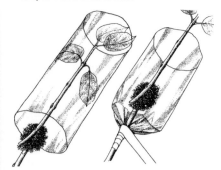

Secure a tube of polythene below the cut

Pack the tube tightly with sphagnum moss, and seal the opening

Serpentine layering

Method used in layering young shoots of such plants as clematis. Slanting cuts, about 2 in. long, are made at intervals along the stem, close behind a node. The stem is then layered into a series of pots filled with sandy compost, or directly into the ground. Cover the cuts with soil and fix them securely with pins; leave the intervening lengths above ground. If clematis is layered in this manner in June, new plants will have formed at each of the joints by early autumn. Sever the new plants and pot them up separately until the following spring, or plant straight out in their growing positions.

Serpentine layering

Tip layering

Simple method of layering loganberries and cultivated blackberries. During summer, peg the tips of healthy shoots into loose soil or

Tip layering (blackberry)

into pots sunk into the ground, and keep the layers moist. Sever the rooted tips from the parents in November and plant out.

Piping

A young tip growth or stem cutting of a carnation or pink. A piping differs from other stem cuttings in that it needs no trimming. Hold the stem of a non-flowering shoot firmly, and pull the tip of the shoot from just above a node. Dip the stem in a rooting powder, and insert in sandy compost to root.

Piping (carnation)

Rootstock

A vigorous rooting plant—often a wild species, used in grafting and budding. The success of grafting depends on a clean, healthy rootstock, which will provide vigour to a grafted choice variety of fruiting trees and shrubs. In recent years research stations have developed rootstocks whose characteristics are suitable for and compatible with scions of other varieties. Rootstocks, some of which are now immune or resistant to pest and virus attacks, are classified into fruit stocks, quince stocks and rose stocks.

Fruit stock

The rootstocks for apple grafting have been developed by the East Malling Research Station, and are known as Malling II, IX, XII, according to certain qualities in the development of the tree. Malling IX stock, for example, denotes a dwarfing rootstock, which will produce a quick-cropping tree of dwarf habit. It is suitable for a small garden and is used for cordons, dwarf pyramids and other restricted forms.

Cherries are grafted on rootstocks of the wild cherry or gean (*Prunus avium*), or on the Mazzard stock, which has a very hard stem.

Quince stock

Also known as Malling Quince A, B and C, and used as rootstocks for pear budding and grafting. There are various rootstocks used for working pears. The Myrobalan B stock, a wild plum rootstock, is suitable for large trees grafted with dessert plum varieties. Peaches and nectarines are grafted on Brompton stock, while ornamental members' of the prunus family (flowering almonds, peaches and plums) are grafted on to Mussel stock.

Roses may be grafted or budded on to a variety of rootstocks. Rooted main stems of the wild brier (*R. canina*) make fine standard roses but, as they are hard to obtain in quantity, most commercial standards are budded on to *R. rugosa* stocks. They can be budded early in the season and have a clean ready workable neck. *R. multiflora* is an alternative for floribunda bush roses.

Scales
The outer covering of flower bulbs. Scales taken from mature bulbs after flowering or in the autumn are used to propagate lilies. Place the scales upright in boxes or pots of compost, consisting of 2 parts loam, 1 part leaf-mould and 1 part sharp sand, with a sprinkling of charcoal. Place the boxes in a cool greenhouse and keep the compost moist. In a few weeks a small bulblet will have formed at the base of each scale.

The new bulbs can then be potted up in suitable compost and be grown on.

Scion
Any shoot taken from a choice variety plant and used for grafting on to a rootstock to form a new plant. A scion transmits the flowering or fruiting qualities of the variety from which it has been taken.

Seed
An embryo plant, formed by the fertilisation of a flower. It will remain dormant until provided with suitable conditions of warmth, moisture and air. Increase of plants by seed (seminal propagation) is the best and cheapest method of raising plants in quantities, and is also the main propagation method for annuals and biennials. Seeds may be harvested from clean, healthy plants on a dry, sunny day. Pick the pods or seedheads before they begin to open, and leave them to ripen properly. When the seeds are dry, clean them thoroughly, and store them correctly labelled in paper bags in a cool, airy place. Seeds purchased from seedsmen and not intended

for immediate sowing must be stored under the same cool, airy conditions.

Seeds differ in shape and size, and these variations determine their cultural needs. The main groups are as follows: 1. Small, dust-like seeds. 2. Hard-coated seeds. 3. Fleshy seeds. 4. Oily seeds. 5. Winged seeds.

1. SMALL, DUSTLIKE SEEDS
These seeds, such as those of begonias and calceolarias, quickly lose their germinating powers, and should therefore be sown as soon as they are fully ripe. Sow the seeds thinly on the surface of firm, even soil, and cover with a fine sprinkling of soil. Cover the receptacle with a pane of glass and brown paper until germination has taken place.

2. HARD-COATED SEEDS
These include the seeds of sweet peas and peaches, and may require some treatment to the hard outer shell before sowing. Chip the seeds of sweet peas with a sharp knife on the side opposite to that of the eye (where the seed was attached in the pod). Hard seeds, such as peach stones, should be stratified before sowing (see *Stratification of seeds*).

3. FLESHY SEEDS
Broad beans, runner beans and garden peas are examples of fleshy seeds. They develop a hard outer skin when stored for any length of time. Soften this seed coat by soaking the seeds in tepid water for 48 hours before sowing. This will speed up the process of germination.

4. OILY SEEDS
Magnolia and camellia, carrot and parsnip seeds contain oil and do not store well. As soon as the oil in the seeds dries up, the seeds will shrivel and fail to germinate. Magnolia and camellia seeds must be sown as soon as they are ripe, and carrot and parsnip seeds should not be kept from one year to another.

5. WINGED SEEDS
Remove the wings or keys from seeds of sycamore, ash and lime before sowing.

Stratification of seeds
The process of hastening germination of hard and fleshy seeds by exposing them to frost before sowing. Seeds of most trees and shrubs are stratified, to soften the hard seed coats. Place the seeds in layers in pots or boxes of sand, or sand and peat, and stand the receptacles outdoors in an exposed position during the winter. Cover with wire netting against attack by birds or mice. Some hard-

coated seeds, such as peach stones, may be left for a year. When the time for sowing arrives, empty the containers into a sieve to separate the softened seeds from the sand.

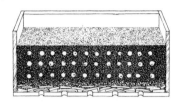

Stratification of hard seeds

Seed sowing
Successful germination of seeds depends on moisture, warmth, air, and eventually light. Generally seeds should be sown to a depth equal to their thickness; though fleshy seeds, such as broad beans, runner beans and garden peas, should be sown 2 in. deep, as they tend to move towards the soil surface as they germinate. Small seeds require only a very fine soil covering, and dust-like seeds, especially when sown under glass, need no other covering than a pane of glass and a sheet of brown paper.

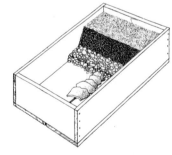

Seed box

Outdoor sowing
Before seeds are sown in the open garden, the soil must be in a suitable condition, which is governed by the weather. Prepare the soil or seed beds by firming the soil and raking it evenly to create a fine tilth. Heavy soils can be made more friable by the addition of sand or weathered boiler ashes. Do not sow in cold, clogged soil, as this will delay or prevent germination.

When the seed bed is ready, sow seeds in drills or broadcast. Mark out sowing distances between the drills, and place small sticks to indicate the ends of rows. Stretch garden lines across the bed from stick to stick, and then draw out flat-bottomed seed drills along the lines to the correct depth. A shallow drill may be taken out simply by pressing the handle of a hoe lightly on the surface; deeper seed drills are drawn out with the blade of a draw hoe.

Watering an outdoor seed bed is usually unnecessary, but in very dry weather the drills may be watered before the seeds are sown; hot water is often an aid to quicker germination, as in the case of drills being prepared for parsley seeds.

Sow seeds thinly and evenly in the drills. Thick sowings cause overcrowding and weak seedlings, and entail eventual heavy thinning of the seedlings. After sowing, draw the soil over the drills with the back of a rake; firm the drill gently and rake over the surface. Label each drill correctly, and give the date of sowing.

Seeds may also be sown broadcast, especially where annuals are to be grown in informal groups. Prepare the soil as above, and scatter the seeds thinly and evenly in irregular patches. Cover broadcast seeds thinly with fine soil, or merely rake the surface.

Sowing under glass
This is a method employed for raising plants under controlled conditions. By sowing seeds of half-hardy plants in a warm greenhouse or frame during late winter or early spring, a good supply of summer bedding plants can be produced. The ideal conditions of moisture, warmth and air are the same as for outdoor sowing; but the outside climatic conditions can be discounted. Seeds sown under glass do not require high temperatures: most greenhouse and half-hardy plants germinate at an average temperature of 13°C (55°F).

Sow the seeds in boxes, pots or seed pans, which are covered with panes of glass to prevent evaporation, and sheets of thick brown paper to exclude light, until germination takes place. Clean the receptacles thoroughly, and soak clay pots for several hours in water to absorb as much moisture as possible. Wooden seed boxes should previously be treated with a wood preservative. Good drainage is essential.

Cover the drainage holes in seed pots and pans with crocks (pieces of broken pots), small stones or dried leaves. Cover spaces between the boards of seed boxes with doubled sheets of newspaper covered with a layer of dried leaves or peat.

Use a home-made compost comprising, by volume, 2 parts sifted soil, 1 part peat and 1 part coarse sand or 1 part peat and 1 part perlite, or a commercial soilless (peat) compost, or John Innes seed compost.

Before sowing the seed, water the pots and boxes thoroughly, by placing them in an old bath filled with water to just below the rim of the containers. When the water has risen through the compost and moistened the soil surface, lift the receptacles and allow them to drain.

Now sow the seeds evenly and thinly to their appropriate depths. Sprinkle some fine silver sand over the surface and firm the soil gently before covering with glass and paper. As soon as the little seedlings have germinated, remove paper and glass. If necessary, shade the new little plants during the day from strong sunshine.

When the seedlings are large enough to handle, they should be carefully pricked out into boxes or pots of John Innes potting compost. Prepare the boxes as previously described, and dampen the potting compost before transplanting the seedlings. Use a small stick or V-notched label to prise the seedlings loose, and prick them out individually, taking care that the roots are dropped well down into the prepared holes. Space the seedlings evenly to 2 in. between each, and 3 in. between each row. Grow the seedlings on in their boxes under the same greenhouse conditions as those under which they were raised, and gradually expose them to more air and light until they are sufficiently hardened to outdoor conditions.

As the new plants grow, it may become necessary to pot them singly before transplanting outdoors.

Sowing in cold frames
Early crops of vegetables may be raised by sowing seeds either in pots or boxes (as sown under glass) or by sowing directly into a seed bed in a well ventilated cold frame. Prepare the seed bed in the frame as for outdoor sowing, and sow into drills. As the seeds germinate and seedlings grow stronger, allow more ventilation to harden off the plants prior to transplanting. Biennials, such as pansies and sweet williams, can be sown in cold frames in late summer for planting out the following spring.

Snag
The portion of the stock (see **Grafting**) above the point where it has been grafted or budded. Snagging consists of removing the stock above the union as soon as the graft or bud has taken.

Stock and scion compatibility
The necessity of using stocks and scions of the same genera for successful grafting. There are a few exceptions: syringa, for example, may be grafted on to *Syringa vulgaris* (common lilac) or on to *ligustrum* (privet) stock.

Union
The junction of scion and rootstock.

Protection
Cultivated plants need protection from extreme weather conditions and other hazards.

Greenhouses, frames and cloches protect plants from frost damage, from being buffeted and dried by winds, from excessive rain and, if shaded, from strong sunlight. Newly planted or tender shrubs can be sheltered from frost and bitter winds with wattle hurdles or screens of hessian nailed to upright posts. The crowns of tender plants in the herbaceous border can be protected from frost with a covering of straw or bracken, or with heaps of coarse ashes. Woolly leaved alpines need protection against the damp of winter. Cover the plants with panes of glass supported on wire pegs.

Protection (wattle hurdles)

Glass protection for alpines

Fruit cage

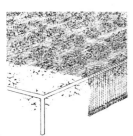

Strawberry netting

Straw on tender plants

Fruit often needs protection against birds. Peaches grown on walls may be covered with netting, and currants and raspberries may be grown in fruit cages, with wire-netting sides and string-netting roofs. Strawberries are often protected by fish netting stretched over a low frame.

Pruners: see **Tools (secateurs)**

Pruning

The practice of cutting back such woody plants as roses, fruit trees and ornamental trees and shrubs. Pruning has three main objectives: to regulate growth; to improve the quality of the flowers and fruits; and to remove damaged, diseased or dead wood.

The removal of part of the top growth of a plant causes a reaction in the root system, resulting in new stem growth. The vigour of the new growth, controlled by the severity and timing of the pruning, must be anticipated so that it may be used advantageously in the development of the plant.

Generally, pruning for growth regulation consists of severe cutting back during the early stages of a plant's development to arrest formation of the basic framework. However, some specially trained trees, such as cordons, need to be pruned annually to keep them in shape. Once the plants are established, pruning is often limited to restricting their size and to removing growths that prevent air and light circulating through the branch system. Lateral shoots, which may rub against and damage the leaders, should also be cut out.

Pruning of mature fruiting and flowering plants is directed chiefly towards improving or maintaining the quality of fruits and flowers. If left unpruned, such trees and shrubs may be so productive that the overall quality suffers. The tree may exhaust itself to such a degree that it needs to rest the following season, producing little or nothing.

Damaged, dead or diseased shoots must be pruned back to healthy, clean wood, and this should be done before any other pruning is carried out. After cutting the damaged shoots flush with a main branch or stem, paint large wounds with a proprietary sealing compound to prevent disease spores entering the wounds.

All pruning cuts should be made cleanly so as not to damage the plant cells in the cambium layer, for the healing of the pruning

Pruning cuts, the right and wrong way

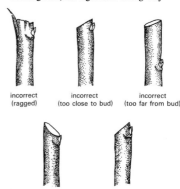

incorrect (ragged) incorrect (too close to bud) incorrect (too far from bud)

incorrect (sloping the wrong way) correct

Pruning terminology (tree)

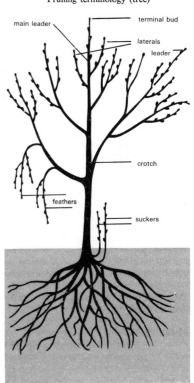

main leader terminal bud laterals leader crotch feathers suckers

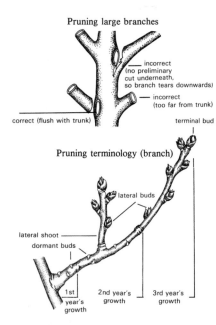

Pruning large branches

incorrect
(no preliminary
cut underneath,
so branch tears downwards)

incorrect
(too far from trunk)

correct (flush with trunk)

terminal bud

Pruning terminology (branch)

lateral buds

lateral shoot

dormant buds

1st year's growth

2nd year's growth

3rd year's growth

wounds and the development of new strong growth depend on these cells. Prune just above a node, beginning the cut opposite to a healthy bud and extending it at an angle so that it finishes just above the bud. Make the cuts above outward pointing buds so that new shoots will grow away from the centre of the plant. Prune lateral and main branches flush with the bark.

The timing of pruning is of great importance and it is essential to know the habits of trees and shrubs before starting to prune. As a general rule fruit trees and ornamental trees and shrubs are pruned hard at the time of planting. Young roses, planted in March, should be pruned hard back at the time of planting. This will encourage development of a good head of branches in a standard tree, and a bushy base in the case of a shrub. Established ornamental trees and shrubs are pruned according to their flowering habits. Deciduous flowering shrubs, which may require pruning in order to restrict size, maintain shape or improve their flowering qualities, may be divided into two categories: those which flower on the current year's wood, and those which produce flowers on one-year-old, two-year-old or older wood.

Shrubs which fall into the former category are cut hard back to old wood, or sometimes almost to ground level, during the dormant season from late autumn to early spring. Plants in the latter category, which flower on older wood, are pruned immediately after flowering by cutting the flowering shoots back to wood of the current year.

Stone fruits, such as plums, and related ornamental trees are exceptions to the general rules; these trees may bleed if pruned hard during the dormant season, and they should therefore be pruned when they are in full leaf, when cuts will heal quickly.

Evergreens and conifers generally need little pruning. Shortening and thinning of shoots to maintain the overall shape should be done in late March or April before new growth begins. Established evergreens, such as laurels and yews, will produce vigorous growth even in exceptional cases where most of the top growth has been pruned away, while other evergreens, such as camellias and magnolias, may die as a result of drastic pruning. Evergreen flowering shrubs which benefit from moderate and light pruning are pruned in the same manner as deciduous flowering shrubs.

The shape of an established hedge is maintained and restricted by pruning during the summer—generally by clipping with shears or a mechanical trimmer.

Hard pruning

The practice of drastically cutting back growing shoots, in some cases to within three or four dormant buds above ground level. Hard pruning of top growth causes a vigorous reaction in the root system and results in strong new growth. Old and overgrown trees and shrubs can be rejuvenated by hard pruning, which also encourages newly planted shrubs to produce robust shoots.

Heading back

Cutting back overgrown trees and shrubs by shortening all or some of the main branches. The shoots are pruned to just above well developed dormant buds.

Light pruning

Moderate shortening of laterals or leaders during early spring, before the new growing season begins, to encourage the development of flower buds or young shoots. The removal of spent flower heads is also classed as light pruning.

Heading back

Lopping

Severely cutting back the upper, large branches of a tree. Lopping should be undertaken only when absolutely necessary, as the operation will often destroy the symmetry and shape of the tree.

Pinching back

Pruning young shoots of trees and shrubs by nipping out the soft tips between forefinger and thumb. Pinching back encourages new and stronger growth and the development of flower buds.

Pollarding

Severe pruning of a tree, so that only the trunk and the stubs of the main branches are left. Pollarding, which results in the formation of extensive new shoots, is often practised on willows and poplars to provide young growths for basket making.

Root pruning

Severing some or all of the main roots of fruit trees, especially plums, to encourage fruitfulness by reducing the vigour of their vegetative growth. When shortening or removing these thick roots, care must be taken not to damage the fibrous feeding roots. The introduction of dwarf rootstocks for many fruit trees has decreased the necessity for root pruning.

Spur pruning

The practice of shortening lateral shoots to two or three growth buds. This form of pruning, commonly used on apple trees, restricts vegetative growth and encourages the formation of spurs—clusters of fruit or flower buds. Spur pruning is carried out in the autumn, when summer-pruned shoots are cut back to two or three buds.

Summer pruning

The shortening of lateral shoots of trained fruit trees grown in a restricted form. Summer pruning, carried out from July onwards, reduces the size of vegetative growth without encouraging new growth. Current year's shoots of cordons, espaliers and dwarf pyramid trees are cut back to about five leaves.

Thinning out

Reducing the number of shoots of shrubs and trees, particularly fruit trees. Removal of lateral shoots, in July, from the centres of fruiting and flowering trees, allows air and light to circulate round the developing fruits or flowers.

Thinning out. The light-tinted branches are removed

Winter pruning

The main cutting back of deciduous trees, especially fruit trees, from November onwards, the severity of the pruning depending on the age of the trees. Newly planted trees require hard pruning to encourage strong growth; on established trees, prune away crowded lateral shoots and shorten leaders to maintain or improve the shape of the trees.

Puddling in

Filling a planting hole with water before setting out new plants or seedlings during hot, dry weather. This helps the plants to withstand the initial exposure to the heat.

Pyrethrum

Insecticide derived from pyrethrum flowers. It is available in the form of a dust or as a dry powder which is soluble in water; it quickly destroys a number of garden pests, notably greenflies and other aphids. The chief value of pyrethrum lies in its quick-acting effect, which is, however, short-lasting, as sunlight renders it ineffective.

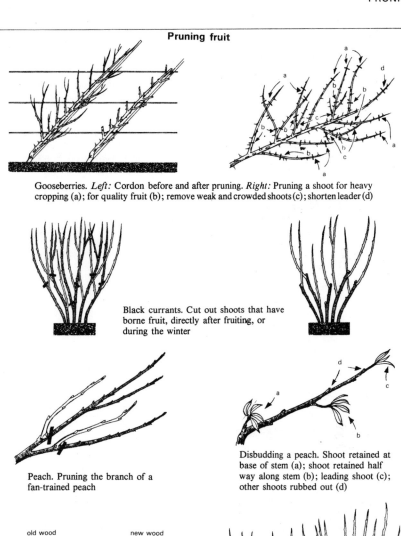

Pruning fruit

Gooseberries. *Left:* Cordon before and after pruning. *Right:* Pruning a shoot for heavy cropping (a); for quality fruit (b); remove weak and crowded shoots (c); shorten leader (d)

Black currants. Cut out shoots that have borne fruit, directly after fruiting, or during the winter

Peach. Pruning the branch of a fan-trained peach

Disbudding a peach. Shoot retained at base of stem (a); shoot retained half way along stem (b); leading shoot (c); other shoots rubbed out (d)

old wood   new wood

Tying in loganberry or blackberry canes

Red and white currants. Pruning newly planted (a) and established (b) plants

485

Pruning fruit

Pruning a newly planted black currant

Pruning the lateral shoots of red and white currants

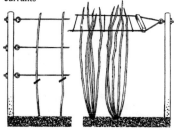

Pruning raspberries. *Left:* Newly established canes. *Right:* Training raspberry canes

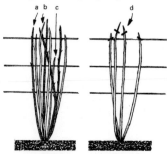

Pruning established raspberries.
Prune old canes (a); leave new, vigorous canes (b); prune new weak canes (c); prune new canes in February (d)

Q

Quintozene
A soil fungicide, also known as PCNB, that is obtainable in dust and wettable-powder forms. Worked into the soil, it offers long-lasting resistance to damping-off of brassicas and reduces the incidence of a number of bulb diseases. Do not plant cucumbers or marrows in soil treated with quintozene, nor sow tomato seed in compost treated with it less than two weeks after application.

R

Raceme
A compound flower head consisting of a central, often pendulous stem with numerous stalked flowers arranged regularly along it. The flower heads of wisteria and laburnum are racemes.

Raceme (wisteria)

Rainfall: see **Weather**

Rakes: see **Tools**

Raking: see **Soil (soil operations)**

Recurved
Applied to petals which are curved backwards from the face of the flower. Many lilies have recurved petals.

Reflexed petals (tiger lily)

Reflexed
Applied to flower petals which curve sharply backwards and downwards. The term is used of lilies and particularly of certain types of chrysanthemums, for example 'Autumn Tints'.

Re-potting: see **Potting**

Reversion
1. Virus disease of black currants. 2. The change of a hybrid or highly selected plant to its prototype. A grafted tree may produce suckers, which, if not removed, supersede the choice variety grafted on it. An ornamental cherry, for example, may then appear to have reverted from a pink-flowering to a white-flowering form. Mutations which are not genetically stable may also revert, as can happen with chrysanthemums. A planting of lupins may appear to have reverted if some of the choice varieties die out, and seedlings of the common blue type germinate.

Rhizome
Thickened underground stem with roots and leaf buds. The stem, which is the plant's storage organ during the dormant season, grows horizontally, and is sometimes, as with bearded irises, partly above ground. (See also **Propagation**.)

Rhomboidal: see **Leaf shapes**

Ridging: see **Soil (soil operations)**

Ring culture
A method of greenhouse cultivation, mainly of tomatoes and chrysanthemums (see also *Greenhouses and frames*, APRIL).

Ring culture (bed and ring)

Take out a trench about 6 in. deep, and line it with polythene. Fill it with a free-draining aggregate of weathered boiler ash or clinkers, and on this bed place the rings (bottomless, non-porous containers, 9 in. in diameter, and made of bituminised paper, roofing felt, linoleum or other material). Fill the rings with John Innes potting compost No. 3, and set a plant in the ring. Place the rings 18 in. apart on the aggregate, and water in the plants. The young plants will develop two root systems: fibrous roots in the ring, where the plants obtain their food; and water-seeking roots in the aggregate.

To encourage root development in the aggregate, water sparingly for about ten days, and then keep the aggregate moist by frequent watering. The rings should not be watered, but fed with liquid fertiliser after the first flower trusses have set. This cultural method encourages steady growth and early cropping, and reduces the danger of soil-borne diseases.

Ringing: see **Bark ringing**

Rogue

A plant which is not true to character. It may appear as an exception in a batch of seedlings, as for example a yellow antirrhinum in a batch of orange ones. The term is also applied to varieties which have become mixed by accident. Rogueing consists of removing these inferior or unwanted plants.

Roller: see **Tools**

Rolling: see **Soil (soil operations)**

Root pruning: see **Pruning**

Rootstock: see **Propagation**

Rotation: see **Crop rotation**

Runner

Horizontally extending shoot or stolon. Strawberries, for example, produce these rooting stems, which form new plants where they touch the soil. These can be severed from the parent and planted out when rooted.

THE YEAR AT A GLANCE

Rhododendrons and azaleas

MARCH

Prepare ground for planting.
Start planting as soon as cold weather ceases.
Water young plants when growth starts, if weather is dry.

APRIL

Transplant plants that need moving.
Complete planting new bushes.
Water newly planted bushes if weather is dry.
Remove dead heads on early-flowering plants.

MAY

Pick off dead flowers to allow new growth to form.
Mulch with peat or leaf-mould to prevent soil drying out.

JUNE

Watch for Japanese lace-wing fly and control with contact or systemic insecticide.
Watch for bud blast. Remove affected shoots and burn them or spray with a non-lime fungicide.
Water young plants in dry weather.

JULY

Spray against Japanese lace-wing fly and bud blast.
Watch for leaf hopper and control with HCH, malathion or derris.
Remove any suckers found on grafted plants.

AUGUST

Propagate rhododendrons by layering.

SEPTEMBER

During rainy weather, transplant bushes which need moving.
Continue to increase stock by layering.
Heel in plants arriving from nurseries if the ground is not ready for planting, but do not allow them to become dry.

OCTOBER

Prepare ground for planting, and plant new bushes.
Mulch plants which are not making healthy growth with peat, leaf-mould or well rotted manure.
Spray buds with a bird deterrent.

NOVEMBER

Spray buds with a bird deterrent.
Continue planting in fine weather.
Lift and pot suitable small plants for indoor decoration.

DECEMBER

Planting is possible if weather is fine.
Spray buds with a bird deterrent.

JANUARY

Lightly cover dwarf rhododendrons and Japanese azaleas with dead bracken to protect from severe frost; remove protection during mild spells.

FEBRUARY

Prepare ground for planting during periods of fine weather; incorporate manure. Leave ground to weather.

THE YEAR AT A GLANCE

Roses

MARCH

Complete planting as soon as possible.
Prune hybrid teas, floribundas, established miniatures, repeat-flowering climbers and repeat-flowering shrubs. Begin at the start of the month in the south; at the end of the month elsewhere.
Cut out diseased or frost-damaged wood and look out for diseased patches in healthy stems.

Under glass

Maintain ventilation.
Spray with water on bright days.
Water systemic insecticide into the soil.
Feed with liquid or soluble plant food.

APRIL

Complete pruning.
Feed with rose fertiliser and hoe it into the surface soil.
Tie new growths of climbers and ramblers to separate canes.
Water newly planted roses during prolonged dry weather.
Mulch rose beds with manure, garden compost or moist peat, or apply $\frac{1}{2}$ in. of grass cuttings.
Water beds with paraquat weedkiller.
Buy and plant container-grown roses from garden centres.

Under glass

Keep temperature to 21°C (70°F) during the day and to 16°C (61°F) at night.
Water pot-grown roses and feed once a week with liquid fertiliser.
Shade the glass of the greenhouse and keep ventilators open.
Spray foliage with dinocap or benomyl to prevent mildew.

MAY

Spray regularly against greenfly, using a systemic insecticide. Spray with benomyl or captan and dinocap against black spot and mildew, with zineb against rust.
Remove rolled-up leaves containing tortrix caterpillar or sawfly grub, and destroy.

Under glass

Damp down on sunny days and ventilate.
Cease feeding when flower buds colour.
After flowering, move roses outdoors; water during dry weather.

JUNE

For quality blooms, remove small side buds from flower shoots.
Hoe regularly.
Pull away brier shoots and suckers.
Spray with systemic insecticide against aphids, and also spray against black spot, mildew and rust.

JULY

Cut blooms for home decoration and remove dead heads.
After the first flush of blooms, feed rose bushes with rose fertiliser and hoe it into the soil.
Continue to spray against greenfly, black spot, mildew and rust.

AUGUST

Remove blooms as they fade.
Cease applying fertilisers.
Continue spraying.
Place orders for new roses for November delivery.

SEPTEMBER

For quality blooms on hybrid teas, remove small side buds from flower stems.
Scatter wood ash or sulphate of potash on the rose beds and hoe it in.
Tie the shoots of climbers into a fan shape.
Prune climbers and ramblers which have only one flush of blooms, and also weeping standards.
Take cuttings of mature side shoots from climbers and ramblers; and of this year's growth from floribundas and hybrid teas.
Insert cuttings in trenches outdoors.
Continue to spray against greenfly and fungus diseases.

OCTOBER

Prepare new rose beds for planting.
Continue to spray against greenfly and fungus diseases.

NOVEMBER

Plant out roses in a planting mixture containing bone-meal and peat or humus.
Heel in plants which cannot be planted straight away.
For standard roses, drive in a stout stake and secure near the top of the rose.
Plant climbers and ramblers 15 in. or more away from a wall or fence.

Under glass

Pot roses for flowering next April and May, and leave them outside in the garden until December.

DECEMBER

Complete planting, but not if the soil is wet and sticky, or if there is frost or snow on the surface.
If conditions are unsuitable for planting, heel the roses in.
Prepare established rose beds for winter, shortening long growths to $2\frac{1}{2}$ ft., collecting and burning fallen leaves which show traces of black spot, and chopping up the top inch of compacted soil.
Ensure that September-planted cuttings are firm in the ground.

Under glass

Bring pot roses into the greenhouse and prune hard.

JANUARY

Support bushes lashed by winter gales and firm the soil around them.
Prepare ground for planting in February and March.

Under glass

Maintain a night temperature of 5°C (41°F) and water roses once a week.

FEBRUARY

Under glass

Maintain temperatures of 16°C (61°F) during the day and 7°C (45°F) at night.
Water well once a week.

S

Sagittate: see **Leaf shapes**

Saprophyte
Any living organism growing on a dead organism. Saprophytic fungi in the soil are beneficial to the decay of dead matter. (See also **Parasite**.)

Scale: see **Propagation**

Scion: see **Propagation**

Scissors: see **Tools**

Scrambling plant
Fast-growing climber which sends shoots upwards through other plants. Prickles or thorns often keep the shoots in position, and such plants are suitable to screen a fence. *Polygonum baldschuanicum* (Russian vine) is a prolific scrambling plant.

Scree
Alternative name for moraine.

Screen
A wall, fence or hedge that encloses a garden or hides an ugly view. Walls and fences can be made more attractive by planting climbing or scrambling plants against them. A few climbers, such as the many varieties of *Hedera helix* (common ivy) and Virginia creeper, will cling to bare walls and fences. Twining plants, like *Actinidia chinensis* (Chinese gooseberry) and wisteria, need the support of wires or rods against a wall or fence. A temporary summer screen can be

Screen (perforated concrete)

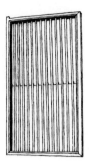

Screen (corrugated PVC)

provided by training *Lathyrus latifolius* (ever-lasting pea) against a fence or a double row of canes, up to 6 ft. high.

Seaweed: see **Fertilisers and manures**

Secateurs: see **Tools**

Seed: see **Propagation**

Seedboxes: see **Tools**

Seed leaf
The first leaf, or pair of leaves, produced by a germinating seed. (See **Cotyledon**.)

Seedling
A young plant with a single, soft and un-branched stem. The term is also used to distinguish a plant raised from seed from one raised vegetatively.

Seed pans: see **Tools**

Seed sower: see **Tools**

Self-coloured
Applied to a flower of a single colour. Self carnations have one colour only, in contrast to fancy carnations.

Self-fertile
Applied to a plant which will set seed when fertilised with its own pollen. Self-fertile fruit trees are suitable for the small garden, as no pollinating partner is needed.

Self-sterile
Applied to a plant, especially sweet cherry and many varieties of apple, which needs a pollinating partner to produce seeds and fruits.

Semi-double
Applied to a flower with more than the normal number of petals. Some but not all of the stamens and pistils have developed into petals, as in a fully double flower.

Sepal
One of the leaf-like growths which form the calyx of a flower.

Sequestrene
Organic chemical compound used to correct iron or other mineral deficiencies in the soil.

Serrate: see **Leaf shapes**

Set
1. Small onions, shallot bulbs or potato tubers, which are planted out early in the season. 2. Applied to fruit blossom which has been fertilised.

Sewage sludge: see **Fertilisers and manures**

Shade
Although light is essential to all green plants, some plants require less than others. Many plants need to be shaded from strong sun-light, particularly if they are grown under glass. During the summer shade greenhouses with blinds of lath, canvas or split bamboo, or cover the panes with a lime wash. Individual plants may be temporarily shaded with sheets of paper. Plants in the open can be shaded with wattle hurdles, hessian screens, hedges and walls. Cuttings and seedlings particularly need shading until they have become established.

Shears: see **Tools**

Shelter: see **Protection**

Shelter belt
One or more rows of trees left to grow un-hindered to their full height and spread.
The shelter belt's effectiveness as a wind-break depends on its height, thickness and length. Wind speeds are reduced at up to ten times the height on the lee side of the belt. A thin shelter belt filters the wind and reduces its strength; a thick belt of trees diverts the wind, but may cause turbulence and wind

eddies on the lee side. Wind speeds are increased at the ends of a shelter belt, and deflected winds blow round the lee side for a short distance. A shelter belt should therefore be two to three rows wide, and at least ten times as long as its ultimate height. (See also **Weather.**)

Evergreen species, such as varieties of *Chamaecyparis lawsoniana* (Lawson's cypress), are more suitable for a windbreak than deciduous trees, though many species of poplar can be relied on to produce a fairly effective shelter. Shelter belts are suitable only for large gardens exposed to the full force of wind. Hedges provide adequate shelter for most gardens.

Shoddy: see **Fertilisers and manures**

Shrub

A plant with woody stems and branches, and with no central trunk. Shrubs may vary in height from a few inches to 15–20 ft.

Side shoot: see **Lateral**

Sieves: see **Tools**

Simazine: see **Weeds and weedkillers**

Single

Applied to a flower with the normal number of petals.

Singling: see **Thinning**

Smith period: see **Weather**

Snag

A stub of a shoot or branch left after pruning. It becomes isolated from the main sap flow and will die, often allowing fungal diseases, such as die-back, to enter the tree. (See also **Pruning.**)

Sodium chlorate: see **Weeds and weedkillers**

Soil

Treatment and improvement of the soil can be carried out correctly only when the components of the soil and their functions are understood. Exposing the 'soil profile', by digging down 3 ft. or more, reveals the existence of two distinct layers. The lower layer, the subsoil, is lighter in colour and harder in texture than the dark upper layer, the topsoil.

Subsoil

There is considerable variation in the depth at which this soil layer begins, but it is easily identified by its marked difference in texture and colour from the layer above. The character of the subsoil can have considerable bearing on the fertility of the topsoil, and it is not necessarily of the same type. A sticky clay subsoil obstructs drainage of the topsoil, which will consequently be cold and sour; a gravel subsoil beneath a clay topsoil ensures good drainage; clay under sand will prevent the sand drying out too quickly. Although the subsoil is much less fertile than the topsoil, due to the absence of organic matter, it can be improved by deep cultivation and by the addition of manure or garden compost; it should never be mixed with the topsoil or placed over it.

Topsoil

This dark, fertile soil layer is composed of mineral particles, organic matter (humus), air and water. The topsoil is also inhabited by living organisms in the form of bacteria and fungi, worms and insects.

Types of soil

The texture of each soil layer is determined by the proportion of sand, silt or clay particles. The higher the proportion of coarse sand grains, the lighter the texture; a high proportion of clay particles gives a heavy soil. A soil layer is rarely all sand, silt or clay but, depending on the relative proportions of such particles, soils can generally be classified within four main categories: chalky, clay, loam and sandy soil.

Chalky soil

A light soil formed for the most part from the impure residues of the original calcium carbonate which weather action has broken down during the centuries. A chalky soil is usually shallow and warms up quickly in spring. It allows water to drain through easily. The slightest drought, however, dries up the thin topsoil, and retention of water and plant nutrients is poor. Brassicas, salad vegetables, some flowering plants and shrubs will thrive in a chalky, alkaline soil, but growth is usually restricted; rhododendrons, azaleas and other lime-hating plants cannot be grown.

A chalky soil can be improved by breaking up the subsoil to assist the penetration of water-seeking roots. The depth of the topsoil can be increased by adding organic materials, such as farmyard manure, garden compost or peat. This organic matter decomposes rapidly and must be replenished frequently. In summer, mulch liberally with a moisture-retaining top dressing, such as peat.

Clay soil

A heavy soil made up of minute mineral particles, which give the soil its sticky texture. The tiny particles are crowded together in compact masses, so that both drainage and aeration are poor, and the soil consequently takes a long time to warm up in spring. During droughts, a heavy clay soil will set rock-hard and crack into wide fissures. A soil with the correct clay balance can be highly fertile, for it retains moisture and the chemical nutrients necessary for plant growth. Improvements of a heavy clay soil are chiefly carried out by deep cultivation. Correct timing is important, because the clods formed when digging wet clay will later dry out into cement-hard lumps unless they are first exposed to frost. Late autumn and early winter are ideal for either single or double digging, preferably the latter. If double digging is carried out, fork over the subsoil and leave the top spit rough and unbroken, so that as large an area as possible is exposed to weather action. If the soil is liable to water-logging, drainage can be improved by incorporating grit, sand or weathered boiler ashes and clinkers when the subsoil is forked over. In extreme cases of waterlogging the installation of pipe drainage may be necessary. The soil can be lightened and made more crumbly by forking well rotted manure, garden compost or sedge peat into the topsoil, or by adding horticultural gypsum to the top 6 in. of soil. Clay soils are often acid, and therefore need regular liming. The addition of lime makes the soil less sour and also helps to break down the clay into crumbly granules.

Loam soil

A mixed soil containing both clay and sand, with a high proportion of humus. A loam soil is normally well aerated and free-draining, and therefore warms up readily and allows easy cultivation. Plant nutrients are retained for long periods.

The texture of a loam soil is determined by the proportion of sand to clay. A loam with a high sand content is termed a light loam, while a heavy loam contains a high proportion of clay. A medium loam has a content of 50–60 per cent sand to 30 per cent clay. This is generally considered the ideal garden soil, having enough sand to keep the soil open and porous, and sufficient clay to keep it moist.

The remaining bulk of a loam soil consists of humus and lime. The higher the lime content the quicker does the organic matter decompose. Where the lime content is high, an annual application of manure or compost is necessary to maintain fertility. If the loam is acid, the organic matter will need to be replenished less often; if desired, excessive acidity can be corrected by the addition of lime.

Sandy soil
This is a light, open soil composed largely of coarse sand particles. A handful of sandy soil feels gritty, and even when moist fails to stick together. Such a soil has many advantages: the light porous texture ensures good drainage and aeration, enabling the soil to be worked nearly all the year round. It warms up quickly in spring, and roots penetrate easily. The drawbacks of a sandy soil also arise from its light texture, for it is unable to retain water for any length of time, thus causing young plants to wilt from drought. Plant nutrients, particularly potash and lime, are rapidly washed out of the soil, so that frequent applications are necessary. A sandy soil can be improved by digging in manure or compost; as these materials decompose rapidly in such soil, applications need to be frequent and liberal. During summer, mulches of compost or sedge peat will retain moisture round plants.

Air and water
Oxygen, which circulates through fissures and cavities in the soil, is essential for the existence of soil bacteria and for the respiration of plant roots.

Water, whether as rain or supplied artificially, penetrates the soil, some of the moisture being retained between the soil granules. Water is essential as a solvent of plant nutrients and as a carrier of hydrogen and oxygen. In well drained soil the surplus water leaches through the subsoil, its upper level at any given time being known as the water table. The depth at which the water table is located may vary from a few inches to several hundred feet, according to the area;

in low-lying areas the water table may be quite near the surface during winter. There is no air in waterlogged soil, and consequently root restriction occurs where drainage is bad and the water table high. During the growing season, plants draw constantly on the water held in the soil, so that an adequate supply must be available at all times. It is important to water the soil to a depth of at least 12 in., otherwise the moisture will merely evaporate from the surface. Ideally, watering should be carried out in the evening. On dry soils, loss of moisture can be reduced by mulching.

Humus
The spongy, dark brown substance which is left after the decomposition of bulky organic matter and soil bacteria. The production in the soil of humus is a slow, continuing process, which constantly releases nutrients for plants to absorb. Few soils, however, contain enough organic material to provide a stable supply of humus, and bulky manures must be added to make up this deficiency.

Organic matter
The decomposed remains of plants and animals, which provide plant nutrients in the form of carbon, nitrogen and trace elements. Organic matter also provides food for the living soil organisms. The presence of bulky organic matter improves the physical condition of the soil—it adds bulk to a porous, sandy soil and opens up a heavy clay soil.

Soil life
Numerous small and microscopic creatures, of both animal and vegetable origin, inhabit the soil. Most of the bacteria and many fungi are beneficial; they help to break down organic matter and on their decomposition release nutritional elements, necessary for plant growth, into the soil. There are, however, many harmful pests, such as slugs, wireworms and cutworms, as well as parasitic fungi, in the soil. Control of these is necessary to obtain good garden crops.

Soil testing
A number of chemical elements must be present in the soil if plants are to make healthy growth. Of these chemicals, nitrogen, phosphorus and potassium are the most vital; if lacking, they must be supplied in the form of fertiliser or manure. The nutritional value of a soil can be determined by testing. Samples of soil taken from different parts of the garden and mixed together, making sufficient in all

to fill a pint carton, can be sent to the county horticultural adviser, who will then recommend the type and quantity of fertiliser or manure required. Alternatively, there are soil-testing kits which can be used to determine both the chemical content of the soil and its acidity. Autumn is generally the best time for soil testing.

pH scale
A soil is either acid (sour), neutral or alkaline (sweet), the degree of acidity or alkalinity, determined by test, being measured against a scale of values known as the pH scale. The neutral point—where a soil is neither acid nor alkaline—is pH 7·0; readings below this denote an acid soil; readings above denote an alkaline soil. A soil with a pH reading of between 6·5 and 7·0 is suitable for growing most plants, slight acidity generally being an advantage. Below 6·0, a soil is suitable only for such plants as rhododendrons and azaleas. At the other end of the scale, a soil with a pH reading of 8·0 will support few plants, due to its deficiency of vital minerals.

Soil operations
Cultivation of the soil is generally considered essential to ensure worthwhile results from crops, in spite of successes claimed by advocates of no-digging techniques. Digging or forking improves the aeration of the soil; during the winter, weather action breaks it down so that raking in the spring is sufficient to produce a fine tilth. However, frequent digging without the addition of organic matter to provide humus will eventually lead to a poor soil.

Digging
Digging has two main objects: to break up the soil and to destroy weeds. Breaking the soil assists penetration of air and rainwater, speeding the natural processes of decay and promoting fertility. Incorporation of bulky organic materials at the time of digging increases the depth of fertile topsoil. Digging —with a spade or a fork—can be done to a depth of one spit (plain digging), to a depth of two spits (double digging or bastard trenching) or three spits deep (trenching).

Plain digging
At one end of the plot, take out a trench across the plot a spade's width and depth, removing the soil to just beyond the far end of the plot. Mark out a second trench alongside the first and turn over the soil, to a spade's

depth, into the first trench. If manure is to be incorporated, add this to the bottom of the trench before filling in.

Double digging (or bastard trenching)
Cultivated soils benefit from double digging once every three years; neglected or badly aerated soils should be double dug before being brought into cultivation.

Mark off and dig out a trench 24 in. wide and one spit deep across one end of the plot, removing this top spit to just beyond the far end of the plot. Dig or fork over the spit beneath, mixing in manure or compost. Dig out the next 24 in. trench, throwing the soil on top of the lower spit in the first trench. Repeat this operation until the whole plot has been dug over, filling the last trench with the soil removed initially from the first trench. Leave the soil clods as they fall, as the rough surface exposes a greater area to weather action during the winter.

Trenching
Take out a trench 3 ft. wide and one spit deep across one end of the plot, removing the soil to just beyond the far end of the plot. Divide the trench longitudinally into two strips, each 18 in. wide. Dig out the soil from the strip nearer the end of the plot and remove it to the far end of the plot, to make a second heap alongside the topsoil already removed. Fork over the third spit to loosen the subsoil, adding manure. Now turn over the second of the 18 in. wide strips on to the manured third spit, forking over and manuring the soil so exposed. Mark out a new trench, this time only 18 in. wide, and turn the top spit on to the first strip in the first trench. Move the second spit to cover the forked-over second strip in the first trench, then loosen and manure the bottom spit in the second trench. Continue this process until the whole plot is dug; when the soil is returned to the last trench, care must be taken to replace it in its original layers: second spit first, topsoil last.

Drainage
It is important that all soil should be well drained. Proper drainage allows the free passage of water, and without it air is excluded and beneficial bacteria and plant roots are destroyed. Badly drained soil is also cold and retards plant growth. Good drainage is primarily dependent upon an open soil texture, which can be achieved by the inclusion in the soil of coarse, gritty materials, and humus in the form of compost, straw or farmyard manure. The drainage of clay soils is usually poor, but may be improved by adding lime to the soil, which binds the fine clay particles together into larger granules. Clay can be ridged or can have grit and humus added to it. Seriously waterlogged soil, which cannot be improved by cultural methods, may require pipe drains. The pipes should be laid in trenches, and in a herring-bone fashion, so as to drain all parts of the area covered. The trenches should have a slight slope towards a natural outlet, such as a stream or ditch, or towards a soakaway, consisting of a large hole partly filled with stones or clinkers.

Forking
Cultivation of the soil in an established bed or border, for example in a shrubbery, is usually done one spit deep, or less, to loosen the topsoil. This is best carried out with a fork, especially on a heavy clay soil.

Hoeing
Cultivating the surface of the soil with a hoe so as to aerate the soil and destroy weeds. Hoeing should be done regularly from spring until the end of the summer. Use a Dutch hoe, or one of patent design, between rows of vegetables and in herbaceous beds and borders to destroy weed seedlings before they begin to germinate. On larger weeds, use a draw hoe to cut through the soil, chopping out the weeds.

Manuring
The addition to soil of bulky organic materials (see also **Fertilisers and manures**). Manures, such as garden compost or farmyard manure, not only help to replenish plant materials but also improve the soil's texture and condition. The addition of manure to a heavy clay soil opens up the fine, sticky particles and thus improves aeration. In a sandy soil the coarse particles are bound together by the humus, retaining moisture and plant nutrients for a longer period as a result.

Mulching
Top-dressing the soil with an organic material—farmyard manure, straw, peat, compost, leaf-mould or spent hops. A layer, or mulch, is spread on the soil surface to conserve moisture, to keep plant roots cool, to supply them with nutrients as the material decomposes and to smother weeds. Do not

---

Plants to suit different soils

Flowers for chalky soil

Acanthus	Eupatorium	Perilla
Aconitum	Euphorbia	Petunia
Anchusa	Filipendula	Pulmonaria
Artemisia	Gaillardia	Pyrethrum
Campanula	Galega	Reseda odorata
Centaurea	Helipterum	Salvia
Chelone	Hemerocallis	Scabiosa
Dianthus	Inula	Sedum
Dictamnus	Iris	Tradescantia
Digitalis	Linum	Verbascum
Doronicum	Matthiola	Zinnia
Echinops	Nemesia	

Trees and shrubs for chalky soil

Berberis	Cornus	Phlomis
Buddleia	Euonymus	Prunus (ornamental
Carpinus	Fagus	cherries and
Cercis	sylvatica	plums)
Choisya	Griselinia	Pyracantha
Clematis	Juniperus	Senecio
montana	Olearia	Sorbus
C. patens	Philadelphus	Taxus saccata

Flowers for sandy soil

Achillea	Dianthus	Montbretia
Alstroemeria	Echinops	Oenothera
Alyssum	Eryngium	Papaver
Anthemis	alpinum	Salvia
Armeria	Geranium	Scabiosa
Aubrieta	Gypsophila	Sedum
Bergenia	Helianthemum	Stokesia
Catananche	Iberis	Verbascum
Coreopsis	Limonium	Veronica
Cynara	Macleava	

Trees and shrubs for sandy soil

Berberis	Cytisus	Lavandula
Buddleia	Deutzia	Olearia
Ceanothus	Elaeagnus	Phlomis fruticosa
Cistus	Genista	Potentilla
Corylopsis	Hebe	Romneya
Cotoneaster	Hypericum	Spartium
microphylla	calycinum	Tamarix

Flowers for clay soil

Aquilegia	Helenium	Polygonum
Aruncus	Hemerocallis	Rudbeckia
Astilbe	Hosta	Solidago
Dicentra	Ligularia	Trollius
Erigeron	Lysimachia	
Geranium	Physostegia	

Trees and shrubs for clay soil

Arundinaria	Forsythia	Ribes
Berberis	Laburnum	Spiraea bumalda
Cornus	Mahonia	Syringa
Deutzia	Philadelphus	Weigela

mulch cold or frozen soils, and in dry weather soak the soil thoroughly before mulching it. In spring or early summer spread a layer of leaf-mould, peat or garden compost, several inches thick, over the roots of herbaceous plants, trees and shrubs. Soft fruits may be mulched with thick layers of straw, and this will also keep the fruits of strawberries clean. Runner beans and peas can be mulched with grass clippings; the mulch, however, should never exceed a depth of $\frac{1}{2}$ in. Black poly-thene film may also be used as a mulch.

Peat is sometimes sold in dry, compressed bales and should be thoroughly wetted before use. When straw is used as a mulch, or incorporated in the soil, a nitrogenous fertiliser, such as sulphate of ammonia or Nitro-chalk, should be sprinkled on top at 1 oz. per sq. yd. This will prevent depletion of nitrogen caused by the decomposition process of the straw.

Raking
Breaking down the soil surface to a fine tilth before sowing. Work the teeth of the rake evenly back and forth over soil already loosened by digging until the surface soil is completely broken down into fine particles.

Ridging
A method of cultivating heavy, badly drained soils in winter so as to expose a greater surface area to the action of frost and rain. Mark off the plot in strips $2\frac{1}{2}$ ft. wide, and remove the soil from the first trench, one spit deep, to the far end of the plot. Working backwards, dig each trench so that the first two spadefuls are thrown forward next to each other in the trench ahead, and the third spade-ful is placed on top of the first two. In this way parallel ridges are formed along the whole length of the plot. In spring, level the surface before sowing or planting.

Rolling
Firming the soil in spring before planting. This may be done either by pulling a light roller over the soil or by treading it carefully. Rolling also breaks down lumpy soil.

Soil capacity: see **Weather**

Soil warming: see **Greenhouses**

Sowing: see **Propagation (seed)**

Spades: see **Tools**

Spathulate: see **Leaf shapes**

Species: see **Classification**

Specimen plant
A plant which is grown so that it can be seen from all angles. An example is a tree planted in the centre of a lawn.

Sphagnum moss: see **Moss**

Spike
A compound flower head consisting of a central stem along which are arranged numerous stalkless florets.

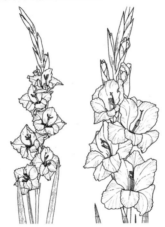

Spikes (gladiolus)

Spit
One spade's depth—a depth of 10–12 in. Digging is done one, two or three spits deep.

Spore
1. The minute reproductive bodies of ferns and mosses. Fern spores appear on the backs of the leaves; moss spores in fruiting bodies are borne on stalks above the plant. 2. The reproductive cells of fungi.

Sport: see **Mutation**

Sprayers: see **Tools**

Spraying
Applying chemicals in spray form to destroy insects or fungi on plant foliage. Spraying should be carried out during dry, still weather,

as rain will wash the spray off and wind will blow it away. Plants are sometimes sprayed with plain water to prevent flagging.

Sprinklers: see **Tools**

Sprout
A young shoot, particularly on a germinating seed or tuber. Potato tubers are encouraged to form sprouts in a light, cool and frost-free place, before they are planted. Faulty tubers are easily recognised; sprouted tubers will make earlier growth.

Spur
1. A short lateral branch bearing clusters of fruit buds. On old fruit trees such spurs may become large and unwieldy and need thinning out by drastic autumn pruning. 2. Tubular appendage in some flowers, such as aquilegia (columbine), in which nectar is produced.

Spur (apple tree)

Spur pruning: see **Pruning**

Staging: see **Greenhouses**

Staking
Supporting plants with posts or canes to keep them upright or within bounds. Many of the more highly developed plants, such as giant-flowered dahlias, are unable to support themselves, and standard forms of trees need stout stakes for their first few years. Stakes must be strong enough for their purpose, be as inconspicuous as possible, and preferably be covered by the growth of the fully grown plant. Trees should be staked to strong larch poles; herbaceous plants can be supported by bamboo canes or birch twigs, linked with ties. Dahlias and standard roses need 1 in. square stakes, terminating below the flowers. Runner beans, which present a great deal of

wind resistance, are usually staked and trained to a double row of hazel sticks, or grown up strings stretched between horizontal wires.

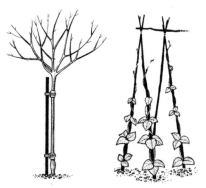

Staking (tree, runner beans)

Stamen
The male reproductive organ of a flower. It consists of the pollen-bearing anther at the end of the filament.

Standard
One of the upright petals of the bearded iris, in contrast to one of the falls.
Standard tree. Any tree or shrub with a bare stem several feet high before the first branches. Standard fruit trees are usually 6–7 ft. high.
Half-standard tree. Any tree or shrub with a clear stem of 4–5 ft. before the head of branches.

Starting
Encouraging plants into growth, particularly tubers such as begonias and gloxinias, after the dormant period. Begonia tubers are started in a mixture of peat and sand, and given water and warmth until they have formed enough roots to be potted on before being planted out.

Stem
That part of a plant above the root system, which carries leaves, buds and shoots.
Stem-rooting. Applied to a bulb which roots from the base, and later produces roots from the stem above the bulb. Most Asiatic species of lilies are stem rooting and require deeper planting than basal-rooting species.

Sterile
1. Unable to breed; the term is often applied to plants which produce fertile pollen but no seed. Many double flowers are sterile, as the necessary reproductive organs have become petaloid. Other plants, such as sweet cherries, cannot set fruit without a pollinating partner.
2. Applied to potting composts, which are partially sterilised by heat or chemical means to destroy weed seeds, fungi and harmful soil organisms.

Sterilisation
The act of destroying fungi, weed seeds and harmful bacteria in the soil. Sterilisation, either by heat or by chemical treatment, is only partial: complete sterilisation would render the soil lifeless and infertile. Loam, used in composts and in greenhouse borders, can be sterilised by subjecting a quantity of soil to steam treatment for approximately 20 min. at a temperature of 82°C (180°F). There are several electric steam sterilisers available, or the soil may be sterilised by chemical means. Diluted cresylic acid, dazomet or formaldehyde is watered on to the greenhouse soil, which is then covered with polythene to trap the poisonous fumes. A heat-treated soil is ready for immediate use; soil treated chemically cannot be worked for several weeks.

Stigma
The tip of the female reproductive organ of a flower. It becomes sticky when the ovules are ready for fertilisation, so that pollen adheres to it.

Stolon
A rooting stem, or runner, on the surface of the soil. Strawberries and mint produce stolons which root themselves.

Stone
The seed of a plum, cherry, peach or other member of the *Prunus* family. Stone formation is necessary in fruit development; adequate fertilisation of the flowers and sufficient water and minerals in the soil are essential for stoning.

Stool
Any plant which is used solely for propagating purposes. A chrysanthemum stool consists of the old roots and basal shoots, which are taken as cuttings. Magnolia and apple stock stools are used for rooting layers.

Standard

Half-standard

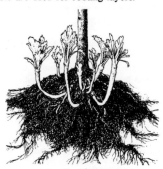

Stool (chrysanthemum)

Stopping

Removing or pinching out the growing tips, especially of chrysanthemums and carnations. This encourages the formation of breaks, or side shoots, and controls the flowering. Late-flowering chrysanthemums often produce better blooms after a second stopping.

Stopping (chrysanthemum)

Storing

Apples and pears, potatoes, carrots and other roots are the garden crops usually stored. Also stored are dahlia tubers and gladioli corms. They require cool, airy, frost-free and dry conditions. Apples need a damp atmosphere to prevent them from shrivelling; they are best kept in a shed with a beaten earth floor, or packed, four layers deep, in boxes stored on top of each other. Potatoes and roots may be kept in clamps.

Strain

A variation or a plant variety raised from seed. Seedsmen select their seed plants for certain desirable characteristics, and a particular flower variety bought from two different seedsmen may be of different strains.

Stratification: see **Propagation (seed)**

Stub: see **Snag**

Style

The stem which joins the stigma to the ovary in a female flower.

Sub-shrub

An intermediate between a shrub and a herbaceous plant. It produces some woody growth at the base, but the herbaceous top growth dies back annually. An example is *Hypericum calycinum* (rose of Sharon).

Subsoil: see **Soil**

Sub-tropical

Applied to a type of summer bedding plant originating from tropical regions. Especially applied to those plants which will grow outdoors during the summer months, but are destroyed by the slightest frost. Such plants include cannas, coleus and abutilons.

Succulent

Any plant with thick, fleshy leaves or stems. The foliage and stems retain large amounts of moisture, and are adaptations to the arid climates in which succulent plants grow naturally. Cacti and sempervivums are succulents. (See **Cacti**.)

Sucker

A shoot which arises from below ground, at the base of a plant. On grafted plants suckers come from the rootstock and must be removed, by cutting them off at their point of origin on the roots. This prevents the stock taking over the plant from the choice variety grafted on to it. (See also **Propagation**.)

Sulphate of ammonia: see **Fertilisers and manures**

Sulphate of potash: see **Fertilisers and manures**

Sulphur

Chemical used in one form or another as a fungicide and acaricide. It is obtainable as a wettable powder (colloidal sulphur) for spray application, or in dust form (dispersible sulphur) to be applied with a powder blower. Sulphur is frequently burnt in greenhouses against mildews; but burning sulphur is harmful to all plant life, and the greenhouse must be cleared before it is treated. A number of fruits are sulphur-shy, and their foliage is liable to damage by sulphur applications. 'Cox's Orange Pippin' apples, 'Wellington XXX' black currants, 'Leveller' gooseberries and all plums are sulphur-shy.

Superphosphate of lime: see **Fertilisers and manures**

Support

Most climbing and scrambling plants need some form of support on which to climb. This can be provided by training them on trellis, on wires fixed to a wall, or over a pergola. (See also **Staking**.)

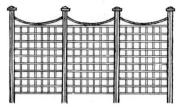

Support (trellis and posts)

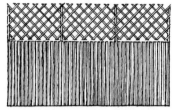

Support (trellis attached to close-board fencing)

Symbiosis

A state in which two different organisms live together, each contributing something to the other's nutrition. Lichen, which is formed of algae and fungi living together, is one such example. Mycorrhizal fungi, which are often found in association with the roots of beech trees and conifers, also live symbiotically with their host plants.

Syringes: see **Tools (sprayers)**

Systemic insecticide

Chemical compound, which when watered on the soil or sprayed on plants enters the plant sap. Sap-sucking insects are consequently destroyed, and beneficial insects are left unharmed. Vegetable crops sprayed with a systemic insecticide should not be harvested for at least thirty days.

T

Tap root

A long anchoring root, which grows vertically downwards. Vegetables such as carrots and parsnips form tap roots.

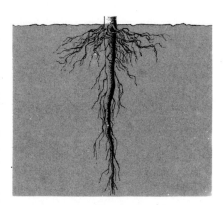

Tap root

Tar oil

Chemical preparation, used as a winter-wash to destroy the eggs of aphids, scale insects and hibernating caterpillars. Tar oil solutions are also effective in cleaning tree bark of lichen and moss. The compounds contain phenol, and are poisonous to humans, animals and fish. Care must be taken to prevent the chemical from touching exposed skin. Apply the spray only during still and frost-free weather, and keep it away from painted surfaces, as it may cause discoloration. Tar oil should be applied during the dormant season on the following: apples, pears, peaches, nectarines, damsons, cherries, black and red currants, gooseberries, blackberries, vines and roses.

Taxonomy

The study and science of classification of plants into families (genera).

Temperature: see Weather

Temperature conversion: see Weights and measures

Tender

Applied to plants which are liable to frost damage when grown outdoors. In winter tender plants, for example pelargoniums and begonias, should be removed to a frost-free room or greenhouse. Some plants are tender in their young stages, but are moderately hardy as they mature and become woody.
Tender annual. See Annual.

THE YEAR AT A GLANCE

Sweet peas

MARCH

Plant out autumn-sown seedlings in double rows where they are to be grown on the cordon system. Plant bush-grown seedlings in single rows, supported with 6 ft. canes.
Put slug bait round plants when they are set out.

Under glass

Make spring sowings and place seed pans in a cold frame or greenhouse.

APRIL

Plant out March-sown seedlings.
Start restricting growth on plants grown as cordons, removing all tendrils and side shoots.

MAY

Hoe round the plants frequently.
Mulch the plants in dry weather.
Tie cordons regularly as they grow.

JUNE

Syringe the plants with a mist-like spray of water in dry weather.
Spray monthly with a systemic insecticide against sap-sucking insects.
Remove any plants whose leaves turn yellow or brown.
Continue to pinch out side shoots and tendrils from cordons.

JULY

A liquid feed may be necessary every 12 days.
Spray monthly with a systemic insecticide against sap-sucking insects.
Continue pinching out tendrils and side shoots from cordons.
Layer cordon-grown plants when they reach a height of 5 ft.

AUGUST

Mulch, feed and water if necessary.
Hoe regularly if no mulch has been applied.
Cut blooms regularly.
Spray monthly with a systemic insecticide.

SEPTEMBER

Purchase seed for sowing next month.
Order some of the old-fashioned varieties to provide scent among the modern ones.

OCTOBER

Sow sweet peas in the open ground.

Under glass

Sow sweet peas under glass in pots or boxes, treating them beforehand with a proprietary fungicidal dressing.
Place the pots or boxes in a cold frame and remove lights when seedlings appear.

NOVEMBER

Prepare next season's planting site by double digging.
Apply 3–4 handfuls of bone-meal per sq. yd. to the top spit.

Under glass

Prick out seedlings from October sowings into 3 in. pots.

DECEMBER

Cover frames with matting after severe frosts to avoid rapid thawing.
Pinch out the tips of seedlings after the second or third pair of leaves has been formed.

JANUARY

Dress beds prepared for planting with hydrated lime.

Under glass

Sow seed in slight heat.

FEBRUARY

Break down and tread soil on planting site.
Erect supports for plants to be grown on the cordon system.
Sow seeds outdoors in their flowering position.

Tendril

A thin, stem-like, curling outgrowth arising from the stem or leaf stalk of a climbing plant. Members of the pea family climb by twining their tendrils round convenient supports.

Tendril climber. A plant, such as passiflora (passion flower) and grape vine, which clings to its supports by means of tendrils.

Tendrils (sweet pea)

Terminal

Applied to a shoot or bud at the end of the extending plant growth.

Thermometer: see **Tools**

Thinning

1. Reducing the number of seedlings so that the remaining young plants have room to develop. Thinning may be done in two stages: first, as soon as the seedlings can be handled, leaving twice as many seedlings as are ultimately required; and second, thinning a few weeks later. 2. Reducing the number of flowers or fruit buds to prevent overcrowding and to improve the fruit quality. (See also **Pruning**.)

Thiram

Fungicide, obtainable as a wettable powder, and used as a spray against grey mould on lettuces, tomatoes and pot plants. Thiram, used as a seed dressing in powder form containing HCH, protects seeds against soil-borne diseases; bulbs dressed in the same mixture will withstand attacks of tulip fire.

Ties: see **Tools**

Till

To cultivate the soil by digging, forking, raking, or hoeing, or with a mechanically powered plough or a rotary or tined cultivator. See **Soil (soil operations)**.

Tilth: see **Soil**

Tine

One of the prongs of a garden fork or rake, or of a mechanical cultivator.

Tip bearing

Applied to fruit trees which produce fruit buds at the tips of shoots. This can stop growth of the tree, and such buds should be removed while building up the tree. 'Worcester Pearmain' is a tip bearer.

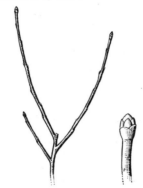

Tip bearing (apple)

Tools, machines and equipment
Aerators

Tools designed for spiking and aerating the surface of the lawn, in order to assist surface drainage and root growth. The simplest models, with three or four pointed tines, are pushed into the ground with the foot; others, more thorough in action, have hollow tines which cut and extract cores of turf. For larger areas, there are wheeled aerators with either spikes or star-shaped wheels, which cut into the surface of the lawn as the machine is pushed or mechanically propelled along.

Cloches

Crops protected with cloches can be sown or planted earlier in the year than similar crops receiving no protection. The date of fruiting or flowering may also be advanced. Glass cloches, consisting of sheets of glass secured by clips, shaped wires, or patent holders of various sorts, are available in various sizes and shapes, generally 24 in. long. The simplest kinds, made from two sheets of glass forming an inverted V, are suitable for lettuces and other low-growing crops; other types, for taller crops or multiple rows, are formed from three or four sheets, sometimes with provision for adjusting the ventilation. Plastic cloches of clear polythene or rigid transparent PVC are generally in the form of a tent or curved tunnel. They are much lighter than glass cloches, less fragile and cheaper, and safer in gardens where children play.

Compost bins

Wooden or metal containers used to hold compost-making materials. Wooden bins are made from slats spaced a few inches apart to allow free entry of air. Metal bins are usually of open wire mesh, some designs being collapsible. Heavy-gauge polythene netting is sometimes used instead of wire mesh.

Cultivators, hand

Long-handled cultivators, generally with three or five hooked tines, are useful with loosening compacted soil and for breaking lumps. The number of tines is not critical on easily worked soils, but three-tined models are best for heavy land. There are also patent cultivating tools, designed for preparing seed beds, which employ star-shaped rotors to produce a fine tilth. A third type of cultivator consists of a wheel-mounted toolbar, with long handles attached, to which cultivating tines, hoe blades or a small plough are bolted. Wheeled cultivators work best on light or well cultivated soil and are particularly useful for ridging and for hoeing between crops grown in rows.

Cultivators, mechanical

Powered cultivators are particularly useful during the earlier stages of garden construction, for digging and inter-row cultivation in a vegetable garden, and for digging borders from which plants have been lifted. Assorted attachments are available for grass cutting, hedge trimming and other tasks. Working with a rotary action, the power-driven tines cut into and mince the soil, incorporating manure or fertiliser distributed on the surface. On many models the number of tines, and hence the width of cultivation, can be varied.

Some cultivators have power-driven tines, mounted under or in front of the engine, and either trailing wheels or no wheels at all. These machines are cheaper than cultivators with power-driven wheels, and are capable of deep digging on most soils. Cultivators with power-driven wheels have rear-mounted tines. They are easier to operate and produce the finest seed beds, but may not dig quite so deeply as those with power-driven tines.

Most cultivators can also be fitted with such implements as ploughs, ridgers and hoes, and will provide power for hedge trimmers and grass cutters. The power is transmitted to the workhead by a flexible drive shaft or, in the case of grass cutters, through a system of belts and pulleys.

Dibbers
Hand tools for making planting holes. The smallest are pencil-sized sticks used for inserting plants or cuttings in pots or seed-boxes. For planting vegetables, there are much larger dibbers with pointed, metal-shod shafts 1 in. or so in diameter.

Distributors
Mechanical distribution of fertiliser and grass seed is quicker and more accurate than spreading by hand. The material is carried in a wheel-mounted hopper and dispensed evenly as the machine is pushed along. It is possible to vary the flow to suit different materials and rates of application.

Dusters
Mechanical applicators for insecticidal and fungicidal dusts are of two types. The simplest and least expensive consists of a bellows, with handle attached, which, when shaken, expels the powder. The other type employs a fan, operated by a geared handle, to distribute the powder from a hopper.

Flame guns
Paraffin-burning appliances, which emit an intensely hot flame, used for burning weeds and debris. Most flame guns have a built-in pump for pressurising the fuel. Some are mounted on wheels and may have detachable hoods, which are helpful for concentrating the flames when working between rows of crops or close to glass.

Forks
Garden forks are sold under a variety of names, depending on their size (for example, 'large digging', 'border', 'lady's'). As these names do not correspond to standard speci-fications, it is important when purchasing to compare the weight and balance of several models. Most digging forks have square prongs, tapering to a point; forks with flat prongs are used for potato lifting; for spread-ing manure, there are five-pronged forks

with round, curved prongs. D-shaped handles are now the most popular, and an increasing number are made of polypropylene, a tough, lightweight plastic. Straight-handled forks, known as weed forks or bedding forks, are useful for surface cultivations between grow-ing plants. They have three or four short prongs, with shaft lengths of from 14 in. to 4 ft. Hand forks, often sold in matching sets with trowels, are useful for weeding.

Garden lines
Available as hanks or bundles of tough, rot-proof twine or nylon, or attached to a reel mounted on an earth spike. Lengths vary from 15 to 60 yd.

Hedge trimmers
Mechanical hedge trimmers are available with integral motors, either electric or petrol; as attachments for electric power tools; or as workheads driven by a flexible drive shaft from a motor mower or cultivator. Electric hedge trimmers are further subdivided into mains and battery-operated types. The latter are becoming increasingly popular for use with battery-driven lawn mowers; they require a comparatively short length of cable, whereas supplementary cable generally has to be purchased for mains-voltage models. Hedge trimmers with integral petrol engines are heavier and more expensive than electric trimmers, but are useful for hedges remote from a mains power point and too long for continuous cutting by a battery-powered trimmer. Hedge-trimming attachments for electric power tools are satisfactory for short lengths of hedge, but for continuous use they are less convenient than purpose-built trim-mers. Workheads powered by a flexible drive from a mower or cultivator are lighter than self-contained trimmers and are just as effec-tive. However, the drive shaft, available in 10–15 ft. lengths, is an inconvenience if the hedge is at the rear of a border or other planted area. Blade lengths of powered hedge trimmers range from 1 to $2\frac{1}{2}$ ft. Long blades save time and make for easier cutting on tall or broad hedges.

Hoes
In addition to conventional Dutch and draw hoes, there are a number of proprietary types designed for lightness and ease of use. Most work on the same principle as the Dutch hoe, but have sharpened edges on both sides of their blades, which are often of stainless steel.

Shafts are generally lightweight, some having moulded handgrips. The Dutch hoe, used with a push–pull action, has a D-shaped blade from 4 to 7 in. wide, attached to a long shaft, and is a useful tool for general surface hoeing. For hoeing between seedlings and rock plants, the short-handled onion hoe is both accurate and easy to use. The draw hoe, consisting of a 5–8 in. blade attached by a swan-necked stem to a long shaft, is ideal for taking out drills, for drawing earth around plants, and for loosening heavy weed growth. Dutch and draw hoes are cheaper than patent types.

To avoid unnecessary stooping, it is impor-tant to buy hoes with handles of adequate length. As a rough guide, the top of the handle should be level with the user's ear when the hoe is placed vertically on the ground.

Hose reels
The simplest designs consist of metal reels, sometimes plastic-covered, either free-stand-ing or on legs. More expensive models are attached to wheeled trolleys or have mount-ing plates which can be secured to the wall of a shed or garage. They have a secondary hose-pipe connecting the axle of the reel to the supply tap, enabling the main hose to be wound or unwound while the water is turned on.

Hoses
Most hoses are nowadays made from plastic, though rubber hoses are still obtainable. Plastic hoses are lighter and more durable. There are three standard diameters—$\frac{1}{2}$ in., $\frac{3}{4}$ in. and 1 in. The $\frac{1}{2}$ in. size is the most popular. There is a wide range of patent con-nectors, which enable joints to be made and accessories added.

Incinerators
Metal containers, open at the base and sides, in which to burn prunings and other woody or tough growth that cannot be rotted down on a compost heap. The open design ensures a good flow of air through the material, producing a fierce flame with the minimum of smoke. Some incinerators are round, with sides and base of expanded metal mesh; others are collapsible, with square sides of welded steel mesh. There is also an enclosed type, similar to a dustbin, with small legs and a chimney lid.

Irrigation systems
Permanent installations, consisting of under-ground pipes connecting a number of sprinklers to the mains supply, save a great

deal of time in gardens where frequent watering is necessary. Conventional types of sprinklers or perforated hose pipe can be used, as can pop-up sprinklers, which rise from their mountings when the water is turned on, and sink back flush with the ground when it is turned off. Most permanent irrigation systems are controlled by hand; electronic control systems, operated by time clock, are also obtainable. (See also **Sprinklers.**)

Semi-rigid plastic pipe, used with plastic connectors, is excellent for permanent irrigation systems. The pipe may be buried in the ground or laid on the surface.

Labels

Available in wood, metal and plastic in a wide range of sizes and designs. Metal and plastic labels are the most durable and can be marked permanently with special inks and scribers. A labelling machine, which prints embossed lettering on tape or soft metal, is a worthwhile investment where large numbers of plants are grown.

Lawn edgers

An edging tool with a half-moon blade, used in conjunction with a garden line, is invaluable for cutting a straight, vertical edge at the beginning of the season. Subsequent trimming of overhanging grass is carried out with long-handled shears, or with a mechanical edging tool designed to cut grass only. Hand-pushed mechanical edging tools have star-shaped cutters which overhang the lawn edge and rotate as the tool is pushed along. There are also powered trimmers.

Leaf sweepers

Designed primarily for collecting fallen leaves, mechanical sweepers are also useful for collecting mowings left by a rotary grass cutter, removing worm casts, and sweeping paths and drives. They have bristle brushes which revolve at high speed as the machine is pushed forwards, lifting the debris and ejecting it into a container at the rear. The brushes, which are adjustable for height, have widths ranging from 14 to 24 in.

Mowers

Hand mowers have cutting widths of 10–14 in. There are two distinct types—roller mowers and side-wheel mowers. In the former, the drive to the cutting cylinder comes from a large metal roller at the rear. Though generally more expensive, roller mowers are easier to handle, cut right up to

lawn edges, and leave the banded finish which looks so attractive on a close-mown lawn. Side-wheel mowers have only a small wooden roller at the rear, the drive to the cylinder being from large wheels on either side. Because the wheelbase is wider than the cutting cylinder, side-wheel mowers will not cut right up to a lawn edge. They do not leave such pronounced bands as a roller mower, but are more efficient for cutting rough or overgrown lawns. One type of side-wheel mower has flexible cutting blades which are particularly efficient on tall or wet grass.

Powered mowers may have cylinder cutters similar to those of hand-pushed mowers, or high-speed rotary blades. Cylinder mowers, other than side-wheel types, give a closer cut and better finish than rotary types, but will not cut grass that is more than about 3 in. high. Rotary mowers will deal with grass considerably taller than this. Powered side-wheel mowers are generally used in orchards or on roadside verges.

Powered cylinder mowers can be further subdivided into petrol-driven, mains electric and battery electric types, all with cutting widths of 12 in. upwards. The chief advantage of petrol-driven mowers is their independence of electricity supplies. Mains electric mowers can be used only within reach of a power point; battery mowers, too, require a power point in a shed or garage for re-charging after use. A disadvantage of petrol-driven mowers is the increased risk of mechanical breakdown compared with electric mowers. Mains electric mowers require a minimum of maintenance, and start at the touch of a switch, but have the disadvantage of a trailing cable. Battery mowers are self-contained and simple to use. Given a convenient power point, battery maintenance is little trouble; if recharged regularly (the charger is generally an integral part of the mower), and kept topped up with distilled water, each battery should last for perhaps four years before requiring replacement. An average 12 in. battery mower will cut up to about 800 sq. yd. on a single charge; an 18 in. battery mower will cut 2,000 sq. yd. or more.

Rotary grass cutters, with cutting widths ranging from 14–27 in., vary from relatively lightweight machines, designed primarily for lawn use, to heavy-duty models capable of cutting tall, dense growth and

weeds. Most rotary grass cutters have petrol motors, but there are also mains electric models. These are designed primarily for lawn use. There are as yet no battery-powered rotary grass cutters.

Nets

Used for training climbing plants, to provide protection from birds, as screening and to form windbreaks. Garden netting is made from a variety of materials, including cotton, twine, nylon and high-density polythene. Polythene netting, offered in a variety of gauges and meshes, is particularly versatile. Lightweight polythene netting is an excellent material for shading greenhouses; heavy-gauge, large-mesh polythene netting is sufficiently stout for use in the construction of a compost bin. Cotton and nylon netting, for protecting crops from birds, is available in rolls 3–6 ft. wide, or as individual pieces for covering fruit cages. Twine netting, for supporting peas and beans, is proofed to resist rot and generally has a 6 in. mesh.

Oilers

To safeguard tools against corrosion, metal surfaces should be cleaned and coated with oil after use. A special gadget is available which applies oil through an impregnated felt block, supplied from an oil reservoir in the plastic handle. Rust-proofing fluids are available in aerosol cans.

Pots

Plastic pots are tending to supersede earthenware types. They are more durable, although they may break if lifted by the rim; they are easier to clean, do not dry out so rapidly and are not affected by frost. Available in diameters of $2–12\frac{1}{2}$ in. The smallest earthenware pots also have a diameter of 2 in., the largest about 18 in.

Rakes

Heads with 10 or 12 teeth are the most suitable for general seed bed preparation and soil levelling. Lightweight alloy shafts make easier work of raking, but cost more than ordinary ash handles.

Lawn rakes for removing moss and dead leaves are also useful for collecting fallen leaves. There is an electrically powered lawn rake that is adjustable for removing moss and sweeping up leaves.

Rollers

Frequent rolling is unnecessary, and even harmful, where the lawn is cut with a mower which has its own built-in roller. In spring a roller may be used on turf loosened by frost. A roller is also useful in the preparation of ground for a new lawn. The latest designs incorporate adjustable scrapers, nylon bearings, moulded handgrips and means of adjusting the weight. Widths of 13–18 in., and diameters of 13–16 in., are average.

Scissors
Vine scissors, used for grape thinning, have sharply-tapered blades. Blunt-ended scissors are available for flower gathering, and there are stubby, sturdy models for light pruning.

Secateurs
Some hand secateurs have a single blade which cuts against an anvil; others have two blades which work with a scissors action. Both types are effective and will make clean cuts, provided that the blades are kept sharp and rust-free. There are also long-handled secateurs, some with a double-lever action, for cutting through thicker branches. For tree lopping there are long-arm pruners, with shafts up to 14 ft. long; a metal rod connects a hand lever to the cutting head.

Seedboxes
Plastic seed trays are easier to clean and more durable than wooden seed boxes and are tending to replace them. Typical dimensions are 9 in. by 15 in. by 2½ in. deep. Standard measurements for wooden seed boxes are 8½ in. by 14 in. by 2 or 3 in.

Seed pans
Available in both earthenware and plastic. Popular sizes have diameters of 5 in., 6 in., and 7 in., with depths that are usually equal to about half the diameter.

Seed sowers
The least expensive type consists of a hand-held container, with a spout down which the seeds are shaken into a drill prepared previously. Larger, wheel-mounted models are pushed over a prepared seed bed, the seeds being dispensed from a drum at pre-determined spacings. Seed sowers of this type incorporate devices to open up the drill ahead of the drum, to fill in behind it, and also to mark the position of the next drill parallel to the one being sown.

Shears
Refinements to look for when choosing shears include hollow-ground blades, simple methods of blade adjustment, rubber shock absorbers and a pruning notch at the base of the blades.

There are ladies' models which are lighter and a few inches shorter in both blade and handle length. One-handed shears are useful for trimming grass in confined spaces or close to an obstruction. Some types have blades which can be adjusted for either vertical or horizontal cutting. Long-handled shears have blades angled vertically for cutting lawn edges, or horizontally for general grass trimming.

Sieves
Used principally to prepare fine soil for compost or covering seeds. Both the circular, timber-framed sieves, and the square, metal types, are satisfactory. Mesh sizes are ⅛–½ in. There are also oblong sieves, sometimes called screens, which serve the same purpose as hand sieves but are used in a somewhat different fashion. The screen is mounted at an angle over a wheelbarrow, or on the ground, and the material thrown against it, whereas hand sieves are held horizontally and shaken with a circular motion.

Spades
A blade measuring about 6½ in. wide by 10½ in. long is adequate for most gardeners. Larger spades, with blades up to 8 in. by 12 in., make heavy work of digging on all but the most easily-worked soils. Stainless steel spades, the most costly, remain permanently free from corrosion, so reducing friction to a minimum. Chrome-armoured blades also resist rust for many years. The effort required for digging can be reduced by using a semi-automatic spade with a pivoted blade. This eliminates bending and lifting and saves time. There are also special spades, with toothed blades, for digging clay, and spades with long, tapering blades for digging post holes and drainage trenches.

Sprayers and syringes
Syringes of all-brass construction are excellent for general spraying. The more elaborate types have a continuous double action: the liquid is expelled whether the plunger is pushed or pulled, with the supply drawn by plastic tube from a bucket or watering can.

There are numerous types of hand sprayer, with capacities of ½ pt. upwards. Some are pressurised by pumping before use. Others have to be activated continuously by a trigger or plunger. Hand sprayers are ideal for use in greenhouses and are adequate for most outdoor applications in small and medium sized gardens. Where a larger spraying capacity is

required—for fruit trees, vegetable crops, large rose beds—knapsack or free-standing sprayers, with a capacity of one gallon or more, are available. The whole range of sprayers is now available with easily cleaned, non-corroding plastic containers.

Sprinklers
The simplest types have no moving parts. They consist of a metal or plastic nozzle, attached to skids or an earth spike, which directs a curtain of spray upwards from a central hole. More elaborate models have revolving or oscillating heads capable of distributing a fine spray of water over considerable areas. For watering in strips—particularly useful between rows of vegetables and on narrow borders—there are perforated hose-pipes for attaching to the end of the main hose. (See also **Irrigation systems**.)

Staging trays
These are large, shallow containers, made from plastic or galvanised metal, which are placed on the greenhouse staging, part filled with sand or gravel, and used as a standing area for pot plants. The aggregate is moistened frequently to maintain a humid atmosphere around the plants.

Thermometers
The cheapest and simplest types have a single scale covering a temperature range of −12 to 49°C (10–120°F). Considerably more useful, especially for greenhouse work, are models which register maximum and minimum temperatures. Most are re-set with a magnet. There is also a thermometer which gives advance warning of frost.

Ties
Materials for tying plants range from rust-proof garden twine, available in balls and spools, to plastic raffia and patent ties made of soft metal. For trees and shrubs there are sturdy, plastic ties, some working on the belt and buckle principle, with a plastic buffer between the stem and the support, and others with slotted fastenings for easy adjustment. For training shrubs and fruit trees to walls and fences, there are patent vine eyes and wire strainers which are simple to fix and give lasting support.

Trowels
A trowel is the best tool for setting out small plants, bulbs and corms. Narrow blades are preferable to broad ones. Some trowel blades are graduated as a guide to planting depths.

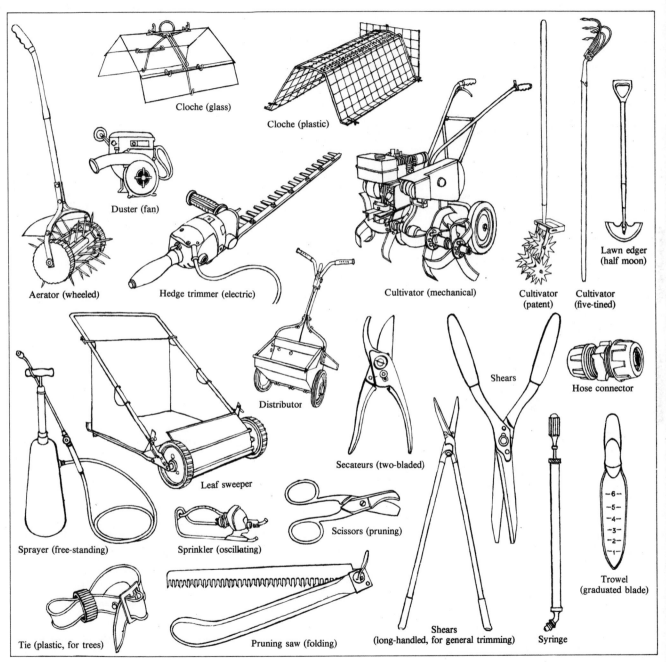

Cloche (glass)

Cloche (plastic)

Duster (fan)

Aerator (wheeled)

Hedge trimmer (electric)

Cultivator (mechanical)

Cultivator (patent)

Cultivator (five-tined)

Lawn edger (half moon)

Leaf sweeper

Distributor

Secateurs (two-bladed)

Shears

Hose connector

Sprayer (free-standing)

Sprinkler (oscillating)

Scissors (pruning)

Trowel (graduated blade)

Tie (plastic, for trees)

Pruning saw (folding)

Shears (long-handled, for general trimming)

Syringe

Trugs

The Sussex trug, a shallow basket made from thin willow boards fastened to a strong framework of ash or chestnut, is a most useful container for carrying garden tools, cut flowers, packets of seeds and so on. Dimensions vary from about 10 in. by 18 in. to 14 in. by 26 in. Containers of similar design are available in coloured plastic.

Turfing irons

Used for undercutting and lifting turves after the sides have been cut vertically. These tools have heart-shaped blades and long, cranked handles.

Watering cans

There is a wide range of metal and plastic types, the latter being lighter to handle and especially suitable for use with corrosive liquids. For greenhouse work, choose a can with a long, narrow spout and a fine rose. Spray-bar attachments, for applying weed-killers and liquid fertilisers, are available for both metal and plastic cans. Capacities range from three pints to three gallons.

Wheelbarrows

Most garden wheelbarrows have a capacity of 3–4 cu. ft., but it is possible to increase the capacity by adding an extension piece to the top. Wheelbarrows usually have galvanised metal bodies, with either solid or pneumatic tyres, but there are some with strong polythene bodies. In addition to conventional single-wheel barrows, in which the weight is distributed between the wheel and the handles, there are also several models in which the whole weight is borne by two wheels mounted directly under the container.

Topiary

The art of clipping and training trees and shrubs into intricate shapes and patterns.

Topsoil: see Soil

Trace element

Certain chemical elements, such as iron, manganese, boron, copper and zinc, are essential for plant growth. Lack of any of these chemicals, which are present in fertile soil in small quantities, can lead to deficiency diseases. (See PESTS AND DISEASES, p. 411.)

Training

Inducing plants, particularly fruit trees and climbing plants, to conform to a certain shape. By careful, selective pruning and tying in to a framework plants can be trained to cover a wall or fence, to form a screen, or to grow in a restricted space. Wall-trained peach trees, for example, are trained to a fan shape; apples may be grown as cordons, espaliers or dwarf pyramids to take up little room.

Transpiration: see Weather

Transplanting

Moving plants from one place to another in order to provide them with more growing space, or to check their root growth. Plants such as cabbages and wallflowers are transplanted for both reasons. Shrubs and trees raised in nurseries are transplanted annually to keep their roots compact, so that they will establish more readily after lifting.

Treading

Firming recently cultivated soil by walking heavily on it, before preparing it for sowing or planting. In firm soil, plant roots are in close contact with the soil particles and are able to take up water and nutrients in solution. Transplanted trees and shrubs should be firmed by treading round them.

Tree

Any plant with a central woody trunk or main stem. (See Bush; Shrub.)

Trenching: see Soil (soil operations)

Trifoliate: see Leaf shapes

Trowels: see Tools

True breeding

Applied to plants whose flowers, after being fertilised with their own pollen, set seeds which germinate into seedlings indistinguishable from the parent plant.

Trumpet

Applied to Division I of the narcissus family (those known as daffodils), in which the

Trumpet, cross-section (daffodil)

tubular, trumpet-like corolla is as long as or longer than the calyx.

Truncate: see Leaf shapes

Trunk

The main stem of a mature tree.

Truss

A loose cluster of flowers or fruits at the end of a stem, as in rhododendrons and tomatoes.

Tuber

Swollen underground root or stem used for the storage of food, and producing shoots. These shoots produce new plants, which in turn develop underground branches that swell and become tubers. Potatoes are tubers; dahlias and begonias are tuberous plants.

Tufa

Porous type of hard limestone, found in England only at Matlock in Derbyshire. Because of its ability to absorb and retain moisture, tufa is often used in rock or sink gardens, where small alpines may be induced to grow on it.

Turf

A grass sward maintained for ornamental purposes. Pieces of turf cut and lifted for laying a lawn elsewhere are usually supplied in sods, 3 ft. by 1 ft., and $1\frac{1}{2}$ in. thick. Good-quality turves should be of even thickness, well rooted and free of weeds and coarse grasses. Turf, which is a more expensive way of obtaining a new lawn than seeding, is best laid during October. (See *Lawns*, OCTOBER.)

Turfing irons: see Tools

Turion

Winter bud or resting shoot of certain aquatic plants, such as *Hydrocharis* and *Utricularia*. The shoots become detached from the parent plant, and spend the winter either resting on the bottom of the pool or floating. In the spring turions form individual roots and develop into independent plants.

2,4,5-T: see Weeds and weedkillers

Type

That specimen of a species which was first described and accepted for the purpose of botanical classification. Species which differ from the type are considered to be variants of it. The natural species does not invariably correspond to the type, as in a few cases a variant was described and accepted as the type, before the natural species was discovered.

U

Umbel
A flower cluster in which the stalked flowers all arise from the same point on the plant's stem, as in polyanthus.

Umbel (rhododendron)

Undulate: see Leaf shapes

Unisexual
Applied to a plant which has either male or female flowers, but not both.

Urea: see Fertilisers and manures

V

Variegated
Applied to leaves (and occasionally flowers) of two or more colours. The absence of chlorophyll from part of the leaf results in pale, often creamy-coloured patches, or deep reddish tints, as in coleus. In some plants, such as dahlias suffering from mosaic disease, variegation is a symptom of virus infection. The characteristics of variegated plants, which are often highly decorative, can only be reproduced vegetatively, and very

rarely by seed (*Aloe variegata* reproduces its variegations from seed). White margins on the leaves of certain types of pelargoniums represent another kind of variegation, and are not caused by lack of chlorophyll. These variegations, known as chimaeras, are caused by the existence of two separate tissue systems: the green leaf tissue is overlaid by a colourless skin (epidermis), which alone forms the edge of the leaf.

Variety
A variant of a species which has arisen either naturally or as a result of selection. (See **Classification**.)

Ventilation: see Greenhouses

Vermiculite
A natural substance, allied to mica, which, when heated, expands and produces air-filled granules. This light and absorbent material is used as a rooting medium for cuttings and seeds. Dried-off dahlia tubers are often stored in vermiculite.

Vernalisation
Subjection of seeds or bulbs for a time to a particular range of temperatures—low temperatures for temperate plants, particularly alpines, and high temperatures for tropical plants. This causes them to pass more quickly from their vegetative to their reproductive phase, so that when seeds are sown or bulbs planted they will grow or flower more quickly, or out of season. This practice is used by nurserymen in preparing bulbs sold for forcing (see **Forcing**). Hyacinths, subjected to a period of high temperature during storage, will flower earlier when forced. Daffodils, stored for a time at low temperature, will, when forced, flower two months earlier than daffodils that have not been pre-cooled.

W

Watering
Supplying plants, particularly those grown under glass, with their water requirements is one of the most important garden operations. Excess water causes waterlogged, oxygen-deficient soil, and suffocates plant roots. Insufficient watering results in retarded

growth, as plants can absorb food only in solution. It is essential to wet the soil deeply enough to reach the plant roots. Frequent but insufficient watering merely damps the soil surface, and does not penetrate to the soil layer where roots are formed. Outdoors the moisture content of the soil can be ascertained by boring it with an auger, which removes a typical soil sample. In the greenhouse, borders to be planted with tomatoes may be flooded in February to build up a reserve of water in the subsoil. When watering seedlings, always attach a rose to the can. Use rainwater when watering such lime-hating plants as rhododendrons and camellias. (See also **Weather**.)

Watering cans: see Tools

Water shoot
Alternative term for breastwood.

Weather
Plant growth is influenced by temperature, sunshine, humidity, rainfall and wind. Overall weather trends are recorded at a network of official stations, but local variations in climate, which may affect the gardener just as much as the general climate, depend on such factors as distance from the sea or large lakes, aspect to north or south, the presence of sheltering hills and proximity to large towns.

Air frost: see Frost

Beaumont period
A period (48 hours or more) of high humidity (over 75 per cent) and mild temperatures (over 10°C, 50°F), associated with the infection of potatoes by blight. (See also **Disease infection weather**.)

Disease infection weather
The type of weather which determines the risk of disease infection and epidemics. The significant weather has been defined for certain diseases. (See **Beaumont period, Mills period** and **Smith period**.)

Drought
A continuous period of 15 days during which there has been no measurable rain. A drought is considered to occur in a garden when the soil moisture in the plants' root zone is exhausted and the plants wilt or die.

Trees and shrubs

MARCH

Plant deciduous trees and shrubs until the end of the month in fine weather.
Top-dress young and newly planted trees and shrubs with old manure, peat or compost.
Plant pot-grown clematis and other wall shrubs.
Many newly planted shrubs should be staked and tied for a time.
Protect tender young shrubs with sacking, straw or netting, and newly planted trees with a windbreak of wire or plastic netting laced with pine branches or bracken.
Begin planting evergreens in prepared ground at the end of the month.

Propagation in the open

Layer shoots of amelanchier, chimonanthus, celastrus, rhus and syringa in pots of sandy loam sunk near the parent plant.
Divide roots of *Hypericum calycinum* and lathyrus, and re-plant.
Separate rooted suckers of kerria and plant in flowering positions.

Propagation under glass

Sow seeds of clematis, cotoneaster and other shrubs in a cold frame or cool greenhouse. Sow seeds of eccremocarpus and *Lavatera olbia rosea* in a greenhouse propagating frame at 13–18°C (55–64°F).
Prick out seedlings in pots and keep in a cold frame until autumn.
Increase camellias by leaf cuttings inserted in pots of sandy peat in a propagating frame at 13–16°C (55–61°F).
Take root cuttings of *Campsis radicans*, *Rhus typhina* and romneya, inserting in pots of sandy compost in a propagating frame at 13°C (55°F).

Pruning

Lightly prune shrubs damaged by heavy snowfalls and frost, removing dead and damaged wood.
Thin out old wood from berberis.
Cut hard back previous year's shoots of *Caryopteris clandonensis,* deciduous ceanothus and *Hypericum calycinum.*
Cut fuchsias and *Lavatera olbia rosea* back to live wood.
Lightly prune *Lonicera fragrantissima* after flowering.
Cut hard back willows grown for winter bark colour.

APRIL

Plant evergreen shrubs during showery weather.
Continue planting pot-grown wall shrubs.
Water newly planted trees and shrubs in dry weather and mulch with lawn mowings or black polythene sheeting.

Propagation

Sow seeds of *Cytisus scoparius* and genista where they are to flower.
Layer shoots of *Hydrangea paniculata grandiflora* in pots of peaty soil, and young magnolia shoots by pegging into peaty soil.

Pruning

Lightly prune trees and shrubs which have finished flowering.
Cut back *Forsythia suspensa* after flowering to within two buds of old growth.
Sever rooted stems and re-plant elsewhere.
Cut hard back those shrubs which flower on current season's growth.
Cut romneya shoots back to ground level and shorten growths of *Spartium junceum.*
Cut back straggly branches of lavenders and *Magnolia grandiflora.*

MAY

Plant out shrubs that are tender when young (arbutus, choisya, fuchsia and hydrangea) and keep well watered.
Complete planting evergreens in showery weather.
Keep newly planted shrubs moist at the roots and spray foliage with water in dry weather.

Keep lilacs to a single stem and mulch heavily to induce them to flower.

Pruning

Cut off dead flower heads and thin out weak shoots from shrubs that have finished flowering.
Remove dead wood and thin shoots to keep old forsythias shapely.
Clip *Laurus nobilis* (bay) where grown as a formal bush.

JUNE

Keep a space 4 ft. in diameter clear of grass around newly planted subjects.
Remove self-sown ash and sycamore seedlings.

Propagation in the open

Layer shoots of chaenomeles and clematis in pots of sandy peat.

Propagation under glass

Take soft or half-ripe cuttings and insert in sandy soil in an open, shaded cold frame.
Root cuttings of fuchsia and philadelphus in a greenhouse propagating frame at 16°C (61°F).
Take half-ripe cuttings of magnolia and viburnum.

Pruning

Cut out shoots which have just flowered from deciduous shrubs such as deutzia.
Cut hard back flowering shoots of brooms to prevent them seeding.
Remove spent flower heads from lilacs and thin out weak shoots.
Remove dead flower clusters from laburnums.
Remove flower buds from senecio.

JULY

Keep an eye on hedges for aphids, white-fly and other pests, and control.

Propagation

Layer passiflora and wisteria shoots.
Root cuttings of *Buddleia alternifolia* and callicarpa in a cold frame.
Root cuttings of *Camellia japonica* and *Elaeagnus pungens* in pots of sandy soil

in a propagating frame at 13–16°C (55–61°F).
Insert heel cuttings of hibiscus and *Jasminum officinale* in pots of sandy soil in a cold frame.

Pruning

Prune deciduous shrubs such as jasmine and philadelphus after flowering.

AUGUST

Continue taking cuttings of callicarpa, cistus and escallonia.

Propagation under glass

Insert softwood cuttings of choisya and *Polygonum baldschuanicum* in pots of sandy soil in a cold frame.
Put half-ripe cuttings of garrya and wisteria in pots of sandy loam in a propagating frame at 13–16°C (55–61°F), transferring to a cold frame when rooted.
Take stem cuttings of *Hydrangea macrophylla*, using a shaded, closed frame and giving ventilation as they root.

Pruning

Prune shrubs that have finished flowering. Cut back established wisterias.

SEPTEMBER

Prepare ground for planting later in the month or in October.
Start planting evergreen shrubs during showery weather at the end of the month.
Support standard shrubs with stakes until they become established.
Water newly planted shrubs during dry weather and spray their foliage with water.

Propagation under glass

Take hardwood and half-ripe cuttings of berberis, juniper and privet, rooting them in sandy soil in a cold frame. Leave them to grow on in the frame during the winter. Cover cuttings in open ground with cloches during cold weather.

Pruning

Lightly prune phlomis after flowering.

OCTOBER

Start planting deciduous trees and shrubs towards the end of the month, but avoid frosty or wet conditions.

Untie plants arriving from nurseries during inclement weather and stand them in a dry shed. If planting is halted for some time by bad weather, heel in shrubs.
Plant scrambling plants, such as ivy, clematis and winter jasmine, as ground cover.
Firmly stake and tie newly planted standard trees.

Propagation

Take hardwood cuttings of *Buddleia davidii*, forsythia and philadelphus, inserting them in sandy soil in a cold frame or in the open.
Layer shoots of *Daphne cneorum* in pots of peaty loam plunged round the parent plants.
Separate and re-plant rooted suckers of poplar, forsythia and *Rhus typhina*.
Divide and re-plant *Euonymus fortunei* and spiraea.

Pruning

Cut back the spurs of wall-trained hibiscus after flowering.

NOVEMBER

Continue planting deciduous trees and shrubs in fine weather.
Protect tender species such as campsis and garrya with a screen of wire netting and bracken.

Propagation

Take hardwood cuttings of ivy, poplar and ribes, and insert in a cold frame or in the open ground.
Layer firm young shoots of actinidia in pots sunk round the parent plant.
Re-firm cuttings lifted by frost.

Propagation under glass

Take heel cuttings of winter jasmine and insert in a cold frame.

DECEMBER

Plant deciduous trees and shrubs during mild weather, firming soil round the roots.
Re-firm soil around newly planted shrubs loosened by frost.
Tie branches of young conifers together

with sacking to prevent snow breaking them down.
Gather leaves and put on compost heap to provide a top dressing next spring.
Bring tub-grown fuchsias and hydrangeas into a cold greenhouse or shed in cold districts.

JANUARY

Stand shrubs arriving from nurseries during hard weather in a frost-free shed with straw around their roots.
Continue planting in suitable weather.

Propagation

Sow seeds of camellia under glass at 16°C (61°F).

Pruning

Thin out dead and diseased branches from established trees and shrubs.
Winter prune wisterias by cutting back young shoots to within 3 in. of old wood.

FEBRUARY

Continue planting deciduous trees and shrubs in favourable weather.
Firm any newly planted shrubs which have been loosened by frost.
Clear moss and lichen from tree trunks with tar-oil wash.

Propagation in the open

Separate and plant out rooted suckers of poplars.

Propagation under glass

Sow seeds of cytisus and spartium in pots of sandy peat in a propagating frame at 18°C (64°F).

Pruning

Prune hard back to within a few inches of old wood such shrubs as *Campsis radicans*, spiraea and tamarisk.
Cut back all shoots which have just flowered of chimonanthus and winter jasmine, and thin old and weak wood from *Jasminum officinale*.
Remove inward-growing branches of crab apples.
Thin out climbers such as celastrus and solanum by removing weak growth and shortening main shoots.

THE YEAR AT A GLANCE

Vegetables

MARCH

Sow seeds for main crop of Brussels sprouts, and set out hardened-off plants.
In the north, plant out over-wintered Brussels sprouts.
Sow parsnips.
In the south, plant early potatoes from the middle of the month.
Sow salad onions and radishes.
Sow seeds of late summer cabbages.
Continue sowing early round-seeded peas.
Sow leeks if raising your own plants.
Sow summer spinach.

Under glass

Sow carrots under cloches, after dressing the seed.

Less common vegetables

Complete shallot planting.
In the south, sow kohl rabi seeds.
Plant asparagus. Dress established asparagus beds with farmyard manure.
Plant Jerusalem artichokes.

APRIL

Plant onion sets and sow salad crops.
In the north, plant early potatoes.
Sow late summer cauliflowers, wrinkled-seeded peas and maincrop carrots.
Cover potato foliage if frost threatens.
Sow globe beetroot.
Plant out late summer cabbages.
Sow winter cabbages, and purple-sprouting and spring-heading broccoli.
Order tomato plants for planting outdoors in June.
Remove rhubarb flowers as soon as seen.

Under glass

In the south, sow french beans and cover with cloches.

Less common vegetables

Replace soil on earthed-up globe artichokes by manure or compost, and plant new artichokes.
Cut asparagus from beds at least two years old.
In the north, sow kohl rabi.

MAY

Cover potatoes if frost threatens.
Prepare sites for growing marrows and pumpkins outdoors, sowing and thinning the seeds later in the month.
Prepare sites for outdoor tomatoes.
Sow french beans for growing outdoors.
Set out late summer cauliflowers.
In the north, plant out Brussels sprouts.
Make further sowings of summer spinach and salad crops.
Sow long-rooted beetroot for storing for winter use.
Sow runner beans and erect canes or poles to support them.

Under glass

Gradually remove cloches from spring cabbages, carrots, lettuces and broad beans.
Prepare sites for growing cucumbers in frames or under cloches.
In the north, sow runner beans under glass for planting out in June.

Less common vegetables

Continue cutting asparagus.
Order self-blanching celery plants for June planting.
Sow seakale beet, scorzonera and salsify.
Sow sweet corn in well manured soil.

JUNE

Plant Brussels sprouts, winter cabbages, savoys, and purple-sprouting and spring-heading broccoli.
Plant marrows if seeds were not sown earlier.
Plant outdoor tomatoes on prepared sites and support with 4 ft. stakes, except for bush varieties.
Continue sowing salad crops, peas and french beans.

In the north, sow swedes, dusting the seedlings with HCH.
Plant leeks.
Water lettuces and other salad crops if prolonged dry weather is forecast.
Sow spinach beet.

Under glass

Shade frames and cloches with whitewash or shading liquid.
Remove the tips from cucumber plants when seven leaves have formed, and give a weekly feed of liquid manure.

Less common vegetables

Plant self-blanching celery.
Sow chicory.
Complete cutting asparagus and support ferns by means of canes and string.

JULY

Complete leek planting.
In the south, sow swedes or hardy turnips.
Complete planting late Brussels sprouts, winter cabbages, sprouting and spring broccoli.
Sow spinach beet.
Pinch out side shoots from tomatoes, except on bush varieties, which should be strawed to keep the fruits clean.
Make late sowings of round-seeded peas and globe beetroot.
Continue watering shallow-rooted crops in dry weather.
Lift and store onions.

Under glass

Cut cucumbers as they swell.

Less common vegetables

Lift and dry off shallots as their tops yellow, separate the bulb clusters, remove the loose skins, and store in bags in a dry, cool shed or room.
Sow winter radishes and thin to 6 in. apart.

AUGUST

Sow seeds of spring cabbages.
Sow lettuces for early winter use.
Sow Japanese onions.

In the north, sow lettuces for over-wintering without cloche protection, and Brussels sprouts seed for an early crop next year.

Less common vegetables
Pick sweet corn cobs.
Start using self-blanching celery.

SEPTEMBER
In the south, sow lettuces for over-wintering with cloche protection.
In the north, plant spring cabbages.
Lift maincrop carrots and store sound ones in layers in deep boxes.

Under glass
Protect lettuces and spring cabbages with cloches.
Sow carrots under cloches.

Less common vegetables
Cut off the tops of chicory, before blanching.

OCTOBER
In the south, plant out spring cabbages.
Pick and take indoors the last of the tomatoes.
Plant winter lettuces.
Cut remaining marrows, squashes and pumpkins, and store in a dry, frost-proof place.
Clear away pea and bean haulm, and dig vacant ground.
Lift beetroot and store in a clamp.
In the north, set out Brussels sprout plants in a nursery bed.

Under glass
Sow lettuces for growing under cloches.
Cover spring cabbages and early carrots with cloches.
Force rhubarb in a warm greenhouse.

Less common vegetables
Store winter radishes in a clamp.

NOVEMBER
In the south, sow broad bean seeds for an early crop.

Under glass
Apply a pre-emergence weedkiller to broad beans sown under cloches.
In the south, complete sowings of lettuces.
Force chicory under the staging in a warm greenhouse.

Less common vegetables
Trim the outer growths of globe artichokes and draw soil round the crowns.
Detach suckers from the plants, and grow on in pots to increase stock.

DECEMBER
In the north, lift turnips and swedes and store in clamps.
Prepare the site for next year's runner beans.

Under glass
Lift rhubarb and chicory for forcing.

JANUARY
Plant rhubarb and spread strawy manure over each station after planting. Cover established plants with boxes to encourage early growth.
Sow peas in sheltered southern districts and cover with cloches if available.
Sow broad beans for an early crop.

Less common vegetables
In the south, plant shallots on well drained soil.
Lift Jerusalem artichokes as required.

FEBRUARY
Sow early peas and beans.
Buy potato tubers for early crops, and sprout them in a light, frost-proof room or shed.

Under glass
Sow carrots in light, fertile soil in a cold frame.

Less common vegetables
Plant shallots.
Order asparagus plants.

Frost
A frost occurs when the temperature falls below 0°C (32°F). An air frost is measured with a thermometer in a white, louvred container 4 ft. above the grass surface; a ground frost is measured with an exposed thermometer placed near the ground with its bulb just touching the tips of short grass. Ground frosts are more frequent than air frosts, but most plants will survive slight ground frosts in the early autumn or late spring when the period of low temperature is fairly short. See also **Soil (mulching).**

Ground frost: see **Frost**

Humidity
The amount of water vapour present in the atmosphere, usually expressed as a percentage of the maximum that would be present if the air were saturated.

Micro-climate
The climate immediately surrounding the plants, which influences their growth. It is partly determined by the design of the garden and by the layout of beds.

Mills period
The duration of leaf wetness, combined with certain temperature levels, which are together associated with the infection of apples by scab. (See **Disease infection weather.**)

Rainfall
The amount of rain falling in a particular area in a given time. It is measured by a rain-gauge, which consists of a funnel resting on a collecting vessel. The measuring jar which accompanies the gauge is normally graduated in hundredths of an inch. (See also **Watering.**)

Shelter from the wind
A hedge or belt of trees allows part of the surface wind to filter through and has a noticeable effect for a long distance down wind (about 20 times the height of the hedge). A stone wall or solid fence cuts down the wind abruptly over a shorter distance (about 10 times the height of the hedge), but creates considerable turbulence on the sheltered side.

For this reason the width of a walled garden should not exceed about 10 times the height of the surrounding wall.

Smith period
The duration of high humidities following rainfall, together with certain temperature levels, which are together associated with the

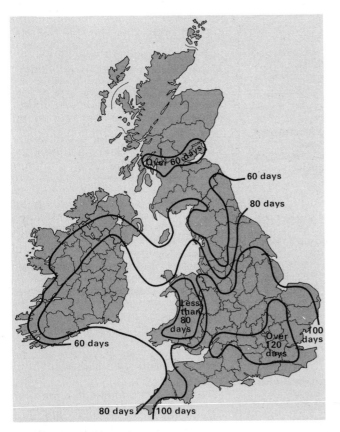

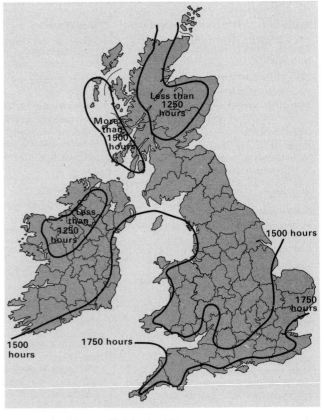

Average length of summer

A day when the maximum temperature exceeds 18°C (64°F) is generally regarded as a summer day. The map shows the distribution of the number of days in an average year when the temperature is higher than this. Summer is longest in inland areas of southern England, where it lasts about a third of the year. Areas in the north and north-west do not often have long periods of summer

Average annual hours of bright sunshine

The pattern of distribution of bright sunshine over the British Isles varies little from month to month. It is greatest in the south and near the coast, and decreases as the height above sea level increases. The only exception to this distribution pattern is in May and June, when high sunshine values are often recorded in the west of Scotland

infection of apples by scab. Closely analogous to the Mills period. (See also **Disease infection weather**.)

Soil capacity

A soil is said to be at capacity when it contains all the moisture it can hold in the soil particles against the pull of gravity. If the soil contains more water than this, the air spaces between the particles are filled and the soil becomes waterlogged. Well drained soil is usually at capacity in March, unless the winter has been exceptionally dry.

Soil moisture deficit

The amount of water which must be added to the soil to bring it back to capacity (see **Soil capacity**), usually stated in inches (1 in. of water equals about $4\frac{1}{2}$ gal. per sq. yd.).

Temperature

Degree of warmth or coldness. Official air temperatures are measured by thermometers placed 4 ft. above a grass surface in a white, louvred box of a standard size. Temperatures below this height are usually higher by day and lower by night.

Transpiration

The evaporation of water into the air which takes place from the leaves of all plants. Water entering a plant's roots from the soil is carried to all parts of the plant, taking mineral nutrients with it. The amount of transpiration varies with latitude and time of year, and in summer it is greater on sunny than on cloudy days. The potential transpiration, or the total amount of water that the heat of the sun could extract from plants by transpiration, can be calculated from weather observations.

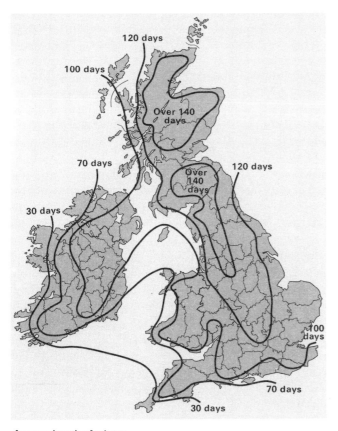

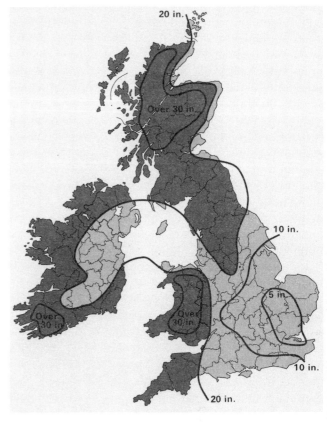

Average length of winter
A day when the mean temperature is below 6°C (43°F) is generally regarded as a winter day. The map shows the distribution of the number of days in an average year when the temperature is lower than this and little plant growth can be expected. The longest non-growing periods occur in the north and on higher ground in central England and Wales

Amount of winter leaching
The greater the leaching of plant nutrients from the soil due to excess winter rain, the more the gardener must put back into the soil in the form of dressings of lime and other fertilisers in the spring. The map shows the average excess winter rainfall which is liable to leach the garden soil. The shaded areas are danger spots where excessive leaching occurs

Watering, amount required
The amount of water which should be added to the soil to ensure that plants have all the moisture they need; it is equal to potential transpiration minus rainfall. Weekly amounts of potential transpiration are given in the introductions to the months from April to September, and rainfall should be measured each week either with a home-made rain-gauge or one bought from a garden sundries-man. Most gardeners find it convenient to water during the weekend, so measure rainfall at the same time.

A gauge can be made by putting a small household funnel in a cylindrical can or jar having the same diameter as the top of the funnel. Set the container firmly in an exposed place in the garden, away from the shelter of trees or walls and preferably in the middle of the lawn, and leave for a week. Measure the rainfall collected by removing the funnel and holding a ruler with $\frac{1}{10}$ in. divisions vertically on the bottom of the container; if the bottom edge of the ruler does not represent 0 in., either saw the end off to the beginning of the scale, or add the appropriate number

of tenths of an inch to the amount of rainfall measured. Empty the container, replace the funnel and leave in place to collect next week's rain. If the total rainfall for the week is less than the potential transpiration, subtract rainfall from potential transpiration and water by this amount over the weekend: $\frac{1}{10}$ (0·1) in. is roughly equal to $\frac{1}{2}$ gal. per sq. yd. For instance, if rainfall is 0·30 in. and the garden is situated between the lines marked 0·55 and 0·50 in. on the map for the month concerned, the amount of watering required is 0·55−0·30, that is, 0·25 in.—or roughly $1\frac{1}{4}$

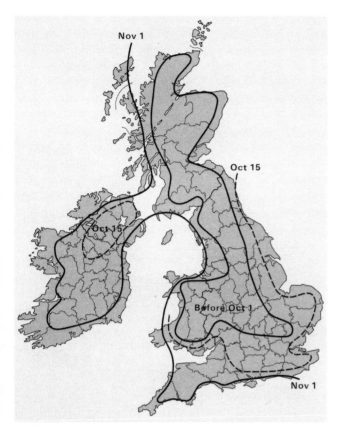

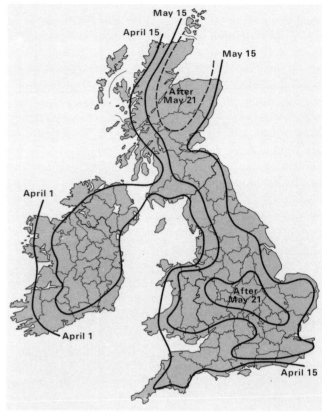

The first autumn air frost
The first widespread ground frost of the autumn, over much of inland Britain as far south as Hertfordshire, usually occurs in September. The map shows the date before which the first autumn air frost is unlikely to occur more than one year in five, except in frost pockets. The first widespread frost of autumn generally occurs after drying north-westerly to northerly winds

The likelihood of late frost
The dates after which a late frost is unlikely to occur four years out of five, except in frost pockets, are shown here. Late frosts are worst well inland over dry, light soils; damp soils freeze less quickly than dry. They are least likely in gardens close to the coast. In some years frost never occurs in areas close to the Atlantic, even as far north as the Outer Hebrides

gal. per sq. yd. If the amount of watering needed is less than 0·1 in., it may be more convenient not to water that weekend, but to add this amount to the next week's total.

Weeds and weedkillers
Weeds compete with cultivated plants for the available light, moisture and plant food, and also encourage the spread of pests and diseases. Shepherd's purse, for example, harbours the flea beetle and cabbage root fly, which attack many types of green vegetable; thistles serve as a host for the mangold fly,

which attacks garden beet, and for the bean aphis. Also, many diseases, such as botrytis, thrive in cold and damp conditions, and if the circulation of air round the plants is impeded by weeds, the humidity in the immediate vicinity is increased and the fungi can thrive.

Weeds in lawns are not only unsightly but can sometimes cause bare patches, since they are unable to withstand treading and wear to the extent that grass does.
Weed control
Mechanical and cultural methods
Weed destruction by hoeing and digging

stimulates plant growth by allowing air and moisture to get to the roots. Regular hoeing round vegetables, and between roses and perennial plants in the border, should keep weeds under control for most of the season.

Weed control by cultural means includes the growing of such crops as potatoes, classed as smother crops, which prevent sunlight from reaching the weeds. Weeds can also be destroyed by preparing seed beds several weeks before sowing. This gives time for the weeds to germinate and be hoed off before the actual crop is sown. In addition, rotation of crops can discourage the predominance of particular weeds.

Chemical weedkillers

There are three main types of chemical weedkiller. These are generally used where control by other means would be too slow or has proved ineffective. Some chemicals fall into more than one category.

Sprayed on to bare ground, pre-emergence weedkillers will kill the germinating weed seedlings without detriment to the cultivated seedlings, which should emerge in a weed-free bed.

Total weedkillers destroy plants and weeds of all types; some are long-lasting, and are therefore more suitable for use on paths; while others are less persistent, and are intended primarily for use on cultivated ground, such as borders.

Selective weedkillers kill weeds in a crop without harming the crop itself.

Pre-emergence weedkillers

Pre-emergence weedkillers are usually based on mixtures of chlorpropham, fenuron or monuron. If applied to annual flowers and most vegetable crops immediately after sowing, they are effective for up to three months. An overdose of the chemical, or excessive rainfall which washes it too far into the soil, may harm the crop. Pre-emergence weedkillers can also be used to treat soil before transplanting.

Total weedkillers

Simazine, a total weedkiller especially suitable for pathways, can also be used selectively to control weeds in rose beds and between rows of soft fruits, such as strawberries and raspberries. This chemical is effective for about 12 months, and does not spread sideways in the soil (on sloping ground in wet weather, for example) to affect neighbouring plants.

Paraquat kills all forms of growth by destroying the green chlorophyll in plants, although repeated applications may be needed to control deep-rooted perennial and shrubby weeds. It is inactivated by contact with the soil and can be used to control weeds among growing plants. It is combined with diquat to give greater effect on broad-leaved plants.

Sodium chlorate, a total weedkiller with no selective use, destroys plants and weeds of all types and will keep land, paths, and drives weed-free for six months or more. However, plants cannot be grown in treated ground for up to a year, and there is a significant fire risk attached to using this liquid, unless a brand containing a fire suppressant is used. Sodium chlorate tends to move sideways in the soil.

Selective weedkillers

2,4,5-T is a hormone weedkiller used to control woody or shrubby plants such as gorse, brambles and young sapling trees. Spray the weeds in early spring, or paint them in winter, with 2,4,5-T diluted with paraffin. This compound is very powerful, and must not be allowed to drift to cultivated plants. Treated plants die completely, but leave a dead skeleton, which should be destroyed.

Dalapon is a selective weedkiller which will control annual and perennial grasses. Tolerance to this chemical varies considerably, and the manufacturer's instructions should be followed exactly. Uncropped land must be left unused for a minimum of four to six weeks after treatment.

All hormone weedkillers used on lawns are selective. An overall spray of a hormone-type weedkiller, based on 2,4-D, MCPA or mecoprop, will control most broad-leaved weeds but leave the grass unharmed. Apply these chemicals on a fine day in late spring, when the grass is growing actively. Normally, it should have been established for at least six months.

A recently introduced hormone compound known as ioxynil will kill weeds in newly established lawns with complete safety. Follow the manufacturer's instructions carefully, and do not allow the liquid to drift on to flower beds, fruit foliage or vegetables.

2,4-D and MCPA will control most lawn weeds, such as daisies, thistles, dandelions, plantains and buttercups, while mecoprop is especially effective against clovers. Proprietary brands of lawn weedkillers are often sold in mixture to provide a wide range of control.

Pearlwort can be controlled by mecoprop or MCPA, but heavy infestations may need an application of lawn sand containing ammonium sulphate and ferrous sulphate.

Ordinary lawn weedkillers are ineffective against moss, which must be controlled by mercurised lawn sand or compounds containing calomel (mercurous chloride) applied in spring or autumn, followed by an application of fertiliser to stimulate the grass to grow into the bare patches. Large patches of moss may be due to too much shade, poor drainage, lack of aeration, or thin soil, and these patches will recur unless the underlying cause is removed.

Chickweed (*Stellaria media*)
Annual. White flowers. Abundant everywhere, especially in gardens, it is found on all types of soil, but is particularly troublesome on heavy, rich soils.

Coltsfoot (*Tussilago farfara*)
Perennial. Tufted rootstock with penetrating, creeping habit. Yellow flowers. Abundant everywhere, especially in waste places and gardens.

Common sorrel (*Rumex acetosa*)
Perennial. Moderately deep-rooted. Reddish-green flowers. Abundant everywhere and found particularly on acid soils, heathland and in fields and gardens.

Corn sow-thistle (*Sonchus arvensis*)
Perennial. Spreads by root shoots; the main roots may penetrate to a depth of 6 ft. Yellow flowers. Common on arable land and in gardens.

Couch grass, twitch (*Agropyron repens*)
Perennial. Creeping rootstock of long wiry rhizomes with sharply pointed ends. White flowers. Common in gardens and waste land.

Creeping buttercup (*Ranunculus repens*)
Perennial. Creeping, stoloniferous stems, which root rapidly at every node. Bright yellow flowers. Common in damp pastures, particularly if the soil is heavy, and in waste places and gardens.

Creeping thistle (*Cirsium arvense*)
Perennial. Creeping rootstock; the lateral roots, which grow out horizontally from the tap-root, are fleshy and rather brittle. Rose-purple flowers. Flourishes in almost any soil, but is particularly common on grassland. It is difficult to eradicate.

Daisy (*Bellis perennis*)
Perennial. Short rootstock. White, pink-tinged flowers with a yellow disc. Common in lawns and short grass.

Dandelion (*Taraxacum officinale*)
Perennial. Thick penetrating rootstock forming a deep tap-root. Rich golden-yellow flowers. Found in grassland, waste places, and in gardens, particularly in lawns.

Fat hen (*Chenopodium album*)
Annual. Green or mealy-white flowers. Frequently found on manure heaps; also in gardens and waste places.

Germander speedwell (*Veronica chamaedrys*)
Perennial. Creeping rootstock. Blue flowers with a white eye. Found on roadsides and grassland, and in woods, hedges and gardens.

Great plantain (*Plantago major*)
Perennial. Short thick rootstock. Brownish flowers. Common on grassland, and in gardens, lawns and waste places.

Ground elder, gout weed, bishop's weed (*Aegopodium podagraria*)
Perennial. Creeping rootstock; thin white roots. White flowers. Common in gardens and on waste land.

Groundsel (*Senecio vulgaris*)
Annual. Fibrous roots. Yellow flowers. One of the most common weeds, found in gardens, fields and waste places, particularly on heavy and moist soils.

Hoary plantain, lamb's tongue (*Plantago media*)
Perennial. Short thick rootstock. Whitish flowers with purple stamens. Common on grassland, in gardens, lawns and waste places, particularly on calcareous soils.

Horsetail (*Equisetum arvense*)
Perennial. Creeping rootstock penetrating to a depth of several feet. Bears no flowers. Found in most parts of England, Ireland, and in south-east and west Scotland, especially on sandy and clay soils.

Knotgrass, knotweed (*Polygonum aviculare*)
Annual. Tough, branching tap-root. Pinkish flowers. Common in gardens and on waste land, especially on sandy soils.

Mouse-ear chickweed (*Cerastium vulgatum*)
Annual. White flowers. Common in cultivated and waste land. Troublesome in lawns.

Prostrate pearlwort (*Sagina procumbens*)
Perennial, sometimes annual. This procumbent and branching plant takes root wherever a stem touches the soil. Inconspicuous flowers. Abundant in gardens, paths, lawns, sandy, dry or wet places and on waste ground.

Purple dead-nettle (*Lamium purpureum*)
Annual or biennial. In winter produces prostrate shoots which may root at the joints.

Chickweed

Coltsfoot

Common sorrel

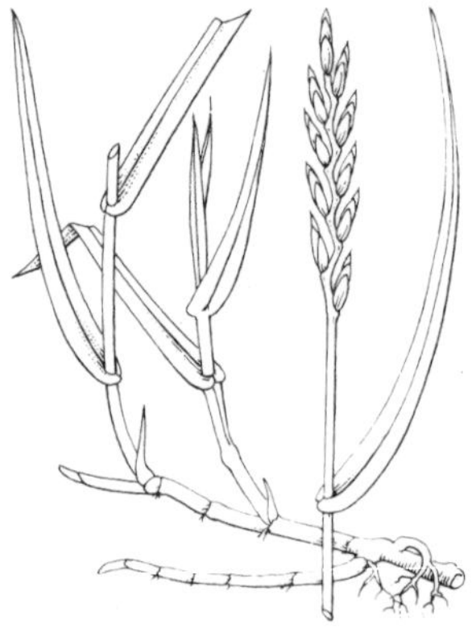

Couch grass

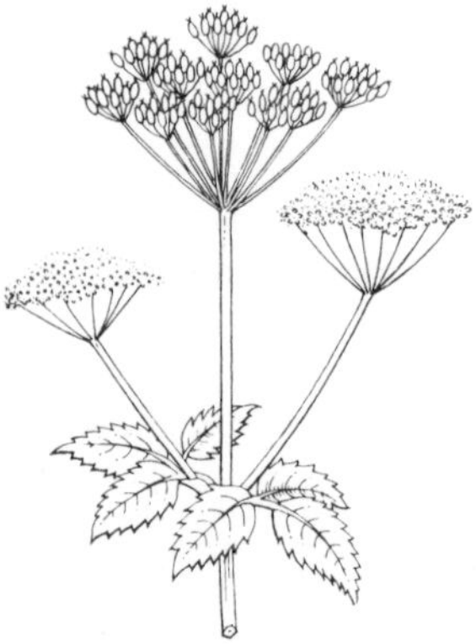

Ground elder

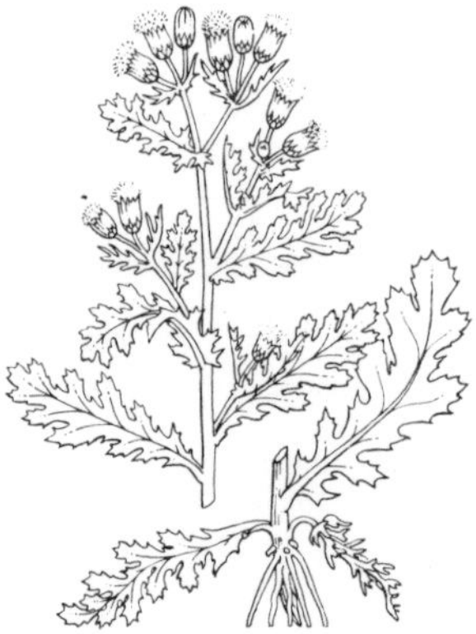

Groundsel

Horsetail

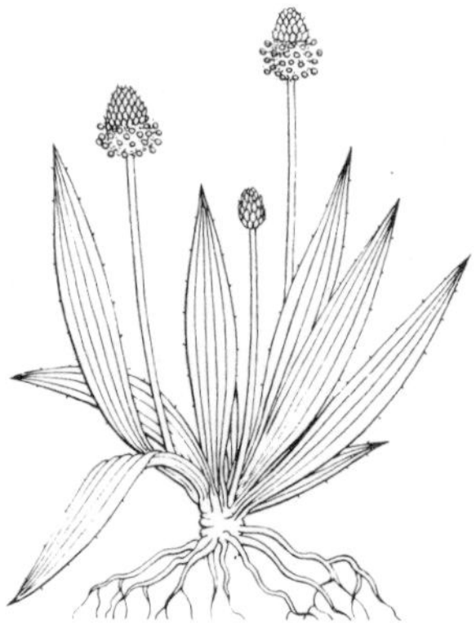

Ribwort plantain

Mauve-pink flowers. Very common in gardens and waste places.

Ragwort (*Senecio jacobaea*)
Perennial. Short thick rootstock. Yellow flowers. Common on roadsides, in fields and waste places, but not so frequent in gardens.

Ribwort plantain (*Plantago lanceolata*)
Perennial. Short thick rootstock. Brownish flowers. Common on grassland, and in gardens, lawns and waste places.

Rose-bay willow-herb, fireweed
(*Chamaenerion angustifolium*)
Perennial. Creeping, rather fleshy rootstock. Deep rose flowers. Found in woodland clearings and gardens, and on waste ground.

Shepherd's purse (*Capsella bursapastoris*)
Annual. Long tapering root. White flowers.

Abundant on waste ground and also common in lawns.

Small bindweed, cornbine (*Convolvulus arvensis*)
Perennial. Creeping rootstock; the root system can cover an area of about 30 sq. yd. in one season. Pink, sometimes white flowers. Found chiefly in England and Wales, in gardens and on arable land.

Stinging nettle, perennial nettle (*Urtica dioica*)
Perennial. Stoloniferous creeping rootstock. Greenish flowers. Common on roadsides, and in hedgerows, waste places and gardens.

Yarrow, milfoil (*Achillea millefolium*)
Perennial. Creeping stoloniferous roots. White or pink flowers. Common in meadows and waste land; sometimes found in lawns.

Weeping
Applied to a tree and shrub of a pendulous habit. *Salix babylonica* (weeping willow) is well known, and there are weeping forms of ash and beech trees, as well as weeping standard roses, for example 'Crimson Conquest'.

Weights and measures
Cement and concrete mixes
Concrete is made from cement, sharp sand, crushed stone or gravel (known as aggregate), and water. The proportions vary according to its purpose.

Cement is now sold by builders' merchants in 50 kg. (110.25 lb.) bags. Smaller amounts can be obtained in do-it-yourself shops and hardware stores, but at comparatively high prices.

Sand and aggregate are sold by builders' merchants, and at local sand and gravel pits, by the cubic metre, or tonne (1.3 cu. yds). The minimum amount that will be delivered is not usually less than $\frac{1}{2}$ cu. m.; but since sand and aggregate do not deteriorate, any surplus to the job in hand can be stored indefinitely for future use.

The following mixes for garden use are recommended by the Cement and Concrete Association. Proportions, which are by volume, can be measured by filling and partly filling an old bucket or similar receptacle.

Mix A (suitable for foundations, garage floors, drives and thick walls): 1 part cement, $2\frac{1}{2}$ parts sharp sand, 4 parts aggregate. One 50 kg. bag of cement so mixed yields about $6\frac{3}{4}$ cu. ft. of concrete.

Mix B (suitable for paths, steps, the sides of garden frames and edging): 1 part cement, 2 parts sand, 3 parts aggregate. One 50 kg. bag of cement so mixed yields about $5\frac{1}{2}$ cu. ft. of concrete.

Mix C (suitable for artificial rocks, formal or crazy paving less than 2 in. thick): 1 part cement, 3 parts sharp sand. The substitution of soft sand (builders' sand) for sharp sand results in mortar, which has a smoother finish but will not stand hard wear. One 50 kg. bag of cement so mixed yields about $3\frac{3}{4}$ cu. ft. of concrete or mortar.

To find the number of cubic feet of concrete required to cover a given area, multiply the area in square feet by the thickness in inches, and divide by 12. To calculate the

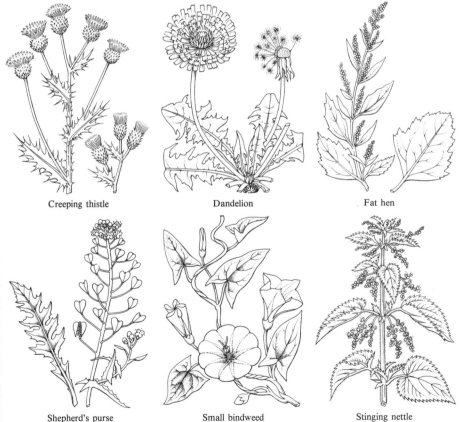

Creeping thistle

Dandelion

Fat hen

Shepherd's purse

Small bindweed

Stinging nettle

number of bags of cement needed, divide the number of cubic feet of concrete required by the number of cubic feet of concrete produced by a 50 kg. bag of cement in the particular mix used. For example, if 20 cu. ft. of mix B is needed, buy 4 bags, since 20 divided by $5\frac{1}{2}$ equals approximately $3\frac{2}{3}$.

Estimating areas, volumes and weights
Areas
Any area bounded by straight lines is either a triangle, or is divisible into triangles. To find the area of a **triangle**, draw a line from one of the angles to meet the side opposite to it at right angles. Call this line the height and the side it meets the base; multiply the length of the height by the length of the base and divide by 2 to find the area.

To calculate the area of a **circular bed**, multiply the radius by itself, then multiply the result by 22 and divide by 7.

To find the area of an **oval bed**, multiply the extreme length by the extreme width, multiply the result by 11 and divide by 14.

The area of a **crescent bed** is too difficult to calculate directly, but the area of any unusually shaped bed can be estimated by spreading a piece of square-meshed netting over the bed, counting the number of holes over the bed, and dividing by the number of holes per square foot of netting. To find the number of holes per square foot, measure the number of holes per foot length, and multiply this number by itself. For example, 3 in. mesh netting has 4 holes per foot; $4 \times 4 = 16$; therefore divide the number of holes over the bed by 16 to obtain the answer in square feet.

To find the area **covered by 1 cu. yd. of material,** divide the thickness in inches of the layer into 36. For example, if 1 cu. yd. of gravel is spread 3 in. thick, divide 36 by 3; the answer, 12, is the number of square yards covered.

Most **paving stones** weigh about 2 tons per cu. yd. If the thickness of the paving in inches

---

THE YEAR AT A GLANCE

Water plants and pools

MARCH
When the ice has thawed, drain most of the water and replace with fresh.
Remove algae.
Remove the tops of marginal plants that were left on for winter protection.
Top-dress water lilies and marginals, if growth was poor last year.
Plant a new bog garden.
Begin regular feeding of fish if they are lively.
Construct new garden pools in an open, sunny position, providing depths of $1\frac{1}{2}$–2 ft. for water lilies, oxygenating plants and fish, and 6–9 in. for marginals.

APRIL
Start planting in pools, either direct or in containers, when weather is warm.
Saturate all soil before planting.
Set rhizomes or tubers of water lilies at about 15° to the horizontal.
Push the lower ends of the stems of oxygenators $\frac{1}{2}$–1 in. into soft soil.
Plant iris and calla rhizomes horizontally.
Place floating plants on the water surface.

MAY
Plant all types of water plants.
Control algae by removing with a stick, or by using chemicals (copper sulphate or potassium permanganate); but remember that if concentrated these are toxic to fish and plants.
Thin overgrown clumps of water lilies and re-plant the crowns in fresh soil.
In warm, dry weather, flood the pool occasionally to keep plants in the bog garden cool and moist.

JUNE
Finish planting aquatics this month for a display in their first season.
In sultry weather, keep the water oxygenated by occasionally adding fresh water from a hose and spray.
Watch for the appearance of aphids and deal with them immediately, being careful how chemicals are used where fish are present.
Control *Chironomas* midge, which eats the leaves of water lilies and aponogeton (water hawthorn).
Continue to remove algae before large masses form.
Reduce the growth of surface plants to allow light to penetrate to underwater plants.
Prick out seedlings of February-sown primulas in seed boxes, ready for planting in September.

JULY–AUGUST
Continue to spray against aphids and other pests.
In warm weather, replace water lost by evaporation, from a garden hose fitted with a spray.
Cut off large water lily leaves hiding the flowers.
Thin heavy growth of oxygenating plants.
Remove weeds from the bog garden.

SEPTEMBER
Collect the winter buds of hydrocharis and utricularia before they sink to the bottom of the pool, and keep them in an unsealed jar of water in a cool place until spring.
Pot up waterside primulas pricked out in June, or plant them in their permanent positions.
Feed the fish, as live food is now becoming scarce.

OCTOBER
Thin out underwater oxygenating plants and remove old water lily leaves.
If the water appears dark, drain off half of it and replace with fresh.
Remove old leaves and debris from the bottom.
Plant waterside plants in the bog garden.
Continue feeding fish as long as they are eating.

is divided into 18, the answer gives the number of square yards covered by a ton of paving.

Volumes

To find the volume of a **greenhouse**, multiply the average height by the width and the length. If the height of the house is 7 ft. to the ridge and 4 ft. to the eaves, the average height is $(7+4) \div 2 = 5\frac{1}{2}$ ft.

The volume of a **cylinder** is the area of the circle at one end multiplied by the length. An easier way to find the capacity of a small vessel is to weigh the amount of water it will contain, remembering that 1 pt. of water weighs $1\frac{1}{4}$ lb.

NOVEMBER

Finish preparing for winter by removing old leaves and thinning oxygenators.
Leave foliage on marginal reeds and rushes as winter protection.
Protect the pool against falling leaves by covering it with small-mesh netting.
Overhaul pumps used for waterfalls and fountains, removing submersible types from the water and storing.

DECEMBER

Keep a small area of the pool free of ice to permit toxic gases to escape.
Alternatively, cover a small area with boards or rush matting to prevent thick ice from forming.
Melt ice if necessary by standing a can of boiling water on its surface.

JANUARY

Continue to protect pools from ice.
Check water levels for indications of loss caused by cracking of the lining.
Check covering on protected plants.
Feed fish with light food such as daphnia in mild weather.

FEBRUARY

Continue to protect pools against ice.
Remove weeds from the bog garden.
Sow moisture-loving primulas in seed boxes.

The volume of a **bushel** is about 2,220 cu. in.; therefore a box 10 in. by 10 in. by 22 in. holds approximately a bushel (so does a cube with a side of 33 cm.). Roughly, a bushel of soil is sufficient to pot about 120 plants in $3\frac{1}{2}$ in. pots or about 40 plants in 5 in. pots. When re-potting from $3\frac{1}{2}$ in. pots to 5 in. pots, a bushel will be enough for about 50 plants. It will almost fill about 12 standard seed boxes 14 in. by 8 in. by 2 in.

Weights

The weight of a given volume of **absorbent material** varies according to how much water it contains. A ton of very light soil in fairly dry condition can be as much as 1 cu. yd., but wet, heavy soil could have only half this volume. 1 cwt. of John Innes potting compost usually measures about $1\frac{1}{2}$ bushels. A ton of gravel is about $\frac{2}{3}$ cu. yd. No reliable estimate can be given for peat and leaf-mould. A ton of potting sand is about $\frac{8}{9}$ cu. yd., or 24 cu. ft. 1 cwt. is just short of a bushel.

1 cwt. per acre is equivalent to 7 lb. per 10 sq. rods (the usual size of an allotment). To express 1 cwt. per acre as 1 lb. per 40 sq. yd. or 2 oz. per 5 sq. yd., results in an excess of about 10 per cent, but this is a tolerable error for most purposes.

Temperature conversions

Convert temperatures as follows:
$°C$ *to* $°F$. Multiply by 9, divide by 5 and add 32. Thus, $25°C \times 9 = 225$; $\div 5 = 45$; $+ 32 = 77°F$; and $-10°C \times 9 = -90$; $\div 5 = -18$; $+ 32 = 14°F$.
$°F$ *to* $°C$. Subtract 32, multiply by 5 and divide by 9. Thus, $86°F - 32 = 54$; $\times 5 = 270$; $\div 9 = 30°C$: and $23°F - 32 = -9$; $\times 5 = -45$; $\div 9 = -5°C$.

°C	°F		°C	°F		°C	°F
−10	= 14		5	= 41		20	= 68
−9	= 15/16		6	= 42/43		21	= 69/70
−8	= 17/18		7	= 44/45		22	= 71/72
−7	= 19/20		8	= 46/47		23	= 73/74
−6	= 21/22		9	= 48/49		24	= 75/76
−5	= 23		10	= 50		25	= 77
−4	= 24/25		11	= 51/52		26	= 78/79
−3	= 26/27		12	= 53/54		27	= 80/81
−2	= 28/29		13	= 55/56		28	= 82/83
−1	= 30/31		14	= 57/58		29	= 84/85
0	= 32		15	= 59		30	= 86
1	= 33/34		16	= 60/61		31	= 87/88
2	= 35/36		17	= 62/63		32	= 89/90
3	= 37/38		18	= 64/65			
4	= 39/40		19	= 66/67			

Wheelbarrows: see **Tools**

Wilt

Plants in full growth may flag or droop for a number of reasons. Wilting may be caused by lack of moisture in the soil, by physical damage to the roots, or by pest or disease damage, especially fungal diseases, which attack the water-conducting tissues in the plant stems. (See PESTS AND DISEASES, p. 410.)

Windbreak

A hedge, fence or wall which lessens the force of strong winds. Wind may cause severe damage to plants, particularly in gardens on high ground or near the coast; plants which are undamaged may still suffer retardation of growth. Exposed gardens should be protected by a windbreak. (See **Shelter belt**.)

Winter-wash

Any insecticide or fungicide applied to plants in the dormant season. The term is chiefly applied to tar oils and other chemicals sprayed on fruit trees in late winter to destroy over-wintering insects and their eggs.

Wood ash: see **Fertilisers and manures**

Wood bud

Alternative name for a growth bud. (See **Bud**.)

Worms

Worms in the cultivated parts of the garden are beneficial, as they aerate the soil and help to produce humus. In lawns worms should be discouraged, as they produce ugly, slippery casts that spoil the appearance of the turf. Control measures should be taken in autumn and spring. Proprietary worm eradicators including derris, chlordane or carbaryl are effective. Water a solution on the lawn in the evenings, when worms are feeding. In a dry spell, water the lawn well before applying the eradicator.

Z

Zineb

Fungicide, effective against downy mildews, leaf diseases and rusts. It is available as a wettable powder or as a dust, and is safe to use, though it may cause skin irritations.

Designing a garden

Thanks to our equable climate, a greater range of plants can be grown in Britain than in any other country in the world, and our lawns are the envy of visitors from overseas. With a background of several centuries of accumulated gardening experience, it is no wonder that British gardens are, in the main, so beautiful.

Designing and planting a garden offers an exciting challenge, the result being a highly individual creation which reflects the taste and interests of its owner. Often its scope is dictated by size, shape and environment, but such is the enormous selection of plants available that something can always be found that will flourish.

Town gardens
It is difficult to generalise about town gardens, because conditions vary so much from town to town—and even within a single town. With the introduction of smokeless zones, it is possible to grow plants which would have been considered quite unsuitable even a few years ago. At one time, town gardeners were advised to grow bulbs and herbaceous plants, which have little foliage during the winter, together with deciduous trees and shrubs. But now, with the cleaner air, many evergreens can be grown successfully.

Full use should be made of walls, especially in towns. House walls clad with magnolias, climbing roses, honeysuckles and other flowering shrubs add enormously to the appearance of a garden.

There are many attractive materials available for paving patios and courtyards, and for the construction of low retaining walls. Particularly popular are prefabricated concrete slabs, which may be had in many colours, and imitation York stone. Brick paths, though of pleasing appearance, tend to become slippery.

With the advent of glass fibre and other plastics, there are numerous types of plant containers from which to choose, including imitation lead urns. The latter are almost indistinguishable from the real thing. Container gardening is particularly useful in towns, where soil is often of poor quality. Using a few bushels of good compost, and a selection of both upright and trailing plants, a rather bare terrace or courtyard can be transformed throughout the spring and summer.

Trellises and screens
In most gardens there is a need somewhere for a screen or trellis, either to secure privacy or to hide an ugly view. The traditional wooden trellis is still probably the most attractive, but it does require regular painting or treatment with wood preservative. Plastic-covered wire mesh panels provide a labour-saving alternative. They are available in various colours and can either be erected on posts or attached to a wall for supporting climbing plants of all kinds. These panels eliminate the need for tying; as the young shoots grow, they are simply pushed in and out of the mesh. If the panels are fixed against a wall, using vine eyes or wooden battens, they can be removed if the wall has to be repainted. Afterwards, they can be tied back in position.

Rock gardens
In every garden, large or small, there is a place for rock plants. A rock garden can be made of massive bluffs of stone with soil pockets placed to suit the requirements of particular plants, some needing shade, others full sun. Even in a small garden, a rock garden on a more modest scale can be constructed to provide a home for many plants that will bloom not only in the spring, when the great flush of alpine flowers occurs, but throughout the summer and into the autumn.

Alpine plants can also be grown in stone sinks and in raised beds. Such beds are a great boon for people who cannot stoop. The walls of a raised bed can be made of flat stones, or even peat blocks, with plants placed between the stones to decorate the sides.

Water in the garden
With modern aids to plumbing, such as rigid plastic pipes and fittings, and by making use of an electric pump and plastic pool liner, it is very easy to construct an attractive water feature. In small gardens, which are usually rectangular or square in shape, it is better to follow the garden's contours and install a formal pool. Informal pools are more attractive in large gardens.

With any type of pool it is always desirable to create a boggy area around the margins, so that irises, primulas and other moisture-loving plants can be accommodated.

Specimen planting
A suitable place can always be found for a specimen tree or shrub. Evergreen subjects, in particular, will give pleasure throughout the year. Do not overlook the value of coloured bark, provided by silver birches and red or yellow stemmed willows. Alternatively, the silvery foliage of such plants as *Senecio laxifolius* and dwarf golden conifers gives enjoyment throughout the dull months of winter.

Though specimen trees and shrubs are often planted in the middle of the lawn, in small gardens they are better placed to one side.

GENERAL AND PLANT INDEX

This index includes subjects, genera, species and varieties described in THE GARDENING YEAR. English common names are cross-referenced to the Latin names of the plants. The only exceptions are fruits, vegetables and herbs. Figures in bold type indicate the main reference to the subject concerned; figures in brackets refer to illustrations.